W9-ATN-381

SOCIOLOGY

IAN ROBERTSON

SOCIOLOGY

WORTH PUBLISHERS, INC.

Sociology

Manufactured in the United States of America

Library of Congress Catalog Number: 76–52248

ISBN: 0–87901–070–3

Designed by Malcolm Grear Designers

Composition by New England Typographic Service

Picture Editor: June Lundborg

Second Printing: August, 1977

Cover: *Vue de l'Arène à Arles,* Vincent Van Gogh
The Hermitage Museum, Leningrad
Photo courtesy of M. Knoedler & Co., New York

Worth Publishers, Inc.

444 Park Avenue South

New York, New York 10016

Preface

There are two basic premises behind this book. The first is that sociology is both a humanistic art and a rigorous science; in fact much of its excitement arises from the insights offered by this unique blend of two intellectual traditions. The second premise is that sociology can be, and should be, a profoundly liberating discipline. By challenging the conventional wisdoms of the past and by dissolving the myths about social reality, the discipline provides an acute awareness of the social authorship of and responsibility for both the social world and much of our personal experience and identity. Sociology thus offers that crucial sense of options and choice that is essential to human freedom.

The impetus to write this book grew out of several years' experience as a teacher and professional journalist in radically different societies in North America, Europe, and Africa. I will count the book successful to the extent that it conveys to the reader the fascination and sheer pleasure that I draw from sociology myself.

Coverage

I decided at the outset not to write a slender "core" text covering a few selected topics. The problem with such an approach, of course, is that one person's core may be another's apple—or vice versa—with the result that some instructors are left without text discussion of material they consider essential. Instead, I have tried to give a broad and thorough coverage of the main fields of the discipline, while keeping the text sufficiently flexible to be adapted to the needs of individual instructors. The book thus provides full coverage of the "traditional" material in the introductory sociology course. It seemed to me important, however, that the text should do much more: that it should also convey a strong sense of the "cutting edge" of the discipline, of the vital issues and trends in contemporary sociology. For this reason, I have included much material that is unusual or even unique in an introductory book. A full chapter, for example, is devoted to the sociology of science, a subject of great potential interest to any student in modern society and perhaps of particular interest to those science majors who may take only one sociology course. There is also an entire chapter on the micro order, in which symbolic interactionist and dramaturgical approaches are applied to the ordinary routines of everyday life. A chapter is devoted, too, to the sociology of sexual behavior, a subject of high student interest and one admirably suited to illustrate the interplay of biological, social, and cultural factors in the shaping of human behavior. There are also discussions of many other fields of current interest, such as ecological concerns, body language, the sociology of death, and ethical problems in sociological research. A full chapter is also accorded to the topic of sex roles—and I have taken care throughout the book to avoid sexist language, with its unintended yet inevitable implication that it is only men who do, and act, and create the social world.

Organization

The book has been divided into five units. Unit I provides an introduction to sociology and to the methods of sociological research. Unit II deals with the individual, culture, and society, and focuses on the influence of social and cultural forces on personal experience and social behavior. The chapters in this unit cover culture, society, socialization, social interaction, social groups, deviance, and sexual behavior. Unit III discusses various forms of social inequality, and emphasizes the role of ideology as well as coercion and tradition in the maintenance of inequalities. The first chapter in the unit deals with the general problem of social stratification and introduces basic concepts; the second deals with social class in the United States; the third, with race and ethnic relations; and the fourth, with sex roles. Unit IV discusses several important social institutions: the family, education, religion, science, the economic order, and the political order. Finally, Unit V focuses on some issues of social order and social change; it contains chapters on population and ecology, urbanization and urban life, collective behavior and social movements, and on the general problem of social change itself.

I have taken great care, however, to structure the book in such a way that instructors can, if they wish, omit some chapters and present others in a different order. Nearly all instructors will want to cover the first five chapters, in which the most important terms and concepts of the discipline are introduced. The sequence of the remaining chapters can then be freely rearranged to suit the convenience of the individual instructor, and there are ample cross-references to the five basic chapters and to relevant topics in other chapters to facilitate any alternative sequence.

Features

The book contains a number of distinctive features that have been included to enhance its effectiveness as a teaching and learning tool.

Cross-cultural material. While this book is not in any sense intended as an exercise in comparative sociology, I have started from the assumption—a surprisingly unusual one—that sociology is something more than the study of American society. Throughout the text there are occasional references to other cultures and to the historical past. This material is intended to serve two purposes. The first is to enliven the text, for the ways of life of other peoples—particularly in so-called "primitive" societies—are inherently fascinating. The second purpose, more serious, is to undermine ethnocentric attitudes by highlighting, through comparison, distinctive aspects of American society that might otherwise pass unnoticed or be taken for granted.

Theory. A basic sociology text should not, in my view, be a heavily theoretical one. But conversely, a sound introduction to sociological theory should be an essential feature of the introductory course, and we fail both the discipline and our students if we do not provide it. The treatment of theory in this book is shaped by two convictions. The first is that theory can be presented in a clear, concise, interesting, and understandable manner, and that its practical value can be readily appreciated by the student. The second conviction is that theory must not, as happens all too often, be briefly introduced in the first chapter and then hastily buried: this tactic can only confirm the student's worst suspicions that theory is an irrelevant luxury.

I have taken a fairly eclectic approach to sociological theory and have utilized all three of the main perspectives in the contemporary discipline: functionalist theory (primarily for issues of social order and stability), conflict theory (primarily for issues of social tension and change) and interactionist theories (primarily for "micro" issues). Above all, I have carried these perspectives throughout the book—not by applying them mechanically to everything, but by introducing particular theoretical perspectives where they will genuinely enhance understanding of a specific problem. Where the perspectives complement one another, as they often do, this is made clear; where they seem contradictory, the problem is discussed. I have drawn extensively, of course, on the ideas of contemporary sociologists; but in keeping with the current resurgence of interest in classical thinkers I have given due emphasis to such writers as Marx, Durkheim, and Weber.

Readings. A number of readings from original sources are included at appropriate places in the text. These readings have been chosen for their interest and relevance, and are designed to give the student a deeper, more firsthand experience of sociological writing and research.

Pedagogical aids. Several features of the book are designed to aid the learning process. Each chapter begins with a brief overview of its major topics and closes with a numbered, point-by-point summary of the contents. All important terms are italicized and defined where they first appear, and unfamiliar terms are illustrated by an example.

These terms are also listed for end-of-chapter review. Throughout the book there are occasional "boxes" containing short and relevant items of interest. The book is abundantly illustrated with photographs, many of them in full color. The photographs have been carefully selected for pedagogical rather than merely decorative reasons, and are accompanied by unusually full captions that reinforce and amplify the text material. Numerous tables and charts, up-to-date and easy to read, are used to aid the student's understanding of concepts and sociological data. Each chapter also contains an annotated list of suggestions for further reading.

Glossary. The book contains an extensive glossary—virtually a mini-dictionary—of over three hundred important sociological terms. The glossary can be used both for ready reference and for reviewing purposes.

Library research techniques. I have included a brief appendix on techniques of library research. This appendix is intended as a handy guide to library facilities; it offers many suggestions for tracking down sources and information and should prove useful to students working on term papers or research projects.

Supplementary materials

A Study Guide is available to help students in both their understanding and their reviewing of the course. The guide, prepared by Diana K. Harris and William E. Cole (University of Tennessee, Knoxville), includes learning objectives, a chapter synopsis, multiple-choice questions, word scramble questions, true-false questions, completion questions, and a term finder.

The text also is complemented by a comprehensive *Instructor's Manual* by Donald P. Irish (Hamline University) and a *Test Bank* of 1000 four-choice multiple-choice questions.

Thanks

Many people have helped in the preparation of this book. I am especially grateful to a number of my colleagues who evaluated various parts of the manuscript for accuracy, coverage, readability, currency, and teachability. The book owes a great deal to the many constructive criticisms and suggestions they offered. The reviewers were:

Robert Antonio, University of Kansas
Helen Arbini, University of California, Davis
E. M. Beck, University of Michigan
William Bruce Cameron, University of South Florida
Janice G. Crumrine, University of Georgia
Donna K. Darden, University of Georgia
Ken Donow, Stockton State College
Robert A. Ellis, University of Georgia
David Fabianic, Montana State University
William Feigelman, Nassau Community College
James Fishkin, Yale University
Charles Y. Glock, University of California, Berkeley
Patricia A. Hartman, California State University, San Diego
Barbara Heyns, University of California, Berkeley
Arlie Hochschild, University of California, Berkeley
David E. Hunter, Southern Connecticut State College
Donald P. Irish, Hamline University
Lewis Killian, University of Massachusetts, Amherst
Edward C. McDonagh, Ohio State University
George A. Miller, University of Utah
Lawrence A. Propper, Suffolk County Community College
Roland Robertson, University of Pittsburgh
Edward Sagarin, City College of New York
Randall G. Stokes, University of Massachusetts, Amherst
Steven Rosenthal, Boston University

Two of these reviewers deserve a special word of thanks, Donald Irish and Edward Sagarin. Both kindly consented to read the entire manuscript, and I benefited enormously from their wisdom. A number of students from different colleges and universities also critiqued the manuscript from the student viewpoint or helped with the research for the book, and I am especially grateful to Elizabeth Hasen, Katja Ocepek, Larry Stern, and Kevin Williams.

Of course, I have not always agreed with the reviewers (nor have they always agreed with one another!) and the responsibility for the final manuscript is entirely my own.

Finally, I have been fortunate to be associated with Worth Publishers, a young and vigorous company with a well-deserved reputation for its commitment to quality at every stage of the publishing process. My sincere thanks go to the staff of Worth for the effort they put into this book.

New York City
February, 1977

IAN ROBERTSON

Contents

UNIT 1 *Introduction to Sociology* 1

CHAPTER 1 *Sociology: A New Look at a Familiar World* **3**

Sociology as a Perspective 4
- The Basic Insight 4
- The Sociological Imagination 5

What Is Science? 7

Sociology as a Science 8
- The Scientific Status of Sociology 8
- Sociology and Common Sense 9

The Social Sciences 10

The Development of Sociology 11
- The Origins 11
- Early Sociologists 12
- Modern Developments 15

Theoretical Perspectives 16
- The Functionalist Perspective 16
- The Conflict Perspective 18
- The Interactionist Perspective 20
- An Evaluation 21

The Problem of Objectivity 22

READING: "Invitation to Sociology" by Peter L. Berger 26

CHAPTER 2 *Doing Sociology: The Methods of Research* **29**

The Logic of Cause and Effect 30
- Variables 30
- Correlations 30
- Controls 32

Difficulties in Sociological Research 33

Basic Research Methods 35
- Experiments 35
- Surveys 36
- Observational Studies 38
- Existing Sources 41

A Research Model 43

Ethical Issues 45
- "Project Camelot" 45
- "Tearoom Trade" 45

UNIT 2 *The Individual, Culture, and Society* 49

CHAPTER 3 *Culture* **51**

The Human Species: What Kind of Animal? 52
- The Evolutionary Background 52
- The Significance of Culture 54
- "Human Nature" 55

Norms 57
- Folkways and Mores 58
- Social Control 58

Values 59
- The Importance of Values 59
- American Values 59

Cultural Variation 61
- The Functionalist Approach 61
- The Ecological Approach 62
- Cultural Universals 64
- Ethnocentrism 64
- Cultural Relativism 66

Cultural Integration 67
- Real Culture and Ideal Culture 67
- Subcultures and Countercultures 67

Language 68
The Importance of Language 70
Linguistic Relativity 70
Cultural Change 71
Are We Prisoners of Culture? 73
READING: "The One Hundred Percent American" by Ralph Linton 75

CHAPTER 4 *Society* **77**

Social Structure 78
Statuses 78
Roles 79
Groups 80
Institutions 81
Types of Societies 81
Hunting and Gathering Societies 82
Pastoral Societies 83
Horticultural Societies 84
Agricultural Societies 85
Industrial Societies 87
Industrial and Preindustrial Societies: A Comparison 89
READING: "Pathology of Imprisonment" by Philip Zimbardo 93

CHAPTER 5 *Socialization* **95**

"Nature" and "Nurture" 97
Effects of Childhood Isolation 98
"Feral" Children 98
Children Raised in Isolation 99
Institutionalized Children 99
Monkeys Raised in Isolation 100
Theories of Learning 101
The Behaviorist Approach 101
The Developmental Approach 101
The Emergence of the Self 102
Freud's Theory 103
Cooley's Theory 104
Mead's Theory 105
Cognitive Development 105
The Sensorimotor Stage 106
The Preoperational Stage 106
The Concrete Operational Stage 107
The Formal Operational Stage 107
Agencies of Socialization 108
The Family 108
The School 108
The Peer Group 109
The Mass Media 110
Other Agencies 110
Socialization and the Life Cycle 110
Types of Socialization 110
The Life Cycle 111
Socialization and Free Will 113

CHAPTER 6 *Social Interaction in Everyday Life* **117**

The Self in Everyday Life 119
Roles and the Self 119
The Dramaturgical Approach 120
Aligning Actions 122
Nonverbal Communication 123
Body Language 123
Physical Proximity 125
The Micro Order: Some Studies 127
Becoming a Marijuana User 127
Male Doctor and Female Patient 128
Helping Others 129
Hurting Others 131
Dying 133
The Social Construction of Reality 135

CHAPTER 7 *Social Groups* **139**

Primary and Secondary Groups 140
Small Groups 141
The Importance of Size 142
Leadership 143
Group Decision Making 144
Group Conformity 145
Ingroups and Outgroups 146
Reference Groups 147
Formal Organizations 147
Bureaucracy 149
Weber's Analysis 149
The Informal Structure of Bureaucracy 152
Dysfunctions of Bureaucracy 153
The Problem of Oligarchy 155
The Future of Formal Organizations 157

CHAPTER 8 ***Deviance*** **161**

Deviance and Social Control 164
Theories of Deviance 166
- Biological Theories 166
- Anomie Theory 168
- Cultural Transmission Theory 169
- Labeling Theory 171

Crime 173
- Types of Crime 174
- Who Are the Criminals? 176
- Selecting the Criminal 176
- Prisons 179

The Social Consequences of Deviance 180
- Dysfunctions of Deviance 180
- Functions of Deviance 180

READING: "The Saints and the Roughnecks" by William J. Chambliss 183

CHAPTER 9 ***Sexuality and Society*** **187**

The Nature of Human Sexuality 189
Sexual Behavior in Other Cultures 189
- Concepts of Beauty 190
- Restrictiveness and Permissiveness 190
- Heterosexual Behavior 190
- Homosexual Behavior 191
- Evaluation 192

Sexual Behavior in the United States 192
- Traditional Values 194
- Contemporary Practices 196

The Incest Taboo 199
Homosexuality 201
- Incidence of Homosexuality 201
- The Homosexual Community 203
- Causes of Homosexuality 204

Prostitution 205
- Types of Prostitution 206
- Prostitution as an Occupation 208
- Reasons for Prostitution 209
- Can Prostitution Be Eliminated? 210

UNIT 3 ***Social Inequality*** **213**

CHAPTER 10 ***Social Stratification*** **215**

The Analysis of Stratification Systems 217
- Caste and Class 217
- Social Mobility 218
- Criteria of Class Membership 219

Stratified Societies: Three Examples 222
- India: A Caste Society 222
- Britain: A Class Society 223
- The Soviet Union: A Classless Society? 224

Maintaining Stratification: The Role of Ideology 225
Theories of Stratification 228
- The Functionalist Approach 228
- The Conflict Approach 229
- The Evolutionary Approach 231

READING: "Caste and Conflict in South Africa" by Ian Robertson 234

CHAPTER 11 ***Social Class in the United States*** **237**

Social Inequality in the United States 237
- Wealth 238
- Power 239
- Prestige 240

The American Class System 241
- Problems of Analysis 241
- The Social Classes 242
- Correlates of Class Membership 247

Social Mobility in the United States 249
Poverty in the United States 251
- Defining Poverty 251
- Who Are the Poor? 251
- The Causes of Poverty 252
- Attitudes Toward Poverty 254

READING: "Blaming the Victim" by William Ryan 258

CHAPTER 12 ***Race and Ethnic Relations*** **261**

The Concepts of Race and Ethnicity 262
- Race 262
- Ethnicity 263

Minority Groups 263
Patterns of Race and Ethnic Relations 267
Racism 269
- The Nature of Racism 269
- The Causes of Racism 269
- The Ideology of Racism 271

Prejudice and Discrimination 273
The Psychology of Prejudice 275
Forms of Discrimination 277
Race and Ethnic Relations in the United States 278
Blacks 279
Native Americans 282
Hispanic Americans 282
Asian Americans 284
White Ethnics 284
The Future of American Race and Ethnic Relations 285

CHAPTER 13 *Sex Roles* **289**

How Different Are the Sexes? 290
Biological Evidence 291
Psychological Evidence 291
Cross-Cultural Evidence 292
A Sociological Analysis 294
Sexism 296
Sexist Ideology 296
Attitudes Toward Sexism 297
Sex Roles in the United States 299
Sex and Personality 300
Sex and the Division of Labor 301
Socialization into Sex Roles 302
The Family 303
The Schools 304
The Mass Media 305
The Costs and Consequences of Sexism 306
Sex Roles in the Future 308
READING: "The Door-Opening Ceremony" by Laurel Richardson Walum 310

UNIT 4 *Social Institutions* **313**

CHAPTER 14 *The Family* **315**

Why Is the Family Universal? 316
The Biological Basis 316
The Functions of the Family 317
Family Patterns 318
A Cross-Cultural Perspective 318
The Analysis of Family Patterns 321
The Transformation of the Family 323
Marriage and Family in the United States 325
The American Family 325
Romantic Love 326
Courtship and Marriage 327
Marital Breakdown 329
Causes of Divorce 331
The Future of the Family 332
Experimental Alternatives 332
READING: "Does Marriage Have A Future?" by Jessie Bernard 337

CHAPTER 15 *Education* **341**

Characteristics of American Education 342
Commitment to Mass Education 342
Faith in Education 345
Utilitarian Emphasis 345
Community Control 346
Inside the School 346
The Formal Structure of the School 346
Competitiveness 348
The Self-Fulfilling Prophecy 348
Student Peer Groups 349
Education: The Functionalist Perspective 350
Cultural Transmission 350
Social Integration 351
Personal Development 351
Screening and Selection 352
Innovation 352
Latent Functions 353
Education: The Conflict Perspective 353
Education and Social Mobility 353
Class, Race, and Education 355
Class, Race, and Intelligence 357
Equality of Educational Opportunity 358
The Coleman Report 358
Jencks's Analysis 362

CHAPTER 16 *Religion* **365**

The Sociological Approach to Religion 367
Types of Religion 368
Religion: A Functionalist Analysis 369
The Work of Durkheim 369
The Functions of Religion 371
Functional Equivalents of Religion 371
Religion: A Conflict Analysis 372
The Work of Marx 372
Religion and Social Conflict 373
The Medieval Witch Craze 374

Millenarian Movements 375
Religion and Social Change: The "Protestant Ethic" 377
Types of Religious Organization 379
Religion in the United States 380
Some Characteristics 381
Correlates of Religious Affiliation 382
Civil Religion in the United States 383
Secularization 384

CHAPTER 17 ***Science*** **389**

The Institutionalization of Science 390
The Historical Background 390
The Modern Institution 393
The Norms of Science 394
The Social Process of Innovation 395
Paradigms in Science 396
Competition in Science 397
Resistance to Innovation 398
Case Study: The Theory of Evolution 399
Technology and Society 401
Technological Determinism 401
Technology and the Rate of Social Change 403
The Social Control of Science and Technology 404

CHAPTER 18 ***The Economic Order*** **409**

The Division of Labor 410
Increased Specialization 410
Anomie and the Division of Labor 412
The Sociology of Occupations 414
Primary, Secondary, and Tertiary Sectors 414
Professionalization 415
Work and Alienation 416
The Concept of Alienation 416
Worker Alienation in the United States 418
"Human Relations" in Industry 418
Capitalism and Socialism 420
The Concept of Property 420
Capitalism 421
Socialism 422
Democratic Socialism 424
Communism 424
Corporate Capitalism in the United States 424
Corporations and the American Economy 425
Multinational Corporations 427
Industrialism and Modernization 429
The Modernization Process 429
The Social Effects of Modernization 429
The Future of Industrial Society 430

CHAPTER 19 ***The Political Order*** **435**

Power 435
Types of Authority 436
Traditional Authority 436
Legal-Rational Authority 437
Charismatic Authority 437
The State 440
The Functionalist Approach 442
The Conflict Approach 443
Evaluation 445
Democracy 445
Prerequisites for Democracy 447
Liberty and Equality 449
The American Political Process 450
Interest Groups 450
Political Parties 452
Who Rules? 453
The Power-Elite Thesis 454
The Pluralist Thesis 454
Empirical Studies 455
Revolutions 460

UNIT 5 ***Social Change in the Modern World*** **467**

CHAPTER 20 ***Population and Ecology*** **469**

The Study of Population 470
The Science of Demography 470
The Dynamics of Demographic Change 470
The World Population Problem 475
The Malthusian Trap 475
The Causes of Rapid Population Growth 477
The Theory of Demographic Transition 479
Population in the United States 482
American Demographic Characteristics 482
Do We Have a Population Problem? 483
What Can Be Done? 484
Population and the Environment 486
The Science of Ecology 486
The Elements of Ecology 487

Pollution 488
Resource Depletion 488
The Limits to Growth 489

CHAPTER 21 ***Urbanization and Urban Life*** **493**

The Urbanization Process 494
The Preindustrial City 495
The Industrial City 496
The American City and Its Problems 497
The Suburbs 499
The Central Cities 500
City Planning 501
The Nature of Urban Life 502
Gemeinschaft and Gesellschaft 502
The Chicago School 502
Urbanism: A Reassessment 504
Urban Ecology 504
The Ecological Approach 504
Patterns of Urban Growth 506

CHAPTER 22 ***Collective Behavior and Social Movements*** **511**

A Theory of Collective Behavior 513
Rumors 514
The Yippie Invasion of Chicago 515
The Death of Paul McCartney 516
Fashions and Fads 518
Fashions 518
Fads 518
Panics 520
Mass Hysteria 521
The Martian Invasion of Earth 521
The Phantom Anesthetist of Mattoon 522
The Seattle Windshield-Pitting Epidemic 522
Crowds 523
Crowd Characteristics 523
Types of Crowds 523
Theories of Crowd Behavior 524
Mobs 526
Riots 527
Publics and Public Opinion 528
Publics 528
Public Opinion 528
Social Movements 531
Types of Social Movements 531
Social Movements and Social Problems 532
READING: "Massacre at My Lai" by Seymour M. Hersch 535

CHAPTER 23 ***Social Change*** **539**

Theories of Social Change 540
Evolutionary Theories 541
Cyclical Theories 543
Functionalist Theories 545
Conflict Theories 546
Some Sources of Change 547
The Physical Environment 547
Ideas 548
Technology 549
Population 550
"Events" 550
Cultural Innovation 551
Human Action 552
Conclusion 554
Prospects for a General Theory 554
Interacting Factors in Social Change 554
Predicting the Future 555

APPENDIX: ***Techniques of Library Research*** **557**
GLOSSARY **560**
REFERENCES **570**
ACKNOWLEDGMENTS **589**
INDEX **594**

UNIT 1 *Introduction to Sociology*

Like any subject that deals with people, sociology is inherently fascinating. This introductory unit explains what sociology is, what sociologists do, and how they go about their work. In it you will discover sociology's distinctive perspective on human society and social behavior.

The first chapter offers you a general overview of the discipline, presenting sociologists as "strangers" in the familiar landscape of their own society: in other words, as people who look afresh at the world others take for granted. The chapter explains the "sociological imagination"—the vivid awareness you will gain of the close link between personal experience and wider social forces. It discusses also the scientific nature of sociology, the relationship of sociology to other social sciences, the history of the discipline, and the major theoretical approaches that sociologists use to make sense of their subject matter.

The second chapter discusses the methods that sociologists use to investigate the social world. Sociological research is essentially a form of detective work, in which the sociologist tries to find out what is happening in society and why. The value of the sociologist's conclusions is obviously influenced by the accuracy and reliability of the methods that are used to collect and analyze the evidence. The chapter thus examines the problems of tracing cause and effect in social behavior, the unique difficulties that sociologists face in their research, and the methods that they use to uncover the facts about social life.

NO
STANDING
ANY
TIME

CHAPTER 1 Sociology: A New Look at a Familiar World

CHAPTER OUTLINE

Sociology as a Perspective
The Basic Insight
The Sociological Imagination

What Is Science?

Sociology as a Science
The Scientific Status of Sociology
Sociology and Common Sense

The Social Sciences

The Development of Sociology
The Origins
Early Sociologists
Modern Developments

Theoretical Perspectives
The Functionalist Perspective
The Conflict Perspective
The Interactionist Perspective
An Evaluation

The Problem of Objectivity

Alone among living creatures, human beings are self-aware—capable of inquiring and reflecting about themselves. Throughout history, our ancestors pondered human nature as it is revealed in the social life of our species. Why do human beings form families and why do they worship gods? Why is the way of life of one group so different from that of another? What makes some people break social rules while others obey them? Why are some people rich when others are poor? What makes one group go to war with another? What might a human being be like who had not been raised in the company of other people? What holds societies together, and why do all societies constantly change over time?

Until quite recently the answers to these and similar questions came from intuition, from speculation, and from the dead weight of myth, superstition, and traditional "folk wisdom" handed down from the past. Only in the course of the last century or so has a new method been applied to the study of human society and social behavior: the method of science, which provides answers drawn from facts collected by systematic research.

This new mode of inquiry has produced the lively but still infant discipline of sociology. *Sociology is the scientific study of human society and social behavior.* The subject matter of sociology is huge, complex, and varied, and the knowledge produced by sociological research is still imperfect in many ways. Yet, in the brief century and a half that the discipline has been in existence, it has taught us a great deal about ourselves that we could never have learned by relying on speculation alone. We have learned to conceive of human beings and social life in an entirely new way—a way that you will find sometimes disconcerting but always fascinating.

Sociology as a Perspective

The world does not consist of a reality that everyone sees in exactly the same way. A house may seem to be simply a house, but different people will look at and interpret it quite differently. The architect will see it in one way, the realtor in a second, the prospective buyer in a third, the artist in a fourth, the demolition expert in a fifth, and so on. Each of these people brings a distinctive perspective to bear on the same subject and sees quite different things as a result. In the same way, sociology offers a particular perspective on society and social behavior, a perspective quite unlike that of, say, the poet, the philosopher, the theologian, the lawyer, or the police officer.

The sociological perspective invites us to become strangers in the familiar landscape of our society. It allows us to look afresh at a world we have always taken for granted, to examine our own surroundings with the same curiosity and fascination that we might bring to an exotic, alien culture. As Peter Berger (1963) has observed, sociology is nothing less than a special form of consciousness. It encourages us to focus on features of our social environment that we have never noticed before and to interpret them in a new and richer light. Sociology gives us a window on the wider world that lies beyond our immediate experience, leading us into areas of society that we might otherwise have ignored or misunderstood. Our own view of the world is shaped by our personal experience of it. Sociology shows us the worlds of the rich and the powerful, the poor and the weak, the worlds of slum dwellers and addicts, religious zealots and criminal gangs. Because these people have different social experiences, they have quite different definitions of social reality. Sociology enables us to appreciate viewpoints other than our own, to understand how these viewpoints came into being, and in the process, to better understand ourselves, our attitudes, and our own lives.

Figure 1.1 To an outsider, the appearance and behavior of this New Guinea tribesman may seem bizarre. In the context of his own society, however, the ritual in which he is taking part is perfectly understandable. Legend has it that members of the tribe once hid from their enemies in a riverbed. When they emerged, covered with white mud, their enemies mistook them for ghosts and fled. The ritual commemorates this event. The sociological perspective invites us to apply the same curiosity to our own society that we might apply to others, examining with fresh insights the behavior that we have always taken for granted. Sociologists are in a sense "outsiders" in their own society.

The Basic Insight

Sociology starts from the premise that we are basically social animals—not just from force of habit but because we could not otherwise survive. We live out our brief lives, for better or worse, in a society that existed long before we were born and will exist long after we are gone. We are all born into human groups and derive our identities, hopes, fears, troubles, and satisfactions from them. The basic insight of sociology is this: *human behavior is largely shaped by the groups to which people belong and by the social interaction that takes place within those groups.* We are what we are and we behave the way we do because we happen to live in particular societies at particular points in space and time. If you had been born, say, a modern Chinese peasant, or an

African pygmy, or an ancient Greek, or a feudal aristocrat, your personality, your options in life, and your social experience would be utterly different. This fact seems obvious enough, but it is easily overlooked. People everywhere tend to take their social world for granted, accepting their society and its customs as unquestioningly as they do the physical world that also surrounds them. But the sociological perspective enables us to see society not as something to be taken for granted as "natural" but as a temporary social product, created by human beings and therefore capable of being changed by them as well.

The main focus of sociology is the group, not the individual. Studies of particular individuals are useful to sociologists, but the sociologist is mainly interested in the *interaction* between people—the ways in which people act toward, respond to, and influence one another. All social behavior, from shaking hands to murder, and all social institutions, from religion to the family, are ultimately the product of social interaction. The group, then, provides the sociologist's main frame of reference—whether the group being studied is as small as a gang or a rock band, as large as a city or an ethnic community, or as vast as a modern industrial society.

The Sociological Imagination

This emphasis on the group always leads back to the individual, however, for it is only by understanding society that we can fully understand ourselves. C. Wright Mills (1959) described the perspective of the discipline as "the sociological imagination"—a vivid awareness of the relationship between private experience and the wider society. People usually see the world through their limited experience in a small orbit of family, relatives, friends, and fellow workers. This viewpoint places blinkers on their view of the wider society. But it does more than that. Paradoxically, it also places blinkers on their view of their own personal worlds, for those worlds are shaped by broader social forces that can easily pass unrecognized. The "sociological imagination" allows us to escape from this cramped personal vision—to stand apart mentally from our own place in society and to see with a new clarity the link between private troubles and social events.

When a society becomes industrialized, rural peasants become urban workers, whether they like it or not. When

Strangers in a Familiar World

Anthropologists use the term "culture shock" to describe the impact of a totally new culture upon a newcomer. In an extreme instance such shock will be experienced by the Western explorer who is told, halfway through dinner, that he is eating the nice old lady he had been chatting with the previous day. Most explorers no longer encounter cannibalism in their travels today. However, the first encounters with polygamy or with puberty rites or even with the way some nations drive their automobiles can be quite a shock to an American visitor. With the shock may go not only disapproval or disgust but a sense of excitement that things can *really* be that different from what they are at home. To some extent, at least, this is the excitement of any first travel abroad. The experience of sociological discovery could be described as "culture shock" minus geographical displacement. In other words, the sociologist travels at home—with shocking results. He is unlikely to find that he is eating a nice old lady for dinner. But the discovery, for instance, that his own church has considerable money invested in the missile industry or that a few blocks from his home there are people who engage in cultic orgies may not be drastically different in emotional impact. Yet we would not want to imply that sociological discoveries are always or even usually outrageous to moral sentiment. Not at all. What they have in common with exploration in distant lands, however, is the sudden illumination of new and unsuspected facets of human existence in society.

People who like to avoid shocking discoveries, who prefer to believe that society is just what they were taught in Sunday School, who like the safety of the rules and the maxims of what Alfred Schutz has called the "world-taken-for-granted," should stay away from sociology. People who feel no temptation before closed doors, who have no curiosity about human beings, who are content to admire scenery without wondering about the people who live in those houses on the other side of that river, should probably also stay away from sociology. They will find it unpleasant or, at any rate, unrewarding. People who are interested in human beings only if they can change, convert or reform them should also be warned, for they will find sociology much less useful than they hoped. And people whose interest is mainly in their own conceptual constructions will do just as well to turn to the study of little white mice. Sociology will be satisfying, in the long run, only to those who can think of nothing more entrancing than to watch and to understand things human.

Source: Peter L. Berger, *Invitation to Sociology* (New York: Doubleday & Company, Inc., Anchor Books, 1963).

Figure 1.2 *The "sociological imagination" enables us to trace the connection between individual experience and social forces. The options and life-styles of these people from the upper and lower classes of the United States, a village in India, and rural China, are very different. People's lives are shaped by historical and social forces over which they have little personal control.*

a nation goes to war, women are widowed and children grow up as orphans, for reasons that are beyond their personal power to control. When an economy sags, workers are thrown out of their jobs, no matter how efficiently they have performed them. When a youth culture emerges and wins over the young, many parents cannot understand their children, for nothing in their experience has prepared them to do so. The "sociological imagination" permits us to trace the intricate connection between the patterns and events of our own lives and the patterns and events of our society. As Mills expressed it:

> The sociological imagination enables us to grasp history and biography and the relationship between the two within society. That is its task and its promise.... It is by means of the sociological imagination that men now hope to grasp what is happening to themselves as minute points of the intersection of biography and history within society.

What Is Science?

Science refers to logical, systematic methods by which knowledge of the universe is obtained and to the actual body of knowledge produced by these methods. The sciences are conventionally divided into two main branches: the *natural sciences,* which study physical and biological phenomena, and the *social sciences,* which study various aspects of human behavior. There are important differences between the two branches, but both have the same commitment to the scientific method.

All science, natural and social, assumes that there is some underlying order, or regular pattern, in the universe. Events, whether they involve molecules or human beings, are not haphazard. They follow a pattern that is sufficiently regular for *generalizations* to be made about them. It is possible to generalize, for example, that hydrogen and oxygen will always form water if they are combined at an appropriate temperature. Similarly, it is possible to generalize that all human societies will create some system of marriage and the family. Generalizations are crucial to science because they place isolated, meaningless events in patterns that we can understand. It then becomes possible to analyze relationships of cause and effect and thus to *explain* why something happens and to *predict* that it will happen again under the same conditions in the future.

Science relies for its generalizations, explanations, and predictions on careful, systematic analysis of verifiable evidence—that is, evidence that can be checked by others and will always yield the same results. Nonscientific, "common sense" explanations are based on *belief,* but scientific explanations are based on *fact.* Scientists do not accept evidence that comes from simple faith; they insist on evidence that comes from verified observations. The ancient Romans believed as a matter of faith that the sun was drawn across the skies each day by a god in a chariot, although none of them had actually seen this happening. Scientists have observed as a matter of fact that the apparent movement of the sun is caused by the daily rotations of the earth, and any competent scientist can verify this observation by using the same methods. In short, the scientific approach gives a more reliable interpretation of reality.

This does not mean that common sense cannot provide accurate explanations and predictions; it can, and often does. The problem is that without using the methods of science, there is no way to tell whether common sense is correct. For centuries common sense told people that the world was the center of the universe and that the earth was flat. Using scientific methods, Copernicus found that the world is simply one planet among others, and the investigations of Columbus and other geographers proved that the earth is round. In making their factual investigations, these men and others like them risked their reputations and sometimes even their lives, for their findings were at odds with important social beliefs of the time. But their challenge to ideas held dearly by their societies tells us something else about science: there are no areas so sacred that science cannot explore them. Any question that can be answered by the scientific method is, in principle, an appropriate subject for scientific inquiry—even if the investigation and the findings outrage powerful interests or undermine cherished values. Yet science is not arrogant: it recognizes no ultimate, final truths. All scientific knowledge is provisional. The body of scientific knowledge at any particular moment represents nothing more than the most logical interpretations of the existing data. It is always possible that new facts will come to light or that the available data will be reinterpreted in a new way, shattering the existing assumptions. Science therefore takes nothing for granted: everything is always open for further testing, reinterpretation, correction, and even refutation.

Sociology as a Science

Sociology uses the same general methods of investigation as all sciences. Social life does not consist of a series of random events. Under most conditions society and its processes are ordered and patterned, so that reasonably reliable generalizations are possible. Like natural scientists, sociologists construct theories, collect and analyze data, conduct experiments and make observations, keep careful records, and attempt to arrive at precise and accurate conclusions.

The Scientific Status of Sociology

Like the other social sciences, however, sociology is relatively less advanced as a discipline than most of the natural sciences. There are two reasons for this. First, the scientific method has been applied to the study of social behavior only in recent times, whereas the scientific method has been applied to the natural world for centuries. Second, the study of human behavior presents many problems that natural scientists do not have to confront. Sociologists are dealing with people: in other words, with subjects who are conscious, self-aware, and capable of changing their behavior when they choose to. Unlike rocks or molecules, people may be uncooperative. They may behave in unforeseen ways for private reasons of their own. They may radically change their behavior when they know they are being studied. They cannot be made the subject of experiments that affront their dignity or infringe on their basic human rights. And their behavior usually has extremely complex causes that may be difficult to pinpoint. We will explore these problems more fully in Chapter 2 when we discuss how sociologists go about their research, but it is clear that the subject matter of sociology poses tricky problems that natural scientists do not have to face.

Although both natural and social scientists recognize on philosophic grounds that it may be impossible to prove that there are "universal laws" that apply to any thing or event in all circumstances, the natural sciences can generally offer more precise explanations and predictions than can sociologists. But sociology is still young. Its research methods are constantly being improved, and we can expect that they will achieve greater precision in the future.

Sociology, then, is not less "scientific" than biochemistry or astronomy: it simply faces greater problems of generalization, explanation, and prediction. Yet the suspicion persists in some quarters that sociology is not "really" a science. In part this is because the popular image of the scientist is often that of someone working in a laboratory in a white coat, something sociologists rarely do. But the origin of the suspicion probably lies deeper. Few people are experts in molecular biology or planetary motions, but all of us can consider ourselves experts on society, because everyone has years of experience of social living. Sociologists, it is suggested, merely state the obvious in complicated language, telling us virtually nothing that common sense does not tell us already.

It is true that the language of sociology is sometimes a little strange to the beginner. The sociologist uses a specialized vocabulary and often employs everyday words, such as "status," "role," and "culture," in precise but unfamiliar ways. Sociologists use a precise vocabulary for the same reason that all scientists must do so: unless terms have an agreed-upon, definite meaning, communication will be ambiguous and confusing, and findings will be difficult to verify. We do not expect a chemist to say, "I took some white crystals, mixed in a bit of black powder, chucked in some yellow stuff, threw in a match, and blew the place up." Unless the chemist tells us that he or she was using potassium chlorate, carbon, and sulfur in specific quantities under particular conditions, the information is useless.

Similarly, it is not enough for a sociologist to say, "I showed this violent movie to some kids, and afterward they started acting much rougher than before." We need to know what is meant by "violent": what sort of violence, in what context, involving what kind of people? We need to know about the "kids": how old, what sex, what background? We need to know what is meant by "rougher than before": what is "roughness," how is it measured, how rough were they, in what ways, under what circumstances, for how long afterward, and toward whom? Only when the experiment is described with precision does it have any value as science, for it can then be repeated by other scientists to test and confirm the original findings. The need for precision means that, as a general rule, sociological writing will not have you chewing your fingernails in suspense or guffawing out of your armchair at an author's wit and humor—but you will find sociological writing interesting to read.

Sociology and Common Sense

But does sociology merely state the obvious by reporting what common sense already tells us? Here are some widely held common sense views about society and social behavior. As you read through them, you might like to check them off as true or false.

1. Human beings have a natural instinct to mate with the opposite sex. (T/F)
2. Lower-class youths are more likely to commit crimes than middle-class youths. (T/F)
3. On average, high-income people in the United States pay a greater proportion of their income in taxes than low-income people. (T/F)
4. Revolutions are more likely to occur when conditions remain very bad than when previously bad conditions are rapidly improving. (T/F)
5. Exposure to pornography has a detrimental effect on the moral character, sexual orientation, and attitudes of young people. (T/F)
6. The amount of money that is spent on a school's equipment and facilities is a strong determinant of the academic success of its pupils. (T/F)
7. A substantial proportion of people on welfare could work if they really wanted to. (T/F)
8. One thing that is found in every society is the romantic love between a boy and a girl. (T/F)
9. People who are regular Christian churchgoers are less likely to be prejudiced against other races than people who do not attend church. (T/F)
10. The best way to get an accurate assessment of public opinion is to ask as many people as possible. (T/F)

All these assumptions may seem to be in accord with common sense, but sociological research has shown that every single one of them is false.

Human beings do not have an instinct to mate with the opposite sex; our sexual preferences are entirely learned (Chapter 9). In fact, if an instinct is defined as a complex inherited behavior pattern, human beings do not have any instincts at all (Chapters 3 and 5). Lower-class youths are not more likely than middle-class youths to commit crimes. If anything, middle-class youths engage in more delinquent acts, but they are less likely to be arrested and therefore do not show up in court statistics (Chapter 8). High-income people pay roughly the same proportion of their income in direct and indirect taxes as low-income people do. The reasons are that the rich can use many tax loopholes and that sales and other indirect taxes take a relatively larger percentage of a poor person's earnings (Chapter 11). Revolutions are actually more likely to occur when conditions have been bad but are rapidly improving. When conditions are bad and stay bad, people take their misfortune for granted, but when conditions suddenly improve, people develop higher aspirations and become easily frustrated (Chapter 19). On the basis of a large number of studies, a presidential commission found that pornography does not have a detrimental effect on young people's moral character, sexual orientation, or attitudes (Chapter 9). The amount of money spent on a school's facilities seems to have little influence on pupil achievement. Their performance is primarily related to their family and social class background (Chapter 15). Less than 2 percent of the people on welfare are adult males who have been out of work for several months. Nearly all welfare recipients are children, old people, handicapped people, or mothers who have to stay at home to look after their families and have no other source of income (Chapter 11). Romantic love may seem a part of "human nature" to us, but in many societies it is unknown and in many others it is regarded as ridiculous or tragic (Chapter 14). Regular churchgoers are generally not less racially prejudiced than nonchurchgoers; in fact, they tend to be more prejudiced (Chapter 16). And the number of people involved in an opinion poll is largely irrelevant. What matters is that the sample should be fully representative of the population whose opinion is wanted. A properly chosen sample of two or three thousand Americans can give a highly accurate test of national opinion; a poorly chosen sample of 3 million could be hopelessly off target (Chapter 2).

Sometimes sociological findings confirm the common sense view; sometimes they do not. The only way to test common sense assumptions about society is to do it scientifically. This does not mean that there is no place for intuition or common sense in sociology. These approaches are a rich source of insights. But they can provide only hunches. The hunch must be tested by the methods of science.

The Social Sciences

We have already referred to the social sciences, a related group of disciplines that study various aspects of human behavior. The social sciences are sociology, economics, psychology, political science, and anthropology. Of course, human behavior does not come in such neat compartments, and in practice the boundaries between the social sciences are vague and constantly shifting. Each of the disciplines has different historical origins, and the distinctions between them have since been preserved largely as a matter of convenience. Nobody could possibly be an expert in all of them, and the fragmentation of the social sciences permits specialization. But social scientists realize how much the concerns of the various disciplines overlap, and they freely "invade" each other's territory whenever it seems useful to do so.

Economics

Economics studies the production, distribution, and consumption of goods and services. Economists examine, for example, how prices are determined or what effects taxes will have. Economics is in many ways the most advanced of the social sciences. Its subject matter is often more easily measured than that of the other disciplines, and economists have developed extremely sophisticated mathematical tools for their explanations and predictions. But the economy is also a part of society: goods and services do not produce, distribute, and consume themselves. These social aspects of economic life are the subject of the sociology of economics.

Psychology

Psychology studies human mental processes, such as emotion, memory, perception, and intelligence. This discipline, more than any other social science, focuses on the individual. Partly because it has its roots in natural sciences such as biology, it also relies more heavily on laboratory and clinical experiments. Psychology shares one major field of interest with sociology: *social psychology,* the study of how personality and behavior are influenced by the social context. Social psychology is a genuine hybrid discipline. In many colleges and universities, in fact, it is taught in sociology rather than in psychology departments.

Political Science

Political science has traditionally focused on two main areas: political philosophy and actual forms of government, with special emphasis on how the two are related. In recent years, however, the discipline has been strongly influenced by political sociology, which analyzes political behavior and studies the social interaction involved in the process of government. Political scientists are now asking more "sociological" questions, such as why people vote the way they do, why some people are more likely to take part in politics than others, or what happens "behind the scenes" in the informal manipulation of power. Sociological research, too, is increasingly used in shaping government policies. The interests of political scientists and political sociologists have been gradually converging and in many instances they now overlap.

Anthropology

Anthropology is sociology's sister discipline. It differs from sociology mainly in that it usually focuses on entire, small-scale, "primitive" societies, whereas sociology concentrates more on group processes within large modern industrial societies. Anthropology has several branches: archaeology, which deals with the remains of extinct civilizations; linguistics, which deals with certain aspects of language; physical anthropology, which deals with human evolution; and *cultural anthropology*, which studies the ways of life of other peoples. A study made by a cultural anthropologist is called an *ethnography,* and sociologists often find ethnographic evidence useful when they want to compare modern societies with other societies that have very different ways of life. Cultural anthropology and sociology have many concepts in common and are steadily converging. Now that "primitive" societies are rapidly becoming extinct, many cultural anthropologists are studying groups in modern industrial societies. Sociologists and cultural anthropologists now draw freely on one another's work.

In this book we will draw on findings from the other social sciences whenever this would be helpful for the understanding of social behavior. We will place particular emphasis on information from social psychology and cultural anthropology. The research of social psychologists often throws light on the ways in which the social environment influences behavior, and the ethnographies of cultural anthropologists enable us to highlight aspects of our own society by comparing our practices with those of other peoples.

The Development of Sociology

Sociology began to emerge as a separate discipline only around the middle of the nineteenth century, and it took another fifty years before the subject began to assume the scientific character that it has today. Before the mid-1800s the study of society was the domain of social philosophers, thinkers who were often less concerned about what society actually *is* like than what they thought it *ought* to be like. Yet in a relatively short period this entire emphasis was reversed.

The Origins

Sociology emerged in the context of the sweeping changes that the Industrial Revolution brought to Europe. No social changes in history had been as widespread or as far-reaching, and this transformation—which is still taking place in the less developed nations of the world—cried for analysis and explanation.

Industrialization threw into turmoil societies that had been relatively stable for centuries. New industries and technologies changed the face of the social and physical environment. Peasants left rural areas and flocked to the towns, where they worked as industrial laborers under appalling conditions. Cities grew at an unprecedented rate, providing an anonymous environment in which the customs and values of the small, tight-knit traditional community could scarcely survive. Social problems became rampant in the teeming cities. The ancient view that the social order was preordained by God began to collapse. Aristocracies and monarchies crumbled and fell. Religion began to lose its force as an unquestioned source of moral authority. For the first time in history, rapid social change became the normal rather than an abnormal state of affairs, and people could no longer expect that their children would live much the same lives as they had done. The direction of change was unclear, and the stability of the social order seemed threatened. An understanding of what was happening was urgently needed.

Figure 1.3 Sociology emerged as a separate discipline during the early stages of the Industrial Revolution, when traditional societies were suddenly thrust into an era of rapid social change and unprecedented social problems. Sociology was born out of the attempt to understand the transformations that seemed to threaten the stability of European society.

Two other factors operating at the time also encouraged the development of sociology. One was the example of the natural sciences—if their methods could make so much sense of the physical world, could they not be applied successfully to the social world as well? The second factor was the exposure of Europe to the radically dif-

Figure 1.4 Auguste Comte

Figure 1.5 Herbert Spencer

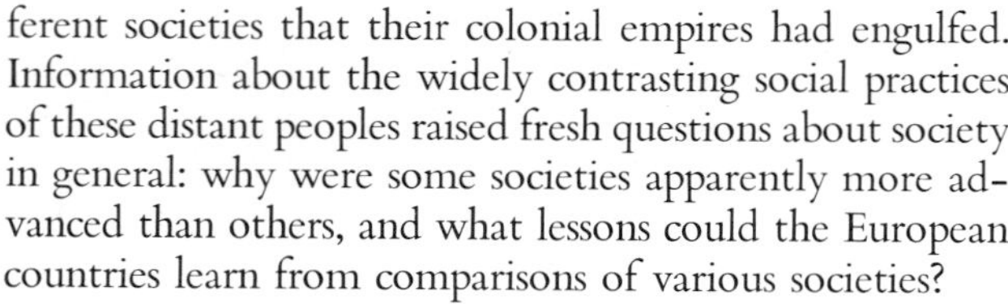

ferent societies that their colonial empires had engulfed. Information about the widely contrasting social practices of these distant peoples raised fresh questions about society in general: why were some societies apparently more advanced than others, and what lessons could the European countries learn from comparisons of various societies?

Early Sociologists

The title "father of sociology" usually goes to Auguste Comte (1789–1857), a French thinker who first coined the term "sociology" and who argued, in 1838, that the methods of science should be applied to the study of society. Comte saw sociologists as a "priesthood of humanity," experts who would not only explain social events but who would also guide society in the direction of greater progress. He also established two specific problems for sociological investigation, social statics and social dynamics. *Social statics* refers to the problem of order and stability—how and why do societies hold together and endure? *Social dynamics* refers to the problem of social change—what makes societies change and what determines the nature and direction of the changes? Sociologists have wrestled with these problems ever since.

Herbert Spencer

Another important nineteenth-century figure was Herbert Spencer (1820–1903), who took up the problems of social statics and dynamics and believed he had found the answer. Spencer compared human societies to living organisms. The organs of an animal are interdependent and contribute to the survival of the total organism. Similarly, Spencer argued, the various parts of society, such as the state and the economy, are also interdependent and work to ensure the stability and survival of the entire system. This theory took care of the problem of statics. To explain dynamics, Spencer pushed his analogy even further. Applying Darwin's theory of evolution to human societies, he argued that they gradually evolve from the forms found in the "primitive" societies of the world to the more complex forms found in the industrializing societies of his own time. Spencer believed that evolution meant progress, and he strongly opposed attempts at social reform on the grounds that they might interfere with a natural evolutionary process. Many of Spencer's ideas have become outmoded and seem rather strange today, but they remain influential in a very modified form. Many sociologists still see society as a more or less harmonious system whose various parts contribute to overall stability. Many also

Figure 1.6 Karl Marx

Figure 1.7 Emile Durkheim

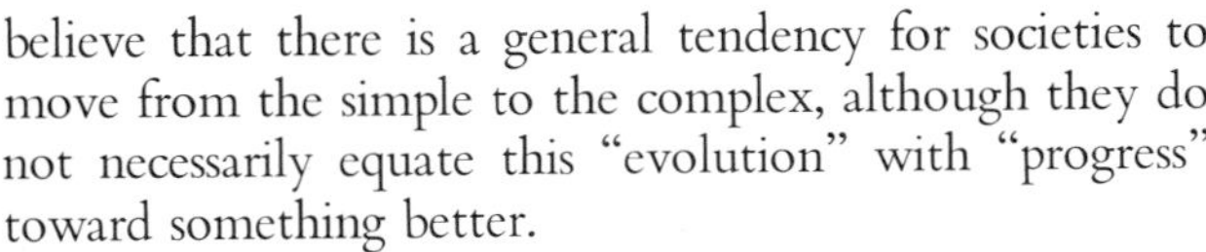

believe that there is a general tendency for societies to move from the simple to the complex, although they do not necessarily equate this "evolution" with "progress" toward something better.

Karl Marx

The third and most important of the nineteenth-century thinkers was Karl Marx (1818–1883). Marx was born in Germany, but after being expelled from various countries for his revolutionary activities, he eventually settled in England. An erratic genius, he wrote brilliantly on subjects as broad and diverse as philosophy, economics, political science, and history. He did not think of himself as a sociologist, but his work is so rich in sociological insights that he is now regarded as one of the most profound and original sociological thinkers. His influence has been immense. Millions of people accept his theories with almost religious fervor, and modern socialist and communist movements owe their inspiration directly to him. It is important to realize, however, that Marxism is not the same as communism. Marx would probably be dismayed at many of the practices of communist movements, and he cannot be held responsible for policies pursued in his name decades after his death.

To Marx, the task of the social scientist was not merely to describe the world: it was to change it. Whereas Spencer saw social harmony and the inevitability of progress, Marx saw social conflict and the inevitability of revolution. The key to history, he believed, is *class conflict*—the bitter struggle between those who own the means of producing wealth and those who do not, a struggle that would end only with the overthrow of the ruling exploiters and the establishment of a free, humane, classless society. Marx placed special emphasis on the economic base of society. He argued that the character of virtually all other social arrangements is determined by the way goods are produced and by the relationships that exist between those who work to produce them and those who live off the production of others. Modern sociologists, including many who reject other aspects of Marx's theories, generally recognize the fundamental influence of the economy on other areas of society.

Emile Durkheim

The French sociologist Emile Durkheim (1858–1917) has strongly influenced the discipline. Durkheim dealt with the problem of social order, arguing that societies are held together by the shared beliefs and values of their members,

Figure 1.8 Max Weber

Figure 1.9 George Herbert Mead

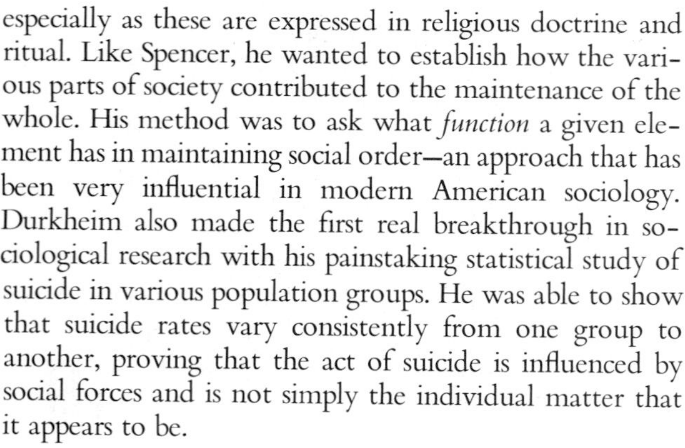

especially as these are expressed in religious doctrine and ritual. Like Spencer, he wanted to establish how the various parts of society contributed to the maintenance of the whole. His method was to ask what *function* a given element has in maintaining social order—an approach that has been very influential in modern American sociology. Durkheim also made the first real breakthrough in sociological research with his painstaking statistical study of suicide in various population groups. He was able to show that suicide rates vary consistently from one group to another, proving that the act of suicide is influenced by social forces and is not simply the individual matter that it appears to be.

Max Weber

The German sociologist Max Weber (1864–1920), a contemporary of Durkheim, has perhaps had a stronger influence on Western sociology than any other single individual. He was a man of prodigious learning whose sociological investigations covered such diverse fields as law, economics, music, cities, and the major world religions. Throughout his adult life Weber felt a great tension between his role as a scholar, dispassionately observing society, and his desire to influence events through political leadership. This tension may have contributed to a severe mental breakdown that incapacitated him for several years of his academic career. Weber remains an enigmatic and somewhat melancholy figure in sociological history. He viewed the direction of social change in industrial societies with distaste, feeling that the world was being "disenchanted" by the cold rationality of petty experts who knew no value other than efficiency.

Much of Weber's work can be seen as "a debate with the ghost of Karl Marx." Although he deeply admired much of Marx's work, Weber took issue with him on several points. He regarded moves toward greater social equality as inevitable, but he did not particularly welcome them, because he foresaw that such moves would involve an increase in the power of the state over the individual. Weber did not believe that social change could always be directly traced to changes in the economy, as Marx had implied. He suggested that other factors, such as religious ideas, could also play an independent role. Perhaps most important, Weber believed that sociologists should be *value-free* in their work—that is, personal convictions or biases should never creep into sociological research or conclusions. His stance in this respect was quite unlike that of Marx.

Figure 1.10 Talcott Parsons

Figure 1.11 Robert Merton

Modern Developments

The major development of sociology in this century has taken place in the United States, where the discipline has sunk roots far deeper than in any other country. Lester Ward (1841–1913) repeated Comte's call for social progress guided by sociological knowledge, and under his influence the discipline rapidly became committed to social reform. William Graham Sumner (1840–1910) studied the minute aspects of daily life found in the ordinary customs of the people. Under the influence of these men, American sociologists lost most of their interest in the larger problems of social order and social change and concentrated instead on the study of smaller and more specific problems.

Until about 1940 the University of Chicago's sociology department dominated the discipline in the United States. Sociologists such as George Herbert Mead developed the new discipline of social psychology, and others such as Robert E. Park and Ernest Burgess turned their attention to social problems and the lives of criminals, drug addicts, prostitutes, and juvenile delinquents. Many of the "Chicago School" sociologists were Protestant ministers or the sons of Protestant ministers, and under their leadership sociology became strongly identified with social reform.

Figure 1.12 C. Wright Mills

From the forties until the early sixties, the center of attention shifted from Chicago to such universities as Harvard, Columbia, Michigan, and Wisconsin, and from reform to the much more neutral field of theory building. Talcott Parsons influenced a generation of American sociologists, such as Kingsley Davis and Robert Merton, with his highly abstract models of society as a fairly stable, harmonious system of functionally interrelated parts. Other sociologists concentrated on perfecting research methods and statistical techniques, and the earlier activist strain in the discipline was almost lost. C. Wright Mills, a vociferous critic of this trend, seemed to be crying in the wilderness. The social turmoil of the sixties, however, encouraged a revival of the activist tradition in American sociology.

The question of whether the sociologist should remain detached and value-free or activist and committed is still controversial. Some sociologists take the view that the science should be "ethically neutral," that it should attempt only to understand social processes and add to the sum of scientific knowledge. Others take a more activist position, arguing that sociological knowledge should be used to criticize and reform existing social arrangements. The latter view seems to have won increasing support in recent years. One survey of American sociologists found that over 70 percent felt that one part of the sociologist's role is to be a critic of society and acknowledged that they were not always value-free in their own work (Gouldner and Sprehe, 1965).

Theoretical Perspectives

A crucial element in sociology, as in all science, is theory. A *theory* is a statement that organizes a set of concepts in a meaningful way by explaining the relationship between them. If the theory is valid, it will correctly predict that identical relationships will occur in the future if the conditions are identical. Although it is sometimes thought that "the facts speak for themselves," facts do nothing of the kind. They are silent. They have no meaning until we give meaning to them, and that meaning is given by theory.

We are often prone to poke fun at "theorists" and to regard more highly the "practical" person. But theory and practice cannot be separated; virtually every practical decision you make and every practical opinion you hold has some theory lying behind it. A person may reject the views of prison reformers as being mere "theory" and may prefer the "practical" approach that criminals should be severely punished in order to discourage crime. But this practical approach is based on theory—on the theory that people can exercise a choice over whether to commit a crime or not, on the theory that people try to avoid punishment, on the theory that the most severe punishments make the best deterrents to crime. Even the most practical gadgets of everyday life, from can openers to automobiles, could not be constructed or used without some theory of how they operate. Theory is not an intellectual luxury practiced only by academics in their ivory towers, aloof from the real world.

Theory makes the facts of social life comprehensible. It places meaningless events in a general framework that enables us to determine cause and effect, to explain, and to predict. Sociological theories vary greatly in their scope and sophistication. Some attempt to explain only a small aspect of reality (such as why some people become heroin addicts). Others are more sweeping and confront large-scale, societal problems (such as those of social order and social change). The leading figures in the early development of sociology, including Spencer, Marx, Durkheim, and Weber, offered grand theories of the latter type. Later sociologists, with the notable exception of Talcott Parsons, have generally felt that such attempts involve biting off more than one can chew and have concentrated instead on narrower theories aimed at explaining more specific social issues.

Despite this preference for more limited theories, most sociologists are guided in their work by major *theoretical perspectives*—broad assumptions about society and social behavior that provide a point of view for the study of specific problems. There are three of these general perspectives in modern sociology, and you will meet them repeatedly throughout this book. They are the functionalist, the conflict, and the interactionist perspectives. Let's look at each in turn.

The Functionalist Perspective

The *functionalist perspective* draws its original inspiration from the work of Herbert Spencer and Emile Durkheim.

As we have seen, Spencer compared societies to living organisms. Any organism has a *structure*—that is, it consists of a number of interrelated parts, such as a head, limbs, a heart, and so on. Each of these parts has a *function* to play in the life of the total organism. In the same way, Spencer argued, a society has a structure—it also consists of interrelated parts, such as the family, religion, the state, and so on. Ideally, each of these components also has a function that contributes to the overall stability of the social system. Modern structural-functionalism (usually called "functionalism") does not press the analogy between a society and an organism. But it does retain the same general idea of society as a system of interrelated parts. Functionalism in modern American sociology is associated particularly with the work of Talcott Parsons (1951) and Robert Merton (1968).

The Social System

Functionalist theory implies that society tends to be an organized, stable, well-integrated system, in which most members agree on basic values. Under normal conditions all the elements in the social system—such as the schools, the family, or the state—tend to "fit together," with each element making a contribution to overall societal stability. The family, for example, *functions* to regulate sexual behavior, to transmit social values to children, and to take care of young and aged people who could not otherwise survive.

In the functionalist view, a society has an underlying tendency to be in equilibrium, or balance. Social change is therefore likely to be disruptive unless it takes place relatively slowly, because changes in one part of the system usually provoke changes elsewhere in the system. If the economy, for example, requires an increasing number of highly trained workers, the schools and colleges will adapt their policies and practices to supply them, and the state will pour more money into education. But if the economy expands so rapidly that the other elements in the social system cannot "catch up," social disequilibrium will result.

Functions and Dysfunctions

How does one determine what the functions of a given element in the social system are? Essentially, the sociologist asks what its *consequences* are—not what its *purposes* are

Figure 1.13 The functionalist perspective focuses on the functions, or consequences, that a given element has in society. Economic activity, for example, functions to provide the goods and services on which our society depends for its existence. It also gives people roles in life, enabling them to earn a living and to draw a sense of identity from the work that they do. These functions contribute to the stability of the social system as a whole.

believed to be. The supposed purposes of some component in the social system do not necessarily tell us what its functions are, because that component can have consequences other than those that were intended. Robert Merton (1968) distinguishes between *manifest functions*—those that are obvious and intended—and *latent functions*—those that are unrecognized and unintended. The schools, for example, have the manifest function of teaching literacy and other skills that are essential if a modern industrial society is to survive. But they also have latent functions that are not intended or generally recognized. For example, they keep children in an industrial society occupied, in the way that farm work kept them occupied in an earlier agricultural society. In the same way, the welfare system has the manifest function of preventing the poor from starving, but it also has the latent function of averting the civil disorder that might result if millions of people had no source of income.

Merton also points out that not all elements in the social system are functional at all times: on occasion some element may actually disrupt the social equilibrium and may therefore be *dysfunctional.* The high birth rate in the less developed countries of the world, for example, is very dysfunctional for those societies because it has created a serious problem of overpopulation. Sometimes an element in the social order can be functional in one respect and dysfunctional in another. American industry, for example, has the manifest function of providing the goods on which our way of life depends, but it also has the latent function of polluting the environment and is therefore dysfunctional in this sense. The full implications of any element in the social system therefore have to be carefully explored.

A sociologist who uses the functionalist perspective, then, is likely to ask specific kinds of questions: what are the consequences of the feature being studied and what effects, positive or negative, does it have on the social system as a whole? This perspective is obviously useful in explaining why some elements in a society exist and persist, but it also has some disadvantages. An important criticism of the perspective is that it tends in practice to be inherently conservative. Because their main emphasis is on social order and stability, functionalists risk the temptation of dismissing disruptive changes as dysfunctional, even if those changes are necessary, inevitable, and beneficial in the long run.

The Conflict Perspective

The *conflict perspective* in modern sociology derives its inspiration from the work of Karl Marx, who saw the struggle between social classes as the "engine" of history and the main source of social change. Although the conflict perspective has dominated Western European sociology ever since, it was largely neglected in American sociology until the sixties. The social and political turmoil of the sixties was more readily analyzed through the conflict than the functionalist perspective, and conflict theory has been popular among American sociologists since that time. Modern conflict theory, which is associated with such sociologists as C. Wright Mills (1956) and Lewis Coser (1956), does not simply focus, as Marx did, on class conflict; it sees conflict between many other groups and interests as a fact of life in any society. These conflicts may involve, for example, the old versus the young, producers versus consumers, urbanites versus suburbanites, or one racial or ethnic group against another.

Conflict and Change

The assumptions of the conflict perspective are different from those of the functionalist perspective. Conflict theorists assume that societies are in a constant state of change, in which conflict is a permanent feature. "Conflict" does not necessarily imply outright violence; it includes tension, hostility, competition, and disagreement over goals and values. This conflict is not an occasional event that disrupts the generally smooth workings of society: it is a constant process and is an inevitable part of social life. The things that people desire—such as power, wealth, and prestige—are always scarce, and the demand for them exceeds the supply. Those who gain control of these things are able to protect their own interests at other people's expense. The general consensus on values that the functionalists see is regarded by conflict theorists as a fiction: what actually happens is that those who have power are able to enforce compliance from everyone else.

Conflict theorists do not see social conflict as a necessarily destructive force, although they admit that it may sometimes have that effect. They argue that conflict can often have positive results. It binds groups together as they pursue their own interests, and the conflict between competing groups focuses attention on social problems and

Figure 1.14 The conflict perspective focuses on tensions, disagreements, and competition in society. Conflict is assumed to be a permanent and inevitable aspect of social life and an important source of change. Conflict over the place of women in American society, for example, has led to significant changes in our traditional sex roles.

leads to beneficial changes that might otherwise not have occurred. In this way social movements—such as those for civil rights or women's liberation—become an important source of change. The changes caused by social conflict prevent society from lapsing into stagnation.

Who Benefits?

The conflict perspective, then, also invites the sociologist to ask specific kinds of questions: whose interests are involved and who benefits or suffers from existing social arrangements? In analyzing social inequality, for example, conflict theorists would argue that this inequality exists not because it is functional for society as a whole but because some people have been able to achieve political and economic power and have managed to pass on these advantages to their descendants. In the same way, conflict theorists would not see environmental pollution as a "latent dysfunction" of industrialism. Instead, they would point to the fact that powerful corporate interests make their profits from manufacturing processes that pollute the environment. Tobacco, an addictive drug that has been conclusively linked to lung cancer, is freely marketed in the United States, but the use of marijuana, which on present evidence does not seem to be physically harmful, is illegal. Why? A conflict perspective would point out that wealthy and influential interests benefit by manufacturing and marketing tobacco, while marijuana use is largely confined to the young and the powerless. As marijuana usage spreads to more influential groups in society, and as large corporations become interested in marketing the drug themselves, pressures to legalize the use of marijuana in the United States are likely to increase. Social change, in this area as in others, is influenced by the shifting relationships and interests of competing groups.

A modern society contains a wide spectrum of opinions, occupations, life-styles, and social groups. On any social issue there are some people who stand to gain and some who stand to lose. Social processes cannot be fully understood without referring to this conflict of interest, a conflict whose outcome always favors the stronger party. To understand many features of our own society, then, we must pay particular attention to the values and interests of those who exercise power—primarily people who are white, middle-aged, Protestant, wealthy, male, and of Anglo-Saxon background.

The conflict perspective has the advantage of highlighting aspects of society that the functionalist perspective, with its emphasis on consensus and stability, tends to ignore. But this fact also suggests an important criticism of the conflict perspective. By focusing so narrowly on issues of competition and change, it fails to come to grips with the more orderly, stable, and less politically controversial aspects of social reality.

The Interactionist Perspective

The *interactionist perspective* in sociology was initially influenced by Max Weber, who emphasized the importance of understanding the social world from the viewpoint of the individuals who act within it. Later developments in interactionist theory have been strongly influenced by social psychology and by the work of early leaders in the Chicago School of sociology, particularly George Herbert Mead. The important difference between this perspective and the two we have considered is that it does not focus on such large structures as the state, the economy, or social classes. Instead, it is concerned primarily with the everyday social interaction that takes place as people go about their daily lives.

Interaction: The Basis of Social Life

Interactionist theorists are often wary of the emphasis that other sociologists place on the major components of society and on such large-scale issues as social order and social change. Concepts such as "the economy" or "the state" are, after all, merely abstractions; they cannot exist or act by themselves. It is people that exist and act, and it is only through their social behavior that society can come into being at all. Society is ultimately created, maintained, and changed by the social interaction of its members.

The interactionist perspective is a broad one, containing a number of loosely linked approaches. Erving Goffman (1959), for example, takes a "dramaturgical" approach to social interaction. In other words, he sees social life as a form of theater, in which people play different parts and "stage-manage" their lives and the impressions they create on others. George Homans (1961) takes an "exchange" approach. He focuses on the way people control one another's behavior by exchanging various forms of rewards and punishments for approved or disapproved behavior. Harold Garfinkel (1967) adopts what he calls an "ethnomethodological" approach. This formidable term simply implies an attempt to scrape below the surface of social behavior to find out how people themselves understand the routines of daily life. The most widely used approach is that of "symbolic interaction" (Mead, 1934; Blumer, 1969), and this is the one that we shall emphasize here and elsewhere in this book.

Figure 1.15 The interactionist perspective focuses on social behavior in everyday life. It tries to understand how people create and interpret the situations they experience, and it emphasizes how countless instances of social interaction produce the larger structures of society—government, the economy, and other institutions.

Symbolic Interaction

Symbolic interaction is the interaction that takes place between people through symbols—such as signs, gestures, shared rules, and, most important, written and spoken language. Much of this interaction takes place on a face-to-face basis, but it can also occur in other forms: symbolic interaction is taking place between you and the author as you read this sentence, and it occurs whenever you obey (or disobey) a traffic signal or a no-trespassing notice. The essential point is that people do not respond to the world directly: they place a social meaning on it and respond to that meaning. The words of this book, the red light of a traffic signal, or a wolf whistle in the street have no meaning in themselves. People learn to attach symbolic meaning to these things, and they order their lives on the basis of these meanings. We live in a symbolic as well as in a physical world, and our social life involves a constant process of interpreting the meanings of our own acts and those of others.

The interactionist perspective, then, also invites the sociologist to ask specific kinds of questions: what kinds of interaction are taking place between people, how do they understand and interpret what is happening to them, and why do they act toward others as they do? Sociologists using this perspective usually focus on the more minute, personal aspects of everyday life. By what process, for example, does someone become a prostitute? Why is it that strangers in elevators so scrupulously avoid eye contact with each other, staring anywhere—at their shoes, at the ceiling, at the nearest wall—rather than directly into another passenger's face? How does someone learn to experience marijuana smoking as pleasurable? What unspoken tactics are used by a male doctor and a female patient to minimize embarrassment during a pelvic examination? What processes are involved in group decision making? What happens, and why, if you stand too close to someone during a conversation?

The interactionist perspective provides a fascinating insight into the basic mechanics of everyday life, and it has the advantage of revealing fundamental social processes that other perspectives easily ignore. But the perspective is open to the important criticism that it neglects larger social institutions and societal processes of stability and change—institutions and processes which, after all, have powerful effects on social interaction and on our personal experience.

An Evaluation

Each of these perspectives starts from different assumptions, each leads the investigator to ask different kinds of questions, and each viewpoint is therefore likely to produce different types of conclusions. In many respects the theories seem quite contradictory. But this does not mean that one of them is "better" than the others, or even that they are always incompatible. The reason is that each perspective focuses on a different aspect of reality: functionalism, primarily on social order and stability; conflict theory, primarily on social tension and change; and interactionism, primarily on the ordinary experiences of everyday life. Each of the perspectives has a part to play in the analysis of society. In fact, there is nothing unusual in a scientist's using apparently incompatible theories to study the same subject. Physicists sometimes find it useful to regard light as a continuous wave and sometimes as a series of particles, and they gain a better understanding of the nature of light than would be possible from taking one viewpoint alone.

Thus all three perspectives could be applied, for example, to the study of education, although each would focus on a different aspect of the institution. A functionalist approach would emphasize the functions that education plays in maintaining the social system as a whole. It would point out how education provides the young with the skills they need in later life, how it sorts and selects people for different kinds of jobs, how it transmits cultural values from one generation to the next, and even how it keeps millions of young people off the streets and out of trouble. A conflict approach would emphasize that education is believed to be an important avenue to social and financial success in life. It would point out how social class background affects a pupil's academic achievement, how more resources are channeled to the schools of the wealthy than to those of the poor, and how education is used by different groups jockeying for competitive advantage. An interactionist approach would emphasize the daily activities within the school. It would point to the forms of interaction between teachers and pupils, the influence of

Figure 1.16 People's views of the world are largely shaped by their own experience of it. Their age, race, sex, nationality, social class, and personal histories all affect their values, attitudes, and interpretations of reality. These two groups of Americans, each from different walks of life, probably interpret many social issues in different ways.

the student peer group over its individual members, or the ways in which the school rules are broken or followed. None of these approaches gives answers that are any more "true" than the other, and taken together they provide a broader and deeper understanding of the entire institution of education.

In this book you will encounter all three perspectives. The interactionist perspective will be used particularly in the discussion of "micro" (small-scale) processes, the functionalist and conflict perspectives in the discussion of "macro" (large-scale) processes. Sometimes the perspectives will contradict each other. When this happens we will evaluate their respective merits. At other times they will complement each other, giving a fuller and richer understanding of the subject.

Some sociologists, however, argue forcefully that one or another of the perspectives gives a generally superior understanding than the others. These sociologists systematically try to apply their chosen perspective to all or most problems. No such approach is adopted here—not just because the author does not accept that any one perspective is always the most useful, but because it would be a disservice to the introductory student to offer only one viewpoint.

The Problem of Objectivity

We have seen that people in different walks of life may interpret the same phenomenon—whether it is a house, a riot, a president's conduct in office, or fashions of long hair and short skirts—in very different ways. In other words, people tend to see the world from a *subjective* viewpoint, one that is based on their own opinions, attitudes, and experiences. We have also seen that sociologists themselves can adopt varying perspectives on the same problem and can come to different and even contrasting conclusions as a result. This fact raises a very important issue: is an *objective* understanding of society possible? In other words, is there any way of interpreting the facts in such a way that personal judgments are eliminated?

If the world consisted simply of some self-evident reality that everyone perceived in exactly the same way, there might be no disagreement among observers. But the truth

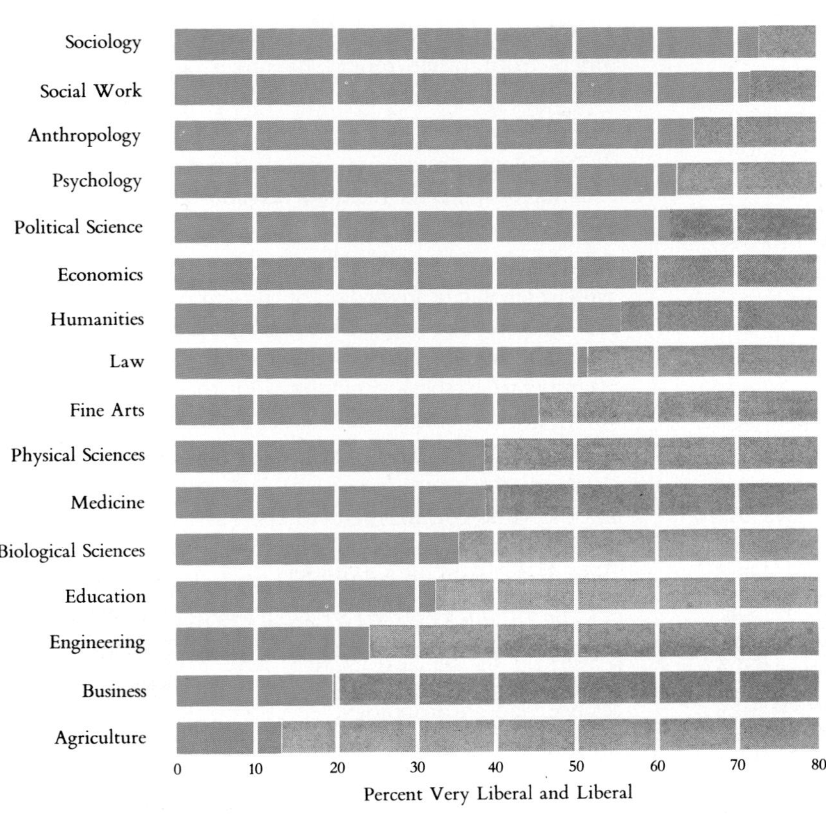

Source: Adapted from Seymour Martin Lipset and Everett Carll Ladd, Jr., "The Politics of American Sociologists," *American Journal of Sociology*, 78 (1972), p. 71, Table 2.

Figure 1.17 American sociologists are more liberal in their political outlooks than scholars in any other discipline. These findings are drawn from an extensive survey of college faculty in 1969.

of the matter is that what we see in the world is not determined by what exists "out there." It is determined by what our past experience has prepared us to see and by what we consciously or unconsciously want to see. Knowledge and belief about the world do not exist in a vacuum; they are social products whose content depends on the social context in which they are produced. A black in an urban ghetto will see American race relations in one way; a Ku Klux Klan member, in another way; a white liberal college student, in yet another. Each is inclined to perceive facts selectively and to interpret them in particular ways.

The same is inevitably true of sociologists, whose outlook on the world is also influenced by their background, training, and prior experiences. Most American sociologists are well-educated, urban, white, middle class, and male, and they naturally interpret reality differently from people who do not share these characteristics. Their background and interests, for example, make sociologists overwhelmingly liberal in political orientation: as Figure 1.17 shows, sociologists are more liberal than scholars in any other discipline. Inevitably, then, sociologists, like anyone else, will be guilty of some measure of *bias*—the tendency, often unconscious, to interpret facts in ways that are influenced by subjective values and attitudes. This problem occurs in all sciences, but it becomes particularly acute in the social sciences, whose subject matter often involves issues of deep moral and human concern. How can the problem be resolved?

The first step is to recognize that subjectivity and objectivity are not two neat and separate categories; they are really matters of degree. By exercising scrupulous caution the sociologist can attempt to be as objective as possible. This caution involves a deliberate effort to be conscious of one's own biases so that they can be kept out of the process of research and interpretation. The ethical code of the discipline requires that sociologists be intellectually honest—that they attempt to be aware of their own values, that they not allow these values to distort their work, that they relentlessly hunt down the relevant facts and not ignore those that are inconvenient for their pet theories, that they not manipulate data to prove a point, and that they not use research to suppress or misuse knowledge. Moreover, the sociological community does not have to rely entirely on the integrity of the individual to ensure that objectivity is strived for. The community has its own elaborate procedures for pursuing the same goal. When sociological research is published it becomes available for the critical scrutiny of the entire community. Other sociologists can assess the findings and attempt to verify them by repeating the research to see if it yields the same results. This procedure provides an extremely effective check against gross distortions.

Since some bias is always unconscious, it can never be entirely avoided. But a self-conscious attempt to be as objective as possible will produce vastly less biased results than research that does not make this attempt. Total objectivity is probably impossible to achieve in any science. But if objectivity is defined as thought that is sufficiently disciplined to minimize the distortions caused by personal bias, then it is certainly possible. The pursuit of objectivity does not necessarily mean that sociologists should not express personal opinions, or *value judgments*. It means that these judgments should be clearly labeled as such and that they should not intrude into the actual process of research and interpretation. It would be perfectly legitimate, therefore, for a sociologist to give as objective an account as possible of a social problem, and then to add a personal, subjective judgment—provided that judgment was presented as a matter of personal opinion.

Summary

1. Sociology is the scientific study of human society; it differs from other modes of understanding the social world in that it relies on systematic observation of verifiable facts.

2. Sociology provides a unique perspective on society, enabling us to see the intimate relationships between social forces and individual experience.

3. Science refers to the logical, systematic methods by which reliable knowledge of the universe is obtained and also to the actual knowledge produced by these methods. Science assumes order in the universe, and it attempts to establish generalizations that can be used for the purposes of explanation and prediction.

4. The subject matter of sociology poses many problems that natural sciences do not face, but sociology nonetheless has the same commitment to the scientific method. Sociological explanations are therefore more reliable than those based only on common sense.

5. The social sciences are a related group of disciplines that study various aspects of human behavior. The main social sciences are sociology, economics, psychology, political science, and anthropology.

6. Sociology emerged in the middle of the nineteenth century, in the context of the changes caused by the Industrial Revolution.

7. Early sociologists, such as Comte, Spencer, Marx, Weber, and Durkheim, concentrated on problems of social order and social change. The subsequent development of sociology, which has taken place largely in the United States, has focused primarily on more restricted theories and studies and on the refinement of research techniques. Particularly since the sixties, there has been a major controversy over whether sociologists should be value-free or socially committed.

8. There are three major theoretical perspectives in modern sociology. The functionalist perspective focuses primarily on processes of order and stability; the conflict perspective, on processes of competition and change; the interactionist perspective, on processes of everyday social behavior. These three perspectives are not necessarily incompatible.

9. Complete objectivity is particularly difficult to achieve in the social sciences. By rigorously excluding personal biases and by submitting research findings to the criticism of the sociological community, however, sociologists can guard against subjective distortions and can reach a high degree of objectivity.

Important Terms

sociology	theoretical perspective
science	functionalist perspective
social sciences	structure
economics	function
psychology	manifest function
social psychology	latent function
political science	dysfunction
anthropology	conflict perspective
cultural anthropology	interactionist perspective
ethnography	symbolic interaction
social statics (order)	objectivity
social dynamics (change)	subjectivity
value freedom	value judgment
theory	

Suggested Readings

BART, PAULINE, AND LINDA FRANKEL. *The Student Sociologist's Handbook.* Cambridge, Mass.: Schenkman, 1971.

A useful and comprehensive guide to sociological literature and sources of information.

BATES, ALAN P. *The Sociological Enterprise.* Boston: Houghton Mifflin, 1967.

A clear discussion of sociology as both an academic pursuit and a professional field.

BERGER, PETER L. *Invitation to Sociology.* New York: Doubleday, 1963.

A brief and elegantly written introduction to the field. Berger provides an absorbing account of the distinctive "sociological perspective."

INKELES, ALEX. *What Is Sociology?* Englewood Cliffs, N.J.: Prentice-Hall, 1967.

A short but comprehensive summary of the development of sociological thought. The book includes a discussion of the relationship of sociology to the other social sciences.

MILLS, C. WRIGHT. *The Sociological Imagination.* New York: Oxford University Press, 1967.

Written from a conflict perspective, this book has become a classic introduction to sociology. Mills elaborates on the intimate connection between private experience and social context.

Reading

Invitation to Sociology *Peter L. Berger*

In this reading, Berger describes the inherent fascination of sociology and invites the newcomer to this "very special kind of passion."

The sociologist . . . is a person intensively, endlessly, shamelessly interested in the doings of men. His natural habitat is all the human gathering places of the world, wherever men come together. The sociologist may be interested in many other things. But his consuming interest remains in the world of men, their institutions, their history, their passions. And since he is interested in men, nothing that men do can be altogether tedious for him. He will naturally be interested in the events that engage men's ultimate beliefs, their moments of tragedy and grandeur and ecstasy. But he will also be fascinated by the commonplace, the everyday. He will know reverence, but this reverence will not prevent him from wanting to see and to understand. He may sometimes feel revulsion or contempt. But this also will not deter him from wanting to have his questions answered. The sociologist, in his quest for understanding, moves through the world of men without respect for the usual lines of demarcation. Nobility and degradation, power and obscurity, intelligence and folly—these are equally *interesting* to him, however unequal they may be in his personal values or tastes. Thus his questions may lead him to all possible levels of society, the best and the least known places, the most respected and the most despised. And, if he is a good sociologist, he will find himself in all these places because his own questions have so taken possession of him that he has little choice but to seek for answers.

It would be possible to say the same things in a lower key. We could say that the sociologist, but for the grace of his academic title, is the man who must listen to gossip despite himself, who is tempted to look through keyholes, to read other people's mail, to open closed cabinets. Before some otherwise unoccupied psychologist sets out now to construct an aptitude test for sociologists on the basis of sublimated voyeurism, let us quickly say that we are speaking merely by way of analogy. Perhaps some little boys consumed with curiosity to watch their maiden aunts in the bathroom later become inveterate sociologists. This is quite uninteresting. What interests us is the curiosity that grips any sociologist in front of a closed door behind which there are human voices. If he is a good sociologist, he will want to open that door, to understand these voices. Behind each closed door he will anticipate some new facet of human life not yet perceived and understood.

The sociologist will occupy himself with matters that others regard as too sacred or as too distasteful for dispassionate investigation. He will find rewarding the company of priests or of prostitutes, depending not on his personal preferences but on the questions he happens to be asking at the moment. He will also concern himself with matters that others may find much too boring. He will be interested in the human interaction that goes with warfare or with great intellectual discoveries, but also in the relations between people employed in a restaurant or between a group of little girls playing with their dolls. His main focus of attention is not the ultimate significance of what men do, but the action in itself, as another example of the infinite richness of human conduct. So much for the image of our playmate.

In these journeys through the world of men the sociologist will inevitably encounter other professional Peeping Toms. Sometimes these will resent his presence, feeling that he is poaching on their preserves. In some places the sociologist will meet up with the economist, in others with the political scientist, in yet others with the psychologist or the ethnologist. Yet chances are that the questions that have brought him to these same places are different from the ones that propelled his fellow-trespassers. The sociologist's questions always remain essentially the same: "What are people doing with each other here?" "What are their relationships to each other?" "How are these relationships organized in institutions?" "What are the collective ideas that move men and institutions?" In trying to answer these questions in specific instances, the sociologist will, of course, have to deal with economic or political matters, but he will do so in a way rather different from that of the economist or the political scientist. The scene that he contemplates is the same human scene that these other scientists concern themselves with. But the sociologist's angle of vision is different. When this is understood, it becomes clear that it makes little sense to try to stake out a special enclave within which the sociologist will carry on business in his own right. Like Wesley, the sociologist will have to confess that his parish is the world. But unlike some later-day Wesleyans he will gladly share this parish with others. . . . Any intellectual activity derives excitement from the moment it becomes a trail of discovery. In some fields of learning this is the discovery of worlds previously unthought and unthinkable. This is the excitement of the astronomer or of the nuclear physicist on the antipodal boundaries of the realities that man is capable of conceiving. But it can also be the excitement of bacteriology or geology. In a different way it can be the excitement of the linguist discovering new realms of human expression or of the anthropologist exploring human customs in faraway countries. In such discovery, when undertaken with passion, a widening of awareness, sometimes a veritable transformation of consciousness, occurs. The universe turns out to be much more wonderful than one had ever dreamed. The excitement of sociology is usually of a different sort. Sometimes, it is true, the sociologist penetrates into worlds that had previously been quite unknown to him--for instance, the world of crime, or the world of some bizarre religious sect, or the world fashioned by the exclusive concerns of some group such as medical specialists or military leaders or advertising executives. However, much of the time the sociologist moves in sectors of experience that are familiar to him and to most people in his society. He investigates communities, institutions and activities that one can read about every day in the newspapers. Yet there is another excitement of discovery beckoning in his investigations. It is not the excitement of coming upon the totally unfamiliar, but rather the excitement of finding the familiar becoming transformed in its meaning. The fascination of sociology lies in the fact that its perspective makes us see in a new light the very world in which we have lived all our lives. This also constitutes a transformation of consciousness. Moreover, this transformation is more relevant existentially than that of many other intellectual disciplines, because it is more difficult to segregate in some special compartment of the mind. The astronomer does not live in the remote galaxies, and the nuclear physicist can, outside his laboratory, eat and laugh and marry and vote without thinking about the insides of the atom. The geologist looks at rocks only at appropriate times, and the linguist speaks English with his wife. The sociologist lives in society, on the job and off it. His own life, inevitably, is part of his subject matter. Men being what they are, sociologists too manage to segregate their professional insights from their everyday affairs. But it is a rather difficult feat to perform in good faith.

The sociologist moves in the common world of men, close to what most of them would call real. The categories he employs in his analyses are only refinements of the categories by which other men live—power, class, status, race, ethnicity. As a result, there is a deceptive simplicity and obviousness about some sociological investigations. One reads them, nods at the familiar scene, remarks that one has heard all this before and don't people have better things to do than to waste their time on truisms—until one is suddenly brought up against an insight that radically questions everything one had previously assumed about this familiar scene. This is the point at which one begins to sense the excitement of sociology. . . . It can be said that the first wisdom of sociology is this—things are not what they seem. This too is a deceptively simple statement. It ceases to be simple after a while. Social reality turns out to have many layers of meaning. The discovery of each new layer changes the perception of the whole. . . . To be sure, sociology is an individual pastime in the sense that it interests some men and bores others. Some like to observe human beings, others to experiment with mice. The world is big enough to hold all kinds and there is no logical priority for one interest as against another. But the word "pastime" is weak in describing what we mean. Sociology is more like a passion. The sociological perspective is more like a demon that possesses one, that drives one compellingly, again and again, to the questions that are its own. An introduction to sociology is, therefore, an invitation to a very special kind of passion.

Source: Peter L. Berger, *Invitation to Sociology* (New York: Doubleday & Company, Inc., Anchor Books, 1963).

CHAPTER 2 Doing Sociology: The Methods of Research

CHAPTER OUTLINE

The Logic of Cause and Effect
Variables
Correlations
Controls

Difficulties in Sociological Research

Basic Research Methods
Experiments
Surveys
Observational Studies
Existing Sources

A Research Model

Ethical Issues
"Project Camelot"
"Tearoom Trade"

Sociological research is inherently interesting and exciting: it offers the stimulation and challenge of going as a "stranger" into the familiar world, often to find one's assumptions shattered by the facts that one discovers: Research in sociology is really a form of systematic detective work—it poses the same early puzzles and suspicions, the same moments of inspired guessing and routine sifting through the evidence, the same disappointments over false leads and facts that do not fit and, perhaps, the same triumph when the pieces finally fall into place and the answer emerges. Research in sociology is where the real action takes place. It is in the field, far more than in the lecture room, that the sociologist comes to grips with the subject.

There are two sides to the sociological enterprise: theory and research. Both are essential, and each thrives on the other. Facts without theory are utterly meaningless. Theories without facts are unproved speculations of little use to anybody, because there is no way to tell whether they are correct. Theory and research are thus parts of a constant cycle. A theory inspires research that can be used to verify or disprove it, and the findings of research are used to confirm, reject, or modify the theory, or even to provide the basis of new theories. The process recurs endlessly, and the accumulated body of sociological knowledge is the result.

Guesswork, intuition, and common sense all have an important part to play in sociological research, but they cannot produce reliable evidence on their own. Reliable evidence can be produced only by using a reliable research methodology. *A methodology is a system of rules, principles, and procedures that guides scientific investigation.* The sociologist is interested in discovering what happens in the social world and why it happens. Research methodology provides guidelines for collecting evidence about what takes place, for explaining why it takes place, and for doing so in such a way that the findings can be checked by other researchers.

The methods of sociology can be applied only to questions that can be answered by reference to observable, verifiable facts. The sociologist cannot tell us if God exists, because there is no way to prove or disprove theories on the subject by testing them against the facts. But the sociologist can tell us what percentage of Americans claim to believe in God, or what reasons they have for believing in God, because these facts can be established by using appropriate research methods, methods that other sociologists can use later to check the original researcher's conclusions.

The Logic of Cause and Effect

To explain any aspect of society or social behavior, the sociologist must understand relationships of cause and effect. It is a basic assumption of science that all events have causes—whether the event is a ball rolling down a hill, an atomic bomb exploding, a nation going to war, an electorate choosing a Republican over a Democrat, or a student passing an examination. If we did not assume that all events have causes, the world would be utterly unpredictable and therefore unintelligible to us. The problem facing the sociologist is to sort out cause from effect and to determine which of several possible causes, or which combination of causes, is producing a particular effect.

Variables

Like all scientists, the sociologist analyzes cause and effect in terms of the influence of variables on one another. A *variable* is simply a characteristic that can vary—across time, across space, or from one individual or group to another. Age, sex, race, and social class are variables. So are rioting, marrying, stealing, and committing suicide. So are intelligence, nationality, income, and a sense of humor. Causation occurs when one variable, such as drunken driving, influences another variable, such as the likelihood of traffic accidents. A theory simply attempts to generalize about the influence of one variable on another: "Drunken driving contributes to traffic accidents." "Wealthy voters tend to support the Republican Party." "Malnutrition causes children to perform poorly in schoolwork." All these statements serve to link variables in a cause-and-effect relationship.

The variable that causes the effect is called the *independent variable,* and the variable that it influences is called the *dependent variable.* Being drunk is one independent variable (though not necessarily the only one) that can produce the dependent variable of a traffic accident. Being wealthy is an independent variable (though, again, not necessarily the only one) that can influence people to vote Republican. The same variable can, of course, be independent in one context and dependent in another. Being drunk is an independent variable where the quality of driving depends on it; it is a dependent variable where the extent of drunkenness depends on the amount of liquor consumed.

A *generalization* is a statement about the recurrent relationships between particular variables. A generalization applies to the whole class of variables that is being considered, not to any particular case within it. Medical scientists can predict what proportion of Americans (barring the intervention of some unforeseen factor) will get lung cancer this year, but they cannot tell us precisely which Americans will contract the disease. A sociologist can tell us that most wealthy Americans (again, barring the intervention of an unforeseen factor) will vote Republican at the next election but cannot say precisely which wealthy people will do so. All generalizations in science are statements of *probability*—not certainty—for the entire category of variables under consideration. The generalizations will hold good only under specific conditions because if circumstances change, other variables might come into play and influence the existing relationship. If, for example, preventative measures against lung cancer suddenly became available, fewer people would contract the disease. If the Republican party for some reason nominated a leftist candidate, fewer wealthy people would vote Republican.

Correlations

Determining cause and effect, then, involves tracing the effect of variables upon one another. But how does the sociologist find out if such a relationship exists between variables?

The basic method is to establish whether there is a *correlation* between the variables—that is, whether they are associated together in a regular, recurrent fashion. By analyzing the statistics, the sociologist can easily establish if there is a correlation between malnutrition and school performance or between drunken driving and traffic accidents. In both cases, the evidence shows conclusively that the correlation is very high. This seems to prove the case. But does it?

Logically, no. The fact that two variables correlate highly does not prove that one caused the other, or even that they are related in any way at all. A different example will make this clearer. In the United States there is a high correlation between the sale of ice cream and the incidence of rape. The more ice cream that is sold, the more likely it is that rapes will occur. If a high correlation between these two variables were sufficient to prove a causal connection, we would have to conclude that eating ice cream causes rape or, alternatively, that rape causes people to eat huge amounts of ice cream. Clearly, neither of these conclusions is true. But what explains the correlation? A moment's thought suggests the answer, in the form of a

Basic Statistical Terms

Although some sociological research uses sophisticated mathematics, introductory students will be able to find their way through most sociological writing by relying on a few basic statistical concepts. The concepts you will encounter most frequently are those of averages and correlations.

Averages. The word "average" is often used loosely in ordinary conversation. There are actually three different ways of calculating averages, or *central tendencies,* and each method can produce a different figure from the same data.

Suppose a researcher has studied nine individuals and finds that their annual incomes are:

$3000	$3800	$9000
$3000	$6500	$9000
$3500	$9000	$150,000

For some purposes it may be sufficient to present all this information in the form given above, but it is often more useful to provide a single figure that reveals the central tendency of all the numbers involved.

The *mode* is the number that appears most often in the data. In our example the mode is $9000. The mode is useful when the researcher wants to show which figure recurs most frequently. It has the disadvantage, however, that it does not give any idea of the range in the data as a whole.

The *mean* is the figure obtained by dividing the total of all the figures by the number of individual cases involved. In this case the total is $196,800; divided by nine, it gives a mean figure of $21,866.66. The mean has the advantage of taking account of all the data, but it can give misleading results. In our example, the central tendency is distorted by the presence of one extreme figure, $150,000, which hides the fact that all the other individuals earn $9000 a year or less. (The mean is the measure of central tendency that we usually call the "average" in ordinary speech.)

The *median* is the number that falls midway in a range of numbers; in our example, it would be $6500. If the number of cases was an even rather than an odd number—say, ten instead of nine—the median would be the mean ("average") of the two numbers in the middle, namely the fifth and sixth items. The median is sometimes useful because it does not allow extreme cases, such as the income of $150,000, to distort the central tendency. Sociologists often present an average in more than one form, particularly when a single measure might give a misleading impression.

Correlations. A correlation expresses the strength of a relationship between two variables; it is usually expressed as a number called a *correlation coefficient.* When two variables have absolutely no consistent relationship to one another, the correlation coefficient is zero. When there is a perfect *positive* correlation, so that one variable is always associated with the other, the correlation coefficient is 1.0. Weak positive correlations of around 0.2 or 0.3 are not very significant, but stronger correlations of around 0.6 and above indicate an increasingly significant relationship between the variables. When there is a perfect *negative* correlation, so that the presence of one variable is always associated with the absence of the other, the correlation coefficient is -1.0.

A high correlation may suggest a causal relationship between the variables involved, but it is always possible that the correlation is coincidental or is produced by a third variable that influences the other two. Correlations therefore have to be interpreted with great care.

third variable that influences the other two: the American summer. People eat more ice cream when it is hot than when it is cold. Rapes are far more likely to occur in the summer than in the winter, partly because people are more likely to venture out of their homes at night and partly because the nature of rape is such that the act is not easily performed in freezing weather. The rape–ice cream correlation exists, but it is *spurious.* In other words, it is merely coincidental and does not imply any causal relationship whatever.

Controls

How, then, can we determine whether a correlation between two variables is a causal one? To find out, sociologists must apply *controls*—ways of excluding the possibility that some other factors might be influencing the relationship that interests them. It might be, for example, that most people who drive when they are drunk do their drunken driving after dark and that poor visibility, not alcohol consumption, is the real cause of the accidents. The sociologist has to control this variable by comparing the accident rates of both drunken and sober drivers during daylight and at night. If the drunken drivers are still proportionately more likely to become involved in traffic accidents under both driving conditions, the possibility that visibility is an influencing variable is eliminated. Similarly, it might be that children who are malnourished typically do not have a father in the home and therefore lack fatherly encouragement in their academic work. Again, the sociologist has to control for this possibility by comparing the school performance of both well-nourished and malnourished children with and without a father in the home.

Only when the sociologist has applied controls to the other possibilities—often a difficult task, because some possibilities are not immediately obvious and may be overlooked—can it be said with confidence that a causal connection exists between the variables. In the cases of our drunken drivers and malnourished children, a high correlation still exists when other possible independent variables have been eliminated. Have we now proved conclusively that malnutrition causes poor school performance and that drunken driving causes traffic accidents?

Not necessarily. The fact that variable A has a causal connection with variable B does not necessarily mean that A causes B. Until we probe deeper, we can equally justifiably conclude that B causes A. In other words, the fact that a causal relationship exists between two variables does not tell us which is the independent and which is the dependent variable. That remains to be established, by one or both of two methods.

The first method is to make a logical, realistic assessment about which of the two possibilities is more likely. Either drunken driving causes traffic accidents, or traffic accidents cause some drivers to immediately become drunk. Either malnutrition causes poor school performance, or poor school performance causes malnutrition. In each case the latter conclusion is logically impossible—ridiculous, in fact—and we can dismiss it, leaving the former conclusion as the only remaining possibility.

Sometimes, however, this kind of analysis does not yield such an obvious answer. We may find, for example, that there is a high correlation between drug abuse and dropping out of college. We may be able to eliminate the possibility that some third variable has produced the other two and that the relationship between drug abuse and dropping out of college is causal, not spurious. But which causes which? One person's hunch might be that dropping out makes people more likely to abuse drugs; another person's hunch might be that drug abuse makes people more likely to drop out. Both conclusions seem reasonable. To determine which is the independent and which is the dependent variable, a second logical approach is needed: one that considers the variable of *time.* An event that causes another event must always precede it. If students drop out first and use drugs afterward, then dropping out tends to cause drug abuse; if they abuse drugs first and then drop out, drug abuse is the independent variable. We can also use this method to validate further our conclusions about malnourished children and drunken drivers, by asking which came first—the malnutrition or poor school performance, the drunkenness or the accidents?

Misinterpretation of cause-and-effect relationships between variables is a major source of sloppy thinking, not only in everyday common sense understandings of the world but sometimes also in scientific writings. An association between variables must be studied very carefully before valid conclusions about a cause-and-effect relationship can be drawn.

Difficulties in Sociological Research

As we noted in Chapter 1, the sociologist's subject matter presents some difficult research problems of a kind that natural scientists rarely have to deal with. The sociologist's subjects are not inanimate objects or unreflecting animals. They are people who are self-aware, who have complex individual personalities, and who are capable of choosing their own courses of action for both rational and irrational reasons. The fact that the sociologist is studying human beings poses five major problems to research methodology.

1. *The mere act of investigating social behavior may alter the very behavior that is being investigated.* When people know that they are being studied, they may not behave as they normally would do. Suppose, for example, that a sociologist who was studying family interaction patterns visited your home: would your family behave in exactly the same way as usual? The presence, personality, and actions of the observer can disrupt the behavior that is under investigation. Sometimes the problem is compounded when the subjects know or guess (correctly or incorrectly) what the sociologist is trying to find out: they may try to "help" by consciously or unconsciously behaving in ways that they feel will conform to the researcher's expectations.

2. *People—unlike bacteria or hydrogen atoms—have emotions, motives, and other highly individual personality characteristics.* They may give false information deliberately, to put themselves in a better light, or unintentionally, because they misinterpret a question or do not understand the reasons for their own behavior or attitudes. They may also behave in unpredictable ways for a variety of peculiar reasons of their own, something inanimate objects do not do. As a result, sociological explanations and predictions are often less precise than those of the natural sciences.

3. *The origins of social behavior are almost always extremely complex, involving many social, psychological, historical, and other factors.* It is usually much more difficult for the sociologist than for the natural scientist to sort out cause and effect because so many more variables tend to be involved. It is relatively easy to establish why water boils or what the effect of pressure is on the volume of a gas. It is much more difficult to establish why people fall in love, or why they fall in love with the people that they do. The causes of social behavior are usually multiple and intricate.

Figure 2.1 "Streaking," a fad of the early seventies, offers an example of some specific difficulties that confront social scientists in their research. (1) By observing, photographing, or interviewing a streaker, the researcher might alter the very behavior that is being studied. (2) The streaker's behavior, unlike that of a virus or a molecule, is a highly personal and unpredictable act. (3) The reasons for the emergence of the fad are extremely complex and difficult to untangle. (4) Streaking is essentially spontaneous and is therefore difficult to study under controlled conditions. (5) The researcher may have a personal attitude toward streaking—perhaps of amusement, perhaps of disgust—and this may hamper objective analysis. Natural scientists rarely face problems like these.

4. *It is not permissible, for ethical reasons, to perform certain kinds of experiments on human beings.* The natural scientist has no moral qualms about experimenting with rays of light and often few qualms about experimenting with animals. But the dignity and privacy of human beings must be respected. We cannot deliberately raise boys as girls to see what effect the experience would have on their later sex-role adjustment, however interesting and valuable the findings might be. We cannot arrange to have parents ill-treat their children so that we can trace the effects on child personality, however useful the results might be to social workers or psychiatrists. Ethical considerations place severe limitations on the methods the sociologist can use.

5. *The sociologist, unlike the natural scientist, is part of the very subject he or she is studying.* It is therefore much more difficult to maintain a detached attitude, and objectivity becomes harder to achieve. The geologist may be interested in establishing the composition of a particular rock sample but is unlikely to be emotionally involved in the findings. The sociologist, who may be studying such issues as race relations or poverty, can become passionately involved in the outcome of the research. The researcher may identify strongly with the problems and experiences of the subjects, and there is a risk that the process of investigation and interpretation will be distorted as a result.

All sociologists recognize these problems, but not all are agreed on how to deal with them. Some focus on refining statistical and similar techniques, modeling their methodology as closely as possible after the example of the natural sciences. They aim to make sociology as exact and precise a science as possible. Others protest that a total dependence on these methods produces mounds of figures but very little understanding. Instead, they rely heavily on their own subjective descriptions and interpretations of social behavior, even when these may be difficult for others to verify. Debate between the more zealous advocates of each approach has at times become heated. Advocates of a more interpretative approach have referred to sociologists relying on computers and statistical techniques as "the IBM mafia," while advocates of the latter approach have dismissed the descriptive writings of the other camp as a "sociology of pot smokers." Most sociologists, however, probably accept the viewpoint expressed by Max Weber many decades ago. Weber believed that sociology must model itself as far as possible on the natural sciences but that its subject matter, being so different, sometimes also calls for an interpretative, subjective approach.

Figure 2.2 John Calvin, whose religious doctrines gave rise to Puritanism. In attempting to establish a connection between "the Protestant Ethic" and the development of capitalism, Max Weber tried to gain a subjective understanding of the psychology of the early Puritans. These insights enriched Weber's work, but (as he himself emphasized) subjective interpretations on their own are no substitute for scientific analysis. Such interpretations have a place in sociology, but they must be tested where possible against verifiable facts.

Subjective interpretation—which Weber called *Verstehen*, or sympathetic understanding—is in no sense a substitute for the scientific method. Wherever possible, the conclusions drawn from subjective interpretation must be verified by the scientific method. But intuitive understandings of social behavior have their place. Weber himself used *Verstehen* when he was trying to prove a causal link between the beliefs of early Puritans and the development of capitalism. The Puritans, he argued, felt that they were predestined to either heaven or damnation. They could not know what their actual fate would be, but they all had the duty of working for the greater glory of God. In their anxiety to find out if they were to be saved or not, they took signs of success in work as an indication of God's favor, and so worked all the harder. But their Puritan ethic forbade them to spend the money they earned on luxurious living, so they simply reinvested it. By accumulating and reinvesting wealth—instead of immediately spending it, as others were prone to do—they unintentionally created modern capitalism. This argument seems plausible, but there is no way to prove it scientifically because we cannot know whether the Puritans really did experience this "salvation panic." Weber's method was to place himself in the Puritans' shoes in order to understand their feelings and motives. By combining his subjective interpretations of Puritan psychology with a rigorous analysis of the development of capitalism, he enhanced the richness (but not necessarily the reliability) of his study.

Basic Research Methods

At the heart of the research process are the actual procedures that sociologists use to collect their facts. One or more of four basic methods can be used: the experiment, the survey, the observational study, and the use of existing sources of information. Each of these has its advantages and its drawbacks, and the success of a research project depends largely on the researcher's choice of an appropriate method.

Experiments

The experimental method provides a reliable way of studying the relationship between two variables under carefully controlled conditions. Experiments can be conducted either in the laboratory or in the field. In a *laboratory experiment* the subjects and any necessary materials are brought into an artificial environment that can be carefully regulated by the researcher. A *field experiment* takes place outside the laboratory under somewhat less artificial conditions, perhaps in a prison, hospital, or factory. The laboratory experiment is more appropriate when the researcher wants to control the situation in minute detail, whereas the field experiment is more suitable when the researcher wants to minimize the possibility that people will change their typical behavior in the artificial laboratory experiment.

The Experimental Method

In the typical experiment, an independent variable is introduced into a carefully designed situation and its influence on a dependent variable is recorded. Let's say the researcher is interested in the effects of racial integration in schools on white students' attitudes and decides to run a small experiment on the subject. The researcher must first measure the white students' attitudes, then introduce black students into the class, and then, after a suitable period, measure the white students' attitudes again to find out if any change has taken place. But this procedure is not enough to establish a causal link between the two variables. Any changes in the students' attitudes might have been caused by coincidental factors—racial disturbances in the neighborhood, perhaps, or a mass media campaign against racism that happened to take place while the experiment was in progress.

The researcher therefore has to control the situation in such a way that other possible influences can be discounted. The standard method of doing this would be to divide the white students into two groups whose members are similar in all relevant respects. Both groups are then tested on their racial attitudes, but only one group, the *experimental group,* is exposed to classroom integration. The other group, the *control group,* is not subjected to this variable, but its experience is the same in all other respects. Finally, both groups are again tested on their racial attitudes, and any difference between the groups is assumed to be the result of the independent variable.

The "Hawthorne Effect"

One of the best-known experiments in sociology was conducted before World War II at the Hawthorne plant of Western Electric (Roethlisberger and Dickson, 1939). The management was anxious to improve productivity and wanted to know what kind of incentives would encourage the workers to increase output. The researcher who investigated the problem, Elton Mayo, separated a group of women from the other workers and systematically varied their lighting, coffee breaks, lunch hours, methods of payment, and so on. At first, Mayo and his associates were delighted: each new change increased levels of productivity. But when the researchers found that productivity rose no matter which variables were involved, they became suspicious. When the workers were finally returned to their original conditions, their productivity rose yet again! Something was seriously wrong with the researchers' assumptions. Whatever had caused the changes in the dependent variable—productivity—it was not the independent variables that the experimenters had introduced, and from this point of view the experiment was a failure. But the reasons for the experiment's failure have taught sociologists a great deal. Production rose, it seems, because the women enjoyed all the attention they were getting: they became a tight-knit, cooperative group, they knew what effects the sociologists were trying to produce, and they did their best to please. This phenomenon—the contamination of the experiment by the subjects' assumptions about what the sociologist is trying to prove—is still known as the *Hawthorne effect.*

The experimental method is useful because it allows the sociologist to investigate specific topics that often cannot be systematically examined under everyday conditions, where so many other influences might conceal or distort the processes involved. The method has some disadvantages, however. It can be used only for very narrowly defined issues. People may behave very differently in the artificial experimental situation than they would in the world beyond. And experimenters may sometimes unwittingly produce the effect that they are looking for.

Surveys

Surveys are frequently used in sociological research, either simply for the purpose of getting facts (such as the political opinions of college students) or for finding out about the relationship between facts (such as how sex, parental opinions, or social class influence students' political views).

The total group of people whose attitudes or behavior the sociologist is interested in is called the *population.* It may consist of all students in college, all mothers with children under the age of five, all twins in the state of Nevada, or the entire nation. In some cases it is possible to survey the entire population, but time and expense make this procedure impractical unless the population is a small one. In most cases it is necessary to survey a *sample,* a small number of individuals drawn from the larger population. This sample must accurately represent the population in question. If it does not, then any conclusions are valid only for the actual people who were surveyed—the *respondents*—and cannot be applied to the entire population from which the sample was drawn.

In 1936, the popular magazine *Literary Digest* conducted an opinion poll to predict the outcome of that year's presidential election. Millions of names were selected from telephone directories and automobile registration lists, and 2 million responses were obtained. The results pointed to a landslide victory for the Republican candidate, Alfred E. Landon, who had a lead of nearly 15 percentage points over his Democratic opponent. If you have never heard of Alfred E. Landon, you need not be unduly concerned by your ignorance. He was beaten by Franklin D. Roosevelt in every state except Maine and Vermont and disappeared into the footnotes of the history texts. The correct outcome of the election was predicted, however, by a young man named George Gallup, who used a very much smaller sample for his purposes. The *Literary Digest* became a national laughingstock and soon went out of business, while the Gallup poll has become a regular feature of the American scene.

What happened? The answer, of course, is that Gallup's small sample was more *representative* than the larger *Literary Digest* sample. During the Depression years only middle- and upper-class people could afford telephones and automobiles, and these people tended to be Republican. As a result, lower- and working-class people, who were overwhelmingly Democratic, were largely excluded from the sample. In effect, the poll was a survey of how a predominantly Republican sample intended to vote, and so it produced a wildly inaccurate prediction for the nation as a whole. Gallup was able to predict the result more accurately because his sample faithfully represented the proportions of Democrats and Republicans in the electorate.

Figure 2.3 Harry S Truman, on the night of his victory over Thomas E. Dewey in the 1948 presidential election. The Chicago Daily Tribune *went to press before the results were announced, relying for its unfortunate headline on earlier opinion polls. In this case the polls were inaccurate primarily because polling stopped too soon before the election. In the closing stages of the campaign the great majority of the "undecideds" swung to Truman, but this trend went undetected. Modern opinion polls continue until the final days of a presidential election campaign.*

Random Samples

Whether a sample is representative has very little to do with its size. A representative sample of two or three thousand Americans can be used to predict the outcome of a presidential election to within 2 percentage points of the actual result; an unrepresentative sample of several million could be hopelessly off target. The standard method of ensuring that the sample is representative is to make a *random* selection of subjects from the population concerned, that is, to make the selection in such a way that every member of the population has the same chance of being selected. The simplest way to do a random sample is perhaps to pull names out of a hat, but sociologists can use more sophisticated techniques for drawing random samples from large populations.

One method of ensuring that the sample is random is to systematically take, say, every tenth or thirty-ninth person from the population. This must be done with care: if you were surveying your college student population, for example, you could not obtain a random sample by asking every tenth person who walks up the library steps. All you would get would be a random sample of students who use the library and who happened to be using it at the time you made the survey. To make your sample representative you would have to draw it from a complete listing of all students. A second method of obtaining a random sample is to assign a number to each member of the population and then to select the sample by using random numbers produced by a computer. This method is the most reliable because it eliminates most sources of human error. Sometimes it is useful to divide the population into various categories—perhaps according to age, race, sex, or any other variable that might be relevant—and then to draw a random sample from each category. This technique, known as *stratified random sampling,* ensures that the categories will be represented in the sample in precisely the same proportion as they occur in the population. Stratified random sampling guarantees, for example, that if people in a very high income bracket constitute 1 percent of the population, they will constitute 1 percent of the sample. The slight margin of error in ordinary random sampling may produce a sample containing virtually no people in this category, and the results of the survey may be slightly biased as a result.

Questionnaires and Interviews

A survey may use questionnaires, interviews, or a combination of the two. If the questionnaire is self-administered without an interview, the respondents are asked to complete it and often to return it by themselves. If the interview technique is used, the researcher asks the questions directly. In a *structured interview* the researcher has a checklist of questions and puts them to the respondents in exactly the same form and exactly the same order. The respondent is asked to choose between several predetermined answers, such as "yes/no/don't know" or "very likely/likely/unlikely/very unlikely." The structured interview is very inflexible, but it enables the researcher to make careful tabulations and comparisons of the answers. If other information about the respondents is included, such as income, geographical location, or age, all these variables can be fed into a computer, and correlations between them can be extracted in a few seconds. By using statistical controls on the data, the researcher can often establish causal links between the different variables in the survey. The *unstructured interview* is much more flexible and "open-ended." The researcher puts more general questions to the respondents, allows them to answer freely, and follows up on their comments. This approach allows the researcher to get insights that a structured interview may overlook, but it has some disadvantages. The answers are often extremely difficult to compare: if people are asked, for example, "Do you intend to vote at the next election?" they will give such answers as "Maybe," "I might if I feel like it," "Depends on who's running," "I suppose so," "I haven't decided yet," and so on. The researcher also has to be on guard against influencing the respondents' answers by such subtle signals as choice of words, tone of voice, and facial expressions.

To be useful, survey questions must be put in straightforward, unemotional language and must be phrased so that all respondents will understand them in the same way. The question "Are you religious?" is almost useless, because it will be interpreted in different ways by different people; it is necessary to ask more specific questions about church attendance, belief in God, and so on. Questions should be stated in a neutral manner: one that begins "Do you agree that . . . ?" will draw a higher proportion of affirmative responses than one that begins "Do you think that . . . ?" Double-barreled questions, such as "Do you think that marijuana and heroin should be legalized?" inevitably produce confusion because people may have different opinions about the two subjects. The word "not" should be avoided if possible: if the researcher asks "Do you think the United States should not get militarily involved in the Rhodesian situation?" many people will read over the word "not" and misunderstand the question.

The survey is an indispensable source of information about social characteristics and the relationships among them. It is particularly useful for tracing changes in these characteristics over time, for questionnaires or interviews can be repeated at suitable intervals. The method has its disadvantages, however. People will sometimes express opinions on subjects they know nothing whatever about. (Even if people are asked to express opinions on a nonexistent law—say, the "Hodge Act"—a large minority will declare themselves for or against it!) They frequently fail to return self-administered questionnaires, and response rates of less than 50 percent are common. An unsatisfactory response rate introduces bias into the sample because those who do return questionnaires may be different in important respects from those who do not—in particular, they are more likely to have strong views on the topic or issue. To complicate matters, about 10 percent of American adults are not sufficiently literate to complete a questionnaire. Respondents may also give false information, particularly in face-to-face interviews. People may deny their racist views, for example, because they know that these views are not "respectable." Surveys rarely give the opportunity for in-depth study of social behavior, and they are often expensive to conduct.

Observational Studies

Observational studies usually involve an intensive examination of a particular group, event, or social process. The researcher does not attempt to influence what happens in any way but aims instead at an accurate description and analysis of what takes place. The analysis usually involves tracing cause-and-effect relationships, but some sociologists are content merely to give a precise account of their observations. This information alone adds to the sum of sociological knowledge and can be used by other sociologists for other purposes.

Like the experiment, an observational study can be conducted in the laboratory or in the field. In a laboratory observation, for example, the sociologist might bring a group of subjects together and present them with a problem in order to observe the processes by which leaders emerge and decisions are made. The researcher may choose to tape-record the interaction and to watch and film it through a two-way mirror rather than risk influencing the course of events by joining the group and taking notes on the spot. In the field observation the

How To Read a Table

Sociologists make considerable use of statistical tables, both as a source of data and as a way of presenting the results of their own research. You will be able to grasp the information in a table quickly if you follow a systematic procedure. Here are the main steps you should follow (using the accompanying table as a model).

1. *Read the title.* The title should tell you exactly what information the table contains. Our table tells about the circumstances of murders that occurred in the United States over the six-year period 1969–1974.
2. *Look for headnotes.* Immediately below the title you will sometimes find a headnote. The headnote may give information about how the data were collected, how they are presented, or why they are presented in a particular way. (In this case, as in many tables, there is no headnote.)
3. *Examine the source.* At the bottom of a table you will find a statement of the source of the data. The source helps you to judge the reliability of the information and tells you where to find the original data if you want to check the statistics further. In the example the source is a reliable one, the FBI's *Uniform Crime Reports.*
4. *Read the labels.* There are two kinds of labels in a table, the column headings at the top and the headings along the left-hand side. You must make sure that you understand the labels, and you will have to keep both column and side headings in mind as you read the table. In our table the column headings represent different types of murder circumstances, while the side headings indicate the years in which the murders took place.
5. *Find out what units are used.* The statistics in a table may be presented in hundreds, thousands, percentages, rates per 1000, rates per 100,000, and so on. Sometimes this information is not contained in the headnote and appears instead in the column or side headings. In our table, as the overall column head has already indicated, figures are presented as percentages.
6. *Make comparisons.* Compare the data in the table, both horizontally and vertically, and notice any differences, similarities, or trends in the statistics. If you read our table horizontally, you will be able to compare the percentage of murders involving, say, parents and children with the percentage involving romantic quarrels. If you read the table vertically, you will be able to compare the percentage of murders in any category from one year to another.
7. *Draw conclusions.* Finally, draw conclusions about the data and consider any questions that the statistics raise. You will notice, for example, that some categories of murder represent a greater percentage of all murders in 1974 than they did in 1969, whereas this trend is reversed for other categories. You will also notice that a high proportion of murders involve people who presumably love one another, such as spouses, relatives, and lovers, and you may want to investigate this further.

Table 2.1 CATEGORIES OF MURDER IN THE UNITED STATES, 1969–1974

Year	Percentages of Total Murders by Category							
	Spouse Killing Spouse	Parent Killing Child	Other Relative Killings	Romantic Quarrels	Other Arguments	Known Felony Type	Suspected Felony Type	Percent
1969	13.1	3.7	8.4	7.0	41.3	19.3	7.2	100.0
1970	12.1	3.1	8.1	7.1	40.8	20.4	8.4	100.0
1971	12.8	3.5	8.4	6.3	41.5	20.4	7.1	100.0
1972	12.5	2.9	8.9	7.1	41.2	22.1	5.3	100.0
1973	12.3	3.2	7.7	7.5	40.3	21.6	7.4	100.0
1974	12.1	2.7	8.0	6.2	43.2	22.2	5.6	100.0

Source: Adapted from *Crime in the United States: Uniform Crime Reports, 1974* (Washington, D.C.: U.S. Government Printing Office), p. 19.

sociologist studies something that is happening or has happened without attempting to structure the conditions of observation. Most observational studies take place in the field.

Case Studies

The most common form of field observation is the *case study*—a complete and detailed record of an event, group, or social process. Some case studies deal with events that have already taken place. The sociologist reconstructs these events through extensive interviews with the participants and by referring to other sources of data, ranging from police records to newspaper files. This method is often used for the analysis of infrequent, temporary events such as riots. Other case studies involve intensive observation at the time that the action is taking place. These "eyewitness" case studies are an exceptionally rich source of sociological information and insights.

The sociologist involved in a case study may choose to be either a detached or a participant observer. The *detached observer* remains as aloof from the process under study as possible, and the subjects may not know that they are being studied. Observing from a distance may obscure the view, however. Many sociologists therefore prefer to become *participant observers*, taking part in all the activities of the people they are studying. Sometimes the participant observer makes it clear to the subjects at the outset that he or she is a sociologist; at other times the sociologist pretends to be an ordinary member of the group. The latter approach has the advantage that people will behave in more typical ways if they do not know they are being observed, and it also enables the sociologist to gain access to groups—such as some religious sects—that would not normally allow themselves to be studied. Concealing one's identity can raise serious ethical problems, however, because the sociologist is using deceit to observe the details of people's lives.

The case-study tradition in American sociology is full and varied. An influential early study was that of Robert and Helen Lynd (1929), who participated fully in the life of the small town of Muncie, Indiana. Their case study provided fascinating details about the daily life of this community and has inspired a long series of similar studies. William Whyte (1943) became a participant observer in an Italian slum neighborhood of an American city. Sociologists had previously assumed that such a slum community would not be highly organized. Whyte showed that it was, although not along the lines dictated by middle-class values. Leon Festinger and his associates (1956) penetrated a cult whose members believed that the earth

Figure 2.4 Infrequent, spontaneous events, such as the campus riots of the sixties, usually have to be studied after they have taken place. It would be almost impossible to make an objective analysis on the spot, even if a trained researcher happened to be there at the time. Such events can often be reconstructed and analyzed through a retrospective case study.

was doomed to imminent destruction but that a select few would be saved by aliens in a flying saucer. He eventually found himself on a hilltop awaiting the event with members of the cult, and he detailed their reactions when the prophecy failed. Erving Goffman (1961) spent many months as an observer in a mental hospital. His account of how the organization of an asylum systematically depersonalizes the patients and may even aggravate their problems has been influential. Ned Polsky (1964) spent long periods as a participant observer with poolroom hustlers, noting how they "set up" their victims and analyzing their code of ethics. Elliot Liebow (1967), a white man, joined a group of apparently aimless black men who "hung out" on street corners. He was eventually able to win the confidence of the group and to provide a detailed account of its members' lives.

Observational studies of this kind place a heavy obligation on the sociologist. The identities of informants must be protected, especially when their behavior is disreputable. Systematic notes must be kept each day while memory is fresh. The observer must be careful not to influence the behavior that he or she is studying. Gaining access to the group and winning the trust of its members can be extremely difficult, especially if the backgrounds of the sociologist and the subjects are dissimilar. The assumption behind participant observation is that some things can be fully understood only by intimate experience of them, but the method relies heavily on the skills and subjective interpretations of the observer.

Observational studies have the advantage that they come to grips with real-life situations and so offer insights that years of experimenting and surveying might overlook. They have the disadvantage, however, of sacrificing scientific precision to some extent. The observer may misinterpret events, may unwittingly ignore things that are relevant and focus on things that are trivial, and may become so emotionally involved with the lives of the subjects that objectivity suffers. Another disadvantage is that the findings of a single observational study cannot be generalized to all apparently similar cases. The phenomenon that has been studied may have been exceptional in unknown but important ways, and the findings cannot be uncritically applied to what seem on the surface to be parallel situations.

Existing Sources

Sometimes the sociologist does not have to generate new information through experiments, surveys, or observational studies. The relevant data may already exist and merely has to be collected and analyzed. A great deal of useful information is available in published or unpublished form, whether it consists of the statistics issued by government agencies, film newsreels, diaries, letters, court records, works of art and literature, or the research findings of other social scientists.

One of the most important sources of information for the American sociologist is the population census report published every ten years by the Bureau of the Census and supplemented annually with estimates and compilations of data on specific topics. Census records provide a wealth of information on subjects ranging from birth and death rates to details of income, sex ratios, and urbanization trends. Other government departments issue statistical data every year on subjects as diverse as education, trade, health, transport, and military spending.

An equally important source of existing information is the accumulated body of sociological research. Information from this source can be collected and reinterpreted; findings of previously isolated reports can be related to one another in new and revealing ways; the data that one sociologist collected to answer one question can often be used by another sociologist to answer a different question.

Durkheim's Study of Suicide

Emile Durkheim's classic study of suicide, first published in 1897, remains an outstanding example of the use of existing sources. Durkheim wanted to find out why people commit suicide, and he suspected that explanations focusing on the psychology of the individual were inadequate. Experiments on suicide were obviously out of the question. Case studies of past suicides would be of little use, because they could not provide reliable generalizations about all suicides. Survey methods were hardly appropriate, because one cannot survey dead people. But statistics on suicide were readily available, and Durkheim chose to analyze them.

Durkheim was able to dismiss some theories of suicide—such as the possibility that suicidal tendencies are

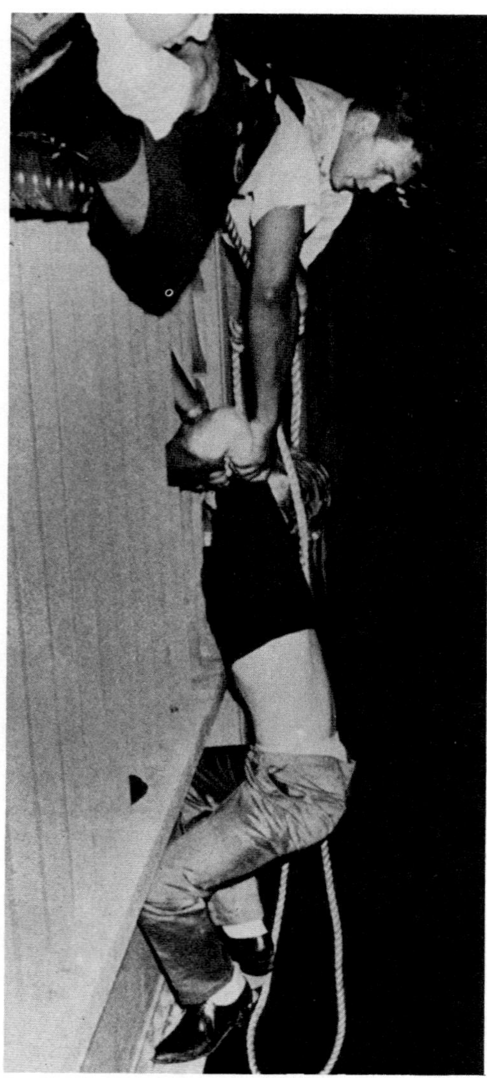

Figure 2.5 Suicide is a highly individual act, yet the motives for a suicide can be fully understood only by reference to the social context in which it occurs. The Vietnamese Buddhist monk is publicly burning himself to death as a form of political protest; his act is one of principled self-sacrifice for a moral cause. The young American attempting suicide probably has very different reasons, stemming from loneliness, despair, and a lack of close and meaningful bonds with other people.

inherited—by applying statistical controls to the data and eliminating these variables. He was left with an interesting and suggestive pattern: the incidence of suicide varied from one social group to another and did so in a consistent manner over the years. Protestants were more likely to commit suicide than Catholics; people in large cities were more likely to commit suicide than people in small communities; people living alone were more likely to commit suicide than people living in families. Durkheim isolated one independent variable that lay behind these differences: the extent to which the individual was integrated into a social bond with others. People with fragile ties to their community are more likely to take their own lives than are people who have stronger ties.

Durkheim then considered a form of suicide that is more typical of traditional societies: the suicide that takes place because it is expected by the community. In ancient Rome or traditional Japan, for example, a suicide was regarded as a highly honorable act under some circumstances. In traditional Indian society, a widow was sometimes expected to throw herself on her husband's funeral pyre and was considered a dutiful wife if she did so. In these cases it is not the weakness but the strength of the individual's ties to the community that accounts for the suicides. People in these societies may actually take their own lives in response to social expectations that they themselves share, whereas in our society they may take their lives because they do not share social expectations with anybody.

Durkheim was thus able to show that suicide—surely the most individual act that anyone is capable of—can only be fully understood in its social context, particularly in terms of the presence or absence of shared social expectations that influence individual behavior. To understand why a specific person commits suicide, of course, we must look at that person's personality and the pressures to which he or she has been subjected. To understand why suicide rates are higher for some groups than for others, however, we have to look at the larger social forces that predispose individuals to suicide. Durkheim's insight—that individual behavior can be fully understood only by referring to the social environment—has become the basis of the modern sociological perspective.

A Research Model

Suppose that you want to conduct a piece of sociological research. Exactly how would you go about it? Most research in sociology follows the same basic, step-by-step procedure. The procedure outlined here is merely an ideal model, and not all sociologists stick to it in every detail, but it does provide the guidelines for most research projects.

1. *Define the problem.* The first step is to choose a topic for research. The general area will usually be one in which the sociologist takes a personal interest. The specific topic can be chosen for a variety of reasons: perhaps because it raises issues of fundamental sociological importance, perhaps because it has suddenly become a focus of controversy, perhaps because research funds have become available to investigate it.

2. *Review the literature.* The existing sociological research bearing on the problem must be tracked down and reviewed. Knowledge of the relevant literature is essential. It provides background information, suggests theoretical approaches, indicates which areas of the topic have already been covered and which have not, and saves the sociologist the labor and embarrassment of unwittingly duplicating research that has already been done.

3. *Formulate a hypothesis.* The research problem must be stated in such a way that it can actually be tested. This is achieved by formulating a *hypothesis,* a tentative statement that predicts a relationship between variables. The hypothesis must be stated in clearly defined terms that the researcher can operate with effectively; these terms are called *operational definitions.* The hypothesis might be "Exposure to antiracist propaganda reduces racist attitudes in the subjects." Each of these terms must then be given an operational definition: "exposure" might be an intense ten-minute session repeated once a week for three weeks; "antiracist propaganda" might consist of a film with a specific content; "racist attitudes" might be measured by a specific test; "subjects" might be volunteer sociology students or a random sample of American housewives. Different researchers may produce different operational definitions of the same terms, which is one reason why investigations of what seems to be the same subject may produce varying conclusions.

4. *Choose a research design.* The sociologist must now select one or more means of gathering data—a survey, an experiment, an observational study, the use of existing sources, or a combination of these. The advantages and disadvantages of each method must be very carefully weighed because the *research design*—the actual plan for the collection and analysis of the data—is the crux of the research process.

5. *Collect the data.* The final conclusions will be no better than the data on which they are based, so the researcher must take great care in collecting and recording information. If the survey method is used, the sociologist must ensure that as many of the sample as possible are contacted and respond. If the experimental method is used, the sociologist must scrupulously control the conditions of the experiment and exclude variables that might influence the result. If the observational method is used, the sociologist must guard against biases of interpretation and must not influence the subjects in any way. If existing

Figure 2.6

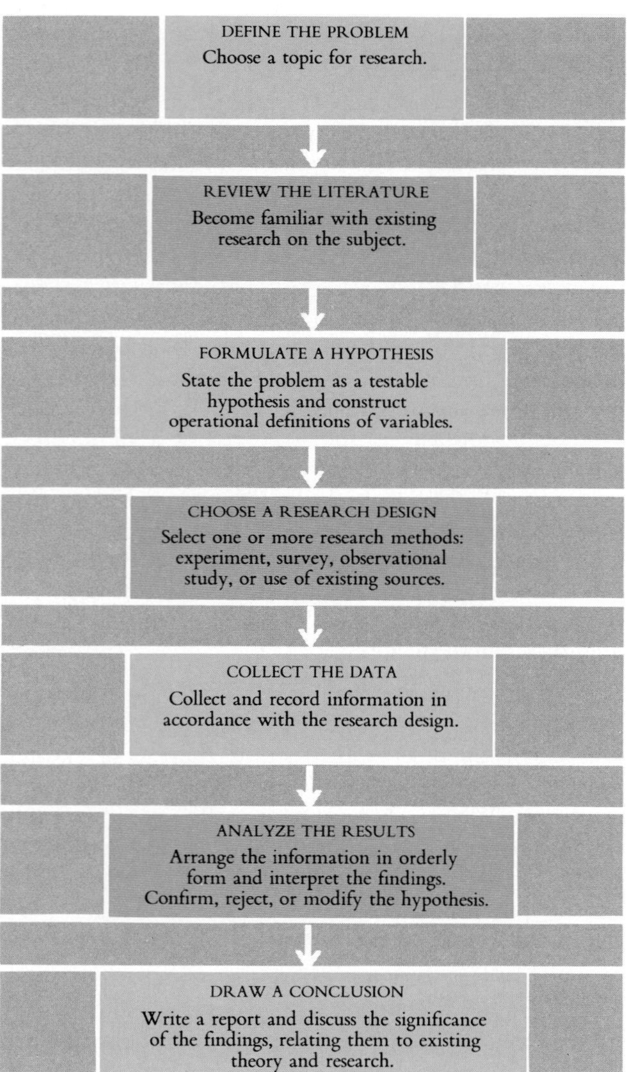

sources are used, the sociologist must try not to overlook relevant information and must evaluate the material with great care.

6. *Analyze the results.* When all the data are in, the sociologist can begin to classify the facts into an orderly form, clarifying trends and relationships and tabulating the information in such a way that it can be accurately analyzed and interpreted. This task requires considerable skill, for the data need not automatically suggest a particular interpretation. The same facts can often be interpreted in several different ways, and the researcher has to evaluate each of these possibilities with as much objectivity and as little bias as possible. The theory, as expressed in the hypothesis, can now be confirmed, rejected, or modified.

7. *Draw a conclusion.* Assuming that all has gone as planned, the sociologist can now draw a conclusion. At this stage he or she will draw up a succinct report of the project, tracing the steps already mentioned and concluding with a discussion of the findings. The report will relate the conclusions to the existing body of theory and research, suggesting where existing assumptions should be modified to take account of the new evidence. The report may also identify unanswered questions that seem to call for further research, and the sociologist may suggest new hypotheses that others can explore. If the research makes a significant contribution to sociological knowledge, it may be published, probably in the form of an article in a scholarly journal. It then becomes the common property of the scientific community, whose members can attempt to *replicate* the study—that is, repeat it to verify the findings—if they wish to do so.

This model is only an ideal outline; the actual process of research is often a good deal more messy. The model tells us nothing about the sheer frustrations, the inspired guesses, or the pure luck involved in research. Some researchers hardly use the model at all; they are more interested in simply describing social behavior and leaving it at that. Some researchers do an exploratory study once they have devised a research design; this study shows up any defects in the design before it is too late. Some researchers do not start with a clearly defined hypothesis but continually modify it and their operational definitions as they go along. Sometimes the data disprove the hypothesis that the researcher had in mind at the beginning but seem to prove some other hypothesis he or she had not thought of. The researcher may then try to fit the facts to the new hypothesis. The final report, however, should make clear what happened and why.

Ethical Issues

Sociological research sometimes runs into serious ethical problems. One of two types of dilemmas is usually involved. The first concerns the use to which the sociologist's work is put. Sociological research on propaganda techniques, for example, might be used by advertisers to sell worthless goods, or research on political movements could be used by people who are interested in suppressing those movements. Such possibilities may also raise questions about the relationship between the researcher and those who fund the research, particularly when the funders specify the research topic. The second kind of dilemma concerns the sociologist's intrusions into people's private lives, especially when the subjects are engaged in deviant or illegal behavior. Sociologists who do not declare their professional identities to their subjects may be gathering information under false pretenses, and a violation of trust may be involved. An example of each type of problem will illustrate the issues.

"Project Camelot"

The U.S. military has long been a major source of funds for scientific research at universities and elsewhere. These research funds have been used to support the research projects of natural scientists, often for the purpose of refining military technology and weaponry. In 1964, however, the army made a major attempt to recruit social scientists for research on "Project Camelot."

The objective of this project was "to devise procedures for assessing the potential for internal war within national societies" and "to identify . . . those actions which a government might take to relieve conditions which are assessed as giving rise to a potential for internal war." Moreover, it was intended that "the geographical orientation of the research will be toward Latin American countries." In other words, the army wanted to know how to predict and avoid revolutions in Latin America. The results of the research, then, could clearly be used to interfere in the domestic affairs of other nations. Several million dollars were made available for the project, and many social scientists agreed to participate in it.

The project was aborted within a year. News of the research and the source of its funds was leaked in Chile, where it caused an immediate furor. The U.S. ambassador complained to the federal government, and both Congress and the State Department applied pressure to have the project canceled. The military backed down, and "Project Camelot" was abandoned. But the affair contributed to a persistent wariness in other countries about the motives of American social scientists. American sociologists conducting research abroad still encounter the suspicion that they are working for the CIA or some other branch of the U.S. government.

Why did the social scientists allow themselves to become involved in the project? Irving Louis Horowitz (1967) found that they did not regard themselves as "spies," nor were they interested in maintaining antidemocratic regimes in Latin America. They saw themselves as "reformers" whose insights into the real causes of revolutions—poverty and oppression—might "educate" the army. None of them actually believed, however, that the military would take their recommendations seriously. They had been presented with an opportunity to do major research with almost unlimited funds, and they simply overlooked some of the ethical issues involved.

Sociological research is not self-supporting. It depends on the grants of public and private institutions, and the line between accepting a grant from them and working for them is a thin one. Sociologists have to be aware that their research may be put to questionable uses, including uses they could not have foreseen.

"Tearoom Trade"

In 1970, Laud Humphreys published *Tearoom Trade,* an observational study of homosexual acts that took place between strangers in certain men's rest rooms that were used almost exclusively for that purpose ("tearooms"). The participants on the scene wanted to avoid any involvement with the police, and for that reason one person always served as a lookout. By taking the role of lookout Humphreys was able to observe hundreds of sexual encounters without his identity as an outsider becoming known. Only a tiny minority of people with homosexual inclinations participate in this highly impersonal form of sexual activity, and Humphreys was interested in finding out more about the special characteristics of these subjects.

To get further information, Humphreys noted the automobile registration numbers of the participants and traced their addresses. After waiting a year to ensure that he would not be recognized, he visited their homes under the guise of a survey researcher looking for information on a quite different topic. He was thus able to obtain a great deal more information about them, including, for example, the surprising fact that the majority of them were married and living with their wives. Humphreys's ingenious study won the C. Wright Mills award of the Society for the Study of Social Problems for outstanding research, but it was strongly criticized by some sociologists and in the press.

One criticism was that Humphreys was a "snooper," delving into a subject unworthy of professional study. This is a criticism few sociologists would accept—all sociologists are in some sense "snoopers," and a research topic cannot be excluded simply because some people find its subject matter distasteful. A second criticism was that Humphreys had endangered his subjects by recording details of their illegal acts and by keeping lists of their names and addresses. If the material had fallen into the wrong hands, blackmail, extortion, or arrest could have followed. Humphreys replied that he had kept only one master list of names in a bank deposit box, that he once allowed himself to be arrested rather than disclose his identity to the police, that he eventually destroyed his data, and that he took every precaution to conceal the identities of the participants in his report. Humphreys's attitude seems to have been a responsible one, but the fact remains that other researchers would not necessarily have been as careful. The third and most serious criticism was that Humphreys had used systematic deception, both to observe the sexual encounters and later to gain entry to the subjects' homes. In the second edition of his book (1975), Humphreys acknowledges the force of this criticism and agrees that he should have identified himself as a researcher, even at the cost of sacrificing some sources of information. His dilemma highlights a problem that keeps recurring in sociological research: the distinction between legitimate investigation and unjustified intrusion is often difficult to judge.

Summary

1. Research methodology refers to the system of rules, principles, and procedures that regulates scientific investigation. Reliable research findings can be produced only by the use of a reliable research method.

2. All events have causes, and the task of science is to trace these causes in the form of the influence of variables upon one another. Generalizations are statements of probability about relationships between particular variables and can be used for the purposes of explanation and prediction.

3. Cause and effect can be traced by establishing correlations between variables. It is necessary, however, to apply controls to analysis—ways of excluding the possibility that some other variable is influencing the relationship concerned. Logical analysis is also necessary to establish that a relationship is causal, not spurious.

4. Sociological research presents several difficulties that derive from the nature of the subject matter: the act of investigating behavior may change the behavior; people may behave in unpredictable ways; the origins of social behavior are extremely complex; certain kinds of experiments cannot be performed on human beings; and the sociologist's personal involvement with the subjects can introduce bias.

5. Some of these problems can be resolved by combining a rigorous scientific methodology with subjective interpretation, which Weber called *Verstehen*. Subjective interpretation on its own, however, is no substitute for the scientific method.

6. There are four basic methods of sociological research. The experiment is useful for narrowly defined issues in which independent variables can be introduced into controlled situations. The survey is useful for obtaining facts about a population, but the sample must be random if it is to be representative. Observational studies, particularly case studies, are useful for in-depth analyses of social processes but rely heavily on the skills of the researcher. Existing sources can often be used to establish new relationships between facts.

7. An ideal research model consists of the following basic steps: defining the problem, reviewing the literature, formulating a hypothesis, choosing a research design, collecting the necessary data, analyzing the results, and drawing a conclusion.

8. Sociological research poses important ethical problems, notably those involving the use to which research is put and those involving intrusion on the privacy of others. "Project Camelot" and "Tearoom Trade" illustrate problems of each type.

Important Terms

methodology
variable
independent variable
dependent variable
generalization
correlation
spurious correlation
controls
Verstehen
experiment
experimental group
control group
Hawthorne effect
survey
population
sample
respondent
random sample
stratified random sample
structured interview
unstructured interview
case study
detached observation
participant observation
hypothesis
operational definition
research design
replication

Suggested Readings

GLAZER, MYRON. *The Research Adventure.* New York: Random House, 1972.

An interesting account of several sociological research projects. Each example is chosen to illustrate the challenges and problems that the researchers had to overcome.

HAMMOND, PHILIP E. (ED.). *Sociologists at Work.* New York: Basic Books, 1964.

A collection of firsthand essays by sociologists on how they conducted their own research projects.

HUFF, DARRELL, AND IRVING GEIS. *How To Lie with Statistics.* New York: W. W. Norton, 1954.

A short and readable volume on the use and abuse of statistics. The writers alert the reader to the many ways statistics can be misleadingly presented or interpreted.

LABOVITZ, SANFORD, AND ROBERT HAGEDORN. *Introduction to Social Research.* New York: McGraw-Hill, 1971.

A concise introductory text outlining the major methods of sociological research, with clear illustrations of their use.

MADGE, JOHN H. *The Origins of Scientific Sociology.* New York: Free Press, 1962.

An account of the development of sociological theory and research. Madge devotes a chapter to each of several classic research projects, carefully analyzing the methods used.

UNIT 2 *The Individual, Culture, and Society*

The theme of this unit is the dynamic interrelationship among individuals, their society, and its culture. The personality and social behavior of individuals are deeply influenced by the culture and society in which they happen to live, while culture and society are themselves produced and maintained by the interaction of countless individuals.

The first chapter in the unit discusses culture—that is, the total way of life of a society. The second focuses on society itself, showing how every society has a social structure that helps it to "work" in a fairly smooth and predictable way. We then explore socialization, the process through which the human animal becomes a fully social being by learning the culture of its society. Then we take a close-up view of social interaction, showing how sociological analysis can throw fascinating light on the taken-for-granted reality of our everyday lives. The following chapter discusses social groups, both small and large, and the ways in which groups can influence the behavior of their members. The next chapter turns to the problem of deviance—that is, behavior that violates the cultural expectations of a society. Finally, we discuss human sexuality as a specific example of the complex process by which individual, culture, and society interact in the shaping of human behavior and social life.

DEPT OF TRAFFIC
INTERNATIO
SUPER
BUS STOP
NO

CHAPTER 3 *Culture*

CHAPTER OUTLINE

The Human Species: What Kind of Animal?
The Evolutionary Background
The Significance of Culture
"Human Nature"

Norms
Folkways and Mores
Social Control

Values
The Importance of Values
American Values

Cultural Variation
The Functionalist Approach
The Ecological Approach
Cultural Universals
Ethnocentrism
Cultural Relativism

Cultural Integration
Real Culture and Ideal Culture
Subcultures and Countercultures

Language
The Importance of Language
Linguistic Relativity

Cultural Change

Are We Prisoners of Culture?

Human beings, unlike other animals, are not born with complex, "wired-in" behavior patterns that enable them to survive in specific environments. Instead, they must learn and invent ways of adapting to many different environments, ranging from arctic snows to desert wastelands and teeming cities. These learned ways of life, which are modified and passed on from one generation to the next, are what sociologists call "culture." An understanding of culture is basic to the understanding of human social life.

In ordinary speech, the word *culture* is often used to refer to sophisticated tastes in art, literature, or music. The sociological use of the term is much wider, for it includes the entire way of life of a society, and in this sense everyone who participates in society is "cultured." To the sociologist, *culture consists of all the shared products of human society*. These products are of two basic kinds, material and nonmaterial. *Material culture* consists of all the artifacts or physical objects human beings create—wheels, clothing, schools, factories, cities, books, spacecraft, totem poles. *Nonmaterial culture* consists of more abstract creations—languages, ideas, beliefs, rules, customs, myths, skills, family patterns, political systems.

It is possible, at least conceptually, to distinguish "culture" from "society." Culture consists of the shared *products* of society; society consists of the interacting *people* who share a culture. But the two are closely interrelated. A society could not exist without culture, for it would simply disintegrate. A culture cannot exist without a society to maintain it (except, perhaps, in the form of archaeological ruins and historical records). Society and culture are closely linked, and because the English language does not have a word meaning "culture-and-society," sociolo-

Figure 3.1 Modern Egyptians enact a cultural ritual by praying in the direction of Mecca, and in doing so, they turn their backs on the idols of ancient Egypt. Culture and society are interwoven, and neither can exist without the other—although cultural artifacts may outlast the society that created them.

gists often use either word interchangeably to refer to the complex whole. In this chapter, however, we will try as far as possible to keep the two concepts distinct and will use the term "culture" in its more specific sense.

The anthropologist Clifford Geertz (1968) observes that noncultured human beings "do not in fact exist, never have existed, and most important, could not in the nature of the case exist." Without culture, neither individual human beings nor human society as a whole could survive. To understand why this is so, we must examine the unique characteristics of our own species.

The Human Species: What Kind of Animal?

"What a piece of work is man!" exclaims Hamlet in Shakespeare's play. "How noble in reason! How infinite in faculty! In form, how moving, how express and admirable! In action, how like an angel! In apprehension, how like a god! The beauty of the world! The paragon of animals! And yet . . . What is this quintessence of dust?"

What are we? Hamlet's question is probably as old as the unique human capacity for self-awareness, a capacity that extends back tens and perhaps hundreds of thousands of years into prehistory. There is no simple answer to the question, for we are a remarkable and extraordinarily complex species—the most intelligent, resourceful, and adaptable that has ever existed on the planet. In the Western world until very recently we tended to regard ourselves as set completely apart from the rest of nature—as beings created in the very image of God, a little lower than the angels but far removed from the rest of the animal world. Today we have a better understanding of our place in nature. We know that we are related by ancient common ancestry to apes and eagles, sharks and lizards, that we are social animals whose bodily form and behavioral potentials have been shaped by millions of years of evolution in changing environments.

Modern science cannot yet give a comprehensive answer to Hamlet's question. But we do know infinitely more about the human species than we did even a few years ago, and we know that many traditional ideas about "human nature," some of them still very popular, are hopelessly naive and misguided. This book is about a particular animal, *Homo sapiens,* about the societies that this animal forms and about social behavior within those societies. Before we proceed to the study of culture and society, then, we must try to establish exactly what kind of animal we are talking about and which of its characteristics make this animal unique.

The Evolutionary Background

In 1859, Charles Darwin published *On the Origin of Species,* a book that has dramatically and permanently altered the human self-concept. With careful argument and a mass of detailed evidence, Darwin showed that all life forms are shaped by an endless process of physical evolution. Far from being created in the literal image of God, we are a recent product of an evolutionary process that can be traced back to the very beginnings of life on earth more than 3 billion years ago.

How does this process of evolution work—how do living organisms adapt to their environment from one generation to the next? Darwin expressed the essence of the process in the phrase "the survival of the fittest." All species tend to produce far more offspring than their environment can support, and an extremely high proportion fall victim to starvation, predators, disease, and other perils. But there is great physical variation among the individuals in any species: some are swifter, some more resistant to disease, some equipped with better eyesight, some better camouflaged. Those that have any advantage in the struggle for survival are more likely to live longer and to breed, and they therefore tend to pass on their characteristics to the next generation. Nature thus "selects" the fittest members of each species to survive and reproduce, a process that Darwin termed "natural selection." In time, the characteristics that are selected tend to spread throughout the entire species.

Tracing the evolution of the human species is no easy task. We have to rely for the most part on fossil evidence, and this evidence is often scanty. As a result, there are sometimes gaps of millions of years in our knowledge of our own evolutionary origins. Peering into our ancestral past is like peering into a landscape covered with mist. The mist parts periodically to reveal the dim outlines of creatures like us yet not like us, but growing more recognizably human with the passage of time.

We do know, however, that we are a member of the primate order, a group of related species that emerged relatively late in evolutionary time. The planet earth is about 4.7 billion years old. The first living organisms emerged approximately 3 billion years ago. The earliest land animals, amphibian creatures, appeared about 400 million years ago and eventually evolved into reptiles. Mammals, which evolved from reptiles about 180 million years ago, are a recent but very successful evolutionary development, primarily because they are more intelligent and adaptable than other life forms. They have an exceptional capacity to learn from experience, and in the higher mammals learning becomes progressively more important in the determination of behavior. This development reaches its climax in human beings. Our almost total reliance on learned behavior is the single most important characteristic distinguishing us from other creatures.

The first primates appeared about 70 million years ago, and our own line began to diverge from that of our closest relatives, the great apes (the chimpanzee, gorilla, and orangutan) about 14 million years ago. The higher primates share a number of common characteristics, all of which give us clues to our own evolutionary background. First, they tend to be very *sociable:* they live in groups with a high degree of affection and interaction among the members. Second, they have high *intelligence,* with brains that are exceptionally heavy in relation to body weight. This is especially true of human beings, whose brains have evolved to an unparalleled complexity. Third, primates have *sensitive hands.* In other mammals the hands have become highly specialized: the horse has a hoof, the porpoise a flipper, the bat a wing. Other animals can only paw or nuzzle at objects, but primates can use their hands as instruments for lifting, gripping, and manipulating things. In the higher primates the thumb can be placed opposite the forefinger to give a firm, precision grip. The importance of this single characteristic cannot be overestimated: try writing, sewing, or using any tool efficiently without opposing the thumb to the forefinger! Fourth, primates are extremely *vocal;* they are among the noisiest of all species and constantly call and chatter to one another. In human beings, this characteristic has developed into the capacity for language. Fifth, primates have a potential for *upright posture.* Many primate species are capable of walking on their hind legs, although they do so only rarely and for short distances. In human beings, however, bipedal (two-footed) standing and walking have become normal.

These, then, are the basic physical and behavioral characteristics that were the heritage of the first humans, who appeared in the fossil record between 1 and 2 million years ago. In the course of their evolution, our ancestors developed two additional characteristics. The first, found in no other animal, is the *year-round* sexual accessibility of the female. Human beings do not have a breeding season, a fact that encourages mates to form stable, permanent bonds. The second, found to a much greater extent in human beings than in any other animal, is the *long period of dependence* of the human infant on adults. This lengthy

Figure 3.2 Our three closest relatives: the chimpanzee, the gorilla, and the orangutan. For some 14 million years, our own line has evolved separately from that of the great apes, and we have become very unlike them in several important ways. Apart from obvious physical differences (such as our hairlessness and habitual upright posture), we have very much larger brains. As a result we are capable of abstract thought and language, and our behavior is shaped by learning rather than by "instinct."

dependence encourages a division of labor between adult females and males. Females tend to take responsibility for domestic and child-rearing activities, and males tend to concentrate on other activities, such as hunting and defense. The dependency period also provides the young human being with the opportunity to learn the cultural knowledge that is necessary for survival as an adult.

By about 35,000 years ago the modern human form of *Homo sapiens* was achieved. The long evolutionary process made us what we are: an almost hairless, bipedal, tool-using, talking, family-forming, self-aware, highly intelligent social animal. Our physical form bears the evidence of our ancestral heritage, and not always in ways convenient to us. Our upright posture has been achieved at the cost of a contortion of the spine into a somewhat S-shaped column, making us liable to that frequent human complaint, lower back pain. Our pelvis and rib cage no longer provide much support for the stomach, leaving us susceptible to hernias and other ruptures. Bipedalism has narrowed the pelvis and brought the legs closer together, and our infants have a very large head in relation to body size. As a result of these two factors, human females experience more difficulty than any other animal in giving birth.

The Significance of Culture

These physical adaptations and the behavioral flexibility offered by our huge brains have made us the most creative species in the planet's history. *Homo sapiens* has spread to every continent, sometimes driving other animal species to extinction in the process. It has become the most widely dispersed species on the planet, occupying mountains and jungles, arctic wastelands and arid deserts, yet always finding some specialized means of living in these widely differing environments. The total weight of all living members of the species far exceeds that of any other animal, and the human population is now growing so rapidly that it will double within the next thirty-eight years.

What accounts for the unprecedented success of our species? The answer, in a word, is culture. We create culture, but culture in turn creates us. We are consequently no longer the helpless victims of the natural environment. We make our own social environment, inventing and sharing the rules and patterns of behavior that shape our lives, and we use our learned knowledge to modify the natural environment as well. Our shared culture is what makes our social life possible. Without a culture transmitted from the past, each new generation would have to solve the most elementary problems of human existence over again. It would be obliged to devise a family system, to invent a language, to discover fire, to create the wheel, and so on.

Clearly, the contents of culture cannot be genetically transmitted. There is no gene that tells us to dance the polka, to drive on the right, to believe in a particular god, to get married, or to build houses. Everything in culture is learned. Culture is thus a substitute for "instinct" as a means of responding to the environment, and it provides a vastly superior method of doing so. The emergence of a species that depends for its survival on a learned culture is perhaps the greatest breakthrough in evolutionary history. Culture frees us from reliance on the slow, random, accidental process of physical evolution by offering us a new, purposive, efficient means of adapting to changing conditions. If we waited for natural selection to enable us to live at the North Pole, to fly to the moon, or to live under the sea, we would wait forever. But cultural inventions enable us to be insulated from the cold of the arctic, to travel in outer space, and to live in submarines—all without any recourse to physical evolution. Unlike other animals, we can self-consciously adapt to our environments and can adapt the environment to meet our own needs. Culture is the secret of our success.

"Human Nature"

A recent Harris poll found that a substantial majority of Americans agree with the statement, "Human nature being what it is, there will always be wars and conflict." This finding indicates the persistence of popular but utterly misguided views about our species. The problem with such ideas about "human nature" is that they are deeply colored by the cultural beliefs of the societies in which they are found. In the industrialized countries of

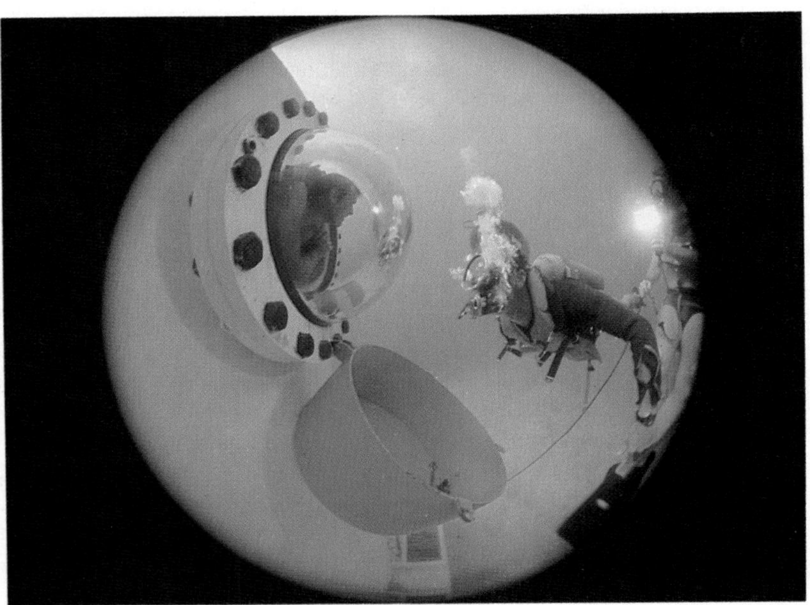

Figure 3.3 The significance of culture is that it enables us to invent and learn ways of adapting to our environments and changing situations. All other animals must rely on the slow and accidental process of biological evolution to adapt them to the environment, but human beings can adapt quickly to radically different environments.

Figure 3.4 The Tasaday, a recently discovered "stone age" tribe in the Philippines, apparently do not have words in their language to express enmity or hatred. Competition, acquisitiveness, aggression, and greed are all unknown among these gentle people. The existence of societies like the Tasaday challenges Western assumptions about "human nature."

the world, particularly in the West, we tend to think of people as being "naturally" self-seeking, selfish, competitive, and even aggressive. But this kind of behavior is virtually unknown among many of the "primitive" peoples of the world, such as the Arapesh of New Guinea, the pygmies of the Ituri forest in central Africa, the Shoshone of the western United States, or the Lepchas of Sikkim in the Himalayas. There are many societies that never fight wars at all, and there is even one group, the Tasaday of the Philippines, that apparently does not even have words in its language to express enmity or hatred. These people presumably have a very different conception of "human nature."

In fact, "human nature," if there is such a thing at all, is highly flexible. Our genetic heritage merely sets limits on what we can do and provides the potential framework for our actual behavior. Human behavior itself is a product of an interaction between our basic biological heritage and the learning experiences of the particular culture in which we happen to live. For example, we have the biological capacity to speak, but which language we use and how we use it depends on our cultural environment. We have the biological capacity to laugh, to cry, to blush, to become angry, but the circumstances under which we might do any of these things are learned in society. Nature provides us with legs, but we are not obliged to use them only for walking. We can use them to kick footballs, or to kick other people, or to ride bicycles, or to do a war dance or a fox-trot, or to sit cross-legged while contemplating.

Most modern psychologists believe that human beings do not have any "instincts." An instinct is a *complex* pattern of behavior that is genetically determined, such as nest building in birds or termites. Any "instincts" that we once had have been lost in the course of our evolution. The idea that we do not have any "instincts" is difficult for some people to accept, because it seems to run counter to "common sense." One reason for the difficulty is that the word "instinct" is often used very loosely in ordinary speech. People talk about "instinctively" stepping on the brake or "instinctively" mistrusting someone, when these actions and attitudes are, in fact, culturally learned. Another reason is that much of our learned behavior is so taken for granted that it becomes "second nature" to us. The behavior seems so "natural" that we lose the awareness that it is learned, not inherited.

We do have some genetically determined behaviors, of course, but these are *simple reflexes*—starting when we hear a loud noise, throwing up our arms when we lose our balance, removing our hand when it touches a hot surface. We also have a few inborn, basic *drives*—needs for self-preservation, for food and drink, for sex, and perhaps for the company of other people. But the way we actually satisfy these drives is learned through cultural experience. We all periodically experience hunger, but we have to learn what can be eaten and what may be eaten. Human beings are not genetically programmed to eat very specific kinds of food. We have to learn through experience that some things are edible and some are inedible. We also have to learn that some edible foods may not be eaten. Roaches, pigs, dogs, snails, cows, crabs, butterflies, and human beings are all edible and nutritious. Each of these animals is regarded as "food" in some societies, while in other societies it would be unthinkable to eat them. Similarly, we experience drives for sexual satisfaction, but the form this satisfaction takes is learned. Some people learn to derive satisfaction from the opposite sex, some from the same sex, some from both, some from inanimate objects, some from other species, and some from one or more of various other possibilities. Most people, of course, learn to satisfy their drives in the way that their own culture tells them to. But we are not genetically programmed to satisfy them in any particular way. If we were, we would all fulfill our drives in a rigid, identical manner. In fact, unlike all other species, we can even override our drives completely. We can ignore the drive for self-preservation by committing suicide or by risking our lives for others. Protestors can go on hunger strikes, even if it means starvation. Priests and others can suppress the sex drive and live out their lives in celibacy.

Within very broad limits, "human nature" is what we make of it, and what we make of it depends on the culture in which we happen to live. One of the most liberating aspects of the sociological perspective is that it strips away myths about our social behavior, showing that what seems "natural" or "instinctive" is usually nothing more than a cultural product of human society.

Norms

When Captain Cook asked the chiefs in Tahiti why they always ate apart and alone, they replied, "Because it is right" (Linton, 1945). If we ask Americans why they eat with knives and forks, or why their men wear pants instead of skirts, or why they may be married to only one person at a time, we are likely to get similar and very uninformative answers: "Because it's right." "Because that's the way it's done." "Because it's the custom." Or even "I don't know."

The reason for these and countless other patterns of social behavior is that they are controlled by social *norms*—shared rules or guidelines that prescribe the behavior that is appropriate in a given situation. Norms define how people "ought" to behave under particular circumstances in a particular society. We conform to norms so readily that we are hardly aware they exist. In fact, we are much more likely to notice departures from norms than conformity to them. You would not be surprised if a stranger tried to shake hands when you were introduced, but you might be a little startled if he or she bowed, curtsied, started to stroke you, or kissed you on both cheeks. Yet each of these other forms of greeting is appropriate in other parts of the world. When we visit another society whose norms are different, we quickly become aware that we do things *this* way, they do them *that* way.

Some norms apply to every member of society. In the United States, for example, nobody is permitted to marry more than one person at the same time. Other norms apply to some people but not to others. There is a very strong norm in American society against the taking of human life, but this norm does not apply to policemen in shootouts, soldiers in combat, or innocent people acting in self-defense against armed attackers. Other norms are even more specific and prescribe the appropriate behavior for people in particular situations, such as college students in lecture rooms, shop clerks serving the public, or marijuana smokers rolling and sharing a joint.

Folkways and Mores

Norms ensure that social life proceeds smoothly, for they give us guidelines for our own behavior and reliable expectations for the behavior of others. This social function of norms is so important that there is always strong social pressure on people to conform. But although most of us conform to most norms most of the time, all of us tend to violate some norms occasionally. In the case of certain norms, the folkways, a fair amount of nonconformity may be tolerated, but in the case of certain other norms, the mores, very little leeway is permitted (Sumner, 1906).

Folkways

The *folkways* are the ordinary usages and conventions of everyday life; they are, quite literally, the "ways of the folk." Conformity to folkways is expected but is not absolutely insisted upon. We expect people to keep their lawns mowed, to refrain from picking their noses in public, to turn up on time for appointments, and to wear a matching pair of shoes. Those who do not conform to these and similar folkways are considered peculiar and eccentric, particularly if they consistently violate a number of folkways. But they are not considered immoral or depraved, nor are they treated as criminals. People are not deeply outraged by violations of folkways and on the whole are tolerant of a certain amount of nonconformity to them.

Mores

The *mores* (pronounced "mor-ays") are much stronger norms. People attach a moral significance to them and treat violations of them much more seriously. (The word "mores" was a Latin term for the ancient Romans' most respected and even sacred customs.) A man who walks down a street wearing nothing on the upper half of his body is violating a folkway; a man who walks down the street wearing nothing on the lower half of his body is violating one of our most important mores, the requirement that people cover their genitals and buttocks in public. Theft, drug abuse, murder, rape, desecration of the American flag, or contemptuous use of religious symbols all excite a strong social reaction. People believe that their mores are crucial for the maintenance of a decent and orderly society, and the offender may be strongly criticized, punched, imprisoned, committed to a mental asylum, or even lynched. Some violations of mores are made almost unthinkable by *taboos*—powerful social beliefs that the acts concerned are utterly loathsome. In the United States, for example, there is a very strong taboo against eating human flesh, a taboo so effective that most of our states do not even bother to have laws prohibiting the practice.

Not all norms can be neatly categorized as either folkways or mores. In practice, norms fall at various points on a continuum, depending on how seriously they are taken by society. There is also a constant shift in the importance attached to some norms. The fashion of short hair for men was apparently regarded by many Americans as one of our mores for most of this century. Youths who grew their hair long in the early sixties were sometimes insulted, attacked, and even shot at. In the 1970s, however, long hair on young males has almost become a folkway. In many parts of the country a youth with a crewcut might draw curious glances, at least from his own age group.

Some norms, particularly mores, are encoded in law. A *law* is simply a rule that has been formally enacted by a political authority and is backed by the power of the state. The law usually codifies important norms that already exist, but sometimes political authorities attempt to introduce new norms by enacting appropriate laws. Civil rights legislation in the United States, for example, was aimed at destroying some traditional norms of race relations and replacing them with new ones. Attempts to introduce new norms in this way are not always successful, as the American attempt to legislate the prohibition of liquor proved. Laws that run counter to cultural norms, particularly in the area of personal morality, are often ineffectual and tend to fall into disuse. For example, many of our drug laws and laws prohibiting sports and entertainments on Sundays are now widely disregarded.

Social Control

Every society must have a system of *social control,* a set of means of ensuring that its members generally behave in socially expected and approved ways. Some of this social control over the individual can be exercised by others, either formally through such agencies as the police and government inspectors or informally through the reactions of other people in the course of everyday life. All norms, whether they are codified in law or not, are supported by *sanctions,* social rewards for conformity and social punishments for nonconformity. The positive sanctions may range from an approving nod to a ceremony of public acclaim; the negative sanctions may range from mild disapproval to imprisonment or even execution. Only a tiny fraction of social behavior can be policed by formal agencies of control, and most sanctions are applied informally. If you help your neighbors and are polite to them, you will be rewarded with smiles and popularity. If you use "bad" language in the wrong company or offer your left hand rather than your right when someone wants to shake hands with you, you will receive raised eyebrows, glares, stares, or comments designed to make you uncomfortable and more likely to conform to social expectations in the future.

Most social control, however, does not have to be exercised through the direct influence of others. We do it ourselves, internally. In the process of growing up in society we unconsciously *internalize* the norms of our culture, making conformity to them a part of our personality and following social expectations without question. Like the chiefs on Tahiti and like people all over the world, we are controlled by society without even realizing it. For the most part, we behave the way we do because "That's the way it's done."

Values

The norms of a society are ultimately an expression of its *values*—socially shared ideas about what is good, right, and desirable. The difference between values and norms is that values are abstract, general concepts, whereas norms are behavioral rules or guidelines for people in particular kinds of situations.

The Importance of Values

The values of a society are important because they influence the content of its norms. If a society values education highly, its norms will make provision for mass schooling. If it values a large population, its norms will make provision for big families. If it values monogamy, its norms will not permit people to marry more than one partner at a time. In principle at least, all norms can be traced to a basic social value. The norms that prescribe the routines of office work and assembly-line production, for example, reflect the high value we place on efficiency. The norms that require a student to be more polite and formal to a professor than to fellow students express the value our society places on respect for authority and learning. The norms that insisted on short hair for men reflected the very high value placed on men's "masculinity" in American culture; until it became fashionable, long hair was regarded as "effeminate."

Although all norms express social values, many norms persist long after the conditions that gave rise to them have been forgotten. The folkway that requires a male to walk on the side nearest the street when accompanying a female, for example, dates back to a time when the sidewalk was regularly splashed with mud as horses trotted along the unpaved streets. The norm simply reflected the high value placed on chivalry in the male and dependence in the female. The folkway that requires us to shake hands, especially when greeting a stranger, seems to have originated long ago in the desire to show that no weapon was concealed in the right hand. Our folkway of showering a new bride and groom with rice or confetti as they emerge from the wedding ceremony may seem rather meaningless, but it actually reflects the high value that earlier ages placed on fertility. Newlyweds were once showered with fruit, nuts, and seeds as symbols of fertility; today we substitute bits of paper, rarely understanding why we behave as we do.

American Values

Unlike norms, whose existence can easily be observed in everyday behavior, values are often more difficult to identify. The values of a society have to be inferred from its norms, so that any analysis of social values relies heavily on the interpretations of the observer concerned.

One of the most influential attempts to identify the major values of American society is that of Robin Williams (1970), who detects fifteen basic "value orientations" that are expressed in the norms that guide our behavior.

Figure 3.5 Social norms reflect social values. The American norm requiring marijuana to be shared reflects the high value placed on intimacy and solidarity in those nonconformist groups in which marijuana use first arose. A tobacco cigarette, in contrast, is rarely shared in the same way, because cigarette smoking does not have the same cultural origins and is generally regarded as an individual affair. A tobacco smoker may, however, offer other cigarettes from the pack to those present, a folkway that expresses the value we place on small acts of generosity.

1. *Achievement and success.* Our society is highly competitive, and we place great value on the achievement of power, wealth, and prestige.

2. *Activity and work.* Regular, disciplined work is highly valued for its own sake; those who do not work are considered lazy and even immoral.

3. *Moral orientation.* Americans tend to be moralists, seeing the world in terms of right and wrong and constantly evaluating the moral behavior of others.

4. *Humanitarian mores.* We regard ourselves as a kindly, charitable people, always ready to come to the aid of the less fortunate or the underdog.

5. *Efficiency and practicality.* We believe that problems have solutions and are an intensely practical people; the ability to "get things done" is widely admired.

6. *Progress.* We look to the future rather than the past, sharing a conviction that things can and should get better; our outlook is fundamentally optimistic.

7. *Material comfort.* Americans value the "good life," which they define in terms of a high standard of living and the possession of material goods.

8. *Equality.* Americans claim to believe in human equality, particularly in equality of opportunity; they generally relate to one another in an informal, egalitarian way.

9. *Freedom.* The freedom of the individual is regarded as one of the most important values in American life; Americans believe devoutly that they are and should remain "free."

10. *External conformity.* Despite their expressed belief in "rugged individualism," Americans tend to be conformist and are suspicious of those who are not.

11. *Science and rationality.* Americans believe deeply in a scientific, rational approach to the world and in the use of applied science to gain mastery over the environment.

12. *Nationalism–patriotism.* Americans are proud of their country and its achievements; the "American way of life" is highly valued and "un-American" behavior is viewed with suspicion and distrust.

13. *Democracy.* Americans regard their form of government as highly democratic, and believe that every citizen should have the right of political participation.

14. *Individual personality.* To be a responsible, self-respecting individual is very important, and Americans are reluctant to give the group priority over the individual.

15. *Group-superiority themes.* A strong countervalue to that of individual personality is the one that places a higher value on some racial, ethnic, class, or religious groups than on others.

It is obvious that many of these values are not entirely consistent with each other. Many of them, too, are changing or are accepted by some Americans but rejected by others. It is also clear that Williams's list does not exhaust all of the possibilities. Other writers have identified rather different sets of values. James Henslin (1975), for example, includes several items on Williams's list but adds other important values, such as education, religiosity, male supremacy, romantic love, monogamy, and heterosexuality. Although these and other analyses may be overlapping and imprecise, they give us useful insights into our culture and thus into the norms that guide our social behavior.

Cultural Variation

The set of norms and values that exist in the United States is unique to our society. The same is true of the culture of every other society. Each culture is distinctive and contains elements, or combinations of elements, found nowhere else. Americans eat oysters but not snails. The French eat snails but not locusts. The Zulus eat locusts but not fish. The Jews eat fish but not pork. The Hindus eat pork but not beef. The Russians eat beef but not snakes. The Chinese eat snakes but not people. The Jalé of New Guinea find people delicious. We spend our lives accumulating private possessions; the BaMbuti of the Congo forests spend their lives sharing their goods; the Kwakiutl of the Pacific Northwest periodically gave them away or even destroyed them at great ceremonies. Our norms have traditionally valued premarital chastity; the norms of the Mentawei of Indonesia require women to become pregnant before they can be considered eligible for marriage; the norms of the Keraki of New Guinea require premarital homosexuality in every male. Women in traditional Arab societies must cover the entire body and even the face; American women may expose their faces but must keep their breasts and the entire pelvic region concealed; women in many parts of Africa may expose their breasts and buttocks but not the genital region; women in Tierra del Fuego may not expose their backs; and Tasaday women in the Philippines proceed about their daily lives stark naked. The range of cultural variation is so immense that there is probably no specific norm that appears in every human society. How can we account for this variation?

The Functionalist Approach

One way of analyzing the components of culture is to look for the *functions* that these components have in maintaining the social order as a whole. Functionalist theorists regard society and culture as a system of interdependent parts. They argue that no one cultural element can be understood in isolation from the social and cultural whole. To explain a particular cultural trait, therefore, one has to establish its functions in making the entire system "work." The functionalist approach has long been popular in studies of other cultures (for example, Radcliffe-Brown, 1935, 1952; Malinowski, 1926, 1948) and has been influential in American sociology during much of this century (for example, Parsons, 1951; Merton, 1968).

In traditional Eskimo society, hospitality to a traveler was very highly valued. A host was obliged to do everything possible to make a traveler comfortable, even if he found the man personally offensive. There was even a norm requiring a host to offer his wife to a guest for the night. This culture trait of obligatory hospitality is an unusual one, entirely unknown in urban, industrial societies. But it was highly functional in Eskimo culture. Travel through snows and arctic blizzards would be utterly impossible unless the traveler could rely on the certainty of food, warmth, and rest at the next settlement, and the host in turn could expect the same hospitality when he next traveled. Without the norm of universal hospitality, communication and trade between various Eskimo groups might have been too hazardous to undertake. A similar norm does not exist in the United States today, where it would make no sense. We have institutionalized other arrangements, such as restaurants and motels, to serve the same function, and the need for protection from the environment is not so pressing.

Figure 3.6 Many of the variations among cultures can be explained in ecological terms. The way of life of the Eskimos of the Arctic Circle differs radically from that of these New Guinea villagers, for each people faces very different environmental pressures. The clothing of the Eskimo, for example, reflects the need for protection against the intense cold. In the tropical climate of New Guinea, where elaborate clothing would be a hindrance, more emphasis is given to body ornaments.

The Cheyenne Indians periodically gathered for a Sun Dance ceremony. Why? The activity brought no obvious rewards and seemed only to distract the various Cheyenne bands from the more mundane activities of making a living in their own areas. A functionalist analysis again suggests the reason. The Sun Dance gave the entire tribe an opportunity to gather together for a common purpose, to reestablish social bonds with one another, and to confirm their sense that they were not simply a scattering of isolated bands but rather a tribe united by similar cultural practices. In the same way, the high value that Americans place on competition and success can be explained in terms of its function in maintaining the capitalist system on which American economic life is believed to depend.

Functionalist theory can thus help us to understand why a particular culture trait is present in one society but not in others. It sometimes has the disadvantage, however, that it focuses on how things "fit together" at a particular moment in cultural history and tends to neglect the process of cultural change. Changes—the introduction of a new religion, for example—may throw other parts of the cultural system into some disorder, and there is always a temptation to see these changes as "dysfunctions," as irritants to the system rather than as useful adaptations to changing conditions.

The Ecological Approach

A second approach has recently become increasingly popular, particularly among anthropologists studying other cultures (for example, Harris, 1974, 1975). These writers attempt to explain a great deal of the variation in human cultures by taking an *ecological* approach, that is, by analyzing cultural elements in the context of the total environment in which the society exists. Culture, as we have seen, is a means of adapting to the environment, and a people's cultural practices are necessarily linked to the pressures and opportunities of the environment in which they live.

The traditional culture of the Eskimo offers an obvious example of this kind of adaptation because their harsh environment set such severe limits on their cultural options. Eskimos lived in homes built of stones, driftwood, and mud, not in open tents or skyscrapers; they had no choice. Their culture was centered around fishing and the hunting of large sea mammals, for there was little else to eat; naturally, their religion did not include gods of rain or agriculture. Their material culture was necessarily based on their limited environmental resources. They had to use snow for building temporary shelters, or igloos, animal skins for clothing, bones for harpoons and other artifacts, and seal or whale blubber for lighting. Almost every important element in traditional Eskimo culture can be traced back to the influence of the environment in which they lived.

The relationship of other cultural practices to the total environment is not always as obvious, but the ecological approach has been successfully used to explain several otherwise puzzling practices. Marvin Harris (1974), for example, applies the ecological perspective to the apparently irrational veneration that Indians have for cows. Although only one Indian in fifty has an adequate diet, the Hindu religion forbids the slaughter of cows. As a result, over 100 million cows roam freely through the countryside and cities of India, snarling traffic and defecating in public places. Western observers are apt to regard most of these cows as "useless." They are scrawny animals, yielding little milk and apparently contributing nothing of value to Indian life.

Harris points out, however, that the cows perform a number of irreplaceable economic functions. A large part of the Indian population lives on small farms, and at least one pair of oxen is needed for ploughing purposes on each farm. These farming families live on the brink of starvation and cannot afford tractors. They must use oxen, and oxen are produced not by factories but by cows. Widespread cow slaughter would worsen the already critical shortage of draft animals, making the existing farms too unproductive and driving as many as 150 million impoverished and unemployable people into the already crowded cities. Moreover, the cows provide India annually with some 700 million tons of manure. About half of this total is used as fertilizer by farmers who could not possibly afford chemical substitutes. The remainder is used as cooking fuel, a vital resource in a country that has very little oil or coal and an acute shortage of wood. And when the cows finally die they are eaten, not by Hindus but by outcastes who are not bound by the Hindu religion and are generally even poorer and hungrier than the rest of the population. The hides of the animals are then used in India's huge leatherworking industry. The cows themselves do not compete with human beings for food. Unlike American cattle, which are often fed grain, they scavenge what they can from roadsides and other unproductive land. In short, the sacred cow is an important element in the entire Indian ecology. As Harris observes, the Indians would probably rather eat their cows than starve, but they would surely starve if they did eat them.

The ecological approach is useful because it can take full account of cultural change. It can readily explain, for example, the changes that have taken place in modern Eskimo culture following the introduction of snowmobiles, central heating, and synthetic materials. It differs from the functionalist approach mainly in that it takes fuller account of the external factors that might influence or change culture. But the two approaches are not incompatible; their interpretations are often simply a matter of emphasis. We could say, for example, that Eskimo hospitality is functional for Eskimo society, or we could say that it results from ecological pressures. By combining the approaches we gain a better overall understanding of cultural variation.

Different societies, of course, may adopt different solutions to similar functional requirements or ecological problems. Many societies face the problem that their environment does not offer enough food resources to maintain a growing population. The Eskimo solved the problem by deliberately leaving a proportion of female infants and many aged, unproductive people out in the snow to die. The Yanamamö of Brazil keep their population down by killing or deliberately starving female infants and by practicing incessant and bloody warfare between their males. The Keraki of New Guinea limit population increase by requiring males to engage in exclusively homosexual relations for several years after puberty. The United States restricts population growth by valuing relatively small families, by permitting abortion, and by using such cultural artifacts as birth-control pills. In Bangladesh and many overpopulated developing nations, the cultural response is not nearly as effective. Little attempt is made to restrict population growth, with the result that as many as half of the children die in the first few years of life of starvation or diseases related to malnutrition.

It must also be recognized that not all cultural elements can be readily explained in functional or ecological terms.

Some practices may diffuse from one culture to another as a result of invasion, migration, or trading, and these alien elements may be adopted as long as they are not dysfunctional or counterecological in the long run. Cultural elements may also persist for decades or centuries after the conditions that gave rise to them have vanished. Culture always tends to be conservative, and traditions may be followed long after their origins are forgotten and the need for them has disappeared.

Cultural Universals

Are there any *cultural universals* in the midst of this variety—practices that are found in every single culture? The answer is that there are a fairly large number of *general* cultural universals, but there do not seem to be any *specific* universal practices. Every culture, for example, has norms prohibiting murder, but different cultures have very different ideas about which homicides constitute murder and which do not. We would consider human sacrifice murder, but the Aztecs did not. Vietnamese peasants no doubt considered our systematic bombing of their communities as murder, but many Americans did not. We would consider the slaughter of an inoffensive stranger as murder, but there are still some small, isolated societies in which the norms permit any outsider to be slaughtered on the spot.

Cultural universals derive from our basic biological heritage and from the common problems that the environment poses for our species. The weather is often too hot or too cold for comfort, and clothing and housing arrangements must be made to adapt us to the climate. Children need care and attention, and some cultural provision must be made for this requirement. Human hair grows, and something must periodically be done about it. People become sick, and attempts must be made to cure them. Individuals must be distinguished from one another, and so they are given names. Life is often hard and death awaits us all, and people everywhere invent myths and religious beliefs to explain the human predicament.

The anthropologist George Murdock (1945) compiled a lengthy list of general traits found in every culture, including the following: athletic sports, bodily adornment, cooking, cooperative labor, courtship, dancing, dream interpretation, family, feasting, folklore, food taboos, funeral ceremonies, games, gift giving, incest taboos, laws, medicine, music, myths, numerals, personal names, property rights, religion, sexual restrictions, toilet training, toolmaking, and attempts to influence the weather. But these are only general traits; their specific content varies from one culture to another.

Ethnocentrism

Cultures may vary, but most human beings spend their entire lives within the culture in which they were born. They readily assume that their own cultural arrangements are inevitable, "natural," and "normal," a part of "human nature." Knowing little about alternative ways of life, they see their own norms and values as necessities rather than options. As one anthropologist (Linton, 1936) has observed:

> It has been said that the last thing which a dweller in the deep sea would discover would be water. He would become conscious of its existence only if some accident brought him to the surface and introduced him to air. Man, throughout most of his history, has been only vaguely aware of the existence of culture. . . . The ability to see the culture of one's own society as a whole . . . calls for a degree of objectivity which is rarely if ever achieved.

For this reason, people in every society are to some extent guilty of *ethnocentrism*—the tendency to judge other cultures by the standards of one's own. People everywhere are apt to assume that their morality, their marriage forms, their clothing styles, or their concepts of beauty are right, proper, and the best of all possible alternatives. Here are some examples of ethnocentric thinking. Our women put rings through their ears and cosmetics on their faces because it enhances their beauty; their women put bones through their noses and scars on their faces because, in their pitiful ignorance, they don't realize how ugly it makes them. We won't eat cats or worms because that would be cruel or disgusting; they won't eat beef or drink milk because of some silly food taboo. We cover our private parts because we are decorous and civilized; they walk around naked because they are ignorant and shameless. Our brave soldiers achieve glorious victories over the enemy; their fanatical soldiers perpetrate bloody massacres on us. Our sexual practices are moral and decent; theirs are primitive or perverse. Our religion is the one true faith; theirs is heathen superstition.

Ethnocentrism is particularly strong in isolated societies that have little contact with other cultures. But even in modern industrial societies, where citizens have the advantages of formal education, mass communications, and international travel, ethnocentric attitudes still prevail. As Linton observes, one reason for the persistence of ethnocentrism is that it is almost impossible to view one's own culture objectively; but another reason is that ethnocentrism can be functional to a society. Ethnocentrism provides faith and confidence in one's own cultural tradition, discourages penetration by outsiders, and thus ensures the solidarity and unity of the group. But under some conditions ethnocentrism can have many undesirable effects. It can encourage racism, it can cause hostility and conflict between groups, and it can make a people unwilling to recognize the need for changes in their own culture.

Ethnocentrism also poses a severe problem for social scientists analyzing other cultures, because they often bring to the task unconscious and often unfounded assumptions about other people and their practices. Even trained observers experience "culture shock" when confronted with cultures radically unlike their own. Napoleon Chagnon, an anthropologist who studied the Yanamamö of Brazil, was aghast when he first met his subjects. They stank to his nostrils (though not, of course, to their own), the heads of the men were covered with scars from their incessant fighting, and they were under the influence of a local psychedelic drug—one of whose effects was to produce strings of green mucous that hung from their noses and were rarely wiped away. Chagnon (1967) recalls:

> I am not ashamed to admit . . . that had there been a diplomatic way out, I would have ended my fieldwork there and then. I did not look forward to the next day when I would be left alone with the Indians: I did not speak a word of their language, and they were decidedly different from what I had imagined them to be. The whole situation was depressing, and I wondered why I had ever decided to switch from civil engineering to anthropology in the first place.

Yet Chagnon was eventually able, after living among the Yanamamö for many months, to adjust to their culture and to develop a sympathetic understanding of their way of life.

Figure 3.7 The norms and values of a culture cannot be arbitrarily judged by those of another culture. From the viewpoint of American culture, the traditional Middle Eastern practice of hiding the entire female body from view seems silly; from the point of view of this Bedouin woman from Oman, the American practice of exposing so much of the female body to public view would be shameful and obscene. Neither viewpoint is objectively "right," for each practice can be fully understood only in its own context.

Cultural Relativism

The ability to achieve a full understanding of another culture depends largely on one's willingness to adopt the position of *cultural relativism,* the recognition that one culture cannot be arbitrarily judged by the standards of another. We are quick to complain when foreign critics—the Russians, for example—judge our culture in terms of their own values, for we feel that such a judgment distorts the reality of our culture and society. We have to be equally on guard against using our own standards to judge other cultures, for the real meaning of their practices can only be fully understood in their terms.

It is probably never possible to be entirely free of bias in favor of one's own culture. However hard we try, the sneaking feeling is likely to persist that our standards of judgment *are* better. Yet we must recognize that judgments about good and bad, moral and immoral, depend very much on who is doing the judging; there is no universal standard to appeal to. People everywhere may *feel* that their own standards are superior, but there is no logical way they can *prove* it. Failure to adopt the position of cultural relativism is simply another example of ethnocentrism, and the problem with ethnocentrism is that it works both ways. We are shocked at the traditional Eskimo practice of leaving the aged in the snow to die, but the Japanese are appalled at our practice of excluding aged parents from the family and leaving them to die in old-age homes. We are shocked at the Yanamamö practice of infanticide, but the San ("Bushmen") of the Kalahari could not begin to comprehend how we can permit poverty and malnutrition in our own society when we have so much surplus wealth. Our own practices can only be fully understood in the total context of our culture, and the same applies to other people.

Cultural relativism does not mean that we can never pass judgment on the practices of another society. No responsible social scientist, for example, could fail to condemn the mass murders perpetrated by the Nazis. What cultural relativism means is that the practices of another society—including Nazi Germany—can only be fully understood in terms of its own cultural norms and values. For the practical purpose of understanding human behavior it is vital that observers try, as far as possible, to remove the blinkers of their own culture when they are looking at another.

Figure 3.8 The entire culture of the Plains Indians centered around the buffalo. Their religion focused on the buffalo hunt, and the prestige of individual males was linked to their skills and courage as hunters. The carcass of the buffalo provided most of the items in the Indians' material culture—hides, tendons, bones, and membranes were all put to use for various purposes, including clothing and shelter. The Indians' nomadic way of life was based on the need to follow the migrations of the animals on which they depended for a living. When white settlers used their superior technology to systematically slaughter the buffalo, the culture of the Plains Indians disintegrated and their societies collapsed. When the Indians were settled on reservations and given cattle to raise, they sometimes turned the animals loose and hunted them like buffalo: there was nothing in their culture that prepared them to tend and milk cows.

Cultural Integration

A culture clearly does not consist of a random collection of different elements. The skills, customs, values, beliefs, practices, and other characteristics of a culture tend to complement one another or to be *integrated* into a complex whole. If a culture is to survive, it must be integrated to a considerable extent, although in practice some cultures are more integrated than others.

In traditional, preindustrial societies, culture is usually highly integrated. These societies tend to be relatively small, and people share similar values. Culture is generally homogeneous and the rate of cultural change is often very slow. In modern industrial soceities, on the other hand, the various cultural elements are not as well integrated. Industrial societies are often large and contain many different groups that have somewhat different ways of life. Culture is relatively heterogeneous, and there is often considerable dispute over values. Social and cultural change occur rapidly and unevenly, with the result that different components of the culture are constantly having to adjust to changes elsewhere in the system.

The fact that cultures tend to be integrated is often not apparent until changes occur in one part of a culture, throwing other parts into disorganization or generating widespread resistance to change. This was the fate of the culture of the Plains Indians (see Figure 3.8).

Real Culture and Ideal Culture

One common source of strain in a culture is the discrepancy that sometimes exists between *ideal culture,* as expressed in the values and norms a people claim to believe in, and *real culture,* as expressed in their actual practices. In the United States, for example, we claim to believe in equality, yet our society contains people who are millionaires and people who are impoverished. We place a very high value on honesty, yet citizens who would never dream of shoplifting or picking pockets routinely evade payment of part of their taxes if they can get away with it. There is often a considerable gap between our ideal norms and our real norms: we have a traditional norm, for example, that sexual intercourse should take place only in the context of marriage, but the statistical data on premarital and extramarital intercourse show that this norm is violated by the great majority of Americans at one time or another.

A society is often able to overlook the contradictions between real and ideal culture. As devout Buddhists, fishermen in Burma are forbidden to kill anything, including fish. Yet they must fish to live. How do they overcome the contradiction? What happens is that the fish are first caught and then "are merely put on the bank to dry after their long soaking in the river, and if they are foolish or ill-judged enough to die while undergoing the process, it is their own fault" (Lowie, 1940). In a similar way, Americans often tolerate highly questionable commercial and advertising practices on the grounds that "business is business," and is somehow exempt from many of the usual norms of morality. Sometimes, however, the strains between real and ideal culture become so great that changes must be made to integrate the two more closely. The strains between the American value of equality and the reality of racial discrimination became so great that a civil war and widespread disturbances took place before our society was brought into a state of greater, but by no means complete, cultural integration.

Subcultures and Countercultures

A second source of strain in a culture arises from the existence of groups that do not participate fully in the dominant culture of the society. These groups are especially common in large, heterogeneous modern industrial societies, in which there are many cultural differences between members of different regional, religious, occupational, and other communities.

Subcultures

A *subculture* is a group that shares in the overall culture of the society but also has its own distinctive values, norms, and life-style. In the United States, for example, we have subcultures of the young, of the rich and the poor, of different racial and ethnic groups, and of different regions of the country. Smaller subcultures exist in the military, in prisons, on college campuses, among drug addicts, or among street-corner gangs. People in each of these subcultures tend to be ethnocentric in relation to other subcultures, for membership in a subculture colors one's view of reality. A member of a wealthy, "jet-set" subculture doubtless has a different perspective on American social reality than a member of a subculture of Hell's Angels or Chicano migrant laborers. If the differences between subcultures are sufficiently great, the results may be *value conflict,* deep disagreements over goals, ideals, and policies.

It is important that sociologists—and this includes sociology students—should adopt a position of cultural relativism toward subcultures as well as toward other cultures. It is all too easy for sociologists—most of whom are white and middle class—to adopt ethnocentric attitudes toward subcultures within American society, arbitrarily judging other groups by the standards of the dominant culture. The practices of any subculture, whether it is made up of ghetto blacks, poor whites, heroin addicts, or the very rich, can only be fully understood by reference to its own norms and values.

Countercultures

A *counterculture* is a subculture that is fundamentally at odds with the dominant culture: it consciously rejects some of the most important norms of the wider society and is usually proud of it. The youth movement of the sixties is a good modern example of a counterculture; its "dropout" hippie wing and its "activist" political wing together challenged a whole range of treasured American norms and values, including those centered on success, hard work, material comfort, conformity, scientific rationality, white superiority, and sexual restrictiveness (Roszak, 1969). A large counterculture inevitably generates strain and value conflict in society, as the turmoil of the sixties showed. In this particular case, a measure of cultural integration was finally achieved partly because the mainstream culture incorporated some countercultural values and norms and partly because young people themselves abandoned many countercultural norms and values (Kunen, 1973).

Figure 3.9

"Daddy, this is my man."

Language

One of the most important of all human characteristics is our capacity to communicate with one another through language. Although chimpanzees can be taught to construct "sentences" from a small "vocabulary" of physical objects (Mounin, 1976), only human beings have spoken language. Language is a form of communication that differs radically from the forms used by other species. Other animals can communicate with sounds, gestures, touch, and chemical emissions, but the meaning of these signals is fixed, and their use is limited to the immediate situation. With the exception of the sign languages that chimpanzees have been taught to use in artificial situations, the signals in animal communication are genetically predetermined and are merely automatic responses to given conditions. These signals can be used to warn of danger, to indicate the presence of food, to claim territory, or to express fear, aggression, and sexual arousal—but little else. The signals cannot be combined in new ways to produce different or more complex information. A monkey can signal "food!" but not "bananas, tomorrow!"

Language, on the other hand, does not consist of fixed signals: it consists of learned symbols. A *symbol* is simply something that meaningfully represents something else. Gestures, facial expressions, drawings, or numbers are all symbols, but the most useful and flexible symbols of all are spoken or written words. Words are arbitrary symbols for objects and concepts, and every human language consists

Helen Keller: The Importance of Language

Although we usually think of our sight as our most important sense, people who are born deaf are more often disadvantaged than people who are born blind: for example, they are more likely to be intellectually retarded. The reason is that deafness makes it difficult for them to learn language, and thus cuts them off from the symbolic world of other human beings. The achievements of Helen Keller, who was left blind and deaf by a serious disease in infancy, are therefore all the more remarkable. Although she was unable to see or hear the world around her, she was able, at the age of seven, to learn the use of spoken language. Language gave her an intelligent understanding of an environment that until then had been almost meaningless to her. She was later able to write books and even to conduct orchestras, responding to the vibrations of the musical instruments. This is Helen Keller's moving account of how she first discovered language.

The most important day I remember in all my life is the one on which my teacher, Anne Mansfield Sullivan, came to me. I am filled with wonder when I consider the immeasurable contrast between the two lives which it connects. It was the third of March, 1887, three months before I was seven years old.

The morning after my teacher came she led me into her room and gave me a doll. The little blind children at the Perkins Institution had sent it and Laura Bridgman had dressed it; but I did not know this until afterward. When I had played with it a little while Miss Sullivan slowly spelled into my hand the word "d-o-l-l." I was at once interested in this finger play and tried to imitate it. When I finally succeeded in making the letters correctly I was flushed with childish pleasure and pride. Running downstairs to my mother I held up my hand and made the letters for doll. I did not know that I was spelling a word or even that words existed; I was simply making my fingers go in monkey-like imitation. In the days that followed I learned to spell in this uncomprehending way a great many words, among them *pin, hat, cup,* and a few verbs like *sit, stand,* and *walk.* But my teacher had been with me several weeks before I understood that everything has a name.

One day, while I was playing with my new doll, Miss Sullivan put my big rag doll into my lap also, spelled "d-o-l-l" and tried to make me understand that "d-o-l-l" applied to both. Earlier in the day we had had a tussle over the word "m-u-g" and "w-a-t-e-r." Miss Sullivan had tried to impress it upon me that "m-u-g" is *mug* and that "w-a-t-e-r" is *water,* but I persisted in confounding the two. In despair she had dropped the subject for the time, only to renew it at the first opportunity. I became impatient with her repeated attempts and, seizing the new doll, I dashed it upon the floor. I was keenly delighted when I felt the fragments of the broken doll at my feet. Neither sorrow nor regret followed my passionate outburst. I had not loved the doll. In the still, dark world in which I lived there was no strong sentiment or tenderness. I felt my teacher sweep the fragments to one side of the hearth, and I had a sense of satisfaction that the cause of my discomfort was removed. She brought me my hat, and I knew I was going out into the warm sunshine. This thought, if a wordless sensation may be called a thought, made me hop and skip with pleasure.

We walked down the path to the well-house, attracted by the fragrance of the honeysuckle with which it was covered. Some one was drawing water and my teacher placed my hand under the spout. As the cool stream gushed over one hand she spelled into the other word *water,* first slowly, then rapidly. I stood still, my whole attention fixed upon the motions of her fingers. Suddenly I felt a misty consciousness as of something forgotten—a thrill of returning thought; and somehow the mystery of language was revealed to me. I knew then that "w-a-t-e-r" meant the wonderful cool something that was flowing over my hand. That living word awakened my soul, gave it light, hope, joy, set it free! There were barriers still, it is true, but barriers that could in time be swept away.

I left the well-house eager to learn. Everything had a name, and each name gave birth to a new thought. As we returned to the house every object I touched seemed to quiver with life. That was because I saw everything with a strange, new sight that had come to me. On entering the door I remembered the doll I had broken. I felt my way to the hearth and picked up the pieces. I tried vainly to put them together. Then my eyes filled with tears; for I realized what I had done, and for the first time I felt repentance and sorrow.

I learned a great many new words that day. I do not remember what they all were; but I do know that *mother, father, sister, teacher,* were among them—words that were to make the world blossom for me, "like Aaron's rod, with flowers." It would have been difficult to find a happier child than I was as I lay in my crib at the close of that eventful day and lived over the joys it had brought me, and for the first time longed for a new day to come.

Source: Helen Keller, *The Story of My Life* (New York: Doubleday, 1903).

of hundreds of thousands of words whose meaning is socially agreed upon. These words can be combined according to grammatical rules to express any idea of which the human mind is capable.

The Importance of Language

Language is the keystone of culture. Without it, culture could not exist. Culture, by definition, is shared, and complex cultural patterns of thought, emotion, knowledge, and belief could not be passed from individual to individual or generation to generation without the medium of the spoken word. When an animal dies, everything it has learned from experience perishes with it. But language gives human beings a history—an access to the accumulated knowledge and experience of the generations that have gone before. Through language we are introduced to the collective experience of our society.

Equally important, language enables us to give meaning to the world. Events in themselves have no meaning; we impose meaning on them by interpreting the evidence of our senses. Without language, all but the most rudimentary forms of thought are impossible. With language, we can apply reason to the world. We can think logically from premises to conclusions: we can categorize; we can order our experience; we can contemplate the past and the future, the abstract and the hypothetical; we can formulate and utter ideas that are entirely new. Nearly all that we learn in human culture is learned through language in the course of social interaction with others. It is through language that we become cultured and thus fully human.

Linguistic Relativity

Shortly after World War II, George Orwell published a futuristic novel, *1984*, about a totalitarian dictatorship in which every aspect of social behavior was strictly controlled. The rulers of the state had even constructed a new language, Newspeak, whose vocabulary and grammar made it impossible for the subjects to think certain thoughts (Orwell, 1949):

> The word *free* still existed in Newspeak, but it could only be used in such statements as "This dog is free from lice" or "This field is free from weeds." It could not be used in the old sense of "politically free," or "intellectually free," since political and intellectual freedom no longer existed as concepts, and were therefore of necessity nameless. . . . Countless other words such as *honor, justice, morality, internationalism, democracy, science,* and *religion* had simply ceased to exist. A few blanket words covered them, and, in covering them, abolished them. All words grouping themselves around the concepts of liberty and equality, for instance, were contained in the single word *crimethink,* while all words grouping themselves around the concepts of objectivity and rationalism were contained in the single word *oldthink.*

Is it possible for the language we speak to structure our reality in this way? For many centuries it has been generally accepted that all languages reflect the same basic reality in the same basic way and that words and concepts can be freely and accurately translated from one language to another. But in the course of this century some social scientists have raised the intriguing possibility that this assumption is unfounded. Studies of many of the thousands of languages in the world have revealed that they often interpret the same phenomena in quite different ways, and several writers have suggested that languages do not so much mirror reality as structure it for us in differing ways.

The Linguistic-Relativity Hypothesis

The *linguistic-relativity hypothesis* holds that speakers of a particular language must necessarily interpret the world through the unique grammatical forms and categories that their language supplies. This hypothesis was strongly propounded by two American linguists, Edward Sapir and his student Benjamin Whorf, and is sometimes known as the "Sapir-Whorf hypothesis." Sapir (1929) argued forcefully that "the worlds in which different societies live are distinct worlds, not merely the same world with different labels attached."

In what ways do languages "slice up" and organize the world differently? The most common differences are in vocabulary: some languages have words for objects and concepts for which other languages have no words at all. The Aztecs, for example, had only one word for snow, frost, ice, and cold, and presumably tended to see these as essentially the same phenomenon. We have only one word for snow; the Eskimo have no general word for snow at all, but have over twenty words for different kinds of snow—snow on the ground, snow falling, snow drifting, and so on. Their language forces them to perceive these distinctions, while our language predisposes us to ignore them. The Koya of South India do not distinguish among snow, fog, and dew, but their language forces them to make distinctions among seven types of bamboo—distinctions that are very important to them but that we would be very unlikely to notice.

Even the color spectrum is dissected in different ways by different languages. The human eye can make between 7 and 10 million different color discriminations, but all languages recognize only a handful of different colors. Most European languages recognize black, white, and six basic colors—red, orange, green, blue, yellow, and purple. Many languages, however, recognize only two colors: the Jalé of New Guinea, for example, divide the spectrum into the colors *hui* and *ziza*, representing the warm and cold colors of the spectrum respectively. Other cultures, such as the Arawak of Surinam, the Toda of India, and the Baganda of Uganda, recognize only three colors (Berlin and Kay, 1969). Different peoples see the same color spectrum, but they divide it up in different ways.

Other differences exist in the grammatical constructions required in different languages. Many European and other languages require a speaker to indicate the relative social statuses of the speaker and the person spoken to. In French, for example, the word *tu* is used for "you" by someone addressing a person considered to be socially equal or inferior, but the word *vous* is used to signify formality and respect. These languages thus oblige speakers to determine the nature of their relationships as soon as they begin to speak, a requirement that English speakers can avoid. The language of the Navajo Indians contains no real equivalent to our active verbs; in Navajo thought people do not so much act on the world as participate passively in actions that are taking place. This linguistic feature is perhaps related to the extremely passive nature of the Navajo people. Even more startling to us is the language of the Hopi Indians, which does not recognize the categories of time and space that we do. The Hopi language lacks the equivalent of past, present, and future tenses, and organizes the universe instead into categories of "manifest" (everything that is or has been accessible to the physical senses) and "manifesting" (everything that is not physically accessible to the senses). If this concept is difficult to understand, it is because our language is poorly equipped to express it, just as the Hopi language has difficulty expressing our concepts of time and space.

Evaluation

The linguistic relativity hypothesis does not imply that speakers of different languages are *incapable* of expressing the same ideas or seeing the world in the same way, although Sapir and Whorf did take this position in some of their earlier writings. All normal human beings are biologically capable of similar perceptions and reasoning (Lévi-Strauss, 1966). What the hypothesis does mean is that the language we speak *predisposes* us to make particular interpretations of reality. We need only consider the likely attitudes of a white child who is taught to call blacks "niggers" or of a black child who is taught to call whites "honkies" to see the truth of this statement. Another contemporary example may remind us of the peculiar use to which the word "free" was put in the society described in Orwell's novel *1984*. Americans commonly use the phrase "the free world" to refer to all noncommunist societies. In reality, most of the societies in the "free world" are anything but free in the sense that we understand the word in our own country. The "free" world has at various times included dictatorships and brutal regimes in Spain, Portugal, Brazil, Chile, South Korea, South Africa, Haiti, and many other countries. But the phrase predisposes us to gloss over these uncomfortable facts and to adopt what is really a very simplistic and often distorted view of international politics. Language and culture, then, are in constant interaction: culture influences the structure and use of language, and language influences cultural interpretations of reality.

Cultural Change

No culture is ever static. All cultures change, although they do so in different ways and at different rates. Culture always tends to be inherently conservative, especially in its nonmaterial aspects—people are reluctant to give up old values, customs, and beliefs in favor of new ones. Changes in one area of a culture are usually accompanied, sooner or later, by changes elsewhere in the culture. If this were not the case, cultures would inevitably become poorly integrated over time. Some of the most important changes are

Figure 3.10 A great deal of cultural change takes place through diffusion of cultural traits from one society to another. Around the turn of the century, Indian women in Bolivia adopted the European upper-class male fashion of the bowler hat and still combine this headgear with their more traditional garb.

those involving the ways in which a society earns its living and exploits the environment. This economic activity is so basic to human life that all other cultural elements have to adapt to it.

Three distinct processes are involved in cultural change: discovery, invention, and diffusion. *Discovery* is the perception of an aspect of reality that already exists—the hallucinogenic properties of peyote, the social structure of a termite colony, the functions of the heart, the cultural practices of another society. *Invention* is the combination or new use of existing knowledge to produce something that did not exist before—the compass, the United Nations, the atomic bomb, rock music. All inventions are based on previous discoveries and inventions. *Diffusion* is the spread of cultural elements from one culture to another and is probably the source of most cultural change. As "The One Hundred Percent American," the reading at the end of this chapter, implies, countless cultural elements that we consider distinctively our own are in fact derived from other cultures and often have histories of many hundreds or even thousands of years.

Inventions, discoveries, and diffused cultural traits become part of a culture only if they are accepted and shared by the society in question. It is easier to demonstrate the usefulness of material artifacts than of new norms and values. For this reason, artifacts such as can openers or the wheel are more readily accepted into a culture than new ideas or religions. Moreover, an innovation must be compatible with the basic values of the culture and must "fit" into its total environment. For this reason, the wearing of skirts by men remains unacceptable in the United States, and automobiles cannot be successfully introduced into a society that lacks roads, gas stations, traffic regulations, or mechanics.

Are We Prisoners of Culture?

The culture into which we are born profoundly affects our behavior, values, attitudes, and personalities. It influences our sense of who we are, what we believe, what our goals in life should be. As the anthropologist Clyde Kluckhohn (1962) has pointed out, "Culture regulates our lives at every turn; from the moment we are born until we die there is, whether we are conscious of it or not, constant pressure on us to conform to certain types of behavior." But where does this leave human freedom? Are we simply the prisoners of our cultures?

The answer is no. Culture makes us, but we also make culture. As Karl Marx (1969, originally published 1852) declared:

> Men make their own history, but they do not make it just as they please; they do not make it under circumstances chosen by themselves, but under circumstances directly encountered, given, and transmitted from the past.

Culture sets certain limitations on our options and behavior, but it cannot control us completely. If it did, there would be no cultural change, for we would all conform rigidly to existing norms and values. Culture provides general guidelines for behavior, but in specific situations people act in ways that often require individual ingenuity, interpretation, and choice. There are times when human beings must be creative, imaginative, and ready to improvise. The broad limits within which they do these things are determined by culture, but their specific acts often break with tradition and generate cultural changes. As individuals, few of us have the opportunity to modify culture; collectively, we do it all the time. Culture has no independent existence apart from ourselves. It is created, sustained, and changed by the acts of human beings, and that is the measure of our freedom.

Summary

1. Culture consists of all the shared products of human society, both material and nonmaterial. Culture and society are closely related and cannot exist independent of one another.

2. Human beings are the most advanced of the primates. Our distinctive characteristics include sociability, high intelligence, sensitive hands, language, upright posture, year-round sexual accessibility of the female, and lengthy infant dependence on adults. We have lost our instincts in the course of evolution, but culture provides a superior mode of adaptation to the environment. It enables us to adapt quickly to changed conditions, or even to change the environment to meet our needs.

3. Human nature is extremely flexible and is the product of an interaction between biological potentials and cultural learning.

4. Norms are shared rules or guidelines that prescribe appropriate behavior. Violations of folkways are more readily tolerated than violations of mores. Some acts are prohibited by taboos and some by laws. Norms are an important element in the system of social control through which a society ensures that its members behave in approved ways. Norms are formally or informally enforced through positive or negative sanctions.

5. Values are shared ideas about what is good or desirable. Norms express social values, although the origin of the norms may be forgotten. The United States has a unique set of important values, some of them contradictory and some of them shared by certain subcultures but not by others.

6. Cultures vary widely and each is unique. Cultural variation can be explained in terms of the functions that particular elements serve in maintaining the social system, and in terms of their ecological significance as an adaptation to the total environment. Cultural traits may also result from diffusion from one culture to another.

7. There are a number of general cultural universals, but no specific practices are found in every society. We tend to be ethnocentric toward other cultures, judging them in terms of our own standards. It is important that a social scientist adopt a position of cultural relativism and attempt to understand other cultures and subcultures in their own terms.

8. Cultures, particularly in preindustrial societies, tend to be integrated. Changes in one area of culture often provoke changes in other areas. One source of cultural strain is the gap between real and ideal culture. Another is value conflict between the dominant culture and subcultures or countercultures.

9. Language is fundamental to society and culture; it permits the transmission of culture and the interpretation of reality. Different languages interpret reality in different ways. The linguistic-relativity hypothesis holds that different languages predispose speakers to interpret reality in different ways.

10. Cultural change is inevitable, although its rate is variable. It stems mainly from discovery, invention, and diffusion. Changes tend to be accepted into a culture only if they are compatible with its existing norms and values. Changes in material culture are usually more readily accepted than changes in nonmaterial culture.

11. We are not the prisoners of culture. Culture shapes us, but collectively we shape and change the culture that we pass on from generation to generation.

Important Terms

culture
material culture
nonmaterial culture
norms
folkways
mores
taboos
law
social control
sanctions
internalize
values
functionalist approach
ecological approach
cultural universals
ethnocentrism
cultural relativism
cultural integration
real culture
ideal culture
subculture
counterculture
symbol
linguistic relativity
discovery
invention
diffusion

Suggested Readings

BENEDICT, RUTH. *Patterns of Culture.* Boston: Houghton Mifflin, 1961.

A classic work that uses examples from several societies to illustrate the impact of culture on personality and social behavior.

HARRIS, MARVIN. *Cows, Pigs, Wars, and Witches: The Riddles of Culture.* New York: Random House, 1974.

An entertaining and provocative application of the ecological perspective to a variety of peculiar and apparently inexplicable cultural practices.

PILBEAM, DAVID R. *The Ascent of Man.* New York: Macmillan, 1972.

A readable account of human evolution and the characteristics that distinguish us from other animals, for the student interested in exploring this topic further.

ROSZAK, THEODORE. *The Making of a Counter Culture.* New York: Doubleday, 1969.

A sociologist's analysis of the youth culture of the sixties. The optimism of the book now seems a little dated, but it remains an interesting analysis of the value conflict between culture and counterculture.

SLATER, PHILIP. *The Pursuit of Loneliness.* Boston: Beacon Press, 1970.

A penetrating critique of American culture, which Slater believes is so contradictory in some respects that it is at the "breaking point."

WILLIAMS, ROBIN. *American Society: A Sociological Interpretation.* New York: Random House, 1970.

A useful text that examines both American society and culture. It contains an influential analysis of American norms and values and their impact on social life.

Reading

The One Hundred Percent American *Ralph Linton*

This classic essay pointedly demonstrates that many cultural traits that we consider distinctively American have in fact diffused from other cultures and often have histories of thousands of years.

There can be no question about the average American's Americanism or his desire to preserve this precious heritage at all costs. Nevertheless, some insidious foreign ideas have already wormed their way into his civilization without his realizing what was going on. Thus dawn finds the unsuspecting patriot garbed in pajamas, a garment of East Indian origin; and lying in a bed built on a pattern which originated in either Persia or Asia Minor. He is muffled to the ears in un-American materials; cotton, first domesticated in India; linen, domesticated in the Near East; wool from an animal native to Asia Minor; or silk whose uses were first discovered by the Chinese. All these substances have been transformed into cloth by a method invented in Southwestern Asia. If the weather is cold enough he may even be sleeping under an eiderdown quilt invented in Scandinavia.

On awakening he glances at the clock, a medieval European invention, uses one potent Latin word in abbreviated form, rises in haste, and goes to the bathroom. Here, if he stops to think about it, he must feel himself in the presence of a great American institution; he will have heard stories of both the quality and frequency of foreign plumbing and will know that in no other country does the average man perform his ablutions in the midst of such splendor. But the invidious foreign influence pursues him even here. Glass was invented by the ancient Egyptians, the use of glazed tiles for floors and walls in the Near East, porcelain in China, and the art of enameling on metal by Mediterranean artisans of the Bronze Age. Even his bathtub and toilet are but slightly modified copies of Roman originals. The only purely American contribution to the ensemble is the steam radiator.

In this bathroom the American washes with soap invented by the ancient Gauls. Next he cleans his teeth, a subversive European practice which did not invade America until the latter part of the eighteenth century. He then shaves, a masochistic rite first developed by the heathen priests of ancient Egypt and Sumer. The process is made less of a penance by the fact that his razor is of steel, an iron-carbon alloy discovered in either India or Turkestan. Lastly, he dries himself on a Turkish towel.

Returning to the bedroom, the unconscious victim of un-American practices removes his clothes from a chair, invented in the Near East, and proceeds to dress. He puts on close-fitting tailored garments whose form derives from the skin clothing of the ancient nomads of the Asiatic steppes and fastens them with buttons whose prototypes appeared in Europe at the close of the Stone Age. This costume is appropriate enough for outdoor exercise in a cold climate, but is quite unsuited to American summers, steam-heated houses, and Pullmans. Nevertheless, foreign ideas and habits hold the unfortunate man in thrall even when common sense tells him that the authentically American costume of gee string and moccasins would be far more comfortable. He puts on his feet stiff coverings made from hide prepared by a process invented in ancient Egypt and cut to a pattern which can be traced back to ancient Greece, and makes sure they are properly polished, also a Greek idea. Lastly, he ties about his neck a strip of bright-colored cloth which is a vestigial survival of the shoulder shawls worn by seventeenth-century Croats. He gives himself a final appraisal in the mirror, an old Mediterranean invention, and goes downstairs. . . .

He places upon his head a molded piece of felt, invented by the nomads of Eastern Asia, and, if it looks like rain, puts on outer shoes of rubber, discovered by the ancient Mexicans, and takes an umbrella, invented in India. He then sprints for his train—the train, not the sprinting, being an English invention. At the station he pauses for a moment to buy a newspaper, paying for it with coins invented in ancient Lydia. Once on board he settles back to inhale the fumes of a cigarette invented in Mexico, or a cigar invented in Brazil. Meanwhile, he reads the news of the day, imprinted in characters invented by the ancient Semites by a process invented in Germany upon a material invented in China. As he scans the latest editorial pointing out the dire results to our institutions of accepting foreign ideas, he will not fail to thank a Hebrew God in an Indo-European language that he is a one hundred percent (decimal system invented by the Greeks) American (from Americus Vespucci, Italian geographer).

Source: Ralph Linton, *The American Mercury,* 40 (April, 1937), pp. 427–429.

SWEENEY MFG. CO.

CHAPTER 4 *Society*

CHAPTER OUTLINE

Social Structure
- *Statuses*
- *Roles*
- *Groups*
- *Institutions*

Types of Societies
- *Hunting and Gathering Societies*
- *Pastoral Societies*
- *Horticultural Societies*
- *Agricultural Societies*
- *Industrial Societies*

Industrial and Preindustrial Societies: A Comparison

Human beings are social animals. The quality we call "humanity" can be achieved only through social living, for there is no such thing as a person whose behavior and personality have not developed in the context of some human society. We take social living so much for granted that we sometimes fail to recognize the immense influence society has over us. But in the complex interaction between the individual and society, society is usually the dominant partner. Society exists long before we are born into it, and it exists long after we are gone. Society gives content, direction, and meaning to our lives, and we, in turn, in countless ways, reshape the society that we leave to the next generation.

We are not social animals just because we happen to find social living convenient. Without society we could not survive. No infant could reach maturity without the care and protection of other people, and no adult could remain alive without using the vast store of information about the world that has been learned and transmitted through society. Almost everything that we do is social in some sense—learned from others, done with others, directed toward others. Even those very rare individuals who attempt to escape from society carry with them into isolation the identities, the ideas, and the techniques that they have learned from others. Hermits in their caves live with society in their memories.

What exactly is a society? Several conditions must be met before people can be said to be living in one society. First, they must occupy a common territory. Second, they must not only share this territory but must also interact with one another. Third, they must to some extent have a common culture and a shared sense of membership in and commitment to the same group. We may say, then, that *a society is a group of interacting individuals sharing the same territory and participating in a common culture.* A society is not necessarily the same as a nation-state, although in the modern world the two are often identical. Many nation-states include smaller societies within their own borders. Most of the countries of South America, for example, contain smaller societies of indigenous Indian peoples who have not been integrated into the larger society.

Many insect, fish, bird, and mammal species are also social animals—such as ants and bees, herrings and sardines, starlings and jays, wolves and elephants. But nonhuman societies depend for their survival and functioning primarily on unlearned ("instinctive") patterns of behavior. As a result, different societies of any one species, be they termites or zebras, are virtually identical. Their societies may differ somewhat in size, but there is little or no difference in the social behavior of their members from one society to another. When you have seen one nest of a particular termite species, you have for most purposes seen all the nests of that species.

Human societies are radically different. The organization and characteristics of each human society are not based on the rigid dictates of its members' "instincts." They are created by human beings themselves and are learned and modified by each new generation. Consequently, although all human beings are members of the same biological species, every human society is different—so different that an individual suddenly transplanted from, say, the United States to a jungle tribe of Brazil (or vice versa) would have very little idea of how to behave appropriately. Each society therefore presents a fresh and exciting challenge to the sociologist's understanding.

In this chapter we will look at two main topics. First, we will examine the *social structure* that underlies all human societies. Our societies are not simply a collection of randomly interacting individuals who happen to occupy the same area. Each society has its own distinctive character, the product of its history and environment, but all societies have an underlying pattern of relationships, a social structure that makes social life relatively smooth and predictable. Second, we will consider some basic *types* of human societies, showing how and why they differ from one another. In particular, we will examine the radical differences between modern industrial societies and the traditional, preindustrial societies that they are rapidly replacing all over the world.

Social Structure

Despite our great capacity for flexible behavior, social life is not a haphazard affair: it is generally stable, patterned, and predictable. We know more or less what kind of behavior is expected of us in most situations, and on the whole we conform to these social expectations. There is an underlying regularity to the behavior of both individuals and groups, a regularity that makes society orderly and workable. This patterned nature of society is based on social structure.

Social structure refers to the organized relationships between the basic components in a social system. These basic components are found in all human societies, although their precise character and the relationships between them vary from one society to another. The most important of the components of social structure are statuses, roles, groups, and institutions. These concepts are of fundamental importance in sociology, and you will encounter them throughout this book.

Statuses

A society consists ultimately of individuals. Each of these individuals has one or more socially defined positions in the society—woman, carpenter, teacher, son, old person, and so on. Such a position is termed a *status.* A person's status determines where that individual "fits" in society and how he or she should relate to other people. The status of daughter, for example, determines the occupant's relationships with other members of the family; the status of corporation president determines the occupant's relationships with employees, shareholders, other corporation presidents, or tax collectors. Naturally, a person can occupy several statuses simultaneously, but one of them, usually an occupational status, tends to be the most important, and sociologists sometimes refer to it as the person's "master status."

The word "status" can be used either to refer simply to one of the many socially defined positions in a society, or it can be used to refer to the fact that some positions rank higher or lower than others. In most societies there is considerable inequality between different statuses. The person who has the status of Supreme Court Justice, for example, enjoys more wealth, power, and prestige than

Figure 4.1 Some statuses are ascribed *to the individual by society on grounds over which he or she has no control; others are* achieved *by the individual through personal effort. This woman has several ascribed statuses, such as female person, black person, and daughter, but she also has an achieved status as a college graduate.*

the person who has the status of janitor. People of roughly equivalent status in an unequal society form a *class:* they enjoy greater access to the society's wealth and other resources than do those with lower statuses, and they have less access than do those with higher statuses. It is usually clear from the context whether sociologists are using the term "status" simply to refer to a position in society in general or to refer to a position of social rank.

We have little control over some of our statuses. If you are young, female, or black, for example, there is nothing you can do about it. Such a status is said to be *ascribed*, or arbitrarily given to us by society. But we have a certain amount of control over other statuses. At least partly through your own efforts you can get married, become a college graduate, a convict, or a member of a different religion. Such a status is said to be earned, or *achieved*. We occupy achieved statuses partly or wholly as a result of our own efforts, and society recognizes our changed status.

Roles

Every status has one or more roles attached to it. The sociological concept of *role* is taken directly from the theater; it refers to the part or parts you play in society. The distinction between status and role is a simple one: you *occupy* a status, but you *play* a role (Linton, 1936). Every position or status in society carries with it a set of expected behavior patterns, obligations, and privileges—in other words, norms specifying how the role attached to the status should be played. Status and role are thus two sides of the same coin.

The presidency of the United States, for example, is a status. Attached to this status is a presidential role, defined by social norms prescribing how the occupier of the status should behave. The status of president is a fixed position in society, but the role is more flexible, for there is considerable variation in how occupants of the position actually play it. In practice a single status may involve a number of roles. The status of college professor, for example, involves one role as teacher, one role as colleague to other professors, one role as researcher, and perhaps other roles, such as student advisor or writer of scholarly articles. A cluster of roles attached to a single status is sometimes called a "role set."

The roles we play in life depend on the status we happen to be occupying at the time. If you are talking to your professor as a student, you will both behave very differently than you would if, for example, you were sitting on a jury together and playing the roles of jurors. If in later years you return to visit the campus as a wealthy alumnus, your role relationship to your old professor will be changed again. If someone playing the role of physician asks you to undress, you will comply; if the same person asks you to undress when playing the role of host at dinner, you will interpret the situation quite differently.

We play many different roles during the course of each day. The content of our role behavior is determined primarily by *role expectations,* the generally accepted social norms that define how a role ought to be played. Our

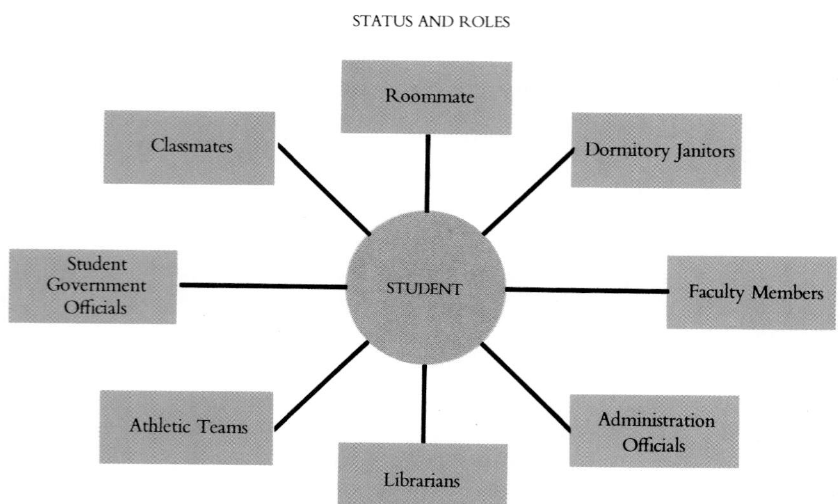

Figure 4.2 The status of student carries with it a number of different roles, some of which are illustrated here. As a student, you will adopt somewhat different roles in your interaction with people who have other statuses and are playing other roles. They will also interact with you in accordance with your student status and with the particular role you present to them. The status of student is only one of your statuses, although it is probably your most important status, or master status, *at present. You also have other statuses—such as male or female, black or white, son or daughter—and each of these has different roles attached to it. The complex of roles that are carried by your particular status form a* role set.

actual role behavior is called *role performance,* and it may or may not conform to role expectations. President Nixon's role performance, for example, violated public role expectations of how the occupant of his status should behave.

The fact that people may have several different statuses, each with several different roles attached, can obviously cause problems when role expectations conflict. Sometimes conflicting expectations are built into a single role. A factory supervisor, for example, is expected to maintain good relations with the workers but is also expected to enforce regulations that the workers may resent. When conflicting demands like this are built into a role, or when a person for some reason cannot meet role expectations, a situation of *role strain* exists. Another problem arises when a person plays two or more roles whose requirements are difficult to reconcile. For example, police officers sometimes find themselves in a situation where they are required to arrest their own children: in such circumstances, the role expectations of a parent and a police officer can be at odds with one another. When two or more roles clash in this way, a situation of *role conflict* exists. But although role expectations may sometimes cause strains and conflicts in role performances, they do for the most part ensure the smooth and predictable course of social interaction. Roles enable us to structure our own behavior along socially expected lines. We can anticipate the behavior of others in most situations, and we can fashion our own action accordingly.

Groups

A society is not simply a series of interacting individuals. People constantly form and re-form groups, and a great deal of social behavior takes place within and between groups. A *group* consists of people interacting together in an orderly way on the basis of shared expectations about each other's behavior. Put another way, a group is a number of persons whose relationships are based on interrelated statuses and roles. A group therefore differs from a mere aggregate of people who just happen to be temporarily in the same place at the same time.

Groups can be classified into two main types, primary and secondary. A *primary group* consists of a small number of people who interact over a relatively long period on an intimate, face-to-face basis. The members know one another personally and interact in an informal manner. Examples of this kind of group are families, cliques of friends and peers, and small communities. These groups are important building blocks of social structure; in fact, the primary group is the very basis of some small-scale, traditional societies in which social organization rests almost entirely on kinship.

A *secondary group,* in contrast, consists of a number of people who interact on a fairly temporary, anonymous, and impersonal basis. The members either do not know one another personally or, at best, know one another only in terms of particular formal roles rather than as whole people. Secondary groups are usually established to serve specific functions, and people are generally less emotionally committed to them than they are to their primary groups. Examples of secondary groups are formal organizations such as General Motors, political parties, or government bureaucracies. These large organizations are not found in the simplest of human societies, but they are an increasingly important element in the social structure of large modern societies.

Because human beings are essentially cooperative social animals, most social behavior takes place in the context of groups. Groups are therefore a vital part of social structure, and the distinctive characteristics of any society depend largely on the nature and activities of the groups that it contains.

Institutions

Every society has to meet certain fundamental requirements if it is to survive and provide a satisfying life for its members. These requirements are sometimes termed the *functional prerequisites* of the society; they represent important social functions that must be fulfilled in all societies (Parsons, 1951). For example, every society must have some means of replacing its members and of teaching them the culture that has been handed down over the generations. Every society must be able to protect its members against outside enemies, and, if possible, against domestic problems such as disease and food shortage. Every society must find some way of producing goods and distributing them to its members. Every society must have some system of social control—some means of ensuring that people act in socially approved ways. Every society must have some system of shared values and of rituals to reaffirm them, so that the solidarity of its members can be confirmed and enhanced. These functional needs are met by institutions.

Institutions are the stable clusters of values, norms, statuses, roles, and expectations that develop around the basic needs of a society. For example, the family institution takes care of the replacement of members and the training of the young. The political and military institutions take care of the protection of the society against outside enemies and assume some of the responsibility for social control within the society. The economic institution organizes the production and distribution of goods and services. The religious institution provides a set of shared values and the rituals that reaffirm them. The educational institution passes on cultural values from one generation to the next and trains the young in the more sophisticated knowledge and skills that they will need in later life. These institutions tend to be closely interrelated within the social structure. Changes in any one of them—especially in the economic institution—tend to be followed by adjustments in the others.

Like the other elements in social structure, institutions help make social life orderly and predictable. Roles, statuses, groups, and institutions are interwoven in a complex network of norms and relationships that makes human society stable and thus possible.

Types of Societies

If we compressed the entire history of life on the planet into a single year, the first modern human being would not appear until December 31 at about 11:53 PM, and the first civilizations would have emerged only about a minute before the end of the year. Yet our cultural achievements in the brief time that we have occupied the planet have been remarkable. Some 15,000 years ago our ancestors were practicing religious rituals and painting superb pictures on the walls of their caves. Around 11,000 years ago, some human groups no longer relied solely on the food that they could hunt and gather; instead, they began to domesticate animals and plants. About 6000 years ago people began to live in cities, to specialize in different forms of labor, to divide into social classes, and to create distinct political and economic institutions. Within a few thousand years empires were created, bringing millions of people under centralized rule and opening up communication between previously isolated groups. Advanced agricultural technologies improved the productivity of the land, resulting in growing populations and the emergence of large nation-states. A mere 250 years ago the industrial revolution began, thrusting us into the modern world of factories and computers, jet aircraft and atomic reactors, instantaneous global communications and terrifying military technologies.

Thousands of different human societies have existed in this time, but they can be classified into a limited number of basic types depending on the technologies that they use to exploit the natural environment. There has been a general historical trend of *sociocultural evolution,* a process that has some similarities with biological evolution. Like an organism, a society has to adapt to its environment in order to exploit food resources. Different societies have used different subsistence strategies, and those societies that have found more productive strategies have tended to grow larger and more complex, often enjoying their success at the expense of societies using more primitive technologies. This process of sociocultural evolution is not in any sense a "law" applicable to all societies: it represents only a general trend that has been observed in the historical and archaeological evidence. Some societies have evolved further and faster than others; some have become "stuck" at a particular level; and all have changed in ways that are unique to themselves. In general, however, societies can be classified according to their reliance on one of five basic subsistence strategies: hunting and gathering, pastoralism, horticulture, agriculture, or industrialism, with social structure growing increasingly complex at each succeeding level.

The *ecological* approach views human society in the context of its environment and its strategy for exploiting that environment. By using this approach, we can account for many of the differences in the complexity of the social structure of human societies, and also for much of the cultural variation that exists among them.

Hunting and Gathering Societies

For almost all of the time that human beings existed, they have relied on hunting and gathering for their survival. All societies used this subsistence strategy until only a few thousand years ago, and even today there are still a handful of isolated peoples, such as the Aranda of the central Australian desert, who retain this way of life.

Figure 4.3 The San of the Kalahari desert in southern Africa are one the few hunting and gathering peoples that have survived into the modern world. The San live in nomadic groups based mainly on kinship. Accustomed to a more affluent life-style, we are inclined to regard their life as one of constant hardship. But the San feel very few "needs," and they are able to satisfy them with only a few hours' work each day. Like other hunting and gathering peoples, most of their time is spent in leisure activities. Their way of life is doomed, however, for their society is rapidly being absorbed by the industrial societies of the surrounding region.

Hunting and gathering societies tend to consist of very small, scattered groups. The reason is simple: the environment cannot support a large concentration of people who rely on whatever food they can find or catch from one day to the next. Hunting and gathering peoples therefore live in small primary groups that rarely exceed about forty members. These groups are based on kinship, with most of their members being related by ancestry or marriage. Each group may require several hundred square miles of territory to support itself, and so contact between groups is infrequent and short-lived. Contrary to popular belief, the life of hunting and gathering peoples is not usually one of constant hardship on the brink of starvation. Their needs are simple and easily satisfied, and they spend less time working for their food than the average inhabitants of any other type of society. They are among the most leisured people on earth (Lee, 1968; Sahlins, 1972).

The family is the only clearly defined institution in these societies. It assumes responsibility for many of the functions that are provided by more specialized institutions in other societies, such as economic production, the education of the young, and the protection of members of the group. Political institutions are absent: statuses in these societies are essentially equal, and although a part-time headman with very limited authority may sometimes be recognized, most decisions are made through group discussion. Hunting and gathering peoples are constantly on the move because they have to leave one area as soon as they have exhausted its food resources. As a result, possessions are a hindrance to them, and they own very few goods. No individual can acquire wealth, because there is no wealth to be acquired. People who do find a substantial food resource are expected to share it with the whole community. Warfare is extremely uncommon among hunting and gathering peoples, partly because they have few possessions and therefore have very little to fight about.

There is very little division of labor in these societies except along lines of age and sex. The roles performed by men and women, and by the young and the old, are somewhat different, but there are no other specialized occupational roles. Most people do much the same things most of the time, and as a result of their common life experiences they share almost identical values. Their religion almost never includes a belief in a powerful god or gods who are active in human affairs; instead, they tend to see the world as populated by unseen spirits that must be taken account of, but not necessarily worshipped.

The use of hunting and gathering as a subsistence strategy thus has a very strong influence on social structure and culture. The social structure of these societies is necessarily very simple, and their cultures cannot become elaborate and diversified.

Pastoral Societies

Between ten and twelve thousand years ago, some hunting and gathering groups began to adopt a new subsistence strategy based on the domestication of herds of animals. This strategy has been adopted by many peoples living in deserts or other regions that are not suited to the cultivation of plants, but which contain animals—such as goats or sheep—that can be readily tamed and used as a food source. Many pastoral societies still exist in the modern world, particularly in Africa and in the Middle and Near East.

Pastoralism is a much more productive strategy than hunting and gathering: it provides an assured food supply and permits the accumulation of surplus resources. As a result societies can grow much larger, including hundreds or even thousands of people. Some individuals become more powerful than others and pass on their status to their descendants. Patterns of chieftainship begin to appear as powerful and wealthy families secure their positions.

Pastoralists are usually nomadic because they must constantly take their herds to new grazing grounds. As a result, their material possessions are few in number but are more elaborate than those of hunting and gathering peoples because they can be carried by animals. Cultural artifacts in these societies therefore consist of items that are easily transportable—tents, woven carpets, simple utensils, and so on. Their nomadic way of life often brings pastoralists into contact with other groups. One consequence is the development of systematic trading; a second is that disputes over grazing rights frequently lead to warfare. Slavery, unknown in hunting and gathering societies, makes its appearance as captives in war are put to work for their conquerors.

Pastoral peoples tend to develop a belief that is found in very few religions: they commonly believe in a god or gods who take an active interest in human affairs and look

Figure 4.4 Pastoralists in the Sahara desert water their camels. The camel is well suited to the nomadic life of these pastoralists, as the animal can go without food and water for long periods and is also an excellent beast of burden. The pastoralists take their herds from one place to another in search of grazing and water, using the camels for meat and milk. Surplus camels are sold or traded for other items that the people need. Not all pastoralists, however, are nomadic; those that live in areas that can support continuous grazing are able to form small, settled communities.

after the people who worship them. This belief seems to have been suggested by the pastoralists' experience of the relationship between themselves and their flocks (Lenski and Lenski, 1974). It is no coincidence that the few modern religions based on this view of the relationship between human beings and a god—Judaism and its offshoots, Christianity and Islam—originated among pastoral peoples.

The subsistence strategy of these societies thus provides distinctive social and cultural opportunities and limitations. Populations become larger, political and economic institutions begin to appear, and both social structure and culture become more complex.

Horticultural Societies

Horticultural societies first appeared at about the same time as pastoral societies. Horticulturalists specialize in the domestication of plants, which they cultivate manually with hoes or digging sticks in relatively small gardens. Unlike pastoralists, they are relatively settled, although they must periodically move short distances. Their subsistence strategy is typically based on a "slash and burn" technology, in which they clear areas of land, burn the vegetation they have cut down, raise crops for two or three years until the soil is exhausted, and then repeat the process elsewhere. Horticulture is essentially an alternative to pastoralism, and the choice of one strategy or the other depends primarily on environmental factors. Horticulture is much more likely to be adopted if the soil and climate favor crop cultivation. Many horticultural societies still exist in Africa, Asia, South America, and Australasia.

Like pastoralism, horticulture is much more efficient than hunting and gathering because it provides an assured food supply and the possibility of a surplus. Again, this surplus allows some wealthy individuals to become more powerful than others, and political institutions emerge in the form of chieftainships. The existence of a surplus also means that some people no longer have to work at food production, and so specialized statuses and roles appear, such as those of shaman, trader, or craft worker.

Warfare is extremely common in horticultural societies, partly because it is often more convenient to steal one's neighbors' goods than to produce one's own. The rare practices of cannibalism, headhunting, and human sacrifice are found almost exclusively in a few horticultural societies. Cannibalism usually involves either eating one's deceased relatives as an act of piety or eating one's slain enemies as an act of ritual revenge. The successful hunting of heads is taken as evidence of the courage and skill of the warrior. The emergence of human sacrifice coincides with a change in the nature of religious belief. Advanced horticultural peoples tend to believe in capricious gods who must be worshipped and propitiated, a development that is probably associated with their own experience of chieftainship and social inequality.

Because they live in relatively permanent settlements, horticulturalists can create more elaborate cultural artifacts than can hunters and gatherers or pastoralists. They can produce, for example, houses, thrones, or large stone sculptures. Their settled way of life and relatively large populations also permit greater complexity in social structure and a more diverse and elaborate material culture. In the more advanced horticultural societies, political and economic institutions become well developed as conquest and trade link various villages together.

Agricultural Societies

About six thousand years ago the plough was invented and the agricultural revolution was under way. The use of the plough greatly improves the productivity of the land; it brings to the surface nutrients that have sunk out of reach of the roots of plants, and it returns weeds to the soil to act as fertilizers. The same land can be cultivated almost continuously, and fully permanent settlements become possible. The use of animal power to pull the plough enables one person to achieve far more productivity than several horticulturalists could. As a result, food output is greatly increased and a substantial surplus can be produced.

The potential size of societies practicing agriculture is much greater than that of horticultural or pastoral communities; it can run to several million people. A fairly large part of this population is freed from the necessity to work on the land and can engage in highly specialized, full-time activities, most of which are conveniently performed among concentrations of other people. Cities appear for the first time, consisting essentially of people who trade their specialized skills for the agricultural products of those who still work the land. The society itself often consists of

Figure 4.5 Lacking draft animals, horticulturalists have to tend their gardens by hand, a laborious process that limits the productivity of the land. The soil quickly becomes exhausted, so horticulturalists must either leave some of their gardens fallow every two or three years or find new areas for cultivation. These horticultural people in the Amazon jungle are using a "slash and burn" technology: they cut down the vegetation, burn it, grow crops until the land is exhausted, and then repeat the process elsewhere. Horticulture permits relatively settled communities, and it can also generate enough food to support fairly large populations in the same area.

Figure 4.6 Agriculture can be a highly productive subsistence strategy. Agriculturalists, like these Asian peasants, cultivate the soil with ploughs instead of hoes and digging sticks. Nutrients are thus returned to the surface of the soil, and the land can be continuously cultivated year after year. The high productivity of agriculture frees a large part of the population from the need to toil on the land, permitting them to engage in other specialized roles.

several such cities and their hinterlands, loosely welded together by periodic shows of force.

Political institutions become much more elaborate. Power is increasingly concentrated in the hands of a single individual, and a hereditary monarchy tends to emerge. The power of the monarch is usually absolute, and he or she literally has the power of life and death over their subjects. In the more advanced agricultural societies an elaborate court and government bureaucracy is established, and the state emerges for the first time as a separate social institution. For the first time, too, distinct social classes make their appearance. The wealth of agricultural societies is almost always very unequally shared, with a small minority enjoying the surplus produced by the working majority; one example of this pattern is the old feudal system of Europe. Religion also becomes a separate social institution, with full-time officials and often with considerable political influence. The religions of agricultural societies often include a belief in a "family" of gods, one of whom, the "high god," is regarded as more powerful than other lesser gods. This belief probably stems from peoples' experience of different levels of political authority, ranging from local rulers to the absolute monarch. A clearly defined economic institution also appears; trade becomes more elaborate and money is used as a medium of exchange. The necessity for accurate records of crop harvests, taxation, and government transactions provides a powerful incentive for the development of writing, and some system of writing is found in virtually all advanced agricultural societies.

Agricultural societies tend to be almost constantly at war and sometimes engage in systematic empire building. These conditions generate the need for an effective military organization, and full-time, permanent armies appear for the first time. The need for efficient transport and communications in these large societies leads to the development of roads and navies, and previously isolated communities are brought into contact with one another. The relative wealth of agricultural societies and their settled way of life permit resources to be invested in new cultural artifacts—paintings and statues, public buildings and monuments, palaces and stadiums.

A society relying on agriculture as a subsistence strategy thus has a far more complex social structure and culture than any of the less evolved types of societies. The number of statuses multiplies, population size increases, cities appear, new institutions emerge, social classes arise, political and economic inequality becomes built into the social structure, and culture becomes much more diversified and heterogeneous.

Industrial Societies

The industrial mode of production originated in England about 250 years ago and proved so immensely successful that it has since spread all over the world, absorbing, transforming, or destroying all other types of society in the process.

Industrialism is based on the application of scientific knowledge to the technology of production, enabling new energy sources to be harnessed and permitting machines to do the work that was previously done by people or animals. It is a highly efficient subsistence strategy, for it allows a relatively small proportion of the population to feed the majority. Because inventions and discoveries build upon one another, the rate of technological innovation in industrial societies is very rapid indeed. New technologies—such as the steam engine, the internal combustion engine, electrical power, or atomic energy—tend to bring about social changes as the economic and other institutions constantly adjust to altered conditions. Unlike other societies, therefore, industrial societies are in a continual state of rapid social change.

Industrial societies may be very large, with populations running into tens or hundreds of millions. They are also highly urbanized; in all the advanced industrial societies a majority of the population lives in urban areas, where most jobs are located. The population growth rate rises sharply in the early stages of industrialism as new medical technologies and improved living standards extend life expectancy, but population size tends to stabilize in the later stages of industrialism as the birth rate drops. The division of labor becomes highly complex as tens of thousands of new, specialized jobs are created. More and more statuses are achieved rather than ascribed: a person becomes a lord or peasant through circumstances beyond

Figure 4.7 Industrial societies rely on an advanced technology and mechanized production for their subsistence. This strategy is so efficient and produces so much wealth that industrialism is rapidly becoming the dominant mode of production all over the world. Despite its many advantages, however, industrialism poses a range of new problems to human society: pollution, resource depletion, overpopulation, and a rapid rate of social change that causes continuing social disorganization.

personal control but can actively achieve such new statuses as teacher, politician, or auto mechanic.

Family and kinship become progressively less important in the social structure. The family loses many of its earlier functions. It is no longer a unit of economic production, and it no longer has the main responsibility for the education of the young. Kinship ties are weakened, and people live with their immediate family but apart from more distant kin. The influence of the religious institution also shrinks markedly. People no longer share similar life experiences and consequently hold many different and competing values and beliefs. Inevitably, religion loses its hold as an unquestioned source of moral authority. Science, however, emerges as a new and very important social institution, for technological innovation depends on the growth and refinement of scientific knowledge. Similarly, education becomes a distinct institution. An industrial society requires a literate and sophisticated population, and for the first time formal education becomes compulsory for the many rather than a luxury for the few.

In the early stages of industrialism there is usually a yawning gap between the incomes of the rich and the poor as the rural peasantry is transformed into an urban work force, often under the most wretched conditions. The general trend in industrial societies, however, is toward a steady reduction in social inequalities, although there are

Figure 4.8 A characteristic feature of industrial societies is the anonymous, impersonal character of many everyday social relationships. This painting, "Government Bureau," by the American artist George Tooker, captures the anonymity that prevails in the large formal organizations that dominate industrial society. (Formal organizations are discussed in detail in Chapter 7, Social Groups.)

some notable exceptions (Lenski, 1966a). Hereditary monarchies pass away and tend to be replaced by more democratic institutions. The state assumes an increasingly important role in society, becoming involved in such diverse areas as education, welfare, and the regulation of economic activity. Although preparedness for warfare may reach new heights of intensity, actual outbreaks of war are relatively infrequent. One study of preindustrial European societies found that over periods of several centuries, they were at war, on the average, almost every second year (Sorokin, 1937). In contrast, most European societies have been at war only twice in the course of this century, and some have not been at war at all. Warfare can be ruinous for an advanced industrial society, largely because it involves such devastating weaponry and economic dislocation.

Secondary groups multiply throughout industrial societies—corporations, political parties, government bureaucracies, and special-purpose organizations and associations of every kind. More and more social life takes place in the context of secondary rather than primary groups, and a good deal of social interaction occurs in an anonymous, impersonal fashion. The range of new life-styles and values creates a much more heterogeneous culture than that found in other types of societies. The overall characteristics of industrial societies tend to be broadly similar, however, partly as a result of the effects of global mass communication and partly because industrialism imposes certain basic requirements on social structure and culture.

Industrial society is rapidly becoming the dominant social form in the modern world. Its success is due to its unprecedented effectiveness in exploiting the natural environment, but this success has caused a variety of problems. Industrial societies have to contend with pollution, depletion of scarce resources, overpopulation, the destruction of traditional communities, the disruption of kinship systems, mass anonymity, and a breakneck rate of social change that constantly threatens to disorganize the existing social structure.

Industrial and Preindustrial Societies: A Comparison

The most radical discontinuity in the course of sociocultural evolution occurs between the various preindustrial societies on the one hand and modern industrial society on the other. The changes involved are profound, and a major task of sociology has been to identify their nature.

In 1887, for example, the German sociologist Ferdinand Tönnies distinguished between the *Gemeinschaft,* or "community," and the *Gesellschaft,* or "association." The former type of society, he argued, is characterized by intimate, face-to-face contact, strong feelings of social solidarity, and a commitment to tradition. The latter is marked by impersonal contacts, individualism rather than group loyalty, and a slackening of traditional ties and values. Around the turn of the century, in 1893, the French sociologist Emile Durkheim distinguished between societies based on *mechanical solidarity,* in which the society is held together by the fact that people perform the same tasks and share similar values, and societies based on *organic solidarity,* in which the society is held together by the fact that people are highly specialized and are therefore mutually dependent on one another. More recently, in 1941, the American anthropologist Robert Redfield distinguished between the *folk society,* which is small and bound by tradition and intimate personal links, and the *urban society,* a large-scale social unit marked by impersonal relationships and a pluralism of values. All these writers were trying to describe essentially the same phenomenon: the differences between what in this book we will call "traditional" or "preindustrial" societies, and societies of the "modern" or "industrial" type.

What are the basic differences between preindustrial and industrial societies? Some of the most important are the following:

Figure 4.9 Industrialism has radically changed the way of life of human societies. By freeing the bulk of the population from work on the land, it has permitted the growth of densely populated cities in which daily life is utterly different from that in preindustrial villages. These two pictures—of a New Guinea village in a horticultural society and of a single street in Manhattan—give some idea of the sweeping transformation that has taken place.

1. The social structure of preindustrial societies is relatively simple; there is comparatively little division of labor, and there are fewer statuses and roles. Social institutions, except for family and kinship, tend to be absent or very rudimentary. The social structure of industrial societies is very complex; there is a high degree of division of labor and a vast number of statuses and roles. The importance of family and kinship in the social structure is reduced, but a series of new institutions emerges.

2. Most social life in preindustrial societies takes place in the context of primary groups and small communities; social relationships are conducted on an intimate, personal basis. A great deal of social life in industrial societies occurs in the context of secondary groups and large, anonymous urban communities; social relationships often take place on an impersonal basis.

3. Most statuses in preindustrial societies are ascribed: a person's "station in life" is usually determined by the circumstances of birth. Many statuses in industrial societies can be achieved at least partly through personal effort or failings.

4. In preindustrial societies there is a general agreement on social values, especially as expressed in religion, and culture tends to be homogeneous. In industrial societies the diversification of life-styles and the wide range of different groups leads to a pluralism of values and beliefs, and a wide range of subcultures appears.

5. Individual behavior in preindustrial societies is regulated by social custom and tradition, which are rarely questioned. People tend to think of themselves as members of their group first and as individuals second. In industrial societies custom and tradition lose much of their force, and people act primarily as individuals, often taking

Figure 4.10

THE GREAT TRANSFORMATION

	Preindustrial Society	Industrial Society
Community Size	Typically small (villages)	Typically large (cities)
Social Relationships	Mostly primary (personal, intimate)	Mostly secondary (impersonal, anonymous)
Division of Labor	Relatively little, except on grounds of age and sex	A great deal: occupations are highly specialized
Statuses	Mostly ascribed	Some ascribed, but many achieved
Social Structure	Relatively simple: few statuses, and few clearly defined institutions other than the family	Complex: many statuses and many clearly defined institutions
Social Control	Mostly informal, relying on spontaneous community reaction	Often formal, relying on laws, police, and courts
Values	Tradition-oriented, religious	Future oriented, secular
Culture	Homogeneous: most people share similar norms and values	Heterogeneous: many subcultures hold different norms and values
Technology	Primitive, based mainly on human and animal power	Advanced, based mainly on machines
Social Change	Slow	Rapid

more account of their personal interests than the needs of the group.

6. The rate of social change in preindustrial societies is usually very slow, and change is regarded with suspicion as an unusual feature of social life. In industrial societies rapid social change becomes a normal state of affairs. People expect change and sometimes even welcome it, for change is often identified with "progress" toward a better life.

All these changes are entirely new in the history of the human species, and industrial societies are still in the difficult process of adjusting to them. In this book we will be dealing primarily with the most technologically advanced industrial society in the world, the United States. But from time to time we will refer to preindustrial and other industrial societies—both to give some sense of the immense and fascinating variety of human social behavior and to offer a greater awareness of the distinctive features of our own society.

Summary

1. Human beings are social animals, by habit and by necessity. A society is a group of interacting individuals occupying the same territory and participating in a common culture.

2. Social processes are generally patterned and predictable. The basic components of a social system tend to be linked in an organized relationship, termed social structure.

3. A status is a socially defined position in society. Some statuses rank higher or lower than others; people of roughly equivalent status form a class. Ascribed statuses are arbitrarily assigned by society; achieved statuses are earned by the individual.

4. A role is a part played by the occupant of a given status. Social norms prescribe how particular roles should be played. Role performance, however, may differ from role expectations. Role strain occurs when conflicting demands are built into the same role; role conflict occurs when two or more of a person's roles impose conflicting demands.

5. A group consists of a number of people interacting on the basis of shared expectations. A primary group is small and intimate; a secondary group is more anonymous. Groups are important building blocks of social structure.

6. Institutions are stable clusters of norms, values, statuses, roles, and expectations that develop around basic needs of society. They tend to be closely interrelated within social structure.

7. Societies can be classified according to their basic subsistence strategies. There has been a general trend of sociocultural evolution from small and simple societies to large and complex ones. The main types of societies are hunting and gathering societies, pastoral societies, horticultural societies, agricultural societies, and industrial societies. Culture and social structure grow more complex at each stage in this process.

8. Industrial societies are radically unlike preindustrial societies. They experience a rapid rate of social change, and virtually all aspects of culture and social structure are transformed by the modernization process that accompanies industrialization. Sociologists are still attempting to grasp the full significance of these changes.

Important Terms

society
social structure
status
class
ascribed status
achieved status
role
role expectation
role performance
role strain
role conflict
functional prerequisite
institution
sociocultural evolution
hunting and gathering society
pastoral society
horticultural society
agricultural society
industrial society
Gemeinschaft/Gesellschaft
mechanical solidarity
group
primary group
secondary group
organic solidarity
folk society
urban society

Suggested Readings

GREER, SCOTT A. *Social Organization.* New York: Random House, 1955.

A short book dealing with the elements of social structure and the relationships between individuals and groups within society.

HOROWITZ, IRVING L. (ED.). *Society.*

A useful sociological journal containing readable articles on a variety of sociological topics, including many current problems of American society. The journal can be used to supplement texts and other course materials with up-to-date commentary and analysis on social issues.

LENKSI, GERHARD, AND JEAN LENSKI. *Human Societies.* New York: McGraw-Hill, 1974.

This book examines societies from the perspective of sociocultural evolution and traces the changes that take place in social structure and institutions in the course of the process.

NISBET, ROBERT. *The Social Bond.* New York: Alfred A. Knopf, 1970.

This book addresses the problem of order and cohesion in society. It includes a careful analysis of groups, norms, roles, and statuses, showing how the "social bond" derives from the relationships between them.

PLOG, FRED, AND DANIEL G. BATES. *Cultural Anthropology.* New York: Alfred A. Knopf, 1975.

A concise account of human societies from an anthropological perspective. The book includes sections on hunting and gathering, pastoral, horiticultural, agricultural, and industrial societies.

SKOLNICK, JEROME H., AND ELLIOTT CURIE. *Crisis in American Institutions.* Boston: Little, Brown, 1976.

A collection of readings on modern American social problems. The book systematically relates these problems to strains and failures in American institutions and stresses the value conflicts involved in many of the problems.

WILLIAMS, ROBIN. *American Society: A Sociological Interpretation.* 3rd ed. New York: Alfred A. Knopf, 1970.

A text specifically devoted to the sociological analysis of contemporary American society. Williams discusses American social structure and its relationship to culture.

Reading

Pathology of Imprisonment *Philip Zimbardo*

Philip Zimbardo, a social psychologist, set up a mock "prison" in which students played the roles of prisoners and guards. The results were frightening. Zimbardo's report shows how the roles that we play deeply influence our social behavior.

In an attempt to understand just what it means psychologically to be a prisoner or a prison guard, Craig Haney, Curt Banks, Dave Jaffe and I created our own prison. We carefully screened over 70 volunteers who answered an ad in a Palo Alto city newspaper and ended up with about two dozen young men who were selected to be part of this study. They were mature, emotionally stable, normal, intelligent college students from middle-class homes throughout the United States and Canada. They appeared to represent the cream of the crop of this generation. None had any criminal record and all were relatively homogeneous on many dimensions initially.

Half were arbitrarily designated as prisoners by a flip of a coin, the others as guards. These were the roles they were to play in our simulated prison. The guards were made aware of the potential seriousness and danger of the situation and their own vulnerability. They made up their own formal rules for maintaining law, order and respect, and were generally free to improvise new ones during their eight-hour, three-man shifts. The prisoners were unexpectedly picked up at their homes by a city policeman in a squad car, searched, handcuffed, fingerprinted, booked at the Palo Alto station house and taken blindfolded to our jail. There they were stripped, deloused, put into a uniform, given a number and put into a cell with two other prisoners where they expected to live for the next two weeks. The pay was good ($15 a day) and their motivation was to make money.

At the end of only six days we had to close down our mock prison because what we saw was frightening. It was no longer apparent to most of the subjects (or to us) where reality ended and their roles began. The majority had indeed become prisoners or guards, no longer able to clearly differentiate between role playing and self. There were dramatic changes in virtually every aspect of their behavior, thinking and feeling. In less than a week the experience of imprisonment undid (temporarily) a lifetime of learning; human values were suspended, self-concepts were challenged and the ugliest, most base, pathological side of human nature surfaced. We were horrified because we saw some boys (guards) treat others as if they were despicable animals, taking pleasure in cruelty, while other boys (prisoners) became servile, dehumanized robots who thought only of escape, of their own individual survival and of their mounting hatred for the guards.

We had to release three prisoners in the first four days because they had such acute situational traumatic reactions as hysterical crying, confusion in thinking and severe depression. Others begged to be paroled, and all but three were willing to forfeit all the money they had earned if they could be paroled. By then (the fifth day) they had been so programmed to think of themselves as prisoners that when their request for parole was denied, they returned docilely to their cells. Now, had they been thinking as college students acting in an oppressive experiment, they would have quit once they no longer wanted the $15 a day we used as our only incentive. However, the reality was not quitting an experiment but "being paroled by the parole board from the Stanford County Jail." By the last days, the earlier solidarity among the prisoners (systematically broken by the guards) dissolved into "each man for himself." Finally, when one of their fellows was put in solitary confinement (a small closet) for refusing to eat, the prisoners were given a choice by one of the guards: give up their blankets and the incorrigible prisoner would be let out, or keep their blankets and he would be kept in all night. They voted to keep their blankets and to abandon their brother.

About a third of the guards became tyrannical in their arbitrary use of power, in enjoying their control over other people. They were corrupted by the power of their roles and became quite inventive in their techniques of breaking the spirit of the prisoners and making them feel they were worthless. Some of the guards merely did their jobs as tough but fair correctional officers, and several were good guards from the prisoners' point of view since they did them small favors and were friendly. However, no good guard ever interfered with a command by any of the bad guards; they never intervened on the side of the prisoners, they never told the others to ease off because it was only an experiment, and they never even came to me as prison superintendent or experimenter in charge to complain. . . . By the end of the week the experiment had become a reality.

Source: Philip G. Zimbardo, "Pathology of Imprisonment," *Society*, 9 (April 1972), pp. 4–8.

17

CHAPTER 5 Socialization

CHAPTER OUTLINE

"Nature" and "Nurture"

Effects of Childhood Isolation
"Feral" Children
Children Raised in Isolation
Institutionalized Children
Monkeys Raised in Isolation

Theories of Learning
The Behaviorist Approach
The Developmental Approach

The Emergence of the Self
Freud's Theory
Cooley's Theory
Mead's Theory

Cognitive Development
The Sensorimotor Stage
The Preoperational Stage
The Concrete Operational Stage
The Formal Operational Stage

Agencies of Socialization
The Family
The School
The Peer Group
The Mass Media
Other Agencies

Socialization and the Life Cycle
Types of Socialization
The Life Cycle

Socialization and Free Will

At birth the human infant is a helpless organism. It knows nothing, does not even know that it knows nothing, and cannot survive for more than a few hours without the help of other people. Unlike other animals, its later patterns of behavior will not be determined by any genetic program; they will have to be learned. Somehow this biological being must be transformed into a fully human being, a person able to participate effectively in society. That transformation is achieved through the complex and lengthy process of socialization.

Socialization is the process of social interaction through which people acquire personality and learn the way of life of their society. Socialization is the essential link between the individual and society—a link so vital that neither individual nor society could survive without it. Socialization enables the individual to learn the norms, values, language, skills, beliefs, and other patterns of thought and action that are essential for social living. And socialization enables the society to reproduce itself socially as well as biologically, thus ensuring its continuity from generation to generation.

One of the most important outcomes of socialization is individual personality. In ordinary speech we use the word "personality" rather loosely to refer to a person's character or temperament, but the sociological use of the term is both more broad and more precise. *Personality refers to the fairly stable patterns of thought, feeling, and action that are typical of an individual.* Personality thus includes three main components: the *cognitive* component of thought, belief, perception, memory, and other intellectual capacities; the *emotional* component of love, hate, envy, sympathy, anger, pride, and other feelings; and the *behavioral* component of skills, aptitudes, competence, and other abilities. Nobody is born a great mathematician, an anxious neurotic, or a

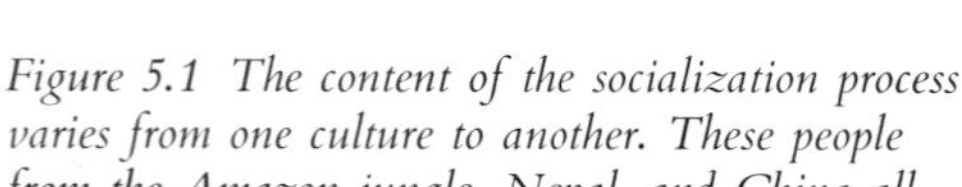

Figure 5.1 The content of the socialization process varies from one culture to another. These people from the Amazon jungle, Nepal, and China all learn very different norms, values, and ways of life. Within each society, there are typical personality patterns that differ from those in other societies.

skillful carpenter. People may be born with the potential to become any of these things, but what they actually become is primarily the product of their unique socialization experiences.

Social interaction takes place according to the norms and values of the culture in question. The content of socialization therefore differs greatly from one society to another, so that the personality types that are most admired and imitated vary among cultures. Many attempts have been made to pinpoint these differences in "national character," but they have met with only limited success. One difficulty is that we do not have sufficiently sophisticated tools for measuring personality, especially tools that are valid cross-culturally. Another difficulty is that our ideas of what other people are like are often ethnocentric and influenced by our emotional attitude toward the people concerned. During World War II, for example, Americans viewed Japanese as cruel and treacherous, but now that they are our allies we regard them as civilized and industrious.

In spite of these difficulties we find characteristic personality patterns in every society—patterns that result from a common experience of socialization in a unique culture. Within every society, however, each person is different, and these differences are also the product of socialization. Each one of us has a unique personal history. We are born and live not only in a society but also in a specific part of it, and we are therefore influenced by the particular subcultures of our family, friends, class, race, religion, or region. Distinctive new experiences in these contexts are continually blended with old ones, so every person's biography and personality is unique. The socialization process thus helps to explain both the general *similarities* in personality and social behavior within a society and the many *differences* that exist between one person and another.

Socialization is a lifelong process, for we continually encounter new or changing conditions and must learn how to adjust to them. The most important socialization, however, occurs in the early years of infancy and childhood when the basic foundations of later behavior and personality are laid. For this reason we will concentrate primarily on early socialization.

"Nature" and "Nurture"

From the middle of the last century until relatively recently, social scientists debated the issue of whether our personalities and social behavior are the product of heredity ("nature") or of learning ("nurture"). The debate led nowhere and is now recognized as one of the most futile controversies in the history of social science.

The "nature" viewpoint was dominant in the late nineteenth and early twentieth centuries. Charles Darwin's book *On the Origin of Species,* published in 1859, had upset the earlier view of the human species as a product of divine creation and had shown us instead to be simply one animal among all others. The behavior of other animals was obviously largely or wholly determined by inherited factors, and it seemed to follow that the same should be true of human beings. A few theorists, such as Karl Marx, emphatically rejected this view, but their arguments were for the most part ignored. Some sociologists applied a simpleminded Darwinism to human society, arguing that classes, nations, or races were superior or inferior to one another because of their inherited qualities. A number of psychologists began to compile endless lists of supposed human "instincts." Warfare was attributed to an "aggressive" instinct, society to a "herding" instinct, capitalism to an "acquisitive" instinct, and so on. The problem with this enterprise was that it soon got out of hand. One researcher reviewed the existing literature and found that over ten thousand supposed instincts had already been "discovered" by various authors (Bernard, 1924). To make matters worse, evidence mounted to show that behavior that seemed to be "instinctive" in Western cultures often did not appear at all or was reversed in other cultures. The situation was becoming ludicrous, and the old concept of "instinct" went out of fashion. Most contemporary psychologists do not regard the term as useful and refuse to use it in discussing human behavior.

Throughout most of this century, the "nurture" viewpoint held sway. At the turn of the century Ivan Pavlov, a Russian physiologist, noticed that dogs salivate not only at the sight of food but also at anything they have learned to associate with food, such as their food dish or even the ringing of a bell. No dog "instinctively" salivates when it hears a bell; the behavior is obviously learned. And if dogs could learn by association, would not human beings have an even greater capacity to do so? Pavlov's theories were taken up by the American psychologist John B. Watson, who argued that human behavior and personality were completely flexible and could be molded in any direction. Watson triumphantly taught an infant to call its milk bottle "mama" by offering it a bottle whenever it uttered the word. He capped his performance by teaching a little boy named Albert to fear white rabbits by frightening the boy with a loud noise whenever the rabbit was presented. In a widely quoted statement Watson (1924) declared:

> Give me a dozen healthy infants, well-formed, and my own specified world to bring them up in, and I'll guarantee to take any one at random and train him to become any type of specialist I might select—doctor, lawyer, artist, merchant-chief and, yes, even beggar, and thief, regardless of his talents, penchants, tendencies, abilities, vocations, and race of his ancestors.

Although some psychologists still seem to accept this view, most regard it as hopelessly naive. The current consensus is that the "nature versus nurture" debate was a pointless one, for it opposed two factors that are closely interrelated and cannot be separated. We are not the product of either heredity or learning but rather of a complex interaction between the two.

We can readily see that this is the case with some of our physical features. Height and weight are partly determined by heredity. But people born with genes for tallness or fatness may not actually become tall or fat. If they are inadequately nourished, they will be shorter and thinner than they might otherwise have been. The same appears to be true of many aspects of personality. So far scientists have not found any genes that can be shown to influence personality, but it is suspected that such complexes of genes might exist. Even from the moment of birth some infants are active, some passive; some are irritable, some easily pleased. Many aspects of personality, such as intelligence and artistic abilities, appear to be partly influenced by hereditary factors. But these factors provide only a basic potential. People learn to develop and satisfy their potentials in a social setting, and it is primarily their social experience that will determine whether they realize or fall short of these potentials. A placid baby, if systematically ill-treated, can become an irritable and neurotic adult; a person born with a capacity for high intelligence, if raised in a stultifying environment, can become an adult dullard. Biology may set the broad outlines and limits of our potential, but the use to which that potential is put is determined by the environment in which we live. The key to understanding the interaction of "nature" and "nurture" is the process of socialization, where biology and culture meet and blend.

Effects of Childhood Isolation

For many centuries people have wondered what human beings would be like if they were raised in isolation from human society. Some people speculated that such children would be mere brutes, revealing the essence of our real "human nature." Others felt that they would be perfect beings, perhaps speaking the language of Adam and Eve in the Garden of Eden. Today there are obvious ethical considerations that make any experiment involving the deliberate isolation of children impossible, but earlier ages were not always under such moral inhibitions. In the thirteen century the Emperor Frederick II conducted just such an experiment, recorded by a medieval historian in these terms (quoted in Ross and McLaughlin, 1949):

> His . . . folly was that he wanted to find out what kind of speech and what manner of speech children would have when they grew up, if they spoke to no one beforehand. So he bade foster mothers and nurses to suckle the children, to bathe and wash them, but in no way to prattle with them or to speak to them, for he wanted to learn whether they would speak the Hebrew language, which was the oldest, or Greek, or Latin, or Arabic, or perhaps the language of their parents, of whom they had been born. But he laboured in vain, because the children all died. For they could not live without the petting and joyful faces and loving words of their foster mothers.

The unhappy fate of the children comes as no surprise to modern social scientists, for it has been proved beyond doubt that children need more than mere physical care if they are to survive and prosper. They need close emotional attachments with at least one other person; without this attachment socialization is impaired, and irreversible damage may be done to the personality. Evidence for this view comes from four main sources: reports of so-called "feral" (untamed) children who were allegedly raised by wild animals; studies of children who were deliberately

Figure 5.2 There is overwhelming evidence that infants need to develop a warm, intimate relationship with at least one other person (not necessarily the mother). If such a relationship is not formed in early childhood, severe damage to later personality is likely to result.

reared in isolation by their own families; studies of children in institutions; and experiments that study the effects of isolation on other primates.

"Feral" Children

The evidence relating to feral children is highly dramatic but also highly unreliable. Many societies have myths about children being raised by animals. The Romans, for example, believed that the founders of Rome, Romulus and Remus, had been raised by a wolf. In the late nineteenth and early twentieth centuries, however, a few cases were reported from India and elsewhere of the discovery of children whose behavior seemed more like that of animals than human beings (Singh and Zingg, 1942). In every case the children could not speak, reacted with fear or hostility toward other human beings, slouched or walked on all fours, and tore ravenously at their food. Attempts to socialize the children are said to have met with little success, and all died at a young age.

There are two difficulties with these reports. The first is that the subjects were never systematically examined by trained investigators, and the second is that we have no way of knowing anything about the previous history of the children before they were discovered. It seems highly improbable that they had been raised by wild animals. It is far more likely that they had been abandoned by their own parents shortly before they were discovered by other people. It is also possible that the children were already mentally disturbed, autistic, or had been raised in some form of isolation before being abandoned.

Children Raised in Isolation

Much more convincing evidence comes from studies of children who were deliberately raised in isolation by their own families. Two such instances, both occurring in the United States, have been reported by Kingsley Davis (1940, 1947, 1948).

The first child, Anna, was discovered at the age of six. She had been born illegitimate, and her grandfather had insisted that she be hidden from the world in an attic room. Anna received a bare minimum of physical care and attention and had virtually no opportunities for social interaction. When she was found she could not talk, walk, keep herself clean, or feed herself; she was totally apathetic, expressionless, and indifferent to human beings. In fact, those who found and worked with her believed at first that she was deaf and possibly blind as well. Davis (1948) comments: "Here, then, was a human organism which had missed nearly six years of socialization. Her condition shows how little her purely biological resources, when acting alone, could contribute to making her a complete person."

Attempts to socialize Anna had only limited success. The girl died four-and-a-half years later, but in that time she was able to learn some words and phrases, although she could never speak sentences. She also learned to use building blocks, to string beads, to wash her hands and brush her teeth, to follow directions, and to treat a doll with affection. She learned to walk but could run only clumsily. By the time of her death at almost eleven years of age she had reached the level of socialization of a child only two or three years old.

The second child, Isabelle, was discovered about the same time as Anna and was approximately the same age, six-and-a-half. She too was an illegitimate child, and her grandfather kept her and her mother—a deaf-mute—in a dark room most of the time. Isabelle had the advantage, over Anna, of social interaction with her mother, but she had no chance to develop speech; the two communicated with gestures. When Isabelle was discovered, her behavior toward other people, especially men, was "almost that of a wild animal." At first it was thought that she was deaf, for she did not appear to hear the sounds around her, and her only speech was a strange croaking sound. The specialists who worked with her pronounced her feebleminded and did not expect that she could ever be taught to speak.

Unlike Anna, however, Isabelle had the advantage of training by a highly skilled team of doctors and psychologists. After a slow start, she suddenly spurted through the stages of learning that are usually characteristic of the first six years of childhood, taking every stage in the usual order but at much greater speed than normal. By the time she was eight-and-a-half years old she had reached an apparently normal level of intellectual development and was able to attend school with other children. Her greater success seems to be related to the skills of her trainers, the fact that her mother was present during her isolation, and the fact that, unlike Anna, she was able to gain the use of language.

Institutionalized Children

The socialization process of children who are raised in orphanages and similar institutions differs from that of other children in one very important respect. They rarely have the opportunity to develop close emotional ties with specific adults, because attendants simply do not have the time to devote much personal attention to any one individual. The standard of nutrition and other physical care in institutions is sometimes good and comparable to that in private homes, but relationships between child and adult are usually minimal.

In 1945, the psychologist René Spitz published an influential article on the effects of institutionalization on children's personalities. Spitz compared some infants who were being raised by their own mothers with infants of the same age who had been placed in the care of an orphanage. The infants living with their mothers had plenty of opportunity for close social interaction, but those in the institution received only routine care at mealtimes and when their clothing and bedding was changed. Spitz found that the infants in the orphanage were physically, socially, and emotionally retarded compared with the other infants—a difference that grew steadily greater as the children grew older.

Spitz's report was followed by a large number of studies on the effects of institutionalization on infants and children, most of which have arrived at similar conclusions (Bowlby, 1969). William Goldfarb (1945), for example, compared forty children who had been placed in foster homes soon after birth with forty children who had spent the first two years of life in institutions before being transferred to foster homes. He found that the institutionalized children suffered a number of personality defects that persisted even after they had left the institutions. They had lower IQ scores, seemed more aggressive and distractible, showed less initiative, and were more emotionally cold toward others. Many other studies have confirmed the depressing effects of institutionalization on physical, cognitive, emotional, and social development (for example, Provence and Lipton, 1962; Yarrow, 1963; Dennis, 1960; Dennis and Najarian, 1957).

Monkeys Raised in Isolation

Harry F. Harlow and his associates at the University of Wisconsin have conducted a series of important experiments on the effects of isolation on rhesus monkeys (Harlow, 1958, 1965; Harlow and Harlow, 1962; Harlow and Zimmerman, 1959). Harlow's work has shown that even in monkeys social behavior is learned, not inherited. The monkeys raised in isolation in his labs behave in a way similar to that of human psychotics. They are fearful of or hostile to other monkeys, make no attempt to interact with them, and are generally withdrawn and apathetic. Monkeys reared in isolation do not know how to mate with other monkeys and usually cannot be taught how to do so. If female monkeys who have been isolated from birth are artificially impregnated, they become unloving and abusive mothers, making little or no attempt to take care of their offspring. In one experiment Harlow provided isolated monkey infants with two substitute mothers—one made of wire and containing a feeding bottle and one covered with soft cloth but without a bottle. The infant monkeys preferred the soft, cuddly "mother"

Figure 5.3 In his experiments with monkeys raised in isolation, Harry Harlow has found that the animals prefer a soft, cuddly "mother" substitute to a "mother" that feeds them but is made of wire. The young monkeys clung to this cuddly "mother" for much of the time, especially if they were frightened. The wire "mother" was used only as a source of food. Harlow's study shows that the little monkeys placed greater priority on intimate physical contact than on food.

to the one that fed them. This wretched substitute for affection seemed more important to them even than food. Harlow has found that the damage resulting from lack of early socialization in monkeys is often irreversible.

Like all animal studies, Harlow's experiments must be treated with caution when inferences are made for human behavior. After all, we are not monkeys. His studies show, however, that without socialization monkeys cannot develop normal social, sexual, emotional, or maternal behavior. Since we know that human beings rely much more heavily on learning than monkeys do, it seems fair to conclude that the same would be true of us.

The evidence from these varied sources, then, points overwhelmingly in the same direction: we can become social and thus fully human only by learning through interaction with other people.

Theories of Learning

Learning refers to a change in an individual's thought, emotion, or action that results from previous experience. All animals have some capacity for learning, an ability that is very limited in the lower animals but highly developed in mammals and especially in human beings. But exactly how do human beings learn? Two general theories have been proposed: the behaviorist and the developmental.

The Behaviorist Approach

The behaviorist school in psychology is founded on the work of Ivan Pavlov and John B. Watson, and it has found favor with American psychologists throughout most of this century. Behaviorism arose as a reaction to the early theories of "instinct" that focused on invisible processes in the mind. Advocates of the new school argued that the concept of "mind" is merely an abstraction that cannot be scientifically studied; one person's guess about what goes on inside it is as good as another's. Learning theory, they argued, could be scientific only if it focused on something that could be observed and analyzed, namely actual behavior—hence the term *behaviorism.*

The essence of the behaviorist approach is that all learning takes place as a result of *conditioning* through rewards and punishments. If an animal is repeatedly rewarded for a particular response—such as getting food every time it presses a lever—the response will recur. If the animal is repeatedly punished for making a particular response—such as getting an electric shock every time it presses the lever—the response will not recur. This pattern of rewards or punishments is called *reinforcement,* and learning takes place through *association* once the animal makes the connection between its behavior and the consequences.

By using these techniques, behaviorists have produced impressive displays of learning in laboratory animals: pigeons have been taught to play table tennis, and rats have learned to make their way through highly complicated obstacle courses to get food. Behaviorist psychologists, most notably B. F. Skinner (1971), have argued that virtually all human learning can be explained in terms of conditioning. Skinner has even advocated a utopian society based on behaviorist principles. Under the appropriate learning conditions, he argues, human behavior could be regulated in such a way that a perfect society would result. Skinner does not confront the problem, however, of precisely who would decide what kind of behavior the rest of us would be conditioned into performing.

Other psychologists in the behaviorist tradition have modified the approach by introducing the concept of *social learning* (Bandura and Walters, 1963). They point out that some learning does not result from any obvious rewards. In traveling from one location to another, for example, we learn something about surroundings en route, even though we are not rewarded for doing so. They also argue that a good deal of behavior seems to be learned as a result of imitation of other human models, especially if the models are seen to be rewarded. People, they point out, often learn from their social environment even in the absence of any obvious rewards.

The Developmental Approach

The developmental school in modern psychology is a broad one, loosely linked by a belief that processes of conditioning cannot in themselves adequately account for human learning. Unlike the behaviorists, the developmentalists are not disturbed by the concept of "mind." They place great emphasis on the individual's internal *interpretation* of situations rather than on such external factors as punishments and rewards. Learning, they argue, is a matter of the continual development of the mind through different *stages;* more advanced forms of learning are possible only when the basis has been laid in the mind by earlier experiences and personal interpretations. The leading exponent of the school is the Swiss philosopher and psychologist Jean Piaget (1950, 1954, 1969). Piaget points out, for example, that a child of three simply cannot learn about the concept of speed. Children at this age will say that a car traveling in front of another is going faster, even if the one behind is rapidly catching up. The minds of very young children are not capable of understanding speed as a relationship between time and distance, and no amount of rewards and punishments can make them understand it.

In the same way, the American linguist Noam Chomsky (1957, 1968, 1971) argues that the behaviorist approach cannot explain how children learn language. Most of the sentences we speak are novel ones that have never been spoken by anyone before. If children had to learn how to construct sentences by a process of association, it would take them forever. What actually happens, Chomsky argues, is that children of a certain age are able to interpret basic rules of grammar. Once they understand these, they can construct original sentences that any other speaker of the language can understand. Similarly, the American psychologist Lawrence Kohlberg (1966) has argued that children do not learn sex roles primarily by being rewarded for the appropriate masculine or feminine behavior. Although this conditioning is important, the crucial part of the process comes when the children define themselves as male or female. Once they think of themselves as boys or girls, they deliberately seek out the behavior that is most rewarding.

The difference between the two approaches, then, lies mainly in the importance they attach to the inner workings of the individual's mind. The behaviorists tend to see people as essentially passive, with their behavior the outcome of conditioning by the environment. The developmentalists acknowledge that a good deal of learning occurs in this way, but insist that people are essentially active—judging, interpreting, defining, and personally creating their behavior. The developmental approach, which is winning increasing acceptance among modern social scientists, is more humanist, for it places greater emphasis on human free will and choice.

The Emergence of the Self

At the core of personality lies the *self*—the individual's conscious experience of a distinct, personal identity that is separate from all other people and things. Unlike other animals, we are self-conscious, capable of thinking as subjects about ourselves as objects. You can be "proud of yourself" or "ashamed of yourself"; you can "love yourself," "change yourself," or "lose control of yourself"; and you can even "talk to yourself."

The concept of "self" is perhaps a rather vague one. But we certainly experience it as real; each of us has some fairly definite conception of who and what he or she is. Our sense of self seems to consist primarily of the various roles that we play and the various qualities of character that we believe we possess. If people are asked to write down as fast as possible twenty answers to the question "who am I?" the initial answers are usually roles—student, female, Catholic, black, brother, and so on. The subsequent answers are usually character traits—generous, friendly, honest, humorous, hard-working, and the like (Kuhn and McPartland, 1954). But whatever our sense of self consists of, where does it come from? The answer is that it is a social product, created and modified throughout life by interaction with other people.

At the time of birth the infant has no sense of self, no awareness of a separate identity. The infant does not show any recognition of other people as distinct beings until around six months of age and does not begin to use words such as "I," "me," and "mine" until at least the age of two. Only in the years that follow do young children gradually come to realize that other people also have distinct selves, with needs and perspectives that are different from their own. And only then can the child fully appreciate that his or her own self is an identity separate from all others.

How does the self emerge in childhood and how is it continually modified throughout the life cycle? This question has been of great interest to sociologists, psychologists, and social psychologists. Three major theories have been proposed: by Sigmund Freud, Charles Horton Cooley, and George Herbert Mead. Although the details of the theories are different, each emphasizes that concepts of the self are learned through social interaction with others.

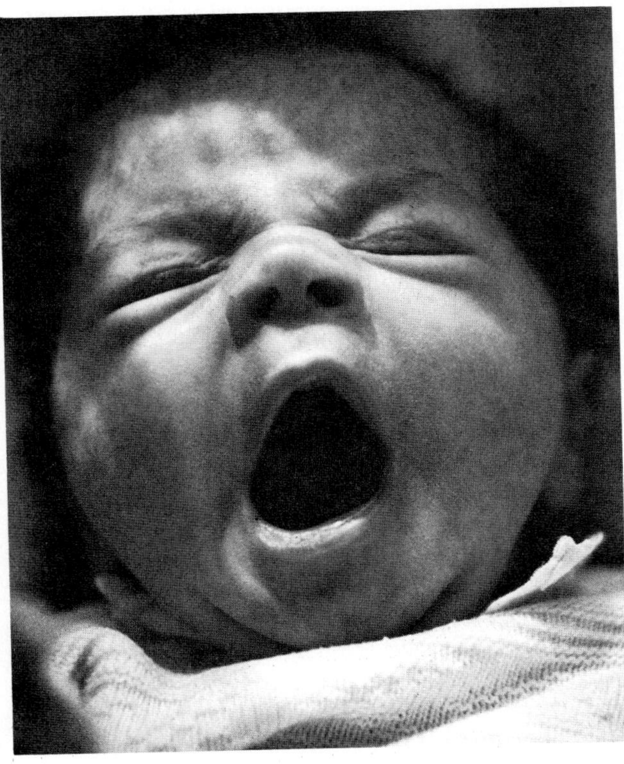

Figure 5.4 At birth, the human infant has no sense of self, no awareness of an identity separate from those of everyone else. The self emerges slowly in the course of socialization, and an awareness of self is essential for effective social interaction. Once children are aware that they have selves, they can appreciate that other people also have selves. By taking the role and viewpoint of other people, they can predict how other people are likely to respond to their own behavior.

Freud's Theory

Sigmund Freud (1856–1939) was one of the founders of modern psychology. He is regarded as one of the most profound and original thinkers of the past century, and various versions of his theories are still influential. Freud's major insight into personality was that the motives for much if not most human behavior are *unconscious:* we are very often unaware of the real reasons for our actions. Freud believed that early childhood experiences, though often lost to conscious memory in later years, are of fundamental importance for later development of the personality. The unconscious motives that guide a good deal of human behavior, he argued, can sometimes be detected through analysis of dreams, slips of the tongue, and prolonged, probing interviews with a trained expert—an approach that he called *psychoanalysis.*

Freud believed that the relationship between the individual and society is essentially one of conflict. He argued that people are born with basic drives, such as those for sex and aggression, and that social order would be impossible unless these drives were controlled. Society therefore imposes its will on the individual, suppressing and channeling the drives into socially acceptable outlets—but often doing so in ways that lead to later neuroses and personality disturbances. Freud placed particular importance on the social control of the sex drive. He believed this drive is present even in young infants and that it leads to constant conflicts between the individual and society.

Personality, Freud proposed, can be divided into three basic, interacting parts. The *id* is the reservoir of drives present in the individual at birth and throughout life; it is entirely unconscious and demands continual, instantaneous satisfaction. The self of the very young child consists almost entirely of the id, but the child soon learns through interaction with others that the demands of the id cannot always be satisfied and must often be repressed. Accordingly, the *ego* emerges—the conscious part of the self that rationally attempts to mediate between the demands of the social environment and the deep, unconscious urges of the id. The child learns about the demands of society from other people, particularly from parents, and finally internalizes these demands into the personality in the form of the *superego,* which is roughly equivalent to the person's conscience. The superego is thus an internal version of the moral authority of the society, and it works through feelings of shame and pride to influence the decisions of the ego.

The ego, or conscious self, thus has two tasks. The first is to counterbalance the demands for self-gratification that come from the id with the demands for socially acceptable behavior that come from the superego. The second task is to mediate between the personality as a whole and the

Figure 5.5 Sigmund Freud, the founder of psychoanalysis and one of the most influential thinkers in the history of psychology.

social environment. If the conscious self achieves a harmonious balance within the personality, and between the entire personality and society, the individual is well adjusted; if not, personality and self-concept may be severely impaired.

Of course, Freud did not argue that the brain is physically divided into these three categories. He merely proposed his theory as a useful way of understanding the development of the self and personality. Some psychologists still find his model useful; others do not. But Freud did make valuable contributions. He stressed that personality is a product of the interaction between the human organism and the social forces that surround it, and he emphasized the crucial influence of early childhood socialization on later conscious and unconscious motives and behavior.

Cooley's Theory

Charles Horton Cooley (1864–1929) was an American economist turned social psychologist. Like Freud, Cooley (1902) maintained that the self is essentially a social product, but he believed that it emerges through a very different process.

The central concept in Cooley's theory is the *looking-glass self*. The "looking glass" is society, which provides a mirror in which we can observe the reactions of others to our own behavior. Our concept of ourselves is derived from this reflection. It is through seeing the attitudes of others that we learn whether we are attractive or ugly, popular or unpopular, respectable or disreputable. By observing the responses of others—or by imagining what their response would be like to some behavior we are contemplating—we are able to evaluate ourselves and our actions. If the image that we see or imagine in the social mirror is favorable, our self-concept is enhanced and our behavior is likely to be repeated. If the image is unfavorable, our self-concept is diminished and our behavior is likely to change. We are defined by other people; we perceive this definition; and thus we learn our identity from them. There can be no self without society, no "I" without a corresponding "they" to provide our self-image.

Of course, people may misjudge the way others see them. We do not gain a direct impression of the reactions of others but must interpret those reactions for ourselves. All of us are guilty of misinterpretations at times, and some people habitually misjudge the opinion of others and have unrealistically high or low self-concepts as a result. But whether we misread the image in the "looking glass" or not, our sense of personal identity arises through social interaction.

Like Freud, Cooley believed that the self-concepts formed in childhood are more stable and lasting than those formed later in life and provide the basis for subsequent personality development. He emphasized, however, that the process of self-evaluation continues throughout life whenever a person enters a new situation. But unlike Freud, Cooley did not accept the idea that individual and society are in a state of eternal conflict. He saw the two as inseparable: society cannot exist without interacting individuals, and the individual self is an impossibility without social interaction.

Mead's Theory

George Herbert Mead (1863–1931) is one of the most important figures in American social science. A philosopher and social psychologist, Mead was by all accounts a fascinating lecturer, yet he never wrote a book—his attempts to commit his ideas to paper led him to agonies of frustration. His students and colleagues, however, compiled and published his work from lecture notes and other sources.

Mead (1934) explicitly intended his work to be seen as an elaboration of Cooley's ideas. His major innovation was to introduce for the first time the concept of *symbolic interaction,* the interaction between people that takes place not through simple physical or other sensory contact but through symbols such as gestures, facial expressions, and, above all, language. Language is socially learned and is essential for all but the most simple forms of thought. In this sense the mind—through which we interpret our own behavior and that of others—is a social product.

To Mead the essence of the socialization process is the ability to anticipate what others expect and to evaluate and control one's own behavior accordingly. This capacity is achieved by *role taking*—pretending to take or actually taking the roles of other people, so that one can see oneself from their perspectives. In early childhood children are able to internalize the expectations of the *particular other,* that is, specific individuals such as parents. But as they grow older they learn to internalize the expectations of the *generalized other,* the attitudes and viewpoint of society as a whole. This internalized general concept of social expectations provides the basis for self-evaluation and hence for self-concept.

Mead illustrated this idea by pointing to the childhood progression from mere play to organized games. *Play* is typical of very young children: they play at taking the roles of specific other people. They walk about in their parents' shoes, pretend to be an adult and scold a doll, or play "house," "doctors and nurses," and so on. In this kind of play the children are merely pretending to take the roles of specific other people, but in doing so they learn to see the world from a perspective that is not their own. Later, the children play organized *games*—preludes to the "game" of life—in which their roles are real and fixed and in which they must simultaneously take account of the roles and perspectives of all the participants. A baseball pitcher, for example, must be aware not only of his or her own role and expectations but also of the roles, expectations, and likely actions of every other player—and of the symbolic system of rules that guides the conduct of the game. Very young children cannot play organized games, for they do not understand the rules, cannot take the role of other players, and thus cannot anticipate how others will respond to their own actions.

Mead pointed out, however, that the socialization process is never perfect or complete. He distinguished between what he called the "I" (the spontaneous, self-interested, impulsive, unsocialized self) and the "me" (the socialized self that is conscious of social norms, expectations, and the individual's social responsibility). Although Mead did not regard the individual and society as being in conflict, he felt that the "I" was never completely under the control of the "me." The socialized self is usually dominant, but we all have the capacity to break social rules and violate the expectations of others.

Cognitive Development

One of the most important achievements of socialization is the development of *cognitive* abilities—intellectual capacities such as reasoning, remembering, perceiving, calculating, believing. Our knowledge of this process is based largely on the work of Jean Piaget. Piaget was born in 1896, published his first scientific papers in his early teens, and has maintained a prodigous and highly influential annual output of books and articles ever since. Like all developmental theorists, Piaget (1950, 1954, 1969) emphasizes the internal processes of the mind as it matures through interaction with the social environment. He sees the individual as actively trying to make sense of the world rather than being passively conditioned by it.

Piaget's many experiments with children have shown that human beings gradually pass through a series of different *stages* of cognitive development, with their skills at each stage being dependent on their successful completion of the previous stage. Piaget outlines four basic stages of cognitive development, each of them characterized by the particular kind of "operations," or intellectual processes, that a person at that stage can perform.

The Sensorimotor Stage

The *sensorimotor stage* lasts from birth until about the age of two. The intelligence of children at this stage is termed "sensorimotor" because it is expressed purely in terms of sensory and physical contact with the environment. Lacking language, the infant cannot "think" about the world in any meaningful way, and its intelligence is inseparable from its actions. The child does not know that it exists as a separate object, and therefore does not distinguish among itself, its actions, and the objects it acts upon. The infant is thus unaware of the consequences of its acts; it does not realize, for example, that its own movements cause a rattle to make a sound. Similarly, the child does not realize that objects have a permanent existence. If a toy is removed from a child's vision, or if a parent leaves the room, the child reacts as though the toy or parent has ceased to exist. Only at the end of the sensorimotor stage does the child begin to look for a missing object. This is a considerable achievement, for it shows that the child now sees the world as a stable, permanent, predictable environment, not simply a shifting chaos of impressions.

The Preoperational Stage

The *preoperational stage,* on which Piaget has focused most of his attention, lasts from the ages of about two to about seven. Piaget uses the term "preoperational" because the children are incapable of performing many simple intellectual operations, largely because they have no real understanding of such elementary concepts as speed, weight, number, quantity, or causality. Particularly during the early years of this stage, for example, children invariably assume that the larger of two objects must be the heavier. (They will typically state that a pound of feathers weighs more than a pound of lead.) Although they may be able to count, they do not really understand the concept of number. They assert that a long row of beads contains more beads than a shorter row, even if the short row is more densely packed with a greater number of beads. They have a very limited understanding of cause and effect—often believing, for example, that trees waving in the wind are actually making the wind. They attribute life to inanimate objects, such as the sun and moon, and may believe that a table is "hurt" when it is bumped.

Figure 5.6 Children at the preoperational stage have great difficulty in realizing that the quantity of water does not change in volume when it is poured from one container to another of a different shape. If water is poured before the childrens' eyes from a tall, thin bottle into a short, fat flask, they insist that there is now less water than before. Children at this stage judge the volume of the water only by the height of the water level and cannot understand that its volume remains constant no matter what the shape of the container is.

Children in the preoperational stage have an increasing command of language and therefore of thought, and they are capable of thinking about concrete objects that are not actually present. But they are also highly *egocentric:* they see the world entirely from their own perspective because they are unable to take the roles of others. If a young boy is asked "How many brothers do you have?" he may correctly answer "One." But if he is asked "How many brothers does your brother have?" he is likely to answer "None," because he cannot see himself from his brother's point of view. Similarly, if young children are asked to draw an object from their own part of the room, they can do so. But if they are asked to draw the same object from the point of view of someone sitting elsewhere in the room, they will draw it exactly as before, being incapable of taking another person's perspective. Young children are also unable to explain their reasoning processes to others, because to examine one's own thought involves taking an "outside" look at it.

The Concrete Operational Stage

The *concrete operational stage* lasts from the ages of seven to about twelve and is so named because the thinking of children is still tied to the concrete world. They think mainly in terms of real situations, not abstract or purely hypothetical ones. If children of this age are asked to talk about abstract concepts, such as death or the afterlife, they have great difficulty in doing so without referring to concrete events or images, such as the death of a pet or the physical appearance of God and heaven.

Children at this stage, however, are able to handle the concrete world with much the same cognitive skill as an adult. They can perform the various operations related to weight, speed, number, or quantity that were not possible in the previous stage. They can also understand cause and effect, can take the roles of others and appreciate their perspectives, and can participate effectively in games and other organized social relationships.

The Formal Operational Stage

The *formal operational stage* begins at the onset of adolescence. People at this stage of cognitive development are able to achieve formal, abstract thought. They can think in terms of theories, concepts, and hypotheses and can manipulate and solve problems, such as those of mathematics or morality, that are not tied to the immediate environment. They are able to use general rules to solve whole classes of problems, and they can reason logically from premises to conclusions with a sophistication that would not be possible in earlier stages. They can think about abstract personal goals and even utopian social conditions, a capacity that is often expressed in adolescent idealism (see Figure 5.7).

Piaget believes that the *process* of cognitive development is universal in all societies: people everywhere advance through the same stages in the same order. But the *content* is culturally variable. If one's culture believes that the earth is flat or that cause and effect are related to magic and witchcraft, then that is how one will interpret the world. Moreover, not everyone advances to the final stage; many adults never progress beyond the stage of concrete operational thought and have great difficulty in understanding abstract concepts. This is particularly true of people who have little exposure to formal thinking in their social environment. As Piaget comments, "Social life is necessary if the individual is to become conscious of his own mind." If the relevant social experiences are lacking, the mind will not develop beyond a certain stage.

Figure 5.7

"Who's going to tell them that utopia is still in the talk stage?"

Drawing by Alan Dunn; © 1970 The New Yorker Magazine, Inc.

Agencies of Socialization

The socialization process involves many different influences that affect the individual throughout life. The most important of these influences are *agencies of socialization,* institutions or other structured situations in which socialization takes place, particularly in the early years of life. Four agencies of socialization are especially important in modern societies, for they affect almost everyone in a powerful and lasting way. These agencies are the family, the school, the peer group, and the mass media.

The Family

The family is without doubt the most important single agency of socialization in all societies. One reason for the importance of the family is that it has the main responsibility for socializing children in the crucial early years of life. The family is where children establish their first close emotional ties, learn language, and begin to internalize cultural norms and values. To young children the family is all-encompassing. They have little social experience beyond its boundaries and therefore lack any basis for comparing and evaluating what is learned from family members. A great deal of the socialization that takes place in the family is conscious and deliberate, but much of it is quite unintentional. The patterns of social interaction within the family, for example, may provide unintended models for the later behavior and personality traits of the children.

A second reason for the importance of the family is that the family is located somewhere in the social structure. From the moment of birth, therefore, the children have an ascribed status in a subculture of race, class, ethnicity, religion, or region—all of which may strongly influence the nature of later social interaction and socialization. For example, the values and expectations that are learned by children depend very much on the social class of the parents. To appreciate the significance of family background for socialization and personality, we need only consider the likely differences between the experiences of, say, a child born into a poor family of fundamentalist Baptists living in rural Alabama and a child born into a wealthy professional family living in the exclusive suburbs of Los Angeles.

Figure 5.8 The family is the most basic agency of socialization in all societies. In the family environment the young child learns important cultural norms and values and acquires language and other skills essential in later life.

The School

The school is an agency formally charged by society with the task of socializing the young in particular skills and values. We usually think of the school as being mainly concerned with teaching skills and knowledge, and this is certainly one of its major functions. But the schools in every society also engage in outright indoctrination in values. We may find this fact more readily apparent in societies other than our own—until we consider the content of civics classes or the daily ritual of the pledge of allegiance. The school socializes not only through its formal academic curriculum but also through the "hidden curriculum" implicit in the content of school activities, ranging from regimented classroom schedules to organized sports. Children learn that they must be neat and punctual. They learn to sit still, keep quiet, wait their turn, and not be distracted from their work. They learn to respect and obey without question the commands of those who have social authority over them.

In the school, children come for the first time under the direct supervision of people who are not relatives. The children learn to obey other people not because they offer love and protection but because a social system requires uniform adherence to rules. The individual child is no longer considered somebody special; he or she is now one of a crowd, subject to the same regulations and expectations that everyone else is subject to. Personal behavior and academic achievements or failures become part of a permanent official record, and the children learn to evaluate themselves by the same standards that others apply to them. Participation in the life of the school also lessens the childrens' dependence on the family and creates new links to the wider society beyond.

The Peer Group

As children grow older they spend more and more time in the company of their peers, children of roughly the same age and usually of similar background and interests. As the influence of the peer group increases, that of the parents diminishes. In the United States young people of school-going age spend on average twice as much time with peers as with parents, and most of them prefer to spend their time this way (Bronfenbrenner, 1970).

Membership in a peer group places children for the first time in a context where most socialization is carried out unintentionally and without any deliberate design. Individuals are able at last to choose their own companions and friends and to interact with other people on a basis of equality. Unlike the family or school, the peer group is entirely centered on its own concerns and interests. Its members can explore relationships and topics that are tabooed in the family and the school, and they can thus learn to break away from the influence of these two agencies and establish separate (and often disapproved) roles and identities. In modern industrial societies, the generations are often highly compartmentalized, with the youthful peer group claiming the primary loyalty of its members and often demanding that they reject the values

Figure 5.9 The peer group is an important agency of socialization throughout life, but it is particularly influential during adolescence. Young people at this age are establishing relatively settled identities, a process that may involve a reaction against earlier patterns learned in the family and at school. The peer group provides new norms and values for its members and offers them the opportunity to interact with others as equals.

and authority of parents and teachers. The influence of the peer group climaxes in adolescence, when young people are apt to form a distinctive subculture with its own tastes, dress, jargon, symbols, values, and heroes. By rewarding members for conformity to peer-group norms and by criticizing or ostracizing them for nonconformity, the group exerts a very strong influence on their social behavior and personality.

The Mass Media

The mass media are the various forms of communication that reach a large audience without any personal contact between the senders and the receivers of the messages: newspapers, magazines, books, television, radio, movies, and records. The mass media are unquestionably a powerful socializing influence, although their precise impact is difficult to gauge. The most influential medium is probably television. There is a TV set in 95 percent of American homes, and the average American between the ages of three and sixteen spends more time in front of the TV set than in school.

The media provide instant coverage of social events and social changes, ranging from news and opinions to fads and fashions. They offer role models and glimpses of life-styles that people might otherwise never have access to. Through the media, children can learn about courtroom lawyers, cowboys, police detectives, or even such improbable characters as Batman. These images are not necessarily very realistic, but this failing need not lessen their influence. Through media advertising, too, the young learn about their future roles as consumers in the marketplace, and about the high value our society places on youth, success, beauty, and materialism. Changing social norms and values are quickly reflected in the media and may be just as quickly adopted by people who might not otherwise be exposed to them. The rapid spread of youth culture in the sixties, for example, depended very heavily on such media as records, FM radio, and underground newspapers and comics.

Other Agencies

The individual may be influenced by many other agencies of socialization—religious groups, Boy Scouts and Girl Scouts, youth organizations, and, later in life, by such agencies as the military, corporations or other employment settings, and by voluntary associations such as clubs, political movements, and retirement homes. It is obvious that the influences of the various agencies are not always complementary and can often be in outright conflict. The church, for example, may hold quite different values from the military, the peer group quite different values from the school. It is also obvious that people do not always learn what they are supposed to learn. The socialization process may fail in certain respects, and people may come to behave in ways that were never anticipated or intended. Personality and behavior are never entirely stable; they change under the influence of socialization experiences throughout the life cycle.

Socialization and the Life Cycle

Socialization is never complete; it continues from the moment of birth throughout maturity and old age until death. The more complex the social structure of a society and the more rapid the pace of its social change, the more intensive and varied is the continuing socialization process.

Types of Socialization

The socialization that a person encounters in the course of a lifetime may be one or more of four different types: primary socialization, anticipatory socialization, developmental socialization, and resocialization.

Primary Socialization

This is the kind of basic learning that we have concentrated on in this chapter: the socialization that takes place in the early years of life. It focuses on the teaching of language and cognitive skills, the internalization of cultural norms and values, the establishment of emotional ties, and the appreciation of other roles and perspectives.

Anticipatory Socialization

This kind of learning is directed toward a person's future roles rather than those that the person has at the time of learning. When children play at "house" they are involved in anticipatory socialization for their future roles as parents. Much of the socialization in the school anticipates

Figure 5.10 Military trainees are subjected to systematic resocialization, a form of socialization that involves an abrupt break with earlier experiences. Resocialization often takes place in the context of "total institutions," such as army camps, traditional boarding schools, prisons, and mental asylums. In these institutions the inmates are strictly segregated from the rest of society, placed in uniforms and treated alike, and are made subject to the almost absolute authority of the officials in charge.

the pupils' roles in their occupational careers. Training programs in business, industry, or the armed forces have similar intent.

Developmental Socialization

This kind of learning is based on the achievements of primary socialization. It builds on already acquired skills and knowledge as the adult progresses through new situations—such as marriage or new jobs—that require new expectations, obligations, and roles. New learning is added to and blended with old in a relatively smooth and continuous process of development.

Resocialization

This kind of learning involves a sharp break with the past and the internalization of radically different norms and values. It frequently takes place in a context where people have been partly or wholly isolated from their previous background. Resocialization occurs, for example, in prisons, in the army "boot camp," in the process of conversion to a different religion, in the experience of an anthropologist who lives among an alien people, or in"brainwashing" situations where the victim's personality is systematically stripped away and rebuilt.

The Life Cycle

The human life cycle seems at first sight to be purely a matter of biology. But our sequence of birth, childhood, maturity, old age, and death is also a social one, for its length, stages, and distinctive problems depend very much on the society in which one lives. Among the malnourished Ik of Uganda, for example, old age sets in by the late twenties; among the better nourished citizens of North America, people are not considered old until they are in their sixties or seventies.

The Stages of the Life Cycle

The stages of the life cycle are very much a matter of social definition. The concept of childhood, for example, did not exist at all in Europe in the Middle Ages. Children were dressed like adults, took part in the same games, did the same jobs, and were even portrayed in paintings as "little adults" with small bodies but mature faces (Aries, 1962; Plumb, 1971). Child labor was not generally considered a scandal in the early stages of the Industrial Revolution, because children were not regarded as very significantly different from adults. The concept of adolescence, which we take so much for granted today, did not appear in the Western world until the Industrial Revolution was well under way, and in fact the word came into common usage only at the beginning of this century. Like "childhood," the stage of "adolescence" is a social creation. It was introduced into our version of the life cycle because extended education has for the first time produced a large category of people who are physically and sexually mature but who are denied adult responsibility, especially participation in the work force. Kenneth Keniston (1970) suggests that another stage is now being introduced into the life cycle, that of "youth." This stage is an optional one that runs from about eighteen to thirty and contains those young people who refuse to "settle down" into the defining characteristics of mature adulthood—a steady job, a marriage, a mortgage, and so on (see Figure 5.11).

Personality and social behavior are therefore strongly affected at different ages by social as well as biological forces. The United States is a very child-centered society, and Americans often look back on childhood as a particularly happy time in which they were shielded, as children in many other parts of the world are not, from many of the harsh realities of life. Adolescence, however, is typically regarded as a time of great turmoil and problems of identity (E. Erikson, 1964). In many traditional, preindustrial societies, in contrast, the stage of adolescence is unknown. In these societies the transition from childhood to adulthood is an abrupt one, often marked by initiation ceremonies involving great pain or feats of endurance. As soon as the ceremony is over, however, the child becomes an adult, with full adult rights and responsibilities.

Failures of the Socialization Process

Unlike the socialization process in simple, preindustrial societies, socialization in complex, modern societies often fails to prepare people for the challenges of the life cycle.

The American socialization process equips people poorly for the challenges of adolescence. The media, for example, extol the virtues of sexual satisfaction and the value of money, but adolescents are usually denied full access to either even though they have the physical maturity to do both. Adolescence in our society is therefore often experienced as a time of confusion and personality crises.

Mature adulthood in our society also brings its problems, particularly in the middle years of the forties and fifties. American women are socialized to value their youth, their beauty, and their roles as mothers. When their youthfulness fades and their children leave home, they may feel desolate and purposeless. Similarly, American men are socialized to value occupational and financial success, but a man who has not achieved these goals by the early forties must face the uncomfortable fact that he probably never will, and his self-concept may suffer accordingly.

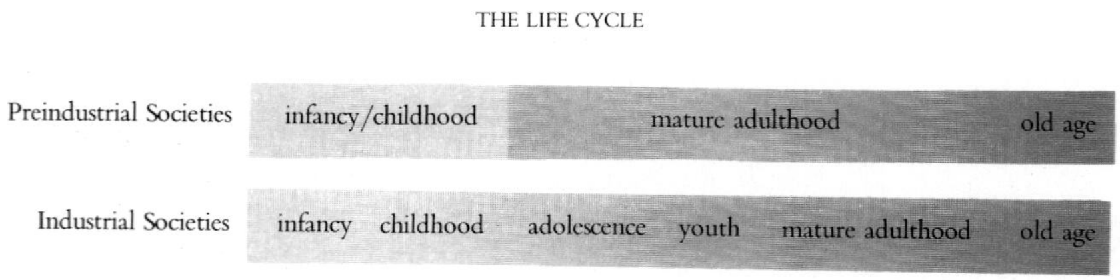

THE LIFE CYCLE

Preindustrial Societies	infancy/childhood		mature adulthood			old age
Industrial Societies	infancy	childhood	adolescence	youth	mature adulthood	old age

Figure 5.11 The stages of the life cycle are influenced by social as well as biological factors. Preindustrial societies generally did not recognize separate stages of infancy, childhood, and adolescence. Childhood was not recognized in Europe until after the Middle Ages, and adolescence has been recognized in industrial societies only in this century. More recently, an additional, optional stage, that of youth, has appeared in the life cycle of advanced industrial societies.

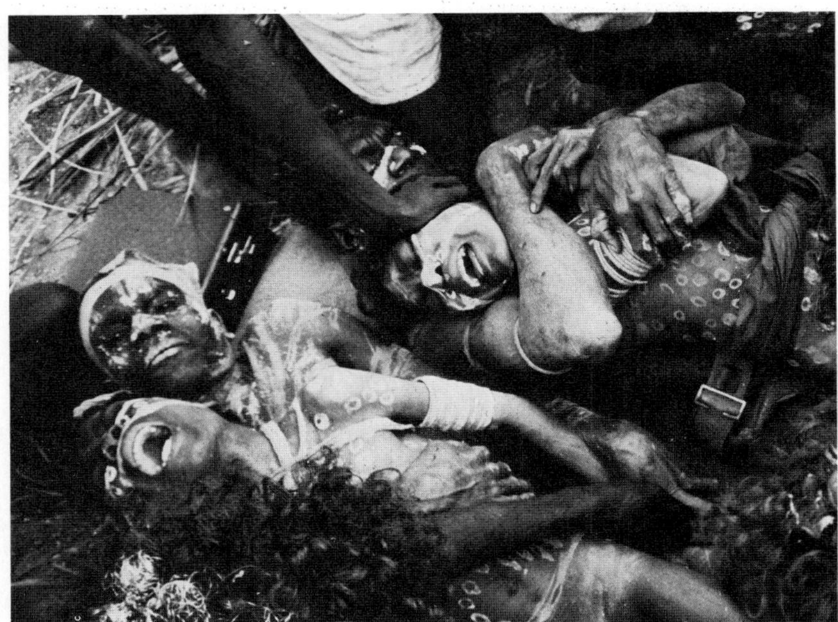

Figure 5.12 In many preindustrial societies the transition from childhood to adulthood is very abrupt. This transition usually takes place at puberty and is often marked by a social ceremony, the puberty rite. These aboriginal boys in Australia are undergoing a painful circumcision ceremony, after which they will be able to take their place as adult members of the society.

Perhaps the greatest failure of the American socialization process is its inability to equip people adequately to face old age and death. Preindustrial societies were generally oriented toward the old rather than the young; the aged were respected for their wisdom and held an honored place in the family. In modern societies their knowledge is obsolete, their authority is negligible, they are frequently unwanted by their children, and the best they can do is attempt not to "be a burden." The old generally do not so much withdraw from society as have social roles withdrawn from them (Riley *et al.,* 1969). They have little part to play in the family or the economy, have fewer and fewer links with society, and may suffer severe personality disorganization resulting from feelings of isolation and rejection rather than from the aging process itself.

Socialization for death is almost nonexistent in the United States. In preindustrial societies deaths usually took place at home in the context of the family, and young people grew up with a close understanding of the experience. In the modern United States death is very much a taboo subject. We speak of death in hushed tones and use such euphemisms as "passed away." We have sanitized death and removed it as far as possible from everyday experience by ensuring that old people die in formal organizations such as old-age homes and hospitals. When someone is dying, there is often a conspiracy between relatives and medical personnel to hide the fact from the dying person. Recent research into the sociology of death and dying, however, has produced an impressive and growing body of evidence to suggest that people die far more happily—even contentedly—if death is openly and honestly discussed with them beforehand (Glaser and Strauss, 1965, 1968; Kubler-Ross, 1969, 1972; Brim *et al.,* 1970; Powers, 1971).

Socialization and Free Will

If our social acts and personalities depend so much on the content of our individual socialization, what becomes of human free will? Do we have any choice over our personal behavior, or is it all shaped for us by our past experiences?

Dennis Wrong (1961) has drawn attention to what he calls the "oversocialized conception" of human beings—the view that we are little more than the predictable products of a harmonious socialization into the social order. Wrong points out that people often feel coerced by society into doing things they do not want to do. Yet if they were perfectly socialized, this should never happen. Socialization, he argues, can never completely wipe out any basic personality traits with which we are born. Our innate drives for food, sex, and security are not as easily channeled as some people might like to think, nor are our socially acquired desires for power, wealth, or prestige.

Wrong also points out that the experiences of past socialization do not simply add up; they are blended and integrated in unique ways by each person. Everyone faces the problem that different socializing influences contradict one another. Parents may tell us one thing, friends something else, the media something else again. And the different roles that a person plays may also be in conflict. As a student, you should stay home and work on your term paper; as a member of your peer group, you should go to a party. The individual is pushed this way and that and constantly has to make personal judgments and decisions in new and unanticipated situations. Our personal histories may strongly influence our choices of action, of course. That is why courts are often willing to take an offender's past background into account before passing sentence, particularly when dealing with juvenile delinquents. But in practice the courts, like the rest of society, always insist at some point that people (unless they are mentally disordered) are capable of deciding on alternative courses of action and of "reforming" their personalities. We hold people responsible for their behavior precisely because they *can* exercise choice over what they do. Our socialization experiences are not necessarily imposed on us; sometimes we actually choose them.

For whatever reasons, everyone violates social norms at some time or another, often in novel and sometimes in socially disapproved ways. Hearing a "different drummer," we do not keep pace with our companions—or, in Mead's more sociological terms, the unsocialized "I" is never completely subservient to the socialized "me." Within very broad limits, we are free to fabricate ourselves and our behavior as we wish—particularly if we understand the social process through which we became what we are.

Summary

1. Socialization is necessary for people to acquire personality and to learn the way of life of their society. The process is essential for the survival of both individual and society. People in the same culture tend to display general similarities in personality, but because their experiences are unique their personalities are different.

2. The "nature versus nurture" debate is now recognized as a pointless one. Human personality and social behavior are the outcome of an interaction between biological potentials and cultural learning.

3. Evidence concerning children reared in isolation, children reared in institutions, and monkeys reared in isolation indicates that intimate social interaction is essential if later personal development is not to be severely impaired.

4. There are two main theories of learning. Behaviorist theory regards learning as the outcome of conditioning through punishments and rewards, although some social-learning theorists point out that learning can take place incidentally or through imitation. Developmental theorists acknowledge that a great deal of learning takes place in this way but believe that learning can be fully explained only as the outcome of personal interpretations of reality as the mind matures through different stages.

5. The emergence of the self is crucial for the development of personality. Freud argued that the self is composed of three parts, the id, ego, and superego. Cooley argued that the self emerges through the "looking glass" supplied by the reactions of other people. Mead emphasized symbolic interaction, particularly through language, and the development of the ability to take the role of others.

6. According to Piaget, cognitive or intellectual abilities develop through four basic stages: the sensorimotor stage, the preoperational stage, the concrete operational stage, and the formal operational stage.

7. In the United States and most industrial societies, there are four main agencies of socialization: the family, the school, the peer group, and the mass media. Other agencies also socialize the individual throughout life.

8. There are four possible types of socialization in the life cycle: primary socialization, anticipatory socialization, de-

velopmental socialization, and resocialization. The content and stages of the life cycle are influenced by social as well as biological factors. American socialization often fails to equip people adequately for certain stages of the life cycle, particularly adolescence and old age.

9. There is a danger of accepting an "oversocialized conception" of human beings. Socialization is never fully successful. We still retain a measure of free will and are responsible for our acts.

Important Terms

socialization
personality
learning
behaviorism
conditioning
social learning
developmental approach
self
psychoanalysis
id
ego
superego
looking-glass self
symbolic interaction
role taking
particular other
generalized other
cognitive development
sensorimotor stage
preoperational stage
concrete operational stage
formal operational stage
agencies of socialization
primary socialization
anticipatory socialization
developmental socialization
resocialization
life cycle

Suggested Readings

BECKER, HOWARD S., et al. *Boys in White.* Chicago: University of Chicago Press, 1961.

A classic account of the socialization process of medical students, showing how their early idealism is modified by the harsh reality of their work.

ELKIN, FREDERICK, AND GERALD HANDEL. *The Child and Society.* New York: Random House, 1972.

A brief but excellent overview of the process of socialization. The book incorporates both sociological and social psychological material.

ERIKSON, ERIK H. *Childhood and Society.* New York: W. W. Norton, 1964.

A classic work that deals with the interaction between the social environment and personality during the socialization process. The book includes a discussion of the life cycle and of the "identity crises."

FREUD, SIGMUND. *Civilization and Its Discontents.* New York: W. W. Norton, 1962.

Freud presents his theory concerning an intrinsic conflict between the inborn drives of the individual and the demands imposed by society in the socialization process.

KUBLER-ROSS, ELISABETH. *On Death and Dying.* New York: Macmillan, 1969.

An important work by one of the pioneers in the sociology of dying and death. The author presents a persuasive case for a more frank and open attitude toward death and toward dying people.

PIAGET, JEAN, AND BARBEL INHELDER. *The Psychology of the Child.* New York: Basic Books, 1969.

A concise account of Piaget's theory of cognitive development, with descriptions of many of his experiments with children.

CHAPTER 6 Social Interaction in Everyday Life

CHAPTER OUTLINE

The Self in Everyday Life
Roles and the Self
The Dramaturgical Approach
Aligning Actions

Nonverbal Communication
Body Language
Physical Proximity

The Micro Order: Some Studies
Becoming a Marijuana User
Male Doctor and Female Patient
Helping Others
Hurting Others
Dying

The Social Construction of Reality

The most basic unit of human behavior is an *act*. Anything you can do is an act—waking in the morning, getting dressed, going to class, reading this sentence. Like the boxes in a Chinese puzzle, acts are contained within acts. Reading this book, for example, is part of the larger act of taking a sociology course, which is part of the larger act of getting a college degree, and so on. Some of our acts have implications for nobody but ourselves, but most of them involve some relationship to other people. When one person's acts influence or are influenced by the acts of another person, social *interaction* takes place. This continuous interaction between people provides the basis for all social life, and thus for society itself.

Social interaction is the process by which people act toward or respond to other people. It includes any and all social behavior—smiling at a friend, asking a professor a question, moving aside so that you do not bump into an oncoming pedestrian, writing a letter to your parents, buying a cup of coffee, or leaving personal "markers" at your place in the library so that nobody will take it while you are away. Human social interaction is extraordinarily flexible and varied and in this respect is quite unlike that of other social animals, such as ants or swallows. Animals in other social species interact with one another in an unreflecting and rather rigid manner, for most of their behavior is "instinctive." In other words, they respond to various stimuli from their environment in ways that have been programmed into them at birth.

Our social interaction is utterly different for the reason that we live in a *meaningful* world, one that we can consciously reflect on and interpret. We respond to the natural and social environment according to the meaning that objects and events have for us. To us, a piece of wood is

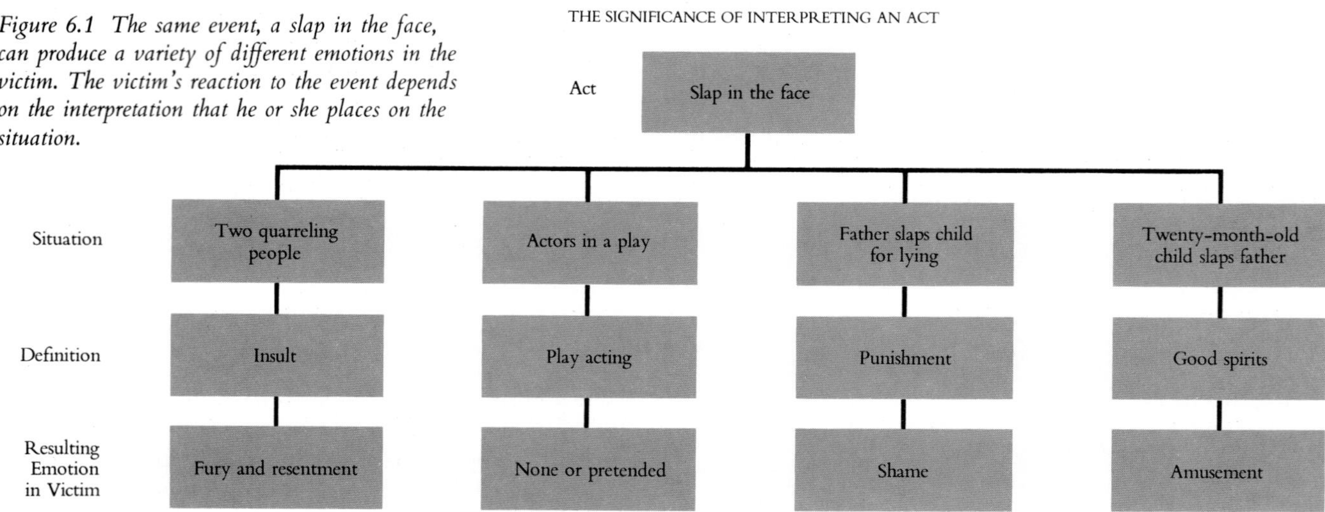

Figure 6.1 The same event, a slap in the face, can produce a variety of different emotions in the victim. The victim's reaction to the event depends on the interpretation that he or she places on the situation.

Source: Alfred Lindesmith, Anselm Strauss, and Norman Denzin, *Social Psychology,* 4th ed. (New York: Holt, Rinehart and Winston, 1975), p. 213.

not simply an object: the same item can be a hockey stick, a potential weapon, or firewood, and we will act toward it in terms of the meaning we place on it. The same is true of our interaction with other people: we have to interpret what they are doing or their actions are meaningless to us. We cannot respond to an outstretched hand until we decide whether it is extended in friendship or is about to deliver a karate chop. A person's act in jumping up and down is meaningless in itself; we cannot respond unless we know whether the person is doing a rain dance, is training for an athletic event, or has just stubbed a toe. Social interaction can take place in an orderly manner only if we and other people are able to define and interpret the situations in which we find ourselves.

How is it possible for us to interpret the actions and even the intentions of others? The key to the process lies in the fact that we develop, in the course of socialization, a concept of *self*—of an "inner person" that we can think about and reflect upon, almost as though our "self" were someone else. The self is the basic mechanism through which we confront the social world, for our awareness of our own selves enables us to appreciate that other people also have selves. We can then *take the role of other people* in our imaginations: that is, we can try to see things from their point of view, understand how they feel, predict how they are likely to behave, and anticipate their responses to our own actions. This shared ability to interpret the behavior of others makes meaningful social interaction possible, because each person can align his or her behavior to fit shared definitions and expectations.

We inhabit a meaningful world because our environment is not merely physical; it is also symbolic. A *symbol* is something that can meaningfully represent something else. Anything can be a symbol—hair length, a laugh, a gesture, a style of clothing, a crucifix, a piece of colored cloth marked with stars and stripes. A symbol has meaning only because people arbitrarily assign meaning to it and agree on that meaning. Your college insignia, for example, represents your college simply because people share the same interpretation of an otherwise meaningless design. The richest and most flexible system of symbols is language. The words of a language represent something other than the sounds themselves, for they are symbols that are arbitrarily attached to agreed-upon meanings. Through language and other symbols people define and interpret the world, piece together the buzz and confusion of life into meaningful patterns, and negotiate their social interactions with others.

This insight into the unique nature of human social life is the basis of the *symbolic interactionist* perspective on society. Herbert Blumer (1962), one of the leading exponents of this perspective, summarizes it this way:

> The term "symbolic interaction" refers, of course, to the peculiar and distinctive character of interaction as it takes place between human beings. The peculiarity consists in the fact that human beings interpret or "define" each other's actions instead of merely reacting to each other's actions. Their "response" is not made directly to the actions of one another but instead is based upon the meaning which they attach to such actions. Thus, human interaction is mediated by the use of symbols, by interpretation, or by ascertaining the meaning of one another's actions. This mediation is equivalent to inserting a process of interpretation between stimulus and response in the case of human behavior.

In short, we do not respond to other people directly: we interpret the events of daily life in terms of categories and definitions supplied by our culture and learned through interaction with others.

The interactionist perspective focuses primarily on the *micro order,* the intricate web of minute, day-to-day activities that make up the ongoing life of society. Many of these countless events easily pass unnoticed because they are so much taken for granted, yet cumulatively they produce and make possible what we call society. Roles, institutions, cultures, and societies have no independent existence. They do not have life and they cannot act or change on their own: it is people who live, act, and change society (Garfinkel, 1967). Although social institutions—such as religion, the state, the economy, the family—reach back into and influence social interaction, they are themselves the product of that interaction. The study of the micro order, then, provides a useful complement to the usual sociological emphasis on major structures and institutions. And when we subject the taken-for-granted reality of the micro order to sociological analysis, the supposedly familiar and obvious suddenly takes on a new and fascinating appearance.

The Self in Everyday Life

Whatever you think your "true" self may be, you can hardly deny that the self you present to others varies from one situation to another. From early childhood we are taught to "behave" when guests come to dinner, or not to do such-and-such "in front of the neighbors." The self you present to your parents is different from the one you present to your friends or to the police officer who stops you for a traffic violation. This does not necessarily mean that we are habitually insincere; insincerity arises only when we present a self that we do not ourselves believe in. The nature of social life is such that we have to present different aspects of ourselves in different situations. If everyone behaved in exactly the same way to everyone else, social chaos would result. We would be unable to fulfill our various roles as teachers, students, sons, daughters, employers, workers, and so on.

We are so used to presenting ourselves in particular ways in particular situations that we are usually not even aware we are doing it, for much of this behavior becomes an everyday routine. It is only when we realize that we are being scrutinized by others—when we are introduced to a stranger, perhaps, or, most excruciatingly of all, when we attend a job interview—that we become conscious of what we are doing. Yet social interaction is a continuous process in which people mutually interpret one another's behavior, actions, personality, and intentions. What determines the actual content of the self that we present in various situations, and how do people actually go about creating the impressions that they offer to others?

Roles and the Self

The self that you present to others is closely linked to the *role* you happen to be playing at the time. As we saw in Chapter 4 (Society), each person has certain *statuses* in society—socially identified positions such as man, woman, student, truck driver, artist, and so on. Various roles are attached to each of these statuses. As a student, for example, you play different roles in relation to your professor, your roommate, your dormitory janitor, or your seminar group. Each of these audiences consequently sees a different aspect of your self.

In many types of social interaction the norms governing the behavior of people in particular roles are fairly clearly defined. When you pay a cashier for a meal, for example, the interaction is usually a routine one for both participants. In other situations the definitions of appropriate behavior can be ambiguous or even absent. You may not be quite sure how to behave, for example, if a professor wants to see you about a poor term paper, or if you find an intruder in your room. We do not simply play our roles, then, as though we were puppets; we often have to actively devise a role performance by imaginatively exploring various possibilities and choosing those that seem most suitable (Turner, 1962).

In devising a role performance, we take account of the expectations that others have of us. These shared expectations provide countless little rules and assumptions that we hardly ever think about. An example is the unspoken rule of what Erving Goffman (1963a) calls "civil inattention" toward strangers: we behave in a way that shows we are aware of their presence, but we avoid eye contact with them at close quarters. In effect, we politely ignore them. Goffman points out how the role of street pedestrian often involves civil inattention:

> In performing this courtesy the eyes of the looker may pass over the eyes of the other, but no "recognition" is typically allowed. Where the courtesy is performed between two persons passing on the street, civil inattention may take the form of eyeing the other up to eight feet . . . and then casting the eyes down as the other passes—a kind of dimming of the lights. In any case, we have here what is perhaps the slightest of interpersonal rituals, yet one that constantly regulates the social intercourse of persons in our society.

Figure 6.2

"I'm crazy about your image, Ray. Who designed it?"

Drawing by Wm. Hamilton; © 1972
The New Yorker Magazine, Inc.

These rules are so much taken for granted that we usually realize they exist only when somebody breaks them. You could, for example, reveal the rules governing eye contact between strangers by staring directly into the face of the next stranger you encounter in an elevator. If you are brazen enough to keep up the performance—and you probably won't be—the reaction will soon show that you have violated an apparently trivial but very important norm governing the role performance of elevator passengers. Harold Garfinkel (1967) has used a number of experiments of this kind to reveal the presence of unspoken expectations that people in particular roles have of one another. In one experiment, for example, he asked his students to behave at home as though their role was that of guest, not son or daughter. The students addressed their parents as "Mr." and "Mrs.," displayed gracious table manners, politely asked for permission to use the refrigerator or bathroom, and so on. The resulting disruption of family interaction patterns was so intense that few of the students could keep up the role for long. Parents interpreted the behavior as signs of arrogance, rudeness, or even emotional instability caused by fatigue, and it took some time to soothe their angers and anxieties.

The Dramaturgical Approach

Much of our knowledge of the unspoken rules of social interaction comes from the writings of Erving Goffman (1959, 1963a, 1966, 1969). Goffman's work often seems to lie beyond the mainstream of sociological research. His eye for the minute and subtle details of social behavior is more like that of a novelist than a scientist, yet his writing seems so remote, aloof, and impersonal that he might almost be an ethologist describing the behavior of another species. Goffman's methods of gathering data are obscure, but his insights into the "little salutations, compliments, and apologies that punctuate social life" are often brilliant and convincing. The essence of his position is that orderly social life is made possible by the unspoken rules of social interaction. A fully accurate picture of society must therefore include an account of these rules in addition to the more explicit ones that people consciously recognize.

Goffman (1959) takes the concept of "acting" a role seriously. He applies a *dramaturgical approach* to social interaction, studying it as though the participants were actors in a theater—playing their various parts and scenes, following the script where they can, and improvising their performances when the script is unclear or absent. People, Goffman argues, are deeply concerned with *impression management:* they attempt to control the impressions they make on others by presenting themselves in the most favorable light. In managing their impressions people are careful to construct their "scenery," perhaps with posters on the wall or a lavishly illustrated book on the coffee table, and they make use of personal "props," such as a pipe or an expensive briefcase. People are careful to wear appropriate clothing for particular social occasions, presenting a different self by dressing casually for a friend, fashionably for a party, formally for a job interview.

Goffman suggests that people may have both a "back stage" and a "front stage" for their performances. Waiters in restaurants, for example, play one role while attending to their customers, switch to another more relaxed role in the private back stage of the kitchen, and then revert to their original performance when they return to the customers. Similarly, a husband and wife who are entertaining the boss and his wife at dinner may seize a private moment, when their guests are otherwise occupied, to exchange thoughts on their own performance and how it might be improved. A good deal of impression management, in fact, involves "teamwork" of this kind. Parents collaborate to prevent children knowing about their quarrels. Professors who loathe each other take care to hide this fact when students are present. Political campaigners and their staffs radiate a common air of confidence about the forthcoming election results.

The attempt to present the self in a favorable light is not always successful, because the audience knows perfectly well what the actor is trying to do. The audience carefully evaluates the performance, noting both the impressions the actor "gives" deliberately and the impressions he or she "gives off" without intending to. The actor may sweat, stutter, blush, laugh too heartily, tremble, stand too close, cower, or drop things. If an orator's gestures seem too carefully rehearsed or too awkwardly coordinated with the verbal part of the presentation, the audience may suspect insincerity. Sometimes, of course, people are able to claim a response—such as respect, trust, or a favor—to which they are not entitled. In this case, a "con" has been achieved. Sometimes, in fact, all parties to an encounter

Figure 6.3 By using various "props," people create particular impressions of the kind of personality they have and the social status that they occupy. This Englishman offers various cues in his dress and appearance (particularly his bowler hat and umbrella) that enable others to make some assessment of his personality and place in society. On the basis of these cues, would you guess that he belongs to the upper class or the middle class? Would you say he is conservative or liberal? What kind of job do you think he has?

may manage to convince the others that the selves they are portraying are authentic, even when they are not.

Although an audience is able to use various cues to assess a performance, people rarely challenge the credentials of an actor even when they suspect that a false impression is being created. The reason is that all participants in an encounter shoulder a common responsibility to maintain one another's "face." An encounter is a perilous

Figure 6.4 People carefully "manage" the impressions they create, presenting different aspects of themselves in different situations. These women are clearly unconcerned about the particular impression that their hair curlers make in the supermarket—but the hair curling is a preparation for a very different impression that they intend to make in some other context later on.

Figure 6.5

"Tonight, by the way, I for one could do without hearing about how your Rhodes Scholarship was no big deal to you again."

exercise, liable to be disrupted at any time if an actor "loses face" by being successfully challenged. The discredited performer's acute embarrassment is highly embarrassing to everyone else as well. People therefore participate in what Goffman calls a "studied nonobservance" of potentially embarrassing particulars—the stomach rumble of the guest, the secretive nose picking of the new dating partner, the physical appearance of the disfigured or crippled person, the slightly slipped hairpiece of the employer, the obviously fictitious excuse of the student who has handed in a late term paper. Much of what we call "polite behavior" consists of an implicit bargain among actors to help one another "keep face" by not questioning the performances they offer.

Aligning Actions

A problem arises in social interaction when one actor's behavior has violated or seems likely to violate the unspoken rules of conduct. When the normal routines are disrupted in this way, the guilty actor often attempts to "save face" by minimizing the significance of the disruption, usually by making it appear that the behavior is uncharacteristic and thus not relevant to the general impression he or she is trying to create. Strategems of this kind are termed *aligning actions,* for they attempt to bring the audience's impressions of the actor's self back into line with the impression intended (Stokes and Hewitt, 1976).

One form of aligning action is the *account* (Scott and Lyman, 1968). An account is an excuse or justification for inappropriate behavior that has taken place. A typical account begins with such phrases as "I realize I shouldn't have done it, but . . . ," "You've got me all wrong; what I'm trying to say is . . . ," "I know I'm creating a bad impression at the moment, but. . . ." A second form of aligning action is the *disclaimer* (Hewitt and Stokes, 1975). A disclaimer is an excuse or justification for inappropriate behavior that is about to take place. A typical disclaimer, then, might begin with "I know this sounds stupid, but . . . ," "Hear me out before you explode . . . ," "This may sound crazy, but I think I saw . . . ." These aligning actions smooth the course of social interaction by allowing the audience, if it so wishes, to overlook acts that might otherwise be interpreted as disruptive, ruining the impression the actor is trying to make.

Nonverbal Communication

A great deal of human interaction is *nonverbal.* That is, it takes place not through the medium of language but through other symbols. Two important forms of nonverbal communication are "body language," such as gestures and facial expressions, and the manipulation of the physical space between the actors.

Body Language

The human face is capable of about 250,000 different expressions, many of them extremely subtle (Birdwhistell, 1970). The head, fingers, hands, arms, shoulders, trunk, hips, and legs can all be used to signify meaning. All these potential sources of communication can be used in multiple combinations, meaning that literally millions of messages can be transmitted through the "language" of body movement. If two people were enclosed in a box and every aspect of their behavior recorded down to microscopic levels, it would be possible to isolate as many as 5000 separate bits of information every second (Birdwhistell, 1970). Nearly all this behavior passes unnoticed, of course, but some of it "gives off" information that the audience consciously or unconsciously is aware of. (The lie detector works on the principle of recording some of this information. The assumption is that the stress of lying will cause heightened physical reactions in the liar, who is usually unaware of and unable to control those signals.)

The most obvious forms of body language are facial expressions and physical gestures made with the hands. The facial expressions that convey such basic emotions as anger, fear, sadness, amusement, puzzlement, and disgust are culturally universal; they appear to be innate in our species and can be understood by people socialized in any culture (Ekman and Friesen, 1971). Gestures, however, are culturally relative, and there does not seem to be any gesture that has the same meaning in all societies. Not all peoples point with the hand the way that we do; some use the eyes, the chin, or the angle of the head for that purpose. Nor do nodding and shaking the head have the same meaning in all cultures. In the Admiralty Islands, for example, a decisive "no" is indicated by a quick stroke of the nose with a finger of the right hand, and a less decisive "no" by a slower stroking. We beckon someone by moving our hands toward our own bodies, but the Islanders beckon by moving the hand in the direction of the person being beckoned (Hillier, 1933).

Figure 6.6 The facial expressions that convey the most basic of human emotions are innate in our species. These expressions of anger and grief can be understood by people in any culture.

Figure 6.7 One of the most important forms of body language is eye contact. Prolonged eye contact between two people usually signifies interpersonal attraction, particularly if no words are spoken. If mutual attraction does not exist, intensive eye contact of this kind is embarrassing. In such a situation the person who does the staring is considered rude, and the person stared at will break the contact and try to avoid it in future.

Gestures, then, can only be understood by people of similar cultural background who attribute the same symbolic meaning to them. As Birdwhistell (1970) points out, a gesture cannot stand alone; it has meaning only in a particular context. A soldier's salute can signify respect, but it can also signify ridicule or insult in some circumstances. The American gesture of "giving the finger" is meaningless in Britain, where the same message is conveyed by holding up the middle and forefinger with the palm facing inward. An American who was urinated upon by another person would not take the gesture kindly, but in parts of Africa the act symbolizes a welcome transference of healing powers. Staring at a stranger does not have the same meaning in many other parts of the world that it does for Americans, who have particularly rigid rules calling for "civil inattention" toward people they do not know. American travelers to Latin America often have great difficulty in adapting to the experience of being scrutinized at close quarters by complete strangers.

Other forms of body language, such as posture, positioning of the legs, or inclination of the body toward or away from the other actor, are not as readily noticed as facial expressions and overt gestures, nor does the actor

Figure 6.8 A common gesture of distress, discomfort, uncertainty, or embarrassment is fidgeting. This fidgeting often takes the form of "grooming"—stroking or fiddling with one's own hair or scratching one's head.

have the same degree of control over them. Yet these signals can convey powerful messages even when neither participant in an encounter is consciously aware of them. Sexual interest on the part of one actor, for example, causes the pupils of his or her eyes to dilate. The other actor may well sense the nature of the message without being able to pinpoint its source. You will find it revealing to focus on the subtle messages that people "give off" by the way they move their bodies. You might try observing the different ways of walking that are apparent on any street, or you can look around your lecture hall and notice how students communicate their degree of interest in what the professor is saying by the inclination of their heads, the positioning of the limbs, and how much they fidget.

Physical Proximity

Another way that people can communicate with one another is through the manipulation of the space between them. People have a very strong sense of some *personal space* that surrounds them and are greatly discomforted if it is invaded. Crowded subway cars, for example, are experienced as psychologically stressful even if they are not actually physically uncomfortable, and outbreaks of aggression are more likely in crowded situations than in less crowded situations that are otherwise similar. Edward T. Hall (1959, 1966), who made extensive studies of attitudes toward physical proximity in several cultures, found that Americans require a distance of at least thirty to thirty-six inches between themselves and other people, unless the relationship between the actors is a very intimate one. Other cultures vary in the amount of physical proximity that their members will tolerate from strangers or acquaintances, but Americans seem to require more personal space than any other people. American travelers to other countries, particularly in South America and the Middle East, find that the inhabitants stand almost offensively close. But people in these cultures are apt to consider Americans—who are always backing away when one tries to talk to them—disdainful and rude.

Hall suggests that there are four distinct zones of private space. The first is *intimate distance* (up to 18 inches), which is reserved for intimate personal contacts. The second is *personal distance* (18 inches to 4 feet), which is reserved for friends and acquaintances; there is some intimacy within this zone but there are definite limits. The third is *social distance* (4 feet to 12 feet), which is maintained in relatively formal situations, such as interviews. The fourth is *public distance* (12 feet and beyond), which is maintained by people wishing to distinguish themselves from the general public, particularly speakers addressing audiences. Invasion of intimate or personal space always excites some reaction on the part of the person whose

Figure 6.9 The proximity of these girls, the expressions on their faces, and the inclinations of their bodies all convey a definite impression to the observer: they are sharing a secret or telling some gossip.

Figure 6.10 The physical distance between people in encounters both reflects and preserves the social distance between them. In one group, very close friends are accepted into one another's intimate distance. In the other group, tenants of the same apartment block who are meeting in the lobby interact at the outer limits of personal distance. If they stood two or three feet farther apart, their interaction would be even more formal.

space is being invaded. People in this situation will, for example, pull their elbows in, lean away from the invader, construct physical barricades (of library books or other convenient objects), avoid eye contact with or else glare at the invader, make "distress" gestures such as scratching the head or fidgeting, or, if all else fails, will actively increase the distance by outright retreat (Garfinkel, 1964; Patterson *et al.,* 1971; Felipe and Sommer, 1966; Argyle and Dean, 1965; McBride *et al.,* 1965).

The physical environment has some influence over standing and seating arrangements. The larger the area in which an interaction takes place, the closer the participants will approach one another. Living room seating is generally arranged within an arc of 8 feet, as this is the maximum distance for comfortable conversation. Within such physical constraints, the proximity of the actors in an encounter is influenced by their precise relationship to one another. People generally approach closer to a friend than to an acquaintance or stranger, and maintain greater distance between themselves and others who are of a different age, race, or social status (Burgoon and Jones, 1976). Pairs of females sit closer than pairs of males; the average distance between male pairs is as much as a foot greater than between female pairs (Pederson, 1973; Rosengrant, 1973). The distance between opposite-sexed pairs is more variable, for it depends on the degree of intimacy that they have established. Seating arrangements are closely linked to the nature of the interaction taking place between the participants. When the relationship is a friendly or cooperative one, the partners usually choose adjacent or corner seating; when it is competitive or formal, they tend to sit opposite one another (Cook, 1970; Norum *et al.,* 1967; Sommer, 1965). All these manipulations of physical space convey subtle symbolic messages, for they reflect and maintain the social intimacy or distance that exists between the actors.

The Micro Order: Some Studies

Sociologists and social psychologists have studied an extraordinary variety of topics in social interaction, ranging from the behavior of poker players, subway passengers, telephone users, and nudist-camp enthusiasts to the social difficulties faced by the dwarf, the teetotaler, and the cab driver (Zurcher, 1970; Levine *et al.*, 1973; Ball, 1968; Weinberg, 1965; Truzzi, 1968; Birenbaum and Sagarin, 1973, Henslin, 1968). Let's look at some examples of this kind of research.

Becoming a Marijuana User

How does somebody become a regular user of marijuana? Howard Becker (1953, 1963b) addressed this problem at a time when marijuana smokers were still widely regarded as "dope fiends." The common sense assumption at the time was that people were motivated to use marijuana by some underlying personality disturbance. Becker's findings challenged this view, and his account of the process by which somebody becomes a marijuana user provided many insights which are now common knowledge.

Becker spent many years as a professional jazz musician, participating in a subculture in which the use of marijuana was common. He drew freely on his observations of jazz musicians for his study, and supplemented these data with in-depth interviews with individual marijuana smokers. He concluded that marijuana use is not the result of psychological disturbance on the part of the smoker, nor is it something that "just happens." Becker found that several conditions must be met before a person becomes a habitual marijuana user and that each of these conditions is fulfilled through a complex social interaction between the novice and more experienced users.

First, the novice must learn that the drug exists and that other people find its use pleasurable. Contact with experienced users increases the novice's curiosity about marijuana, and eventually he or she accepts an invitation by users to try it. But trying marijuana is not the same as getting high. The novice usually fails to perceive any effects on the first attempt to smoke the drug, and several repetitions may be necessary before he or she actually notices any symptoms. Unless the novice is willing to persevere, use of the drug is likely to be abandoned at this point. Typically, however, other users provide constant reassurance. They instruct the novice in techniques for inhaling the smoke and holding it in the lungs, and the novice's own observations of their obvious pleasure in the drug provide faith that it will eventually have an effect.

In due course the novice begins to notice physical and mental symptoms that follow inhalation of marijuana smoke. But perceiving symptoms is not the same as getting high, either. The novice must not only consciously connect these symptoms with the fact of having smoked the drug but must also learn to experience the symptoms as

Figure 6.11 The process of becoming a marijuana user is a learning experience that typically takes place in interaction with other users. Merely smoking the drug is not enough to get the new user high, and getting high is not enough to make the user enjoy the drug. The novice's reactions to the drug are shaped by interpretations learned from others.

pleasurable. If this interpretation is not made, marijuana usage is likely to be discontinued, on the grounds that "It does nothing for me." As Becker points out, the effects of marijuana are not automatically or necessarily pleasurable. The user's scalp may tingle; time and distance are easily misjudged; and there may be sensations of dizziness, faintness, thirst, and hunger. The novice is by no means sure that these and similar experiences are pleasant and has to learn to interpret them as enjoyable. Becker (1963b) suggests that this definition "occurs, typically, in interaction with more experienced users, who, in a number of ways, teach the novice to find pleasure in this experience which is at first so frightening." Social definitions of a rather ambiguous experience predispose the new user to interpret the drug's effects as pleasant, and only at this point does the novice become a habitual user. He or she begins to secure a supply of marijuana, to develop any routines of secrecy that may be necessary, and to redefine earlier notions about the morality of marijuana use. Again, these techniques and justifications are learned in social interaction with others.

Becker (1963b) concludes that marijuana use cannot be explained in terms of supposed failings in individual personality: habitual use of the drug results from resocialization through interaction with existing users:

> Instead of the deviant motives leading to the deviant behavior, it is the other way around; the deviant behavior in time produces the deviant motivations. Vague impulses and desires—in this case, probably most frequently a curiosity about the kind of experience the drug will induce—are transformed into definite patterns of action through the social interpretation of an act which is in itself ambiguous.

Male Doctor and Female Patient

A pelvic examination, especially when it is performed by a male physician, involves an extremely delicate and problematic social interaction. Women in our society are socialized from early childhood to regard the vagina as a singularly private part of the body, and legitimate access to it is normally granted only to the husband or other highly specific individuals in an intimate and sexually charged context. As a result, many women find the experience of a pelvic examination to be threatening—so much so that a high proportion of patients put off such examinations even when they know there is a pressing medical reason for having one. The examination therefore requires an elaborate ritual on the part of the doctor, nurse, and patient to desexualize the interaction and to maintain the fiction that nothing out of the ordinary is happening.

James Henslin and Mae Briggs (1971) have analyzed this ritual, drawing their information from several thousand pelvic examinations observed by Briggs, a trained nurse. Using Goffman's dramaturgical approach, they analyze the interaction as though it consisted of a series of scenes in a play, in which the participants shift roles in order to maintain their definitions of reality. In the "prologue" to the play, the woman enters the doctor's reception room, casting off her previous role and preparing to assume the role of patient. When she is summoned into the consulting room, she fully takes on this new role, and the first "scene" opens. In this part of the performance, the doctor presents himself as a competent physician, responding to the patient role that the other is acting. The doctor treats the patient as a full person, maintaining eye contact with her and discussing her medical problems in a courteous and professional manner. If he decides a pelvic examination is necessary, he announces his decision and leaves the room.

The second "scene" then opens with the nurse's appearance. Her appearance and the disappearance of the doctor both serve important purposes. The nurse is essentially "a stagehand for the scene that is to follow." Her role is to transform the patient from a "person" to a "nonperson," a "pelvic" to be clinically examined. The nurse soothes any anxieties that the patient might express: many women, for example, make such comments as "The things we women have to put up with!" and the nurse sympathetically agrees. The nurse supervises the patient's undressing and prepares the clinical "props" for the examination. Nearly all women are anxious to conceal their discarded underclothing before the doctor returns, and the nurse facilitates these wishes. The doctor's absence is highly significant, for it ensures that the patient does not undress in his presence and thus eliminates any suggestion that a striptease is being performed. By the time the nurse summons him back into the room, the patient is lying on an examination couch with a sheet over most of her body.

In this crucial "scene" all three actors are present. The presence of the nurse has two purposes. It serves to desexualize the interaction by introducing a third party, and it protects the doctor's interests by providing a legal witness if the patient should interpret his performance as unprofessional. The patient is now "dramaturgically transformed for the duration of this scene into a nonperson." The drape sheet separates her pubic area from the rest of her body. From her position on the couch, she can see only the drape sheet and can maintain the sense that she is almost fully covered. More important, she cannot see the doctor's face. He sits out of view on a low stool, and there is no eye contact between them. The doctor may address occasional questions or instructions of a medical nature to the patient, but he can otherwise ignore her completely. The patient "plays the role of object," engaging in a studied nonobservance of the entire scene. She typically initiates no conversation, avoids eye contact even with the nurse by staring at the wall or ceiling, and tries to present an image of immobility and self-control.

The next "scene" begins as soon as the examination is over. The doctor departs, allowing the patient to dress in his absence. The nurse helps the patient make the transition back to the role of "person" once more. The two engage in conversation, with the patient often making such comments as "I'm glad that's over with." The nurse again provides sympathetic reassurance. Once the patient is recostumed and regroomed, the last "scene" takes place. The doctor reenters for a final interview, interacting with the patient in terms of the more normal role she is now playing. His manner, courteous and professional as before, affirms that nothing out of the ordinary has occurred and that his view of her self is essentially unaffected by the interaction that has just taken place. In the "epilogue" to the whole performance, the patient departs, resuming her everyday roles in the world beyond.

As Henslin and Briggs point out:

> The ritual of the vaginal examination allows the doctor to approach the sacred without profaning it or violating taboos by dramaturgically defining the vagina as just another organ of the body, and disassociating the vagina from the person, while desexualizing the person into a cooperative object.

Helping Others

In 1964, a woman named Kitty Genovese was murdered outside her home in New York in the early hours of the morning. Her assailant took half an hour to murder her, and her screams were heard by at least thirty-eight of her neighbors. These people watched the entire scene from their windows, but not one of them came to her aid or even bothered to call the police. Their behavior was an extreme example of a tendency that is not in itself at all unusual—the reluctance of people to "get involved" in the problems of others under certain circumstances. Although people will readily help friends or acquaintances in private, they often become apathetic bystanders when the emergency takes place in public and affects a stranger. The case of Kitty Genovese stimulated a considerable amount of research into the phenomenon of *bystander apathy*, and this apparently callous behavior is now well understood.

If you encountered someone unconscious on the steps of your home or your college dormitory, you would probably do something about it, either by attending to the person yourself or by drawing someone else's attention to the situation. But if you notice someone lying unconscious at the side of a crowded city sidewalk, it is very likely that you will ignore the person, just as everybody else seems to be doing. Why?

Two factors seem to operate in these situations. The first is that many emergencies are somewhat ambiguous. A person lying in the street might be ill or dying, but then he or she might also be asleep or drunk. Smoke pouring from a window might be from a fire, but then it might be steam from a radiator. People will not act in these situations until they have interpreted them, and this is where the second factor comes into play. In order to interpret the situation, people look for cues from other bystanders. If other people appear unconcerned, the individual is unlikely to define the situation as an emergency. Each person is hesitant about "overreacting," because he or she will "lose face" and appear foolish if the wrong interpretation is made. In many situations, of course, everyone is attempting to appear calm and composed so as to avoid possible ridicule by others. As a result, the bystanders collectively mislead one another. Just as an entire crowd can panic when some of its members define a situation as dangerous, so it can maintain a collective unconcern when none of its members make such a definition. Only when one person takes on the responsibility to act do others tend to follow suit. But the larger the crowd, the less likely it is that any single individual will assume this responsibility. If

Figure 6.12 Bystander apathy, or the unwillingness of bystanders to "get involved" in the problems of others, is especially common in cities and other crowded environments. People are reluctant to interpret a situation as an emergency unless "someone else" does so first, with the result that they all tend to ignore the problem.

you encounter an emergency on your own, there is no way of escaping the moral responsibility to do something about it. But if a number of people are present, moral responsibility is much more diffused; everyone tends to wait for "someone else" to take the initiative.

A number of experiments have demonstrated this process quite clearly (for example, Latané and Darley, 1968, 1969; Darley and Latané, 1968; Latané and Rodin, 1969; Zimbardo, 1969; Lerner and Simmons, 1966). In one such experiment, Bibb Latané and John Darley (1968) tested the reactions of college students to an apparent emergency. Student volunteers were shown singly into a room, where they were left alone and asked to complete a questionnaire. The students believed that this was simply a preparation for some undisclosed experiment to be conducted in due course, but soon after they were seated the experimenters, watching through a one-way mirror, introduced a stream of smoke into the room through an air vent. The smoke continued to pour into the room for several minutes, until it finally obscured vision. The typical subject would notice the smoke, show a distinct startle reaction, and undergo a brief period of indecision. Most subjects would then walk over to the source of the smoke, sniff it and feel its temperature, and then calmly leave the room and report the situation. Some 75 percent of the subjects reported the smoke within two minutes of first noticing it.

Latané and Darley then varied the experimental conditions by showing students into the room in groups of three. In this situation, individual reaction to the potential emergency was markedly inhibited. In the three-person groups the great majority of subjects ignored the smoke after noting it. In only 38 percent of the cases did even one member take the responsibility of reporting the potential emergency, and on average it took them much longer to do so than the subjects who had been tested individually.

In an even more revealing experiment, Bibb Latané and Jean Rodin had single subjects enter a room and fill out a form on the instructions of a female receptionist. The receptionist then left the room. A few moments later she turned on a tape recorder in the next room, and the subjects could clearly hear an apparent emergency. A loud crashing noise was followed by cries of "Oh my God, my foot . . . I . . . I . . . can't move . . . it. Oh . . . my ankle . . . I can't get this thing . . . off me." The cries continued for about a minute longer and finally grew more subdued. Some 70 percent of the subjects intervened and came to the receptionist's help. Latané and Rodin then varied the experiment by having two people present. In this case, only 40 percent came to the aid of the lady in distress. They then varied the experiment further by pairing individual subjects with another who, unknown to the subject, was actually an accomplice of the experimenters. The accomplice was instructed to ignore the screams. Under these conditions, only 7 percent of the subjects went to the receptionist's aid—a mere tenth of those who did so when there was nobody else in the room. Interpretations of the situation, derived from cues transmitted by other participants, were the decisive factors in determining whether one person would help another in distress.

Hurting Others

Would you deliberately apply severe electric shocks to an inoffensive stranger, even if he were screaming in agony, begging you to stop, and had a heart condition? You probably would, under the appropriate circumstances. That is the disturbing conclusion to be drawn from research by Stanley Milgram (1973), who has conducted a series of studies of people's willingness to obey authority. Milgram has shown that a substantial majority of subjects in his experiments are quite willing to apply electric shocks to someone they believe is screaming in pain, provided they define their behavior as an appropriate response to an order by a legitimate authority.

Milgram secured volunteers by advertising in a newspaper for subjects to take part in a psychological experiment. The experiment took place in a Yale University laboratory, where each subject was introduced to the experimenter and to another volunteer. The experimenter explained that the research was designed to test the effects of negative reinforcement—in this case, punishment by electric shock—on learning. By pulling pieces of paper from a hat, the experimenter assigned one volunteer to the role of "teacher" and the other to the role of "learner." In fact, however, this draw was rigged. The "learner," unknown to the subject, was actually an accomplice of the experimenter.

The experimenter then explained that the teacher was to read word pairs to the learner, and to give him an electric shock of increasing voltage every time he failed to recall a word pair correctly. The learner protested at this point that he had a heart condition, but the experimenter replied that the test would be painful but not dangerous. The learner was then strapped into a chair in an adjoining room and the teacher was given an "electric shock generator". The control board of the generator was scaled from 15 volts at one end to 450 volts at the other, and there were verbal descriptions above the shock levels, ranging from "slight shock" at one end to "intense shock" in the middle and "danger—severe shock" at the other end. Milgram wanted to find the shock level at which volunteers would refuse to cooperate further.

First, Milgram pretested the experiment on Yale University students. To his complete astonishment, they all applied shocks right up to the maximum level. Before beginning his experiments on his nonstudent volunteers, Milgram varied the experiment by introducing tape-recorded protests from the learner. At 125 volts, the learner shouted "I can't stand the pain." At 180 volts, he complained of heart trouble. At 195 volts, he gave an agonized scream. At 315 volts he did not answer at all, and further shocks were greeted by an ominous silence. Under these conditions, 65 percent of the subjects obediently pulled the levers all the way to 450 volts. Milgram, who was incredulous at this point, varied the experiment again. He put the learner in the same room as the teacher and required the teacher physically to force the learner's hand down onto a "shock plate" in order to receive the punishment. Under these rather gruesome conditions—with the learner struggling violently, screaming at the top of his voice, and complaining about his heart condition—30 percent of the subjects still applied shocks all the way to 450 volts.

How can this apparent cruelty in ordinary American citizens be explained? Milgram rejects any suggestion that his subjects were brutal or sadistic. They did not enjoy what they were doing. They often sweated, trembled, and protested to the experimenter, who met their complaints with a firm "The experiment requires that you continue." The behavior can only be explained, Milgram contends, in terms of the meaning that people placed on the situation. No action contains meaning in itself; the meaning is derived from a definition of the situation in which the act takes place. A substantial part of the population will simply do what they are told to do, irrespective of the content of the act and without any limitations of conscience, as long as they believe the commands come from a legiti-

Complying with Authority

This is a transcript from one of Stanley Milgram's experiments, in which the subject is told by authority to give electric shocks to a person whom he believes is in great pain and is suffering from a heart condition.

LEARNER *(who, from the teacher's point of view is heard but not seen, an offstage voice):* Ow, I can't stand the pain. Don't do that. . . .

TEACHER *(pivoting around in his chair and shaking his head):* I can't stand it. I'm not going to kill that man in there. You hear him hollering?

EXPERIMENTER: As I told you before, the shocks may be painful, but—

TEACHER: But he's hollering. He can't stand it. What's going to happen to him?

EXPERIMENTER *(his voice is patient, matter-of-fact):* The experiment requires that you continue, Teacher.

TEACHER: Aaah, but, unh, I'm not going to get that man sick in there . . . know what I mean?

EXPERIMENTER: Whether the learner likes it or not, we must go on, through all the word pairs.

TEACHER: I refuse to take the responsibility. He's in there hollering!

EXPERIMENTER: It's absolutely essential that you continue, Teacher.

TEACHER *(indicating the unused questions):* There's too many left here, I mean, Geez, if he gets them wrong, there's too many of them left. I mean who's going to take the responsibility if anything happens to that gentleman?

EXPERIMENTER: I'm responsible for anything that happens to him. Continue please.

TEACHER: All right. *(Consults list of words.)* The next one's "Slow—walk, truck, dance, music." Answer, please. *(A buzzing sound indicates the learner has signaled his answer.)* Wrong. A hundred and ninety-five volts. "Dance." *(Zzumph!)*

LEARNER: Let me out of here. My heart's bothering me! *(Teacher looks at experimenter.)*

EXPERIMENTER: Continue, please.

LEARNER *(screaming):* Let me out of here, you have no right to keep me here. Let me out of here, let me out, my heart's bothering me, let me out! *(Teacher shakes head, pats the table nervously.)*

TEACHER: You see, he's hollering. Hear that? Gee, I don't know.

EXPERIMENTER: The experiment requires. . . .

TEACHER *(interrupting):* I know it does, sir, but I mean—hunh! He don't know what he's getting in for. He's up to 195 volts! *(Experiment continues, through 210 volts, 225 volts, 240 volts, 255 volts, 270 volts, delivered to the man in the electric chair, at which point the teacher, with evident relief, runs out of word-pair questions.)*

EXPERIMENTER: You'll have to go back to the beginning of that page and go through them again until he's learned them all correctly.

TEACHER: Aw, no. I'm not going to kill that man. You mean I've got to keep going up with the scale? No sir. He's hollering in there. I'm not going to give him 450 volts.

EXPERIMENTER: The experiment requires that you go on.

TEACHER: I know it does, but that man is hollering in there, sir.

LEARNER: Ohhh. I absolutely refuse to answer any more. *(Shouting urgently, now)* Let me out of here. You can't hold me here. Get me out. Get—me—out—of—here.

EXPERIMENTER: Continue. The next word is "Green," please.

TEACHER: "Green—grass, hat, ink, apple." *(Nothing happens. No answering buzz. Just gloomy silence.)*

TEACHER: I don't think he is going to answer.

EXPERIMENTER: If the learner doesn't answer in a reasonable time, about four or five seconds, consider the answer wrong. And follow the same procedures you have for wrong answers. Say "Wrong," tell him the number of volts, give him the punishment, read him the correct answer. Please continue, Teacher. Continue, please. *(Teacher pushes lever. Zzumph!)*

TEACHER *(swiveling around in his chair):* Something's happened to that man in there. *(Swiveling back)* Next one. "Low—dollar, necklace, moon, paint." *(Turning around again)* Something's happened to that man in there. You better check in on him, sir. He won't answer or nothing.

EXPERIMENTER: Continue. Go on, please.

TEACHER: You accept all responsibility.

EXPERIMENTER: The responsibility is mine. Correct. Please go on. *(Teacher returns to his list, starts running through words as rapidly as he can read them, works through to 450 volts.)*

Source: From the film *Obedience,* distributed by the New York University Film Library. Copyright 1965 by Stanley Milgram.

Figure 6.13 In preindustrial societies people were intimately acquainted with death. Like these members of the Xhosa tribe in South Africa, they saw their relatives die and personally took care of the funeral arrangements. In modern societies, however, the dying are segregated from society in hospitals and geriatric institutions, and funerals are arranged by specialists and professionals.

mate authority. In this case, they accepted the experimenter as a legitimate authority and accepted his interpretation of the situation—that the shocks were not dangerous and that the research was justified in the interests of science.

Dying

Until a few generations ago, death in our society typically took place in the home. People were familiar with death from an early age. They saw their kinsfolk die, were often with them to offer comfort at the time of death, and participated in the preparation and disposal of the corpses. In the United States today, however, the dying are effectively segregated from society, and the fact of death is insulated from common experience. More than two-thirds of all deaths take place in hospitals and geriatric institutions, with professional personnel rather than relatives in attendance, and funeral arrangements are made by experts. Many people grow to adulthood or even spend their entire lives without ever seeing a dead body. Death has become a taboo subject in our society; it is spoken of in embarrassment and hushed tones as though it were somehow indecent.

Barney Glaser and Anselm Strauss (1968) have made extensive studies of the process of dying in the relatively impersonal environment of the modern hospital. The hospital is organized to hide the fact of death from both inmates and visitors. When a death is expected, the dying person is removed to a private room out of sight of the other patients. Drugs are often given to the patient to minimize the disruption that the dying person might cause, even when there is no reason for medication in terms of treatment of symptoms or relief of pain. Relatives are forewarned that the patient "has taken a turn for the worse" so that they can be prepared for the event of death. The staff attempts to avoid announcing deaths abruptly to waiting visitors because friends and relatives are apt to break down emotionally, creating the kind of "scene" the staff is anxious to avoid. Some deaths, of course, occur unexpectedly, and these are regarded as particularly troublesome. They are often noticed by other patients before they come to the attention of the hospital staff. They may even occur during visiting hours when outsiders are present, and elaborate procedures are considered necessary to remove the corpses without causing offense or distress to other patients.

The hospital's attempt to deny the fact of death influences more than its internal organization. It also affects the nature of the social interaction between the staff and the dying patient, because the staff typically attempts to keep the patient in ignorance of his or her impending death. Glaser and Strauss refer to this situation as a "closed-awareness context," one in which one actor does not know the facts of his or her identity as someone who is dying. This situation differs from an "open-awareness context," perhaps more typical of deaths in earlier times, in which all participants share an awareness of the impending death.

Several factors make it possible for the interaction between the dying person and the hospital staff to take place in a closed-awareness context. First, patients are not experienced at interpreting their own symptoms. Second, the hospital is organized to hide the relevant information

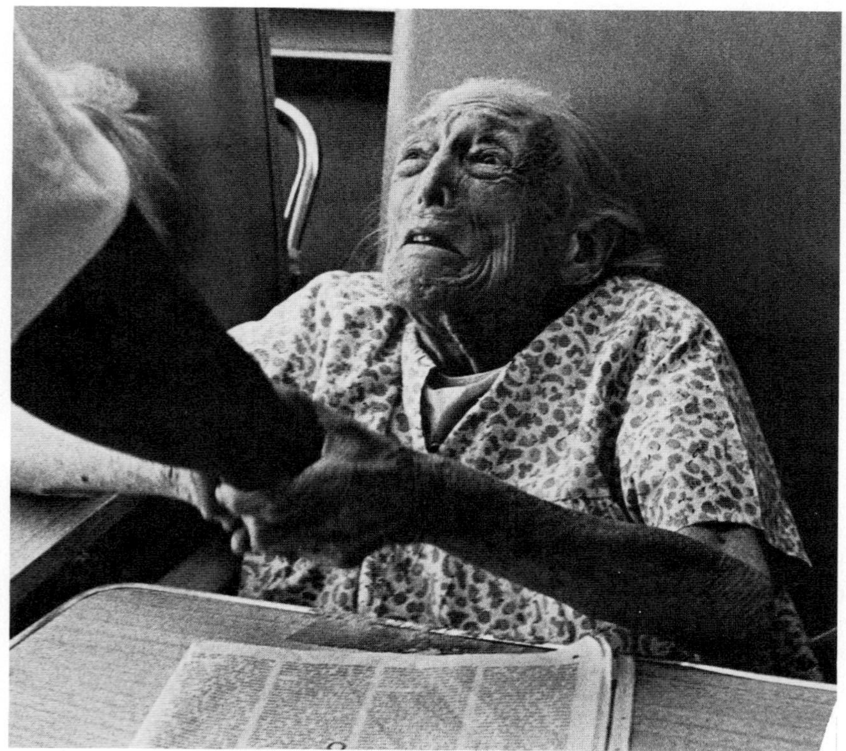

Figure 6.14 The elderly had an honored and respected role in traditional societies, and typically spent their last years living with their children and grandchildren. In the modern United States, however, the old are often segregated from the rest of society, typically by being placed in old-age homes or geriatric institutions. More than two-thirds of all deaths now take place in hospitals and geriatric institutions.

from the patient. Records are kept out of reach, and nurses and doctors engage in "teamwork" to deceive the patient: nurses deliberately withhold or falsify information, while doctors minimize their contact with the patient and discuss the diagnosis "backstage" in private. Third, the patient usually has no allies who can help in discovering the staff's secret, because family and friends generally join in the conspiracy as well.

The staff tries to maintain a "situation as normal" atmosphere around dying patients. They act in the patients' presence as though they were going to live—for example, by talking about the future or by telling stories of other people who made splendid recoveries from much worse illnesses. They take care to prevent the patients' overhearing chance remarks that might ruin the illusion, they carefully manage the impression created by their facial and physical gestures, and they control expressions of their own distress. But this false presentation is difficult to maintain, and patients often begin to suspect the truth.

Dying patients may notice that hospital personnel, who are increasingly embarrassed by their own pretense, are minimizing their personal contacts with them. The "teamwork" of night and day staffs may be poorly coordinated, so that patients hear a different story from each. The personnel may fail to reassure patients sufficiently, talk only about the present instead of the future, or use awkward phrases that reveal more than they conceal. Patients may also overhear remarks that give the game away. They may become more knowledgeable about the hospital and realize that it is organized to deny the fact of approaching death.

A complex and confusing drama can result. The patients cannot act toward others as though they were dying, being unsure of whether others are aware of the fact. Relatives, trying to maintain the illusion that all will be well, also cannot act toward the patients as if they were dying. As a result, the patients cannot act toward themselves as though they were dying either. Relatives are denied the rituals of farewells with the dying person; the dying person is denied the opportunity to arrange his or her affairs and to face up to the reality of death.

A growing body of research indicates that death is more easily accepted if the dying person faces the end in an open-awareness context, is able to discuss the fact of death frankly with friends and relatives, and is able to share mutual comfort with them. The more typical death, in the emotional isolation of a closed-awareness context of mutual deception, may be very much more stressful for the dying person, however compassionate are the motives of all involved.

The Social Construction of Reality

Up to this point, we have talked about how people interpret the immediate situation in which they find themselves. But the interactionist perspective on society has far wider implications, extending to our interpretation of reality itself.

People generally take the world "out there" for granted. Its components—categories such as time and space, cause and effect, animal and vegetable, the United States and Canada—appear to be prearranged long before we arrive on the scene, merely awaiting our discovery. "Reality" seems just to be there, presenting the same face to everyone: in short, it seems to be self-evident (Schutz, 1962). Yet this is not the case. The "reality" that we encounter is merely the interpretation we place on the evidence of our senses, and people in different cultures may interpret that reality very differently (Lindesmith *et al.,* 1975):

> The world out there is not reacted to directly but through the mediation of symbols. So, even if different groups live on the same physical terrain and under the same sky, it is not necessarily the same terrain or the same sky for all of them. The sky, for instance, can be the abode of a family of gods, the container for a hierarchy of seven ascending heavens, or the small segment of an expanding universe that is available to the naked eye from one small body called earth.

We are not born with any sense of time, of place, of cause and effect, or of the society in which we live. We learn about these things through social interaction, and what we learn depends on the society in which we live and our particular place within it. As W. I. Thomas remarked, "If men define situations as real, they are real in their consequences." If members of a society believe that the earth is flat, that Jupiter rules the heavens, that illness is caused by witches, or that there are such things as X-rays, then the supposed flatness of the earth, the rule of Jupiter, the presence of witches, and the existence of X-rays will become as much a part of reality to people in that society as any other feature of their world. A person's location within a particular society also influences his or her perceptions of reality. A millionaire, for example, might interpret the reality of the American economic system very differently from a welfare mother. All knowledge and belief, including our own, is relative to the time and place in which it is produced. Our own conceptions of the universe might (who knows?) seem laughable a hundred or a thousand years from now, or our understandings of human psychology primitive and naive.

In an influential analysis, Peter Berger and Thomas Luckmann (1963) have described the process by which reality is *socially constructed*. This process involves three distinct stages:

Externalization occurs when, through their social interaction, people produce cultural products. These products are of many different kinds—material artifacts, social institutions, ideas about the nature of reality. When these products have been created, they become in a sense "external" to those who have produced them.

Objectivation occurs when these externalized products appear to take on a reality of their own, becoming independent of the people who created them. In other words, people lose the awareness that they themselves are the authors of their social and cultural environment and of their interpretations of reality. They are confronted by their products as though these things had an "objective" existence, like mountains or the moon. The products become just another part of reality to be taken for granted.

Internalization occurs when, through the socialization process, people learn the supposedly objective facts about reality, making them part of their own subjective, "internal" consciousness. People socialized in similar cultures or subcultures thus share the same perceptions of reality, rarely questioning the origins of their beliefs or understanding the process by which these beliefs arose in the first place.

Reality is thus constructed through a complex process of social interaction, in which people collectively act on the world and are influenced in turn by the results of their own actions. Seen in this light, the routines and "realities" of everyday life take on a new and enhanced significance.

Summary

1. Social interaction is the process by which people act toward or respond to other people. This interaction is possible because people have an awareness of self and an ability to take the roles of others in their imaginations, and so can make meaningful interpretations of one another's behavior. Human interaction is mediated through symbols and is thus primarily symbolic interaction.

2. The self we present at any moment depends primarily on the role we are playing. Roles are not always routinely enacted; they often have to be improvised.

3. Social life is made predictable by shared rules and expectations. Erving Goffman has studied these through a dramaturgical approach that focuses on unspoken social assumptions, on the way people manage the impressions they create, and on the way these impressions are interpreted by others. Aligning actions are used by social actors to readjust potentially disruptive interactions.

4. A great deal of human communication is nonverbal. Some of this communication is through body language, which includes facial expressions and physical gestures, many of them unconscious and unintended. Information can also be communicated through the manipulation of physical space between the actors, which reflects and maintains the social intimacy or distance between them.

5. Studies of the micro order provide insights into situations that are beyond the reach of functionalist or conflict analyses. The processes of becoming a marijuana user, maintaining definitions of reality in the course of a vaginal examination, helping others, hurting others, and dying in a hospital all involve social interpretations of potentially problematic situations. These interpretations are created through social interaction among the participants.

6. Reality is socially constructed. People do not perceive a reality "out there" directly; they create shared interpretations of reality. This process involves three stages: externalization, objectivation, and internalization.

Important Terms

social interaction	role taking
self	symbol

symbolic interaction
micro order
dramaturgical approach
impression management
aligning actions
account
disclaimer
nonverbal communication
personal space
bystander apathy
social construction of reality
externalization
objectivation
internalization

Suggested Readings

BERGER, PETER L., AND THOMAS LUCKMANN. *The Social Construction of Reality.* New York: Doubleday, 1963.

An influential analysis of the way in which interpretations of reality are created and sustained through social interaction.

BIRENBAUM, ARNOLD, AND EDWARD SAGARIN (EDS.). *People in Places.* New York: Praeger, 1973.

A lively collection of articles detailing research on social interaction in various situations. Many of the articles are strongly influenced by Goffman's work.

BROWN, ROGER. *Social Psychology.* New York: Free Press, 1965.

An excellent general introduction to social psychology for the student who wants to explore the discipline and its relationship to sociology.

GOFFMAN, ERVING. *Behavior in Public Places.* New York: Free Press, 1963.

A shrewd and acute description and analysis of social behavior in public settings. Goffman illuminates many aspects of interactive behavior that we normally take for granted or do not notice.

GOFFMAN, ERVING. *The Presentation of Self in Everyday Life.* New York: Doubleday, 1959.

The classic statement of Goffman's dramaturgical perspective on social interaction.

HALL, EDWARD T. *The Silent Language.* New York: Doubleday, 1959.

A readable and entertaining account of "body language" and the way physical space is manipulated to convey subtle messages.

NASH, JEFFREY E., AND JAMES P. SPRADLEY. *Sociology: A Descriptive Approach.* Chicago: Rand McNally, 1976.

An anthology of articles on various aspects of the micro order. The topics cover a very wide range and the articles use many different perspectives.

CHAPTER 7 *Social Groups*

CHAPTER OUTLINE

Primary and Secondary Groups

Small Groups
The Importance of Size
Leadership
Group Decision Making
Group Conformity

Ingroups and Outgroups

Reference Groups

Formal Organizations
Bureaucracy
Weber's Analysis
The Informal Structure of Bureaucracy
Dysfunctions of Bureaucracy

The Problem of Oligarchy

The Future of Formal Organizations

"No man is an island," wrote the poet John Donne several centuries ago. He was drawing attention to one of the most distinctive of all human characteristics: we are social animals whose lives are inextricably bound up with one another's. Our social behavior and personalities are shaped by the groups to which we belong, for the lifelong socialization process takes place almost entirely in group contexts. Throughout life, most of our daily activities are performed in the company of others. Whether our purpose is working, raising a family, learning, worshipping, or simply relaxing, we usually pursue it in groups, even if the group is as small as two or three people. Our need for meaningful human contacts is not merely a practical one; it is a deep psychological need as well. If people are deprived of the company of others for prolonged periods, mental breakdown is the usual result. Even the Geneva Convention, an international agreement that regulates the treatment of prisoners of war, recognizes this need. It regards solitary confinement for more than thirty days as a cruel and barbarous form of torture.

In its strictest sense, *a group is a collection of people interacting together in an orderly way on the basis of shared expectations about each other's behavior.* As a result of this interaction, the members of a group feel a common sense of "belonging." They distinguish members from nonmembers and expect certain kinds of behavior from one another that they would not necessarily expect from outsiders. A group differs from an *aggregate,* a collection of people who happen to be in the same place at the same time, such as the passengers in a bus or a crowd in a street. The members of an aggregate do not interact together to any significant extent and do not feel any common sense of belonging. A group also differs from a *category,* a number of people who may never have met one another but who share similar characteristics, such as age, race, or sex. Although sociologists sometimes uses the word "group" loosely to refer to aggregates and categories, we will use the term in this chapter only in its stricter sense.

The essence of a group is that its members interact with one another. As a result of this interaction, a group, unlike an aggregate or category, develops an internal structure. Every group has its own boundaries, norms, values, and interrelated statuses and roles, such as those of leader, follower, joker, or scapegoat. In some groups this structure is very rigid and explicit: members may hold official positions, and values and norms may be embodied in written objectives and rules. In other groups the structure may be much more flexible. Values and norms may be vague and shifting, and statuses and roles may be subject to negotiation and change.

People form groups for a purpose, generally one that the members cannot achieve satisfactorily through individual effort. The purpose of a group may be an explicit one, such as raising money for charity or waging war against an enemy, or it may be a less clearly defined one, such as having a good time. The fact that groups share common goals means that the members tend to be generally similar to one another in those respects that are relevant to the group's purpose. If the goals of the group are political, the members tend to share similar political opinions. If the goals are leisure activities, the members tend to be of similar age, social class, race, and leisure interests. The more the members interact within the group, the more they are influenced by its norms and values and the more similar they are likely to become.

Primary and Secondary Groups

There are two basic types of social groups, primary and secondary.

A *primary group* consists of a small number of people who interact in direct, intimate, and personal ways. The relationships between the members have emotional depth, and the group tends to endure over time. Primary groups are always small because large numbers of people cannot interact in a highly personal, face-to-face manner. For this reason large groups tend to break down into smaller, more intimate cliques. Typical primary groups include the family, the gang, or a college peer group.

A *secondary group* consists of a number of people who have few if any emotional ties with one another. The members come together for some specific, practical purpose, such as making a committee decision or attending a convention. There is limited face-to-face contact among the members, and they relate to one another not as full persons but only in terms of specific roles, such as chairperson, sergeant, or supervisor. Secondary groups can be either small or large. Any newly formed small group is a secondary group initially, although it may become a primary group if its members come to know one another well and begin to interact on a more intimate basis. A

Figure 7.1 A primary group contains a small number of people who interact in direct and intimate ways, usually over a long period of time. In preindustrial societies virtually all social life took place in the context of primary groups. This small fishing community in Ghana is a primary group. Its members know one another well and interact together as full persons, not in terms of specific roles.

Figure 7.2 A secondary group contains a number of people who have few emotional ties to one another. They usually meet together for some practical purpose, and they interact with one another in terms of specific roles rather than as full persons. Secondary groups, such as these employees in a large modern organization, are characteristic of modern industrial societies.

college seminar group, for example, may start out as a secondary group, but after a while it may become a primary group, or smaller primary groups may develop within it. All large groups, however, are secondary groups. These groups, which are often called *associations,* include organizations such as business corporations, large factories, government departments, political parties, and religious movements. Large secondary groups always contain smaller primary groups within them, however. Colleges and army camps, for example, are secondary groups, but they may contain hundreds of smaller primary groups when friendships are established among specific individuals.

In traditional, preindustrial societies almost all social life took place in the context of primary groups, such as the kinship network or small village. In modern industrial societies, however, dense urban populations and the proliferation of large associations have made social life much more anonymous. Many of our daily interactions involve secondary relationships with people we encounter in limited and specific roles and may never meet again. As we saw in Chapter 4 (Society), the growth of secondary groups and the multiplication of secondary relationships is one of the outstanding features of modern societies.

Small Groups

A *small group* is one that contains sufficiently few members for the participants to relate to one another as individuals. Whether a small group is primary or secondary depends on the nature of the relationships between the members. A gathering of old friends is a primary group; a number of previously unacquainted people trapped in an elevator for half an hour is a small secondary group.

Half a century ago the German sociologist Georg Simmel suggested that the interaction within small groups would prove to be an important subject for sociological research. His suggestion was largely neglected until the years after World War II, when Robert Bales and his associates began an influential series of studies of small group processes (Bales, 1950, 1970; J. Davis, 1969; Hare *et al.,* 1965; Hollander, 1964; T. Mills, 1967). Most of these studies took place in a laboratory setting, in which groups of volunteers were given some task to work on while researchers observed the interaction that took place. Although there is some question whether it is valid to apply the findings of these studies to "real-life" situations, this research has illuminated many aspects of small group interaction.

Figure 7.3 The size of a group has a strong influence on the kind of interaction that can take place within it. When a group contains less than about seven members, the interaction can be direct and personal. Beyond that point relationships tend to become more formal, and a leader usually has to regulate the interaction among the members. Larger groups, like this cocktail party, tend to break down into smaller and more intimate groups.

The Importance of Size

The single most important feature of small groups is probably their size, for this characteristic determines the kinds of interaction that can take place among the members. The smaller the group is, the more personal and intense the interaction can become.

The smallest possible group, a *dyad,* contains two people. A dyad differs from all other groups in that its members have to take account of one another. If one member ignores the conversation of the other or begins daydreaming, the interaction is disrupted, and if one member withdraws from the group, it simply ceases to exist. If a third member is added, to form a *triad,* the situation changes significantly. Any one member can ignore the conversation of the others without destroying the interaction in the group. Two members can form a coalition against one, so that any individual member can become subject to group pressure. As more members are added, the nature of the interaction continues to change. People can take sides in discussions, and more than one coalition can be formed. In a group of up to about seven people, all the members can take part in the same conversation, but beyond that point it becomes progressively more likely that smaller groups will form, with several conversations taking place at the same time.

If the group becomes larger than about ten or twelve people, it is virtually impossible for them to take part in the same conversation unless one member assumes the role of leader and regulates the interaction so that everyone has a chance to contribute. In groups of this size the style of conversation changes because people can no longer talk to each other as individuals. They cannot tailor their speech to meet the expectations of specific people, and so they tend to talk in a more formal and less conversational way. The members are inclined to make pronouncements in rather impersonal language, restricting their ordinary conversation to "asides" directed at those people nearest to them. Individuals no longer "talk" to the group; they "address" it, with a grammar and vocabulary unlike that used in ordinary conversation. The interaction at this point is markedly different from that in our original dyad.

Sudden changes in group size tend to be disruptive, particularly if there is a rapid increase in the number of new members. This disruption is partly caused by the fact that interaction grows more difficult as the group becomes larger, but another factor is that group members often resist the assimilation of newcomers. The presence of new members threatens the norms of interaction that the group has already developed, and old members are discomfited until new norms of interaction have evolved (Berelson and Steiner, 1964).

Leadership

One element is always present in groups, even in those groups that try to avoid it: leadership. A *leader* is a person who is able to influence the behavior of others. Groups always have leaders, even if the leaders do not hold formal positions of authority.

Research has indicated that there are two distinct types of leadership in small groups (Bales, 1953; Slater, 1955). *Instrumental leadership* is the kind necessary to organize the group in pursuit of its goals. An instrumental leader proposes courses of action and influences the members to follow them. *Expressive leadership* is the kind necessary to create harmony and solidarity among the members. An expressive leader is concerned to keep morale high and to minimize conflicts within the group. The expressive leader is well liked by the group. When a newly formed group is asked to choose a leader, it usually gives both roles to the same person, for the reason that individuals who are well liked also tend to dominate group activities. Leaders generally do not fill both roles for long, however, because people who direct group activities tend to lose popularity. In one experiment on small groups, Philip Slater (1955) found that most members gave top rating to the same individual for both expressive and instrumental leadership at the first meeting, but by the end of the fourth meeting, only 8 percent of the members still considered the leader likeable. The original leader may retain the instrumental leadership role, but another group member emerges to assume the expressive leadership role.

Do leaders have distinctive characteristics that are not shared by their followers? While there are certainly no hard and fast rules, it seems that leaders are likely to be taller than the average group member, to be judged better looking than other members, to have a higher IQ, and to be more sociable, talkative, determined, and self-confident than the others. They also tend to be more liberal in outlook, even in conservative groups (Berelson and Steiner, 1964; Stouffer, 1955). The style of leadership may be one of three basic kinds: *authoritarian,* in which the leader simply gives orders; *democratic,* in which the leader attempts to win a consensus on a course of action; and *laissez-faire,* in which the leader is easygoing and makes little attempt to direct or organize the group. In the United States, at least, democratic leaders seem to be most effective in holding small groups together and seeing that they accomplish their tasks. Authoritarian leaders are much less effective, because the work of the group becomes bogged down in internal conflicts. Laissez-faire leaders are usually ineffectual, for the group lacks directives and tackles problems in a very haphazard way (White and Lippitt, 1960). This does not mean, however, that democratic leadership is the most effective in all situations. Research on American subjects, who have been socialized to react negatively to authoritarian leaders, cannot be generalized to cultures where authoritarian leadership is expected and where there is no experience of democratic decision making.

One cannot talk of "good" or "bad" leaders without specifying the conditions in which the leader is operating. A person who is ineffectual in one situation may be highly effective in another (Fiedler, 1969). An authoritarian leader, for example, is more effective in emergency situations, where speed and efficiency outweigh other considerations. For this reason, leadership in armies, police forces, and hospital emergency rooms is typically authoritarian. Democratic leaders are more effective in situations where group members are concerned about individual rights or where there is disagreement over goals.

Group Decision Making

There is a general assumption in our society that when it comes to making decisions, two heads, or preferably several heads, are better than one. We have great faith in democratic decision making, believing that group decisions are likely to be wiser than decisions made by individuals acting alone. How valid is this belief?

The answer depends to some extent on the problem that has to be solved. In "determinate" tasks—problems that have only one correct solution, such as a crossword puzzle—group effort increases the chances of finding the answer. As a matter of simple probability, a group is more likely to come up with the correct solution than a single person. If the problem is a complex one involving specialized knowledge, the efficiency of the group is far superior to that of the individual, because group members can contribute a broader range of expertise and skills. The situation is rather different in the case of "indeterminate" tasks—problems that have no necessarily correct solution, such as selecting one of several applicants for a job or deciding on how to handle an aircraft hijacking. In these cases different groups may arrive at very different decisions, probably because each group is influenced by the opinions of particular dominant members. Sometimes group decisions in indeterminate problems seem better than those of individuals, but sometimes they seem worse.

Figure 7.4

"What do you say we shred this stuff and go have a beer?"
Copyright William Hamilton.

It is often thought that individuals are more likely than groups to make bold and imaginative decisions. As Roger Brown (1965) comments, "the academic committees on which one has served . . . do not leave one breathless with their daring." Indeed, the initial step to "appoint a committee" is frequently made because someone is reluctant to take the responsibility for an individual decision on a controversial issue. There is considerable evidence, however, that committees do sometimes make more risky decisions than individuals. J. A. Stoner (1961) asked individual subjects to come to tentative decisions on hypothetical problems, and he then combined the subjects into groups to consider these problems. He found a strong tendency toward what he called "the risky shift," a change to a decision for a more daring course of action. More recent research has shown that the risky shift is by no means universal; some groups are more cautious than their individual members would be. Research on the problem is continuing, both to account for the risky shift and for the fact that it occurs in some groups but not in others. One plausible hypothesis for the risky shift is that in group decisions, responsibility is diffused among the members. No individual feels personally guilty if the decision was the wrong one (Kogan and Wallach, 1964).

Irving Janis (1972) has pointed out that in some cases of group decision making, individual loyalty to the group prevents members from raising controversial and uncomfortable questions. The members become so concerned with maintaining group harmony and consensus, particularly when a difficult moral problem is involved, that they withhold their reservations and criticisms. The result is what Janis calls "groupthink," a decision-making process in which members ignore information and alternatives that do not fit with the group's original assumptions. As an

Figure 7.5 Group decision-making processes have been studied extensively by sociologists. One surprising finding has been that groups are often willing to make much more risky decisions than any of their individual members would. Another finding is that individual members sometimes suppress criticisms of controversial proposals as a result of their loyalty to the group.

example of groupthink Janis cites the decision of President Kennedy and his top advisors to launch the ill-fated Bay of Pigs invasion of Cuba in 1961. This decision, which produced a military and diplomatic fiasco, was based on strategic assumptions that were almost ludicrous. Several members of the decision-making group had very strong private objections to the plan, yet the decision to launch the invasion was unanimous. Janis quotes one of the participants as commenting afterward: "Our meeting was taking place in an atmosphere of assumed consensus. Had one senior advisor opposed the venture, I believe Kennedy would have canceled it. Not one spoke up." (The ancient Persians seem to have been aware of the groupthink phenomenon. The historian Herodotus tells us that whenever they made an important decision in a sober, rational frame of mind, they always reconsidered the matter later while thoroughly drunk!)

Most group decision making on controversial issues, however, does involve debate and even antagonisms between the participants. The process of decision making in small groups generally proceeds through a sequence of stages. The first stage is that of collecting information; the members orient themselves to the problem by analyzing the facts. The second stage is that of evaluating the information; at this point members express opinions and react to the opinions of others. The third stage is that of reaching a decision. Emotional tensions may rise at this stage as coalitions form and an emerging majority imposes its view on the minority. The fourth stage occurs once the decision is made; it involves a general effort to restore harmony in the group. The members react more positively to one another, and there may be a certain amount of joking and frivolity. In this way the continuing solidarity of the group is assured (Bales and Strodtbeck, 1951).

Group Conformity

The pressure to conform to social expectations is strong in every area of life, but it seems to be particularly powerful in the intense atmosphere of a small group (Festinger *et al.*, 1956). One of the most dramatic examples of this tendency comes from some classic experiments by Solomon Asch (1955), who found that people are willing to disavow the evidence of their own senses if other members of the group interpret reality differently.

Asch assembled groups consisting of eight college students, but only one of the students in each group was actually a subject in the experiment; the other seven were secret confederates, or accomplices, of the experimenter. In the experiment, each group was told that it was taking part in a test of visual discrimination and would judge and compare the lengths of lines drawn on cards. Asch displayed two large cards like the ones shown in Figure 7.6. One card contained a single standard line and the other contained three lines of significantly different lengths, one of which was the same length as the standard. The members of the group were asked one by one to state out loud which of the lines matched the standard line in length.

When the first pair of cards was presented the group

STANDARD AND COMPARISON LINES IN THE ASCH EXPERIMENT

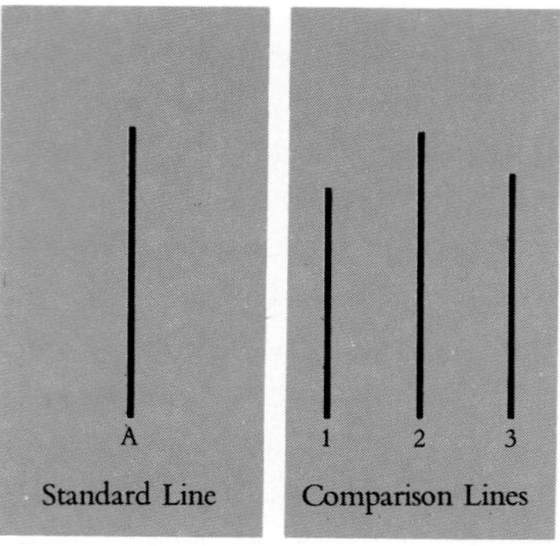

Source: Adapted from Solomon Asch, "Effects of Group Pressure upon the Modification and Distortion of Judgments," in H. Proshansky and B. Seidenberg (eds.), *Basic Studies in Social Psychology* (New York: Holt, Rinehart and Winston, 1965), pp. 393–401.

Figure 7.6 The lines presented to subjects in one trial in Asch's experiment. Asch asked the subjects to state which of the comparison lines appeared to be the same length as the standard line. Control subjects (who made the judgment without any group pressure) chose the correct line over 99 percent of the time, but experimental subjects who were under group pressure to choose the wrong line did so in nearly a third of the cases.

gave a unanimous judgment. The same thing happened on the second trial. When the third pair of cards was presented, however, all seven of Asch's confederates agreed on what was clearly an incorrect answer, asserting that two lines matched when they obviously did not. This happened on six out of eighteen trials. How did the real subject of the experiment react to this uncomfortable situation? In about a third of the cases, the subject yielded to the majority and conformed to its decision. In separate experiments with a control group, Asch found that people made mistakes less than 1 percent of the time, which indicates how much the experimental subjects were influenced by group pressure to conform.

In subsequent interviews with those who yielded to the majority, Asch found that very few of them had actually perceived the majority choice as correct. Although these few subjects actually disbelieved the evidence of their own senses, most of the yielders admitted that they thought they had judged the length of the lines correctly but did not want to be the "odd one out" by giving the right answer. His experiment shows vividly the power of groups to influence their members.

Ingroups and Outgroups

Every group must have some boundaries, for there would otherwise by no way of distinguishing between members and nonmembers. Sometimes these boundaries are formal and clearly defined, with access to the group available to "members only" on the basis of some predetermined criterion. In such cases the boundary may be maintained by symbols, such as badges, membership cards, or even secret signs. A police department, a family, or a labor union has no difficulty in maintaining boundaries, because the criteria for membership are formally defined. In other cases the boundaries are not nearly as clear. A high-school or college peer group, for example, has no specific criteria for membership, and the boundary between actual members and hangers-on may be a very blurred one.

All groups, however, tend to maintain their boundaries by developing a strong sense of the distinction between the "we" of the group and the "they" who are outside the group. Members tend to regard their own group, the *ingroup,* as being somehow special, whereas any *outgroup* to which other people belong is regarded as less worthy and may even be viewed with hostility. A common way of maintaining boundaries between groups, in fact, is through some form of conflict between them. The presence of a common enemy (real or imaginary) draws the members together and increases the solidarity and cohesion of the group (Coser, 1956).

An experiment by Muzafer Sherif (1956) illustrates how ingroup loyalties can help to maintain group boundaries and solidarity. Sherif's subjects were eleven-year-old American boys, all from stable, white, middle-class, Protestant backgrounds. None of them knew each other before the experiment began. Sherif took his subjects for an extended stay at a summer camp, where they soon began to form friendship cliques. Once these groups had been formed, Sherif randomly divided the boys into two main groups that lodged in separate cabins some distance apart. In doing so, he disrupted the cliques that had already formed, but the boys soon began to develop strong loyalties to their new groups. Next, Sherif pitted the two groups against each other in various sporting and other competitive activities. The result was considerable antagonism and hostility between the groups, including those members on either side who had earlier been in the same friendship cliques. Rivalry between the two groups grew steadily more intense, with each ingroup holding a very negative attitude toward the other outgroup. Finally, Sherif created some emergency situations, such as a disruption of the water supply, that required both groups to cooperate as a team. Within a short period, members of the two groups began to interact as a single group, their old hostilities forgotten. Sherif's experiment shows clearly how feelings of group loyalty contributed to the maintenance of group boundaries, how the presence of conflict between the groups heightened these loyalties, and how ingroup feelings lessened and disappeared once the members of both groups were obliged to unite in pursuit of common goals.

Reference Groups

There is one kind of group which people may feel they "belong" to even if they are not actually members. This is the *reference group,* a group to which people refer when making evaluations of themselves and their behavior.

We constantly evaluate ourselves—our behavior, our appearance, our values, our ambitions, our life-styles, and so on. In making these evaluations, we always refer to the standards of some group. The group may be one of which we are a member, such as the family or the peer group. But it may also be one that we do not actually belong to. People may judge themselves, for example, by the standards of a community they previously lived in or of a community they hope to join in the future. A sociology student who hopes eventually to take a graduate degree may evaluate his or her progress in terms of the standards of graduate students rather than an undergraduate peer group. A medical student may refer to the standards of physicians rather than fellow students.

Our evaluations of ourselves are strongly influenced by the reference groups we choose: if a student who obtains a "B" in an examination compares the result with that of "A" students, the self-evaluation will be very different than if the result is compared with that of "C" students. Whether people are members of these groups or not, they refer to the norms and values of the groups in evaluating their own behavior. Reference groups are therefore an important element in the socialization process, for they can shape individual behavior and personality no less powerfully than any other group to which a person feels loyalty.

The influence of reference groups on individual behavior and attitudes is illustrated by a long-term study conducted by Theodore Newcomb (1958) at Bennington College, a liberal women's college in New England. Most of the students, Newcomb found, came from conservative families, and the values they brought with them from these backgrounds conflicted with those they met in the college. The longer the students stayed at the college, the more liberal most of them became, although a minority retained their earlier conservative outlook. Those who became liberal appeared to use their new peers or the faculty as a reference group, whereas those who remained conservative continued to refer to the values and standards of their families. Adoption of a new reference group or loyalty to an old one correlated closely with the political opinions of the students.

Formal Organizations

Until a century or so ago, nearly all social life took place within the context of small primary groups, such as the family, the church congregation, the schoolhouse, the farm or small workplace, and the village community. Today the social landscape is dominated by large, impersonal organizations that influence our lives from the moment of birth, such as hospitals, colleges, large factories, business corporations, government departments. Some of these organizations are *voluntary,* in the sense that people may freely join them or withdraw from them. Examples include religious movements, political parties, and professional associations. Some are *coercive,* in the sense that people are forced to join them—for example, prisons, ele-

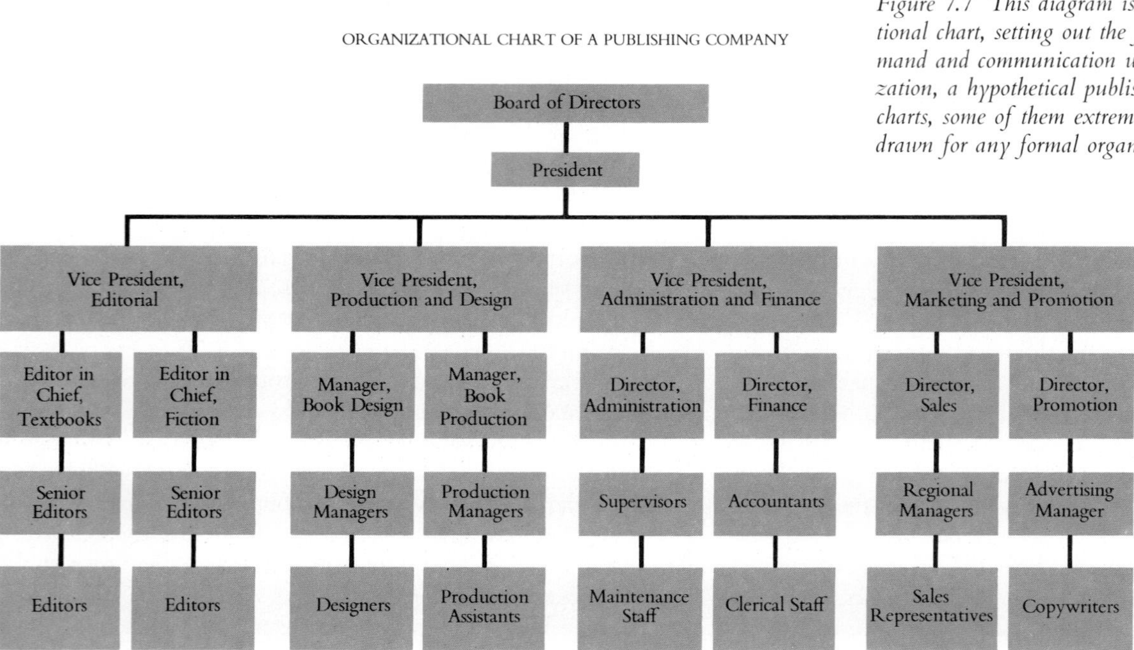

Figure 7.7 This diagram is a typical organizational chart, setting out the formal chains of command and communication within a formal organization, a hypothetical publishing company. Similar charts, some of them extremely complex, can be drawn for any formal organization.

mentary schools, or, for draftees, the army. Other organizations are *utilitarian,* in the sense that people join them for practical reasons: they join business enterprises, for example, in order to earn a living (Etzioni, 1961). But whichever organizations we belong to and whatever our reasons for joining them, we spend a substantial part of our lives within these large, impersonal groups.

Secondary associations of this type are generally formal organizations. A *formal organization* is a large social group that is deliberately and rationally designed to achieve specific objectives. Unlike primary groups, which are informal, these organizations have a carefully designed structure that coordinates the activities of the members in the interests of the greatest possible efficiency. The relationships between the members of a formal organization are based on the positions that they hold. Rights and responsibilities are attached to the office a person occupies, not to the person as an individual. It is possible to draw a chart of any formal organization, showing the relationship of the various positions to one another, without any reference to the actual individuals involved. (See Figure 7.7.)

Most people seem to have an ambiguous attitude toward formal organizations. On the one hand, our material affluence and our very way of life are clearly dependent on the existence of formal organizations, such as corporations, colleges, government departments, and large factories. On the other hand, the size, impersonality, and power of formal organizations are often seen as dehumanizing and threatening. Formal organizations, in fact, have been held responsible for much of the feeling of alienation that is said to characterize modern industrial society (Roszak, 1969). As Amitai Etzioni (1964) points out:

> Without well-run organizations our standard of living, our level of culture, and our democratic way of life could not be maintained. Thus, to a degree, *organizational rationality and human happiness go hand in hand.* But a point is reached where happiness and efficiency cease to support each other. . . . Here we face a true dilemma.

Bureaucracy

The larger and more complex a formal organization becomes, the greater is the need for a chain of command to coordinate the activities of its members. This need is fulfilled by a *bureaucracy,* a hierarchical authority structure that operates under explicit rules and procedures. Understanding bureaucracy is the key to the analysis of formal organizations.

The word "bureaucracy" usually carries negative connotations in everyday speech. It conjures forth images of forms in triplicate, "red tape," lost files, incorrect bills, unanswered letters, counter clerks blinded by petty regulations, and runarounds as the victim of some bureaucratic bungle tries in vain to find an official capable of taking or reversing a decision rather than "passing the buck" to someone else. Yet although "bureaucracy" often seems synonymous with "inefficiency" from the point of view of the individual, the bureaucratic form has thrived for the simple reason that it is, for most purposes, highly efficient. It is the most effective means ever devised of making a large organization work. Sociologists therefore use the word bureaucracy in a neutral sense, without the overtones that it usually has in ordinary speech.

This does not mean, however, that sociologists refrain from passing judgment on the bureaucratic form. In fact, there is a deep current of distaste for bureaucracy running through Western sociology right back to such early thinkers as Karl Marx and Max Weber. Marx (1843) loathed bureaucracy, which he saw as an "excrescence" on society. Weber, whose writings have provided the foundation for almost all later research on bureaucracy, declared in 1909:

> The passion for bureaucracy is enough to drive one to despair. . . . The great question is . . . not how we can promote and hasten it, but what we can oppose to this machinery in order to keep a portion of mankind free from this parcelling out of the soul, from this supreme mastery of the bureaucratic way of life.

Despite his misgivings about bureaucracy, however, it was Weber who first systematically analyzed the system and demonstrated its efficiency.

Weber's Analysis

To Max Weber (1922), the master trend in the modern world was the process that he called *rationalization.* By this concept he meant the way in which traditional, spontaneous, rule-of-thumb methods of social organization are replaced by abstract, explicit, carefully calculated rules and procedures. This rationalization process can be seen in

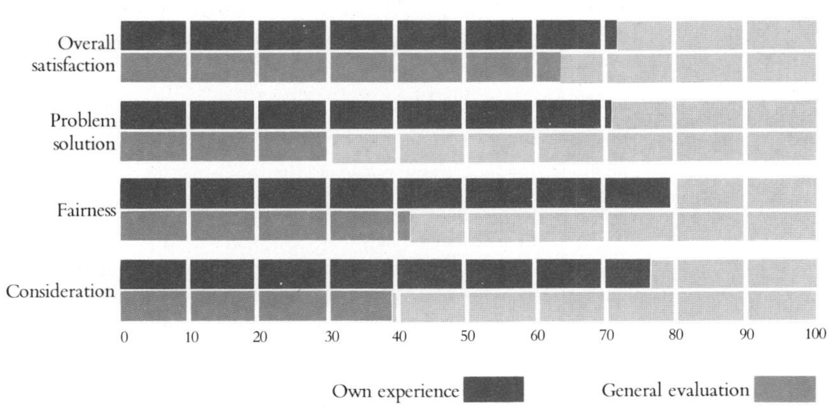

Source: Adapted from Robert L. Kahn *et al.,* "Americans Love Their Bureaucrats," *Psychology Today,* 9 (June 1975), p. 71.

Figure 7.8 When asked to give an overall evaluation of government bureaucracies, most Americans are unenthusiastic. This general evaluation is not consistent with their personal experience, however. Americans report high levels of satisfaction with the treatment they actually receive from these organizations.

Figure 7.9 The bureaucratic form is efficient because it relies on highly rationalized procedures. Officials do not, for example, retain information in their heads or in the form of jottings on odd scraps of paper. All information is carefully coded in a uniform manner and filed away so that it is readily accessible.

nearly every aspect of modern social life. In education, the tutor with a small circle of students is replaced by the vast modern university, with lectures supplied on videotape and multiple-choice examinations graded by computer. The traditional market of small stalls is replaced by the modern supermarket. The "justice" meted out by a village headman is replaced by an intricate system of laws and courtroom procedures. Individual craft workers disappear, to be replaced by laborers on the assembly line. Varied forms of architecture give way, in country after country, to the familiar oblong office building. In each case, the result of the rationalization process is a marked increase in efficiency, but this efficiency is bought at a cost. The world, Weber felt, was becoming dull, drab, and "disenchanted," its mystery and beauty subverted by the new value of technical rationality. Weber believed bureaucracy was an especially threatening form of rationalization. Unlike other forms of rationalization, which involve the manipulation of physical objects (such as machinery) or of procedures (such as the legal system), bureaucracy involves the calculated organization and subordination of *human beings* in the interests of impersonal, technical goals. As a result, Weber felt, people are becoming imprisoned in an "iron cage" of their own making.

Weber analyzed bureaucracy in terms of what he called an ideal type. An *ideal type* is simply an abstract description, constructed by the sociologist from observations of a number of real cases in order to reveal their essential features. Weber's ideal type of a bureaucracy therefore shows us the essential characteristics of the bureaucratic form, although any individual bureaucracy will not necessarily conform to the ideal type in all respects.

According to Weber, a bureaucracy has the following typical features.

1. There is a clear-cut division of labor among the various officials. Each member of the organization has a specialized job to do and concentrates on this specific task.

2. There is a hierarchy of authority within the organization. This hierarchy takes the shape of a pyramid, with greater authority for the few at the top and less for the many at the bottom. The scope of an individual's authority is clearly defined; each official takes orders from the officials immediately above and takes responsibility for those immediately below in the hierarchy.

3. The day-to-day functioning of the bureaucracy is governed by an elaborate system of rules and regulations. Decisions are based on these rules and on established precedents.

4. Officials treat people as "cases," not as individuals. The members of the organization remain impersonal in their contacts with the public. They also adopt a detached attitude to other members of the organization, interacting with them in terms of their official roles. Personal feelings are thus excluded from official business and do not enter into or distort the decision-making process.

5. A bureaucracy includes a specialized administrative staff of managers, secretaries, record keepers, and others. Their sole function is to keep the organization as a whole running smoothly.

GO 73 (Rev. 1-65)

ILLINOIS DEPARTMENT OF LABOR
BUREAU OF EMPLOYMENT SECURITY

MEMORANDUM

Date: April 30, 1971

To: David Gassman, Statistician

From: Benjamin Greenstein, Chief
Research and Statistics

Subject: Hazardous Use of Coffee Pot

The afternoon of April 29, while Mr. Arthur Haverly was on vacation, an electric coffee pot was plugged in his office and left unattended. It spread noxious fumes through the office and scorched a table belonging to the State.

You admitted that you plugged in that coffee pot and that you did it, although Mr. Haverly had told you that I had requested that it should not be done due to previous adverse experience. When I asked you why you plugged in that coffee pot, although I had requested that it should not be done, you stated that you did not take it that seriously.

I may note also that Mr. Haverly informed me the previous day that he had not authorized you to connect the coffee pot in his office.

The following facts, therefore, emerge:

1. You had used your supervisor's office for cooking coffee without his authorization.
2. You did so, although you knew that I had requested that it should not be done.
3. You had left the coffee pot unattended. For that matter, there may have been a conflict between performing agency work and attending to the coffee pot.
4. You created a fire hazard for your fellow workers and subjected them to noxious fumes.
5. When I asked you why you plugged in the coffee pot in spite of my request to the contrary, you stated that you did not take it seriously. This is a rejection of supervision.
6. Your disregard of my authority has resulted in discomfort to your fellow workers and damage to State property.
7. On April 30, the day following the above actions and conversation, at 8:25 in the morning, I noted that you had again plugged in the coffee pot. When I pointed out that you were aware that I had asked you not to plug it in, you replied that it is not 8:30 yet. I then told you that I am in charge of the section, even though it is not 8:30 yet.

What should be done with respect to your actions, as specified above, is under consideration. In the meantime, you are emphatically requested not to repeat the hazard you created by plugging in the coffee pot.

Source: The Washington Monthly, 1974, reprinted in Rafael Steinberg, *Man and the Organization* (New York: Time-Life Books, 1975), p. 115.

Figure 7.10 This memo reveals several features that distinguish formal organizations from more informal groups. (1) The communication is in writing. Composing, dictating, typing, and transmitting it may have taken hours of official time. (2) The people involved are communicating in their official roles, as "Chief, Research and Statistics" and "Statistician." (3) The superior official is deeply concerned that the appropriate hierarchical relationship between the two members of the organization should be observed. (4) The junior official has attempted to disobey the senior official by bending the rules. (5) An excessive amount of effort has been put into resolving an issue that would be regarded as trivial in a less formal group, where it would be handled with a few spoken words. The goals of the organization have become temporarily forgotten while energies are devoted to this internal problem.

Figure 7.11

"Mr. Bradshaw, today is my retirement day, and I want you to know that I've saved every single memo you've ever sent me."

Drawing by Stan Hunt; © 1970 The New Yorker Magazine, Inc.

6. Employees usually anticipate a career with the organization. Candidates for positions in the hierarchy are appointed on the basis of seniority or merit, or some combination of the two—not on the grounds of favoritism, family connections, or other criteria that are irrelevant to organizational efficiency.

Weber argued that such an organization would be highly efficient at coordinating the activities of its members and achieving specific objectives. In general, his analysis has stood the test of time. Later researchers have found it necessary to make one major modification, however, to take account of the informal, primary relationships that exist in all bureaucracies.

The Informal Structure of Bureaucracy

The formal structure of a bureaucracy is easily determined by a glance at its organizational chart, which will show the lines of authority along which communcations flow from one official to another, usually in writing. In practice, however, no bureaucracy ever works quite that way. People get to know one another as individuals, not simply as officials. They establish primary relationships with one another, they bend and break the rules, they develop informal procedures for handling problems, and they take shortcuts through the hierarchy whenever they can (Blau, 1963; Blau and Meyer, 1971; Blau and Scott, 1962).

The existence of these informal networks was established in the course of research carried out between 1927 and 1932 at the Hawthorne plant of the Western Electric Company. Industrial sociologists were attempting to find out which incentives were likely to make workers increase their production. In a classic study of fourteen men involved in wiring telephone switchboards, the researchers found that the output of the workers was not determined by the official rules or even by financial incentives. Output was determined instead by informal norms among the men themselves. The men worked rapidly in the mornings, but slackened off in the afternoons. In order to make their work more interesting and varied they often traded tasks among one another, although this practice was against the regulations. The workers had strong informal norms against working too hard; anyone who attempted to do so was called a "rate buster." They also had norms against working too slowly; anyone who appeared to slack was called a "chiseler." They had an informal norm, too, against telling a superior about the failings of any individual; anyone who did so was considered a "squealer." The output of the workers was determined by an informal, unspoken agreement on what they felt was reasonable—not by what the management, for all its rational and careful calculations, believed they could do (Roethlisberger and Dickson, 1939).

More recent research has confirmed that the formal structure of a bureaucracy always breeds informal relationships and practices. Employees establish their own norms about how long a "lunch hour" should be. They trade tasks to make their work more varied and take over one another's duties when someone wants unofficial "time off." They develop norms about the type and amount of company property that they can "take home" for their private use. Because information travels slowly through the official channels and because some decisions at the executive level are deliberately concealed from subordinates, an informal channel of communication develops—the "grapevine." People who ought not to be in possession of important information, at least in terms of the organizational chart, often gain access to it.

Members of a bureaucracy are never treated entirely in terms of the offices they hold. One person may be known as an incompetent whose advice should never be taken; another as an "old-timer," valuable for his or her knowledge of rules and precedents and how to bend them; another as a "crown prince" marked out for future promotion and worth cultivating in the meanwhile. Following the tortuous route of the official channels is no less irritating to members of a bureaucracy than it is to outsiders, and they quickly learn to short-circuit the process by informal contact with friendly officials elsewhere in the hierarchy. Government officials, for example, do not always adopt the impersonal orientation to the public that their roles require. They may bend the rules to help someone who has gained their sympathy, or they may subtly obstruct a case involving a member of the public who has been rude or offensive. In short, bureaucrats are human as well, and they do their best to establish informal, primary relationships within the artificial constraints of the formal organization.

Dysfunctions of Bureaucracy

Although Weber did not make it explicit, his analysis of bureaucracy was essentially a *functionalist* one. He analyzed bureaucracy as a functional response to a problem in social organization, showing how the various elements in bureaucratic structure promote the efficiency, survival, and goals of the organization as a whole. Weber did not elaborate on the *dysfunctions* of bureaucracy, although he was certainly aware of them. Other sociologists have subsequently identified a number of dysfunctions that are built into the bureaucratic form and may hinder its efficiency.

The most obvious of all bureaucratic dysfunctions is one that is an inevitable by-product of the overall efficiency of the system. Bureaucracies are efficient because their rules are designed for *typical* cases and problems. Officials can handle these cases quickly and effectively by applying uniform rules and procedures to them. Yet this means that the bureaucracy is ill equipped to handle *unusual* cases—the taxpayer whose file has been lost, the illiterate who cannot complete the necessary forms, the American citizen who was born in Romania sixty years ago, wants a passport, but cannot produce or trace the necessary birth certificate. When an unprecedented case arises that does not fit the rules, the bureaucracy is stumped. The problem may then circulate from desk to desk for weeks, months, or even years before it finally reaches an official who is authorized and willing to make a decision on the problem.

Blind adherence to existing bureaucratic rules and procedures may result in what Thorstein Veblen caustically termed "trained incapacity"—the previous training of the bureaucrats makes them incapable of any new, imaginative response. An example of trained incapacity was the typical reaction of college bureaucracies to student disturbances in the sixties and early seventies. Faced with this unanticipated situation, college administrators fell back on the only procedures they knew. They set up committees and commissioned reports, as administrators so often do when they are presented with a problem that might involve changes in established routines. This response was frequently interpreted by the students as nothing more than a stalling device or an attempt to "co-opt" their leaders into the campus bureaucracy, and it merely served to increase campus tensions.

Another dysfunction of bureaucracies is that they may become bogged down in their own internal problems to such an extent that they lose sight of their original goals. The running of a large organization generates problems that may be entirely unconnected to its original purpose, but day-to-day behavior becomes centered on handling these problems. Members of the organization, whose livelihoods depend on its continued existence, may become more concerned with preserving the organization and their own prospects within it than with the original goals (Selznick, 1943). There is often pressure to keep an organization going long after its purpose has been served—either by claiming that there is still work to be done or by finding new work to do. The National Foundation for Infantile Paralysis, for example, was established to combat polio. The discovery of the Salk vaccine virtually eliminated polio within a few years, but the organization did not disband. It looked for other goals and now combats arthritis and other ills (Sills, 1957). Government agencies are particularly notorious for finding a new reason for existence once their original program has either been achieved or abandoned.

The formal communications system of bureaucracies also has its dysfunctions. In theory, communications flow upward and downward through the appropriate channels. In practice, the communications flow almost entirely downward and are often distorted at the middle levels during the process. Those at the top of the hierarchy are very unlikely to be aware of the problems or feelings of those at the bottom. Because the structure of a bureaucracy is essentially authoritarian, officials at lower levels may conceal defects, mistakes, and inefficiences from their superiors.

The authoritarian structure generates further problems. A bureaucracy is by nature a hierarchy of unequals. The level of an official's position may be indicated by such things as the nature of his or her parking space, the presence of a secretary, the type of carpeting in the office, and the size of the desk and the amount of paper on it (the less paper and the bigger the desk, the higher the official). There is consequently always a tendency for an "us against them" attitude to develop at different levels in the hierarchy, causing all the problems that the presence of "ingroup" versus "outgroup" conflicts can create. Victor Thompson (1961) writes of the "bureaupathology" of large organizations. He found that bureaucracies are characterized by tensions, anxieties, and frustrations caused by the authoritarian nature of the bureaucratic hierarchy.

Robert Merton (1968) has suggested another dysfunction of bureaucracy—its effects on the personalities of the bureaucrats. Merton argues that the pressures for conformity and the rigid routines found in large organizations may stifle individual creativity and imagination. This view, though controversial, is widely accepted. The title of William Whyte's book *The Organization Man* (1956), which presented a roughly similar picture, has entered popular speech to describe people so involved in an organization that other areas of their personal experience are distorted and impoverished. This picture may be overdrawn, but there is little doubt that a bureaucracy can produce feelings of alienation among its members. Peter Blau and Richard Scott (1962) comment:

Figure 7.12

"That may be your point of view down there, Hodgins. It's not our point of view up here."

Drawing by Ed Fisher; © 1976 The New Yorker Magazine, Inc.

> The most pervasive feature that distinguishes contemporary life is that it is dominated by large, complex, and formal organizations. Our ability to organize thousands and even millions of men in order to accomplish large-scale tasks—be they economic, political, or military—is one of our greatest strengths. The possibility that free men become mere cogs in the bureaucratic machines we set up for this purpose is one of the greatest threats to our liberty.

"Parkinson's Law" and the "Peter Principle"

Bureaucracies have been the subject of many satirical criticisms. The two best-known onslaughts are expressed in "Parkinson's Law" and the "Peter Principle."

Parkinson's Law is named after the writer who proposed it, C. Northcote Parkinson. The law is a simple one: In any bureaucracy, "work expands to fill the time available for its completion." The natural tendency of any formal organization, Parkinson points out, is to grow. Officials have to appear busy, and therefore they create tasks for themselves. In due course they have so much work to do that they need assistants. When an official has an assistant, however, the burden of work on the official actually increases, because he or she now has to supervise the subordinate. Much of the subordinate's time is taken up in turn with submitting reports to the superior official. As work continues to expand, more assistants and officials are added, some of whom are responsible solely for supervising others or handling the flow of communications between the multiplying personnel. An immense amount of time and effort is then spent on form filling, memo writing, and file keeping and on checking the form filling, memo writing, and file keeping of others. Parkinson argues that virtually all of this activity is unnecessary.

The Peter Principle is named after its discoverer, Lawrence Peter. This principle, too, is a simple one: "In any hierarchy every employee tends to rise to his level of incompetence." Peter points out that officials who are competent at their jobs tend to be promoted. If they are competent at their new jobs, they are promoted again. This process continues until they finally reach a job that is beyond their abilities—and there they stay. The result is expressed in "Peter's corollary": "In time, every post tends to be occupied by an employee who is incompetent to carry out its duties." Bureaucracies are able to function, Peter suggests, only because at any given time there are enough officials who have not yet reached their level of incompetence and are capable of performing their jobs efficiently.

Sources: C. Northcote Parkinson, *Parkinson's Law* (Boston: Houghton Mifflin, 1957); Lawrence J. Peter and Raymond Hull, *The Peter Principle* (New York: William Morrow, 1969.)

The Problem of Oligarchy

The relationship between human freedom and bureaucracy is a complex one, for it involves much more than the subordination of individuals to the needs of organizations. Bureaucracy tends to result in *oligarchy*, or rule by the few officials at the top of the hierarchy. In a society dominated by large formal organizations, therefore, there is a danger that social, political, and economic power will become concentrated in the hands of those who hold high positions in the most influential formal organizations.

This issue was first raised in 1911 by Robert Michels, a German sociologist and friend of Max Weber. Michels was a dedicated socialist at the time and was dismayed to find that the new socialist parties of Europe, despite their democratic structure and provisions for mass participation in their decision making, seemed to be dominated by their leaders just as much as the traditional conservative parties were. Michels came to the conclusion that the problem lay in the very nature of large organizations. "Who says organization," he stated, "says oligarchy." According to his "Iron Law of Oligarchy," democracy and large-scale organizations are incompatible.

Any large organization, Michels pointed out, is faced with administrative problems that can only be solved by creating a bureaucracy. A bureaucracy, in turn, must be hierarchically organized, because the many decisions that must be made every day cannot be made in practice by large numbers of people. The effective functioning of an organization must therefore involve the concentration of power in the hands of a few people.

This situation is aggravated by certain characteristics of both the leaders and the masses. People achieve leadership positions precisely because they have unusual political skills; they are adept at getting their way and persuading others. Once they hold high office, their power and prestige are further increased. They have access to knowledge and facilities that are not available to the rank-and-file members of the organization, and they can control the information that flows down the channels of communication. The leaders are strongly motivated to maintain their own position and to persuade the organization of the rightness of their own views, and they use all their skills and opportunities to do so. They also tend to promote junior officials who support their viewpoints, so that the oligarchy becomes a self-perpetuating one.

The masses, on the other hand, tend to admire the leaders, whose prestige is enhanced by their office as well as by their personal qualities. Unlike the leaders, who work in the organization full time, the members may have only a part-time commitment to it and are prepared to allow the leaders to exercise their own judgment on most matters. The members tend to be less sophisticated and not as well informed as the leaders, and they look to the leaders for policy directives. The very nature of large-scale organization, Michels concluded, makes oligarchy inevitable. The socialist dream of human equality, he concluded, was therefore merely a dream of utopia: "The socialists might triumph, but not socialism, which would perish in the moment of its adherents' triumph." Michels became progressively more disillusioned and, when teaching in Italy later in his life, became for a time an ardent supporter of the Fascist party and an admirer of Mussolini.

Michel's argument is a persuasive one, but it should not be accepted uncritically. Although he was correct in his view that power in organizations tends to be concentrated among the top officeholders, he neglected certain checks on the power of the leadership. In many organizations, from corporations to political parties, there are usually two or more competing groups. If the dominant group gets too far out of line with mass opinion, it risks being displaced by another group, as happened to the Democratic Party establishment when it was routed by the McGovern forces in 1972. Similarly, it is often possible for the mass membership to defect if the leadership no longer reflects its will, as millions of Republicans did when the party convention nominated Barry Goldwater for president in 1964. Michels also overlooked another vital aspect of organizations—whether they are oligarchic or not, they are often the best means of achieving a given goal. Many of the democratic advances of the last century have resulted, directly or indirectly, from the campaigning efforts of large-scale organizations.

Figure 7.13 Many areas of society are now dominated by large bureaucracies, and the bureaucracies themselves tend to be dominated by oligarchies of high-ranking officials. The individual is thus separated from control over the decision-making processes that affect so many aspects of private and public life.

The relationship between bureaucracy and freedom is a paradoxical one. Human freedom in a modern industrial society is dependent on bureaucracy, yet bureaucracy tends to undermine human freedom. Max Weber pointed out that the trend toward greater liberty requires bureaucratization of social institutions. We cannot have impartial justice if decisions are handed down in an arbitrary way on the basis of whim or favoritism. There must be a rational system of laws and a judicial bureaucracy to ensure that everyone is treated in the same way. We cannot have free elections without a representative list of voters, but then we need a formal bureaucracy to register voters and keep the lists up to date. We cannot prevent some people from infringing on the liberties of others unless there are formal organizations, ranging from police forces to federal regulatory agencies, to protect those liberties. In short, the preservation of liberty requires impartial rules and procedures and formal organizations to apply them.

Yet bureaucracy may undermine as well as protect human freedom. The reason is that bureaucracy separates individuals from control over the decisions that affect their lives. Government departments, for example, are theoretically responsible to the electorate, but this responsibility is almost entirely fictional. It often happens, in fact, that the electorate—and even Congress—does not know what these bureaucracies are doing. Government departments are now so large and complex that they often cannot be effectively supervised. In the mid-seventies, largely as a result of investigations following the Watergate scandal, it was discovered that government agencies such as the CIA and the FBI had been guilty of many thousands of crimes over the preceding years, ranging from burglaries of the homes of members of legitimate opposition groups to the experimental administration of LSD to unsuspecting subjects. It also emerged that for a period of at least fifteen years, the United States had been involved in attempts to assassinate the heads of state of foreign countries through plots that included the use of Mafia "hit men." Very few of the elected representatives of the American people had any idea that these policies were being pursued. These cases are merely dramatic examples of a permanent problem, that of making large organizations responsive to the needs and wishes of the people whose interests they are supposed to be serving.

Our democratic theories have their roots in the small-scale world of the eighteenth century. The thinkers and revolutionaries who created those theories could not anticipate the growth and spread of vast, formal organizations. Despite the democratization of other areas of life, formal organizations have further separated us from control over major social, political, and economic decisions. In this respect, as in many others, the radical changes that have taken place in the group basis of social life present a range of new problems.

The Future of Formal Organizations

How are formal organizations likely to develop in the future? A fairly safe prediction would be that they will tend to grow bigger and more complex. Governmental bureaucracies will grow simply because the demands that we make on government, and the range of public services that we require, are also growing. Corporate organizations will grow because large organizations appear to be profitable—although it is entirely possible that there is some optimal limit beyond which their growth will become dysfunctional, leading to difficulties in supervision and coordination, inefficiencies, and reduced profits.

Some writers have predicted that bureaucracies will tend to become less centralized, perhaps through being reorganized into self-contained, more temporary units. Alvin Toffler (1970) argues that the traditional, impersonal organization is not capable of meeting the challenges of modern society. Rapidly changing or temporary conditions demand a more fluid organization—what Toffler calls an "ad-hocracy," a special-purpose unit that is dissolved when its task is done. Warren Bennis (1966) suggests that future organizations will contain "task forces" brought into being in response to specific problems; organizational charts would then consist of a series of project groups rather than traditional hierarchies. This prospect is perhaps more tempting than persuasive. Although organizations may have to modify their structures to deal with new problems, many of their traditional concerns will remain, and their traditional structures are likely to remain also.

One potentially significant trend is the increasing reliance of formal organizations on professional advice—from economists, physicists, sociologists, and other highly trained experts. These professionals do not readily fit into the hierarchical structure of the bureaucracy. Their knowledge and expertise are individual properties, attaching to them as people rather than to their offices. These professionals require the freedom to innovate, experiment, and take risks, and they expect their work to be judged by others in their own reference group—not by a bureaucrat who has no knowledge of their field of expertise. For this reason, there is often tension between, say, administrators and physicians in a hospital or administrators and faculty in a college. As formal organizations come to rely more and more on highly advanced technologies and expert advice, there is likely to be some change in the traditional hierarchical relationships within formal organizations.

The growing resistance of the young to the impersonality of formal organizations is also likely to bring changes in organizational structure and relationships. The humanistic trends that have been present in American society since the emergence of the "counterculture" of the sixties have had a subtle but lasting effect on American culture, and formal organizations have not been immune to this influence. Weber held forth the hope that an excess of rationalization would cause a reaction in favor of greater informality and spontaneity, and the values of the sixties "counterculture" can be seen as just such a reaction to the rationalization of American institutions.

Finally, we will have to confront the problem that formal organizations pose for democratic values. A challenge in the future will be to develop better means of social control over bureaucracy and thus to ensure that we will not be dominated by the organizations that we have established for our own convenience.

Summary

1. Human beings are social animals who spend much of their time in groups. Groups are distinguished from aggregates and categories by the fact that their members interact.

2. Primary groups consist of a small number of people who interact on an intimate basis. Secondary groups may be large or small, but their members interact without any emotional commitment to one another.

3. Extensive research has been devoted to small-group interaction. The size of groups is an important factor in determining the kind of interaction that can take place. Leadership in groups may be instrumental or expressive. Democratic leaders are more effective than authoritarian or laissez-faire leaders, at least in American laboratory experiments. Groups are more effective than individuals at solving determinate problems. Group performance on indeterminate problems varies. There is sometimes a tendency toward a "risky shift" and sometimes toward "groupthink." Most group decisions proceed through a regular sequence of stages. As Asch's experiments reveal, there is strong pressure for conformity in groups.

4. Members of groups tend to regard their group as an "ingroup" and other groups as "outgroups." Conflict and tension between groups heightens feelings of group solidarity and loyalty, as Sherif's experiment shows.

5. Reference groups are those to which an individual refers when making self-evaluations. One need not be a member of a reference group in order to identify with it.

6. Large secondary groups, or associations, generally take the form of formal organizations. These social groups dominate modern life.

7. Formal organizations are coordinated through bureaucracies. Weber saw bureaucracy as a form of rationalization, and by constructing an ideal type, analyzed the way they operate. His analysis has since been modified to take account of the informal structure that exists in all bureaucracies. Although bureaucracies are highly efficient, they have many dysfunctions as well, particularly when faced with unprecedented or unfamiliar situations.

8. Bureaucracies tend to be oligarchic, a feature that Michels argued was incompatible with democracy. Although bureaucracies are necessary for a mass democracy, they also undermine liberty by separating people from the decision-making processes that affect their lives.

9. Although some modifications are likely in formal organizations in the future, they are an indispensable social tool. The increasingly bureaucratic nature of social institutions continues to present many problems, however.

Important Terms

group
aggregate
category
primary group
secondary group
association
small group
dyad
triad
leader
instrumental leadership
expressive leadership
ingroup
outgroup
reference group
formal organization
bureaucracy
rationalization
ideal type
oligarchy

Suggested Readings

BLAU, PETER, AND MARSHALL W. MEYER. *Bureaucracy in Modern Society*, 2nd ed. New York: Random House, 1971.

Blau, perhaps the foremost sociologist in the field, offers a brief but comprehensive analysis of the functions, dysfunctions, workings, and social implications of bureaucracies.

DAVIS, JAMES H. *Group Performance.* Reading, Mass.: Addison-Wesley, 1969.

A comprehensive discussion of group processes, with particular emphasis on decision making and problem solving in small groups. Davis summarizes all of the major research that has taken place on this topic.

ETZIONI, AMITAI. *A Sociological Reader on Complex Organizations.* New York: Holt, Rinehart and Winston, 1969.

A useful collection of articles on formal organizations; the selection includes excerpts from Weber's work as well as contributions from modern sociologists.

HOLLANDER, EDWIN P. *Leaders, Groups, and Influence.* New York: Oxford University Press, 1964.

A good overview of leadership, small-group dynamics, and the processes of group influence on individual behavior.

MICHELS, ROBERT. *Political Parties.* New York: Free Press, 1967.

Although this book was first published more than half a century ago, it remains a readable and relevant analysis of the relationship between democracy and oligarchic organizations.

PARKINSON, C. NORTHCOTE. *Parkinson's Law.* Boston: Houghton Mifflin, 1957.

A satirical account of the inefficiencies of large organizations. The book includes an account of "Parkinson's Law," which states that in any organization, work expands to fill the amount of time available for its completion.

CAL
578241

CHAPTER 8 *Deviance*

CHAPTER OUTLINE

Deviance and Social Control

Theories of Deviance
Biological Theories
Anomie Theory
Cultural Transmission Theory
Labeling Theory

Crime
Types of Crime
Who Are the Criminals?
Selecting the Criminal
Prisons

The Social Consequences of Deviance
Dysfunctions of Deviance
Functions of Deviance

In the preceding chapters we have emphasized the basically orderly nature of society. Most people conform to most norms most of the time, and social life therefore takes on a fairly regular and predictable pattern. Yet this picture is incomplete. We need only look at the newspapers or at the social world around us to see that social norms are often violated as well as adhered to. People rob, rape, and defraud others. They wear peculiar clothing, shoot heroin, and take part in riots. They embrace alien religions, become mentally disordered, and commit bigamy. A full picture of society, therefore, must take account of deviance from social norms as well as conformity to them.

What exactly is deviance? One sociologist put the question "Who is deviant?" to a number of people from different backgrounds and obtained more than two hundred and fifty different answers. Predictably, the range of responses included alcoholics, drug addicts, homosexuals, radicals, prostitutes, and criminals. But it also included liars, women, Democrats, reckless drivers, atheists, young folks, card players, bearded men, straights, prudes, the President, divorcees, modern people, artists, pacifists, smart-aleck students, and know-it-all professors (Simmons, 1969). Alexander Liazos (1972) found that college students state the matter more succinctly: the deviance course in sociology departments is often known as "nuts, sluts, and 'preverts.' "

This list certainly tells us something about deviants and deviance: obviously, the terms refer to people and acts that other people strongly disapprove of. But it hardly provides us with a working definition, particularly one that can help us determine who is a deviant and who is not. A review of the sociological literature on the topic will not

Stigma

Dear Miss Lonelyhearts—

I am sixteen years old now and I don't know what to do and would appreciate it if you could tell me what to do. When I was a little girl it was not so bad because I got used to the kids on the block makeing fun of me, but now I would like to have boy friends like the other girls and go out on Saturday nites, but no boy will take me because I was born without a nose—although I am a good dancer and have a nice shape and my father buys me pretty clothes.

I sit and look at myself all day and cry. I have a big hole in the middle of my face that scares people even myself so I cant blame the boys for not wanting to take me out. My mother loves me, but she crys terrible when she looks at me.

What did I do to deserve such a terrible bad fate? Even if I did do some bad things I didn't do any before I was a year old and I was born this way. I asked Papa and he says he doesnt know, but that maybe I did something in the other world before I was born or that maybe I was being punished for his sins. I dont believe that because he is a very nice man. Ought I commit suicide?

Sincerely yours,
Desperate

Source: Nathanael West, *Miss Lonelyhearts* (New York: New Directions, 1962), pp. 14–15.

provide a precise and generally accepted definition either, because sociologists also find the concept a slippery one to pin down. Howard Becker (1963b) tries to resolve the issue by defining deviance as "behavior that people so label." Kai Erikson (1966) tells us that deviance is behavior that people feel "something ought to be done about." Some sociologists restrict the concept of deviance to behavior that people can presumably choose whether to engage in or not, such as prostitution or robbery, but others extend the concept to cover characteristics over which people have no control. Fred Davis (1961), for example, includes blacks and cripples in the category of deviants, and Erving Goffman (1963b) includes lepers and the badly scarred.

Strictly speaking, deviance is any behavior that does not conform to social norms. But this definition is not very helpful, because many norms can be stretched or even broken without the people concerned actually being regarded or treated as deviants. Many norms tend to be fairly elastic, and varying degrees of deviance from them are tolerated or even ignored. Many norms are not regarded as particularly important, and nobody cares much whether people abide by them or not. The social reaction you get if you turn up late for appointments, don't eat three meals a day, or occasionally wear mismatched socks is very different from the reaction you get if you mug an old lady in the streets, participate in orgies, or announce that you are Napoleon.

Minor deviations from norms, or deviations from norms that nobody bothers much about, have few if any social consequences and are not of particular sociological interest. The sociology of deviance is primarily concerned with deviations that arouse a strong negative reaction in a large number of people. The one characteristic shared by all people who are widely regarded as deviant is *stigma*—the mark of social disgrace that sets the deviant apart from those who consider themselves "normal." Erving Goffman (1963b) has perceptively remarked that the stigmatized person has a "spoiled identity" as a result of negative evaluations by others. For our purposes, then, we may say that *deviance refers to behavior or characteristics that violate significant social norms and expectations and are negatively valued by large numbers of people as a result.* This definition brings us closer to an understanding of deviance, and three additional points will clarify the concept further.

First, social deviance should not be confused with statistical rarity. People whose behavior or characteristics are found only in a minority of the population are statistically unusual, but that does not necessarily make them socially deviant. To jog for a mile before breakfast is to be statistically unusual, and to run for the U.S. Senate even more so, but people who do these things are not socially deviant for that reason. Although most forms of deviance are practiced by a minority of people, it occasionally happens that a majority of the population deviates from a significant norm. Since no society can survive for long if most of its members violate important norms, the usual result is that the norm itself is modified or abandoned. American society has always had a norm prohibiting premarital sex, but for many years a majority of Americans have deviated from this norm. As a result the norm has been losing its

Figure 8.1 In some cases, the line between conformity and deviance is blurred. Some people would consider these young men deviant; others would consider them merely eccentric.

force—so much so that it is questionable if it can still be considered a norm at all in its traditional form.

The second point is that society cannot be divided neatly into the sheep and the goats, the "normals" who conform and the "deviants" who do not. The popular notion that people can be categorized in this way is completely false. Although a majority of people usually conform to any specific norm that is important to society, most people have violated one or more important norms at some time in their lives. If we were to subtract from "normal" society all the people who have engaged in prohibited sexual acts, all the people who have ever stolen something, all the people who have suffered a mental disorder, and all the people who have used illegal drugs, to mention just a few out of hundreds of possibilities, we would have very few "normal" people left. Most people, however, escape discovery of their deviant behavior, are not stigmatized as deviants, and generally do not even regard themselves as deviant at all.

The third point is that deviance is relative. No act is inherently deviant. It becomes deviant only when it is socially defined as such, and definitions vary greatly from time to time, place to place, and group to group. The heretic of one age may be the saint of the next; the "freedom fighter" of one group may be a "terrorist" to another; conservative views in one society may seem dangerously radical in a different society. The determination of who and what is deviant depends on who is doing the defining and who has the power to make the definition stick.

It is even possible for the same act to be differently interpreted depending on the precise context in which it takes place. If you talk to God in a synagogue or church you are considered a moral and respectable citizen; if you talk to God in a bus or a restaurant, or if God talks back to you, you are considered mentally disordered. It is quite acceptable for you to "do nothing" at home, but our society demands that you be "doing something" in public. If you stand around a street corner for long enough, you will probably be arrested for loitering. The police are entitled to ask what you are doing, and "nothing" is not an acceptable answer. A similar act may also draw dif-

Figure 8.2 Deviance is never an absolute matter; it all depends on the viewpoint of the people making the definition. These women are clearly reacting negatively to the young man (note, incidentally, the "body language" of their elbows as well as their faces), but his own peer group would not respond in this way.

ferent reactions depending on the social status of the person concerned. If a lower-class male exposes himself in a park, he will probably be charged with public indecency. If a corporation president does the same, he has an excellent chance of being referred to a psychiatrist for treatment of a "nervous breakdown." A bank teller who steals a thousand dollars from the bank will almost certainly go to prison. If a member of the bank's board of directors steals a thousand dollars from the government by misrepresenting his or her income to the tax collector, the matter will probably be settled through private negotiation with the Internal Revenue Service. Deviance is never absolute. The definition of any act depends on the prevailing cultural interpretations that are applied to the act itself, to the context in which it takes place, and to the social characteristics of the person involved.

Deviance and Social Control

Under most conditions society and its processes are remarkably orderly and predictable. You can generally rely on your sociology professor to show up for class, and you can expect that he or she will talk about sociology and not something else. Public transport will run more or less on time, mail will be delivered, and Congress will follow its usual procedures. Your bank will be open during working hours, not closed because the tellers became bored and decided to throw a private party instead. People will wear much the same clothes tomorrow as they did yesterday, and will not appear on the streets half naked or painted with blue dye. In short, people generally fulfill their roles in accordance with social expectations. In doing so they make social order, and therefore society, possible.

Social order can exist only if there is an effective system of *social control,* that is, some set of mechanisms to ensure that rules are learned and generally followed. No society can function without rules. Not all rules are necessary, of course, and many of them are petty, arrogant, outdated, or oppressive. But there must be some rules to guide individual behavior in such a way that people meet their social responsibilities and fulfill their obligations toward one another. Social control starts with the socialization process, which ideally ensures that everyone internalizes the norms of the society and behaves in accordance with them. On the whole, socialization is highly successful: people conform to social norms most of the time through sheer habit, and rarely question why they act as they do. But socialization is always to some extent imperfect and incomplete. People may be born with different potentials; they are exposed to different socializing influences; they interpret these influences in different ways; and they are often faced with novel situations in which they must improvise new behavior on their own.

To the extent that socialization cannot guarantee sufficient conformity, further means of social control are necessary. Society has to enforce its norms through *sanctions,* or rewards for conformity and punishments for deviance. Both types of sanction can be applied either formally, in a patterned and organized way, or informally, through the spontaneous reactions of other people. A *formal positive sanction,* for example, might be the presentation of a medal or graduation certificate; a *formal negative sanction* might be imprisonment or execution. An *informal positive sanction* might be a pat on the back or a congratulatory handshake; an *informal negative sanction* might be a gesture of disapproval or simply avoidance of the offender. The award of positive sanctions indicates that social control is working effectively and that people are fulfilling the expectations others have of them. But the use of negative sanctions implies that social control has failed and deviance has occurred.

Paradoxically, however, the presence of deviance can actually contribute to the effectiveness of social control. Emile Durkheim (1964a, originally published 1893) strongly argued that deviance is *functional* for society—so functional that if deviants did not exist, they might have to be invented. The reason for the paradox is that the existence of deviants helps to define the boundaries of permissible behavior. When society stigmatizes thieves or prostitutes, it does more than punish them. It also reaffirms the existing norms and implicitly warns other people what their fate will be if they stray from the rules. The public example of the stigmatized deviant provides evidence that social control has failed, but it also demonstrates the consequences of deviance and thus restrains others from deviating. In applying sanctions to deviants, moreover, other people are able to become conscious of and to reaffirm their own conformity, to feel solidarity as the normal "us" against the deviant "them."

There can be little question that deviance does serve this function, provided it is kept within reasonable limits, and there is also evidence that many groups do, in fact, invent deviants where none exist. In highly conformist societies such as China, periodic purges take place against political deviants whose ideological differences with the "party line" are minimal. The early American Puritans invented deviants in the form of witches and reaffirmed their own moral purity in the process (K. Erikson, 1966). In the fifties the United States was seized with an almost hysterical witch hunt against supposed "communists," whom the late Senator Joe McCarthy alleged were infesting the State Department. McCarthy brandished "lists" of nonexistent "reds," indiscriminately accused his critics of communist sympathies, and ruined many reputations before the Senate finally summoned the courage to pass a vote of censure on him.

Figure 8.3 In modern industrial societies, social control is often applied through formal sanctions involving police, courts, and other agencies. This situation contrasts with that in traditional, preindustrial societies, where social control is usually applied through spontaneous community reactions.

Deviance thus arises from the very nature of society and the necessity for social order. Without rules there can be no rule breakers, but where there are rules there will always be people tempted to break them. The individual deviant may be abnormal, but deviance itself is intrinsic to society.

Figure 8.4 The seventeenth-century Puritans of Massachusetts created deviants where they did not exist, in the form of witches. The picture shows one old woman being arrested and charged with witchcraft; by the time the witchhunt came to an end, several women had been executed. In persecuting "witches," the Puritans reaffirmed their own solidarity as a community and enhanced their sense of righteousness.

Theories of Deviance

The extent and the content of deviant behavior vary a great deal from one society to another and from group to group within a society, a fact that requires explanation. Psychologists have investigated the personal characteristics of individual deviants, explaining their behavior in terms of a weak ego, an inability to take the role of other people, a failure to identify with parental authority, a process of social learning, a reaction to frustration, and so on. These explanations provide an adequate account of why particular people adopt the deviant practices that they do. But the sociological problem is not to explain why a particular person becomes deviant: it is to understand why deviance arises at all, why it follows specific patterns, and why some acts rather than others are defined as deviant in the first place. Four main theories have been offered; the first three have focused primarily on one of the most socially disruptive forms of deviance, crime.

Biological Theories

Early approaches to deviance started from the assumption that there was something basically "wrong" with the deviant. The distinction between deviant and normal behavior was regarded as absolute and self-evident, and the failure of some people to follow social rules was explained in terms of sin, wickedness, degeneracy, or "moral insanity." The problem of why some people should be more prone to these vices than others was addressed by the Italian criminologist Cesare Lombroso (1911), whose research convinced him that he had found the answer: criminal behavior was inborn.

By using a number of crude tests to measure the physical characteristics of convicted criminals, Lombroso was able to isolate certain recurring "stigmata," features typically found in the criminal population. Among these stigmata, he announced, were shifty eyes, receding hairlines, red hair, strong jaws, whispy beards, and the like. Lombroso came to the conclusion that criminals were a form of evolutionary throwback to a more primitive human type. The criminal, it seemed, was a

> being who reproduces in his person the ferocious instincts of primitive humanity and the inferior animals. Thus were explained [the characteristics] found in criminals, savages, and apes: insensitivity to pain, extremely acute sight, tatooing, excessive idleness, love of orgies, the irresistible craving for evil for its own sake, the desire not only to extinguish life in the victim, but to mutilate the corpse, tear its flesh, and drink its blood.

Lombroso's work attracted a number of admirers, none of whom noticed the fatal flaw in the criminologist's methodology. He had neglected to measure noncriminals as well, and therefore had not established that his "stigmata" appeared more frequently in criminals than in the general population. A British physician, Charles Goring (1913), corrected this oversight and disposed of Lombroso's theory by showing that the physical characteristics of criminals did not differ in any detectable way from those of ordinary citizens.

Biological theories of criminal deviance have reappeared periodically since Lombroso's time. The psychologist William Sheldon (1940) attempted to classify people in terms of three basic body types: the *endomorph,* who is round and stout; the *mesomorph,* who is muscular and agile, and the *ectomorph,* who is skinny and delicate. After investigating a small number of juvenile delinquents in Boston, Sheldon (1949) concluded that the muscular and agile mesomorphs were disproportionately represented in his sample. Sheldon Glueck and Eleanor Glueck (1956) used Sheldon's typology to compare five hundred juvenile delinquents with a carefully matched sample of five hundred nondelinquents. They also found that mesomorphs predominated in the delinquent sample, although all three body types were present in both groups. The Gluecks concluded that body type, in conjunction with other personal characteristics and experiences, might predispose certain people toward crime. This finding has to be interpreted very carefully, because it is easy to overlook the interaction that takes place between biological and social factors in the shaping of behavior. People respond to others in subtle ways on the basis of their physical appearance, and these responses in turn influence the behavior of the individuals concerned. The delicate youth, for example, is not likely to be selected by his peers for a gang fight, nor the stout youth for a burglary that might involve climbing a drainpipe or a headlong flight from the police. The muscular and agile youth is presumably more likely to become involved in adventurous and high-spirited behavior of the kind that is readily defined as delinquency, but this hardly means that his body type is a *cause* of his criminal tendencies.

SHELDON'S BODY TYPES

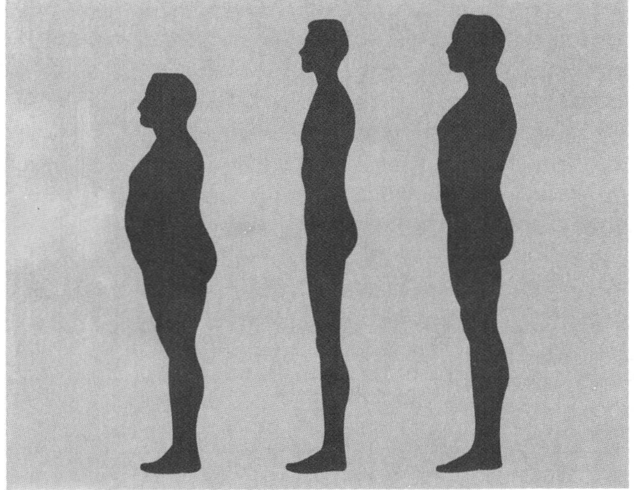

Figure 8.5 William Sheldon identified three basic body types: the round and stout, the skinny and delicate, and the muscular and agile. Sheldon's research convinced him that the muscular and agile type was more prone to criminal behavior, but this conclusion has since been called into question.

Interest in biological factors was revived more recently when it was discovered that some violent criminals have a chromosome disorder. Normal males have an XY chromosome makeup, but these criminals had an extra chromosome, giving them the combination XYY. Subsequent studies indicate that XYY criminals are not more violent than other criminals, but they have shown that XYY males do appear more often in criminal than in noncriminal groups (Owen, 1972). The great majority of XYY males have never been convicted of a crime, however, and appear to lead normal lives. Research on the issue is continuing, but it seems unlikely that the extra chromosome is a cause of criminal behavior. XYY individuals often have low intelligence and are unusually tall; they may therefore be stigmatized by society. They may turn to crime as a reaction against the stigma imposed on them by others, not as a result of their genetic makeup (I. Taylor *et al.,* 1973).

Although biological factors may be isolated for very specific kinds of deviance—particular forms of mental disorder, for example—they are of little use in the explanation of deviance in general. Every society defines crime and other forms of deviance differently, and a highly deviant act in one society may be a conforming and virtuous one in another. Absolute characteristics of an inborn nature cannot be used as a comprehensive explanation of culturally relative forms of behavior.

Anomie Theory

The concept of *anomie* was introduced to modern sociology by Emile Durkheim (1964, originally published 1893) to describe the confused condition that exists in both individuals and society when social norms are weak, absent, or conflicting. A society with a high level of anomie risks disintegration, for its members no longer share common goals and values. Individuals in a state of anomie lack guidelines for behavior, for they feel little sense of social discipline over their personal desires and acts. Robert Merton (1938, 1968) has modified this concept and applied it to deviant behavior.

Merton writes from a *functionalist* perspective and regards deviance as the outcome of an imbalance in the social system. To Merton, anomie is the situation that arises when there is a discrepancy between socially approved goals and the availability of socially approved means of achieving them. If a society places a high value on material goods and affluent living for all but denies people equal access to socially approved ways of reaching these goals, it invites theft, fraud, and similar crimes. As Merton (1968) explains:

> It is only when a system of cultural values extols, virtually above all else, certain *common* success goals for the *population at large,* while the social structure rigorously restricts or completely closes access to approved modes of reaching these goals *for a considerable part of the same population,* that deviant behavior ensues on a large scale.

In small, traditional communities the goals offered to the general population are usually matched to the opportunities for achieving them. But in large modern societies, many people may not have access to the approved means of achieving valued social goals. Americans are readily socialized into the belief that one has to "make it" in the world or be a "failure." But they are not always as easily socialized into accepting socially approved ways of "making it" as being the only possible ways of achieving success.

People who accept the goal of success but find approved avenues to success blocked may fall into a state of anomie and seek success by disapproved methods. As Merton puts it, "in this setting, a cardinal American virtue, 'ambition,' becomes a cardinal American vice, 'deviant behavior.' " The strength of Merton's approach is that it locates the source of deviance squarely within culture and social structure, not in the failings of individual deviants. Society itself—through discrepancies between its institutionalized goals and its institutionalized opportunities to reach them—exerts a definite pressure on some people to behave in deviant rather than conformist ways.

Merton suggests that people may respond to this situation in one of five different ways, depending on their acceptance or rejection of the socially approved goals or the socially approved means of achieving them.

Conformity occurs when people accept both the approved goals and the approved means. Conformists want to achieve the goals of success and materialism. They work hard, save money, and generally use approved means of seeking the goals—even if they are unsuccessful.

Innovation occurs when people accept the approved goals but resort to disapproved means. This is the most common form of deviance: it occurs, for example, when a student wants to pass an examination but resorts to cheating; when a candidate wants to win an election but uses "dirty tricks" to discredit an opponent; when a man wants sexual satisfaction but resorts to a prostitute.

Ritualism occurs when people abandon the goals as irrelevant to their lives but still accept and compulsively enact the means. The classic example is the bureaucrat who becomes obsessed with petty rules and procedures, losing sight of the objectives that the rules were designed to achieve. Ritualism is the mildest form of deviance, and except in extreme cases is not usually regarded as such.

Retreatism occurs when people abandon both the approved goals and the approved means of achieving them. The retreatist is the "double failure" in the eyes of society—the vagrant, the chronic narcotics addict, the "skid-

MERTON'S TYPOLOGY OF DEVIANCE

Modes of Adapting	Accepts Culturally Approved Goals	Accepts Culturally Approved Means
Conformist	yes	yes
Innovation	yes	no
Ritualist	no	yes
Retreatist	no	no
Rebel	no (creates new goals)	no (creates new means)

Source: Adapted from Robert K. Merton, *Social Theory and Social Structure* (New York: Free Press, 1968), p. 194.

row bum," or anyone else who has lost commitment to both the goals and the means that society values.

Rebellion occurs when people reject both the approved goals and means and then substitute new, disapproved ones instead. The rebel, for example, may reject the goal of personal wealth and the means of capital accumulation as the way to achieve it, substituting instead the goal of an egalitarian state achieved through revolution.

Applications

Anomie theory has been usefully applied to several forms of deviance, particularly that of delinquent juvenile gangs. Albert Cohen (1955) points out that gangs are generally composed of lower-class boys. These youths lack the social and educational background that would enable them to achieve success via the approved channels that are open to middle-class youth. Consequently, they attempt to achieve status in other ways—by gaining the respect of their peers through "hell-raising" and other forms of behavior that conform to gang norms. Gang members, Cohen suggests, are "denied status in the respectable society because they cannot meet the criteria of the respectable status system. The delinquent subculture deals with these problems by providing criteria of status which these children *can* meet." Richard Cloward and Lloyd Ohlin (1960), also applying anomie theory to delinquent gangs, point out that the gangs may take one of three basic forms. The youths' access to legitimate channels of achievement is blocked, but the opportunities to use illegitimate channels are also unevenly distributed. Cloward and Ohlin suggest that there are three types of delinquent subcultures. The *criminal* type is organized for material gain through theft, robbery, and the like; the *conflict* type is concerned with territorial defense and gang warfare; and the *retreatist* type emphasizes less visible activities, such as drug and alcohol abuse, as its source of "kicks."

Evaluation

Merton's theory of deviance is an elegant, thoughtful, and influential one. It has the virtue of locating the cause of deviance in society, not the deviants themselves, and it provides a very plausible explanation of why people commit certain deviant acts, particularly crimes involving property. It is less useful, however, for explaining other forms of deviance, such as homosexuality, exhibitionism, or marijuana use. And because Merton shares the implicit functionalist assumption that there is a general consensus on values in society, he largely ignores the process by which some people are defined as deviant by others—a process that often involves a conflict of values between those who have the power to apply these definitions and those who do not.

Cultural Transmission Theory

Earlier in this century two researchers at the University of Chicago, Clifford Shaw and Henry McKay (1929), found that high crime rates had persisted in the same Chicago neighborhoods for twenty years, even though the character of these neighborhoods had changed in other ways as different ethnic groups had come and gone. How could this finding be explained? The answer, they felt, was that deviant behavior must be *learned.* If deviant behavior already exists as a cultural pattern in some group or community, it will tend to be transmitted to newcomers and the young. New arrivals in a high-crime neighborhood, Shaw and McKay reasoned, were learning deviant behavior in play groups, in teenage gangs, and in other contexts of social interaction with the people who lived there.

Another sociologist working in Chicago at the time, Edwin Sutherland, produced a theory to explain exactly how this process of *cultural transmission* takes place. According to Sutherland (1939), deviant behavior is learned through a process of *differential association.* Sutherland's concept is really a sophisticated version of the old "bad companions" formula ("he was such a good boy until he fell in with that lot"). Just as people will tend to be conformist if their socialization emphasizes a respect for the prevailing norms, so they will tend to become deviant if their socialization emphasizes a contempt for these norms. As Sutherland put it, "A person becomes delinquent because of an excess of definitions favorable to violation of the law over definitions unfavorable to violation of the law."

Sutherland begins with the assumption that criminal behavior is learned and that, like all social behavior, it is learned from other people. Nobody is exposed exclusively to conformists or deviants, and several factors determine whether conformist or deviant influences will be the stronger. The first is the *intensity* of contacts with others; a person is more likely to be influenced by deviant friends or family members than by deviant acquaintances or other more distant associates. The second is the *age* at which the contacts take place; influences in childhood and adolescence are more powerful and enduring than those that occur later in life. The third is the *frequency* of the contacts; regular association with deviant people is more likely to encourage deviance than infrequent contacts. The fourth is the *duration* of contacts with others; long periods of association with deviants are more likely to produce deviant tendencies than shorter contacts. The fifth factor is the *number* of contacts; the more deviants a person associates with, the more likely that individual is to become deviant as well. In short, the ordinary person does not have the knowledge, the techniques, or the justifications that are available to the deviant. These things must be learned, and they can only be learned from others.

Applications

An interesting implication of cultural transmission theory is that deviance will tend to be more common when a society is culturally heterogeneous and contains a number of distinctive subcultures (Wirth, 1931; Sellin, 1938; Sorokin, 1941; Cohen, 1955; Nisbet, 1953). When culture is homogeneous, as is usually the case in small, traditional communities, deviance—particularly crime—is rare. The members of these communities share the same norms and values and have little difficulty in passing them on to succeeding generations. They place little reliance on formal methods of social control, such as statutes, police, courts, or prisons; people are kept "in line" by the overwhelming force of public opinion. A large and heterogeneous modern society, on the other hand, may contain a range of subcultures based on such characteristics as race, ethnicity, religion, age, or economic status. The members of these subcultures may feel a greater loyalty to their own groups than to the common culture. Subcultural norms may differ in significant respects from those of the dominant culture, and they may be defined as deviant by the society as a whole. The very heterogeneity of a large modern society thus guarantees that some people will become deviant merely by learning the norms of their own group.

Walter Miller (1958) uses this insight in his analysis of gang delinquency, arguing that mere acceptance of certain lower-class norms and values can put juveniles in trouble with the law. Miller identifies several "focal concerns" of lower-class culture: *toughness,* an emphasis on physical strength; *smartness,* the capacity to be "streetwise" as a way of holding one's own in the world; *excitement,* in the form of gambling or other "kicks" as a way of relieving the routine of a life in which one never "gets ahead"; *autonomy,* the wish to be free of external controls and authority; and *fate,* the sense that what happens to a person is less a matter of personal responsibility than luck or fortune. The gang, Miller argues, offers an environment in which these values can be expressed. It provides security, stability, and support for juveniles who have internalized the norms of their own community rather than those of the predom-

Figure 8.6 Cultural transmission theory implies that people raised in a particular subculture may become deviant simply through learning the values and norms of their own subculture. Living in a slum environment, these boys learn patterns of behavior that are readily defined as deviant by the mainstream culture.

inantly middle-class culture beyond. Simply by accepting the values of their own community, lower-class juveniles may become delinquent in the eyes of the wider society.

Evaluation

Cultural transmission theory has the merit of drawing attention to the fact that deviant behavior is learned. People do not find out how to shoot heroin or forge checks on their own. But it is possible to learn deviant behavior without any actual contact with deviants, a fact that differential association theory does not take account of. Many forms of deviant behavior are learned through contact with ideas, not people. A check forger or heroin shooter need not have had personal instruction in how to perform the acts, and a child molestor almost certainly will not have learned the behavior directly from others. The theory does not explain why some people who have prolonged contacts with deviants—as lawyers do with criminals—may resist becoming deviant themselves. Nor does it take account of the fact that some forms of deviant behavior are actually learned in contact with conforming citizens. One can learn the techniques of embezzlement, for example, by taking a course in bookkeeping (Sagarin, 1975). Most important, cultural transmission theory explains only how deviance is culturally transmitted, not how it arose in the culture or why it was defined as deviance in the first place.

Labeling Theory

A newer theory confronts some of the problems that earlier theories ignored or were unable to explain. This theory emphasizes the relativity of deviance and the fact that nothing is inherently deviant. A person or act becomes deviant only when the *label* of "deviance" has been succesfully applied by other people. Labeling theorists argue that the *process* by which people are labeled as deviants, not their acts, should be the focus of sociological attention. The theory draws heavily on the insights of the *interactionist* perspective in modern sociology for its understanding of the labeling process, and in recent years it has drawn on the *conflict* perspective to explain why some people and acts rather than others are labeled as deviant at all.

Labeling theory is associated primarily with the work of Edwin Lemert (1951, 1967) and Howard Becker (1963b). They point out that virtually everyone behaves in a deviant manner at some time or another. Most of this deviant behavior is temporary, exploratory, trivial, or easily concealed and falls into the category of *primary deviance.* The primary deviant may be a wealthy man who periodically misrepresents his income to the tax collector, an overburdened mother who sometimes becomes hysterical, an adolescent who occasionally has homosexual relations with a friend, or a youth who tries an illicit drug "to see what it's like." This behavior may pass unnoticed, and the individuals concerned do not regard themselves as deviants and are not regarded as such by others. But if these acts are discovered and made public by significant other people—friends, parents, employees, school principals, or even the police and the courts—the situation changes radically. The offender is confronted by the evidence, often in a situation that Harold Garfinkel (1956) calls a "degradation ceremony." In this "ceremony" the person is accused of the deviant act, lectured to and perhaps punished, and forced to recognize the moral superiority of the accusers. Most important, the person is now labeled by others as a deviant—as a "nut," "whore," "queer," "weirdo," "crook," "dope addict." Other people begin to respond to the offender in terms of this label. As a result, the offender consciously or unconsciously accepts the label, develops a new self-concept, and begins to behave in accordance with it. The behavior now takes the form of *secondary deviance.* The label proves prophetic, and the deviance becomes habitual.

Once people have been labeled as deviants, their biographies are significantly altered. "Normal" people apply stigma to the deviants, often forcing them into the company of other deviants. The result is that the sanctions have the effect of reinforcing the very behavior they were intended to eliminate. The deviants live up to the labels, frequently because they have no options, and are thrust into a *deviant career.* Deviance then becomes their *master status,* and much of their behavior is interpreted by others in the light of this single characteristic, however irrelevant it may actually be to ordinary day-to-day interactions (Goffman, 1963b). This interpretation may even be applied retrospectively, and often incorrectly, to the individual's past behavior. The earlier friendliness of the person who is now labeled a homosexual is reinterpreted as a sexual advance; the request for employment by the person who is now known to be an ex-convict is reinterpreted as an attempt to "go straight"; the mild tantrum by the person who is now known to have been a mental patient is reinterpreted as a sign of underlying instability.

Applications

Why are certain people and acts rather than others labeled as deviant? Several labeling theorists argue that the answer is to be found in the conflict of interests and values between those who have the power to label and those who are powerless to reject the label (for example, Lemert, 1974; Liazos, 1972; Lofland, 1969). As Edwin Schur (1965) points out, people with high social, economic, and political resources have a high ability to resist charges of deviance; a high ability to resist sanctions such as arrest, conviction, and imprisonment; and a high ability to impose the actual rules that define deviance. Conversely, those with lesser resources have a lower ability to achieve these things. Alexander Liazos (1972) points out that the concept of deviance is rarely applied to the politician who starts a war or the corporate executive whose decisions lead to environmental pollution. These acts have far more serious social consequences than those of the bicycle thief or the habitually unwashed person, but the latter offenders, not the former, attract the stigma of deviance. Begging in the streets is considered deviant, but living in idleness off inherited wealth is not. These and similar anomalies can only be explained in terms of the fact that it is the rich and the powerful, not the poor and the powerless, who are able to define deviance and to have that definition socially accepted. The prevailing interpretations of reality in any society are the interpretations of those who hold social, political, and economic power; they are able to impose absolute definitions on what is really a relative matter.

Figure 8.7 Labeling theorists argue that definitions of who and what is deviant can only be fully understood in terms of the power relationships between different or competing groups. Powerful groups are able to use social control agencies to enforce their own definitions and to uphold their own interests. Less powerful groups, however, cannot successfully apply the label of deviance to those with superior power.

Jock Young (1971) uses a similar argument to explain the social reaction to different forms of drug use. The National Commission on Marijuana and Drug Abuse (1973) reported that alcohol abuse "is without question the most serious drug problem in the country today." Between 5 and 9 million Americans are compulsive alcoholics, and over half the crimes recorded each year by the FBI are alcohol-related. Yet the Commission found that only 7 percent of American adults consider alcohol abuse a problem, and less than 40 percent even regard alcohol as a "drug" at all. Tobacco is causally linked to lung cancer, emphysema, and heart disease. It is also highly addictive: of those people who smoke more than one cigarette in adolescence, 70 percent continue smoking for the next forty years (Russell, 1971). Yet both these drugs are accepted in the most respected circles and are manufactured, advertised, and distributed by large and legitimate corporations. Marijuana use, on the other hand, is generally illegal, and hundreds of thousands of young people are arrested each year for smoking or possessing it; some of them have received harsh prison sentences. Although it is possible that research will disclose some adverse effects of marijuana (Maugh, 1974), there is currently a general agreement among experts that it is not as harmful to health as alcohol or tobacco.

How can this differential treatment of drug users be explained? Part of the reason is that alcohol and tobacco use is already entrenched and institutionalized in society, but Young suggests that the real reason lies deeper. The social reaction to drug use, he argues, has little or nothing

SUBSTANCES REGARDED AS DRUGS

	Adults (Percent)	Youth (Percent)
Heroin	95	96
Cocaine	88	86
Barbiturates	83	91
Marijuana	80	80
Amphetamines	79	86
Alcohol	39	34
Tobacco	27	16
No opinion	1	1

Source: Drug Abuse in America: Problem in Perspective, Second Report of the National Commission on Marijuana and Drug Abuse (Washington, D.C.: U.S. Government Printing Office, 1973), p. 10.

Figure 8.8 Public attitudes toward drugs bear very little relationship to the properties of the drugs themselves. The main killer drugs in the United States are alcohol and tobacco, yet a large majority of American adults and youth do not regard them as drugs at all. In contrast, the only substance on this list that is neither addictive nor potentially lethal—marijuana—is regarded as a drug by 80 percent of adults and young people.

to do with the characteristics of the drug in question: it has to do with the social characteristics of the people who use it. Marijuana use was associated in the past with such "disreputable" groups as blacks and jazz musicians, and more recently with "hippies" and the rebellious young. Society identifies the drug with the people who use it, and if the people are disapproved, so is the drug.

Evaluation

Labeling theory has the important advantage that it can explain why only certain people and acts are considered deviant. Yet the theory runs into several difficulties. It cannot adequately account for the phenomenon of habitual but secret deviance—the deviance of people who have not been discovered and labeled but who behave in a consistently deviant way and may regard themselves as deviants. Some people, it seems, may become secondary deviants by labeling *themselves* in terms of their own ideas about how others would see them. Labeling theory also ignores the fact that discovery and labeling may actually jolt the primary deviant out of deviance altogether. In other words, a "degradation ceremony" may reform the deviant rather than reinforce the deviance (Mankoff, 1971). Another problem with labeling theory is that it tends to encourage an indiscriminate sympathy for the "underdog" as the helpless victim of definitions arbitrarily imposed by the powerful. But not everyone who is in a prison or an asylum is there simply because somebody chose to label them, although that was certainly part of the process that put them there. Some deviant acts are so socially disruptive that society must impose severe sanctions if social order is to be maintained, and the extreme relativism of labeling theory sometimes obscures this fact.

Each of these theories, then, has some part to play in the explanation of deviance. Let's turn now to an examination of crime, one of the most widespread forms of deviance in contemporary American society.

Crime

A *crime* is an act that has been prohibited by a political authority, usually through the enactment of a law. By defining certain acts as crimes, political authorities ensure that the social reaction to them takes place in an orderly and predictable form. The law is thus used to specify the nature of the crime, to indicate which categories of persons are prohibited from performing the act, and to organize the process through which formal negative sanctions are applied to the offender. An act tends to be defined as a crime when two conditions are present. First, the act must be regarded as so socially disruptive that it should be prohibited; second, it must be considered one that cannot be adequately controlled through informal sanctions.

Although many forms of deviance are defined as crimes, not all crimes are regarded as forms of deviance. Some crimes, such as jaywalking, are committed so frequently and ignored by social control agencies so often that stigma does not attach to the offender, even in the rare cases where an arrest does take place. Other acts are crimes only in the technical sense that they are prohibited by a law that has fallen into disuse. A majority of Americans could doubtless be imprisoned if existing laws governing nonmarital sexual behavior or Sunday sport and entertainment were actually enforced. But as the American experiment with the prohibition of alcohol so conclusively demonstrated, any law that does not enjoy public support tends to become unenforceable and to fall into disuse.

Like all forms of deviance, crime is a relative matter. In Singapore it is illegal for males to have long hair; in medieval Iceland it was illegal to write verses of more than a certain length about another person; in the Soviet Union it is illegal to form a new political party; in South Africa it is illegal to consume alcohol with a member of another race unless a government permit has been obtained for the specific occasion. Although certain acts, such as murder, are regarded as criminal in all societies, each society defines these crimes in different ways. What may be murder in one society is regarded as a justifiable and even praiseworthy act in another. People in every society tend to regard their distinctions between criminal and noncriminal behavior as absolute and beyond question, but these distinctions are based entirely on the prevailing social definitions of the time.

Types of Crime

The major types of crime in the United States can be conveniently classified into five main categories, although there is inevitably considerable overlap among them: juvenile delinquency, crimes without victims, white-collar crime, organized crime, and crimes against property and persons.

Juvenile Delinquency

Crime by juveniles is regarded with particular social concern—partly because it appears to be so common and seems to be on the increase, and partly because society has a strong interest in treating young delinquents in such a way that they will not become persistent offenders in later life. Some 43 percent of all serious crimes are committed by persons under the age of eighteen, and almost 20 percent by persons under the age of fifteen. The overwhelming majority of arrested juveniles are male, and convicted juveniles are far more likely than other juveniles to become adult offenders.

Crimes Without Victims

Offenses from which nobody suffers, except perhaps the offender, include gambling, prostitution, vagrancy, illicit drug use, homosexual acts between consenting adults, and the like (Schur, 1965). These acts are defined as crimes not because they do any demonstrable social damage but because they are regarded as morally repugnant. The United States invests immense resources in its attempts to control victimless crime; well over a third of the arrests each year involve offenses of this kind. The 1975 *Uniform Crime Reports* of the FBI records over 1 million arrests for public drunkenness and about 40,000 for vagrancy, 250,100 for juvenile runaways, 62,600 for gambling, 68,200 for prostitution, and 416,100 for marijuana offenses. Victimless crime is notoriously difficult to control. One reason is that there is no aggrieved victim to bring a charge or give evidence. Another is that the offenders typically hold the law in contempt and feel no guilt at violating it.

White-Collar Crime

The term "white-collar crime" was first used by Edwin Sutherland (1940) to refer to offenses "committed by a person of respectability and high status in the course of his occupation." Sutherland documented the existence of this

Figure 8.9

"In examining our books, Mr. Mathews promises to use generally accepted accounting principles, if you know what I mean."

form of crime by investigating seventy large and respected corporations and establishing that they had accumulated a total of 890 criminal convictions. Behind these offenses of false advertising, copyright infringement, swindling, stock manipulation, price fixing, and so on, were highly respectable citizens. Many sociologists now use the concept of white-collar crime to refer to all the crimes typically committed by high-status people, such as tax evasion, smuggling of articles through customs, embezzlement, and fraud. White-collar crime is generally regarded with more tolerance than most other forms of crime, yet its economic impact is often greater. The President's Commission on Law Enforcement and the Administration of Justice (1967) compared the annual cost of four major categories of white-collar crime (embezzlement, forgery, tax evasion, and fraud) with the annual cost of four major categories of property crime (auto theft, robbery, burglary, and larceny) and found that the total cost of the white-collar crime was almost three times that of the property crimes. Since most white-collar crime probably goes either undetected or unreported, the total cost is doubtless much greater than these figures indicate.

Organized Crime

Organized crime is one of America's largest industries; its gross income is estimated to be twice that of all other forms of illegal activity. This form of crime is dominated by the Mafia, or Cosa Nostra, which is believed to be a loose network of about twenty-four regional syndicates, or "families" (Cressey, 1969). Organized crime depends primarily on the supply of illegal goods and services such as gambling, prostitution, and narcotics to others who are willing to pay for them, but in recent years it has been entering legitimate businesses, where it uses ruthless methods to gain monopoly control. Organized crime depends for its existence and success on the implicit support of otherwise "respectable" citizens—both those who purchase its services and those who protect it from successful prosecution. It is impossible to accept that crime on this scale could flourish without the active connivance of many law enforcement officers, judges, and public officials, and indeed, a 1971 Harris poll found that 80 percent of American adults believe that "organized crime has corrupted and controls many of the politicians in this country."

Crimes Against Property and Persons

These are the crimes that Americans fear most. The cry for "law and order" rarely refers to middle-class tax dodgers or senators accepting illegal campaign donations. The FBI crime reports show that in the United States a theft occurs every 5 seconds, a burglary every 10 seconds, an auto theft every 32 seconds, an aggravated assault every 65 seconds, a robbery every 68 seconds, a rape every 9 minutes, and a murder every 26 minutes. Violence is the crime that is viewed with the most fear and concern, but it constitutes only 9 percent of all serious crime and only a very small proportion of crime as a whole. Part of the fear of violence is anxiety about being attacked by a complete stranger, but in fact most people who are murdered, assaulted, or raped are already acquainted with the attacker. Most murders and assaults arise in the course of family arguments and romantic entanglements. The United States is, however, an extremely violent society, in which the general availability of guns and other weapons contributes to a homicide rate without parallel in other modern industrial societies. A city such as Detroit, Chicago, or New York records more murders in a year than the whole of England, where even the police do not carry guns.

Figure 8.10 The homicide rate in the United States is without parallel in any other modern industrial society. The main reason appears to be the ready availability of handguns, the weapons used in most murders.

Who Are the Criminals?

At first sight it seems easy enough to establish who the criminals are: we need only look at the annual compilation of statistics published by the FBI in its *Uniform Crime Reports.* Recent issues of these reports tell us that the average age for arrest is sixteen, that most offenders are male, that they are much more likely to live in large cities than in small towns or rural areas, and that they are disproportionately likely to be black—in fact, black adults are arrested five times more often than white adults.

The problem is that crime statistics are highly suspect. A 1966 national opinion poll and a 1974 Census Bureau survey of residents and business executives in thirteen cities found that a great deal of crime is not reported at all, even if it is detected. The actual crime rate is probably two or three times as high as the official statistics indicate. The problem is compounded by the fact that the FBI reports statistics for only twenty-nine categories of crime and concentrates on seven crimes: murder, rape, robbery, aggravated assault, burglary, larceny, and auto theft. White-collar crimes such as tax evasion, price fixing, environmental pollution, bribery of officials, and embezzlement are omitted from the reports. The inclusion of statistics on these crimes might substantially alter our picture of the "typical" criminal, who would become significantly whiter, older, and more "respectable."

Most significantly, the crime statistics exclude the most successful criminal of all—the one who escapes detection and arrest. And the disconcerting fact is that this category of criminal includes virtually all of us. This does not mean, of course, that there are not important differences between people who are habitually law-abiding and people who are habitually criminal, or between people who commit minor crimes and people who commit serious ones. But a large number of self-report studies, in which people are asked to give anonymous details of any crimes they have committed, indicate that close to 100 percent of Americans have committed some kind of offense (Doleschal and Klapmuts, 1973). One study of 1678 New Yorkers, for example, found that 91 percent admitted they had broken at least one law, excluding juvenile offenses, for which they could have been fined or imprisoned (Wallerstein and Wyle, 1947). A national survey of youths between the ages of thirteen and sixteen found that 86 percent admitted delinquent acts, although only 4 percent had criminal records; studies of high school populations have uncovered thousands of violations by students with no police records; and it seems that over 90 percent of illegal acts reported by juveniles go undetected by the police (Empey and Erickson, 1966; Dentler and Monroe, 1961; Gold, 1970). These studies have a disturbing implication for our traditional distinctions between criminal and law-abiding citizens. The "typical" criminal is not the typical criminal at all, but rather the one who typically gets arrested, prosecuted, and convicted. The tiny proportion of offenders who actually suffer formal negative sanctions for their acts are the product of a long process of social selection.

Selecting the Criminal

The process of selecting the criminal involves several stages. Only a proportion of crimes are detected, only a proportion of those detected lead to an arrest, only a proportion of arrests lead to prosecution, only a proportion of prosecutions lead to conviction, and only a proportion of convictions lead to imprisonment. The evidence is overwhelming that the attrition rate at each stage depends largely on the social status of the offender.

Many crimes, as we have seen, either go undetected or go unreported even if they are detected. These are predominantly petty crimes against property and crimes committed by "white-collar" citizens, such as inflated insurance claims or tax evasion. When a crime is actually detected, the social status of the offender, all other things being equal, appears to be the main factor in determining whether an arrest and prosecution will follow. This tendency is especially apparent in the treatment of juvenile offenders. The great majority of juveniles in the arrest statistics are lower-class males, but this does not mean they commit most juvenile crimes—only that they are more likely to be arrested. Self-report studies of juveniles have found either no relationship between the incidence of delinquent acts and the social class of the offenders, or else have found that middle-class juveniles are actually more likely to commit crimes, including thefts and assaults (Doleschal and Klapmuts, 1973; Dentler and Monroe, 1961; Short and Nye, 1957; Gold, 1970; Hirschi, 1969; Williams and Gold, 1972; Voss, 1966). Studies have also shown that contrary to popular assumptions and even the earlier assumptions of sociologists, juvenile crimes are more likely to be committed by people acting alone rather than in gangs (M. L. Erickson, 1971, 1973; Hindelang, 1971a). As David Matza (1964) points out, the distinction between delinquents and nondelinquents is a tenuous one at best; many young people are in a state of "drift" between basically conformist behavior and occasional misbehavior.

Why, then, are lower-class youths more likely to be selected for arrest? Two researchers, Irvin Piliavan and Scott Briar (1964), spent nine months riding in police cars of the juvenile bureau of a West Coast police department. They found that more than 90 percent of the incidents that came to police attention were very minor. In these cases the police were reluctant to take official action unless they gauged that the offender had a basically "bad character." In making this assessment the police were guided by such cues as race, dress, and demeanor. Of those who were polite, contrite, and cooperative, less than 1 percent were arrested; but of those who were defiant, nonchalant, and uncooperative, fully two-thirds were arrested. William Chambliss (1973) did a careful study of two teenage gangs in the same town, a lower-class gang that he called the "Roughnecks" and a middle-class gang that he called the "Saints." The Saints committed far more delinquent acts than the Roughnecks, but the Roughnecks were defined by the community as delinquents and were constantly in trouble. (His analysis appears in the reading at the end of this chapter, "The Saints and the Roughnecks.")

This pattern of selective perception and labeling appears to be fairly typical. Two separate incidents occurring at the same time in adjoining California neighborhoods illustrate this tendency further. In the first incident a group of high-school seniors went on a rampage, committing crimes of arson, rape, auto theft, assault, and breaking and entering. In the second incident a nine-year-old boy stole a nickel from a schoolmate. But the high-school seniors were from wealthy white families, and after a conference between community leaders and the police they were simply returned to their parents for private discipline. The child who stole the nickel was from a black ghetto, and spent six weeks in a detention center awaiting a hearing of his case (Mitford, 1973). Another example of differential treatment is provided by an experiment conducted in Los Angeles by Frances Heussenstamm (1971). At the time, members of the Black Panther Party were complaining of victimization by the police, who, they alleged, were bombarding them with traffic citations, a charge the police denied. Heussenstamm recruited twenty university students, all of whom had exemplary driving records and had received no citations in the previous year. The students were asked to attach "Black Panther Party" stickers

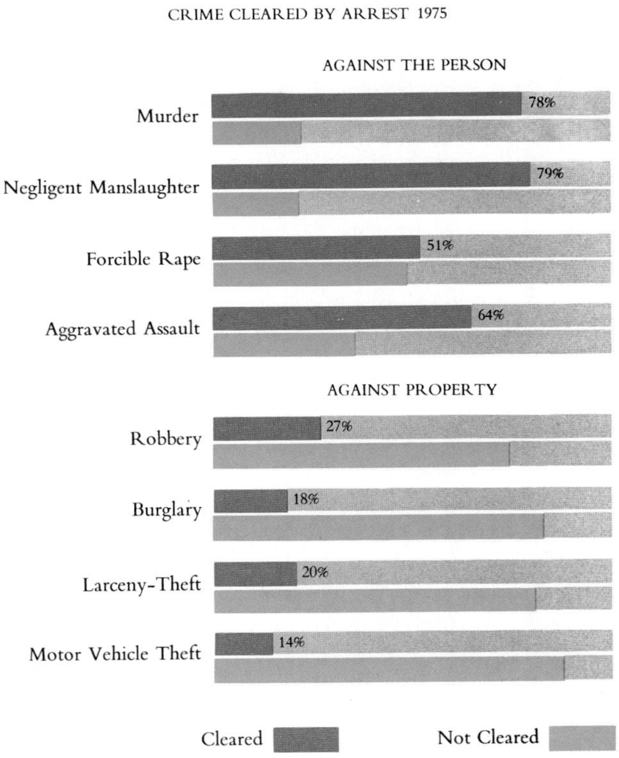

CRIME CLEARED BY ARREST 1975

AGAINST THE PERSON

Murder 78%

Negligent Manslaughter 79%

Forcible Rape 51%

Aggravated Assault 64%

AGAINST PROPERTY

Robbery 27%

Burglary 18%

Larceny-Theft 20%

Motor Vehicle Theft 14%

Cleared Not Cleared

Source: Crime in the United States: Uniform Crime Reports (Washington, D.C.: U.S. Government Printing Office, 1975), p. 40.

Figure 8.11 Only a proportion of those who commit crimes are arrested, as this graph shows, but not all of those arrested are prosecuted. In 1975, 20 percent of adults arrested were not prosecuted. The selection process continues in the courts. In the case of forcible rape, for example, arrests were made in 51 percent of the cases reported, but 46 percent of those prosecuted were acquitted or had their cases dismissed.

Figure 8.12 The social status of the offender seems to be the most significant determinant of whether a person will be arrested and convicted for an offense and of the kind of penalty that will be applied. In this picture, a police officer is preventing a black male from falling asleep in a public place. Would the officer be likely to do the same if the "offender" were a well-dressed, middle-aged white person?

to their cars and to take great care to drive carefully. Their vehicles were also carefully checked to make sure they were not defective. Within seventeen days the students had received a total of thirty-three traffic citations, and in several cases their cars were thoroughly searched as well. The experiment came to an end at this point because a fund to pay fines had been completely exhausted.

The process of selecting the criminal continues when the offender appears in court. Although every accused person has the right to counsel, to pretrial bail, to a jury trial, and to appeal to higher courts, the system does not work this way in practice. Many people cannot afford bail and may spend weeks or months awaiting trial; the President's Commission on Law Enforcement and Administration of Justice (1967) found that in New York City 25 percent of those arrested could not come up with the $25 that would have allowed them to go free on bail. The commission also reported that people who are not released on bail before a trial are likely to receive heavier sentences for the same offense than people who are freed. Actual courtroom procedure rarely follows the stylized confrontations seen in TV dramas. Over 90 percent of the people who appear in lower courts plead guilty and are sentenced on the spot. One reason is that the poor, unlike the rich, cannot afford their own lawyers. They have to rely on overworked court-appointed lawyers, who frequently urge them to plead guilty. Those who demand a jury trial and are eventually convicted tend to receive a more severe sentence than those who plead guilty. In effect, they are punished for wasting the court's time.

In comparison with judges in other countries, American judges have exceptional discretion in determining the severity of the sentence, and there is strong evidence that the race and social class of the offender influences judicial decisions (Seymour, 1973; D. A. Bell, 1973). In one experiment, three dozen judges were given fact sheets on hypothetical cases and asked to determine an appropriate sentence. The sheets contained the following basic information.

> "Joe Cut," 27, pleads guilty to battery. He slashed his common-law wife on the arms with a switchblade. His record showed convictions for disturbing the peace, drunkenness, and hit-and-run driving. He told a probation officer that he acted in self-defense after his wife attacked him with a broom handle. The prosecutor recommended not more than five days in jail or a $100 fine.

On half of the fact sheets, however, "Joe Cut" was described as white and on the other half as black. The judges who thought he was white gave him sentences of three to ten days, while those who thought he was black gave him sentences of five to thirty days (D. Jackson, 1974).

Judges also tend to take the social status of a convicted criminal into account before passing sentence, frequently reasoning that a higher-status offender has "already suffered" through damage to reputation and perhaps loss of employment (Oelsner, 1972). Although most convicted car thieves go to prison for three years, white business executives accused of white-collar crimes involving much larger sums are more likely to be fined or to receive very short sentences. An outstanding example of differential treatment of offenders was provided by the trials that followed the Watergate and related scandals. Vice-President Agnew pleaded "no contest" to a charge of tax evasion and received a fine, without even having to face the more serious charges that the money on which he had not paid taxes was obtained through bribery and extortion. High-status offenders in the Watergate cases generally received fines or light sentences or were still out on bail years after they were charged, but low-status offenders—such as the actual burglars who followed their superiors' instructions—were still in prison years later.

Prisons

Prisons are a relatively recent innovation. Until two centuries ago convicts were more likely to be executed, tortured, deported, or exposed to public ridicule in the stocks. The original idea behind the prison was that it would provide the convict with the opportunity for solitary repentance and thus for rehabilitation, but this goal has certainly not been achieved in practice. Imprisonment is now regarded as having several distinct functions: *punishment* for the crime, *deterrence* for others who might be tempted to commit the crime themselves, *incapacitation* of the offenders by removing them from society, and *rehabilitation* by giving them the attitudes and skills that will enable them to take up a law-abiding life on release. A recent Harris poll showed that nearly 80 percent of the American public believes that rehabilitation should be the main aim of the prisons, but they are clearly failing in that task. Although the United States spends more than $1 billion a year on penal institutions, only five cents in each dollar is spent on rehabilitation. The FBI's 1975 crime report shows that 74 percent of offenders released after serving their prison time were rearrested within four years. Since other released prisoners presumably also returned to crime but were not arrested, the actual rate of crime among released convicts is probably even greater.

About 1.3 million offenders are held each day in the nation's 5000 local and county jails and 400 state and federal prisons. About half of these inmates have not been convicted of any crime, and of these, four out of five are eligible for bail but cannot raise the cash. Because its custodial function takes priority over all other goals, a prison is organized as what Erving Goffman (1961) terms a *total institution*. Such institutions, which include army camps, traditional boarding schools, and mental asylums, are places of residence where the inmates are confined for an entire period of their lives. The inmates are all in a similar situation, are cut off from the rest of society, and are under the absolute control of the administrative authorities. Entry into a total institution is a process of transition in which people give up their former, self-determining roles and assume the roles of inmates. The new entrants are identified, examined, and coded and are

PERCENT REPEATERS BY TYPE OF CRIME

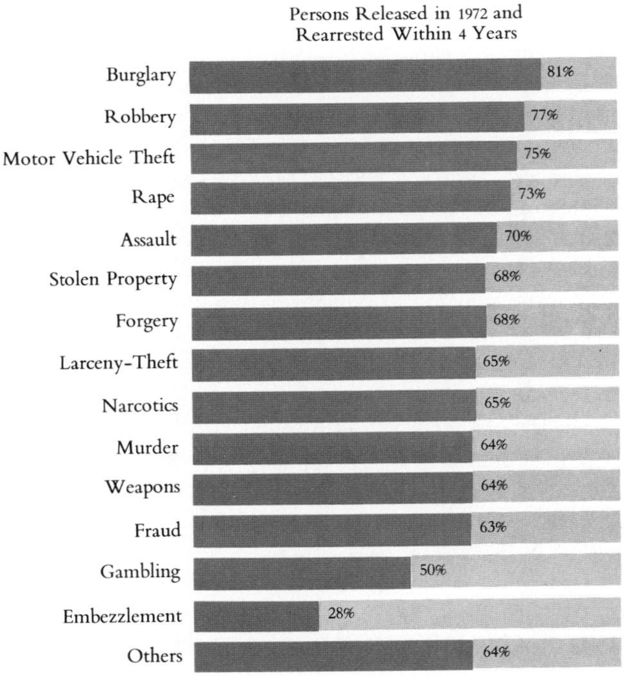

	Persons Released in 1972 and Rearrested Within 4 Years
Burglary	81%
Robbery	77%
Motor Vehicle Theft	75%
Rape	73%
Assault	70%
Stolen Property	68%
Forgery	68%
Larceny-Theft	65%
Narcotics	65%
Murder	64%
Weapons	64%
Fraud	63%
Gambling	50%
Embezzlement	28%
Others	64%

Source: Crime in the United States: Uniform Crime Reports (Washington, D.C.: U.S. Government Printing Office, 1975), p. 45.

Figure 8.13 A substantial proportion of convicted offenders repeat their crime within a few years of conviction. The existing system of treating offenders is clearly failing in what most Americans, according to opinion polls, consider its main task to be: the reform of criminals.

stripped of their personal possessions and issued uniforms. There is an absolute cleavage between the administrators and the residents; the latter surrender all personal control of their lives and are deprived of liberty, heterosexual outlets, and personal autonomy. Goffman argues forcefully that the very nature of a total institution is such that it aggravates the existing problems of the inmates and in the long run makes them incapable of assuming normal social responsibilities.

Advocates of prison reform also point to the effects of the differential association with other criminals that the prison environment guarantees. A Harris Poll taken in the early seventies revealed that nearly two-thirds of American adults believe that "jails are the real breeders of crime," a view that probably has considerable validity. Prison inmates can scarcely fail to learn about new possibilities and techniques for crime. Separated from the rest of society and thrown into the company of criminals, they encounter "an excess of definitions favorable to violation of the law" and may become predisposed toward further crime, and not rehabilitation. The argument that radical reform of the corrections system is desirable does not mean, of course, that society should be "soft" on all criminals: some may be so dangerous and unreformable that imprisonment is the only alternative. James Q. Wilson (1975), for example, offers the interesting argument that society should stop wasting its energies on the counterproductive practice of imprisoning petty offenders, for whom other forms of correction might be more appropriate, but should concentrate on incapacitating dangerous and persistent offenders by locking them up for very long periods if necessary.

The Social Consequences of Deviance

Deviance has a number of social consequences. Some of these consequences are dysfunctional and some of them are functional to society.

Dysfunctions of Deviance

The most obvious dysfunction of deviance is that widespread violation of significant social norms can disrupt social order. A society can survive only if its members generally behave in expected and socially approved ways. Major and extensive deviations from important norms make social life unpredictable and can cause tensions and conflict between conformist and deviant groups. What is true of society as a whole is also true of smaller groups within society. The idle worker can disrupt the flow of the assembly line, the psychotic can disrupt the family, the embezzler can disrupt the commercial enterprise.

A second dysfunction of widespread deviance is that it diverts social resources into efforts at social control when those resources could more usefully be directed elsewhere. Crime control in the United States is a case in point. Our society would benefit considerably if the resources devoted to controlling this form of deviance could be channeled instead to more productive uses.

A third dysfunction of deviance is that it undermines trust. Social relationships are based on the assumption that people will behave according to accepted norms of conduct: that they will not break contracts, not exploit friendships, not molest children left in their care, not rob strangers they meet in the street. Widespread deviance undermines this trust and generates anxiety in everyone, conformists and deviants alike.

A fourth dysfunction of deviance is that if it goes unpunished in some people, it undermines other people's will to conform. The example of the stigmatized deviant is a powerful incentive to others to abide by the rules, and if deviants are seen to "get away with it," other people may be tempted to do the same. Many forms of deviance are pleasurable and profitable for the individual but disruptive for society, and unless deviance is closely controlled it can spread, with disruptive consequences.

Functions of Deviance

The most important function of deviance is probably the one identified by Durkheim: the existence of deviance helps to clarify social norms and indicate the limits of social tolerance. It might be said that if there were no deviants, there could be no conformists; there can be no "we" without a corresponding "they."

The second function of deviance is implied by the first. By collectively reacting against deviants and deviance, conforming members of society reaffirm their norms and values and sense their group solidarity. Provided it is kept within reasonable limits, deviance has the function of maintaining social integration and cohesion.

A third function of deviance is that it serves as a safety valve for social discontent; people can violate the rules rather than attack the rules themselves. Resorting to prostitution, for example, allows men to find sexual satisfaction outside the marriage system without directly attacking the system. Prostitution involves an anonymous relationship without any emotional attachments. If the institution did not exist, nonmarital sexual relations would be more likely to involve emotional attachments and the marriage system itself would be threatened. Deviance can thus function to take the strain off the social order by preventing an excessive accumulation of discontent (Cohen, 1959).

A fourth function of deviance is that it may serve to signal some defect in social organization. In certain circumstances *institutionalized evasion* of norms occurs—large-scale, patterned deviance involving many or most people in society. The institutionalized evasion that accompanied Prohibition or "blue laws" forbidding Sunday entertainment are useful examples; they showed that existing legislation was simply unenforceable. Other forms of deviance—such as excessive rates of alcoholism in some social group or truancy from a particular school—also provide a signal that something is amiss (Cohen, 1959; Coser, 1962).

A final function of deviance is that it is often a source of social change: what is deviant today may be comformist tomorrow. Any person or group that sets out to change existing norms risks stigmatization for deviance, but these changes may be necessary and may not come about as effectively or as quickly unless people are prepared to take this risk. A contemporary example is offered by the early women's liberation movement. Its leaders were initially ridiculed, scorned, and accused of lesbianism or sexual frustration, but the "deviant" roles and attitudes they espoused are rapidly becoming "conformist." In some social groups today, a woman who adheres to traditional sex roles may well risk being regarded as somewhat deviant herself.

Deviance is not intrinsically "good" or "bad." It can be socially useful or threatening, depending on the circumstances. Nor is it a rare or temporary phenomenon that suddenly afflicts a society. It is an inevitable—and sometimes constructive—product of social living.

Summary

1. Deviance refers to socially disapproved violations of important norms and expectations; deviants share the characteristic of stigma. Deviance is a relative matter, because the determination of who is deviant depends on who makes the definition.

2. Deviance signals a failure of social control. Social control is applied through the socialization process and through sanctions, which may be formal or informal, positive or negative. Some measure of deviance, however, reinforces social control by demonstrating the consequences of deviance to the rest of society.

3. Biological theories attempt to explain deviance in terms of inherited characteristics. Lombroso proposed that criminal tendencies are inherited. Sheldon proposed that they are linked to body type. Recent research suggests that some specific deviant tendencies, such as some forms of mental disorder, may have hormonal or chromosomal origins, but no general category of deviance has been linked to inherited characteristics.

4. Anomie theory, as propounded by Merton, explains deviance as the result of a discrepancy between socially approved goals and access to socially approved means of achieving them. Individual reaction to this situation may take the form of conformity, innovation, ritualism, retreatism, or rebellion. This theory has been usefully applied to juvenile gangs.

5. Cultural transmission theory, especially as expressed in the concept of differential association, regards deviant behavior as learned through intensive and regular contacts with other deviants. In a culturally heterogeneous society, people's acceptance of subcultural values may make them deviant in the eyes of the wider society.

6. Labeling theory explains deviance as a process through which some people successfully label others as deviant. People who engage in primary deviance may become habitual, secondary deviants after being labeled. Labeling often involves a conflict of values and interests; the socially powerful are able to label others as deviant in accordance with their own values.

7. Crimes may be conveniently classified into the categories of juvenile delinquency, crimes without victims, white-collar crime, organized crime, and crimes against

property and persons. Crime statistics are suspect, for they reflect only the crimes most likely to be reported and the criminals most likely to be arrested.

8. The selection of criminals involves a long process in which higher-status offenders are disproportionately more likely to escape sanctions. Only a small minority of offenders are ultimately imprisoned. Prisons are total institutions, and their nature is such that they are ineffective at rehabilitation.

9. Deviance has several dysfunctions: it disrupts social order, diverts social resources, undermines trust, and, if deviants go unpunished, undermines the will of others to conform. Deviance also has several functions: it clarifies social norms, maintains social integration among conformists, serves as a "safety valve" for discontent, signals defeats in social organization, and is a source of social change.

Important Terms

deviance
stigma
social control
sanctions
positive sanctions
negative sanctions
formal sanctions
informal sanctions
anomie
conformity
innovation
ritualism
retreatism
rebellion
cultural transmission
differential association
labeling
primary deviance
secondary deviance
deviant career
crime
total institution

Suggested Readings

BECKER, HOWARD S. *Outsiders.* New York: Free Press, 1963.

A highly influential book in which Becker outlines the labeling theory of deviance and applies the theory to various "outsiders," such as marijuana smokers.

CLINARD, MARSHALL B. *Sociology of Deviant Behavior.* Englewood Cliffs, N.J.: Prentice-Hall, 1974.

A comprehensive text on the sociology of deviance. The book is recommended for the student who wants to study the subject in detail.

DOUGLAS, JACK D. *Observations of Deviance.* New York: Random House, 1970.

A useful collection of articles on many different types of deviant behavior, many of them by researchers who used the method of participant observation.

ERIKSON, KAI T. *Wayward Puritans.* New York: Wiley, 1966.

A study of the early Puritans in Massachusetts. Erikson shows that the Puritans created deviants where none really existed and thus affirmed their own normality and solidarity.

MITFORD, JESSICA. *Kind and Usual Punishment.* New York: Alfred A. Knopf, 1973.

A critical look at the American criminal justice system. The book is interestingly written and contains many illustrations of failures in the system.

SZASZ, THOMAS. *The Manufacture of Madness.* New York: Harper & Row, 1970.

A highly controversial book, in which Szasz argues forcefully that the label of "mental illness" is often used by society as a means of social control over certain types of deviants.

Reading

The Saints and the Roughnecks *William J. Chambliss*

Two youth gangs in a small community were equally delinquent. Yet one gang was perceived by the community as nothing more than a group of high-spirited youths having a good time; while the other was perceived as delinquent. Chambliss uses labeling theory to explain why.

Eight promising young men—children of good, stable, white upper-middle-class families, active in school affairs, good pre-college students—were some of the most delinquent boys at Hanibal High School. The Saints were constantly occupied with truancy, drinking, wild driving, petty theft and vandalism. Yet not one was officially arrested for any misdeed during the two years I observed them.

This record was particularly surprising in light of my observations during the same two years of another gang of Hanibal High School students, six lower-class white boys known as the Roughnecks. The Roughnecks were constantly in trouble with police and community even through their rate of delinquency was about equal with that of the Saints. What was the cause of this disparity?

By midnight on Fridays and Saturdays the Saints were usually thoroughly high, and one or two of them were often so drunk they had to be carried to the cars. Then the boys drove around town, calling obscenities to women and girls; occasionally trying (unsuccessfully so far as I could tell) to pick girls up; and driving recklessly through red lights and at high speeds with their lights out. Occasionally they played "chicken."

Searching for "fair game" for a prank was the boys' principal activity after they left the tavern. The boys would drive alongside a foot patrolman and ask directions to some street. If the policeman leaned on the car in the course of answering the question, the driver would speed away, causing him to lose his balance. The Saints were careful to play this prank only in an area where they were not going to spend much time and where they could quickly disappear around a corner to avoid having their license plate number taken.

Construction sites and road repair areas were the special province of the Saints' mischief. A soon-to-be-repaired hole in the road inevitably invited the Saints to remove lanterns and wooden barricades and put them in the car, leaving the hole unprotected. The boys would find a safe vantage point and wait for an unsuspecting motorist to drive into the hole. Often, though not always, the boys would go up to the motorist and commiserate with him about the dreadful way the city protected its citizenry.

Leaving the scene of the open hole and the motorist, the boys would then go searching for an appropriate place to erect the stolen barricade. An "appropriate place" was often a spot on a highway near a curve in the road where the barricade would not be seen by an oncoming motorist. The boys would wait to watch an unsuspecting motorist attempt to stop and (usually) crash into the wooden barricade. With saintly bearing the boys might offer help.

Abandoned houses, especially if they were located in out-of-the-way places, were fair game for destruction and spontaneous vandalism. The boys would break windows, remove furniture to the yard and tear it apart, urinate on the walls and scrawl obscenities inside.

The Saints were highly successful in school. The average grade for the group was "B," with two of the boys having close to a straight "A" average. Almost all of the boys were popular and many of them held offices in the school. One of the boys was vice-president of the student body one year. Six of the boys played on athletic teams.

At the end of their senior year, the student body selected ten seniors for special recognition as the "school wheels"; four of the ten were Saints. Teachers and school officials saw no problem with any of these boys and anticipated that they would all "make something of themselves."

How the boys managed to maintain this impression is surprising in view of their actual behavior while in school. Their technique for covering truancy was so successful that teachers did not even realize that the boys were absent from school much of the time. Occasionally, of course, the system would backfire and then the boy was on his own. A boy who was caught would be most contrite, would plead guilty and ask for mercy. He inevitably got the mercy he sought.

The local police saw the Saints as good boys who were among the leaders of the youth in the community. Rarely, the boys might be stopped in town for speeding or for running a stop sign. When this happened the boys were always polite, contrite and pled for mercy. As in school, they received the mercy they asked for. None ever received a ticket or was taken into the precinct by the local police.

Hanibal townspeople never perceived the Saints' high level of delinquency. The Saints were good boys who just went in for an occasional prank. After all, they were well dressed, well mannered and had nice cars. The Roughnecks were a different story. Although the two gangs of boys were the same age, and both groups engaged in an equal amount of wild-oat sowing, everyone agreed that the not-so-well-dressed, not-so-well-mannered, not-so-rich boys were heading for trouble.

The fighting activities of the group were fairly readily and accurately perceived by almost everyone. At least once a month, the boys would get into some sort of fight, although most fights were scraps between members of the group or involved only one member of the group and some peripheral hanger-on.

More serious than fighting, had the community been aware of it, was theft. Although almost everyone was aware that the boys occasionally stole things, they did not realize the extent of the activity. Petty stealing was a frequent event for the Roughnecks. Sometimes they stole as a group and coordinated their efforts; other times they stole in pairs. Rarely did they steal alone.

The thefts ranged from very small things like paperback books, comics and ballpoint pens to expensive items like watches. The nature of the thefts varied from time to time. The gang would go through a period of systematically shoplifting items from automobiles or school lockers. Types of thievery varied with the whim of the gang. Some forms of thievery were more profitable than others, but all thefts were for profit, not just thrills.

Roughnecks siphoned gasoline from cars as often as they had access to an automobile, which was not very often. Unlike the Saints, who owned their own cars, the Roughnecks would have to borrow their parents' cars, an event which occurred only eight or nine times a year. The boys claimed to have stolen cars for joy rides from time to time.

There was a high level of mutual distrust and dislike between the Roughnecks and the police. The boys felt very strongly that the police were unfair and corrupt. Some evidence existed that the boys were correct in their perception.

The main source of the boys' dislike for the police undoubtedly stemmed from the fact that the police would sporadically harass the group. From the standpoint of the boys, these acts of occasional enforcement of the law were whimsical and uncalled for. It made no sense to them, for example, that the police would come to the corner occasionally and threaten them with arrest for loitering when the night before the boys had been out siphoning gasoline from cars and the police had been nowhere in sight. To the boys, the police were stupid on the one hand, for not being where they should have been and catching the boys in a serious offense, and unfair on the other hand, for trumping up "loitering" charges against them.

Over the period that the group was under observation, each member was arrested at least once. Several of the boys were arrested a number of times and spent at least one night in jail. While most were never taken to court, two of the boys were sentenced to six months' incarceration in boys' schools.

The Roughnecks' behavior in school was not particularly disruptive. During school hours they did not all hang around together, but tended instead to spend most of their time with one or two other members of the gang who were their special buddies. Although every member of the gang attempted to avoid school as much as possible, they were not particularly successful and most of them attended school with surprising regularity. They considered school a burden—something to be gotten through with a minimum of conflict.

Teachers saw the boys the way the general community did, as heading for trouble, as being uninterested in making something of themselves. Some were also seen as being incapable of meeting the academic standards of the school. Most of the teachers expressed concern for this group of boys and were willing to pass them despite poor performance, in the belief that failing them would only aggravate the problem.

Why did the community, the school and the police react to the Saints as though they were good, upstanding, nondelinquent youths with bright futures but to the Roughnecks as though they were tough, young criminals who were headed for trouble? Why did the Roughnecks and the Saints in fact have quite different careers after high school—careers which, by and large, lived up to the expectations of the community?

Differential treatment of the two gangs resulted in part because one gang was infinitely more visible than the other. This differential visibility was a direct function of the economic standing of the families. The Saints had access to automobiles and were able to remove themselves from the sight of the community. In as routine a decision as to where to go to have a milkshake after school, the Saints stayed away from the mainstream of community life. Lacking transportation, the Roughnecks could not make it to the edge of town. The center of town was the only practical place for them to meet since their homes were scattered throughout the town and any noncentral meeting place put an undue hardship on some members. Through necessity the Roughnecks congregated in a crowded area where everyone in the community passed frequently, including teachers and law enforcement officers. They could easily see the Roughnecks hanging around the drugstore.

On their escapades the Saints were also relatively invisible, since they left Hanibal and travelled to Big City. Here, too, they were mobile, roaming the city, rarely going to the same area twice.

To the notion of visibility must be added the difference in the responses of group members to outside intervention with their activities. If one of the Saints was confronted with an accusing policeman, even if he felt he was truly innocent of a wrongdoing, his demeanor was apologetic and penitent. A Roughneck's attitude was almost the polar opposite. When confronted with a threatening adult authority, even one who tried to be pleasant, the Roughneck's hostility and disdain were clearly observable. Sometimes he might attempt to put up a veneer of respect, but it was thin and was not accepted as sincere by the authority.

In the eyes of the police and school officials, a boy who drinks in an alley and stands intoxicated on the street corner is committing a more serious offense than is a boy who drinks to inebriation in a nightclub or a tavern and drives around afterwards in a car. Similarly, a boy who steals a wallet from a store will be viewed as having committed a more serious offense than a boy who steals a lantern from a construction site.

Visibility, demeanor and bias are surface variables which explain the day-to-day operations of the police. Why do these surface variables operate as they do? Why did the police choose to disregard the Saints' delinquencies while breathing down the backs of the Roughnecks?

The answer lies in the class structure of American society and the control of legal institutions by those at the top of the class structure. Obviously, no representative of the upper class drew up the operational chart for the police which led them to look in the ghettoes and on streetcorners—which led them to see the demeanor of lower-class youth as troublesome and that of upper-middle-class youth as tolerable. Rather, the procedures simply developed from experience—experience with irate and influential upper-middle-class parents insisting that their son's vandalism was simply a prank and his drunkenness only a momentary "sowing of wild oats"—experience with cooperative or indifferent, powerless, lower-class parents who acquiesced to the laws' definition of their son's behavior.

The community responded to the Roughnecks as boys in trouble, and the boys agreed with that perception. Their pattern of deviancy was reinforced, and breaking away from it became increasingly unlikely. Once the boys acquired an image of themselves as deviants, they selected new friends who affirmed that self-image. As that self-conception became more firmly entrenched, they also became willing to try new and more extreme deviances. With their growing alienation came freer expression of disrespect and hostility for representatives of the legitimate society. This disrespect increased the community's negativism, perpetuating the entire process of commitment to deviance. Lack of a commitment to deviance works the same way.

Selective perception and labeling—finding, processing and punishing some kinds of criminality and not others—means that visible, poor, nonmobile, outspoken, undiplomatic "tough" kids will be noticed, whether their actions are seriously delinquent or not. Other kids, who have established a reputation for being bright (even though underachieving), disciplined and involved in respectable activities, who are mobile and monied, will be invisible when they deviate from sanctioned activities. They'll sow their wild oats—perhaps even wider and thicker than their lower-class cohorts—but they won't be noticed. When it's time to leave adolescence most will follow the expected path, settling into the ways of the middle class, remembering fondly the delinquent but unnoticed fling of their youth. The Roughnecks and others like them may turn around, too. It is more likely that their noticeable deviance will have been so reinforced by police and community that their lives will be effectively channelled into careers consistent with their adolescent background.

Source: William J. Chambliss, "The Saints and the Roughnecks," *Society,* (November 1973), pp. 24–31.

CHAPTER 9 *Sexuality and Society*

CHAPTER OUTLINE

The Nature of Human Sexuality

Sexual Behavior in Other Cultures
Concepts of Beauty
Restrictiveness and Permissiveness
Heterosexual Behavior
Homosexual Behavior
Evaluation

Sexual Behavior in the United States
Traditional Values
Contemporary Practices

The Incest Taboo

Homosexuality
Incidence of Homosexuality
The Homosexual Community
Causes of Homosexuality

Prostitution
Types of Prostitution
Prostitution as an Occupation
Reasons for Prostitution
Can Prostitution Be Eliminated?

For centuries, the societies of the Western world have shrouded sexuality in myth, taboo, and ignorance. Even sociologists, supposedly dedicated to studying social behavior regardless of the prejudices and obstacles in the way, have hesitated until recently to accept human sexuality as a legitimate field of research. A distinctive sociology of sex has emerged only since World War II, and although the subdiscipline is now growing rapidly, it is still often regarded as a marginal sociological concern. Yet the fact remains that every society contains two sexes, a feature that obviously has important and far-reaching implications for personal behavior and social life.

Sexuality is a significant ingredient of individual personality. Our self-concepts are strongly influenced by our feelings about our own sexuality—feelings that may range from ones of competence or incompetence to ones of guilt or moral self-righteousness. Much of our leisure time is occupied with sexual acts, thoughts, feelings, or even fears. Even in situations that are not defined as sexual—the street, the workplace, the college dining hall—undertones and overtones of sexuality are often present. Interpersonal communications and relationships are often rich in various forms of sexual expression, ranging from overt acts to the most subtle glances, gestures, and other signals.

Sexual relationships have an even greater importance in the broader societal context, especially when they are institutionalized in the form of marriage. The sexual bond between husband and wife is the basis of the marital arrangement, and marriage, in turn, is the basis of the family. The family is the fundamental unit in the social structure of all societies. It is responsible for, among other things, legitimate birth, primary socialization, the allocation of many ascribed statuses to its members, economic consumption, and the transmission of property and other rights from generation to generation. It is small wonder, then, that every society carefully regulates the sexual behavior of its inhabitants, channeling their biological potentials into socially acceptable outlets that are defined and generally accepted as natural, normal, and moral.

The public discussion of sexuality in the Western world is barely three-quarters of a century old. It dates primarily from the work of the psychoanalyst Sigmund Freud (1856–1939), who shocked many of his contemporaries when he claimed that sexual impulses are present in human beings from the time of birth and are a crucial factor in adult personality. Other sex researchers, such as Havelock Ellis (1859–1939), amassed a great deal of data on sexual behavior, much of it impressionistic and sometimes inaccurate. These early researchers were continually harassed by critics who regarded the mere investigation of the subject as immoral. The breakthrough in sex research came in 1948, when the zoologist Alfred Kinsey published a massive volume on the sexual behavior of American men, followed in 1953 by a companion volume on American women. Kinsey's surveys, which were sociological in method and presentation, became best sellers and led to a series of specifically sociological investigations into many aspects of sexual behavior.

The sociological perspective on human sexuality may at first seem to run counter to common sense and everyday experience. The sex drive appears to be essentially biological in its character and mode of expression. It involves the use of specific bodily organs and is linked to the biological process of maturation. To most people nothing seems more natural, or even more "instinctive," than they they should mate in a particular way with a member of the opposite sex. But this popular view is simply wrong. *Human sexual behavior is learned through the socialization process and conforms to (or deviates in a patterned way from) the prevailing norms of the society concerned.* Sexual behavior and feelings are learned through interaction with other people. Unlike most other animals, we do not make our sexual responses in a manner dictated by our genes. We talk, think, and learn about sex. We place complex meanings on physical acts and personal emotions, and we do so according to the cultural

Figure 9.1 Sexuality is an important element in both personal and social life. As this picture suggests, sexual thoughts and feelings are present even in everyday situations that are not usually defined as sexual. Although taboos against the public discussion of sex hampered sociological research in the area for many decades, the sociology of sex is now a rapidly growing field.

definitions offered by our society. Ideas about what is sexually appropriate or inappropriate, moral or immoral, erotic or offensive, are purely social in origin. Even people who deviate from the prevailing norms tend to do so in predictable ways that are typical of each society.

Many aspects of human sexuality are still imperfectly understood. One reason is that continuing social inhibitions on sex research have hindered the accumulation of the necessary information. Another reason is that sex research, like most research in the social sciences, has been affected by the sexist bias of our culture; we know far more about male sexuality than female sexuality. But there is now sufficient knowledge about sexual attitudes and behavior, in our own society and in many others, to provide an intelligent understanding of the subject. In this chapter we will first examine the nature of human sexuality, especially as it is revealed in the widely varying practices of different societies. Then we will review what is known about contemporary American sexual values and sexual behavior. Finally, we will apply the sociological perspective to three specific topics: the incest taboo, homosexuality, and prostitution.

The Nature of Human Sexuality

There is now a general agreement among researchers in several disciplines that human sexual behavior is extremely flexible and that we are capable of learning to attach our erotic desires to almost anything—human beings, animals, inanimate objects such as shoes or underwear, or even the experience of pain and humiliation. Kingsley Davis (1971), one of the first sociologists to study sexual behavior, states flatly that "like other forms of behavior, sexual activity must be learned. Without socialization, human beings would not even know how to copulate." John Gagnon and William Simon (1973), two prominent modern sociologists of sex, observe that "the very experience of sexual excitement that seems to originate from hidden internal sources is in fact a learned process and it is only our insistence on the myth of naturalness that hides these social components from us." Alfred Kinsey (1953), a zoologist, wrote that "It is not so difficult to explain why a human animal does a particular thing sexually. It is more difficult to explain why each and every individual is not involved in every type of activity." Similar views have been expressed by psychologists, anthropologists, and medical scientists (for example, Money and Ehrhardt, 1972; Coleman, 1976; Ford and Beach, 1951). The same principle seems to apply to some higher primates as well. Harry Harlow's experiments with rhesus monkeys (discussed in Chapter 5, Socialization) have shown that if monkeys are raised in isolation, they do not know how to copulate in later life, and it is extremely difficult, especially in the case of the males, to teach them how to do so.

The human sex drive can usefully be compared to the hunger drive. We all have an innate tendency to feel hungry periodically, but we have to learn through the socialization process what we may eat and what we may not eat, although different societies teach rather different lessons in this regard. By taking various objects into its mouth, the infant soon learns which are edible and which are not. But the growing child also learns through interaction with other people that some items, although edible, are taboo and may not be eaten. Unlike the inhabitants of some societies, the well-socialized American who encounters a dog, roach, or woodlouse does not for one moment consider the creature as "food": we have what seems to be an "instinctive," but is in fact a learned, aversion to the idea. The process by which we learn norms of sexual conduct is similar. We start with a basic, undirected drive and learn through the socialization process to recognize some stimuli as nonsexual, some as sexual and appropriate, and some as potentially sexual but taboo. The fact that our sex drive is so flexible is, of course, the reason every society goes to such lengths to regulate it. If we would all behave in a rigid and predictable manner without the guidelines supplied by powerful norms and taboos, there would be no need for these controls and they would not exist (McKee and Robertson, 1975).

Sexual Behavior in Other Cultures

There are great variations in the sexual practices institutionalized by other societies, but two general norms are universal. First, in no society may people mate at random. Every society has an *incest taboo* that specifies certain classes of relatives as being ineligible as sexual partners. Second, every society insists on some degree of conformity to a norm of genital, heterosexual intercourse within the context of marriage. Without this norm there might be so much nonreproductive sexual activity that both the family and the society's capacity to reproduce itself would be undermined.

The most comprehensive study of cross-cultural variations in sexual behavior is that of Clellan Ford and Frank Beach (1951), who analyzed data from the United States and from 190 traditional, preindustrial societies. The data for these small-scale societies were drawn from the ethnographic reports of visiting anthropologists, and the societies themselves were selected to provide as diverse a cultural and geographical sample as possible. The following data are drawn from the Ford and Beach study unless otherwise indicated.

Concepts of Beauty

There is little data on the standards by which the attractiveness of men is judged in other cultures. One reason may be that anthropologists did not ask about or record this kind of information. Another reason is that most cultures have more specific ideas about female than about male beauty, for men are much more likely to be valued for characteristics other than physical appearance. Data on concepts of female beauty are plentiful, however. There appear to be few if any universal standards of female beauty and sexual attractiveness. Some peoples regard the shape and color of the eyes as the main determinant of beauty; others are more concerned about the formation of the mouth, nose, or ears. In some societies small, slim women are admired, but there is a strong cross-cultural tendency for men to prefer plump women; in some African societies the sexy woman is one who is positively fat. The Thonga of eastern Africa admire a woman who is tall and powerful, while the Tongans of Polynesia are more concerned that her ankles should be small. The Masai of eastern Africa prefer women with small breasts, while the Apache prefer women with very large breasts. In many tropical societies women do not cover their breasts, but this does not mean that the men are in a constant state of erotic frenzy. The breasts are simply not considered a sexual stimulus at all, and attention may focus instead on the legs, buttocks, back, or elsewhere. Notions of beauty have also changed over time in Western culture: the ideal female form depicted in the work of Reubens, Rembrandt, or Raphael is, to modern eyes, distinctly plump.

Restrictiveness and Permissiveness

Most societies in the Ford and Beach sample were permissive rather than restrictive in their attitudes toward sexual behavior. Only ten of the societies wholly disapproved of both premarital and extramarital intercourse. Like the United States, these *restrictive* societies practice a public conspiracy to keep sexual knowledge from children, but some of them carry their restrictions even further. Among the Arapaho Indians, for example, the sexes were strictly segregated from childhood and could not play together; in later adolescence they could meet only in the presence of chaperones. Among the Gilbertese Islanders of the Pacific a girl who was seduced could be put to death with her seducer, and among the Vedda of Ceylon a man seen merely talking to an unmarried woman could be killed by her relatives.

These attitudes contrast sharply with those of more *permissive* societies. Well over a third of the societies in the sample allow some form of what we would call adultery. The Siriono of Bolivia permit a man to have sexual relations with his wife's sisters and with his brother's wives and their sisters. Among the Toda of southern India married men and women are free to form sexual liaisons with others; their language contains no word for adultery. Among many peoples, such as the Lesu of the Pacific, sexual knowledge is fully available to young children, and the parents openly copulate in front of them. The Trukese of the Carolines encourage sexual experimentation by their children, and little huts are constructed outside the main compound for the purpose. The Lepcha of the Himalayas believe that small girls will not mature without the benefit of sexual intercourse, and Trobriand Island parents gave their children sexual instruction at a very early age, enabling them to begin full intercourse at the age of six to eight for girls and ten to twelve for boys.

Heterosexual Behavior

The norms governing adult *heterosexual behavior* are subject to very wide cross-cultural variation. Even the position that the partners adopt in sexual intercourse differs from one society to another. The usual position in the United States and most Western societies is for the couple to lie face to face with the male on top; Kinsey found that 70 percent of American couples had never tried any other position. In the South Sea Islands this Western habit was laughingly termed the "missionary position" by incredulous women who had had sexual intercourse with visiting missionaries, for the position was quite unknown to them. In a survey of the evidence from 131 other societies, the anthropologist Clyde Kluckhohn (1948) found that the "missionary position" was customary or preferred in only 17 cases. Other peoples conduct intercourse from the side, from the rear, with the female on top, with the male kneeling over the female, and in many other possible positions.

The context and content of heterosexual intercourse is also highly variable. Some peoples regard full nakedness as desirable or obligatory; others, as quite improper or even dangerous. The Hopi Indians insist that intercourse take place indoors; the Witoto of South America insist that it take place outside. The Masai of eastern Africa believe that intercourse in the daytime can be fatal; the Chenchu of India believe that intercourse at night can lead to the birth of a blind child. Some people insist on privacy; others are indifferent to the presence of observers. Some, such as the Trobriand Islanders, believe that women are sexually insatiable and expect them to take the initiative in sexual contact; others, such as the Chiricahua Indians, assume and expect that a woman will remain completely passive. Kissing is unknown in some societies; the Siriono consider it a particularly disgusting act. Foreplay before intercourse is unknown among the Lepcha but may occupy several hours among the Ponapeans of the Pacific. Kinsey (1948) found that the great majority of American males reach orgasm within two minutes of starting intercourse, but the Marquesan men of the Pacific habitually perform for hours. Even the frequency of intercourse is related to cultural norms. The Keraki of New Guinea are reported to average once a week, Americans two or three times a week, and the Aranda of Australia three or five times a night; the Chagga of eastern Africa are alleged to manage ten episodes in a single night. Some peoples have learned to experience violence during intercourse as erotically exciting. The Siriono find pleasure in poking their fingers into each others' eyes; Choroti women in South America spit in their partners' faces; Ponapean men tug out tufts of their mates' hair; and Apinaye women in the Brazilian jungle are reported to bite off pieces of their lovers' eyebrows, noisily spitting them aside to enhance the erotic effect.

Figure 9.2

"What's new on the sexual front? Are our chaps still on top?"

Homosexual Behavior

Attitudes toward *homosexual behavior* vary widely. In a minority of the societies in the Ford and Beach sample homosexual behavior is thoroughly disapproved of; some peoples react only with ridicule, but others, such as the Rwala Bedouins, consider the death penalty an appropriate response. In 64 percent of the societies, however, homosexuality is tolerated, approved, or even required—either for some members of the community all the time, or for all males in the community for some of the time. Male homosexuality is almost everywhere more common and more likely to be accepted than female homosexuality. All societies that permit very extensive homosexual practices also expect the practitioners to be heterosexual or bisexual at some point in the life cycle.

Some societies, such as the Lango of eastern Africa, the Koniag of Alaska, and the Tanala of Madagascar, make provision for marriages between men. In a few societies, particularly in Siberia and among some Indian peoples of North and South America, the homosexual role was institutionalized and specific social duties were attached to it, often those of the tribal shaman. Clyde Kluckhohn (1948) found that male homosexuality was accepted by 120 American Indian peoples and rejected by 54; in many of the former groups the homosexual had high social status. In some societies, such as the Aranda of Australia, the Siwans of northern Africa, and the Keraki of New Guinea, every male is required to engage in exclusively homosexual behavior during adolescence but is expected to be bisexual after marriage. Among the Keraki, for example, the initiation ceremony for adolescent males requires them to take the passive role in anal intercourse for a full year; thereafter they spend the remainder of their youth initiating younger boys in like manner. The ethnographic literature appears to record only two societies in which homosexuality is actually preferred to heterosexuality, although both these societies have also institutionalized heterosexual marriage. The Etero of New Guinea place a taboo on heterosexual intercourse for 295 days a year, while the neighboring Marindanim people are so strongly homosexual that they sometimes have to kidnap children from surrounding tribes to maintain their population (Kottak, 1974).

Evaluation

This cross-cultural evidence can be misleading in one respect, for it deals only with the sexual practices of small, preliterate societies. No comparable study of sexual practices in modern industrial societies has been made, but it seems very likely that sexual behavior in these societies, like most other aspects of their cultures, is subject to much less variation. Since the great majority of the world's population lives in industrialized or industrializing societies, it seems safe to conclude that the sexual practices of most people in the world no longer differ as radically from our own as do the practices recorded in preindustrial societies. The available cross-cultural evidence is very valuable, however, for it reveals the potential diversity of human sexual conduct.

The cross-cultural evidence also shows the interplay between our basic biological potentials and the cultural norms that we learn through the socialization process. The conclusion from the cross-cultural data is perhaps disconcerting, but it is inescapable. If you were an Alorese mother in Indonesia, you would habitually masturbate your infants to pacify them. If you were a Siwan male in northern Africa, you would engage freely in both heterosexual and homosexual intercourse, and you might lend your son to other men for sexual purposes. If you were a male Copper Eskimo, you might have intercourse with live or dead animals. If you were a Chewa parent in central Africa, you would encourage your preadolescent daughter to have intercourse in the belief that she would otherwise be infertile when she grew up. If you were a Kwoma male in New Guinea, you would have learned to regard sex as so forbidding that you would never touch your own genitals, even when urinating. If you were an adolescent girl in traditional Mohave society, you would expect your first heterosexual intercourse to involve anal penetration. You would do these things with the full knowledge and approval of your community, and if your personal tastes ran counter to the prevailing norms, you might be considered distinctly odd. Being no less ethnocentric than people in other societies, you would also regard American sexual attitudes and practices as most peculiar, to say the least.

Sexual Behavior in the United States

The most striking feature of sexuality in the United States is the tension between a tradition of highly restrictive standards, on the one hand, and a climate that values individuality and personal freedom, on the other. Restrictive patterns of sexual behavior have long been regarded as the cornerstone of public and private morality, yet the pleasures of sexual gratification are constantly extolled, implicitly and explicitly, through the mass media, through commercial advertisements, and through the exhortations and examples of social groups and movements

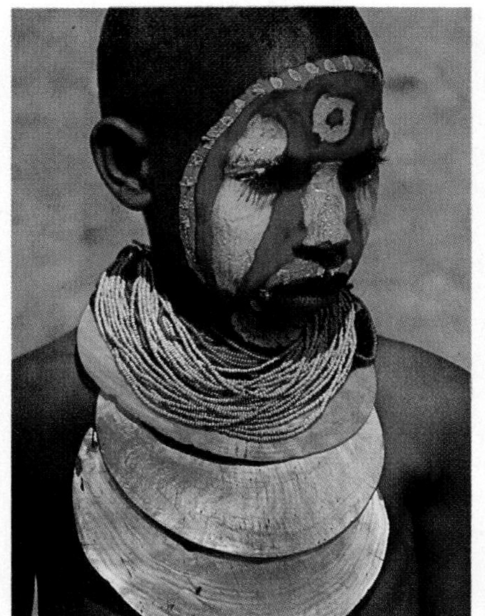

Figure 9.3 Concepts of beauty and sexual attractiveness are culturally learned; in fact, what may be attractive in one culture may be repulsive in another. The hair styles and other adornments displayed by these people show widely varying conceptions of beauty and appeal—a boy from New Guinea, white American beauty queens, a man from an Amazon jungle tribe, a couple from Nigeria, an Indian woman, and a black American woman.

that reject the traditional values. Not surprisingly, the attempt to maintain the standards of earlier generations is largely unsuccessful. As a result, there is a considerable discrepancy between the sexuality portrayed in the *ideal culture* of norms and values and the sexuality actually practiced in the *real culture* of everyday life.

Traditional Values

The traditional sexual values of American society, and of Western society in general, have their roots in a particular interpretation of ancient Judeo-Christian morality. Sexual activity can have two basic purposes: reproduction and pleasure. The Western tradition has strongly emphasized the former and has taken a generally negative attitude toward the latter. In short, sex has tended to be regarded as legitimate only if it takes place within the context of marriage and only if its primary purpose is reproduction.

The tradition that sex should be mainly for reproductive purposes comes from the Old Testament, with its strong injunction on the faithful to "be fruitful and multiply," its censure of those who "waste" their seed, and its severe penalties for those who engage in bestiality or homosexuality. Sexuality itself, however, was not regarded as sinful, and the Old Testament permitted premarital and extramarital sex under certain circumstances. (The commandment forbidding adultery refers only to adultery with someone else's spouse; under some conditions married men could have intercourse with unmarried women,

Figure 9.4 Traditional Western attitudes toward sexuality derive from a particular interpretation of Judeo-Christian morality. The Genesis tale of the sin of Adam and Eve and their subsequent expulsion from the Garden of Eden, depicted in this painting by the Italian artist Masaccio, has strong sexual overtones; forever after, the human species was sinful and nakedness was shameful. Under the influence of Saint Paul, the medieval church took a strongly negative attitude toward any sexual activity that was not aimed at reproduction; sexual activity for pleasure alone was considered immoral. Traces of this attitude still persist today.

particularly household servants.) The emphasis on premarital virginity and the blanket prohibition on sex outside of marriage comes from the New Testament—not from the teachings of Jesus, who had very little to say about sex, but from those of Saint Paul. Saint Paul recommended total abstention from sex. He believed that celibacy was preferable even to marriage and tolerated marriage only on the grounds that it was "better to marry than to burn." This view was strongly endorsed by such theologians as St. Augustine and is the source of the Catholic Church's requirement of celibacy in its priests. By the early Middle Ages sex was virtually equated with sin; the doctrines of the medieval church "were based, quite simply, upon the conviction that the sexual act was to be avoided like the plague, except for the bare minimum necessary to keep the race in existence. Even when performed for this purpose it remained a regrettable necessity. Those who could were exhorted to avoid it entirely" (G. Taylor, 1970). The church even attempted to limit the number of days on which a married couple could copulate. Sex on Sundays, Wednesdays, and eventually Fridays was forbidden, so that sexual activity was prohibited for the equivalent of about five months of the year.

Subsequent centuries were marked by alternating periods of restrictiveness and relative permissiveness, with the most restrictive attitudes occurring among the early Puritans and among the Victorians of the last century. Prudery reached its climax with the middle-class Victorians, who were unable to refer to anything remotely sexual except in the most discreet terms. Sweat became "perspiration" and then "glow"; legs became "limbs"; underwear became "unmentionables"; chicken breast became "white meat"; prostitutes became "fallen women"; pregnancy became "in an interesting condition." Women were careful to cover even their ankles from the gaze of men, and some zealots took to covering the legs of their furniture from the public view. Masturbation was regarded as a dreadful vice that rendered its practitioners liable to such maladies as deafness, blindness, heart disease, epilepsy, hair on the palms, and insanity. Some lunatic asylums even had separate wards for inmates whose condition was believed to be caused by this "self-abuse."

To the concern for reproduction and the sense of the erotic as sinful, one further ingredient was added in medieval times: the *double standard* of conduct for men and women. The tradition of chivalry and courtly love in the Middle Ages emphasized the purity and chastity of women, while acknowledging and tolerating the baser desires of men. Sex came to be seen as woman's noble duty and man's brutal pleasure. Women were expected to remain virtuous and innocent while men, although formally expected to do the same, were in reality allowed much greater freedom. The notion of the inherent purity of women led to a widely accepted myth that (with the

Figure 9.5 Although the general tendency throughout Western European history has been toward a strongly negative view of sexuality, there have been occasional periods and occasional groups in which more permissive attitudes have prevailed—as this illustration from a medieval manuscript suggests.

possible exception of prostitutes) they were essentially sexless. William Acton, a nineteenth-century expert on marriage, wrote that "the belief that women have a sexual appetite is a vile aspersion"; a surgeon-general of the United States stated that "nine-tenths of the time decent women feel not the slightest pleasure in intercourse"; and an eminent gynecologist felt that "sexual desire in a woman is pathological" (Hunt, 1959). The double standard has persisted until the present, particularly in the working class of the Western world. Premarital intercourse is frequently seen as a matter of surrender by the female and conquest by the male, with the woman's status being cheapened in the process and the man gaining status and respect among his peers.

These traditional values remain powerful in the United States today. Sex is still often regarded as somehow dirty and unmentionable, and practices that do not potentially lead to reproduction are widely considered to be perverted. Despite the introduction of sex education programs into some schools, a conspiracy of silence often still prevents the young from obtaining accurate and objective information about sex. Parents, if they discuss the subject with their offspring at all, often do so with embarrassment, and most information is acquired from the peer group. Whatever else these attitudes achieve, they certainly contribute to many problems of sexual adjustment in later life. The young are often brought up to view sex as a forbidden and taboo subject, but upon marrying they are expected to unlearn these prohibitions without difficulty. This transition is not always smoothly achieved. Frigidity in women is generally the result of earlier attitudes that sex is dirty and frightening, and impotence in men often stems from feelings of anxiousness and guilt (Cooper, 1969; Masters and Johnson, 1970, 1975).

The United States still attempts to control the private sexual behavior of consenting adults by law. About half of our states have laws against extramarital intercourse. Prostitution is illegal in every state except Nevada, where local counties can decide for themselves whether they will permit it. In addition, the great majority of states have "sodomy" laws, directed at what are often referred to as "crimes against nature." Oral-genital and anal-genital contacts, even between husband and wife, are illegal in about forty states, with penalties of up to twenty years' imprisonment. Homosexual acts were illegal in all states until the late sixties, and they still carry severe penalties in most states. Until recently Connecticut banned the use or sale of contraceptives, and Indiana has a law against encouraging anyone under twenty-one to masturbate. Some states regard any position for intercourse other than the "missionary position" as a crime against nature. Until the sixties, half the states of the Union prohibited interracial sexual relations, another interesting example of how temporary norms are confused with absolute morality. Most of these laws have fallen into disuse, but prosecutions under some of them are by no means uncommon. These laws have few parallels in the modern world outside the Soviet Union and some of its satellites. Western European nations have generally abandoned similar legislation, in some cases as long as a century ago. In 1976, however, the Supreme Court upheld the rights of states to make laws regulating the private sexual behavior of consenting adults.

Contemporary Practices

Research into the sexual practices of Americans is very limited and often unreliable. The greatest obstacle to obtaining fuller knowledge is the difficulty of surveying a representative, random sample of the population. It is easy enough to use standard surveying techniques to discover how Americans will vote or which brand of soap they use, but it is much more difficult for researchers to inquire in depth into the sex lives of complete strangers. Understandably, a large proportion of the respondents will refuse to answer such questions. Since these people may differ in unknown but perhaps significant ways from those who are willing to answer, the results of the survey may be biased. No sex researchers have yet been able to overcome this problem as far as the general population is concerned, although there are many useful studies of specific groups—prostitutes, "swingers," homosexuals, transvestites, and so on. Even these studies, however, run into the difficulty that people may not tell the truth when asked for details of their sexual practices.

The first major research into the sexual behavior of Americans was that of Alfred Kinsey, who despite considerable harrassment was able to obtain full histories of the sex lives of more than 16,000 Americans. Kinsey relied on two main sources: individual volunteers and specific groups of people, ranging from prison populations to sports clubs, which he was able to persuade to take part in his research. By trying to select people and groups from every walk of white American life, he attempted to put together a fairly representative cross-section of the white American population. His study was not statistically perfect by any means, but it remains the most ambitious and reliable sex survey ever undertaken. Only two attempts at a national survey have been made since, and both are methodologically much less satisfactory. *Playboy* magazine commissioned a random survey, reported by Morton Hunt (1974). But the actual survey did not reach a random sample of the population: it left out "strongly deviant" individuals, and, worse, some 80 percent of the respondents refused to cooperate. *Psychology Today* magazine also asked its readers to return a detailed questionnaire, whose results were reported by Robert Athanasiou *et al.* (1972). The findings, however, are presumably representative only of those readers of the magazine who responded. In addition, Robert Sorensen (1973) tried to get information from a random sample of teenagers aged thirteen to nineteen. But the parents of 40 percent of the respondents refused to allow their children to cooperate, and about 20 percent of those who were permitted to cooperate refused to do so, with the result that Sorensen's findings may also be biased in some way.

Despite these difficulties, all the evidence points overwhelmingly in the same direction. There is a glaring gap between the moral norms specifying how Americans ought to behave and the statistical norms revealing how they behave in practice. Nowhere is this more evident than in Kinsey's volumes, *Sexual Behavior in the Human Male* (1948) and *Sexual Behavior in the Human Female* (1953). Kinsey's findings stunned American society with revelations of widespread deviation from moral norms, and his work became a major element in the American popular culture of the fifties.

Kinsey found, for example, that 85 percent of all men had experienced premarital intercourse. Nearly 70 percent of the men had visited a prostitute. One man in six had as much homosexual as heterosexual experience. Over 90 percent of the men had masturbated, and nearly 60 percent had engaged in heterosexual oral-genital contacts. Half the married men had committed adultery, and a further 25 percent favored the idea of doing so. About 8 percent of the men had engaged in sexual contacts with animals, and among some rural populations the incidence rose as high as 50 percent. In accordance with the double standard, 40 percent of the men required that their wives be virgins at the time of marriage. Nearly half the women had experienced premarital intercourse, although in the great majority of cases their only partner had been their prospective husband. A quarter of the married women had committed adultery, 28 percent had had homosexual experience or desires, nearly 60 percent had masturbated, nearly 60 percent had engaged in heterosexual oral-genital contacts, and nearly 4 percent had taken part in sexual activities with animals. On the basis of the evidence, Kin-

AMERICAN ATTITUDES TO PREMARITAL SEX, 1969 and 1973

	Percent Saying Premarital Sex Is "Wrong"	
	1969	1973
Nationwide	68	48
Under 30 years	49	29
30–49 years	67	44
50 and over	80	64
Men	62	42
Women	74	53
Married	X	51
Single	X	27
College background	56	41
High school	69	45
Grade school	77	60
Protestants	70	53
Catholics	72	45
East	65	38
Midwest	69	51
South	78	58
West	55	41

Source: Gallup Poll.

Figure 9.6 Attitudes toward premarital sex have changed markedly in recent years. In 1973 some 20 percent fewer Americans believed premarital sex was "wrong" than in 1969. The 1973 data show that American values are now conforming more closely with American practices. A substantial majority of Americans have practiced premarital sex for many decades, but until recently their expressed values bore little relationship to their actual behavior.

sey (1948) concluded that "a call for a cleanup of sex offenders in the community is in effect a proposal that 5 percent of the population should support the other 95 percent in penal institutions."

Recent studies all confirm that sexual behavior in the United States is much more permissive than the moral norms would suggest. Morton Hunt's study, for example, found that 95 percent of the males and 85 percent of the females under the age of twenty-four had experienced premarital intercourse. He also found that only a quarter of his sample considered anal intercourse "wrong" and that nearly a quarter of married couples under the age of thirty-five have used the technique. Robert Sorensen's survey of teenagers found that by the age of nineteen, 59 percent of the boys and 45 percent of the girls had experienced intercourse; 13 percent of the sample had done so by the age of twelve or younger.

These findings, together with such highly publicized phenomena as readily obtained abortions, nudity in the theater, gay liberation, and the availability of pornography, appear to indicate that the United States has been undergoing a sexual revolution. But appearances can be deceptive, and closer examination of the evidence suggests that the revolution is primarily one of attitudes, not behavior. The real sexual revolution began, largely unnoticed, much earlier in the century—certainly before World War II. Developments since that time have simply been a continuation of the trend that was rather abruptly established then. Social norms and values are now finally catching up with social behavior; what was previously concealed and private is now becoming open and public. The trend toward greater permissiveness is a long-term one, propelled by a complex of factors. The most important factors are the development of birth-control techniques, which guarantee a separation of the reproductive and the pleasurable aspects of intercourse, and the general erosion of traditions that is characteristic of all industrial societies.

The changes that have taken place in recent years are probably fewer than are generally realized. One is the rapid decline of the double standard. Although men are still permitted greater promiscuity than women, there has unquestionably been an increase in the incidence of premarital sexual activity among women, and the stigma that previously attached to this behavior is disappearing. Norms of female chastity make little sense from a functional point of view when contraception enables females to be sexually active with the kind of freedom that was previously the prerogative of males.

Figure 9.7 A couple dancing the Charleston in the 1920s. The real sexual revolution began during this era, but because people still professed values that they did not practice, it passed largely unnoticed. The sexual "revolution" of recent decades is primarily a revolution of attitudes and values, not behavior.

Another obvious change is in the amount and availability of pornography in the United States: more than 85 percent of adult men and 70 percent of adult women have been exposed to it. Most regular users of pornography are male, middle-aged, white, middle class, and married, and well over a quarter of the adult male population has frequent experience of pornographic material. Although there is some concern that pornography may stimulate sex crimes, the reverse appears to be the case. Pornography may actually serve as an outlet for people who might otherwise find satisfaction in less acceptable ways. After considering a mass of research and other evidence, the

Figure 9.8 Considerable value conflict still exists in the United States over sexual standards and attitudes. Opinion polls and other research indicate that these different values are related to age, with older people generally adhering to more conservative standards and young people becoming increasingly permissive in their attitudes and behavior.

Figure 9.9 Pornography is much more evident in the United States today than at any time in our history. There is no convincing evidence that pornography leads to sex crimes or has any other detectable adverse effects on those who use it, but many people find these public displays highly offensive.

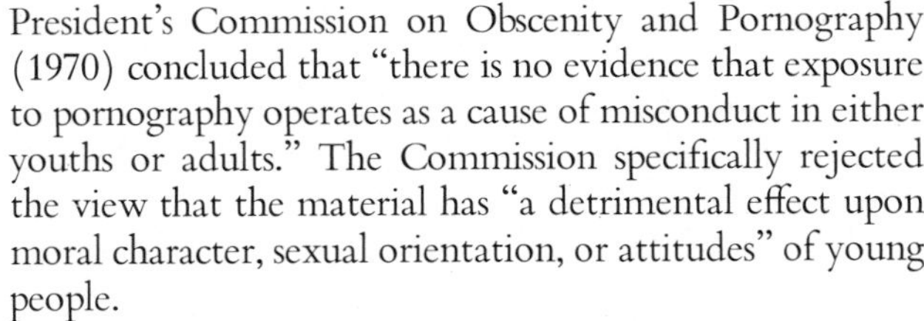

President's Commission on Obscenity and Pornography (1970) concluded that "there is no evidence that exposure to pornography operates as a cause of misconduct in either youths or adults." The Commission specifically rejected the view that the material has "a detrimental effect upon moral character, sexual orientation, or attitudes" of young people.

The most important change in recent years appears to be a redefinition of sexual morality. Right and wrong in matters sexual are now being defined less and less in terms of the absolute rules handed down by earlier generations. Instead sexual morality is being judged in accordance with the attitude that any behavior is acceptable as long as it involves mutual respect, is experienced as pleasant, and does not do any physical or psychological harm to those involved.

The Incest Taboo

The problem of the incest taboo offers a useful example of how sociological analysis can explain an otherwise puzzling practice. Every known society has had an incest taboo that prohibits sexual relations between specific classes of relatives. The taboo is almost always applied to relations between parent and child and between brother and sister, and it is always applied to other classes of relatives as well, although different societies have different rules in this regard.

The exceptions to the parent–child and brother–sister rule are few and far between. Brother and sister were expected to marry in the royal families of ancient Egypt, Hawaii, and Peru, probably to prevent defilement of the royal lineage by commoners. The Thonga of West Africa permit a father to have ritual intercourse with his own daughter before he goes on a lion hunt; the Azande of central Africa expect their highest chiefs to marry their own daughters; and the mothers of Burundi are expected to cure impotence in their adult sons by having intercourse with them. There is also evidence that brother-sister and parent-child marriages were occasionally practiced at certain periods in ancient Egypt and Iran, perhaps as a means of keeping property within the family (Ford and Beach, 1951; Murdock, 1949; La Barre, 1954; Albert, 1963; Middleton, 1962). The general cross-cultural rule, however, is that people regard intercourse with certain close relatives as utterly immoral and even unthinkable. Why?

A popular response might be that the taboo is instinctive, because we certainly experience our reaction to the idea of incest as though it were an "instinct." But this view is clearly wrong, for several reasons. First, no other animal observes an incest taboo, and it is highly unlikely that we, who rely less than any other species on inherited behavior, would have evolved an instinct that all other animals lack. Second, if the attitude to incest were instinctive, there would be no need for the taboo—yet every society finds it necessary to institute one. Third, definitions of incest vary from one society to another. In some societies it is incestuous to marry any cousin; in other societies all cousins are eligible. In some societies it is incestuous to marry the child of one's father's brother or one's mother's sister, but it is obligatory to marry the child of one's father's sister or one's mother's brother, even though all these cousins are equally closely related. The Mundugumor of New Guinea recognize blood relationships in such a complex way that three-quarters of all women in the society are ineligible as sex partners for any given man, and seven women out of eight are ineligible as wives. It would be a very strange instinct indeed that turned up in such different guises in different societies, scrupulously observing local and national boundaries in the process.

A second popular response might be that the incest taboo exists to prevent the physical and mental degeneration that comes from inbreeding. This explanation sounds plausible, but for several reasons it is also incorrect. First, inbreeding does not necessarily produce degeneration: it merely intensifies certain traits, good or bad, that are already present in the related partners. Agricultural scientists use selective inbreeding, in fact, to produce healthier stock. Second, any ill effects of inbreeding usually take place too slowly and too haphazardly to be noticeable over a few generations. People living in simple, traditional societies would not be likely to link cause and effect, especially when other explanations, such as illness or witchcraft, are more readily available. Third, some peoples apparently failed to recognize that pregnancy is the result of intercourse: the Trobriand Islanders, for example, denied that intercourse led to birth, and other peoples attribute pregnancy to the work of their dead ancestors. Yet these societies have some of the most complex incest taboos ever recorded.

Then why the incest taboo? There are three main reasons, and they are social, not biological. The first is that early human beings—living primarily in small kinship groups of hunters and gatherers—needed to protect themselves by forming alliances with other groups. By forcing their children to marry into other families, each group widened its social links and provided itself with allies in time of conflict and help in time of famine or other hazards. These groups, it has been said, faced the alternative between marrying out and dying out. Marriage in most traditional societies is a bond between groups, not individuals. That is why marriages are arranged by the parents, often when their offspring are still children and sometimes even before they are born (White, 1969).

The second reason for the incest taboo is that the family itself could not function without it. As Kingsley Davis (1948) points out: "The confusion of statuses would be phenomenal. The incestuous child of a father-daughter union, for example, would be a brother of his own mother, i.e. the son of his own sister; a stepson of his own grandmother; possibly a brother of his own uncle; and certainly a grandson of his own father."

The third reason is that without an incest taboo sexual rivalry between family members would disrupt the normal roles and attitudes of the various relatives. The father, for example, might experience role conflict as both the disciplinarian and the lover of his daughter; the mother might be jealous of both. Faced with constant conflict and tension of this kind, the family institution might simply disintegrate.

Of course, neither traditional nor modern societies consciously appreciate the reasons for the taboo. They and we simply accept it as natural and moral.

Homosexuality

Homosexuality, much more evident in the United States now that the gay liberation movement has encouraged its adherents to "come out" and openly declare their preference, is one of the most stigmatized forms of sexual variance in our society. The ancient Greeks, in the cradle of Western civilization, regarded male homosexual love as a higher value than heterosexual love and institutionalized a system of sexual and spiritual liaisons between boys and older men. Since then, however, Western attitudes toward homosexuality have generally been negative. Homosexuality was tolerated for a few periods in the Roman Empire and the Middle Ages, usually at times when emperors, kings, and popes themselves had homosexual tastes, but homosexuals have generally been persecuted until modern times. The persecution reached its climax in Nazi Germany, when hundreds of thousands of suspected homosexuals were sent to the gas chambers along with Jews and political dissidents.

Figure 9.10 Homosexuality has become much more noticeable in recent years as a result of the emergence of the gay liberation movement. The movement has demanded an end to discrimination against homosexuals and the repeal of laws against homosexual acts between consenting adults. A major objective of the movement has been to give homosexuals a sense of pride rather than guilt in their sexual orientation.

Why has homosexuality attracted this negative reaction? The reason lies yet again in the Western moral tradition that recognizes sexual acts as legitimate only if they occur within marriage and can potentially lead to reproduction. Homosexual acts are pursued for their own sake and are necessarily nonreproductive; and if homosexuality serves as an exclusive outlet, it is impossible to reconcile with the central institutions of marriage and the family. For this reason homosexuality has traditionally been regarded as immoral, as a vice even worse than such nonreproductive heterosexual acts as oral-genital contacts, which can at least be used as a supplement to reproductive intercourse. Until the global population explosion of the present century, widespread exclusive homosexuality would have been highly *dysfunctional.* Preindustrial societies had a very high death rate, especially among children, and a society that did not encourage high birth rates might risk extinction. In a world faced with a crisis of overpopulation, however, homosexuality is no longer dysfunctional from this point of view: it may even be functional. The growing tolerance of homosexuality (and of abortion, contraception, masturbation, and nonreproductive forms of heterosexual activity) is probably related to this fact.

Incidence of Homosexuality

How common is homosexuality in the United States? The question is not easily answered, for it depends on the definition of homosexuality. In the United States we tend to see homosexuality and heterosexuality as "either/or" categories and to assume that they are mutually exclusive. This idea seems to have arisen in seventeenth-century England (McIntosh, 1968). It is incorrect, however, for many people fall on a continuum between the two. Any attempt to divide the population into two distinct categories must fail because of the countless ambiguous cases that arise—people whose desires are heterosexual but whose behavior is homosexual, people who have homosexual histories but whose current behavior is heterosexual, people who alternate between both forms of behavior, and so on.

No findings of the Kinsey studies caused a greater furor than his data on homosexuality, which indicated that only 50 percent of the male population could be considered exclusively heterosexual in terms of both their sexual acts and their feelings since puberty. Kinsey found that 37 percent of males had experienced at least one homosexual contact to the point of orgasm and that a further 13 percent had experienced homosexual desires but had not acted on them. Some 18 percent of the men had as much homosexual as heterosexual experience, and 8 percent had engaged in exclusively homosexual relationships for at least three years since adolescence. The proportion of lifelong exclusive homosexuals, however, was much smaller: 4 percent. The incidence of homosexuality in women was significantly lower; 13 percent had experienced homosexual contacts, a further 15 percent had experienced homosexual desires but had not acted on them, and only about 2 percent of the female population was exclusively homosexual. The lower incidence of female homosexuality is probably related to the great emphasis placed in female socialization on comformity and on the joys of motherhood. Kinsey (1948) concluded that

> the world is not divided into sheep and goats. . . . Only the human mind invents categories and tries to force facts into separated pigeon holes. The living world is a continuum in each and every one of its aspects. The sooner we learn this concerning human sexual behavior the sooner we will reach a sound understanding of the realities of sex.

Kinsey accordingly constructed a seven-point rating scale, with exclusive homosexuality at one end and exclusive heterosexuality at the other end (see Figure 9.11).

How accurate are Kinsey's figures? Kinsey himself reported that he was "totally unprepared" for his findings, and he lists twelve separate methods by which he checked them to test their reliability; he found much the same pattern emerging in group after group in his study. But

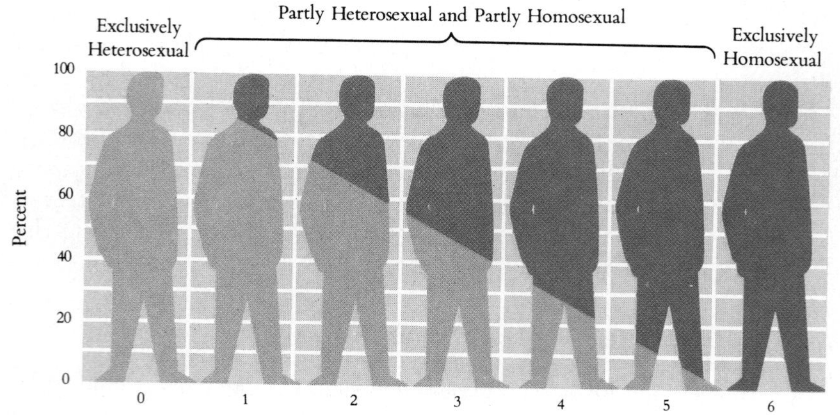

Source: Adapted from Alfred C. Kinsey *et al., Sexual Behavior in the Human Male* (Philadelphia: W. B. Saunders, 1948), p. 638.

Figure 9.11 Alfred Kinsey's research established that homosexuality and heterosexuality are not mutually exclusive categories. Elements of both are found in most people in varying degrees. Kinsey's seven-point scale provides a way of measuring the balance in particular individuals. The scale runs from one extreme of exclusively heterosexual acts or feelings through to the other extreme of exclusively homosexual acts or feelings.

Kinsey's was not a fully representative sample. In his zeal not to exclude homosexual cases from his study, he may have included too many. Wardell Pomeroy (1972), one of Kinsey's research associates, believes that the figures are somewhat high and suggests that a 33 percent figure for the total proportion of males who have had at least one homosexual experience since puberty would be more accurate. Subsequent studies are not very helpful. The *Psychology Today* survey found precisely the same figures as Kinsey's—37 percent of the sample had experience of homosexual acts and 4 percent were exclusively homosexual throughout their lives—but the sample was so unlike Kinsey's that this finding is probably coincidental. The *Playboy* study is also of little help. Morton Hunt admits that it specifically omitted "many, if not most" of the "committed homosexuals," but he believes that the Kinsey figures are a little high. Even a conservative estimate, however, indicates that around 20 million Americans are exclusively or substantially homosexual (APA *Monitor,* 1974), a minority almost as large as that of American blacks and one that also suffers much prejudice and discrimination.

The Homosexual Community

It is barely a quarter of a century since no American newspaper would dare print the world "homosexual." In the absence of informed discussion of the subject, homosexuality has been surrounded by myths, many of which are still widely believed. The sociological research of recent years has made a more objective picture possible, at least in the case of males; female homosexuality is still inadequately researched.

It is not true that homosexuals are typically "effeminate" in the case of men and "masculine" in the case of women. The great majority are indistinguishable in manner and appearance from heterosexuals, and there is no evidence to suggest that "effeminacy" and "masculinity" are any more common in homosexual than in heterosexual men and women. Nor is it true that homosexuals typically suffer from gender confusion, believing or wishing that they were members of the opposite sex. This myth stems from a confusion between homosexuality and *transvestism,* the wearing of the clothing of the opposite sex. A transvestite is sexually aroused by cross-dressing in this way, but many transvestites are otherwise normal heterosexuals. In fact, the evidence available suggests that most transvestites are heterosexual married men (Buckner, 1970; Newton, 1972). It is not true that homosexuals typically assume a "passive" or an "active" role in their relationships; most alternate between the two. The preferences of the small minority who do prefer a particular role cannot be inferred from their physical appearance, any more than any specific sexual preferences of heterosexuals can be inferred from their appearance (Hooker, 1965). It is not true that homosexuals pose a particular menace to the young; child molestation by heterosexuals is proportionately much more frequent. And it is not true that homosexuals as a group have disturbed or even characteristic personality patterns; except for their sexual orientation they are psychologically indistinguishable from heterosexuals (Hooker, 1957; Thompson *et al.,* 1971; Weinberg and Williams, 1974; Freedman, 1975). One popular belief about homosexuals, however, is probably true: that as a category they are more promiscuous than heterosexuals. This is probably due in part to the lack of institutional supports for stable homosexual relationships—particularly marriage, with its implied social approval, its ritual mutual commitments, its tax breaks, and its possibilities for adoption of children.

Some homosexuals attempt throughout their lives to "pass" as heterosexuals, but a growing number, perhaps a majority, participate in the homosexual community that is centered in urban America. Most large cities contain definable areas that are occupied primarily by homosexuals and in which shops, restaurants, and other amenities cater almost exclusively to the homosexual community. Membership in the homosexual community provides entrance to a subculture in which the individual can learn new roles, norms, and values. The community provides a context in which people who have identified themselves as homosexual can be resocialized. The climate of the community neutralizes earlier concepts of homosexuality as perverted, sinful, and abnormal and enables homosexual people to rebuild positive self-concepts (Hooker, 1962; Leznoff and Westley, 1956; Humphreys, 1972; Warren, 1974). A central institution in the community is the gay bar, of which there are dozens or even hundreds in large cities. The bar provides opportunities for social interaction, for the exchange of information, for the making of sexual contacts, and above all for the sense that one belongs to a worthwhile and accepting group. As one homosexual recalls (quoted in Dank, 1971):

> I was resigned to the fact that I was a foul, dirty person, but I wasn't actually calling myself a homosexual yet. . . . The time I really caught myself coming out is the time I walked into this bar and saw a whole crowd of groovy, groovy guys. And I said to myself, there was this realization, that not all gay men are dirty old men or idiots, silly queens, but there are some just normal looking and acting people, as far as I could see. I saw gay society and I said, "Wow, I'm home."

Causes of Homosexuality

Why do some people become homosexual in the face of so much social discouragement? Several theories have been offered.

Biological Factors

Some people, including some homosexuals, assume that homosexuals are simply "born that way." But since we know that even heterosexuals are not "born that way," this explanation seems unlikely. Numerous attempts have been made to find genetic or hormonal factors that might predispose individuals toward homosexuality, but there is no plausible evidence that homosexual tendencies are inherited (D. Rosenthal, 1970) or caused by hormones (Tourney *et al.,* 1975). Since homosexuals have a low rate of reproduction, any inherited causes would quickly be bred out of a population. Moreover, biological factors cannot explain the different extent of homosexuality in different societies at different times, or the changes that may take place during the lifetime of an individual. Homosexuality, like other sexual behavior, is learned.

Early Experiences

A common popular view is that homosexuality is caused by early childhood experiences, particularly seduction. But while this may be true in some specific instances, it cannot provide a comprehensive explanation. The great majority of American preadolescents and a substantial proportion of adolescents have had some homosexual experience, but only a small minority of them become exclusive homosexuals. Other people who have never had any homosexual experience in their entire lives may still privately define themselves as homosexual (Dank, 1971).

Family Environment

Psychoanalysts have attempted to isolate factors in the family background of homosexuals, usually in the belief that homosexuality is a form of mental disorder or "sickness" resulting from pathological family interactions. The principal modern statement of this theory is that of Irving Bieber (1962), whose work led him to believe that homosexual males typically had domineering, possessive mothers and ineffectual or hostile fathers. Bieber's study was widely acclaimed when it was published but has since been criticized as a badly compromised piece of research. His sample consisted entirely of patients in psychiatric care and was thus no more representative of the general homosexual population than a group of similar heterosexuals would be of the general heterosexual population. A study of heterosexuals in psychiatric care would doubtless reveal problems in their family background, but these could hardly be taken as an explanation for their heterosexuality. Other studies (for example, Hooker, 1969) have found no consistent personality differences between homosexuals and heterosexuals. This fact is now accepted by the American Psychiatric Association, which in 1973 removed homosexuality from its list of mental disorders, offering this "sick" community an instant cure. Although family background may predispose some individuals toward homosexuality, this theory is yet to be proved.

Social Learning

John Gagnon and William Simon (1973) offer what is essentially a behaviorist or social-learning account of homosexuality. The orientation, they argue, is learned through rewards and punishments. A person who finds an initial homosexual experience pleasurable may repeat the experience, find it pleasurable again, and have the orientation further reinforced. Particularly if heterosexual experiences are simultaneously experienced as unpleasant or threatening, a homosexual identity may result. This approach is helpful, but it still has two major defects. First, why should some specific rewards overcome the many punishing responses that the homosexual receives from the total social environment? The balance of rewards and punishments in society heavily favors a heterosexual orientation, and it is difficult to see how specific rewards in a limited context would counter this powerful social experience. Second, some homosexuals clearly do not find their orientation rewarding. They may wish to abandon their homosexual life-style but are unable to do so. It is difficult to see how their sexual preference can be fully explained in terms of the punishments and rewards it offers them.

Self-Definition

A new approach to the problem avoids many of these difficulties. It sees homosexual identity as the result of a false self-definition that people impose on themselves. This definition can be made consciously or unconsciously, voluntarily or involuntarily, but it is made in accordance with the prevailing beliefs of the culture concerned (Sagarin, 1973, 1975; Blumstein and Schwartz, 1974). In this view, both heterosexual and homosexual behavior are learned through a similar process. People who experience heterosexual acts or desires achieve a sense that they are heterosexual and define themselves accordingly. Believing that heterosexuality and homosexuality are mutually exclusive, they also define themselves as not homosexual. A similar process applies to people who become homosexual. As a result of early homosexual experiences or desires, they come to think of themselves as homosexual. They become trapped within this self-definition and—irrespective of social rewards and punishments—cannot escape from it. If they are labeled as homosexuals by others, the self-definition is further reinforced. As Sagarin (1973) suggests,

> it might be useful to start from the premise that . . . there is no such thing as a *homosexual,* for such a concept is . . . an artificially created entity that has no basis in reality. What exists are people with erotic desires for their own sex, or who engage in sexual activities with same-sex others, or both. The desires constitute feeling, the acts constitute doing, but neither is being. . . . However, people become entrapped in a false consciousness of identifying themselves as *being* homosexuals. They believe that they discover what they are. . . . Learning their "identity" they become involved in it, boxed into their own biographies. . . . There is no road back because they believe there is none.

Cultural beliefs determine the self-definition that the individual makes. It is quite possible to engage in homosexual acts without defining oneself as or becoming homosexual, provided one's culture or subculture offers this option. In many contemporary Arab societies, for example, people would tend to regard their homosexual desires and acts as evidence not of homosexuality but of potential bisexuality, because the category of bisexuality is recognized and accepted in these cultures. Male homosexuality is very common in American prisons, but the prison community defines the dominant partner as heterosexual (even though he achieves sexual gratification from his acts) and the submissive partner as homosexual (even if he is unwilling and even if he is raped). The participants in the acts learn to accept these definitions (Kirkham, 1971; Davis, 1968). Similarly, many homosexual prostitutes define and think of themselves as fully heterosexual, because their subculture permits them to believe that they are "just doing it for the money" (Reiss, 1961; Benjamin and Masters, 1964; Gandy and Deisher, 1970; Humphreys, 1971). In general, exclusive homosexuality is found only in societies that define heterosexuality and homosexuality as mutually exclusive. In societies that offer bisexuality as a cultural option, people with homosexual tendencies are more likely to define themselves and to be defined by others as bisexual and to behave accordingly (Duberman, 1974). The precise content of the homosexual role and the process by which people come to assume it can only be understood in terms of the prevailing cultural definitions.

Prostitution

Prostitution is the relatively indiscriminate exchange of sexual favors for economic gain. Not all exchanges of sex for gain are prostitution: the woman who "marries for money," the kept mistress, the actress who sleeps with film directors en route to stardom, or the wife who "holds out" on her husband until he parts with his paycheck are not prostitutes. What distinguishes the prostitute is a willingness to perform sexual services for virtually anyone in return for some gain. In theory four forms of prostitution are possible: women for men, men for men, women for women, and men for women. In practice the last two types are very rare indeed. Male homosexual prostitution is common in large cities, but by far the greatest number of prostitutes are women offering their services to men.

In some preindustrial societies the prostitute enjoyed high social status. In ancient Greece high-class prostitutes, the *hetairae,* were welcomed in literary and political circles. They appeared in public with leading statesmen, and their

Figure 9.12 Prostitution has often been called "the world's oldest profession." These prostitutes and their rather elegant surroundings were painted by the Italian artist Carpaccio in the sixteenth century. Despite numerous attempts to stamp out the profession, prostitution has continued to thrive.

portraits and statues adorned public buildings. In many ancient societies of the Middle and Far East, prostitution assumed a sacred form and was practiced in the temples. In some societies, such as ancient Cyprus, all women were expected to prostitute themselves in a temple at least once in their lives as a religious ritual. Sacred prostitution even occurred among the early Hebrews, although the Old Testament later forbade the practice. But the social status of the prostitute since early Christian times has been anything but a respected one. Although she may consort on the most intimate terms with politicians and bank presidents, judges and bishops, the prostitute's status is very low.

The reason can again be traced to the Judeo-Christian moral tradition. Men engage in prostitution for pleasure alone, and neither they nor the prostitute have any intention that the relationship should lead to reproduction. By definition, prostitution can take place only outside the context of marriage. To violate social norms even further, the prostitute offers her services for money, not for love, in a society that regards love as a prerequisite for legitimate sex. And to make matters worse still, she flouts the double standard with her promiscuity.

Types of Prostitution

The main types of female prostitute today are the streetwalker, the housegirl, and the call girl; there are also various types of male prostitute (Greenwald, 1958, 1970; Winick and Kinsie, 1971; Benjamin and Masters, 1964).

The Streetwalker

The streetwalker has the lowest status and earnings of all prostitutes. She solicits clients in public places, usually in the street or the lobbies of hotels, and her fee rarely exceeds $20. Some streetwalkers, including teenage runaways, are newcomers to the occupation, but many are older women who can no longer compete at the higher levels of the market. Because the streetwalker is the most visible of all prostitutes, she attracts the most public criticism and attention from the police.

The Housegirl

The housegirl works and sometimes lives in a brothel, an organized house of prostitution. Before World War II most prostitution took place in brothels, often in notorious "red light" districts of large cities. Some of the houses of prostitution in Chicago, Galveston, and New Orleans won international fame for the elegance and splendor of their decor. The brothels were usually run by a "madame," often a retired prostitute, who organized the house and took a percentage of the housegirls' earnings. These brothels are largely a thing of the past; they have been replaced by houses of prostitution disguised as "massage parlors" or "clubs."

The Call Girl

The call girl has the highest status and earnings in the occupation; she may charge several hundred dollars for an evening's services and is generally more attractive and better educated than the other types of prostitute. The call girl is a relatively new phenomenon, and her competition is partly responsible for the decline of the brothel. She may work on her own from a hotel room or apartment, or she may be part of a call-girl network disguised as an "escort agency." In either case, she makes her contacts through personal introductions. In addition to their sexual services, call girls are also available for companionship on semi-public occasions and may come to know their clients on a more personal and regular basis than other prostitutes. Many call girls see their occupation as a potential avenue to higher social status as the mistress or perhaps ultimately the wife of a wealthy man.

The Male Prostitute

Male prostitution is more common than is generally realized in the United States, partly because youths "hanging out" on a street corner do not attract the same attention as young women, and partly because many local laws are directed only at female prostitution, enabling the males to operate with relative freedom. The lowest status in the profession is that of the "street hustler," generally a teenager who offers his services for under $30 on certain streets of the city. The "bar hustler" is often slightly older and solicits clients in specific gay bars where the proprietor tolerates prostitution. Most of these hustlers regard their activities as a temporary means of earning money, and many consider themselves basically heterosexual. The "houseboy" works but rarely lives in a male house of prostitution, of which there are a few in some large cities. The "call boy" has the highest status and earnings in the profession, although he can rarely command the fees of his female counterpart. A male prostitute may hope to become a "kept boy," the homosexual equivalent of a mistress, under the guise of being a wealthy man's "secretary," "chauffeur," or "nephew."

V.I.P. SERVICE
A residential service
catering to the
sophisticated gentleman.
Beautiful, young, discreet
girls to visit you at your
Apartment, Hotel or Office.
For an appointment Call:
661-6869

YOUR BODY IS
OUR BUSINESS
$5.00 Summer Sale
TOPLESS BODY RUBS AND
DOMINANT SESSIONS
Air Conditioned, Color TV, &
Refreshments are Free
The Pink Pussy Cat
200 E. 14th St. 533-5719

Beautiful Boys
for your Pleasures
& Joys
Your Place
7 Days 541-7788

Figure 9.13 The traditional brothel has almost disappeared from American society. Instead, commercial sex now often takes the form of organized call-girl networks, "escort agencies," or "massage parlors." Advertisements like these are printed in sex-oriented magazines in all large American cities.

Figure 9.14 American prostitutes attending the "First Hookers' Convention" in San Francisco in 1974. The prostitutes formed a new organization called COYOTE ("call off your old tired ethics"), which is now working for reform of the nation's vice laws.

Prostitution as an Occupation

Recruitment into the role of prostitute is rarely the consequence of an abrupt decision. People tend to drift into the role and to serve a period of apprenticeship before finally defining themselves as prostitutes and relying on the occupation as a major or sole source of income (Bryant, 1965; N. Davis, 1971). Most female prostitutes come from lower-class or lower-middle-class backgrounds. They often have histories of considerable promiscuity in adolescence and are frequently alienated from their families, especially their fathers.

Drift into prostitution may begin when a woman accepts a casual offer from a man, or when she meets another prostitute or a pimp who suggests that she enter the career. A pimp is a man who lives off the proceeds of female prostitution. He systematically introduces women to their new role and serves as lover, business manager, and protector afterward. He arranges contacts, paying court fines and bail, and safeguards the prostitute's territory against competitors. Housegirls, call girls, and male prostitutes have little need of pimps, but a high proportion of streetwalkers participate in the arrangement. They generally take pride in the life-style that they provide for the pimp, while the pimp's own affluence provides evidence of the prostitutes' occupational success. The relationship between prostitute and pimp is a curious one. It involves a reversal of the usual sex-role definitions, for the female partner or partners are more promiscuous than the male and serve as breadwinners for him.

The new entrant to the occupation is resocialized by pimps and other prostitutes. She learns various techniques—how to solicit in public, how to recognize plainclothes police officers, how to handle difficult customers, and how to service her clients and get rid of them as soon as possible. She also acquires a new set of values that serve to alienate her further from her previous life. She learns to hold "respectable" women in contempt, to view her clients as mere exploiters, to regard society as hypocritical, and to justify her own activities as socially valuable. Despite the stigma attached to the occupation and the fact that it is inherently a dead-end job—the prostitute's only real asset is her vanishing youth and beauty—prostitutes seem to be reasonably satisfied with their work. One study found that although only one-fifth of prostitutes would advise other women to become prostitutes, two-thirds of them expressed no regret about their choice of occupation (Pomeroy, 1965).

From Call Girl to Streetwalker

I was about fifteen, going on sixteen. I was sitting in a coffee shop in the Village, and a friend of mine came by. She said: "I've got a cab waiting. Hurry up. You can make fifty dollars in twenty minutes." Looking back, I wonder why I was so willing to run out of the coffee shop, get in a cab, and turn a trick. It wasn't traumatic because my training had been in how to be a hustler anyway.

I learned it from the society around me, just as a woman. We're taught how to hustle, how to attract, hold a man, and give sexual favors in return. The language that you hear all the time, "Don't sell yourself cheap." "Hold out for the highest bidder." "Is it proper to kiss a man good night on the first date?" The implication is it may not be proper on the first date, but if he takes you out to dinner on the second date, it's proper. If he brings you a bottle of perfume on the third date, you should let him touch you above the waist. And go on from there. It's a market place transaction.

Somehow I managed to absorb that when I was quite young. So it wasn't even a moment of truth when this woman came into the coffee shop and said; "Come on." I was back in twenty-five minutes and I felt no guilt. . . . It was a tremendous kick. Here I was doing absolutely nothing, *feeling* nothing, and in twenty minutes I was going to walk out with fifty dollars in my pocket. That just made me feel absolutely marvelous. I came downtown. I can't believe this! I'm not changed, I'm the same as I was twenty minutes ago, except that now I have fifty dollars in my pocket. It really was tremendous status. How many people could make fifty dollars for twenty minutes' work? Folks work for eighty dollars take-home pay. I worked twenty minutes for fifty dollars clear, no taxes, nothing! I was still in school, I was smoking grass, I was shooting heroin, I wasn't hooked yet, and I had money. It was terrific.

After that, I made it my business to let my friend know that I was available for more of these situations. (Laughs.) She had good connections. Very shortly I linked up with a couple of others who had a good call book. . . . At the beginning I was very excited. But in order to continue I had to turn myself off. I had to disassociate who I was from what I was doing.

It's a process of numbing yourself. I couldn't associate with people who were not in the life—either the drug life or the hustling life. I found I couldn't turn myself back on when I finished working. When I turned myself off, I was numb—emotionally, sexually numb. . . . When I was a call girl I looked down on streetwalkers. I couldn't understand why anybody would put themselves in that position. It seemed to me to be hard work and very dangerous. . . . I had to work an awful lot harder for the same money when I was a streetwalker. I remember having knives pulled on me, broken bottles held over my head, being raped, having my money stolen back from me, having to jump out of a second-story window, having a gun pointed at me. . . . I looked terrible. When I hit the streets, I tried to stick to at least twenty dollars and folks would laugh. I needed a hundred dollars a night to maintain a drug habit and keep a room somewhere. It meant turning seven or eight tricks a night. I was out on the street from nine o'clock at night till four in the morning. I was taking subways and eating in hamburger stands. . . . I once really got trapped. It was about midnight and a guy came down the street. He said he was a postal worker who just got off the shift. He told me how much money he had and what he wanted. I took him to my room. The cop isn't supposed to undress. If you can describe the color of his shorts, it's an invalid arrest. Not only did he show me the color of his shorts, he went to bed with me. Then he pulled a badge and a gun and he busted me. . . . I did time for that—close to four years.

Source: Studs Terkel, *Working* (New York: Pantheon Books, 1974), pp. 57–65. (Quotation from a former prostitute.)

Reasons for Prostitution

Why does prostitution exist, despite the stigma that attaches to the institution? The reason is that both men and women have found sound reasons for entering into the relationship. From the point of view of the prostitute, the occupation offers far higher earnings, even after the pimp has taken his share, than would be available in a "straight" job. Nor is the work particularly difficult. It can be much less tedious or time-consuming than many alternative occupations, such as those of waitress, keypunch operator, or assembly-line worker. The occupation offers the woman considerable freedom; she may work more or less when she pleases. There is always the possibility, too, of meeting and forming relationships with high-status men whom the prostitute would normally never encounter.

From the point of view of the prostitute's client, prostitution offers a convenient opportunity for sexual contacts that might otherwise be unavailable or difficult to come by. The prostitute's services often cost less than the price of entertaining a woman for an evening in the hope of seducing her. Relationships with a prostitute involve no complications, obligations, or emotional entanglements. Men who are away from home may find the prostitute a convenient substitute for their wives, and men whose sexual preferences are somewhat unusual may find that prostitutes will cater to tastes that their wives would not. And for the old and the physically unattractive, prostitution may offer the only means by which a man can enjoy sex with a young and attractive woman. As Kingsley Davis (1932) points out, prostitution is functional. It provides men with a variety of sexual outlets that do not undermine the family system in the way that more affectionate extramarital relationships would do.

Can Prostitution Be Eliminated?

For centuries prostitution has survived every effort to eradicate it; the institution seems to thrive despite all attempts at social control. Many countries have legalized prostitution, and they have done so for several reasons. First, prostitution is a victimless crime. There is no aggrieved party to complain to the police or to give court evidence, and so convictions are difficult to obtain—unless the police resort to the morally questionable tactic of posing as potential clients in order to make arrests. Second, prostitution involves a private act by consenting adults, and many people feel that what happens in private beds is no business of the state. Third, when prostitution is legalized it is largely taken out of the hands of organized crime and becomes just another commercial enterprise. Fourth, it is possible to submit legalized prostitution to public regulation. For example, prostitutes can be licensed, taxed, and periodically checked for venereal disease. Fifth, police attention can be focused on public nuisances associated with prostitution (such as blackmail, theft, and blatant soliciting) rather than on the thankless task of trying to suppress the institution itself. The idea that prostitution should be legalized is strongly resisted in the United States, however, mainly on the grounds that this would legitimate the institution, encourage more use of prostitutes' services, and so undermine public morality.

As Kingsley Davis (1932, 1976a) points out, however, prostitution cannot be eliminated in a sexually restrictive society, for it arises in response to those very restrictions. In the more permissive societies in the Ford and Beach cross-cultural sample, prostitution is extremely rare, for the reason that men have considerable opportunity for legitimate outlets beyond marriage. As Davis points out, prostitution could be completely eliminated only in a society that was totally permissive and in which sexual relations were freely available to all. Such a society could never exist, for total sexual freedom would imply a breakdown of the family system. The more restrictive a society is, the greater the pressure for prostitution to provide outlets for men who are not married or who find that exclusive sexual relationships with their wives are unsatisfactory.

There is also an economic reason why prostitution cannot be eliminated. Police crackdowns on prostitution might temporarily reduce the number of prostitutes. In such circumstances, the supply of prostitutes would decrease while the demand for their services would remain constant. The result would be an immediate increase in the fees for prostitution, which in turn would attract more women into the profession—including some who would not otherwise have considered it (Benjamin and Masters, 1964).

The sociological perspective on prostitution, as on all other forms of human sexual expression, offers a more acute insight into this aspect of social behavior—and with that understanding, perhaps, comes a more tolerant attitude to the varied ways of men and women in our own society and elsewhere.

Summary

1. Sexuality is an important element in social life. Human sexual behavior is not innate, but learned through the socialization process. The subject has been poorly researched until recently.

2. Human sexuality is extremely flexible; for this reason,

every society makes strong efforts to regulate it in culturally approved ways.

3. There are considerable variations in sexual practices in other societies, particularly preindustrial societies. Societies vary in their concepts of beauty, their permissiveness or restrictiveness, their norms of heterosexual conduct, and their attitudes toward homosexuality. This variation reveals the interplay of biological potentials and cultural learning.

4. Sexual behavior in the United States is marked by a contrast between real and ideal norms and values. Traditional values emphasize sex as legitimate only in the context of marriage and only if its primary purpose is reproduction, but they tolerate a double standard of behavior for males and females. The work of Kinsey and others indicates that these norms and values are extensively violated. Recent permissive trends appear to signal changes in attitudes rather than practices.

5. Some form of incest taboo is universal. The taboo is not instinctive, nor does it exist to prevent any ill effects of inbreeding. It exists to encourage alliances between groups through marriage, to prevent confusion of statuses in the family, and to prevent sexual jealousies between family members.

6. Homosexuality has long been stigmatized in Western societies. Homosexual and bisexual behavior is, however, fairly common. Many traditional beliefs about homosexuality are inaccurate. Homosexual life, particularly in urban centers, focuses on a defined homosexual community. Several theories of causation have been offered: biological factors, early experiences, family environment, social learning, and self-definition in terms of cultural beliefs.

7. The practice of prostitution violates several traditional values and is stigmatized in the United States, although it was approved of in some ancient societies. The main types of prostitute are the streetwalker, the housegirl, the call girl, and the male prostitute. Entry into the occupation is usually a matter of drift, often involving contact with a pimp. Prostitution offers certain advantages for both prostitutes and their clients and is functional in relieving potential strains on the family system. It cannot be eliminated in a sexually restrictive society, since it arises in response to those restrictions.

Important Terms

incest taboo
restrictiveness
permissiveness
heterosexual behavior
homosexual behavior
ideal culture
real culture
double standard
prostitution

Suggested Readings

FORD, CLELLAN S., and FRANK A. BEACH. *Patterns of Sexual Behavior.* New York: Harper & Row, 1951.

An important study of sexual behavior in other cultures and in other species. The authors use this material to draw basic conclusions about human sexuality.

GAGNON, JOHN, and WILLIAM SIMON. *Sexual Conduct.* Chicago: Aldine, 1973.

A sociological interpretation of human sexual behavior from a social-learning perspective.

HENSLIN, JAMES M. (ED.). *Studies in the Sociology of Sex.* New York: Appleton-Century-Crofts, 1971.

A collection of articles on various aspects of the sociology of sex. The book provides a useful overview of research in this field.

HUMPHREYS, LAUD. *Out of the Closets.* Englewood Cliffs, N.J.: Prentice-Hall, 1972.

A sociological account of the gay liberation movement. Humphreys includes descriptive material on the American homosexual community.

KATCHADOURIAN, HERANT P., and DONALD T. LUNDE. *Fundamentals of Human Sexuality.* New York: Holt, Rinehart and Winston, 1975.

A readable and up-to-date college text that provides a good overview of human sexuality. The book integrates material from several disciplines.

WINICK, CHARLES, and PAUL M. KINSIE. *The Lively Commerce: Prostitution in the United States.* Chicago: Aldine, 1971.

A useful sociological analysis of prostitution, containing both historical and modern data on the institution and those who participate in it.

UNIT 3 *Social Inequality*

Social inequality exists when some people have a greater share of power, wealth, or prestige than others. Such inequality is as old as society itself, and throughout history it has been a constant source of tension, conflict, violence, injustice, and oppression. In most societies, social inequality is built into the social structure in such a way that it is passed down from generation to generation. When this happens, whole categories of a population are denied a fair share of their society's resources virtually from the moment of birth.

The first chapter in this unit deals with the general problem of social stratification, or the ranking of a population into unequal "strata." The second chapter takes up the issue of social class in the United States, a country that is formally committed to human equality but in which there are severe inequalities among different segments of the population. The third chapter discusses race and ethnic relations, focusing on social inequalities between peoples who are physically or culturally different from one another. The last chapter discusses sex roles, showing how traditional roles have ensured the dominance of men over women. Throughout the unit, it is stressed that these social inequalities are rarely maintained primarily through force. Instead, they are sustained by the power of ideas. Members of both the dominant and the subordinate group are inclined to accept unquestioningly the ideologies, or sets of ideas, that justify the inequalities and make them seem "natural" and even moral.

CHAPTER 10 Social Stratification

CHAPTER OUTLINE

The Analysis of Stratification Systems
Caste and Class
Social Mobility
Criteria of Class Membership

Stratified Societies: Three Examples
India: A Caste Society
Britain: A Class Society
The Soviet Union: A Classless Society?

Maintaining Stratification: The Role of Ideology

Theories of Stratification
The Functionalist Approach
The Conflict Approach
The Evolutionary Approach

All societies differentiate among their members, treating people who have certain characteristics differently from other people. Every society, for example, differentiates between the old and the young and between males and females. In addition, a society may also treat its members differently on a variety of other grounds, such as religion, skin color, physical strength, or educational achievement. The usual result of this differentiation is social inequality.

Social inequality exists when people have different access to social rewards (such as money, influence, or respect) because of their personal or group characteristics. Inequality of this kind is universal in human societies. In all societies known to us, large or small, modern or extinct, there have been distinct differences in the statuses of the individual members. When a society values males over females, the rich over the poor, Christians over Moslems, or whites over blacks, then people who have the preferred characteristic enjoy a higher status than those who do not. Those with the higher status have a superior access to whatever rewards the society offers, and those with the lower status are deprived of these advantages.

In a very few simple, preindustrial societies, social inequality (other than that based on age and sex) is restricted to differences in the status of specific *individuals.* In these societies a person may have higher status than others because of some personal quality, such as wisdom, hunting skill, or beauty. In all other societies, however, social inequality takes a much more elaborate and structured form, in which entire *categories* of people have higher or lower status than other categories. In these societies inequality is built into the social structure, and unequal statuses are passed down from generation to generation. Like the

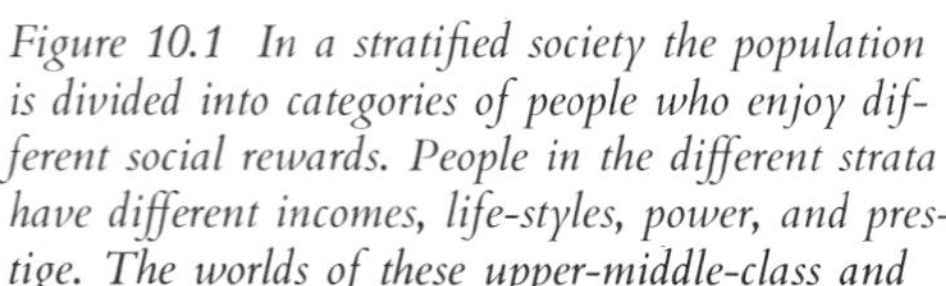

Figure 10.1 In a stratified society the population is divided into categories of people who enjoy different social rewards. People in the different strata have different incomes, life-styles, power, and prestige. The worlds of these upper-middle-class and working-class Americans are very different. The members of each group, too, will tend to transmit their statuses to their children, so that inequalities will be passed on from generation to generation.

layers of rock that we can see in the cliffs of the Grand Canyon, people in these societies are grouped into "strata." People in any one stratum have a different access to social rewards than people in any other stratum, so the society as a whole is said to be *stratified. Social stratification is the structured inequality of entire categories of people, who have different access to social rewards as a result of their status in the social hierarchy.* Individuals within a particular stratum share similar *life chances,* or probabilities of benefiting from the opportunities that their society offers. They generally view others within their stratum as equals, those in any stratum above as in some way their superiors, and those in any stratum below as in some way inferior.

Throughout history social stratification has been a source of tensions, revolutions, and social change. It has generated bloody conflict between slave and master, peasant and noble, worker and capitalist, poor and rich. Ever since Karl Marx brought the issue of social stratification to the forefront of political debate with his *Communist Manifesto* in 1848, these tensions have assumed global importance. Today the nuclear powers of East and West are divided mainly by their different attitudes about the way wealth should be distributed in society. If these powers ever came into open conflict, that conflict could wipe out human life on the planet within minutes.

Social stratification is a central concern of sociology, and not only because it can lead to conflict and change. Sociologists have found that a person's status in a stratified society correlates closely with many other variables. Almost every aspect of our lives is linked to our status in the social hierarchy: our scores on IQ tests, our educational achievements, the size of our families, our standards of nutrition and health care, the likelihood that we will be imprisoned or committed to a mental institution, our tastes in literature and art, and even the probability that we will keep the light on during sexual intercourse.

The Analysis of Stratification Systems

Systems of stratification vary a great deal from one society to another. There are obvious differences, for example, between the system in the modern United States and that in feudal Europe or ancient Rome. Let's look at social stratification systems in more detail.

Caste and Class

A stratification system may be either closed or open. In a *closed system,* the boundaries between the strata are very clearly drawn, and there is no way for people to change their statuses. A person's status in the hierarchy is determined at birth, perhaps by such criteria as skin color or ancestry, and the status is a lifelong one. In an *open system,* on the other hand, the boundaries between the strata are more flexible. People can change their statuses through their own efforts or failings. A person's original status in an open system is the same as the status of the family into which he or she was born, but this status can be changed later in life—for example, by making money or losing it, or by marrying someone of a different status.

Figure 10.2 The racial segregation pattern of the American South was a form of caste stratification. The system was a closed one; blacks could not enter the upper stratum, nor whites the lower stratum, for their status was ascribed at birth. As in all caste systems, the upper stratum was deeply concerned about "ritual pollution" through eating, drinking, or sexual contact with the lower stratum.

Caste Systems

A system of the closed type is called a *caste* system. These systems are very rigid, for people are automatic and lifelong members of the caste into which they were born. A person's status is determined entirely by birth; one's social status is always that of one's parents. A feature of caste systems is that they are *endogamous:* people may marry only within their own caste. Endogamy helps to keep up the boundaries between the castes, for it prevents the confusions that would arise if a person were born to parents of different castes. An individual's status in a caste society is said to be *ascribed,* since it is attached to the person on grounds over which he or she has no control.

Caste systems existed in several ancient societies, but they are uncommon in the modern world. There is still a caste system in India, but it is being steadily undermined. The South African stratification system, which is based on racial segregation, can also be regarded as a caste system. Status in that society is ascribed at birth on the grounds of color, and intermarriage between blacks and whites is forbidden by law. The segregation system in the United States was also a form of caste stratification, particularly in the South before the abolition of slavery. Under this system, too, status was ascribed on the grounds of color and intermarriage between the strata was outlawed. Despite many changes in patterns of American race relations, structured inequality between blacks and whites in the United States still has caste-like features.

Class Systems

A system of the open type is called a *class* system. In a class system stratification takes a more flexible form, for the boundaries between the strata are more blurred and people may pass from one stratum to another. An individual's status usually depends on the economic position of the family breadwinner, but a person can rise or fall in the hierarchy through individual efforts or failings. Status in a class society is said to be at least partly *achieved,* for it depends to some extent on characteristics over which the individual has some control. It is possible for people to become members of a social class other than that of their parents, and there are no formal restrictions against marriages between people of different classes.

Class systems are found in almost all agricultural and industrial societies. In agricultural societies, such as those found in feudal Europe and in some of the least developed nations of the modern world, there are usually two main classes, a very wealthy class of landowners and a very poor class of peasants. In industrial societies there are usually three main classes, an elite upper class, a fairly large middle class of professionals and skilled white-collar workers, and a large working class of less skilled workers. (The socialist societies of the world claim to have virtually abolished classes, but this is a claim that most American sociologists would reject, for reasons we will discuss shortly.)

In practice, stratification systems do not fall neatly into either category. There is usually a small amount of achieved status even in caste societies, for a few people may manage to move from one caste to another. There is always a great deal of ascribed status in class societies, for in even the most open systems some people are trapped in a particular class because of characteristics, such as skin color or the poverty of their parents, over which they have no control. Virtually all modern societies, however, have stratification systems that are basically of the open, class type, and we will concentrate mainly on class systems in this chapter.

Social Mobility

We have seen that an important difference between caste and class systems is the extent to which people can change their social statuses. Such movement from one social status to another is called *social mobility*. The more social mobility there is in a society, the more open its stratification system is.

Types of Social Mobility

Social mobility can take one of three forms. *Horizontal mobility* involves a change in an individual's lifetime from one status to another that is roughly equivalent, say, from that of a plumber to that of a carpenter. *Vertical mobility* may be either upward or downward. It involves a change within the lifetime of an individual to a higher or lower status than the person had to begin with. Movement from the status of plumber to that of corporation president, or vice versa, is an example of vertical mobility. The third form of social mobility is *intergenerational mobility*. This is a change in the status of family members from one generation to the next, as when a plumber's child becomes a corporation president or vice versa. Intergenerational mobility is the most important of the three forms, because the amount of this mobility in a society tells us to what extent inequalities are being passed on from one generation to the next. If there is very little intergenerational mobility, inequality is clearly deeply built into the society, for people's life chances are being determined at the moment of birth. If there is a good deal of intergenerational mobility, people are clearly able to achieve new statuses through their own efforts, regardless of the circumstances of their births.

Determinants of Mobility

The extent of social mobility in a society is determined by two factors: the total amount of mobility the society can support and the conditions under which people are allowed to be mobile.

The *amount* of mobility that a society can support depends on how many different statuses there are in the society. The more statuses there are, the greater the opportunities for a person to move from one status to another. In traditional agricultural societies, for example, there were a very limited number of different statuses, and high-status positions, such as those of nobles and landowners, were very few. If the eldest son inherited the property and title of a high-status father, the younger sons had to seek their fortunes elsewhere, perhaps in the military or the clergy. Or, if the property of the father was evenly divided among the offspring, each was left with a lower status than the father enjoyed. In these societies the number of high-status positions remained fairly constant, and there was a steady downward mobility of the surplus offspring of high-status families. There were few high statuses for people of low status to move into, and so there was virtually no upward mobility.

Industrial societies offer greater opportunities for mobility because they contain a very large number of different statuses. Social mobility in these societies is influenced by the level of development and condition of the economy. In times of economic depression, for example, the proportion of high-status positions decreases and the proportion of lower-status positions increases. This results in a general downward trend in mobility as people lose their jobs and as new entrants to the labor market are unable to find employment of the kind that their family background and education has prepared them to expect. In a rapidly expanding economy, on the other hand, new high-status positions constantly become available. The demand for workers to fill these positions causes a general upward trend in social mobility. The long-term trend in industrial societies has been toward an increase both in wealth and in the proportion of upper-status positions, leading to the growth of a large middle class whose members were originally drawn from the lower strata (Lipset and Bendix, 1959).

The second factor affecting social mobility is the *conditions* under which people are allowed to be mobile. Some societies place greater restrictions on changes in status than other societies do. If most statuses in a society are ascribed, the rate of mobility is likely to be much lower than if the society emphasizes individual achievement. In preindustrial societies there was very little upward mobility because legal and traditional restrictions made it almost impossible for a peasant to become a member of the landowning class: once a peasant, always a peasant. In industrial societies, which place high value on individual merit, the rate of mobility is very much greater. Some categories of people in industrial societies still suffer, however, from the effects of ascribed status. In the United States the rate of social mobility for blacks is lower than that for whites, and the mobility of women is lower than that of men (although women can compensate by marrying socially mobile men).

Criteria of Class Membership

What is your social class? You may hesitate about the answer, and you may find that other people would not agree about your precise position in the American class system. Determining the social status of a person in a caste system is easy. The boundaries between the castes are so clearly drawn that the matter is rarely in any doubt. But it is much more difficult to pinpoint a person's social status in a class system. The boundaries between the classes are blurred, and people may have no very clear idea of precisely where they fit in the system.

Marx's Analysis

An analysis of the problem can usefully begin with the work of Karl Marx (1967, originally published 1867–1895). Although social class was the main focus of Marx's writings, he never dealt with the issue systematically. The unfinished third volume of his book *Capital* breaks off, in fact, at precisely the point where he seems to have intended to present his ideas on the subject in rigorous detail. The general principles of his theory have to be extracted from a lifetime's work of voluminous, diffuse, and sometimes contradictory writings.

Marx defined a class as all those people who share a common relationship to the means of economic production. Those who own and control the means of production—slaveowners, feudal landowners, or the owners of property such as factories and capital—are the dominant class. Those who work for them—slaves, peasants, or industrial laborers—are the subordinate class. The relationship between the classes is not only one of dominance and subordination but also of *exploitation.* The workers produce more wealth in the form of food, manufactured products, and services than is necessary to meet their basic needs. In other words, they produce *surplus wealth.* But they do not enjoy the use of the surplus they have created. Instead, those who own the means of production are able to seize this surplus wealth as "profit" for their own use. This, in Marx's view, is the essence of exploitation and the main source of conflict between the classes that has occurred throughout history.

Marx linked this analysis to the idea that the economic base of society influences the general character of all other aspects of culture and social structure, such as law, religion, education, and government. The dominant class is able to control all of these institutions and to ensure that they protect its own interests. The laws therefore protect the rich, not the poor. The established religion supports the social order as it is, not as it might be. Education teaches the virtues of the existing system, not its vices. Government upholds the status quo rather than undermines it.

The Marxist definition of class has been a very influential one. Many sociologists still find it convenient to regard as a class any category of people who have a similar degree of control over and access to basic economic resources. Yet Marx's definition can be misleading in many marginal cases. This is particularly true in advanced industrial societies, which have changed a great deal since Marx's time. When Marx wrote, industry was owned and controlled primarily by individual capitalists, but this is no longer the case today. Most industry is now run by large corporations, which are owned by thousands or even hundreds of thousands of stockholders but controlled by salaried managers. As a result, the *ownership* and the *control* of the means of production have been largely separated (Berle and Means, 1933; Burnham, 1941). Executives, technicians, scientists, and other professionals may control the means of production, but they do not own it. They are on the payroll like any other workers. Marx's definition does not help very much in determining their social class.

Other cases also present problems. What is the social class of a dropout, who does not own or control the means of production but does not work either? What is the social class of an impoverished member of the European aristocracy, who enjoys high social prestige because of ancestry rather than any relationship to the means of production? What is the class of a wealthy black surgeon who suffers racial prejudice and discrimination almost every day of his or her life? In Cambridge, Massachusetts, police officers are paid more than assistant professors at Harvard University in the same city. How do we assess their relative social statuses when the police officers have considerably more income but considerably less prestige and influence than the professors? The Marxist analysis does not handle these ambiguous cases very satisfactorily.

Weber's Analysis

The German sociologist Max Weber (1946) offered a very influential analysis that confronts these problems. Weber's approach is a multidimensional one. He breaks the single concept of class down into three distinct but related elements, which we may translate as political status, or *power,* economic status, or *wealth,* and social status, or *prestige.* Clearly, a person may be politically powerful but have little wealth (like Ralph Nader), or may be very wealthy but have no prestige (like a Mafia boss), or may have prestige but not wealth (like an impoverished aristocrat). The multidimensional approach enables us to take account of many inconsistencies that the Marxist approach overlooks. Instead of trying to decide whether a Cambridge police officer is of a higher or lower class than a Harvard assistant professor, we can rank them on all three dimensions. In this case the police officer would have economic status superior to that of the professor, but the professor would have political and social status superior to that of the police officer.

Power, wealth, and prestige can thus be independent of each other. In practice, however, they are usually very closely associated. The reason is that any one can often be "converted" into any of the others. This is particularly true of wealth, which can readily be used to acquire power or prestige. The prestige ratings given by the public to various occupations have been studied by sociologists since 1927 through opinion polls in the United States and several other industrialized societies. These ratings have been very consistent over the years, both within the United States and among the various countries that have been studied (Hodge, Siegel, and Rossi, 1964; Hodge, Treiman, and Rossi, 1966; Inkeles and Rossi, 1956; Reiss *et al,* 1961; Armer, 1968).

As the data in Figure 10.3 suggest, prestige is closely linked to the income of workers in different occupations, and the holders of political power tend to be ranked highly. There are a few exceptions, however. Professionals who earn relatively low incomes, such as ministers and teachers, seem to draw their prestige from their professional identity and educational achievements rather than their income. Slightly stigmatized workers, such as funeral undertakers and nightclub singers, have a lower prestige than their incomes would predict. Despite these minor discrepancies, the overall trend is clear. Wealth, power, and prestige are closely linked.

Many sociologists recognize this fact, and assess people's social positions through a measure called *socioeconomic status* (SES). This measure takes into account a complex of factors, such as educational background and place of residence, as well as income. An SES rating thus includes the dimensions of power and prestige as well as that of wealth.

Weber's distinction is useful in many ambiguous cases. For many other purposes, however, the Marxist analysis of class in terms of economic position alone is adequate. We will discuss the difficulties of determining social class membership more fully in Chapter 11 (Social Class in the United States).

PRESTIGE RATINGS OF OCCUPATIONS IN THE UNITED STATES

Occupation	Score	Occupation	Score
U.S. Supreme Court Justice	94	Newspaper columnist	73
Physician	93	Policeman	72
Nuclear physicist	92	Reporter on a daily newspaper	71
Scientist	92	Bookkeeper	70
Government scientist	91	Radio announcer	70
State governor	91	Insurance agent	69
Cabinet member in the federal government	90	Tenant farmer—one who owns livestock and machinery and manages the farm	69
College professor	90	Local official of a labor union	67
U.S. Representative in Congress	90	Manager of a small store in a city	67
Chemist	89	Mail carrier	66
Diplomat in the U.S. Foreign Service	89	Railroad conductor	66
Lawyer	89	Traveling salesman for a wholesale concern	66
Architect	88	Plumber	65
County judge	88	Barber	63
Dentist	88	Machine operator in a factory	63
Mayor of a large city	87	Owner-operator of a lunch stand	63
Member of the board of directors of a large corporation	87	Playground director	63
Minister	87	Corporal in the regular army	62
Psychologist	87	Garage mechanic	62
Airline pilot	86	Truck driver	59
Civil engineer	86	Fisherman who owns his own boat	58
Head of a department in a state government	86	Clerk in a store	56
Priest	86	Milk route man	56
Banker	85	Streetcar motorman	56
Biologist	85	Lumberjack	55
Sociologist	83	Restaurant cook	55
Captain in the regular army	82	Singer in a nightclub	54
Accountant for a large business	81	Filling station attendant	51
Public schoolteacher	81	Coal miner	50
Building contractor	80	Dock worker	50
Owner of a factory that employs about 100 people	80	Night watchman	50
Artist who paints pictures that are exhibited in galleries	78	Railroad section hand	50
Author of novels	78	Restaurant waiter	49
Economist	78	Taxi driver	49
Musician in a symphony orchestra	78	Bartender	48
Official of an international labor union	77	Farmhand	48
County agricultural agent	76	Janitor	48
Electrician	76	Clothes presser in a laundry	45
Railroad engineer	76	Soda fountain clerk	44
Owner-operator of a printing shop	75	Sharecropper—one who owns no livestock or equipment and does not manage farm	42
Trained machinist	75	Garbage collector	39
Farm owner and operator	74	Street sweeper	36
Undertaker	74	Shoe shiner	34
Welfare worker for a city government	74		

Source: Robert W. Hodge *et al.*, "Occupational Prestige in the United States, 1925–1963," *American Journal of Sociology*, 70 (November, 1964), pp. 286–302.

Figure 10.3 This table shows the prestige ratings given by Americans to various occupations. The most prestigious jobs appear to be those that yield high income, offer political power, or require specialized knowledge.

Stratified Societies: Three Examples

Our discussion up to this point has been mostly theoretical. Let's look now at stratification in practice in three very contrasting modern societies: India, in which there is still a caste system; Britain, which is perhaps the most class-conscious of the advanced industrial societies; and the Soviet Union, a society that claims to have abolished classes altogether.

India: A Caste Society

The Indian caste system is a very ancient one: it has been a fundamental feature of Indian life for over 2500 years. Although the system was officially abolished by the Indian government in 1949, it is still an important element in the social life of the country, especially in rural areas that are comparatively unaffected by modernization.

In theory there are four main castes, or *varnas,* which were originally based on racial or ethnic distinctions between segments of the Indian population. The highest *varna* is that of the *Brahmins,* or priests and scholars; next are the *Kshatriyas,* or nobles and warriors; below them are the *Vaishyas,* or merchants and skilled artisans; and finally there are *Shudras,* or common laborers. Beyond the actual castes are the *Harijans,* or outcastes. The outcastes are often called "untouchables" because merely to touch an outcaste, or even to be touched by an outcaste's shadow, is a form of ritual pollution for members of the higher *varnas.* The rules concerning ritual pollution and the ritual purification that must follow it are highly elaborate. In some regions the glance of a *Shudra* or *Harijan* at a cooking pot is sufficient to defile the food, and the passage of a low-caste person over a bridge may pollute the entire stream beneath. In some areas untouchables are not allowed in the villages during the early morning and late afternoon hours, because their bodies cast such long shadows at these times and make them a ritual danger to others. Some low-caste groups are not only untouchable but also unseeable. There is one group of washerwomen who work only at night so as not to show themselves in the daytime.

In practice there are not so much four castes in India as literally thousands of subcastes, or *jati.* These *jati* are sometimes confined to local areas, but membership in some of them is spread across India. Many *jati* contain only a handful of members; others contains millions. A *jati* is often linked to a particular occupation—scavenging, silkworm raising, or even snake charming—and all members of the *jati* are expected to follow the same occupation. No individual can ever change his or her status, since status is determined by caste and one's caste is that of one's parents. Intermarriage between castes is taboo, and intermarriage between members of different *jati* is strongly disapproved of and rarely takes place.

Figure 10.4 This woman is a member of the outcaste category of Indian society. The social status of the outcastes is so low that they are not even included in the caste system. Members of higher castes may consider it a form of ritual pollution even to be touched by the shadow of an outcaste—and in some cases, even to be looked at by such a person.

The Indian caste system is closely interwined with the Hindu religion, which is explicitly concerned with maintaining the stratified social order. Each of the *varnas* and *jati* has rules of behavior that every member must follow.

According to Hindu doctrine, each person is reincarnated again and again through a series of lifetimes, and one's status in the next lifetime depends entirely on how well one observes the required behavior in this one. Failure to live up to the obligations of the stratification system may result in reincarnation as a member of a lower varna, or perhaps as an outcaste, or even as an animal. The Hindu religion is both an expression of the caste system and the basic mechanism for maintaining it.

The Indian caste system is breaking down fairly rapidly in urban areas, where the difficulty of determining another person's caste in a crowded and anonymous environment makes it impossible to observe the complicated rules of ritual distance or to avoid constant ritual pollution. Industrialism has caused many changes in the urban occupational structure, and it is no longer considered a sacred obligation to do the work traditionally done by members of one's *jati.* Industrial development has also brought about considerable social mobility, both upward and downward, and there are now many poor *Brahmins,* many rich *Shudras,* and even wealthy outcastes. In the rural areas, however, a highly rigid and closed system still dominates the lives of millions of Indians (Hutton, 1963; Bergel, 1962; Zinkin, 1962; Berreman, 1960, 1973; Taylor *et al.,* 1965; Robertson, 1976; Srinivas *et al.,* 1959).

Britain: A Class Society

Modern British society is stratified along the lines of class. The number of classes in a class system and the exact boundaries between the classes are always a matter of some debate. Most observers would probably agree, however, that the country has a very small upper class consisting mostly of families that have been wealthy for some generations; a small upper-middle class consisting of professionals and other more recently wealthy people; a fairly large lower-middle class containing skilled white-collar workers; and a large working class containing somewhat more than half of the total population.

Unlike most other European societies, Britain survived the transition from feudalism to industrialism without a revolution. The monarchy was never abolished, and an intricate system of prestige awards—knighthoods, peerages, earldoms—survives intact. The parliamentary system still reflects feudal arrangements. There are two legislative assemblies, the elected House of Commons and the largely hereditary House of Lords. Although the power of the monarch and of the House of Lords has been whittled away to insignificance, rituals of pomp still surround these aspects of British life. The mere presence of people entitled to put "Sir," "Lady," or "Lord" before their names obviously heightens differences between the upper class and the bulk of the population, and people in Britain are acutely aware that theirs is a class society.

Despite the efforts of post-World War II leftist governments, wealth remains very unequally distributed in British society. Tax laws have been very effective in reducing differences in income. Incomes over $35,000 are taxed at a rate of nearly 90 percent, and tax loopholes are almost nonexistent. Yet there are still glaring disparities between the rich and the poor because most wealth in the country is acquired not through salaried income but through inheritance. A 1976 Royal Commission reported that the richest 1 percent of the population owned 25 percent of the nation's wealth, the richest 5 percent owned nearly 50 percent, and the richest 10 percent owned over 60 percent of the wealth. These inequalities are being gradually reduced through heavy inheritance taxes, but the process is a slow one because it must await the deaths of the rich.

Class differences in life-styles and behavior are far more evident in Britain than in the United States. Men of very high status, for example, are likely to wear bowler hats; men of low status, cloth caps. The upper classes are enthusiastic about cricket; the lower classes, about soccer. The single most important indicator of social class, however, is accent. There are very distinct differences among the accents of the upper, middle, and lower classes, and there are minute variations of accent within these classes. Any person in Britain can pinpoint the social status of another the moment that person utters a sentence, and this indicator overrides any others that might be inconsistent with it, such as style of dress. The observant American tourist will notice that the British tend to respond to one another quite differently on the basis of accent. A salesperson, for example, will call someone with an upper-class accent "sir" or "madam," but may address a person with a lower-class accent as "dear," "love," or "mate."

Apart from the inheritance of wealth, the principal mechanism for maintaining the class system is education.

Figure 10.5 Modern British society is marked by very noticeable class divisions. Despite attempts by successive socialist governments to redistribute the wealth of the society, there is still an affluent upper class that lives mainly off inherited wealth and capital investments. Members of this tiny class dominate most British institutions.

Approximately 5 percent of the nation's children attend what are called "public" schools. These schools are not public; they are private and charge very high fees, and most of them are single-sex boarding schools. Children of the upper classes share a common experience in these schools and benefit from their superior academic facilities. Attendance at these schools confers great advantages later in life. No less than eighteen former pupils of the most prestigious private school, Eton, have become prime ministers (Baltzell, 1958), and as recently as the sixties, half of the members of the cabinet came from this one school alone. The pattern is repeated at the college level. Two universities, Oxford and Cambridge, enjoy far greater prestige than the others, and about half of their entrants come from the private schools. Graduates of Oxford and Cambridge are very disproportionately represented at the upper levels of British society and dominate politics, law, the church, the media, corporations, and the civil service. The country's elite maintains its contacts through exclusive men's clubs and forms what is known in Britain as "the establishment" or "the magic circle."

Social mobility in Britain compares unfavorably with that in the United States and in several other industrialized societies (Treiman and Terrell, 1972; Lipset and Bendix, 1959). One study found that a person of manual-worker origins has a better chance of reaching the elite in the United States than does a person of middle-class origins in Britain (Fox and Miller, 1965b). Although the country's depressed economy has heightened class tensions in recent years, many members of the lower classes remain deferential toward the middle and upper classes. More than a quarter of manual workers, in fact, identify themselves as middle class (Runciman, 1966). Although nearly 60 percent of the population is working class, the right-wing Conservative Party has ruled the country for most of this century. It has been able to do so because it has consistently drawn the support of about a third of the working-class voters.

The Soviet Union: A Classless Society?

The government of the Soviet Union has abolished private ownership of the means of producing and distributing wealth and claims to be working toward the creation of a totally egalitarian, communist society. Although the Soviet Union is often described as "communist" in the West, there is actually no society that regards itself as communist. The Soviet Union claims only to have reached the intermediate stage of socialism, in which classes have been formally abolished but strong centralized government is still needed to guide the transition to the future society.

There is no doubt that the Soviet Union does not have a dominant, profit-making class such as those found in all capitalist societies. Large amounts of wealth cannot be inherited, special privileges such as private education cannot be bought for the next generation, and the amassing of private profit is illegal. In fact, "profiteering" is punishable in some instances by the death sentence. But whether the Soviet Union has successfully abolished classes is a matter of some debate (Parkin, 1971; Lane, 1971). In the Soviet Union, as in all other East European socialist societies, the incomes of officials in the upper levels of the communist party and government bureaucracy are several times the incomes of ordinary people. The bureaucrats enjoy many privileges denied to the masses, such as better housing, luxurious vacation facilities, and the use of free automobiles (Djilas, 1957).

The Soviet Union is ruled by a small elite of officials who have only a fictional responsibility to the general population. This ruling elite is significantly more powerful than any comparable elite in the West, for two reasons. First, it has both political and economic power concentrated in its hands, whereas in capitalist societies power is more diffuse. Second, the Soviet elite does not have to face periodic free elections, and its policies are not subject to public criticism.

There is little doubt that power, wealth, and prestige are very unequally distributed in Soviet society, and that occupational status is often passed down from one generation to the next (Lipset, 1973). Whether the Soviet elite actually constitutes a class is perhaps a matter of definition. If we define a class in terms of its control over basic national resources, then the Soviet elite is clearly a class, and a very powerful one. If, however, we specify that the ruling class must use its control of resources primarily for its own benefit, as is the case in all other stratified societies, then the Soviet elite cannot be considered a class. The Soviet system certainly differs from all other stratification systems in that there is no "leisure class" that lives off accumulated wealth, and, perhaps more significantly, people cannot inherit large sums of wealth from their parents. There also seems to be more social mobility and less of a gap between the strata in the Soviet Union than we find in Western capitalist societies. The issue of whether the Soviet Union is a class society is still unsettled, and it remains to be seen whether that country—or any other society with a different interpretation of communism, such as China—can arrive at an unambiguously classless society.

Maintaining Stratification: The Role of Ideology

How does any stratification system survive? At first sight, it seems highly unlikely that any stratification system would last for very long, because in every case a small minority enjoys unequal access to scarce resources and thus deprives the majority of a fair share in what the society produces. Yet stratification systems do persist, and some of the most rigid and inegalitarian—such as the European feudal system and the Indian caste system—last for many centuries. How are these systems maintained?

Any successful system requires some kind of *legitimacy*. If the bulk of the people do not regard the social order as legitimate—that is, as valid and justified—the system is inherently unstable and will soon collapse. The ruling elite in any stratified society can apply force to try to maintain the system, but in fact most stratification systems survive without much use of force. The reason is simple. The system is accepted because it is taken for granted and regarded as "natural" by all concerned. The legitimacy of the system rests on its habitual, unthinking acceptance by the people, including the subordinate as well as the dominant strata.

A political system is legitimated by the dominant *ideology* of the society, the set of beliefs that explain and justify the existing order. Karl Marx systematically explored the role of ideologies in legitimating social stratification, and his views are now widely accepted, even by sociologists who reject some of his other theories. Marx's argument was simple. The dominant ideology in any society is always the ideology of the ruling class, and it always justifies that class's economic interests. Of course, other ideologies may exist in a society, but an ideology can never become dominant or widely accepted until the class that

Figure 10.6 Black South Africans riot during the widespread disturbances that took place in the country in 1976. Although many members of the older generation of South African blacks opposed the rioting, young blacks appear to have developed a general consciousness of oppression. In Marxist terms, a large part of the older generation still accepts the legitimacy of the South African caste system, but the younger generation has developed a class consciousness. Inevitably, conflict between the dominant and subordinate castes has resulted.

holds it, and whose own interests it justifies, becomes the dominant class. In a society dominated by capitalists, therefore, the dominant ideology will be capitalism, not socialism. In a society dominated by socialists, the dominant ideology will be socialism, not capitalism. In a society dominated by slave owners, the dominant ideology will justify the institution of slavery, not the idea of human equality.

It is easy to see why members of the dominant group should believe in the dominant ideology, but what about the members of the subordinate group? They usually also accept the legitimacy of the system, a phenomenon Marx called *false consciousness*—a subjective consciousness that does not accord with the objective facts of one's situation. The oppressed class fails to understand that the life chances of its individual members are linked to their common circumstances as an exploited group. Instead, they attribute their low status to fate, luck, the will of god, or other factors beyond their control. Thus the feudal peasant accepts the legitimacy of the class system, the low-caste Indian accepts the legitimacy of the caste system, and the industrial laborer accepts the legitimacy of the capitalist system. Only if members of the subordinate stratum gain a *class consciousness*—an objective awareness of their common predicament and the reasons for it—do they begin to question the legitimacy of the system. They then develop a new ideology, one that justifies their own interests and consequently seems revolutionary to the dominant class. According to Marx, *class conflict* will then follow.

An ideology is a complex belief system. It may include religious, political, economic, and other elements. The advanced feudal system, for example, was legitimated by the political and religious doctrine of the divine right of kings. This was the notion that the monarch derives authority directly from God. When the king delegated some of this authority to the nobles, it followed logically that the peasants were under a divine imperative to obey them also. The peasants seem, on the whole, to have accepted this doctrine as unquestioningly as their masters did. The feudal system was eventually overthrown when a new class emerged. This was a class of urban capitalists, armed with a new ideology of political democracy and economic freedom. In much the same way, the ideology of colonialism provided a justification for the acts of the colonists. They saw themselves not as exploiters of raw materials and sweated labor but as bearers of the "white man's burden," the noble but demanding task of bringing Christian civilization to "inferior" peoples. The subject peoples seem to have accepted the colonists' view that they were genuinely inferior. Their acceptance of the legitimacy of the colonial system made it easier for tiny European minorities to dominate vast populations until a new nationalist ideology emerged in the colonies after World War II. The Indian caste system is yet another example. It is legitimated primarily by religion and has been almost unquestioningly accepted by all castes, even outcastes, for thousands of years.

Like the inequalities of feudal, colonial, or Indian societies, the inequalities of American society are also legitimated by an ideology, and this ideology also tends to be accepted unquestioningly by the dominant and subordinate classes alike. In the American ideology, inequality is justified as a means of providing incentives and rewarding achievement. The class system is legitimated by the belief (though not the fact) that people have an equal opportunity to improve their status. Everyone is supposed to have

Figure 10.7 Like the subordinate strata in other stratified societies, working-class Americans generally appear to accept the legitimacy of the American system. Workers have frequently demonstrated against radical changes in the system and appear to accept the American ideological belief that inequality is justified by equality of opportunity. Marx called attitudes and behavior of this kind "false consciousness," a subjective understanding of one's position that does not accord with the objective facts.

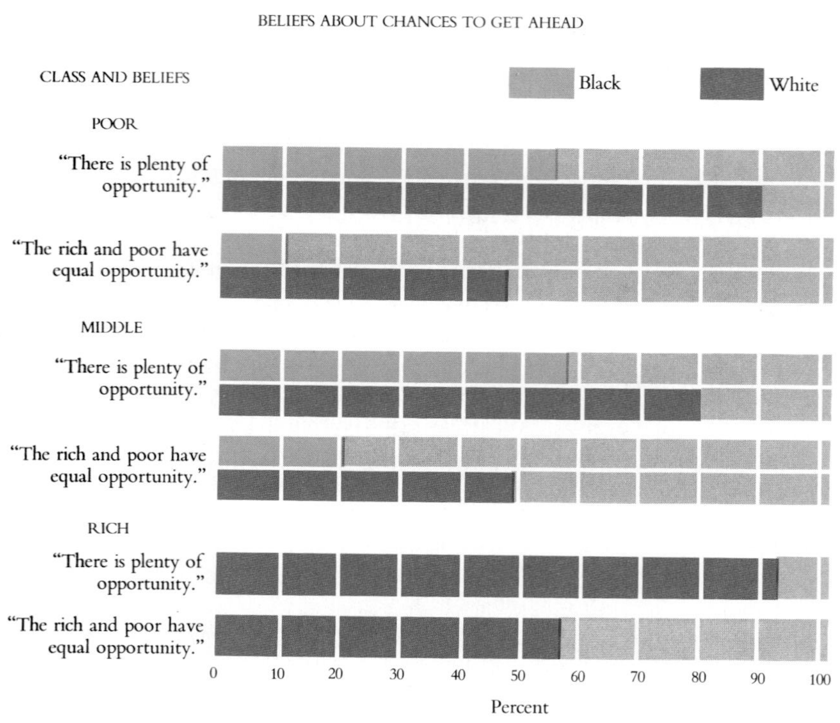

Source: Joan H. Rytina *et al.*, "Income and Stratification Ideology: Beliefs about the American Opportunity Structure," *American Journal of Sociology*, 75 (January, 1970), p. 708.

Figure 10.8 Lower-class white Americans are almost as convinced as upper-class Americans that there is "plenty of opportunity" in the United States and that the rich and the poor have equal opportunity—a belief that sociological research has shown to be entirely incorrect. Black Americans, however, seem to have a more realistic assessment of the opportunities available to members of different classes.

the same chance to get rich by working hard. Those who do not get rich (that is, most of us, and especially those who started out from a low-status family) therefore have only bad luck or themselves to blame. The well-socialized American who becomes a "failure" in the class system is inclined to attribute the fault to fate or to personal failings—not to the elite, and not to the system as a whole (Robertson, 1976).

Theories of Stratification

Why are virtually all societies stratified? Sociologists have tended to take one of two distinct positions on the problem. The *functionalist* perspective, adopted mainly by theorists influenced by Talcott Parsons (1937, 1940), sees stratification as an inevitable and even necessary feature of society. The *conflict* perspective, taken by theorists under the direct or indirect influence of Karl Marx, sees stratification as avoidable, unnecessary, and the source of most human injustice. More recently Gerhard Lenski (1966a) has offered a third perspective, an *evolutionary* approach that combines elements of the other two.

The Functionalist Approach

Functionalist theory analyzes elements in culture and social structure in terms of their effects or functions for other parts of the system. It is usually assumed that these functions contribute to the stability and survival of society as a whole. Functionalists have argued that if stratification exists in all societies, it must have some useful function in maintaining those societies. The classic statement of this position is that of Kingsley Davis and Wilbert Moore (1945), who contend that some form of stratification is a functional necessity. They emphasize, however, that they are merely trying to explain this situation, not to justify it.

Davis and Moore point out that some social roles require scarce talents or prolonged training. Not everyone can be a surgeon, a nuclear physicist, or a military strategist. If a society is to function effectively, it must find some way of matching these roles with the people who have the talents and skills to fill them. The roles that require scarce talents or lengthy training usually involve stress, considerable sacrifice, and heavy responsibilities. Those who assume these important roles must therefore be rewarded with wealth, power, prestige, or some combination of the three, or else they would have no motive for performing their tasks. Thus a society that values senators above garbage collectors will give higher status and rewards to senators; one that values film stars above carpenters will give higher status and rewards to film stars; one that values warriors more than priests will give higher status and rewards to warriors. This unequal distribution of social rewards is functional for society because roles that demand scarce talents are filled by the most able individuals. Social stratification, however, is the inevitable result.

This analysis was very popular among American sociologists for many years, perhaps because it fitted so well with American cultural values about individual achievement. Some critics have argued, however, that the analysis contains serious flaws (Tumin, 1953, 1955, 1963, Buckley, 1958; Wrong, 1959).

The principal criticism of the theory is that it seems to lose touch with reality in several respects. Stratification systems simply do not work in practice the way Davis and Moore have them working in theory. A quick glance at any stratification system reveals some of the weaknesses in their argument. Some people whose roles have no apparent value to society are often highly rewarded, such as the jet-setting inheritors of family fortunes. Some people whose roles are of limited value, such as film stars, may earn very much more than people whose roles are very important, such as the President of the United States. Above all, many people have low rewards because their social status is ascribed on the basis of characteristics over which they have no control: blacks in the United States, outcastes in India, and so on. Others have high rewards for the same reason: wealthy aristocrats in Britain, Brahmins in India.

The functionalist argument is at its weakest in all cases where social status is inherited, not achieved by the individual. This is the situation in all caste societies, and to a large extent it is the situation in all class societies. Even in the most open class systems, the rate of intergenerational mobility is very low (Lipset and Bendix, 1959). In general, social stratification does not function to ensure that the fittest people train for and fill the most important roles. It functions to ensure that most people stay where they are. It is true that some people in some stratified societies can gain high status through personal efforts. But these people, like the poor, then pass their status on to their descendants. Inequality thus spreads and diffuses with the passage of time, until its ultimate form bears no relationship to its origins, functional or otherwise.

Davis and Moore overlook the *dysfunctions* of stratification for society. In practice, social stratification ensures that people do not have equal access to social roles, so it *hinders* the allocation of roles on merit. All stratification systems offer entire categories of people different life chances because of the circumstances of their birth, and therefore stratification does not make the best use of the talents of the population. And if the lower stratum comes to believe that the system is unjust, social conflict will result. In such cases stratification does not contribute to the maintenance of the social system. It can, and frequently does, lead to the disruption of the entire social order.

The Conflict Approach

Conflict theorists reject the functionalist model of society as a fairly harmonious, well-integrated system whose various features contribute to overall social stability. Instead, they regard conflict over social values and group interests as intrinsic to any society. The conflict approach to stratification has always found favor with European sociologists, perhaps because their societies have a long history of class conflict and still have more noticeable class hostilities than those found in the United States.

Karl Marx argued that history is essentially the story of class conflict between the exploiters and the exploited. Social stratification is created and maintained by one group in order to protect and enhance its economic interests. Stratification exists only because the rich and power-

FUNCTIONALIST AND CONFLICT VIEWS OF STRATIFICATION: A COMPARISON

The Functionalist View	The Conflict View
(1) Stratification is universal, necessary, and inevitable.	(1) Stratification may be universal without being necessary or inevitable.
(2) The social system shapes the stratification system.	(2) The stratification system shapes the social system.
(3) Stratification arises from the need for social integration and coordination.	(3) Stratification arises from group conquest, competition, and conflict.
(4) Stratification is an expression of shared social values.	(4) Stratification is an expression of the values of powerful groups.
(5) Tasks and rewards are equitably allocated.	(5) Tasks and rewards are inequitably allocated.
(6) Stratification facilitates the optimal functioning of society and the individual.	(6) Stratification impedes the optimal functioning of society and the individual.

Figure 10.9 This table compares and contrasts the essential ingredients of the functionalist and the conflict views of stratification.

ful are determined to preserve their advantages. Marx saw class conflict as the key to historical change: every ruling class is eventually overthrown by the subordinate class, which then becomes the new ruling class. This process repeats itself until the final confrontation between workers and capitalists in industrial society. Writing in England at a time when workers were subjected to appalling conditions in the factories, Marx predicted that the capitalists would grow fewer and stronger as a result of their endless competition, that the middle class would disappear into the working class, and that the growing poverty of the workers would spark a successful revolution. The workers would then create a new socialist society in which the means of producing and distributing wealth would be publicly and not privately owned. Socialism would lead ultimately to a communist society, in which inequality, alienation, conflict, and human misery would be things of the past.

Marx's theories have tended to be neglected by American sociologists for most of this century. One reason is that Marx has been associated, rather unfairly, with the corruption of his doctrines by the Soviet Union and other societies of Eastern Europe. Another reason is that his predictions about the future of industrial capitalism were hopelessly wrong. He did not foresee that individual capitalists would be largely replaced by corporations. He did not anticipate that the wealth of industrialism would create a much larger middle class or that the poor would be better off, both relatively and absolutely, than they were in his own time. He was even wrong in predicting that successful socialist revolutions would take place in highly industrialized societies. Without exception, these uprisings have taken place in advanced agricultural societies, such as Russia, China, and Cuba at the times of their revolutions. Very few Western sociologists accept Marx's view that historical forces will lead us inevitably to a classless society.

Despite the recognition of the flaws in Marx's theory, there has recently been a great renewal of interest in his work. Sociologists now appreciate that Marx's failure as a prophet does not necessarily invalidate his basic insight: that conflict over scarce resources leads to the creation of caste and class systems and that in every case the interests of the dominant class are served by the ideology and the power of the state. The implication of the conflict perspective is clear. Stratification is not a functional necessity at all—although it is certainly convenient for those who benefit by it.

The Evolutionary Approach

The debate between conflict and functionalist theorists became at times very heated, especially during the sixties. Several writers have pointed out, however, that the two perspectives are not necessarily incompatible (for example, Dahrendorf, 1958; Van den Berghe, 1963). The most promising attempt at a synthesis of the two positions is that of Gerhard Lenski (1966a), who emphasizes both conflict and functionalist elements in the evolution of stratification systems.

Lenski starts with the idea that people generally find it more rewarding to fulfill their own wants and ambitions than those of others. He agrees that this tendency may be regrettable and that it may be possible to socialize human beings so that they do not behave in this way, but he points out that it remains an almost universal feature of social life. Most of the things that people want are scarce: the demand for them exceeds the supply. Inevitably, therefore, there will be some conflict over the distribution of these rewards in all societies. And because people are unequally equipped for the competitive struggle, social inequality will inevitably result. Sometimes these inequalities will be functional for society, but forms of stratification will tend to persist long after they have ceased to be useful. A certain amount of inequality, then, is inevitable and perhaps even necessary, but most societies are much more stratified than they need to be.

Lenski then traces the evolution of social stratification, showing how the form it takes is related to the society's means of economic production. In hunting and gathering societies there is no stratification. Populations are small and intimate, and the members are essentially equal. There is no surplus wealth, and so there is no opportunity for some people to become wealthier than others. In horticultural and pastoral societies a surplus product is possible, and chieftainships emerge as powerful families gain control over the surplus. These societies are not stratified, however, because inequalities exist only among specific individuals, and there are no distinct castes or classes. But with the development of advanced horticulture into agriculture, the picture changes radically. Agriculture allows people to produce a considerable surplus, and a dominant elite makes claim to this wealth. The society becomes divided into strata according to their access to wealth and other rewards. Power becomes concentrated in the hands

Figure 10.10 Lenski's evolutionary approach shows how the nature of stratification varies from one type of society to another. In ancient Egypt, an agricultural society, there was a vast gap between the upper class and the peasants. Tens of thousands of members of the lower class toiled for years simply to create enormous burial monuments for their rulers. In modern Egypt such inequalities would be inconceivable, as they would be in any industrializing or industrialized society.

of a monarch, who typically has almost absolute control over the subjects.

These rigid divisions are undermined, however, when a society shifts to industrialism. Industrial production requires a skilled and mobile labor force, and its efficiency is impaired if people are prevented from using their talents to the full. In the early stages of industrialism there is a vast gap between the rich and the poor as a rural peasantry is transformed into an urban work force. This situation still prevails in the less industrialized nations of the world. In the more advanced industrial societies, however, the lower class shrinks in size and the middle class expands rapidly, because the entire society shares, however unequally, in the great wealth that industrialism produces. Governments become more democratic, and measures such as welfare and progressive income taxes limit excessive inequalities in wealth. The rate of social mobility increases as a variety of new jobs are created.

Lenski's theory is not a rigid one, and he accepts that there may be some exceptions to the general trend he outlines. He also notes that independent factors, such as external threats or the role of particular leaders, may have an impact on the way stratification systems evolve. In general, however, he believes that the long-term trend in all industrial societies will be toward less social inequality. His theory explains why inequalities are so often far more extreme than could ever be necessary from a functional point of view: once stratification is built into a society, privileged groups use their advantages to gain even more advantages. While he acknowledges the importance of conflict in stratification systems, he does not reduce all explanations to this one factor alone. He accepts that some inequalities may be unavoidable and even useful.

Whichever view one accepts, one must recognize that social stratification cannot simply be taken for granted. Castes and classes are socially constructed in society after society by countless men and women. Since social stratification is socially created it must, in principle, be socially modifiable as well—provided only that people are conscious of their own ability to change the systems they have built.

In this chapter we have considered the general principles of social stratification. In the next chapter we apply these principles to a specific stratification system, social class in the United States.

Summary

1. All societies differentiate among their members. This differentiation leads to social inequality. In most societies social inequality is built into the social structure, resulting in social stratification. Under social stratification, entire categories of a population have different life chances.

2. Stratification systems may be closed or open. In closed systems the boundaries between strata are fixed and status is ascribed and lifelong. In open systems the boundaries are flexible and new statuses can be achieved. Closed systems take the form of castes; open systems, of classes.

3. Change from one status to another is called social mobility. Mobility may be horizontal, vertical (upward or downward), or intergenerational. The extent of mobility in a society depends on the amount of mobility the society can support and the conditions under which people are allowed to be mobile.

4. It is often difficult to determine an individual's status in a class society. Marx argued that economic factors are decisive; those who own and control the means of production are the dominant class; those who do not, and are exploited, are the subordinate class. Weber broke the concept of class into three related dimensions: power, wealth, and prestige. In practice, these three variables correlate strongly.

5. India is a caste society, in which the different *varnas* and *jatis* are endogamous and have different access to valued resources. The system has been maintained in the past by the Hindu religion, but it is tending to break down. Britain is a class society in which wealth is unequally shared and in which a small elite enjoys disproportionate power and prestige. Education is an important factor in maintaining the system. The Soviet Union claims to have virtually abolished classes, but in fact there are many disparities in power, wealth, and prestige between the bureaucratic elite and the rest of the population. It is doubtful whether the Soviet Union has really abolished classes.

6. An ideology is a belief system that explains and justifies, or legitimates, some situation. Stratification systems are legitimated by ideologies that are usually accepted by both dominant and subordinate groups. If the subordinate group rejects the ideology, class conflict will follow.

7. Functionalists argue that stratification is functional because it matches important roles with scarce talents. In practice, however, stratification prevents the allocation of roles on merit. Conflict theorists argue that stratification arises because it serves the economic interests of some groups in society; the privileged group maintains the system and transmits its advantages to the next generation. Lenski's evolutionary theory shows how the nature of stratification is influenced by the complexity of a society and its mode of economic production; his theory combines elements of both functionalist and conflict theories.

Important Terms

social inequality	intergenerational mobility
social stratification	exploitation
life chances	surplus wealth
closed system	power
open system	wealth
caste	prestige
endogamy	socioeconomic status
ascribed status	legitimacy
class	ideology
achieved status	false consciousness
social mobility	class consciousness
horizontal mobility	class conflict
vertical mobility	

Suggested Readings

BENDIX, REINHARD, AND SEYMOUR MARTIN LIPSET (EDS.). *Class Status and Power.* New York: Free Press, 1966.

An important and comprehensive collection of articles on social stratification. The selections include many classic contributions to the field and cover virtually all the major issues raised by social stratification.

BOTTOMORE, T. B. *Classes in Modern Society.* New York: Pantheon, 1965.

An excellent and clearly written short introduction to the class systems of modern industrial societies, including Britain, the United States, and the Soviet Union.

HELLER, CELIA (ED.). *Structured Social Inequality.* New York: Macmillan, 1969.

A collection of several important articles on social stratification in the United States and elsewhere. These essays provide an excellent overview of the field.

HUTTON, J. H. *Caste in India: Its Nature, Functions, and Origins.* New York: Oxford University Press, 1963.

This book is the classic analysis of the Indian class system. Hutton shows how the caste system evolved and how it is closely intertwined with Hindu religion. The book includes interesting information about the rituals surrounding the caste system.

LENSKI, GERHARD. *Power and Privilege: A Theory of Social Stratification.* New York: McGraw-Hill, 1966.

Lenski outlines his original and influential theory of stratification. The book contains much fascinating detail about social inequalities in preindustrial as well as industrial societies.

MATRAS, JUDAH. *Social Inequality, Stratification, and Mobility.* Englewood Cliffs, N.J.: Prentice-Hall, 1975.

A detailed and comprehensive text that summarizes research and theories on social stratification and mobility. The book includes material on the United States but also contains a good deal of comparative data.

Reading

Caste and Conflict in South Africa *Ian Robertson*

South Africa offers one of the few examples of a caste system in the modern world. In the past the system has been maintained by an ideology of white superiority, but blacks are now rejecting this ideology, and conflict between the strata is intensifying.

In South Africa's dual economy, a thriving industrial sector coexists with a traditional horticultural and pastoral sector. The population consists of some 17 million blacks, some 4 million whites, and about 3 million members of other minorities, primarily Asians and persons of mixed ancestry. The society is dominated by the white minority, which exerts total political control over all other groups through the most rigid system of racial segregation in history—*apartheid.*

Blacks have no vote in national elections and no representation in the central parliament. Their only political rights are in impoverished reserves occupying 13 percent of the land area of the country. Blacks may leave these areas only to work for the whites but may not bring their spouses and children with them unless they too can obtain work permits. All skilled and most unskilled jobs are reserved by law for whites, and it is a criminal offense for black workers to strike. The average income of black workers is less than a seventh of the whites', who in turn enjoy one of the highest standards of living in the world.

Apartheid segregates the races in every conceivable sphere of human activity. Schools, transport, residential areas, eating places, beaches, and even footbridges are strictly segregated by law. Marriage across the color line is illegal, and sexual relations between blacks and whites carries a punishment of up to seven years imprisonment and a whipping of up to a dozen strokes. Civil liberties are few for whites and virtually nonexistent for blacks. The police may detain any person indefinitely in solitary confinement without trial.

The politically dominant group are the Afrikaners, descendants of early Dutch settlers. The Afrikaners are mostly members of a fundamentalist Calvinist sect, the Dutch Reformed Church, which teaches that racial segregation is God's will. The ideology of the Afrikaners includes the following basic ideas: the Afrikaner people are chosen by God to work his will on the African continent; Western civilization is inextricably linked to white skin color; the blacks are racially inferior; race purity is a moral imperative, to be maintained at any cost; and evil forces are at work in the world, determined to subvert white, Christian South Africa.

Statements by prominent Afrikaner leaders provide some insight into their view of the South African stratification system. The last Prime Minister, Dr. H. F. Verwoerd (subsequently assassinated) explained his policies to parliament in these terms: "We want to make South Africa white. . . . Keeping it white can mean only one thing, namely white domination, not 'leadership,' not 'guidance,' but 'control,' 'supremacy'." His predecessor as Prime Minister, Dr. D. F. Malan, spoke as follows about the special role of the Afrikaner in God's plan for the universe:

The history of the Afrikaner reveals a determination and a definiteness of purpose which make one feel that Afrikanerdom is not the work of man but a creation of God. We have a divine right to be Afrikaners. Our history is the highest work of art of the Architect of the ages.

The Afrikaner elite is well aware that international opinion is highly critical of *apartheid,* but this criticism is taken as evidence that there is something seriously wrong with the rest of the world, not South Africa. The leading Afrikaner newspaper comments:

In Britain and America, the spiritual capitulation of the White man is the order of the day, to such an extent that the British are apparently prepared to become a bastard race within a few generations. . . . The liberalistic sickness will not continue. . . . When liberalism disappears and a normal situation rules again, common South Africa will be praised because it did not want to go with the stream.

The socialization process for white children makes the *apartheid* system seem a legitimate and moral one. School textbooks systematically justify the system. One high-school book declares:

Our forefathers believed that like must seek like. Also, the non-whites do not like the bastardizing of their people. During the years gone by the whites therefore remained white and the non-whites, non-white. It has become the traditional principle that although white and non-white share a common fatherland, there is no blood-mixing, and there is no eating, drinking, or visiting together. This principle is also entrenched in various laws. The living together of white and non-white is not only a great shame, but it is also forbidden by law.

The religious legitimation of *apartheid* as

a manifestation of God's will is explained in another school text:

The Creator has a purpose in the placing of a people in a determined place. We as a people are not fortuitously here in Africa. It is the will of our Father who is in Heaven.... Taking all the circumstances into account, the coming into existence of the white Christian civilization, in spite of the mass of the non-whites, can be seen as nothing less than a providence of the Almighty. We believe that Providence planted us more than three centuries ago on the Southern corner of Africa because He had a definite purpose with us.

How does the black majority perceive this system? The growing unrest among blacks, which in 1976 led to riots throughout the country and cost hundreds of lives, indicates that the system is not considered legitimate by the majority of the population. Although black South Africans seemed to accept the legitimacy of white rule earlier in this century, this no longer seems to be the case. Nelson Mandela, the man generally acknowledged as leader of the black resistance movement, is currently serving a life sentence for attempting to overthrow the regime. His remarks at his trial present a sharply contrasting view of the stratification system:

South Africa is the richest country in Africa, and could be one of the richest countries in the world. But it is a land of extremes and remarkable contrasts. The Whites enjoy what may well be the highest standard of living in the world, while Africans live in poverty and misery . . . under conditions similar to those of serfs in the Middle Ages. The complaint of the Africans . . . is not only that they are poor and the Whites are rich, but that the laws that are made by the Whites are designed to preserve this situation. . . . The lack of human dignity experienced by Africans is the direct result of the policy of White supremacy. . . . Whites tend to regard Africans as an inferior breed. They do not look upon them as people with families of their own; they do not realize that they have emotions—that they fall in love like White people do, that they want to be with their wives and children like White people want to be with theirs, that they want to earn enough money to support their families properly, to feed and clothe them and send them to school. . . . Africans want a just share in the whole of South Africa.

In sociological terms, South Africa is a caste society. Status is ascriptive: it is determined at birth on the basis of skin color and is lifelong and unchangeable. The society is a completely closed one; there is no social mobility whatever between the strata. The system reflects and maintains the economic interests of the dominant caste. Through *apartheid,* the whites are able to keep black wages at a low level and to monopolize wealth, power, and prestige. They have created an elaborate ideology to legitimate their privileged position.

The various segregation practices are used to maintain social distance between the castes and thus to enhance awareness of the differences that exist. The concern over intermarriage and interracial sex represents a deep fear of ritual pollution in an important area of life, for endogamy (marriage within a caste) is fundamental to the preservation of the system. Unlike many other stratification systems, *apartheid* is based on observable physical differences between the dominant and subordinate groups. Inbreeding would blur the boundaries between the castes and prevent the hereditary transmission of status. Naturally, not all contact between the castes is avoided—only that which suggests racial equality. It is considered a matter of ritual pollution for a white to eat with a black, but it is considered permissible, and indeed it is expected, that the black should cook the meal, serve it, and then wash the dishes.

Like the dominant ideologies of most stratified societies, the ideology of *apartheid* is closely intertwined with religion. When Calvinist Dutch settlers first arrived on the "dark continent" three centuries ago, they faced many challenges and surmounted them with great courage. Believing already in the predestination of individuals, they readily came to believe also in the predestination of entire peoples and became convinced that their destiny was to rule South Africa. The result has been the creation of a very authoritative and ethnocentric group, clinging desperately to its precarious control of a country in which it is a tiny minority.

It is now apparent that the blacks are developing both a general consciousness of oppression and a new ideology that calls for the radical reconstruction of the social order. The future will therefore inevitably be one of conflict between the dominant and subordinate strata. If the subordinate group in any society lacks faith in the legitimacy of the system, only the threat or use of force can preserve the existing order—but not indefinitely.

Source: Adapted from Ian Robertson, "Social Stratification," in David E. Hunter and Phillip Whitten (eds.), *The Study of Anthropology* (New York: Harper & Row, 1976).

ENIGADES
HARLEM

CHAPTER 11 Social Class in the United States

CHAPTER OUTLINE

Social Inequality in the United States
Wealth
Power
Prestige

The American Class System
Problems of Analysis
The Social Classes
Correlates of Class Membership

Social Mobility in the United States

Poverty in the United States
Defining Poverty
Who Are the Poor?
The Causes of Poverty
Attitudes Toward Poverty

The founders of the United States declared in ringing tones that "all men are created equal," and this value has been a central one in American culture ever since. Yet slavery was practiced in the United States for nearly a century after the Declaration of Independence, and legal discrimination against blacks persisted until the 1960s. For decades after the new republic was founded, the vote was restricted to adult white males who owned property; women were not permitted to vote until early in the twentieth century. Despite our professed belief in equality, the United States now contains over 180,000 millionaires while about 26 million people live below the official poverty line.

The reality of American life, then, has fallen far short of the ideal. In practice, the value of equality has always been contradicted by other values, such as those of white superiority, male superiority, economic competition, and individual achievement. As a result, the modern United States is a very unequal society. We will reserve our discussion of race and sex inequalities until later chapters and will focus here on the economic inequalities of American society. These economic inequalities have become structured into society and are passed on from generation to generation. Entire categories of the population have different *life chances,* or probabilities of benefiting from the opportunities the society offers. In short, American society is *stratified* into *social classes* on the basis of economic inequalities.

Social Inequality in the United States

As we saw in Chapter 10 (Social Stratification), social inequality can take many different forms. All forms of inequality, however, involve an unequal distribution of wealth, power, or prestige. The evidence shows that all three, particularly wealth and power, are very unequally distributed in American society.

Wealth

It seems to be generally true that the distribution of wealth (such as capital and other property) and income (such as salaries and wages) becomes steadily more equal as a society becomes more industrialized (Lenski, 1966a; Cutright, 1967). There is general agreement among researchers, however, that the United States is an exception to this trend (Rossides, 1976). There has been little or no equalization of wealth or income in the United States for at least the last quarter century. Moreover, the economic inequalities that exist between the rich and the poor are enormous.

The information on the distribution of wealth in the United States in the past is rather sketchy. The available data for the period 1810 to 1900 show no major changes (Gallman, 1969), and separate data for the period 1922 to 1953 show only a slight drop in the percentage of wealth held by the top 2 percent of families (Lampman, 1962). As Figure 11.1 shows, the poorest fifth of Americans owns only 0.2 percent of the national wealth and the next poorest fifth owns only 2.1 percent. The richest fifth, however, owns 76.0 percent of the national wealth. To put this another way, while the richest fifth owns more than three-quarters of the nation's wealth, the poorest fifth owns only one-five hundredth of it. More than half of the country's wealth, in fact, is owned by one-twentieth of the population (Gans, 1973).

We have rather better information on the distribution of income during this century. There was a small decline in differences in the earnings of families during the early thirties and forties (Kuznets, 1953), but there has been virtually no redistribution of income since that time (H. P. Miller, 1972; Glenn, 1974). As Figure 11.3 shows, there is a huge gap between the incomes of the very rich and the very poor. The bottom fifth of American families receives only 5.4 percent of the income, while the highest fifth receives 41.0 percent. These shares have hardly changed at all since the end of World War II.

Despite these marked disparities in wealth and income, the rising standard of living in the United States has brought benefits to virtually the entire society. The median income of Americans has doubled over the last quarter century. The poor are probably better off in absolute terms than they were earlier in the century, even if their

THE DISTRIBUTION OF WEALTH IN THE UNITED STATES: FIFTHS OF CONSUMER UNITS RANKED BY WEALTH

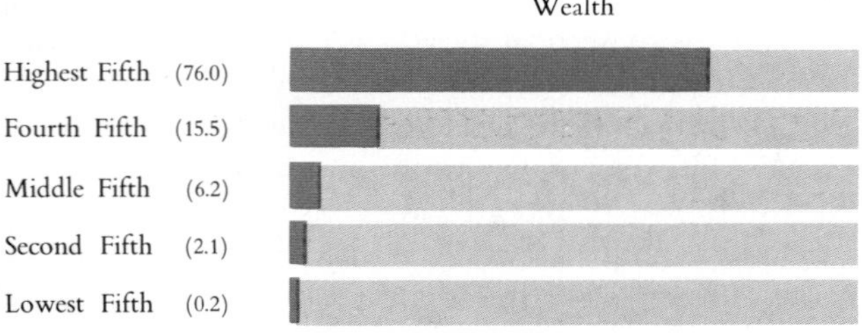

Source: Executive Office of the President, Office of Management and the Budget, *Social Indicators, 1973* (Washington, D.C.: U.S. Government Printing Office, 1973), Chart 5/15.

Figure 11.1 Wealth—that is, property and other capital—is very unequally distributed in the United States. As this chart shows, the richest fifth of consumer units (families and single individuals) owns more than three-quarters of the wealth of American society.

Figure 11.2

"I guess people are just going to have to tighten their belts and fall back on their trust funds for awhile."

relative earnings have changed little. The proportion of the nation that is living in poverty has declined from about 27 percent in the late forties to about 12 percent today. There are still some 37 million Americans, however, who are so poor that they are entitled to food stamps (although millions of these are apparently unaware of and do not make use of the program).

We know much less about the very rich than about the very poor, a fact that probably reflects the ability of the wealthy to keep inquisitive sociologists at arm's length. We do know, however, that the rich consist mainly of two overlapping elements: those living largely on inherited capital investments and those holding high executive positions in major corporations. The private ownership of stock is highly concentrated among a few wealthy individuals and families. The top 1 percent of individuals and families own more than half of the total market value of all privately owned stock and receive nearly half of the total dividend income from stocks (Blume *et al.*, 1974). In a 1976 survey of the nation's largest corporations, *Fortune* magazine found that chief executives enjoyed an annual median income of $209,000, about fifteen times greater than the median family income for the nation as a whole.

The evidence, then, points to a very unequal distribution of the country's economic rewards. As a result of these inequalities, the life chances of those in the upper strata of society are very different from the chances of those in the lower strata. To give but one example, the United States, despite its great affluence, ranks in eighteenth place among the nations of the world in the prevention of infant mortality. The great majority of these preventable childhood deaths occur among the impoverished (Chandler, 1969).

Power

Like wealth, power is very unequally distributed in the United States. The extension of voting rights to the poor, to women, and to blacks seems at first sight to represent a steady broadening of the power base to include different groups in society. Progress in this area, however, has been offset by the growth of vast federal bureaucracies and powerful corporate interests. As a result, power has become concentrated more and more at the upper levels of

PERCENTAGE SHARE OF TOTAL INCOME RECEIVED BY EACH FIFTH AND TOP 5 PERCENT OF FAMILIES, 1957 TO 1974

	Percent Distribution of Aggregate Income					
Year	Lowest Fifth	Second Fifth	Middle Fifth	Fourth Fifth	Highest Fifth	Top 5 Percent
1974	5.4	12.0	17.6	24.1	41.0	15.3
1973	5.5	11.9	17.5	24.0	41.1	15.5
1972	5.4	11.9	17.5	23.9	41.4	15.9
1971	5.5	12.0	17.6	23.8	41.1	15.7
1970	5.4	12.2	17.6	23.8	40.9	15.6
1969	5.6	12.4	17.7	23.7	40.6	15.6
1968	5.6	12.4	17.7	23.7	40.5	15.6
1967	5.5	12.4	17.9	23.9	40.4	15.2
1966	5.6	12.4	17.8	23.8	40.5	15.6
1965	5.2	12.2	17.8	23.9	40.9	15.5
1964	5.1	12.0	17.7	24.0	41.2	15.9
1963	5.0	12.1	17.7	24.0	41.2	15.8
1962	5.0	12.1	17.6	24.0	41.3	15.7
1961	4.7	11.9	17.5	23.8	42.2	16.6
1960	4.8	12.2	17.8	24.0	41.3	15.9
1959	4.9	12.3	17.9	23.8	41.1	15.9
1958	5.0	12.5	18.0	23.9	40.6	15.4
1957	5.0	12.6	18.1	23.7	40.5	15.8

Source: U.S. Bureau of the Census, *Current Population Reports,* Series P–60, no. 97, "Money Income in 1973 of Families and Persons in the United States" (Washington, D.C.: U.S. Government Printing Office, 1975); U.S. Bureau of the Census, *Statistical Abstract, 1975,* Table 636.

Figure 11.3 The distribution of income—salaries, wages, and similar earnings—has remained virtually unchanged since the end of World War II. The richest fifth of American families has consistently received over 40 percent of the total income during this period, while the poorest fifth has consistently received around 5 percent.

the executive branch of government and the corporate economy.

Sociologists have tended to take one of two basic views of the distribution of power. Some, such as C. Wright Mills (1956), argue that American society is dominated by a *power elite* consisting of high officials in government and corporations. This elite operates informally and makes most of the important decisions that affect political and economic life. These decisions are usually made "behind the scenes," and even Congress often has little influence over them. Other sociologists, such as David Riesman (1961), argue that the power structure is more *pluralistic.* In this view, a variety of powerful interest groups struggle for advantage but counterbalance one another in the long run. Different groups compete over different issues, and they often attempt to win the support of the public to further their own interests. We do not yet have enough information to prove or disprove either of these views, but it is significant that the ordinary voter does not figure at all in the power-elite model and is an insignificant element in the pluralistic model. In addition, studies of thirty-three American communities have shown that power at the local level is always exercised either by a small elite or by powerful interest groups (Walton, 1966). A recurrent complaint in American life over the last decade or so—heard not only from radicals but also from the conservative "silent majority"—is that the ordinary citizen is powerless to influence major decisions.

Those with political power in the United States tend to be white, middle-aged, male, Protestant, and, perhaps most significantly, wealthy. Several studies (for example, Domhoff, 1967, 1971; Anderson, 1974a) have shown that there is a tight-knit "establishment" or "governing class" that has a strong informal influence on policy decisions, particularly in economic and foreign affairs. Investigations following the Watergate scandals also uncovered many cases of bribes and payoffs to public officials by commercial interests, including dozens of the most powerful corporations in the United States. These payments were intended to bring about policy decisions favorable to the corporations concerned. (The power structure of the United States is discussed in more detail in Chapter 19, The Political Order.)

An outstanding example of the successful use of behind-the-scenes influence can be found in our tax laws, which contain numerous loopholes that were inserted under pressure from powerful interests. In theory, our tax system is progressive; that is, it should take away a progressively greater proportion of earnings as income rises. In fact, however, the tax laws place a heavier burden on the poor than the rich, because the wealthy are able to exploit a wide range of loopholes. The result is that the wealthy—those earning over $50,000—pay much the same proportion of their income in direct and indirect tax as those earning only a few thousand dollars a year. Philip Stern (1969, 1972, 1973) claims that loopholes have turned the American tax system into "Uncle Sam's welfare program for the rich." Stern found that in one recent year there were 381 people with incomes over $100,000—twenty-one of them with incomes exceeding $1 million—who did not pay any income taxes, quite legally. In another year John Paul Getty, who enjoyed a daily income of $300,000 and who would otherwise have paid a tax of no less than $70 million, used loopholes so effectively that his tax bill was only a few thousand dollars. Many tax deductions, of course, are socially and economically useful and justifiable. They provide, for example, incentives for investment and for gifts to charity. Some deductions, however, are widely used by the rich to avoid taxes. In 1976 Congress finally passed a new tax reform package designed to plug some of these loopholes, but it remains to be seen how effective these new provisions will be.

Prestige

The main determinant of a person's social prestige appears to be occupation. Occupations are valued largely in terms of the incomes of those who hold them, although other factors also affect the prestige of various jobs. The most important of these factors are the amount of control over other people that the job involves and the amount of education necessary to hold the job (Reiss *et al.,* 1961). As Figure 10.3 in Chapter 10 (Social Stratification) suggests, prestige correlates closely with the income level of workers in particular occupations, and the holders of political power tend to be highly ranked.

Unlike power and wealth, which do not seem to be becoming more equally shared, the symbols of prestige have become available to an increasing number of Americans. The main reason is the radical change in the nature of jobs over the course of this century. In 1900 nearly 40 percent of the labor force were farm workers and less than 20 percent held more prestigious white-collar jobs. By the end of the sixties, however, only 5 percent of the labor force worked on farms, and white-collar workers were the largest single occupational category. Blue-collar workers, the largest category in the mid-fifties, now represent a steadily shrinking proportion of the labor force and will constitute less than a third of all workers by 1980. The increase in the proportion of high-prestige jobs has allowed a much greater number of Americans to enjoy more prestigious occupational statuses and the life-styles that go with them.

The American Class System

It is inevitable that there will be some inequalities in any human group, if only because different people have different talents, skills, looks, personalities, physical strength, and so on. Inequality becomes a major sociological concern when it is *structured* into society. When this happens, entire categories of the population have unequal access to wealth, power, and prestige, and these inequalities are transmitted from one generation to the next. This kind of inequality is deeply entrenched in American society in the form of the class system. But how many classes are there in the United States, and what are the characteristics of the different classes?

Problems of Analysis

Social classes do not exist "out there," any more than inches, gallons, or tons do. The concept of class, like the concept of an inch, is something people impose on reality. What exists "out there" is social inequality, but different observers may draw the precise boundaries of class in quite different ways. Just as we could create many different ways of measuring off the length of a piece of wood, so we can create many different ways of categorizing a population into classes.

A sociologist can use three basic methods to analyze the class structure of a society. The first is the *reputational method,* in which the researcher asks people what class they believe other people belong to. The second is the *subjective method,* in which the researcher asks people what class they believe they themselves belong to. The third is the *objective method,* in which the researcher fits people into an arbitrary number of classes on the basis of some predetermined criterion, such as annual income. All three methods have been used in the United States, and they have given a generally similar picture of the class system. The precise details vary, however, depending not only on which method is used but also on the wording of the questions and the kind of community in which the respondents live.

The Reputational Method

One of the most influential studies using the reputational method was made by W. Lloyd Warner and Paul Lunt (1941) in the Massachusetts town of Newburyport.

Warner and Lunt conducted in-depth interviews with many residents of this small community, which had a population of about 17,000 at the time. In these interviews, they tried to find out how many classes the residents saw in their community and why they believed that specific people belonged to one class rather than another. It was soon clear that this small town was anything but classless. Respondents continually described other people as "old aristocracy," "the folks with the money," "snobs trying to push up," "nobodies," "society," "poor folk but decent," or "poor whites." Using these and other cues, Warner and Lunt divided the community into six social classes: an upper, a middle, and a lower, each containing an internal upper and lower level.

The reputational method is useful in small communities where people know one another. In these cases it can provide fascinating insights into people's concepts of the class system. The method has two main disadvantages, however. First, it is difficult or even impossible to apply it to a large community where people do not know one another or to an entire society. Second, the method depends heavily on the personal interpretations of the observer. By analyzing their data differently, Warner and Lunt might have been able to find, say, four or ten classes.

The Subjective Method

The subjective method, in which people are asked to locate themselves in the class system, has been used in several studies. These studies have shown, however, that the precise phrasing of the question that is asked can influence the results.

In the late forties a *Fortune* magazine poll found that 80 percent of the respondents claimed to be middle class. The magazine took this finding as evidence that the United States was a truly middle-class society. Richard Centers (1949) objected to this conclusion. He pointed out that the poll had offered the respondents only three choices: "upper class," "middle class," or "lower class." Using a national random sample, Centers added a fourth choice, "working class." Approximately half of his respondents placed themselves in this category—a finding that suggested that the United States was primarily a working-class society. The *Fortune* poll had not shown that the United States is a middle-class society; it had simply shown that Americans have a distaste for the term "lower class." Low-income people will proudly identify themselves as "working class" but will call themselves "middle class" rather than "lower class" if only these two options are given.

The proportion of Americans identifying themselves as working class has shrunk since Centers did his research. In a more recent study (Hodge and Treiman, 1964), a national sample of Americans was given this question: "If you were asked to use one of these names for your social class standing, which would you say you belonged to: the middle class, lower class, upper-middle class, working class, or upper class?" The answers were:

Upper class	2.2 percent
Upper-middle class	16.6 percent
Middle class	44.0 percent
Working class	34.3 percent
Lower class	2.3 percent
Don't believe in classes	.6 percent

The subjective method has the advantage that it can be applied to a large population by polling a random sample. But the method also has its disadvantages. First, the results are influenced by the form of the question that is asked. Second, people may have a mistaken view of their class status. People often rank themselves higher than their incomes and life-styles seem to justify.

The Objective Method

This method carries a misleading label, for it implies that the approach is more "scientific" and unbiased than the others. In fact, however, it is a purely arbitrary way of analyzing a class system. The sociologist first sets a basic criterion for determining class membership and then divides the population into a number of classes on this basis.

The objective method was pioneered by August Hollingshead (1949) in a study of New Haven, Connecticut. Using the criteria of place of residence, occupation, and level of education, he divided the families in the community into five classes. Lloyd Warner (1949) also used the objective method to analyze the class system of Morristown, Illinois. He constructed an "index of status characteristics," based initially on six main indicators: occupation, type of house, area of residence, source of income, amount of income, and amount of education. All these factors, however, were found to correlate fairly strongly. Later investigators have often found it sufficient to use the income of the family breadwinner as the main or sole criterion of class membership.

The objective method has the advantage that it gives clear-cut results and usually requires no painstaking collection of data. The relevant statistics are readily available from the Bureau of the Census and other agencies and merely have to be interpreted. The main disadvantage of the method is that it is so arbitrary. Different sociologists may use different criteria for determining class membership and may divide the same population into very different class categories. The method also ignores the beliefs that the people themselves have about the class system. There is some debate about whether a sociologist can validly classify people as, say, "working class" when those people are convinced that they belong to another class.

The Social Classes

What, then, is the structure of the American class system? Most sociologists would probably accept, at least in general outline, the picture drawn by Daniel Rossides (1976). He suggests that there is an upper class consisting of about 1 to 3 percent of the population, an upper-middle class of 10 to 15 percent, a lower-middle class of 30 to 35 percent, a working class of 40 to 45 percent, and a lower class of 20 to 25 percent (see Figure 11.4). Other researchers (for example, Coleman and Neugarten, 1971) have come to similar conclusions. Let's look at the characteristics of these classes in more detail. The portraits presented are, of course, broad generalizations. There are many individual exceptions to these overall patterns.

The Upper Class

The *upper class* is a very small one, yet it has huge wealth and influence. Its members own at least a quarter of the nation's wealth, and they are very disproportionately represented at the highest levels of political and economic power. This class consists of two main elements. The *upper-upper class* consists of the old aristocracy of birth and wealth. To be fully respectable in America, money, like wine, must age a little. One can become a member of the upper-upper class only by being born into it. The names of

THE AMERICAN CLASS SYSTEM IN THE TWENTIETH CENTURY: AN ESTIMATE

Class (and Percentage of Total Population)	Income	Property	Occupation	Education	Personal and Family Life	Education of Children
Upper class (1–3%)	Very high income	Great wealth, old wealth	Managers, professionals, high civil and military officials	Liberal arts education at elite schools	Stable family life Autonomous personality	College education by right for both sexes
Upper-middle class (10–15%)	High income	Accumulation of property through savings	Lowest unemployment	Graduate training	Better physical and mental health	Educational system biased in their favor
Lower-middle class (30–35%)	Modest income	Some savings	Small business people and farmers, lower professionals, semiprofessionals, sales and clerical workers	Some college High school	Longer life expectancy	Greater chance of college than working-class children
Working class (40–45%)	Low income	Some savings	Skilled labor	Some high school	Unstable family life	Educational system biased against them
			Unskilled labor	Grade school	Conformist personality	Tendency toward vocational programs
Lower class (20–25%)	Poverty income (destitution)	No savings	Highest unemployment Surplus labor	Illiteracy	Poorer physical and mental health Lower life expectancy	Little interest in education, high dropout rates

Source: Adapted from Daniel W. Rossides, *The American Class System* (Boston: Houghton Mifflin, 1976), p. 26.

Figure 11.4 An illustration of the general outlines of the American class system and the characteristics of each class. There is always disagreement on where the boundaries between the strata fall in any class system, but this broad outline would be accepted by most American sociologists. It was constructed from a variety of sources, including government statistics, sociological studies of various communities and of the national population, and interpretative works.

people in this class are familiar ones: the Chryslers, Rockefellers, Fords, Roosevelts, Kennedys, Astors, Vanderbilts. The founding ancestors of many of the present clans were never accepted into the upper-upper class because their origins were too humble and their wealth was too recently acquired. Only a generation ago Mrs. David Lion Gardiner, the "empress" of the aristocratic Gardiner family of New York, forbade her grandson to play with the Rockefeller grandchildren on the grounds that "No Gardiner will ever play with the grandchild of a gangster" (Lundberg, 1968). Similarly, the author once heard a dowager of an ancient Boston lineage refer to the newly wealthy Kennedy family, at a time when one of them had become president of the United States, as "those low street-Irish." The members of the upper-upper class tend to know one another personally, to attend the same schools, to visit the

Figure 11.5 This photograph of two successive Presidents of the United States illustrates a distinction between the upper-upper and the lower-upper class. President Kennedy, with a pained expression, is apparently restraining then Vice-President Johnson from behaving in what Kennedy seems to regard as a vulgar way. Kennedy was a member of the upper-upper class: he was born to great wealth and the attendant "social graces." Johnson entered the upper class through his own efforts. Throughout his career Johnson was suspicious and resentful of the "Eastern Establishment" that, he felt, looked down upon him because of his origins.

same resorts, and to intermarry. Their names are included in the *Social Register* or the *Blue Book*—volumes that self-consciously imitate *Debrett's Peerage,* a listing of the British aristocracy.

The *lower-upper class* are those who have become very wealthy more recently. They may actually have more money, better houses, and larger automobiles than the upper-uppers, but they lack the right "breeding" to win full acceptance into the very highest social circles.

The distinctions between the two upper classes are not generally recognized by the rest of society, and they are of little importance outside the elite circles in which they are found. The upper class as a whole has great power and prestige from its ownership and control of economic resources. It has such a great influence on both domestic and foreign policy that it affects the lives not only of other classes but also of other nations throughout the world (Domhoff, 1971).

The Middle Class

The *middle class* lacks the cohesion of the upper class but has a distinctive life-style that distinguishes it from the upper and lower classes. In fact, the values of the middle class form the dominant morality of the United States. Middle-class attitudes and tastes are respected and endorsed by politicians, media, advertisers, and schools. This class also contains two fairly distinct elements.

The *upper-middle class* consists primarily of high-income business and professional families. Like the upper class, this group contains a disproportionate number of people from white, Protestant, Anglo-Saxon backgrounds. Members of the upper-middle class are highly "respectable," but they are not "society." They tend to live in comfortable suburban homes, to enjoy a stable family life, and to have a high sense of civic duty. They are very active in political life and dominate community organizations. They are concerned with personal career advancement and have very high aspirations for their children, who receive a college education as a matter of course.

The *lower-middle class* share most of the values of the upper-middle class, but they lack the educational or economic advantages that would let them enjoy the same life-style. This class consists of people whose diverse jobs do not involve manual labor. It includes small-business oper-

Figure 11.6 The upper-middle and lower-middle classes differ primarily in the life-styles that their different incomes make possible. While both classes enjoy a comfortable standard of living, the higher occupational status of the upper-middle class permits its members to pursue a more affluent and leisured way of life.

ators and sales representatives, teachers and nurses, police officers, and middle-management personnel. The lower-middle class is very concerned about respectability and "proper" behavior, about decency and the value of hard work. Members of this class, who usually must work hard to achieve and retain what they have, are often politically and economically conservative.

The Lower Class

The *lower class* consists essentially of those whose jobs and educational levels prevent them from enjoying the status and life-style of that "typical" American family portrayed in schoolbooks and the media. Racial and ethnic minority groups are disproportionately represented in this class. The lower class can also be divided into two strata.

The upper-lower, or *working class,* consists primarily of blue-collar workers—small tradespeople, service personnel, and semiskilled workers of various kinds. Their jobs typically involve manual labor and have little public prestige. Although some of these workers earn incomes that are higher than those of some members of the middle class, their jobs typically lack the "fringe benefits" of pensions, insurance, sick leave, paid vacations, and job safety. Most

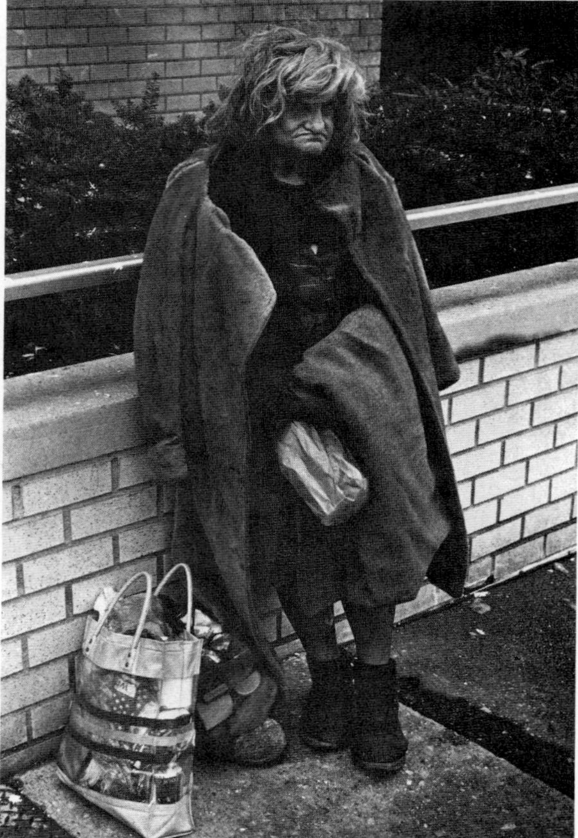

Figure 11.7 The upper-lower or working class consists primarily of blue-collar workers who earn a modest income from their semiskilled jobs. Members of this class place great value on respectability and the virtues of hard work. The lower-lower class (usually just termed the lower class) consists primarily of the "disreputable poor." This class of people are habitually unemployed or underemployed, and are often stigmatized by other Americans.

members of the working class have very modest incomes. Few of them are able to save money, and many live on credit. The members of this class live in less desirable residential areas but take great pride in being "respectable." Much of their self-image as respectable people derives from the sense that they work hard—at "real" work done with the hands. Home ownership is a big achievement to them, and they are sharply aware of the differences between them and the stratum below. They often feel antagonistic toward this stratum, especially when they feel that their taxes are being used to support people who "choose to be" on welfare.

The *lower-lower class* (usually simply called the "lower class" to distinguish it from the working class) consists of the "disreputable poor." This class includes the permanently unemployed, the homeless, the illiterate, the chronic welfare recipient, and the impoverished aged. They are virtually worthless on the labor market and so are virtually worthless in terms of power and prestige as well (Rossides, 1976). Members of this class are poorly regarded by other Americans. Their supposed laziness, promiscuity, or reliance on public handouts are contrasted with the morality of the middle class. They tend to lack a common class consciousness, to be alienated from and cynical about society, and to be fatalistic about their own chances in life.

Since a person's class status depends primarily on the income of the family breadwinner—usually the father—it is easy to see why class distinctions tend to be handed down from generation to generation. As William Goode (1964) comments, "The family is the keystone of the stratification system, the social mechanism by which it is maintained." The social class of the family strongly influences the opportunities of the children. A child in a high-status family, for example, has a good opportunity to acquire the values, attitudes, personal contacts, education, and skills that make for success in American life. A child from a low-status family is raised in an atmosphere of poverty, interacts only with low-status peers, and lacks the opportunities and career ambitions that children in other classes take for granted. As a result, most people are likely to remain for a lifetime in their class of origin.

Correlates of Class Membership

One of the many reasons why social class is important is that class membership correlates with a variety of other aspects of social life.

Political Behavior

The higher a person's social class, the more likely he or she is to register as a voter, to vote, and to take an interest in political affairs. Party affiliation also correlates with social class. People higher in the social hierarchy are more likely to be Republican; people lower in the hierarchy are more likely to be Democrats. The working class is liberal on many economic issues that affect its own interest, but on most other issues it is more conservative than the other classes. Tolerance in attitudes toward issues of civil liberty tends to increase as social class rises.

Marital Stability

Divorce is more common at the lower social levels, perhaps because unemployment and economic problems generate friction between the partners (Goode, 1965). Traditional sex roles are most entrenched in the lower class, and there is evidence that marital relations at this level are relatively lacking in warmth (Komarovsky, 1962). Female-headed families are found predominantly in the lower class, particularly in the black community.

Religious Affiliation

There is a strong correlation, at least among whites, between Protestantism and high status—perhaps because Protestants were the first to establish themselves in the United States and to gain wealth and political power. Within the Protestant churches there is a fairly close correlation between income and membership in a particular denomination. The upper classes prefer denominations that offer quiet and restrained services, while the lower classes are disproportionately represented in revivalist and fundamentalist sects. The most prestigious Protestant denomination appears to be the Episcopalian, followed in rough order by the Congregational, Presbyterian, Methodist, Lutheran, and Baptist denominations (Gockel, 1969).

Educational Achievement

Social class membership has a strong influence on IQ and on educational achievement. Only 20 percent of high-school graduates from families with incomes below $3000 go on to college, compared with 87 percent of those from families with incomes of $15,000 or more. This discrepancy is not necessarily related to differences in intellectual ability. Less than 10 percent of students with high incomes and high abilities fail to enter college, but about 25 percent of low-income students with comparable abilities do not manage to get to college. A college graduate, incidentally, earns an average of $236,000 more in the course of a lifetime than a person who goes to work straight from high school (Jencks, 1972).

Health

In almost all other industrialized countries, medicine is socialized and health care is available either free or for a low sum. These countries take it for granted that the quality of one's medical attention should depend on how sick one is and not how wealthy one is. In the United States, however, people have to pay for their health care, either directly or through some form of health insurance. About 24 million Americans are not covered by health insurance of any kind. Fear of the expenses involved often makes people reluctant to seek early treatment of medical problems or even to leave some problems unattended.

Rich people are very much healthier than poor people. The incidence of most diseases, including diabetes, heart disease, and cancer, is significantly higher in the lower social classes (Ornati, 1966).

Life Expectancy

The higher one's social status, the longer one is likely to live (Kitwanger and Hauser, 1967). Infant mortality rates in particular are strongly influenced by social class. Infant deaths are three times more common among families with annual incomes of less than $3000 than among families with incomes exceeding $10,000 (U.S. Department of Health, Education, and Welfare, 1972).

Mental Disorder

The incidence of mental disorder is closely linked to social class, and the treatment received varies according to the class of the patient. One study (Hollingshead and Redlich, 1958) found that hospitalization for schizophrenia was eleven times more common for lower-class than for upper-class persons. Upper-class patients were more likely to be treated with psychotherapy and to be hospitalized for only brief periods. Lower-class patients were more likely to be treated with drugs and electric shock therapy and to be hospitalized for long periods. Another study in Manhattan (Srole *et al.*, 1962) found that nearly one person in every two in the lowest class was psychologically impaired, although only 1 percent of these people were receiving treatment.

Social Participation

The middle and upper classes participate extensively in community activities and organizations—charities, parent-teacher associations, women's groups, civic associations, and the like. The upper class tends to play high-prestige roles, such as that of honorary president. The middle-class members are more likely to do the routine work of the organizations. In the working and lower class, on the other hand, social relationships center around family, kin, and neighbors (Bott, 1971; Komarovsky, 1962).

Values and Attitudes

Middle- and upper-class people feel a relatively strong sense of control over and responsibility for their lives. They are generally prepared to defer immediate gratification in the hope of greater future rewards. Although their values and attitudes set the general moral standards of the whole society, they are somewhat more tolerant of ambiguity in sexual behavior, religion, and other areas than are members of the working and lower classes. Members of the working and lower classes are less likely to defer gratification, and the working class is inclined to be particularly intolerant of unconventional behavior and attitudes. People in the lowest class tend to have a strongly fatalistic attitude toward life. They often see their chances as determined by luck and other forces beyond their personal control.

Child-Rearing Practices

Middle- and upper-class child-rearing practices are more concerned with teaching principles of behavior and helping children to decide for themselves how to act in accordance with these principles. Working- and lower-class practices tend to focus on teaching children to obey the rules and stay out of trouble. Middle- and upper-class

Figure 11.8

"It's not what you know, it's who *you know. And who do* I *know?* You!"

training often uses withdrawal of love as a control device, which may cause anxieties and guilt in the children. Working- and lower-class training is more disciplinarian and may involve more physical punishment (M. L. Kohn, 1969; Walters and Stinnett, 1971). These child-rearing practices inevitably color the later personalities of people in different classes.

Criminal Justice

Lower-class people are more likely to be arrested for criminal offences, denied bail, found guilty, and given longer sentences than members of other classes. This does not necessarily mean that lower-class people commit more crimes; it means that they are more likely to be caught and more likely to be harshly treated. A large number of self-report studies have concluded that almost every American has committed some kind of criminal offense (Doleschal and Klapmuts, 1973). Typical lower-class crimes, however, such as robbery, larceny, auto theft, and burglary, are regarded as much more serious than typical middle- or upper-class crimes, such as embezzlement, forgery, tax evasion, and fraud.

Social Mobility in the United States

Abraham Lincoln was born in a log cabin but served in the White House. Andrew Carnegie, John D. Rockefeller, and J. P. Morgan started life in poverty but became millionaires. These tales are a treasured part of our folklore. It is easy to overlook the countless would-be millionaires or presidents who remained in poverty or obscurity despite their ambitions and efforts.

In European societies, with their long feudal histories and obvious social divisions, people tend to regard their class systems as rigid. They recognize that *social mobility*, or movement from one status to another, is no easy matter. In the United States, with its deep commitment to the ideal of human equality, the belief that one can get ahead with hard work is a central part of the national ethic. What are the facts?

Research on social mobility since the twenties has shown that the American dream of ambition and hard work as the key to success rarely becomes a reality. In one early study, Pitirim Sorokin (1927) found that most men

Figure 11.9 Despite the American ideology of equality of opportunity, social status tends to be transmitted from generation to generation, and the rate of social mobility between the classes is rather low. A family's class background has a profound effect on the attitudes, motivations, educational achievement, prospects for inheriting wealth, and social opportunities of its children. Do these two young people—one from the upper class and one from the lower class—really have equal opportunity to "make it" in American society?

started their occupational careers at about the same level as their fathers and that only a very few made significant advances thereafter. In their study of Muncie, Indiana, Robert and Helen Lynd (1929) found that whatever an ordinary worker's chances of becoming a foreman might be in theory, in practice they were minimal. Ely Chinoy (1955) drew similar conclusions from his study of auto workers. Seymour Martin Lipset and Reinhard Bendix (1959) studied the backgrounds of business executives born between 1770 and 1920 and found that some 70 percent of them had come from the upper class, 20 percent from the middle class, and only 10 percent from the working class.

These findings do not mean that there is no social mobility from one generation to the next in American society. In fact, there is a great deal, but most of this mobility involves relatively minor changes in status, not great leaps from lowly origins to lofty positions. Joseph Kahl (1961) estimates that the total amount of *intergenerational mobility* (changes in the status of sons relative to the status of their fathers) between 1920 and 1950 was about 67 percent. In other words, 67 percent of the sons were mobile relative to the fathers. Most of this mobility, however, was very moderate and did not involve very significant changes in social status. Moreover, a great deal of the mobility was due to the expansion of the economy and the creation of new white-collar jobs. Kahl found that only 18 percent of the executive elite in the early fifties came from working-class origins. Another study of professional people in the sixties found that some 40 percent of them were the offspring of professional fathers—nearly five times as many as would be expected in a perfectly open system (Jackson and Crockett, 1964).

The most detailed work on social mobility in the United States was conducted by Peter Blau and Otis Dudley Duncan (1967), who collected data from 20,000 men. By analyzing information on the educational and occupational background of the fathers and of the sons, they were able to show that 37 percent of the men in white-collar jobs had fathers who held blue-collar jobs. Blau and Duncan also established that a person's own educational achievement has more influence on social mobility than does the father's occupation or education. A person's educational achievement is related to the social background of the family, of course, but Blau and Duncan found that a well-educated son of a working-class father has much the same chance of upward mobility as the poorly educated son of a middle-class father.

The general pattern in American society, then, is one of moderate upward mobility from one generation to the next. Blau and Duncan suggest three reasons for this trend. First, the American economy has been expanding steadily throughout this century. The proportion of white-collar jobs has been increasing and the proportion of blue-collar jobs has been shrinking. Inevitably, many people from working-class origins have filled the new middle-class jobs. Second, the higher classes have lower birth rates than the lower classes. The higher classes thus fail to supply the personnel needed to fill new high-status jobs, so that people lower down in the social hierarchy are able to move upward. Third, immigration of unskilled workers from other parts of the world and from rural areas within the United States has tended to push existing urban groups into higher occupational statuses.

What makes one person more likely than another to achieve a higher status? Several factors have been identified, and most of them are characteristics over which individuals have little or no control. They include willingness to postpone marriage, willingness to defer immediate gratification in favor of long-term goals, residence in an urban rather than a rural area, high IQ, level of education, racial or ethnic background, childhood nutrition, physical appearance (especially among women), and, of course, class of origin (Blau and Duncan, 1967; Lipset and Bendix, 1959; Lassiter, 1966; Coleman, 1966; Porter, 1968).

How does intergenerational mobility in the United States compare with that in other industrialized societies? In a classic study of this question, Seymour Martin Lipset and Reinhard Bendix (1959) compared rates of mobility from blue- to white-collar occupations in several industrial societies. They concluded that there was very little difference among them. In the United States the mobility rate from blue- to white-collar occupations was about 34 percent, compared with 32 percent in Sweden, 31 percent in Britain, 29 percent in France, and 25 percent in West Germany and Japan. In this respect, at least, the United States does not seem to be a land of especially great opportunity.

There is one respect, however, in which mobility in the

United States is higher than that in other industrial societies. Working-class Americans have a significantly greater chance of entering the professional elite than do members of the working class in other societies (S. M. Miller, 1960; Fox and Miller, 1965; Blau and Duncan, 1967). About 10 percent of Americans of working-class origins enters the professional elite, compared with about 7 percent in Japan and the Netherlands, less than 3 percent in Britain, less than 2 percent in Denmark, West Germany, and France, and less than 1 percent in Italy. Even so, a working-class American's chances of mobility into the highest strata of society are very small.

There is only very limited truth, then, to the American belief that this is a country of equal opportunity. The fact is that most people remain at or near the level of the families into which they were born and that many of the factors that determine individual social mobility are beyond personal control.

Poverty in the United States

Most Americans are so accustomed to affluence that they may find it hard to believe that one American in ten lives in poverty. "Poverty" does not simply mean that the poor do not live quite as well as the other members of society. It means that the federal government considers their incomes inadequate to meet basic needs for food, clothing, and shelter. Poverty means the deaths of thousands of infants every year, malnutrition in hundreds of thousands of American children, and aged people eating dog food in order to survive. It means illiteracy and ignorance, disease and misery, and the stunting of human lives and potential.

Defining Poverty

How do we determine if someone is "poor?" There are two basic ways of defining poverty: in terms of *absolute deprivation,* the lack of basic necessities; or in terms of *relative deprivation,* the inability to maintain the living standards customary in the society.

Absolute Deprivation

This concept refers to a situation in which people cannot afford the basic standards of health care, nourishment, housing, and clothing (Kolko, 1962). This is the definition of poverty that is most often used in the United States. Analysts simply determine an annual income below which an individual or family will be deprived of the basic necessities of life. There is naturally some debate about exactly what this level is, but the official poverty line as determined by the federal government in 1975 was $5500 for a nonfarm family of four. This level is determined by calculating the cost of maintaining adequate nutrition under emergency or temporary conditions, and then trebling that figure to cover other necessities, such as clothing, housing, heating, and medical care. Adjustments are made for differences in family size, place of residence, and other factors. Rural families, for example, are expected to be able to live on a lower income because they can grow some of their own food.

Relative Deprivation

This concept refers to a situation in which people may be able to provide themselves with basic necessities but are unable to maintain the standard of living that is considered normal in the society. In some ways this definition is a more realistic one, because the poor evaluate their poverty not only in relation to their needs but also in relation to the affluence that they see around them. Electricity may not be an absolute necessity in the home—most people in the world get by without it—but it is considered a necessity, not a luxury, in our society. It would be hard not to regard an American family living without electricity as impoverished, even if the family's income were somewhat above the poverty line. Under this definition of poverty, the poor are arbitrarily defined as some proportion of the lowest income earners in society, often the bottom fifth or tenth. Their poverty is then considered not in terms of how their incomes compare with the poverty line but rather in terms of how their incomes compare with those of the rest of society. This approach assumes that poverty cannot be eliminated as long as there are significant economic inequalities in society.

Who Are the Poor?

As we might expect, poverty in the United States is not randomly distributed. It is concentrated in specific groups and specific areas.

Figure 11.10 These people are living in what some social scientists regard as a "culture of poverty." Oscar Lewis, for example, maintains that the poor remain poor because of the attitudes and values that they learn from their impoverished families and communities. Other social scientists are critical of this approach. They charge that it involves "blaming the victim" for poverty, rather than blaming the society that permits poverty to exist.

Data from the 1970 Census show that over 40 percent of the families living in poverty are headed by women. About half of the poor families live on small farms in rural areas, where they are unable to compete against modern large-scale agriculture. Some 40 percent of the poor are children; in fact, about 16 percent of American children live in poverty. Poverty is also found disproportionately among the aged; about 20 percent of people over the age of sixty-five are poor. More than half of the native American population lives below the poverty line. Although nearly 70 percent of the poor are white, only 9 percent of the total white population is impoverished, compared with 33 percent of the black population. Some 20 percent of families in the South live in poverty. It is clear, then, that poverty is concentrated in depressed areas, among minority groups, among fatherless families, and among the very old and the very young.

The Causes of Poverty

Poverty has no single cause. It is produced by a number of interrelated factors.

Economic Factors

Poverty is usually associated with high unemployment. High unemployment rates are found in specific areas and specific sectors of the economy and are usually the result of structural changes in economic life. Small farmers and agricultural laborers, for example, have been steadily displaced over the last few decades by mechanized agriculture, and they can no longer earn a decent living on the land. Automation in many industries has displaced unskilled workers, but these workers lack the training that would enable them to compete for jobs in industries using advanced technologies. Many workers are trapped in the less-skilled service industries—as shoe shiners, domestic cleaners, dishwashers, or car-park attendants. The poor, if they are able to find employment at all, are concentrated in those jobs that offer only low wages and little security.

Discrimination

Poverty is found disproportionately among minority group members and among families headed by women. Nonwhites generally earn less than whites, even when they have similar qualifications, and women generally earn less than men. Black women suffer from double discrimination on grounds of both race and sex. More than half the black families headed by women are in poverty. These inequalities are not caused primarily by discrimination in employment practices, although this is a factor. The origins lie deeper, in the many subtle influences which prevent both women and minorities from acquiring the education, training, and attitudes that are necessary for success in a competitive society.

Cultural Factors

Poverty tends to be transmitted from one generation to the next. This fact has alerted investigators to the possibility that the cultural values of the poor may make it even more difficult for them to enter the mainstream economy. Oscar Lewis (1966, 1968), an anthropologist, has argued that a distinctive *culture of poverty* exists among poor groups in capitalist societies all over the world. According to Lewis, the poor have a strong sense of fatalism, helplessness, and inferiority. They are oriented to the present and do not plan for the future. They have a narrow outlook and do not see their problems in a broader social context. They also make little use of and are hostile to major social institutions. A person growing up in such a culture and internalizing its norms will be ill-equipped to participate in the wider society. This general argument was widely accepted during the short-lived "War on Poverty" of the sixties. Immense efforts were devoted to changing the culture of the poor, primarily through education, but these efforts had little apparent impact on the problem. Although most sociologists would accept that the poor do have their own cultural norms,

many argue that this culture is mainly a consequence rather than a cause of poverty. Middle-class norms make little sense to an impoverished person, and the culture of poverty can be seen as an adaptive response to prolonged impoverishment. Cultural factors no doubt contribute to the persistence of poverty, but their precise influence is still a matter of debate.

Political Factors

Poverty exists because our society is an unequal one, and there are overwhelming political pressures to keep it that way. Any attempt to redistribute wealth and income in the United States will inevitably be opposed by powerful middle- and upper-class interests. People can be relatively rich only if others are relatively poor, and since power is concentrated in the hands of the rich, public policies will continue to reflect their interests rather than those of the poor.

As Herbert Gans (1973) has pointed out, poverty is actually functional from the point of view of the nonpoor. Poverty ensures that "dirty" work gets done. If there were no poor people to scrub floors and empty bedpans, these jobs would have to be rewarded with high incomes before anyone would touch them. Poverty creates jobs for many of the nonpoor, such as police officers, welfare workers, pawnbrokers, and government bureaucrats. Poverty makes life easier for the rich by providing them with cooks, gardeners, and other workers to perform basic chores while their employers enjoy more pleasurable activities. Poverty provides a market for inferior goods and services, such as day-old bread, run-down automobiles, or the advice of incompetent physicians and lawyers. Poverty legitimizes middle-class values. To the middle class, the fate of the poor—who are supposed to lack the virtues of thrift, honesty, monogamy, and a taste for hard work—only confirms the desirability of qualities the poor are thought to lack. Poverty also provides a group that can be made to absorb the costs of change. For example, the poor bear the brunt of unemployment caused by automation, and it is their homes, not those of the wealthy, that are demolished when a route has to be found for a new highway. There is no deliberate, conscious "conspiracy" of the wealthy to keep the poor in poverty. It is just that poverty is an inevitable outcome of the American economic system, which the poor are politically powerless to influence or change.

Attitudes Toward Poverty

It has been calculated that the United States could eliminate absolute poverty by spending $12 billion per year to raise all impoverished families above the poverty line (Bureau of the Census, 1973). This sum is less than 2 percent of our gross national product. It represents less than a fifth of our annual expenditure on defense, or a little more than we spend each year on tobacco. The United States could wipe out poverty easily by placing an income floor under those who cannot earn enough, instead of deliberately keeping welfare payments to a minimum. The reason for this policy lies in a peculiar American myth: that the poor are poor because they are idle and prefer not to work. This attitude was clearly expressed by former President Nixon (1971):

> I advocate a system that will encourage people to take work, and that means whatever work is available. If a job puts bread on the table, if it gives you the satisfaction of providing for your children and lets you look everyone else in the eye, I don't think, that it is menial. . . . Low income workers feel somehow that certain kinds of work are demeaning—scrubbing floors, emptying bedpans. . . . It is not enjoyable work, but . . . there is as much dignity in that as there is in any work to be done in this country, including my own.

This attitude implies that the poor should not be pampered with too much welfare in case it destroys their incentive to work. The attitude is very widely held. A 1972 Harris poll found that nearly nine out of ten Americans favored the idea of "making people on welfare go to work," and another poll in the same year found that more than half of the population regards the poor as responsible for their own poverty (Feagin, 1972).

These attitudes bear virtually no relationship to reality. A quarter of the poor are actually engaged in full-time employment but simply do not earn enough to bring their incomes up to the poverty line. What about those on welfare, the supposed freeloaders who choose not to work? An analysis of 1970 Census data reveals the following about their composition:

Children under 14	34.4 percent
Elderly, 65 and over	18.2 percent
Ill and disabled	4.7 percent
In school, 14 and over	6.6 percent
	63.9 percent

Thus nearly 64 percent of the poor on welfare were incapable of working anyway. Of the remaining 36.1 percent, 23.8 percent worked and 12.3 percent did not. Of this 12.3 percent who could have worked, 10.9 percent were female, the vast majority of whom were at home caring for small children. Thus only 1.4 percent of all those on welfare were able-bodied unemployed males, many of them lacking skills and many of them living in areas of high unemployment. Yet our reluctance to support the poor is so acute that every application for welfare is investigated for possible fraud. In contrast, only one income tax return in sixty is investigated, although tax fraud costs the nation vastly greater sums.

One further little-known fact deserves mention: we pay out far more in welfare to the wealthy than to the poor. This fact is little known because these massive government handouts are not called "welfare." As Dale Tussing (1974) points out:

> Two welfare systems exist simultaneously in this country. One is explicit, poorly funded, stigmatized and stigmatizing, and is directed at the poor. The other, practically unknown, is implicit, literally invisible, is nonstigmatized and nonstigmatizing, and provides vast but nonacknowledged benefits for the nonpoor. Our welfare systems do not distribute benefits on the basis of need. Rather, they distribute benefits on the basis of legitimacy. Poor people are viewed as less legitimate than nonpoor people.

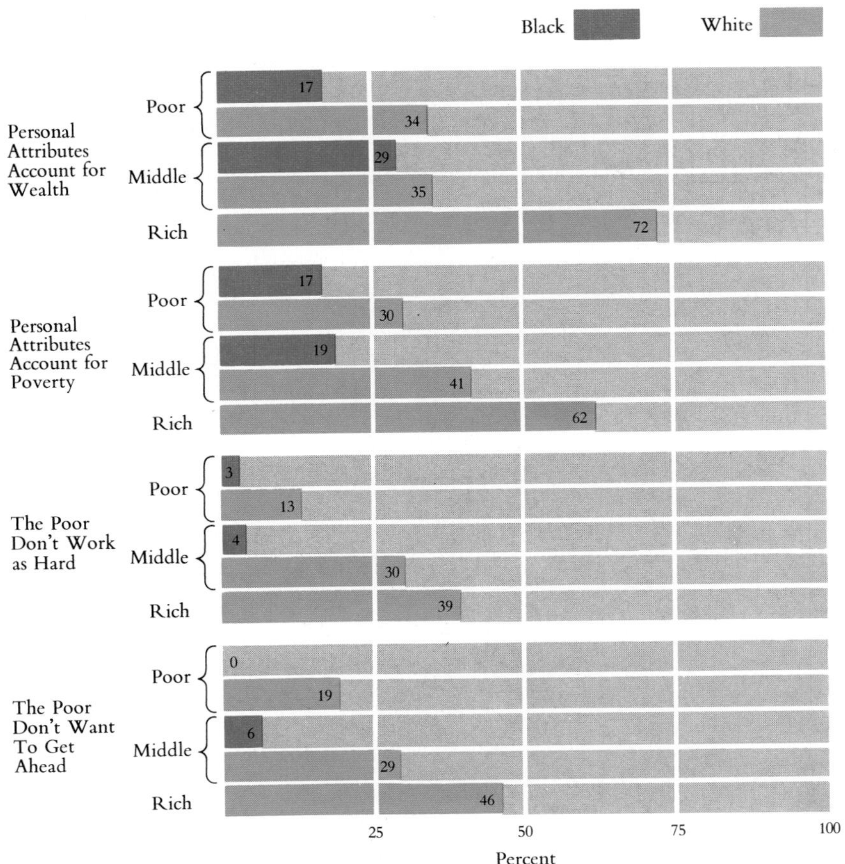

Figure 11.11 Can poverty and wealth be explained in terms of personal attributes? Americans have very different opinions on this question, but their opinions are related to their own social status and race group membership. Significantly, nearly a third of poor whites believe that poverty can be explained in terms of personal characteristics, a fact that suggests they share the common American belief that they are responsible for their own plight. But blacks, perhaps because they have a greater class consciousness, are much less inclined to share this view. Although nearly half of the rich whites believe that "the poor don't want to get ahead," none of the poor blacks hold this view.

Source: Adapted from Joan H. Rytina *et al.*, "Income and Stratification Ideology," *American Journal of Sociology*, 75 (January, 1970), p. 713.

One example of these "welfare" payments to the nonpoor is tax relief for interest on home mortgages and for property taxes. In effect, these tax deductions are rent supplements to homeowners that cost the federal government more than $5 billion a year, or more than four times the amount of all money spent on housing programs for the poor. Some 85 percent of the benefits of this "supplement" goes to people with incomes in excess of $10,000, while those with incomes under $3000 receive 0.1 percent of the handout. Another example is the tax relief obtained by people with incomes of over $1 million per year through the use of tax loopholes. The average annual saving for each of these superrich Americans is a handsome $720,000, and it makes little difference to the rest of us whether it is termed "tax relief" or "welfare." In either case the U.S. Treasury is $2.2 billion poorer, and other taxpayers have to make up the difference (Stern, 1972). Similar disguised benefits for the nonpoor are to be found in many other areas of public expenditure.

Poverty is only one sign of social inequality in America. Like all other forms of social inequality, it is built into the very structure of society and legitimized by a set of beliefs that justify its existence. In the next two chapters we will see the same processes at work in the fields of race and ethnic relations and sex roles.

Summary

1. Although equality is a core value in American culture, the United States is a very unequal society. It is stratified along lines of social class.

2. Wealth and income are very unequally distributed in the United States, and there has been little change in the distribution of these rewards since the end of World War II. Power is also unequally distributed. Ordinary citizens have little influence over political decisions, but there is debate as to whether power is exercised by an elite or by powerful interest groups that struggle for advantage on specific issues. Prestige, however, has become available to an increasing number of Americans, largely because of the increase in the proportion of white-collar jobs.

3. The structure of the class system has been analyzed by the reputational method (asking people where they think others fit), the subjective method (asking people where they think they fit), and the objective method (establishing criteria for class membership and dividing the population into preselected classes). Each has its advantages and disadvantages, but all give a generally similar picture of the class system.

4. Most sociologists view the American class system as containing six strata: the upper-upper class, the lower-upper class, the upper-middle class, the lower-middle class, the upper-lower (working) class, and the lower-lower class. Each class has distinctive characteristics and life-styles that are related to the economic inequalities between the classes.

5. Class membership correlates with a variety of other aspects of life, including political behavior, marital stability, religious affiliation, educational achievement, health, life expectancy, mental disorder, social participation, values and attitudes, child-rearing practices, and criminal justice.

6. Research on social mobility indicates that there is a fair amount of intergenerational mobility in the United States, but most of it involves minor changes in status and results from the increase in the proportion of white-collar jobs. Opportunities for social mobility are not significantly greater in the United States than in other industrial societies, except that working-class people have a rather better chance of reaching the professional elite. Most people, however, remain at or near the status of their parents.

7. One American in ten is officially regarded as poor. Poverty may be defined in terms of absolute deprivation (lack of basic necessities) or relative deprivation (inability to maintain customary living standards). Poverty is concentrated in depressed areas, among minority groups, among fatherless families, and among the very old and the very young. Among the causes of poverty are economic factors, discrimination, and political factors, and possibly also the culture of the poor. Americans are inclined to blame the poor for their poverty, an attitude that is not justified by the facts.

Important Terms

life chances	objective method
wealth	class system
power	social mobility
power-elite model	intergenerational mobility
pluralistic model	poverty
prestige	absolute deprivation
reputational method	relative deprivation
subjective method	culture of poverty

Suggested Readings

DOMHOFF, G. WILLIAM. *Who Rules America.* Englewood Cliffs, N.J.: Prentice-Hall, 1967.

Domhoff presents convincing evidence for the existence of a "governing class" in the United States, which owns most of the nation's corporate wealth and holds key decision-making positions throughout the country.

GANS, HERBERT J. *More Equality.* New York: Pantheon, 1973.

A useful examination of social inequality in the United States and the reasons for its persistence. Gans makes a realistic assessment of the prospects for bringing about more equality.

LIPSET, SEYMOUR MARTIN, AND REINHARD BENDIX. *Social Mobility in Industrial Society.* Berkeley, Calif.: University of California Press, 1959.

A classic study of social mobility in the United States and several other industrial societies. Despite many methodological problems, Lipset and Bendix were able to compare mobility rates in these societies and to establish that there was little variation among them.

ROACH, JACK et al., (EDS.). *Social Stratification in the United States.* Englewood Cliffs, N.J.: Prentice-Hall, 1969.

An excellent collection of articles on social inequality and social class in the United States. The book contains useful introductions to the various topics and is recommended for an overview of the subject.

ROSSIDES, DANIEL W. *The American Class System.* Boston: Houghton Mifflin, 1976.

A very thorough and sophisticated text on social stratification in the United States. The book is strongly recommended to the student who wants to pursue the subject in some depth.

STERN, PHILIP M. *The Rape of the Taxpayer.* New York: Random House, 1973.

A highly readable yet detailed account of the inequities built into the American tax system. Stern shows how the superrich are able to use many loopholes to their advantage, thus escaping much and sometimes all of their tax liability.

Reading

Blaming the Victim *William Ryan*

Americans frequently blame the poor for their poverty, the uneducated for their lack of education, the unemployed for their reliance on welfare. This practice, Ryan argues, is part of a deep-rooted tendency to blame the victim for failings that are actually caused, in many cases, by social forces over which the victim has no control.

Twenty years ago, Zero Mostel used to do a sketch in which he impersonated a Dixiecrat Senator conducting an investigation of the origins of World War II. At the climax of the sketch, the Senator boomed out, in an excruciating mixture of triumph and suspicion, "What was Pearl Harbor *doing* in the Pacific?" This is an extreme example of Blaming the Victim.

Twenty years ago, we could laugh at Zero Mostel's caricature. In recent years, however, the same process has been going on every day in the arena of social problems, public health, anti-poverty programs, and social welfare. A philosopher might analyze this process and prove that, technically, it is comic. But it is hardly ever funny.

Consider . . . the miseducated child in the slum school. He is blamed for his own miseducation. He is said to contain within himself the causes of his inability to read and write well. The shorthand phrase is "cultural deprivation," which, to those in the know, conveys what they allege to be inside information: that the poor child carries a scanty pack of cultural baggage as he enters school. He doesn't know about books and magazines and newspapers, they say. (No books in the home: the mother fails to subscribe to *Reader's Digest.*) They say that if he talks at all—an unlikely event since slum parents don't talk to their children—he certainly doesn't talk correctly. . . . If you can manage to get him to sit in a chair, they say, he squirms and looks out the window. (Impulse-ridden, these kids, motoric rather than verbal.) In a word he is "disadvantaged" and "socially deprived," they say, and this, of course, accounts for his failure (*his* failure, they say) to learn much in school.

Note the similarity to the logic of Zero Mostel's Dixiecrat Senator. What is the culturally deprived child *doing* in the school? What is wrong with the victim? In pursuing this logic, no one remembers to ask questions about the collapsing buildings and torn textbooks, the frightened, insensitive teachers, the six additional desks in the room, the blustering, frightened principals, the relentless segregation, the callous administrator, the irrelevant curriculum, the bigoted or cowardly members of the school board, the insulting history book, the stingy taxpayers, the fairy-tale readers, or the self-serving faculty of the local teachers' college. We are encouraged to confine our attention to the child and to dwell on all his alleged defects. Cultural deprivation becomes an omnibus explanation for the educational disaster area known as the inner-city school. This is Blaming the Victim.

The generic process of Blaming the Victim is applied to almost every American problem. The miserable health care of the poor is explained away on the grounds that the victim has poor motivation and lacks health information. The problems of slum housing are traced to the characteristics of tenants who are labeled as "Southern rural migrants" not yet "acculturated" to life in the big city. The "multiproblem" poor, it is claimed, suffer the psychological effects of impoverishment, the "culture of poverty," and the deviant value system of the lower classes; consequently, though unwittingly, they cause their own troubles. From such a viewpoint, the obvious fact that poverty is primarily an absence of money is easily overlooked or set aside. . . . Every important social problem—crime, mental illness, civil disorder, unemployment—has been analyzed within the framework of the victim-blaming ideology.

I have been listening to the victim-blamers and pondering their thought processes for a number of years. That process is often very subtle. Victim-blaming is cloaked in kindness and concern. . . . In this way, the new ideology is very different from the open prejudice and reactionary tactics of the old days. Its adherents include sympathetic social scientists with social consciences in good working order, and liberal politicians with a genuine commitment to reform.

Blaming the Victim is, of course, quite different from old-fashioned conservative ideologies. The latter simply dismissed victims as inferior, genetically defective, or morally unfit; the emphasis is on the intrinsic, even hereditary, defect. The former shifts its emphasis to the environmental causation. The old-fashioned conservative could hold firmly to the belief that the oppressed and the victimized were born that way—"that way" being defective or inadequate in character or ability. The new ideology attributes defect and inadequacy to the malignant nature of poverty, injustice, slum life, and racial difficulties. . . . But the stigma, the defect, the fatal difference—though derived in the past from environmental forces—is still located *within* the victim, inside his skin. . . . It is a brilliant ideology for justifying a perverse form of social action designed to change, not society, as one might expect, but rather society's victim.

We must particularly ask, "To whom are social problems a problem?" And usually, if truth were to be told, we would have to admit that we mean they are a problem to those of us who are outside the boundaries of what we have defined as the problem. Negroes are a problem to racist whites, welfare is a problem to stingy taxpayers, delinquency is a problem to nervous property owners.

Now, if this is the quality of our assumptions about social problems, we are led unerringly to certain beliefs about the causes of these problems. We cannot comfortably believe that *we* are the cause of that which is problematic to us; therefore, we are almost compelled to believe that *they*—the problematic ones—are the cause. . . .

Blaming the Victim . . . is central in the mainstream of contemporary American social thought, and its ideas pervade our most crucial assumptions so thoroughly that they are hardly noticed. Moreover, the fruits of this ideology appear to be fraught with altruism and humanitarianism, so it is hard to believe that it has principally functioned to block social change.

A major pharmaceutical manufacturer, as an act of humanitarian concern, has distributed copies of a large poster warning "LEAD PAINT CAN KILL!" The poster, featuring a photograph of the face of a charming little girl, goes on to explain that if children *eat* lead paint, it can poison them, they can develop serious symptoms, suffer permanent brain damage, even die. The health department of a major American city has put out a coloring book that provides the same information. While the poster urges parents to prevent their children from eating paint, the coloring book is more vivid. It labels as neglectful and thoughtless the mother who does not keep her infant under constant surveillance to keep it from eating paint chips.

Now, no one would argue against the idea that it is important to spread knowledge about the danger of eating paint in order that parents might act to forestall their children from doing so. But to campaign against lead paint *only* in these terms is destructive and misleading and, in a sense, an effective way to support and agree with slum landlords—who define the problem of lead poisoning in precisely these terms. . . .

It is not accurate to say that lead poisoning results from the actions of individual neglectful mothers. Rather, lead poisoning is a social phenomenon supported by a number of social mechanisms, one of the most tragic by-products of the systematic toleration of slum housing. In New Haven, which has the highest reported rate of lead poisoning in the country, several small children have died and many others have incurred irreparable brain damage as a result of eating peeling paint. In several cases, when the landlord failed to make repairs, poisonings have occurred time and again through a succession of tenancies. And the major reason for the landlord's neglect of this problem was that the city agency responsible for enforcing the housing code did nothing to make him correct this dangerous condition.

The cause of the poisoning is the lead in the paint on the walls of the apartment in which the children live. The presence of the lead is illegal. To use lead paint in a residence is illegal; to permit lead paint to be exposed in a residence is illegal. It is not only illegal, it is potentially criminal since the housing code does provide for criminal penalties. The general problem of lead poisoning, then, is more accurately analyzed as the result of a systematic program of lawbreaking by one interest group in the community, with the toleration and encouragement of the public authority charged with enforcing that law. To ignore these continued and repeated law violations, to ignore the fact that the supposed law enforcer actually cooperates in lawbreaking, and then to load a burden of guilt on the mother of a dead or dangerously-ill child is an egregious distortion of reality. And to do so under the guise of public-spirited and humanitarian service to the community is intolerable.

But this is how Blaming the Victim works. The righteous humanitarian concern displayed by the drug company, with its poster, and the health department, with its coloring book, is a genuine concern, and this is a typical feature of Blaming the Victim. Also typical is the swerving away from the central target that requires systematic change and, instead, focusing in on the individual affected. The ultimate effect is always to distract attention from the basic causes and to leave the primary social injustice untouched. And, most telling, the proposed remedy for the problem is, of course, to work on the victim himself.

Source: William Ryan, *Blaming the Victim* (New York: Pantheon, 1971), pp. 3–24.

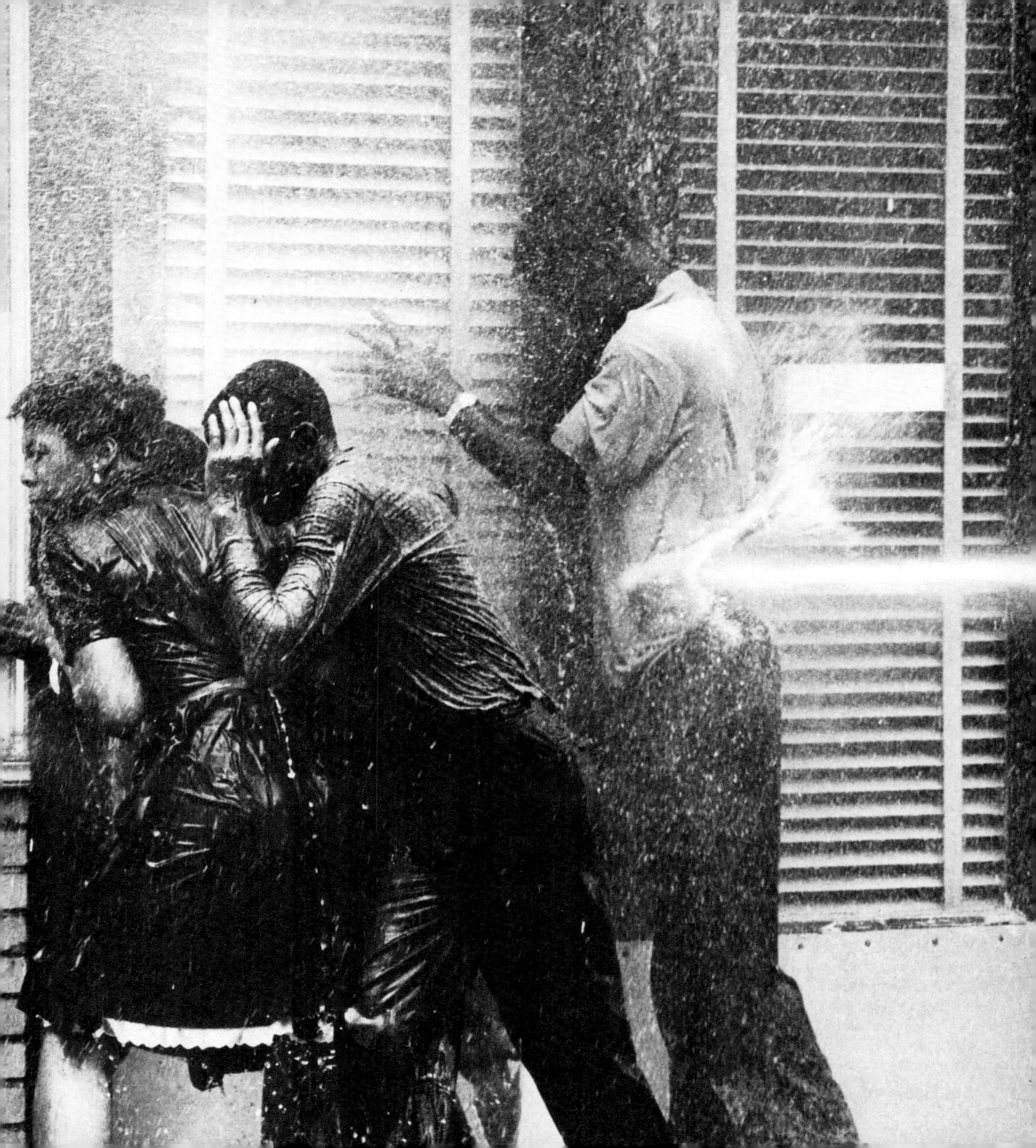

CHAPTER 12 *Race and Ethnic Relations*

CHAPTER OUTLINE

The Concepts of Race and Ethnicity
Race
Ethnicity

Minority Groups

Patterns of Race and Ethnic Relations

Racism
The Nature of Racism
The Causes of Racism
The Ideology of Racism

Prejudice and Discrimination
The Psychology of Prejudice
Forms of Discrimination

Race and Ethnic Relations in the United States
Blacks
Native Americans
Hispanic Americans
Asian Americans
White Ethnics

The Future of American Race and Ethnic Relations

One of the most fascinating aspects of our species is the extraordinary physical and cultural diversity of its members. Yet this diversity is often a source of conflict and inequality, because human relationships are all too often conducted on the basis of the differences rather than the similarities between groups.

As we saw in Chapter 10 (Social Stratification), all societies differentiate among their members, and these distinctions are usually translated into social inequalities. One common way of differentiating among people is to do so on the basis of their physical characteristics or cultural traits. As a result of these social distinctions, the groups in question come to regard themselves and to be regarded and treated by others as "different." *Race and ethnic relations are the patterns of interaction among groups whose members share distinctive physical characteristics or cultural traits.* Those people who share similar physical characteristics are socially defined as a "race," and those who share similar cultural traits are socially defined as an "ethnic group."

Throughout history, relationships between racial and ethnic groups have been marked by prejudice, antagonism, warfare, and social inequality. Even in the course of the present decade, hundreds of thousands of people have been slaughtered, and millions more subjected to cruelty and injustice, for no apparent reason other than their membership in some despised group. In the United States, a country formally committed to human equality, the physical and cultural differences among various groups still have a strong influence on their members' social status.

The Concepts of Race and Ethnicity

The term "race" refers to the genetically transmitted physical characteristics of different human groups, and the term "ethnicity" refers to culturally acquired differences. Both words are often misused in ordinary speech, and we must examine their meaning more closely.

Race

As a biological concept, the word "race" is almost meaningless. There are over 4 billion people in the world, and they display a wide variety of skin colors, hair textures, limb-to-trunk ratios, and other characteristics, such as distinctive nose, lip, and eyelid forms (see Figure 12.2). Although the human animal can be traced back for well over a million years, the racial differences that we see today are of comparatively recent origin—50,000 years at the most.

These physical differences have resulted from the adaptations that human groups have made to the environments in which they lived. For example, populations in tropical and subtropical areas tend to have dark skin, which protects them against harmful rays from the sun. Populations in high altitudes tend to have large lung capacity, which makes breathing easier for them. Populations in very cold climates tend to have relatively short limbs, which enable them to conserve body heat. So far as is known, these evolutionary differences affect only physical characteristics. There is no convincing evidence that different groups inherit different psychological characteristics, whether these be general traits such as intelligence or more specific ones such as artistic ability.

Confronted with this vast range of physical types, anthropologists have tried for decades to create some kind of conceptual order by dividing the human species into races and subraces. The number of races that is discovered, however, depends very much on the particular anthropologist who is doing the discovering: estimates range from three races to well over a hundred. The reason for the confusion is that there is no such thing as a "pure" race. Different population groups have been interbreeding for tens of thousands of years, and categories of "race" are a creation of the observer, not of nature.

The classification that has won broadest acceptance in the past divides the human species into three major categories: the Caucasoids, with fair skin and straight or wavy hair; the Mongoloids, with yellowish skin and a distinctive fold around the eyes; and the Negroids, with dark skin and woolly hair. Unfortunately, however, there are many people who cannot be neatly fitted into this classification. The Indians of Asia have Caucasoid features but dark skin. The Ainu of Japan have Mongoloid facial features but Caucasoid hair and skin color. The aborigines of Australia have dark skin, but their woolly hair is often blond. The San of Africa have coppery skin, woolly hair, and Mongoloid facial features. There are also many millions of people, such as those of Indonesia, whose ancestry is so mixed that they cannot possibly be fitted into one of the main categories. Many, if not most, anthropologists have now abandoned the attempt to classify the human species into races and consider the term "race" to have no scientific meaning at all.

The physical differences between human groups, then, are simply a biological fact. As such, they are of no particular interest to the sociologist. The intense sociological interest in race derives from its significance as a *social* fact, because people attach meanings to the physical differences, real or imagined, between human groups. If people believe that a certain group forms a biological unity, they will act on the basis of that belief. The members of the group will tend to develop a common loyalty and to intermarry with one another, and members of other groups will regard them as "different." From the sociological point of view, then, a *race* is a large number of people who, for social or geographical reasons, have interbred over a long period of time; as a result, they have developed visible physical characteristics and regard themselves and are regarded by others as a biological unity.

Whether social beliefs about race have any biological basis is of little relevance. It is people's beliefs about race rather than the facts about race that influence race relations, for better or worse. Many people, for example, consider the Jews a race. In biological terms, this view is nonsense. Jews have always interbred to some extent with their host populations, and many Jewish people are blond and blue-eyed in Sweden, small and swarthy in eastern Europe, black in Ethiopia, or Mongoloid in China. Even in Nazi Germany, which attached such great importance to the distinctions between Jews and non-Jews, the Jewish population was obliged to wear yellow stars so that their persecutors could distinguish them from the rest of the population. Yet when any group is arbitrarily defined as a race, as Jews were in Nazi Germany, important social consequences may follow.

Ethnicity

Race refers only to physical characteristics, but the concept of ethnicity refers to cultural features. These features may include language, religion, national origin, dietary practices, a sense of common historical heritage, or any other distinctive cultural trait. Many groups, such as blacks or native Americans, are both racially and ethnically distinct. Such groups are regarded as doubly "different." In other cases, ethnic groups cannot be distinguished from the rest of the population by their physical characteristics. German and Polish Americans, for example, are physically indistinguishable, but members of the two groups may form distinct subcultures based on their different ethnic backgrounds.

From the sociological viewpoint, then, an *ethnic group* is a large number of people who, as a result of their shared cultural traits and high level of mutual interaction, come to regard themselves and to be regarded as a cultural unity. Unlike racial differences, ethnic differences are culturally learned and not genetically inherited—a point that seems obvious enough, until we remember how often the supposed "intelligence," "industriousness," "warlikeness," "inscrutability," "laziness," or other characteristic of some group is assumed to be an inborn trait of its members. But no ethnic group has any inborn cultural traits; it acquires them from its environment. The Japanese of Japan and Americans of Japanese ancestry share the same genetic heritage, yet they display very different cultural norms and values.

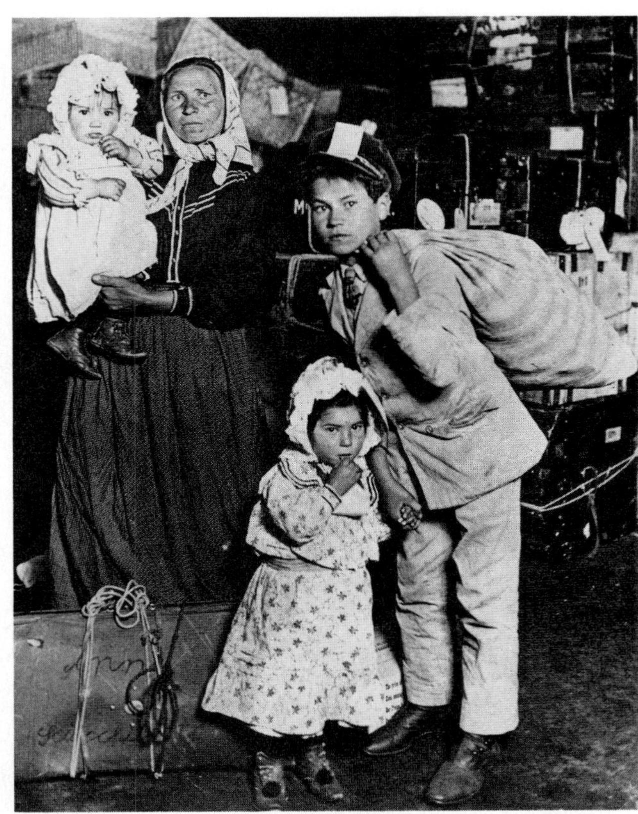

Figure 12.1 An Italian mother and her children arriving in the United States at the turn of the century. As a result of massive immigration during the latter part of the nineteenth and the early twentieth centuries, the United States contains several ethnic minorities. Each new wave of immigrants from Europe encountered prejudice and discrimination on arrival; this was particularly true of Catholic groups or groups from southern and eastern Europe.

Minority Groups

The simple, preindustrial societies of the past were usually small and homogeneous. Within these societies everyone spoke the same language, shared the same values, worshipped the same gods, and had very similar physical characteristics.

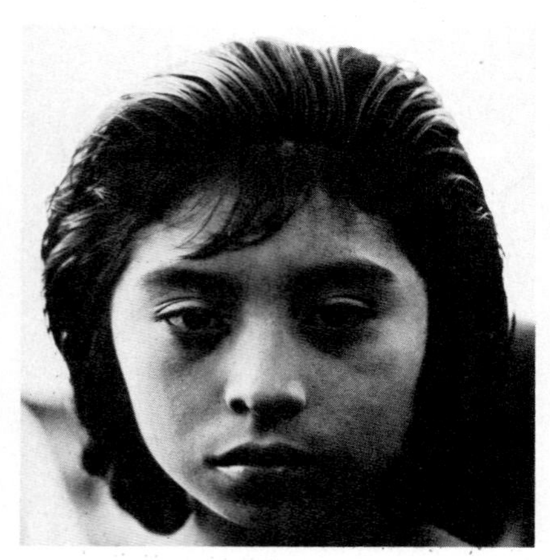

Figure 12.2 As a result of their adaptations to the particular environments in which they have lived, different human populations display a fascinating variety of physical characteristics.

In the modern world, however, many societies are large and heterogeneous. As a result of colonial settlements, missionary work, migrations, and the flight of refugees from famine, poverty, and persecution, these societies frequently contain minorities whose physical appearance and cultural practices are unlike those of the dominant group. The dominant group in these societies often differentiates between its own members and the minority. It treats minority group members in an unequal way, typically by denying them equal access to the power, wealth, and prestige that its own members enjoy.

The concept of a *minority group* is an important one in sociology, and sociologists use it in a very specific sense. There are many numerical minorities in American society—such as people of Scottish extraction, blue-eyed people, or auto mechanics—but these are not regarded as minority groups. The term is used only in the sense in which it was first defined by Louis Wirth (1945):

> We may define a minority as a group of people who, because of their physical or cultural characteristics, are singled out from the others in the society in which they live for differential and unequal treatment and who therefore regard themselves as objects of collective discrimination.

This concept of a minority group has since been further refined, and sociologists now regard a part of the population as a minority group if it has the following distinguishing features (Wagley and Harris, 1964; Williams, 1964; Vander Zanden, 1972):

1. *The members of a minority group suffer various disadvantages at the hands of another group.* This disadvantage does not only mean that the minority is denied equal access to power, wealth, and prestige. The minority's disadvantage is an important source of the dominant group's advantage. The dominant group exploits the minority, relegating its members to low-status positions in society and draining off its labor and resources. And the members of the minority group are not merely exploited: they are the victims of prejudice, discrimination, abuse, humiliation, and deeply held social beliefs that they are somehow "inferior."

2. *A minority is identified by group characteristics that are socially visible.* The characteristics and boundaries of a minority group are socially defined on arbitrary grounds. All people sharing some visible or noticeable characteristic, such as skin color, religion, or language, are lumped together into a single category. No matter what characteristic is used to make this differentiation, it is believed to be of great social importance. Individual characteristics of a minority group member are regarded as less significant than the supposed characteristics of the group to which the individual belongs.

3. *A minority is a self-conscious group with a strong sense of "oneness."* Members of a minority, such as Jews, American blacks, or Palestinians, tend to feel a strong affinity with one another. Their "consciousness of kind," or sense of common identity, is often so strong that differences within the group become submerged in a common loyalty to "the people." The minority group's shared experience of suffering heightens these feelings; in fact, the more its members are persecuted, the more intense their group solidarity is likely to become.

4. *People usually do not become members of a minority group voluntarily; they are born into it.* The sense of common identity usually comes from an awareness of common ancestry and traditions. It is often difficult for a member of a minority group to leave the group, for the reason that the dominant group regards anyone with minority group ancestry as a permanent member of that minority. In the United States, for example, a person with one black parent—or even a person with white parents and only one black grandparent—is still regarded as black rather than white.

5. *By choice or necessity, members of a minority group generally marry within the group.* This practice (called endogamy) may be encouraged by the dominant group, by the minority group, or by both. Members of the dominant group are typically reluctant to marry members of the stigmatized minority group, and the minority group's consciousness of kind predisposes its members to look for marital partners within the group. As a result, minority status within a society tends to be passed on from generation to generation.

There is one aspect of the sociological use of the term "minority group" that may seem rather peculiar at first: a minority group can sometimes be a numerical majority. Minority group status is not a matter of numbers; it is determined by the presence of the distinguishing features outlined above. In practice, of course, it is very rare for a numerical majority to be a minority group in their own society, but examples of this situation do exist. In the African country of Burundi, the small Tutsi tribe dominates the large Hutu tribe, and in South Africa the small white population dominates the much larger black population. Some sociologists have also argued that women in the United States can be regarded as a minority group, although they slightly outnumber men.

Patterns of Race and Ethnic Relations

Race and ethnic relations may follow many different patterns, ranging from harmonious coexistence to outright conflict. George Simpson and Milton Yinger (1972) have provided a useful typology of six basic patterns of intergroup hostility or cooperation. This typology covers virtually all the possible patterns of race and ethnic relations, and each pattern exists or has existed in some part of the world.

1. *Assimilation.* In some cases a minority group is simply eliminated by being assimilated into the dominant group. This process may involve cultural assimilation, racial assimilation, or both. Cultural assimilation occurs when the minority group abandons its distinctive cultural traits and adopts those of the dominant culture; racial assimilation occurs when the physical differences between the groups disappear as a result of inbreeding. Brazil is probably the best contemporary example of a country following a policy of assimilation. With the exception of some isolated Indian groups, the various racial and ethnic groups within the society interbreed fairly freely. Portugal attempted a policy of assimilation in the African colonies that it ruled until the mid-seventies. The Portuguese even created a special status, *assimilado,* for those Africans or people of mixed race who were considered sufficiently Portuguese in color or culture to share the privileges of the dominant group.

2. *Pluralism.* Some minorities do not want to lose their group identity; their members have a strong consciousness of kind and pride in their own heritage, and are loyal to their own group. The dominant group in the society may also be willing to permit or even to encourage cultural variation within the broader confines of national unity. Tanzania, for example, is a pluralistic society that respects the cultural distinctions among its African, Asian, European, and Middle Eastern peoples. In Switzerland four ethnic groups, speaking German, French, Italian, and Romanche, retain their sense of group identity while living together amicably in the society as a whole.

3. *Legal protection of minorities.* In some societies, significant sections of the dominant group may have hostile attitudes toward minority groups, but the minorities may enjoy the protection of the government. In such cases the government may find it necessary to introduce legal measures to protect the interests and rights of the minorities. In Britain, for example, the Race Relations Act of 1965 makes it illegal to discriminate against any person on racial grounds in employment or housing. It is also a criminal offense to publish or even to utter publicly any sentiments that might encourage hostility between racial and ethnic groups in the population.

4. *Population transfer.* In some situations of intense hostility between groups, the problem is "solved" by removing the minority from the scene altogether. This policy was adopted, for example, by President Amin of Uganda, who simply ordered Asian residents to leave the country in which they had lived for generations. In a few cases, population transfer may involve outright partition of a territory. Hostility between Hindus and Muslims in India was so intense that the entire subcontinent was divided between them in such a way that a new Muslim state, Pakistan, was created. There are signs that Cyprus is becoming permanently divided into Greek and Turkish territories, and Lebanon into Muslim and Christian territories. Voluntary and forced population transfers have been taking place in both countries.

5. *Continued subjugation.* In some cases the dominant group has every intention of maintaining its privilege over the minority group indefinitely. It may be fully willing to use force to achieve this objective, and it may even physically segregate the members of the various groups. Historically, continued subjugation has been a very common policy. In the early colonial empires, for example, it was implicitly assumed that colonial domination over the

Figure 12.3 The Nazis attempted the systematic genocide of the Jewish population of Germany and of several countries that they occupied in World War II. This scene is from the concentration camp at Dachau, one of several centers where up to six million Jews were murdered.

subject peoples was to be a permanent state of affairs. The climate of world opinion is now such that few countries dare to endorse openly a policy of continued subjugation, but the pattern does persist in some cases. The outstanding example is South Africa, where, under the policy of *apartheid,* the white minority proposes to keep its power over the black majority forever, and has openly declared its willingness to use all necessary force to achieve this goal. Less overt policies of continued subjugation are found in several Latin American countries, where dominant Hispanic groups continue to oppress the indigenous Indian minorities.

6. *Extermination.* The extermination of entire populations, or *genocide,* has been attempted and even achieved in several parts of the world. The methods of genocide include systematic slaughter by force of arms and the deliberate spreading of infectious diseases, particularly smallpox, to peoples who have no natural immunity to them. Dutch settlers in South Africa entirely exterminated the Hottentots and came close to exterminating the San, who at one point in South African history were actually classified as "vermin." British settlers on the island of Tasmania wiped out the local population, whom they hunted for sport and even for dog food. There is strong evidence that economic interests in Brazil, with the connivance of the Brazilian government, have slaughtered the Indian occupants of land that is wanted for agricultural development. Between 1933 and 1945 several million Jews were murdered in Germany. The most recent example of attempted genocide occurred in the African state of Burundi in 1972, when the dominant Tutsi tribe massacred nearly 100,000 members of the Hutu tribe.

These patterns are not necessarily mutually exclusive, and a society can adopt more than one of them at the same time. It is interesting to note that at some point in its history the United States has made use of every single one of these six strategies. Immigrant groups, particularly those from Scandinavia and other parts of northern Europe, have been *assimilated* into the mainstream of American life. There is a strong trend toward *pluralism* at present, with different groups, such as blacks and native Americans, asserting pride in their own cultural traditions. *Legal protection of minorities* has been entrenched in law through a series of civil rights acts. *Population transfer* was used extensively against the native Americans, who were often forced to leave their traditional territories and to settle on remote reserves. *Continued subjugation* was practiced against blacks, particularly through slavery in the South. *Extermination* was used against the native Americans, and several tribes were in fact hounded out of existence.

Racism

Some racial and ethnic groups, then, are able to live together in harmony and mutual respect, but others are in a state of constant antagonism and conflict. Clearly, there is no inherent reason why different groups should be hostile to one another. Poor relations among racial and ethnic groups have social causes. But what are these causes? How and why do racial and ethnic hostilities develop?

The Nature of Racism

As we saw in Chapter 3 (Culture), most human groups tend to be *ethnocentric;* that is, they unquestioningly assume that their own values and way of life are superior to all others. They use their own standards to judge other groups and, not surprisingly, find those that they are judging deficient in some respects. To most people, it is self-evident that their own norms, religion, attitudes, values, and cultural practices are right and proper, while those of other groups are peculiar, bizarre, or even immoral. A certain amount of ethnocentrism is almost inevitable in any racial or ethnic group. In fact, it may even be *functional* for the group's survival. Ethnocentric attitudes ensure the solidarity and cohesion of the group that holds them. Such attitudes discourage outsiders from penetrating the group and provide group members with faith and confidence in their own cultural tradition.

The difficulty is, of course, that ethnocentric attitudes that are functional for the group that has them may be highly *dysfunctional* for another group that suffers from them. Under certain conditions, ethnocentric attitudes can take an extreme and aggressive form and can be used to justify the oppressive treatment of other racial or ethnic groups. This is the phenomenon of *racism,* in which a group that is seen as inferior or different is exploited and oppressed by a dominant group (Blauner, 1972). Racism is not an inevitable result of contact between different groups. It is perfectly possible to identify with one's own group and take pride in its heritage while respecting the culture and traditions of other groups. Ethnocentrism develops into racism only under certain conditions, and a major task of sociology has been to specify what those conditions are.

The Causes of Racism

The most useful approach to the problem of racism is to view it from the perspective of *conflict* theory. Seen in these terms, racism is the outcome of a competition between different groups for scarce resources.

For racism to develop, three basic conditions must usually be met (Noel, 1968; Vander Zanden, 1972):

1. There must be two or more social groups, identifiable by their visible physical characteristics or cultural practices. Unless people are aware of differences between the groups and are able to identify people as belonging to one group rather than another, racism cannot develop.

2. There must be competition between the groups for valued resources, such as power, land, or jobs. In this situation, members of one group will be inclined to secure their own interests by denying members of other groups full access to these resources.

3. The groups must be unequal in power, so that one of them is able to make good its claim over scarce resources at the expense of the other group or groups. At this point inequalities become structured into the society.

From this point on, events follow a fairly predictable course. The more the groups compete, the more negatively they view one another. The dominant group develops racist views about the supposed inferiority of the minority group or groups, and it uses these notions to justify its continued supremacy. Attempts by the minority group to assert its own interests are likely to be regarded as threatening by the dominant group, and further oppression may follow.

From the conflict perspective, economic inequalities underlie racism. The disputes between groups are not so much about racial or ethnic distinctions as about the use of supposed distinctions to preserve an unequal society. Racism may even arise when competition is expected at some point in the future: white settlers in the United States quickly developed racist attitudes toward the native population, whom they saw as potential competitors for possession of land and other resources. And because social attitudes, like any other part of culture, tend to be inherently conservative, racism may persist long after the conditions that gave rise to it have disappeared. Negative concepts about the native Americans, for example, have persisted for many decades after they were finally defeated and their lands were seized. In short, racism may be rapidly institutionalized but only slowly eradicated. It tends to disappear only when competition among the various groups has declined.

The European colonial period offers a good case study of the relationship between racism and economic interests. There was very little racism in the European powers before they started building their respective colonial empires. In fact, occasional visitors from exotic foreign lands were often treated with honor and sometimes with awe. Under the colonial system, however, a few European nations seized control of almost half of the land area and population of the world and developed a strong economic interest in oppressing the colonial peoples. The colonists relied on the indigenous populations for cheap labor and on their countries as a source of raw materials and as a market for manufactured goods. This era of colonial expansion was marked by an intense race consciousness among European peoples.

The European powers, particularly those that practiced slavery, risked a severe moral dilemma. Their treatment of colonial peoples was clearly incompatible with their avowed Christian beliefs. Since no Christian could legitimately make a slave of another human being, an obvious justification presented itself: to classify the colonial peoples as subhuman. In the 1840s one of the early anthropologists, James Pritchard, found it necessary to devote considerable effort to the question of whether "primitive" peoples were truly human (quoted in Lienhardt, 1966):

> If the Negro and Australian are not our fellow creatures and of one family with ourselves but beings of an inferior order, and if our duties toward them were not contemplated . . . in any of the positive commands on which the morality of the Christian world is founded, our relations with these tribes will appear to be not very different from those which might be imagined to subsist between us and a race of orangutans.

Darwin's theory of evolution was also used by those who wanted to prove the subhuman status of nonwhite peoples. Some argued that the colonial peoples were at a lower point on the evolutionary ladder than whites; others that they were products of a completely separate process of evolution and were thus half animal.

These attitudes became deeply embedded in western European culture and were transported by white settlers to the United States, where many traces of them remain

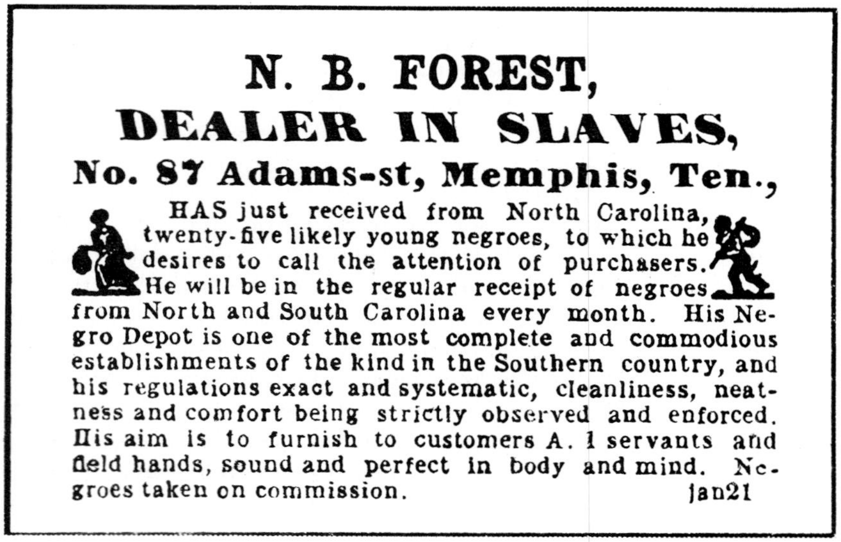

N. B. FOREST,
DEALER IN SLAVES,
No. 87 Adams-st, Memphis, Ten.,

HAS just received from North Carolina, twenty-five likely young negroes, to which he desires to call the attention of purchasers. He will be in the regular receipt of negroes from North and South Carolina every month. His Negro Depot is one of the most complete and commodious establishments of the kind in the Southern country, and his regulations exact and systematic, cleanliness, neatness and comfort being strictly observed and enforced. His aim is to furnish to customers A. 1 servants and field hands, sound and perfect in body and mind. Negroes taken on commission. jan21

Figure 12.4 As this advertisement from a slave dealer suggests, slaves were regarded as less than human: the advertiser might as well have been talking about livestock. This racist attitude helped to lessen any moral qualms about the institution of slavery. It would have been much more difficult to make slaves of other people if their full humanity were recognized.

to this day. Racist beliefs provided a convenient justification for slavery in the South and for the slaughter and dispossession of native Americans. Blacks were considered suitable for slavery "by nature," and the destruction of native American society by a "superior" white civilization was seen as a matter of "manifest destiny."

The racism of the Western powers was notable for its international scale and systematic theoretical justification by theologians and scientists alike. But racism is by no means restricted to Western whites. It is found throughout the world, invariably in situations of economic competition between different groups. The East African nations of Kenya and Uganda, for example, have expelled tens of thousands of their Asian residents. In both societies, the Asian minorities had an economic status far superior to that of the indigenous Africans, who took over their jobs and businesses after they had left. Similarly, many of the conflicts between blacks and Arabs in sub-Saharan Africa are related to the struggle for scarce resources as the desert steadily spreads into drought-stricken lands that were once fertile.

Intergroup conflicts generally do not subside until economic inequalities are overcome, as the history of American race relations suggests. The strong prejudices that existed against Japanese, Chinese, Irish, Italian, and other immigrants have gradually lessened as these groups have gained entry to the middle class. Prejudice is still greatest against those groups, such as blacks or Hispanic Americans, who remain impoverished. There is strong evidence that the greatest prejudice against minority groups in America is found among low-status whites who feel most threatened by the economic progress and competition of the minorities (Selznick and Steinberg, 1969; Cohen and Hodges, 1963). The evidence from other countries has also shown a consistent pattern of racial intolerance among low-status members of the dominant group (Lipset, 1959a).

The Ideology of Racism

A dominant group always tries to legitimate its interests by means of an *ideology,* or set of beliefs, that defines the existing system as just and moral (see Chapter 10, Social Stratification). Racist theories about the supposed inferiority of oppressed groups are one such ideology. No group can systematically exploit and debase another group without using some values to justify this behavior. The ideology of racism serves to legitimate the social inequalities between the groups by making them seem "natural," or "right." If one can believe that "slaves are happy," or that native Americans are so subhuman that "the only good Indian is a dead Indian," then slavery and slaughter become more acceptable policies.

The ideology of racism does not only justify the existing inequalities, it also reinforces them by the social process of the *self-fulfilling prophecy* (Merton, 1968). One of the founders of American sociology, W. I. Thomas, first expressed this idea in a simple but profound statement that has since become famous as the "Thomas theorem": "If men define situations as real, they are real in their consequences." Thus, to cite an example given by Merton, if people wrongly believe that a bank will go bankrupt, they will rush to withdraw their money—with the result that the bank *will* go bankrupt. The self-fulfilling prophecy is a false definition of a situation, but the definition leads to behavior that makes the prediction come true. The actual course of events then seems to justify and confirm the original prophecy.

In the field of race and ethnic relations, the self-fulfilling prophecy works as follows. The racist ideology of the dominant group defines the minority as inferior. Because the members of the minority group are considered inferior, they are believed to be unsuited for high-status jobs, advanced education, or responsible positions in society. Accordingly, they are not given access to these opportunities. Since they are denied the opportunities, they naturally hold low-status jobs, are poorly educated, and fill few responsible positions in society. This situation is then cited as an objective fact to "prove" that the minority group is inferior, and the racist ideology is confirmed.

It often happens, too, that the minority group shares the beliefs that the dominant group holds about them, for it is quite common for an oppressed group to accept the ideology that justifies their oppression. There is little doubt, for example, that colonial peoples accepted the colonizers' view of their inferiority, at least until the surge of nationalism in these countries after World War II. In such cases the minority is in a state of what Marx called

Racism

IN THE SUPERIOR COURT OF THE STATE OF CALIFORNIA IN AND FOR THE COUNTY OF SANTA CLARA JUVENILE DIVISION

HONORABLE GERALD S. CHARGIN, Judge

In the Matter of PAUL PETE CASILLAS, JR., a minor.

STATEMENTS OF THE COURT

San Jose, California September 2, 1969 10:25 a.m.

APPEARANCES

For the Minor: FRED LUCERO, ESQ. Deputy Public Defender

For the Probation Department: WILLIAM TAPOGNA, ESQ. Court Probation Officer

The Court: There is some indication that you more or less didn't think that it was against the law or was improper. Haven't you had any moral training? Have you and your family gone to church?

The Minor: Yes, sir.

The Court: Don't you know that things like this are terribly wrong? This is one of the worst crimes that a person can commit. I just get so disgusted that I just figure what is the use? You are just an animal. You are lower than an animal. Even animals don't do that. You are pretty low.

I don't know why your parents haven't been able to teach you anything or train you. Mexican people, after 13 years of age, it's perfectly all right to go out and act like an animal. It's not even right to do that to a stranger, let alone a member of your own family. I don't have much hope for you. You will probably end up in State's Prison before you are 25, and that's where you belong, any how. There is nothing much you can do.

I think you haven't any moral principles. You won't acquire anything. Your parents won't teach you what is right or wrong and won't watch out.

Apparently, you sister is pregnant; is that right?

The Minor's Father, Mr. Casillas: Yes.

The Court: It's a fine situation. How old is she?

The Minor's Mother, Mrs. Casillas: Fifteen.

The Court: Well, probably she will have a half a dozen children and three or four marriages before she is 18.

The County will have to take care of you. You are no particular good to anybody. We ought to send you out of the country—send you back to Mexico. You belong in prison for the rest of your life for doing things of this kind. You ought to commit suicide. That's what I think of people of this kind. You are lower than animals and haven't the right to live in organized society—just miserable, lousy, rotten people.

There is nothing we can do with you. You expect the County to take care of you. Maybe Hitler was right. The animals in our society probably ought to be destroyed because they have no right to live among human beings. If you refuse to act like a human being, then, you don't belong among the society of human beings.

Mr. Lucero: Your Honor, I don't think I can sit here and listen to that sort of thing.

The Court: You are going to have to listen to it because I consider this a very vulgar, rotten human being.

Mr. Lucero: The Court is indicting the whole Mexican group.

The Court: When they are 10 or 12 years of age, going out and having intercourse with anybody without any moral training—they don't even understand the Ten Commandments. That's all. Apparently, they don't want to.

So if you want to act like that, the County has a system of taking care of them. They don't care about that. They have no personal self-respect.

Mr. Lucero: The Court ought to look at this youngster and deal with this youngster's case.

The Court: All right. That's what I am going to do. The family should be able to control this boy and the young girl.

Mr. Lucero: What appalls me is that the Court is saying that Hitler was right in genocide.

The Court: What are we going to do with the mad dogs of our society? Either we have to kill them or send them to an institution or place them out of the hands of good people because that's the theory—one of the theories of punishment is if they get to the position that they want to act like mad dogs, then, we have to separate them from our society.

Well, I will go along with the recommendation. You will learn in time or else you will have to pay for the penalty with the law because the law grinds slowly but exceedingly well. If you are going to be a law violator—you have to make up your mind whether you are going to observe the law or not. If you can't observe the law, then, you have to be put away.

false consciousness, a subjective understanding of one's situation that does not accord with the objective facts.

White racist theory reached its most extreme forms during the course of this century in the rantings of Adolf Hitler (1948), a short, dark man who believed that the tall, blond "Aryan" race was infinitely superior to all others:

> All the human culture, all the results of art, science, and technology that we see before us today, are almost exclusively the product of the Aryan.... He is the Prometheus of mankind from whose singing brow the divine spark of genius has sprung at all times.... It is no accident that the first cultures arose in places where the Aryan, in his encounters with lower peoples, subjugated them, and bent them to his will.... History has shown with terrible clarity that each time Aryan blood has become mixed with inferior peoples the result has been the end of the culture-sustaining race.

This view neglected several uncomfortable facts. First, there is no such thing as a "pure" race, and certainly no such thing as an "Aryan" race. Second, complex civilizations existed thousands of years ago in India, Egypt, Mesopotamia, and China at a time when northern Europeans had still to invent the alphabet, the wheel, the plough, or the city. Third, it is a matter of scientific fact that interbreeding between different human populations is likely (as is the case with other plant and animal species) to produce offspring that are healthier than either parental stock (Simpson and Yinger, 1972). Hitler's theories led to gas chambers and concentration camps, to the murder of up to six million Jews, and to a global war. One outcome, however, was that racist ideology was made utterly disreputable, and few people or governments today, whatever their private attitudes, dare to openly endorse a racist attitude. It is worth noting, however, that the United States fought Hitler with a racially segregated army and that German prisoners of war ate in canteens in which black American soldiers were refused service.

Prejudice and Discrimination

Prejudice and discrimination are found in any situation of hostility between racial and ethnic groups. The two terms are often used interchangeably in ordinary speech, but in fact they refer to two different, though related, phenomena. *Prejudice* is a "prejudged" *attitude* toward members of another group. These people are regarded with hostility simply because they belong to a particular group, and they are assumed to have the undesirable qualities that are supposed to be characteristic of the group as a whole. *Discrimination,* on the other hand, refers to *action* against other people on the grounds of their group membership—particularly the refusal to grant members of another group the opportunities that would be granted to similarly qualified members of one's own group.

In a classic study conducted in the thirties, Richard LaPiere showed the importance of distinguishing between the two concepts. He traveled around the United States with a Chinese couple, stopping at over 250 restaurants and hotels on the way. In only one case were they refused service—that is, discriminated against. Six months later, LaPiere wrote to each of the establishments he had visited and asked if they were willing to serve "members of the Chinese race." Over 90 percent of the replies indicated that Chinese would not be welcome—that is, there was prejudice against them. Clearly, prejudice was not necessarily translated into discrimination. There is also the possibility that many of those who replied to LaPiere were not even prejudiced against Chinese, but thought it would be good for business to pretend that they were. LaPiere's study is one of many examples of sociological research that reveals the discrepancy between what people say and what they do (Deutscher, 1973).

Robert Merton (1949) has proposed a prejudice/discrimination typology containing four different types of persons and their characteristic responses. A particular individual may not necessarily fit neatly into the model, but it does cover all the possibilities.

The *unprejudiced nondiscriminator* accepts the formal values of American democracy and adheres to the ideal of equality in both theory and practice. Such a person is not prejudiced and does not discriminate against others on racial or ethnic grounds.

The *unprejudiced discriminator* has no personal prejudices, but may discriminate when it is convenient to do so. For example, an employer may have no personal hostility toward members of another group, but may not hire them for fear of offending customers.

Figure 12.5 Racial prejudice is still very common in the United States, although it has lost its "respectability." These pictures show some extreme examples: a demonstration by the American Nazi Party; a protest by white residents of Chicago against open housing; and a ceremony of the Ku Klux Klan.

The *prejudiced nondiscriminator* is a "timid bigot" who is prejudiced against other groups but who, because of legal or social pressures, is reluctant to translate attitudes into action.

The *prejudiced discriminator* does not genuinely believe in the values of freedom or equality (at least as far as minority groups are concerned) and discriminates on the basis of prejudiced attitudes. Such a person may, however, attempt to hide his or her prejudice by using other justifications for discriminatory acts. For example, the prejudiced discriminator may refuse to rent a room to a minority group member on the grounds that "it's already been taken," or may inflate the rent to discourage minority group applicants.

The Psychology of Prejudice

A major focus of the work of social psychologists, particularly in the decade after World War II, has been the psychology of prejudice. How and why do people become prejudiced, and what are the characteristic features of prejudiced thought?

Stereotypes

Prejudiced thought always involves the use of a rigid mental image that summarizes whatever is believed to be typical about a group. This kind of image is called a *stereotype.*

Like ethnocentrism, stereotyped thinking is an almost unavoidable feature of social life. The ability to form general categories is essential if we are to make sense of the world. The use of these categories allows us to respond to the general rather than the particular and thus to simplify greatly the complexity of our surroundings. You probably have your own stereotype of what an Australian aborigine or an Eskimo is like. The essence of prejudiced thinking, however, is that the stereotype is not checked against reality. It is not modified by experiences that contradict the rigid image. If a prejudiced person finds that an individual member of a group does not conform to the stereotype for the group as a whole, this evidence is simply taken as "the exception that proves the rule" and not as grounds for questioning the original belief. Robert Merton (1968) shows how the same behavior can be interpreted differently to fit an existing stereotype.

> Did Lincoln work far into the night? This testifies that he was industrious, resolute, perserverant, and eager to realize his capacities to the full. Do the out-group Jews or Japanese keep the same hours? This only bears witness to their sweatshop mentality, their ruthless undercutting of American standards, their unfair competitive practices. Is the in-group hero frugal, thrifty, and sparing? Then the out-group villain is stingy, miserly, and penny-pinching. All honor is due to the in-group Abe for his having been smart, shrewd, and intelligent, and, by the same token, all contempt is owing the out-group Abes for their being sharp, cunning, crafty, and too clever by far.

The "Authoritarian Personality"

Do some people have personality patterns that make them more prone to prejudice than others? In the late forties, Theodore Adorno and his associates (1950) tried to answer this question.

Adorno tested his subjects on three different dimensions: an F (fascism), and E (ethnocentrism), and an A-S (antisemitism) scale. His method was to present the subjects with a series of reactionary, ethnocentric, and antisemitic statements. The subjects then indicated their degree of agreement or disagreement with each statement. The significant finding was that people who scored high on any one of the scales also tended to score high on the others. In other words, those who were prejudiced against Jews were also likely to be prejudiced against blacks and other minorities, to favor strong, authoritarian leadership, and to have a very ethnocentric view of their own customs and values.

Adorno concluded that some people have a distinct set of personality traits which together make up what he called the *authoritarian personality.* People who have this personality pattern are intolerant, insecure, highly conformist, submissive to superiors, and bullying to inferiors. They tend to have anti-intellectual and antiscientific attitudes; they are disturbed by any ambiguity in sexual or religious matters; and they see the world in very rigid and stereotyped terms. The authoritarian personality, Adorno claimed, was primarily a product of a family environment in which the parents were cold, aloof, disciplinarian, and themselves bigoted.

Adorno's work has since inspired over a thousand pieces of research and critical articles. Some writers have pointed out that Adorno's methodology was weak in certain respects; others that he neglected the possibility of an authoritarian personality among radicals as well as conservatives; others that his concept is too general and sweeping in its scope. Some critics have suggested that a third variable—such as lack of exposure to different values and norms—is responsible for both authoritarianism and prejudice (Selznick and Steinberg, 1969). Despite these and other criticisms, however, it is now generally accepted that some people are psychologically more prone to prejudiced thinking than others.

One interesting finding of Adorno's research was how irrational and inconsistent prejudiced thought is. In one of their measures of antisemitism, the researchers deliberately inserted pairs of mutually contradictory statements. One series of pairs, for example, dealt with the alleged "seclusiveness" and the alleged "inclusiveness" of Jews. Here are two such pairs:

> Much resentment against Jews stems from their tending to keep apart and exclude gentiles from Jewish social life.
>
> The Jews should not pry too much into Christian activities and organizations nor seek so much recognition and prestige from Christians.

and:

> Jews tend to remain a foreign element in American society, to preseve their old social standards and resist the American way of life.
>
> Jews go too far in hiding their Jewishness, especially such extremes as changing their names, straightening their noses, and imitating Christian manners and customs.

The researchers found that nearly three-quarters of those who were prejudiced against Jews for being too seclusive were also prejudiced against them for being too intrusive. Similarly, those who disliked them for being too capitalistic and for controlling business also disliked them for being too communistic and subversive of the capitalist system. Those who disliked Jews for begging and scrounging also disliked them for giving money to charity as a means of gaining prestige, and so on. Clearly, prejudiced people are not concerned about genuine group characteristics; they simply believe any statement that feeds their existing attitude.

A fascinating study by Eugene Hartley (1946) throws further light on this phenomenon. Hartley gave his subjects a list of thirty-five racial and ethnic minorities and asked them to select their reactions to these groups from a wide range of options. Again, people who were prejudiced against one minority group tended to be prejudiced against others. Nearly three-quarters of those who disliked Jews and blacks also disliked such people as the Wallonians, the Pireneans, and the Danireans. Some of the subjects even recommended that members of the latter three groups be expelled from the United States. As it happens, however, the Wallonians, the Pireneans, and the Danireans do not exist and never have. Their names were concocted by Hartley to see if people who were prejudiced against existing groups would also be prejudiced against groups they could never have met or even heard of. His study suggests that prejudice is learned not through contact with the groups against whom prejudice is directed but through contact with other prejudiced people.

Scapegoating

A psychological mechanism that has been identified in some situations of racial or ethnic antagonism is *scapegoating,* or placing the blame for one's troubles on some individual or group incapable of offering resistance. Scapegoating typically occurs when the members of one group feel threatened but are unable to retaliate against the real source of the threat. Therefore they vent their frustrations on some weak and despised group. Low-status whites, for example, may resent their low social and economic status, but they cannot strike at the source of the problem—the employer or "the system." Instead, they direct their hostility at minority group members whom they believe to be competing for jobs at the same level. The outstanding example of a scapegoated group were the Jews of Nazi Germany, who were conveniently blamed for Germany's economic troubles after World War I. Scapegoating another group also has the psychological function of enhancing the self-image of the group that does the scapegoating, for it proves that they are at least superior to someone.

Projection

Another psychological element present in many situations of racist interaction is *projection,* which occurs when people

Figure 12.6 Chinese immigrants to the western United States often served as scapegoats for the frustrations of low-status whites, who saw them as competitors for jobs. This engraving shows an anti-Chinese riot in Denver, Colorado, in 1880.

attribute to others the characteristics they are unwilling to recognize in themselves. The myth of the superior sexual appetite of the black male, especially as directed toward white women, has its origins in projection. Lillian Smith (1949) explains:

> Because [the slaveowners] were Puritan, they succeeded in developing a frigidity in their white women that precluded the possibility of mutual satisfaction. Lonely and baffled . . . they could not resist the vigor and kindliness and gaiety of these slaves. And succumbing to desire, they mated with these dark women whom they had dehumanized in their minds. . . . The race-sex-sin spiral had begun. The more trails the white man made to the back-yard cabins, the higher he raised his white wife on her pedestal when he returned to the big house. The higher the pedestal, the less he enjoyed her whom he had put there, for statues are after all only nice things to look at. More and more numerous became the little trails of escape . . . and more and more intricately they began to weave in and out of southern life. Guilt, shame, fear, lust spiralled after each other. Then a time came . . . when white man's suspicion of white woman began to pull the spiral higher and higher. It was of course inevitable for him to suspect her of the sins he had committed so pleasantly and often. *What if,* he whispered, and the words were never finished. . . . White man . . . in jealous panic began to project his own sins on to the Negro male.

The lynchings of black men in the South, often on the merest suspicion of their desire for white women, can only be fully understood as a result of the projection of the white man's own lusts onto his black victim.

Forms of Discrimination

Discrimination occurs when the dominant group regards itself as entitled to social advantages and uses its power to secure those advantages at the expense of minority groups. These advantages may be of many different kinds. The dominant group may, for example, reserve positions of political power for itself; it may establish a claim over desirable residential areas; it may demand the exclusive use of certain recreational facilities and schools; it may claim a right to high-status jobs. In extreme cases, it may even enforce the physical segregation of the minority group from the rest of society.

Discrimination takes two basic forms: *de jure,* or legal, discrimination encoded in laws; and *de facto,* or informal, discrimination entrenched in social customs. *De jure* discrimination was applied in all the colonies established by the European powers, where the laws reserved certain rights and privileges for the dominant group. Similar laws existed in many parts of the United States until the 1960s, when they were gradually repealed or struck down by the Supreme Court. *De facto* discrimination is always present in any situation in which a dominant group maintains advantages over a minority. Unlike *de jure* discrimination, which can be eliminated by law, *de facto* discrimination is very difficult to eradicate. Those who hoped that the repeal of discriminatory laws in the United States would be the end of discrimination have been sorely disappointed.

De facto discrimination has persisted in the United States because it has become deeply entrenched in our customs and other institutional arrangements. This *institutionalized discrimination* pervades many areas of society. For example, informal barriers to residential integration have resulted in a pattern of urban racial segregation. As a result, whites and blacks tend to use segregated schools and other facilities. Similarly, there is a strong tendency toward discrimination in hiring practices, so that blacks have much higher unemployment rates and consistently earn less than similarly qualified whites. Blacks are underrepresented in all high-status positions in society—for example, in Congress, in the judiciary, or at the upper levels of military and corporate power. In the same way, there is institutionalized discrimination within the legal system: blacks are likely to receive more severe sentences than whites convicted of the same crimes.

Race and Ethnic Relations in the United States

The American Declaration of Independence, signed on July 4, 1776, proclaimed to the world:

> We hold these truths to be self-evident, that all men are created equal, that they are endowed by their Creator with certain inalienable rights, that among these are life, liberty, and the pursuit of happiness.

Thomas Jefferson, who wrote these words of stirring idealism, was a slaveowner, and so were many of the men who appended their signatures to the document.

As the Swedish sociologist Gunnar Myrdal pointed out in 1944 in his classic study of American race relations, *An American Dilemma,* there has always been a deep tension between the expressed ideals on which the United States was founded and the actual treatment that minorities have received at the hands of the dominant group. This tension, Myrdal predicted, would ultimately have to be resolved, and we are still a long way from a final resolution. American society remains a substantially racist one, in which inequalities of power, wealth, and prestige tend to follow the lines of racial and ethnic divisions.

Unlike most societies, we are primarily a nation of relatively recent immigrants; our forebears came here as

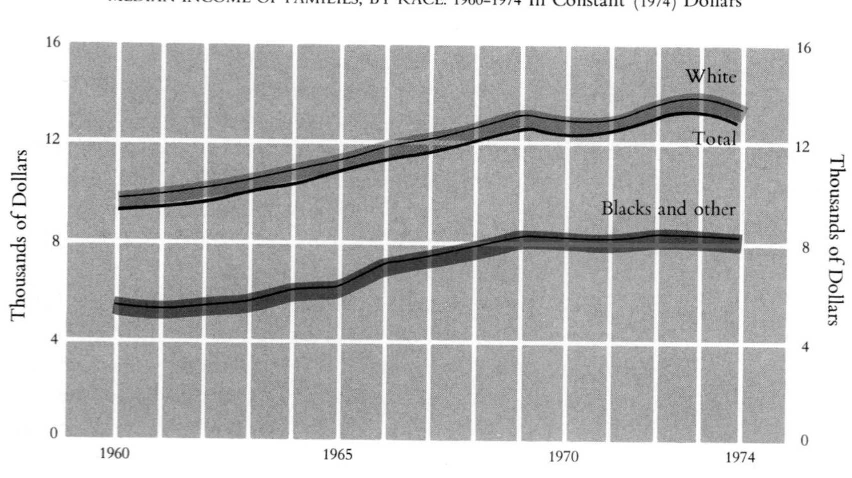

Figure 12.7 This chart gives some indication of the nature and extent of institutionalized discrimination in the United States. Although blacks have made economic gains in recent years, their earnings relative to those of whites have changed hardly at all. In a situation of truly equal opportunity, there would be no discrepancy between the average earnings of different population groups.

explorers, adventurers, colonizers, refugees, deported criminals, or captive slaves. It is a cherished American belief that our society has served as a "melting pot" for these diverse peoples. The essence of this credo was captured in *The Melting Pot,* a popular Broadway success of 1908 (Zangwill, 1933):

> America is God's crucible, the great Melting Pot, where all the races of Europe are melting and re-forming! Here you stand, good folk, think I, when I see them at Ellis Island, here you stand in your fifty groups, with your fifty languages and histories, and your fifty blood hatreds and rivalries. But you won't long be like that, brothers, for these are the fires of God you've come to . . . Germans, and Frenchmen, Irishmen and Englishmen, Jews and Russians—into the Crucible with you all! God is making the American.

The truth, however, is very different. The first settlers on our shores came mostly from "Anglo-Saxon" northern Europe, and they quickly assumed control of political and economic power. To a considerable extent, they have managed to keep this power ever since, and their cultural values have become the dominant ones of the entire nation (Graham and Gurr, 1969). Successive waves of immigrants have often had to struggle long and hard to be assimilated into the American mainstream, and many have failed. Those who were racially or ethnically akin to the dominant "WASP" (white, Anglo-Saxon Protestant) group, such as the Scandinavians and Germans, were assimilated fairly easily. Those who were racially akin but ethnically different, such as the Catholic Irish and Poles, faced much more prejudice and discrimination. Those who were racially and ethnically very dissimilar to the dominant group, such as blacks and Hispanic Americans, have been systematically excluded by formal and informal barriers from equal participation in American society.

Let's look at the background and the contemporary situation of some of our minority groups: blacks, native Americans, Hispanic Americans, Asian Americans, and "white ethnics."

Blacks

Black Americans are the largest minority group in the United States; they number over 24 million and represent about 12 percent of the population. Their history in the United States has been one of sustained oppression and discrimination.

The first Africans were brought to North America in 1619, and within a few decades the demand for their cheap labor had created a massive slave trade that ultimately brought some 400,000 Africans to our shores. Contrary to popular belief, the slaves were not captured by whites on the West African coast. They were captured by other blacks from the slave-owning kingdoms of the interior and sold to white traders at the coastal ports. The slaves were then chained wrist to wrist and ankle to ankle for a two-month sea voyage, during which they were often packed so tightly that they could not even sit up. To prevent the risk of mutiny and suicide among the captives, they were often kept in this position for days or weeks on end, lying in their own blood and excrement (Elkins, 1963; Cheek, 1970). Many of the slaves tried to starve themselves to death and were force fed through metal funnels that were jammed into their mouths for the purpose. For many years an intense economic debate raged between two groups of slave traders: the "tight packers," who held that profits would be greater if as many slaves as possible were crammed aboard, and the "loose packers," who argued that crowded conditions caused so many deaths that, on balance, it was better to allow the captives a little more space. On arrival in the United States the slaves were sold at public auction and set to work on the plantations. Their culture offered few guidelines in this new situation, and their old traditions, language, and religion were quickly eliminated. (One cultural feature that did survive in modified form, however, was the rhythm of West African traditional music. Transformed over the generations into blues, jazz, soul, rhythm and blues, and ultimately rock music, it has become a major contribution to contemporary American and world culture.)

Slavery was initially based not so much on racism as on the need for cheap labor in the cotton and tobacco fields. Slavery, in turn, led to the creation of a racist ideology that depicted blacks as subhuman: the slaveowners propagated myths about the irresponsibility, promiscuity, stupidity, laziness, and even the happiness of the slaves as a justification for continued subjugation. The experience of slavery set the stage for all the subsequent interaction between black and white in the United States.

Figure 12.8 Some stages in the changing relationship of the white and black groups in the United States: a slave auction in the 1860s; a lynching during the 1930s; institutionalized discrimination in the 1950s; a civil rights march in the 1960s; and members of the black power movement of the early 1970s.

The Northern states began to outlaw slavery in 1780, but it persisted in the South until it was ended by the Civil War and legislation that followed Lincoln's emancipation of slaves in 1863. During the period of Reconstruction, which lasted for just over a decade after Lincoln's declaration, there was a concerted attempt to establish the equality of the newly freed slaves. White political dominance was reasserted, however, by the use of terror tactics and by depriving the blacks of the vote. Segregation became the rule and was gradually encoded into law. Throughout the country, including supposedly liberal metropolitan areas of the North, segregation in hotels, restaurants, and other public facilities was common. In 1954, however, the Supreme Court ruled in the historic *Brown* v. *Board of Education* case that segregated schools were inherently unequal and ordered nationwide school desegregation "with all deliberate speed." Progress toward greater equality was painfully slow until the emergence of a powerful civil rights movement and a series of violent and costly riots in Northern cities during the sixties. As conflict theory would suggest, this heightened tension between the competing groups generated rapid changes. A series of civil rights acts was passed, and blacks did make certain economic gains. According to the 1970 census, the incomes of black families rose by nearly 70 percent in the sixties—although that of white families rose by nearly 100 percent.

Institutionalized discrimination against blacks is still rife in the United States—perhaps more so in the North (where more than half the blacks now live, primarily in urban ghettos) than in the South, which has adjusted relatively rapidly to the changing relationships between black and white. Largely because of institutionalized discrimination in education and employment opportunities, black median income is still only about 60 percent of the median income of whites, and in the recession years of the middle seventies this gap has actually widened.

One of the most significant outcomes of the racial turmoil of the sixties has been the change in both black goals and black self-image. From the early days of slavery onward, many blacks and their white liberal sympathizers had hoped for an integrated society—in effect, one in which blacks would be accepted into the WASP middle-class culture. The rise of a black power movement, with its emphasis on the validity of black culture and black pride, marks an important change in direction. Blacks are now demanding a pluralist society rather than assimilation into the dominant culture. The self-image of blacks has been radically revised as a result, and the black community shows signs of unprecedented self-confidence.

PRIVATE POOL
MEMBERS ONLY

Native Americans

Few groups in the United States have been as cruelly treated or as absurdly stereotyped as the native Americans, the original inhabitants of the country. Today, about two-thirds of the 790,000 native Americans live in a handful of largely impoverished reservations. They comprise over 300 tribal groups, and about fifty of their original languages are still in use.

When the first white settlers arrived on the northeast coast, the native Americans befriended and helped them. But the two groups were soon in open conflict as the settlers, armed with a superior military technology, started their relentless drive westward. On any objective analysis of the facts, the invading whites were morally in the wrong in their dispossession of the Native Americans, but since our history has been written primarily by whites, a grossly distorted picture of the events has been handed down to us. The ethnocentrism of the standard historical accounts is remarkable: the whites are described as "pioneers," not "invaders"; the native Americans' defense of their way of life and economic assets is "treacherous," not "courageous"; the military successes of the whites are "victories," but those of the native Americans are "massacres."

The policy toward the native Americans was frequently one of outright genocide. As early as 1755 the following proclamation was issued in Boston against the Penobscot Indians (Paine, 1897):

> At the desire of the House of Representatives . . . I do hereby require his majesty's subjects of the Province to embrace all opportunities of pursuing, captivating, killing and destroying all and every of the aforesaid Indians. . . . The General Court of this Province have voted that a bounty . . . be granted: For the capture of every male Penobscot Indian above the age of twelve and brought to Boston, fifty pounds. For every scalp of a male Indian above the age aforesaid, brought in as evidence of their being killed as aforesaid, forty pounds. . . . For every scalp of such female Indian or male Indian under the age of twelve years that shall be killed and brought in as evidence of their being killed as aforesaid, twenty pounds.

It is a curious fact of history that settlers who were willing to pay large sums for the scalp of a murdered child under the age of twelve were able to portray successfully the native Americans as savages and themselves as entirely righteous. (The practice of scalping, in fact, originated among the settlers, not the native Americans.) Yet this stereotype, much reinforced during the present century by western movies, has persisted almost unchallenged until very recently.

The westward advance of the whites shattered the cultures of the diverse tribes. Treaty after treaty was broken by the federal government, and entire tribes were hounded from one area to another as the land they had been promised became coveted by settlers. Thousands of Cherokee, for example, died when they were forced to travel on foot from Carolina and Georgia to Oklahoma in mid-winter. After 1871, all native Americans were made wards of the federal government, and not until 1924 were the original inhabitants of the land granted the right of citizenship in it.

The current social and economic position of the native Americans is probably worse than that of any other minority group in the United States. Unemployment averages 45 percent, and the average family income is a little over $1500 a year. The average native American has only five years of schooling, and the average life expectancy of forty-four years is more than twenty-five years below the national average. The infant mortality rate among native Americans is by far the highest of any minority group; among Alaskan Eskimos, one child in four dies before the age of four. Many, if not most, reservation dwellings are substandard: thousands of people are living in unheated log houses, tarpaper shacks, old tents, caves, and even abandoned automobile bodies (Burnette, 1971; P. Rose, 1974).

Inspired by the success of the civil rights and black power movements, native Americans have become militant in their demands for equality. A "red power" movement has arisen, intertribal organizations have been created, and the American Indian Movement (AIM) has campaigned vigorously for the interests of native Americans. Like black Americans, native Americans are now demanding not assimilation but respect for their own culture, and with it the right to self-determination on their reservations.

Hispanic Americans

There are approximately five million Mexican Americans, or Chicanos, in the United States. Many have come as

Figure 12.9 Chicano leader Cesar Chavez organizing a strike by migrant farm laborers. Chicano demands for better pay and better working conditions have led to bitter conflicts with farm owners in southern California and the Southwest.

legal or illegal immigrants; others are descendants of the people who have occupied the Southwest of the United States for over four centuries and who were involuntarily included into our society by conquest. Their position as a Spanish-speaking, Catholic people in an English-speaking, predominantly Protestant country has always been a difficult one, and their problems have been aggravated by a tacit assumption that they are not "really" Americans at all, but rather Mexicans.

The Chicanos have traditionally worked as migrant farm laborers, but the mechanization of agriculture has steadily driven them into urban areas, where over 80 percent now live in *barrios,* or ghettos. The average family income is about $6000 per year, and over a third of the Chicanos live on incomes below the federal poverty line (Womack, 1972). Nearly a third of the Chicano population has not completed high school. Their often limited facility in the English language increases the difficulties that the Chicanos already face as a result of institutionalized discrimination in employment opportunities, housing, and education.

Like other minority groups, the Chicanos are rapidly becoming more militant. Migrant workers have been unionized by the Chicano leader Cesar Chavez, and they have organized nationwide boycotts of fruit picked by underpaid workers. A political party, Raza Unida (United People), has been founded and has had success in local elections. There are strong signs of a growing pride in the Chicano cultural heritage and a reluctance to be assimilated into the mainstream American culture.

Another Spanish-speaking minority are the Puerto Ricans, a people of mixed Spanish, Indian, and Negroid origins. The island of Puerto Rico has been an American possession since the Spanish-American war, and Puerto Ricans have been United States citizens since 1917. A great many Puerto Ricans have migrated to the continental United States in search of better job opportunities, and there are now more than a million Puerto Ricans in the country, three-quarters of them in New York City. Living primarily in urban ghettos, they constitute a fast-growing and impoverished minority group in American society.

Asian Americans

Asian Americans are perhaps the only racial minority in the United States that has approached any real degree of equality with the whites, although they are still often regarded as intruders into American life.

Over 300,000 Chinese settled in the United States between 1850 and 1880, most of them imported to California as laborers in the mining industry and in railroad construction. Their presence aroused violent anti-Chinese feeling, especially among low-status whites who feared job competition from them. Frequent anti-Chinese riots took place. There were a number of lynchings of Chinese in California and even a wholesale massacre of Chinese in Wyoming in 1885. Fears of the "yellow peril" led Congress to pass the discriminatory Chinese Exclusion Act of 1882 that restricted the number of Chinese immigrants, and the entry of Chinese laborers to the United States was totally prohibited between the turn of the century and World War II. The Chinese have remained largely isolated from the mainstream of American life ever since. Living in their own very closed communities, they remain largely inconspicuous to other Americans, who seem to value them primarily for their cuisine.

Figure 12.10 Prejudice against Japanese Americans reached its height during and immediately after World War II. Similar antagonisms were not directed at German or Italian Americans, although the United States was at war with their ancestral countries as well. This photograph was taken in Hollywood, California.

Japanese began to immigrate to the United States somewhat later than the Chinese, and most of them settled in Hawaii and California. During World War II the entire Japanese American population of the West Coast, including tens of thousands of second-generation U.S. citizens, was interned in "security camps" (actually, concentration camps, complete with barbed wire and gun turrets) in the Western deserts and the Rocky Mountains. Many of them suffered economic ruin as a result. The reasoning behind this drastic infringement of civil liberties was that the Japanese Americans might be disloyal to the United States, but the racist implications of the step can be gauged by the fact that no discriminatory action was taken against Italian and German Americans at the time. Today, however, the Japanese have been relatively well assimilated into American society. Although some prejudice against them persists, they have the highest per capita income and educational achievements of any racial minority and are the only one that does not live mainly in neighborhood ghettos.

White Ethnics

One of the most remarkable and unexpected events in American intergroup relations of the last decade has been the sudden resurgence of group consciousness among the "white ethnics," or Americans of Polish, Italian, Greek, Irish, and Slavonic extraction (Greeley, 1974). The appearance of this ethnic consciousness seems to be closely related to the militancy among other minority groups and the new emphasis on pluralism rather than assimilation as a desirable goal in the United States.

When the various ethnic groups from southern and eastern Europe first immigrated to the United States, they tried to overcome the considerable hostility against them by attempting as far as possible to be assimilated into the mainstream culture. Middle and upper-class ethnic group members have been absorbed fairly readily into WASP society, but the working-class ethnics, particularly in large

Figure 12.11 White ethnic groups in the United States are now displaying an unprecedented pride in their cultural heritage, and many seem less concerned with being assimilated into the WASP culture than with asserting their ethnic identity. This pattern is in keeping with the general trend toward an acceptance of pluralism in American society.

cities, have tended to live in close-knit communities and to retain some traditional ethnic loyalties. They have also felt resentful of the dominant WASP culture, whose members have much easier access to social, political, and economic opportunity.

This resentment was greatly increased in the sixties, when it seemed to many white working-class ethnics that the WASP-dominated political authorities were favoring blacks over other disadvantaged groups. Michael Novak (1971), himself of Slavonic ancestry, writes caustically of the WASP liberal who does not feel for the ethnic groups

> that same sympathy that the educated find so easy to conjure up for black culture, Chicano culture, Indian culture, and other cultures of the poor. . . . Why do the educated classes find it so difficult to want to understand the man who drives a beer truck, or the fellow with a helmet working on the site across the street with plumbers and electricians, while their sensitivities race easily to Mississippi or even Bedford-Stuyvesant?

Black power, it seems, has been indirectly responsible for the growth of white ethnic feeling. The blacks were the first minority group in recent years to assert their right to be different, rather than their right to be assimilated, and the white ethnics now also see their ethnicity as a potential source of pride and strength.

The Future of American Race and Ethnic Relations

There is some indication that American intergroup relations are improving, but we still have a long way to go. Opinion polls of white Americans show a steady trend in the direction of greater tolerance and less prejudice. In 1942, only 35 percent of whites would not have objected to a black neighbor, but by 1968 fully 65 percent declared themselves willing to have a black next door (Skolnick, 1969). Harris polls show that the number of whites who feel that blacks are "inferior" dropped from 31 percent in 1963 to 22 percent in 1971, and the number of whites who think blacks are moving "too fast" fell from 63 percent in 1966 to 47 percent in 1972. On the other hand, these polls show that as recently as 1976 only 28 percent of whites favored "full integration" of the races, with a further 48 percent favoring "integration in some areas." The overwhelming majority of blacks, too, believe that they are discriminated against in many important institutional areas, but whites do not share this view. For example, 72 percent of blacks felt there was discrimination in the way they were "treated as human beings," but only 40 percent of whites held this opinion; 72 percent of blacks felt they were not "getting full equality," but only 40 percent of whites agreed; 61 percent of blacks thought there was "discrimination in wages paid," but only 22 percent of whites believed this to be the case. These data suggest that there is considerable scope for increased hostility between the dominant and the minority groups in the United States if the rate of progress toward equality slows down.

The future pattern of race relations in the United States is difficult to predict because there is no consensus on what our goals should be. Many Americans are no longer criticizing our society for its failure to provide a "melting pot" for the assimilation of the various groups. Instead, they consider a "melted," homogeneous nation undesirable and would prefer a pluralist society in which the groups interact on the basis of mutual equality and respect.

Several years ago Milton Gordon (1961) outlined three main options that are open to the United States: Anglo-conformity, melting pot, and cultural pluralism. His analysis is still relevant today.

Anglo-conformity assumes that it is desirable to maintain modified English institutions, language, and culture as the dominant standard in American life. In practice, "assimilation" in the United States has always meant Anglo-conformity.

Melting pot is a rather different concept, involving a totally new blend, culturally and biologically, of all the racial and ethnic groups in the United States. In practice, the melting pot has been of limited significance in the American experience.

Cultural pluralism assumes a series of distinct but coexisting groups, each preserving its own tradition and culture, but each loyal to broader national unity. In practice, there has always been a high degree of cultural pluralism in the United States, but this pluralism has been marked by severe inequalities among the various racial and ethnic groups.

Current indications are that, for the foreseeable future at least, our race and ethnic relations will be conducted primarily within a pluralist framework—although the melting pot may well be our ultimate destiny. Pursuit of cultural pluralism may be a dangerous course, for it presumes some degree of ethnocentrism on the part of the participating groups, and it can provide a workable solution only if it is based on equality, respect, and interdependence. But if we can achieve that, we may finally, after three centuries, resolve our "American dilemma."

Summary

1. Race and ethnic relations are the patterns of interaction among groups whose members share distinctive physical characteristics or cultural traits. People who have similar physical characteristics are socially defined as a race; people who share similar cultural characteristics are socially defined as an ethnic group.

2. A minority group is one that is differentiated from the rest of the population and treated unequally. Minorities (a) suffer social disadvantages, (b) are socially visible, (c) have a consciousness of kind, (d) consist mainly of people born into the group, and (e) generally marry within the group.

3. Six possible patterns of race and ethnic relations are assimilation, pluralism, legal protection of minorities, population transfer, continued subjugation, and extermination. All have been attempted in the United States.

4. Racism refers to a situation in which one group is regarded as inferior to and dominated by another. From the conflict perspective, racism arises as a result of competition among different social groups for scarce and valued resources. Intergroup tensions tend to decline as competition subsides. The domination of one group by another is justified by an ideology of racism, which defines the situation as just and the minority group as unfit for equal status.

5. Prejudice refers to negative attitudes toward members of other groups; discrimination refers to negative actions against them. Prejudice is not necessarily translated into discrimination. Several psychological processes are involved in prejudiced thinking: stereotypes, authoritarian personality patterns, scapegoating, and projection. Discrimination may be both *de jure* (encoded in law) and *de facto* (entrenched in custom). Institutionalized discrimination may pervade many areas of life and is very difficult to eradicate.

6. The United States has never been a "melting pot" for all its peoples; those racially or ethnically unlike the dominant group have been excluded to some extent from equal participation in American society. Important mi-

norities in the modern United States are the blacks, native Americans, Hispanic Americans, Asian Americans, and white ethnics. All have suffered in various ways and in various degrees from prejudice and discrimination.

7. There are signs that American race and ethnic relations are improving, but considerable hostility and resentment still remains. The most likely trend for the foreseeable future is one of cultural pluralism, in which different groups preserve their own traditions and culture.

Important Terms

race
ethnic group
minority group
genocide
ethnocentrism
racism
ideology
self-fulfilling prophecy
false consciousness
prejudice
discrimination
stereotype
authoritarian personality
scapegoating
projection
de jure discrimination
de facto discrimination
institutionalized discrimination

Suggested Readings

ALLPORT, GORDON W. *The Nature of Prejudice.* Reading, Mass.: Addison-Wesley, 1954.

A classic work on the psychology of prejudice. Allport discusses stereotypes, the authoritarian personality, and the irrational character of prejudiced attitudes.

BROWN, DEE. *Bury My Heart at Wounded Knee.* New York: Bantam, 1972.

An account of the early relationships between white settlers and native Americans, told from the point of view of the latter. The book is a useful corrective to the usual treatments of this era of American history.

FANON, FRANZ. *The Wretched of the Earth.* New York: Grove Press, 1963.

A trenchant and often passionate account of racism around the world, particularly in its colonial and neocolonial forms.

KNOWLES, LOUIS L., AND KENNETH PREWITT (EDS.). *Institutional Racism in America.* Englewood Cliffs, N.J.: Prentice-Hall, 1969.

An important collection of essays that show how deeply discrimination is built into American institutions, despite the existence of civil rights and other laws designed to protect minorities.

ROSE, PETER. *They and We: Racial and Ethnic Relations in the United States,* 2nd ed. New York: Random House, 1974.

A short and very readable account of intergroup relations in the United States. Rose includes material on the history and current circumstances of each of the major groups.

SIMPSON, GEORGE E., AND MILTON YINGER. *Racial and Cultural Minorities: An Analysis of Prejudice and Discrimination,* 4th ed. New York: Harper & Row, 1972.

An authoritative general text on race and ethnic relations, providing a full treatment of facts and theories.

80
60
57
62
77

CHAPTER 13 *Sex Roles*

CHAPTER OUTLINE

How Different Are the Sexes?
Biological Evidence
Psychological Evidence
Cross-Cultural Evidence
A Sociological Analysis

Sexism
Sexist Ideology
Attitudes Toward Sexism

Sex Roles in the United States
Sex and Personality
Sex and the Division of Labor

Socialization into Sex Roles
The Family
The Schools
The Mass Media

The Costs and Consequences of Sexism

Sex Roles in the Future

In societies all over the world, the first question parents ask at the birth of child is always the same: is it a boy or a girl? The urgency of the question reveals the great importance that all human societies attach to sex differences. Every society differentiates among its members on the basis of sex, treating men and women in different ways and expecting different patterns of behavior from them. This differentiation does not necessarily imply that one sex should have superior status to the other, but in practice sexual differentiation is always translated into sexual inequality. In fact, the inequality of the sexes is probably the oldest form of structured social inequality; it certainly existed long before social castes or classes first appeared.

In every society known to us, certain rights and opportunities have been denied to women on the basis of a social assumption that the talents and potentials of the sexes are different in many respects. Throughout history the inferior status of women has been seen as a self-evident fact of nature. Both the men and the women in each society tend to share this assumption, which is passed on from generation to generation as a part of culture.

Every social status has one or more roles, or expected patterns of behavior, attached to it. A person who occupies the status of male or female is expected to play certain roles whose content is specified by cultural norms. *Sex roles are the learned patterns of behavior expected of the sexes in any society.* Because the social status of males is superior to that of females, the roles that each sex plays both reflect and reinforce a pattern of male dominance and female subordination.

The division of the human species into the categories of "male" and "female" is based on a biological fact, *sex.* All societies, however, elaborate this biological fact into secondary, nonbiological differences of *gender*—that is, notions of "masculinity" and "femininity." Masculinity and femininity refer not to biological characteristics but to purely social ones, such as differences in hair styles, clothing patterns, occupational roles, or culturally approved personality traits. In every society, however, people assume that their own concepts of masculinity and femininity are as much a part of "human nature" as the biological distinctions between males and females.

It is precisely this notion that is now under such strong attack in the United States and many other modern societies. The structured inequality of the sexes, so long taken for granted, is now being vigorously challenged. What was once regarded as an unalterable fact of life is now seen by millions of people to be nothing more than a cultural product of human society. Although women still occupy a subordinate status in nearly every area of our society, there is a growing consensus that this situation is irrational and unjust.

How Different Are the Sexes?

Just how different are the sexes? Any attempt to change traditional roles must confront the question of whether there are any inborn differences between the sexes and, if so, how important these differences are. Are sex roles completely flexible, as some people suggest, or are there some natural, genetically determined, boundaries beyond which change is impossible?

To answer this question, sociologists have drawn on evidence from three other disciplines. These disciplines are biology, which tells us about the physical differences between men and women and their possible effects on behavior; psychology, which tells us about any personality differences between the sexes and how those differences arise; and anthropology, which tells us about any variations in the sex roles that exist among the many cultures of the world. We will look first at the evidence from each of these disciplines and will then make a sociological analysis of the problem.

Figure 13.1 The women's liberation movement of the sixties and seventies has strongly challenged traditional American sex roles. Although feminist movements existed earlier in the century, they lost most of their impetus after the vote was granted to women. The new women's movement has renewed earlier calls for total equality of the sexes. Largely as a result of the movement's work, discrimination against women is now regarded as a major social problem for the first time.

Biological Evidence

Men and women differ from one another anatomically, genetically, and hormonally.

The *anatomical* differences are those in the physical structure and appearance of the sexes. The most important anatomical differences are those in the reproductive systems of men and women. As a result of these differences, it is women who become pregnant and suckle children, a biological responsibility that places periodic restrictions on their social and economic activity. Men, in contrast, are never subject to restrictions of this kind. There are also other anatomical differences in such characteristics as height, weight, amount of body hair, distribution of body fat, and musculature. These differences are socially important, both because they make it easy for others to recognize the sex of an individual and because they make men more physically powerful than women, at least in short-term feats of exertion. Their greater strength gives men the potential to dominate women by force, a fact that helps to explain why there has never been a society in which women have superior political status to men.

The *genetic* differences between the sexes are based on differences in the makeup of their sex chromosomes. Females have two similar sex chromosomes (XX), while males have two dissimilar chromosomes (XY). Scientists do not yet know whether this difference affects the personalities or abilities of the sexes. The difference does, however, have important biological effects. Except in the area of short-term feats of physical strength, the male's lack of a second X chromosome makes him in many respects the weaker sex. Male infants are more likely than females to be stillborn or malformed. Over thirty hereditary disorders, such as hemophilia and webbing of the toes, are found only in men. Throughout the life cycle, the death rate for men is higher than it is for women. Although in the United States about 106 males are born for every 100 females, the ratio of the sexes is equal by the time a generation has reached the mid-twenties, and among people over sixty-five there are only 85 males for every hundred females. Women are more resistant than men to most diseases and seem to have a greater tolerance for pain and malnutrition (Greenberg, 1957; Yorburg, 1974).

The effects, if any, of *hormonal* differences have not yet been determined. A hormone is a chemical substance that is secreted by glands in the body, and it is known that hormones can influence both physical development and certain forms of behavior. Both sexes have "male" as well as "female" hormones, but the proportion of male hormones is greater in men and the proportion of female hormones is greater in women. Experiments with some animals have shown that artificially increased levels of male hormones can produce a heightened aggressiveness and sex drive, even in females. This evidence cannot be uncritically applied to human beings, however. Nearly all human behavior is learned, not inborn. The increase in the size of the brain during the course of evolution has led to a corresponding decrease in the influence of hormones and other inborn factors on our behavior (Ford and Beach, 1951). The present consensus among natural and social scientists is that hormonal differences probably do have some influence on the behavior of men and women but that this influence is a minor one.

Psychological Evidence

The typical personality patterns of adult men and women are clearly different in many ways. But are these differences the result of inborn or learned factors? In the case of adults, this question cannot be answered, for it is impossible to untangle the effects of biological and social influences on personality. For this reason, psychologists have focused much of their research on very young infants. Babies have had very little exposure to learning situations, and the earlier sex-linked differences in behavior appear, the more likely it is that they are the result of inborn factors.

Many studies of young infants have found sex-linked personality differences early in life. Even in the cradle, for example, male babies are more active than females; female babies smile more readily and are more sensitive to warmth and touch than males. These are only general tendencies, however. Many male babies show traits that are more typical of female babies, and vice versa (Maccoby and Jacklin, 1974). These and other findings seem at first sight to indicate some inborn personality differences between the sexes, but the case is not proved. It remains possible that even these early differences are learned. From the time a child is born, the parents treat it in subtly different ways according to its sex: girl babies are cooed over; boy babies are bounced on the knee. Parents handle infant girls more affectionately and warmly and are more tolerant of restlessness and aggression in boys (Sears, Maccoby, and Levin, 1957). The infants may learn to behave differently even in the first few weeks of life.

Some of the most important research on the sex-linked behavior of children concerns people who have been mistakenly assigned to the wrong sex at birth or who for some other reason have been raised as a member of the opposite sex. If a child is biologically a boy but is raised as a girl, what happens? If sex roles were determined by biological factors, it should be impossible to socialize a child into the "wrong" sex role. But research by John Money and his associates (Green and Money, 1969; Money and Ehrhardt, 1972) indicates that this is not the case. Money's studies of misassigned children show that people can easily be raised as a member of the opposite sex. In fact, beyond the age of about three or four they strongly resist attempts to change their gender and have great difficulty making the adjustment, in exactly the same way as a girl or boy raised in the "right" role would do. Money concludes that the human species is "psychosexually neuter at birth" and that sex roles are independent of biological sex.

The present consensus among psychologists is that there may be some *predispositions* toward minor differences in the behavior of the sexes at birth but that these differences can easily be overriden by cultural learning (Diamond, 1965; Beach, 1965; Maccoby and Jacklin, 1974). It is also worth noting that the differences so far discovered are relatively minor and certainly provide no justification for the elaborate sex-role distinctions found in human societies all over the world.

Cross-Cultural Evidence

If anatomy were destiny and if sex roles were largely determined by inborn differences, we would expect the roles of men and women to be much the same in all cultures. On the other hand, if sex roles vary a great deal from one culture to another, then they must be much more flexible than we have assumed in the past.

Anthropologists have reported a number of societies whose sex roles are very unlike our own. The classic study in this field was done by Margaret Mead (1935) among three New Guinea tribes. In one tribe, the Arapesh, Mead found that both sexes conformed to a personality type that we would consider feminine. Both males and females were gentle, passive, and emotionally warm. Aggression, competitiveness, and possessiveness were strongly discouraged in both sexes. Men and women were believed to have identical sex drives, and both were responsible for child care. In contrast, the neighboring Mundugumor tribe were a cannibalistic, headhunting people who expected both men and women to be violent and aggressive. The Mundugumor women showed little trace of what we sometimes call the "maternal instinct." They dreaded pregnancy, disliked nursing their children, and were especially hostile toward their daughters. Both sexes conformed to a personality type that we would consider masculine. The third tribe, the Tchambuli, differed from the other two in that there were strong differences in their sex roles. But these roles were the reverse of those that we would consider "normal." The women were domineering and energetic, wore no ornaments, and were the major economic providers. The men, on the other hand, were artistic, gossipy, expressive, and nurturant toward children. Mead concluded that gender traits of masculinity and feminity have no necessary connection to biological sex. Since then, anthropologists have studied a number of other societies in which there are minimal differences in sex roles or in which the roles that we consider "normal" tend to be reversed (D'Andrade, 1966; Barry, Bacon, and Child, 1957).

These cases, however, are exceptional, and the overall cross-cultural evidence points to a very strong pattern of male dominance. Despite mythical tales of societies ruled by Amazons or other warrior females, there is no society in which men are not politically dominant, even if they allow women greater authority in the household. The general cross-cultural tendency is for men to have more domineering personalities than women and for women to be more passive and nurturant than men. These personality characteristics do not develop "naturally," however; they are the product of socialization experiences in each society. In every culture, children are systematically socialized into acceptance of the prevailing sex roles (Barry, Bacon, and Child 1957).

In all societies there is some division of labor between men and women. Child rearing and home maintenance are usually considered a woman's task, while hunting and fighting are always reserved for the man. Men are gener-

THE DIVISION OF LABOR BY SEX: A CROSS-CULTURAL COMPARISON

	Number Of Societies In Which Activity Is Performed By:				
Activity	Men Always	Men Usually	Either Sex Equally	Women Usually	Women Always
Pursuing sea mammals	34	1	0	0	0
Hunting	166	13	0	0	0
Trapping small animals	128	13	4	1	2
Herding	38	8	4	0	5
Fishing	98	34	19	3	4
Clearing land for agriculture	73	22	17	5	13
Dairy operations	17	4	3	1	13
Preparing and planting soil	31	23	33	20	37
Erecting and dismantling shelter	14	2	5	6	22
Tending fowl and small animals	21	4	8	1	39
Tending and harvesting crops	10	15	35	39	44
Gathering shellfish	9	4	8	7	35
Making and tending fires	18	6	25	22	62
Bearing burdens	12	6	35	20	57
Preparing drinks and narcotics	20	1	13	8	57
Gathering fruits, berries, nuts	12	3	15	13	63
Gathering fuel	22	1	10	19	89
Preserving meat and fish	8	2	10	14	74
Gathering herbs, roots, seeds	8	1	11	7	74
Cooking	5	1	9	28	158
Carrying water	7	0	5	7	119
Grinding grain	2	4	5	13	114

Source: Adapted from George P. Murdock, "Comparative Data on the Division of Labor by Sex," *Social Forces* 15 (May, 1935), pp. 551–553.

Figure 13.2 There is great cross-cultural variation in the tasks that are considered appropriate for men and women. In many cases, in fact, the division of labor is quite unlike our own. The general tendency, however, is for men to be responsible for tasks involving strenuous effort and for women to be responsible for tasks that can be performed near the home. The data in this table come from a survey of 224 traditional preindustrial societies.

ally given tasks that require vigorous physical activity or travel away from the home, such as hunting or herding. Women, on the other hand, are responsible for tasks that require less concentrated physical effort and can be performed close to home. Beyond these basic patterns, however, there is great cross-cultural variation in the kind of labor that is considered appropriate for men and women (see Figure 13.2).

Interestingly, our own view that women are exceptionally delicate is a rather unusual one and does not fit the general cross-cultural trend. Although there have been many laws in the United States restricting the amount of weight a woman may carry at work, the bearing of heavy burdens is considered a woman's job in most traditional societies. In most of sub-Saharan Africa, agricultural labor is considered unsuitable for a man's talents, and in these regions husbands typically travel on horseback while their wife or wives proceed on foot, bearing burdens on their heads. In many traditional societies, too, a man is fully entitled to beat his wife if she displeases him; in our culture, such behavior would be considered distinctly brutish. Our own concept of the female as a delicate creature arose among the upper classes in twelfth-century Europe and has persisted in various forms ever since. Traces of this medieval chivalry are still to be found, for example, in the male practice of taking off hats, giving up seats, and opening doors for females.

Sex roles in the other modern industrialized societies of the world are much the same as in the United States, except that the ideal male is typically much less aggressive than his American counterpart and the ideal female is typically much more submissive. Only in the socialist countries of Eastern Europe and Asia has any formal attempt been made to equalize the statuses of men and women. Sex roles in these societies, however, are not very different from our own. In the Soviet Union, women are encouraged to take up independent careers, and they have made inroads into many professions previously dominated by men. About three-quarters of Soviet physicians are women, but their entry into the profession has been accompanied by a decline in the status of doctors, who earn less than two-thirds of the salaries of skilled nonprofessionals. Although 42 percent of Soviet scientists are women, only two of the 204 members of the prestigious Soviet Academy of Scientists are female (Safilios-Rothschild, 1974). Again, high political positions are very much a male preserve, and the Soviet woman still has the main responsibility for housework.

The general conclusion from the cross-cultural evidence is that male dominance is the norm, although there are many societies whose sex-role arrangements are very unlike our own. It seems that sex roles, like any other learned behavior, are highly flexible. We have only to look at the recent history of our own culture, in fact, to see that this is the case. It is not so very long ago that a due concern with wigs, perfumes, and silk stockings was a characteristic of every self-respecting upper-class male in Western culture.

A Sociological Analysis

It is clear from our survey of the evidence that anatomy is not destiny. Human beings can be socialized into a very wide range of sex roles with their accompanying gender characteristics. It is equally evident, however, that most societies have adopted a fairly consistent pattern in their sex roles. Why?

A Functionalist View

The answer seems to lie originally in the fact that it was highly *functional* in traditional, preindustrial societies for men and women to play very different roles. A society functions more efficiently if there is a division of tasks and responsibilities and if its members are socialized to fill specific roles. This division of labor need not necessarily be among sex lines, but sexual differences do offer an obvious and convenient means of achieving it.

The human infant is helpless for a longer period after birth than any other animal, and it has to be looked after. It is convenient if the mother, who bears and suckles the child and who may soon become pregnant with another, stays home and takes care of it. Since she is staying at home, domestic duties tend to fall on her as well. Likewise, it is convenient if the male, who is physically more powerful and who is not periodically pregnant or suckling children, takes on such tasks as hunting, defending the family against enemies or predators, and taking the herds to distant pastures.

Because the female is dependent on the male for protection and food and because the male is physically capable of enforcing his will on the female, he inevitably becomes the dominant partner in this arrangement. Because he is the dominant partner, his activities and personality patterns become more highly regarded and rewarded. Over time, these arrangements become institutionalized. They become deeply structured into the society and are passed down from generation to generation. Men accept their role as "natural," and women submit not because they are coerced by the men but because submission has become the custom. The social origins of sex roles are lost to human consciousness, and the roles are regarded instead as being inextricably linked to biological sex.

Are these traditional sex roles still functional in a modern industrial society? Two functionalist theorists, Talcott Parsons and Robert Bales (1953), have argued that they are. Parsons and Bales claim that a modern family needs two adults who will specialize in particular roles. The "instrumental" role, which is usually taken by the father, focuses on relationships between the family and the outside world. The father, for example, is responsible for earning the income that supports the family. The "expressive" role, which is usually taken by the mother, focuses on relationships within the family. The mother is thus responsible for providing the love and support that is needed to hold the family together. The male's instrumental role requires that he be dominant and competent; the female's expressive role requires that she be passive and nurturant. The family unit functions more effectively than it would if the roles were not so sharply defined.

A Conflict View

The theory of Parsons and Bales has been much criticized, mainly on the grounds that it seems to be an example of functionalism defending the status quo. Critics have argued that the traditional sex roles may have been functional in a traditional society, but they make little sense in a diversified modern society, where the daily activities of men and women are far removed from these primitive origins. Apart from the roles directly linked to childbirth, few of the gender characteristics expected of the sexes in modern society are functionally related to the biological differences between men and women (Epstein, 1976). Functional theory says nothing about the strains that the traditional roles place on women who want to play an "instrumental" role in society or on men who would prefer to play an "expressive" role. It also says nothing about the dysfunctions to society of preventing half of the population from participating fully in economic life.

A functionalist analysis can explain how sex-role inequalities arose, but a *conflict* analysis may offer a better explanation of why they persist. Helen Hacker (1951) has argued that women can be regarded as a minority group in society, in much the same way as racial or other minorities that suffer from discrimination. She draws a number of convincing comparisons between the situation of women and the situation of blacks in American society, showing that both groups are at a disadvantage as a result of a status ascribed on the arbitrary grounds of sex or race (see Figure 13.3). The parallel is not an exact one, however, because women, unlike blacks, are found in equal proportion to the dominant group in every social class—for the simple reason that their economic status is linked to that of their

Figure 13.3

THE SOCIAL STATUS OF BLACKS AND WOMEN: A COMPARISON

	Blacks	Women
Social status	Ascribed on grounds of race.	Ascribed on grounds of sex.
Social visibility	High—based on skin color and other physical characteristics.	High—based on anatomy and other physical characteristics.
Supposed attributes	Inferior intelligence, smaller brain, scarcity of geniuses. More free in instinctual gratifications, more emotional, "primitive" and childlike. Imagined sexual prowess is envied.	Inferior intelligence, smaller brain, scarcity of geniuses. Irresponsible, inconsistent, emotionally unstable, lacks strong will. Seen as sexual "temptress."
Common stereotype	"Inferior."	"Weaker."
Justifications of status	"All right in their place." Myth of the contented black—happy in a subordinate role.	"Woman's place is in the home." Myth of the contented woman —happy in a subordinate role.
Attitudes to superior group	Deferential manner. Concealment of real feelings. Outwit "white folks." Careful study of points at which dominant group is susceptible to influence. Fake show of ignorance.	Flattering manner. "Feminine wiles." Outwit "menfolk." Careful study of points at which dominant group is susceptible to influence. Fake appearance of helplessness.
Discrimination	Limitations on education—should fit "place" in society. Confined to traditional jobs—barred from supervisory positions. Their competition feared. No family examples for new aspirations. Deprived of political importance. Social and professional segregation. Unwelcome in facilities used by dominant group—hotels, swimming pools, etc.	Limitations on education—should fit "place" in society. Confined to traditional jobs—barred from supervisory positions. Their competition feared. No family examples for new aspirations. Deprived of political importance. Social and professional segregation. Unwelcome in facilities used by dominant group—clubs, bars, etc.
Similar problems	Roles not clearly defined, but in flux as a result of social change. Conflict between achieved and ascribed status.	Roles not clearly defined, but in flux as a result of social change. Conflict between achieved and ascribed status.

Source: Adapted from Helen Hacker, "Women as a Minority Group," *Social Forces*, 30 (October, 1951), pp. 60–69.

husbands or fathers. The stratification of men and women therefore takes an unusual form. Women are found at every position in the class hierarchy, but at any position they have inferior status to the men who are at a similar position.

Randall Collins (1971) argues that sexual inequalities, like any other structured social inequality, are based on a conflict of interests between the dominant and subordinate group. Sexual inequalities prevent the lower-status group from making the best use of its talents and thereby provide greater opportunities for the upper-status group to do so. Men can enjoy superior status only if women have inferior status, and the existing sex-role patterns allow them to maintain their political, social, and economic privileges. This does not mean, of course, that there is a deliberate, conscious conspiracy by men to maintain the prevailing inequalities. It simply means that the dominant group benefits from the existing arrangements and has little motivation to change them. Since the cultural arrangements of any society always reflect the interests of the dominant group, sex roles continue to reinforce the pattern of male dominance.

Conflict and functionalist theories are not as contradictory on the issue of sex roles as they might seem to be at first sight. Many conflict theorists accept that sex inequalities may have arisen because they were functional, even if they are functional no longer. Many functionalist theorists would also accept that traditional sex roles are becoming dysfunctional in the modern world. More important, both perspectives agree on one point: that existing sex-role patterns are primarily social in origin, not biological.

Sexism

As we saw in our earlier discussion of economic and racial inequalities, the domination of one group by another is always justified by an *ideology*, a set of beliefs that legitimates the existing arrangements and makes them seem natural and morally acceptable. Just as the Indian caste system is legitimated by Hindu religion or as racial discrimination is legitimated by racist beliefs, so is the inequality of the sexes legitimated by an ideology that is generally accepted by the dominant and the subordinate groups alike. This is the ideology of *sexism.*

Figure 13.4

"Sexism! *For heaven's sake, Nancy, I'm not even over* racism *yet.*"

Sexist Ideology

The sexist ideology of Western culture is based on the view that the different roles of the sexes and the superiority of men over women are rooted in the natural order. This belief has been ingrained in our cultural tradition for thousands of years. Even our language reflects the dominance of men. We speak of "man" and "mankind" when we mean human beings and humanity. The English language does not even have a pronoun meaning "he/she," and so we usually use "he" when referring to someone whose sex is not specified. Whenever we talk about people in general, our language predisposes us to talk only of men. (This linguistic usage is actually reasonably easy to avoid; no such sexist language is used by the author in this book.)

Even the image of God in our culture is male. According to the Genesis story, God made man in his own image, with woman as a subsequent and secondary act of creation. Like most ideologies that justify social inequality, the ideology of sexism is to some extent endorsed by religion. There is a very strong antifeminist bias in the Judeo-Christian religious tradition. The ancient Israelites were a strongly patriarchal people, and even today a male orthodox Jew is expected to say this prayer every morning:

> Blessed art thou, oh Lord our God, King of the Universe, that I was not born a gentile. Blessed art thou, oh Lord our God, King of the Universe, that I was not born a slave. Blessed art thou, oh Lord our God, King of the Universe, that I was not born a woman.

This bias was transmitted into Christianity. Jesus himself seems to have been remarkably free from the patriarchal attitudes of his time, but Christianity as we know it today has been strongly influenced by the later teachings of Saint Paul, whose antifeminism was almost fanatical. Paul was quite explicit about the inferior role of women:

> A man . . . is the image of God and reflects God's glory; but woman is the reflection of man's glory. For man did not come from woman; no, woman came from man; and man was not created for the sake of woman, but woman was created for the sake of man (I Corinthians 11:7–9).

And elsewhere in the New Testament we find:

> Wives should regard their husbands as they regard the Lord, since as Christ is head of the church and serves the whole body, so is a husband the head of his wife; and as the Church submits to Christ, so should wives submit to their husbands, in everything (Ephesians 5:22–23).

Even today many Christian churches and denominations reserve their priesthoods or equivalent positions for men.

Sexist beliefs are still expressed in the strong consensus found in the United States and many other countries about the different qualities and abilities of men and women. The sexes are believed to be "naturally" different in many respects, and their roles are believed to reflect those inborn differences. Moreover, the characteristics attributed to men are more highly valued than those attributed to women. Beliefs about "masculinity" and "femininity" are uncritically accepted by millions of people of both sexes and are incorporated into their self-concepts, shaping the way they relate to one another and go about their private lives.

Attitudes Toward Sexism

As Karl Marx pointed out, both the dominant and the subordinate groups in any situation of structured social inequality tend to accept the ideology that legitimates the system. The dominant group does so for the obvious reason that the ideology supports its own interests. It is hardly surprising, then, that slaveowners believed in slavery, that feudal lords believed in the feudal system, that white supremacists believe in their racial superiority, or that wealthy capitalists believe in capitalism. Nor is it surprising that men have always tended to believe in their "natural" superiority over women.

The subordinate group also usually accepts the legitimacy of the system. They, too, see the existing arrangements as "natural" and do not question them. Marx called this kind of attitude *false consciousness,* a subjective understanding of one's situation that does not accord with the objective facts. Only when the subordinate group loses this false consciousness does it challenge the existing system. For the first time, it questions the ideology that justifies the superior status of the dominant group, and demands that changes be made in the system. This is precisely what has been happening in the United States since the early sixties. The women's liberation movement has challenged the inequalities that are built into existing sex roles. By using "consciousness-raising" techniques and other methods, it has tried to make women aware that they are unjustly discriminated against.

Although the women's movement has scored many successes, it is clear that many women remain in a state of false consciousness and continue to accept the system that puts them at a disadvantage. There is considerable evidence that women have tended to internalize the social image or *stereotype* of themselves as inferior and incompetent. Research has shown that as girls grow up they come to value boys more and more and themselves less and less (McKee and Sherriffs, 1956; Mendelsohn and Dobie, 1970). In one study, women were asked to choose from a long list of adjectives the words that they felt applied most clearly to themselves. The women strongly felt that they were uncertain, anxious, silly, dull, nervous, childish, helpless, sorry, timid, clumsy, domestic, and careless, as well as tender, understanding, sympathetic, affectionate, kind, and patient (Bennet and Cohen, 1959). Another study of female college students revealed that they were prejudiced against academics of their own sex. The women were divided into two groups and were given identical sets of booklets containing scholarly articles. In the sets given to one group, however, the author was identified as "John T. MacKay" and in the sets given to the other group as "Joan T. MacKay." When the students were asked to rate the articles for their value, persuasiveness, profundity, writing style, and general competence, they overwhelmingly preferred the articles by "John." This was true even of articles in traditionally "female" fields, such as dietetics (Goldberg, 1968). Another study using the same method found that female students have similar attitudes toward the work of "male" and "female" artists (Pheterson *et al.,* 1971).

In one widely reported experiment, Matina Horner (1968, 1969) gave a simple test to male and female college students. The male students were asked to make up a story on the cue "After first term exams, John finds himself at the top of the medical school class." The female students were given the same cue, but with the name "Anne'" substituted for "John." When the male students made up a story, over 90 percent of them showed strongly positive feelings about John's success and predicted a bright future for him. Some 65 percent of the women, however, were troubled or confused. Anne's academic achievement was clearly associated with loss of femininity, and most of the stories revealed negative feelings toward Anne or predicted unpleasant consequences for her. One response was:

> Anne will deliberately lower her academic standing next term, while she does all she subtly can to help Carl. . . . His grades come up and Anne soon drops out of medical school. They marry and he goes on in school while she raises their family.

Another response was:

> Aggressive, unmarried, wearing Oxford shoes and hair pulled back in a bun, she wears glasses and is terribly bright.

To find out how male students would react to female academic success, Horner also gave them the cue with "Anne" substituted for "John." Their responses were generally negative:

> Anne is paralyzed from the waist down. She sits in a wheelchair and studies for medical school.

and:

> Anne is not a woman. She is really a computer, the best in a new line of machines.

Attitudes of this kind appear to be changing rapidly, however, probably because of the effect of the women's liberation movement. When Marlaine Katz (1972) tried to replicate Horner's study, she found that only a third of her sample, compared with two-thirds of Horner's, showed this fear of success. Black women, too, do not display a fear of success when they are given a similar test, probably because competence, independence, and resourcefulness are not regarded as unfeminine in the black subculture (Watson and Mednick, 1970).

Research on the attitudes of housewives has shown that many of them believe that housework should be their main source of fulfillment, even if they do not find the work very satisfying. One housewife interviewed by Ann Oakley (1974) commented:

> I like housework. I'm quite domesticated really. I've always been brought up to be domesticated—to do the housework and dust and wash up and cook—so it's a natural instinct really.

Asked whether she was satisfied or dissatisfied with her life as a housewife, another woman responded:

> Satisfied, I suppose. I suppose I have to be. What's the point in being the other way when you know you've got to be satisfied?

And another woman, asked about her attitude toward a reversal of sex roles in the home, replied:

> Oh, that's ridiculous—it's up to the woman to look after the kids and do all the housework. It wouldn't be my idea of a man. I think a man should go out to work and a woman should look after the house. I don't agree with men doing housework—I don't think it's a man's job. . . . I certainly wouldn't like to see my husband cleaning a room up. I don't think its mannish for a man to stay at home. I like a man to be a man.

A fairly large number of women, then, do not consider themselves disadvantaged by the existing sex roles, although attitudes are changing rapidly. In a 1970 Gallup poll, some 65 percent of women agreed that "women get as good a break as men in this country." In a 1971 poll, a slight plurality of women (42 to 40 percent, with the rest

COLLEGE AND NONCOLLEGE WOMEN'S BELIEFS ABOUT SEX ROLES

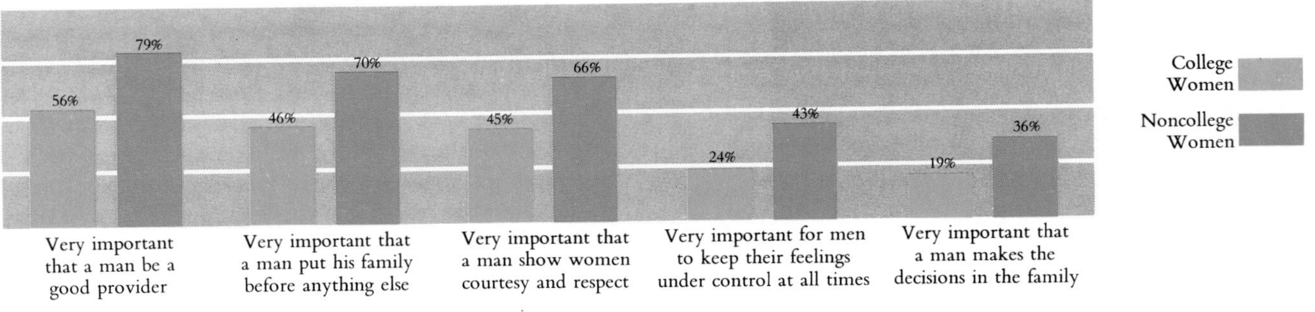

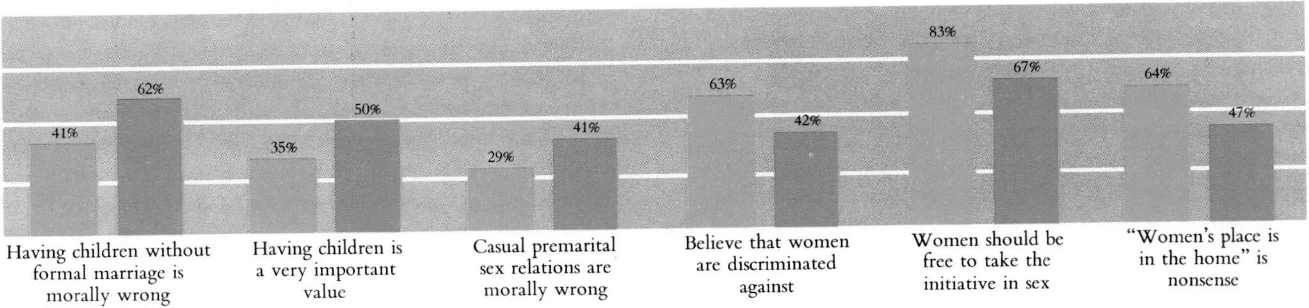

Source: Daniel Yankelovich, *The New Morality: A Profile of American Youth in the '70s* (New York: JDR 3rd Fund, 1974), pp. 34–35.

Figure 13.5 Opinion poll data on the attitudes of women toward traditional sex roles show that a substantial number of them still accept these roles. College women, however, appear to be much more "liberated" than women who have not been to college.

undecided) were actually opposed to "efforts to change women's place in society." By 1972, however, such efforts were finally supported by a small plurality of women (42 to 38 percent), although the women still opposed the women's liberation movement by a large plurality of 49 to 35 percent. Even as recently as 1976, a proposal to guarantee the equal rights of men and women in New York State was defeated at the polls, largely through the opposition of women voters. Attitudes such as these reveal how deeply sexist ideology is engrained in our culture and in the consciousness of the subordinate group.

Sex Roles in the United States

American sex roles are very much more flexible than those found in most other societies. There are still many traditional norms, however, that structure the experience of men and women and provide the basic options within which they live out their lives. An increasing amount of deviance from these norms is permitted, but if the deviance is too great it usually leads to a strong negative reaction. The woman who is too "masculine" and, more particularly, the man who is too "effeminate" in manner, dress, or interests still invite ridicule. The strength of the reaction to deviance from the norms is a good indication of the strength of the norms themselves. Clearly defined sex roles still exist, and they are reflected in the temperament, attitudes, interests, clothing, family responsibilities, and economic activities of men and women. Let's look at these roles more closely.

Sex and Personality

Despite the changes of recent years, there is still a strong consensus in the United States about the personality traits that are most desirable for each of the sexes.

The American women is still widely expected to be conformist, passive, affectionate, sensitive, and dependent. She is not supposed to be too assertive, ambitious, or interested in sports, politics, and economics. She should not take the initiative in sexual relationships but instead should entrap the male by shrewd psychological manipulation. She is expected to be deeply concerned about her physical appearance, and her life should revolve primarily around the home. The self-image of a woman comes not from any achievement in the occupational world but rather from a satisfactory fulfillment of a nurturant role for her children and a supportive role for her husband.

The American man, on the other hand, is still expected to be self-reliant, competent, independent, and in certain circumstances aggressive. He should keep his emotions under fairly strict control and is expected to have firm opinions on public affairs. In his relationships with the opposite sex he is supposed to take the initiative, and he is often more interested in sexual gratification than romantic involvement. He may give some authority in the home to his wife, but on major domestic issues, such as relocating to a different neighborhood, his decision is final. His self-image comes mainly from his achievements in the outside world, and his work is a major focus on his life. He has a moral duty to be the family breadwinner, and his self-image may be severely undermined if his wife takes that role, or even if she earns more than he does.

These portraits, of course, represent only the traditional ideal types. Millions of American men and women reject them, and millions more deviate from them in significant ways. There are also important subcultural variations from these patterns along lines of both race and class. Generally speaking, the lower a person's social class, the more likely

Figure 13.6 There is a strong tendency in the United States, as in many other societies, to value women as "sex objects" rather than as people with individual personalities. Playboy Bunnies have been criticized by the women's movement on the grounds that they encourage these attitudes.

Figure 13.7 Under the existing sex-role arrangements, adventurous activities are almost exclusively reserved for men. American men are inclined to take pride in their physical achievements, competitiveness, and their active rather than passive relationship to the world around them.

he or she is to conform to the traditional stereotypes. The reason is probably that poorer and less educated people have less freedom and effective choice in their lives. Working-class men may have a greater need to maintain an image of toughness, and working-class women are inclined to be more passive and emotional than their middle-class counterparts (Yorburg, 1974; Rainwater *et al.*, 1959). Black Americans are the least male-dominated of the racial and ethnic groups in the United States, partly because slavery shattered the black family and with it the father's role. Today, a disproportionate number of family breadwinners in the black community are female. Black women also tend to be more aggressive than white women, irrespective of social class. Black men, too, are often more emotionally expressive in their relations with one another and with women than are white men (Centers *et al.*, 1971; Scanzioni, 1971). But despite these variations, the traditional patterns still provide the standard against which all others are measured.

Sex and the Division of Labor

Sex is a major determinant of occupational roles in the United States. In general, the jobs that are reserved for women are those that do not compete with but rather aid the work of men: secretaries and salespersons, prostitutes and nurses, social workers and telephone operators. Women represent only 32 percent of writers, artists, and entertainers, 23 percent of college teachers, 20 percent of accountants, 9 percent of physicians, and 1 percent of engineers. On the other hand, they account for 70 percent of teachers (mostly in elementary schools), 83 percent of librarians, 87 percent of cashiers, 96 percent of nurses and child-care workers, and, not very surprisingly, 99 percent of secretaries (*U.S. News and World Report,* 1974). Although women are often thought to be innately suited for these tasks, their supposed talents are very selectively interpreted. Women's deft fingers equip them admirably for sewing, but not for surgery; their intuitive understanding makes them good mothers, but not psychiatrists; their nurturant skills suit them to be nurses, but not doctors.

Although the average American woman spends only 3 percent of her entire life in the reproductive functions of pregnancy and suckling children, it is still widely felt that the woman's place should be the home. Employers are reluctant to promote single women in case they get married and become housewives, and they are reluctant to promote married women in case they become pregnant and stay home to bring up their children. To make matters worse, the self-fulfilling prophecy that a female child

Figure 13.8 Although sex roles are becoming increasingly flexible in the United States, the division of labor is still largely based on sex. Professional and semiskilled positions are dominated by men, while jobs requiring lower skills and paying lower wages are more likely to be filled by women.

will not enter a professional career has its effect. Women are much less motivated than men to spend extra years in education, so they are poorly equipped to compete at the upper levels of the labor market. The unemployment rate for women seeking work is about a third higher than that for men, and it is twice as high for women who are the family breadwinners as a result of the absence of the husband.

In almost every major field of public and professional life, men hold the dominant positions. In 1976 every seat in the U.S. Senate, every seat in the cabinet, every mayorship of a large city, every chairmanship and presidency of a major corporation, every presidency of a major university, and all but two state governorships were held by men. Women represent only 8 percent of our scientists—an advance from 2 percent over the last forty years—and only 3 percent of our lawyers, although over 40 percent of our total work force is female. Even today, women receive only 8.5 percent of medical degrees, 5.6 percent of law degrees, and 3.9 percent of graduate degrees in business (Howe, 1973).

The median income of women is lower than that of men, even for people holding similar qualifications in the same occupations. Some 41.6 percent of men earn more than $10,000 a year, but only 7.9 percent of women do so. The average earnings of women are less than two-thirds those of men, and in the late seventies the gap is actually widening. Discrimination by employers is not the only or even the main reason for this discrepancy. The underlying cause is the institutionalized sexism of our society, which makes it unlikely that women will be trained or motivated for occupational achievement. The cultural emphasis on the male as breadwinner and the female as homemaker has implications throughout our social life.

Socialization into Sex Roles

Like any other roles, sex roles are learned in the course of the socialization process. The basic patterns of behavior expected of the sexes are learned in the family environment very early in life. They are then reinforced in the schools, in peer groups, in the mass media, and in many other specific agencies, ranging from sports teams to workplaces. Let's look at the sex-role socialization that

Figure 13.9 The people in every culture are inclined to take their own sex roles for granted as part of "human nature." It comes as a surprise to many Americans, accustomed to regarding women as physically delicate, to find that most traditional societies expect women to be responsible for carrying heavy weights. It would be almost unthinkable for an American woman to be required to bear a heavy load on her head, but for this Indian woman it is part of a normal day's work. Similarly, it would be distinctly abnormal for an American man to wear a skirt, but in traditional cultures the practice of women wearing pants and men wearing skirts is as common as the reverse arrangement. Traces of this pattern are to be found in the Scottish male custom of wearing kilts, which is still practiced in the military and in rural regions.

takes place through the family, the schools, and the media, bearing in mind that from the childhood years onward the peer group and other agencies reinforce the patterns that have already been established.

The Family

From the time that a child is born, the parents treat it differently on the basis of its sex. Little boys are dressed in blue, little girls in pink. Girls are treated protectively, boys are given more freedom. Girls are valued for their docile and pleasing behavior and are not required to be achieving or competitive. They need not be bright; charm and attractiveness are more important. As Ruth Hartley (1970) notes, this kind of treatment is likely to produce timid, conformist personalities. Boys, on the other hand, are given much more rigorous sex-role training. The little girl may be allowed some tomboyish behavior, but the little boy cannot be allowed to be a sissy. Parents view any "effeminate" behavior or interests with great alarm, and if these tendencies persist they may be seen as a sign of psychological disturbance. The boy is constantly expected to prove his masculinity, particularly by performing well at sports. He is taught to "act like a man," in other words, to suppress his emotions and particularly his tears. Hartley points out that the requirement that the boy avoid anything "sissy" can breed a hostility toward femininity that may later develop into a contempt for the opposite sex.

As a result of this training, children learn their sex roles quickly and effectively. In fact, they are certain of the existence of two sexes and of their own identification with one of them long before they are aware of the biological basis for these distinctions (Katcher, 1955). By the age of three, nearly all children know whether they are male or female, and by the age of four, they have very definite ideas of what masculinity and femininity should involve (Gessell, 1940).

The psychological process by which children learn their sex roles is a complex one, but it contains three main elements. The first is *conditioning* through rewards and punishments, usually in the form of parental approval or disapproval. The child who behaves in the "right" way is

Figure 13.10 Children learn their sex roles early in the family environment. Parents reward sex-appropriate behavior and discourage behavior that is not appropriate. By giving the children sex-related objects, for example, they encourage them to make the "right" sex-role identification. Once the children have identified themselves as members of a particular sex, they use this self-definition as a basis for selecting their later interests and activities.

encouraged, but the boy who plays with dolls or the girl who plays with mud is strongly discouraged. The parents also deliberately arrange conditioning experiences—for example, by giving children sex-related toys. The second element is *imitation.* Young children tend to imitate older children and adults and are inclined to imitate those whom they regard as most like themselves. Young children thus use other people of the same sex as models for their own behavior. The third and perhaps the most important element is *self-definition.* Through social interaction with others, children learn to categorize the people around them into two sexes and to define themselves as belonging to one sex rather than the other. They then use this self-definition to select their future interests and to construct their personalities and social roles (Kohlberg, 1966). (This is why children who have been assigned to the wrong sex at birth have such difficulty in identifying with the correct sex after the age of about three or four. The boy who has been raised as a girl "knows" that he is not a boy and naturally resists attempts to make him into one.)

The Schools

The schools reinforce traditional sex-role stereotypes in many ways. Perhaps the most obvious is the manner in which many school activities—academic courses, hobbies, sports, and so on—tend to be segregated by sex. Girls are channeled into the cooking class, boys into the mechanics class; girls play softball, boys play hardball. The pressures for conformity are, as usual, stronger for the boy. It is possible, though difficult, for a girl to gain entry to the printing workshop, but the boy who wants to take sewing classes faces the likelihood of discouragement from his teachers and ridicule from his peers. The girl who aspires to "masculine" pursuits is at least behaving in an understandable way, for she is seeking a status that is acknowledged to be superior, if inappropriate. But the boy who has "effeminate" interests is behaving almost incomprehensibly, for he is deliberately seeking an inferior status for which he ought to have contempt.

Because the boy is destined to be the family breadwinner, his education is considered more important than that of the girl, and the school tends to be much more concerned with his academic success and the chances of his going on to college. Counsellors are likely to make much greater efforts to persuade boys to undertake further education; there is a lingering belief that a woman's advanced education will be "wasted" if she gets married and stays at home. Unlike boys, girls gain little prestige from being bright, and although they are on average better achievers than boys in school, far fewer of them go on to college and fewer still to graduate school. Lacking the confidence that they will be good at science or at other subjects that might lead to a professional career, they are more likely to concentrate on courses that will prepare them for their housewifely duties.

School textbooks also encourage acceptance of the traditional sex roles. Several recent studies have shown that the literature for children, from preschool onward, presents sex-typed images of how children and adults should behave. In a study of picture books that had been awarded prizes for "excellence" by the American Library Association, Lenore Weitzman and her associates (1972) found that a third of the books had no female characters at all. In the total sample of books, males outnumbered females in a ratio of eleven to one, and in the case of animals with obvious sex identities the ratio was even higher: ninety-five to one. The ratio of titles featuring males and females was eight to three. Throughout the books, boys were presented as active and girls as passive. The boys took part in adventurous and varied activities; the girls were more likely to be helping their mothers in the kitchen or taking care not to soil their clothes at play. In another study of school textbooks, Marjorie U'Ren (1971) found that only 15 percent of the illustrations that featured people included women. As she points out, "We tend to forget the simple fact that the female sex is half the human species, that women are not merely a ladies' auxiliary to the human species." Florence Howe (1971) found that school readers overwhelmingly presented a stereotyped version of the American family—with a father who goes to work, a mother who does not, and two children, an older brother and a younger sister. Again, the girls were usually depicted in eager pursuit of their household chores, while the boys were typically taking part in adventurous activities. This picture of a domesticated, home-loving mother is hardly accurate. Nine out of ten married women work outside the home at some point in their lives, and over a third of mothers with children are currently at work.

The Mass Media

The mass media—films, books, magazines, comics, television, radio, and records—are a powerful agency for socialization. In all forms of mass media, from television soap operas to the lyrics of popular tunes, there is a strong emphasis on traditional sex-role stereotypes.

Perhaps the most insidious of these media presentations is the image of women in magazine and television advertising. Women are typically portrayed either as sex objects, in an attempt to market various products to men, or as domesticated housewives, in order to market home maintenance products to women. Advertisers have found that one of the most effective ways of reaching a male audience is to associate their product, however remotely, with a seductively smiling female. The sexuality of women is thus exploited by having buxom models stroking new automobiles, cradling bottles of whiskey, or sent into raptures by the odor of a pipe tobacco. Advertising

Figure 13.11

"I married Momma because her towels were soft and fluffy and her dishes were bright and clean."

directed at women, on the other hand, shows females delighted beyond measure at the discovery of a new canned soup, or thrilled into ecstasy by the blinding whiteness of their wash. As Lucy Komisar (1971) comments:

> Advertising ... legitimizes the ideal, stereotyped roles of woman as a temptress, wife, mother, and sex object, and portrays women as less intelligent and more dependent than men. It makes women believe that their chief role is to please men and that their fulfillment will be as wives, mothers, and homemakers. It makes women feel unfeminine if they are not pretty enough and guilty if they do not spend most of their time in desperate attempts to imitate gourmet cooks.... It makes women believe that their own lives, talents, and interests ought to be secondary to the needs of their husbands.

The Costs and Consequences of Sexism

Our existing sex roles are maintained at a heavy economic and psychological cost. They deny the full use of the talents of half of our population, and they require an adherence to norms of conduct that are increasingly irrelevant in modern society.

One of the most obvious consequences of sexism is the limitation it places on the options of women. As Sandra and Daryl Bem (1970) suggest:

> Consider the following—when a boy is born, it is difficult to predict what he will be doing twenty-five years later. We cannot say whether he will be an artist or a doctor or a college professor because he will be permitted to develop and fulfill his own identity. But if the newborn child is a girl, we can predict with almost complete certainty how she will be spending her time twenty-five years later. Her individuality does not have to be considered; it is irrelevant.

The economic costs to women are great. It is no accident that women earn less than similarly qualified men or that more than 40 percent of the families living in poverty in the United States today rely on a female breadwinner. But the nation suffers too. Any society that ascribes low status to some of its members on such arbitrary grounds as race, caste, or sex is artificially restricting the economic contribution of part of the population. To be fully efficient, a modern industrial economy must allow social mobility on the grounds of merit, not restrict it on the grounds of an irrational, ascribed status.

Equally important, however, are the psychological costs to women. One of the most important features of our species, and one that distinguishes us from all other animals, is our creative capacity, our ability to act on and shape the environment. In our society this fundamental human experience is largely restricted to men. Women experience it only second hand, through their supportive role of the men who act, and do, and shape the world. The core of women's experience becomes passive rather than active; they tend to be objects, not subjects, in the social environment.

The cult of motherhood cuts women off from many educational, political, cultural, and economic opportunities, leaving them to spend a lifetime impersonating an absurd notion of the feminine ideal—the Playboy beauty and perfect housewife. If they accept these stereotypes, they must surrender all possibility of fully exploring their talents. If they reject them, they risk severe role conflicts and the accusation that they are unfeminine. Because the female self-concept depends so much on physical appearance and a motherhood role, the process of aging is one that many women face with distaste and even shame. Growing old is not such a trial for a man. He may still hope to attract younger women even when he is in his forties and fifties, and his job provides a continuing source of identity that is denied to the mother when her children mature and leave home. Women in our society may find the last two-thirds of their lives something of an ordeal as their youth and their children are slowly lost to them.

These psychological costs to women have received a great deal of attention in recent years, but the strains placed on men have been neglected. In fact, however, the male role is a very stressful and demanding one, and there is no shortage of hard data to bear this out. Men are five times more likely than women to commit suicide. They are three times more likely to suffer from severe mental disorders. They are disproportionately likely to suffer from all stress-related illnesses, such as ulcers, asthma, hypertension, and heart disease. They are fourteen times more likely than women to become alcoholics, and the overwhelming majority of narcotics addicts are male. Men are far more frequently involved in acts of violence: they commit eight times as many murders as women do and

He Is Playing Masculine. She Is Playing Feminine

He is playing masculine because she is playing feminine. She is playing feminine because he is playing masculine.

He is playing the kind of man that she thinks the kind of woman she is playing ought to admire. She is playing the kind of woman that he thinks the kind of man he is playing ought to desire.

If he were not playing masculine, he might well be more feminine than she is—except when she is playing very feminine. If she were not playing feminine, she might well be more masculine than he is—except when he is playing very masculine.

So he plays harder. And she plays . . . softer.

He wants to make sure that she could never be more masculine than he. She wants to make sure that he could never be more feminine than she. He therefore seeks to destroy the femininity in himself. She therefore seeks to destroy the masculinity in herself.

She is supposed to admire him for the masculinity in him that she fears in herself. He is supposed to desire her for the femininity in her that he despises in himself.

He desires her for her femininity which is his femininity, but which he can never lay claim to. She admires him for his masculinity which is her masculinity, but which she can never lay claim to. Since he may only love his own femininity in her, he envies her her femininity. Since she may only love her own masculinity in him, she envies him his masculinity.

The envy poisons their love.

He, coveting her unattainable femininity, decides to punish her. She, coveting his unattainable masculinity, decides to punish him. He denigrates her femininity—which he is supposed to desire and which he really envies—and becomes more aggressively masculine. She feigns disgust at his masculinity—which she is supposed to admire and which she really envies—and becomes more fastidiously feminine. He is becoming less and less what he wants to be. She is becoming less and less what she wants to be. But now he is more manly than ever, and she is more womanly than ever.

Her femininity, growing more dependently supine, becomes contemptible. His masculinity, growing more oppressively domineering, becomes intolerable. At last she loathes what she has helped his masculinity to become. At last he loathes what he has helped her femininity to become.

So far, it has all been symmetrical. But we have left one thing out.

The world belongs to what his masculinity has become.

The reward for what his masculinity has become is power. The reward for what her femininity has become is only the security which his power can bestow upon her. If he were to yield to what her femininity has become, he would be yielding to contemptible incompetence. If she were to acquire what his masculinity has become, she would participate in intolerable coerciveness.

She is stifling under the triviality of her femininity. The world is groaning beneath the terrors of his masculinity.

He is playing masculine. She is playing feminine.

How do we call off the game?

Source: Betty and Theodore Roszak (eds.), *Masculine and Feminine* (New York: Harper & Row, 1970).

are also responsible for 95 percent of violent crimes.

The emotional insensitivity required of men also has its costs. Men find it embarrassing to reveal signs of anxiety or distress, and they cannot show too much affection for other men. Because their masculine image is defined by the rejection of anything that smacks of femininity, they often develop a contempt for women and are unprepared for the emotional closeness that is increasingly expected of a lover or husband. Their frequent assumption that women are in some ways inferior makes truly meaningful relationships with women difficult for them, for such relationships cannot be conducted on a basis of inequality. In their relationships with women, many American men feel obliged to adopt a "cowboy" role as the strong, silent, 100 percent American he-man and are virtually incapable of showing tenderness to the opposite sex. Others adopt a "playboy" role, treating females as commodities and avoiding personal involvement with them; the emphasis is on "playing it cool" and on sexually manipulating women (Balswick and Peek, 1971). The male's nurturant potential as a husband and father is undermined by his continual need to strive, compete, and achieve.

Sex Roles in the Future

American sex roles are changing very rapidly. This change is inevitable, for it is the product of many powerful social forces. As the family loses more of its traditional functions to other institutions, the motherhood role in the family is becoming more unrewarding. As our economy becomes more diversified, the old sex-based division of labor is being steadily undermined. The trend toward sexual permissiveness is freeing women from the ancient double standard of sexual morality. The increasingly higher levels of female educational achievement are encouraging greater freedom of choice for women and greater motivation to exercise that choice. The male role as major economic provider is being steadily eroded, and with it the male's dominant role in the family and in other areas of society. The mood of the times is against artificial restrictions on equality of opportunity, and we are probably more sensitive to charges of discrimination than at any other time in our history. Many of our states have laws guaranteeing equal rights for men and women, and an Equal Rights Amendment to the U.S. Constitution is now awaiting final ratification. Much of the tension that surrounds our sex-role patterns is caused by the lag in the adjustment of our institutions to these other social changes.

There remain some barriers to change. One difficulty will obviously be the necessity for the male population to modify its roles and attitudes to fit the changing circumstances. Like the members of any privileged group, men may be reluctant to surrender their superior status. At present, many men seem to find their role obligations rather confused (Komarovsky, 1973). At a trival level, men wonder whether they should open a door for a woman. Some women still expect it, but others might be insulted. At a more serious level, men are now finding their sexual obligations more difficult to define. The burden for a successful sexual relationship has shifted from women to men within the last few years, and college psychiatrists now report far fewer women concerned about frigidity and far more men concerned about impotence. Thanks largely to the effects of the sixties "counterculture," however, men now find it very much easier to be gentle, tender, and emotional, and the John Wayne image has less and less appeal to them.

Another barrier to change will be the attitudes of women themselves. A great many women are still dedicated to their traditional roles and do not regard themselves as being disadvantaged by the system at all: they "enjoy being feminine" or being "treated like ladies." This kind of attitude is common in disadvantaged groups all over the world and throughout history, and indeed the first task of any new liberation movement is always to alert the consciousness of its own group. Black power had first to convince the black community that "black is beautiful"; gay liberation had first to convince the homosexual community that "gay is good"; and women's liberation has had to concentrate, in a similar way, on raising the consciousness of women.

What will the final shape of our sex roles be? Sexual equality does not necessarily mean sexual similarity or a "unisex" society. It does not necessarily mean that women will gradually adopt the characteristics of men or that the two existing roles will converge on some happy medium. The most probable pattern is one in which many alternative life-styles and roles will be acceptable for both men and women. Our society is individualistic and highly open to change and experimentation, and it is likely that men and women will explore a wide variety of possible roles. True liberation from traditional sex roles would mean that all possible options would be open and equally acceptable for both sexes. A person's individual human qualities, rather than his or her biological sex, would be the primary measure of personal worth and achievement.

Finally, it is worth noting that the changes that have taken place and will take place result, in a sense, from the application of the sociological perspective to sex roles. What was once regarded as an unalterable part of the natural order is now recognized as a social creation, and therefore as something that we can refashion in accordance with social goals.

Summary

1. All societies differentiate among their members on the grounds of sex, creating notions of gender (masculinity and femininity) that are usually believed to be linked to biological sex. Sex roles are the learned patterns of behavior expected of the sexes in any society.

2. The biological differences between the sexes are anatomical, genetic, and hormonal. Apart from reproductive functions, these differences have few inevitable implications for sex roles. Some minor psychological differences between the sexes have been established in young infants, although it remains possible that even these are learned. The general cross-cultural trend is toward male dominance and female subordination, although there are many cultures whose sex roles are unlike our own in certain respects.

3. Sociologists generally accept that sex roles are social, not biological, in origin. Sex-role differences appear to have been functional in traditional societies, and some theorists argue that this is still the case today. Others see the differences as reflecting a conflict of interest between men and women.

4. Sexism, like other ideologies, is a belief system that upholds existing arrangements. It tends to be shared by both men and women, who are both inclined to regard sexual inequalities as being rooted in biology. Many women are in a state of false consciousness in this respect.

5. There are still distinct sex-role differences in the United States. These differences are expressed in the culturally approved personality traits of each sex and in the sex-based division of labor. Men are expected to have more dominant personalities and to play the more important and better-rewarded economic roles.

6. Several agencies of socialization systematically ensure that the sexes learn the appropriate roles. The most important of these agencies are the family, the schools, and the mass media; each reinforces the existing patterns.

7. Sexism has important costs and consequences. Like other systems of inequality that prevent people from fulfilling their potential on the grounds of ascribed status, traditional sex roles prevent part of the population from playing an effective part in the economy. Sex roles also have undesirable psychological effects on both men and women, although the effects on men are not as well recognized.

8. American sex roles are changing rapidly as a result of several social forces. Sex roles in the future are not likely to be "unisex"; they are more likely to offer both men and women a wider range of acceptable options.

Important Terms

sex roles
sex (male/female)
gender (masculine/feminine)
sexism
ideology
stereotype
false consciousness

Suggested Readings

GORNICK, VIVIAN, AND BARBARA K. MORAN (EDS.). *Women in Sexist Society: Studies in Power and Powerlessness.* New York: Basic Books, 1971.

An excellent collection of readings on the role of women in a society that institutionalizes sexual discrimination. The book includes articles on a very wide range of subjects, including sexism in textbooks and advertising.

GREER, GERMAINE. *The Female Eunuch.* New York: McGraw-Hill, 1971.

One of the best known of the many lively and readable of books by spokeswomen of the women's liberation movement. Greer discusses sexism and its implications in a trenchant and perceptive manner.

MACCOBY, ELEANOR E. (ED.). *The Development of Sex Differences.* Palo Alto, Calif.: Stanford University Press, 1966.

A collection of sophisticated scholarly articles. Most are on the psychological aspects of sex roles, but the selection includes valuable material on sex roles in cross-cultural perspective.

PETRAS, JOHN W. *Sex: Male/Gender: Masculine.* Port Washington, N.Y.: Alfred Publishing Co., 1975.

A very useful anthology of articles on men, masculinity, and the male sex role. The selection includes material on male liberation and likely trends in "masculinity."

THEODORE, ATHENA (ED.). *The Professional Woman.* Cambridge, Mass.: Schenkman, 1971.

Of particular interest to female college students, this collection contains fifty-three articles about professional women and the problems they face in their careers.

YORBURG, BETTY. *Sexual Identity: Sex Roles and Social Change.* New York: Wiley, 1974.

A short and readable sociological introduction to sex roles. Yorburg discusses both male and female sex roles and integrates a considerable amount of psychological information into her presentation.

Reading

The Door-Opening Ceremony *Laurel Richardson Walum*

Should a man open a door for a woman? In the past, this ceremony was taken for granted; today, many people are questioning its meanings and are uncertain about their role obligations in the ritual. Writing from an interactionist perspective, Walum analyzes the social meanings of the door-opening ceremony and the confusions that it arouses in contemporary college students.

A young woman and a young man, total strangers to each other, simultaneously reach the closed classroom door. She steps slightly aside, stops, and waits. He positions himself, twists the handle, pulls open the door, and holds it while she enters. Once she is safely across the threshold, he enters behind her. An everyday, commonplace social ceremony has been performed. It is not accidental that their performance in this ceremonial ritual of "door opening" has gone so smoothly, although they have never rehearsed it with each other. Nor is it by chance that such trivial, commonplace ceremonies between the sexes occur day after day.

Of the multitude of such ceremonial occasions between the sexes in middle-class society—occasions wherein the interplay of cultural values and self-image are displayed—the "Door Ceremony" is probably the most common. And nearly as often as we confront the door, we are in a social situation in which a ceremonial ritual concerning it may occur.

Goffman has paid special attention to these ceremonial occasions. In our everyday associations we abide by rules of conduct. The rules of conduct bind actors and recipients in appropriate interaction, encourage their interaction, and serve in a daily pedestrian way to hold together the social order. The ceremony, then, affirms the nature of the social order, the morality of it, as well as the properness of the self who is engaged in the action. As Goffman succinctly states, "The gestures which we sometimes call empty are perhaps, in fact, the fullest things of all." To be "masculine" means to be "active"; to be "feminine" means to be "passive." This distinction pervades the entire ceremony. The male is the active party in the encounter; the female waits passively for the door to open and for the door to close. The passivity is closely linked to another prescribed feminine trait, namely "dependence." By waiting for the service to be performed, the woman communicates that she *needs* someone to help her through her daily round of activities. The male, in turn, communicates his independence by actively meeting the challenge of the door and overcoming it. If Joe College goes through his routine without mishap, he has engaged all these traits culturally associated with masculinity, and of course, he does *feel* masculine. And Betty Coed, by acting out her expectations, has drawn upon the perceptions of femininity recognized by the culture: frailty, weakness, ineptitude, and protectibility. She *feels* womanly.

As more and more women and men "recognize" the meaning that common courtesies have for the perpetuation of the patriarchal ideology, the world which has been taken for granted, the rules of conduct once abided by, are called into question. Ceremonial rituals, once performed with propriety, are perceived by some as insulting, assaulting, and degrading. As a consequence, the once routine, matter-of-fact, door-opening ceremony becomes situationally problematic to increasing numbers of people. What are some of the responses to the altered consciousness? I offer a kind of typology of such stances based on empirical observations and student reports.

The *confused,* . . . confronted for the first time with a ceremonial profanation, are uncertain what to do about it. They have practiced the standard behaviors and do not know how to respond when one of the actors is out of "character." A woman reports the following:

> *I approached a door ahead of a fellow and then with common courtesy, I held it open for him to go through. He bumped right into me even though he could see me. He looked awfully puzzled and it took him forever to get through.*

The "confused" man could indeed see her, but he could not perceive what was "happening" and was unable to make sense out of it. He acted along his normal path—destined for collision. Confusion is even more explicit in another reported episode:

> *I came to a door at the same time as this guy. He reached to open it for me but then I started to open it myself and he just let me do it. It was like neither of us knew what to do.*

The confused, embarrassed, and awkward literally don't know yet how to make sense out of the situation.

The *tester,* unlike the confused, recognizes that the routine rules of conduct in any given encounter are violatable and yet wants to maintain proper demeanor as well as proper deference. For example, a woman reports that "A man opening a door holds it open for me, asking, 'Are you a liberated woman? If not, I'll hold this door open for you.'" Or, take the following overheard conversation:

> *Female: Well, aren't you going to open the door for me?*
> *Male: I didn't know that girls still liked for boys to do that.*
> *Female: I'm not in Woman's Lib.*

Often, the tester has other motives in mind, such as wanting to act properly in order to "score." This excerpt from a male student's journal is illustrative:

> *It's almost like discovering a third sex to deal with liberated women. In the past I would make advances to my date almost as a matter of course. Now, I must "discover" if my date is sexually traditional or not before I decide on the conduct of our date. I can't just open doors and light cigarettes and expect to score. In fact, if I do treat those so-called liberated women like chattels, we never make it.*

This male has found, then, that the whole course of his sexual life can hinge on the perception of appropriate deference.

The *humanitarian,* like the tester, recognizes that the situation is changing but has drawn upon other cultural values to explain and guide behavior, particularly the values of "sensitivity" and of "considerateness" of all people. For example, one male states,

> *A male shouldn't circle the car to open the door for a woman. I believe each sex should treat the other with mutual courtesy. If a woman reaches the car first, there is nothing wrong with her opening it.*

Or, as another male student writes,

> *I had a 15-second encounter with a pro-libber which has left a bad taste in my mouth all day. She had a large stack of papers and I pushed open and held the door for her. I would have done this for a woman or a man. Instead of thank you I got the coldest, bitterest, most glaring stare that went right through me. I resent being seen as a Pig when I was being courteous to her as a* person.

The *defender* recognizes there is change afoot in the land but wants no part of it. For example, one woman relates:

> *I opened a door to enter a building and a boy walked in ahead of me. It was just like he expected me to open the door for him. My first reaction was frowning and thinking some people have a lot of nerve. I believe in manners that did not enter the mind of the boy. I wondered if most boys now take it for granted that girls are woman's liberationists and will want to hold the door open for boys.*

And a male student observes:

> *It happens many times in this University that the female purposefully beats the male to the door and opens it herself. To the male, this is a discourtesy and an example of bad manners. To him it appears that the female is a hard and calloused woman who has never been taught proper manners. They are trying to assert their person over their sex.*

The *rebel* recognizes that the rules of conduct are changing and is anxious to speed the change on its way. Rebels . . . report pleasure in their sacrilege. One woman states:

> *I had a date with this same fellow [previously referred to as a gentleman] and this time I deliberately opened the door. He looked distressed. So I rubbed it in and told him I was capable of opening the door myself. I never wanted to go out with him in the first place. Ha!*

Males appear also in the rebel ranks. Says one,

> *I don't open doors for women. I'm glad not to. I don't want to serve them just because they're women. If they had their heads screwed on right they wouldn't trade doing laundry for me lighting their cigarettes.*

Where do we go from here? Durkheim and Goffman argue that the social order is dependent on the routine daily acting-out of the morality of people who are simultaneously being bound together and providing living testimony of the cultural values. If altered consciousness continues and courtesies are rebuked, then ceremonial profanations will increase in frequency. A potential substantive change, then, might be forthcoming. If patriarchal values, which now govern the ceremonial conduct between the sexes, cannot be routinely enacted, these values cannot persist. Looking to changing values in other realms, and speaking optimistically, we might even be able to foresee ceremonial occasions dominated by a humanitarian perspective. If so, we might all get through our daily rounds with increased efficacy and joy.

Source: Laurel Richardson Walum, "The Changing Door Ceremony: Notes on the Operation of Sex Roles," *Urban Life and Culture* 2 (January, 1974), pp. 506–515.

UNIT 4 *Social Institutions*

Every society must meet certain basic social needs if it is to survive and to offer a satisfying life to its members. In each society, therefore, people create social institutions to meet these needs.

An institution is a fairly stable cluster of norms, values, statuses, and roles, all of them centered around some social need. The family, for example, is an institution built around the needs to regulate sexual activity and to provide care and protection for the young. The educational institution focuses on the need to give young people formal training in the skills that they will require later in life. The economic institution centers on the social need for an orderly way of producing and distributing goods and services. Within these broad social institutions there are, of course, many smaller ones: high schools are institutions within the educational institution, churches are institutions within the wider religious institution.

The study of social institutions is important because institutions are a central part of social structure, and there is an intimate relationship between a society's institutional framework and the private experience of its members. In this unit we will focus on several of the most important institutions in modern society: the family, education, religion, science, the economic order, and the political order. As you will see, American social institutions are currently in a state of considerable flux as they attempt to respond to new demands and constant social change.

CHAPTER 14 *The Family*

CHAPTER OUTLINE

Why Is the Family Universal?
The Biological Basis
The Functions of the Family

Family Patterns
A Cross-Cultural Perspective
The Analysis of Family Patterns

The Transformation of the Family

Marriage and Family in the United States
The American Family
Romantic Love
Courtship and Marriage
Marital Breakdown
Causes of Divorce

The Future of the Family
Experimental Alternatives

The family is the most basic of all social institutions. It existed among our ancestors long before the human species evolved to its present physical form, and it remains the basic social unit in every society. Yet there are many people in the United States today who predict—some with despair and some with enthusiasm—the doom of the family system as we know it. The family, it is contended, is breaking down, the victim of moral decay or irresistible social forces. A mass of evidence is cited to support this view: a soaring divorce rate, an increase in illegitimacy, the changing role of women, the spread of sexual permissiveness, and the many new experimental alternatives to traditional marriage. In this chapter we will begin with a sociological analysis of the institution, and we will then apply the sociological perspective to the plight of the family in America today.

What exactly is a family? Our idea of the family tends to be a very ethnocentric one, for it is often based on that middle-class ideal family so faithfully portrayed in TV commercials. We usually think of a family as consisting of a husband, a wife, and their dependent children. This particular family pattern, however, is far from typical. It is, in fact, a relatively recent development in human history. A more accurate conception of the family must take account of the many different family forms that exist both within the United States and in other cultures, as well as family forms that have existed here and elsewhere in the past.

What, then, are the characteristics of a family? First, it consists of a group of people who are in some way related to one another. Second, its members live together for long periods. Third, the adults in the group assume responsibility for any offspring. And fourth, the members of the family form an economic unit—often for the production of goods and services (as when all members share agricultural tasks) and always for the consumption of goods and services. We may say, then, that *the family is a relatively permanent group of people related by ancestry, marriage, or adoption, who live together and form an economic unit and whose adult members assume responsibility for the young.* If this definition seems a little cumbersome, it is only because it has to include such a great variety of family forms.

Most of us spend most of our lives in two families: the family of *orientation,* into which we are born, and the family of *procreation,* which we later create ourselves. In every society a family is expected to be formed through marriage. *Marriage is a socially approved sexual union of some permanence between two or more people.* This union is usually inaugurated through some socially approved ceremony, which may be very elaborate or quite informal. The offspring from such a union are considered *legitimate,* because society can allocate the social roles of mother and father to specific persons who are then responsible for the care and protection of the young. Children born into a family that has not been formed through marriage may be considered *illegitimate,* because although their mother is known, there may be nobody to assume the social role of father.

The family is a unit within a much wider social network of relatives, or kin. *Kinship refers to a network of people related by common ancestry, adoption, or marriage.* In many traditional societies, kinship is an important or even the most important basis of social organization, but in modern societies the family tends to become isolated from all but the closest kin. Many of us do not even know the names of our second cousins or similarly distant relatives. Even close kin may gather, if at all, only for a few ceremonial occasions such as Thanksgiving or funerals.

A kinship network is a highly complicated affair, as you will know if you have ever tried to construct your own family tree. Your primary relatives—mother, father, brother, sister, spouse, daughter, and son—give a total of seven possible types. Your secondary relatives—the primary relatives of your primary relatives, excluding your own primary relatives—provide 33 additional types, ranging from mothers-in-law to nephews. If you further include tertiary relatives—the primary relatives of your secondary relatives, excluding your own primary and secondary relatives—you have 151 more types, giving a grand total of 191. Since many people can occupy several of these positions at once, the number of primary, secondary, and tertiary relatives can run to many hundreds. A kinship network of this size is more than people can deal with, socially or even conceptually, and so every society finds a way of arbitrarily excluding some categories of relatives from its concept of kin. The most common way of doing this in other societies, odd as it may seem to us, is simply to recognize as kin only those relatives on either the father's or the mother's side of the family and to ignore the others. In the United States we recognize the relatives of both father and mother as kin, but we solve the problem of numbers by generally regarding all tertiary and many secondary relatives as too distant to be considered real kinfolk.

Why Is the Family Universal?

Why does every society institutionalize some family system? There are two main reasons, one lying in the biological nature of our species and the other in the social functions that the family performs in human society.

The Biological Basis

At the most basic level, the institution of the family derives from a set of biological imperatives that are unique to our species. Unlike the females of other species, the human female is sexually accessible throughout virtually the entire year. The fact that sexual relations are not restricted to a brief breeding season encourages the formation of stable, long-lasting bonds between mates. In other species, moreover, the offspring are generally able to fend for themselves quite soon after being born or hatched. The human infant, however, is helpless and in need of constant care and protection for several years after birth. This period of dependency is far longer, in both relative and absolute terms, than that found in any other animal. The fact that women bear and suckle children restricts their activity during this period, making them dependent on the protection and economic support of males. In the past, every society has found it convenient (or at least the men in every society have found it so) to assign responsibility for child rearing to women as well, while the men concentrate on such activities as hunting, heavy agriculture, or fighting. The result has been a universal pattern in which men and women establish permanent bonds which maximize the efficiency of their child-rearing and economic activity through a sex-based division of labor.

The Functions of the Family

The institution of the family arose around basic biological imperatives. But we are not merely biological animals. We are social animals as well. A full understanding of the universality of the family must take into account the *functions* that the institution performs for the maintenance of the entire social order, as well as for the survival of individuals. The family has several basic social functions.

Regulation of Sexual Behavior

No society allows people to mate at random, and no society regards sexual behavior purely as a matter of private choice. The marriage and family system provides a means of regulating sexual behavior by specifying who may mate with whom and under what circumstances they may do so.

Replacement of Members

A society cannot survive unless it has a system for replacing its members from generation to generation. The family provides a stable, institutionalized means through which this replacement can take place, with specific individuals occupying the social roles of mother and father and assuming defined responsibilities.

Socialization

Newborn infants do not become fully human until they are socialized, and the primary context for this socialization is the family. Because the child is theirs, the parents normally take particular care to monitor its behavior and to transmit to it the language, values, norms, and beliefs of the culture. Although many of these socialization functions have been taken over by other institutions in modern society—such as the schools, the churches, or the media—the family remains the earliest and most significant agency of socialization.

Figure 14.1 One of the most crucial functions of the family is socialization. In every society, the family takes the primary responsibility for the early training of the young in cultural knowledge and values.

Care and Protection

The family is able to offer the care, protection, security, and love that are vital to its members. Infants need warmth, food, shelter, and affection. The family provides an intimate atmosphere and an economic unit in which these needs can be provided. The adult family members, too, provide one another with material and emotional support that cannot be readily obtained outside the family context. The productive members take care of those who, through reasons of age or other incapacity, cannot care for themselves.

Social Placement

Legitimate birth into a family gives the individual a stable place in society. We inherit from our family of orientation not only material goods but also our social status. We belong to the same racial or ethnic group and usually to the same religion and social class as our parents belong to. Our family background is the most significant single determinant of our status in society.

All these functions are necessary. As many critics have suggested, however, the family is not the only conceivable means through which they could be fulfilled. Other institutions could perhaps be created to perform these functions, but the family fulfills them so effectively that it takes primary responsibility for them in every human culture.

Figure 14.2 Some form of marriage ceremony is found in every society. These ceremonies differ a great deal from one society to another, yet most of them contain some similarities that we can easily recognize. These pictures show (a) a marriage in Indonesia, (b) a Greek Orthodox marriage ceremony, (c) a Hindu wedding in India, (d) a Buddhist ceremony in Cambodia, and (e) an informal "pop" wedding in the United States.

Family Patterns

Each society views its own patterns of marriage, family, and kinship as self-evidently right and proper, and usually as God-given as well. Much of the current concern about the fate of the American family stems from this kind of ethnocentrism. If we assume that there is only one "right" family form, then naturally any change will be interpreted as heralding the doom of the whole institution. New family patterns that deviate from the "typical" form are frequently regarded as inherently immoral or undesirable rather than as potential alternatives in their own right. It is important to recognize, therefore, that there is an immense range in marriage, family, and kinship patterns; that each of these patterns is, at least in its own context, perfectly viable; and above all that the family, like any other social institution, must inevitably change through time.

A Cross-Cultural Perspective

The family patterns of other cultures challenge many of our assumptions about the nature of marriage, family, and kinship.

Incest Rules

There is one universal norm in all family patterns: people may not mate with anyone they choose. In every society there is an *incest taboo* that prohibits sexual intercourse between certain relatives. As we saw in Chapter 9 (Sexuality and Society), the revulsion felt by people everywhere against incest is of course not in any sense "instinctive"; like any other social norm, it is learned in the socialization process. This fact becomes fully apparent when we realize that different societies extend the incest taboo to quite different sets of relatives.

The incest taboo is almost universally applied to relations between parent and child and between brother and sister, the exceptions being in the royal households of the ancient Eygptian, Hawaiian, and Incan societies and among a few isolated African tribes. Beyond this, the boundaries of the taboo vary considerably from one culture to another. In the United States, all fifty states prohibit marriage between an individual and his or her parent, grandparent, uncle or aunt, brother or sister, and niece or nephew; an additional twenty-nine states regard marriage between first cousins as incestuous, but the remainder do not. There are a number of societies, however, that do not make any distinction between *siblings* (brothers and sisters) and cousins—the Shoshone Indians, for example, lump all brothers and male cousins into one category and all sisters and female cousins into another. Separate terms for "brother" and "cousin" do not even exist; they are regarded as the same kind of relative. In these societies, the incest taboo is naturally extended to first, second, third, and even more distant cousins as well. Other societies consider it incestuous to marry one's mother's sister's or father's brother's children, but may expect or even require that one should

(a)

(b)

(c)

(e)

(d)

marry one's mother's brother's or father's sister's children. Biologically, of course, each type of cousin is equally close; but social norms define one union as revolting and incestuous and the other as desirable or even obligatory. A few societies actually extend the taboo to social as well as sexual behavior. Among the Nama Hottentots, a brother and sister could not speak to one another or even be alone together, and a Crow husband could not speak to or even look at his mother-in-law.

The origin of the incest taboo is not, as is often assumed, the fear of mental or physical degeneration that may result from inbreeding. This degeneration is by no means inevitable; inbreeding can sometimes reinforce desirable as well as undesirable traits. Moreover, any ill effects of inbreeding would take place too slowly to be observable within the life span of a generation or two, and it is unlikely that primitive peoples would have made a causal connection. The incest taboo arose for three main reasons. First, it prevents rivalries and hostilities within the family. If incest were permitted, a father, for example, might be simultaneously the lover and disciplinarian of his daughter, and his daughter might be the rival of his wife. Second, the taboo prevents role confusions within the family. Without it, the offspring of a father-daughter union, for example, might be simultaneously the son and grandson of his own father. The family might be so dislocated that it could barely survive. Third, the incest taboo ensures that offspring marry into other kinship networks, thus creating wider social and economic alliances between families that might otherwise remain isolated.

Other Variations

Some societies are very specific about whom people may or should marry as well as whom they may not. Among some Arab peoples, a man has an absolute right to marry his father's brother's daughter, and he may demand a substantial gift from her family if he chooses not to exercise the right. In several societies, a widow is automatically expected to marry her brother-in-law. Among some Australian aborigines, a man may marry only a woman in a specific group within a particular subsection of the opposite half of his tribe.

We assume that the social role of father should be taken by the biological father, but in many societies this role is allocated instead to the mother's eldest brother. In these cases the biological father may not have responsibility for the children, although he is married to the mother, but he may have to take responsibility for the children of his sisters. An extreme example of this practice existed in the last century among the Nayar of southern India. Before puberty, Nayar sisters were simultaneously married to the same man. He was not allowed to have sexual relations with any of them, and after three days the partners were divorced. The husband received gifts from the girls' family and then had nothing more to do with them. The women could then receive any number of lovers, and their eldest brother assumed responsibility for any offspring (Gough, 1959).

We assume that a man will have only one wife and a woman only one husband at a time, but this ideal is held by a minority of the societies of the world. In a survey of evidence from 238 societies, George Murdock (1949) found that only 43 insisted on restriction to one mate at a time. In 4 of the remaining societies a woman was permitted to have more than one husband, and in all the rest a man was permitted to have more than one wife. In practice, of course, most men do have only one wife, as there are not enough women to go around.

We assume that marriage is founded on romantic love between the partners and that the choice of a mate should be left to them. But the concept of romantic love is entirely unknown in many societies and is considered laughable or tragic in many others. In most traditional societies marriage is considered a practical economic arrangement or a matter of family alliances, not a love match. The marriage is accordingly negotiated by the parents of the partners, often with little or no consideration of their wishes. If love is a feature of these marriages at all, it is expected to be a consequence and not a cause of the union. The economic aspect of traditional marriages is especially apparent in those societies in which an intending groom must pay a bride-price to his prospective father in law. This practice is especially widespread in sub-Saharan Africa, where over 90 percent of the tribes expect a groom to exchange cattle for the bride.

We have a traditional assumption that people should not have premarital or extramarital sexual experience, a value still very strongly held by many people in the United States and other Western countries. In cross-cultural terms, however, this belief is something of an exotic curiosity. From a survey of the evidence from a sample of some 250 societies, Murdock concluded: "It seems unlikely that a general prohibition of sexual relations outside marriage occurs in as many as five percent of the peoples of the earth." Most societies accept premarital sexual experimentation with indifference or little disapproval. As Bronislaw Malinowski (1922) pointed out in his study of the Trobriand Islanders of the western Pacific, this experimentation is functional, for it provides a test of compatibility before the partners enter the full responsibilities of marriage.

Children born of these nonmarital unions do not necessarily present a problem. They are legitimated either through subsequent marriage (not necessarily to the biological father) or through the social role of father being taken by the mother's brother or father. In a few societies, such as the Mentawei of Indonesia, a woman is required to give birth to a child before she can marry, for she is expected to demonstrate her fertility to potential husbands. In most societies, the idea of virgin marriage is ludicrous; historically the concept has been largely restricted to the Middle East and to those cultures whose religions derive from that area—Judaism, Christianity, and Islam. Many societies also make provision for married partners to obtain sexual gratification outside marriage, although the privilege is far more often granted to the husband than to the wife. The Eskimos are one of several peoples that have practiced spouse-sharing under certain circumstances. As a good host, the traditional Eskimo husband would automatically offer his wife to a male guest for the night, and both husband and wife would be deeply offended if the offer were refused. A number of societies have institutionalized provisions for the sexual gratification of widowed people, usually by giving them right of access to close relatives of the deceased spouse. In our own society, by contrast, widowed persons, even if very young, are supposed to cease sexual activity unless they remarry.

We generally assume that married partners should be of much the same age, although we make occasional exceptions for an older man and a younger woman. We also assume that the partners should be adult at the time of marriage. Some societies offer strikingly contrasting patterns. The Kadara of Nigeria marry infants to one another; the Tiwi of Australia may marry babies at birth or even before they are born (annuling the marriage if the child turns out to be the wrong sex); and the Chuckchee of Siberia allow adult women to marry males of only two or three years of age. The women take care of the boys until they are old enough to assume their husbandly duties, believing that parental care is the best way of cementing the subsequent marriage bond.

Many of these practices may appear very peculiar to us. But we must recognize that our own practices would appear no less quaint and bizarre to other peoples and that our existing family system cannot be taken for granted as the only sensible or "right" one.

The Analysis of Family Patterns

How can we impose some conceptual order on the range of family patterns that exist in the world and even within our own society? Sociologists find that it is possible to analyze all family types in terms of six basic dimensions.

Marriage Form

A marriage may be either *monogamous,* involving one man and one woman, or *polygamous,* involving one person of one sex and two or more persons of the opposite sex. If the husband has more than one wife, the marriage form is termed *polygyny;* if the wife has more than one husband, it is termed *polyandry.* Although most societies favor polygyny rather than monogamy, most men in the world have only one wife—partly because the societies that insist on monogamy are generally larger and contain the bulk of the world's population, and partly because there are not enough women to permit widespread polygyny even in societies that favor it. Polyandry occurs only under exceptional conditions. The Toda of India, for example, practice female infanticide, and so have a large surplus of males.

Preferred Partners

Some groups expect or require members to marry outside the group, a pattern termed *exogamy.* The Aranda of Australia, for example, divide their entire society into two sections, and individuals may marry only into the opposite section. Exogamy is useful in building alliances between different groups. Other groups expect or require their

Figure 14.3 Polygamy is still widely practiced in many parts of the world, and in fact is the favored family pattern in most societies. This picture shows a man in the Upper Volta with several of his wives and their children. In such traditional societies, a man's prestige is linked to the number of his wives, and a large family is often an economic asset.

members to marry within the group, a pattern termed *endogamy*. Religious, racial, and ethnic groups generally practice endogamy, either because of prejudice or lack of contact between them and other groups, or as a means of maintaining their group solidarity.

Family Form

All family systems can be roughly categorized into one of two types. In the *extended family*, more than two generations of the same kinship line live together, either in the same dwelling or in adjacent dwellings. The head of the entire family is usually the eldest male, and all adults share some responsibility for child rearing and other tasks. The extended family, found in most traditional societies, can be very large; it may contain several adult offspring of the head of the family, together with all their spouses and children. In the *nuclear family*, which is the dominant pattern in virtually all industrialized societies, the family group consists only of the parents and any dependent children they may have, and it lives apart from other relatives.

Residence Pattern

A newly married couple may be expected to live in an extended family with the father of the husband, the *patrilocal* pattern. Or they may be expected to live with the family of the wife, the *matrilocal* pattern. Increasingly commonly, they may establish a nuclear family in a new place of residence of their own, the *neolocal* pattern. Neolocal residence is the usual practice in modern industrialized societies.

Authority Relationships

Patterns of authority between husband and wife are always affected by the personalities of the spouses, but they generally follow the norms of the surrounding society. In nearly all societies a *patriarchal* pattern prevails, in which the husband has the final say in family matters. There is no true *matriarchal* family system in which women have authority over their husbands, although several societies give the wife greater authority than the husband in some domestic areas. Some matriarchal families are found in many societies, however, although never as the norm. They are matriarchal usually by default, through the death or desertion of the husband. A third and newly emerging pattern is that of the *egalitarian* family. In this pattern, which is becoming increasingly common in the modern world, husband and wife have a more or less equal say in family matters.

Descent and Inheritance

Descent may be traced and property passed on in one of three basic ways. Under the *patrilineal* system, descent and inheritance pass through the male side of the family. The mother's relatives are ignored and are not considered kin, and females do not inherit property rights. Under the *matrilineal* system, the reverse is the case; the father's relatives are not regarded as kin, and property passes only through the female line. Under the *bilateral* system—more familiar to us but practiced by only about 40 percent of the cultures of the world—descent and inheritance are traced through both sides of the family. The relatives of both parents are considered kin and property may pass to both males and females.

The Transformation of the Family

Over the past two centuries or so, there has been a major, worldwide change in family patterns. This transformation has involved the collapse of the ancient extended family system and its general replacement by the new nuclear system. As a result, neolocal residence has rapidly replaced patrilocal or matrilocal residence; the ideal of polygamy has steadily given way to the ideal of monogamy; patriarchal families have become more egalitarian. In all industrialized countries, the small, isolated nuclear family is rapidly becoming or has already become the norm, and in the developing countries the extended family is facing disintegration as industrialization advances. Kinship is everywhere becoming less important as an organizer of social life, and marriage is seen by the partners more in terms of personal goals and less in terms of an economic arrangement or kinship alliance.

The extended family is highly functional in a traditional, preindustrial society. It usually serves as a self-contained productive unit in which tasks can be divided among the members to ensure the optimum economic cooperation in agriculture, hunting, craft work, or other means of subsistence. Large families are highly desirable under these conditions because every able-bodied member is an economic asset. The extended family also provides a stable environment for its members. If one of them is ill, others may take his or her place; if a spouse dies, the other family members are close at hand to give emotional support to the bereaved. Old people usually have an honored and respected role in the extended family and spend their last years in the close company and care of the social group that matters to them the most.

In the urban environment that is characteristic of modern industrial societies, however, the extended family becomes dysfunctional and tends to disintegrate. The nuclear family emerges, a far more functional institution in the changed environment. William Goode (1963), a sociologist who has studied the transformation of the family in several societies, points out that there are a number of reasons why industrialization and the shift to the nuclear family must go hand in hand.

1. Life in an industrial society requires geographic mobility—workers must go to where the jobs and promotions are. They cannot do so if kinship obligations tie them to a particular area and prevent prolonged separation from relatives.

Figure 14.4 The small nuclear family of parents and dependent children has become the dominant form in the modern world. The traditional extended family, in which many relatives live together, is no longer functional in a rapidly changing society.

Figure 14.5

"Well, summer's over. You go on rambling in your boots of Spanish leather. For me, it's political science at Smith."

2. An industrial society offers a wide range of economic opportunities and with it the prospect of social mobility. Socially mobile people have different life experiences, education, interests, and tastes from those whose status is traditional and static. The bonds of common interest between the relatives—who in the extended family would all live much the same lives—are therefore loosened and even shattered.

3. In an urban environment, people turn to agencies and institutions other than the family to meet many of their needs. Formal, nonkin organizations and institutions—corporations, schools, hospitals, governments, and media—assume many of the functions, including some child care and socialization, that were once the prerogative of the family. As the bonds that kept the extended family together as a unit begin to dissolve, people seek a new foundation for married life—close companionship with a single spouse and a deepened appreciation of their children as individuals rather than as productive assets.

4. Industrialism emphasizes personal achievement, not the circumstances of one's birth, as the route to success. This emphasis reverses the traditional pattern and reduces the importance of kinship as the main determinant of social status. Individual goals become more important than kinship obligations, and people expect personal freedom in their choice of mate and place of residence.

5. In a modern society, children cease to be an economic asset and become an economic liability instead. The parents receive no economic gain from the vast expense they incur in feeding and educating their offspring. Almost as soon as the young are able to earn a living, they leave home and prepare to found their own separate families. People find it convenient to restrict the size of their families and their households, preferring to live in isolated, independent units away from other relatives.

Yet although the nuclear family is functional in modern society, it suffers from a number of dysfunctions as well—and this is the key to understanding many of its present difficulties. The modern family has been stripped of many of its former functions, but it has had new burdens imposed on it. In the extended family, the individual could turn for support to an array of relatives. Today the married partners can turn only to each other, and sometimes demand more from one another than either can provide. A death, disablement, or mental disorder in one member of an extended family could be absorbed with relatively little disruption, but the nuclear family may become severely disorganized if it has to handle such problems in one of its members. If a member of an extended family were for some reason unable to perform his or her tasks, other members could take them over. In the nuclear family, on the other hand, the loss of a job or a period of prolonged illness on the part of a breadwinner can throw the entire family into severe crisis. In the extended family, people rarely had expectations of romantic love with their spouses; marriage was a practical, common sense affair. In the nuclear family, far higher expectations exist, and if they are not fulfilled—and often they cannot be—discontent and unhappiness may result. The old had a meaningful role in the extended family, but they may have no role in the nuclear family. In our society a widowed person whose children live elsewhere faces the final years of life alone, perhaps in an institution filled with other unwanted old people. In such a situation feelings of isolation, loneliness, and loss of personal worth are all too common.

Marriage and Family in the United States

"Love and marriage," an old popular song tells us, "go together like a horse and carriage." A compelling assumption in American society is that everyone will fall in love, will marry, will have children, and will have an emotionally satisfying lifetime relationship with the chosen partner. It is probably true that most of us fall in love at some point; it is certainly true that nearly all of us marry and have children; but it is likely that a great many of us—perhaps the majority—find that married life falls below our expectations. To find out what goes wrong and why our existing system is under so much criticism, let's look in more detail at American family patterns and at love, courtship, marriage, and marital breakdown.

The American Family

How does the "typical" American family fit into the family patterns we outlined? First, it is *monogamous:* we may marry only one person at a time. Second, it is *endogamous,* in that most people marry within their own racial, ethnic, religious, and class group. Third, our family system is *nuclear,* although occasionally a grandparent or other relative may be permitted to reside with the family group. Fourth, it is *neolocal,* with newlyweds almost always establishing a home of their own away from their families of orientation. Fifth, it is increasingly *egalitarian;* there are still strong patriarchal tendencies, but wives are becoming much more assertive than they were even a decade ago. Sixth, the American family is *bilateral.* Relatives of both husband and wife are regarded as kin, and property generally passes to both sons and daughters. There is one patrilineal element, however: both wife and children usually take the last name of the husband.

There have always been exceptions to this ideal pattern in the United States. In early colonial times there were many extended families, although the nuclear form has always been the dominant one in America. Polygamy was practiced by the Mormons for many years, and the acceptance of monogamy was a condition of the admission of Utah into the Union in 1896. A number of communes in the nineteenth century advocated and practiced free love, and similar communes exist today, most of them created in the sixties or the early seventies. Before the Civil War,

Arrival of a new batch of lambs for the Mormon fold at Salt Lake City, Utah—the Deacons, Elders, Saints, and Prophets of the "New Dispensation" selecting additions to their family.

Figure 14.6 There have always been exceptions to the general American pattern of the monogamous nuclear family. The Mormons institutionalized polygamy, a practice that scandalized many other Americans. This anti-Mormon propaganda cartoon was published in 1880.

slaves were treated as the property of the master, to be bought, bred, and sold at will. They were denied formal marriage, but mating among them was encouraged because children were economic assets for the slaveowner. There remain many social class differences between families in the United States, as is true elsewhere in the world. For example, lower-class families are more likely to be matriarchal by default and to retain stronger ties with other kin than middle- and upper-class families (Gans, 1962b).

The most marked divergence from the ideal pattern is probably to be found among black Americans. In a controversial report prepared for the federal government on the basis of data collected in the early sixties, Daniel Moynihan (1965) argued that a major factor behind the plight of black Americans was their high rate of family disorganization. Moynihan pointed out that in 23 percent of all black homes the father was absent, that 24 percent of black births were illegitimate, and that 36 percent of black children were living in broken homes. Moynihan argued:

> The fundamental source of weakness in the black community is an unstable family structure caused by the experience of slavery, the absence of husbands, and a high rate of illegitimacy. The modal family type, then, is matriarchy. A matriarchal form of family is detrimental because it is at variance with the standard pattern in American society. It is especially harmful to boys, who will be denied adequate sex role models. Thus, the institution of the black family is assumed to be defective. Black culture produces a weak and disorganized form of family life, which . . . is the obstacle to full realization of equality.

Moynihan recommended that attempts to bring about racial equality in the United States should concentrate on changing the black family structure.

This view has been heavily criticized. Moynihan's data, viewed another way, indicate that the overwhelming majority of blacks do have a stable family environment: 77 percent of the families have a father present, 76 percent of the children are legitimate, and 64 percent of the children are living with both parents—yet we still have to explain the many social disadvantages suffered by this majority. Moynihan's thesis seems to be a classic case of unintentionally blaming the victim for a fault that lies elsewhere, in this case in the institutionalized prejudice and discrimination of American society. One reason that so many black families are fatherless is that the death rate for black males between the ages of 20 and 40 is twice that of whites, primarily because of differences in nutrition and health-care facilities (Eitzen, 1974). The higher rate of illegitimacy does not necessarily mean that blacks are more promiscuous; it results largely from a limited access to contraception information and techniques, an inability to pay for abortions, and a lower willingness than whites to enter forced marriages. The problem with Moynihan's approach is that it locates a social pathology within the black community, not within the society that discriminates against them and thus undermines their family system.

Romantic Love

Romantic love is a culture trait found primarily in the industrialized societies of the world. It is recognized as an occasional phenomenon in most other cultures but is completely unknown in many. Elsewhere in the world, pragmatic considerations rather than flights of fancy are used in determining choice of partner, and romantic love is seen as an unfortunate inconvenience that gets in the way of the ordinary, rational process of mate selection. Traces of this attitude persist in the American upper classes. Daughters at least are expected to marry "well," that is, to a male who is eligible by reason of family background and earning potential. But for most other Americans, romantic love is seen as the essential prerequisite for a successful marriage, and we tend to look askance at anyone who marries for a more practical reason in which love plays no part.

The phenomenon of romantic love occurs when two young people meet and find one another personally and physically attractive. They become absorbed in one another, start to behave in what appears to be a flighty, irrational, and abnormal manner, decide that they are right for one another, and may then proceed to form a nuclear family whose success is expected to be guaranteed by their enduring mutual love (Greenfield, 1965; Reiss, 1971). Behavior of this kind is portrayed and warmly endorsed throughout American popular culture, in books, magazines, comics, records, movies, and TV presentations. If the couple is to live happily ever after, it will be primarily because of their love, which will solve the many problems that life has in store for them.

Romantic love is a noble ideal, and it can certainly provide a basis for a successful marriage. But a marriage can equally well be founded on much more practical considerations—as indeed they have been in most societies throughout most of history. Why is romantic love of such importance in the nuclear family system of the modern world?

The reason seems to be that romantic love is *functional* in maintaining the institution of the nuclear family (Goode, 1959). Romantic love has the following basic functions:

1. Romantic love helps the young partners to sever their bonds with their family of orientation, a step that is essential if a new neolocal nuclear family is to be created. By becoming totally absorbed in one another and transferring commitment from the family of orientation to the new family of procreation, they are able to break the powerful ties to the parents that exist under the extended family system.

2. Romantic love provides the couple with emotional support in the difficulties that they face in establishing a new life on their own. This romantic love would not be so necessary in an extended family, where all of the relatives are able to confront problems cooperatively and lend mutual support to one another. In an extended family, in fact, romantic love might even be dysfunctional, for it could distract the couple from their wider obligations to other kin.

3. Romantic love serves as a bait to lure people into marriage. In the modern world, people have considerable choice over whether they will get married or not—whereas in the extended family system of traditional societies, it is automatically assumed that they will marry. Marriage into a nuclear family may offer many disadvantages—support obligations for the husband, overdependency for the wife—and without feelings of romantic love, many people might have no incentive at all to marry.

To most of us, particularly to those who are in love, romantic love seems to be the most natural thing in the world, but sociological analysis shows that it is a purely cultural product, arising in certain societies for specific reasons. In a different time or in a different society, you might never fall in love, nor would you expect to.

Figure 14.7 Romantic love, captured in this idealistic painting by the artist Pierre Auguste Cot, is a culture trait found primarily in the industrial societies of the world. Although Americans take romantic love for granted, it is unknown in many other societies, where far more practical considerations determine who will marry whom.

Courtship and Marriage

A courtship system is essentially a marriage market, although different systems vary according to how much choice they permit the individual. The United States probably allows more individual freedom of choice than any other society. A parent who attempts to interfere in the choice of a son or daughter is considered meddlesome and is more likely to alienate than persuade the young

Figure 14.8 Young people in the United States have exceptional freedom to pursue courtship in privacy and to make their own choice of marital partners. In many other societies courtship is closely supervised by the parents of the young people, but such intervention would be regarded as meddlesome by most young Americans.

lover. In our predominantly urban and anonymous society, young people—often equipped with automobiles—have an exceptional degree of privacy in their courting.

The practice of dating enables young people to find out about one another, to improve their own interpersonal skills in the market, to engage in sexual experimentation if they so wish, and finally to select a marriage partner. The metaphor of the "market" may seem a little unromantic, but in fact the participants do attempt to "sell" their assets—physical appearance, personal charms, talents and interests, and career prospects.

Who marries whom? In general, the American mate selection process is *homogamous:* individuals marry others much like themselves. Among the characteristics that seem to attract people to one another are the following:

Similar Age

Married partners are usually of roughly the same age. Husbands are on average older than their wives, though rarely by more than five years, and even this difference in age is gradually declining (Parke and Glick, 1967). The 1970 census showed that the median age difference between partners was only two to four years.

Social Class

Most people marry within their own social class. The reasons are obvious: we tend to live in class-segregated neighborhoods, to meet mostly people of the same class, and to share class-specific tastes and interests (Udry, 1971). Interclass marriages are relatively more common, however, among college students.

Proximity

People tend to marry people who live in the same area, even in the same neighborhood. In part this is because they are more likely to meet, in part because their common environment provides them with similar experiences and interests.

Religion

Most marriages are between people sharing the same religious faith: 93 percent of Jews, 91 percent of Catholics, and 78 percent of Protestants marry partners of the same religion (Blood, 1962). Interreligious marriages within Protestant denominations, however, are fairly common. Religious bodies generally oppose interfaith marriages, on the grounds that they may lead to personal conflicts, disagreements over the faith in which children should be raised, and an undermining of belief in a particular doctrine. Many intending spouses change their religion to that of their partner before marriage.

Education

Husbands and wives generally have a similar educational level. Since the number of years of schooling correlates strongly with social class, it is difficult to disentangle the influence of educational level from class status, but some degree of intellectual parity seems to be demanded by marital partners. The college campus is, of course, a marriage market in its own right, and college-educated people are especially likely to marry people of similar educational achievement.

Racial Background

Interracial marriages are extremely rare. Several states had laws prohibiting interracial marriages until the sixties, and even today such marriages attract considerable social disapproval. Interracial marriages between blacks and whites are particularly rare; in the majority of these cases, the husband is black and the wife white.

Ethnic Background

Members of the white ethnic groups are more likely to marry within their own group than outside it, but with the halt in new immigration and the steady assimilation of the ethnic groups into mainstream American society, this tendency is declining markedly.

Physical Characteristics

People tend to marry partners who are physically similar to themselves in height, weight, and even in hair color, state of health, and basal metabolism (Burgess and Wallin, 1973).

Cupid's arrow, then, does not strike at random. We know very little about the personality characteristics that attract partners to one another. If a general psychological pattern exists, no researchers have yet been able to determine it with any certainty. But the social characteristics of marriage partners are much easier to establish, and all research findings point in the same direction: we tend to choose as mates people who have social characteristics similar to our own.

Marital Breakdown

The divorce rate in the United States is believed to be the highest in the world. The precise divorce rate, however, is not easy to establish. One method is to take a representative sample of couples married in a given year and to trace the subsequent fortunes of their marriages over the years that follow; their divorce rate is then assumed to represent a typical national pattern. Another method is to compare the number of divorces in any given year with the number of marriages. This measure can be quite misleading because the population that is eligible for divorce contains everyone who is married, but the population that is eligible for marriage is much smaller, consisting primarily of those between eighteen and thirty years of age. Moreover, the divorce rate and the marriage rate are influenced by a number of external factors. Growing employment opportunities for women or easing of the divorce laws may tend to push up the divorce rate. The marriage rate, on the other hand, is influenced by the proportion of the population between eighteen and thirty at a given time and by current social attitudes toward the desirability of marriage rather than some alternative. The general consensus of researchers, however, is that about three out of every ten American marriages end in divorce. There is also no question that the divorce rate is increasing fairly rapidly. And these figures do not tell the whole story. Many people have separated from their partners without bothering to go through the process of divorce, and an unknown number of marriages are merely "empty shells," in which the unloving partners stay together out of mere habit, because of religious scruples, or "for the sake of the children."

Divorce constitutes official social recognition that a marriage has failed, and it can be a traumatic experience for all concerned. Until recently, most states granted a divorce only if the "guilt" of one partner could be proved. Ugly and acrimonious court cases resulted, with one spouse accusing the other of desertion, cruelty, adultery, or failure to provide economic support, but the actual grounds on which the divorce was granted often had little relationship to the real reasons for the marital breakdown. Many states now offer a "no fault" divorce on grounds of simple incompatibility, but there is still room for fierce resentment over the determination of alimony payments

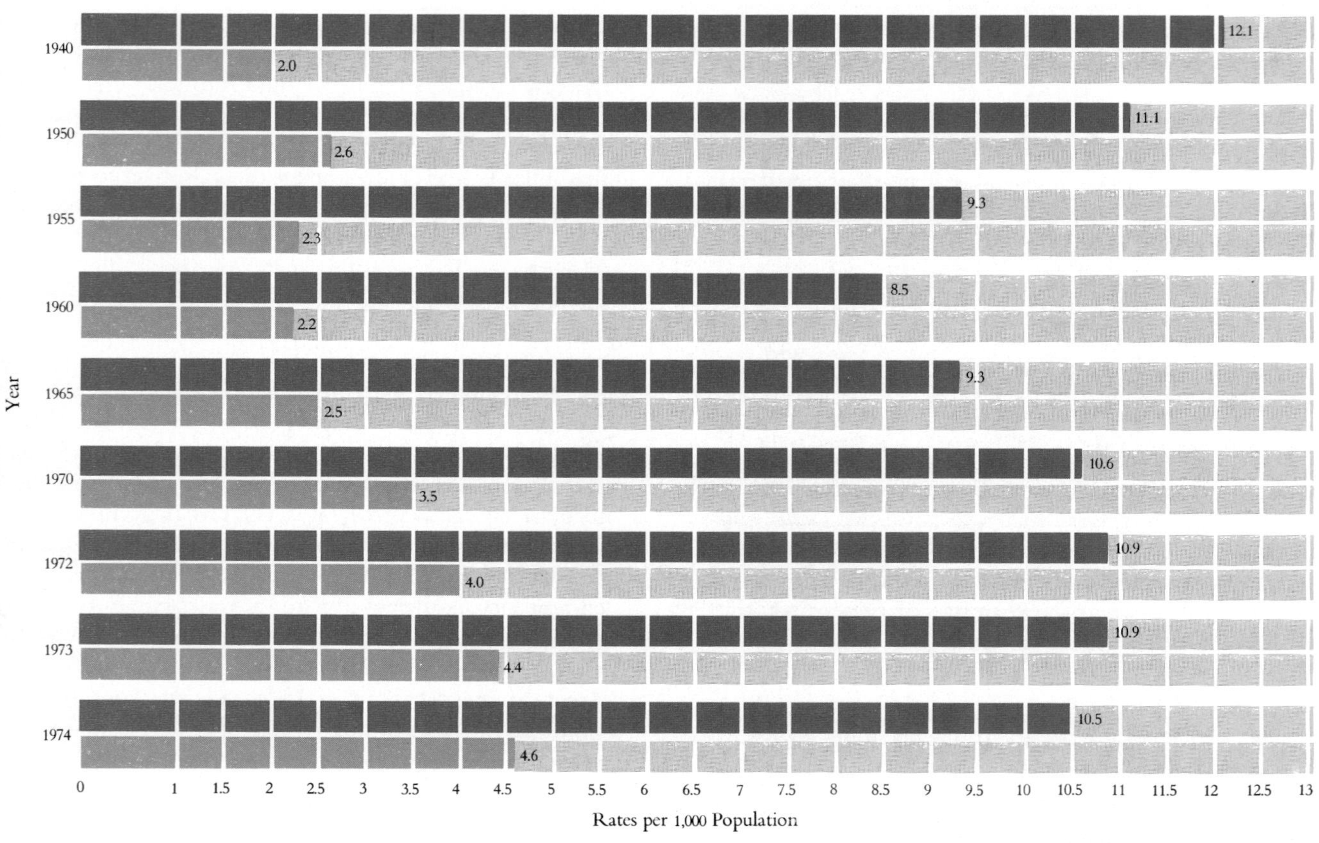

Figure 14.9 In 1940 Americans married at a rate of 12.1 per 1000 people. The rate of divorce per 1000 population was a mere 2.0. As this graph indicates, the rate of divorce has steadily increased over the last three decades, and the rate of marriage has fluctuated and decreased only slightly. By 1974 the rate of divorce was nearly one-half the marriage rate.

and the award of custody of offspring. Children are present in two-thirds of the families that break up through divorce.

The children inevitably suffer through the divorce of their parents, although there is growing evidence that it is even more emotionally disturbing for them to remain in a home where the marriage is deeply unhappy (for example, Landis, 1962). The wife may face severe economic problems, especially if she has to raise young children. Nearly half the American families in which the husband is absent live below the poverty line; mothers who have to stay at home to take care of their children may have to become permanent welfare recipients. Former husbands frequently default on their alimony and child-support obligations. A recent survey found that nearly 47 percent of all families that should have been receiving court-ordered payments were receiving nothing at all (King, 1974). American social life is tailored to the needs of couples, and divorced partners may experience great loneliness and isolation. Divorce ruptures one's personal universe; it is no coincidence that men are much more likely to be fired from their jobs after divorce, nor that the death rate for divorced people is significantly higher than that for married people, at all age levels (Goode, 1956; Plateris, 1970).

Who gets divorced? The social characteristics of divorce-prone partners have been well established. Divorces are especially common among urban couples, among those who marry very young, among those who marry after only short acquaintance, and among those whose relatives and friends disapprove of the marriage (Goode, 1956). In general, the people who are most likely to get divorced are those who are least likely to marry. Differences in religion, in social class, and in educational level all make a marriage less likely to succeed (Udry, 1971). Partners who have been married before are more likely to become involved in subsequent divorce. Most divorces take place within the first few years of marriage; the longer a marriage lasts, the less likely it is to end in divorce.

Figure 14.10 Americans are socialized to regard romantic love as the basis of marriage. When a marriage settles down into the ordinary routines of housework and job, romantic love may fade, and many Americans interpret this as a sign that their marriage is failing.

Causes of Divorce

There are many causes for the breakup of marriages, but the following seem to be the main ones.

Stress on the Nuclear Family

As we have seen, the nuclear family has many dysfunctions in modern society, although it is more functional in this context than the extended family. The nuclear family is highly vulnerable if the breadwinner is for any reason unwilling or unable to meet economic obligations. This is especially true in the United States; in most other advanced industrial societies the state offers much more support to the family in the form of family allowances, preferential housing, child-care programs, free childhood medical and dental care, and free college education. The spouses in a nuclear family have a very strong mutual dependency, especially after the children have left home, and may make extremely heavy demands on one another for emotional support. The failure of one partner to meet the expectations of the other jeopardizes the marriage in a way that would hardly be possible under the extended family system.

The Fading of Romantic Love

Americans are thoroughly socialized into the expectation that romantic love will make their marriage happy ever after. But the heady joys of romantic love are usually short-lived, and the excitement of the earlier relationship is diminished or lost in the daily routines of job and housework, diapers and dishwashing, mortgages and bills. This does not mean that the partners no longer love one another, but their love is likely to be of a different kind. It can be mature, companionable, and deeply fulfilling—but Americans are not socialized to recognize or appreciate it. Believing that romantic love is the only possible basis for a successful marriage, many people assume that the fading of their romance is a symptom of marital failure. They lose faith in their marriages and may start looking for romance elsewhere.

The Changing Role of Women

In the past, the role of the wife in an American marriage was assumed to be that of housekeeper, child rearer, and nurturant supporter of a husband who was active in the world beyond the home. More and more American women are rejecting this role, and in doing so are challenging the established structure of the nuclear family. Women are no longer confined to the home for much of their lives through pregnancy and the care of infants. The average family now has only 2.3 children, and the average woman now has her last child at the age of only twenty-six. Our family norms make little provision for the woman who wants an independent career, and even less for the family in which the wife earns more than the husband and becomes the primary breadwinner. The growing economic independence of women makes it much easier for them to divorce their mates, and it undermines the role relationship on which the nuclear family has been based.

Sexual Permissiveness

The development and widespread availability of contraceptives has separated two quite different functions of sexual relations—procreation and recreation. It made sense for sexual intercourse to be restricted to marital partners in the days when intercourse was likely to lead to pregnancy, for our society makes little provision for the proper care of illegitimate children. But if the prospect of pregnancy is removed, many of the inhibitions against the use of sex for recreation are removed also, and people feel much freer to engage in premarital and extramarital sexual intercourse. The nuclear family is founded on an assumption of monogamous fidelity, but the growing permissiveness of our society encourages many people to look outside their marriages for sexual satisfaction or, if they are unmarried, to enjoy sexual experience before marriage. The great majority of American men have engaged in premarital and extramarital intercourse, as have about half of American women. This experience gives the partners a standard by which to measure the performance of their spouses—an opportunity that the partners in a traditional virgin marriage did not have—and the spouses may be found wanting. Our nuclear family system is based on the assumption that the partners will have an exclusive and mutually gratifying sexual relationship, but this central assumption is being undermined by changing sexual norms.

The Future of the Family

The American family is changing. These are not changes that can be halted by laws or sermons, for they are the inevitable products of much more encompassing changes in the social order. But what will become of the family? Some writers consider the nuclear family an anachronism that will eventually disappear. Barrington Moore (1958), for example, writes that in the modern world there are new conditions that "make it possible for the advanced industrial societies of the world to do away with the family and substitute other social arrangements that impose fewer unnecessary and painful restrictions on humanity."

Experimental Alternatives

Many alternatives to the established nuclear pattern already exist in the United States. The following alternatives seem to be most common.

Serial Monogamy

A growing number of people marry more than once. In fact, the great majority of divorced partners marry someone else within a few years of the divorce. Until fairly

Modern Marriage: A Critique

Parents, teachers, and concerned adults all counsel against premature marriage. But they rarely speak the truth about marriage as it really is in modern middle-class America. The truth as I see it is that contemporary marriage is a wretched institution. It spells the end of voluntary affection, of love freely given and joyously received. Beautiful romances are transmuted into dull marriages, and eventually the relationship becomes constricting, corrosive, grinding, and destructive. The beautiful love affair becomes a bitter contract.

The basic reason for this sad state of affairs is that marriage was not designed to bear the burdens now being asked of it by the urban American middle class. It is an institution that evolved over centuries to meet some very specific functional needs of a nonindustrial society. Romantic love was viewed as tragic, or merely irrelevant. Today it is the titillating prelude to domestic tragedy, or, perhaps more frequently, to domestic grotesqueries that are only pathetic.

Marriage was not designed as a mechanism for providing friendship, erotic experience, romantic love, personal fulfillment, continuous lay psychotherapy, or recreation. The Western European family was not designed to carry a lifelong load of highly emotional romantic freight. Given its present structure, it simply has to fail when asked to do so. The very idea of an irrevocable contract obligating the parties concerned to a lifetime of romantic effort is utterly absurd. . . .

The purposes of marriage have changed radically, yet we cling desperately to the outmoded structures of the past. . . . Our schools, both high schools and colleges, teach sentimental rubbish in their marriage and family courses. The texts make much of a posture of hard-nosed objectivity that is neither objective nor hard-nosed. The basic structure of Western marriage is never questioned, alternatives are not proposed or discussed. Instead, the prospective young bride and bridegroom are offered housekeeping advice and told to work hard at making their marriage succeed. . . . If taught honestly, these courses would alert the teenager and young adult to the realities of matrimonial life in the United States and try to advise them on how to survive marriage if they insist on that hazardous venture. . . .

The cool adolescent finishing high school or starting college has a skeptical view of virtually every institutional sector of his society. He knows that government is corrupt, the military dehumanizing, the corporations rapacious, the churches organized hypocrisy, and the schools dishonest. But the one area that seems to be exempt from his cynicism is romantic love and marriage. When I talk to teenagers about marriage, that cool skepticism turns to sentimental dreams right out of *Ladies' Home Journal* or the hard-hitting pages of *Reader's Digest.* They all mouth the same vapid platitudes about finding happiness through sharing and personal fulfillment through giving (each is to give 51 percent). They have all heard about divorce, and most of them have been touched by it in some way or another. Yet they insist that their marriage will be different.

So, clutching their illusions, young girls with ecstatic screams of joy lead their awkward brooding boys through the portals of the church into the land of the Mustang, Apartment 24, Macy's, Sears, and the ubiquitous drive-in. They have become members in good standing of the adult world.

The end of most of these sentimental marriages is quite predictable. They progress, in most cases, to varying stages of marital ennui, depending on the ability of the couple to adjust to reality; most common are (1) a lackluster standoff, (2) a bitter business carried on for the children, church, or neighbors, or (3) separation and divorce, followed by another search to find the right person. . . .

Now, the absurdity of much of this lies in the fact that we pretend that marriages of short duration must be contracted for life. Why not permit a flexible contract perhaps for one to two or more years, with periodic options to renew? If a couple grew disenchanted with their life together, they would not feel trapped for life. They would not have to anticipate and then go through the destructive agonies of divorce. They would not have to carry about the stigma of marital failure, like the mark of Cain on their foreheads. Instead of a declaration of war, they could simply let their contract lapse, and while still friendly, be free to continue their romantic quest. Sexualized romanticism is now so fundamental to American life—and is bound to become even more so—that marriage will simply have to accommodate itself to it in one way or another. For a great proportion of us it already has. . . .

The braver and more critical among our teenagers and youthful adults will still ask, But if the institution is so bad, why get married at all? This is a tough one to deal with. . . . How do you marry and yet live like gentle lovers, or at least like friendly roommates? Quite frankly, I do not know the answer to that question.

Source: Mervyn Cadwallader, "Marriage as a Wretched Institution," *The Atlantic Monthly* (November, 1966).

recently, divorce was quite infrequent, for the law made it difficult and social disapproval discouraged it. Today divorce carries little stigma in the United States, however, and many people now embark on a career of "serial" marriages. One sociologist, Jessie Bernard, suggests that under this system there are probably more people practicing plural marriages in our society than in those that actually favor polygamy. Serial monogamy allows the partners to maintain the ideal of romantic love in marriage by simply divorcing when romantic loves fades and remarrying.

Communes

There have been many experiments in the United States aimed at establishing communal groups whose members may share both sexual relations and the task of raising children. There is great variation in the norms that operate within these communes. A few insist on free love, but in most of them the adults tend to pair off with one another, at least for periods of a few weeks or months. The limited evidence available suggests that "group marriages" are highly unstable (Ellis, 1970), and despite the range of family systems found in other cultures, anthropologists have never found a society that has institutionalized group marriage. Communes with rather more restrictive sexual patterns have persisted for years and even decades, however. Although the appeal of communes seems to be rather limited, there is little doubt that they do represent an alternative family system.

Exchange of Partners

"Swinging," or the mutually-agreed-to exchange of partners for the purposes of periodic extramarital sex, has become a popular pastime in some restricted sections of American society. The practice seems to appeal to people who wish to maintain their marriage but are dissatisfied with the sexual exclusiveness of their relationship. Little research has been conducted on the phenomenon of "swinging," but it appears that the participants are primarily middle class, middle-aged, and rather conservative in other matters, ranging from politics to tastes in furnishing. An elaborate communications network exists for "swingers," based on advertisements in a number of specialized magazines. It has been estimated that hundreds of thousands of Americans participate in the activity (Bartell, 1974; Denfield and Gordon, 1974).

Trial Marriage

A rapidly growing number of Americans engage in an informal "trial marriage" by cohabiting together for some time before deciding whether to marry or not. Many, in fact, participate in serial trial marriages. Cohabitation of this kind differs from simple promiscuity, in that the partners have considerable affection for and commitment to one another, and their sexual relationship is usually an exclusive one. In Poland the law makes provision for a recognized trial marriage, which is followed by a standard marriage if the trial is successful. It has been suggested that other countries might experiment with a similar pattern, with an "experimental" marriage followed by a "parental" marriage only if the former has been mutually satisfying to the partners for perhaps two or three years.

Remaining Single

A great many Americans no longer consider marriage a prerequisite for legitimate sex, and a growing number do not wish to have children. The birth rate in the United States has been dropping steadily throughout this century and is now one of the lowest in the world. If people are willing to obtain sexual gratification outside of marriage and if they do not want children, then marriage offers few advantages over simple cohabitation. The stigma attached to illegitimacy is also very much weaker than it used to be, for both the mother and the child, and growing numbers of women are willing to raise illegitimate children rather than enter into a loveless marriage with the father. The number of single-parent families is likely to continue to increase, both because of the increasing divorce rate and the small but growing number of mothers who choose to raise adopted or illegitimate children.

The emergence of patterns such as these does not mean, however, that the nuclear family is about to disappear. Some 94 percent of all Americans get married at some point in their lives, and even the divorced are still deeply committed to marriage. Their marriage rate at all ages is higher than that for single or widowed persons (Plateris, 1970). What is more likely is that the United States, a pluralist society with a strong emphasis on individualism, will increasingly tolerate a range of alternative marriage

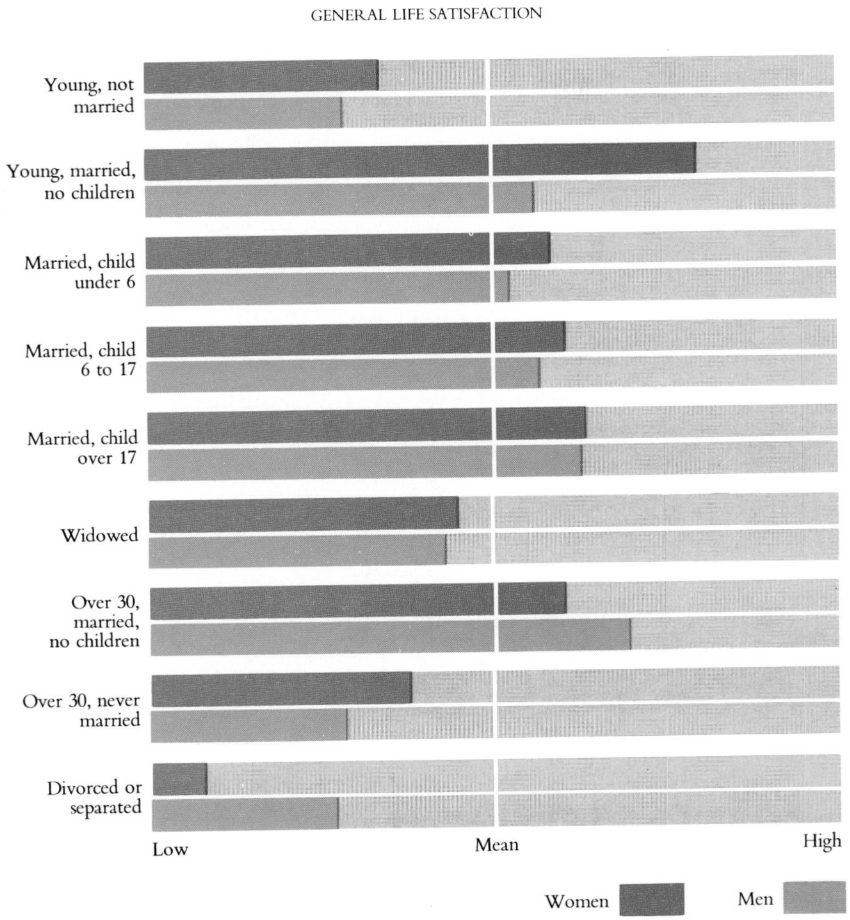

Source: Angus Campbell, "The American Way of Mating," *Psychology Today,* 8 (May, 1975), p. 40.

Figure 14.11 Married people are more happy and satisfied with their lives than all categories of the unmarried: singles, widowed, and divorced. The highest levels of satisfaction were reported by young married women without children, the lowest levels by divorced or separated women. Despite the many criticisms that have been made of modern nuclear marriage, those who are married seem significantly more satisfied with life than those who are not.

and family styles. No other society has ever endorsed more than one family form at a time, but no other society has been both as heterogeneous and as rapidly changing as the contemporary United States. The family in the sense that we defined it earlier—a relatively permanent group of related people, living together, forming an economic unit, and sharing responsibility for offspring—is here to stay as a permanent feature of human society. The most popular form of the family for the foreseeable future is the nuclear family. Whatever its disadvantages, it seems to be the most functional and satisfying family form in the modern world. The nuclear family will probably undergo internal structural changes, but it seems destined to remain the preferred and dominant system in all industrial societies.

Summary

1. The family is the most basic of all social institutions. It consists of a relatively permanent group whose members are related by ancestry, marriage, or adoption, who live together and form an economic unit, and whose adult members assume responsibility for the young. The family is expected to be formed through a marriage which legiti-

mates any offspring. The family is part of a wider network of relatives, or kin.

2. The family is universal partly because of biological features unique to our species and partly because it is highly functional. The main functions of the family are the regulation of sexual behavior, the replacement of members, socialization, care and protection, and social placement.

3. Family patterns vary widely from one society to another; even the incest taboo takes different forms in different cultures.

4. Family patterns can be analyzed in terms of their variation along six basic dimensions: marriage form, preferred partners, family form, residence pattern, authority relationships, and descent and inheritance.

5. Industrialism and urbanization have been accompanied by a worldwide transformation of the family; the extended family is dysfunctional in the modern environment and is giving way to the nuclear form. The nuclear family, however, experiences distinctive problems resulting from the extensive reliance that the husband and wife have on one another.

6. The American family is monogamous, endogamous, nuclear, neolocal, increasingly egalitarian, and bilateral, although there are some class and racial variations on this pattern. Americans place high emphasis on romantic love, which is functional for a nuclear family system.

7. American marriage tends to be homogamous: in other words people generally marry others with similar social characteristics.

8. The American divorce rate is very high; the partners most likely to get divorced are those whose social characteristics differ markedly. The main causes of divorce are stress on the nuclear family, the fading of romantic love after marriage, the changing role of women, and certain effects of sexual permissiveness.

9. There are a number of current experimental alternatives to traditional marriage, such as serial monogamy, communes, exchange of partners, trial marriage, and remaining single. The great majority of Americans continue to marry, however, and although a range of alternative marriage and family styles are likely to be tolerated, the nuclear family seems to be here to stay.

Important Terms

family
marriage
legitimate
illegitimate
kinship
incest taboo
sibling
monogamy
polygamy
polygyny
polyandry
exogamy
endogamy
extended family
nuclear family
patrilocal
matrilocal
neolocal
patriarchal
matriarchal
egalitarian
patrilineal
matrilineal
bilateral
homogamy

Suggested Readings

BERNARD, JESSIE. *The Future of Marriage.* New York: Bantam, 1973.

A lively discussion of current and future changes in marriage and the family.

MURDOCK, GEORGE. *Social Structure.* New York: Macmillan, 1949.

A classic cross-cultural analysis of family patterns, based on data from 250 societies.

SKOLNICK, ARLENE, AND JEROME SKOLNICK. *Family in Transition.* Boston: Little, Brown, 1971.

A careful analysis of some of the problems facing the contemporary family, with an analysis of changes that are taking place in sexual behavior, marriage patterns, and child rearing.

SPIRO, MELFORD. *Children of the Kibbutz.* Cambridge, Mass.: Harvard University Press, 1958.

A study of the Israeli kibbutz, or commune, with special attention to the process and consequences of child rearing in this novel setting.

WINCH, ROBERT F. *The Modern Family.* New York: Holt, Rinehart and Winston, 1971.

A useful text on the family institution. Winch summarizes sociological literature on the topic and adds a number of original arguments of his own.

Reading

Does Marriage Have a Future? *Jessie Bernard*

Jessie Bernard, a leading sociologist of marriage and the family, takes a critical look at the future of the institution. Although she is critical of existing marriage patterns, she is optimistic about the prospects for new and satisfying forms of marriage in the future.

The answer to this question is an unequivocal yes. The future of marriage is, I believe, as assured as any human social form can be. There are, in fact, few human relationships with a more assured future. For men and women will continue to want intimacy, they will continue to want the thousand and one ways in which men and women share and reassure one another. They will continue to want to celebrate their mutuality, to experience the mystic unity that once led the church to consider marriage a sacrament. They will therefore, as far into the future as we can project, continue to commit themselves to each other. There is hardly any probability that such commitments will disappear and that all relationships between them will become merely casual or transient. The commitment may not take the form we know today, although that, too, has a future. But some form of commitment there will be. It may change its name; people may say they are "pair-bound" rather than married, but there will be such "paired" men and women bound to each other in one way or another. Still, I do not see the traditional form of marriage retaining its monopolistic sway. I see, rather, a future of marital options.

Not only does marriage have a future, it has many futures. There will be, for example, options that permit different kinds of relationships over time for different stages in life, and options that permit different life styles or living arrangements according to the nature of the relationships. There may be, up to about age twenty-five, options for childless liaisons; for the years of maturity, stable and at least "temporarily permanent" marriages involving child rearing; for middle age and beyond, new forms of relationships, perhaps even polgynous ones. People will be able to tailor their relationships to their circumstances and preferences. The most characteristic aspect of marriage in the future will be precisely the array of options available to different people who want different things from their relationships with one another.

Traditional marriage will of course be among the options available, for there is little likelihood that lifelong commitments and vows of sexual exclusivity will be discarded entirely. For a long time to come, millions of people will prefer this form of marriage, whatever the costs. But it will not have a monopoly; it will not be the only choice open.

Some couples may even want to relate to each other in the nineteenth-century manner. They will wait to marry until the young man has established himself in a well-paying job; and the young woman will either go directly into marriage without ever holding a job of her own, or give up her job upon marriage and devote herself exclusively to her household forever after. Her husband will make all the important decisions, and she will accept them, glad to be free of the responsibility. Since an increasing number of married women do enter the labor force, however, this style of marriage will predictably be of declining importance.

At the other extreme, the future will permit freewheeling relationships which will allow both partners a maximum of individuality and independence, relying wholly on emotional commitment, and limited only by their own feelings of responsibility. They may specify the length of their commitment, with an option for extension, if they so desire, as the proposed bill in the Maryland legislature specifies; or they may want only a partial commitment, spelled out in detail. Some may want specifications that strike us as outré and outrageous—separate households, for example, or weekend marriages. They may become matter-of-fact, quite acceptable choices for those who prefer them, with no raised eyebrows on anyone's part.

There will, in brief, be marriages in the future as different from conventional marriages of today as those of the present are from those of our forebears in the nineteenth century. Individual men and women will make different demands on their relationships. It is fallacious, then, even to speak of "*the* future of marriage." We should rather speak of "marriage in the future."

It is not, however, the specific forms the options will take that is important but rather the fact that there will be options, that no one kind of marriage will be required of everyone, that there will be recognition of the enormous difference among human beings which modern life demands and produces. It will come to seem incongruous that everyone has to be forced into an identical mold. . . . For good or ill, then, there *will* be options—a wide gamut of options, in fact. But are there not certain intrinsic limits to the forms that such options may take—in human nature, in the nature of societies, in the nature of culture? . . . Is there anything about marriage that is demanded or prescribed by human nature, or even proscribed? Are some forms "unnatural" or contrary to human instincts?

Neither "human nature" nor any of our instincts demand any special form of marriage. Just how "natural" marriage is can be gleaned from the diverse forms it has taken and the enormous literature on how to come to terms with it that has been necessary.

The variety of ways in which husbands and wives can relate to each other in marriage, and have, is so staggering as to boggle the imagination. Human beings can accept almost any kind of relationship if they are properly socialized into it. Just as people learn to accept fasts, painful rites, scarification, sacrifices of the most difficult kinds as a matter of course, so also can they accept lifelong celibacy or lifelong virginity—and they do—if that is defined as their lot. Girls accept doddering old men as husbands if that is what their parents tell them to. Wretched, miserable, quarreling spouses remain together no matter how destructive the relationship if that is what their community prescribes. Almost every kind of relationship has occurred somewhere, sometime—monogamy, polygyny, polyandry, exogamy, endogamy, matrilocal residence, neolocal residence, arranged marriages, self-selection of mates, parental selection of mates, marriage for love, marriage for convenience. . . . There is literally nothing about marriage that anyone can imagine that has not in fact taken place, whether prescribed, proscribed, or optional. All these variations seemed quite natural to those who lived with them. If any of them offends our "human nature," we have to remind ourselves that "human nature" as we know it this moment in this country is only one kind of human nature. . . . The question raised here is, actually, unanswerable. We will never know if there is anything intrinsic in human nature that limits the way the sexes can relate to one another because no one has ever survived outside of any culture long enough to teach us. We imbibe the sex-role behavior required by marriage in our culture long before we marry. We can, therefore, find no blueprint for marriage in pristine "uncontaminated" human nature. Human nature seems to be able to take almost any form of marriage—or unable to take any form.

For although human nature may not place rigid limits on the forms that marriage takes, it can, and does, place limits on the happiness experienced in marriage. We have referred many times to the incompatible demands that human beings make on life, for excitement, freedom, new experiences on the one hand, along with security and stability on the other. But they cannot have it both ways. Any commitment, however desirable, imposes restraints. What seems to be reflected here is an inevitable part of the human condition: people shaking their fists at the restraints they need and know they must have. Marriage, whatever form it takes, is for most, therefore, a compromise between conflicting impulses.

Most people come to terms with this conflict. The price they pay for marriage seems to them inconsequential as compared with the value received. Some find the costs too high; they feel that they sacrifice too much in the form of independence, freedom, adventure. Some of the options proposed for the future are designed to minimize the intrinsic conflict. It is conceivable that they might succeed, at least to a certain extent. They can mollify some conflicts by making possible the dissolution of commitments which are clearly untenable, in which the cost of either security or freedom is too high for one or both partners. But even if there were no commitments required, or if commitments could be abrogated at will, some people would long for the security that they represent along with the freedom that would come in their absence. There isn't much we can do about that. . . . One of the most common grievances expressed by young people today is the pressure they feel they are under to perform certain roles which they find uncongenial. The whole matter of roles is anathema to them. They believe that roles interfere with spontaneity, and force them into stereotypical behavior that does not really fit them.

One could argue that precisely the reverse is happening. Men and women are evolving a host of relationships with one another without corresponding clarification of their nature. One could even say that it is a major problem in our day that we do not have definitions for them, not to use as weapons against them but as tools to secure them.

As an example, while traveling around the world one runs into young couples living together who are not in the conventional status of marriage. They sometimes find it awkward to know how to refer to each other. She is not his wife; he is not her husband. "Girl friend" or "boy friend" does not convey the meaning of the relationship either. Nor does "roommate" or "housemate." "Lover" or "mistress" gives a misleading impression. "Companion" is not accurate. We have no term for this relationship, nor is there any clear-cut recognition of precisely what status it implies. . . . Are the new options that young people are now proposing a final solution? If we come to terms with them, can we then relax and close the book and say that we have solved the problems of marriage? Will we be able to say that although we cannot make every marriage a happy one, we have at least guaranteed that we have made it possible for most to be happy? Alas, no.

Every generation is the last in the sense of most recent, but not in the sense of final, generation. There will never be an ultimate or last in the sense of final form of marriage. It will go on changing as the times and the people change and as the demands on it change. There is no Ideal Marriage fixed in the nature of things that we will one day discover, toward which we are groping, slowly finding our way, and which we finally achieve. Every age has to find its own. We are only now getting used to the idea that any form of marriage is always transitional between an old one and a new one. It was easier to get used to change in the past because it took a very long time, even centuries, to make the transition, to accommodate to new conditions. It took close to two hundred years, for example, for the thinking about marriage which began during the Enlightenment among a minuscule avant-garde to percolate down to the men and women in the street. It is less than a quarter of a century since the "two-role" pattern of marriage for women recognizing both her worker and her domestic roles, which was the accommodation to the urban industrial order, achieved official sanction. Such a fast pace of change is hard to come to terms with.

But we have no choice. Change is bound to come whether we like it or not. We might as well come to terms with it gracefully. And to those who show us the way, I would even add that I am grateful, glad that there are men and women willing to pioneer the path for those of us who are not willing to pioneer it ourselves.

Source: Jessie Bernard, *The Future of Marriage* (New York: Bantam, 1973), pp. 301–323.

CHAPTER 15 *Education*

CHAPTER OUTLINE

Characteristics of American Education
Commitment to Mass Education
Faith in Education
Utilitarian Emphasis
Community Control

Inside the School
The Formal Structure of the School
Competitiveness
The Self-Fulfilling Prophecy
Student Peer Groups

Education: The Functionalist Perspective
Cultural Transmission
Social Integration
Personal Development
Screening and Selection
Innovation
Latent Functions

Education: The Conflict Perspective
Education and Social Mobility
Class, Race, and Education
Class, Race, and Intelligence

Equality of Educational Opportunity
The Coleman Report
Jencks's Analysis

The word "school" comes from an ancient Greek word meaning "leisure." The link between the two words may not seem obvious today, but in preindustrial societies schooling, if it existed at all, was reserved for the children of a privileged elite. Until fairly recently, no society could afford more than a handful of educated people. Schooling did little or nothing to increase a person's productivity and was thus, in an economic sense, wasteful. Education had little practical use and was undertaken only by those with the time and money to pursue the cultivation of the mind for its own sake. The rest of the population entered adult economic roles at the time of adolescence or even earlier. Most people acquired all the knowledge and skills they needed in the world through an informal socialization process consisting mostly of ordinary, everyday contacts with parents and other kin.

With the rise of industrialism, however, mass schooling became a necessity. Knowledge expanded rapidly, the pace of social change increased, and many new economic roles were created. Members of a modern industrial society need specialized knowledge and skills if they are to fill their adult roles competently. All modern societies recognize that the learning of this knowledge and these skills cannot be left to chance. It requires lengthy attendance at specialized formal organizations such as elementary schools, high schools, and colleges. In all industrial societies, education is a central social institution.

In its broadest sense, "education" is almost synonymous with "socialization," since both processes involve the transmission of culture from one person or group to another. The distinguishing feature of education in modern industrial societies, however, is that it has become an institutionalized, formal activity. Modern societies deliberately organize the educational experience, make it compulsory for people in certain age groups, train specialists to act as educators, and provide locations and equipment for the teaching and learning process. We have already dealt with informal socialization in Chapter 5 and will concentrate here on the more formal socialization that takes place in the schools. For our present purposes, then, *education is the systematic, formalized transmission of knowledge, skills, and values.*

In terms of the number of people involved, education is the largest single industry in the United States. If we include students, teachers, and administrators and other staff, almost one American in three currently participates in the institution—a figure without parallel anywhere else in the world. There are two main reasons for our remarkable emphasis on education. First, a modern industrial society such as the United States could not survive without a very large number of skilled and educated people. Second, Americans have historically had a deep faith in the virtues of mass education, even if it means educating millions of people to levels far above those demanded by most occupational roles in the economy. We tend to regard education as a cure-all for a variety of social ills, and it is no accident that in recent years our schools have become involved in controversial issues of social and racial equality. In the sixties and early seventies in particular, many efforts were made to use the schools as a tool for social change. As we shall see, the results have been somewhat disappointing, largely because of a failure to make a realistic sociological assessment of the potential role of education in society.

Characteristics of American Education

Education in the United States has several characteristics not found in the same combination in any other society. Many of the virtues and problems of our educational system stem from this unique blend of features. Let's look at some of the more important of these characteristics.

Commitment to Mass Education

In the United States it is taken for granted that everyone has a basic right to at least some formal education and that the state should therefore provide free elementary and high-school education for the masses. The belief that every child should attend school is a relatively recent one, and it was pioneered by the United States. As early as 1647, Massachusetts passed a law requiring towns of a certain size to establish elementary schools, and by the time of the Civil War most states were offering free education to their white citizens. This development took place long before similar systems were introduced in Europe. European countries were much less inclined to regard mass education as a virtue in itself; they have always been more inclined to tailor their educational planning to the economic demands of their respective societies.

The expansion of mass education in the United States in the course of this century has been unequaled in any other country. In 1900, about 7 percent of Americans in the appropriate age group were graduated from high school; by 1920 this figure had risen to 17 percent; by 1940, to 50 percent; and it stands today at over 80 percent. More than two-thirds of the present American population has a high-school diploma, and the population has a median of twelve years of education. The proportion of high-school graduates attending college has also risen steeply, from 4 percent in 1900 to 16 percent in 1940 to about 40 percent in the mid-seventies.

This extension of educational opportunities has not been without its cost, for mass education on this scale inevitably means some lowering of academic standards. Other industrialized countries, such as Britain and France, have generally insisted on high standards, even though this has meant denying educational opportunities to the less academically able. Until the late sixties, for example, British schoolchildren were required to take a tough examination at the age of eleven, and on the basis of their results were sent to one of two quite different kinds of schools. The "secondary modern" schools, to which the vast majority of children went, offered vocational training and only a rudimentary academic curriculum; most of these children left school at the age of fifteen or sixteen. The "grammar" schools, to which a very small minority of

Figure 15.1 The average American has significantly more years of schooling than the average inhabitant of any other country. The United States has a particularly strong commitment to formal education, which is believed to be a great benefit to both the individual and society. Education has developed rapidly into one of our major social institutions.

children were sent, had very high academic standards, emphasized such subjects as Latin or ancient Greek, and prepared their students for university entrance. Less than a decade ago a young black in the American South had a better chance of getting to college than the average young person in England (Wattenburg and Scammon, 1967). In Europe today only about 20 percent of the sixteen- and seventeen-year-olds are still in school, compared with about 80 percent in the United States, and only about 10 percent of European children proceed to college, compared with about 40 percent here. Although the developing nations of the world attempt to provide elementary education to all children, only a small minority obtain secondary education, and a person's chances of a college education are minimal. More than half of the world's population can neither read nor write, and the absolute number of illiterates is actually increasing (see Figure 15.2).

Formal education in the United States is not merely freely available: it is actually compulsory. There are still many societies where schooling is either not compulsory or where it is compulsory for only the first few grades of elementary school. In the United States, parents are legally obliged to send their children to school, although they may choose between private and public education and between secular and religious education, choices that are not offered in many other countries. Education in the United States is financed by taxes on everybody, not merely those who use the service. People without children, people whose children attend private schools, and even people who oppose formal schooling are all required to support public education. The implication is that public education is for the benefit of the entire society, not merely those who happen to receive it. This deep commitment to mass education has given us the most extensive educational system in the world, and we take it for granted that every child is entitled to at least twelve years of schooling at public expense. We even expect some skilled professionals to spend twenty years or more in school—a period equal to half the life expectancy in some other countries.

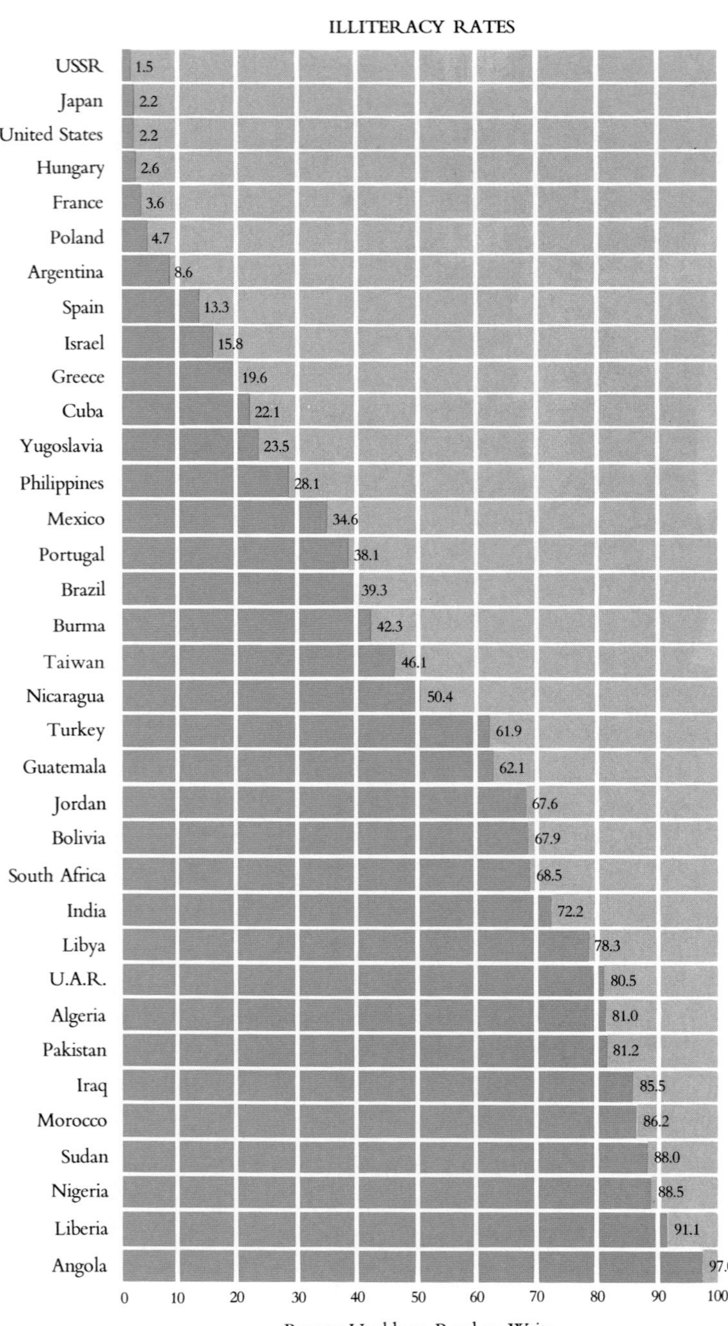

Source: Statistical Office of the United Nations, *Statistical Yearbook* (New York, 1969); and United Nations Educational, Scientific, and Cultural Organization, *Statistical Yearbook* (Paris, 1969 and 1972).

Figure 15.2 As this figure shows, many countries have very high illiteracy rates. At present, more than half of the world's population can neither read nor write. The absolute number of illiterate people is actually increasing, primarily because educational facilities in the developing nations cannot keep pace with their population growth.

Faith in Education

Our commitment to mass education stems not only from our recognition of the economic necessity for a skilled, literate population but also from our historic belief that education is valuable and desirable in itself. Much of this tradition derives from the Jeffersonian ideal of a wise, informed, and sophisticated electorate that could be relied upon to make a democracy work. If the voters were merely an ignorant rabble, Jefferson believed, the American experiment was doomed.

Since the nineteenth century there has been a deep belief in American society that education can be used to solve a variety of social problems, including many that were once considered a more appropriate concern for the family or the church. Education was first used as a tool for social engineering in attempts to "Americanize" immigrants and to "civilize" native American children. Since then we have laid greater burdens on the schools. If the crime rate increases, we expect schools to teach students not to become criminals. If drug addiction spreads, we immediately institute drug programs in schools. In the sixties the "war on poverty" placed great emphasis on education, in the belief that the culture of the poor, not their lack of money, was the source of their poverty. We attempted for years to cut down the appalling traffic fatalities on our roads through driver-education programs rather than through compulsory wearing of seat belts, although the former was calculated to save lives at an average cost of $88,000 each, the latter at $87 each (Etzioni, 1972). There is little evidence that these and similar programs have had much effect and a good deal of evidence that they have not, but our faith in education as a cure-all for social problems persists anyway. Other societies, of course, have used education to change attitudes and behavior—the outstanding examples are probably Nazi Germany and modern China—but they have done so in conjunction with sweeping changes in other social institutions at the same time. The faith that the schools *alone* can change attitudes and behavior and remedy social ills is distinctively American. As sociologists of education are increasingly pointing out, there seems to be very little empirical justification for this faith, and it may be that we have cherished expectations of the institution that it cannot fulfill alone.

Utilitarian Emphasis

Educational philosophers have always made a distinction between "education" and "training." "Education" in this sense refers to a broad, humanistic process that encourages creativity and critical thinking. "Training" refers to a much narrower process that aims at providing technical competence and a store of specific information.

The schools in the United States have always concentrated primarily on training, on imparting specific skills and information rather than on the development of the whole person. The school curriculum generally emphasizes material that is directly relevant to the students' future occupational roles. Classroom discussions are rarely tailored to the students' own interests, even when these concern pressing public issues. Charles Silberman (1970) cites one example:

> All over the United States, that last week of November, 1963, teachers reported the same complaint: "I can't get the children to concentrate on their work; all they want to do is talk about the assassination." The idea that the children might learn more from discussing President Kennedy's assassination—or that, like most adults, they were simply too obsessed with the horrible events to think about anything else—didn't occur to these teachers. It wasn't in that week's lesson plan.

A similar attitude is revealed in a recommendation from a National Teachers' Association manual: "Plan the lesson. Be ready to use the first minute of class time. If you get Johnny right away, he has not time to cook up *interesting* ideas that do not fit into the class situation" (quoted with italics added in Silberman, 1970).

When the Gallup poll asked Americans in 1972 why they want their children to get educated, the most frequent response was, "to get a better job"; only 15 percent felt that education was "to stimulate their minds." When the respondents were asked what the schools should pay the greatest attention to, their most common answer was "teaching students to respect law and authority." A 1969 Harris poll found that a majority of students believed that there should be more discussion of racial issues in the classroom, but only 36 percent of teachers and only 27 percent of parents agreed. Most teachers and parents felt that the schools "are not the place to foster controversy or to challenge prevailing standards"—a far cry from Jefferson's idea that education should equip the people to inquire critically into social and political issues.

This *utilitarian emphasis* in American education has been challenged from time to time, most notably by the "progressive" schools movement inspired by the writings of the educational philosopher John Dewey (1859–1952). Dewey argued for a person-centered education in a democratic school environment. Pupils, he believed, should take an active role in constructing their educational experience. The progressive movement had some limited success in the thirties and forties, and educational practices that owed a good deal to Dewey's thought flourished again briefly in the sixties. The pendulum now seems to be swinging back strongly in the direction of formal training centered around the subject rather than the child. Rightly or wrongly, many people blame the "permissive" educational environment of the sixties for the sharp drop in student reading levels that is now evident throughout our educational system, including the colleges.

Community Control

Most other countries regard education as a national enterprise, and many have uniform national curricula, teacher salaries, funding policies, and examinations. Not long ago it was said, a little cynically, that the national minister of education in France could state exactly which book every child at a given grade was using during a particular hour of any school day. In the United States, however, the schools are regarded as the concern of the community they serve, and most decisions are in the hands of a local school board elected by the voters of the community. At present the individual states provide about 40 percent of the funding for the schools, the federal government provides about 10 percent, and the remainder comes from local school districts—most of it derived from property taxes.

This tradition of *community control* is highly valued and zealously guarded. But it has the result that schools in wealthy neighborhoods are far more lavishly funded than schools in poorer areas. When taxable property per pupil is measured, some school districts have as much as ten thousand times the fiscal capacity of others (Reischauer *et al.*, 1973). Thus, in the early seventies, one district in South Dakota was spending $175 per pupil per year, while another district in Wyoming was spending $14,554. The average class size in Tennessee was over 23 pupils, while in Vermont it was nearer 16. As Figure 15.3 shows, there are wide variations in the per pupil expenditures of the different states. Compared with control from a distant national government, community control has many obvious advantages. But it has the very serious drawback that the quality of a child's educational experience may depend on the neighborhood in which the parents happen to live. Most other countries believe that this kind of situation is intolerable. They have chosen instead to rely on regional or national funding of the schools, even though local community influence is reduced as a result.

Inside the School

Every school is a miniature social system, with its own social structure, system of statuses and roles, subcultures, values and traditions, and rituals and ceremonies. Each school, classroom, and clique is an interacting social unit. The study of what actually goes on inside the school has been an important focus of sociological research.

The Formal Structure of the School

Perhaps the most obvious feature of the school is that it is a formal, *bureaucratic* organization (Roberts, 1970). The school is no longer housed in a single room and staffed by a schoolmarm who teaches all pupils and all subjects; the educational process has been rationalized in the interests of efficiency. Pupils are grouped according to age, subject, and, in many schools, according to ability; teachers are specialists and some of them, such as department chairpersons, have formal authority over others; and an administrative staff supervises the entire operation. Procedures are kept as uniform as possible so that the school can be run in an orderly and predictable way.

A result of the bureaucratization of the school is that the atmosphere is necessarily repressive to some degree. Pupils are obliged to remain silent, to line up and march on command, to sit still for hours, to be punctual, and even to request permission to use the toilet. In elementary and high schools, the degree of regimentation is greater than any that the students, except those who later enter

ESTIMATED PUBLIC SCHOOL EXPENDITURES AND PERSONAL INCOME, BY STATES

State	Current Expenditures, 1975 Average per Pupil	Per Capita Personal Income, 1974
U.S.	$1,250	$5,434
Alabama	871	4,198
Alaska	1,624	7,023
Arizona	1,176	4,989
Arkansas	896	4,280
California	1,210	5,997
Colorado	1,188	5,343
Connecticut	1,507	6,471
Delaware	1,485	6,227
Florida	1,147	5,235
Georgia	869	4,662
Hawaii	1,384	5,882
Idaho	910	4,934
Illinois	1,376	6,337
Indiana	1,074	5,263
Iowa	1,240	5,302
Kansas	1,444	5,406
Kentucky	864	4,470
Louisiana	1,034	4,310
Maine	918	4,439
Maryland	1,369	5,881
Massachusetts	1,136	5,731
Michigan	1,547	5,928
Minnesota	1,423	5,450
Mississippi	834	3,764
Missouri	1,078	5,056
Montana	1,269	4,776
Nebraska	1,211	4,877
Nevada	1,101	6,073
New Hampshire	1,095	5,143
New Jersey	1,294	6,384
New Mexico	1,052	4,137
New York	2,005	6,244
North Carolina	1,052	4,612
North Dakota	1,032	5,547
Ohio	1,144	5,549
Oklahoma	1,009	4,566
Oregon	1,425	5,270
Pennsylvania	1,446	5,490
Rhode Island	1,493	5,376
South Carolina	984	4,258
South Dakota	973	4,218
Tennessee	903	4,484
Texas	894	4,790
Utah	942	4,452
Vermont	1,095	4,588
Virginia	1,054	5,265
Washington	1,199	5,651
West Virginia	910	4,390
Wisconsin	1,323	5,210
Wyoming	1,322	5,156

Source: U.S. Bureau of the Census, *Statistical Abstract, 1975,* p. 133.

Figure 15.3 There is great variation in the per capita expenditure on public schools from one state to another. These variations are closely related to the per capita income in each state. The quality of the school environment is therefore dependent on the relative wealth of the state concerned.

the military or the prisons, will encounter again in their lifetimes. The college atmosphere, particularly since the changes that followed the student demonstrations of the sixties, is much more permissive, but college students' lives are still subject to many rules and regulations. Classrooms in colleges are often fairly informal, but no student who has been through the veritable circus of form filling known as "registration" can doubt the basically bureaucratic nature of college organization. It is easy to overlook the fact, too, that teachers are themselves subject to some measure of regimentation. Unlike other professionals, such as doctors and lawyers, teachers are not entitled to professional privacy. Elementary and high-school teachers are regarded as public servants, and their work is closely supervised by other officials.

To be efficient a bureaucracy must fit individuals to its own administrative needs, not its administrative procedures to the needs of individuals. As a result the elementary and high schools tend to emphasize conformity and obedience, and they have difficulty accommodating spontaneity, energy, excitement, and individual creativity. Although the schools pay lip service to the ideal of encouraging students to think critically, they are generally authoritarian; although they preach the value of democratic participation, they are reluctant to practice this value within the school walls. Controversial topics are avoided: American social problems are often ignored, and school textbooks, typically portraying "nice" and "typical" middle-class white Americans, are as notable for what they fail to teach as for what they do teach (Silberman, 1971). The emphasis on obedience and conformity has been held responsible by many educators for the widespread apathy of students, particularly in high schools (e.g., Holt, 1964, 1972; Goodman, 1970; Friedenberg, 1969; Farber, 1970).

Figure 15.4 A characteristic feature of American education is competitiveness. From the earliest school years, children are taught to compete against one another. This emphasis on competition helps to socialize the children for the competitiveness they will encounter later in almost every aspect of American life.

Competitiveness

Another universal feature of American schools, from the elementary level through college, is competitiveness (R. Johnson *et al.,* 1973). Like our economic system, our educational system prizes individualism and competition. The use of grading encourages students to vie with one another for academic achievement, and the losers in the competition are gradually eliminated from the system altogether and sent into the work force. In many other cultures, this kind of competitive behavior in school is unknown or considered antisocial. In China, for example, members of a class are expected not to compete with but to help one another, but in our society mutual help may be regarded as cheating. Jules Henry (1963) points to this cultural contrast between ourselves and other societies:

> Boris had trouble reducing "12/16" to the lowest terms, and could only get as far as "6/8." The teacher asked him quietly if that was as far as he could reduce it. She suggested he "think." Much heaving up and down and waving of hands by the other children, all frantic to correct him. Boris pretty unhappy, probably mentally paralyzed. The teacher, quiet, patient, ignores the others and concentrates with looks and voice on Boris. . . . After a minute or two, she becomes more urgent, but there is no response from Boris. She then turns to the class and says, "Well, who can tell Boris what the number is?" A forest of hands appears, and the teacher calls Peggy. Peggy says that four may be divided into the numerator and the denominator. Thus Boris's failure has made it possible for Peggy to succeed; his depression is the price of her exhilaration; his misery the occasion of her rejoicing. This is the standard condition of the American elementary school. . . . So often somebody's success has been bought at the cost of our failure. To a Zuni, Hopi, or Dakota Indian, Peggy's performance would seem cruel beyond belief, for competition, the wringing of success from somebody else's failure, is a form of torture foreign to those noncompetitive redskins.

The Self-Fulfilling Prophecy

The results of this competition—the success or failure of individual students—become part of an official record, so that particular individuals are labeled as bright or dull and treated accordingly (P. Jackson, 1968). One manifestation of this differential treatment is the tracking system, which segregates students on the assumption that they will learn better if they are grouped with others of similar ability. This assumption is widely held, but the evidence for its validity is doubtful at best. Some forty-one separate studies have found favorable results from tracking, usually indicating that higher-ability students benefit from it, but seventy-seven other studies have found either mixed or unfavorable results (National Education Association, 1968).

The labeling of students as "bright" or "dull" can have important consequences for their later academic careers. Teachers' expectations and attitudes are influenced by these labels, and so are the self-concepts of the students concerned. The process of labeling may involve a *self-fulfilling prophecy*. Believing that certain children will fail, the school treats them as failures, with the result that they do fail; the prophecy is confirmed by the result. Some important experiments by the psychologist Robert Rosenthal suggest the possible effects of this kind of labeling. In one experiment, Rosenthal (1966) divided a number of rats at random into two groups and told his introductory psychology students that one group contained fast learners and the other slow learners. He then asked the students to perform various experiments with the rats to determine their learning ability. The students reported that the "fast learners" were indeed much more "intelligent" than the "slow learners." The reasons for this finding are not entirely clear. Perhaps the students gave the "fast learners" the benefit of the doubt in ambiguous situations, perhaps they treated them more gently and made the rats more confident. In any case, there is no doubt that the students' expectations influenced their assessments of the rats' behavior.

Rosenthal (1969) next tried a similar experiment in an elementary school. He told the teachers at the school that he had developed a new test that would identify those children whose learning abilities were likely to spurt ahead during the next year. The children were duly tested and the teachers were given a list of "spurters" with instructions to watch their progress without revealing their expectations to the children or the children's parents in any way. In actual fact, the test had no predictive value whatever, and the names that Rosenthal provided had merely been selected at random. The only characteristic that distinguished these children from their classmates, then, was the teachers' expectation that their work would improve. A year later, Rosenthal found marked academic gains among the "spurters." They showed an average IQ increase of 12.22 points, compared with an increase of 8.42 among a control group of "nonspurters." The most dramatic gains were in the first and second grades, where individual "spurters" made gains of up to 27.4 and 16.5 points, respectively, compared with 12 and 7 points among the "nonspurters." Rosenthal concluded that the teachers had changed their attitudes toward the children in subtle ways and had influenced the pupils' progress as a result. Rosenthal's findings remain controversial, however, as later attempts to replicate his experiment have produced varying results. His findings have been confirmed by some studies but not by others, suggesting that more research is needed to discover the precise conditions under which the self-fulfilling prophecy operates (Rist, 1970; Thorndike, 1968; Rosenthal, 1969; Gephart, 1970; Barber *et al.*, 1969; Leacock, 1969; Rubovits and Maehr, 1971, 1973; Brophy and Good, 1970).

Grading, tracking, and counseling all gradually eliminate from the educational system those students who are not considered bright enough to benefit from further schooling. Unlike other educational systems, such as the British one discussed earlier, we do not abruptly separate our academic sheep from the goats. Instead, we use a more subtle process of "cooling out" unwanted students (Clark, 1960). Students thus learn slowly that the social prizes that a good education brings are restricted to the few, and that hard work is not enough to bring success. Since the vast majority of the students who are "cooled out" are from the lower social classes, the educational system legitimates social inequality by making academic failure seem the result of individual inadequacies alone. The idea is that everyone is supposed to have the same chance but that only some are able to make use of it.

Student Peer Groups

Despite the importance of good grades in the educational system, academic success is rarely linked to high status among peers. In fact, student peer groups typically play down the pursuit of knowledge in favor of other goals, and status is more likely to be achieved among males by athletic prowess and among females by popularity or looks (J. S. Coleman, 1961). Peer groups and cliques are of great importance in the culture of a school or college and may exert far more influence over the behavior and attitudes of individual students than do the efforts of the teachers, counselors, or administrators. In particular, students who

Figure 15.5 The youthful peer group is an important element in the social structure of any school. From early adolescence on, young people tend to feel greater loyalty to the norms of their peers than to those of adults. Peer-group values may contradict those of the school, and children may seek high status in the peer group to compensate for low academic status.

are not academically gifted or interested in schoolwork may find alternative sources of gratification among their peers. Status within the peer group may thus compensate for academic failure in the school.

In colleges, which draw their students from much more diverse backgrounds than do local elementary and high schools, there are often a number of distinct subcultures, and membership in one of these colors the entire college experience of the student. Burton Clark and Martin Trow (1966) identify four different college subcultures. The *collegiate* subculture fits the traditional stereotype. Its interests revolve around fun, drinking, dating, football, and fraternities. The *vocational* subculture is more serious. It emphasizes the necessity of hard work as a means of getting a good degree and thus a good job in later life. The *academic* subculture has a less utilitarian outlook on education and is more concerned with exploring the world of ideas for its own sake. Finally, the *nonconformist* subculture is critical of existing social arrangements and may adopt deviant forms of dress and behavior. These distinctions refer to types of subculture, not types of student; an individual student may participate in more than one of them.

Education: The Functionalist Perspective

The functionalist perspective provides a useful way of explaining the central importance of the schools in maintaining the social order as a whole. Several important functions of education can be identified.

Cultural Transmission

If a society is to survive, its culture must be transmitted from one generation to the next. In a complex modern society this process cannot be left to chance, and the schools are used to provide the young with the knowledge, skills, and values that the society considers especially important. Thus we learn about our history, geography, and language. We learn how to read, write, and manipulate numbers. We learn about patriotism, the virtues of our political system, and our society's norms of behavior and morality. This function of education is an essentially conservative one, for the schools are transmitting the culture of the past, or, at best, the present. In a traditional society, this conservatism does not matter much, because culture changes very slowly. In a rapidly changing modern society, however, teachers of the older generation may find it impossible to adequately equip students of a younger generation to face a future that can never be fully anticipated. In their transmission of cultural values, too, the schools in all societies engage, deliberately or otherwise, in indoctrination. We are well aware of this practice in totalitarian societies but tend to overlook it in our own because we are hardly aware of our attempts to indoctrinate. But if a teacher in an elementary or high school fails to teach accepted values—if, for example, he or she tries to present the life and thought of Karl Marx in a favorable light, or discusses sexual practices that are accepted in other societies but are considered highly deviant in our own—a community furor is likely to result. The cultural-transmission function of education very often tends to reinforce existing ethnocentrism.

Social Integration

Modern industrial societies, which are usually far larger and more populous than traditional preindustrial societies, frequently contain many different ethnic, racial, religious, or other subcultures. Education may serve to integrate the young members of these subcultures into a common culture, encouraging the development of a relatively homogeneous society with shared values. In the United States the schools have always been considered an important factor in the "melting-pot" process. Children of immigrants may arrive in the first grade unable to speak more than a few words of English, but they emerge from school, at least in theory, able to take their place in the mainstream of American life. This *social integration* function is particularly important in many of the developing nations of the Third World. The borders of these countries were often established by European colonial powers without any reference to tribal, linguistic, or ethnic barriers, and some of the new nations contain literally hundreds of different language groups that have no common cultural tradition and often have a history of mutual hostility. These countries explicitly use the schools to generate a common sense of national loyalty among the young.

Personal Development

The schools provide opportunities for students to acquire knowledge, skills, and perspectives that are not available elsewhere. In both the formal curriculum and in informal interaction with peers and teachers, students learn a great deal about themselves and about the world that surrounds them. Some of this learning is relevant to their future occupational roles, but much of it is more valuable for personal emotional, social, and intellectual development. To take but one example, level of education has a strong impact on attitudes and opinions. A "don't know" response to questions in national opinion polls has consistently been found to be related to low educational attainment, irrespective of the subject of the poll. The

Figure 15.6 Chinese children's pageants under portraits of Chairman Mao immediately suggest "indoctrination" to an American audience. But is the American practice of pledging allegiance to the flag (often beneath portraits of national heroes) really any different?

higher one's level of education, the more likely one is to reject prejudice and intolerant thinking (Clark, 1962; Selznick and Steinberg, 1969). Each additional year of college appears to make a student more democratic in outlook and more tolerant toward civil-liberties issues (Selvin and Hagstrom, 1960).

Screening and Selection

Education is an important avenue to social mobility in the United States and other industrial societies. By screening the academic performance of students, the schools effectively select particular types of students for particular types of occupations. From the elementary years onward, the schools constantly test students and evaluate their achievements, channeling some toward technical vocations, some toward academic subjects, and failing some while passing others. The credentials that people possess at the end of their education have a strong influence on their life chances. As we shall see, however, the influence of family background on a person's chances in life still remains highly significant, for family background appears to be the main determinant of individual educational achievement. The screening and selection process, however objective and impartial it may seem, generally serves to give further advantages to those who already have them as a result of the higher social and economic status of their parents.

Innovation

Educational institutions do not merely transmit existing knowledge; they add to the cultural heritage by developing new knowledge and skills as well. This function arises partly because the experience of education stimulates intellectual curiosity and critical thought, and partly because college and university teachers are usually expected to conduct research that will increase scientific knowledge. A good deal of research now takes place outside the schools—in government, industry, and specialized research institutes—but the college professor has a double role both as teacher and researcher. This role can generate many tensions, as it is not always possible for the same individual to perform both tasks competently in the limited time available; in fact, many professors complain that

Figure 15.7 An important function of education is personal development. The schools provide many opportunities for developing skills that might not otherwise be acquired.

Figure 15.8 The schools screen and select students for their later occupational roles. Examinations and grading serve to distinguish the academically able from the less able, and those who fail to meet the required standards are gradually eased out of the educational system and into the work force.

they face the choice of neglecting either their research or their students. Colleges remain primarily responsible for *basic* research, which is concerned with establishing new knowledge. *Applied* research, which is concerned with finding practical uses for knowledge, is increasingly pursued outside the college context.

Latent Functions

The functions discussed so far are of the type that sociologists call *manifest,* that is, they are recognized and intended. But education also has functions of a *latent* type, functions that are not generally recognized and were never intended (Merton, 1968). For example, schools serve as "baby-sitting" agencies. They free mothers from their child-rearing tasks and permit them to work outside the home. Schools, particularly colleges, also serve as a "marriage market," by giving young people of fairly similar background and opposite sex a chance to interact with one another in a way that would not be possible if their social orbits were restricted to the home and workplace. By isolating young people from the rest of society in segregated institutions, the schools also have the latent function of permitting distinctive youth cultures to form. In the sixties and early seventies, for example, many college students adopted political and social norms that were often radically at odds with those of the wider society, and the college campus became a focus of unrest. In addition to their formal curricula, the schools also teach habits of punctuality, docility, and obedience to authority, a latent function that has a useful payoff when young people enter offices and factories. One further latent function of education in the United States, which we shall shortly discuss in more detail, is that of perpetuating the class and racial inequalities of our society.

Figure 15.9 The schools have many latent, or unrecognized, functions. One latent function of the colleges is to segregate young people from adults in an atmosphere where critical thinking is encouraged. As a result, college campuses in the United States and elsewhere are often centers of political dissent.

Education: The Conflict Perspective

A functionalist analysis of education gives a useful understanding of the role that this institution has in society. But the analysis does not tell the whole story, for it tends to ignore the fact that education can become deeply involved in social conflict. The conflict perspective, on the other hand, focuses on the ways different social groups use education as a means of getting or keeping power, wealth, and prestige.

Education and Social Mobility

If you turn to Figure 10.3 in Chapter 10 (Social Stratification), which lists the prestige rankings of various occupations, you will notice that the most prestigious jobs tend to be not only those that yield the highest incomes but also the ones that require the longest education. The more education people have, the more likely they are to obtain good jobs and to enjoy high incomes. In their study of

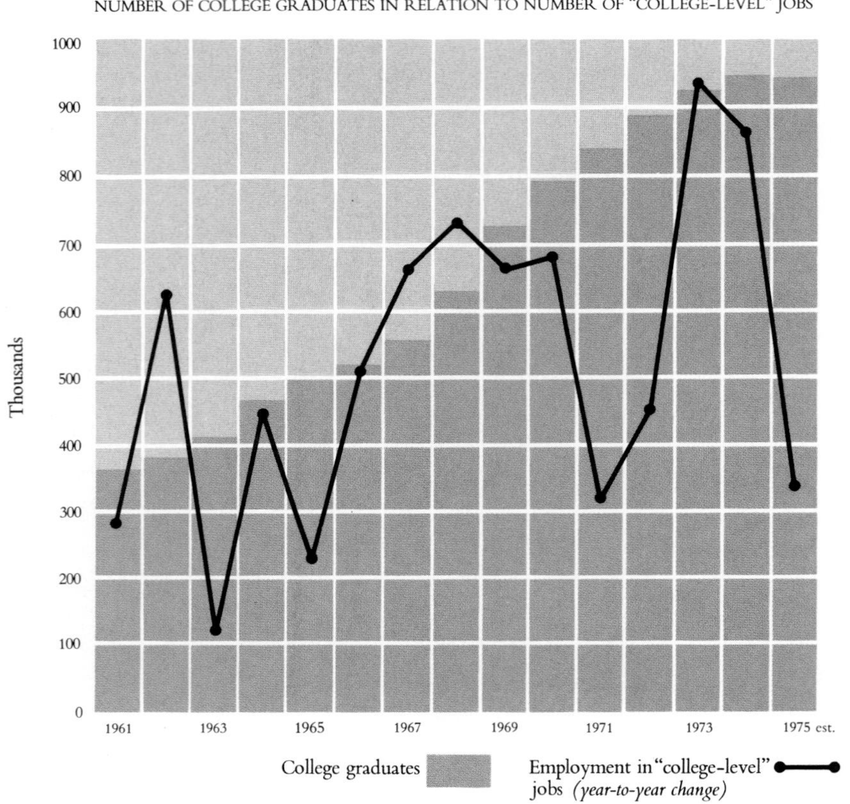

Source: Walter Guzzardi, Jr., "The Uncertain Passage from College to Job," *Fortune* Magazine, (January, 1976), p. 129.

Figure 15.10 Until 1975, the number of new college graduates increased steadily every year. The economy's demand for these graduates, however, has declined rapidly in recent years. The Department of Labor projects that of the 13 million new college graduates expected between now and 1985, at least 1 million will remain unemployed or will work at jobs not requiring a degree.

social mobility in the United States, Peter Blau and Otis Duncan (1967) found that the most important factor affecting whether a son moved to a higher social status than his father's was the amount of education the son received. A high level of education is a scarce and valued resource, and one for which people compete vigorously.

The rapid growth in the number of Americans with college degrees, including higher degrees at the master's and doctoral level, is not simply a result of the increasing technological sophistication of our economy. As Figure 15.10 shows, the number of new college graduates is now far greater than the number of "college-level" jobs available. In fact, it has been calculated that only 15 percent of the increase in educational requirements for jobs during the course of this century can be attributed to the replacement of low-skill jobs by new jobs requiring greater expertise (Collins, 1971). What has actually happened is that the "educational threshold" has risen: people need higher qualifications to get jobs that previously required much lower educational credentials. It is very doubtful whether these extra years of education are really necessary for most occupations. There is evidence that educational achievement has no consistent relationship to later job performance and productivity (Gintis, 1971). What is significant, however, is that the lack of these qualifications restricts the social mobility of those people who, for one reason or another, have been unable to obtain them. The crucial insight of the conflict perspective is that people do not have equal opportunity to achieve educational success. In practice, their chances are very strongly influenced by the social class of the family into which they were born. Social stratification distributes educational opportunities as unequally as it distributes wealth, power, and prestige. By reinforcing the advantages that some people already have over others as a result of an accident of birth, the schools preserve the social inequalities that already exist (Rist, 1973).

Class, Race, and Education

It is obvious that educational level is related to income, but it is not always so obvious that social class affects educational level. The average higher-status child stays in school longer and achieves better results while there than the average lower-status child, a fact that can only be explained in terms of unequal opportunity to benefit from the educational experience. The superior educational achievement of the upper-status person is then translated into further social and economic advantages.

The influence of social class is so strong that educational achievement may not be the critical factor in later occupational achievement. There is no shortage of evidence on the differential achievements of children from different social classes. In a major study, William Sewell (1971) followed the fortunes of some randomly selected high-school pupils for fourteen years. He divided his sample into four groups on the basis of their socioeconomic status and found that those in the highest group were four times more likely to attend college, six times more likely to graduate, and nine times more likely to receive graduate

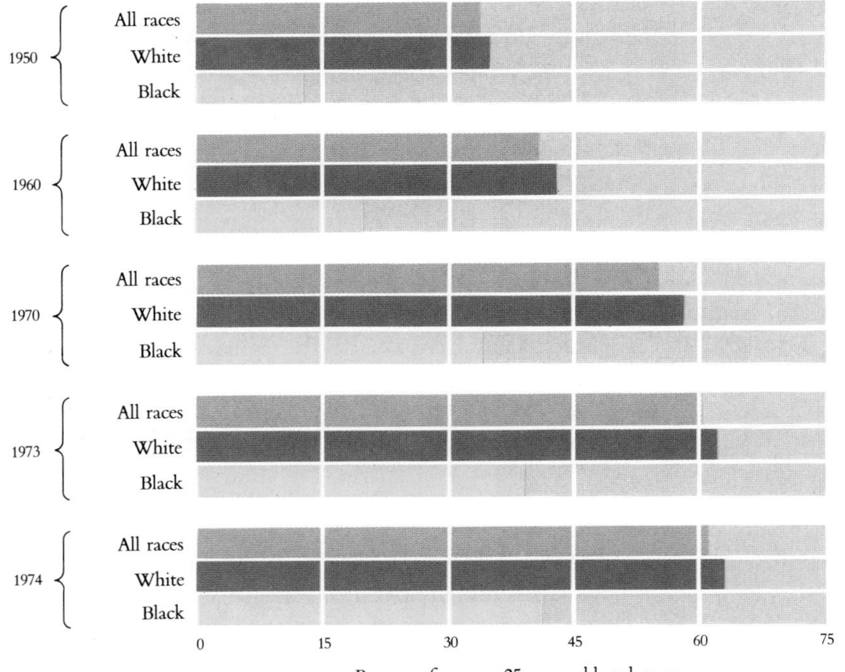

Source: U.S. Bureau of the Census, *Statistical Abstract, 1975.*

Figure 15.11 A far greater proportion of whites than blacks have completed four years of high school, although the gap between the races has been narrowing in recent years. A similar pattern is found at the college level.

or professional training than those in the lowest-status group. In general, white lower-class children receive about 1.5 fewer years of high-school education than their middle-class counterparts (Jencks, 1972). Because race and class overlap to a great extent, minority groups also have a lower average educational achievement than whites (see Figure 15.11 on page 355).

These discrepancies are magnified at the college level. Almost one-fourth of all whites in the eighteen to twenty-four age group are enrolled in college, compared with less than one-fifth of blacks. Some 5.5 percent of the black population has completed college, compared with 14.0 percent of the white population (*Statistical Abstract, 1975*). Intelligence is not the only or even the main determinant of who goes to college and finally gets a degree. In fact, a high-school graduate of high intelligence but low social status is no more likely to attend college than a graduate with low intelligence but high social status. Less than 10 percent of students with high incomes and high abilities fail to enter college, whereas a quarter of low-income students with comparable abilities do not continue their education beyond high school.

How can we account for these discrepancies? It seems that several factors are operating:

Costs of Education

To keep a child in high school and to put a student through college is an expensive undertaking, especially when indirect costs, such as the loss of the student's immediate earning capacity, are taken into account. The more wealthy a family is, the more able it is to bear these costs.

Family Expectations

If the family expects that a child will remain in high school and attend college, the expectation will influence the motivation of the student. Middle- and upper-class families are inclined to take it for granted that their children will do well academically; lower-class families are much less likely to make the same assumption.

Cultural Background

Middle- and upper-class children are socialized in a way that maximizes their learning potential. For example, their families are smaller, their homes are more likely to be stocked with books, they are more likely to be given educational toys, and they are encouraged to defer immediate gratification in favor of long-term goals. The lower-class child is likely to be born into a larger family in a smaller home, to have less experience of the world of ideas and books, and to have lower commitment to the values needed for educational success.

Childhood Nutrition

Children raised in impoverished surroundings face serious physical obstacles to educational success. There is mounting evidence that malnutrition, particularly in the prenatal period and infancy, can do irreparable damage to later intellectual growth by stunting the development of the brain. Malnutrition is not a problem restricted to distant underdeveloped nations; it is surprisingly common in the United States and is particularly widespread in the black rural "underclass" (Coles, 1969).

Language Problems

Schools teach pupils in "standard," middle-class American English. Some students from minority groups—particularly Mexican Americans—enter school scarcely able to speak any English. They inevitably suffer an initial setback, from which they may never recover. Black English and lower-class white English also differ in important respects from "standard" American English, and the pupils may be penalized for language that appears "ungrammatical." Moreover, they may actually fail to understand much of what the teacher says to them (Bernstein, 1971). (In fact, these variants of English are not in any sense "ungrammatical." They have a perfectly regular system of grammatical rules and are valid dialects of the English language, just as valid as those of the Australians, the Irish, the Queen of England, or, for that matter, middle-class Americans.)

Teacher Attitudes

Most teachers have middle-class values and attitudes and may unintentionally penalize students who fail to display them. Teachers tend to appreciate students who are punctual, clean, "moral," neat, hardworking, obedient, and ambitious. Pupils who do not behave according to middle-class norms risk being considered "bad" students, irrespective of their intelligence and ability.

Labeling

Once a child is labeled as a dull student, a self-fulfilling prophecy may follow. Lower-ability children are often put in slower tracks and counseled to make "realistic" career choices. If the child internalizes the self-concept that the school offers, his or her academic motivation may be undermined. There is also strong evidence that the quality of counseling in school is directly related to the social class of the pupil, irrespective of individual talent (Cicourel and Kitsuse, 1963) and that class and race strongly affect the high-school track to which a student is assigned, regardless of IQ or earlier achievement (Schafer *et al.*, 1967).

Peer-Group Influence

Peer groups in schools or colleges strongly influence the academic motivation and career plans of their members. These peer groups are usually composed of people of similar social background. The importance of college plans to individual students is very closely linked to the aspirations of their friends (Campbell and Alexander, 1964; Krauss, 1964). In working-class peer groups, the norm may be to enter the work force at high-school graduation or even before (S. M. Miller, 1964).

Class, Race, and Intelligence

Educational achievement is highly correlated with intelligence as measured on IQ (*Intelligence Quotient*) tests. Again, however, it seems that intelligence is not the critical factor influencing achievement: IQ scores are strongly influenced in turn by social class background. Lower-class whites score less well on IQ tests than middle- and upper-class whites, as do members of disadvantaged minority groups. Blacks, for example, score on the average ten to fifteen points below whites on these tests. Individual members of both races are found at every point on the entire ability range, however, and middle-class northern blacks generally do better than lower-class southern whites. The issue of race and intelligence has become highly controversial since the late sixties, when the psychologist Arthur Jensen (1969) implied that the differences in IQ between blacks and whites could be partially explained by an inborn intellectual inferiority on the part of blacks.

To evaluate this argument we must look at both "intelligence" and at IQ tests. Exactly what "intelligence" is, nobody knows. Psychologists have been attempting to define the concept throughout this century without much success. It is accepted, however, that intelligence is a combination of two factors: an innate, *inherited* element that sets a limit on a person's intellectual potential and a learned, *environmental* element that determines how far that potential will be fulfilled. Since there is no such thing as a person who has not been exposed to socialization in some environment, there is no experimental method for measuring either the innate or the learned component on its own. Both are inextricably mixed in any individual.

"Intelligence" is usually measured by an IQ test, which compares the performance of the subject with that of the rest of his or her age group. The IQ test is misnamed, however, for it is not really a test of "intelligence" at all, whatever intelligence may be. It is actually a test of academic aptitude in a very limited range of fields, primarily in linguistic, spatial, symbolic, and mathematical knowledge and reasoning. The tests ignore many other intellectual abilities that are not directly relevant to the school curriculum—such as creativity, social skills, persuasiveness, literary imagination, art appreciation, or the ability to compose music.

Because IQ tests use language and assume basic information on the part of the person being tested, they are *culture-bound.* That is, they require a familiarity with knowledge and assumptions that are more likely to be shared by one group than by another. Children reared in a culture or subculture other than that of the white middle-class America assumed by the tests are consequently at a disadvantage. The fact that a child does not know who discovered America, or cannot select an eggplant, having never heard of or seen one, as the "odd one out" in a series of fruits, does not mean that the child is unintelligent. An American child would not do well on a test that required the subject to select the poisonous insect from a series of four scorpions, but a child reared in the Kalahari Desert would have little difficulty in getting the answer right. What is often tested in IQ tests, then, is not "intelligence" but rather culturally acquired knowledge, which is a very different thing. The middle-class child has greater access to the kind of knowledge, experience, and skills demanded by these tests.

There is also strong evidence that blacks find the testing situation more stressful than whites and that this stress affects their performance. If blacks are tested by a black tester, they do better than if tested by a white. If they are told that their results will be compared with those of other blacks, they do better than if told their results will be compared with those of whites. The average difference in IQ scores between these situations of greater and less stress is about eight points, meaning that this single factor alone can account for more than half of the difference found between the average scores of blacks and whites. For these reasons, very few social scientists accept Jensen's argument. Racial and social class differences in IQ test results are adequately explained by cultural factors. The problem is, however, that IQ tests are widely used as a basis for labeling and tracking students, so that a self-fulfilling prophecy of academic success or failure often follows.

Equality of Educational Opportunity

In a situation of *equal educational opportunity,* we would expect that a random member of any given social class or racial group would have the same probability of ending up in college as a random member of any other group. Accidental factors such as sex, race, or class would not affect educational achievement. A major thrust of recent American domestic policy has been to equalize educational opportunity, particularly between black and white children. The ultimate objective of this policy has been to provide blacks with the educational channels to social mobility that they have been denied in the past.

In 1954, the U.S. Supreme Court ruled that segregated schools were inherently unequal and ordered school systems to desegregate. But progress was painfully slow. By the beginning of this decade, nearly 50 percent of black schoolchildren were attending schools that were over 90 percent black, and almost 80 percent of white children were attending schools that were over 90 percent white. Surprisingly, school desegregation has been much more readily accomplished in the South than in the North, even though most northern states have never had segregated schools by law. The problem in the North has proved much more difficult because school segregation there is largely caused by segregated residential patterns. Black migrants from the South moved to the North in large numbers after World War II and settled primarily in inner-city ghettos. Around the same time the suburbs began to expand rapidly, and whites deserted the city centers—partly, it seems, to avoid sending their children to integrated urban schools. The predominantly black and predominantly white neighborhoods that resulted have now spawned a series of highly segregated local school systems.

This pattern was tolerated until the civil rights movement and the racial disturbances of the sixties finally provoked the federal government into action. The elimination of social inequality between the races became a pressing national concern and, true to form, Americans looked to the schools to do the job.

The Coleman Report

The Civil Rights Act of 1964 directed the Commissioner of Education to investigate inequalities in educational opportunities for the major racial groups, and a team of sociologists led by James Coleman was asked to conduct a major study on the subject. The researchers gathered data from nearly 4000 schools and surveyed some 570,000 students and 60,000 teachers. There was a general expectation that the study would find important differences in the quality of education offered to whites and blacks. Coleman himself predicted that the differences would be "striking" (Hodgson, 1973).

The popular assumption was soon challenged. Coleman (1966) did find a major gap in the achievement of black and white students: 84 percent of blacks performed below the median level of whites. But to his astonishment, he found relatively little difference between predominantly black and predominantly white schools in virtually every factor he analyzed, including expenditure per pupil, age of buildings, library facilities, laboratory facilities, number of books, class size, and teacher characteristics. Although there were some differences in the quality and quantity of the facilities at predominantly black and predominantly white schools, Coleman did not consider that these differences were sufficient to account for differences in pupil achievement. In fact, most of the individual variation in pupil achievement was not between one school or another but

A "Culture Bound" Intelligence Test

These test items were constructed by a black psychologist. The tone is humorous, but the underlying intention is more serious; to show how a person's performance on an IQ test is influenced by cultural knowledge. If you are white, you may find yourself unable to answer a single question.

1. Who did "Stagger Lee" kill?
   (A) His mother, (B) Frankie, (C) Johnny, (D) His girlfriend, (E) Billy.

2. A "gas head" is a person who has a . . .
   (A) Fast-moving car, (B) Stable of "lace," (C) "Process," (D) Habit of stealing cars, (E) Long jail record for arson.

3. If a man is called a "blood," then he is a . . .
   (A) Fighter, (B) Mexican-American, (C) Negro, (D) Hungry hemophile, (E) Redman or Indian.

4. If you throw the dice and 7 is showing on the top, what is facing down?
   (A) Seven, (B) Snake Eyes, (C) Boxcars, (D) Little Joes, (E) 11.

5. Cheap chitlings (not the kind you purchase at a frozen-food counter) will taste rubbery unless they are cooked long enough. How soon can you quit cooking them to eat and enjoy them?
   (A) 45 minutes, (B) 2 hours, (C) 24 hours, (D) 1 week (on a low flame), (E) 1 hour.

6. "Down home" (the South) today, for the average "soul brother" who is picking cotton (in season) from sunup until sundown, what is the average earning (take home) for one full day?
   (A) $.75, (B) $1.65, (C) $3.50,(D) $5, (E) $12.

7. A "handkerchief head" is . . .
   (A) A cool cat, (B) A porter, (C) An Uncle Tom, (D) A hoddi, (E) A preacher.

8. "Jet" is . . .
   (A) An East Oakland motorcycle club, (B) One of the gangs in "West Side Story," (C) A news and gossip magazine, (D) A way of life for the very rich.

9. "And Jesus said, 'Walk together, children . . .' "
   (A) "Don't get weary. There's a great camp meeting," (B) "For we shall overcome," (C) "For the family that walks together talks together," (D) "By your patience you will win your souls" (Luke 21:19), (E) "Mind the things that are above, not the things that are on earth" (Col. 3:3).

10. If a pimp is up tight with a woman who gets state aid, what does he mean when he talks about "Mother's Day"?
    (A) Second Sunday in May, (B) Third Sunday in June, (C) First of every month, (D) None of these, (E) First and fifteenth of every month.

11. Jazz pianist Ahmad Jamal took an Arabic name after becoming really famous. Previously he had some fame with what he called his "slave name." What was his previous name?
    (A) Willie Lee Jackson, (B) LeRoi Jones, (C) Wilbur McDougal, (D) Fritz Jones, (E) Andy Johnson.

12. What is Willie Mae's last name?
    (A) Schwartz, (B) Matsuda, (C) Gomez, (D) Turner, (E) O'Flaherty.

13. What are the "Dixie hummingbirds"?
    (A) A part of the KKK, (B) A swamp disease, (C) A modern gospel group, (D) A Mississippi paramilitary group, (E) Deacons.

14. "Bo Diddley" is a . . .
    (A) Game for children, (B) Down home cheap wine, (C) Down home singer, (D) New dance, (E) Mojo call.

15. "Hully Gully" came from . . .
    (A) East Oakland, (B) Fillmore, (C) Watts, (D) Harlem, (E) Motor City.

16. Which word is most out of place here?
    (A) Slib, (B) Blood, (C) Gray, (D) Spook, (E) Black.

The Answers

1. (E) 3. (C) 5. (C) 7. (C) 9. (A) 11. (D) 13. (C) 15. (C)
2. (C) 4. (A) 6. (D) 8. (C) 10. (E) 12. (D) 14. (C) 16. (C)

Source: *New York Times,* July 2, 1968.

Figure 15.12 In most American communities, the busing of children to ensure racial balance in the classroom has passed without incident. In some cases, however, the white community has reacted with hostility and even violence. The picture shows white New Yorkers protesting the entry of black children to their neighborhood school.

between pupils within the same schools. The kind of facilities a school had at its disposal and the amount of money spent per pupil did not have any significant effect on pupil performance. The cause-and-effect relationship between input of resources and output of achievement, so long taken for granted, hardly existed.

What, then, accounted for the differences in black and white academic achievement? Coleman's crucial finding was that achievement in all schools is related not to the characteristics of the schools but to the social class background of the pupils themselves. He concluded:

> Schools bring little influence to bear on a child's achievement that is independent of his background and general social context. . . . This very lack of independent effect means that the inequalities imposed on children by their home, neighborhood, and peer evaluation are carried along to become the inequalities with which they confront adult life at the end of school.

Black students, it seemed, were underachieving simply because they came from predominantly lower-class homes. White students were doing better because they came from predominantly middle-class homes, where they were better prepared and motivated for the academic demands of school life. When blacks attend desegregated schools their performance improves, Coleman found, because these schools have a more "middle-class" atmosphere. White pupils' achievement in desegregated schools is unaffected by the presence of blacks. Later research has indicated, however, that the achievement of black children in desegregated schools is affected by the level of interracial harmony within the school. Desegregation in an atmosphere of hostility has no beneficial effects on minority group pupils (Pettigrew and Cohen, 1966).

Coleman's findings stimulated interest in *compensatory education* programs for minority group students—programs designed to "compensate" them for supposed deficiencies in family and neighborhood background. The assumption behind these programs was that many members of minority groups suffered from *cultural deprivation* and needed preschool and other training if they were to have an equal chance in the educational system and hence in the world beyond. Although some of these programs were successful, most have proved disappointing, perhaps because the programs were not sufficiently intensive or prolonged. The idea that minority groups are "culturally deprived" has also come in for strong criticism. This notion may simply be another example of white middle-class ethnocentrism toward subcultures whose characteristics are assumed to be inferior simply because they are different.

Coleman's finding that black pupils do better in desegregated schools seemed to provide a strong argument for the busing of pupils from one neighborhood to another to correct racial imbalances in segregated school systems. The great majority of busing programs have been put into effect without difficulty. In some areas, however, particularly where blacks have been bused into such tight-knit "white ethnic" neighborhoods as the Irish community in South Boston, strong resentment and even outright violence have resulted. Opinion polls throughout the seventies have shown that a very large majority of the public favors school integration but that an equally large majority opposes busing as the means to achieve it—even though busing is probably the only means of ensuring a fully integrated school system. There is no doubt that much of this opposition stems from attitudes of outright racism. It is also clear, however, that many whites oppose busing because they fear that the presence of lower-class children in the schools will lower educational standards and because they resent state interference in local community control over education.

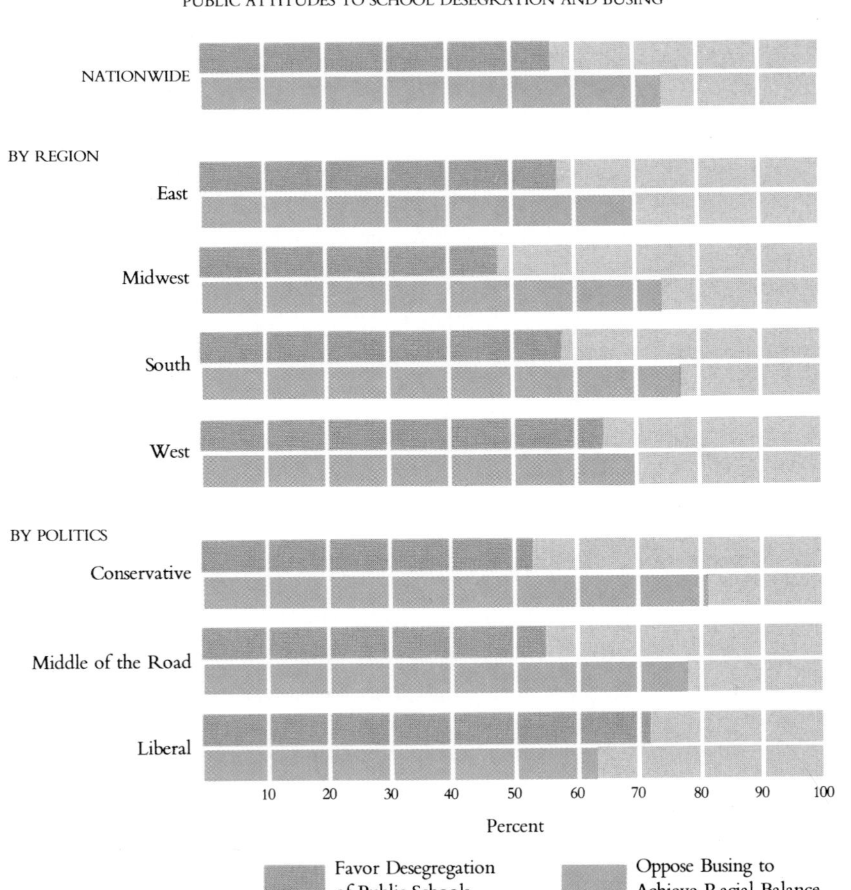

Source: The Harris Survey, "Desegregation? Yes. Busing? No." (October 2, 1975).

Figure 15.13 As these data from a 1975 national opinion poll show, Americans have very different attitudes toward the desirability of school desegregation and the desirability of busing as a means of achieving it. People in every region of the country and in every position on the political spectrum favor the desegregation of schools, but most also oppose busing.

Jencks's Analysis

Faith in the view that social inequality can be reduced by equalizing educational opportunity was further shaken when Christopher Jencks (1972) published his controversial book *Inequality*. After a careful analysis of the available data, Jencks came to the conclusion that the schools have hardly any effect on social inequality. The source of the inequality lies beyond the schools, and the schools merely reflect the situation in the wider society. Equalizing the quality of all elementary schools, he found, would reduce inequalities in measured intelligence by 3 percent or less; equalizing the quality of high schools, by 1 percent or less. Americans, Jencks charges, have a "recurrent fantasy" that schools can solve their problems and are guilty of "muddleheaded ideas about the various causes and cures of poverty and inequality." Attempts to equalize educational opportunity, he contends, will have virtually no impact on student academic performance or on social equality. Economic inequality is certainly related to educational achievement—but it is not caused by it.

Jencks does not argue against spending more money on the schools. But money should be spent, he suggests, in order to make the schools a more pleasant place in which to spend twelve years of life—a highly desirable goal—and not in the misguided belief that social inequality can be reduced in this way. Much more drastic steps are necessary if the goal is to reduce inequality (Bane and Jencks, 1972):

> If we want to eliminate economic inequality, we must make this an explicit objective of public policy rather than deluding ourselves into thinking that we can do it by giving everyone equal opportunity to succeed or fail. . . . This strategy was rejected during the 1960s for the simple reason that it commanded relatively little public support. The required legislation could not have passed Congress, nor could it pass today. That does not mean it is the wrong strategy. It simply means that, until we change the political and moral premises on which most Americans now operate, poverty and inequality will persist at pretty much their present level. . . . If we want to move beyond this tradition, we must establish political control over the economic institutions that shape our society. What we will need, in short, is socialism. Anything less will end in the same disappointment as the reforms of the 1960s.

The findings of Coleman and of Jencks challenge a cherished American belief and have noticeably dampened enthusiasm for using the schools to bring about social change. Their work echoes that of Emile Durkheim, who made the first systematic sociological analysis of education around the turn of the century. The schools, Durkheim pointed out, are primarily concerned with transmitting the culture of the past and perhaps of the present. They are shaped by existing forces in society and therefore cannot be a significant instrument for social change in themselves. The schools will change as other institutions change, and if change is to be brought about, policy makers must focus on other areas of society, particularly the political and economic institutions. The schools will then change, reinforcing the social and cultural changes that have taken place.

Equality of *opportunity* cannot ensure social equality, because people are differently equipped to take advantage of opportunities. It is like giving everyone an equal chance in a footrace, even though some are limp, lame, or have never trained for an athletic event. The "equal" chance merely ensures that those who are already better equipped are able to maintain their advantage. Jencks suggests that a fairer conception of equality would involve equality of *results*, which would require a major redistribution of the nation's wealth. But this is not a concept to which, as a people, Americans have very much commitment. Americans do not really believe in equality, preferring instead to see life as a race to be won by the "fittest"—and our present educational system reflects our values.

Summary

1. Education is the systematic, formalized transmission of knowledge, skills, and values. Mass education is a recent historical development, made necessary by industrialization.

2. American education has a unique combination of characteristics: commitment to mass education, faith in education as a means of solving social problems, a utilitarian emphasis on training for future occupational roles, and a strong tradition of community control.

3. American schools are organized as formal, bureaucratic structures. They place great emphasis on competition, and students of different ability are treated differently. One

consequence of this may be a self-fulfilling prophecy under which pupils perform according to the school's expectations. Student peer groups are a powerful influence on individual behavior in the schools.

4. Education has several important social functions: cultural transmission, social integration, personal development, screening and selection, innovation, and a number of latent functions.

5. A conflict perspective emphasizes that level of education is closely correlated with social mobility, but educational achievement is in turn influenced by social background. The schools thus reinforce existing inequalities.

6. There are many discrepancies in the educational achievement of individuals of different social classes and races. Class and race distinctions overlap, and the racial differences are the product of class differences. Several specific factors account for these class differences: costs of education, family expectations, cultural background, childhood nutrition, language problems, teacher attitudes, labeling of students, and peer-group influence.

7. Measured intelligence is also to some extent correlated with the class and race of the individual. Racial differences in IQ are not inherited; higher-status blacks, for example, have higher average IQ scores than lower-status whites. IQ tests are an unsatisfactory way of measuring intelligence, as they are culture-bound and tend to test learned knowledge, not innate intelligence.

8. Attempts have been made to equalize educational opportunity in the belief that this will lead to greater social equality. The Coleman report, however, found that the quality of school facilities hardly affects student performance; student achievement is primarily determined by class background. Black students do better in desegregated schools, however, because these schools have a more middle-class atmosphere. Christopher Jencks has strongly argued that the schools cannot be used to change society because they merely reflect existing political and economic arrangements: only when these arrangements are changed will the schools change in consequence.

Important Terms

education
utilitarian emphasis
community control
bureaucracy
self-fulfilling prophecy
cultural transmission
social integration
latent functions
social mobility
IQ
equality of opportunity
compensatory education
cultural deprivation

Suggested Readings

BERG, IVAR. *Education and Jobs: The Great Training Robbery.* New York: Praeger, 1970.

A critical account of the relationship between education and employment.

JENCKS, CHRISTOPHER et al. *Inequality.* New York: Basic Books, 1972.

A devastating critique of the American "myth" that the schools can be used to bring about social equality. Jencks includes some provocative suggestions for how this equality could actually be created.

RICHARDSON, KEN, AND DAVID SPEARS (EDS.). *Race and Intelligence.* Baltimore: Penguin, 1972.

A collection of articles on the issue of race and class differences in IQ. The contributors unanimously reject the view that these differences are genetically determined and present formidable evidence to support their opinion.

ROSENTHAL, ROBERT, AND LENORE JACOBSON. *Pygmalion in the Classroom.* New York: Holt, Rinehart and Winston, 1968.

An account of Rosenthal's experiments on the self-fulfilling prophecy in education.

SILBERMAN, CHARLES E. *Crisis in the Classroom.* New York: Random House, 1970.

A lively and trenchant criticism of current American educational practices.

CHAPTER 16 *Religion*

CHAPTER OUTLINE

The Sociological Approach to Religion

Types of Religion

Religion: A Functionalist Analysis
The Work of Durkheim
The Functions of Religion
Functional Equivalents of Religion

Religion: A Conflict Analysis
The Work of Marx
Religion and Social Conflict
The Medieval Witch Craze
Millenarian Movements

Religion and Social Change: The "Protestant Ethic"

Types of Religious Organization

Religion in the United States
Some Characteristics
Correlates of Religious Affiliation
Civil Religion in the United States

Secularization

Every society that we know of has had religious beliefs and practices. Such beliefs and practices are very ancient, predating even the emergence of modern *Homo sapiens.* Among the fossilized remains of Neanderthal cave dwellers, anthropologists have found evidence of funeral ceremonies in the form of flowers and artifacts buried with the dead. These artifacts were presumably intended to accompany the dead people on the journey to the afterlife. Even the primitive Neanderthals, it seems, had some concept of a supernatural realm that lay beyond everyday reality.

Religion is a universal social institution, but it takes a multitude of forms. There are many thousands of religions in the modern world, and as many ways of expressing religious faith. Believers may worship gods, ancestors, and totems; they may practice solitary meditation, mass frenzy, and solemn prayer. The great variety of religious behavior and belief makes "religion" very difficult to define. Sociologists have offered hundreds of definitions in the past, but many of their attempts have been biased by ethnocentric Judeo-Christian ideas about religion. The Western religious tradition contains a number of central beliefs: that there exists one supreme being or God; that God created the universe and all life and takes a continuing interest in the creation; that there is a life hereafter; and that one's moral behavior in this life determines one's fate in the next. In cross-cultural terms, however, this particular combination of beliefs is very rare. Many religions do not believe in a supreme being, and many do not believe in gods at all. Several religions do not include beliefs about the origins of the universe and life; these problems are dealt with instead in nonreligious myth.

(a)

(b)

(c)

(d)

(e)

(f)

Figure 16.1 Some religious rituals and symbols from various parts of the world: (a) a Waura tribesman of the Amazon jungle preparing for a religious ritual; (b) members of the Hare Krishna sect in urban America; (c) a Hindu shrine in Nepal; (d) a monk cleaning a statue of Buddha; (e) a totem pole from a native American community of the Pacific northwest; (f) a baptism in a fundamentalist sect of the American South.

Many religions assume that the gods take little or no interest in human affairs. Many have almost nothing to say about life after death, and many—perhaps most—do not make any connection between earthly morality and one's fate beyond the grave. Religion cannot be defined simply in Judeo-Christian terms. What, then, are its essential features?

A good starting point is the work of Emile Durkheim, one of the first sociologists to study religion. Durkheim pointed out that one feature is found in all religions, a distinction between the sacred and the profane. The *sacred* is anything that inspires awe, reverence, and deep respect. It has extraordinary, supernatural, and often dangerous qualities and can usually be approached only through some form of *ritual,* such as prayer, incantation, or ceremonial cleansing. Anything can be sacred: a god, a rock, the moon, a king, a tree, or a symbol such as a cross. The *profane,* on the other hand, is anything that is regarded as part of the ordinary rather than the supernatural world. Of course, a rock, the moon, a king, a tree, or a symbol may also be considered profane: something becomes sacred or profane only when it is socially defined as such by a *community* of believers.

We can say, then, that *religion is a system of communally held beliefs and practices that are oriented toward some sacred, supernatural realm.* Without this combination of beliefs, practices, some degree of orientation toward the sacred, and a community of believers, there can be no religion. (An individual's private beliefs about the supernatural are not "religion" if they are not shared with others, for religion is a system of beliefs and practices that has become institutionalized and shared by a community.)

The Sociological Approach to Religion

The sociological investigation of religion inevitably risks offending people of all religions, who tend to accept their own doctrines on faith and to regard them as absolute truths. To the sociologist, religion—like any other aspect of culture—is a social product, created by human beings and not by supernatural forces. It is easy for a believer in any particular faith to apply this perspective to other faiths. An ancient Roman would "know" that Jupiter was father of the gods but that Judaism was simply superstition; a believing Jew "knows" that the messiah will one day come but that Jesus was not he. Ethnocentric attitudes of this kind are summed up in a statement by Mr. Thwackum, a character in Henry Fielding's *Tom Jones:* "When I mention religion, I mean the Christian religion; and not only the Christian religion, but the Protestant religion; and not only the Protestant religion, but the Church of England."

The sociologist regards all religions as social products and sees religious faith as arising from socialization or resocialization into a particular set of beliefs. You may be a devout Christian or Jew, but if you had been raised as a Zulu, a Pakistani, or an ancient Greek, your religious beliefs might be very different, although just as devoutly held. The sociological approach does *not* mean, however, that the sociologist cannot personally believe in the doctrines of a particular religion. Many sociologists of religion (for example, Berger, 1970) combine a sociological approach with a personal religious commitment. What the sociological approach does imply is that the sociologist, *as a sociologist,* cannot be concerned with the truth or falsity of religious faith. Sociology is a science, dealing with verifiable facts; in their professional roles sociologists are not competent to pronounce on questions of faith that cannot be scientifically investigated.

Sociologists of religion focus on the complex interrelationship between society and religion. The sociologist can show, for example, that all religions reflect the cultural concerns of the societies in which they arise. For instance, warlike societies tend to have gods of war; agricultural societies, gods of fertility. Strongly patriarchal societies, such as the ancient Israelites, tend to have masculine gods, and it is from the Israelites that Western societies derived the concept of God as "He" rather than "She." Most Christian Westerners, being white, tend to think of both God and Jesus as white. The idea of a black god is almost unimaginable to them, and portraits of Jesus frequently present him as a blond Caucasian rather than as the Semitic-featured person he no doubt was. In many African churches, on the other hand, statues and portraits of Jesus show him with dark, Negroid features. Religion is closely integrated into the culture in which it is found, and an important task of the sociology of religion has been to identify the roles that religion plays in society.

Types of Religion

Sociologists have tried to bring some conceptual order to the study of religion by classifying different religions into a series of basic types. One of the most useful of these classifications is that of Reece McGee (1975), who divides religions into four main types: religions of simple supernaturalism, animism, theism, or abstract ideals. These types are merely artificial categories, of course, and not all religions will fit neatly into this classification.

Simple supernaturalism. This type of religion, which is fairly common in very simple preindustrial societies, recognizes the existence of supernatural forces in the world. Religions of this kind do not include a belief in gods or spirits, but the believers assume that there are supernatural forces that influence human events for better or worse. One example of simple supernaturalism is the Melanesian belief in *mana,* a diffuse, impersonal force that may exist in both people and natural objects. A person does not necessarily have *mana* but can sometimes gain it by performing the appropriate rituals. *Mana* can be good or bad, perhaps causing arrows to fly straight or to miss their target. The nearest Western approximations to this simple supernaturalism are the gambler's belief in "luck" or a soldier's reliance on a protective charm such as a rabbit's foot.

Animism. This kind of religion recognizes active, animate spirits operating in the world. These spirits may be found both in people and in otherwise inanimate natural phenomena such as rivers, winds, mountains, and the weather. The spirits are personified: they are assumed, like human beings, to have motives, will, and emotions. People must sometimes appease the spirits through rituals and must always take account of their activities. But the spirits are not gods, for they are not worshipped. People may try to influence the spirits by the use of *magic,* or rituals that harness supernatural power for human ends. The spirits of animistic religion may be benevolent or evil, or they may even be indifferent to human beings.

Theism. Religions of this kind center on a belief in gods. A god is presumed to be powerful, to be interested at least to some extent in human affairs, and to be worthy of worship. In cross-cultural terms the most common form of theism is *polytheism,* a belief in a number of gods. There is usually a "high god," often the "father" of the other gods and somewhat more powerful than they. The lesser gods generally have specific spheres of influence, such as war, earthquakes, athletics, rain, and so on. A second form of theism is *monotheism,* or belief in a single supreme being. The monotheistic religions of the modern world have the greatest number of adherents, but very few of the religions in the world are monotheistic. The belief is found only in Judaism and its two offshoots, Christianity and Islam. Yet none of these faiths is purely monotheistic. Different versions of Christianity, for example, still contain a number of semidivine lesser figures, such as the Devil, angels, saints, and the Virgin Mary, and some versions regard God as being composed of three different elements, the Father, Son, and Holy Ghost. The fact that we do not actually call any of these figures "gods" may lead us to overlook their divine status. All three religions place such great emphasis on one supreme being, however, that for most purposes they can be considered monotheistic.

Abstract ideals. This type of religion centers not on the worship of a god but rather on ways of thinking and behaving. The goal is to reach an elevated state of being and consciousness, and in this way to fulfill one's human potential to the utmost. The best-known religion of abstract ideals is Buddhism, which is not concerned with worship but with the attempt to become "at one with the universe" through many years of meditation. Some Western belief systems, such as humanism, bear many similarities to religions of abstract ideals, but these belief systems are not truly religious, for they lack the ritual and the orientation toward the sacred and supernatural that characterizes religions.

Most religions do not attempt to win converts, and their adherents are usually indifferent toward or tolerant of the religions of others. Several of the major world religions shown in Figure 16.3, however, have tried to win converts at some point in their history. A common feature of these world religions is that they have a convincing *theodicy,* an emotionally satisfying explanation for the great problems of earthly existence, namely human origins, suffering, and death (Berger, 1969). We are born, live a brief span of years, often suffer, and then die. This universal sequence can easily seem meaningless, but a

Figure 16.2 Only three of the thousands of religions in the world have developed monotheistic beliefs: Judaism, Islam, and Christianity. The latter two have such a large number of adherents, however, that a majority of the world's population believes in a single God. Michaelangelo's portrayal of the creation of Adam suggests a typical feature of monotheistic religion, the assumption that an all-powerful god created the universe and takes a continuing interest in what he has created.

theodicy tries to give it meaning by explaining or justifying the presence of evil and misfortune in the world.

Theodicies can explain these problems in many ways. The Hindu doctrine of reincarnation explains suffering and evil by extending the life span indefinitely. One's present existence becomes only a tiny link in an endless chain, in which death and misery seem only temporary and insignificant. The mysticism of Buddhism or Taoism allows the believer to achieve salvation at a spiritual level, where earthly cares become unimportant. Christian theodicy offers the hope of eternal salvation in heaven in recompense for the cares of earth. In the Calvinist version, worldy woes are the fault of sinful humans, not of God; God's purposes are unfathomable, and He thus cannot be criticized for human misfortune. The Zoroastrian theodicy sees the universe as a battleground between the evenly balanced forces of good and evil. It is the duty of humans to throw their weight on the side of good, and their misfortunes result from their failure to do so. In Shintoism, which focuses on ancestor worship, one's misfortunes and death are made more tolerable by the knowledge that one's life will be remembered and celebrated forever (Berger, 1969).

Religion: A Functionalist Analysis

Our discussion of theodicies implies that religion has some function in social life, and in fact the functionalist perspective offers many insights into the role of religion in society.

The Work of Durkheim

Emile Durkheim, one of the earliest functionalist theorists, was the first sociologist to apply the perspective to religion in a systematic way. His work on the subject, *The Elementary Forms of Religious Life,* was first published in 1912 and has since become a classic. Many of Durkheim's contemporaries regarded religion as hardly worthy of study. They saw it as nothing more than a remnant from a primitive and superstitious past and generally expected that it would disappear in the more sophisticated modern world. But Durkheim was impressed by the fact that religion is universal in human society, and he wondered why this should be so. His answer was that religion has a vital function in maintaining the social system as a whole.

RELIGIOUS POPULATION OF THE WORLD

Religion	N. America	S. America	Europe	Asia	Africa	Oceania	Total
Total Christian	225,504,750	161,583,500	352,597,100	86,811,000	100,465,100	17,104,000	944,065,450
Roman Catholic	128,884,000	151,600,000	171,748,500	45,122,000	32,039,500	3,188,000	532,582,000
Eastern Orthodox ...	4,115,000	54,000	65,534,600	1,835,000	17,410,000	353,000	89,301,600
Protestant	92,505,750	9,929,500	115,314,000	39,854,000	51,015,600	13,563,000	322,181,850
Jewish	6,346,525	678,700	3,960,700	3,026,150	299,465	75,000	14,386,540
Muslim	235,000	191,200	8,730,000	422,208,000	97,678,500	66,000	529,108,700
Zoroastrian	250	.....	.....	224,650	475	.....	225,375
Shinto	55,000	90,000	.....	62,004	.....	.....	62,149,000
Taoist	16,000	12,000	.....	31,360,700	.....	.....	31,388,700
Confucian	96,000	83,000	30,000	205,725,700	500	41,500	205,976,700
Buddhist	148,000	180,300	220,000	247,951,500	2,000	15,000	248,516,800
Hindu	70,000	502,000	350,000	512,418,000	463,400	629,000	514,432,400
Totals	232,471,525	163,320,700	365,887,800	1,571,729,700	198,909,440	17,930,500	2,550,249,665

Source: Encyclopaedia Britannica Book of the Year, 1975.

Figure 16.3 The major religions of the world have achieved their success largely because they offer a satisfying theodicy, or explanation for eternal human problems such as suffering, death, and the meaning of life.

Durkheim reasoned that if he could understand the social role of the most simple form of religion, he would have the key to understanding the role of all religion. He therefore focused on what he believed was the most simple religion in existence, the totemism of Australian aborigines. The *totem* is usually some commonplace object, such as an animal or a plant, and a symbol representing it is sacred. Each aborigine clan is organized around a particular totem, from which the clan takes its name. The totem, then, is sacred but is also the symbol of the society itself. From this fact Durkheim concluded that when people worship religion, they are really worshipping nothing more than their own society: "divinity is merely society transformed and symbolically conceived."

What happens, Durkheim argued, is that the members of the clan gather periodically. This crowd situation creates emotional excitement in which people feel great ecstasy and elation of a kind they would never feel alone. The participants do not recognize that their fervor comes from society but assume it has a supernatural origin: "Men know well that they are acted upon, but they do not know by whom." They pick on some nearby item, such as a plant or animal, and make this the symbol of both their clan gathering (or society) and their experience of fervor and ecstasy (or religion). Their shared religious belief arises from the society and, in turn, it helps to hold the society together.

The solidarity of the community is further enhanced by the rituals that are enacted on religious occasions. These rituals bring people together, reaffirm the values and beliefs of the group, and help to transmit the cultural heritage from one generation to the next. They also serve to maintain taboos and prohibitions; those who violate important norms may be required to undergo ritual punishment or purification. The rituals also offer aid and comfort to the individual in moments of distress, especially at the time of death. The social function of shared religious beliefs and the rituals that go with them is so important, Durkheim argued, that every society needs a religion or at least some belief system that serves the same functions.

Much of the social disorder in modern societies, he contended, stems from the fact that "the old gods are growing old or are already dead, and others are not yet born." In other words, people no longer believe deeply in religion, but they have found no satisfying substitute. Lacking commitment to a shared belief system, people tend to pursue their private interests without regard for their fellows.

The Functions of Religion

Much of Durkheim's work on religion was purely speculative. His account of the origins of religion, for example, would not be accepted by most modern sociologists. The real value of his analysis is his recognition of the vital social functions that religion plays in society. Modern sociologists have elaborated on Durkheim's ideas, and several of these social functions have been identified.

1. Religion functions as a form of social "cement." It unites a community of believers by bringing them together periodically to enact various rituals and by providing them with shared values and beliefs that bind them together.

2. Religion provides individuals with emotional support in the uncertainty of the world. It offers explanations of common human problems and predicaments and gives people a sense of meaning and purpose in a world that might otherwise seem meaningless.

3. Religion reinforces the most important norms of a society, for these tend to become part of religious doctrine and are therefore regarded as sacred. The teachings found in the Bible, the Talmud, the Koran, or the Upanishads would have far less power if they were regarded as the work of ordinary men and not as sacred scriptures. The most important norms of any society—for example, those relating to murder or incest—tend to be incorporated not only in law but also in religious doctrine.

4. Religion helps people during such major events of the life cycle as puberty, marriage, and death. In most traditional societies each of these occasions in the life cycle is surrounded by religious ritual. Although puberty rites are no longer practiced in the United States (the nearest equivalents are high-school graduation ceremonies and the Jewish bar mitzvah), birth, marriage, and death are almost always associated with religious rituals.

Functional Equivalents of Religion

As Durkheim emphasized, a society needs some shared set of beliefs. Although religion fulfills this function, other belief systems may be *functionally equivalent:* that is, they may serve the same function. Many such belief systems have been proposed, including psychotherapy, the values of the "hippie" counterculture, science, humanism, fascism, or communism. Some sociologists believe that these and other belief systems fill the functions of religion so well that they can actually be regarded as "religions."

It is true that some of these belief systems have features similar to those of traditional Western religion. For example, communism has its founding prophet, Karl Marx. It has sacred texts, the works of Marx, Engels, or, in different versions, Mao or Trotsky. It has its saints among those who were martyred in the cause of socialist revolution, such as Che Guevara, and it has its shrines, such as the tomb of Lenin in Moscow's Red Square. Like traditional religion, communism claims to have access to ultimate truth, and regards all alternative views as false. Like traditional religion, it claims to be able to explain suffering in the world. It is also future-oriented. It offers a vision of a better life based on a moral command—"from each according to his ability, to each according to his needs." Like the great world religions, it has a missionary zeal to convert the world to its principles. The experience of conversion to communism can be similar to conversion to a new religion; the novelist Arthur Koestler describes his own conversion (which he later recanted) in these terms (Crossman, 1952):

> Something had clicked in my brain which shook me like a mental explosion. To say that one had "seen the light" is a poor description of the mental rapture which only the convert knows (regardless of what faith he has been converted to). The new light seems to pour from all directions across the skull; the whole universe falls into pattern like the stray pieces of a jigsaw puzzle assembled by magic at one stroke. There is now an answer to every question, doubts and conflicts are a matter of the tortured past—a past already remote, when one had lived in dismal ignorance in the tasteless, colorless world of those who *don't know.*

The essential difference between such belief systems and religion is, of course, that they are not oriented toward the sacred. It is probably best to keep this distinction, referring

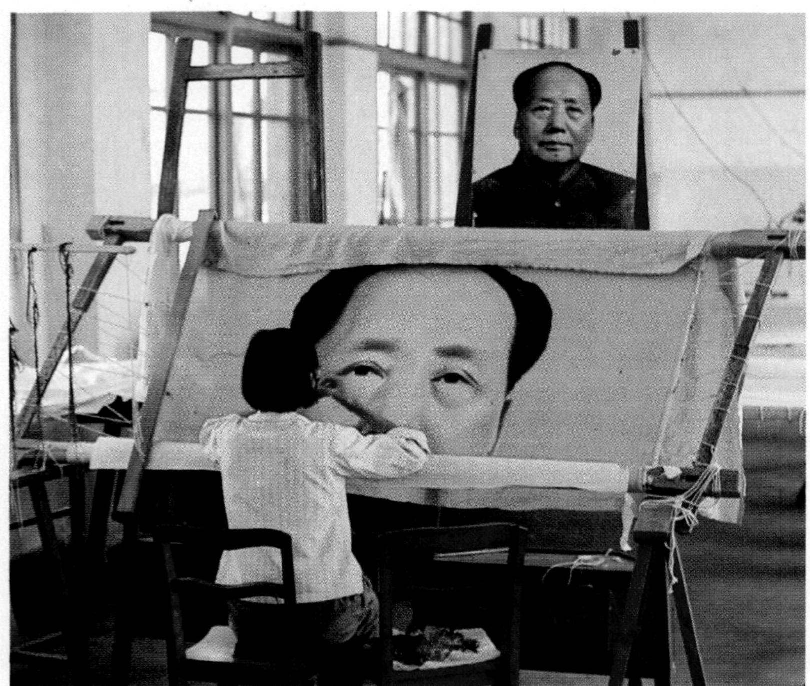

Figure 16.4 Modern communist movements have many similarities with traditional religious movements, and often serve many of the same functions—such as uniting a community through shared rituals and beliefs or providing a sense of purpose in life. Like traditional religions, they also have their "sacred" texts, their martyrs, and their saints. The veneration that communist movements have for their leaders, such as the late Chairman Mao, is also similar to the veneration that religious movements have for their prophets.

to belief systems that are oriented to the sacred as "religion" and worldly belief systems as "functional equivalents" of religion when they seem to serve similar social functions.

Religion: A Conflict Analysis

Although religion may often be functional for society, it can also be deeply implicated in social conflict. A full understanding of the role of religion in society must take account of this fact.

The Work of Marx

The conflict approach to religion derives mainly from the writings of Karl Marx, who saw religion as a form of false consciousness and as a tool of the powerful in the struggles between competing social classes.

To Marx, belief in religion was the profoundest form of human alienation. By *alienation* Marx meant the process through which people lose their sense of control over the social world that they have created, so that they find themselves "alien" in a hostile social environment. Thus, people create systems of government, law, marriage, feudalism, industrialism, or slavery, but they then lose their sense of social authorship of these creations and instead take them for granted as though they were part of an unchanging natural order. Nowhere is this process more poignant than in the field of religion: people create gods, lose their sense of social authorship of religion, and then worship or fear the very gods that they themselves have created. For this reason, declared Marx, "the criticism of religion is the premise of all criticism." In other words, if one can critically understand religion, one can develop a similar understanding of all social institutions.

Moreover, Marx claimed, the *dominant* religion in any society is always the religion of its economically and politically dominant class, and it always provides a justification for existing inequalities and injustices. The dominant religion legitimates the interests of the ruling class and offers "pie in the sky" to the oppressed, thus ensuring that they are satisfied with their lot. Marx proclaimed passionately (1964b, originally published 1848):

> Man makes religion, religion does not make man. . . . Religious suffering is at the same time an expression of real suffering and a protest against real suffering. Religion is the sigh of the oppressed creature, the sentiment of a heartless world, and the soul of soulless conditions. It is the opium of the people.
>
> The abolition of religion, as the illusory happiness of men, is a demand for their real happiness. The call to abandon their illusions about their condition is a call to abandon a condition that requires illusions. . . . The immediate task is to unmask human alienation. . . . Thus the criticism of heaven transforms itself into the criticism of earth, the criticism of religion into the criticism of law, and the criticism of theology into the criticism of politics.

Marx argued that in simple societies, which have no class divisions, religion was simply a matter of superstition. In all other societies, he insisted, the dominant religion supports the *status quo* and diverts the attention of the oppressed from their real problems.

Religion and Social Conflict

There is no shortage of historical examples to justify Marx's view that the dominant religion in any society legitimates the interests of the ruling class. In fact, it is difficult to find a contrary example.

As we saw in Chapter 10 (Social Stratification), the most rigid of all stratification systems has probably been that of India, in which each person is born into and dies a member of a particular caste. This system is intertwined with the Hindu religion and its doctrine of reincarnation. A person's duty is to perform his or her caste obligations; failure to do so will result in reincarnation as a member of a lower caste, or even as an animal. People who believe this are hardly likely to challenge the social order—which is doubtless why the caste system has persisted for several thousand years. In much the same way, the feudal system was justified by the concept of the "divine right" of kings to rule and to delegate some of their authority to the nobles. Revolution against political authority would thus be a revolution against religious authority also, a fact that helped this system to last for several centuries. The institution of slavery was justified by some churches for many years on various biblical grounds, as was the European colonizers' invasion of foreign countries. Missionaries established themselves among "primitive" peoples in the colonies with the *intent* of winning them to Christianity. The *effect,* however, was often to shatter traditional tribal structure and institutions (such as polygamy), to introduce Western values of hard work and deferred gratification, and thus to help transform these independent peoples into a work force for the colonial empires. The conversion of the subject peoples to Christianity often made it easier for the colonists to rule over them: those who believe that the meek shall inherit the earth are not likely to overthrow their rulers.

Religion has also served to legitimate the interests of the dominant class in the United States. Slavery and racial segregation in the South were justified by some churches as being in accordance with God's will, as Kenneth Stampp (1956) notes:

> Through religious instruction the [slaves] learned that slavery had a divine sanction, that insolence was as much an offense against God as against the temporal master. They received the biblical command that servants should obey the masters, and they heard of the punishments awaiting the disobedient slave in the hereafter.

In the North, the possibilities of using religion as a means of social control were also explicitly recognized, although this time religion was directed against potential socialism and radicalism among the millions of impoverished new immigrants. James Hill, the railroad baron, gave a million dollars to the Catholic church on the grounds that for "millions of foreigners" it was "the only authority they fear or respect" (Baltzell, 1958). As Friedrich Engels caustically remarked, religion tends to make the masses "submissive to the behests of the masters it had pleased God to place over them."

Religion is often present, too, in conflicts between societies or between groups of different faiths within a society. A nation at war invariably assumes that its gods are on its side—even when, as in the case of the two World Wars of this century, several of the warring nations worship the same deity. Wars fought on ostensibly religious grounds are often marked by extreme bloodiness and fanaticism, but religious differences are not necessarily the *causes* of the wars, even though the participants themselves may take this view. The medieval crusades, for example, appear at first sight to have been a purely religious conflict between Christians and Muslims. A closer analysis suggests, however, that the crusades were initiated in Europe partly to gain control of the trading routes to the East and partly to divert the considerable unrest that existed among the peasantry at the time. Similarly, the continuing conflict in Northern Ireland seems on the surface to be simply one between Protestants and Catholics, but its roots lie deeper in a conflict between classes and nationalisms. For historical reasons, the Protestants are primarily members of the middle and upper classes and are pro-British, while the Catholics are primarily members of the working class and favor secession from Britain. Religious differences may thus serve as a justification for rather than a cause of conflict: the real origin of the conflict often lies elsewhere.

Let's look at two situations in which religious turmoil masks an underlying social conflict: the medieval witch craze and millenarian movements.

The Medieval Witch Craze

A belief in witchcraft appears in almost all societies, but the reaction to supposed witchcraft in Europe between the fifteenth and seventeenth centuries is without parallel. Basing their action on the biblical text "Thou shalt not suffer a witch to live" (Exodus 22:18), the Protestant and Catholic clergy burned some 500,000 people to death during this period (M. Harris, 1974).

Figure 16.5 The medieval witch craze took the lives of some 500,000 people in Europe between the fifteenth and seventeenth centuries. Once a woman was accused of witchcraft, she was doomed: she would be tortured until she confessed, and then executed; and if she did not confess, she would be executed anyway.

Although the church had discouraged belief in witchcraft for several centuries before this period, the official attitude changed early in the fifteenth century, when it became heretical not to believe in the existence of witches. It was widely believed that thousands of people, mostly old women, had made a pact with the devil. The historian Hugh Trevor-Roper (1967) outlines some of the myths that were accepted at the time:

> Every night these ill-advised ladies were anointing themselves with "devil's grease," made out of the fat of murdered infants, and thus lubricated, were slipping through cracks and keyholes and up chimneys, mounting on broomsticks or spindles or airborne goats, and flying off . . . to a diabolical rendezvous, the Witches' sabbat. . . . They all joined to worship the Devil and danced around him to the sound of macabre music made with curious instruments—horse's skulls, oak logs, human bones, etc. They kissed him in homage, under the tail if he were a goat, on the lips if he were a toad. After which, at a word of command from him, they threw themselves into promiscuous sexual orgies and settled down to a feast. . . . In Savoy, roast or boiled children; in Spain, exhumed corpses, preferably of kinsfolk; in Alsace, fricassees of bats. . . . In the intervals between these acts of public devotion, the old ladies . . . occupied themselves by suckling familiar spirits in the form of weasels, moles, bats, toads, or other convenient creatures.

"Witches" were accused of these and many other crimes—causing hailstorms, crop failures, or sickness. Once the suspects were formally accused of witchcraft there was usually no way out. They were tortured on the rack, often with red-hot irons, until they confessed or died, and if they confessed, they were burned alive. Moreover, the supposed witches were tortured to make them give the names of some of their supposed accomplices—who were tortured in turn until even more people were named. The number of witches naturally multiplied rapidly, and the hysteria about witchcraft grew accordingly. The judges and clergy benefited from the witch craze: they enjoyed the gratitude of the people and even billed the families of the deceased for the cost of the firewood and the celebratory banquets they held after each burning (M. Harris, 1974). For two centuries Europe lived in dread of witches, until more enlightened and rational thought finally gained ascendance on the continent.

How can we explain the witch craze? Again, the conflict perspective is helpful. Two historical factors seem to have played a part. The conflict between Catholicism and Protestantism reached its height during the witch craze, and both churches used the accusation of witchcraft as a means of social control over heretics and potential heretics. More important, however, is the fact that Europe was in a state of deep economic, political, and social unrest at the time. The fear of witchcraft served to divert the attention of the wretched peasantry from the real source of their problems, the church and the state, and onto an illusion instead. As Marvin Harris (1974) suggests:

> The principal result of the witch-hunt system (aside from charred bodies) was that the poor came to believe that they were being victimized by witches and devils instead of princes and popes. Did your roof leak, your cow abort, your oats wither, your wine go sour, your head ache, your baby die? . . . Did the price of bread go up, prices soar, wages fall, jobs grow scarce? It was the work of witches. . . . Against the peoples' phantom enemies, Church and state mounted a bold campaign. . . . The practical significance of the witch mania therefore was that it shifted responsibility for the crisis of late medieval society from both Church and state to imaginary demons in human form. . . . It demobilized the poor and the dispossessed, increased their social distance, filled them with mutual suspicions, pitted neighbor against neighbor, heightened everyone's insecurity, made everyone feel helpless and dependent on the governing class.

Millenarian Movements

A *millenarian movement* is one that prophesies a cataclysmic upheaval within the immediate future, an upheaval that may involve the end of the world, a radical change in the social order, or a return to some golden age of the past. (The word comes from "millenium," the prophesied thousand-year reign of Christ.)

Millenarian movements have been recorded in all parts of the world, but they are found mainly in simple, preindustrial societies that have been colonized by Europeans. The millenarian prophecy often contains a modified version of Judeo-Christian beliefs. The colonized people, for example, may equate themselves with the Israelites in search of the promised land, and the colonizers with the Egyptian oppressors.

A typical millenarian movement arose among the Plains Indians of the United States at the time of their desperate defense of their lands and cultures against the invading settlers. This movement was the Ghost Dance cult, which erupted in the 1870s and again in the 1890s. Various prophets foretold that if the appropriate dances and rituals were performed, the dead ancestors would arise from the grave, the Indians would be immune to the invaders' bullets, and the whites would be driven back to the ocean. The slaughtered buffalo would return in vast numbers, and the old way of life would be restored. Belief in the Ghost Dance cult was destroyed at the Battle of Wounded Knee, where the Indians discovered that they had no immunity whatever to the invaders' bullets (Mooney, 1965).

Figure 16.6 The Ghost Dance cult arose among the Plains Indians after they had been defeated in battle several times. Military attempts to restore their lost lands and shattered culture had failed, and they turned instead to a religious means. Millenarian movements of this kind have frequently occurred in colonial situations.

Another millenarian movement arose among the Xhosa, a tribe of nomadic pastoralists in southern Africa. In the middle of the last century they encountered Dutch settlers, themselves nomadic pastoralists, who were penetrating the continent from the south. The competing groups fought several bloody wars, which the Dutch settlers won as a result of their superior military technology. A prophet arose among the Xhosa, claiming that if the people slaughtered all their cattle and destroyed all their stores of food, the sun would rise blood red the following day. Cattle, grain, and guns would emerge from the ground, the dead ancestors would return, and the whites would be driven back to the ocean from which they had come. The Xhosa accepted the prophecy, destroyed their cattle and food, and waited on the hilltops for the blood-red dawn. At least twenty thousand of them starved to death.

How can we explain these diverse millenarian movements? The conflict perspective is useful here, for it directs attention to the fact that all millenarian movements draw their recruits from disadvantaged members of society. The movements are, in effect, "religions of the oppressed" (Lanternari, 1963). Before adopting the new religion, the members have felt a sense of injustice or deprivation. The religion offers compensation—not as "pie-in-the-sky" in the hereafter, but here and soon on earth. The recruits are people whose traditional norms and values no longer enable them to make sense of their situation. The millenarian movement provides new norms and values and a sense of purpose once more. An important feature of these movements, however, is that they often serve as the forerunner to militant political movements (Cohn, 1962; Worsley, 1968). The millenarian movement provides the basis for group unity and collective organization, which in turn makes political action possible.

Religious values, then, are often a source of radical

Figure 16.7 An interesting form of millenarian movement is the "cargo cult" of Melanesia. When the Melanesians of the South Pacific were colonized by Europeans, they were deeply impressed by the quantity and variety of goods that arrived as cargo into their country. Prophets declared that the cargo was being manufactured and sent to the Melanesians by their own ancestors, but was being intercepted by the colonists. Millenarian movements arose, typically prophesying that if all crops and food were destroyed and if harbors (and later, airstrips) were built, cargo would miraculously appear. In a few cases the prophecies were confirmed: when the Melanesians had destroyed their food stocks, the colonial administration was obliged to ship in fresh supplies to prevent mass starvation —an event that gave added impetus to the movements. Cargo cults persist in Melanesia to this day.

change. Although the conversion of colonial peoples to Christianity may initially have led them to accept colonial rule, their newly acquired Christian values later encouraged them to reject it. Many of the leaders of colonial nationalist movements had been educated in mission schools, where they were taught Christian ideals—and took them seriously. Similarly, religious values have played an important part in many other social movements, such as those to abolish slavery and to bring about civil rights in the United States. While religion may often have a conservative role in maintaining the status quo, it can also provide the impetus for social change.

Religion and Social Change: The "Protestant Ethic"

The role of religion (or any other belief system) in social change is an important topic in sociology. There is a long-standing controversy over whether ideas and beliefs influence changes in culture and social structure or whether culture and social structure instead determine the content of beliefs.

Karl Marx was the first social theorist to address this question. He argued that all human culture can be divided into two basic categories: real or *material* culture (such as the reality of economic life) and the more abstract *ideal* culture (such as ideas, law, philosophy, and religion). The material culture, he believed, is paramount. The economic base of a society influences the character of its belief systems, and these ideas merely justify the existing economic arrangements in general and the class system in particular. Religion thus reflects but does not change society.

Max Weber partially disagreed with this view. He accepted that Marx's approach was useful and might be correct in many instances, but he maintained that under certain circumstances religious or other ideas could influence social change. Weber was fascinated by the growth of modern capitalism, which was rapidly transforming the European and American societies of his time. But why had capitalism first emerged in Europe rather than in, say, China or India? Weber undertook a massive study of the major world religions and the societies in which they are found and concluded that the answer lay in a specific religious belief—Calvinism and other forms of Protestant Puritanism.

Modern capitalism, Weber pointed out, is unlike traditional commercial activity. The pirates or merchants of old earned money in a haphazard way, spent it as it came in luxurious living, and regarded the consumption of wealth as a higher value than the earning of it. Capitalism, on the other hand, requires rational, calculated procedures (such as accounting) in the methodical attempt to accumulate money. Hard work and making money are regarded as high values in themselves, but the spending of money in luxurious living is disreputable. Instead, the capital must be reinvested to earn yet more capital.

Weber argued that this approach stemmed from the "Protestant ethic" of hard work and deferred gratification. The early Calvinists believed that they had been predestined by God to salvation in heaven or damnation in hell since the beginning of time. No one could do anything to change his or her fate, and only a small minority were among the elect who would go to heaven. The duty of believers was to abstain from pleasure and to spend their lives working for the glory of God. But because of their great psychological anxiety about their ultimate fate, the Calvinists looked for "signs" that they were among the elect—and found these signs in their worldly success. The more successful a person was at work, the more likely he or she was to be among the elect—and since profits could not be spent on pleasure, they had to be reinvested. Thus, argued Weber, modern capitalism was born. By a historical irony, the very people who rejected material comforts unwittingly created industrial capitalism, the foundation for the affluence of modern societies. By a further supreme irony, industrialism in turn encouraged the development of the modern rational-scientific world view, in which religion has little place. Modern capitalists, although they are no longer Puritans, have retained the "Protestant ethic" on which their success is largely founded (Weber, 1958a, originally published 1904).

Other religions, Weber argued, did not provide the same incentive for this kind of social and economic change. Catholicism stresses rewards in heaven and encourages people to be satisfied with their lot on earth. Hinduism threatens a lower form of life after reincarnation to anyone who tries to leave his or her caste status. Buddhism stresses mysticism, far removed from earthly goals. Taoism requires the believer to withdraw from worldly temptations. Confucianism emphasizes a static social structure as a part of the natural order. Although Islam is an activist religion, it lacks the emphasis on thrift and hard work. All these religions, according to Weber, served to discourage the growth of capitalist industrialism (Weber, 1951, 1952, 1958b, 1963).

Figure 16.8 Capitalism was quite unlike earlier commercial activity in that profits were not immediately spent on personal gratification. Instead, they were saved and reinvested to produce ever-greater profits. The increased rate of capital investment made possible the historic "takeoff" into modern industrialism. This portrait of a banker and his wife captures the distinctive spirit of early capitalism.

Weber's thesis is often misunderstood and misrepresented, even in college textbooks. Weber did not mean to disprove Marx's view that society usually shapes belief systems rather than vice versa. Nor did he mean to prove that the "Protestant ethic" was the "cause" of capitalism—merely that it was an important influence. And Weber did not believe that he had proved this thesis. He offered it only as a tentative hypothesis.

It is certainly possible that Weber was wrong about the origin of capitalism. Capitalism did not occur in some Calvinist societies, and it sometimes occurred in non-Calvinist societies. England, the birthplace of the Industrial Revolution, was not Calvinist; Scotland, which was Calvinist, failed to develop early capitalism. There is no way of proving that the "salvation panic" of the Calvinists led them to become capitalists. They may have done so for other reasons, such as the fact that they were more likely than Catholics to live in urban areas, or that their religion encouraged hard work, or even that they were not so wedded to tradition as were Catholics of the time. Weber's hypothesis is one of the most provocative in all sociology, but its subject is so vast and complex that his argument is probably unverifiable. Weber simply bit off more than he or anyone else could chew.

Most Western sociologists probably accept Weber's hypothesis as being at least plausible, and they generally agree that religion or other belief systems can influence society. The material and ideal components of culture are best seen as parts of an interacting system, each influencing the other in different ways at different times.

Types of Religious Organization

The "Protestant ethic" arose in a religious movement that had broken away from a larger and more established body, the Catholic church. The Catholic church, in turn, had originated centuries earlier as an offshoot of Judaism. These are but two examples of a constant process by which new and different religious organizations are formed.

Religious organizations can be conveniently divided into one of four basic types: the ecclesia, the denomination, the sect, and the cult. The distinctions are important because participation in one of these types of organization correlates with specific types of belief and practice.

The *ecclesia* is a religious organization that claims the membership of everyone in a society or even in several societies. It is closely intertwined with the state and is considered the "official" religion of the society. The ecclesia is a powerful, bureaucratized organization that gives full support to the state authorities and expects full support from them in return. The Roman Catholic church was such an ecclesia for centuries until Protestantism began to compete with it in many countries. There is probably no pure type of ecclesia in the modern world, but there are several religious organizations that approximate this type—the Anglican church in England, the Lutheran church in Scandinavia, the Catholic church in Spain, and Islam in Saudi Arabia.

The *denomination* is one of two or more religious organizations that claim the allegiance of a substantial part of a population. The denomination cannot claim from and does not provide full support to the state and may be at odds with it on occasion. It is well established and "respectable," and, like the ecclesia, has a formal, bureaucratic structure, with trained clergy and other officials. It is generally tolerant of other denominations, although they may compete for recruits. The Catholic church in the United States and the various Protestant churches are examples of this type.

The *sect* is a less formally organized body, usually one that has split off from a denomination. Its members are generally recruited by conversion rather than born into the faith. The sect is dogmatic and fundamentalist, believing in a literal interpretation of the scriptures and demanding that members give continuing proof of their faith. There is usually no trained clergy. The sect is intolerant of other groups and is indifferent or hostile to political authority. Its members are drawn primarily from the lower social class, and its rituals emphasize emotion and spontaneity. Most sects tend to be short-lived, but some gradually become denominations—always with an accompanying loss of fervor and an increase in social respectability. Christianity was originally a breakaway sect from Judaism, and Mormonism was originally a breakaway sect from Christianity. Contemporary sects include the Jehovah's Witnesses, the Assembly of God, the Seventh Day Adventists, and the various pentecostal and evangelical movements.

The *cult* is the most loosely organized and short-lived

CHARACTERISTICS OF SECTS AND CHURCHES

Characteristic	*Sect*	*Denomination (Church)*
Size	Small	Large
Relationship with other religious groups	Rejects—feels that the sect alone has the "truth"	Accepts other denominations and is able to work in harmony with them
Wealth (church property, buildings, salary of clergy, income of members)	Limited	Extensive
Religious services	Emotional emphasis—try to recapture conversion thrill; informal; extensive congregational participation	Intellectual emphasis; concern with teaching; formal; limited congregational participation
Clergy	Unspecialized; little if any professional training; frequently part-time	Specialized; professionally trained; full-time
Doctrines	Literal interpretation of scriptures; emphasis upon other-worldly rewards	Liberal interpretations of scriptures; emphasis upon this-worldly rewards
Membership requirements	Conversion experience; emotional commitment	Born into group or ritualistic requirements; intellectual commitment
Relationship with secular world	"At war" with the secular world which is defined as being "evil"	Endorses prevailing culture and social organization
Social class of members	Mainly lower class	Mainly middle class

Source: Glenn M. Vernon, *Sociology of Religion* (New York: McGraw-Hill, 1962), p. 174.

Figure 16.9 The two most important forms of religious organization in the United States are the church (denomination) and the sect. The church is more "respectable" than the sect; its members have higher social status, it interprets scriptures more liberally, and it is more inclined to make compromises with secular society.

of all forms of religious organization. It has few coherent doctrines and imposes minimal requirements on believers. There is little demand for moral purity; instead, the cult focuses on the personal benefits and experiences that members gain. Modern examples of the cult might include such very loosely organized groups as believers in astrology, black magic, or transcendental meditation.

The cult and the ecclesia play a relatively unimportant role in society, and most sociologists focus on the distinctions between denominations and sects, often using the term "church" to refer to the denominations. As we will see, there are marked differences in the religious beliefs and practices of the various American churches and sects.

Religion in the United States

Many of the founding fathers of the United States were suspicious of organized religion. In the Europe from which the early settlers had recently emigrated, the church had great political influence and was closely associated with the state. The influence of the church was generally a very conservative one, and organized religion was seen by many radicals of the time as a buttress of the monarchy and its absolute rule. In the two hundred years since then, however, religion has come to be one of the most highly regarded of American institutions, and one of the least politically controversial.

Some Characteristics

Americans consider themselves a deeply religious people, and religion plays an important role in American life. This role is different in many respects from that of religion in other societies, however, for the American institution has several distinctive characteristics.

1. The United States has no official, "established" religion. The Constitution specifically separates church from state, and freedom of religious belief is an important value in America. Unlike many other societies, the United States has no formal, legal, or "official" assumptions that one particular faith is more "true" than any other.

2. Americans have a high degree of tolerance for religious diversity, particularly within the Christian churches. All religions, so long as they are institutionalized and thus "respectable," are considered equally valid and acceptable. Officials of different religions avoid public debates over dogma and other potentially controversial theological issues. Sects and cults, such as the Jehovah's Witnesses, the Jesus freaks, the "Moonies," or the Hare Krishna movement, do not receive quite the same tolerance, but their right to exist and to propagate their beliefs is scarcely questioned.

3. Americans are expected to be religious—not necessarily in the sense of attending church or synagogue and taking part in religious rituals, but in the sense of believing in God and expressing at least some lip service to religious principles. A candidate for public office, for example, would be at a distinct disadvantage if it were known that he or she was a professed atheist. The same is true of other areas of national life. School principals, for example, ought not to be openly irreligious.

4. Senior members of the clergy of all faiths enjoy very high social status. Unlike business or political leaders, they are normally beyond the pale of personal attack; the only major exception to this rule occurs when they become involved in controversial political issues.

5. Religion in the United States is not merely a set of beliefs and practices. It is also an ascribed social status. Many subcultures, particularly Catholic ethnic groups, derive much of their identity from their religion, which is one of the most important features differentiating them from other Americans. These groups make considerable use of church schools instead of public schools, a practice that enhances group identification among younger ethnic group members who might otherwise be more readily assimilated into the American mainstream.

Figure 16.10 Religious sects and cults, such as that of Guru Maharaj Ji, have attracted large numbers of youthful adherents in recent years. Although these religious movements lack the "respectability" of the more established churches, Americans are generally tolerant of the religious diversity they represent.

Correlates of Religious Affiliation

Membership in a particular church or sect has a number of important correlates. One of the most important is the relationship between church or sect and social class. Among whites there is a strong correlation between Protestantism and high social status, and within the Protestant churches there is a close correlation between level of income and membership in the various denominations. The denominations with the largest percentage of upper-income members are the Christian Scientists and the Episcopalians, followed by Congregationalists, Presbyterians, Methodists, Lutherans, and Baptists. People who are upwardly socially mobile tend to switch from one denomination to another as their social status rises (Schneider, 1952; Gockel, 1969).

In an influential but still controversial study conducted in Detroit, Gerhard Lenski (1966b) found that the "religious factor" seemed to have as much influence on attitudes and behavior as social class status. Religious affiliation correlated strongly with many other variables, such as personal values, dropping out of school, and career success. Lenski insisted that religious affiliation did not merely correlate with these characteristics; it actually caused them. This conclusion has been criticized by many sociologists, and it is in any case difficult to prove because so many factors (particularly ethnic group membership) may intervene. Another finding, from a 1971 Gallup poll, illustrates the difficulty of interpreting these kinds of data. The poll found that 40 percent of Jews enter the professions and business, compared with 20 percent of Catholics and 22 percent of Protestants. But this does not mean that the religious affiliation of Jews is the cause of this tendency. American Jews are overwhelmingly an urban subculture, and professional and business opportunities are concentrated in cities. The mere fact that Jews have easier access to these opportunities might explain their disproportionate representation in these fields.

Party political affiliation, too, is closely linked with religion in some instances. A 1971 Gallup poll found that only 6 percent of Jews were Republican, whereas 63 percent were Democratic; 19 percent of Catholics were Republican, and 52 percent were Democratic. Only in the Protestant faith is religion a poor predictor of political attitudes: 33 percent were Republican and 39 percent Democratic. It is likely, however, that race is an important variable in the political attitudes of Protestants, with black Protestants being overwhelmingly Democratic and many white Protestants being Republican.

Religion in the United States is generally, though by no means always, a conservative force in society, and this appears to be particularly true of the Protestant churches. During the social turmoil of the sixties, Rodney Stark and his associates (1971) found that more than a third of a random sample of Protestant ministers in California had never commented in their sermons on the major issue of the day, the Vietnam War. The more literally the clergymen interpreted the Bible, the less likely they were to preach about social problems. Lay members of the organized religions, too, tend to be politically conservative. One national survey found that nearly three-quarters of the lay members would be upset if their minister, priest, or rabbi were to participate in a picket or demonstration.

Another study (Glock and Stark, 1966) found that people who attend church frequently and who believe in orthodox religious doctrine are politically more conservative and more prejudiced against minority groups than people who are less religious on these criteria. A majority of churchgoers were found to be prejudiced against minority groups, including Jews. Half of the churchgoing Christians in the United States, in fact, still blame the Jews for the crucifixion of Jesus, even though this view has no basis in either Christian doctrine or historical fact. On the same page of a questionnaire on which the overwhelming majority of respondents had declared their commitment to Christian brotherhood, more than 40 percent said they would move their homes if several black families came to live in their neighborhoods, and nearly a third said they did not want blacks in their churches. Regular churchgoers were also less likely to give time and money to charity than those who did not attend church regularly. This evidence does not mean, of course, that religious affiliation is a *cause* of these attitudes. It may be that conservative people are more attracted than liberals by organized religion, or even that conservatives tend to live in areas where church attendance is expected by local customs and norms.

The actual content of religious belief also varies from one denomination or sect to another. A study by Charles

RELIGIOUS BELIEFS OF PEOPLE BELONGING TO DIFFERENT CHRISTIAN CHURCHES AND SECTS (IN PERCENT)

Congregational	Methodist	Episcopalian	Disciples of Christ	Presbyterian	American Lutheran	American Baptist	Missouri Lutheran	Southern Baptist	Sects	Total Protestant	Roman Catholic
I know God really exists and I have no doubts about it.											
41	60	63	76	75	73	78	81	99	96	71	81
Jesus is the Divine Son of God and I have no doubts about it.											
40	54	59	74	72	74	76	93	99	97	69	86
Jesus was born of a virgin. Percentage who said "completely true."											
21	34	39	62	57	66	69	92	99	96	57	81
Miracles actually happened just as the Bible says they did.											
28	37	41	62	58	69	62	89	92	92	57	74
There is a life beyond death. Percentage who answered "completely true."											
36	49	53	64	69	70	72	84	97	94	65	75
The Devil actually exists. Percentage who answered "completely true."											
6	13	17	18	31	49	49	77	92	90	38	66

Source: Charles Y. Glock and Rodney Stark, *American Piety: The Nature of Religious Commitment* (Berkeley: University of California Press, 1968), Chap. 2.

Figure 16.11 The extent to which Christians accept some basic doctrines of their religion varies sharply from one denomination or sect to another; sect members are much more likely to accept the truth of the doctrines.

Glock and Rodney Stark (1968) found sharp differences in the extent of belief in basic Christian doctrines among various denominations and sects. For example, only 21 percent of Congregationalists, compared with 96 percent of members of various sects, believe that Jesus was born of a virgin (see Figure 16.11).

Civil Religion in the United States

Weekly church attendance in the United States averaged nearly 50 percent of the population in 1955 and has since dropped slowly to around 40 percent in the seventies. This attendance rate is by far the highest in the advanced industrial societies of the world; in Britain, by comparison, the weekly attendance rate is 10 percent. Does this mean that Americans are a very religious people?

The Bureau of the Census has asked Americans about their religious beliefs only once, in 1966. It found that 96 percent of a representative sample declared some religious faith; only 3 percent claimed to have no religion, and 1 percent refused to answer the question. In another survey, Rodney Stark and Charles Glock (1965) asked people "Do you, personally, believe in God?" Again, 96 percent answered in the affirmative. A 1976 Gallup poll reported a similar finding: 94 percent of Americans claim to believe in "God or a universal spirit." The poll, which surveyed sixty nations, found that the United States ranks behind only one other country, India, in terms of professed religious commitment. In no European country, for example, does a majority of the population believe in life after death (the highest figure is 48 percent among Italians). Nearly 70 percent of Americans, however, profess this belief. The evidence seems to indicate that we are a remarkably religious people.

Or are we? Most sociologists think not. Attendance at church or even a declaration of belief in God are not necessarily good evidence for religious commitment, unless we know why people attend church and what kind of god they believe in. Will Herberg (1960) argues that the United States is "at once the most secular and the most religious of societies" and suggests that, apart from a few sects, the churches of America really worship "the American way of life." Americans tend to use religion primarily for social rather than religious purposes, finding in their church a source of community and in its beliefs a justification for the American values of good neighborliness, self-help, individualism, hard work, and anticommunism. Being a good American involves being religious; President Eisenhower once commented that it did not matter which religion a person believed in, as long as he had one.

Robert Bellah (1970) has suggested that the United States really has a "civil religion," in which religious elements are used to sanctify and celebrate our way of life. The pledge of allegiance declares that we are one nation "under God." Our coins declare: "In God we trust." Americans often seem to believe that their social order and historical mission are specifically sanctioned by God. John F. Kennedy captured this idea in his inaugural address:

> With a good conscience our only sure reward, with history the final judge of our deeds, let us go forth to lead the land we love, asking His blessing and His help, but knowing that here on earth God's work must truly be our own.

Political leaders must always pay at least lip service to religious belief; in fact, every presidential inaugural except one (Washington's second) makes mention of God (Eitzen, 1974). Religion is present at inaugurals, at oaths of office, at party conventions, in courtroom procedures, and indeed at nearly all formal public occasions. Even the Boy Scouts give a "God and country" award, a term that implies, to say the least, a compatibility of interest between the two. Many of our secular symbols also have a sacred quality—the flag, the eagle, the Constitution, the Bill of Rights, "America the Beautiful," "The Star-Spangled Banner," Washington, Jefferson, and Lincoln. This civil religion is not Catholic, Protestant, Jewish, or allied to any other faith; as Stanley Eitzen points out:

> Civil religion is not a specific creed. It is a set of beliefs, symbols and rituals broad enough for all citizens to accept. The God of civil religion is all things to all people.

Secularization

Secularization is the process by which traditional religious beliefs and institutions lose their influence in society. As industrialization advances, the general historical tendency is for societies to become increasingly secular, or worldy, in their values, beliefs, and institutions. What causes this process, how far has it advanced, and what is the future, if any, of religion?

The principal cause of secularization is to be found in the complexity of modern urbanized, industrialized society. In small-scale, simple societies, religion extends to every aspect of experience. It suffuses all social institutions—law, family, art, politics, economic activity. Everyday routines, such as eating, hunting, or caring for the sick, are surrounded with religious ritual. Most people have much the same kind of daily tasks and experiences, and they share readily in a common, unchallenged belief system.

In a complex modern society, however, many new specialized institutions arise. Medical institutions take care of the sick, welfare agencies aid the poor, legal institutions handle deviant behavior, educational institutions transmit knowledge, scientific institutions explain the universe, economic institutions organize the production and distribution of goods, political institutions oversee society. Religion becomes a separate and distinct institution with a limited field of influence, and may even find itself in competition with other institutions, such as science or government. People play highly specific occupational roles and follow different life-styles, and their varying experiences lead them to view the world in different ways. Religious belief is no longer self-evidently true. Religion loses its monopoly of faith and has to compete with alternative belief systems, including even atheism. For the first time, people have a measure of choice about what they will believe, and many opt for different interpretations of reality. Religious values, which once seemed relevant to every area of experience, may appear to have little relevance to many aspects of daily life. Religious commitment, if it exists at all, tends to become part-time rather than total (Luckmann, 1967).

A complex modern industrial society is necessarily based on a scientific, rational view of the world. In many areas of knowledge, science offers a more plausible explanation than traditional religion. The natural sciences have cast in doubt many scriptural teachings, such as the account of God's creation of the earth. The social sciences have also undermined religious belief, by revealing possible sociological and psychological explanations of religion and thus suggesting that religious doctrine is a human and not a divine product. The educated citizen of a modern society, who has access to an unprecedented quantity of historical and cross-cultural information, is much more likely than the inhabitant of a simple, preliterate society to see religious belief in relativistic rather than absolute terms.

The process of secularization may be measured in several ways. One is the extent to which religion becomes a separate and distinct institution with a limited role in society. As religion loses its earlier control over other areas of social life, it becomes a marginal rather than an all-encompassing institution. This process is occurring in all industrial societies.

A second measure of secularization is the extent to which the churches have adapted their teachings and rituals in order to come to terms with secular society. The modern church faces a hard choice: it can either stick to traditional doctrines at the risk of losing members and becoming a sect, or it can modify its teachings and practices and thus become secularized from within. Many churches attempt to become more "relevant" to the modern world—by establishing youth centers or by becoming politically active, for example—but they lose many of their traditional and most distinctive features in the process. As Peter Berger (1970) suggests, the churches and secular society are engaged in a bargaining process, but the compromise inevitably favors the stronger party, secular society. The churches may thus become more concerned with preserving themselves than with their original mission.

A third measure of secularization is the declining membership of the churches and the decreasing attendance at worship and other rituals. This process is in fact difficult to measure and interpret. Figures for church membership are highly unreliable. Some churches count as a member everyone who has been baptized; some, everyone who has affirmed membership as an adult; and some, the entire group that they feel ought to belong. Attendance statistics

Figure 16.12 Many American churches have tried to counter the charge that they are irrelevant by becoming more deeply involved in secular activities, ranging from youth clubs to political activism. Critics of this tendency protest that the churches risk loosing sight of their traditional religious role in society.

are also suspect because they are not necessarily a good measure of how "religious" people actually are. One can attend church for many reasons, ranging from habit to piety to the desire for social status. The evidence from all industrial societies, however, points to a steady decline in church membership and attendance.

What of the future of religion? For many years it was widely felt that as science progressively provided rational explanations for the mysteries of the universe, religion would have less and less of a role to play and would eventually disappear, unmasked as nothing more than superstition. No serious thinker accepts that view today. There are still gaps in our understanding that science can

PERCENTAGE ATTENDING CHURCH IN THE UNITED STATES DURING AVERAGE WEEK

1955	49	1966	44
1956	46	1967	45
1957	47	1968	43
1958	49	1969	42
1959	47	1970	42
1960	47	1971	40
1961	47	1972	40
1962	46	1973	40
1963	46	1974	40
1964	45	1975	40
1965	44	1976	42

Source: Gallup Polls

Figure 16.13 The percentage of Americans who attend church during an average week has been declining fairly steadily for the last two decades, with attendance figures dropping most rapidly among Catholics. Major Protestant denominations have also lost participants, but this trend has been offset by increased participation in fundamentalist Protestant sects, such as the "Jesus freaks." American church attendance is still significantly higher, however, than attendance in any other advanced industrial society.

never fill. On the most ultimately important questions—of the meaning and purpose of life and the real nature of morality—science is utterly silent and, by its very nature, always will be. We can probably anticipate a continuing decline in allegiance to traditional, church-oriented religion, for these belief systems will have to compete with an increasing number of other systems that many people will find at least as rationally or emotionally satisfying. But this does not mean that there will be no place for a belief in the sacred and the supernatural. Few citizens of modern societies would utterly deny the possibility of some supernatural, transcendental realm that lies beyond the boundaries of ordinary experience, and in this fundamental sense religion is probably here to stay.

Summary

1. Religion is a system of communally held beliefs and practices that are oriented toward some sacred, supernatural realm. According to Durkheim, all religions distinguish between the sacred and the profane.

2. The sociological approach to religion is to view it as a social product, like any other part of culture, and to trace the interrelationships between religion and society.

3. Religions can be conveniently classified into four main types: simple supernaturalism, animism, theism, and abstract ideals. The major world religions have convincing theodicies, or explanations of the human predicament.

4. Durkheim analyzed the totemism of Australian aborigines from a functionalist perspective and concluded that religious belief and ritual function to enhance social solidarity. The most important functions of religion are those of "cementing" society, providing emotional support by giving believers meaning and purpose in life, reinforcing social norms, and marking the major points of the life cycle. Some secular belief systems, such as communism, may serve as functional equivalents of religion in some respects.

5. Marx analyzed religion from a conflict perspective. He saw religious belief as a form of alienation and argued that the dominant religion tends to support the status quo in any society. Religion does play this role in many societies and is often an element in social conflict, as the examples of the medieval witch craze and millenarian movements suggest. Religion can, however, sometimes be a source of radical change.

6. According to Weber's "Protestant ethic" thesis, modern capitalism arose partly as a result of the Puritan tendency to work hard and reinvest money rather than spend it. His theory allows a greater role for ideas in social change than Marx's theory does. Marx saw ideas as reflecting rather than causing change.

7. The United States has no established religion, is relatively tolerant of religious diversity, expects at least lip service to religious ideals from its citizens, grants clergy high status, and contains subcultures whose members' statuses are ascribed on religious grounds.

8. There are four main types of religious organization: the ecclesia, the denomination, the sect, and the cult. Membership in various denominations and sects correlates with but does not necessarily have a causal influence on many other variables, including social status, political affiliation and attitudes, and religious beliefs.

9. Although the level of participation in religious organizations is exceptionally high in the United States, Americans are not an especially religious people; the United States has, in effect, a civil religion that exalts American virtues and downplays religious doctrine.

10. Secularization is taking place in all industrial societies as they become more diversified and the influence of the religious institution shrinks. The role of organized religion in a heterogeneous modern society may continue to decline, but religion still addresses important problems that other belief systems ignore, and religious faith is for this reason likely to persist.

Important Terms

sacred	theodicy
profane	totem
ritual	functional equivalent
religion	alienation
simple supernaturalism	millenarian movement
animism	ecclesia
magic	denomination
theism	sect
polytheism	cult
monotheism	secularization
abstract ideals	

Suggested Readings

BERGER, PETER L. *A Rumor of Angels: Modern Society and the Rediscovery of the Supernatural.* New York: Doubleday, 1969.

Thoughtfully and elegantly written, this book argues that there is still a place for religion in the modern world and that a sociological approach to religion can be combined with religious faith.

GLOCK, CHARLES Y. *Religion in Sociological Perspective: Essays in the Empirical Study of Religion.* Belmont, Calif.: Wadsworth, 1973.

An excellent collection of articles by modern sociologists of religion. The selection gives a good overview of current research in the field.

KELLY, DEAN M. *Why the Conservative Churches Are Growing: A Study in the Sociology of Religion.* New York: Harper & Row, 1972.

A sociologist looks at an unexpected phenomenon in modern America: the rapid growth in membership of fundamentalist Christian sects at a time when other denominations are reporting declining participation.

LENSKI, GERHARD. *The Religious Factor.* New York: Doubleday, 1966.

An influential and controversial study in the influence of religious belief and participation on attitudes toward politics, education, work, values, and other subjects.

O'DEA, THOMAS. *The Sociology of Religion.* Englewood Cliffs, N.J.: Prentice-Hall, 1966.

A short but thorough introduction to the sociology of religion, recommended for the student who wants an accessible overview of the field.

CHAPTER 17 *Science*

CHAPTER OUTLINE

The Institutionalization of Science
The Historical Background
The Modern Institution

The Norms of Science

The Social Process of Innovation
Paradigms in Science
Competition in Science

Resistance to Innovation
Case Study: The Theory of Evolution

Technology and Society
Technological Determinism
Technology and the Rate of Social Change

The Social Control of Science and Technology

Science, although unknown to many societies in the past, has become a central institution in the life of all modern industrial societies. A modern society such as our own depends for its very existence on advanced scientific knowledge and its technological applications—aircraft and antibiotics, telecommunications and assembly lines, skyscrapers and synthetic fabrics, computers and automobiles. Nor is it just our material existence that depends on science and technology. Our view of the world has been radically changed over the past century by scientific thought in such various fields as biology, physics, astronomy, psychology, medicine, and sociology. If you try to imagine what our society will be like in the years or generations ahead, your ideas are likely to be based on the assumption that science and technology will continue, for better or worse, to transform our way of life.

The terms "science" and "technology" are often used as synonyms in ordinary speech. But although the two happen to be closely linked in our own society, they are distinct phenomena. *Science refers to the logical, systematic methods by which knowledge of nature is obtained, and to the actual knowledge accumulated by these methods. Technology,* however, refers to the practical applications of knowledge about nature. The goals of science and technology are not the same. Science is concerned with the pursuit of knowledge about nature; technology is concerned with putting knowledge of nature to some use.

Every society has at least a simple technology, even if it is limited to such techniques as making bows and arrows, fire, or canoes. All primitive peoples have some body of practical knowledge on which their technology is based. But this kind of knowledge is not science. It is derived from earlier trial-and-error experience, not from an understanding of the abstract principles involved. The cave dweller may know how to light a fire but does not know why it burns, or why some substances burn while others do not.

Science, unlike technology, is not found in every society. In fact, it has appeared only rarely in human societies in the past. Scientific knowledge requires a logical, systematic understanding of the principles that underlie natural events. A scientific understanding of the world is necessary, however, for an advanced technology. Automobiles or atomic reactors cannot be built without precise knowledge of the relevant scientific principles. The close link between science and technology that we take for granted today is a relatively recent development. Yet it has launched the modernization process that is radically changing societies all over the world.

Paradoxically, the study of science has always been a rather neglected area of sociology. Despite increased interest in the topic in recent years, it still remains a marginal one to most sociologists. One reason for this neglect has probably been the great prestige that science has enjoyed in society from the time of the Industrial Revolution until World War II. Throughout this period, people generally agreed that scientific advance was the route to human happiness. Science was not seen as problematic, and most sociologists took it for granted or ignored it. Faith in science faltered, however, when the atomic bomb was dropped on Hiroshima near the end of World War II, for the explosion brought the abrupt realization that scientific knowledge could now be used to destroy all human life on earth. The prestige of science, though still high, has been further eroded since (Pitzer, 1971; Wiesner, 1973). Many of our most urgent global problems are the unforeseen results of scientific advance and technological innovation. The ecological crisis, for example, is widely seen as the outcome of the uncontrolled application of scientific knowledge to industrial technology. The worldwide population explosion, too, is largely a result of the introduction of new medical technologies to developing countries, and we may watch the harrowing consequences on our TV sets over the next few decades as millions of people starve to death.

Public attitudes toward science now seem to be ambiguous, even though they remain basically favorable (Etzioni and Nunn, 1974). We still acknowledge the extraordinary benefits we derive from science. Ideas of "getting back to nature" have a certain romantic appeal only until we consider the prospect of toothache without painkillers or homes without electricity. But many people are becoming less enthusiastic about headlong scientific and technological advance, and sociologists are now studying science and technology more critically than ever before.

The Institutionalization of Science

Science has emerged only relatively recently as a major social institution (Ben-David, 1971). How and why did this development take place?

The Historical Background

A few ancient peoples, such as the Arabs, the Greeks, and the Mayans, accumulated a considerable amount of scientific knowledge, particularly in the fields of mathematics and astronomy. They had hardly any specialized scientific roles, however, and they made little effort to link science to technology. The Greeks had a particularly elaborate science, which, had they applied it to technology, might have speeded up the modernization process by many centuries. Why did they fail to do so? The reason seems to lie in the values and social structure of ancient Greek society. The Greeks rigidly differentiated between slaves, who were responsible for work, and citizens, who ideally refrained from such lowly activities and instead pursued intellectual pleasures. To the Greeks, science was simply an aspect of philosophy, and they sought knowledge about the natural world as a value in itself, not for any practical purposes (Farrington, 1949). The Romans were less interested than the Greeks in abstract ideas, and although Greek scientific knowledge was available to them, they based most of their own technology on rule-of-thumb methods rather than scientific principles. With the fall of the Roman Empire, scientific advance came to a halt for almost a thousand years, largely because scientific inquiry was discouraged by the medieval church.

The rebirth of learning in the sixteenth and seventeenth centuries marked the beginning of modern science, although there were still no specialized scientific roles. In

Figure 17.1 The earliest forms of systematic science were astronomy and mathematics, which were practiced by peoples in Asia, Africa, the Middle East, Europe, and Central and South America. Although these ancient peoples made some practical use of their scientific knowledge in such fields as agriculture, architecture, and navigation, for the most part they pursued science for its own sake and failed to link science to technology.

Figure 17.2 Until the twentieth century, science was practiced primarily by gentlemen equipped with intellectual curiosity and private wealth. The activity was not very highly valued by society, for its practical purposes were not widely recognized. Few scientists were full-time professionals; the field was dominated by what we would today regard as gifted amateurs. Note that these scientists of the mid-eighteenth century are wearing the formal clothes of the upper class even at work in the laboratory.

England, where much of this scientific innovation took place, science was practiced mainly by gentlemen of leisure. There were only a handful of scientists in this period. They can still be counted and named, and nearly all of them made significant scientific discoveries. The problems that they dealt with were very often the problems that faced their society and economy: the bulk of their research was in fields relevant to warfare, navigation, or industry.

Almost until the beginning of the present century, science remained a respectable leisure activity whose usefulness was not socially recognized. Universities were gradually admitting science to the curriculum, but they continued to concentrate on more prestigious traditional subjects such as classical languages and philosophy. Specialized scientific roles existed mainly in the universities, and scientific research was largely confined to the ivory tower of the academic world.

The Modern Institution

In the course of this century, however, the relationship between science and technology has become fully recognized and exploited. The "little science" of the previous centuries has now become "big science," deeply involved in big organizations, big money, and big politics. The number of scientists in the world has grown so rapidly that over 90 percent of all scientists who have ever lived are alive today (Price, 1963). Nearly 100,000 scientific journals are currently published, and more than 2 million individual scientific papers appear each year.

Largely because American society relies so heavily on advanced technology, science has rapidly emerged—particularly in the years since World War II—as one of our dominant social institutions. The number of scientific roles in the United States has expanded enormously. There are now more than 1 million Americans with scientific degrees and more than 300,000 full-time scientists. These scientists rarely conduct their research in their own private laboratories. Nearly all of them are employed by large formal organizations: the universities are the largest single employer, followed by industry and government. The scientist in a university or college still has considerable freedom to choose the area of research, provided some organization or interest can be persuaded to fund it. In industry and government, however, the scientist's specific tasks are usually set by the organization in accordance with its own political, military, commercial, or other goals.

A technological society such as the United States supports science and scientists because it expects a payoff. The federal government provides more than half of the funds for scientific research, and most of the rest is supplied by industry. Government and industry are more concerned with useful technologies than with the pursuit of knowledge for its own sake. They therefore tend to allocate funds to *applied research,* which aims at finding technological applications for scientific knowledge, rather than for *basic research,* which aims merely at increasing the sum of knowledge. In the "little science" of previous centuries, most scientists were involved primarily in basic research; in the modern United States, however, only 14 percent of scientists are engaged in research of this kind (Bates and Julian, 1975). The determination of how money should be allocated, be it for cancer research or space technology, is the outcome of a political process and has little to do with what scientists themselves regard as the most pressing social or scientific priorities.

The rapid rate of increase in scientific knowledge—about 90 percent of which has been determined within living memory—has had important effects on the scientific community. Science is no longer a field for the gifted amateur. Scientists must spend many years in training for scientific careers and can rarely expect to make a significant contribution until they have mastered a relatively specialized subsection of some scientific field. Scientific

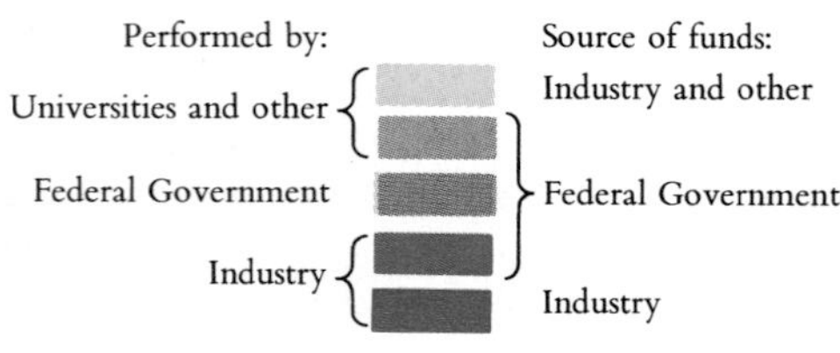

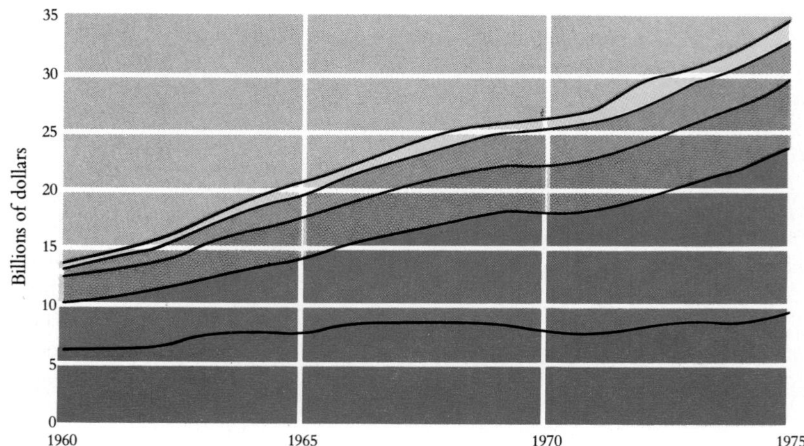

Figure 17.3 The federal government, followed by industry and the universities, is a major source of funds for scientific and technological research and development. The government supports science because it expects a payoff; a modern industrial society is heavily dependent on scientific and technological innovation.

Source: U.S. Bureau of the Census, *Statistical Abstracts, 1975* (Washington, D.C.: U.S. Government Printing Office), p. 547.

disciplines have become more and more specialized, and even within these specialties the scientist may find it difficult to keep up with the literature that reports new advances in the field. To handle this problem, scientists form social organizations of various kinds. These organizations may be either large formal bodies, such as the American Association for the Advancement of Science, or small, informal, "invisible colleges" containing a network of scientists in the same field who share information with one another. Such organizations enable individual scientists to stay abreast of developments, to find answers to specific questions, to sense new trends, and to obtain critical responses to their own work (Price, 1963; Griffith and Mullins, 1972).

The Norms of Science

The scientific community has developed a set of *norms* that are expected to govern the work of its individual members. These norms are nowhere spelled out explicitly, but they can be deduced from the reaction of the community to those who violate them. Robert Merton (1942) identified four principal norms that constitute the "moral imperatives" of science: universalism, communalism, disinterestedness, and organized skepticism.

Universalism emphasizes the universal nature of the scientific enterprise and its findings. The particular characteristics of individual scientists—such as their race, class, or national origin—are irrelevant to the validity of their work. Research findings must be evaluated purely in terms of their scientific worth.

Communalism is the principle that scientific knowledge should not be the personal property of the discoverer. It should be made available instead to the entire scientific community. All science rests on a shared heritage of past discoveries, and no individual can claim property rights over the outcome of research. A few scientists may be fortunate enough to have their discoveries named after them (Boyle's law, the Salk vaccine, Einstein's theory of relativity, Darwin's theory of evolution), but the discoveries are common property. (Technology, in contrast, can become private or corporate property through the use of patents.)

Disinterestedness is the requirement that scientists should be free from self-interest in their professional roles. Of course, scientists may legitimately hope that their work will be recognized and praised by the scientific community. But this recognition should be sufficient reward, and the scientist's main aim should be to contribute to the sum of scientific knowledge. In other careers—in business, say, or politics—it is almost expected that people will distort the facts to serve their own ends, but in the scientific community the dishonest manipulation of data or any other fraudulent practice is intolerable.

Organized skepticism refers to the expectation that scientists will suspend judgment until all the facts are at hand. No theory, however ancient and respected or new and revolutionary, can be uncritically accepted. There are no sacred areas in science that should not be critically investigated, even if political or religious dogma forbids it. The skepticism of the scientific community is "organized" in the sense that it is built into the scientific method itself and is binding on all members of the scientific community.

To the extent that these norms are followed, Merton argues, scientific knowledge will accumulate; if they are violated, scientific inquiry will suffer. Of course, the norms, like any others, are sometimes broken. The norm of universalism was flagrantly violated in Nazi Germany, which attempted to distinguish between "Jewish" and "Aryan" science. Many Jewish scientists lost their jobs, were obliged to leave Germany, or were sent to concentration camps. But scientific facts and theories cannot be repealed by political edict, and German science suffered as a result. The norm of communalism is often violated, particularly in "classified" military research and in research conducted for commercial interests that hope to profit from a monopoly over some item of knowledge. The norm of disinterestedness is also violated, for scientists, after all, may be as greedy or ambitious as anyone else. Outright fraud in science is extremely rare, however, if only because research findings may be carefully checked and verified by other scientists. The norm of organized skepticism is perhaps most frequently violated of all. Like the rest of us, scientists have their private values and prejudices, and may be reluctant to abandon old ideas or to accept new ones—a problem which we will discuss in more detail later.

Figure 17.4 Albert Einstein was perhaps the greatest scientist of the century, but his work was scorned in Nazi Germany because he was Jewish and was highly critical of Hitler. In taking this attitude, the Nazis violated the "moral imperatives" of science; if attitudes of this kind were widespread, scientific progress would be severely hindered.

The Social Process of Innovation

The object of scientific inquiry is *innovation,* the discovery of new knowledge. This innovation does not simply occur in a random fashion. Science is not just the creation of a few curious and inquiring individuals. It is a social institution that is subject to the influence of social forces, both within and beyond the scientific community. These forces strongly affect both the rate and the direction of scientific innovation.

Paradigms in Science

The social process of innovation is the subject of one of the most influential books in the philosophy and sociology of science, Thomas Kuhn's *The Structure of Scientific Revolutions* (1962). Kuhn is concerned with two aspects of the process of innovation: the steady innovation of what he calls *"normal" science,* in which knowledge is gradually increased, and the radical innovation of a *scientific "revolution,"* in which scientists come to look at their subject matter in an entirely different way, or even to establish a new discipline. Most scientific advance is of the "normal" kind, but occasionally—as when Copernican astronomy replaced the old earth-centered view of the universe, or when Einstein's physics replaced the Newtonian model—a scientific revolution takes place.

Kuhn starts with the assertion that science, contrary to popular belief, does not develop merely by a simple accumulation of individual discoveries and inventions. What often happens is that a community of scientists in a particular discipline develops a shared set of concepts, methods, and assumptions about their subject matter. Kuhn calls such a set of beliefs a *paradigm.* These paradigms determine what is regarded as a problem, a solution, a discovery, or an appropriate research method. The work of the scientist is, in effect, an attempt to fit nature into the conceptual box provided by the current paradigm. Physicists committed to the Newtonian paradigm, for example, interpreted physical phenomena in one way; physicists committed to the Einsteinian paradigm interpret them in another way. The training of a scientist is essentially an introduction to the prevailing paradigm. Textbooks, for example, generally do not present a variety of ways of looking at the same phenomenon. They teach the existing assumptions, usually presenting them as accepted truth even though most of them may appear as ludicrous to future generations as pre-Copernican astronomy does to us in the twentieth century.

The paradigm, however, is necessary for "normal" scientific innovation. Nature is much too vast and complex for haphazard, random investigations to be very successful. The paradigm defines the problems that must be solved and the means that should be used to solve them, and it focuses the attention of an entire scientific community upon them. If a science has no paradigm, so that the investigators are making random and uncoordinated efforts to solve problems, little progress will be made. Such was the case, for example, with the investigation of electricity until Benjamin Franklin supplied a set of assumptions that were generally acceptable and fruitful. Research guided by a paradigm produces a rapid accumulation of knowledge and permits the advance of "normal" science.

Why, then, do scientific "revolutions" come about? The reason is that research under a particular paradigm will continually generate new problems, some of which can be solved under the paradigm but some of which cannot. Problems that cannot be fitted to the existing paradigm are called *anomalies.* At first anomalies may be shelved and ignored, or the paradigm may be modified to take account of them. In the end, however, so many anomalies may emerge that the existing paradigm becomes a mere patchwork, incapable of containing or explaining them. At this point the scientific discipline concerned is in a *crisis* situation, and scientists begin to cast around for some entirely new paradigm that will yield better results. When the new paradigm is found, a scientific revolution takes place. Many scientists resist the change, but if the new paradigm makes more sense of reality, it will finally triumph. In this way the Copernican view of the universe finally replaced the centuries-old Ptolemaic system, an unwieldy one that placed the earth at the center of the universe with the sun revolving around it. Endless efforts were made to modify the Ptolemaic system to take account of new astronomical discoveries, but in the end the system simply did not "work" and there was general recognition that a new one was needed. In the same way, Einstein's view of the universe provided answers to anomalies that Newton's view could not explain. At present, even Einstein's system is generating serious anomalies that are leading to continual modifications of his paradigm.

Science is not a matter of a steady accumulation of knowledge. Theories are proposed, used, and abandoned, and the existing knowledge at any period is only provisional, never final and irrefutable. One philosopher of science, Karl Popper (1959), takes the view that it is never possible to *prove* anything in science with absolute finality, since there is always the possibility that an exception will be found to every scientific "law." All that we can do is *disprove* hypotheses, and our scientific knowledge consists entirely of theories that are not yet disproved, although one day they might be.

The way a scientist interprets reality depends on the assumptions of the scientific community at the time, which are in turn influenced by other social forces. Between 1690 and 1769, for example, the planet Uranus was observed on at least seventeen different occasions, but because existing beliefs, influenced by religious doctrine, discounted the possibility of a new planet, it was classified as a star. When the astronomer William Herschel observed the planet on successive days in 1769, he noticed that it moved. Clearly, it could not be a star, and so Herschel assumed that it was a comet—the only other legitimate assumption permitted by the existing paradigm. Only when the "comet" failed to behave like a comet did Herschel finally conclude that Uranus must be a planet—and once the possibility of other planets was recognized, astronomers looked for and found them. What we see in the world depends not just on what we look at but also on what our previous training has taught us to find (Kuhn, 1962).

Competition in Science

Another important factor in the social process of innovation is *competition* between scientists. Fame and honor go to the scientist who arrives first at a discovery. The scientist who gets there second by independent work is ignored, no matter how meritorious his or her work. The socialization of scientists emphasizes the importance of doing original research. Ph.D. dissertations, for example, are expected to make a new contribution to the field, not merely to replicate work that has already been done. (Partly for this reason, many research studies in sociology and other sciences have never been independently verified. Researchers get no acclaim for following in the footsteps of others, so they prefer to break new ground.)

Professional recognition is of great importance to the scientist. In the United States this recognition is closely tied to career prospects in higher education. The scientist must "publish or perish" because tenure and promotion are usually dependent on a continuing output of journal articles and scholarly books. The American scientific community is highly stratified, with the greatest honors going to a very small number of scientists. Social mobility in the scientific community correlates strongly with the volume of an individual's publications. The more original work a scientist publishes, the more honors—in the form of prizes, awards, honorary degrees, promotion, or citation by others in their own publications—he or she receives. The higher a scientist rises in the prestige hierarchy, the easier it becomes to publish and to get funds for further research (Merton, 1973; Cole and Cole, 1972; Allison and Steward, 1974).

The exchange of new information in return for professional recognition is thus an important process in the scientific community. This phenomenon is familiar to sociologists and anthropologists in another guise, gift giving. In every human society, if a gift is offered and accepted, the act of acceptance is an acknowledgment of the enhanced prestige of the giver. Research publications are in effect a gift (they are even called "contributions") from the researcher to the scientific community. If the gift is accepted—that is, if the research is published—the enhanced prestige of the researcher is publicly acknowledged (Hagstrom, 1965). The gift can only be accepted, however, if it

Figure 17.5

"We go to Stockholm, we accept our prize, and then I never want to see your ugly mug again!"

Drawing by Wm. Hamilton; © 1972 The New Yorker Magazine, Inc.

is original and if similar findings have not been published before. For this reason there are often intense *priority disputes* in science, arguments about who made a particular discovery first. The fear of being "scooped," or anticipated, by another researcher is so great that in some disciplines there are special publications consisting entirely of announcements by scientists that they are completing research on a particular topic and intend to publish specific findings in due course. The authors of the announcements thus hope to claim priority over other researchers who might publish fuller results in the interim. One recent study found that more than 60 percent of scientists had been anticipated by others at least once in their careers, 17 percent had been anticipated more than twice, and about a third were worried about being anticipated in their present research (Hagstrom, 1974).

The desire for recognition may be dysfunctional in that it encourages secrecy, but it has several functional effects as well. First, it encourages scientists to publish their findings and communicate their results to others as soon as possible. For example, Darwin developed the theory of evolution seventeen years before he published it; he was finally spurred to write his book, in the space of a few months, only by the realization that he was about to be "scooped" by Alfred Russel Wallace. Second, competition reduces a wasteful duplication of effort, for scientists are motivated to tackle problems that others are not working on. Scientific effort is thus efficiently allocated among the various problems that exist. Third, competition encourages scientists to explore new specialties or even to found new disciplines in existing areas of ignorance, where their chances of making significant contributions are greatest. Many new disciplines were created by applying paradigms from one field to an entirely new field. Sociology, for example, was originally conceived as "social physics," in the novel belief that "laws" analogous to those of nature could be applied to human society. Similarly molecular biology was created primarily by nuclear physicists who deserted their own field in order to apply its paradigm to the science of living organisms (Hagstrom, 1965, 1974; Polanyi, 1951).

Resistance to Innovation

It is often the case that a major new scientific discovery or theory causes an intellectual scandal. Indeed, resistance to radical innovation has been the norm rather than the exception in the scientific community (Kuhn, 1962). Galileo's colleagues refused to look through his telescope to see

Figure 17.6 Galileo on trial by the medieval church. His offense was to support the theory that the earth moves around the sun, and not vice versa. Galileo was forced to recant his view on pain of death, but legend has it that he muttered under his breath, "yet it still moves."

the moons of Jupiter. Giordano Bruno was burned at the stake for proclaiming that the earth revolved around the sun. Pasteur's germ theory was ignored by the surgeons of his time, who could have saved countless lives by washing their hands and instruments before operating on patients. Harvey's theory of the circulation of the blood was greeted with howls of laughter when he delivered a paper on the subject to other physicians. Freud was shouted down by his outraged fellow psychologists when he outlined his theory of childhood sexuality. The discoveries of modern physics, such as gravitation, relativity, wave theory, and quantum theory, were vigorously resisted by many scientists for years after they were first announced. An attempt by a contemporary biologist, Edmund Wilson, to launch a new science, "sociobiology"—the unified study of all social animals, including human beings—has been bitterly opposed by scientists in several fields. Why are so many scientists so reluctant to accept scientific innovation? An examination of a case study will throw some light on the problem.

Case Study: The Theory of Evolution

In 1650, Dr. John Lightfoot, vice-chancellor of the University of Cambridge, determined on the basis of the available "evidence" (all of which he found in the Old Testament) that God created Adam and Eve "on 23 October 4004 BC, at nine o'clock in the morning." This calculation won extremely wide acceptance and became an accepted part of religious dogma for more than two hundred years. Few people in western Europe doubted that the world was more than 6000 years old.

The first challenge to this dogma came from geologists, who increasingly wondered whether what they saw in rock formations could have been the product of a few thousand years of history. The layers of sand, gravel, clay, limestone, and other minerals, many of them containing fossils of extinct animals, could be explained only in terms of natural processes extending over millions of years. The first geologist to present this view systematically was James Hutton. His work, published in 1785, was scorned. Theologians and scientists alike took the view that the extinct creatures had either been killed in Noah's flood, or else had never existed—the fossils had been created by God as part and parcel of the rocks in which they were found. Yet the geological evidence mounted, and it could not be contained within the existing belief that the world was a mere 6000 years old. By the year 1830, opinions had changed sufficiently to allow Sir Charles Lyell's *Principles of Geology*, a book declaring that the earth was millions of years old, to be warmly received by the scientific if not the theological community.

Darwin's Theory

In 1859 Charles Darwin published his sensational work *On The Origin of Species*, in which he argued that life forms had been continually evolving over thousands or millions of years. The inescapable conclusion was that living species could not have been originally created in their present form. Yet the intellectual climate of the time was such that Darwin did not dare to deal with the evolution of the human species in his book. He commented privately, "I think I shall avoid the whole subject, as so surrounded by prejudices, though I fully admit it is the highest and most interesting problem." In only one passage in his book did he obliquely refer to human evolution, merely commenting that "light will be thrown on the origin of man and his history." The implication of Darwin's theory, however, was inescapable. The various primate species, including *Homo sapiens*, had evolved from common ancestors.

The conflict between science and religion, which had been proceeding unabated since Copernicus and Galileo challenged the medieval view of the universe, reached perhaps its final climax in a famous debate at Oxford University in 1860. The debaters were Bishop Wilberforce, who still accepted Lightfoot's calculation of the date of creation, and T. H. Huxley, a scientist who supported Darwin. At a critical moment in the debate, the Bishop turned to Huxley and asked him whether he was "related on your father's or your mother's side to an ape?" Huxley instantly replied that if he had to choose for an ancestor between an ape and someone who could discuss a serious question not with logic but only with ridicule, "I would not hesitate for a moment to prefer the ape." In the "inextinguishable laughter" that followed, the bishop sat down, his speech unfinished. In the succeeding years public opinion swung rapidly to the side of the evolutionists, and since that period organized religion has generally attempted to compromise with rather than suppress the findings of science.

Figure 17.7 A caricature of Charles Darwin, showing him emerging from the jungle. Although Darwin suffered a torrent of abuse when his theory was first published, it fitted the facts that other theories could not explain and was quickly accepted by scientists as a result.

Piltdown Man

At around the time of the publication of Darwin's book, the first fossil of a Neanderthal human was discovered. All that was needed to prove Darwin's theory was the "missing link," an intermediate form between the "brutish" Neanderthal and modern *Homo sapiens.* In 1912 it seemed that this evolutionary link had been discovered in England in the form of Piltdown man, whose fossil skull contained a noble human brow with a cruder, apelike jaw. The fossil fitted perfectly with existing conceptions and its discovery caused immense excitement. Some five hundred essays were written about the creature, and the site of the discovery was designated as a national monument. In fact, however, the skull was the work of an unknown forger and consisted of a relatively modern human head and the jaw of an orangutan. Several tests available to scientists at the time would have proved that the skull was a fraud—the jaw was bone, not stone, and was thus not even a fossil, and the teeth had been filed down to alter their shape. Yet nobody examined the find carefully enough to discover the forgery. A few scientists were suspicious about Piltdown man and published critical articles, but they were almost universally ignored or even ridiculed. Not until 1953, forty years later, did scientists take the trouble to reexamine the original specimen, which was immediately pronounced a forgery.

Why did scientists finally begin to doubt that Piltdown man was genuine? The main reason was the discovery of other hominid fossils of different species that also appeared to be intermediate between *Homo sapiens* and some apelike ancestor. Several of these hominids, particularly the species *Australopithecus,* fitted the "missing link" far more neatly than Piltdown man, which increasingly appeared to be an anomaly in the emerging picture of human evolution (Millar, 1974).

Analysis

These instances of resistance to innovation point again to the importance of paradigms in science. When the geological and fossil evidence contradicted the accepted paradigm of the seventeenth, eighteenth, and early nineteenth centuries—a paradigm based on the Genesis story of creation—the facts were either ignored or reinterpreted to fit the paradigm. But the anomalies mounted, and the paradigm began to collapse. Theories such as those of Lyell in geology and Darwin in biology began to win wide acceptance, for they provided a better explanation of the scientific evidence. Yet once the scientific revolution had taken place, resistance to further innovation set in once more: Piltdown man fitted the new paradigm perfectly. Only after four more decades of research that pointed overwhelmingly to the anomalous position of Piltdown man did scientists finally make the investigations that uncovered one of the most preposterous frauds in scientific history. In most of the period covered by the case study, the "moral imperatives" of science—the four norms outlined by Merton—were widely suspended. What many scientists actually did, as some still do when confronted with radical innovation, was to use the existing paradigm as a norm, rejecting as unacceptable any new theories or discoveries that deviated from or undermined it (Mulkay, 1972). The costs of scientific conservatism often seem far lower than those of scientific radicalism. Scientists may be reluctant to give up ideas that have proved useful in the past, particularly when their reputations and research funds are tied to their work under the existing paradigm.

The case study also reveals the influence of wider social forces on the scientific community. In the seventeenth and eighteenth centuries, scientists were blinded to the facts by the religious dogma of the time. By the late nineteenth and twentieth centuries, the religious world view was no longer uncritically accepted, and there was growing faith that science could unlock the mysteries of nature. New theories quickly gained acceptance. But when it seemed that the problem of human evolution had been solved, scientists were reluctant to admit fresh evidence that would upset their tidy theories—or worse, make them look foolish in the eyes of the public.

The case study raises one further question about the influence of social factors on scientific innovation. The time lag between an innovation and its final acceptance was far greater in the past than it is today. Copernicus's view of the universe was not generally accepted for a century after his death. The principle of the eyeglass was known in 1286, but Galen's theory of sight, which ruled out the artificial correction of vision, was taught in medical schools until 1700. It took centuries for scientists to accept the evidence of the earth's age, but it took only decades before most of them accepted the evidence for the evolution of the species. Fossil finds during the 1960s and the 1970s have upset previous theories of our evolutionary origins, but scientists have modified their paradigm to take account of these discoveries in months rather than years. Why is scientific innovation now so much more readily accepted?

Kingsley Davis (1949) suggests that there are four factors that make a society more or less willing to accept innovation. The first is the society's *attitude toward change.* Western society is no longer suspicious of change; we believe in "progress" and acknowledge the role of scientific innovation in bringing about that progress. The second factor is the *institutionalization* of science. When science becomes a central rather than a marginal activity and when scientists are socially rewarded for new discoveries, innovation takes place much faster. The third factor is *specialization.* Life is short and intellect is limited. If scientists are amateurs in several fields, they are less likely to make discoveries than highly specialized practitioners, who are intimately acquainted with a particular field. The fourth factor is the *methods of communication* available to a society. If new ideas can be conveniently stored and quickly transmitted, information becomes more accessible and can more readily be put to use. All four factors operate to make our own society exceptionally well adapted to accept rather than resist innovation.

Technology and Society

The great store of scientific knowledge in modern industrial societies has been used to create an extremely sophisticated technology. What is the social significance of technological innovation?

Technological Determinism

We have only to look around us to see how our way of life and social behavior are influenced by the technologies available to us, from kitchen gadgets to automobiles. The influence of technology on society seems so powerful that some sociologists have adopted a position of *technological determinism*—the view that the technology available to a society is an important determinant of its social structure and even of its history. There is a strong element of technological determinism in the work of Karl Marx, who called attention to the way technologies of economic production affect the social order. Several American social scientists, notably Thorstein Veblen (1922) and William Ogburn (1950), have also argued that specific historical developments and culture traits are the direct result of particular technologies.

Within limits, this view has considerable validity. It is obvious, for example, that the technology that a society

Figure 17.8 The technology available to a society has a strong influence on its culture and social structure. In a society that relies for its energy on the muscles of its own members, great time and effort must be expended for a relatively small reward. A society that uses the muscle power of animals exploits the environment more efficiently, for it receives greater returns for less effort. A society that uses machines is vastly more efficient and productive; it can become very large and diversified because it can generate an abundant economic surplus.

uses to produce energy sets certain limits on its way of life. A society that relies on the muscle power of its own members is subject to severe restrictions. People must devote most of their time to producing enough food to sustain life, and must live in small, isolated groups. A society that uses the power of animals has far more options. It can develop agriculture, and with it a larger population in a smaller area, an economic surplus, a system of social stratification, and specialized nonproductive roles for some of its members. A society that uses machines driven by natural forces—wind, water, steam, electricity, nuclear fusion—has many more options. The social horizon and the internal complexity of an industrial society are immeasurably greater than those of societies employing only the muscle power of human beings or animals, and mass societies of many millions of people become possible (Davis, 1948; Lenski, 1966a; White, 1959).

When specific social or historical events are explained in terms of technological determinism, however, the case is much harder to prove. William Ogburn attempted to trace connections of this kind. He argued, for example, that the invention of the cotton gin in 1793 promoted the institution of slavery in the United States. The cotton gin greatly increased the productive capacity and thus the profitability of the textile industry, and many more slaves were needed to work on the new cotton plantations that sprang into being. Like Karl Marx, Ogburn divided human culture into material and nonmaterial elements. He acknowledged that a change could initially take place in either element but argued that changes usually occur in the material culture first. People accept new tools much more readily than they accept new ideas, values, norms, or institutions, but these technological innovations inevitably lead to changes in the nonmaterial culture. As a result, there is always a *culture lag* as the nonmaterial elements attempt to "catch up" with changes in the material elements. Ogburn argued that this culture lag is a continuing source of social disorganization and social problems.

Ogburn's argument has a good deal of plausibility, as you will appreciate if you consider the social impact of such innovations as gunpowder, the compass, the printing press, the automobile, the elevator (which makes skyscrapers practical), or the jet engine. But the theory has its limitations. Technological change, such as the introduction of the cotton gin, always occurs in the context of other changes. It is very difficult, if not impossible, to isolate the technological factor from the others as the main cause of social change. Moreover, the precise effect of technological innovation depends on the culture into which it is introduced. Different cultures will accept, reject, ignore, or modify an innovation in accordance with their existing norms, values, and expectations. The theory of technological determinism cannot be pushed too far. It is better to see technological innovation and other elements in society—religious, political, economic, military, familial, and so on—as parts of an interacting system.

Technology and the Rate of Social Change

Technology is undoubtedly an important agent for social change. Most technological innovations are based on existing scientific knowledge and technology. The more advanced a society is in this respect, therefore, the faster the pace of technological change is likely to be. And the more rapid the technological change, the more rapid is the social change that it generates.

A mere sixty-six years elapsed between the first faltering flight of the Wright brothers and the landing of the first astronauts on the moon. The rate of technological change in modern industrial societies has no historical precedent. Throughout most of history, people lived in a world little different from that of their parents, and they expected their children and grandchildren to live much the same lives as they did. Traditional societies assume an almost unchanging social world and are typically very suspicious of change. In the modern world, however, we accept change as the norm. We look for novelty, we are oriented to the future rather than the past, and we expect constant improvements in our material environment. Alvin Toffler (1970) has argued that we are living in a permanent state of "future shock." The future, he contends, continually intrudes into the stability of the present. Ours is a "throwaway" society in which change takes place faster than our ability to adjust to it.

The pace of technological change has implications for every area of society. Medical advances have lengthened life expectancy and slashed the death rate, radically altering our population structure. Innovations in industrial technology displace thousands of workers and render recently manufactured machinery obsolete within a few years. The nature of cultural activities is transformed through such innovations as radio, television, and phonograph records. People require long years of training and education if they are to function effectively in such a society, and increasingly they need reeducation later in life if they are to keep up with advances in knowledge and techniques. The socialization process, which in simple societies consists almost entirely of passing the culture of one generation on to the next, becomes both more complex and more inadequate. Margaret Mead (1970) suggests that the pace of technological change is now so great that the old and the young live in quite different worlds—so much so that, in a sense, the parents have no children and the children no parents. For the first time in history, she points out, the old are no longer the main source of wisdom and knowledge in the community. The young often know far more relevant information about the modern world than their parents. The culture lag between technological change and the cultural adjustment to it is now a permanent and often disruptive feature of our society. Consider, for example, the time lag between the invention of the birth-control pill and the adjustment in sexual norms that were originally designed to prevent illegitimate births by prohibiting premarital intercourse.

Figure 17.9 The rate of technological change in modern societies is without precedent. This glider, piloted by Orville Wright, was considered something of a marvel in 1908; this modern B-52 military airplane is fast becoming obsolete. The reason for the rapid pace of technological innovation is that each innovation builds on previous ones. The greater the accumulation of technology, therefore, the faster the rate of innovation is likely to be.

The Social Control of Science and Technology

Science and technology are not simply the work of isolated individuals, unaffected by wider social forces. The selection of research problems and the rate and direction of innovation are strongly influenced by social forces. It is no accident, for example, that so much applied research in the United States focuses on the development of military and commercial products. It follows that science and technology cannot be regarded as somehow independent of society. Like any other cultural products, they are created and controlled by countless individual men and women. The difficulty is that this control is very haphazard. We have created a complex institution to ensure the development of science and technology, but we have created few means of monitoring and controlling their effects—despite the impact that these effects can have on the social order.

The lack of systematic social control over scientific and technological innovation presents three main problems.

1. A relatively haphazard scientific and technological advance may have many unforeseen social effects, particularly in terms of the quality of the environment. Recently, for example, there have been fears that some food additives may contribute to human cancers; that atmospheric pollution may lead to climatic changes that could cause a new ice age; and that gases from aerosol spray cans may interfere with the planet's ozone layer and allow dangerous radiation to reach the surface of the earth.

2. Unless society ensures that scientific and technological innovation takes place in accordance with defined social goals, there may be distortion in the priorities that are given to research efforts in different fields. Critics argue that under the existing haphazard system, scarce and valuable resources may be devoted to producing such trivia as self-heating shaving cream, when they might

otherwise be devoted to more socially desirable ends, such as medical research.

3. A highly technological society poses a possible threat to democracy. Public participation in the decision-making process may become difficult for the reason that the relevant facts about many important issues—such as the wisdom of building nuclear reactors near urban settlements—may be beyond the comprehension of both voters and their elected representatives. Several writers (for example, Galbraith, 1967) have warned of the dangers of *technocracy,* rule by experts operating behind the scenes. In modern corporations and government departments the real decisions are often made by experts whose specialized knowledge and recommendations are relied upon by those who are officially responsible for the decisions.

Any attempt to apply a more systematic form of social control over science and technology would probably run into severe problems. One such problem involves a conflict of values. The object of science is the pursuit of knowledge, and ideally this activity should take place in an atmosphere of complete intellectual freedom. There are enough unhappy examples in the past of nonscientists attempting to dictate to scientists what they should and should not investigate for us to be wary of doing the same. Should we impose restrictions on research, and if so, what restrictions? A similar conflict of values might arise if society attempted to shift priorities in applied research from the manufacture of trivial commercial products to other social goals. Radical changes in these priorities would inevitably interfere in the workings of the capitalist system that most Americans value so highly.

Another problem involves the moral responsibility for decisions about research that may have far-reaching consequences. The development of the hydrogen bomb is but one example of many cases in which technical and moral issues are not easily separated in practice. At present, scientists usually cannot and do not control the uses to which their work is put, although there are signs that many scientists are now very disturbed about this situation. Ought the responsibility for decisions about new research and technology to rest with scientists themselves, or with government, or with some new control agency such as a "science court" with full legal powers to restrict certain research? The question is a very important one, for scientific and technological advance in the years ahead may change our material and social environment in ways that many people might consider undesirable.

Some of the scientific research currently in progress illustrates the significance of this problem. Scientists are now working on techniques that may make it possible for parents to determine the sex of their children. If a marketable product eventually emerges, commercial interests may encourage widespread sex selection of children. This may sound like a socially useful technology until we consider one factor. Several opinion polls have indicated that a large majority of parents would prefer to have boys rather than girls. The result of sex selection might be a society where males heavily outnumber females, with important effects on population structure, family patterns, and sexual

PUBLIC'S CONFIDENCE IN THOSE WHO RUN SCIENCE: 1966 vs. 1971–1973

	Year of Poll			
Confidence in Science	1966	1971	1972	1973
Great deal	56%	32%	37%	37%
Only some	25	47	39	47
Hardly any or none	4	10	8	6
Not sure	15	11	16	10

Source: Adapted from Amitai Etzioni and Clyde Nunn, "The Public Appreciation of Science in Contemporary America," *Daedalus,* 103 (Summer, 1974), p. 194.

Figure 17.10 Opinion polls between 1966 and 1973 showed a marked decline in public confidence in "those who run science." The reasons for this decline are not clear, but ambiguous feelings about the direction in which scientific advance is leading us may be one factor.

Technology: Servant or Master?

Since technological change forces social changes upon us, this has had the effect of abdicating all control over our social environment to a kind of whimsical deity. While we think of ourselves as a people of change and progress, masters of our environment and our fate, we are no more entitled to this designation than the most superstitious savage, for our relation to change is entirely passive. We poke our noses out the door each day and wonder breathlessly what new disruptions technology has in store for us. We talk of technology as the servant of man, but it is a servant that now dominates the household, too powerful to fire, upon whom everyone is helplessly dependent. We tiptoe about and speculate upon his mood. What will be the effects of such-and-such an invention? How will it change our daily lives? We never ask, do we *want* this, is it worth it? (We did not ask ourselves, for example, if the trivial conveniences offered by the automobile could really offset the calamitous disruption and depersonalization of our lives that it brought about.) We simply say "You can't stop progress" and shuffle back inside.

We pride ourselves on being a "democracy" but we are in fact slaves. We submit to an absolute ruler whose edicts and whims we never question. We watch him carefully, hang on his every word; for technology is a harsh and capricious king, demanding prompt and absolute obedience. . . . We have passively surrendered to every degradation, every atrocity, every enslavement that our technological ingenuity has brought about. We laugh at the old lady who holds off the highway bulldozers with a shotgun, but we laugh because we are Uncle Toms. We try to outdo each other in singing the praises of the oppressor, although in fact the value of technology in terms of human satisfaction remains at best undemonstrated. For when evaluating its effects we always adopt the basic assumptions and perspective of technology itself, and never examine it in terms of the totality of human experience. We say this or that invention is valuable because it generates other inventions—because it is a means to some other means—not because it achieves an ultimate human end. We play down the "side effects" that so often become the main effects and completely negate any alleged benefits. The advantages of *all* technological "progress" will after all be totally outweighed the moment nuclear war breaks out (an event which, given the inadequacy of precautions and the number of fanatical fingers close to the trigger, is only a matter of time unless radical changes are made).

Source: Philip Slater, *The Pursuit of Loneliness: American Culture at the Breaking Point* (Boston: Beacon, 1970), pp. 44–45.

norms. Do we want this kind of situation, and should the decision be left to commercial interests?

Another controversial field of research involves the rearrangement of living molecules, in particular the DNA molecule that determines the hereditary characteristics of all living things. This research can have many uses, ranging from the control of insect pests to the treatment of cancers. The danger exists, however, that new and harmful strains of viruses and bacteria can be created in the course of this research. Human beings would have no natural immunity to these strains. The escape of such new life forms into circulation could lead to catastrophic, worldwide epidemics. Scientists have been quick to recognize this danger and have themselves set up strict guidelines and safety procedures for DNA research. Some scientists, however, believe that even these safeguards are inadequate and have called for a total ban on this kind of research.

The awesome problems posed by science and technology are an example of the "culture lag" problem discussed earlier. Science and technology have developed far faster than have social mechanisms to control them. A century ago, science was marginal to society and technology was relatively undeveloped. Today they offer the prospect of social upheaval and even the destruction of human life—or the prospect of unprecedented social benefits and new levels of civilized existence. An urgent social challenge in the future will be to find some means of ensuring that science and technology develop exclusively in the second direction.

Summary

1. Science has become an important institution in modern society, largely because it has been linked to technology. An industrial society depends heavily on scientific knowledge and its technological applications, although there are signs of concern about the potential effects of headlong scientific and technological advance.

2. Science emerged only recently as a major institution. Until the Industrial Revolution there were few specialized scientific roles, but since that time science has enjoyed extensive social support. The rapid development of scientific knowledge presents many problems to scientists, who may have difficulty in keeping abreast of developments.

3. The scientific community works under four basic norms: universalism, communalism, disinterestedness, and organized skepticism. These norms tend to be violated at times, and scientific advance may suffer in consequence.

4. Innovation in science is not a random matter; it is influenced by social forces. Scientists work under paradigms, or sets of assumptions about the discipline. Normal scientific advance takes place under the paradigm until serious anomalies are generated; at this point, a scientific revolution may take place. Competition between scientists, often expressed in priority disputes, encourages scientists to make original contributions and to explore new areas.

5. Scientists sometimes resist innovation, as a case study of the theory of evolution reveals. Scientists may be reluctant to give up ideas that have proved useful in the past, although this conservative tendency is less noticeable in contemporary industrial societies.

6. Technological innovation is of great social significance, The theory of technological determinism suggests that technological changes are responsible for many social changes, although a culture lag may occur as cultural arrangements slowly adapt to technological innovation. Rapid technological change generates rapid and widespread social change, with important implications in many areas of society.

7. The lack of adequate social control of science and technology presents several problems, for innovation may have undesirable social consequences that were not anticipated. The development of suitable methods of control poses a major challenge for the future.

Important Terms

science	paradigm
technology	anomaly
applied research	priority dispute
basic research	technological determinism
norms of science	culture lag
innovation	alienation
"normal" science	technocracy
scientific "revolution"	

Suggested Readings

KUHN, THOMAS S. *The Structure of Scientific Revolutions.* Chicago: University of Chicago Press, 1962.

A highly influential book. Kuhn outlines his concept of the scientific paradigm and shows the role of paradigms in both "normal" and "revolutionary" scientific innovation.

MERTON, ROBERT K. *Sociology of Science: Theoretical and Empirical Investigations,* Norman W. Storer (ed.). Chicago: University of Chicago Press, 1973.

An important collection of articles on the sociology of science by Robert Merton the leading sociologist in the field.

MILLAR, RONALD. *The Piltdown Man.* New York: St. Martin's Press, 1974.

A readable account of the famous Piltdown man hoax. Millar includes extensive historical background on the resistance to evolutionary theory.

MULKAY, MICHAEL J. *The Social Process of Innovation.* New York: Macmillan, 1972.

A short discussion of the social processes that influence the rate and direction of scientific innovation, with special emphasis on the phenomenon of resistance to new scientific theories.

TOFFLER, ALVIN. *Future Shock.* New York: Alfred A. Knopf, 1970.

A best-selling book on the "throwaway society" created by rapid technological change. Toffler explores the implications of the rapid pace of change in the modern world.

CHAPTER 18 *The Economic Order*

CHAPTER OUTLINE

The Division of Labor
Increased Specialization
Anomie and the Division of Labor

The Sociology of Occupations
Primary, Secondary, and Tertiary Sectors
Professionalization

Work and Alienation
The Concept of Alienation
Worker Alienation in the United States
"Human Relations" in Industry

Capitalism and Socialism
The Concept of Property
Capitalism
Socialism
Democratic Socialism
Communism

Corporate Capitalism in the United States
Corporations and the American Economy
Multinational Corporations

Industrialism and Modernization
The Modernization Process
The Social Effects of Modernization

The Future of Industrial Society

The human animal needs food and shelter in order to survive: these are basic biological necessities. Beyond these requirements, people in all societies feel that they have "needs" for certain other goods and services as well—in one society, perhaps, for bows and arrows and the attention of a witch doctor, in another society, for a color TV set and the skills of an auto mechanic. Whether these needs are biologically determined necessities or socially defined desirables, they can usually be satisfied only by human effort. A few of the material goods and personal services that people want are freely available, like the air they breathe or such care as they receive from adults when they are children. But most goods and services are scarce. People must work to produce them and must find some way of distributing them among the various members of the society. This activity, basic to our species, is the substance of economic life. *The economic order is the institutionalized system for producing and distributing goods and services.*

Economic activity is important not only because it sustains life. Throughout this book we have noted the central importance of economic production for human culture and social structure as well. The principal means of production that a society uses—hunting and gathering, horticulture, pastoralism, agriculture, or industrialism—strongly influences the size and complexity of the society and the character of its culture and social institutions. Changes in the mode of economic production are therefore inevitably accompanied by sweeping changes elsewhere in society. We have also noted, in the work of Karl Marx and others, the close connection between economic and political issues, particularly in the area of social inequality. Goods and services are rarely equally distributed in a society, because the more powerful groups are able to secure a disproportionate supply for themselves and to control the political process by which inequalities are maintained. And we must also recognize the importance of economic activity in personal life. Work occupies a major part of our waking lives, and our occupations usually define our social status. Work is therefore a significant source of personal and social identity: that is why one of the first questions you ask a person you have just met is: "What do you do?"

In this chapter we will be focusing on one of the most basic of all human activities, with implications that extend into many areas of social ife. We will not examine the actual mechanics of the economy in detail; that is the task of economists. We will concentrate instead on the social basis and consequences of economic activity.

The Division of Labor

Every human society, however large or small, establishes some *division of labor* among its members: people are expected to specialize, at least to some extent, in particular economic activities. This division of labor occurs in all societies because it is highly *functional.* It ensures that particular categories of people have specific jobs to do, enabling them to become expert in their assigned activities. The division of labor thus enhances the efficiency of economic life, but it may have other far-reaching effects as well.

Increased Specialization

There has been a general historical trend toward increased specialization in economic activities, a trend that has reached its climax in modern industrial societies.

In small-scale hunting and gathering societies there is little division of labor except on grounds of age and sex. The very young and very old are not expected to do the same work as other members of the community, and men and women always have some specific tasks assigned to them. Apart from these distinctions there is very little specialization. Most members of these communities participate in much the same kind of activities, and there are very few full-time, specialized occupational roles. In the more advanced horticultural and pastoral societies, and especially in agricultural societies, there is a much greater division of labor. These societies can produce an economic surplus, an achievement that has two main results. First, some people are freed from basic subsistence activities and can specialize in other roles—perhaps as artists, traders, or military commanders. Second, powerful groups are able to gain control of the surplus wealth and to live largely from the work of others. In agricultural societies, the division of labor becomes based on class distinctions as well as on individual differences.

Figure 18.1 Unlike preindustrial societies, a modern industrial society like the United States has a very complex division of labor with many thousands of job specialties. The economies of industrialized societies are highly diversified, and it is both more efficient and more convenient if people specialize in particular occupations.

This more elaborate division of labor persists in industrial societies, although class differences become less accentuated in some of the more advanced societies of this type. But industrialism breeds an entirely new form of division of labor: the high degree of specialization found in factories, offices, and other formal organizations, where each individual contributes only a minute part to the final product. The worker no longer creates a total product but is instead merely a minor component in an elaborate mechanized or bureaucratized process. In the most simple preindustrial society, the number of specialized occupational roles—if any exist at all—can probably be counted on the fingers of one hand. In 1850, in the early stages of industrialism in the United States, the census recorded a grand total of 323 occupations. In the contemporary United States, according to the U.S. Department of Labor, there are over 35,000 job specialties. This calculation, incidentally, refers only to legitimate occupations. It excludes such jobs as dope pusher, pimp, pickpocket, counterfeiter, and confidence trickster, all of which, of course, include many further subspecialties. In its *Dictionary of Occupational Titles* the Department of Labor lists such highly specialized occupations as blintze roller, alligator farmer, oxtail washer, cherry-bomb finisher, corset stringer, earmuff assembler, scallop trimmer, and chicken sexer.

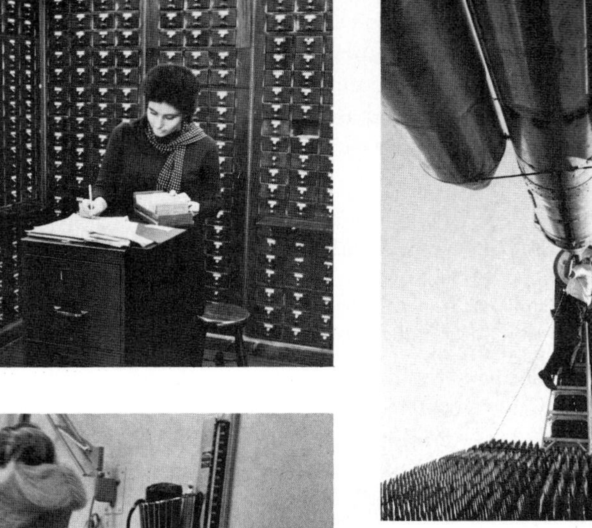

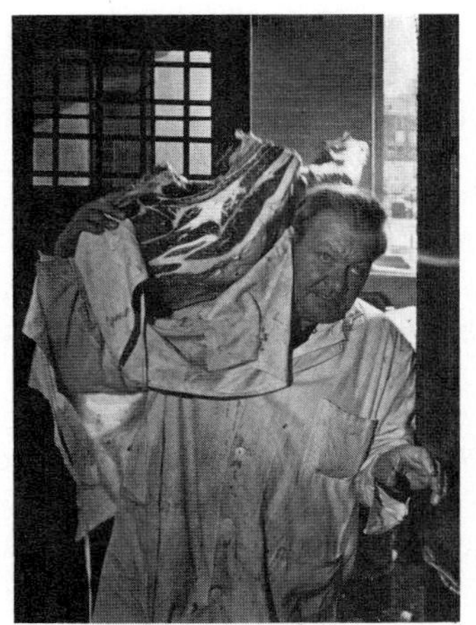

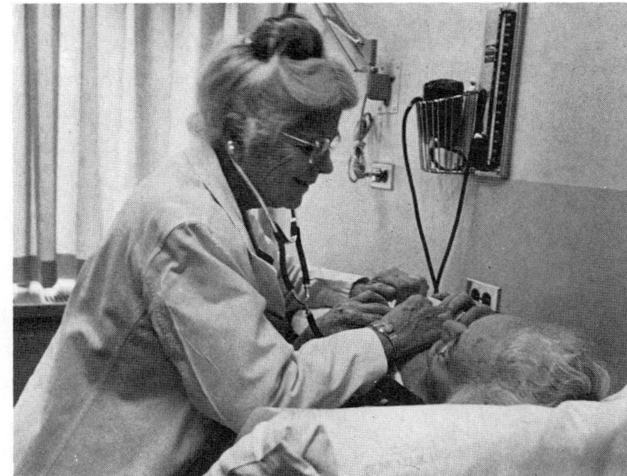

The assembly line of the modern factory has come to epitomize the division of labor in modern industry. This is particularly true in the auto industry, where a worker may tighten identical bolts hundreds of times an hour, day after day and month after month. The potential consequences of this kind of work were suggested as long ago as 1776, when Adam Smith published his classic work, *The Wealth of Nations:*

> The man whose whole life is spent in performing a few simple operations . . . has no occasion to exert his understanding or to exercise his invention. . . . He naturally loses, therefore, the habit of such exertion, and generally becomes as stupid and ignorant as it is possible for a human creature to become.

A more restrained comment was made by Alexis de Tocqueville (1954, originally published 1835), a French observer of early industrial development in the United States:

> What can be expected of a man who has spent twenty years of his life in making heads for pins? And to what can that mighty human intelligence which has so often stirred the world be applied in him . . . ? When a workman has spent a considerable proportion of his existence in this manner, his thoughts are forever set upon the object of his daily toil. . . . The workman becomes more weak, more narrow-minded, and more dependent. The art advances, the artisan recedes.

Such a situation is obviously of great sociological and personal significance, a topic to which we will return when we consider the relationship between work and alienation in industrial society.

Anomie and the Division of Labor

In his important work *The Division of Labor in Society* (1893), the French sociologist Emile Durkheim tried to determine the social consequences of the division of labor in modern societies. A major theme in nearly all Durkheim's writings is the importance of shared social norms and values in maintaining social cohesion and solidarity. He argued that the nature of this social solidarity depends on the extent of the division of labor.

Traditional societies, Durkheim argued, are held together by what he called *mechanical solidarity.* Because these societies are small and because everyone does much the same work, the members are all socialized in the same pattern, share the same experiences, and hold common values. These values, which are mainly religious in nature, form a "collective consciousness" for the community, a set of norms, beliefs, and assumptions shared by one and all. There is little individuality, and the society consists basically of a collection of kinship groups, all with similar characteristics.

Figure 18.2 In a traditional, preindustrial community, such as this village in the Sudan, there is hardly any division of labor except on the grounds of age and sex. People wear similar clothes, reside in similar dwellings, share similar ideas, and live much the same lives. Such a society, Durkheim argued, is held together by "mechanical solidarity," or the basic similarity of its members. A diversified modern industrial society, in contrast, is held together by "organic solidarity," or the dissimilarity of people who have to depend on one another's specialized skills.

Modern societies, on the other hand, are held together by what Durkheim called *organic solidarity,* a much looser bond. Because these societies are large and people engage in a variety of economic activities, the members have quite different experiences, hold different values, and socialize their children in many varying patterns. They have fewer beliefs in common, and religion shrinks in importance. The collective consciousness has much less binding power on the community, and people no longer unquestioningly accept the assumptions it contains. People think of themselves as individuals first and as members of a kinship or wider social group second. The society thus consists of a series of interconnected individuals, each with different characteristics. The basis for social solidarity and cohesion is no longer the *similarity* of the members but rather their *differences.* Because they are now interdependent, they must rely on one another if their society is to function effectively.

The essential problem in modern society, Durkheim argued, is that the division of labor leads inevitably to

feelings of individualism, which can be achieved only at the cost of shared sentiments or beliefs. The result is *anomie*—a state of normlessness in both the society and the individual. Social norms become confused or break down, and people feel detached from their fellows. Having little commitment to shared norms, people lack social guidelines for personal conduct and are inclined to pursue their private interests without regard for the interests of society as a whole. Social control of individual behavior becomes ineffective, and the society is threatened with disorganization or even disintegration as a result.

Durkheim was probably correct in his view that the division of labor and the resulting growth of individualism would break down shared commitment to social norms, and it seems plausible that there is widespread anomie in modern societies. Yet these societies do retain some broad consensus on norms and values, as we can readily see when we compare one society with another, say, the United States with China. Although this consensus seems much weaker than that in preindustrial societies, it is probably still strong enough to guide most individual behavior and to avert the social breakdown that Durkheim feared. Durkheim's analysis remains valuable, however, for his acute insights into the far-ranging effects that the division of labor has on social and personal life.

The Sociology of Occupations

Sociologists who study economic life are especially interested in the changes that industrialization causes in the occupational structure of a society. Their interest focuses primarily on two patterns that accompany the industrialization process in all societies: first, the changing nature and content of occupations; second, the tendency for occupations that were once poorly esteemed to become professionalized. Let's examine each of these patterns.

Primary, Secondary, and Tertiary Sectors

Work in an industrial society takes place in any one of three main sectors, with the proportion of the labor force in any one sector depending on the society's level of industrial development. *Primary industry* involves the gathering and extracting of undeveloped natural re-

Figure 18.3 There are three main sectors of work in an industrial society. Workers in primary industry are involved in extracting raw materials, such as coal, from the environment. Workers in secondary industry transform raw materials, such as cotton, into manufactured objects, such as twine. Workers in tertiary industry supply services, such as that of the secretary, to other members of society. As an industrial society becomes more advanced, the proportion of workers in secondary and, later, in tertiary industry grows larger.

DISTRIBUTION OF PRIMARY, SECONDARY, AND TERTIARY OCCUPATIONAL GROUPS AS PERCENT OF TOTAL LABOR FORCE 1900–1975

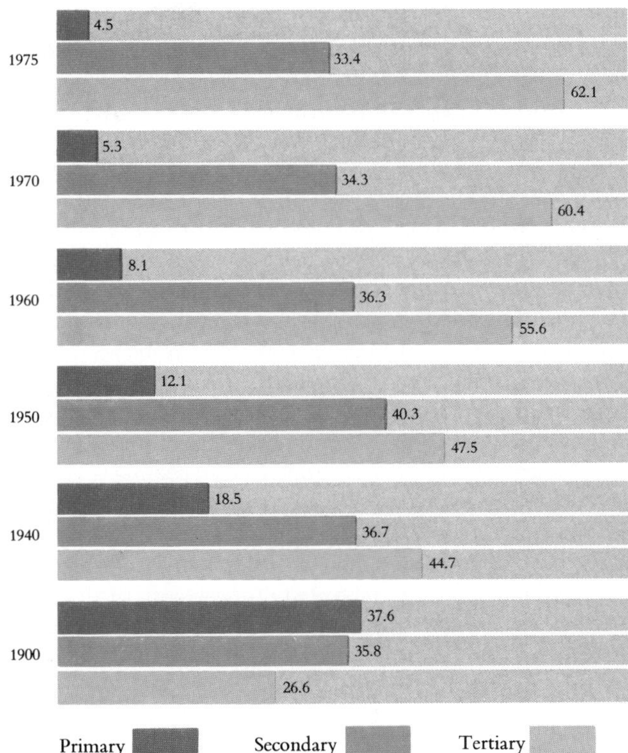

Source: Adapted from Daniel J. Rossides, *The American Class System* (Boston: Houghton Mifflin, 1976), p. 136.

Figure 18.4 The proportion of American workers engaged in primary industry has dropped sharply since the turn of the century; the proportion in secondary industry is now shrinking, and the proportion in tertiary industry is rising rapidly.

sources—for example, mining, fishing, forestry, and agriculture. *Secondary industry* involves turning the raw materials produced by primary industry into manufactured goods—for example, automobiles, furniture, canned foods. *Tertiary industry* involves service activities of some kind or another—for example, medicine, banking, teaching, laundering, automobile maintenance.

In the early stages of industrialism most workers are employed in primary industry, tapping the natural resources on which later industrial development will build. In the later stages secondary industry becomes the dominant sector as more and more economic activity is devoted to the production of manufactured goods. In the most advanced stages of industrialism tertiary industry becomes dominant, with the bulk of the work force becoming involved in service occupations. In the sixties, the United States became the first country in the world to have more than half of its labor force engaged in tertiary industry. White-collar workers are now the largest single occupational category; the blue-collar category is shrinking rapidly; and farm workers, who represented nearly 40 percent of the labor force at the turn of the century, now comprise less than 5 percent of all workers. The immense productivity of industrialism has created a substantial surplus wealth and with it a demand for a variety of new services, while advances in industrial technology have freed many workers from the hard manual labor that was more typical of the earlier stages of industrialism. As a result, more and more people are acquiring professional, technical, or managerial skills, and our occupational structure is now radically unlike that found in less economically developed societies.

Professionalization

A *profession* is an occupation requiring some knowledge of and training in an art or science. Professions are generally the most highly paid and prestigious of occupations, and professionals perform many of society's most important roles—for example, in teaching, research, law, medicine, and technology (Parsons, 1954).

Professions are distinguished from other occupations by several characteristics. First, the skill of professionals is based on systematic, theoretical knowledge, not merely on training in particular techniques. Second, professionals have considerable autonomy over their work. Their clients are presumed to be incompetent to make judgments about the problems with which the profession is concerned: you can give instructions to your hairdresser or tailor but cannot advise a doctor or lawyer on matters of medicine or law. Third, professionals form associations that regulate the conduct of their members and even have the right to strip members of their professional credentials. Fourth, admission to a profession is carefully controlled by the existing members. Anyone can claim to be a salesperson or a carpenter, but someone who claims to be a surgeon or a professor without having the necessary credentials is an imposter. The process of becoming a professional involves taking an examination, receiving a licence, and acquiring a title, and this process is usually regulated by the professional association concerned. Fifth, professions have a code of ethics that all their members are expected to adhere to; the penalty for a breach of this code may be expulsion from the profession (Greenwood, 1962). Most occupations have some of these characteristics to some degree, but only professions place such great emphasis on all of them (Etzioni, 1969).

It is common for nonprofessionals to try to "professionalize" their occupations in the hope of achieving the greater prestige and income that professional status brings. This transformation generally follows a typical sequence. The first step is the creation of a professional association, one of whose first tasks is to define who is qualified to be a member of the profession and who is not. The second step is to change the name of the occupation, perhaps from "plumber" to "sanitary engineer," so that public identification with the old, low-status occupation is broken. The third step is to establish a code of ethics, which serves to raise the esteem in which the occupation is held and provides a means of keeping out "undesirable" members. The fourth step is to persuade political authorities to require all members of the occupation to have formal certification and to ensure that training facilities fall, as far as possible, under the control of the professional association (Caplow, 1954; Wilensky, 1964). Attempts to professionalize jobs in the primary and secondary sectors of industry generally meet with only limited success. These jobs usually do not involve sophisticated training, are often publicly identified as "hard" or even "dirty" work that virtually anyone could do, and continue to have relatively low prestige despite efforts at professionalization. In the more "clean" white-collar jobs of the tertiary sector, however, professionalization tends to be more successful, and the number of jobs whose occupants can claim professional or at least semiprofessional status is expanding rapidly.

Work and Alienation

Whether we see it as a source of fulfillment and satisfaction or as a source of boredom and indignity, whether we view it as enjoyable in itself or simply as a means of making a living, work is a central part of our lives. We derive our social status primarily from our work and from the income that it produces. In American society, the person who is poorly paid or habitually out of work is apt to be dismissed as "worthless," but the holder of a respected, well-paid occupation is honored. Work helps to define the respective social roles of both sexes. The husband who is a breadwinner finds his masculinity and responsibility as a husband and father reaffirmed, while the wife's sense of identity is influenced by whether she has an independent career or is "only a housewife." Retired people often feel a shattering loss of identity and purpose when they stop working, for work integrates us into society, offering a place in the world and a sense of being useful and needed (Berger, 1964). Given the importance of work in social life, it is small wonder that the growing signs of worker alienation in the United States have attracted a great deal of attention.

The Concept of Alienation

The word "alienation" has come into popular usage as a catch-all term for a variety of psychological ills, and we must define its sociological meaning more closely. Essentially, *alienation* refers to the sense of powerlessness, isolation, and meaninglessness experienced by human beings when they are confronted with social institutions and conditions that they cannot control and consider oppressive (Seeman, 1959).

Figure 18.5 Assembly-line work is usually considered one of the most alienating forms of labor. It demands little imagination or commitment from the worker, who is reduced to a mere element in the manufacturing process, a "cog in the machine."

The concept of alienation was introduced to modern sociology by Karl Marx. To Marx, alienation results from the lack of a sense of control over the social world. People lose the recognition that society and social institutions are constructed by human beings and can therefore be changed by human beings. The social world thus confronts people as a hostile thing, leaving them "alien" in the very environment that they have created. Marx applied this perspective to many social institutions, such as law, government, religion, and economic life. In the religious sphere, for example, people create religions, lose the sense that religions are socially created, and helplessly allow their lives to be dominated by the very institution they have constructed. So it is with the economic order. People establish economic systems, find themselves confronted and oppressed by systems they feel powerless to change, and become the victims of their own institutions.

Marx believed that the capacity for labor is one of the most distinctive human characteristics. All other species, he argued, are merely objects in the world; human beings alone are subjects, because they consciously act on and create the world, shaping their lives, cultures, and personalities in the process. In modern societies, however, people have become alienated from their work, and thus from nature, from other human beings, and from themselves.

An important source of this alienation, in Marx's view, is the extreme division of labor in modern societies. Each worker has a specific, restricted, and limiting role. He or she no longer applies total human capacities of the hands, the mind, and the emotions to work. The worker has diminished responsibility, does not own the tools with which the work is done, does not own the final product, does not have the right to make decisions, and becomes a minute part of a process, a mere cog in a machine. Work becomes an enforced activity, not a creative and satisfying one. This situation is aggravated in capitalist economies, in which the profit produced by the labor of the worker goes to someone else. Marx's summary of the nature of alienation at work, written well over a century ago, seems as relevant today as it was then (Marx, 1964a, originally published 1844):

> What, then, constitutes the alienation of labor? First, the fact that labor is *external* to the worker, i.e., it does not belong to his essential being; that in his work, therefore, he does not affirm himself but denies himself, does not feel content but unhappy, does not develop freely his physical and mental energy but mortifies his body and ruins his mind. The worker therefore only feels himself outside his work, and in his work feels outside himself. He is at home when he is not working, and when he is working he is not at home. His labor is therefore not voluntary, but coerced; it is *forced labor.* It is therefore not the satisfaction of a need; it is merely a *means* to satisfy needs external to it. Its alien character emerges clearly in the fact that as soon as no physical or other compulsion exists, labor is shunned like the plague. External labor, labor in which man alienates himself, is a labor of self-sacrifice. Lastly, the external character of labor for the worker appears in the fact that it is not his own, but someone else's, that it does not belong to him, that he belongs, not to himself, but to another.

Worker Alienation in the United States

In 1973, the U.S. Department of Health, Education, and Welfare issued a report, *Work in America,* that captured the public attention as few government reports ever do. The report focused on alienation in the American work force, and its account of the "blue-collar blues" and "white-collar woes" was instantly recognizable to millions of people. Alienation, the report found, is a common, growing, and serious problem in American economic life:

> Significant numbers of American workers are dissatisfied with the quality of their working lives. Dull, repetitive, seemingly meaningless tasks, offering little challenge or autonomy, are causing discontent among workers at all occupational levels. . . . Many workers . . . feel locked in, their mobility blocked, the opportunity to grow lacking in their jobs, challenge missing from their tasks. Young workers appear to be as committed to the institution of work as their elders have been, but many are rebelling against the anachronistic authoritarianism of the workplace.

The extent of worker dissatisfaction varies from job to job and from one social group to another. In terms of income, the most dissatisfied workers are those who earn the least. In technical, managerial, and professional occupations, one person in ten is dissatisfied. In manufacturing, service, and wholesale occupations, the rate is one in four (Herrick, 1972). Differences in income provide only a partial explanation for this difference between job categories, however. Low-income workers have much less control over their working environment than do professional and other high-income workers, a factor that also influences worker satisfaction.

The most dissatisfied social group are black workers, of whom 37 percent express negative attitudes toward their jobs, probably because blacks are concentrated in low-paying, dead-end occupations. The second most dissatisfied group are workers under thirty with some college education, among whom about one in four is dissatisfied. Their dissatisfaction is probably related to the disillusion they experience in the regimented world of work after the relative freedom and idealism of the college environment. The third most dissatisfied group are women under thirty. Younger women are more likely to resent the sex-based division of labor that restricts them to low-paying, uninteresting jobs and denies them the opportunities available to similarly qualified men. The younger the worker, the more dissatisfied he or she is likely to be. Older workers, it seems, have lower expectations of job satisfaction, but younger workers expect their jobs to be interesting and fulfilling. Attitudes of the young toward the authoritarian atmosphere of many workplaces are changing rapidly. As recently as 1968 some 56 percent of students said they did not mind "being bossed around on the job," but this proportion had shrunk to 36 percent by 1971 (Yankelovitch, 1972).

Asking people whether they are satisfied with their jobs is one way of detecting worker alienation. Another way is to ask them if they would choose the same job over again. The answers to this question, the *Work in America* report found, suggest an even higher level of alienation. The great majority of workers would rather have different jobs. Only 43 percent of white-collar workers and only 24 percent of blue-collar workers would choose the same occupation again. Interestingly, the report also found that worker satisfaction is the best predictor of life expectancy. It is a better indicator of longevity than such standard measures as a rating by an examining physician or the extent of tobacco use.

"Human Relations" in Industry

Employers are now keenly interested in redesigning work as a means of reducing alienation, improving labor-management relations, and stepping up production, and they are calling on industrial sociologists to help them. Indeed, many of the attempts to humanize the workplace over the past few decades have been based on insights gained from sociological research into industrial relations. Earlier in the century, the worker in industry was regarded as little more than another machine. "Efficiency experts" ignored the worker's psychological and social characteristics and concentrated instead on the physical aspects of the job to be done. The chief advocate of this approach was Frederick Winslow Taylor, an engineer who fathered "time and motion" studies of work and recommended "scientific management." Taylor believed that maximum efficiency would be achieved if the worker was strictly disciplined and if every physical movement at work was carefully planned in advance down to the tiniest detail.

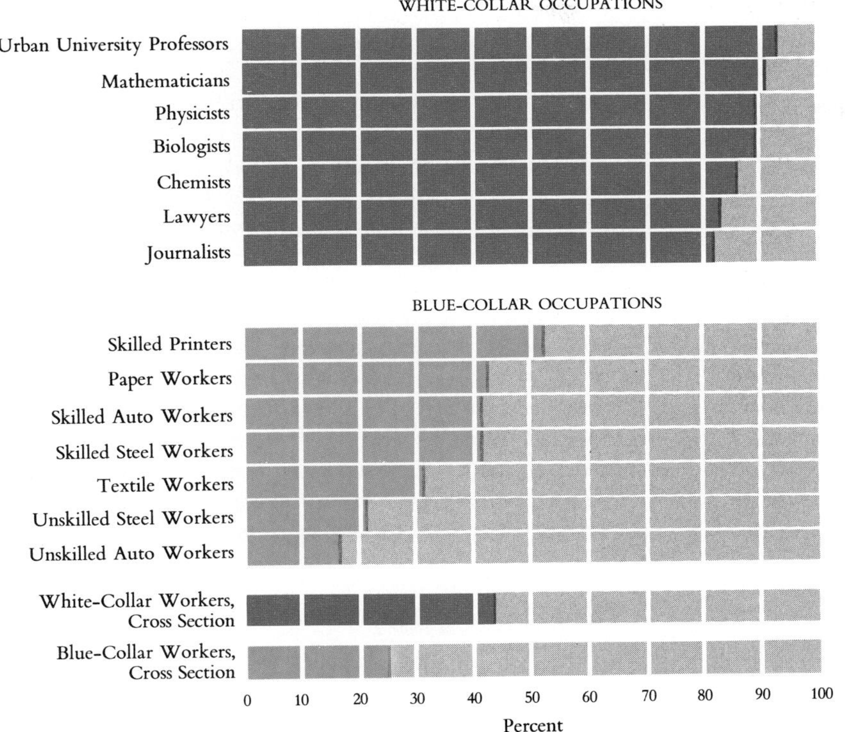

Source: Work in America: Report on a Special Task Force to the Secretary of Health, Education, and Welfare (Cambridge, Mass.: MIT Press, 1973), p. 16.

Figure 18.6 Job satisfaction is closely related to occupational status: those jobs that are professionalized yield higher incomes, more prestige, and a greater sense of control over one's working life.

This view was shattered by the experiments conducted during the thirties by Elton Mayo and his associates at the Hawthorne plant of the Western Electric company. In their most famous experiment, the researchers systematically altered the working conditions of a group of employees to find out how the changes would influence productivity. First, they changed the method of payment to one of group piecework. Production went up. Then they introduced brief rest periods. Production rose again. Next they served refreshments twice a day, and production rose once more. The researchers tried new experiments, introducing new breaks in the working day, or letting the workers go home early. With each change, production rose. Finally, the researchers returned the group to their original working conditions—and production rose to even greater heights! What was happening? The answer—a sociological commonplace now but a revolutionary finding then—is that the workers had formed a close-knit primary group. Flattered by the attention that they were receiving and the variety that was introduced into their working lives, they had established their own norms for productivity and were attempting to please the researchers by working harder (Roethlisberger and Dickson, 1939; Mayo, 1966). Sociologists are now fully aware of the influence of peer-group norms on worker productivity. It is not so much pay or even working conditions that directly affect output; it is the consensus of the workers as to what a reasonable output should be. Individual workers who exceed the output are considered "rate-busters" and are informally pressured into conforming to group norms.

Mayo's findings led to a new "human relations" approach in industry that emphasizes the human concerns of the worker. The growth of labor unions, whose formation was vigorously resisted until the thirties in a series of particularly bloody conflicts, has also given workers considerable influence in determining their working conditions. The environment of the contemporary office or factory is infinitely more congenial than it was even a few decades ago. Why, then, has worker alienation come to the fore as a serious social problem?

One reason is that organizations have grown very much larger, leaving people in an ever more impersonal environment in which their contributions seem meaningless. Another reason is that worker expectations have generally risen, but changes in the organization of work have not kept pace with this trend. The modern worker is much less likely than the worker of a few decades ago to tolerate boring, tedious, meaningless, or authoritarian working conditions. Better educated than ever before and enjoying an affluent leisure life, the worker sees a stark contrast between the conditions within and beyond the place of work. Conditions that would be tolerated by an earlier generation are considered oppressive today.

Employers are beginning to recognize this situation, and we can expect many attempts to improve the human aspects of working conditions in the future. These will include giving workers more responsibility, encouraging group decision making, rotating jobs so that workers do not spend months or years at the same task, modifying the minute division of labor on the assembly line, sharing profits with workers, and offering increased leisure time in return for increased productivity.

Capitalism and Socialism

There are two basic ways in which an industrial society can produce and distribute goods and services: capitalism and socialism. There are strong ideological differences between countries adopting either strategy, and as a result, the differences between these systems have tended to be overemphasized. In fact, however, there is little basis for the common view that capitalism and socialism represent "either/or" alternatives. In practice the American economy, generally regarded as a model of capitalism, has many socialistic features. It is, for example, subject to extensive government regulation and efforts to redistribute wealth. Similarly, the Soviet economy, generally regarded as a model of socialism, has many capitalistic features. There are great differences in individual income and there is an increasing reliance on financial "incentives" for workers.

It would also be grossly inaccurate to regard either all capitalist or all socialist societies as being fundamentally identical. In practice there is a great variety of kinds of economy, ranging from the most capitalist societies, such as the United States and Canada, through intermediate societies, such as Britain, Sweden, and Yugoslavia, to the most socialist societies, such as Albania and China. The terms "capitalist" and "socialist" represent *ideal types*—abstract concepts that are approximated to a greater or lesser extent by existing societies. Before we consider these types in detail, we must examine the concept of property, for the ownership of property is the chief bone of contention between the advocates of each type of economic system.

The Concept of Property

In everyday speech we think of "property" as referring to an object or objects. Strictly speaking, however, *property* refers not to an object but to the *rights* that the owner of the object has in relation to others who are not owners of the object. Property is established in a society through social norms, often expressed in law, that define the conditions under which people may own objects. Property rights are backed by the state and enforced through its legal institutions. We can own private property in the United States, for example, only because the law allows us to. Property not only confers rights on the owner; it may impose duties as well. No society permits unrestricted rights over property. If you own land in a residential area, you may not build a factory or a pig farm on it.

Property exists because resources are scarce; if they were all as unlimited and inexhaustible as the air, nobody would want to claim ownership. Ownership of property may take one of three forms:

1. *Communal ownership* exists when property belongs to the community as a whole and may be used but not owned by any member of the community. Communal

ownership of land is frequently found in small preindustrial societies.

2. *Private ownership* exists when property belongs to specific individuals. Private property is recognized in all societies. In some it may be restricted to a few household possessions; in others it may include assets worth millions of dollars.

3. *Public ownership* exists when property belongs to the state or some other recognized political authority that claims the property on behalf of the people as a whole. A good deal of property in industrial societies (such as highways and schools) is publicly owned.

Ownership does not merely create a relationship between the owner and the object; it also creates a relationship between the owner and other people. Those who own the means of producing goods and services—means such as land, factories, and capital funds—are potentially in a position of power over those who do not. The debate between the advocates of capitalism and socialism hinges on the question of whether the means of production and distribution should be privately or publicly owned. Advocates of capitalism contend that the interests of all are served best if there is a minimum of public ownership of the means of production and distribution. Advocates of socialism argue that private ownership leads to exploitation and inequality, which can be avoided if the means of production and distribution are publicly owned. Let's look at the problem in more detail.

Capitalism

In its ideal form, *capitalism* contains two essential ingredients: the deliberate pursuit of *personal profit* as the goal of economic activity, and *free competition* among both the buyers and the sellers of goods and services. As Max Weber remarked, the outstanding characteristic of capitalism is production "for the pursuit of profit, and ever renewed profit." There is nothing unusual about people seeking their own self-interest, but the distinguishing feature of capitalism is that it defines this activity as normal, morally acceptable, and socially desirable. Competition, however, is also regarded as necessary if the capitalist system is to work effectively. As John D. Rockefeller put it, competition "is not an evil tendency in business. It is merely a working out of a law of nature and a law of God" (quoted in Hofstadter, 1955).

Why is the pursuit of profit and an atmosphere of unrestricted competition so necessary for capitalism? The reason, Adam Smith argued in 1776, is that under these conditions the forces of supply and demand will ensure the production of the best possible products at the lowest possible price. If there is a public demand for some good or service, the profit motive will provide an incentive for individual capitalists to produce what the public wants. Competition among capitalists will give the public the opportunity to compare the quality and prices of goods, so that producers who are inefficient or who charge excessive prices will be put out of business. The "invisible hand" of market forces thus ensures the greatest good of the entire society. Efficient producers are rewarded with profits, and consumers get quality products at competitive prices. For the system to work, however, there should ideally be a minimum of government interference in economic life. If the government attempts to regulate the supply of or demand for goods, the forces of the market will be upset, producers will lose their incentive to produce, and prices will be artificially distorted. The government should therefore adopt a policy of *laissez-faire,* meaning "leave it alone."

In practice, this pure form of capitalism has never existed, although it was perhaps approximated in the early phases of industrial development. Particularly since the Great Depression, when the capitalist system seemed in danger of total collapse, there has been general recognition of the need for government regulation of the economy. The U.S. government now finds it necessary to supervise many details of economic activity. It supports the price of some commodities and puts ceilings on the prices of others. It intervenes in international trade and concerns itself with the balance of payments with other countries. It protects some natural resources and encourages the exploitation of others. It sets minimum wage standards, provides for unemployment benefits, and sometimes supervises labor-management relations. It regulates the level of production and consumption through its budget and its tax policy. The growth of *monopolies,* single firms that dominate an industry, and *oligopolies,* groups of a few firms that dominate an industry, has sometimes eliminated competition and made it possible for these firms to fix

Figure 18.7 Capitalism, at least in its ideal form, assumes free competition among the suppliers of goods and services. In theory at least, this competition results in the production of the best possible goods at the lowest possible price, because consumers are able to select the cheapest and best products. Socialist critics argue, however, that this system involves a waste of resources by firms producing essentially similar products.

prices. For this reason, the government has the authority to prevent the concentration of economic power. Private ownership of firms by individual capitalists is now largely a thing of the past, for the American economy is now dominated by giant corporations owned by many thousands of shareholders.

Modern American capitalism is thus unlike the classical model in many respects. But our ideology still legitimates free competition and the pursuit of private profit, and our government is consequently reluctant to restrict either. Above all, Americans believe that their social and economic interests are best served if the means of production and distribution are privately owned, and they strongly resist any attempt to establish public ownership over them. It is this feature that makes the United States the most capitalistic society in the world.

Socialism

Socialism rests on entirely different assumptions: production should not be for private profit, and competition between different firms producing similar products is a waste of resources. The pursuit of private profit is regarded as fundamentally immoral, because one person's profit is another person's loss. Under capitalism, it is argued, workers are paid less than the value of what they produce, and the surplus wealth is seized as profit by the owners. The result is social inequality and social conflict. Production should not be for profit; it should be designed to serve social goals, and whether it is profitable or not is of secondary importance. Since private owners exploit both workers and consumers and will not produce unprofitable goods or services, whatever the social need for them, it is necessary for the means of production to be taken into public ownership and run in the best interests of society as a whole. Similarly, the means of distribution of wealth must be publicly owned to ensure that goods and services flow to those who need them rather than only to those who can afford them. The aims of a socialist economy are the efficient production of needed goods and services and the achievement of social equality by preventing the accumulation of private wealth. To this end, the government must regulate the economy in accordance with long-term national plans, and it must not hesitate to establish artificial price levels or to run important industries at a loss if necessary.

The economy of modern socialist societies, such as the Soviet Union, conforms in some respects to this classic model. The means of production and distribution—land, machines, factories, capital funds, banks, retail outlets, and so on—are publicly owned. Speculative investment and the pursuit of private profit are not only considered undesir-

Figure 18.8 Under socialism, the government regulates the economy in accordance with social goals, particularly that of economic equality among the people. This Chinese couple is living in an apartment supplied by the state to factory workers, at a rental equivalent to about 5 percent of wages. The apartment may seem inadequate by American standards, but compared to housing standards before the Chinese revolution it is a tremendous improvement. Critics argue, however, that this system discourages individual initiative.

able but are crimes of theft punishable in certain instances with the death penalty. The economy is closely regulated in accordance with national economic plans that are designed to meet specified social goals—even if this means depriving people of more frivolous needs, such as the latest in fashionable clothing, in favor of investment in heavy industry that will generate more wealth in the long run. People are permitted private ownership of personal goods, such as household furniture and automobiles, but may not own property that produces wealth. In the Soviet Union and all other socialist societies, however, there are marked differences in income between ordinary workers and those in managerial and other executive positions, and the distribution of wealth is thus often very unequal. Several socialist societies are also experimenting with "incentive payments" to encourage higher production among workers—a practice not very different from offering them greater "profit" for working harder.

Democratic Socialism

A compromise between the capitalist and socialist models is that of *democratic socialism,* which is practiced by nearly all the countries of Western Europe. Under this system, the state takes only strategic industries and services into public ownership, such as railways, airlines, mines, banks, radio, TV, telephone systems, medical services, colleges, and important manufacturing enterprises such as chemicals and steel. Private ownership of other means of production is permitted or even encouraged, but the economy is closely regulated in accordance with national priorities. Very high tax rates are used to prevent excessive profits or an undue concentration of wealth. A measure of social equality is ensured through extensive welfare services. In Britain, for example, college education and medical services are available free of charge, and about a third of the population lives in heavily subsidized public housing.

Communism

A fourth alternative, which is hypothetical at this point and seems likely to remain so, is *communism.* The socialist societies of Eastern Europe and Asia are usually but incorrectly described as "communist" in the United States, but they never describe themselves in this way. They believe that they are still at the stage of socialism, a preparatory step before a truly communist society is achieved. Since no communist society has ever existed and since the writings of Marx and other advocates of communism are somewhat vague on this point, it is not entirely clear what a communist society would look like. In general, however, it would have some of the characteristics implied in the communal ownership pattern described earlier but currently found only in primitive societies. The role of the state would shrink, there would be an abundance of goods and services, people would no longer regard property as "private," and wealth and power would be shared in harmony by the community as a whole. Under socialism, people are paid according to their work, but under communism individuals would contribute according to their abilities and receive according to their needs. The history of human alienation and strife would be over, and each person would be able to fulfill his or her human potential to the full. The major problem with such a society is that nobody seems to know quite how to arrive there. It has become increasingly evident over the past few decades that the socialist countries of the world are "stuck" in the socialist stage and have virtually no idea of how to get beyond it. Indeed, China seems to be the only socialist society that has not abandoned the effort.

It is important to recognize that when Marx advocated communism, it was the concept of communism we have outlined and not the Soviet version of socialism that he had in mind. Much of the antagonism to Marxist thought in the United States stems from a confusion between his ideas and contemporary Soviet practice, but if Marx's writings are anything to go by, it is highly unlikely that he would regard modern Soviet society with much enthusiasm.

Corporate Capitalism in the United States

The modern American economy, as we have seen, is no longer based on the competitive efforts of innumerable private capitalists. It is now dominated by large *corporations,* formal, commercial organizations that have widely dispersed ownership and that may exert enormous political and economic power.

Corporations and the American Economy

The corporation is a relatively new social invention that first achieved prominence in the late nineteenth century. Corporations have no single owner. They are owned by thousands or even hundreds of thousands of stockholders, and some of these stockholders are other corporations. In fact, most corporate stock in the United States is actually owned by corporate investors and not private citizens. In theory, the stockholders control the corporation by electing a board of directors and by voting on company policies at annual shareholders' meetings. In practice, however, the widely dispersed shareholders cannot effectively control corporate activities, and they merely rubber-stamp decisions that have already been made for them. The boards of directors are essentially self-perpetuating bodies whose recommendations, including nominations for new board members, are approved by stockholders as a matter of course. The day-to-day running of the corporation is in the hands of the management, which not only supervises company operations but also makes most of the major policy decisions, which in turn are usually approved by the board. The most important effect of this situation is that it tends to separate *ownership* of the firm from *control* of the firm. Those who control the corporation—the managers and to a lesser extent the directors—are for most purposes responsible to nobody but themselves. As long as they continue to maximize profits, the shareholders generally remain content.

The size and economic power of the major corporations is immense. The top one hundred corporations, less than 0.01 percent of all corporations in the United States, own more than half of the manufacturing assets in the country. The top 0.5 percent account for 75 percent of assets, and the top 1 percent for 81 percent of assets (Means, 1970; Galbraith, 1973). Of the nearly 14,000 banks in the United States, the largest ten hold over a quarter of all assets and deposits, while ten of the 18,000 insurance companies hold almost 60 percent of all insurance company assets (Anderson, 1974a). In 1975, 173 industrial corporations made profits of more than $50 million a year, more than 90 made profits of more than $100 million, and 3 made profits of over $1 billion. General Motors employs more than half a million people and has sales revenues greater than the entire national product of 130 individual countries (Vernon, 1971).

The domination of the American economy by large corporations has several important consequences. One of them, explored more fully in Chapter 19 (The Political Order), is that these corporations are able to apply political leverage on national policy, winning favors for themselves, influencing the country's tax structure, and successfully blocking efforts to prevent the growth of oligopolies in particular industries. Corporate capitalism, according to the economist John Kenneth Galbraith (1971), has become so large and complex and invests so much time and capital in its enterprises that it can no longer afford the hazards of free competition: the stakes are too high. As a result, government and corporations cooperate informally in running what is in effect a planned economy, with minimal competition among the major enterprises.

At the highest levels of corporate industry there is very little of the competition considered so essential in the classic model of capitalism. Corporations compete not with the quality or price of their products but rather through their advertising (Smelser, 1963). This tendency, which is apparent, for example, in the automobile and airline industries, involves an extraordinary waste of resources on the production of basically similar goods and services and on extensive advertising designed to make them appear different. Most countries have only one airline; the United States has several major airlines and hundreds of smaller ones. The services offered by the major airlines are essentially similar. They often fly the same planes, always charge identical fares to the same categories of passengers on the same routes, and operate under agreements that specify uniformity in the tiniest detail of their services, from the size of seats to the size of drinks. Competition takes place only at the level of advertising and in the splendor of their respective terminal buildings—a duplication of effort that might well be much more productively directed elsewhere but is instead reflected in the costs of air travel to the public. Americans are bombarded with commercial advertising. We receive, on the average, a minimum of 560 advertising messages each day (Toffler, 1970). This advertising, much of it devoted to making otherwise indistinguishable products seem distinctive and to creating artificial demands for products where no demand existed before, represents a diversion of billions of dollars each year from other more socially useful goals.

Figure 18.9 The life-style that corporate capitalism has brought to the United States is highly valued by Americans, but it involves a colossal waste of scarce natural resources. Americans are consuming many mineral and other resources at such a rate that known world reserves of many of these materials may be exhausted within a few decades (see Chapter 20, Population and Ecology).

Large oligopolies are able to use advertising to influence public tastes and preferences. The auto industry, to cite an obvious example, has persuaded Americans that the appearance, though not necessarily the quality and performance, of cars should change every year. Under the policy of "planned obsolescence," American cars are deliberately designed to last only a few years. It is technically feasible to build cars that would last far longer than they do at present, but social values have been so manipulated by auto-industry advertising that possession of a car more than a few years old is almost a social stigma. A former chairman of General Motors explained that "planned obsolescence, in my view, is another word for progress," but the word also represents huge corporate profits, spectacular wastage of scarce mineral resources, and an extra $1000 on every car sold to the American public. This kind of manipulation of public tastes and diversion of scarce resources is perhaps inevitable in any capitalist society.

One further feature of corporate capitalism in the United States merits consideration: what Galbraith (1966) has termed the contrast between "private affluence" and "public squalor." The American public has learned to prefer to spend its money on the consumption of goods and services provided by private enterprise rather than on taxes for goods and services provided by public authorities. The United States therefore has a generally affluent private life in the midst of generally squalid public facilities such as mass-transit systems and urban schools. This ordering of priorities would seem peculiar to many other societies, but it is taken for granted in the United States, where we have learned to value highly the particular life-style that corporate capitalism has made possible.

Multinational Corporations

In the past, corporations concentrated their efforts in a single industry. Today they diversify into a host of other industries by buying controlling shares in other corporations. The largest corporations have now become multinational in scale by establishing industries abroad or taking over existing foreign corporations. The International Telephone and Telegraph company (ITT), which has diversified into hundreds of industries entirely unrelated to telephones and telegraphs, now employs 400,000 workers in sixty-eight countries. Many multinational corporations are wealthier than some of the countries in which they operate. Multinational corporations already account for more than a quarter of total world economic production, a share that will rise to over one-half in the next twenty-five years (Segal, 1973). American corporate industry abroad is now the third largest economy in the world, after the United States and the Soviet Union (Jacoby, 1970). Subject to the authority of no one nation, having a largely fictional responsibility to their far-flung shareholders, dedicated to the pursuit of profit, and run by a tiny elite of managers and directors, these corporations are posing problems on a global scale. Decisions taken by a small group of people in the United States can mean prosperity or unemployment in nations thousands of miles away, and they can also mean direct political interference in other societies. American armaments, aircraft, and oil companies, among others, have not hesitated to bribe government officials elsewhere in the world in order to win contracts or influence the policies of foreign governments. ITT secretly requested the Nixon administration to overthrow the government of Chile, offering up to $1 million to the federal government as a contribution toward the expenses involved (Sampson, 1973). These huge multinational corporations have evolved much more quickly than have any means to apply social control over them. They now represent a disturbing concentration of unscrutinized political and economic power that may have important social impact.

Figure 18.10 Many American corporations are multinational in scale and have become important factors on the world political and economic scene. In many instances, these corporations have greater financial resources than the countries in which they operate, and decisions by corporate executives in the United States can have a profound impact on nations thousands of miles away.

THE LARGEST INDUSTRIAL COMPANIES IN THE WORLD (RANKED BY SALES)

Company	Headquarters	Sales ($ Thousands)	Net Income ($ Thousands)
Exxon	New York	44,864,824	2,503,013
General Motors	Detroit	35,724,911	1,253,092
Royal Dutch/Shell Group	London/The Hague	32,105,096	2,110,927
Texaco	New York	24,507,454	830,583
Ford Motor	Dearborn, Mich.	24,009,100	322,700
Mobil Oil	New York	20,620,392	809,877
National Iranian Oil	Teheran	18,854,547	16,947,071
British Petroleum	London	17,285,854	369,202
Standard Oil California	San Francisco	16,822,077	772,509
Unilever	London	15,015,994	322,108
International Business Machines	Armonk, N.Y.	14,436,541	1,989,877
Gulf Oil	Pittsburgh	14,268,000	700,000
General Electric	Fairfield, Conn.	13,399,100	580,800
Chrysler	Highland Park, Mich.	11,699,305	(259,535)
International Tel. & Tel.	New York	11,367,647	398,171
Philips' Gloeilampenfabrieken	Eindhoven (Netherlands)	10,746,485	152,190
Standard Oil (Ind.)	Chicago	9,955,248	786,987
Cie Francaise des Pétroles	Paris	9,145,778	168,472
Nippon Steel	Tokyo	8,796,902	111,935
August Thyssen-Hütte	Duisburg (Germany)	8,764,899	99,926
Hoechst	Frankfurt on Main	8,462,322	100,972
ENI	Rome	8,334,432	(134,869)
Daimler-Benz	Stuttgart	8,194,271	125,768
U.S. Steel	Pittsburgh	8,167,269	559,614
BASF	Ludwigshafen on Rhine	8,152,318	152,831
Shell Oil	Houston	8,143,445	514,827
Renault	Boulogne-Billancourt (France)	7,831,330	(128,702)
Siemens	Munich	7,759,909	201,275
Volkswagenwerk	Wolfsburg (Germany)	7,680,786	(63,971)
Atlantic Richfield	Los Angeles	7,307,854	350,395
Continental Oil	Stamford, Conn.	7,253,801	330,854
Bayer	Leverkusen (Germany)	7,223,302	128,229
E.I. du Pont de Nemours	Wilmington, Del.	7,221,500	271,800
Toyota Motor	Toyoda-City (Japan)	7,194,139	250,848
ELF-Aquitaine	Paris	7,165,390	199,875
Nestlé	Vevey (Switzerland)	7,080,160	309,365
ICI (Imperial Chemical Industries)	London	6,884,219	424,294
Petrobrás (Petróleo Brasileiro)	Rio de Janeiro	6,625,516	703,586
Western Electric	New York	6,590,116	107,308
British-American Tobacco	London	6,145,979	314,041
Procter & Gamble	Cincinnati	6,081,675	333,862
Hitachi	Tokyo	5,916,135	94,084

Source: Fortune Magazine (August, 1976), p. 243.

Figure 18.11 The economies of Western nations, and of much of the rest of the world, are dominated by a handful of giant corporations. The bulk of these corporations are U.S.-owned.

Industrialism and Modernization

Modernization is the process of economic and social change that is brought about by the introduction of the industrial mode of production into a society. The process is now sweeping the globe as the less developed nations of the world attempt to follow the patterns established by the more advanced industrial societies. Modernization represents one of the most significant social changes in history, for it has implications for almost every other area of social life—a testimony to the powerful influence of the economic order on other institutions.

The Modernization Process

Until a few centuries ago, the human population of the world consisted of a large number of relatively localized and isolated societies, most of whose members lived at a subsistence level in economies based on hunting, gathering, horticulture, pastoralism, or agriculture. The Industrial Revolution ushered in an entirely new type of society, one that produced unprecedented wealth but also undermined or destroyed traditional forms of social organization and created new ones in their place. The modernization process in the early industrial societies of Europe took several generations. In these countries culture and social structure were able to adapt relatively slowly, although not necessarily very easily, to the changing economic order.

In the less developed parts of the world, however, change has come much more rapidly and with much more dislocating effects. Some of the previously undeveloped societies were thrust into the modernization process whether their inhabitants wished it or not. The early industrial powers needed cheap labor and raw materials for their industries and markets for their products, and they used their far-flung colonies to fuel their own economic development. More recently, particularly since the achievement of independence by dozens of former colonial nations after World War II, undeveloped countries have embarked on crash programs of modernization.

These countries are hoping to achieve in the space of a few years the material advantages that the older industrial nations have taken nearly two centuries to gain. The result has often been a tug-of-war between the forces of modernization and the sentiments of tradition, with serious social disorganization as the result. The responses to disorganization have taken many different forms: military coups by army officers determined to impose social order; millenarian religious movements prophesying a return to a golden age of the past or the advent of a new golden age in the future; revolutions aimed at reconstructing society in accordance with a coherent program for social change; or nationalism as a new ideology to unite the people for the challenge of modernization (Smelser, 1973). But whatever the drawbacks of modernization, there are few societies in the world today that are not openly committed to the process.

The Social Effects of Modernization

The modernization process affects virtually every area of society. We have already encountered many of its effects in our discussion of other social institutions and the changes occurring within them. In brief, modernization has the following characteristic effects.

The Family

The extended family system, found in nearly all traditional societies, is shattered. The family is no longer a unit of production, and the extended family becomes dysfunctional in a society requiring geographic and social mobility among its members. The monogamous nuclear family takes its place, and traditional kinship ties are loosened or broken.

Education

Formal organizations, the schools, take over many of the family's earlier socialization functions. Education is extended to the masses, not just to the privileged few, because an industrial work force must be skilled and literate. Universities and research institutes multiply, serving both to transmit and to create specialized knowledge.

Religion

Traditional religion is no longer the central element in a society's belief system. Increasing numbers of people adopt secular belief systems and interpret the world through these rather than religious principles. The process of secularization leaves religion as a marginal rather than a central social institution.

Science

Science emerges for the first time as a major social institution, largely because industrialization relies on the technological applications of scientific knowledge. Rapid technological change leads to rapid social change. Technical efficiency becomes a value—an end, not simply a means—and people look to technology for the solutions to their problems, including the problems that technology creates.

Politics

A strong, centralized state emerges if none existed previously, and it regulates more and more areas of social and economic life. The long-term trend in the older industrialized societies has been toward greater formal democracy, but the newer modernizing societies are almost without exception ruled by new elites who cannot be removed from office by popular vote.

Urbanization

Cities grow rapidly, largely because industries are concentrated in urban areas and people are attracted by job opportunities. In all highly industrialized countries a majority of the population now lives in urban areas, and urbanization is currently taking place even faster in some developing nations than it has in the older industrial countries.

Demography

Death rates decline sharply as modern medical facilities are extended to the population. In the older industrial countries, birth rates have slowly declined as well, but in the developing nations social norms have not yet adjusted to the decline in death rates and large families are still highly valued. The result has been a population explosion unprecedented in human history.

Social Organization

The small, primary group—particularly the kinship network—is no longer able to meet most social or individual needs. For many purposes it is replaced by large, anonymous, formal organizations. Most social institutions become bureaucratized, and large formal organizations, such as industrial corporations or government departments, become new centers of power and influence.

Social Stratification

In the early stages of industrialization there is a yawning gap between the incomes of the privileged few and the masses. As industrialization proceeds, the growing wealth of the society tends to be more equally shared. Rigid forms of stratification based on ascribed characteristics, such as race or caste, tend to dissolve. The rate of social mobility increases, and social status is increasingly achieved by personal effort rather than ascribed on arbitrary grounds.

Personal Values

Individual values and attitudes alter markedly. People are more change-oriented. They look to the future rather than to the past; they are less fatalistic and have faith in the human capacity to dominate and transform the environment. They are also more willing to defer immediate gratification in the hope of greater future reward.

Culture

Culture is no longer maintained and enacted primarily in the small rural community. It becomes a widely shared mass culture, spread not only within the society but from society to society by the mass media and through travel. Within mass cultures, however, a variety of new subcultures appear, so that large modernized societies are more pluralistic in values and outlook than small traditional societies.

The scale, significance, and consequences of these changes are immense—so much so that their implications are still difficult to grasp fully. As we noted in Chapter 4 (Society), the transition from a preindustrial to an industrial mode of production marks the most radical break in the course of sociocultural evolution. This transformation was precisely what the major figures in the sociology of the nineteenth century were trying to understand, and sociologists grapple with the problem to this day.

The Future of Industrial Society

Some observers have taken the view that industrial society is soon to be modified or even replaced by a social order based primarily on a new, highly technological form of

Figure 18.12 Many industries are becoming automated: that is, the manufacturing process is monitored and controlled by machines. Workers become technicians, periodically checking the information provided by the machines and keeping them in working order. This work is less demanding than previous forms of industrial production, and some sociologists believe that automation heralds the arrival of a new, "postindustrial" society.

production. There is no consensus on what this new social order should be called, but among the terms that have been proposed are "technetronic," "postmodern," "superindustrial," and "postindustrial." The term *postindustrial* seems to have won the greatest popularity, and that is the term we shall use here.

The trend to a postindustrial society is said to be based on two main factors. The first is the change in the occupational structure of advanced industrial societies. More and more workers are employed in tertiary industry, providing services for other members of society rather than extracting raw materials or manufacturing goods. Work in the tertiary sector is becoming more professionalized and is generally regarded as more pleasant and less alienating than work in the primary and secondary sectors.

The second factor is technological development, which is making traditional methods of work outmoded, primarily through advances in electronic engineering. A single computer, for example, can take over the work of virtually the entire accounting department of a large firm. In industry, the assembly line is often replaced by automated production. *Automation* is a system in which machines themselves, often guided by computers, monitor and control the manufacturing process. The worker no longer labors on an assembly line, but instead becomes a technician, periodically checking the information provided by machines to ensure that everything is functioning correctly. Work becomes cleaner, lighter, and often requires more skills and greater responsibilities. For this reason workers in automated industries appear less alienated than workers in more traditional industries (Blauner, 1964). Automation also requires fewer workers, although whether this results in unemployment or in increased leisure time for the same number of workers depends on prevailing corporate and national policies. Not all industries can be conveniently automated, but many operate more efficiently and cheaply under the system.

These trends, it is argued, herald a society in which there will be greatly increased leisure time, a heavy reliance on people with skill and knowledge, a central role for technological innovation, and an emphasis on personal development and fulfillment through education and consumption rather than on constant and arduous work (Bell, 1967a, 1967b, 1973; Touraine, 1971).

All this sounds most promising, but it neglects one crucial factor. A postindustrial society would still require a substantial industrial base and a constant supply of raw materials, and there is no reason to suppose that its industries would stop polluting the environment. A research team at the Massachusetts Institute of Technology (MIT) developed a computer model that projected current trends of population increase, resource depletion, food production, pollution, and industrial output well into the next century (Meadows *et al.*, 1972). The computer predicted an inevitable collapse of industrial society within a hundred years, and possibly a good deal sooner—unless population growth and industrial growth are brought to an immediate halt. This highly controversial finding, which is representative of a number of predictions about the future of industrial society, will be dealt with in more detail in Chapter 20 (Population and Ecology). For the present, we should note that global population size and the rate of industrial output are still increasing and that they are doing so in a world that has limited resources. This combination of facts does not encourage optimism about the long-term future of industrialism. Whether the new level of postindustrial civilization can be safely achieved or whether industrial societies will prove, in the MIT team's phrase, to be "self-extinguishing," remains to be seen. Given the importance of the economic order, the answer to the question will have the profoundest implications for social life as we know it—and the answer may be apparent well within the lifetimes of most readers of this book.

Summary

1. The economic order is the institutionalized system for distributing goods and services. Economic activity is important because it sustains life, because a society's main means of economic production influences culture and social structure, because economic and political issues are very closely linked, and because an individual's work is a major source of personal identity and social status.

2. Every society establishes a division of labor among its members. There has been a general trend toward increased specialization, which culminates in modern industrial societies. Durkeim distinguished between societies integrated by mechanical solidarity and those integrated by organic solidarity; the latter are more prone to anomie.

3. One important concern of the sociology of occupations is the changing proportion of workers in primary, secondary, and tertiary industry. A second concern is the growth of professions and the process by which jobs are professionalized.

4. Alienation refers to the sense of powerlessness and meaninglessness experienced by people confronted with social institutions that they consider oppressive and cannot control. Karl Marx linked alienation to the extreme division of labor, which reduces the worker's autonomy and contribution almost to insignificance. Worker alienation has become recognized as a growing problem in the United States, although an attempt has been made to combat the problem through a "human relations" approach to industry.

5. Capitalism and socialism represent two basic ways in which goods can be produced and distributed. Both concepts represent ideal types and are approximated in varying degrees by different societies. The two systems differ primarily over whether economic resources should be privately or publicly owned. Democratic socialism represents a compromise between the two, while communism is a hypothetical advance on socialism.

6. The American economy is dominated by large corporations whose power and influence have important implications for the economy and society. Many corporations have now become multinational in scope and influence, and they represent a disturbing concentration of economic—and therefore political—power.

7. Modernization is the process of social transformation brought about by the introduction of industrialism into traditional societies. The process has profound effects on almost every aspect of social and personal life.

8. Some observers predict that advanced industrial societies are moving into a postindustrial stage marked by extended leisure time and heavy reliance on automation. Others doubt whether the environment will have the capacity to tolerate the pollution and resource depletion that might result from increased industrial output.

Important Terms

economic order
division of labor
mechanical solidarity
organic solidarity
anomie
primary industry
secondary industry
tertiary industry
professions
alienation
property
communal ownership
private ownership
public ownership
capitalism
laissez-faire
monopoly
oligopoly
socialism
democratic socialism
communism
corporations
modernization
postindustrial society
automation

Suggested Readings

MARX, KARL. *Selected Writings in Sociology and Social Philosophy,* Tom Bottomore and Maximilian Rubel (eds.). Baltimore, Md.: Penguin, 1964.

A selection of excerpts from Marx's major works. The selections include Marx's writings on the concept of alienation and his impassioned denunciations of alienated labor.

NADER, RALPH, AND MARK J. GREEN (EDS.). *Corporate Power in America.* New York: Grossman, 1973.

A collection of essays detailing the extent of corporate power and influence in the United States.

SMELSER, NEIL J. *The Sociology of Economic Life.* Englewood Cliffs, N.J.: Prentice-Hall, 1963.

A succinct treatment of the relationship between economy and society.

TERKEL, STUDS. *Working.* New York: Random House, 1974.

A fascinating collection of tape-recorded interviews with workers across the United States. The book, which became a best-seller, has great human interest as well as sociological significance.

Work in America: Report of a Special Task Force to the Secretary of Health, Education, and Welfare. Cambridge, Mass.: MIT Press, 1973.

Written in clear, nontechnical language, this government report recounts the "white-collar woes" and "blue-collar blues" of alienated American workers.

CHAPTER 19 *The Political Order*

CHAPTER OUTLINE

Power

Types of Authority
Traditional Authority
Legal-Rational Authority
Charismatic Authority

The State
The Functionalist Approach
The Conflict Approach
Evaluation

Democracy
Prerequisites for Democracy
Liberty and Equality

The American Political Process
Interest Groups
Political Parties

Who Rules?
The Power-Elite Thesis
The Pluralist Thesis
Empirical Studies

Revolutions

Over 2000 years ago the philosopher Aristotle observed that we are political animals. We are indeed, and necessarily so, for politics is an inevitable consequence of social living. In every society some valued resources are scarce, and politics is essentially the process of deciding "who gets what, when, and how" (Lasswell, 1936). The character of political institutions and behavior varies a great deal from one society or group to another, but the political process itself is universal.

The political order is the institutionalized system through which some individuals and groups acquire and exercise power over others. This chapter will focus primarily on the political process at the highest level of power in modern society, the state. Max Weber (1946), who laid the foundations of modern political sociology, defined the *state* as the institution that successfully claims a monopoly on the right to use force within a given territory. Of course, the state may choose to delegate some of its powers to other agencies, such as local authorities, the police, or the military. In the final analysis, however, the state can override all other agencies and is thus the central and most vital component of the political order. The "state," incidentally, is not quite the same thing as the "government." The state is an impersonal social institution, whereas the government is the collection of individuals who happen to be directing the power of the state at any given moment.

Power

Politics is about power—about who gets it, how it is obtained, how it is used, and to what purposes it is put. Max Weber defined *power* as the ability to control the behavior of others, even in the absence of their consent. Put another way, power is the capacity to participate effectively in a decision-making process. Those who for one reason or another cannot affect the process are therefore powerless. Power may be exercised blatantly or subtly, legally or illegally, justly or unjustly. It may derive from many sources, such as wealth, status, prestige, numbers, or organizational efficiency. Its ultimate basis, however, is the ability to compel obedience, if necessary through the threat or use of force.

The use of power may be either legitimate or illegitimate. Power is considered *legitimate* only if people generally recognize that those who apply it have the right to do so—perhaps because they are elected government officials, perhaps because they are an aristocracy whose commands are never questioned, perhaps because they are believed to be inspired by God. Weber used the term *authority* to refer to legitimate power. Power is considered *illegitimate,* on the other hand, if people believe that those who apply it do not have the right to do so—perhaps because they are acting illegally, perhaps because they hold no public office, perhaps because they are newly successful revolutionaries who have not yet entrenched their regime. Weber called illegitimate power *coercion.*

A simple example will illustrate this distinction more fully. If a judge rules that you must pay a fine, you will probably obey. If you do not, the judge has the power to make you pay or suffer other negative consequences. If an armed mugger in the street demands your money, you will likewise probably hand it over. The mugger also has the power to make you pay or suffer negative consequences. But you regard the judge's demand as legitimate. It rests on judicial authority, and you recognize that the judge has the *right* to fine you even if you disagree with and resent the decision. You do not acknowledge, however, that the mugger has any *right* whatever to take your money. You paid up simply because you were coerced.

Power based on authority is usually unquestioningly accepted by those to whom it is applied, for obedience to it has become a social norm. Power based on coercion, on the other hand, tends to be unstable, because people obey only out of fear and will disobey at the first opportunity. For this reason every political system must be regarded as legitimate by its participants if it is to survive. Most people must consider it desirable, workable, and better than any alternatives. If the bulk of the citizens in any society no longer consider their political system legitimate, it is doomed, for its power can then rest only on coercion, which will fail in the long run. The French, Russian, and American revolutions, for example, were preceded by an erosion of the legitimacy of the existing systems. The authority of the respective monarchies was questioned and their power, based increasingly on coercion rather than unquestioning loyalty, inevitably crumbled.

Types of Authority

Max Weber distinguished three basic types of legitimate authority: traditional authority, legal-rational authority, and charismatic authority. Each type of authority is legitimate because it rests on the implicit or explicit consent of the governed. A person who can successfully claim one of these types of authority is regarded as having the right to compel obedience, at least within socially specified limits.

Traditional Authority

In a political system based on *traditional authority,* power is legitimated by ancient custom. The authority of the ruler is generally founded on unwritten laws and it has an almost sacred quality. Chieftainships and monarchies have always relied on traditional authority, and historically it has been the most common source of the legitimation of power.

People obey traditional authority because "it has always been that way": the right of the king to rule is not open to question. Claim to traditional authority is usually based on birthright, with the status of ruler generally passing to the eldest son of the incumbent. In some cases the power of the ruler over the subjects seems virtually unlimited, but in practice there are always informal social norms setting the boundaries within which power can be exercised. If a ruler exceeds these limits, as many Roman emperors did, people may regard such use of power as illegitimate and coercive. Under these circumstances attempts may be made to depose the ruler. People are likely to remain loyal to the system of traditional authority, however; they will probably still recognize the close kin of the deposed ruler as having the strongest claim to the succession.

Figure 19.1 The power of the rulers of most modern societies is legitimated by legal-rational authority. Their power derives from the office they hold, not from personal characteristics such as ancestry. Holders of public office, like these members of the United States Congress, may exercise power only within the limits defined by the laws and the Constitution.

Legal-Rational Authority

In a system based on *legal-rational authority,* power is legitimated by explicit rules and procedures that define the rights and obligations of the rulers. The rules and procedures are typically found in a written constitution and set of laws that, at least in theory, have been socially agreed upon. This form of authority is characteristic of the political systems of most modern societies.

Legal-rational authority stresses a "government of laws, not of people." The power of an official in a country such as the United States or the Soviet Union derives from the office the person holds, not from personal characteristics such as birthright. Officials can exercise power only within legally defined limits that have been formally set in advance. Americans thus acknowledge the right of a president or even of a minor bureaucrat to exercise power, provided they do not exceed the specific boundaries of authority that attach to their respective offices. When President Nixon did overstep these boundaries, his acts were considered illegitimate—an abuse of power—and he was forced from office. A similar or worse fate would doubtless await a modern Soviet leader who used power in ways considered illegitimate in that country.

Charismatic Authority

In a system based on *charismatic authority,* power is legitimated by the unusual, exceptional, or even supernatural qualities that people attribute to particular political, religious, or military leaders. Weber called this extraordinary quality *charisma.* Typical charismatic leaders are such people as Jesus, Joan of Arc, Hitler, Gandhi, Napoleon, Mao, Castro, Julius Caesar, Alexander the Great, and Churchill. The charismatic leader is seen as a person of destiny who is inspired by unusual vision, by lofty principles, or even by God. The charisma of these leaders is itself sufficient to make their authority seem legitimate to their followers. Whether they can also lay claim to traditional or legal-rational authority is of little relevance.

Charisma is a spontaneous, irrational phenomenon that often poses a threat to systems based on traditional or

Figure 19.2 The power of certain leaders is legitimated by charismatic authority. Other people attribute exceptional and sometimes even supernatural qualities to such leaders, and this charisma alone makes their authority seem legitimate to their followers. Charismatic leaders may, of course, enjoy legitimacy from some other source as well, but this is not relevant to their charismatic appeal. Churchill, Castro, Martin Luther King, John Kennedy, Mao, Napoleon, Joan of Arc, Gandhi, and Franklin Roosevelt are typical examples of charismatic leaders.

legal-rational authority. Revolutions are typically led by charismatic figures who win personal allegiance and are regarded as the symbol of radical changes to come. Yet charismatic authority is inherently unstable. It has no rules or traditions to guide conduct, and because it rests on the unique characteristics of a particular individual, it is undermined if the leader fails or dies. Successful revolutions led by charismatic figures such as Mao or Castro almost always face a problem of succession, for those who take over are unlikely to have such a rare quality themselves. For this reason systems based on charismatic authority are usually short-lived. Many of them collapse. Others are either slowly *routinized* into legal-rational systems based on bureaucratic rules and procedures, or—more commonly in the past than today—into traditional systems in which power passes to the descendants of the original leader.

Each of these forms of authority represents an *ideal type.* In other words, each is an abstraction that is only approximated to a greater or lesser extent by any actual political system. In practice, political systems and political leaders may derive their authority from more than one source. The power of the American presidency, for example, is legitimated primarily by legal-rational authority, but the office has existed for so long that it now seems to have traditional authority as well. Richard Nixon demonstrated this fact in the closing months of his presidency. Nixon lacked personal charisma and his legal-rational authority was being eroded by allegations that he had committed serious crimes during his election and his tenure of the presidency. Yet he was able to stave off his fate for some time by appealing to traditional loyalties to the office of the presidency—a confusion of the office and its temporary occupant more appropriate for a traditional monarchy. John Kennedy, a highly charismatic personality, may be said to have enjoyed legitimacy from all three sources of authority—charismatic, legal-rational, and traditional.

The State

We have noted that the state is a distinct social institution that claims a monopoly of the legitimate use of force within a given territory. That territory comprises a nation, and conversely a nation may be defined as a geographically distinct collectivity of people ruled by a state. The nation-state, however, is a relatively recent historical development. The anthropologist George Murdock (1949) tells us that:

> for 99 percent of the [time] that man has inhabited this earth, he lived, thrived, and developed without any true government whatsoever, and as late as 100 years ago half the peoples of the world—not half the population but half the tribes or nations—still ordered their lives exclusively through informal controls without the benefit of political institutions.

Figure 19.3 The state does not exist in the simplest of preindustrial societies. Among these Iranian pastoralists, for example, all decisions are made through group consensus, and the power of the headman is very limited. The state is present only in societies that are stratified into classes or castes.

The nation-state emerged in Europe only a few centuries ago, spread later to the Americas, and arose in most parts of Africa and Asia only in the course of this century. Before that time the state, if it existed at all, was a very rudimentary affair. Rulers certainly laid claim to authority over large areas, but there was little sense of nationhood, and the rulers could rarely achieve a successful monopoly of authority. Even the early empires, such as that of Rome, were in effect alliances between city-states and small kingdoms, each claiming authority over its own citizens and only grudgingly recognizing the center of power.

The emergence of the state as a separate institution is closely linked to the level of cultural evolution of a society, and in particular to its means of subsistence (Fried, 1967; Lenski and Lenski, 1974). As noted in Chapter 4 (Society), political institutions are absent in hunting and gathering societies. Each group is autonomous and independent, and decisions are made by group consensus. In pastoral and horticultural societies, where populations are larger and there may be a food surplus, some individuals become more powerful and wealthy than others. They pass their status on to their descendants, and patterns of chieftainship emerge. In agricultural societies a very large food surplus is possible, and this can be stored and con-

verted into wealth and power. Entire categories of the population become wealthier than others, and social classes appear for the first time. Societies may contain millions of people, and a central political authority is needed to maintain social order and organize social life. The state thus emerges as a distinct social institution, with power typically concentrated in the hands of a monarch or emperor. The power of the ruler is legitimated by traditional authority, and an elaborate court bureaucracy and full-time military organization is established.

In industrial societies the nature of the state changes radically. The unprecedented wealth produced by industrialism permits the emergence of a large middle class. Rising levels of aspiration, combined with mass education, produce a more politically sophisticated population. Arbitrary rule is no longer acceptable, and traditional authority is replaced by legal-rational authority as the basis of the state's legitimacy. The responsibilities of the state expand enormously because it is explicitly concerned with improving social conditions. The state assumes responsibilities in areas as diverse as welfare, education, medicine, public transport, scientific research, and economic planning. State expenditures rise dramatically: the U.S. government, for example, had an annual budget of about $4.3 million at the end of the eighteenth century, compared with about $350 billion today. The size of the government bureaucracy shows a corresponding increase. A century and a half ago the federal government employed 5000 people; today it employs 3 million, and the total of all federal, state, and local government employees exceeds 13 million people. The state thus becomes one of the most powerful and central institutions in a modern society.

The Functionalist Approach

From the functionalist perspective, the emergence of the state and its dominant position in modern societies can be explained in terms of the *functions* that it serves in the maintenance of the social system as a whole. Four major functions of the state can be identified.

Enforcement of Norms

In small, traditional communities norms are usually unwritten and are generally enforced by spontaneous community action. In a highly complex and rapidly changing modern society such a system would be unworkable. The state accordingly takes the responsibility for codifying important norms in the form of laws. It also assumes responsibility for ensuring that these norms are obeyed by applying formal negative sanctions to offenders. Laws are used to define and suppress certain forms of deviance; these are the criminal laws. Laws are also used to define and protect the rights of individuals and groups; these are the civil laws.

Arbitration of Conflict

The state provides an institutionalized process for determining "who gets what, when, and how." Conflict over the allocation of scarce resources and over national goals must be kept within manageable limits, or society might become a jungle in which different groups pursue their own interests without restraint. The state acts as arbitrator, or umpire, between conflicting interests, establishing means for resolving disputes and determining policies.

Figure 19.4 An important function of the state is the enforcement of norms. In small, traditional societies social control can be applied effectively through informal community reactions. A large modern society, on the other hand, requires a formal system of social control, including laws, policing, and judicial processes.

Planning and Direction

A complex modern society requires coordinated and systematic planning and direction. The economy must be closely monitored and steps taken to prevent unemployment or inflation. The output of trained workers must be geared to the demands of industry and commerce. Research funds must be allocated in accordance with national priorities. The effects of pollution on the environment must be gauged and if necessary counteracted. Highways must be put where people need them. Welfare must be distributed to the poor and pensions to the aged. These and countless other decisions must be based on knowledge derived from reliable data, which have to be systematically collected and analyzed. To a greater or lesser degree the decisions must be centralized if uniform and coherent policies are to emerge.

Relations with Other Societies

The state is responsible for political, economic, and military relations with other societies. It forms alliances with friendly states and participates in international organizations. It forms trading agreements with other societies and attempts to protect its country's foreign investments. It engages in acts of diplomacy and, if necessary, defense or aggression against other states. None of these functions could be met without a high degree of centralized control and authority. If the state is to be effective in its relations with other states, it must have the capacity to be taken seriously.

A single theme underlies all four functions: the preservation of social order. This view of the role of the state is an ancient one, long predating modern sociological theory. It was perhaps best presented by the conservative English philospher Thomas Hobbes (1588–1679), who argued for a strong state with unchallenged legitimacy. Hobbes claimed that in the "state of nature" that supposedly existed before the establishment of political authority, life was "solitary, poor, nasty, brutish, and short." There was no justice or injustice, right or wrong, good or bad, since there was no authority to define, establish, and maintain order. Despairing of the situation, people made a "social contract" to form the state. This contract could never be broken, because no matter how oppressive the state might be, it would always be preferable to the earlier chaos.

Hobbes's analysis was implicitly functional and explicitly conservative. His central notion, although now less philosophically and romantically expressed, is still widely accepted in the United States and elsewhere: that the main duty of the state is to preserve law and order.

The Conflict Approach

An alternative view of the state is that it emerged and exists largely to safeguard the interests of the privileged. In other words, the state protects the "haves" in their conflict with the "have nots."

This view was systematically presented by the French philosopher Jean Jacques Rousseau (1712–1778), whose writings provided much of the inspiration for the French Revolution. Rousseau rejected Hobbes's view that people in the original "state of nature" were brutal and self-seeking. Instead, he saw them as "noble savages," free, happy, and peaceful. The establishment of the state was the source of their problems, not the solution: "Man is born free, yet everywhere he is in chains."

How, then, did the state arise? The answer, claimed Rousseau (1950, originally published 1762), lay in the creation of private property:

> The first man who, having enclosed a piece of ground, bethought himself of saying, "This is mine," and found people simple enough to believe him, was the real founder of civil society. From how many crimes, wars, and murders, from how many horrors and misfortunes might not anyone have saved mankind, by pulling up the stake, or filling up the ditch, and crying to his fellows: "Beware of listening to this imposter; you are undone if you once forget that the fruits of the earth belong to us all, and the earth itself to nobody!"

Once private property had been established the people of the "state of nature" took to fighting among themselves, and eventually agreed on a "social contract" to form the state so that order could be achieved once more. But the state did not apply impartial justice; it merely protected the interests of the wealthy. The state "bound new fetters to the poor, and gave new powers to the rich . . . and, for the advantage of a few ambitious individuals, subjected all mankind to perpetual labor, slavery, and wretchedness."

Figure 19.5

"When my distinguished colleague refers to the will of the 'people,' does he mean his 'people' or my 'people'?"

Drawing by Richter; © 1976 The New Yorker Magazine, Inc.

Since the "state of nature" was preferable to unjust rule by central authority, Rousseau recommended that the state be overthrown and that a new social contract be made—one that gave power to the people, not the state.

The most influential modern conflict theory of the state is of course that of Karl Marx, as put forward in the *Communist Manifesto* (1848) and elsewhere. Marx's analysis draws on Rousseau's insights but is a much more sophisticated one. The key to his analysis is the idea that the nature of economic production in a particular society influences the character of its social structure and institutions. In every society those who control the means of economic production (such as slaves, land, or capital) are the ruling class. All except the most primitive societies, Marx claimed, are divided into two or more classes, one of which dominates and exploits the others. The ruling class always uses social institutions, particularly the state, to maintain its privileged position. For this reason, social institutions always serve to maintain the status quo, not to change it. The state itself is simply the "executive committee" of the ruling class, protecting that class's interests and allowing it to enjoy the surplus wealth produced by the workers.

Class conflict, Marx maintained, is the dynamic force in history (Marx and Engels, 1970, originally published 1848):

> The history of all hitherto existing societies is the history of class struggle. . . . Freedman and slave, patrician and plebeian, lord and serf, guildmaster and journeyman, in a word, oppressor and oppressed, stood in constant opposition to one another, carried on an uninterrupted, now hidden, now open fight, a fight that each time ended, either in a revolutionary reconstruction of society at large, or the common ruin of the contending parties.

Marx traced a series of stages through which human society evolves, according to the means of production that is dominant at each stage. The first is *primitive communism,* in which there is no private property. The second is *slavery,* in which one class owns and exploits the members of another. The third is *feudalism,* in which a class of aristocratic landowners exploits the mass of peasants. The fourth is *capitalism,* in which the owners of wealth exploit the mass of industrial workers. Each of these systems is more economically productive than its predecessor, but the tensions of class conflict lead to a revolution that ushers in the next stage. The fifth stage, *socialism,* occurs when the industrial workers have finally revolted. They establish a temporary "dictatorship of the proletariat" to prevent attempts by reactionaries to return to the old system and to guide social change toward the final stage. This is the stage of *communism,* in which property is communally owned and in which, Marx believed, people would enjoy true freedom and the fulfillment of their human potential for the first time in history.

If the state exists primarily to safeguard the interests of the ruling class, then what happens to the state in the classless communist society? Marx's collaborator, Engels, declared optimistically that it would just "wither away." Modern scholarship indicates that the ideas of Marx and Engels were not nearly as similar as has always been assumed in the past, and it is very doubtful if Marx took such a naive view. Yet Marx's own concept of the state in a classless society is not very clear. He merely commented, rather mysteriously, that "the government of people will be replaced by the administration of things," and that "freedom consists in converting the state from an organ superimposed on society into one completely subordinate to it."

The idea that the role of the state will be significantly reduced in a classless society is perhaps the weakest element in Marx's analysis. In countries that are currently at the stage of socialism, such as the Soviet Union and China, the state clearly has more power than it does in capitalist societies. Nor does it seem that socialist societies have any idea of how to achieve the abolition of the state, even if that remains their goal.

Evaluation

Marx was undoubtedly correct in his view that a *major* function of the state is to protect the interests of the ruling class. As we have noted, the state comes into existence only when classes emerge in society. The historical evidence confirms that the ruling classes in all societies have without exception been the economically dominant classes as well. The sociological evidence confirms that institutions and other cultural arrangements generally tend to support the status quo, and therefore to support the interests of the class that benefits from it.

Marx failed to recognize, however, that the role of the state is not *only* an oppressive one. As our functional analysis shows, the state has several functions that are not necessarily related to class conflict. Many of these functions would have to be fulfilled by a strong central authority in any modern society, class-based or classless. In fact, a socialist or communist society must regulate the lives of its citizens much more closely than a capitalist society, because it supervises not only the production but also the distribution of wealth. For this reason, the power of the state is likely to increase in a socialist society, and even more so in a communist society.

The functionalist and conflict approaches, then, each give us only a partial view of social reality. The functionalist approach demonstrates the necessity for the institution of the state, while the conflict approach reveals the role that the state plays in competition between different social classes and in maintaining social inequality. Taken together, the two perspectives give us a better understanding of the modern state.

Democracy

Democracy comes from a Greek word meaning "rule of the people," and this is no doubt what Lincoln had in mind when he defined democracy as "government of the people, by the people, and for the people." In practice, no such system has ever existed. Pure democracy would mean that every citizen would have the right to participate in every decision, a situation that would lead to complete chaos and the abandonment of all kinds of other activities (Lenski and Lenski, 1974). This ideal form of democracy has been approximated only in very small communities, such as the ancient Greek city-states and early New England towns. Even in these cases, however, certain people were denied the right of participation—women in New England, and both women and slaves in Greece.

In practice, the societies we consider democratic are those that explicitly recognize that the powers of government derive from the consent of the governed. These societies have institutionalized procedures for choosing periodically among contenders for public office. They have a *representative democracy;* that is, the voters periodically elect representatives who are responsible for making political decisions. A characteristic of all democracies is that they have a high regard for the right of the individual to choose between alternatives, which presupposes civil liberties such as freedom of speech and assembly.

Representative democracy is historically recent, rare, and fragile. It is found almost exclusively in a handful of Western European countries and in the countries that they colonized and implanted with their own traditions. In most instances, these transplants were short-lived. Many societies, notably several newly independent African nations and the socialist countries of Eastern Europe, retain the trappings of representative democracy in that there are still periodic elections. The outcome of an election is a foregone conclusion, however, because there is only one party and thus no choice among alternatives. The practice of one-party "democracy" is defended on the grounds that the party already "knows" what the people want, or that party strife would be socially devisive. In the absence of free elections, there is obviously no way of finding out whether this diagnosis is correct. The suspicion must linger that a party that is reluctant to face a free election is afraid it might lose it.

Figure 19.6 Nazi Germany was a dictatorship in which the state assumed totalitarian powers. The Nazis demanded absolute conformity to their racial and other political beliefs and recognized no limits to the power of the state. This picture shows members of the Hitler Youth parading past the dictator (on the balcony at left).

Democracy is one of several possible forms of government. Most societies in the past have been governed by *autocracy,* the rule of a single individual. Autocrats usually hold the hereditary status of emperor, king, or chief. Apart from a few isolated *dictatorships*—nonhereditary rule by a single individual who cannot be removed from office by legal means—autocracy is very rare in the modern world. The most common form of nondemocratic rule is *oligarchy,* or rule by a few. The socialist societies of Eastern Europe and Asia are regarded in the West as oligarchies because they are ruled in practice by a bureaucratic elite. A few Latin American countries are still ruled by oligarchies consisting of a handful of extremely wealthy families. In both Latin America and Africa a new form of oligarchy, the *junta,* or rule by military officers who have achieved a coup, is increasingly common. In some nondemocratic states, the government assumes *totalitarian* powers. A totalitarian government recognizes no ultimate limits to its authority and is willing to regulate any aspect of social life. The outstanding historical example of the totalitarian state is undoubtedly Nazi Germany, but the governments of many other societies, particularly socialist societies and those ruled by right-wing juntas, have strong totalitarian tendencies.

Prerequisites for Democracy

Why is democratic government so rare and why has it been successfully established almost exclusively in societies of a certain type, namely, advanced industrial countries? It seems that democracy can thrive only when most of several basic conditions have been met.

Advanced Economic Development

Seymour Martin Lipset (1959c) surveyed data from forty-eight societies and found a strong correlation between the level of economic development and the presence of democratic institutions. The reasons for this relationship are complex, but two basic factors seem to be particularly important. First, an advanced economy always contains an urbanized, literate, and sophisticated population that expects and demands some participation in the political process. Second, societies with advanced economies tend to be politically stable. This stability probably derives from the presence of a substantial middle class that has a stake in the society and is reluctant to support political upheavals of any kind. Lacking the very large oppressed classes found in agricultural or early industrial societies, these countries can afford to offer their citizens political alternatives without fearing that society would be torn apart in any resulting conflict. In societies with a large lower class, there is likely to be strong opposition from the ruling class to the extension of democratic rights.

Restraints on Government Power

Democracy is best served if there are institutional restraints on the power of the state. These constraints can be of many different kinds: laws limiting the exercise of power, constitutional arrangements for the impeachment of officials, free criticism by the press and other media, or simply informal norms so powerful that they cannot be violated. These norms, which specify the "rules of the game," are easily overlooked, but they are a vital part of any democratic system.

An excellent example of the force of informal norms is provided by Britain, which is unique among modern societies in having no written constitution. Like the United States, the country has two legislative chambers. The House of Commons is elected by popular vote, and the majority party forms the national government. The House of Lords, which has to approve legislation passed in the House of Commons, is not elected. Its members are mostly hereditary aristocrats who generally support the right-wing Conservative Party. When the left-wing Labor Party has a majority in the House of Commons and forms a government, the House of Lords could easily reject all its legislation. But in practice it very rarely attempts to do so. The House of Lords informally recognizes the superior legitimacy of the popularly elected House of Commons, and its Conservative members abstain from voting in sufficiently large numbers to allow the small minority of Labor lords to become a majority. When the Conservatives control the House of Commons, the Conservative lords present themselves for voting and ensure the passage of government legislation.

Absence of Major Cleavages

Democracy is more likely to survive in a society in which there is a general consensus on basic values and a widespread commitment to existing political institutions. A clear-cut political cleavage tends to polarize society into militant camps that are unwilling to make the compromises necessary for democracy to work. The greater the potential or actual conflict in a society, the more pressures are put on the government to become "strong" in order to contain them. In highly polarized societies—such as Lebanon with its religious divisions, South Africa with its racial divisions, or Bolivia with its economic divisions—democratic institutions are either unstable or absent.

Tolerance of Dissent

A tolerance of criticism and of dissenting opinions is fundamental to democracy. Governing parties must resist the temptation to equate their own policies with the national good, or they will tend to regard opposition as disloyal or even treasonable. President Johnson and more particularly President Nixon were inclined to regard opposition to their military policies in Southeast Asia as outright subversion, and both abused government agencies such as the CIA, the FBI, and the Pentagon in an attempt to suppress dissent. One result was that dissenting groups felt they were being denied access to the normal political process and turned to other avenues of protest. Internal conflict in the United States was greatly sharpened as a result.

Figure 19.7 Opposition to the American military involvement in Southeast Asia was initially peaceful, but it grew more violent during the late sixties and early seventies. Because the government was unwilling to heed their protests and in fact attempted to suppress legitimate dissent, many opponents of the war used less legitimate avenues of protest.

Another danger to democracy is that of the "tyranny of the majority." In some cases the democratic process may work in such a way that a small minority, such as blacks in the United States, is a permanent loser. To such groups, democracy might as well not exist if they are to gain little benefit from it, and it is important that government should recognize the grievances of minorities that have little political clout. If the losers in the political process do not recognize the legitimacy of the process under which they have lost, they may resort to more radical tactics outside the institutional framework.

Access to Information

A democracy requires its citizens to make informed choices among alternatives. If citizens are denied access to the information they need to make these choices, or if they are given false or misleading information, the democratic process may become a sham. It is therefore important that the media should not be censored, that citizens have the right of free speech, and that public officials tell the truth.

The practice of some recent presidents of concealing information from or lying to Congress and the public is clearly contrary to democratic values. When President Johnson was running for reelection in 1964 he campaigned against an air war in Vietnam even though he had already taken a decision to launch such a war. When President Nixon took office he promised "to tell the people the hard truth" and to provide "an open administration" (Wise, 1973). Nixon then proceeded to bomb Cambodia for fourteen months while denying that he was doing so, and he secretly sent troops into Laos in violation of specific prohibitions voted by Congress and signed by himself. If neither the voters nor their representatives are aware of the policies their government is pursuing, democratic participation is impossible.

Diffusion of Power

If power is diffuse and no one group can obtain a monopoly over it, the prospects for democracy are enhanced. One way of diffusing power is to distribute it among various branches of government. The U.S. Constitution separates the powers of the executive, legislative, and judicial branches, and they often provide an effective check on one another. The abuses of executive power in the Watergate affair, for example, were investigated and checked by the other two branches. Another way of diffusing power is to distribute it to regional and local governments. Power may also be spread beyond government into other institutions and organizations. The existence of separate centers of power in labor unions, corporations, churches, and elsewhere provides a system of checks and balances and ensures that each group must take account of the others.

Liberty and Equality

The socialist societies of Eastern Europe and Asia claim to be democratic and dedicated to human freedom, although their political systems have few of the features that we have identified as prerequisites for democracy, as we understand the term in the West. Yet the leaders of these societies are not being cynical. They and no doubt many of their citizens believe that they live in democracies and that their people are free. Conversely, they also believe that our societies are undemocratic and unfree. How can this be?

The source of the difficulty lies in the way "freedom" is defined. Capitalist and socialist societies define the word differently, but they believe they are democratic because their systems enhance the kind of freedom they believe in. In our society we are primarily concerned with freedom "of": freedom of speech, freedom of assembly, freedom of the press, freedom of the individual to make a fortune. In their societies they are primarily concerned with freedom "from": freedom from want, freedom from hunger, freedom from unemployment, freedom from exploitation by people who want to make a fortune. Put another way, we interpret freedom as meaning "liberty"; they interpret it as meaning "equality."

Liberty and equality are uneasy bedfellows. In general, the more you have of one, the less you will have of the other. Your liberty to be richer than anyone else violates other people's right to be your equal; other people's right to be your equal violates your liberty to earn more than anyone else. The United States has chosen to emphasize personal liberty, although this emphasis can only lead to social inequality. Socialist societies have stressed equality, although this emphasis can only lead to infringements of personal liberty. Most Western European countries have chosen a middle way, that of "democratic socialism," and attempt to balance the demands of liberty and equality more evenly. There is no way to *prove* that any one of these solutions is more desirable, moral, or "right" than any other. The question is a matter of philosophic preference.

Most people, of course, do not rationally consider the various alternatives. They simply accept the system they have been socialized to believe in. Extensive research on political socialization has shown that people take the legitimacy of their particular political system for granted very early in life, and usually adopt the political views of their parents. By the time they are in elementary school, children take an overwhelmingly favorable view of their country's system and regard their national leaders as wise and benevolent (Easton and Hess, 1962; Easton and Dennis, 1969; Greenstein, 1965, 1968; Hyman, 1969; Langton and Jennings, 1967).

The American Political Process

After several years of high-school civics and history classes you are already familiar with the formal elements of the American political system, such as the electoral process, the role of the presidency, and the way legislation is passed. We will not be concerned with these features of the political system in this chapter. Instead, we will focus on the more informal but no less vital processes of interest-group lobbying and party politics. These processes are "unofficial," that is, they are not included in any formal diagram of how our system "works." But they are very important.

Interest Groups

An *interest group* is an organization or group of people that attempts to influence political decisions that might affect its members. These groups may be small or large, temporary or permanent, secretive or open, but they all try to gain access to and influence those who have power. In general, the larger and better funded the group is, the more influence it has.

Interest groups use a variety of tactics to gain decisions in their favor. They may collect petitions, take court action, bribe officials, advertise in the media, donate money to election campaigns, pledge the votes of their members to certain candidates, organize a flood of letters to legislators on particular issues, or seek direct contact with members of Congress and the executive branch of government. The tactic of directly persuading decision makers is called *lobbying*. Many large interest groups maintain highly paid, full-time professional lobbyists in Washington. The lobbyists meet regularly with legislators and government officials and try to win favors for their particular interest.

Well-organized and well-funded interest groups are often very successful in their efforts, most of which take place without any public knowledge. The highly complicated tax laws of the United States contain a great many provisions and exemptions designed to benefit special interests, and these are almost always included as a result of behind-the-scenes lobbying. Interest groups also apply pressure on both domestic and foreign policy making. The American Medical Association, which represents the country's physicians, has prevented the introduction of socialized medicine through a series of vigorous campaigns, including successful attempts to unseat legislators who favored the proposal by giving funds to their opponents. The National Rifle Association, with an annual budget of $5 million and a membership of over 900,000, has successfully resisted all attempts to introduce effective gun-control legislation. Citizens favoring gun control are not organized to lobby effectively and have therefore never been able to counteract the intensive campaigns of the NRA. As mentioned in Chapter 18 (The Economic Order), the International Telephone and Telegraph Corporation (ITT) successfully persuaded the Nixon administration to try to bring about a coup in another country,

Chile, where ITT feared for the safety of its investments (Sampson, 1973). The Watergate-related scandals revealed many U.S. corporations making illegal campaign donations and outright bribes to legislators; Gulf Oil alone spent over $10 million on bribes and payoffs to public officials in the United States and abroad.

Political sociologists are divided over whether the activities of interest groups are beneficial or harmful to democracy. On the one hand, these groups, frequently operating in secrecy, are often able to win favors that might not be in the public interest. The ordinary voter's influence is thus reduced. What chance, for example, do unorganized individuals have of bringing about change in the nation's tax structure when they are competing with the efforts of wealthy and highly organized groups to keep it the way it is? On the other hand, the existence of a number of interest groups, many of them with conflicting goals, may prevent a monopoly of power and influence by creating a system of checks and balances. Furthermore, the interest group provides an effective means for otherwise powerless citizens to gain political influence. A mass of unorganized citizens concerned about civil rights or ecology, for example, has little means of exerting influence. If they form an organized interest group, they have a potentially far greater access to the decision-making process.

Figure 19.8 The most visible interest groups in American society are those that resort to public demonstrations to further their viewpoints. Yet these interest groups rarely have much influence on political decisions. Far more influential are the wealthy groups, such as corporate interests, that operate behind the scenes by lobbying members of Congress and the executive branch of government.

Political Parties

Political parties are collectivities of people organized for the specific purpose of gaining legitimate control of government. Parties are a vital element in a democracy. They link the voter to government, they define policy alternatives, they transmit public opinion from the level of the citizen to the level of the leadership, they mobilize grassroots political participation, and they recruit and offer candidates for public office.

American political parties are quite unlike parties in any other democracy. Parties in other countries are usually closely tied to either the working class or to the middle and upper classes (Lipset, 1959a). They have very specific programs, which are contained in policy documents issued before elections, and policy differences between parties are usually clear cut and significant. Every member of a party is expected to support the party's program in public, and failure to do so can lead to expulsion from the party. Each party applies strict discipline over its legislators, requiring them to be present for voting and instructing them on how to vote. People may become candidates for a party

Figure 19.9 American political parties are essentially loose coalitions, more interested in gaining control of government than in very specific programs. The parties meet at the national level only once every four years for the purpose of selecting a presidential candidate. In general, they choose a candidate who will appeal to the political center; in the few instances when a party has chosen a strongly left- or right-wing candidate, he has been heavily defeated.

nomination only if they are approved by the party organization. There are no primary elections, and candidates are selected behind closed doors by a small group of party activists. The electorate generally votes for the party, not the individual, because voters are oriented toward policies, not personalities. A politician who is expelled from a party for deviations from its official line has little chance of being reelected, because there is little or no advantage in being an incumbent.

American parties are entirely different. Although there is a strong tendency for the lower and working classes to vote Democratic and the upper-middle and upper classes to vote Republican, both parties have a wide base of support and never introduce class issues into their campaigns. Each party has a liberal and a conservative wing, and it is quite possible for voters to be faced with a choice between a liberal Republican and a conservative Democrat. The parties try to avoid specific programs as far as possible, and their platforms usually consist of vague generalities that are intended to appeal to the political center. There is no expectation that candidates will support every detail of the party platform and no means of disciplining them if they do not. Both parties have weak national organizations. In effect, they are federations of state and local parties that meet together only once every four years to select a presidential candidate. Any member of a party can seek its nomination for office, and where there are primary elections an individual can win the nomination even in the face of opposition from the party. Americans are willing to vote for the individual, not the party; a 1968 Gallup poll found that this was true of 84 percent of the electorate. An incumbent who is well known therefore has a strong advantage in an election.

American parties are essentially loose coalitions, less concerned with ideology and coherent programs than with winning office. Both parties accept the main structural features of American society, including its class system and capitalist economy, and both aim at winning the middle ground in politics. If either party nominates a candidate for national office who veers too far to the left or the right, it invites a landslide defeat, as happened to Barry Goldwater in 1964 and George McGovern in 1972.

The loose nature of American parties and their lack of internal discipline means that a new coalition of congressional votes has to be assembled on each new issue. This feature encourages lobbying activities by interest groups, for they can hope to influence the outcome of any vote. The party systems of other democracies ensure great predictability of legislative voting because most legislators toe the party line and are not so subject to external influence. The American system, although more democratic in some respects, offers greater possibilities for corruption and other abuses. The practice of campaign funding by private interests is often particularly suspect for this reason. Many corporations and other interest groups actually donate money to opposing candidates of each party, a practice that can only be explained in terms of their expectation that they will get some payoff later no matter who wins.

American political culture thus encourages an informal, behind-the-scenes interaction among parties, elected officials, and private interest groups. An understanding of this process gives a much fuller picture of our political life than an analysis of formal institutions and processes alone. But where does power really lie? Who makes the decisions?

Who Rules?

In a democracy, power is theoretically vested in the people, who periodically delegate it to their representatives. The difficulty is, of course, that power may pass to the representatives themselves and to those individuals and interests who have privileged access to the decision-making process. The growth of mass political parties in the late nineteenth and early twentieth centuries appeared at first to promise an end to the ancient pattern of rule by a small elite. Yet disillusion set in early when it seemed that even in these new, theoretically democratic parties, power was concentrated in the hands of the leadership.

Three important social scientists of this period addressed the problem, and they all came to similar conclusions. Robert Michels (1911) argued that any organization would by its very nature have to concentrate power in the hands of its leaders in the interests of efficiency (see Chapter 7, Social Groups). Vilfredo Pareto (1935) pointed out that elites are present in all societies, communities, and organizations. Some people have greater skill, determination, ambition, intelligence, or manipulative ability than others, and they tend to dominate the group. Pareto saw no reason why political life should be any different. He believed it was important, however, that political systems should be "open," permitting new rulers to replace old ones in a continual "circulation of elites." Gaetano Mosca (1939) insisted that every society contains a class that rules and a class that is ruled; the ruling class is always a minority. This situation, he argued, will always be found in any society.

Do these principles apply to the United States? Is there a "ruling class," and do the ordinary voters have much influence over the political decisions that affect their lives? Let's look first at two important theories on the subject, and then at some empirical evidence.

The Power-Elite Thesis

In his book *The Power Elite,* C. Wright Mills (1956) argued that the United States is dominated by a small, informal elite of powerful and influential individuals. This "power elite" is not a conspiracy, and the members have usually not even sought the power that they enjoy. They happen to hold important positions in the great organizations that dominate American society, such as government departments, the military, and large corporations:

> The power elite is composed of men whose positions enable them to transcend the ordinary environments of ordinary men and women; they are in a position to make decisions having major consequences. . . . They are in command of the major hierarchies and organizations of modern society. They rule the big organizations. They run the machinery of state and claim its prerogatives. They direct the military establishment. They occupy the strategic command posts of the social structure, in which are centered the effective means of the power and the wealth and the celebrity which they enjoy.

Our advanced capitalist system, Mills argues, requires highly coordinated, long-range decision making among government, corporations, and the military, which is by far the biggest single spender and consumer in the United States. The leading officials of these organizations are therefore in constant contact with one another, and they often make informal decisions of great social and political importance. The power elite is composed of men of very similar social background. They are mostly born in America of American parents; they are from urban areas; they are predominantly Protestant; and a great number of them have attended Ivy League colleges. Except for the politicians, most of them are from the East. The members of the power elite know one another personally and share very similar attitudes, values, and interests. They sit together on corporation boards and government commissions, and thus form an "interlocking directorate" that coordinates activities and policies.

Mills argues that there are three distinct levels of power and influence in the United States. At the highest level is the power elite, which operates informally and invisibly and makes all the most important decisions in domestic and especially foreign policy. The middle level consists of the legislative branch of government, the various interest groups, and local opinion leaders. Decisions at this level take place mostly through lobbying and the legislative process, but these decisions are usually of secondary importance. At the third and lowest level is the mass of powerless, unorganized citizens, who have little direct influence on decisions and, in fact, are often unaware that the decisions are even being made.

The Pluralist Thesis

Some sociologists reject Mills's argument, mainly on the grounds that they do not believe power is as concentrated as Mills suggests. These sociologists offer a more pluralistic model of the American power structure. They stress the diversity rather than the similarity of the many organizations and groups that exercise power and influence.

TWO PORTRAITS OF THE AMERICAN POWER STRUCTURE

Power Structure	Mills—Power Elite	Riesman—Pluralism
Levels	Unified power elite Diversified and balanced plurality of interest groups Mass of unorganized people who have no power over elite	No dominant power elite Diversified and balanced plurality of interest groups Mass of unorganized people who have some power over interest groups
Operation	One group determines all major policies Manipulation of people at the bottom by group at the top	Who determines policy depends on the issue Competition among organized groups
Basis	Coincidence of interests among major institutions (economic, military, governmental)	Diversity of interests among major organized groups
Consequences	Enhancement of interests of corporations, armed forces, and executive branch of government Decline of responsible and accountable power—loss of democracy	No one group or class is favored significantly over others Decline of effective leadership

Source: Adapted from William Kornhauser, "Power Elite or Veto Groups?" in Seymour Martin Lipset and Leo Lowenthal (eds.), *Culture and Social Character* (New York: Free Press, 1961).

Figure 19.10 This table compares some features of the "power elite" and "pluralist" interpretations of the American power structure. Mills's model emphasizes the concentration of power in the hands of a few people who use it to further their own interests; Riesman's model implies that power is more diversified and that many more groups benefit as a result.

David Riesman (1961) acknowledges that power is unequally distributed in American society but denies that there is any coordinated power elite. The decision makers, he suggests, are not nearly as unified as Mills contends. The conflicting interests of the various groups at the upper levels of power ensure that no one group is able to maintain a monopoly of the decision-making process. Riesman argues that there are two levels of power in the United States. The upper level consists of what he calls *veto groups,* strong interest groups that try to protect themselves by blocking any proposals of other groups that might encroach on their own interests. Power is not highly centralized. Instead, shifting coalitions emerge depending on the issue at stake, and in the long run no one group is favored over the others. At the second level is the unorganized public, which Riesman believes is not so much dominated by the veto groups as sought by them as an ally in their campaigns. Those who seek power must therefore take account of public opinion if they are to be successful. In Riesman's view there is no coordinated elite that dominates society in its own interests.

Empirical Studies

Both of these analyses have won a good deal of support from sociologists. Their validity is difficult to evaluate, however, because they deal with an informal process that cannot easily be studied. But research in some areas can throw light on the problem. Important studies have been made on the backgrounds of the country's political, industrial, and military elite; of the extent of popular participation in the political process; of local community politics; and of the "military-industrial complex."

The "Governing Class"

G. William Domhoff (1967, 1971) has made a systematic attempt to discover whether the United States has a "governing class" of the kind described by Mills. Domhoff tried to find out who the members of the American upper class were. His criteria for membership in this class included being listed in the exclusive *Social Register,* having gone to a select private school, having millionaire status, and belonging to prestigious men's clubs in large cities.

Figure 19.11 This group of corporation executives is typical in significant respects of the most influential decision-making groups in American society. Notice the age, race, and sex composition of the group.

Domhoff found that this uppermost social class consisted of not more than 0.5 percent of the population. The members were not only extremely wealthy. A disproportionate number of them held high-level positions in important social organizations. These included corporations, banks, insurance companies, the diplomatic service, the CIA, charitable foundations, the military, the mass media, the National Security Council, the Council on Foreign Relations, government departments, and the boards of trustees of universities and colleges. Moreover, these people were closely knit through intermarriage, attendance at the same schools and universities, membership in the same clubs, and service on boards of important governmental and economic organizations.

This group clearly bears many similarities to the "power elite" described by Mills, and Domhoff concluded that it constitutes the governing class of the United States. The evidence seems convincing, but the case is not proved. The members of this elite may not necessarily work for their own advantage; there may be severe disagreements among them; and there may be many restraints on the power that they exercise. The fact that the elite exists seems beyond dispute, but how much power it has and how it uses it remains debatable.

Political Participation

To what extent do people at the other end of the power structure—the ordinary voters—participate in the political process? Research has shown that political participation is closely correlated with social class. The lower a person's social status, the less likely that person is to register as a voter, to vote, to be interested in politics, to belong to a political organization, or to attempt to influence the views of others (Erbe, 1964).

The turnout of voters in American elections is strikingly low compared with that in most other democracies. Only about 60 percent of Americans vote in national elections, compared with about 85 percent in Britain and nearly 90 percent in such countries as Denmark, Italy, and West Germany. Furthermore, a substantial number of Americans who are eligible to vote do not bother to register. Only 72 percent of eligible voters were registered at the time of the 1972 presidential election, and one in four of those who were registered did not vote. President Nixon's sweeping majority of 61 percent of the votes cast was thus based on the support of not more than one-third of the potential electorate. Voter turnout was particularly low among blacks and among new voters in the age group

Figure 19.12 Despite the supposed greater commitment of young people to political and social reform, they are significantly less likely than most other age groups to register to vote or to vote. Radical youth groups, such as the "Yippies" (Youth International Party), maintain that the electoral system is a sham.

eighteen to twenty. Over 40 percent of the youth did not register, and less than half of those who did register voted in the election. At the time of the 1976 presidential election, only 71 percent of all adults—and only 50 percent of citizens aged eighteen to thirty—had bothered to register as voters, and only 53.3 percent of them actually voted.

The fact that the young and people of lower social status are less likely to vote is open to varying interpretations. It is possible, for example, that they are quite happy with the system, have no fear that either party will alter it much, and therefore see no real need to vote. It is more plausible, however, that they do not believe that they can influence national policies by voting. Perceiving no relationship between voting and political influence, they do not bother to vote. One study of the opinions of American youth lends support to this view. Six out of ten believe that "special interests" run the government and that the United States is democratic in name only. More than half believe that the corporations are the real centers of power, and nine out of ten believe that business corporations put profits too far ahead of social responsibility (Yankelovitch, 1974). A 1976 poll of nonvoters by Hart Research Associates also found that four out of five of them cite feelings of political alienation as the reason for their apathy.

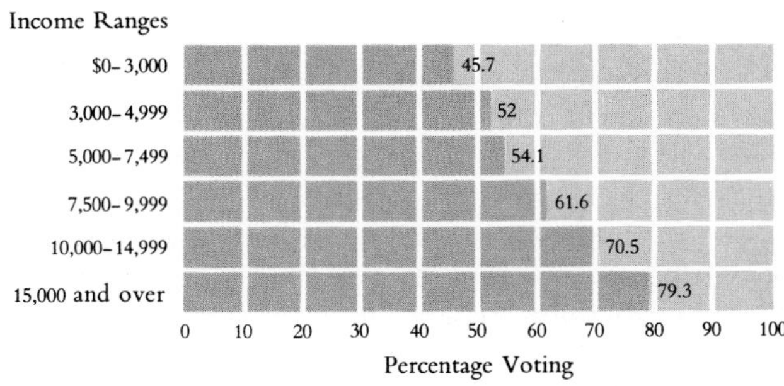

Source: U.S. Bureau of the Census, *Current Population Reports,* Series P-20, no. 253, "Voting and Registration in the Election of November, 1972" (Washington, D.C.: U.S. Government Printing Office, 1973), Table 11, p. 96.

Figure 19.13 The likelihood of voting correlates strongly with the income of the voter. This fact seems to indicate a pervasive apathy among poorer voters toward the political system.

Community Politics

The relatively small scale of towns and cities makes analysis of their political processes easier than analyses at the national level. Several studies of this kind have been conducted, sometimes in the hope that patterns of power and influence in communities will provide insights into those of the wider society.

The general finding of these studies has been that power is exercised by small elites, although the nature of the elites varies from one community to another. In the late nineteenth and early twentieth centuries, for example, large cities such as New York, Philadelphia, Boston, and San Francisco were ruled by the party "machine," the local organization of the dominant party. These machines, headed by a party "boss," effectively traded votes for jobs and other benefits. The base of the machine's power was the lower class, in most cases containing large numbers of new immigrants. Except in Chicago, where the Democratic party machine of the "boss" and the late mayor Richard Daley persisted into the seventies, this system is largely a thing of the past.

More recent studies have reported different patterns. In his study of Atlanta, Georgia, Floyd Hunter (1953) found that most decisions were made by an informal economic elite consisting mainly of corporation executives and bankers. These men communicated informally, shared a similar point of view on major community issues, and determined local policies. Ordinary members of the community were not aware that this elite existed, and they regarded their elected public officials as their real leaders. Hunter found, however, that the elected leaders were not the actual decision makers; they carried out decisions made by others who had the ability to influence them. In a more recent study of New Haven, Connecticut, Robert Dahl (1961) found the community power structure was much less centralized, with a far wider participation in decision making. The upper class, Dahl found, had withdrawn from the community political arena by moving to the suburbs. The lower class was also excluded from decision making, since it had no effective means of asserting influence. The actual power structure was a shifting coalition of public officials and private individuals, with different people participating in decisions on different issues. Men and women from the middle and upper-middle class appeared to have the greatest influence but took part only in decisions affecting their own particular interests. Other community studies reveal no consistent pattern other than that decisions are made by small elites in every case (Walton, 1966). Who these elites are, how much influence they have, and to what extent they are unified are questions that seem to depend on the characteristics of the community itself.

The Military-Industrial Complex

The term *military-industrial complex* was first used by President Dwight Eisenhower in his farewell address to the American people. Eisenhower (quoted in Melman, 1970) warned that:

> The conjunction of an immense military establishment and a large arms industry is new to the American experience. The total influence . . . economic, political, even spiritual . . . is felt in every statehouse, every office of the Federal government. . . . We must not fail to recognize its grave implications. Our toil, resources, and livelihood are all involved; so is the very structure of our society. In the councils of government we must guard against the unwarranted influence, whether sought or unsought, by the military-industrial complex. The potential for a disastrous rise of misplaced power exists and will persist.

The military-industrial complex is an informal system of mutual influence between the Pentagon, which buys armaments, and major U.S. corporations, which sell them. The Pentagon relies heavily on the small number of giant corporations that have the technological expertise to supply sophisticated weaponry. The corporations, in turn, are dependent on the Pentagon, because manufacturing goods for the military is much more profitable than competitive commercial production. Less than 10 percent of Pentagon contracts are open for competitive bidding, and the Pentagon allows corporations to make very large profits and to incur vast "cost overruns" on the original estimated prices of products. The F-111 aircraft, for example, was originally ordered at a price of $2.4 million each; the current price of the plane is now in excess of $13 million apiece. A navy rescue submarine that was ordered at a price of $3 million eventually sold at $125 million. In fact, the price of thirty-eight of our major weapons systems jumped by an average of nearly 50 percent from the price originally agreed on (Sherrill, 1970). Contracts that do not involve competitive bidding and permit huge cost overruns naturally appeal to corporations, and they have flocked to gain a piece of the action: the Pentagon signs agreements with over 20,000 prime contractors and more than 100,000 smaller contractors. Some twenty-four major corporations, however, hold more than 50 percent of the prime contracts.

Inefficiency in the manufacture of American military equipment is now legendary. The B-70 aircraft, developed at a cost of over $1.5 billion, was such a disaster that only two of the planes were ever built. One promptly crashed and the other is now in a museum. The Sheridan tank, which cost $1 billion to develop, is a lumbering monster that will never see a battle. A new atomic submarine launched in California immediately sank to the bottom of the ocean; the salvage costs alone are estimated at $35 million. The nuclear ANP aircraft was abandoned after more than $511 million had been invested to develop it. The Seamaster aircraft was scrapped after an investment of $330 million; the Navaho missile after an investment of nearly $680 million; and the Dyna-soar missile after an investment of $405 million (Sherrill, 1970; Melman, 1970). The F-111 aircraft proved virtually unflyable and unfit for military combat: the planes in the first contingent sent to Vietnam either crashed or were readily shot down, sometimes by rifle fire. The Pentagon canceled its original contract for the F-111 but paid the manufacturer, General Dynamics, compensation of $215.5 million. Why does the Pentagon tolerate these inefficiencies? The reason is that it is not merely the customer but also the captive of the major corporations. If they should collapse into bankruptcy through loss of Pentagon contracts and overrun handouts, the Pentagon would be left without a weapons supply. In any event, the sums involved are a drop in the bucket to the Pentagon, which since World War II has spent well over 1 trillion dollars—that is, 1,000,000 times $1,000,000—on defense.

The Pentagon has immense importance in the U.S. economy. It is the largest single formal organization in world history. It is housed in the world's largest office building. It is the world's largest home builder. It finances half of all federal government research. It owns more property than any one single organization in the world, controls an area of land equal to the size of New York State, and has assets worth $200 billion. One in every nine jobs in the United States is dependent on the military establishment, and over a third of federal civilian em-

THE ANNUAL FEDERAL BUDGET: 1970–1975

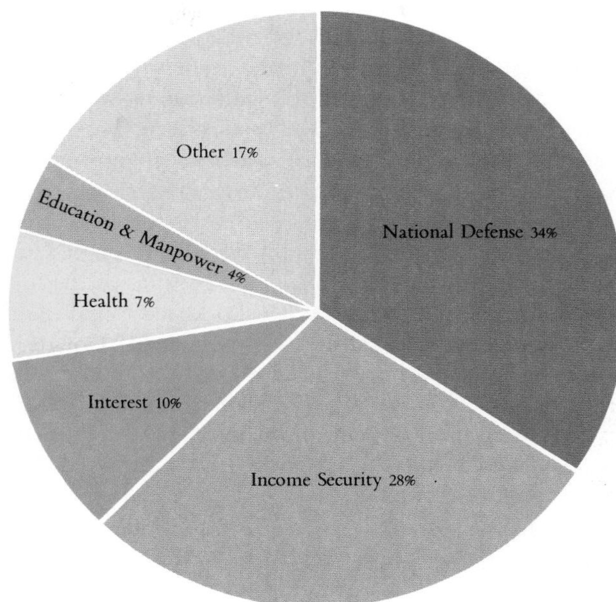

Source: U.S. Bureau of the Census, *Statistical Abstracts, 1975,* p. 224.

Figure 19.14 In the first half of the present decade, the United States spent an average of more than a third of the entire federal budget on defense.

ployees work for the Pentagon. Defense money flows into more than three-fourths of the nation's congressional districts, and some 350 American communities have at least one defense plant or factory. The Pentagon spends over $190 million a year on propaganda, and without any authorization from Congress has kept confidential files on one out of every eight Americans (Eitzen, 1974; Melman, 1970; McDonald, 1970; Kaufman, 1970; Sherrill, 1970; Anderson, 1974b).

Because large corporations such as Lockheed and General Dynamics derive most of their income from defense contracts, they constantly lobby the Pentagon and Congress to spend ever larger sums on defense. Most of the corporations have permanent lobbyists in Washington, and many try to maintain their links with the Pentagon by hiring ex-military officers. By the end of the sixties, the top one hundred military contractors employed some

2072 former officers with the rank of colonel or above, and the ten largest contractors were responsible for more than half of the total. Many of these men presumably retained influence with their former colleagues. Military officials who are responsible for negotiating contracts and who may hope for a corporate appointment when they retire are also, to say the least, put in a compromising situation. The Pentagon itself employs the largest professional lobby in Washington—one lobbyist for every two members of Congress. These lobbyists urge Congress to increase defense expenditures and to take care of the interests of prime contractors. When Lockheed found itself on the brink of bankruptcy in 1971, for example, Congress bailed the company out with a loan of $250 million—an act more typical of a socialist society than one priding itself on free enterprise. The Pentagon worked furiously to win the loan for Lockheed, a company that employed 210 ex-military officers at the time. It is also worth noting that more than half of the company directors of the major defense contractors are members of the tight-knit "governing class" identified by Domhoff.

Mills argued that "military capitalism" is at the heart of the power elite, a view that seems highly plausible. The soaring levels of defense expenditure, at a time when the United States has long had the capacity to destroy life on the planet several times over, can only be fully explained in terms of continuing corporate pressure for profits from often unnecessary weapons production. As Ernest Fitzgerald (1973) sourly comments, "the Pentagon and its supporting cast of contractors unite to pick the public pocket."

What, then, is the nature of the American power structure: a "power elite" or a series of competing "veto groups"? We still lack the detailed information we need to give a definitive answer to this question, but on the basis of the available evidence it seems that both views are too simplistic. It is likely that decision making in foreign policy is controlled by a very small elite but that domestic issues are determined by shifting coalitions of elites. There are probably a number of power elites in American society that are united on some issues but in disagreement on others. What does seem clear, however, is that most important political decisions are made by an elite or elites consisting of a very small and privileged part of the population (Kornhauser, 1966; Rose, 1967).

Figure 19.15 The Cuban revolutionary leader Che Guevara has become a symbol for revolutionaries all over the world. Dedicated to communist revolution throughout the less-developed countries of the world, he left Cuba after the successful revolution in that country and started a new revolutionary movement in Bolivia. He was captured by Bolivian security forces and shot.

Revolutions

Most political change is *evolutionary:* it grows out of existing processes and institutions. Under some circumstances, however, *revolutionary* change takes place, involving the overthrow of existing institutions and the radical reconstruction of the social and political order.

The philosophic justification for revolution in modern times can be traced back to yet another of the "social contract" theorists, John Locke (1632–1704). Like Hobbes and Rousseau, Locke argued that political authority had been created by a social contract made in the original "state of nature." But Locke held that people in the "state of nature" were free and that they had created government for the sole purpose of guaranteeing their freedom. If a government violated this trust, the contract was broken, and the people had the right to rebel in order to restore their freedom. The leaders of the American Revolution were deeply influenced by Locke's writings, and the Declaration of Independence echoes his theory in its specific justification of a people's right to revolt:

> We hold these truths to be self-evident, that all men are created equal, that they are endowed by their Creator with certain inalienable rights, that among these are life, liberty, and the pursuit of happiness. That to secure these rights, governments are instituted among men, deriving their just powers from the consent of the governed. . . . That whenever any form of government becomes destructive of these ends it is the right of the people to alter or abolish it and to institute new government, laying its foundations on such principles and organizing its powers in such form as to them shall seem most likely to effect their safety and happiness.

Unlike a *coup d'etat,* which involves a restricted use of force to replace government leaders with people previously outside the government, a revolution usually involves mass violence. Sociologists have long been interested in the conditions that give rise to such a situation, and several factors have been identified (Brinton, 1960; Davies, 1962). If all the following conditions are present, a revolution is a distinct possibility, although not a certainty. Each situation has its own unique characteristics that may affect the chances for revolution.

1. Alternative channels to change must be blocked, and significant groups in society must feel that they have no access to power. Revolutions are more likely if the rulers refuse to accept change or keep the pace of change too slow, while suppressing efforts by other groups to bring about change.

2. There must be a widespread awareness that valued resources, such as wealth and power, are unfairly distributed. Unless a large part of the population feels a continuing sense of grievance, a revolution is unlikely.

3. People must be aware that there are alternatives to the existing system and must feel that they are entitled to benefits that have been denied them in the past. To be poor or oppressed is not in itself sufficient grounds for revolution. If it were, most of the world would be in revolt at this moment, since well over half the global population is hungry and is denied democratic rights. Revolutions occur only in the context of *rising expectations:* people who have accepted the situation in the past must sense that it is their right to have something better in the future.

4. Existing political institutions must usually be weak or even on the verge of breakdown. The ruling elite in prerevolutionary situations is often divided. The system is failing to "work," and the legitimacy of the form of government is being eroded, so that the system is maintained by coercion. In many revolutionary situations the government is so weak that prolonged or widespread bloodshed is not needed to bring it down: it collapses at the first push.

Revolutions are almost always led not by members of the oppressed class but rather by well-educated members of the middle class. A revolution does not need the support of the majority of the people; it is sufficient if those who support the government are in a minority and most other people are apathetic. Revolutions are usually followed by periods of great uncertainty as the new regime attempts to make policies and establish its own legitimacy. There are often power struggles within the revolutionary movement once the revolution has taken place. The indiscriminate guillotining that followed the French Revolution is a particularly gory example of this trend, but it conforms to a widespread pattern. The final victors are usually the most disciplined and dedicated of the revolutionaries, which is one reason why communists are often able to benefit from revolutions fought largely by liberals

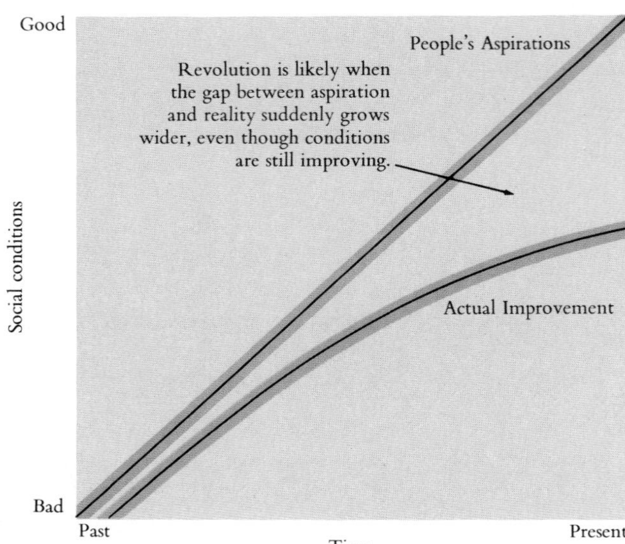

Source: Adapted from James C. Davies, "Toward a Theory of Revolution," *American Sociological Review,* 27 (1962), p. 7.

Figure 19.16 Social unrest is likely when people's aspirations run ahead of improvements in their actual conditions. Oppressive conditions in themselves will not cause a revolution unless people have come to expect better conditions.

Figure 19.17 Like many revolutions, the French Revolution was followed by internal power struggles within the revolutionary movement and by the execution of members of the previous ruling class.

and noncommunist radicals. Revolutions tend to be followed by the creation of nondemocratic and even totalitarian political institutions, largely because the new regime has not achieved full legitimacy and fears challenges to its authority, but these controls are likely to be gradually lessened once the political order becomes stable.

Summary

1. The political order is the institutionalized system through which some people acquire and exercise power over others. The highest level of power is that of the state, the institution that claims a monopoly of the legitimate use of force within a given territory.

2. Power is the ability to compel obedience, even in the absence of consent by those who obey. Power may be regarded as legitimate (authority) or illegitimate (coercion). There are three basic types of authority: traditional, legal-rational, and charismatic.

3. The emergence of the state is linked to the level of evolution of a society; it appears first in agricultural societies and becomes a dominant institution in industrial societies. The functionalist perspective emphasizes the functions of the state in maintaining social order: enforcing norms; arbitrating conflict; planning and giving direction; and regulating relationships with other societies. The conflict perspective emphasizes the role of the state in maintaining the status quo and thus protecting the interests of the dominant class. These approaches are not necessarily incompatible.

4. Democracy is rare and exists only as representative democracy. The prerequisites for democracy are advanced economic development; restraints on government power; absence of major cleavages; tolerance of dissent; free access to information; and diffusion of power. Liberty and equality are to some extent incompatible: capitalist societies emphasize liberty; socialist societies, equality.

5. The American political process involves an important interaction between interest groups and parties. Powerful interest groups may lobby successfully for their own advantage. American parties are loose coalitions, and legislative votes are often unpredictable and subject to the influence of interest groups.

6. Mills argued that the United States is ruled by a power elite. Riesman argued that important decisions are made through the interplay of veto groups. Studies of the governing class, of political participation, of community politics, and of the military-industrial complex all indicate that important decisions are made by powerful interests.

7. Revolutions may occur under certain conditions: when avenues to change are blocked; when there is widespread sense of grievance; when expectations are rising but not being met; and when the legitimacy of existing institutions is crumbling.

Important Terms

political order
state
power
legitimate power
authority
illegitimate power
coercion
traditional authority
legal-rational authority
charismatic authority
ideal type
class conflict
primitive communism
slavery
feudalism
capitalism
socialism
communism
democracy
representative democracy
oligarchy
totalitarian
interest group
lobbying
political party
power elite
veto groups
military-industrial complex
revolution
coup d'etat
rising expectations

Suggested Readings

BRINTON, CRANE. *The Anatomy of Revolution.* New York: Vintage, 1960.

Brinton carefully analyzes some revolutions of the past, attempting to discover common conditions that gave rise to them.

DAHL, ROBERT. *Who Governs?* New Haven, Conn.: Yale University Press, 1961.

A classic study of community politics. Dahl traces the patterns of political influence in New Haven, Connecticut, showing how different interest groups dominate the decision-making process on different issues.

DOMHOFF, G. WILLIAM. *Who Rules America?* Englewood Cliffs, N.J.: Prentice-Hall, 1967.

An important study of the American "governing class," the close-knit group who, Domhoff contends, are able to translate their economic resources into immense political influence in the United States.

MELMAN, SEYMOUR. *Pentagon Capitalism.* New York: McGraw-Hill, 1970.

A fascinating study of the Pentagon, its use of public money, and its relationships with the major corporate weapons suppliers.

MILLS, C. WRIGHT. *The Power Elite.* New York: Oxford University Press, 1956.

This is the book that first raised the issue of "who rules" in the United States. Mills argues forcefully that American political life is dominated by a "power elite" drawn from the executive branch of government, the military, and major corporations.

SAMPSON, ANTHONY. *The Sovereign State of ITT.* Greenwich, Conn.: Fawcett Books, 1973.

A highly readable account of the political activities and influence of one of America's largest corporations, the International Telephone and Telegraph Corporation. Sampson details the various domestic and international intrigues of the organization.

UNIT 5 *Social Change in the Modern World*

Everything changes, and human societies are no exception. Yet throughout most of the history of our species social change has been relatively slow. Most people lived much the same lives as their parents and grandparents before them, and they expected that their children and grandchildren would lead similar lives as well. Today this is no longer true. The modern industrial world is in a state of constant and rapid social change, and we take it for granted that social and technological innovations will continue to transform our lives in the years that lie ahead.

The chapters in this unit deal with some of the issues involved in this process of change. The first chapter confronts one of the most pressing problems of the modern world, that of rapid population growth and environmental destruction, and shows how the dynamic interplay between the two may threaten the human future. The second chapter deals with urbanization and the nature of urban life, a crucial topic in a world that has become heavily urbanized only in the course of the present century. The third chapter in the unit discusses collective behavior and social movements—those concerted acts of large numbers of people that often provoke social changes. The final chapter comes to grips with the more general problem of explaining and directing social change, a problem that sociologists have grappled with since the founding of the discipline.

CHAPTER 20 *Population and Ecology*

CHAPTER OUTLINE

The Study of Population
The Science of Demography
The Dynamics of Demographic Change

The World Population Problem
The Malthusian Trap
The Causes of Rapid Population Growth
The Theory of Demographic Transition

Population in the United States
American Demographic Characteristics
Do We Have a Population Problem?

What Can Be Done?

Population and the Environment
The Science of Ecology
The Elements of Ecology
Pollution
Resource Depletion
The Limits to Growth

The sun sets every night on an additional 200,000 human beings. Some 50,000 years ago the human population was so small that there was an average of 200 square miles of the earth's surface for each individual. If population growth were to continue at its present rate, there would be one hundred people for every square yard of the earth's surface within nine hundred years. Obviously, such an absurd situation could never occur: one way or another, population growth will stop long before that point is reached.

The human population already stands at over 4 billion, and at current growth rates that number will double within thirty-eight years. If the growth rate were to continue unchecked, in fact, global population would reach about 150 billion within two centuries. Yet nearly two-thirds of the existing inhabitants of the earth are undernourished or malnourished, and they are dying of starvation at the rate of more than 10 million every year. There can be little question that unchecked population growth is the most critical social problem in the modern world, with potential consequences in terms of sheer human misery that are almost unimaginable.

In our modern, urbanized society we often feel insulated from nature and confident that our technology can give us mastery over the natural environment. We forget all too easily that human beings are animals, ultimately as dependent on the environment as any other species. No natural environment can withstand an infinite increase in the animal or plant populations that it supports. It is doubtful if the planet can continue to provide the food and other raw materials that huge human populations require, or if it can tolerate the pollution caused by ever-expanding industrial production.

Population growth and environmental problems are thus closely linked. For analytic purposes we will look first at the dynamics of population growth and then at the human relationship to the environment, but throughout our discussion we will bear in mind the close connection between the two.

The Study of Population

No human population is ever completely stable. Some populations grow and some decline. The size of some populations changes rapidly, while that of others changes much more slowly. Some populations have a high proportion of young people, some of old people. Most populations contain more females than males, particularly in the oldest generation, but the exact ratio of the sexes varies over time and from place to place. These and other population characteristics are the result of processes that can be scientifically analyzed.

The Science of Demography

Demography is the study of the size, composition, distribution, and changes in human populations. In the United States the science is usually regarded as a subdiscipline of sociology, for the reason that population dynamics are strongly affected by social factors. If a society places restrictions on abortion or the use of contraceptives, the number of births will tend to increase. If a society places taboos on premarital intercourse or on marital intercourse for some time after childbirth, the number of births will tend to be reduced. Social values that encourage large families exert pressure for population increase. Values that encourage women to pursue independent careers tend to depress population growth, as does a social belief that too many children are an economic burden.

Demography thus consists of more than simply extending lines on graphs. The science must take full account of all factors, social, cultural, and environmental, that may affect population trends. Since these factors cannot always be accurately predicted, demographic projections into the distant future are necessarily inexact. Nor is this the only problem that demographers have to face. Many of the statistics that they have to work with are merely estimates, and these estimates are often unreliable. A number of developing nations do not have an efficient and regular population census, and demographic statistics from many of these countries are based to some extent on guesswork. The United States has an elaborate population census every ten years, but the Bureau of the Census believes that about 5 million people—vagrants, illegal immigrants, illiterates, and others—were omitted from its last census in 1970.

Despite these limitations, however, demographers can use current data to give reasonably accurate projections for the relatively short term—say, the next quarter-century or so. They can also offer long-range projections, but these will hold good only under specified hypothetical conditions.

The Dynamics of Demographic Change

Population growth or decline in a given society is affected by three factors: the birth rate, the death rate, and the rate of migration into or out of the society.

Birth Rate

The crude *birth rate* in a given population is usually expressed as the number of births per year per thousand members of the population. In Bangladesh, for example, the birth rate is high, 47 per thousand; in the United States it is low, 15 per thousand in 1976. This statistical measure is called the "crude" rate because it does not give us specific information about the births. It does not tell us, for example, about the birth ratio of male to female, black to white, middle class to lower class, or any other categories. For such categories a separate statistical measure, the specific birth rate, can be constructed.

The birth rate tells us about the *fertility* of the women in a given society: in other words, it tells us how many children the average woman is bearing. Fertility must be distinguished from *fecundity,* or the potential number of children that could be born to a woman of childbearing age. The fecundity of a physically normal woman during this period is about twenty to twenty-five children. In practice the actual fertility of women in any society does not even approach this level of fecundity, because cultural, social, economic, and health factors prevent such prolific breeding.

Figure 20.1 The fertility of women (the actual number of children they bear) rarely approaches their fecundity (the number they could bear in theory). Although some women, such as this Wisconsin mother in the late nineteenth century, may approach the fecundity level of twenty to twenty-five children, in practice very few women do so.

Death Rate

The crude *death rate* in a given population is usually expressed as the number of deaths per year per thousand members of the population. In Bangladesh the death rate is high, 20 per thousand, while in the United States it is comparatively low, 9 per thousand in 1976. Again, it is possible to construct specific death rates for particular categories in the population. The infant death rate for American blacks, for example, is 26.2 per thousand, while that for whites is 15.8 per thousand.

The death rate in any society is related to the average *life expectancy* of its members at birth, that is, the number of years of life that the average newborn will enjoy. Modern medical advances have greatly increased the life expectancy of people all over the world, primarily by eliminating infectious diseases such as smallpox, cholera, and diphtheria. These diseases once killed off a very high proportion of infants and children—as many as 40 to 50 percent of children under the age of five in preindustrial societies. In the United States life expectancy has increased from about forty years at the turn of the century to about seventy years today. Life expectancy must be distinguished from *life span,* the maximum length of life possible in a particular species. Although human life expectancy in most societies has increased markedly during this century, the life span has increased little, if at all, and very few people live beyond a hundred. We have been unable to extend the life span because we have been unable to combat the diseases of old age—cancer and degenerative conditions of the heart, lungs, kidneys, and other organs—as easily as the infectious diseases of childhood.

Migration Rate

The crude *migration rate* in a given population is usually expressed as the number of immigrants (people entering the population) or emigrants (people leaving the population) per year per thousand members of the population. Again, specific rates can be constructed for particular categories of immigrants and emigrants.

Migration rates obviously do not affect the increase or decrease in global population, but they may be an important factor in specific societies. The United States is a case in point: immigration accounted for 40 percent of our population growth in the first decade of this century alone. Immigration to the United States in the late nineteenth and early twentieth centuries was part of the most massive migration in history, in which some 75 million Europeans left their continent and settled in North and South America, parts of Africa, and Australasia. Migration is the product of two interacting factors. The first is *push,* which refers to the conditions that encourage people to emigrate (such as the potato famine in Ireland). The second factor is *pull,* which refers to the conditions that encourage them to immigrate to a particular place (such as the promise of a new and better life in the United States).

Growth Rate

Changes in population size are measured by the *growth rate,* which represents the number of births minus the number of deaths and is usually expressed as an annual percentage. (In most countries migration is now a negligible factor in population growth, and for this reason migration statistics are often omitted from growth-rate calculations.) The average world growth rate at the moment is about 1.8 percent. The United States now has a relatively low growth rate of 0.8 percent, and a few areas in Europe, such as East Germany and Portugal, actually have negative growth rates, meaning that their populations are shrinking. The industrialized countries of the world generally have low growth rates of less than 1 percent, but the developing nations typically have rates well above 2 percent. Some, such as Kenya and Colombia, have rates above 3 percent.

Expressed in percentage terms, these differences seem small. But their long-term impact is staggering. The reason is that population growth is *exponential:* the increase each year is based not on the original figure but on the total for the preceding year. A population of 10,000 with a growth rate of 3 percent will thus increase in ten years not by 30 percent, to 13,000, but by about 34 percent, to 13,439. A very useful concept in analyzing the effects of exponential growth is *doubling time,* the period it takes for a population to double its numbers. A population growing at 1 percent will double itself in 70 years; a population growing at 2 percent will double itself in 35 years; and a population growing at 3 percent will double itself in 23 years. Thus the population of Austria, currently growing at 0.1 percent each year, will take about seven hundred years to double, but the population of Mexico, growing at 3.5 percent each year, will double within twenty years.

The history of world population growth gives some idea of the dizzying speed of exponential growth. In 8000 B.C. the total human population was probably about 5 million people. By A.D. 1 it had risen to about 250 million. A thousand years later it had increased to around 300 million, and by 1650 to half a billion (Miles, 1971). The current doubling to 4 billion was completed in fifty years,

WORLD POPULATION GROWTH IN HISTORY

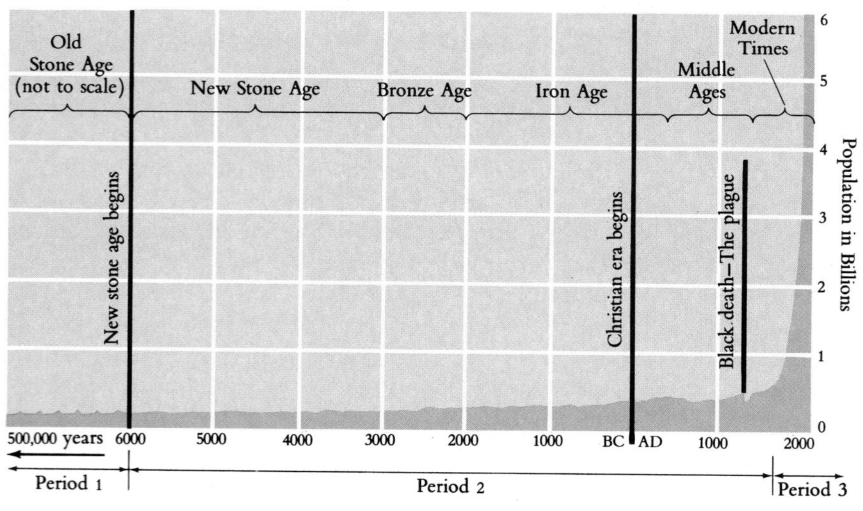

Source: Population Reference Bureau, "How Many People Have Ever Lived on Earth?" *The Population Bulletin,* 18 (February, 1962), p. 5.

Figure 20.2 This graph gives some idea of the implications of exponential population growth. Clearly, growth at this rate will have to come to a drastic halt, either through a decline in the birth rate, an increase in the death rate, or both.

and the next doubling, if the present growth rate continues, will take thirty-eight years. About one person out of every twenty who has ever lived is alive today, and by the year 2000 the world will contain well over twice as many people as when most readers of this book were born.

Obviously, population cannot continue to increase at this rate. The process can be halted only by a sharp decrease in the birth rate, by a sharp increase in the death rate, or by some combination of the two. If each set of parents reproduced only enough children to replace them (about 2.1 children per family, to allow for those who died young or for other reasons did not reproduce themselves), we would ultimately have *zero population growth* (ZPG), a situation in which population size would remain stable.

Age Structure

A stable world population is a long way off, however. Even if every set of parents in the world had only 2.1 children from this moment on, world population would continue to increase for many years. The reason is that the children who have already been born would still have to grow up and reproduce themselves. The *age structure* of a population is therefore an important element in predicting demographic trends.

In most developed societies roughly one-fourth of the population are under the age of fifteen. In Sweden, for example, the figure is 21 percent; in Austria, 24 percent; and in the United States, 27 percent. But in the developing nations the proportion of people under fifteen is very much larger. In Brazil, it is 42 percent; in Uganda, 44 percent; in Togo, 46 percent. These countries consequently have a vast potential for future population growth, regardless of whether their birth rates decline in the next few years. A rapid drop in birth rates therefore offers no immediate solution to the population problem. Even if parents the world over reproduced only enough children to replace themselves from now on, population would still soar to at least 7 billion before it stabilized. But there is little sign of any immediate decline in global birth rates—a fact that makes the alternative "solution," a sharp increase in the death rate through famine, disease, and war, all the more probable.

Let's look at the population problem in more detail, first in the world as a whole, and then in the United States.

The Dangers of Exponential Growth

Common as it is, exponential growth can yield surprising results—results that have fascinated mankind for centuries. There is an old Persian legend about a clever courtier who presented a beautiful chessboard to his king and requested that the king give him in return 1 grain of rice for the first square on the board, 2 grains for the second square, 4 grains for the third, and so forth. The king readily agreed and ordered rice to be brought from his stores. The fourth square of the chessboard required 8 grains, the tenth square 512 grains, the fifteenth required 16,384, and the twenty-first square gave the courtier more than a million grains of rice. By the fortieth square a million million rice grains had to be brought from the storerooms. The king's entire rice supply was exhausted long before he reached the sixty-fourth square. Exponential increase is deceptive because it generates immense numbers very quickly.

A French riddle for children illustrates another aspect of exponential growth—the apparent suddenness with which it approaches a fixed limit. Suppose you own a pond on which a water lily is growing. The lily plant doubles in size each day. If the lily were allowed to grow unchecked, it would completely cover the pond in thirty days, choking off the other forms of life in the water. For a long time the lily plant seems small, and so you decide not to worry about cutting it back until it covers half the pond. On what day will that be? On the twenty-ninth day, of course. You have one day to save your pond.

Source: Donnella H. Meadows *et al., The Limits to Growth* (New York: Signet, 1972).

AGE STRUCTURES OF DENMARK AND EL SALVADOR

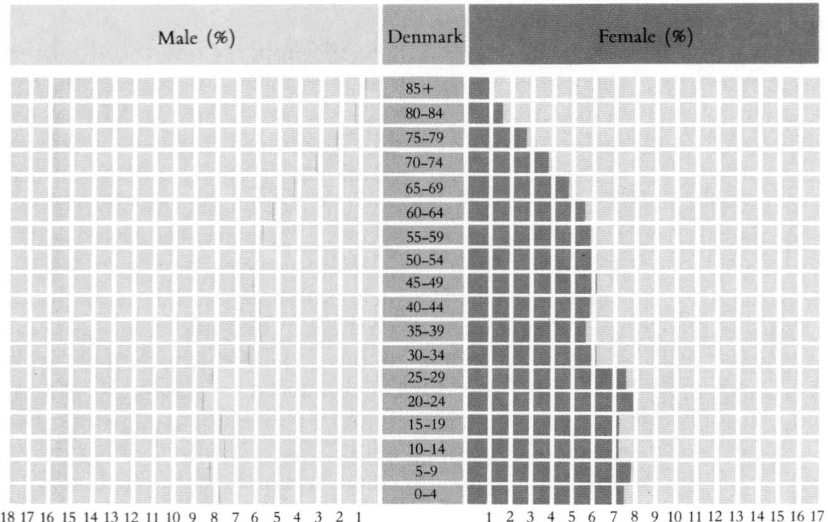

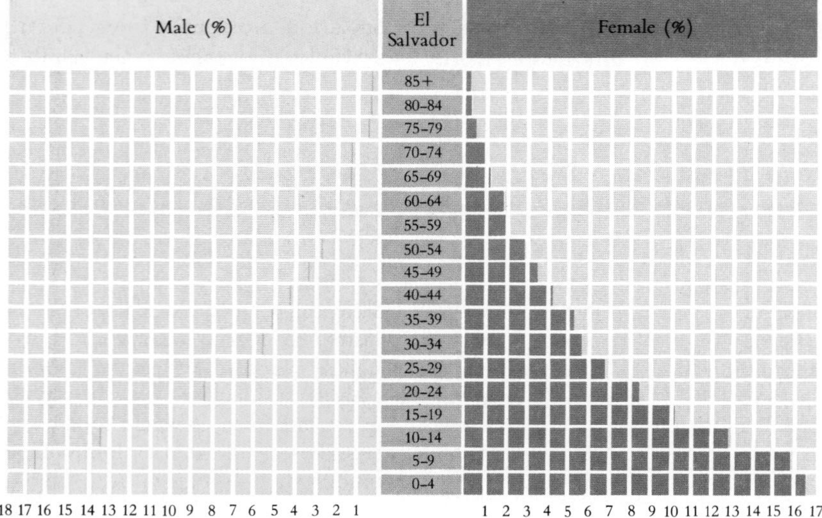

Source: Adapted from Kingsley Davis, "The World's Population Crisis," in Robert K. Merton and Robert Nisbet (eds.), *Contemporary Social Problems* (New York: Harcourt Brace Jovanovich, 1976), p. 276.

Figure 20.3 The age structure of a population tells us a great deal about its demographic future. The proportion of the population under fifteen is very much smaller in Denmark that it is in El Salvador. El Salvador therefore has a far-greater potential for population increase as the younger members of society grow up and reproduce themselves.

The World Population Problem

Birth rates were always very high in preindustrial societies. In most of these societies large families were highly valued. Each new member was an economic asset in groups that had to tend animals or wrest their living from the soil, and the high infant death rate encouraged people to raise large numbers of children in the hope that some of them would survive into adulthood. In the early stages of the Industrial Revolution in England, however, this traditional value was seriously questioned for the first time.

The Malthusian Trap

In 1798, an English parson, Thomas Malthus, published a book entitled *Essay on the Principles of Population,* a work that aroused strong antagonism from his contemporaries. Malthus lived in an age of great optimism, dominated by the idea of the "perfectibility of man." According to this notion, a new golden age of abundance and bliss would be achieved in the future through the marvels of industrial technology. Malthus set out to shatter this idea through a very simple argument, based on his observation that the European population was growing rapidly at the time.

The natural tendency of population growth, Malthus pointed out, is to increase exponentially. But food supply depends on a fixed amount of land, and increases in agricultural production can be made only in a simple, additive fashion by bringing new land under cultivation. Inevitably, therefore, population tends to outrun the means of subsistence. At this point certain factors intervene to keep population within the limits set by food supply—those factors being "war, pestilence, and famine." Human beings, Malthus argued, were destined forever to press against the limits of the food supply. Misery, hunger, and poverty were the inevitable fate of the majority of the human species.

This argument was not a popular one. Malthus became known as the "gloomy parson" and one contemporary critic called his theory "that black and terrible demon that is always ready to stifle the hopes of humanity" (quoted in Heilbroner, 1967). Malthus himself offered little hope. The only suggestions he made were the abolition of poor relief and state support of poor children, in order to cut the growth rate of the lower classes, and "moral restraint" on the part of the rest of the population. But Malthus did not foresee the technical improvements that were later achieved in agriculture, making possible a vastly increased yield from a fixed amount of land, nor did he foresee the decline in birth rates that took place in the industrialized nations in the nineteenth and twentieth centuries. Both Europe and the United States grew in affluence and even in numbers, and it seemed for a while that Malthus had been wrong. Since then, however, an unprecedented population explosion has occurred in the poorer nations of the world, and we have come to recognize that the continuing affluence of the wealthier nations largely depends on their exploitation of the limited resources of the developing countries. The underlying logic of Malthus's argument is

Figure 20.4 Thomas Malthus, who pointed out in 1798 that the human population cannot increase indefinitely in a world of limited resources.

Figure 20.5 Mechanized agriculture, the use of chemical fertilizers, and the introduction of new high-yield grains have all greatly increased food production in the modern world, but global population may soon outstrip the food supply.

difficult to refute: population cannot increase indefinitely in a world that has finite resources. We find ourselves in the Malthusian trap once more.

In demographic terms, the countries of the world fall into two main categories: the developed nations, such as the United States, which have relatively low birth and growth rates, and the developing nations, such as Nigeria, with relatively high birth and growth rates. Between these two lies a third group of countries with intermediate birth and growth rates; these are mostly the smaller and more industrialized of the developing nations, such as Argentina. Rapid population growth is therefore primarily a problem of the poorest nations of the world: in Asia, life expectancy is fifty-six years and the per capita gross national product is $450; in Africa, life expectancy is forty-five years and per capita gross national product is $340. In Europe and North America, by contrast, life expectancy is seventy-one years, while per capita gross national product is $3680 in Europe and $6580 in North America.

Much of this poverty results from the unequal distribution of the world's resources, but even if all the food in the world were equally distributed, there would not be enough to go around—we would *all* be malnourished. And if the entire food supply in the world were distributed at the dietary level that we take for granted in the United States, it would feed only one-third of the current world population. Moreover, the gap between the rich and the poor nations is steadily widening and is likely to continue

THE POPULATION EXPLOSION CURVE

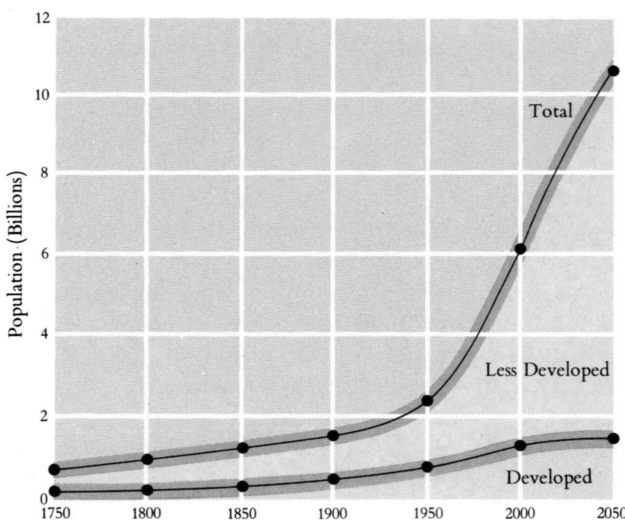

Source: Nathan Keyfitz, "World Resources and the World Middle Class," *Scientific American*, 235 (July, 1976), p. 29.

Figure 20.6 The gap between the per capita incomes of the developed and less developed countries is very wide and is expected to widen even further in the future. The poorer countries, moreover, are the ones that have the greatest and fastest growing populations—and ironically, their population growth is a major reason for their poverty.

to do so. If we project future demographic trends in the developing nations, the picture becomes bleaker still. Kenya, growing at a rate of 3.4 percent a year and with a per capita gross national product of $200, will double its population in 20 years. Mexico, with a 1976 population of 62 million people, would have 2 billion people in 100 years if present growth rates were to continue—a population half as large as the entire present world population.

The Causes of Rapid Population Growth

Why is population increasing at such a speed in the developing nations? The main reason is the change in the ratio of births to deaths. The death rate in these societies has been sharply reduced by the introduction of modern medical techniques, but the birth rate has remained extremely high. In the early industrial societies medical techniques were improved in a slow process extending over many decades, and there was time for cultural values about family size to adjust to the changed material conditions. In the newly developing nations, however, medical knowledge has been introduced with dramatic suddenness, causing a sharp drop in death rates while the birth rates remain at or near their previous levels. Thus Algeria has a birth rate of 49 and a death rate of 15, Mexico a birth rate of 46 and a death rate of 8. As a result, the overall rate of population increase in the developing countries exceeds 2 percent—a rate sufficient to double their populations no less than ten times in 116 years.

A complicating factor is that the developing nations, unlike the early industrial societies, are facing rapid population growth at a time when they already have very large populations. The high rate of growth, operating on this large population base, therefore produces a much greater increase in absolute numbers of people than the comparable population expansions that took place in Europe and the United States in earlier years.

Why have cultural values that emphasize the desirability of large families been so slow to change? The reason is that technological innovations, such as modern medical techniques, have an obvious utility and tend to be rapidly accepted into a society. Cultural values, however, are much more conservative and tend to change only slowly. In many traditional societies a man's virility is gauged by

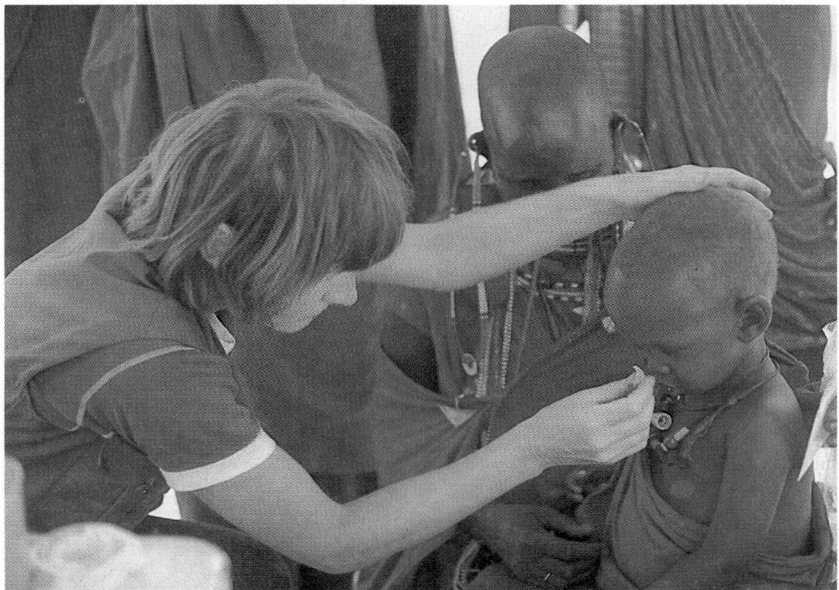

Figure 20.7 The main reason for the rapid population growth rate in the less developed countries is the decline in their death rates, particularly among young children. Modern medical techniques have dramatically reduced the death rate in these societies, but the birth rate remains very high.

Figure 20.8 In traditional, preindustrial societies a large family is still often considered an economic asset. In these societies the family is the main unit of production and each additional child represents another potential worker in the fields.

the number of children he fathers, and most traditional societies emphasize the domestic role of the wife as mother and child rearer. These cultural patterns are not easily changed. A large family was always an asset in a rural economy in the past, and people in a tradition-bound society may have difficulty in appreciating that this situation has changed within the course of a few decades. Even today a large family may serve important functions for parents in developing societies. In countries that lack a system of social security, children provide the only guarantee that one will be looked after in old age.

Many religions, too, emphasize some version of the Judeo-Christian injunction to "be fruitful and multiply." An old Arab proverb declares that "to have many children is to be blessed by Allah," and Islamic religion in several countries is opposed to birth control. The Catholic Church, which is particularly influential in the overpopulated continent of South America, has always opposed the use of contraceptives. To complicate matters further, many peoples regard high birth rates as essential for their economic or political strength. Argentina banned the use of contraceptives in 1974 as part of a planned campaign to double its population as soon as possible, in the supposed interests of economic development. In the wretchedly poor country of Bangladesh, once described by Henry Kissinger as "an international basket case," the first minister of family planning was the father of eighteen children. He was opposed to birth control in principle and his first act was to curtail family-planning programs. Bangladesh, he felt, can be politically secure only if it has as many people as its neighbor, China. Similar arguments about the political desirability of a population increase are heard all over the world—for example, among some Israelis, some white South Africans, and some black Americans. Some black radicals in the United States have maintained that American family-planning programs are directed mainly at blacks, who have a higher average birth rate than whites, and are really a form of genocide. Throughout history, in short, large families and growing nations have been considered a fundamentally good thing. This value has deeply pervaded culture and institutional arrangements, and it is not easily or rapidly changed.

The Theory of Demographic Transition

There is a glimmer of hope in this otherwise bleak picture. We have noted that the early industrial societies faced a rapid population increase as their living standards rose and as improved medical techniques reduced their death rates. We noted also that their population growth rates tended to level off afterward as a result of a fall in the birth rates. This historical sequence has led some demographers to ask whether the same process might occur in other countries as they also industrialize. The theory of *demographic transition* holds that the growth rate of a population tends to stabilize once a certain level of economic development is achieved, primarily because people in urban, industrialized societies prefer small families and voluntarily limit the number of their children. In modern industrial societies children are not an economic asset at all; to feed and educate them places a considerable burden on the parents but yields no economic rewards. According to demographic transition theory, people generally tend to have as many children as they believe they can support. The problem in the developing societies, then, is that peoples' attitudes have not yet caught up with their rapidly changing circumstances.

The demographic transition appears to progress through three basic stages:

Stage one is the situation found in all traditional societies. There is a very high birth rate and a very high death rate, especially among infants. As a result, population numbers remain fairly stable.

Stage two is the situation found in all developing societies in the early stages of industrialism. The birth rate remains high but the death rate drops sharply as a result of improved living standards and medical care. As a result, population grows very rapidly.

THE DEMOGRAPHIC TRANSITION

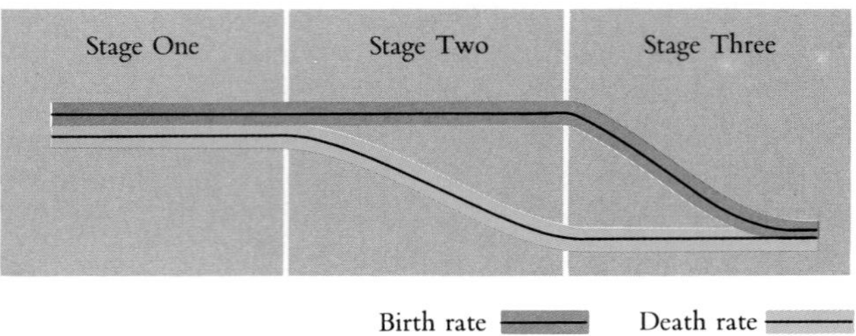

Figure 20.9 According to demographic transition theory, the high population growth rate in the less developed countries should be only a temporary phenomenon. As these societies industrialize, the birth rate should drop to much the same level as the death rate. This has been the pattern in the existing industrialized societies, but there can be no certainty that this pattern will be repeated elsewhere.

Stage three is the situation found in advanced industrial societies. The birth rate drops as large families come to be seen as a liability, and the death rate remains low. As a result, the population growth rate gradually declines toward zero and remains fairly stable.

This transition has been almost completed in Europe, North America, and Japan. Encouragingly, some of the smaller and more economically advanced developing nations—such as Tunisia, Taiwan, Cuba, Puerto Rico, and Costa Rica—are showing signs of a steady decline in birth rates, suggesting that they are in transition between stages two and three. The remaining developing nations, however, are in stage two—and it is these countries that have some of the largest populations in the world and so make the greatest contribution to global population growth. But in time—if the demographic transition theory is correct—they should show signs of a declining birth rate.

How valid is this theory? First, we must recognize that it is merely a hypothesis. The fact that some societies have followed a pattern of demographic transition does not mean that every society will do so. It is possible that specific factors operating in a particular society could speed the transition—or delay it or even "freeze" it at a particular point. The Japanese demographic transition, for example, did not follow the historical pattern of Western societies but was influenced instead by unique factors in Japanese culture and society. The Japanese government started a deliberate policy of population limitation after World War II, relying on abortion as a primary means of birth control. The result was the most spectacular drop in birth rates ever recorded—from 34 per thousand to 14 per thousand in the ten years between 1947 and 1957. Half of the conceptions in Japan during this time were terminated by abortions. But this particular transition was possible only because Japan, unlike many other developing societies, already had a strong central government that had traditionally enjoyed the loyalty of the entire nation and because the Japanese, unlike many other peoples, did not regard abortion as basically immoral. If these factors had not operated, it is doubtful whether Japan could have achieved the transition in the time that it did (Taeuber, 1960).

The second problem with demographic transition theory is that it assumes that an economic "threshhold" must be reached before the transition will take place. Dudley Kirk (1971) points out that there is generally a close connection between a decline in birth rates and the level of socioeconomic development, with per capita income and educational level as important factors. If this view is correct, we cannot expect a transition in the developing nations until they are more economically advanced. Yet the poorest and most populous nations are precisely those that find economic advancement most difficult. The reasons lie in the vicious cycle of poverty and overpopulation.

A country with a rapidly growing population has a disproportionate number of young people, as we have seen. As a result, the work force contains a relatively small part of the population. If, as is the case in most developing nations, 40 to 50 percent of the population is under fifteen, and if a further substantial portion is diseased, disabled, or aged, then the work force must put much or most of its efforts into feeding the unproductive members of society. Per capita income is therefore very low, and living standards and educational levels are consequently depressed. Moreover, capital cannot be accumulated in the quantities necessary to spur economic development. In a society with a stable population, about 3 to 5 percent of national income would have to be invested to create a 1 percent increase in per capita income. In a society with a 3 percent population growth rate, the investment would have to be very much greater—often more than developing countries can afford. As a result, whatever economic advances these countries make may be literally eaten up by their increasing populations and used to accommodate more people rather than improve the living standards of the existing population. A country whose population doubles in twenty or thirty years has to double its national income in that period—a staggering task—merely to keep its population at the same level of subsistence.

To complicate matters still further, the planet may not even have the resources to support huge human populations at anything remotely resembling the standard of living of the advanced industrial societies. To bring everyone up to our economic level would require, for example, that we extract 75 times as much iron, 100 times as much copper, 200 times as much lead, 75 times as much zinc, and 250 times as much tin as we now do every year (Ehrlich and Ehrlich, 1972). Yet there is evidence that, even at present rates of extraction, known supplies of several of these minerals may be exhausted within the next quarter of a century (Meadows *et al.*, 1972). Nor is it easy to see how the environment could tolerate the amount of

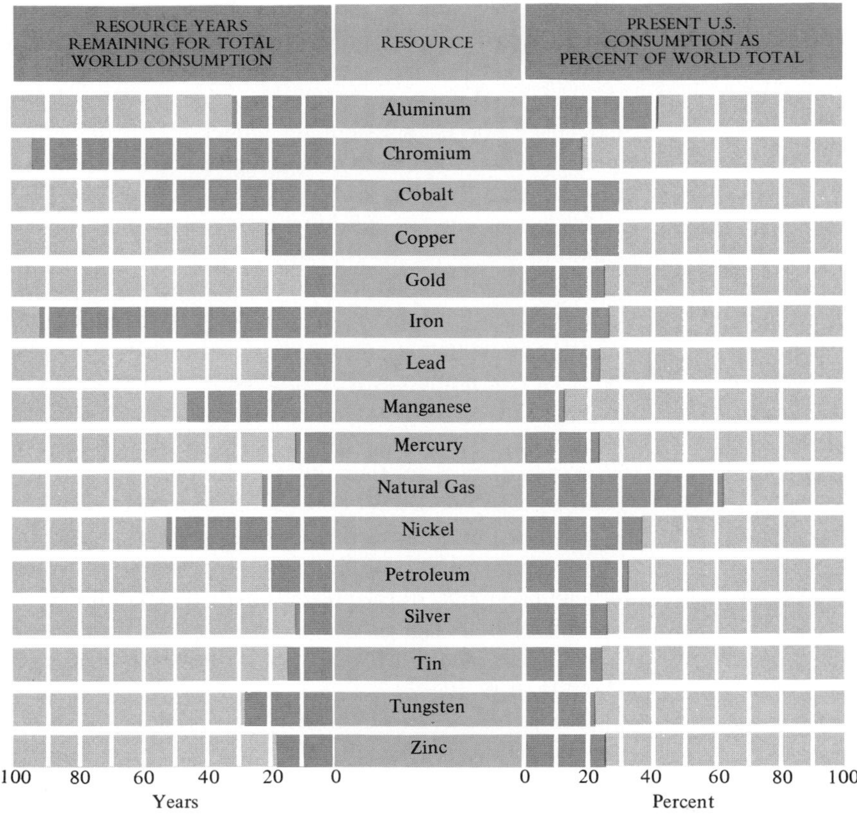

Source: Donella Meadows *et al. The Limits to Growth* (New York: Signet, 1972).

Figure 20.10 As this graph shows, world reserves of many natural resources are rapidly being depleted. The United States accounts for a very disproportionate amount of this resource consumption. Given the shortage of resources, it is possible that the less developed nations will never reach the level of industrial development of the modern United States. It is important to note that these figures are based on the assumption that the world usage rate of every natural resource will continue to grow exponentially, indicating both that more people are consuming resources each year and also that the average consumption per person is increasing annually. The figures may, therefore, be unrealistically gloomy. Not only have new reserves of petroleum, iron, phosphates, and other resources been discovered since these figures were calculated, but new technologies for extracting these resources are constantly being developed. Nevertheless, the basic conclusion that the world is moving rapidly from an age of relative resource abundance to an era of relative resource scarcity remains valid.

pollution involved in a world consisting entirely of heavily populated and fully industrialized societies. It is possible that some of the developing societies will never reach the level of socioeconomic development that has historically been necessary before a demographic transition occurred.

Paul Ehrlich and John Holdren (1971) take an even more pessimistic view of the prospects for a solution through demographic transition. They point out that even if global industrialization could be accomplished in fifty years, which is highly doubtful, a rapid drop in birth rates would not begin until around the year 2020, and global birth rates would not approach the current U.S. level until 2050. At that time world population would be about four times its present size and would continue to double every seventy years.

Population in the United States

The United States is the world's wealthiest nation, fully capable of supporting its population at a very high standard of living. Do we have a population problem? To answer the question, we must first look at the demographic characteristics of the nation.

American Demographic Characteristics

The current population of the United States exceeds 215 million. Females outnumber males by about 5.3 million, or about 2.5 percent, and the population is overwhelmingly white. Blacks represent 11.6 percent of the population. This proportion has held steady for almost fifteen years and represents a marked decrease from the early nineteenth century, when nearly a fifth of the population was black. The median age of the population, 28.1 years, is relatively high, both in comparison with most other countries and with our historical past. Population tends to be concentrated in the coastal and Great Lakes areas, and the nation is becoming increasingly urbanized; some 74 percent of Americans now live in metropolitan areas. Nearly 37 percent of the population changed its place of residence between 1970 and 1974. There is a continuing process of population shift from rural to industrialized states, from small towns to large cities, from low-income to high-income areas, from the Northeast to Florida and the "sun belt" states of the South and Southwest, and, among blacks, from the South to the North and to the West Coast.

The birth rate is low and reflects a consistent trend of declining fertility over the past 150 years. In 1820, the birth rate was 55 per thousand, but this level dropped steadily until it hit a low of 17 per thousand during the Great Depression of the thirties. The years after World War II saw a "baby boom," resulting from a backlog of delayed marriages and a greatly improved economic climate, and the birth rate rose again to around 25 per thousand in the late fifties. Since then it has declined steadily once more, from 23.7 in 1960 to 18.4 in 1970 and 15.0 in 1976. The baby boom was not anticipated by demographers, and neither was the "birth dearth" of the 1970s. The large number of children born in the postwar years has created a "bulge" in the age structure of our population, and the baby-boom generation is now of marriageable age. The result should be an "echo effect" as this large generation reproduces itself, but there are few signs that this is taking place. The reasons are not clear, but the low birth rate seems to be the result of several factors—the economic recession, the tendency of many young adults to postpone marriage, and a growing unwillingness to raise large families.

At present, the average American woman is bearing 1.9 children, somewhat less than the 2.1 percent required for zero population growth. Demographers expect the rate to increase slightly, however, as the economic climate improves and as young adults who have delayed marriage begin to raise families. Census Bureau surveys indicate that young married women expect to have rather more than two children on average. Many of them, too, will have more children than they intend. In one study, Larry Bumpass and Charles Westoff (1970) found that a fifth of all births to American women were unwanted at the time of conception. The birth rate varies considerably between different segments of the population. It is higher for blacks than for whites, higher for the working class than for the middle class, and it is higher for Catholics than it is for Protestants or Jews.

The death rate in the United States is also low, at 9.1 per thousand, and life expectancy is extremely high at 71.3 (67.6 for males and 75.3 for females). Average life expectancy for whites is 72.2 years, significantly higher than that of blacks and other nonwhite groups, whose life expectancy is only 65.9 years. Some 22 percent of the population is sixty-five and over, and this proportion will increase markedly as the baby-boom generation grows older in the years ahead. The death rate will therefore increase noticeably as this generation reaches its seventieth decade.

Do We Have a Population Problem?

An affluent society with a low birth and growth rate may not at first sight appear to have a population problem. But the national Commission on Population Growth and the American Future (1972) reported that our population growth threatens severe problems for American society—and for the rest of the world—and recommended a national policy of zero population growth.

The Commission pointed out that even if reproduction stabilizes now at replacement levels, the population will continue to increase for many years as the existing younger generation enters the childbearing period. If the average American family has only two children, population will rise to 307 million by the year 2020, and if the average family has three children, it will rise to 477 million. Even the lower rate of increase would have enormous consequences. Cities would become more crowded, and more rural land would have to be converted for urban or industrial use. New demands would be made on our already strained energy resources. Pollution of land, sea, rivers, and air would increase—the more so if we expect this larger population to enjoy a higher standard of living than we do at present. Immense sums would have to be spent on

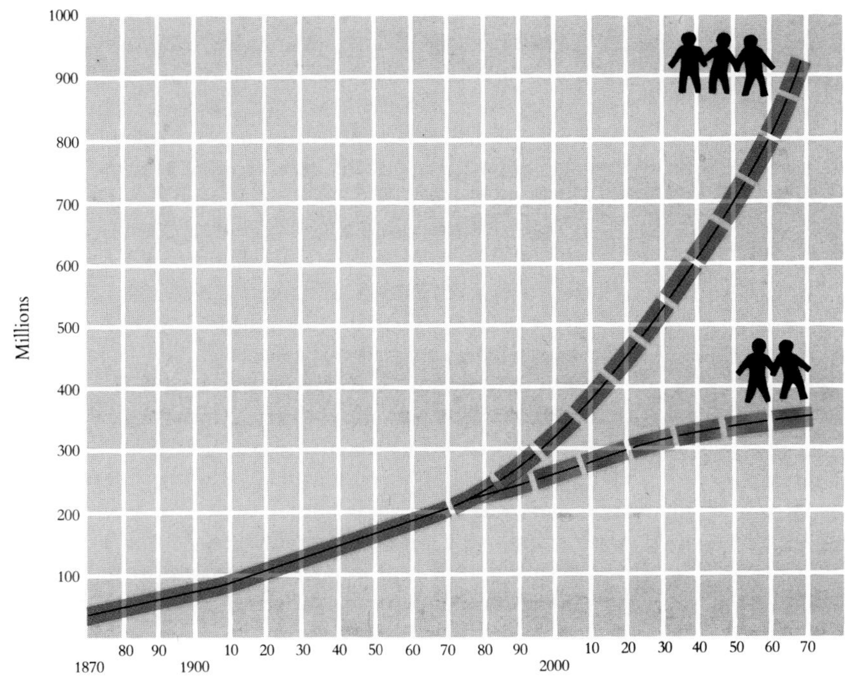

Figure 20.11 The difference in size between families of two and three children may not seem very significant, but the long-term impact would be enormous. These projections were made by a presidential commission, which strongly recommended the limitation of family size in the United States.

Source: Report of the Commission on Population Growth and the American Future, *Population and the American Future* (Washington, D.C.: U.S. Government Printing Office, 1972), p. 23.

duplicating existing facilities, such as schools and hospitals, rather than on improving these facilities and raising living standards. Fresh sources of food, lumber, minerals, and other raw materials—including water, which is already in short supply in many parts of the United States—would have to be found. As demands for these dwindling resources multiplied, prices would skyrocket. The Commission looked for but found no economic advantages in population increase. Instead, it reported, the quality of life in the United States would suffer and a number of serious social problems would be created.

We also have to take into account the global impact of American population growth. In international terms, a new American child is something of a disaster, for he or she presents a greater threat to the ecology of the planet than fifty Asian babies. With less than 6 percent of the world's population, we use more than a third of the earth's energy and material resources and generate almost half of its pollution. We already use, for example, a third of the world's tin, half of its newsprint and rubber, a fourth of its steel, and a fifth of its cotton, and we rely on foreign sources for twenty-two of seventy-four minerals considered essential in industrial societies. Adding another 50 million Americans to the population—which we will probably do by the year 2000—would be the equivalent, in ecological terms, of adding another 2 billion or so Indians to the world. Our population growth cannot be considered in isolation from the rest of the world, for the various nations are increasingly interdependent. We rely on them for raw materials; if those materials are exhausted, or if other peoples need to use them to support their own growing populations, we suffer. Other peoples rely on us, as one of the few countries that periodically produces an agricultural surplus, for their food. If we need that food for our own expanding population, they starve.

For these reasons the Commission strongly recommended a series of measures designed to reduce population growth. The most crucial recommendations were probably the most controversial. These included the removal of formal and informal restrictions against sterilization, the provision of readily available abortion facilities, thorough sex education in the schools, and the removal of restrictions on the distribution of contraceptive information and devices to the public, including minors. President Nixon rejected these recommendations as "immoral."

What Can Be Done?

It is obvious that unless population growth is rapidly halted we face a disaster whose toll in human lives and human misery is barely conceivable. What steps can be taken to avoid this fate? There are three basic strategies that can be used: family planning, incentives, and outright coercion.

Family Planning

This strategy involves the use of contraception by parents to limit the number of their offspring. Nearly all the nations of Asia and many countries in other parts of the world are already committed to population limitation through family planning. But no society has yet managed to achieve a significant drop in its birth rate through this means alone. The main reason is that family planning, by definition, permits parents to determine how large their family is to be, and the parents' concept of the ideal family size may not accord with the needs of society.

The experience of India, the first country to introduce a policy of population limitation, is instructive. At its present growth rates, India will have a population of well over 1 billion by the year 2000, which it could not possibly hope to feed, let alone clothe, house, and educate. Even today, 98 percent of the Indian population has an inadequate diet. The Indian birth rate has declined from 52.4 at the beginning of the century to about 35 today, but the death rate has declined even faster, from 46.8 to 15, resulting in a huge population increase. India started an official family-planning program in 1952 and today devotes 1 percent of its budget to family planning. This is the largest percentage of a national budget that any nation has ever applied to population limitation, yet it represents less than 8 cents a year for each person in the country. An immediate problem, then, is that India seems unable to afford a higher investment in family planning. As a result, information about contraception and sterilization simply does not reach millions of Indians, and neither do the necessary medical facilities. More important, perhaps, is the reluctance of many Indians to take advantage of contraception. Westerners are often guilty of the "technological fallacy," the belief that merely applying technology to a problem will solve it. But people have to be persuaded to make use of contraceptive technology, and they will not do so if the

Figure 20.12 Almost the entire Indian population lives in dire poverty, yet family planning programs have had very little impact on the population growth rate. Several Indian states, however, have recently passed laws imposing severe penalties and even compulsory sterilization on parents who have more than three children.

technology runs counter to their values. Although millions of Indians have been sterilized or have accepted contraceptives, it seems that many of them, perhaps the majority, have done so only *after* they have produced what they believe is a sufficiently large family.

The extension of family-planning facilities is not in itself enough to produce a sharp decline in birth rates. People will make use of the facilities only when they value small families more highly than large ones. For this reason family planning is an important factor in population limitation in the advanced industrial societies, but it has yet to bring about a drop in birth rates in the poorest and most populous nations of the world.

Incentives

This strategy includes various methods of encouraging people to limit the number of their children. Several countries have experimented with the use of gifts or cash rewards to people who accept sterilization or contraceptive devices. Another proposal is to give tax exemptions to people with only a few children, instead of the current practice of giving exemptions to parents of large families. This proposal has the disadvantage, however, that the children of large but poor families would suffer greater hardships. Kingsley Davis (1967, 1976b) has argued that basic changes must be engineered in social values and attitudes to encourage smaller families. Once social norms oppose prolific reproduction, he points out, most people will conform. Women, for example, might be offered satisfying and appealing careers outside the home. Advantages in taxation, housing, and recreation might be given to single rather than to married people. The responsibility of schools for children might be increased, thus diminishing the parents' responsibility and hence the "ego-identity which plays such a strong role in parental motivation." Such steps might limit the birth rate, but no government has yet attempted these or similar social changes with that intention in mind, and none seems likely to do so.

Coercion

This strategy would be the least popular but the most effective means of limiting population. The state would simply determine how many children each set of parents might have and would then proceed, by any of a variety of methods, to enforce its policies. One method might be to issue child licenses to each woman, entitling her to have as many children as a zero population growth permits (Boulding, 1964). Another might be to administer a chemical inhibitor on fertility to the entire population, perhaps by adding it periodically to the water supply in order to regulate births (Ketchel, 1968). Another method, less subtle still, might be to automatically sterilize each couple after the birth of their second child.

These are not very amiable suggestions, and they involve the intrusion of the power of the state into some of the most sacred areas of private life. Yet we have long recognized that individuals do not have absolute rights: their personal liberties are often restricted for the good of society. We cannot fire guns where we choose, or discriminate against anyone we choose, or throw our garbage where we choose, or employ child labor if we choose. Our right to swing our fists ends where someone else's nose begins. In due course we may be forced to consider whether our freedom to bring children into the world is subject to the same principle. Coercion must necessarily be a last resort, undertaken with the most extreme reluctance, but in the end it may prove the lesser of the evils confronting us.

Population and the Environment

Every animal or plant species is the product of a lengthy process of evolution that makes the organism uniquely adapted to the environment that supports it. Each species is able to survive only by exploiting the environment in which it lives, and if for one reason or another it can no longer do so, it becomes extinct. The ultimate extinction of organisms is the rule rather than the exception in the biological world; it is calculated that over 99.9 percent of all species that have ever lived met this fate.

The Science of Ecology

Ecology is the science of the relationship between living organisms and their environments. Ecology emerged as a natural science in the late nineteenth century and is still primarily the domain of biologists and zoologists. In the twentieth century, however, social scientists have been systematically applying ecological principles to the study of human societies and populations. Anthropologists have found the ecological approach a useful means of analyzing human cultural arrangements. As we saw in Chapter 4 (Society), the subsistence strategy that a society uses to exploit its environment—hunting and gathering, pastoralism, horticulture, agriculture, or industrialism—has important effects on social structure and culture. In particular, the subsistence strategy strongly affects the potential size of a population. If all societies still relied on hunting and gathering for their subsistence, world population would have leveled off at around 10 million people (Brown, 1972). But the industrial mode of production, which is always linked to advanced medical and other technologies, permits a small part of the population to feed the rest and thus makes high population growth rates possible. If this method of ex-

Figure 20.13 Although the industrial mode of production has produced unprecedented wealth, it has often disrupted the natural environment in unforeseen ways. Atmospheric pollution, for example, has become a serious public health hazard in many areas, and it may have effects on the global climate that are not yet fully understood.

ploiting the environment were for any reason to become difficult or impossible, a population collapse would follow.

Sociologists have also been deeply interested in *human ecology,* the interrelationship between human groups and their natural environment. Sociologists working in this field have studied both the geographic distribution of the entire species over the planet and the spatial distribution of local populations. We know, for example, that although our species is highly adaptable and can even adapt hostile environments (including the surface of the moon) to meet its needs, about 50 to 75 percent of the earth's land area is inhospitable to us. In fact, world population is so unevenly distributed that about half the population lives on 5 percent of the land area (Hauser, 1969). Some of the most promising work in the human ecology of local populations was conducted at the University of Chicago in the thirties and forties and is discussed in Chapter 21 (Urbanization and Urban Life). More recently, however, an awareness of the "ecological crisis" has led social and natural scientists from several disciplines to focus on the complex interrelationship among population growth, industrialism, and the global environment.

The problem posed by large-scale industrialism is twofold. First, it generates pollution of the natural environment, destroying life in a chain reaction that can run from the tiniest microorganism to human beings. Second, it depletes natural resources such as wood, oil, and minerals, many of which are in short supply and cannot be replaced. Industrialism has made possible high living standards for a minority of the world's population, but at the cost of increasing exploitation and despoilation of the environment. Industrialism has also encouraged a huge increase in human population, and the populous developing nations understandably want to raise their living standards as well. The question that arises is whether a world population that will double in thirty-eight years, and thus produce twice as many people to consume and pollute, can be supported by the environment.

The Elements of Ecology

Life on earth exists only in the biosphere, a thin film of soil, air, and water at or near the surface of the planet. Within this biosphere all living organisms are interdependent, existing in a delicate balance with one another and with the environmental resources that support them. A fundamental ecological concept is that of the *ecosystem,* a self-sustaining community of organisms within its natural environment. An ecosystem may be as small as a drop of pond water or as large as the biosphere itself, but the same principle of mutual interdependence always applies. Energy and inorganic (nonliving) matter are both essential for life. The energy is derived directly or indirectly from the sun, and the inorganic matter in the soil and the air provides the nutrients necessary for living organisms. Green plants convert the energy and nutrients into organic, living matter. The plants are eaten by animals, many of which are consumed in turn by other animals in highly complex food chains. Finally, insects, bacteria, fungi, and other decomposers break down the dead bodies of plants and animals, releasing the nutrients back into the ecosystem and completing the cycle.

We think nothing of the bacteria in the soil at our feet, but if we destroy them we destroy ourselves, for all life depends on these lowly creatures. If we poison insects, that poison may find its way back into our bodies, perhaps many years later, for insects are an element in a food chain that may ultimately concentrate the poison in the bodies of animals, including ourselves, for whom it was never intended. In primitive societies people treat nature with respect, considering themselves a part of, rather than set apart from, the natural world (Redfield, 1953). In industrial society our attitude is different. We consider ourselves the lords of creation and see nature primarily as a resource for exploitation. As our "needs" increase, our capacity for exploitation expands. We do not see our ravaging of the environment as "ravaging" at all; it is "progress" or "development." We are so used to exploiting natural resources and dumping our waste products into the environment that we forget that resources are limited and exhaustible and that pollution can disrupt the ecological balance on which our survival depends.

Pollution

The atmosphere of our cities is heavily polluted. The average citizen in New York inhales the equivalent in toxic materials of thirty-eight cigarettes a day, and pollution cuts out up to 40 percent of Chicago's sunlight (Rienow and Rienow, 1969; Ehrlich and Ehrlich, 1972). We dump more than 200 million tons of waste into the atmosphere every day, almost a ton a day for each American (Auchincloss, 1970). Much of this pollution comes from automobiles, which are being added to our crowded highways in such numbers that the gains made from anti-pollution devices will be reversed by 1980 (Berry, 1970). We have turned rivers into sewers and killed off lakes by using them for the disposal of industrial effluents and by saturating them with pesticides and fertilizers washed in from the land. Some sixty American cities have been listed by the Public Health Service as having water supplies that are "unsatisfactory" or "a potential health hazard" (Ehrlich and Ehrlich, 1972). Every year in the United States we junk 7 million automobiles, 20 million tons of paper, 55 billion cans, 10 million tons of iron and steel, 26 billion bottles, 65 billion bottle caps, and 200 million tons of domestic garbage (Erhlich and Ehrlich, 1972).

American women carry in their breasts up to ten times more of the insecticide DDT than is permitted in dairy milk for human consumption. DDT is an extremely stable chemical that does not break down for decades after it is used. The United States alone has released more than 1 billion pounds of the substance into the environment. Every morsel of food that we eat, even the so-called "organic" food favored by health enthusiasts, is tainted with pesticides and insecticides. These chemicals are found even in polar bears, thousands of miles from the source of the pollution. The combined effects of habitat destruction and pollution have exterminated many species and currently threaten the survival of 280 mammal, 350 bird, and 20,000 plant species (Goldsmith *et al.,* 1972). Pollutants such as industrial emissions, the trails of jet aircraft, dust from mechanized agriculture, and excess carbon dioxide from the burning of fuels and wastes, threaten to alter the earth's atmosphere and with it the global temperature. If the temperature rises by as little as another four or five degrees, the polar icecaps will begin to melt, raising sea levels by as much as 300 feet and flooding coastal areas all over the world. If it drops by a few degrees, we will be plunged into a new ice age that would envelope the Northern Hemisphere. At present, fortunately for us, our atmospheric pollutants have contrary effects. Some, such as carbon dioxide, prevent heat radiating back into space and thus keep the planet warmer. Others, such as dust from agriculture, block out the sun's rays and thus keep it cooler. We have stumbled on this happy balance by accident, however, and there is no reason to suppose it will be maintained indefinitely.

Resource Depletion

The shortage of resources—raw materials and energy—is also a growing problem for industrial societies. The United States alone consumes a third of the world's energy, more than 60 percent of the natural gas, more than 40 percent of the aluminum and coal, one third of the petroleum, platinum, and copper, about a quarter of the gold, iron, lead, silver, and zinc. But it was calculated in 1972 that if current patterns of exploitation are continued, many of these resources will be exhausted very soon. The known reserves of iron and chromium will be gone in less than a hundred years, of nickel in about fifty years, of aluminum in about thirty years, and of copper, lead, tin, and zinc in twenty years or less. (See Figure 20.10, page 481.) It is possible, although by no means certain, that synthetic substitutes for some of these materials might be invented. New resources of these minerals will also no doubt be discovered, but it is likely that most are already known. Despite intensified efforts, the rate of discovery of new mineral deposits has been dropping rapidly in recent years. Low-grade resources that are not economically worthwhile to exploit at present might be used, but the price of these commodities would then soar.

Like much of our pollution, a good deal of resource depletion is unnecessary and results from irresponsibility and greed. But the problem cannot be reduced to a simple conflict between the "bad guys" who ravage the environment and the "good guys" who are committed to environmental preservation. All of us are presumably in favor of protecting the environment, yet all of us are guilty of practices that worsen the problem. Steps to protect the environment are often very costly and very inconvenient, and proposals for environmental preservation often involve hard and uncomfortable choices.

The Limits to Growth

Can industrial growth continue? Only one major research effort has attempted to answer this question, and the response—a very controversial one—was negative. A research team at the Massachusetts Institute of Technology used a computer model to project current trends of population increase, industrial output, food production, resource depletion, and pollution well into the next century. The report, entitled *The Limits to Growth* (Meadows *et al.*, 1972) concluded that industrial society faces an inevitable and disastrous collapse within a hundred years, and possibly a good deal sooner, unless both population growth and industrial growth are brought to an immediate halt.

The MIT team devised various scenarios for the future, but the result of each was the same: collapse. If current trends continue unchanged, a shortage of raw materials will destroy the industrial base of society and produce a sharp rise in the death rate through famine. If huge new resources are discovered and developed, industrialism will advance more rapidly than ever, but the resulting pollution would ravage public health, overwhelm the environment, destroy the agricultural base, and cause a population collapse. If technology succeeds in controlling pollution, population will soar and will outstrip the capacity of the land to produce food. And so on. No matter how the factors were varied, all growth projections ended in mass starvation, the exhaustion of resources, intolerable pollution, or some combination of the three.

The only solution, the MIT team concluded, is for world population to be stabilized and for industrial societies to follow a deliberate antigrowth program. People would have to learn to derive satisfaction from services such as entertainment and education, rather than from accumulating material goods. In a no-growth world, the poor countries would obviously never become rich. If there were to be global equality, it would mean an international sharing of resources and a very sharp drop in the living standards of the wealthier nations. The political problems involved in rejecting the idea of "progress" and accepting a fall in living standards are so great that the adoption of this program in the foreseeable future is scarcely likely.

These gloomy forecasts have attracted a great deal of criticism. Many critics (for example, Kayson, 1972) take the more optimistic view that technology will somehow solve the problems, just as it has solved many apparently insuperable problems in the past. New synthetic materials, for example, might provide substitutes for scarce nonrenewable resources. Other critics (for example, Klein, 1972) have focused on the inadequacies of the MIT computer model. Predicting the future is a risky matter at the best of times, and to project highly complex trends for many decades into the future, when one cannot be aware of subsequent factors that might influence their interaction, is not a very reliable way of making forecasts. If data on agricultural production a century ago had been used to project trends into the 1970s, they would have pointed to global mass starvation at this moment. But the "green revolution" (the introduction of new hybrid species of high-yield grain) and highly mechanized agricultural techniques have greatly increased food production in a way that could not have been anticipated. In 1850, New York City was faced with a "horse crisis." The number of horses was increasing exponentially and the streets were piled with horse dung. A simple projection would have

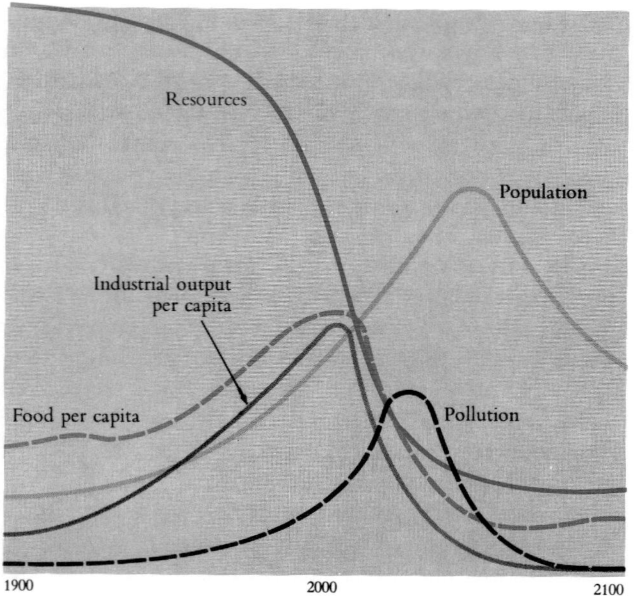

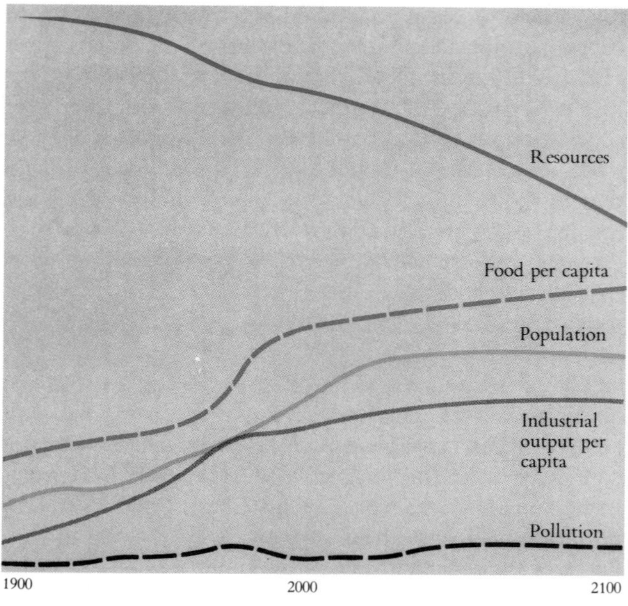

Figure 20.14 These graphs show two of the MIT team's projections for the future of industrial society. The first graph assumes that resource depletion, pollution, food production, industrial output, and population growth will continue at present rates. The result is a collapse of industrial society and a rapid decline in population as the death rate soars. The second graph assumes a "no growth" world, in which all the factors are stabilized. Under these conditions, a balance among the various factors could be achieved, but the poor countries could never become rich unless the more developed nations were willing to share their wealth. These MIT projections have been a matter of controversy, however.

indicated that the streets of New York would by now be piled with dung to a height of fourteen stories, but this prediction could not take account of several intervening factors, most notably the replacement of horses by automobiles.

Yet although the precise calculations of the MIT team are open to criticism, their underlying logic is difficult to dispute. Nobody denies that the planet has a finite amount of resources or that it can tolerate only a limited amount of pollution. If world population continues to grow rapidly, if industrialism spreads around the world, and if pollution and resource depletion continue at an increasing rate—and all these things are happening—where is human society headed? The most optimistic answer to these questions would be that, one way or another, sweeping social changes await us.

Summary

1. Rapid population growth in a context of limited resources is probably the most serious social problem in the modern world.

2. Demography is the study of population composition

and change. The principal factors involved in demographic change are the birth rate, the death rate, and the migration rate. Population growth rate, which takes place exponentially, is also influenced by the age structure of the population concerned.

3. Malthus pointed out that population tends to grow faster than the food supply. This problem has been averted in the past by new technologies and decreased birth rates in advanced industrial societies, but it has now become an acute one in less developed societies.

4. The main reason for rapid population growth is the fact that death rates have declined while birth rates have remained high. Moreover, the highest growth rates are in countries that already have large populations. Cultural values have always emphasized the desirability of large families, and these values have been slow to change.

5. The theory of demographic transition holds that birth rates will decline once developing societies become more industrialized. The theory is only a hypothesis, however, and remains unproved. Specific factors in some societies may inhibit the transition. In particular, the poorest nations may have great difficulty in reaching an adequate level of industrialization.

6. The American birth and death rates are both relatively low, although the birth rate may increase slightly as we experience an "echo effect" from the post–World War II "baby boom."

7. The United States has a population problem. Further U.S. population increases will tax natural resources and will place a disproportionate burden on societies elsewhere in the world.

8. There are three possible strategies for reducing birth rates: family planning, the use of incentives, and coercion.

9. Ecology is the science of the relationship of organisms to their environments. Human ecology applies ecological principles to human populations. All organisms exist in ecosystems that are delicate and easily disrupted.

10. Pollution and resource depletion pose a major challenge to industrial societies. The MIT *Limits to Growth* study predicted ultimate population and economic collapse if current trends continue, although these findings have been strongly criticized. The underlying logic of the report's arguments, however, is difficult to refute.

Important Terms

demography
birth rate
fertility
fecundity
death rate
life expectancy
life span
migration rate
push
pull
growth rate
exponential growth
doubling time
zero population growth
age structure
demographic transition
family planning
ecology
human ecology
ecosystem

Suggested Readings

DAVIS, KINGSLEY. "The World's Population Crisis," in Robert K. Merton and Robert Nisbet (eds.), *Contemporary Social Problems*, 4th ed. New York: Harcourt Brace Jovanovich, 1976.

A succinct analysis of the population problem by one of America's leading demographers. The article includes material on both the United States and the world as a whole.

EHRLICH, PAUL R., AND ANN H. EHRLICH. *Population, Resources, Environment*. San Francisco: W. H. Freeman, 1972.

A readable and forthright account of the interrelationship among population growth, resource depletion, and environmental pollution. The book is one of the most comprehensive on the subject.

MEADOWS, DONELLA H. et al. *The Limits to Growth*. New York: Signet, 1972.

A summary of the main findings of the MIT team's computer projections for the future of industrial society.

WRONG, DENNIS H. *Population and Society*. New York: Random House, 1976.

A short and clear account of the principles of demography, particularly of the dynamics of population growth.

Commission on Population Growth and the American Future. *Population and the American Future*. Washington, D.C.: U.S. Government Printing Office, 1972.

An important summary of data on the present American population, with projections for population growth in the future and an analysis of what those trends would mean.

BANK NEW YORK
NY

CHAPTER 21 *Urbanization and Urban Life*

CHAPTER OUTLINE

The Urbanization Process
The Preindustrial City
The Industrial City

The American City and Its Problems
The Suburbs
The Central Cities
City Planning

The Nature of Urban Life
Gemeinschaft and Gesellschaft
The Chicago School
Urbanism: A Reassessment

Urban Ecology
The Ecological Approach
Patterns of Urban Growth

Urbanization is one of the most significant trends in the modern world. Human beings have inhabited the planet for well over a million years, yet our ancestors lived in small primary groups for all but five or six thousand years of that time. The growth of large cities that contain the bulk of a society's population is a very recent development, yet it is one that is occurring all over the world at an astonishing speed. Our new, highly urbanized social environment offers opportunities and challenges that are without precedent in the history of the species.

A city is a permanent concentration of relatively large numbers of people who do not produce their own food. Large-scale urbanization has occurred only in the course of the past century. Until 1850, not more than 5 percent of the global population was urbanized, and no society had more than half of its members living in cities. In 1850 only one city, London, had more than 1 million inhabitants. Yet today all the industrialized societies of the world are heavily urbanized, and over 140 cities contain more than 1 million people. If present trends continue, there will be 500 cities with over 1 million inhabitants by the end of the century, several of them containing more than 25 million people. By then, more than 80 percent of the world's population will live in cities (Davis, 1965).

The United States is no exception to this trend. You probably live in an urban area: most Americans do. Yet the first U.S. census in 1790 recorded only twenty-four urban places, of which only two had populations of more than 25,000. In 1820, nearly 80 percent of the American people still lived on farms. But by 1920, half the population lived in urban areas; by 1950, 65 percent; and by 1980 the proportion may have risen to 90 percent. Already, more than half of the American population lives on 1

Figure 21.1 Throughout most of human history, communities were rarely much larger than this one in the Niger Republic. The initial growth of the city became possible only after the invention of agriculture, and the emergence of the huge modern city had to await the invention of industrialism.

percent of the nation's land mass (Commission on Population Growth and the American Future, 1972).

The process of urbanization has radically changed the nature of human communities and traditional patterns of social life. A *community* is a social group with a common territorial base and a shared sense of common interests and "belonging." The differences between a community of a few hundred people and one of several millions are so great that some sociologists doubt whether a large city can be usefully described as a "community" at all. An important task of sociology has been to identify the precise nature of urban life and to establish in what ways it differs from the life of traditional communities.

The study of cities is not only important because of the impact that urban life has on the people who actually inhabit cities. Urbanization implies more than the fact that a major part of the population lives in urban areas. It also implies that the culture and values of the city become dominant in the entire society, reaching through economic and political networks and the mass media into the most remote rural villages, so that even traditional communities are affected by the process. And the study of cities is important for an additional reason: the city is the locus of nearly all the social problems that beset modern societies. In the United States the problems of the inner cities have become so severe, in fact, that many people doubt whether they can survive as livable environments at all.

The Urbanization Process

Why did it take so long for cities to develop, and why has urbanization spread so rapidly during the past century? The answer lies in the very nature of the city as a dense concentration of people who do not produce their own food. The emergence of cities depended initially on the development of agricultural techniques that were sufficiently advanced to permit a food surplus. Only when farmers could produce more food than they needed to sustain themselves was it possible for large numbers of people to abandon agriculture and to engage instead in other specialized roles, such as those of merchant or craft worker. These roles, unlike that of the farmer, require minimal land area and are more conveniently performed in a concentrated human population. Thus the city was born. But the subsequent growth and spread of cities was hampered for centuries by poorly developed facilities for the transportation and storage of food. The larger the concentration of people in a city, the more food they require and the greater the distance the food must be transported. Large-scale urbanization had to await the Industrial Revolution, which introduced highly developed facilities for the transportation of food by road, rail, sea, and air and advanced technologies for the storage of food by such means as canning, refrigeration, and the use of chemical preservatives.

The Preindustrial City

The first urban settlements appeared between five and six thousand years ago in the Middle East and in Asia, on the fertile banks of the Nile, Tigris, Euphrates, Indus, and Yellow rivers. In later centuries techniques for domesticating animals and plants were either invented in or diffused to other parts of the world, and urban settlements began to appear elsewhere in Asia and the Middle East, in Europe, in Central and South America, and in North Africa.

By modern standards, the earliest of these settlements were so small that we would hardly consider them cities at all. The biblical city of Ur occupied only about 220 acres, and even Babylon, one of the largest of these ancient settlements, covered a mere 3.2 square miles (Mumford, 1961). The small scale of the ancient cities resulted from several factors. Their still rudimentary agricultural techniques could not produce a very large surplus; on average, it took about seventy-five farmers to support one city inhabitant. Facilities for communication and transport were primitive. Roads hardly existed, the wheel was unknown in many early settlements, and food had to be laboriously carried by human beings or animals from farming areas to the cities. Poor sanitation and a total lack of sewage facilities also encouraged epidemics and plagues, causing drastic periodic declines in urban populations. In the first few centuries A.D., Rome became the largest of all the preindustrial cities, but its population never numbered more than a few hundred thousand people. After the collapse of the Roman Empire urban development came to a standstill for many centuries, until the growth of international trade led to the development of new cities,

Figure 21.2 The preindustrial city, such as this one in Yemen, differs radically from the city in modern industrial societies. It is very much smaller—we would call it a town, not a city—and its social organization is based on kinship networks. There is no "downtown," because commercial operations are spread throughout the city.

such as Venice and Genoa, at the commercial centers of the world.

Small as these preindustrial cities were, they revolutionized human social organization. The concentration of populations required new institutional arrangements. Distinctive political, religious, and economic institutions emerged for the first time. The relatively large market offered by the urban population encouraged occupational specialization and an increasingly refined division of labor. The cities became a crossroads for trade, communication, and ideas, and the center of learning and innovation. The city-state, in which an urban settlement dominated its hinterland, became the typical political unit and the source of legal and military authority.

The preindustrial city differed from the modern industrial city in features other than size. As Gideon Sjoberg (1960) points out, extended family or kinship networks were the principal form of social organization within these cities. Class or caste systems were generally very rigid and there was little social mobility. With rare exceptions, such as some of the ancient Greek city-states, governments were monarchies or oligarchies. There was rarely a separate commercial district; the equivalent of "downtown" was the political and religious center of the community. Traders and artisans worked at home and used their houses as shops, and people following particular trades or crafts often lived and worked in distinct parts of the city. The city itself was commonly divided into "quarters" for various occupational, religious, or other social groups. In many cases the quarters were walled off from one another and their inhabitants locked into their own districts at night. In medieval Europe, for example, Jews were confined to "ghetto" areas of the city. Traces of ancient quarters can still be found in many North African towns today.

The Industrial City

As we have seen, it is no accident that the rapid growth and spread of cities coincided with the advance of the Industrial Revolution. The huge modern city must rest on an industrial base. It relies for its existence on the high productivity of mechanized agriculture, on sophisticated methods of transporting and storing food and other goods, and on the variety of specialized, nonagricultural jobs that industrialism creates. In 1790, only 5 percent of the American population lived in cities; today less than 5 percent work on the farms. Yet our agricultural techniques are so advanced that the remaining 95 percent of the population is able to live in conditions of unprecedented abundance, and we still have a food surplus available for export to other nations.

There are notable differences between the typical cities of advanced industrial societies and the cities found in less developed societies that have only recently embarked on the modernization process. As we saw in Chapter 20 (Population and Ecology), medical advances in less developed societies have resulted in a spectacular population increase, often beyond the capacity of the agricultural base to support. Displaced rural migrants flock to the cities in search of work, only to find that there is none. Industrial development has not yet created enough jobs, and the migrants cannot be absorbed. Many cities in these countries are consequently surrounded by settlements of impoverished squatters, and the city itself may have a very large homeless and unemployed population. In Calcutta, for example, hundreds of thousands of people literally live and die on the streets, unable to find food in the rural areas or jobs and housing in the city.

Cities in the more advanced industrial societies rarely face this problem and continue to absorb rural migrants who have come to the urban area in search of better jobs. The larger cities in these societies generally assume a fairly similar form. The urban area contains a *central city,* often inhabited by a small number of the very wealthy and a large number of the very poor. The central city is typically surrounded by *suburbs,* primarily residential areas that have grown up around the city as the urban population has expanded. This combined area is called a *metropolis,* and it forms an economic and geographic unity. In several advanced industrial societies, metropolitan areas have expanded to such an extent that they have merged with adjacent metropolises. The result is the *megalopolis,* a virtually unbroken urban tract consisting of two or more central cities and their surrounding suburbs. If current trends persist, most inhabitants of industrial societies will eventually live in sprawling megalopolises containing many millions of people and stretching in some instances for hundreds of miles—a far cry from our ancestral communities of a handful of cave dwellers.

Figure 21.3 In many parts of the world, cities are surrounded by squatter settlements. These settlements, like this one in southern Africa, are occupied by people who have left agricultural work in the countryside in search of better jobs. All too often, however, the city, already greatly overpopulated, has no jobs to offer.

The American City and Its Problems

Most Americans live in urban areas, but this does not mean that they live in the central cities. In fact, slightly more Americans reside in the suburbs of metropolitan areas than the central cities themselves, and many others live in urban areas with relatively small populations. The Bureau of the Census regards any locality with more than 2500 inhabitants as an urban area, and it deliberately ignores the boundaries of cities and suburbs in its collection and analysis of urban data. The Bureau recognizes that the political boundaries are less important than the social, economic, and communications network that integrates various urban communities into one unit, and it analyzes large-scale urban settlements through the concept of a *Standard Metropolitan Statistical Area* (SMSA). An SMSA is any area that contains one or more cities and surrounding suburbs and has a total population of 50,000 or more. At present the Bureau recognizes 272 SMSAs, and these urban areas contain nearly 75 percent of the American population.

The Bureau also takes account of the megalopolis, which it terms a *Standard Consolidated Area* (SCA), and it recognizes a total of thirteen areas that have developed or will shortly develop into a continuous urban sprawl of several metropolises. The outstanding megalopolis at present is the chain of hundreds of cities and suburbs on the eastern seaboard from Boston to Virginia—a tract that runs through ten states and contains some 40 million people. Other important megalopolises are currently developing in California (San Francisco–Los Angeles–San Diego), Florida (Jacksonville–Tampa–Miami), Texas (Dallas–San Antonio–Houston), and the Great Lakes area (Chicago–Pittsburgh). (See Figure 21.4.)

URBAN REGIONS: YEAR 2000

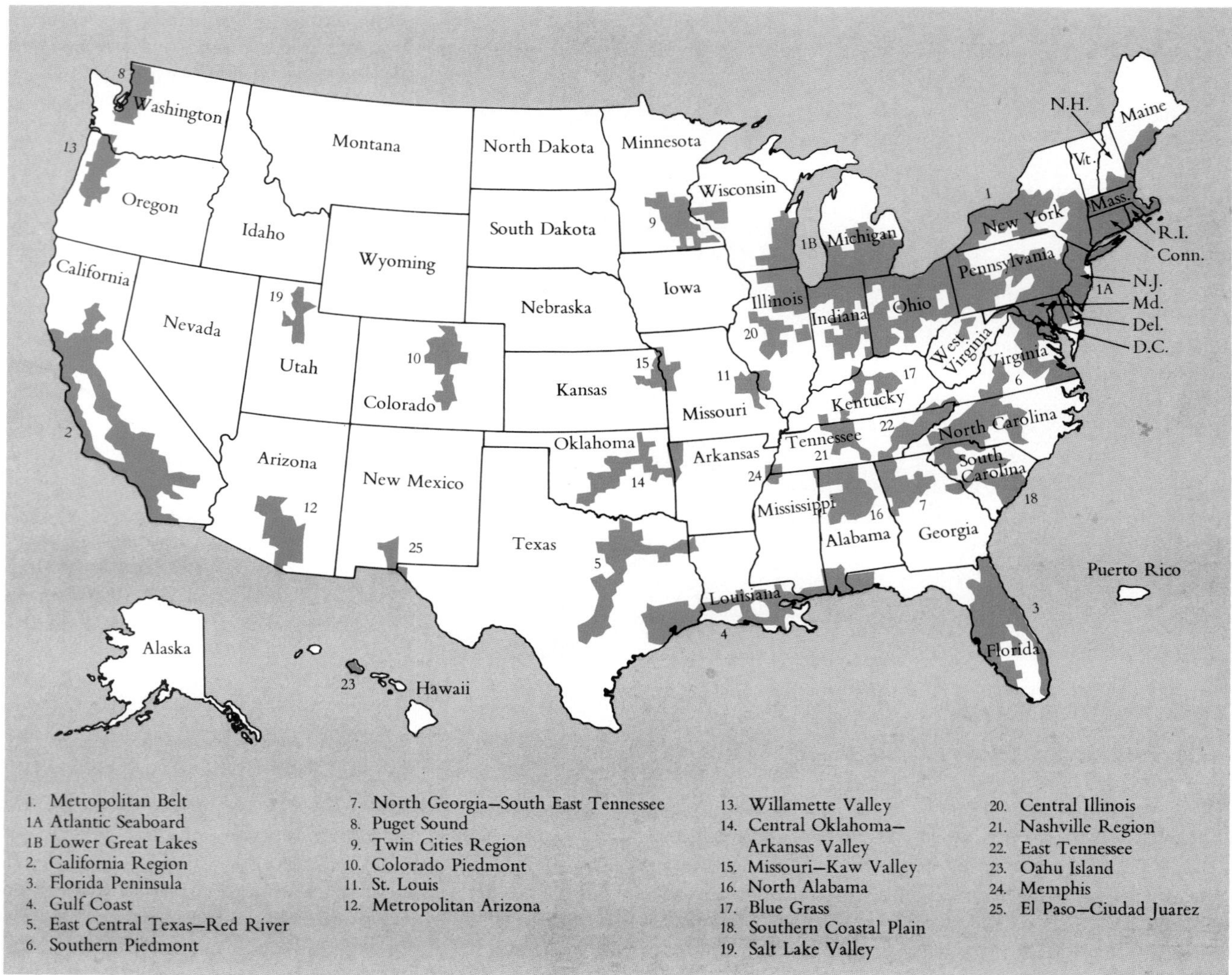

Source: Presidential Commission on Population Growth and the American Future, *Population Growth and the American Future* (Washington, D.C.: U.S. Government Printing Office, 1972).

Figure 21.4 By the year 2000, many regions of the country will contain unbroken urban tracts, or megalopolises, some of them stretching for hundreds of miles and containing tens of millions of people.

The Suburbs

One of the most outstanding features of the urbanization process in the United States is the rapid growth of the suburbs—a development that is largely responsible for the current plight of the central cities. In 1920, some 17 percent of the American people lived in the suburbs; in 1930, 19 percent; in 1940, 20 percent; in 1950, 24 percent. The rate of growth during that period was steady but slow. In the few years after World War II, however, the drift to the suburbs became a mass flight: 33 percent of the population lived in the suburbs in 1960 and 37 percent in 1970. During the sixties the suburban population increased by 15 million, but the overall population of the central cities remained unchanged. In fact, thirteen of the largest twenty-five central cities actually lost population.

Several factors made the flight to the suburbs possible. One was the construction of federally subsidized highways, which made it easier for workers to commute to the city. Another was the shortage of central-city housing after World War II. Land was exhausted in the older cities, and a construction industry that had mastered techniques for mass home building began to exploit the outlying areas. The postwar boom in the American economy made home ownership available to millions of Americans for the first time, and they were aided by ample mortgages from the Veterans Administration and the Federal Housing Authority. Suburban living, too, seemed highly attractive. It offered an ideal compromise between urban and rural life: one could be close enough to the city to enjoy its amenities but far away enough to avoid its inconveniences.

Life in the suburbs has been the object of a great deal of scorn and satire. It is often thought that the suburbs are dull, homogeneous places, in which the residents are obsessed with the neatness of their lawns or with keeping up with the Joneses next door in their material purchases. There may be some truth in this picture, but it is probably exaggerated. Suburban residents in general are doubtless more politically conservative, more morally conventional, and more oriented toward family life and the local community than city residents. But the suburbs—many of which are now predominantly working class—appear to be much more heterogeneous and less unlike some central-city neighborhoods than popular beliefs allow (Berger, 1961; Ross, 1965; Gans, 1967).

Figure 21.5 Suburban living has often been scorned and satirized, yet it has a very strong appeal for many Americans—including, obviously, the millions who have fled the central cities over the last few decades.

The Central Cities

The Greek philosopher Aristotle once described the city as "a common life to a noble end." That is hardly the kind of description we would apply to our own central cities today. The word "city" is more likely to conjure forth images of decaying housing, rundown schools, high rates of crime and drug addiction, racial segregation and tension, overburdened welfare rolls, and deteriorating public services. Why are so many social problems concentrated in the central cities of our metropolitan areas?

An underlying source of these problems is the growth of the suburbs, which has largely removed the middle class from the central cities. As the middle class has fled to the suburbs, it has taken its local tax money with it. The central cities have therefore had to rely for their revenue on a population that consists disproportionately of poor people. The tax base has shrunk as a result, and it has generally not been possible to compensate by raising taxes. The poorer city residents simply cannot afford to pay higher taxes. Wealthier residents and businesses are likely to see higher taxes as a further incentive to move to the suburbs, where property taxes are lower. To make matters worse, the central city has more ancient buildings, a far higher crime rate, older public facilities and schools, and a greater proportion of unemployed residents. As a result, it must spend much more money per capita on fire and police protection, urban renewal, transport systems, schools, and welfare if it is to offer services comparable to those of the suburbs. Central-city residents not only pay more than suburban residents in local taxes; they also get less for their money.

Under these circumstances it is hardly surprising that the urban environment has continued to deteriorate. But the process of decay merely encourages even more people to leave for the suburbs. As the suburbs expand, commerce and industry desert the central cities to take advantage of this new source of customers and labor. The suburbs do not merely take people from the cities; they also take jobs. New York City alone has lost more than a quarter of a million jobs since 1970, a trend that has further narrowed the city's already perilous tax base (Stern, 1974). And because racial and class divisions tend to overlap, the suburbs have been and remain primarily white, while the cities are becoming steadily more black. The 1970 census found that almost three-fourths of black Americans now live in metropolitan areas, and of these, 80 percent live in the central cities, mostly in ghettos. Metropolitan residential patterns have thus created a state of segregation almost as effective as the segregation that was once imposed in the South by law. This segregation, some of whose effects are considered in Chapter 15 (Education), is proving almost impossible to eliminate. Unlike most other forms of segregation, which involve overt acts by some people against others, this residential segregation cannot be abolished virtually overnight through legislation.

The residents of the central cities are rather more heterogeneous than those of the suburbs. The city contains a variety of racial and ethnic groups, and despite the loss of much of its middle class, it has a greater social class heterogeneity than most individual suburbs. Herbert Gans (1962a) distinguishes five basic categories of central-city residents. The *cosmopolites* are those who choose to live in the city because of its unrivaled cultural facilities—artists, students, writers, intellectuals, and professional people. The *unmarried or childless* are mostly young adults who come to the city to be close to job opportunities. They rent apartments until they get married, and then tend to move to the suburbs, where they buy homes and raise their families. The *ethnic villagers* are ethnic groups who retain their traditional ways of life in their own neighborhoods, which may be physically deteriorating but which are socially highly structured. The ethnic villagers have a strong sense of community and tend to limit their contact with the rest of the metropolitan area. The *deprived* are the very poor, the handicapped, and the nonwhite population, who are concentrated in the most undesirable residential areas. The *trapped* are those who would like to leave the central city but cannot. This category consists of people who are downwardly mobile or chronically unemployed, people who are very old or living on small fixed incomes, and people whose neighborhood is being invaded by other ethnic or racial groups but who cannot afford to get out. The cosmopolites and the unmarried or childless are in the city by choice; the ethnic villagers are there partly by tradition and partly by necessity; but the deprived and the trapped are there because they are unable to leave.

City Planning

City planning is not new; the Romans, the Egyptians, and other people practiced it more than 2000 years ago. The object of city planning varies, however, from time to time and place to place. The intention may be to encourage growth or to restrict it, to develop land for building purposes or to preserve it for parks, to make urban life more efficient or to make it more beautiful.

The goals of city planning in the United States have often been vague and inconsistent. Many plans, when finally adopted, are more the outcome of a political conflict between competing interest groups than of reasoned and objective analysis. Any city plan involves clashes of interests and values. Do we construct a new highway from the suburb to the city center in the interests of the suburbanites, or do we refuse to build it in the interests of the central-city working-class residents through whose neighborhoods the highway will run? Do we want our downtown area to be neat, clean, and quiet, or would we prefer a more hectic and colorful scene, complete with street vendors and rows of small stores?

For many years attempts have been made to solve some of the problems of the central cities through *urban renewal*—in other words, through demolishing "undesirable" areas and replacing them with something else. Two problems arise: determining what is "undesirable" and determining what the "something else" should be. In Boston, for example, urban renewal involved the demolition of an "undesirable" residential neighborhood that also happened to be an Italian "ethnic village." Herbert Gans (1962b) found that this renewal program was deeply resented by the residents, some of whom grieved for years at the destruction of their community.

In many cities lower-class residential areas have been demolished only to be replaced by more profitable forms of construction: luxury apartments and high-rise government and corporate office buildings. Urban renewal programs have destroyed more than ten times as many low-income housing units as they have replaced. The result has often been an increased demand for low-income housing that leads to even higher rents for the poor. There is also a concern that many of the "renewed" urban centers are uninteresting and arid places to live or even to walk about in. Jane Jacobs (1961), one critic of many urban renewal programs, writes contemptuously of "cultural centers that are unable to support a good bookstore ... civic centers that are avoided by everyone but bums ... promenades that go from no place to no where and have no promenaders." Planners have been slow to recognize that we cannot tear down neighborhoods and displace their residents without providing alternative accommodations for them and that new construction projects must blend harmoniously with the living city.

Figure 21.6

"It's called grass; it's softer to walk on than concrete."

One major obstacle to urban reform and effective metropolitan planning is the fragmentation of metropolitan governments. The problems of the metropolis—highways, mass transit, pollution, school segregation, police protection, public utilities—are regional. The city and the suburbs are politically separate but interdependent in all other respects. The suburbs are viable only because a very large number of their residents commute to work in the central cities. Moreover, suburban residents rely on many city services that they do not support through their taxes. Yet some metropolitan regions have dozens of different local authorities, each jealously guarding its own domain in the name of the American tradition of "community control." Los Angeles, for example, has a small central city, a county of nine other cities, and sixty-seven smaller self-governing communities.

A rational solution to many problems would be to recognize that the political boundaries between cities and suburbs are outdated. Each of the existing communities could retain some measure of local autonomy while being integrated into a single metropolitan unit with a common tax base. This is precisely the solution, in fact, that has been adopted by the Canadians for the Toronto metropolitan area and by the British for the Greater London area. There are a few examples of this kind of arrangement in the United States, such as the metropolitan government of the seven counties surrounding the Twin Cities of Minnesota, Minneapolis and St. Paul. There is little sign, however, that these examples will be widely adopted in the United States. The suburbanites, who have more political muscle than the central-city residents, usually believe that they have everything to gain by preserving their distance from the troubled central cities.

The Nature of Urban Life

In what ways does the urban community differ from the small rural community? What are the defining characteristics of urban life? A good deal of sociological effort has gone into attempting to answer this question, with some sociologists taking a pessimistic and dismal view of urban life and others delighting in the many advantages that urban living is supposed to offer.

Gemeinschaft and Gesellschaft

Ferdinand Tönnies (1855–1936) was one of the first sociologists to address the question. His analysis, first published in 1887, has become a sociological classic and remains influential. Tönnies made a distinction between two forms of social grouping: the *Gemeinschaft* and the *Gesellschaft,* which we may roughly translate as "community" and "association."

The *Gemeinshaft* is a small community in which most people know each other. Interpersonal relationships are close, people are oriented toward the interests and activities of the group as a whole, and they have a strong feeling of unity. People share the same values, and social control over any deviance is exercised through informal means, such as gossip and personal persuasion. Kinship ties are very strong and social life centers on the family.

The *Gesellschaft,* on the other hand, contains a large population in which most people are strangers to one another. Relationships are impersonal and are often based on the functional need that people have for one another rather than any emotional commitment. People are oriented toward their personal goals rather than the goals of the group, and they do not necessarily hold the same values. Social control cannot be effectively applied by informal methods, and so laws and formal sanctions have to be used to ensure social order. Tradition and custom no longer have a very strong influence on individual behavior, and kinship ceases to be the most important basis of social organization. In short, urbanization implies that the community with strong interpersonal bonds is replaced by an association of individuals, most of whose relationships are temporary and impersonal.

The Chicago School

Tönnies' work influenced sociologists at the University of Chicago in the 1920s and 1930s. These sociologists, notably Robert Park, Louis Wirth, and Ernest Burgess, were especially interested in the problems of the city, and their work laid the foundations for modern urban sociology. The classic statement of the Chicago School's position is contained in an essay, "Urbanism as a Way of Life," published by Wirth in 1938.

Wirth drew not only on the work of Tönnies but also on that of another German sociologist, Georg Simmel (1858–1918). Simmel had pointed out that residents of modern cities receive a constant barrage of stimuli and impressions. If they took every person they met seriously, or responded to each new situation with excitement and surprise, social life would be almost impossible. The high population density in cities, Simmel argued, forces people to take an offhand, matter-of-fact attitude toward their environment and to treat most people they encounter in an impersonal way.

Figure 21.7 According to Louis Wirth, the modern city is characterized by large size, population density, and social diversity. All these characteristics are suggested by this aerial photograph of San Francisco.

In his essay, Wirth isolated three distinctive features of the city: its *size,* its *population density,* and its *social diversity.* These three features combine to produce a style of life that is much more anonymous than that found in small communities. Each individual becomes almost insignificant in the city, and cannot know more than a tiny proportion of his or her fellow urban citizens. The city resident no doubt knows far more people than the villager, but these people are known in a much more superficial and transitory way. City residents interact with one another largely in terms of "segmental roles," for example, as street vendor, banker, grocer, or mail carrier, and not as whole persons. Relationships are generally based not on affection and trust but rather on rational self-interest. The roles that the city resident plays in relation to others are usually a means to pursuing or maintaining economic advantages. "The clock and the traffic signal," Wirth remarked, "are symbolic of the basis of our social order in the urban world." The city, in his view, consists of a large number of people who are essentially alone in the midst of the crowd. Though physically the people are very close to one another, they are socially very distant.

Wirth also pointed out that cities have much more diverse populations than small communities. Urban areas therefore tend to become segregated along class, racial, or ethnic lines as people of similar background congregate together. Moreover, the division of labor in the city is far more elaborate than that in a small community. This specialization of jobs and services leads to the development of areas that have specific functions and characteristics, such as Wall Street, Hollywood, Broadway, Nob Hill, and Greenwich Village. Confronted with this range of life-styles and personalities, the city resident becomes much more tolerant of diversity and deviance than someone living in a small rural community. Urban residents are therefore more *relativistic:* that is, they are less likely to take their own viewpoints for granted and more likely to see the validity of other viewpoints and life-styles. Paradoxically, however, it is sometimes difficult to maintain a sense of individuality in the city, because the city is an anonymous mass environment. Urban services and facilities must be uniform in the interests of efficiency, and as a result they cannot take individual differences into account.

Urbanism: a Reassessment

The work of the Chicago School tended to be rather pessimistic about urban life. In this respect it conformed to a long tradition of anti-urban bias that has existed in American life from the time of Jefferson to the present day. Other peoples, from the Greeks and Romans to the contemporary Europeans, have unstintingly praised the city as the center of cultural, intellectual, and civilized life. Even words in our language such as "civilized" and "urbane" derive from Latin words referring to the city. Americans, on the other hand, have always tended to consider urban life somewhat distasteful, and have felt that the good life is essentially one of good neighborliness in a small, intimate community. The work of the Chicago School may also have been distorted by two other factors. Most of its members had small-town origins themselves, and they did almost all their research in the Chicago central city at a time when it was in a state of severe social disorganization. Several sociologists have argued that Wirth's analysis contains unconscious biases and needs reassessment (for example, Greer, 1962; Stein, 1964).

One important reassessment is that of Herbert Gans (1962a, 1962b, 1968). He suggests that although Wirth's analysis may still have some relevance to the central cities, it does not apply to the outlying metropolitan areas. Even within the central city, Gans finds thriving communities. Some of them are restricted to specific neighborhoods and often take the form of "urban villages." In these communities, which are primarily ethnic neighborhoods, kinship ties remain very strong and there is a genuine sense of community loyalty and shared values. Other communities consist of scattered individuals whose common interests and pursuits give them a sense of community that transcends their physical distance. Urban writers and intellectuals, for example, may form a community without actually living in the same area of the city. More recent work in Chicago by Gerald Suttles (1970) has shown that strong feelings of community solidarity exist in slum neighborhoods. He found that residents were often acutely aware of the boundaries of their communities and strongly identified with their own neighborhoods.

A fair reassessment of the nature of urban life must take account of both its drawbacks and its advantages. There is little doubt that urban life involves more impersonality and possibly more isolation than life in a traditional rural community. Urban life separates people from the web of close community relationships, and it subjects them to the irritations of bureaucratic social organization. It cuts them off from the scenic beauty of the natural environment and exposes them to the overstimulation of too many people, too much noise, and too much pollution. It immerses them in social problems such as poverty, racial conflict, drug addiction, and crime.

But rural life is not all wine and roses. The traditional community lacks many of the comforts and amenities of the city. Large urban populations can support a cultural life of a richness and diversity never found in a small community. The city allows occupational specialization and thus far greater opportunities for fulfilling talents. Its anonymity is something for which many people are grateful. The close relationships of the small community can too often mean that everyone pries into everyone else's affairs. Nonconformists thrive in the more tolerant atmosphere of the city, where behavior that might scandalize a traditional community is ignored or may even be considered acceptable. The city provides a more cosmopolitan outlook, in contrast to the relatively narrow, conservative, and provincial outlook of the small community. Urban living thus offers a much greater opportunity for intellectual and personal freedom.

Urban Ecology

An important contribution of the Chicago School was its emphasis on an *ecological approach* to urban analysis.

The Ecological Approach

Ecology, a natural science concerned with the relationship of living organisms to their environment, has been usefully adapted to the study of patterns of urban development and land use. Cities are not dotted about the earth at random, nor do they grow in random fashion. They come into being and develop in particular ways as the result of a complex interplay of environmental and social factors.

Several factors in the natural environment determine the location of cities. Large cities, for example, are generally not found in inhospitable zones—jungles, deserts, polar

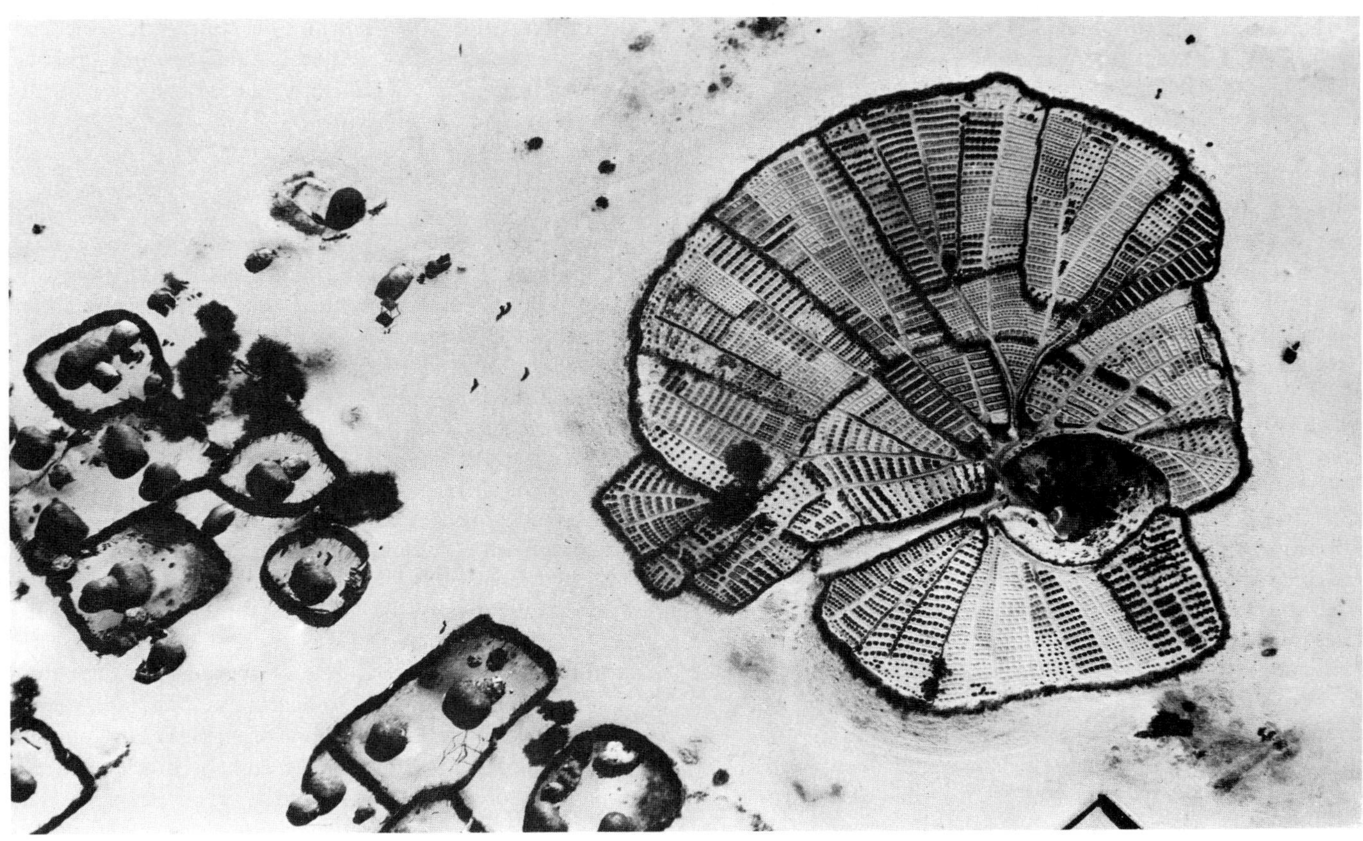

Figure 21.8 The ecological approach to urban analysis focuses on the social and environmental factors that influence the physical arrangements of human settlements. In this photograph of a small community in the Sahara desert, you will notice that the houses (left) are set some distance away from the oasis (right). The reason for this arrangement is that the gardens on which these people depend for food must be situated as closely as possible to the water source, so that the labor of carrying water to the plants is minimized. The factors that affect the physical layout of a large modern city are not so easily determined, but the same ecological principles apply.

regions, or at very high altitudes. Most major cities developed from villages and towns that grew up along shorelines or navigable rivers or, more recently, railroads. These settlements became centers of trade and communication and thus had the potential to grow into cities. The spatial development of an urban settlement is also influenced by factors in the natural environment. For example, mountains must be skirted, lakes and marshes must be avoided if they cannot be drained, and housing and industry must be placed conveniently near water and raw materials.

Social factors also influence the appearance and development of cities. Political decisions, for example, may involve the establishment of a city through colonizing an area—or the destruction of a city by burning it to the ground, as the Romans did to Carthage or the Americans to the German city of Dresden in World War II. Prevailing ideas about architecture and the desirability of town planning also influence the growth patterns of cities. The grid pattern of Manhattan, since copied by many American cities, is the product of a planning decision made in 1811. The actual use to which land is put often depends on economic factors, because owners tend to devote their land to whatever use gives them the greatest gain. Land on a hillside, with a commanding view of a valley below, is of more value for upper-class residential property than for factories, which are more conveniently situated on flat land near major transport arteries.

The spatial distribution of particular social groups is also influenced by ecological factors. Certain kinds of land use, such as parking lots and junkyards, quickly generate urban decay in the area in which they are situated, even if there was little decay there to begin with (Jacobs, 1961). The intrusion of these forms of land use, or the intrusion of a group considered "undesirable" by existing residents, frequently results in a mass departure of the original inhabitants and further deterioration of the area. The mass departure is not an immediate one, however. The first intrusions may pass unnoticed, but at a certain stage, the "tipping point," older residents seem to agree that the character of the neighborhood is irreversibly changed and that they should leave if possible. The spatial distribution of different groups is thus related to such factors as their relative incomes, which determine where they can afford to live, and to their feelings of group solidarity or prejudice against outsiders.

Social inventions such as automobiles and mass transit systems also influence the spatial patterning of cities. If workers have to walk to their factories every day, their homes must be near industrial areas, but if they can drive to work, their homes can easily be fifteen miles away. If enough members of the urban labor force live several miles away, services and facilities will tend to follow them from the city center, perhaps leaving a vacuum that, as in many American cities, is filled by further decay.

Patterns of Urban Growth

Several theorists have attempted to identify and account for patterns in the way people and facilities are distributed within the physical space of a modern city. Three theories have attracted special attention: the concentric-zone theory, the sector theory, and the multiple-nuclei theory. Each of these theories is represented diagrammatically in Figure 21.9.

The Concentric-Zone Theory

Using the large city of Chicago as their principal source of evidence, Robert Park, Ernest Burgess, and R. D. McKenzie (1925) suggested that a modern city typically consists of a series of concentric zones. These zones radiate out from the downtown center, and each successive zone contains a different type of land use. The first zone is the *central business district,* containing retail stores, banks, hotels, theaters, business and professional offices, railroad and bus stations, and city government buildings. The second zone is the *zone in transition.* The transition is caused by the steady encroachment of business and industry into what were once residential neighborhoods, often containing the homes of the wealthy. This process is the classic pattern of growth of the American slum. Wealthy families leave their old homes near the city center under competition for space from the central business district. The residences are then converted to apartment dwellings, rooming houses, and marginal business establishments such as restaurants. These shabby zones readily become ghettos for minority groups or the center of the urban vice trade. The third zone is the *zone of working people's homes,* consisting of aging, relatively inexpensive family residences and apartments. The homes are superior to those in the zone of transition, however, and are often filled with people who have escaped from the second zone. The fourth zone is the *residential zone,* inhabited mainly by small business operators and professionals. Land use here is less intensive than in the more central zones. There are a large number of single-family residences, and the proportion of homes that are owned rather than rented is quite high. The final zone is the *commuters' zone,* consisting of small towns from which the wealthy travel to their work in the city. The neighborhoods in the commuters' zone are beyond the city limits, but most of their inhabitants are economically integrated into the urban area.

This model is, of course, merely an ideal type that stresses the relationship between social status and distance from the city center. Many factors, such as environmental obstacles or determined resistance by residents of one zone to invaders from the next, may influence the actual pattern of development.

The Sector Theory

Homer Hoyt (1939) proposed the sector theory or urban development as a better model for the growth of American cities since the appearance of the automobile. Hoyt recognized that cities grow outward from the center, but he saw growth as taking place largely in "sectors" of land use—wedge-shaped areas that extend from the center to the periphery rather like slices cut from a pie. As the city expands, both low- and high-rent areas move outward, but the area in which they originated may keep its character and is not necessarily abandoned. Nor do upper-class residential areas encircle the city entirely. They tend to cluster at certain points on the boundary, usually on the outer edge of high-rent sectors. Industrial areas, too, do not necessarily form a concentric zone. They may also take a wedge-shaped form because they spread outward along river valleys, watercourses, and railroad lines. Again, Hoyt's theory is merely an ideal type that may provide a better model for at least some cities than the concentric-zone theory. It does not represent a universal pattern, and specific exceptions to it have been found—for example, in the case of Boston (Firey, 1947).

The Multiple-Nuclei Theory

This theory, proposed by C. D. Harris and Edward Ullman, places less emphasis on the downtown business area. Instead, it suggests that a city has a series of nuclei, each of which is the center of a specialized area. In addition to the business district, for example, there may be "bright lights" areas, light or heavy manufacturing areas, or government administrative centers. Each of these nuclei influences the character and development of the surrounding district. The nuclei develop for several reasons. Some activities require specialized facilities—for example, the commercial area needs easy public access, and the port area needs a waterfront. Some activities benefit from being concentrated in one area—for example, retail outlets draw more customers, and financial and business institutions benefit from easy communication. Certain activities, such as industrial manufacturing and entertainments, cannot be reconciled in the same area and therefore tend to be segregated. Like the other models, the multiple-nuclei

THREE MODELS OF THE INTERNAL STRUCTURE OF CITIES

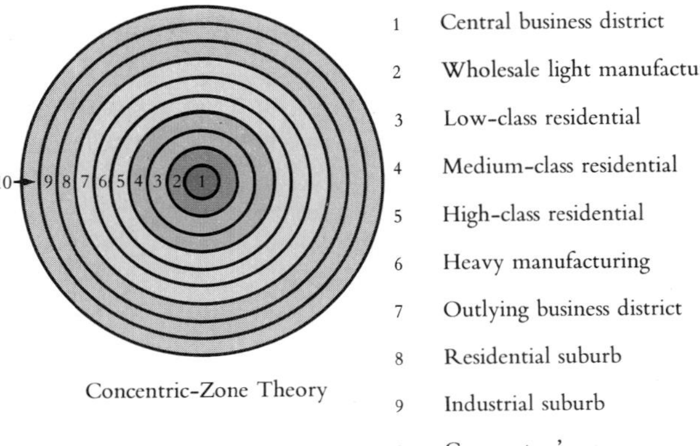

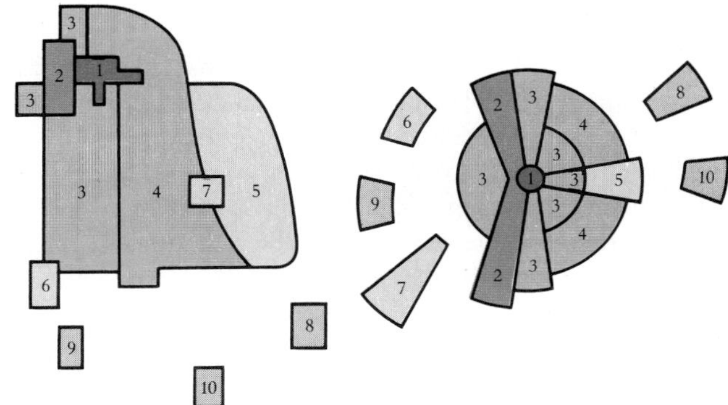

Mutliple-Nuclei Theory

Sector Theory

Source: Adapted from Chauncy D. Harris and Edward L. Ullman, "The Nature of Cities," *Annals of the American Academy of Political and Social Science,* 242 (November, 1945).

Figure 21.9 This diagram shows the three theories that have been proposed to describe typical patterns of development in modern cities: the concentric-zone theory, the sector theory, and the multiple-nuclei theory. The figure shows the total number of categories (zones, sectors, and nuclei, ten in all) presented in all three theories, and places them simultaneously within each of the three models.

theory fits some cities better than others. It seems most applicable to those cities that have developed since the arrival of the automobile and therefore have more decentralization of facilities (Harris and Ullman, 1945).

Each of the theories provides a way of analyzing urban development patterns—no easy task when the cities are constantly changing and when new developments are often being superimposed on older patterns. We have to remember, too, that these models are derived from American data and may not apply to cities in other countries. In societies in the early stages of industrialization, for example, the most prestigious residences are usually at the center of the city, not in the suburbs. The city center is usually focused on religious and political institutions rather than on business. Commercial activity is scattered throughout the city, not concentrated away from private residences.

The ecological approach has great potential value in city planning. Any plan that fails to take account of the social and natural influences that transform the city over time is unlikely to be successful. Some of the most unsuccessful plans, in the United States and elsewhere, have been precisely those that have neglected the human element in the dynamic process that either brings a great city to life or makes it an arid and sterile environment.

Summary

1. A city is a permanent concentration of relatively large numbers of people who do not produce their own food. Urbanization is one of the most significant trends in the modern world. It has radically altered the nature of human communities. Cities are also the primary locus of most modern social problems.

2. Urbanization requires the development of agricultural techniques and means of transporting and storing food. Preindustrial cities remained small, but industrialization has encouraged the growth of large cities. Industrial cities typically contain a central city and suburbs, which together form a metropolis. When metropolises merge, they form a megalopolis.

3. The United States is a highy urbanized society. Suburbs have expanded rapidly and now contain more people than do central cities. The central cities are in a state of crisis, largely as a result of the flight of middle-class residents and their local tax money to the suburbs. The population remaining in the central cities is relatively heterogeneous but also disproportionately poor.

4. City planning has focused recently on urban renewal, but many programs have been criticized for disrupting communities or penalizing the poor. A major obstacle to urban reform is the political boundaries between cities and suburbs. A rational solution would be to integrate all metropolitan communities for local tax purposes.

5. Tönnies' distinction between the small, intimate *Gemeinschaft* and the large, impersonal *Gesellschaft* has influenced theories of urbanism, particularly those of the Chicago School. Wirth emphasized the size, population density, and social diversity of cities, which led to urban anonymity, heterogeneity, and relativism. Reassessments by later writers suggest that intimate communities do, in fact, exist in large cities.

6. The ecological approach attempts to explain the appearance and growth of cities in terms of influences from both the social and natural environment. Three main models of urban growth have been proposed: the concentric-zone theory, the sector theory, and the multiple-nuclei theory.

Important Terms

city
community
preindustrial city
industrial city
central city
suburb
metropolis
megalopolis
Standard Metropolitan Statistical Area (SMSA)
Standard Consolidated Area (SCA)
urban renewal
Gemeinschaft
Gesellschaft
ecological approach
concentric-zone theory
sector theory
multiple-nuclei theory

Suggested Readings

GANS, HERBERT J. *The Urban Villagers.* New York: Free Press, 1962.

An account of the tight-knit communities that are found in American cities. It focuses on a case study of the destruction through urban renewal of an Italian neighborhood in Boston.

GIST, NOEL P., AND SYLVIA F. FAVA. *Urban Society.* New York: Thomas Y. Crowell, 1974.

An extremely thorough and comprehensive text on urban sociology. The book covers urban history, ecology, psychology, social organization, and planning.

GREER, SCOTT A. *The Emerging City: Myth and Reality.* New York: Free Press, 1962.

An excellent discussion of urban trends. Greer shows how political, economic, demographic, and other factors affect urban structure and development.

JACOBS, JANE. *The Death and Life of Great American Cities.* New York: Random House, 1961.

A critical assessment of some urban renewal programs in American cities. Jacobs makes a number of suggestions for more constructive urban planning.

MUMFORD, LEWIS. *The City in History.* New York: Harcourt Brace Jovanovich, 1961.

A rich and fascinating account of the rise and role of cities in history by one of the foremost experts in the field.

VIDICH, ARTHUR, AND JOSEPH BENSMAN. *Small Town in Mass Society.* Princeton, N.J.: Princeton University Press, 1958.

A report of a research study on a small town, showing how the community held a misconceived idea of its own autonomy and freedom from the influence of urban America.

CHAPTER 22 Collective Behavior and Social Movements

CHAPTER OUTLINE

A Theory of Collective Behavior

Rumors
The Yippie Invasion of Chicago
The Death of Paul McCartney

Fashions and Fads
Fashions
Fads

Panics

Mass Hysteria
The Martian Invasion of Earth
The Phantom Anesthetist of Mattoon
The Seattle Windshield-Pitting Epidemic

Crowds
Crowd Characteristics
Types of Crowds
Theories of Crowd Behavior
Mobs
Riots

Publics and Public Opinion
Publics
Public Opinion

Social Movements
Types of Social Movements
Social Movements and Social Problems

Most social behavior follows a regular, patterned, and predictable course. People play their roles and interact with one another according to the social norms that define the behavior expected in various situations. Consider social behavior in your own sociology lecture class. People arrive more or less on time, they seat themselves in an orderly way, they listen and take notes, they ask questions at appropriate points, and they leave when the lecture is over. There are an infinite number of other things that a group of students could do in a room, but in practice everyone behaves in a fairly predictable fashion.

But suppose that a fire suddenly breaks out in the room. Immediately, the normal pattern of behavior is disrupted. The norms that prevailed a few moments before are suspended, and social behavior becomes unstructured and unpredictable. There are few if any generally accepted norms to guide behavior in this new and unanticipated situation. It is possible, although certainly not inevitable, that a panic will result. If this happens, cooperative behavior will break down. There will be a disorderly rush to the exits, even though this will actually reduce any individual's own chance of escape. It is also possible that there will be little panic, particularly if leaders emerge who take charge of the situation, supervise an orderly exit, and attempt to extinguish the fire. But whether the crowd panics or not, its behavior is no longer guided by everyday norms.

Sociologists use the term "collective behavior" to refer to group behavior that is apparently not guided by the usual norms of conduct. Often, in fact, it seems that the people concerned are actually improvising new norms on the spot, and behaving in accordance with these instead. We can say, then, that *collective behavior refers to relatively spontaneous and unstructured ways of thinking, feeling, and acting on the part of large numbers of people.* The concept includes a wide range of social behavior, much of it unusual or even bizarre: a crowd in panic, a lynch mob, a craze, fad, or fashion, rumors, riots, mass hysteria, and the ebb and flow of public opinion.

What all these forms of behavior have in common is that they are relatively unstructured and unpredictable. The participants generally have no clearly defined roles, goals, expectations, or definitions of the situation, and they are subject to few mechanisms of social control. We need only consider social behavior in a much more structured setting—say, in a formal organization such as a government bureaucracy—to appreciate the contrast between the more routine activities of human groups and these outbursts of collective behavior.

There is another form of social behavior that often has many similarities to the kind of collective action just discussed. This is the behavior of social movements, such as those for women's liberation or civil rights. *A social movement consists of a large number of people who have joined together to bring about or resist some social or cultural change.* Some sociologists regard social movements as a form of collective behavior, but others regard them as a separate, though related, phenomenon. The difficulty lies in the varied nature of social movements. Some, such as the "hippie" counterculture of the sixties, seem to fit the definition of collective behavior. Such movements are very unstructured: they are not organized, their norms are flexible and changing, they have few clearly defined roles and statuses, and their goals are diffuse. Other social movements—such as the antiabortion "Right to Life" movement, which ran a candidate for the Democratic presidential nomination in 1976—are much more structured. These movements are highly organized. They are stable and may endure for many years, their goals are clearly defined, they have recognized statuses and roles (including those of leaders), and there are generally accepted norms of conduct for the participants. Still other social movements, such as those for environmental preservation or gay liberation, seem to fall between these two extremes.

In practice there is really a continuum between the most spontaneous forms of collective behavior, such as panics and fads, and the most structured social movements. Treating all these forms of behavior as the same kind of phenomenon presents many difficulties, and for the analytic purposes of this chapter we will regard collective

Figure 22.1 Collective behavior and social movements are of particular sociological interest because they often play an important role in social change. The French Revolution, for example, led to sweeping social changes in France and inspired democratic reforms in many other countries.

behavior and social movements as distinct phenomena, although we will emphasize the often close relationship between them.

Collective behavior and social movements are of great interest to sociologists, and not only because they often take such fascinating forms. Both collective behavior and social movements are an important element in social change. They can serve as the source of new values and norms and even of sweeping changes in human history. Yet it must be frankly admitted that the study of social movements and collective behavior is still in its infancy. Some of the forms of behavior you will encounter in this chapter are now well understood by sociologists, but others still present serious problems of analysis and interpretation.

The study of collective behavior is particularly difficult for three main reasons. The first problem is that collective behavior is so unstructured. It is therefore difficult to find underlying regularities or to generalize from one specific incident to others. The second problem is that collective behavior often occurs as a spontaneous outburst. It cannot easily be created or reproduced for the convenience of the sociologist. Firsthand studies of collective behavior are therefore often difficult to conduct. In analyzing a riot, for example, the researcher may have to rely on the recollections (often contradictory and inaccurate) of untrained observers who were there at the time. The third problem is that the concept of "collective behavior" is something of a grab bag, for it includes such an extraordinary range of social action. It may be that various forms of collective behavior, such as fashions and riots, have so little in common that the field will have to be broken down further if we are to gain a better understanding of its components. Despite these limitations, however, sociological research has already made many otherwise puzzling forms of collective behavior comprehensible.

A Theory of Collective Behavior

The very diversity of collective behavior presents a formidable challenge to sociologists who try to find a general explanation for the phenomena. One of the most promising attempts at a comprehensive theory of collective behavior is that of Neil Smelser (1962).

Smelser argues that collective behavior is essentially an attempt by people to alter their environment when they are under conditions of uncertainty, threat, or strain. These conditions may involve many factors, such as fear, boredom, or a sense of oppression, but people find them stressful and want to change them. The form that their collective behavior actually takes depends largely on how they define the situation that is bothering them. If they do not understand their situation, for example, they can hardly start a social movement to change it and are more likely to respond through, say, a rumor or a riot. The more elaborate their definition of their situation, the more elaborate and structured their form of collective behavior is likely to be.

Smelser identifies six basic conditions that, taken together, provide "necessary and sufficient" grounds for collective behavior to occur. In other words, collective behavior will not take place unless all six conditions are present, and if all six are present, some form of collective behavior is inevitable. The six conditions are:

1. *Structural conduciveness.* This term refers to structural elements in society that make a particular form of collective behavior possible in the first place. The Great Depression, for example, was preceded by a financial panic in which people sold their stock and withdrew money from banks, causing stock values to drop and banks to collapse. This panic was possible only because the United States had a stock market, on which stock could be bought and sold in a short space of time, and a banking system in which banks never had enough ready cash to repay all their depositors. The nature of these economic institutions provided the "structural conduciveness" for the financial panic, which was a classic example of collective behavior.

2. *Structural strains.* Any situation that places a strain on society—poverty, conflict, discrimination, uncertainty about the future—encourages people to make a collective effort to relieve the problem. The civil rights movement and the urban ghetto riots of the sixties, for instance, were two examples of collective behavior that arose because of a structural strain in American society between our social ideal of human equality and our social realities of racial and economic inequality.

3. *Generalized belief.* Structural conduciveness and structural strains are not in themselves sufficient to pro-

voke collective behavior. People must also develop some general belief about the situation—by identifying the problem, determining their opinions about it, and defining appropriate responses. The women's movement, for example, has developed a generalized belief or ideology about the subordinate role of women in American society. This ideology identifies the causes and nature of the problem and is used to justify collective action for social change.

4. *Precipitating factors.* Collective behavior does not "just happen." If the preceding conditions are present, a single incident, often exaggerated by rumor, may be sufficient to trigger collective behavior. The precipitating factor serves to confirm the suspicion and uneasiness that already exist. In all the ghetto riots that have been studied, for example, a specific incident—usually involving a conflict between local residents and the police—precipitated the outbreak of violence. In many cases the violence was fanned by exaggerated rumors concerning the incident.

5. *Mobilization for action.* Once the precipitating incident has taken place, all that is necessary is that the people involved become organized for action. This organization can be of the most rudimentary and unstructured form. Mere physical closeness in a milling crowd creates social interaction and some group cohesion. If leaders emerge and encourage the others to take some action, collective behavior will probably follow. When police raided a gay bar in Greenwich Village in New York in 1969, some of the patrons refused to be arrested and fought back. Their example mobilized other patrons and sympathetic onlookers, and a serious riot followed. The national publicity from this event greatly stimulated the growth of a new social movement for gay liberation.

6. *Mechanisms of social control.* When the preceding conditions have been met, the outcome depends on the success or failure of social control mechanisms. These mechanisms include all the methods by which society reacts to the event, including police behavior, media treatment, and responses of other individuals and groups. The social control mechanisms may be so strong that collective behavior is suppressed, even if the other five conditions are met; or they may be too weak to prevent the behavior; or they may be counterproductive and may actually magnify the behavior. In the campus disturbances of the sixties and early seventies, for example, the different control tactics used by various college administrations served in some cases to prevent or deflect collective protest and action and in other cases to provoke it.

Smelser's theory provides a useful means of analyzing collective behavior. Fads, fashions, and crazes, for example, can be interpreted as a response to conditions of boredom, panics as a response to conditions of threat, or riots as a response to conditions of strain and resentment. Let's look at some forms of collective behavior in more detail, bearing Smelser's approach in mind as we do so.

Rumors

A *rumor* is information that is transmitted informally from anonymous sources. The spreading of a rumor is itself a form of collective behavior, and rumors are in turn an important element in virtually all other forms of collective behavior.

A rumor may be true, false, or a combination of truth and falsehood. Its origin is usually difficult to check, and its method of transmission operates outside the formal communications system of press, TV, government announcements, and the like. Rumors are especially likely to arise in situations where people are deprived of information or where they do not trust the official information they are given. A rumor thus is a substitute for hard news: people want information, and rumor fills their need if reliable information is lacking.

One insight into the importance of rumor in tense situations came after the Detroit riots of 1967, when a newspaper strike eliminated an important source of "official" information. A rumor control center was established in the city, and within less than a month it had received some 10,000 calls from people wanting confirmation of rumors they had heard. These included reports of concentration camps for blacks and incidents of interracial violence and even castration (Rosenthal, 1971). In a strained situation (particularly in a milling, excitable crowd in which it is difficult to check or evaluate rumors) stories such as these can easily provoke violent outbursts.

The process by which rumors are transmitted has been quite thoroughly studied through the use of controlled experiments and analyses of actual cases. Experiments have usually been sophisticated versions of the children's game of "pass it on." People are given a story and asked to spread it to others, and then various versions of the rumor are compared. Gordon Allport and Leo Postman (1947) have shown that what happens to the rumor depends on its content, on the number of people involved in the chain of transmission, and on their attitudes toward the rumor. Some rumors change little, but others, especially those that excite emotions, may be severely distorted. In general, part of the content drops out and the remainder is organized around some dominant theme. The ultimate form of the rumor is often influenced by the special interests of the people involved, because they tend to reshape and transmit those parts of the rumor that fit their preconceptions about the subject matter.

Ralph Turner (1964) and Tamotsu Shibutani (1966) have pointed out that a rumor should not be regarded simply as the transmission and possible distortion of information. It also represents a collective attempt to form a definition of an ambiguous situation. Shibutani points out that many people contribute to the spread of a rumor, and they can play many different roles in doing so. Some take the role of "messenger" by relaying the rumor. Some take the role of "interpreter" by placing it in context and speculating on its implications. Others may be "skeptics" who urge caution and express doubt. Some become "protagonists," forcefully arguing in favor of one interpretation rather than another. Others play the role of "decision makers" and try to initiate action on the basis of the rumor. Most people become an "audience" and are mere spectators in the process. A rumor can thus be seen as a form of communication in which people pool their resources to construct a meaningful interpretation of an ambiguous situation. In doing so they may sometimes improve the accuracy of the rumor rather than distort the truth.

Let's look at two actual cases of rumor transmission.

Figure 22.2 Yippie demonstrators at the 1968 Democratic National Convention in Chicago. In the weeks before the convention, many rumors spread through the city, claiming that the yippies intended to disrupt the convention through such outrageous acts as putting LSD in the Chicago water supply. The unconventional appearance and behavior of the yippies helped to make these absurd rumors seem plausible. Widespread belief in the rumors heightened tensions in the city, and undoubtedly contributed to the violence that followed.

The Yippie Invasion of Chicago

The 1968 Democratic National Convention in Chicago was preceded by dozens of rumors to the effect that members of the Youth International Party ("Yippies") intended to disrupt the convention or even paralyze the entire city. The Yippies themselves, a very small group who wanted to disrupt the convention but apparently had no specific plans for doing so, gleefully promoted some of these rumors and basked for a while in an international spotlight of notoriety. Several rumors spread through Chicago, many of them never mentioned in the official channels of communication. LSD would be put in the city's water supply, sending the entire population on an extended trip. Thousands of young people would engage openly in sexual intercourse in the streets and parks. Gasoline pumps would be broken, the sewers flooded with gasoline, and the city set aflame. "Superpotent" hippies would seduce the wives and daughters of convention delegates. Greased pigs would be released in the main streets of the city. Vehicles would be stalled on bridges and expressways in the rush-hour traffic.

Many of these rumors seem to have been widely believed, and a very tense situation developed. This atmosphere of strain and confusion undoubtedly contributed to a massive overreaction by the Chicago police, who engaged in what was later described as a "police riot" (Walker Commission, 1968). A shocked international television audience watched as the police attacked not only demonstrators but also onlookers and even newspaper and television reporters in the convention hall itself. The publicity provided a severe setback for the Democratic presidential campaign, particularly when the events were compared to the orderly Republican convention that nominated Richard Nixon (Whyte, 1969).

To understand why these absurd rumors about the Yippie invasion seemed believable, we have to look at the social context of the time. The urban ghetto riots and the Vietnam war had placed considerable structural strain on American society. Protest demonstrations, often ending in violence, had taken place at colleges across the country. The youthful "counterculture" was at its height. The generation gap, it seemed, had never been so wide. The clothing, hair styles, music, drugs, politics, and general attitudes of the young seemed so alien to many Americans that almost any rumor of further outrages seemed plausible. Rumors that would have been dismissed a few years earlier or a few years later aroused great anxiety instead, and a self-fulfilling prophecy of violence and disruption followed. The events in Chicago provide an excellent example of rumor as a form of collective behavior in itself, and as a stimulus for other kinds of collective behavior.

The Death of Paul McCartney

In 1969 a Detroit disc jockey referred in passing to a fictitious story, written by an Ohio student, about the death of a member of the Beatles, Paul McCartney. Within a few days the rumor had spread to at least three continents, with knowledge of its origin completely lost. McCartney, it was believed, had died in an auto accident some years previously, but his record company had persuaded the remaining Beatles to hush up the event in the interests of continued sales of new Beatles albums. But the Beatles, faithful to their fans, had inserted various clues about McCartney's death in their records in order to let others in on the secret.

In the following weeks, thousands of people ransacked Beatles albums for confirmation of the rumor. They amassed a great deal of evidence to "prove" the rumor, much of which was printed in the underground press. After playing records in the normal way and discovering many lyrics supposedly referring to the death, ingenious investigators began to play them backward, and found even more startling evidence. On the track "Revolution No. 9," for example, a ghostly voice was heard intoning "turn me on, dead man." On the cover of the *Sergeant Pepper* album, a hand was spotted above McCartney's head—a symbol of death, it was alleged, in ancient Greek or perhaps Indian mythology. In the *Magical Mystery Tour* album photograph, McCartney significantly wore a black carnation, in contrast to the red blossoms sported by the other Beatles.

In a final spurt of enthusiasm, investigators held up Beatles album covers to mirrors, hoping to find some message in the reverse image. They did not go unrewarded: the word "Beatles" on the reversed cover of *Magical Mystery Tour,* if viewed with an appropriate squint, yielded a telephone number. A fresh rumor spread that calls to this number, allegedly in London, would be answered with a full account of McCartney's death. For a period of several days the owner of the number, a British journalist, received hundreds of calls—most of them from the United States and most of them collect—from determined Beatles fans. When repeated denials by record company officials failed to have much impact on the rumor, Paul McCartney finally squashed it himself, while admitting that "If I were dead, I'd be the last to know about it."

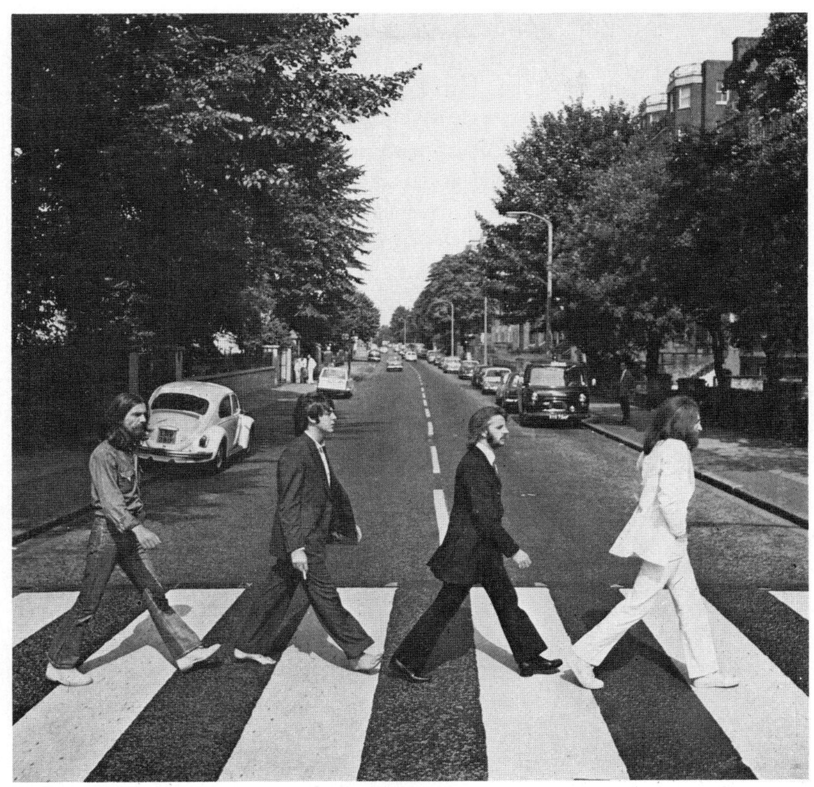

Figure 22.3 In their search for evidence to confirm the death of Paul McCartney, Beatles fans looked for and found hidden meanings on album covers. On the Abbey Road *cover, the Beatles appeared to be walking in funeral procession. John Lennon was in white (the priest), Ringo Starr was in a black suit (the undertaker), McCartney was barefooted, out of step, and had his eyes closed (the corpse), and George Harrison was in working clothes (the gravedigger). To clinch matters, a car in the background had the registration number 28IF, meaning—what else?—that McCartney would be twenty-eight if he were still alive.*

To understand the spread of this irrational rumor we must consider the social role of the Beatles and their relationship to the youth culture of the time. The Beatles were by far the most popular and influential rock group. They had pioneered or spread a number of innovative trends, not only in music but also in fashions (notably long hair for males) and in fads (such as Eastern religion and the use of psychedelic drugs as a route to new consciousness). They had strongly influenced the development of the sixties youth culture and were cult heroes to millions of young people. For this reason, *any* rumor about the Beatles was likely to spread; there was an eager audience for news about all their doings, however trivial. But why should this particular rumor have been so widely believed? Part of the reason was that there was already anxiety about the Beatles. Rumors were circulating—this time correct—that the group was about to break up. The rumor of McCartney's death was made more plausible by the fact that the Beatles had not appeared together in public for several years, so that it would have been at least possible for a fake McCartney to be substituted in their more recent records and photographs. The rock audience was accustomed to analyzing rock lyrics for hidden meanings—if only because the meaning of many lyrics had to be disguised if they were to be on the air—and the surrealistic images of many Beatles songs lent themselves to whatever interpretation people chose to put on them. Moreover, several leading rock stars had died in the eighteen months preceding the McCartney rumor, providing an atmosphere in which the story seemed more credible. Conflict between the generations was particularly acute at the time, and many young people were highly distrustful of the establishment, including the media and record company officials who tried to discount the rumor. The underground press, on the other hand, was often ambiguous about the story and in some cases gave credence to it. Finally, there was growing disillusion in the "counterculture," which was failing to change society to any significant extent and appeared to be disintegrating from within. It is not surprising that this anxiety and disillusion was projected through rumor onto the most prominent symbols of the youth movement, the Beatles.

Fashions and Fads

Fashions and fads are two closely related forms of collective behavior. Both tend to arise fairly spontaneously and to be relatively short-lived, although they may occasionally become more permanently incorporated into a culture.

Fashions

Fashions are the currently accepted styles of appearance and behavior. The fact that some style is termed a "fashion" implies a social recognition that it is temporary and will eventually be replaced by a new style. In small-scale, traditional communities, fashions are virtually unknown. In these communities everyone of similar age and sex wears much the same clothing and behaves in much the same way, and there is little change in styles from year to year or even from generation to generation. In modern societies, however, fashions may change very rapidly indeed: automobile bodies assume new contours every year, and women's hemlines rise and fall with the passage of the seasons.

One reason for the emphasis on fashion in modern societies is that these societies are oriented toward the future rather than the past; novelty is considered desirable rather than threatening. A second reason, closely related, is that changes in fashions are encouraged by powerful commercial interests that profit from producing popular innovations. A further reason is that in a competitive, status-conscious society, fashion is used as a means of indicating one's social characteristics to others. People may wish to appear attractive, distinctive, or affluent, and a new fashion enables them to do so—for a while at least.

Not all fashions are deliberately imposed on the population, however, and people may resist new fashions, even in the face of massive advertising campaigns designed to influence the public taste. The greatest flop in auto industry history was the Ford Edsel, mass-produced in the fifties but almost unanimously scorned by American consumers, who considered it monstrously ugly. Fashions can arise at any level of society, not merely in the upper social strata, and can then spread outward from their point of origin. Blue jeans, for example, are the traditional clothes of the working class, but they are now highly acceptable for young members of the middle and upper classes. A new fashion is generally more likely to be accepted if it does not differ too much from existing fashions. If you consider consecutive changes in automobile styles, for example, you will find few, if any, abrupt changes in appearance. Each new fashion is essentially a modification of its predecessor.

Fads

A *fad* is a temporary form of conduct that is followed enthusiastically by large numbers of people. Fads differ from fashions not only in that they are typically even more temporary but also in that they are usually mildly

Figure 22.4

"I'm so bored! I wish there was a new trend or something."

scorned by the majority of the population. Those who participate in a fad are labeled as faddists; they are believed to follow a fad simply because it has "caught on," not because it has any intrinsic value. Those who are "in fashion," on the other hand, are more positively regarded, for their behavior is appropriate for as long as the fashion lasts.

Some notable fads in recent decades have been the hula hoop, the use of particular catch phrases ("far out," "right on," and so forth), dabbling in mysticism and oriental religion, or "streaking." A fad often provides a means of asserting personal identity. It is a way of showing that one is worth noticing, that one is a little different from everyone else (Klapp, 1969). For this reason, fads tend to appeal primarily to young people, who often have less stable identities than their elders. They also have greater appeal to the affluent than to the poor, for the affluent are better able to afford the luxury of indulging in fads. When a fad becomes so widespread that it no longer offers a distinctive identity to its adherents, it tends to be regarded as something of a bore and is usually abandoned.

Some fads win popularity because they offer the promise—frequently illusory—of personal advantage to their adherents. Of the hundreds of different forms of psychotherapy that are available in the United States, ranging from "orgonomy" to "psychodrama," many have the characteristics of fads. Grandiose claims are made for a new therapeutic technique, such as Janov's "primal scream" therapy; people flock to participate; disillusion sets in; and finally the fad is abandoned by all but a few zealots. A similar form of fad is the financial craze, such as a gold rush or a boom in real estate that turns out to be worthless. One of the most extraordinary of these crazes was the tulip mania that occurred in Holland in 1634. The Dutch suddenly developed a passion for tulips, which rose rapidly in value. People at every level of society invested in tulips and tulip bulbs, and many speculators made vast fortunes. Hoping to get rich quick, many people sold their homes and land to invest even more money in tulips, which at the height of the craze were worth their weight in gold. But suddenly, a rumor spread that the price of tulips was about to fall. Tulip owners desperately tried to sell their bulbs and blooms, but there were no buyers. The price of tulips fell to well below its normal level, and thousands of speculators were ruined. But even today, the Dutch are

Figure 22.5 A short-lived but popular fad of the 1950s, much practiced by college students, was telephone booth cramming. Fads tend to appeal mostly to young people, who are often anxious to assert their personal identity by being a little "different." Once the fad becomes too commonplace, of course, it quickly loses its appeal.

internationally famous for the quality of their tulips—an indication of how a brief episode of collective behavior can leave lingering social effects.

Panics

A *panic* is a form of collective behavior in which a group of people, faced with an immediate threat, engages in an uncoordinated and irrational response. Their behavior is uncoordinated in the sense that cooperative social relationships break down, often creating new problems and dangers. It is irrational in the sense that people's actions are not appropriate for the goals they wish to achieve.

The progress of a panic follows a fairly regular pattern. A sudden crisis occurs; people experience intense fear; normal social expectations are disrupted; each individual tries desparately to escape from the source of danger; mutual cooperation breaks down; and the situation becomes even more threatening as a result. Panics are especially likely to occur in unusual conditions in which everyday norms have little relevance, such as fires, floods, shipwrecks, earthquakes, or military invasions. Some kind of response is necessary in these situations, but there are few, if any, social norms that specify an appropriate reaction. Thus, when a fire breaks out in a crowded room, people may attempt to flee from the source of the threat, but only succeed in hampering themselves and others by creating bottlenecks at the exits. Awareness of the bottlenecks may lead to increased panic, with people fighting and trampling on one another in the effort to escape.

The most dramatic panics are those that occur in temporary situations of extreme emergency, but not all panics are quite so frantic or short-lived. A less dramatic form of this collective behavior is the financial panic, which is typically provoked by rumors that the price of stocks will fall or that a bank will be unable to repay its depositors. As in other forms of panic, the individuals involved try to protect their own interests, and in so doing they worsen the situation for themselves and everyone else. By trying to sell their stocks as quickly as possible, people ensure that the price of stocks *will* fall; by demanding their money back from the bank, they ensure that the bank actually *will* collapse.

Figure 22.6 The stock market collapse of 1929 was a classic example of a financial panic. Fearing that the price of stocks would fall, investors rushed to sell their holdings, thus forcing the price down even lower. As the panic spread, huge fortunes were wiped out in hours or even minutes, and many thousands of investors were ruined.

Mass Hysteria

Mass hysteria is a form of collective behavior involving widespread and contagious anxiety, usually caused by some unfounded belief. In extreme cases mass hysteria can result in panic, particularly if the source of the anxiety is believed to be sufficiently close or threatening. The medieval witch-hunts discussed in Chapter 16 (Religion) are an example of mass hysteria, created in this instance by the illusory belief that many of the problems of late medieval society were caused by witches. McCarthyism, the secular witch-hunt of the fifties which aimed at finding communists in influential positions in American society, also had many of the characteristics of mass hysteria.

Let us look briefly at three instances of mass hysteria that have been closely studied by sociologists.

The Martian Invasion of Earth

In 1938 a radio dramatization of the *War of the Worlds* was broadcast in the New York area. The result was mass hysteria and even outright panic, involving perhaps as many as 1 million of the 6 million people who heard the broadcast.

Although an announcer made the nature of the program clear at the outset, many people tuned in later and did not realize that they were listening to a play. The dramatization itself started innocently enough, with what purported to be a music concert. The music was interrupted with an announcement of strange atmospheric disturbances, followed by an interview with an expert who assured listeners that this could not possibly be the start of an invasion from Mars. The music continued, only to be interrupted again by an eye-witness account of a strange meteorite that had landed near New York (quoted in Cantril, 1940):

> Just a minute! Something's happening! Ladies and gentlemen, this is terrific! . . . The thing must be hollow! . . . Good heavens, something's wriggling out. . . . There, I can see the thing's body. It's large as a bear and glistens like wet leather. But that face. It . . . it's indescribable. I can hardly force myself to keep looking at it. The eyes are black and gleam like a serpent. The mouth is V-shaped with saliva dripping from its rimless lips that seem to quiver and pulsate. The crowd falls back. . . . What's that? There's a jet of flame . . . and it leaps right at the advancing men. . . . Good Lord, they're turning to flame!

This "on-the-spot" transmission ended abruptly, and various "experts," "public officials," and "scientists" then took turns at commenting on the invasion. The listeners were eventually told (quoted in Cantril, 1940):

> Ladies and gentlemen, I have a grave announcement to make. Incredible as it may seem, both the observations of science and the evidence of our eyes lead to the inescapable assumption that those strange beings who landed in the Jersey farmlands tonight are the vanguard of an invading army from the planet Mars. The battle which took place tonight at Govers Mill has ended in one of the most startling defeats ever suffered by an army in modern times; seven thousand men armed with rifles and machine guns pitted against a single fighting machine of the invaders from Mars. One hundred and twenty known survivors.

A very large number of people accepted this broadcast as fact, not fiction. Some of them hid in cellars. Others bundled their children into their cars and drove as fast as they could from the scene of the supposed invasion. Others telephoned their relatives to give them the terrible news and to say farewell. Others simply prayed and waited for the inevitable end. Crowds gathered excitedly in public places, and fresh rumors about the invasion were generated.

Why did such an improbable tale of invasion from outer space have such a devastating effect? One reason was undoubtedly the skill of the dramatists, who used an unusual and imaginative form of presentation. The use of the "bulletin" format, with comments from supposed scientific experts and public officials, gave a certain credibility to the events. Equally important, however, was the fact that in this pretelevision age people relied heavily on the radio for up-to-the-minute news. Much of the news at the time dealt with the growing tensions in Europe, which in 1938 stood on the brink of World War II. Listeners were glued to their radio sets as never before, had learned to expect interruptions of their scheduled programs, and expected that these interruptions might deal with conflict and warfare (Cantril, 1940). In addition, knowledge of other planets was far less extensive than it is today. Observations of Mars had led some astronomers to the mistaken conclusion that its surface was criss-crossed by "canals," presumably constructed by highly intelligent Martians. Belief in the possibility of advanced life forms on Mars was quite widespread among the ordinary public.

The Phantom Anesthetist of Mattoon

In early September 1944, a woman in Mattoon, Illinois, told the police that she and her daughter had been the victims of an unseen intruder who had sprayed them with sweet-smelling gas, which had temporarily paralyzed them and made them feel ill. The local newspaper made the event its page-one story, under the headline "Anesthetic Prowler on the Loose." The day after the report appeared, three similar attacks were alleged to have taken place. Because of a holiday period, these accounts were not printed in the press for two days, and no attacks took place during this time. When the reports were finally printed, the number of attacks rose sharply for nearly a week, with as many as seven incidents being reported in a single evening. In all, the phantom anesthetist claimed twenty-seven victims.

Police efforts to trap the maniac were unsuccessful. Although some people claimed to have seen him fleetingly, or even to have heard him pumping his spray gun, the combined efforts of local police, state police, and bands of armed citizens who patrolled the streets were entirely fruitless. The police were so efficiently organized that they were able to arrive at the scene of a complaint, according to the police chief, "even before the phone was back on the hook," but they found nothing. Scientific experts could find no chemical traces of the gas, knew of no gas that could cause the reported effects, and strongly doubted if a gas of this kind—so potent, yet so quick to disappear without trace—could even exist. Doubts started to set in: was there really an anesthetist on the loose, or were people imagining the attacks? Newspapers began to print articles and interviews on the subject of mass hysteria—and the attacks stopped abruptly, never to be repeated. Medical, scientific, psychological, and police conclusions all pointed in the same direction. There never had been a phantom anesthetist in Mattoon.

How can we account for this episode of mass hysteria? In a careful study of the incident, Donald M. Johnson (1945) found that nearly all the victims were women whose average educational and economic levels were significantly lower than the average for Mattoon as a whole. Three-fourths of the victims, in fact, had not gone beyond elementary school. The husbands of several of the women were away in the army, a fact which presumably left them feeling more isolated and vulnerable. In more than half of the cases for which Johnson could obtain information, there were symptoms of psychological stress: the victims spoke of having "always been nervous," of needing "doctoring for nerves," and of how they "never slept much." In short, the victims of the phantom anesthetist were precisely those whom Smelser's theory predicts might become involved in an unstructured outburst of collective behavior such as mass hysteria—people with a sense of unhappiness or discontent and no clear idea of the cause.

Why did the outbreak of mass hysteria spread in the way that it did? Johnson (1945) concluded:

> [The first victim] had a mild hysterical attack, an event which is not at all uncommon, which is, on the contrary, familiar to most physicians. The crucial point is that her interpretation of her symptoms was rather dramatic . . . with the result that an exciting uncritical story of the case appeared in the evening newspaper. As the news spread, other people reported similar symptoms, more exciting stories were written, and so the affair snowballed.
>
> But such acute outbursts are necessarily self-limiting. The bizarre details which captured the public imagination at the beginning of the episode became rather ridiculous when studied more leisurely. The drama of the story lost tang with time and the absurdities showed through.

One interesting result of the more critical public attitude was that police calls in Mattoon reached a new low for several days after the attacks ceased. The citizens, it seems, were reluctant to risk making fools of themselves, and routine complaints about prowlers and similar incidents dropped off sharply.

The Seattle Windshield-Pitting Epidemic

In late March 1954, Seattle newspapers carried occasional reports of damage to automobile windshields in a city eighty miles to the north—damage that the police suspected was caused by vandals. On the morning of April 14, newspapers reported windshield damage in a town only sixty-five miles away, and later that day similar incidents were reported only forty-five miles from the city limits. On the same evening, the mysterious windshield-pitting agent struck Seattle itself: between April 14 and April 15, over 15,000 people called the Seattle police department to complain about damage to their windshields.

The windshield damage usually consisted of small pitting marks, which often grew into bubbles about the size of a thumbnail. Many people tried to protect their windshields by covering them with cardboard or by garaging their cars, but even these tactics did not guarantee immunity. Clearly, vandals could not be responsible. The most popular culprit was the H-bomb, which had recently been tested in the Pacific. On the evening of April 15, the Mayor of Seattle dramatically announced that the pitting was "no longer a police matter" and called on the state governor and the president of the United States for help. Yet the epidemic ended almost as soon as it had started. Newspapers suggested on April 16 that mass hysteria, not radioactive fallout, was the cause of the problem. On that day the police received only forty-six complaints; on April 17, only ten; and thereafter, none at all.

Careful scientific analysis of the pitted windshields revealed that the amount of pitting increased with the age and mileage of the car in question, and that there was no evidence of pitting that could not be explained by ordinary road damage. What had happened was that the residents of Seattle, for the first time, had started to look *at* their windshields instead of *through* them.

In a study of the epidemic, Nahum Medalia and Otto Larsen (1958) found that for two months before the epidemic, Seattle newspapers had been printing reports about H-bomb tests and fallout, "hinting darkly at doom and disaster." The epidemic, they suggest, may have served to relieve the tensions that had been built up, if only by focusing these diffuse anxieties on a very narrow area of experience, automobile windshields.

Crowds

A *crowd* is a temporary collection of people in close physical proximity. The social structure of a crowd is very simple, rarely consisting of more than a distinction between leaders and others, but crowds are always more than just aggregates of individuals. Physical closeness leads to social interaction, even if the members of the crowd actually try to avoid interpersonal contact. The mere awareness of the presence of others leads to a subtle but rich interchange of impressions, based on eye contact or avoidance, facial expressions, gestures, postures, or even clothing.

Crowd Characteristics

Crowds vary greatly in character and behavior. A crowd of one type—say, a crowd of football spectators—can be quickly transformed into a crowd of a quite different type, such as a rampaging mob. Most crowds, however, have certain characteristics in common:

1. *Suggestibility.* People in a crowd tend to be more suggestible than usual. They are more likely to go along with the opinions, feelings, and actions of the rest of the crowd.

2. *Anonymity.* The individual feels relatively insignificant and unrecognized in a crowd. The crowd often appears to act as a whole, and its individual members are not and do not feel readily identifiable.

3. *Spontaneity.* Members of a crowd tend to behave in a more spontaneous manner than they would on their own. They do not reflect on their actions as much as usual and are more likely to let their behavior be guided by their emotions.

4. *Invulnerability.* Because members of crowds feel anonymous, they are inclined to feel that they cannot be personally "got at." They may behave in ways that would be less likely if they felt social control mechanisms could be applied to them as individuals.

Types of Crowds

Herbert Blumer (1951) has constructed a useful typology of crowds. Blumer distinguishes four basic types of crowds:

Casual crowds are the most loosely structured of all crowds and consist of a collection of individuals who have little or no purpose in common, such as an ordinary crowd in a street. The individual members have little emotional involvement in the crowd, and can easily detach themselves from it. Their physical closeness implies some social interaction, however, and a precipitating incident—such as a traffic accident or attempted suicide leap from a nearby building—can produce greater structure and more social cohesion.

Conventional crowds are deliberately planned and relatively structured; they are "conventional" in the sense that their behavior follows established social norms or con-

(a)

ventions. An audience in a lecture room, for example, is a conventional crowd, although circumstances such as a fire can disrupt the crowd's social structure and conventional behavior.

Expressive crowds are usually organized to permit the personal gratification of their members, an activity that is viewed as an end in itself. A college dance, a religious revival meeting, or a rock festival are all examples of expressive crowds.

Acting crowds, as the term implies, are crowds in action—mobbing, rioting, or engaging in other extreme forms of behavior. The acting crowd is the least common but sometimes the most socially significant of the four basic crowd types. To take an outstanding historical example: the French Revolution, whose impact spread far beyond the borders of France, was precipitated by a mob assault on the notorious Paris prison, the Bastille.

Theories of Crowd Behavior

Crowd behavior, particularly the apparently irrational and often destructive behavior of acting crowds, has always fascinated sociologists. How can this unusual phenomenon, so unlike everyday group behavior, be explained? Smelser's theory gives us a good general explanation, but other theorists have looked for specific factors in the crowd situation that might give us a better understanding of this particular form of collective behavior. Two main theories have been proposed.

The "Contagion" Theory

Some theorists have regarded crowd behavior, especially that of the acting crowd, as the product of a group *"contagion"* in which individuals lose much of their self-identity and even self-control. The earliest systematic version of the theory was proposed in 1895 by a French writer, Gustave Le Bon. He argued that a "collective mind" emerges in crowd situations, with the conscious personality of the individual members almost disappearing.

Le Bon believed that the members of a crowd are dominated by a single impulse and act almost identically. People are less capable of rational thought once they are caught up in the frenzy of the crowd, and the "collective mind" is, in effect, merely the lowest common denomi-

(b)

(c)

Figure 22.7 Four basic types of crowd: (a) a conventional crowd—the behavior of such a crowd is largely governed by social norms and conventions and is therefore relatively predictable; (b) a casual crowd—this kind of crowd is very temporary and loosely structured; (c) an expressive crowd—the members are primarily concerned with expressing their own feelings and interests; (d) an acting crowd—a crowd of this type is not content merely to observe events; it takes concerted action.

(d)

nator of the emotions of the members. Le Bon was an aristocrat, and like most members of upper classes everywhere, he thoroughly disliked crowds drawn from the ranks of ordinary citizens. The reason, of course, is that a dissatisfied crowd readily becomes a militant mob, which is why governments facing popular unrest often go to such lengths to ban all public gatherings, even of as few as three people. Le Bon was firmly convinced that a person in a crowd "descends several rungs in the ladder of civilization. Isolated, he may be a cultivated individual; in a crowd, he is a barbarian; that is, a creature acting by instinct."

We know today that the idea of a "collective mind" is a fallacy. The behavior of a crowd is a patterned aggregate of the behavior of its individual members, and there is no crowd "mind" with an independent existence. We are also more sensitive to the antidemocratic bias in Le Bon's work. Yet other parts of his theory remain influential, and many social scientists have attempted to identify the process of contagion by which individual personality seems to become merged into and influenced by the crowd.

There is no doubt that members of crowds are subject to a certain amount of contagion from others. They are more suggestible, and they feel a strong sense of social integration into the group, with a corresponding loss of personal identity. People in crowds look to others for cues, narrow their field of emotional and intellectual focus, and behave in less critical and reflecting ways. This is particularly true if the crowd is closely packed. For this reason, religious and political speakers whose audience is scattered about a room often ask those present to move to the front and fill any vacant seats. Crowd contagion can also be manipulated by "planting" supporters in the room with instructions to applaud at prearranged points: once a few people start clapping (or laughing or even coughing), others usually do so as well.

The "Emergent-Norms" Theory

One important criticism of the "contagion" theory is that it tends to regard crowd behavior as a unique phenomenon, lying beyond the normal boundaries of social scientific investigation. Some sociologists, notably Ralph Turner (1964), have argued strongly that crowd behavior can be analyzed in terms of ordinary social and psychological processes and that "contagion" is not, in itself, an adequate explanation.

Turner challenges the assumption that all members of crowds tend to behave in almost identical ways. In fact, he argues, there are considerable differences in the motives, attitudes, and actions of crowd members. Some of those present may be impulsive participants, others passive supporters, others passers-by who have become onlookers, others opportunistic individuals who are seeking their own gratification from the crowd situation. The unanimity of crowds is often an illusion. Even in the midst of a riot, people may have very different motives and intentions and may behave in markedly different ways (Turner, 1964; Turner and Killian, 1972).

The *"emergent-norms" theory* is an attempt to incorporate crowd behavior into the framework of existing sociological theory. What actually happens in a crowd, Turner argues, is that new norms emerge in the course of social interaction. These norms define appropriate behavior in the crowd situation and emerge from the visible actions of a few people. In the ambiguous situation that exists in the crowd, these few activists are able to define the norms—whether they are norms regarding applause, violence, or anything else—for most of the other members. Many of the others do not agree with the direction that is being taken. They may not express any opposition, however, out of fear of ridicule, coercion, or even personal injury. As a result, casual observers may believe that the crowd is unanimous. Crowd behavior is thus explicable in the same terms as other social behavior: that is, it is influenced by the prevailing social norms. The only difference is that the norms are improvised on the spot. The crowd itself evolves the norms and then starts to enforce them, informally, on its members.

Mobs

One important form of the acting crowd is the mob. A *mob* is an emotionally aroused crowd bent on violent action. Mobs usually have leaders, are single-minded in their aggressive intent, and impose strong conformity on their members. The mob has immediate and limited objectives and is a particularly temporary and unstable form of collective behavior.

One example of mob behavior, common in American history but extremely rare elsewhere, is the lynch mob. Lynching is part of an American vigilante tradition, in which self-appointed groups of citizens, in order to serve their own version of law and order, kill people whom they define as criminal or undesirable. Lynching is thus a curious combination of moral self-righteousness and brutal sadism. The practice has historically taken place primarily in the West and the South. Until the turn of the century the victims were both white and nonwhite, but during this century they have been increasingly and overwhelmingly black. During the Reconstruction period after the Civil War, "nigger hunts" were organized in which whole groups of freed slaves were rounded up and murdered: in the decade 1889–1899, some 1875 lynchings were reported, and many more doubtless went unrecorded (Cantril, 1963). Between 1900 and 1950, well over 3000 people were lynched in the United States, including just under 200 whites. Contrary to popular belief, lynching of blacks was not usually associated with charges of sexual offenses against white women. Rape or attempted rape was allegedly involved in only one-fourth of the cases. Other blacks were hanged, shot, mutilated, and burned to death for such offenses as "trying to act like a white man," "making boastful remarks," "insisting on voting," "giving poor entertainment," "being too prosperous," and "riding in a train with white passengers" (Raper, 1933).

Virtually all the lynchings recorded in this century have been the result of mob action, often by the Ku Klux Klan and almost always with little or no opposition from law-enforcement agencies. Local social norms, in fact, appeared to expect police and prison officials to give only token resistance to lynching attempts, and even this resistance was tolerated only because it would safeguard the officials in the event of a subsequent inquiry. Participants in lynch mobs have typically been whites of very low socioeconomic level, and their acts may be interpreted as a venting of their frustrations onto a defenseless scapegoat group. Support for this view is provided by the fact that between 1882 and 1930 there was a significant relationship between the price of cotton in southern states and the frequency of lynchings. Poor whites suffered intense frustrations in economic bad times; unable to strike at their social superiors, the white landowning class, they turned their aggression onto the blacks (Raper, 1933). The lynch mob now seems to have faded from the American scene: six lynchings were recorded in the fifties, but none have been reported since.

Riots

A second important form of active crowd behavior is the *riot,* a violent and destructive collective outburst. Rioting crowds differ from mobs in that their behavior is less structured, purposive, and unified; it may even involve a number of different groups in different locations engaging in similar but not necessarily identical behavior. Whereas the mob usually has some specific target—lynching a victim, attacking a police vehicle, burning down a foreign embassy—a riot involves much more generalized behavior with few specific objectives other than the creation of disorder.

The most recent outbreak of rioting in the United States was the series of ghetto riots that shook northern cities in the sixties. But the riot has a much longer history in the United States, and many previous outbreaks were very much more violent. Extensive antidraft riots took

Figure 22.8 Riots were fairly frequent in urban America during the latter half of the nineteenth and the early twentieth century. Although some of these outbursts were race riots, most of them, such as the New York riot of 1889 shown here, were sparked by industrial unrest.

place in New York in 1863 when working-class whites protested attempts to draft them into the Civil War. Labor history in the United States was marked by bitter conflict and riots until the 1930s. Serious race riots took place in many cities earlier in this century, notably in Chicago in 1919 and Detroit in 1943. These race riots were quite unlike the ghetto riots of the sixties. They were initiated by white mobs who engaged mainly in acts of violence on individual blacks.

The ghetto riots of the sixties, in contrast, were primarily directed not against persons but against property. Although the police and national guard who attempted to suppress the riots were mostly white, the ghetto riots were not "race" riots as such; there was little interracial conflict between ordinary citizens. The ghetto riots were essentially *protest* riots, the outcome of frustration and resentment at a society that promised equality but did not deliver it. The worst of these riots took place in 1967 and caused so much concern that a National Commission on Civil Disorders (the Kerner Commission) was appointed to investigate them. Smelser's theory of collective behavior fits the Commision's findings remarkably well.

The Commission reported that riots occurred in more than twenty cities in 1967. There were at least 164 separate instances of disorder, of which 41 were classified as "serious" or "major." Some eighty-three people died in the riots—nearly all of them blacks—and in Detroit alone damage was estimated at more than $40 million. The Commission found that in every instance there had been a reservoir of growing discontent and that a single precipitating factor, usually involving white police, had sparked the riot. Efforts at social control had often aggravated the situation, leading to fresh and more extensive outbursts, and exaggerated rumors had often heightened tension on the part of both rioters and police. The underlying cause of the riots, the commission found, was the institutionalized racism of American society, as evidenced by both the social and economic conditions of blacks and their inability to bring about significant change through normal institutional channels.

One important finding of the Commission was that the riots were not the work of a small minority of "riffraff" or "troublemakers." The typical rioter's social characteristics were not significantly different from those of the typical ghetto inhabitant, and as many as 20 percent of randomly selected ghetto residents admitted taking part in riots. A further substantial part of the ghetto population was sympathetic toward the rioters, and many others believed the riots had been helpful in focusing attention on black complaints. Most riots took place in hot weather after working hours, when large numbers of people were gathering on the streets to escape the heat of crowded tenement buildings.

In Smelser's terms, then, the *structural conduciveness* was the existence of depressed black ghettos in urban areas. The *structural strain* was the discrepancy between American ideals of equality and the reality of institutionalized racism. The *generalized belief* was the blacks' recognition that discrimination was the source of their problem and that decades of peaceful protest had brought little change. The *precipating factors* were isolated incidents of tension or conflict, and rumors about these incidents. The *mobilization for action* took place when some individuals began an outright attack on police or property, setting an example for others. The *mechanisms of social control* were the reactions of police and other elements, including ghetto residents who urged rioters to "cool it." But these mechanisms generally failed to prevent the outburst of collective behavior.

Publics and Public Opinion

Most of the forms of collective behavior we have considered so far involve a certain amount of direct contact and even contagion among the participants. The study of publics and public opinion presents a somewhat different picture, however, because the participants are much more dispersed and much more inclined to make individual decisions.

Publics

A *public* is a substantial number of people with a shared interest in some issue on which there are differing opinions. We sometimes speak loosely of the whole population as "the public," but this concept is really a fiction. In practice, there are as many publics as there are issues, and there is no issue for which the entire population is a public, simply because many people are ignorant of or uninterested in any specific issue. The Gallup Poll, for example, has found that it is very rare for more than 80 percent of the American population to be aware of a particular issue, and the percentage is often very much lower. The public for a single issue—such as abortion, a political scandal, fluoridation of water, or protection of the environment—expands or contracts as more people become involved or lose interest in the topic.

The activities of a public are more rational than those of a crowd. Some members of a public may think and feel alike, but they are individuals making individual decisions and so are less susceptible to contagion and suggestibility. Some of the interaction within a public takes place on a face-to-face basis between friends, associates, and family members, but much of it occurs indirectly through the mass media. A public does not act together (although some of its members may join in collective behavior or social movements), but it does form opinions on the issue around which it is focused.

Public Opinion

Public opinion is the sum of the decisions of the members of a public on a particular issue. Because people may constantly change their views, opinion on many issues is often in a state of flux. An assessment of public opinion is therefore valid only for the time and place in which it was made.

In a society such as our own, considerable importance is placed on public opinion. We are a democratic society in which elected officials must pay some attention to the opinions of their electorates, and we are a capitalist society in which commercial interests must take account of public opinions about various goods and services. A great deal of effort consequently goes into finding out what the public thinks about particular issues—and into influencing or changing these opinions. Billions of dollars are spent annually on public-opinion polls and market surveys and on media campaigns to build favorable public images of candidates, policies, corporations, and products. These campaigns are forms of *propaganda*—information or viewpoints that are presented with the deliberate intention of persuading the audience to adopt a particular opinion. Propaganda may be true or false, but its objective is always the same: to influence public opinion toward a specific conclusion.

Propaganda Techniques

Propagandists can use several very simple methods to persuade their audiences. All these techniques have one element in common: they make an appeal to the values and attitudes of the audience. The next time you watch advertisements on television, you might try to identify the particular techniques being used.

1. *Glittering generalities* is a technique of surrounding a product, candidate, or policy with rather meaningless words that evoke a favorable response. Politicians, for example, become lyrical about "freedom," "democracy," "the individual," or "a better future," and have successfully campaigned on such slogans as "New Frontier," "Great Society," or even "Law and Order."
2. *Name-calling* is a method used in negative propaganda, and attempts to attach an unfavorable label to something that the propagandist opposes. Opponents of plans for a national health insurance program, for example, have successfully branded these plans as "socialized medicine." This phrase conjures up images of socialism, a concept to which the American public reacts very unfavorably.
3. *Transfer* is a method of winning approval for something by associating it with something else that is known to be viewed favorably. The most obvious example is the practice of associating commercial products with attractive female models, however irrelevant the link between the two may be.
4. *Testimonial* is the technique of using famous or respected people to make public statements favoring or opposing something. Commercial advertisers, for example, commonly use sports heroes, movie stars, or even retired astronauts to recommend their products on television and in magazines.
5. *Plain folks* is the method of identifying the propagandist's ideas or product with "ordinary" people. Political and commercial advertisers often use interviews with what appear to be ordinary citizens (they are generally actors) praising a product, policy, or candidate in what seem to be down-to-earth, common sense terms.
6. *Card stacking* is an argument in which the facts (or falsehoods) are arranged in such a way that only one conclusion seems to be logically possible. This method is commonly used in commercial advertisements that compare one brand to another.
7. *Bandwagon* is a method that tries to build support for a particular viewpoint or product by creating the impression that "everyone is doing it." The implication is that the audience is being "left out" of a popular trend and should "get with it."

Source: Adapted from Alfred McClung Lee and Elizabeth Bryant Lee, *The Fine Art of Propaganda* (New York: Harcourt Brace Jovanovich, 1939).

The actual process by which public opinion is formed is an informal and diffuse one, and it is not easily studied. We do know, however, that people are not the passive victims of advertisers and other media persuaders. Opinions are not formed in a vacuum; they are made in the context of existing cultural values and personal preconceptions. Moreover, people do not necessarily get their opinions directly from media sources. Information and viewpoints are sifted through other people, particularly members of one's primary group, such as family, friends, and workmates. For example, we are more likely to be influenced to see a movie by a friend who recommends it to us than by a newspaper advertisement. A public is also influenced by prominent members of the community who act as *opinion leaders.* These individuals usually have higher social status than the public they influence, and they are more interested in the issue in question. They spend more time in studying the controversy, form definite opinions about it, and interpret the issue for others. Labor union officials, for example, are likely to have a strong influence over union members' opinions on economic and labor issues, and this influence may extend to other areas as well. Contagion may also play a role in the formation of public opinion through what is known as the "bandwagon" effect. If it appears that opinion is swinging rapidly in one direction, many people—particularly those who were previously undecided or who had no very strong commitment to the other side—tend to change their viewpoints. This is why commercial advertisers often stress an "everybody is doing it" theme and why candidates in presidential primaries are so eager to do well in the early stages of their campaigns.

Public opinion can now be measured by opinion polls with a high degree of accuracy. A properly chosen sample of as few as 3000 voters can be used to predict the outcome of a national election, usually to within less than 2 percentage points of the final result. The problems of constructing, using, and interpreting opinion polls have already been discussed in Chapter 2 (Doing Sociology: The Methods of Research), and will not be repeated here. It should be noted, however, that opinion polls can themselves be an important influence on public opinion. Publication of poll findings gives people the opportunity to compare their opinions with others, and any strong trend in the findings may have an impact on individual suggestibility. Thus, if polls show that what was previously a minority viewpoint is now becoming more respectable, as was the case in the later stages of opposition to the Viet-

Figure 22.9 Social movements often play an important role in the formation of public opinion. The movements draw public attention to social problems and provoke debate about the issues involved.

nam war, people who originally rejected that viewpoint may take its arguments more seriously. They will tend to reassess their own opinions; leaders who were too timid to support the minority position before will speak out; and public opinion may shift further. Some political scientists are disturbed at the possibility that preelection publication of opinion polls may influence the way people vote, even to the extent of altering the results of elections. If it appears from poll findings that candidate A is ahead of candidate B, undecided voters may join a bandwagon in favor of candidate A, and other voters, particularly the disheartened supporters of candidate B, may choose not to vote at all in the belief that doing so will make little difference to the result.

Social Movements

Social movements are of importance because they actively and deliberately intervene in history. Their members are not content to be the passive playthings of social forces; instead, they attempt to influence the course of human events by collective action. Many social movements, of course, fail in their objectives, but others have brought about social changes—some minor, some far-reaching.

Unlike most other forms of collective behavior, social movements may last for many years or even decades. Unlike other forms, too, social movements are fairly well structured. Their members are not scattered, unorganized individuals but rather people consciously acting together in accordance with a shared belief system, or ideology. The ideology provides a criticism of existing social conditions, a concept of the movement's purpose, a distinction between "us" and "them," and a program for action. Social movements frequently consist of several related organizations. The civil rights movement or women's movement, for example, have contained many separate groups working toward a common goal. In most social movements, however, there are clear role distinctions between leaders and followers, and in many social movements there are other specialized roles—treasurer, newsletter editor, and so on. In fact, some social movements become so organized and structured that they cease to be social movements and instead become formal organizations. The present trend, in keeping with the rationalization process found in all other areas of society, is for social movements to become highly organized and professionalized at an early stage of their existence (McCarthy and Zald, 1973). Many other social movements, however, such as some short-lived religious cults, are loosely structured and relatively spontaneous and unpredictable.

Types of Social Movements

Social movements can be classified into different types according to their objectives.

Regressive movements are those that aim to "put the clock back." Their members view certain social changes with suspicion and distaste, and try to reverse the current trends. The Ku Klux Klan is an example of a regressive movement, in this case one that resists the trends toward racial equality and greater civil liberties that have taken place in the course of this century.

Reform movements are basically satisfied with the existing social order but believe certain reforms are necessary, usually in specific areas of society. The civil rights movement, the women's movement, the ecology movement, and the gay liberation movement are all examples of this type of social movement.

Revolutionary movements are deeply dissatisfied with the social order and work for radical change. Their objective is the reorganization of society in accordance with their own ideological blueprint. Revolutionary movements generally prefer not to use violence, although some of them do (the movements usually turn to violence, in fact, only when the state has already tried to repress them by violent methods of its own). A successful revolutionary movement, such as those that gave birth to the modern United States, Soviet Union, and China, can launch sweeping social and historical change.

Utopian movements are loosely structured collectivities that envision a radically changed and blissful state, either on a large scale at some time in the future, or on a smaller scale in the present. The utopian ideal and the means of achieving it are often vague, but many utopian movements have quite specific programs for social change. Members of these movements often concentrate more on expressive collective behavior than on purposive collective action. The "counterculture" of the sixties and the Hare Krishna sect of the seventies are examples of utopian movements.

Why do people join these various types of social movements? A common assumption is that certain people are psychologically susceptible to the appeal of social movements. In its crudest form, this view implies that there is something "wrong" with people who join social movements: they do so because of their personal frustrations, psychological problems, or deviant tendencies. This approach neglects the possibility that there may be something "wrong" with society, not the people who try to change it. The reason for the emergence of a social movement need not be the same as the reason why people join it. Social movements arise because social conditions create dissatisfaction with existing arrangements. People join specific social movements for an almost infinite variety of reasons—including idealism, altruism, compassion, and practical considerations as well as neurotic frustration.

Social Movements and Social Problems

Social movements play a vital part in the process by which a social problem is brought to public attention. Some undesirable conditions can exist for years or even centuries before they are recognized as social problems. Slavery, the subordination of women, poverty, and pollution were all generally regarded as either unimportant or inevitable until social movements drew these conditions to public attention, mobilized public opinion, and campaigned for change.

The degree of success of a social movement determines not only how the social problem is confronted but also what happens to the movement itself. A number of sociologists (for example, Spector and Kitsuse, 1973) have noted that the interplay of social problems and social movements produces a typical "life cycle" or "natural history" that often ends in either the disappearance or the institutionalization of the movement. In the early stages of the process, there is a growing feeling of discontent over the social condition in question. People become aware that others share their discontent and join together to take collective action. A social movement is born, which tries to bring the problem to public attention and to secure appropriate changes in public policy. The movement soon develops an organizational structure, with leaders and other specialized officials; it also clarifies its ideology and makes specific demands for change. If the movement is successful, it is finally institutionalized, becoming a permanent part of the established order that it originally

Figure 22.10 This picture of child laborers was taken in the United States early in the twentieth century. It gives some idea of the social conditions that the early labor movement crusaded against. Like many social movements, however, the labor movement became more conservative as its original objectives were achieved, and many large unions are now defenders rather than radical critics of the status quo. Social movements and social problems often have an intertwined "life cycle" of this kind.

challenged. Groups that were once spontaneous elements in a collective social movement become formal organizations, complete with bureaucratic structures.

This routinization process is well exemplified by the history of the American labor movement. In the late nineteenth century, American workers were deeply resentful of their low pay, poor working conditions, and lack of the right to form unions. Workers joined together to take collective action, and the labor movement was born. Labor unions emerged, and after many years of tension and violence, they won official recognition from Congress and employers. Many unions grew and prospered, secured many gains for their members, became vast formal organizations, and are now part of the very establishment that the early labor movement set out to attack. The Teamsters' Union, to cite one of the more notorious examples, has a president who enjoys an annual salary of $156,250, an unlimited expense account, and a private jet for his personal use. This particular life cycle of social movements is by no means universal or even typical, however. Most social movements fail in their objectives, and many wither from lack of support in the early stages of their careers. Yet successful social movements, like so many other forms of collective behavior, bring about important social change.

Summary

1. Collective behavior refers to relatively spontaneous and unstructured action by large numbers of people. Social movements collectively attempt to bring about or resist change. Social movements bear many similarities to some forms of collective behavior. Collective behavior and social movements are an important ingredient in social change.

2. Smelser's theory holds that collective behavior can and will take place if six factors are present: structural conduciveness, structural strains, generalized belief, precipitating factors, mobilization for action, and the influence of mechanisms for social control.

3. The content of rumors tends to be shortened and reshaped during the process of transmission. Rumors may be seen as a collective attempt to define an ambiguous situation. The Yippie invasion of Chicago and the "death" of Paul McCartney provide examples of rumors.

4. Fashions are found primarily in modern industrial societies, where they are promoted by commercial interests and used to signal individual status. Fads are short-lived and often provide a means of asserting personal identity.

5. Panics involve irrational and uncoordinated behavior in the face of threat. Some occur in temporary situations of extreme emergency (such as fires), others in more diffuse situations of threat (such as stock-market collapses).

6. Mass hysteria involves contagious anxiety, usually caused by an unfounded belief. Examples are the Martian invasion of earth, the phantom anesthetist of Mattoon, and the Seattle windshield-pitting epidemic.

7. Crowd characteristics include suggestibility, anonymity, spontaneity, and invulnerability. Crowds may be classified as casual crowds, conventional crowds, expressive crowds, or acting crowds. The contagion theory holds that crowd members lose personal identity in crowd situations and are easily influenced by others; the emergent-norms theory holds that crowd behavior involves a collective improvisation of new norms.

8. Mobs are acting crowds bent on violent action; the lynch mob is an example. Riots are destructive collective outbursts but involve less purposive, unified, and structured behavior than mobs. Smelser's theory can be usefully applied to the ghetto riots of the sixties.

9. Publics involve numbers of people with opinions on a controversial issue. Their behavior is more individualistic than those of other forms of collective behavior. Public opinion may be influenced to some extent by advertising and propaganda. Public opinion can be measured by opinion polls, and poll findings may influence public opinion.

10. Social movements may be expressive, reformist, revolutionary, or utopian. They bring social problems to public attention and may thus bring about social change. The "life cycle" of social movements and social problems is often closely interlinked.

Important Terms

collective behavior
social movement
structural conduciveness
structural strains
generalized belief
precipitating factors
mobilization for action
mechanisms of social control
rumor
fashion
fad
panic
mass hysteria
crowd
casual crowd
conventional crowd
expressive crowd
acting crowd
contagion theory
emergent-norms theory
mob
riot
public
public opinion
propaganda
opinion leaders
regressive movements
reform movements
revolutionary movements
utopian movements

Suggested Readings

ASH, ROBERT A. *Social Movements in America.* Chicago: Markham, 1972.

A brief account of social movements in the United States, past and present. The book includes material on the social movements of the sixties.

EVANS, ROBERT R. *Readings in Collective Behavior.* Chicago: Rand McNally, 1969.

A useful anthology of articles on different types of collective behavior and the theories that attempt to explain them. The readings give a good general overview of the field.

SHIBUTANI, TAMOTSU. *Improvised News: A Sociological Study of Rumor.* Indianapolis, Ind.: Bobbs-Merrill, 1966.

A sociological study of rumor, based primarily on research among Japanese Americans who were interned by the federal government in World War II.

SMELSER, NEIL J. *Theory of Collective Behavior.* New York: Free Press, 1962.

A highly influential analysis of various forms in collective behavior. Smelser interprets collective behavior as an attempt by people to alter their social environment.

TURNER, RALPH H., AND LEWIS M. KILLIAN. *Collective Behavior,* 2nd ed. Englewood Cliffs, N.J.: Prentice-Hall, 1972.

A comprehensive treatment of collective behavior. The book includes readings, case studies, and theoretical analysis of a wide range of collective phenomena.

WORSLEY, PETER. *The Trumpet Shall Sound.* London: MacGibbon & Kee, 1957.

An interesting descriptive and analytical account of the various "cargo-cult" movements in the South Pacific. Worsley's account throws light on other, less exotic social movements nearer home.

Reading

Massacre at My Lai *Seymour M. Hersch*

On March 16, 1968, a platoon of American soldiers led by Lieutenant William Calley entered the Vietnamese hamlet of My Lai and systematically murdered several hundred of its inhabitants—most of them women, children, and old men. Although many of the soldiers experienced great guilt and remorse after they had left Vietnam, most of them took part in the massacre of defenseless civilians almost as though it were a routine matter.

This description of the event is a well-documented one, but it is journalistic, not sociological. As you read it, try to apply the sociological concepts you have learned in the chapter (such as emergent-norms theory) to the information Hersch gives, and see if this enhances your understanding. You should know that before the massacre the company was in a very demoralized state; it had lost several of its members through ambushes and booby traps but had never been able to strike back at the enemy.

Some of Calley's men thought it was breakfast time as they walked in; a few families were gathered in front of their homes cooking rice over a small fire. Without a direct order, the first platoon also began rounding up the villagers. There still was no sniper fire, no sign of a large enemy unit. Sledge remembered thinking that "if there were VC around, they had plenty of time to leave before we came in. We didn't tiptoe in there."

The killings began without warning. Harry Stanley told the C.I.D. that one young member of Calley's platoon took a civilian into custody and then "pushed the man up to where we were standing and then stabbed the man in the back with his bayonet . . . The man fell to the ground and was gasping for breath." The GI then "killed him with another bayonet thrust or by shooting him with a rifle. . . ." The youth next "turned to where some soldiers were holding another forty- or fifty-year-old man in custody." He "picked this man up and threw him down a well. Then [he] pulled the pin from a M26 grenade and threw it in after the man." Moments later Stanley saw "some old women and some little children—fifteen or twenty of them—in a group around a temple where some incense was burning. They were kneeling and crying and praying, and various soldiers . . . walked by and executed these women and children by shooting them in the head with their rifles. The soldiers killed all fifteen or twenty of them. . . ."

There were few physical protests from the people; about eighty of them were taken quietly from their homes and herded together in the plaza area. A few hollered out, "No VC. No VC." But that was hardly unexpected. Calley left Meadlo, Boyce and a few others with the responsibility of guarding the group. "You know what I want you to do with them," he told Meadlo. Ten minutes later—about 8:15 A.M.—he returned and asked, "Haven't you got rid of them yet? I want them dead." Radioman Sledge, who was trailing Calley, heard the officer tell Meadlo to "waste them." Meadlo followed orders: "We stood about ten to fifteen feet away from them and then he [Calley] started shooting them. Then he told me to start shooting them. I started to shoot them. So we went ahead and killed them. I used more than a whole clip—used four or five clips." There are seventeen M16 bullets in each clip. Boyce slipped away, to the northern side of the hamlet, glad he hadn't been asked to shoot. Women were huddled against their children, vainly trying to save them. Some continued to chant, "No VC." Others simply said, "No. No. No."

Do Chuc is a gnarled forty-eight-year-old Vietnamese peasant whose two daughters and an aunt were killed by the GIs in My Lai 4 that day. He and his family were eating breakfast when the GIs entered the hamlet and ordered them out of their homes. Together with other villagers, they were marched a few hundred meters into the plaza, where they were told to squat. "Still we had no reason to be afraid," Chuc recalled. "Everyone was calm." He watched as the GIs set up a machine gun. The calm ended. The people began crying and begging. One monk showed his identification papers to a soldier, but the American simply said, "Sorry." Then the shooting started. Chuc was wounded in the leg, but he was covered by dead bodies and thus spared. After waiting an hour, he fled the hamlet. . . .

By this time, there was shooting everywhere. Dennis I. Conti, a GI from Providence, Rhode Island, later explained to C.I.D. investigators what he thought had happened: "We were all psyched up, and as a result, when we got there the shooting started, almost as a chain reaction. The majority of us had expected to meet VC combat troops, but this did not turn out to be so. First we saw a few men running . . . and the next thing I knew we were shooting at everything. Everybody was just firing. After they got in the village, I guess you could say that the men were out of control."

Brooks and his men in the second platoon to the north had begun to systematically ransack the hamlet and slaughter the people, kill the livestock and destroy the crops. Men poured rifle and machine-gun fire into huts without knowing—or seemingly caring—who was inside.

Roy Wood, one of Calley's men who was working next to Brooks' platoon, stormed into a hut, saw an elderly man hiding inside along with his wife and two young daughters: "I hit him with my rifle and pushed him out." A GI from Brooks' platoon, standing by with an M79 grenade launcher, asked to borrow his gun. Wood refused, and the soldier asked another platoon mate. He got the weapon, said, "Don't let none of them live," and shot the Vietnamese in the head. "These mothers are crazy," Wood remembered thinking. "Stand right in front of us and blow a man's brains out." Later he vomited when he saw more of the dead residents of My Lai 4.

Carter testified that soon after the third platoon moved in, a woman was sighted. Somebody knocked her down, and then, Carter said, "Medina shot her with his M16 rifle. I was fifty or sixty feet away and saw this. There was no reason to shoot this girl." The men continued on, making sure no one was escaping. "We came to where the soldiers had collected fifteen or more Vietnamese men, women and children in a group. Medina said, 'Kill every one. Leave no one standing.' " A machine gunner began firing into the group. Moments later one of Medina's radio operators slowly "passed among them and finished them off." . . .

Roberts and Haeberle also moved in just behind the third platoon. Haeberle watched a group of ten to fifteen GIs methodically pump bullets into a cow until it keeled over. A woman then poked her head out from behind some brush; she may have been hiding in a bunker. The GIs turned their fire from the cow to the woman. "They just kept shooting at her. You could see the bones flying in the air chip by chip." No one had attempted to question her; GIs inside the hamlet also were asking no questions. Before moving on, the photographer took a picture of the dead woman. Haeberle took many more pictures that day; he saw about thirty GIs kill at least a hundred Vietnamese civilians. . . .

Haeberle noticed a man and two small children walking toward a group of GIs: "They just kept walking toward us . . . you could hear the little girl saying, 'No, no . . .' All of a sudden the GIs opened up and cut them down." Later he watched a machine gunner suddenly open fire on a group of civilians—women, children and babies—who had been collected in a big circle: "They were trying to run. I don't know how many got out." He saw a GI with an M16 rifle fire at two young boys walking along a road. The older of the two—about seven or eight years old—fell over the first to protect him. The GIs kept on firing until both were dead. . . .

Now it was nearly nine o'clock and all of Charlie Company was in My Lai 4. Most families were being shot inside their homes, or just outside the doorways. Those who had tried to flee were crammed by GIs into the many bunkers built throughout the hamlet for protection—once the bunkers became filled, hand grenades were lobbed in. Everything became a target. Gary Garfolo borrowed someone's M79 grenade launcher and fired it point-blank at a water buffalo: "I hit that sucker right in the head; went down like a shot. You don't get to shoot water buffalo with an M79 every day." Others fired the weapon into the bunkers full of people. . . .

Carter recalled that some GIs were shouting and yelling during the massacre: "The boys enjoyed it. When someone laughs and jokes about what they're doing, they have to be enjoying it." A GI said, "Hey, I got me another one." Another said, "Chalk up one for me." Even Captain Medina was having a good time, Carter thought: "You can tell when someone enjoys their work." Few members of Charlie Company protested that day. For the most part, those who didn't like what was going on kept their thoughts to themselves. . . .

At one point in the morning one of the members of Medina's CP joined in the shooting. "A woman came out of a hut with a baby in her arms and she was crying," Carter told the C.I.D. "She was crying because her little boy had been in front of their hut and . . . someone had killed the child by shooting it." When the mother came into view, one of Medina's men "shot her with an M16 and she fell. When she fell, she dropped the baby." The GI next "opened up on the baby with his M16." The infant was also killed. Carter also saw an officer grab a woman by the hair and shoot her with a .45-caliber pistol: "He held her by the hair for a minute and then let go and she fell to the ground. Some enlisted man standing there said, 'Well, she'll be in the big rice paddy in the sky.' "

One of the helicopters was piloted by Chief Warrant Officer Hugh C. Thompson of Decatur, Georgia. He began seeing wounded and dead Vietnamese civilians all over the hamlet, with no sign of an enemy force. . . . The pilot thought that the best thing he could do would be to mark the location of wounded civilians with smoke so that the GIs on the ground could move over and begin treating some of them. "The first one that I marked was a girl that was wounded," Thompson testified, "and they came over and walked up to her, put their weapon on automatic and let her have it." The man who did the shooting was a captain, Thompson said. Later he identified the officer as Ernest Medina.

Hugh Thompson's nightmare had only begun with the shooting of the girl. He flew north back over the hamlet and saw a small boy bleeding along a trench. Again he marked the spot so that the GIs below could provide some medical aid. Instead, he saw a lieutenant casually walk up and empty a clip into the child. He saw yet another wounded youngster; again he marked it, and this time it was a sergeant who came up and fired his M16 at the child.

"I kept flying around and across a ditch . . . and it . . . had a bunch of bodies in it and I don't know how they got in the ditch. But I saw some of them were still alive." Thompson was almost frantic. He landed his small helicopter near the ditch, and asked a soldier there if he could help the people out: "He said the only way he could help them was to help them out of their misery. . . ." He then saw Calley and the first platoon. . . . "I asked him if he could get the women and kids out of there before they tore it [the bunker] up, and he said the only way he could get them out was to use hand grenades. 'You just hold your men right here,' " the angry Thompson told the equally angry Calley, " 'and I will get the women and kids out.' "

Before climbing out of his aircraft, Thompson ordered Colburn and his crew chief to stay alert. "He told us that if any of the Americans opened up on the Vietnamese, we should open up on the Americans," Colburn said. Thompson walked back to the ship and called in two helicopter gunships to rescue the civilians. While waiting for them to land, Colburn said, "He stood between our troops and the bunker. He was shielding the people with his body. He just wanted to get those people out of here." Calley did nothing to stop Thompson, but later stormed up to Sledge, his radioman, and complained that the pilot "doesn't like the way I'm running the show, but I'm the boss."

One further incident stood out in many GIs' minds: seconds after the shooting stopped, a bloodied but unhurt two-year-old boy miraculously crawled out of the ditch, crying. He began running toward the hamlet. Someone hollered, "There's a kid." There was a long pause. Then Calley ran back, grabbed the child, threw him back in the ditch and shot him.

There were some small acts of mercy. A GI placed a blanket over the body of a mutilated child. An elderly woman was spared when some GIs hollered at a soldier just as he was about to shoot her. Grzesik remembered watching a GI seem to wrestle with his conscience while holding a bayonet over a wounded old man. "He wants to stab somebody with a bayonet," Grzesik thought. The GI hesitated . . . and finally passed on, leaving the old man to die.

Some GIs, however, didn't hesitate to use their bayonets. Nineteen-year-old Nguyen Thi Ngoc Tuyet watched a baby trying to open her slain mother's blouse to nurse. A soldier shot the infant while it was struggling with the blouse, and then slashed at it with his bayonet. Tuyet also said she saw another baby hacked to death by GIs wielding their bayonets.

By nightfall the Viet Cong were back in My Lai 4, helping the survivors bury the dead. It took five days. Most of the funeral speeches were made by the Communist guerrillas. Nguyen Bat was not a Communist at the time of the massacre, but the incident changed his mind. "After the shooting," he said, "all the villagers became Communists."

When Army investigators reached the barren area in November, 1969, in connection with the My Lai probe in the United States, they found mass graves at three sites, as well as a ditch full of bodies. It was estimated that between 450 and 500 people—most of them women, children and old men—had been slain and buried there.

Source: Seymour M. Hersch, *My Lai 4: A Report on the Massacre and Its Aftermath* (New York: Vintage, 1970), pp. 49–75.

CHAPTER 23 Social Change

CHAPTER OUTLINE

Theories of Social Change
Evolutionary Theories
Cyclical Theories
Functionalist Theories
Conflict Theories

Some Sources of Change
The Physical Environment
Ideas
Technology
Population
"Events"
Cultural Innovation
Human Action

Conclusion
Prospects for a General Theory
Interacting Factors in Social Change
Predicting the Future

"Everything changes," observed the ancient Greek philosopher Heraclitus. It was he who pointed out that a man cannot step twice into the same river—for he is not quite the same man, nor is it quite the same river. This principle applies to every phenomenon known to us, from the behavior of subatomic particles to the expansion of the universe, from the growth and decay of living organisms to changes in individual psychology. Societies, as we are only too well aware in the modern world, also change. We have pointed to these changes throughout this book, placing particular emphasis on the social transformation that accompanies industrialization (see Chapter 4, Society, and Chapter 18, The Economic Order). Yet, although social change is a central concern of sociology, the question of how, why, and in what ways societies change remains one of the most intriguing and difficult problems in the discipline.

Social change is the alteration in patterns of social structure, social institutions, and social behavior over time. No society can successfully resist change, not even those that try to do so, although some societies are more resistant to change than others. But the rate, nature, and direction of change differ greatly from one society to another. In the last two hundred years, the United States has changed from a predominantly agricultural society into a highly urbanized and industrialized one. In the same period, the society of the BaMbuti pygmies of the Central African forests has changed hardly at all. Why? In all but the most inhospitable parts of the world we find the ruins of great civilizations. What caused them to flourish, and what caused them to collapse? Why did civilization arise in India long before it appeared in Europe? Why did industrialism arise in Europe rather than in India? Does social change take place in a random, haphazard manner, or are recurrent patterns to be found in different societies? Why is change abrupt or far-reaching in some societies but slow or insignificant in others? Are all human societies moving toward a common destiny and similar social forms, or will they differ in the future as much as they have in the past?

These are important questions, and they are as old as sociology itself. The man who first coined the term "sociology," Auguste Comte, believed that the new science could lay bare the processes of social change and thus make it possible to plan the human future in a rational way. Almost without exception, the most distinguished sociologists of the nineteenth and twentieth centuries have grappled with the problem of social change. But it must be confessed that sociology has, so far, failed to fully overcome the challenge of explaining social change. Many theories have been offered, but none has won general acceptance. As Wilbert E. Moore (1960) comments: "The mention of 'theory of social change' will make most social scientists appear defensive, furtive, guilt-ridden, or frightened."

Why does the study of social change present such problems? There are two basic reasons. The first is that the understanding of social change, or *dynamics,* logically involves an understanding of social order and stability, or *statics.* We cannot know precisely why or how societies change until we know precisely why and how they form relatively stable units in the first place (Parsons, 1951; Moore, 1960). We know that societies—which consist of many different individuals and often of many very different groups—tend to "hang together," or to be integrated. But we still have no generally accepted theory of why this should be so—of why a society should not simply disintegrate into its component parts. Again, many theories have been proposed—such as the functional need of people for one another, the political authority of the state, the inborn sociability of our species, or the existence of shared values that "glue" a society together. None of these theories, however, seems to offer a really satisfactory explanation of why societies are generally orderly and stable. Social order and social change are closely linked, and it is unlikely that we can fully understand the latter without a fully developed theory of the former.

The second reason for the difficulty of developing a general theory is that social change involves such complex and varied factors. If any sample of pure water is heated to 100 degrees centigrade at sea level, it will boil. We can identify heat as the cause of the change, and we can predict that the same thing will happen in all similar circumstances in the future. Changes in human societies are not so easily investigated. Each society is unique, and any changes that take place are likely to result from a whole complex of interacting factors—environmental, technological, personal, cultural, political, religious, economic, and so on. To discover the cause or causes of change is therefore very difficult indeed—especially as we cannot "rerun" history or conduct laboratory experiments in large-scale social change to test our theories. And because each society is unique, we must be hesitant about using the experiences of one society as the basis for confident predictions about changes in another.

These problems are not impossible to overcome; they are merely difficult. In principle, we should be able to understand social change. It is a basic assumption of science that all events have causes. If this were not so, the social and physical world would be unintelligible to us. Sociology is still an infant science, dealing with a very complicated subject, but we already have a good, if partial and tentative, understanding of the processes of social change. In this chapter we will consider two major topics: first, some general theories of social change, and second, some specific factors that can cause social changes. Finally, we will review the present state of our understanding and assess the prospects for predicting social change in the future.

Theories of Social Change

A number of general theories of social change have been proposed, not only by sociologists but also by historians and anthropologists, for all three disciplines have a common interest in social change. The various theories may be grouped conveniently into four main categories: evolutionary, cyclical, functional, and conflict theories. The study of these theories, incidentally, gives us an interesting insight into the sociology of knowledge and belief. Each type of theory won acceptance because it fitted so well with popular assumptions that prevailed at the time the theory was offered.

Evolutionary Theories

Evolutionary theories are based on the assumption that societies gradually change from simple beginnings into ever more complex forms. This assumption rests on both cross-cultural and historical evidence. We know from the cross-cultural evidence that there have been and still are many small-scale, simple societies, such as those of hunters and gatherers, horticulturalists, and pastoralists. We know from the historical evidence that many small, simple societies have grown steadily larger, and some of them have been transformed into the huge industrial societies of the modern world. But how is this evidence to be interpreted?

The Early Theorists: Unilinear Evolution

Early sociologists, beginning with Auguste Comte, believed that human societies evolve in a *unilinear* way—that is, in "one line" of development that recurs in every society. These thinkers also made an assumption that was very radical at the time, although it is familiar to us today: that social "change" meant "progress" toward something better. They saw change as positive and beneficial, because the evolutionary process implied that societies would necessarily reach new and higher levels of civilization.

The middle and late nineteenth century was an era of colonial expansion, in which soldiers, missionaries, merchants, and adventurers from European countries penetrated distant lands whose peoples had been almost unknown in Europe. The new science of anthropology arose, dedicated to the study of the exotic, "primitive" peoples whose cultures were described in letters and books by the early colonists. Few of the early anthropologists, however, engaged in actual field work among the peoples they studied. Anthropology was mainly an "armchair" discipline that relied on the reports—often inaccurate and sometimes irresponsibly imaginative—of untrained observers in other parts of the world. Working primarily from this kind of information, a number of early anthropologists argued that there was a universal evolutionary process. They claimed that all societies passed through a number of stages, begining in primitive origins and climaxing in Western civilization. Lewis Henry Morgan, for example, believed that there were three basic stages in the process: savagery, barbarism, and civilization.

Figure 23.1 This nineteenth century painting of America's "manifest destiny" captures some of the ethnocentric but popular beliefs of the time. It was generally accepted that "change" meant "progress," and that progress was inevitable. The westward advance of "civilization" across the American continent was seen as a matter of destiny, and the destruction of the native American cultures was regarded as unavoidable and necessary.

This evolutionary view of social change drew much of its impetus from Charles Darwin's book *On the Origin of Species,* published in 1859. Darwin had shown that all life forms had evolved from distant origins and that the general direction of biological evolution was toward greater complexity. Other writers immediately applied this theory to human society. If human beings had evolved from some primitive state, it followed that at some time in the past they must have been entirely without culture. The cultures of different societies around the world offered glimpses of what culture must have been like at different stages of the evolutionary process. In this view, the most primitive cultures and peoples were the closest to the original state of the human species, while the cultures and peoples of Western societies were the most advanced.

Herbert Spencer, a sociologist, carried this Darwinian analogy to its outmost limits. He argued that society itself constituted an organism, with its different parts playing roles similar to those of the different organs and limbs of an animal. Spencer even applied Darwin's principle of "the survival of the fittest" to human societies. He claimed that Western "races," classes, or societies had survived and evolved because they were better adapted to face the conditions of life. This view, known as *social Darwinism,* won extraordinarily wide acceptance in the late nineteenth century. It survived in both Europe and the United States until World War I, and was used to justify the dominance of whites over nonwhites, of the rich over the poor, and of the powerful over the weak.

Figure 23.2 The evolutionary theorists of the nineteenth century assumed that all societies evolve in the same unilinear manner through a series of "stages," culminating in Western civilization. As the ethnographic evidence from preindustrial societies mounted, however, it became clear that no such sequence of stages exists. These "primitive" people in the southwestern Pacific, for example, are being introduced directly to Western culture, thereby skipping the various "stages" that, according to this evolutionary theory, they should pass through.

Evaluation

It is easy to see why these early evolutionary doctrines were so readily accepted. The discovery of so many "primitive" peoples whose cultures differed so radically from those of Europe and North America posed a difficult question: why were some societies more "advanced" than others? Evolutionary theory provided not only an answer but also a flattering and convenient justification for colonial rule over "lesser peoples." There was little concept of cultural relativity at the time. People judged other cultures purely in terms of their own culture's standards and, not surprisingly, found them inferior. The ethnocentric belief that all human societies were evolving in a unilinear way toward one crowning achievement—Western civilization—provided an ideology that legitimized the political and economic interest of the colonizers. The enforced spread of Western culture was conveniently thought of as "the white man's burden"—the thankless but noble task of bringing "higher" forms of civilization to "inferior" peoples.

One problem with evolutionary theories of this unilinear type is that they described but did not explain social change. They offered no convincing explanation of how or why societies should evolve toward the Western pattern. A second and fatal problem is that they were based on faulty interpretations of the data. Different theorists grouped vastly different cultures into misleading categories so that they would fit into the various "stages" of evolution. The trends in Western civilization were ethnocentrically equated with "progress," largely because only one aspect of change—technological and economic development—was emphasized. Other peoples might regard Western cultures as more technologically developed yet morally backward, but the evolutionary theorists never considered this more relativistic view. Later systematic gathering of ethnographic data from traditional societies soon showed that they did not follow the same step-by-step evolutionary sequence. They developed in different ways, often by borrowing ideas and innovations from other societies. The San ("Bushmen") of the Kalahari and the aborigines of Australia, for example, are among the most supposedly "primitive" peoples in the world. Yet they are being introduced directly to industrial society, and are thus skipping the "stages" that, according to evolutionary theory, they should first pass through. By the 1920s, unilinear evolutionary theory in sociology and anthropology was dead as the dodo.

A Modern View: Multilinear Evolution

More recently, however, anthropologists have again developed an interest in social and cultural evolution. But this time they see the process as a *tendency*, not a universal "law," and they do not press the analogy between societies and living organisms. They point out, however, that societies generally tend to move from small-scale, simple forms of social organization to large-scale, complex forms. Modern anthropologists (for example, Steward, 1956) agree that this evolutionary process is *multilinear*. In other words, it can take place in many different ways and change does not necessarily follow exactly the same direction in every society. Unlike earlier theorists, modern anthropologists no longer believe that "change" necessarily means "progress." They do not assume that greater social complexity produces greater human happiness. This view, much more tentative than that of the early evolutionists, is now gradually finding its way into the mainstream of anthropological and sociological thought (for example, Lenski, 1966a; Lenski and Lenski, 1974; Fried, 1967; Parsons, 1966).

Cyclical Theories

The senseless slaughter of World War I and the growing signs of social disorganization and unrest in the industrial societies early in this century led many people to wonder whether social "change" really meant social "progress" after all. New theories of social change were now proposed—theories that focused instead on the *cyclical* nature of change as displayed in the rise and fall of civilizations. The assumption that Western civilization was the crowning achievement of history was questioned. Might not our civilization be destined, like all previous civilizations, to extinction? And if so, what forces were responsible for these cycles of change?

Figure 23.3 Cyclical theories of social change focus on the rise and fall of civilizations, attempting to discover and account for these patterns of growth and decay. This picture shows the ancient Inca city of Machu Pichu in Peru. Located on an isolated 8000-foot-high mountaintop in the Andes, it was deserted by its inhabitants several centuries ago, for reasons that are not known. The city remained "lost" until it was discovered in 1911.

Spengler: The Destiny of Civilizations

In 1918, a German schoolteacher, Oswald Spengler, published *The Decline of the West.* His sweeping, poetic account of the rise and fall of civilizations won wide readership and acclaim. The fate of civilizations, Spengler declared, was a matter of "destiny." Each civilization is like a biological organism and has a similar life cycle: birth, maturity, old age, and death. All creative activity takes place in the early stages of the cycle; as the civilization matures it loses its original inspiration, becomes more materialistic, and declines. Spengler studied eight major civilizations, including that of the West. He concluded that Western societies were entering a period of decay—as evidenced by wars, conflict, and social breakdown—that heralded their doom (Spengler, 1926; originally published 1918, 1922). Spengler's theory is out of fashion today. Although no sociologist would be so foolish as to reject the possibility that Western civilization and the societies that share it might ultimately be doomed, "destiny" is hardly an adequate explanation of social change. Spengler's biological analogy is clearly pushed too far, and his work is too mystical and speculative.

Toynbee: Challenge and Response

A somewhat more promising theory was offered by Arnold Toynbee, a British historian with considerable sociological insight. His multivolume work, *A Study of History* (1946), draws on material from twenty-one civilizations. Toynbee set out to discover and account for recurrent patterns in the rise and fall of civilizations. The key concepts in Toynbee's theory are those of "challenge" and "response." Every society faces challenges—at first, challenges posed by the environment; later, challenges from internal and external enemies. The nature of the responses determines the society's fate. The achievements of a civilization consist of its successful responses to challenges; if it cannot mount an effective response, it dies. Toynbee's work is more optimistic than Spengler's, for he does not believe that all civilizations will inevitably decay. History, he argues, is a series of cycles of decay and growth, but each new civilization is able to learn from the mistakes and to borrow from cultures of others. It is therefore possible for each new cycle to offer higher levels of achievement. Unlike Spengler's cycles, Toynbee's cycles build upon one another—rather like a circular staircase. His arguments, however, are not very persuasive. Toynbee uses a large number of illustrations to support his theme, but he uses them selectively and has been accused of ignoring counter-examples. He never fully explains why some societies mount effective responses to their challenges while others do not, or why a society should overcome one challenge but succumb to another. Few sociologists—or historians, for that matter—believe that the complexity of human history and social change can be explained through Toynbee's theory.

Sorokin: "Sensate" and "Ideational" Culture

The Russian American sociologist, Pitirim Sorokin, made another attempt at a cyclical theory of social change. In his book *Social and Cultural Dynamics* (1937), Sorokin argues that Western civilization has always fluctuated between two cultural extremes, the "sensate" and the "ideational." Sensate culture emphasizes those things which can be perceived directly by the senses: it is practical, hedonistic, sensual, and materialistic. Ideational culture emphasizes those things that can be perceived only by the mind: it is abstract, religious, concerned with faith and ultimate truth. Sorokin believed that no society ever fully conforms to either type. For reasons that he never makes quite clear, too much emphasis on one type of culture leads to a reaction toward the other. Between the two lies a third type, "idealistic" culture. This is a happy and desirable blend of the other two, but no society ever seems to have achieved it as a stable condition. Again, this theory has won little support from sociologists. Sorokin's prejudices show through too clearly. He is obviously disgusted by modern society, which he believed to be in an "overripe" sensate condition, and he displays a nostalgic yearning for medieval society, which he believed was primarily ideational. His concepts of sensate and ideational culture are purely subjective, and he neglects evidence that conflicts with his theory. Furthermore, his theory is again purely speculative and descriptive: he offers no convincing account of how or why social change should take this form.

Evaluation

Cyclical theories of social change may at first seem attractive because they deal with an observed historical fact: all civilizations of the past have risen and fallen. But this does not mean that historical and social change is necessarily cyclical. The fact that the sun has risen and set every day in recorded history gives us good reason to suppose that it will do so again tomorrow. Changes in human societies, however, are not subject to such inexorable "laws"—or if they are, the cyclical theorists have failed to discover them. To say that cyclical changes are caused by a tendency for change to occur in cycles explains nothing: it is like explaining the movement of an automobile in terms of its "automotive tendency." Cyclical theories also place too much emphasis on mysterious forces such as "destiny" and too little emphasis on human action. If, as is conceivable, a human society were to develop both the knowledge and the means necessary to control and direct social change, what would become of these supposedly inevitable cycles?

Functionalist Theories

Functionalist theories of social change start with the advantage that they deal with social statics before dealing with social dynamics. In the opinion of some critics, however, their very emphasis on social order and stability has prevented them from giving an adequate theory of social change (for example, Mills, 1959; Dahrendorf, 1958).

The functionalist perspective was introduced into modern sociology by Emile Durkheim, who examined several aspects of society by asking what function they played in maintaining the social order as a whole. Religion, he found, had the function of providing a common set of values that enhanced the social solidarity of the believers; the schools had the function of passing culture from one generation to the next. The American sociologist Talcott Parsons, drawing on the work of Durkheim and other early European sociologists—but not Marx—has tried to develop a general theory of social order based on the functionalist perspective.

Parsons' Theory of Social Order

Parsons' writings are highly abstract and make singularly difficult reading. The basic idea of his early writings, however, is not very complex. In brief, Parsons (1937, 1951) argued that a society consists of interdependent parts, each of which contributes to the maintenance of order and stability in the system as a whole. Society is able to absorb disruptive forces and to maintain overall stability because it is constantly straining for *equilibrium,* or balance. Cultural patterns, particularly shared norms and values, hold the society together. Because these patterns are inherently conservative, they also serve to resist radical changes.

The focus of Parsons' early writings was thus on social statics, not social dynamics. In his major work, *The Social System* (1951), Parsons devoted only one chapter to social change, which he saw as something that must be "introduced into the system." His approach thus failed to account for change: how could disruptions, even revolutions, occur in this stable, self-regulating system? Moreover, changes tended to be regarded as dysfunctions, as unwelcome irritants that disturbed the smooth functioning of the social system.

Throughout the forties and fifties, Parsons' work dominated American sociology. American society was enjoying a period of relative cohesion and stability, and Parsons' emphasis on society as a balanced system that integrated small yet necessary changes won wide acceptance. But the major social conflict in the United States in the late fifties and throughout the sixties raised many doubts about Parsons' assumptions. C. Wright Mills and other sociologists (for example, Lockwood, 1956) questioned whether a theory of equilibrium and stability was relevant to societies that were in a state of constant change and social conflict. In his later writings, Parsons (1961, 1966) confronted this problem and attempted to include social change in his functionalist model.

Parsons' Theory of Social Change

Parsons now sees change not as something that disturbs the social equilibrium but as something that alters the state of the equilibrium so that a qualitatively new equilibrium results. He acknowledges that changes may arise from two sources. They may come either from outside the society, through contact with other societies, or they may come from inside the society, through adjustments that must be made to resolve strains within the system.

Parsons also adopts what amounts to an evolutionary perspective on social change and tries to account for the changes that take place as a society becomes progressively more complex in its social organization. Two processes, he argues, are at work. In simple societies, institutions are undifferentiated: that is, a single institution serves many different functions. The family, for example, is responsible for reproduction, education, economic production, and socialization. As a society becomes more complex, a process of *differentiation* takes place. Different institutions, such as schools and corporations, emerge and take over the functions that were previously undifferentiated within a single institution. But the new institutions must be linked together once more, this time by the process of *integration*. New norms, for example, must evolve to govern the relationship between the school and the home, and "bridging institutions," such as law courts, must resolve conflicts between other components in the system.

Evaluation

Parsons has rather neatly taken account of social change while keeping intact his emphasis on social equilibrium and stability. His work is now an ambitious attempt to explain both social statics and social dynamics, although his focus is still overwhelmingly on the former. Parsons' model remains limited, however, in that it does not presume to cover all possible forms of social change. It deals only with the institutional changes that take place as a society modernizes. Other functionalists have tried to overcome this difficulty by pointing out that there are strains and dysfunctions even in the most harmonious social system and that these tensions may cause social changes of many types. Robert Merton (1968), for example, writes of the "strain, tension, contradiction, and discrepancy between the component parts of social structure" that may lead to changes. In so doing, however, he is borrowing concepts from conflict theories of change.

Figure 23.4 Conflict theorists see tensions and competition as a major source of social change. Thus conflict between capitalists and workers in the United States has led to many changes in industrial organization and working conditions. This engraving shows an 1892 battle between workers and agents hired by the employers.

Conflict Theories

Karl Marx declared that "violence is the midwife of history." In a similar vein, Mao wrote that "change comes from the barrel of a gun." The conflict theory of change, of which Marx is the most prominent and eloquent exponent, holds that change is caused by tensions between competing interests in society.

Marx: Change Through Class Conflict

"All history," Marx and Engels wrote in *The Communist Manifesto* (1848), "is the history of class conflict." Marx believed that the character of social and cultural forms is influenced by the economic base of society—specifically, by the mode of production that is used and by the relationships that exist between those who own and those who do not own the means of production. History is the story of conflict between the exploiting and the exploited classes. This conflict repeats itself again and again until capitalism is overthrown by the workers and a socialist state is created. Socialism is the forerunner to the ultimate social form, communism. Marx's theories have been dealt with in several previous chapters and need not be elaborated here. The essential point is that Marx and other conflict theorists after him see society as fundamentally dynamic, not static. They regard conflict as a normal, not an abnormal process, and they believe that the existing conditions in any society contain the seeds of future social changes.

Other Conflicts as Sources of Change

Later Marxist writers kept Marx's emphasis on class conflict as the source of social change, but other conflict theorists, although influenced by Marx, have focused on conflict between groups other than social classes. An early German sociologist, Georg Simmel (1904, 1955), pointed out that conflict is a permanent feature of society, not just an occasional or temporary event. Simmel regarded conflict as a process that binds people together in interaction. Although hate and envy may drive people apart, they cannot enter into conflict without interacting with their opponents. Moreover, conflict encourages people of similar interests to bind together to achieve their objectives. In this way, Simmel argued, continuous conflict keeps a society dynamic and changing. Ralf Dahrendorf (1958) regards the view that "all history is the history of class conflict" as an "unjustifiable oversimplification." He points to conflicts between racial groups, between nations, between political parties, and between religious groups as examples of conflict involving units other than social classes. All these conflicts, he believes, can lead to social changes.

Evaluation

Conflict over values and scarce resources is clearly a cause of social change. Conflict theory does not account for all forms of social change, but it does give us a means of analyzing some of the most significant changes in history and contemporary society. It can be applied, for example, to the overthrow of feudalism and its replacement by capitalist industrialism, or to the civil rights movement in the United States and recent changes in our patterns of race relations. Yet it is not a comprehensive theory of social change. Conflict theory cannot, for example, tell us why technology is having such a dramatic effect on the rate of social change in the United States. It cannot tell us why forms of family organization are changing. Above all, it cannot tell us much about the future direction of social change—and that is the acid test of a fully satisfactory theory. Even hard-line Marxists have been unable to predict successfully the countries or the periods in which socialist revolutions will occur, although they are able to provide plausible explanations of similar changes in the past. But a fully satisfactory theory must do more than explain history. It must also give us sufficient understanding of social dynamics for us to be able to predict, at least in broad outline, the future implications of present trends.

Some Sources of Change

When we move from the realm of general theory to the problem of finding the specific sources of social changes, our task becomes somewhat easier. There are a number of specific factors that, in their interaction with other factors, may generate changes in all societies. The precise nature and direction of the changes, however, depend very much on the unique conditions of the place and time in which they occur.

The Physical Environment

As we saw in Chapter 3 (Culture), the physical environment has a strong influence on the culture and social structure of a society. People living in mountainous regions must obviously evolve social forms different from those of people living in arid deserts or on tropical islands. The society and culture of Eskimos differ from those of Arab nomads in ways that are clearly related to the environments in which the two peoples live. The environment thus sets limits on the kinds of social changes that can occur. The Australian aborigines live on a continent that had no indigenous animals suitable for domestication and virtually no indigenous plants suitable for systematic cultivation. It is hardly surprising, therefore, that they remained hunters and gatherers and did not become a pastoral, horticultural, or agricultural society. Even in the most advanced industrial societies, which are able to make significant changes in the natural environment, the environment still sets limits. We now realize, for example, that the limited capacity of the environment to tolerate pollution may restrict future industrial growth.

The physical environment, then, may influence the character of a society and its culture, and it may set limits on some forms of social change. But this is not the same as *causing* change. Social change that is directly caused by environmental factors is in fact quite rare. Severe earthquakes, floods, volcanic eruptions, or droughts may cause changes in population structure or may even provoke migrations, but major environmental changes usually take place too slowly to have much impact on social life. Many environmental changes are actually caused by human action: much of the desert of North Africa and the land erosion of the Andes was caused by human interference in the ecology of these regions.

Most environmental influences on social change result from an interaction between social and environmental forces. Societies that have been located at geographic crossroads—such as those at the land bridge between Europe, Asia, and Africa—have always been centers of social change. Societies that have been geographically isolated have tended to change less. It is no accident that the most "primitive" peoples of the world have lived in geographic isolation from other societies. The interaction of social and environmental factors undoubtedly generates social change, but environmental factors on their own rarely do so.

Ideas

What role do ideas, particularly belief systems or *ideologies,* play in social change? This question raises one of the oldest controversies in sociology. Karl Marx, who first raised the problem, argued strongly that social conditions shape people's ideologies, not the other way around. In his view, it is not the ideology of socialism that makes workers resent the oppression of capitalism; it is the oppression of capitalism that makes workers embrace the ideology of socialism. Similarly, Marx saw the ideology of capitalism as nothing more than an attempt to justify the capitalist system. Capitalism itself had been created not by an ideology but by the social forces that had overthrown feudalism and generated a new mode of production.

As we noted in Chapter 16 (Religion), Max Weber contested this view. He argued that the "Protestant ethic" of hard work and deferred gratification had spurred the development of the capitalist system. The failure of other, non-Western societies to develop capitalism, he believed, was partly due to their lack of a similar ideology. Weber thus gave ideas a much greater role in causing social change than did Marx. Durkheim took a broadly similar view. He accepted that ideas derive from social conditions but believed that they could then become independent "social facts" that could act back on society and cause social change.

There can be no question that ideologies are derived from social conditions and that people generally tend to accept belief systems that they believe, rightly or wrongly, conform to their own interests. In this sense Marx was correct. But it seems that Weber and Durkheim were equally correct in their view that ideas can also have a causal influence: that they can become "detached," as it were, from the social conditions in which they originally arose and can then have an independent effect on social action.

For example, Hinduism, a religious ideology, arose in a caste-based society and served to justify social inequality. This ideology is still influential in India, although it is inappropriate for a society that is attempting to modernize. The ban on artificial birth control by the Catholic church, the Seventh-Day Adventists, and other Christian groups stems ultimately from the stern morality of the ancient Israelites. The Israelites were a small people surrounded by enemies, and they placed high value on large families. This value was transmitted to Christianity and disapproval of artificial birth control eventually became part of the official doctrine of several churches, even though the origins of the value had been forgotten. The belief that birth control is somehow immoral is inappropriate, however, in developing nations where resources are limited and population is rocketing. Failure to introduce effective birth control methods will inevitably lead to major social changes in these countries, including changes caused by mass poverty and even mass starvation.

Ideas, often expressed in slogans, have been an important ingredient in many social changes. The cry for "Liberty, equality, fraternity" in the French Revolution influenced political events in that country and in many others. The concept of "the brotherhood of man" was used by those who wished to abolish slavery in the United States and elsewhere. Appeals to the ideal of "democracy" and "civil rights" helped swing American public opinion in favor of extending the vote to women and to blacks. Yet none of these ideas existed in a vacuum; they were influential only in the context of other social forces.

Ideas are a particularly important element in social change in countries that are oriented to change as a way of life. The reason is that we try to shape the future in terms of our ideologies and our concepts of what the future should be like. Our ideas determine what we regard as needs, and we take social action to bring about the changes necessary to meet those needs. This is precisely what is happening in the less developed countries, which are attempting to modernize along the lines of the advanced industrial societies.

Technology

As we saw in Chapter 17 (Science), technology is a major source of social change. The more advanced a society's technology, the more rapid social change tends to be. As William F. Ogburn (1950) pointed out, technological change tends to be followed by changes in other parts of the social system, although there may be a *culture lag* while the other parts adjust. Technological innovations are usually accepted quite readily if they are obviously useful, but social norms and other cultural arrangements are more conservative and adjust much more slowly to changed material conditions.

A classic example of the effects of technological innovation, many of them unanticipated, is the introduction of the automobile to American society. Cars were initially used by the leisure class for recreation and for the ostentatious display of wealth. Their practical value was soon recognized, however, and Henry Ford used mass-production techniques to make them available to ordinary American families. The car has since become one of the most prominent features of the American landscape, with social effects that are almost impossible to calculate.

The automobile industry has become the largest single industry in the United States. The assembly line, first developed in the auto industry, has been duplicated in thousands of other manufacturing processes. Huge multinational corporations have emerged to produce millions of cars each year. New supportive industries have arisen to supply the raw materials for the manufacturing process. The petroleum industry has become a critical factor in

Figure 23.5 Technological change can be a major source of social change. A classic example is the introduction of the automobile to American society. Although the automobile was something of a curiosity in 1914, Henry Ford used mass-production techniques to make cars available to millions of Americans. The effects have been enormous. This innovation has not only changed the face of the landscape, but has also had incalculable social and economic effects. Most of these effects were not foreseen, and many of them were unwanted.

national and international politics and economics. A national system of roads and highways has been created at huge expense, linking communities and facilitating travel in a way that the railroad could never have achieved. Elaborate traffic laws have become necessary, and tens of thousands of Americans are killed in road accidents every year. Cities have become congested with traffic, and urban settlement patterns have drastically changed. New suburbs have been developed, whose residents commute by car to work in cities. The cities, faced with the loss of local taxes as the middle class flees to the suburbs, have been thrown into financial crisis. Motels and gas stations line the roads and highways, and drive-in banks, movies, and churches have appeared. Leisure and dating patterns have changed. Air pollution from auto exhausts has become a major problem, and diseases such as emphysema and lung cancer, whose incidence is closely related to air pollution, have become far more common. Few of these changes were anticipated and few of them were desired, but all can be traced directly or indirectly to a single technological innovation.

Population

Any significant increase or decrease in population size or population growth rates may disrupt social life. A population that grows too large puts impossible demands on resources. The result, as so often in history, may be mass migration, usually resulting in cultural diffusion and sometimes in wars as the migrants invade other territories. Or the result may be social disorganization and conflict over scarce resources within the society itself. A population that grows too slowly or that declines in numbers faces the danger of extinction. The latter problem is not one that most societies have to face, but the former—overpopulation—is probably the most pressing social problem in the contemporary world. If global population continues to increase at anything like its current rate, demands for food and other natural resources will become insupportable. Far-reaching social changes will follow, including an abrupt population decline as the death rate from starvation soars.

The size of a population also has a strong influence on social organization. In small, thinly settled populations, most relationships are primary: people know one another on an informal, face-to-face basis. In larger and more densely settled populations, social organization changes markedly. Secondary relationships multiply, new agencies of social control emerge, new institutions appear, and formal organizations replace informal groups. Population growth thus has important effects throughout social life.

Changes in the demographic structure of a population also cause social changes. The post-World War II "baby boom" in the United States gave our society a disproportionate number of young people, which made a massive expansion of educational facilities necessary in the fifties and sixties. As the "baby-boom" generation grows older, the United States will become "top heavy" with old people, resulting in still further social changes. If, like the old of previous generations, these people become politically conservative in later years, this fact will affect our political life. Medical science will focus increasingly on the problems of the aged, and geriatrics will become a growth area in medicine. New provision will have to be made for the elderly, probably through an extension of old-age homes and similar facilities. Existing schools will stand empty or be converted to other uses, and funeral parlors will enjoy an unprecedented boom.

"Events"

The term "events" is used by the sociologist Robert Nisbet (1969, 1970) to refer to random, unpredictable happenings that affect the course of social change. An assassin's bullet ended the Kennedy presidency, initiating the presidency of Lyndon Johnson and making possible his policies in Southeast Asia and elsewhere. An alert night watchman noticed that a burglary was in process at the Watergate building in Washington, and set in motion a series of investigations that led to the downfall of Richard Nixon and to the presidency of Gerald Ford. Crucial battles have been lost by the mistake of a general, or abandoned because of superstitious fear of a solar eclipse.

Although a few sociologists (for example, McIver, 1942) have tried to deal with this random ingredient in social change, most have been reluctant to do so for the reason that "events" of this kind seem to fall beyond the scope of scientific analysis. As Nisbet points out, however, the actual event need not always be the decisive factor in social change. The system as a whole may sometimes be "ripe" for change and the event may merely "trigger" it. Corruption and deceit in American politics is a problem of long standing. Sooner or later someone was likely to get caught, and that someone happened to be Richard Nixon. The United States has its share of psychopaths and lacks a responsible system of gun control; sooner or later someone was likely to assassinate a president. Attempts were made in recent decades on the lives of Presidents Roosevelt, Truman, Kennedy, and Ford; the president who was fatally shot at was John Kennedy. To at least some extent, then, "events" can be explained in terms of existing social conditions. They are certainly a potential cause of major social change. Imagine, for example, the effect of nuclear war between the major powers as a result of human or electronic error. The often random nature of "events," however, poses a very difficult problem to any general theory of social change.

Cultural Innovation

Changes in a society's culture tend to involve social changes as well. Cultural innovation was discussed in Chapter 3 (Culture), and will only be summarized here. Three distinct processes are involved: discovery, invention, and diffusion.

Discovery

A *discovery* is the perception of an aspect of reality that already exists: the principle of the lever, a new continent, the composition of the atmosphere, or the circulation of the blood. A new discovery, if shared within the society, becomes an addition to the society's culture and store of knowledge. It becomes a source of social change, however, only when it is put to use. Europeans knew of other continents for centuries, but it was only when they colonized parts of these continents that social change resulted, in both the colonies and the countries that colonized them. The Greeks discovered the principle of steam power; in fact, a steam engine was built as a toy in Alexandria around 100 A.D. But the principle was not put to serious use for nearly 1700 years after it was discovered.

Invention

An *invention* is the combination or new use of existing knowledge to produce something that did not exist before. Inventions may be either material (can openers, cigarettes, spacecraft) or social (corporations, slavery, democratic institutions). All inventions are based on previous knowledge, discoveries, and inventions. For this reason, the nature and rate of inventions in a particular society depends on its existing store of knowledge. The cave

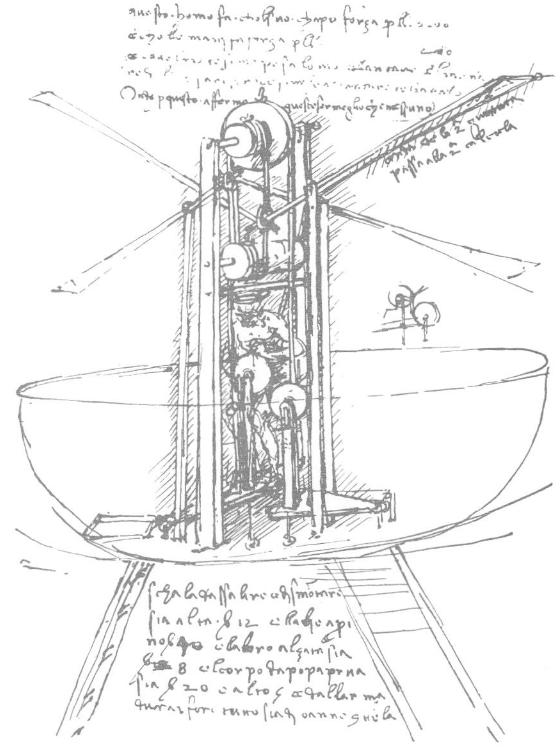

Figure 23.6 Leonardo da Vinci produced this sketch of a helicopter (powered by human muscle) in the fifteenth century. Many of Leonardo's designs for new machines were workable in principle and were centuries ahead of their time. But the machines could not be constructed, for his society lacked the technological knowledge to construct and power them. Rapid technological innovation is possible only in a society that already has a large store of knowledge to draw on, for all inventions are based on previous knowledge.

dweller has little knowledge to work with, and merely to produce a bow and arrow is a considerable intellectual achievement. We are no cleverer than our "primitive" ancestors; we simply have more knowledge to build on. As Ralph Linton (1936) remarked, "If Einstein had been born into a primitive tribe which was unable to count beyond three, lifelong application to mathematics probably would not have carried him beyond the development of a decimal system based on fingers and toes." Leonardo da Vinci, working in the fifteenth century, produced plans for many machines that were workable in principle, including helicopters, submarines, machine guns, air-conditioning units, aerial bombs, and hydraulic pumps, but his society lacked the technology necessary to build them.

SIMULTANEOUS DISCOVERIES AND INVENTIONS

Discovery of the planet Neptune	By Adams (1845) Leverrier (1845)
Discovery of oxygen	By Scheele (1774) Priestley (1774)
Logarithms	By Napier-Briggs (1614) Burgi (1620)
Photography	By Daguerre–Niepe (1839) Talbot (1839)
Kinetic theory of gases	By Clausius (1850) Rankine (1850)
Discovery of sunspots	By Galileo (1611) Fabricius (1611) Scheiner (1611) Harriott (1611)
Laws of heredity	By Mendel (1865) DeVries (1900) Correns (1900) Tschermak (1900)

Source: William F. Ogburn, *Social Change* (New York: Viking, 1922), pp. 90–122.

Figure 23.7 These are some of the 150 discoveries and inventions that William Ogburn found had been made almost simultaneously. In most cases the inventors were unaware of one another's work. They all lived in similar cultures, however, and so had access to the same store of cultural knowledge. Once sufficient knowledge has accumulated in a particular field, new inventions become almost inevitable.

Inventions occur exponentially: the more inventions that exist in a culture, the more rapidly further inventions can be made. To take a simple example: three elements can theoretically be combined into six new combinations, four into twenty-four, five into one hundred and twenty-five, and so on. Given a sufficient cultural store of knowledge, new inventions become almost inevitable. Ogburn (1950) listed 150 inventions that were made almost simultaneously by different scientists living in the same or similar cultures (see Figure 23.7). This fact helps to explain why the modernization process took so much longer in those societies that had to make the necessary discoveries and inventions than it did in those societies that merely had to adopt them from others.

Diffusion

The process of *diffusion* involves the spread of cultural elements—both material artifacts and ideas—from one culture to another. George Murdock (1934) has estimated that about 90 percent of the contents of every culture have been acquired from other societies, and some social scientists (for example, Kroeber, 1937) see diffusion as the main source of cultural and social change. The most outstanding contemporary social change—the spread of the modernization process around the world—represents the diffusion of industrialism from the advanced to the less developed societies. Each culture accepts elements from other cultures selectively, however. Material artifacts that prove useful are more readily accepted than new norms, values, or beliefs. Innovations must also be compatible with the culture of the society into which they diffuse. For these reasons, white settlers in America accepted the Indians' tobacco but not their religion.

Human Action

A final and obvious source of social change is human action, which may bring about social changes whether they are intended and foreseen or not. Two types of human action are particularly important: the acts of powerful leaders and other individuals, and the collective behavior of large numbers of people.

The precise influence of individuals on the course of history and social change is very difficult to judge. Take the case of Julius Caesar. As a general in the army of the

Figure 23.8 Diffusion is the process by which cultural elements spread from one society to another. These judges in the African state of Uganda have adopted the wigs of their former British rulers. Although the judicial wigs have survived in Uganda, British legal principles have not: material artifacts are usually more readily accepted into a culture than nonmaterial elements such as ideas.

Figure 23.9 One of the most important sources of social change is human action, particularly the concerted action by social movements such as that for women's liberation. These movements actively intervene in the course of social history, attempting to influence the direction of change.

Roman republic, he made the historic decision to cross the river Rubicon, march on Rome, and overthrow the republican form of government, replacing it with a dictatorship. His act led directly to an imperial form of government, and the empire passed from him through his adopted son Augustus to tyrants such as Nero and Caligula. If Caesar had not taken that step, the Roman republic might have survived; Augustus, Nero, Caligula, and the rest would not have become emperors; and the entire history of the Western world would have taken a different course. Or would it? We cannot know. We cannot conduct an experiment in which we remove Caesar from the scene and wait to see what happens.

Historians and biographers have often taken what is sometimes called the "great man" theory of history and social change. Sociologists have generally rejected the approach, taking the view that history makes individuals rather than that individuals make history. Sociologists see the personality and ambitions of leaders, like those of anyone else, as being strongly influenced by the culture in which they were born and socialized. From the sociological perspective, the social changes that individuals appear to have created are interpreted as the product of deeper social forces. Caesar could destroy the Roman republic only because it was already on its last legs; fifty years earlier his act would have been impossible and even unthinkable. If he had not acted when he did, others might have done so instead, and later events might have followed a broadly similar course. Similarly, World War II cannot be attributed simply to the personality and ambitions of Adolf Hitler. Hitler certainly influenced the course of events, but if there had not been severe social, ethnic, and economic strains in Germany at the time, he might never have come to power or have had the opportunity to put his policies into effect.

The role of collective action in social change poses less difficulty. Collective behavior, from fads and fashions to riots, social movements, and revolutions, is an attempt by people to change their social environment (Smelser, 1962). Large-scale movements—for women's liberation, civil rights, national independence, religious conversion, and so on—are a vital source of social change. So, too, are the actions of other social agencies and institutions, particularly governments that determine policies in the deliberate attempt to change society.

Conclusion

Where does this survey leave us? Let's look first at the problem of a general theory of change, then at the specific factors that can cause changes, and then at the prospects for predicting change in the future.

Prospects for a General Theory

Some of the theories that attempt to explain social change are clearly unsatisfactory, and no single theory seems able to account for all social change.

Cyclical theories of change seem unacceptable. They are too speculative, too subjective, and they give no explanation of how or why change takes place. *Unilinear evolutionary* theories are also unacceptable, for they are based on faulty data about other cultures. *Multilinear evolutionary* theory, however, may prove more useful. It seems to fit the facts: societies generally tend to evolve from the small and simple to the large and complex. They do so in different ways, but a change in the mode of production is always involved, usually culminating in industrialism. The theory also helps explain why these changes take place. The more elaborate a culture becomes, the greater the probability of new invention and discovery. And the more efficient the mode of production becomes, the greater use a society is able to make of its environment. It is able to produce a steadily greater economic surplus, which permits population growth, urbanization, and modernization. But the theory is not fully satisfactory, for it explains only one dimension of social change—the evolution of societies from simple to complex, from preindustrial to industrial. It tells us nothing, for example, about wars, revolutions, migrations, and other important forms of change.

Functionalist and *conflict* theories seem at first sight to be at odds with one another, and indeed the debate between advocates of each view became quite heated during the sixties. If we look at the basic assumptions of each approach, the contrast seems quite glaring.

1. Functionalist theory holds that every society is relatively stable; conflict theory holds that every society is in a process of continuous change.

2. Functionalist theory holds that every society is well integrated; conflict theory holds that every society experiences continuous conflict and tension.

3. Functionalist theory holds that every element in society contributes to its functioning; conflict theory holds that every element in society contributes to its change.

4. Functionalist theory holds that every society is held together by the common values of its members; conflict theory holds that every society is held together by the coercion of some of its members by others.

As Ralf Dahrendorf (1958) points out, however, each part of all the above statements is true, although they may seem contradictory. The reason for the paradox lies in the paradoxical nature of society itself. Societies *are* stable, enduring systems, but they *do* experience conflict and continuous change. The functionalist and conflict approaches are merely focusing on different aspects of social reality: one mainly on statics, one mainly on dynamics.

There seems to be no logical reason why the two theories cannot be integrated to a considerable extent (Smelser, 1967; Gouldner, 1970; Van den Berghe, 1963). As we have noted, Merton has introduced the concepts of "strain" and "tension" from conflict theory into functionalist theory. In a similar vein, Lewis Coser (1956) has written about the "functions" of conflict in society. Conflict, Coser points out, can be functional for the social system because it prevents stagnation and generates necessary changes.

Evolutionary theory, in its multilinear form, is compatible with either functionalist or conflict theory. If we take an evolutionary perspective on social change and combine it with functionalist or conflict theory—or, where appropriate, with both—we have the best general theory of social change. It remains an imperfect theory, admittedly, but it provides a rich understanding of many forms of social change.

Interacting Factors in Social Change

The essential point about specific sources of change is that change is never the product of any one factor. As Parsons (1966) reminds us: "No claim that social change is determined by economic interests, ideas, personalities of particular individuals, geographic conditions, and so on, is acceptable. All such single-factor theories belong to the kindergarten stage of a social science's development. Any single factor is always interdependent with several others." No change can be explained or understood without reference to a series of interacting factors and to the society and culture in which it takes place. Existing conditions determine which changes will be accepted, which will be rejected, and which will be adopted in modified form. The highly conservative rulers of Tibet were able to keep the wheel out of their mountain kingdom for almost a thousand years. Sub-Saharan African peoples, to whom cattle are a form of wealth, have refused to practice "rational" stock-rearing methods that would give them fewer but healthier cattle. Islam is being accepted more readily than Christianity in many parts of Africa, largely because it is not seen as a "white" religion and because it permits polygyny, which most African peoples practice. A broad range of changes is acceptable in the United States because we are a change-oriented culture with a commitment to science, technology, and the pursuit of a better society.

Predicting the Future

To what extent does our present understanding of social change permit us to predict the future? We are able to do so within limits, particularly for those societies that have not yet reached our level of industrial development. Our society and other advanced industrial societies such as the Soviet Union provide the mirrors in which developing societies can see the outlines of their own futures, and sociological analysis enables us to predict the general lines that social change in these countries will follow. But when we look to our own future we have no example to guide us. We can, however, make fairly confident predictions about specific areas of society. We can anticipate the likely effect of population growth and we can project the future trends in urbanization, for example. When it comes to predicting the overall form of our society in the future, however, we are in real difficulty.

There is no shortage of attempts to predict this future. Daniel Bell (1973) has written about a new "postindustrial" society, characterized by increased affluence, automation, and leisure time. Alvin Toffler (1970) has written about a society in a permanent state of "future shock," where technological and social change takes place much faster than peoples' ability to adjust to it. William Ophuls (1974) describes a "scarcity society," in which depletion of resources leads to a lower standard of living and a strong, authoritarian state that regulates conflict between groups struggling for their piece of the diminishing pie. These are very different predictions, for the reason that each writer focuses on one or a few aspects of change in the modern United States and projects this trend, largely through guesswork, into the future. Lacking any general theory of social change, these and other writers cannot provide a systematic and persuasive picture of the future. Until an adequate theory of social change is produced, such a picture will continue to elude us. The task of producing that theory remains no less a challenge today than it did when the new discipline of sociology was born.

Summary

1. Social change is the alteration in patterns of social structure, institutions, and behavior over time. The process is universal but occurs at different rates and in different ways. Social change is often difficult to analyze because we lack a full understanding of social statics and because changes usually have very complex origins.

2. Evolutionary theories hold that societies evolve from simple to complex forms. Early ethnocentric theorists believed that the process was unilinear and culminated in Western civilization. Social Darwinists believed that some societies or groups prospered because they were better adapted to the conditions of life. Many modern social scientists believe that evolution is multilinear and takes many forms. They also refuse to equate "change" with "progress."

3. Cyclical theories hold that change recurs in cycles over time. Spengler believed societies have life cycles and that their fate was a matter of "destiny." Toynbee believed that societies advance or decline according to their "responses" to "challenges." Sorokin believed that cultures fluctuate between "sensate" and "ideational" forms.

4. Functionalist theories focus mainly on social statics. Parsons, however, sees change as a process by which the

social equilibrium is altered so that a new equilibrium results. This process takes place through differentiation and integration.

5. Conflict theorists, influenced by Marx, see conflict as intrinsic to society and as the main source of social change. The theory explains some change but has not given very accurate predictions in the past.

6. Some specific sources of change are the following: (a) the physical environment, which sets limits on change although it rarely causes change; (b) ideas, which in interaction with other factors can generate change; (c) technology, which generates changes in society and culture, often causing a culture lag; (d) cultural innovation, which takes the forms of discovery, invention, and diffusion; and (e) human action, in the sense that individuals, groups, and agencies such as governments can influence social change.

7. Cyclical theories are too speculative and are not explanatory. Unilinear evolutionary theories were based on faulty data. Multilinear evolutionary theories seem useful but explain only one dimension of change. Functionalist and conflict theories seem to contradict one another but actually focus on different aspects of the same reality. Multilinear, functionalist, and conflict theories may sometimes be combined to explain many forms of social change. Change is never the result of one specific factor; several factors always operate together.

8. Although we can predict the course of change in some aspects of society, a fully satisfactory general theory of change has still to be developed.

Important Terms

social change
dynamics
statics
evolutionary theories
unilinear evolution
social Darwinism
multilinear evolution
functionalist theories
equilibrium
differentiation
integration
ideology
culture lag
discovery
invention
diffusion

Suggested Readings

BELL, DANIEL. *The Coming of Postindustrial Society.* New York: Basic Books, 1973.

A leading prophet of the "postindustrial society" explains why and how we are entering that stage and outlines the characteristics of this new social form.

ETZIONI, AMITAI, and EVA ETZIONI-HALEVY. *Social Change.* New York: Basic Books, 1973.

An important collection of articles on various aspects of social change. The book includes excerpts from the writings of several classical and modern theorists on the subject.

GOULDNER, ALVIN. *The Coming Crisis of Western Sociology.* New York: Avon, 1970.

An important book on sociological theory. Gouldner argues strongly that aspects of conflict and functionalist theory can and should be combined to produce a better understanding of social processes.

MEAD, MARGARET. *Culture and Commitment.* New York: Doubleday, 1970.

An anthropologist examines the effect of rapid technological change on modern societies, placing particular emphasis on the cleavage that change can create between the generations.

OGBURN, WILLIAM F. *Social Change.* New York: Viking, 1950.

A classic work in the field. Ogburn presents his concept of "culture lag" and discusses the social disorganization that technological changes can create.

SWANSON, GUY E. *Social Change.* Glenview, Ill.: Scott, Foresman, 1971.

A survey of theory and research on social change from several disciplines, including history and sociology.

TOFFLER, ALVIN. *Future Shock.* New York: Random House, 1970.

A lively and provocative book, in which Toffler argues that social change is now taking place faster than our capacity to adjust to it. The book has been a best-seller.

APPENDIX

Techniques of Library Research

The library, besides housing the works of novelists, poets, biographers, and playwrights, is also a storehouse of scientific knowledge. Every library is systematically organized so that this knowledge can be easily located and retrieved, and the purpose of this appendix is to acquaint you with some of the ways you can "plug into" the sociological information that the library contains.

Your method of tracking down information will depend very much on the exact kind of information you are looking for. The following categories cover most situations.

If you are looking for a book or article and have the full reference:

First, a word about references. You will find that scientific references are usually given in one of two ways. The first way is to use a *numbered footnote,* usually appearing at the bottom of the page but sometimes at the end of the chapter in which the reference is made. Footnote references to *books* usually look like this:

[1] Edward Sagarin, *Deviants and Deviance* (New York: Praeger, 1975).

[2] T. B. Bottomore, *Sociology: A Guide to Problems and Literature* (New York: Pantheon, 1971), p. 34.

Note that the information is usually given in the same order: first the author's name; followed by the title of the book, generally in italic type; the publisher; the place of publication; and the year of publication. If the person quoting the reference is referring to a specific page, the page number is given also, usually at the end.

References to *articles* generally look like this:

[3] John P. Hewitt and Randall Stokes, "Disclaimers," *American Sociological Review,* 40 (February, 1975), pp. 1–11.

[4] Edwin M. Lemert, "Paranoia and the Dynamics of Exclusion," *Sociometry,* 25 (March, 1962), pp. 2–20.

Again, the information is usually in the same order: first the name of the author; followed by the title of the article, generally in quotation marks; the name of the journal, usually in italic type; the volume number; the month (or season) and the year in which the journal issue was published; and the inclusive page numbers of the article.

The second way of giving a reference is to refer simply to the *author's name and date of the publication.* This kind of reference does not appear in a footnote but is included in the text at the point where the reference is made, thus: (Sagarin, 1975). All references are then listed at the back of the book in alphabetical order, like this:

Bottomore, T. B. 1971. *Sociology: A Guide to Problems and Literature.* New York: Pantheon, p. 34.

Hewitt, John P., and Randall Stokes. 1975. "Disclaimers," *American Sociological Review,* 40, February, pp. 1–11.

Lemert, Edwin M. 1962. "Paranoia and the Dynamics of Exclusion," *Sociometry,* 25, March, pp. 2–20.

Sagarin, Edward. 1975. *Deviants and Deviance.* New York: Praeger.

Note that the order of the reference is the same as before, except that the year of publication appears immediately after the author's name. If an author has published more than one book or article in the same year and more than one of these are referred to, they are distinguished in the text by the use of the letters a, b, c, etc., after the date, thus: (Goffman, 1961a, 1961b). The references then appear at the back of the book like this:

Goffman, Erving. 1961a. *Asylums: Essays on the Social Situation of Mental Patients and Other Inmates.* Chicago: Aldine.

Goffman, Erving. 1961b. *Encounters: Two Studies in the Sociology of Interaction.* Indianapolis, Ind.: Bobbs-Merrill.

The name/date system of referencing is becoming more popular than the footnote system. It has two main advantages: first, references are easier to locate when you cannot remember exactly where in the book they were made—you simply turn to the alphabetical list at the back of the book, rather than having to page through the entire book. Second, the name/date system keeps down the cost of printing because the typesetter does not have to leave spaces for references at the bottom of the page, which are usually set separately in a smaller type, then combined with the rest of the book. The name/date system is used in this book.

If you have a full reference such as those given above, locating the book or article is easy. Every library has a card catalog containing an alphabetical list of authors, with a separate card for each book. The card will tell you exactly where the book is to be found. The library also has a separate listing of journals, and each entry tells you where the journals are kept. To find an article you simply go to the journal, locate the volume containing the article you want, and turn to the particular issue and page numbers that you have been given.

If you are looking for general information on a particular subject:

A useful place to start might be a general encyclopedia such as the *Britannica* or the *Americana;* or you can try the 17-volume *International Encyclopaedia of the Social Sciences,* which contains general reviews written by experts in various fields. Every encyclopedia contains instructions on how to use it, and at the end of each article you will find additional references that you can use for follow-up.

You can also consult the *Reader's Guide to Periodical Literature,* which covers such nontechnical sources as *Time, Newsweek,* and the *New Republic.* The index will direct you to articles that have been published on the subject you are interested in. You should be wary, though, of these nonscholarly sources. They often give a useful introduction to some issue, but they usually lack the objectivity and precision of good sociology. A very useful guide to more scientific articles is the *Social Sciences Index,* which will direct you to more reliable sources in sociology and related fields.

For specifically sociological information, you can start with *Sociological Abstracts,* which arranges all sociological books, articles, and papers presented to professional meetings, according to subject area. The publication includes a brief summary of the content of each item, together with the names of the authors and the source of the material. Similar abstracts are available in related areas, such as *Psychological Abstracts, Crime and Delinquency Abstracts, Education Abstracts,* and *Poverty and Human Resources Abstracts.* There is also a *Dissertation Abstracts,* covering unpublished doctoral dissertations.

You may also wish to refer to major journals covering various aspects of the discipline. Four highly regarded journals that print articles of general sociological interest are the *American Journal of Sociology*, the *American Sociological Review*, *Social Forces*, and the *British Journal of Sociology*. There are also a number of journals on specific areas, such as *Sociology of Education*, *Journal of Health and Social Behavior*, *Social Problems*, *Public Opinion Quarterly*, *Issues in Criminology*, *Journal of Marriage and the Family*, and *Journal of Abnormal and Social Psychology*.

If you are looking for a specific book or article but don't know the name of the author:

Many libraries have a separate card catalog that lists books by title; if your library has such a catalog you can easily trace a book without knowing its author's name. An alternative method is to refer to *Books in Print*, a two-volume annual publication. One volume lists all books in print alphabetically by author; the other volume lists them alphabetically by title. If you are looking for an article but do not know the name of the author, you can look through the articles listed under the relevant subject heading in the *Reader's Guide to Periodical Literature*, *The Social Sciences Index*, or *Sociological Abstracts*.

If you want information about specific events:

A good place to look is in newspaper files. Certain newspapers are known as "journals of record"—in other words, they not only cover "newsworthy" events but also try to preserve a record of significant social events, and print lengthy extracts from government reports and similar material. The two outstanding journals of record in the English-speaking world are the *New York Times* and the London *Times*. Both maintain an index of all names and events that have appeared in their columns, and this index will direct you to any article they have published on the subject you are interested in.

If you want information about particular people:

One obvious source is the newspaper files just mentioned (obituaries in newspapers are a particularly useful source of information about people who are dead). Information can also be obtained from such volumes as *Who's Who*, *Who Was Who*, *Current Biography*, or *American Men and Women of Science*. The latter is in two volumes, one covering the physical and biological sciences and the other covering the behavioral sciences and humanities.

If you want statistical information:

The best place to start is usually *Statistical Abstracts*, an annual publication that contains information about virtually every aspect of American life on which statistics are kept. The *Census Report*, published every ten years, gives many details about the characteristics of the American population. You might also consult *Statistical Sources: A Subject Guide to Data on Industrial, Business, Social, Educational, Financial, and Other Topics for the U.S. and Internationally*. This useful volume will direct you to other sources of information that you may not know about: if you are looking for information on crime trends, for example, it will direct you to such sources as the annual *Uniform Crime Reports* of the FBI.

You will always find that sources generate more sources, because each reference will lead you to several more. Unless you want a broad overview of a topic, then, it is best to have very specific information in mind, or you might be overwhelmed by the richness of the data waiting for you! Above all, remember that when you are in any difficulty, you should not hesitate to *ask the librarian*. Some people are reluctant to "bother" the librarian, or feel that he or she may not know about the specific information that is sought. But the librarian is a professional trained in library science, and has an intimate knowledge of the general methods for locating information and of the specific resources of your library. The librarian will be glad to help, so if you are unable to find what you are looking for, just ask.

Glossary

Absolute deprivation The lack of the basic necessities of life.

Account In social interaction, an excuse or justification for inappropriate behavior that has taken place.

Achieved status A social status that an individual achieves at least partly through personal effort or failings, such as that of college graduate or prison convict.

Agency of socialization An institution or other structured situation in which socialization takes place, such as the family or the school.

Agricultural society A society whose primary subsistence strategy is the cultivation of crops through the use of ploughs and draft animals.

Alienation The sense that one has no control over the social world and so feels like an "alien" within it.

Aligning actions Strategies used by social actors to smooth the course of interaction when their behavior is potentially disruptive.

Anomaly In the sociology of science, a problem that cannot be explained in terms of the existing paradigm.

Anomie A state of normlessness, in either a society or an individual, caused by a conflict or absence of norms and hence of effective social control.

Anthropology A social science that focuses primarily on the cultures of small-scale, preindustrial societies and on the physical evolution of the human species.

Anticipatory socialization Socialization that is directed toward learning future roles.

Applied research Research aimed at finding technological applications for scientific knowledge.

Ascribed status A social status assigned to the individual by society on arbitrary grounds, such as age, race, or sex.

Association A large secondary group, usually taking the form of a formal organization.

Authoritarian personality A set of distinctive personality traits, including conformity, intolerance, and insecurity, alleged to be typical of many prejudiced people.

Authority Power that is regarded as legitimate by those over whom it is exercised (in contrast to coercion).

Autocracy Rule by a single individual.

Automation A system in which machines themselves monitor and control a manufacturing process.

Basic research Research aimed at increasing the sum of knowledge (in contrast to applied research, which is aimed at finding technological applications for knowledge).

Behaviorism A theory of learning that focuses on actual behavior, which is believed to be the result of conditioning through rewards and punishments.

Bilateral system A family system in which descent and inheritance are reckoned through both the male and female lines.

Birth rate A statistical measure, usually expressed as the number of births per year per thousand members of a given population.

Bureaucracy A hierarchical authority structure that operates under explicit rules and procedures; bureaucracies are found in all formal organizations.

Bystander apathy The tendency of witnesses to take no action when confronted by an emergency affecting others.

Capitalism A class-based political and economic system in which most wealth is privately owned and may be reinvested to produce profit for those who own it.

Case study A detailed record of an event, group, or social process.

Caste system A system of social stratification in which status is ascribed at birth and in which there is virtually no social mobility or intermarriage between the strata.

Charisma An unusual, exceptional, or even supernatural quality that people attribute to particular individuals.

Charismatic authority Authority that is legitimated by the unusual, exceptional, or even supernatural qualities that people attribute to those who exercise it.

City A permanent concentration of relatively large numbers of people who do not produce their own food.

Class conflict The struggle between social classes, primarily between the class that owns the means of economic production and the class or classes that do not.

Class consciousness A social class's shared, objective awareness of the common situation and interests of its members.

Class system A system of social stratification in which categories of the population are ranked primarily according to economic status but in which there is some measure of achieved status and social mobility.

Closed system A system of social stratification in which virtually no social mobility is possible.

Coercion Power that is perceived as illegitimate by those over whom it is exercised (in contrast to authority).

Cognitive Refers to intellectual capacities such as perception, reasoning, and memory.

Collective behavior Relatively spontaneous and unstructured ways of thinking, feeling, and acting on the part of a large number of people.

Collective consciousness A set of norms, values, and assumptions shared by a community or society.

Communism A political and economic system in which, ideally, wealth and power are shared equally by the community as a whole because of the common ownership of the means of production and distribution.

Community A social group with a common territorial base and a shared sense of common interests and "belonging."

Concentric-zone theory A theory that cities typically consist of a series of zones radiating concentrically from a downtown center, with each successive zone containing a different type of land use.

Concrete operational stage A stage of cognitive development in which thinking is tied to the physical world and is insufficiently developed to deal with abstract or hypothetical concepts.

Conditioning A process of learning through the association of acts with their consequences.

Conflict perspective A theoretical perspective of society that emphasizes conflict as a permanent feature of social life, an important influence on social structure and culture, and a significant source of social change.

Conformity Adherence to social norms.

Control group A group of subjects in an experiment who are not exposed to the independent variable introduced by the researcher but whose experience is the same in all other respects to that of the experimental group, which is exposed to the variable.

Controls Statistical or experimental methods that serve to exclude the possibility that external factors might influence a relationship that a researcher is studying.

Correlation A regular, recurrent association between variables, generally expressed in statistical terms.

Counterculture A subculture that is fundamentally at odds with the dominant culture.

Crime An act that has been prohibited by political authority, usually through the enactment of a law.

Crimes without victims Crimes such as gambling, prostitution, or illicit drug use that have no direct victim, except possibly the offender.

Crowd A temporary collection of people in close physical proximity.

Cult A loosely organized religious or other social movement that tends to lack coherent doctrines and to impose minimal demands on its members.

Cultural anthropology The scientific study of the cultures of other peoples, particularly in small-scale, preindustrial societies.

Cultural integration A situation in which the various elements in a culture complement one another, or "fit together."

Cultural relativism The recognition that one culture or subculture cannot be arbitrarily judged by the standards of another.

Cultural universals Practices that are found in every culture.

Culture All the shared products of human society, comprising its total way of life. Culture includes material products (houses, cities, etc.) and nonmaterial products (religions, languages, etc.).

Culture lag The time discrepancy between the introduction of a change in material culture and the adaptation of nonmaterial culture to the change.

Culture of poverty A distinctive culture said to exist among the poor in industrialized societies.

Cyclical theories Theories holding that social change tends to recur in cycles over time.

Death rate A statistical measure, usually expressed as the number of deaths per year per thousand members of a given population.

De facto discrimination Discrimination that is entrenched in social customs and institutions.

De jure discrimination Discrimination that is entrenched in law.

Democracy A system of government in which citizens have the right to participate in the decision-making process and in which the rulers acknowledge that their power derives from the consent of the governed.

Democratic socialism A political and economic system that aims at creating a high degree of social equality while preserving the freedom of the individual.

Demographic transition theory A theory that the growth rate of a population tends to decrease and stabilize once a certain level of economic development has been achieved.

Demography The scientific study of the size, composition, distribution, and changes in human populations.

Denomination One of two or more well-established religious organizations that claim the allegiance of a substantial part of a population.

Dependent variable A variable that is changed or influenced by the effect of another variable, termed the independent variable.

Detached observation A case-study method in which the researcher remains aloof from the process involved, often with the result that the subjects do not know they are being studied.

Developmental approach An approach to the psychology of learning that emphasizes the individual's internal interpretations of the world and regards learning as a process of continual development through different stages.

Developmental socialization Socialization that builds on already-acquired skills and knowledge.

Deviance Behavior or characteristics that violate significant social norms and expectations and are negatively valued by large numbers of people in consequence.

Deviant career Permanent and habitual deviance among people who regard themselves and are regarded by others as deviant.

Differential association Refers to a theory that explains deviant behavior in terms of cultural transmission through regular and intensive association with existing deviants.

Differentiation In social theory, the tendency for societies to treat their members differently on such grounds as age, sex, or race. In Parsonian theory, the process by which new institutions emerge to assume functions that were previously undifferentiated within a single institution.

Diffusion The spread of cultural elements from one culture to another.

Disclaimer In social interaction, an excuse or justification for inappropriate behavior that is about to take place.

Discovery The perception of an aspect of reality that already exists.

Discrimination Action against other people on the grounds of their group membership, particularly the refusal to grant such people opportunities that would be granted to similarly qualified members of one's own group.

Division of labor The specialization by particular individuals or categories of individuals in particular economic activities.

Double standard Refers to social norms that tolerate male promiscuity while demanding female chastity.

Dramaturgical approach A term used by Erving Goffman to describe his method of analysis of social interaction, which he studies as though the participants were actors in a theater.

Drive A basic inborn urge, arising either spontaneously or in response to a stimulus from the environment, and temporarily disappearing when it has been satisfied.

Dyad A group consisting of two people.

Dynamics Refers to the phenomenon of social change.

Dysfunction A consequence of some element in a social system that disrupts the equilibrium of the system or the functioning of another element within the system.

Ecclesia A well-established religious organization that claims the allegiance of everyone in a society or in several societies.

Ecological approach An analytic approach that studies social phenomena in the context of the total environment.

Ecology The science of the relationship between living organisms and their environments.

Economic determinism The theory that the economic base of society determines the general character of social structure and culture.

Economic order The institutionalized system for producing and distributing goods and services.

Ecosystem A self-sustaining community of organisms within its natural environment.

Education The systematic, formalized transmission of knowledge, skills, and values.

Egalitarian family A family in which the husband and wife have equal authority in family matters.

Ego In Freudian theory, the conscious, rational part of the self.

Endogamy A marriage pattern in which individuals marry within their own social group.

Equilibrium In functionalist theory, the overall balance that exists among the various elements in a social system.

Ethnic group A large number of people who, as a result of their shared cultural traits and high level of mutual interaction, come to regard themselves and to be regarded as a cultural unity.

Ethnocentrism The tendency to judge other cultures or subcultures by the standards of one's own.

Ethnography A study of the way of life of a human group, usually a small-scale, preindustrial society.

Evolution In biology and physical anthropology, the process by which organisms adapt their physical forms and behavioral patterns to the demands and opportunities of the environment. In sociology and cultural anthropology, the process by which societies become more complex, usually as a result of more efficient technologies for exploiting the environment.

Exogamy A marriage pattern in which individuals marry outside their own social group.

Experimental group A group of subjects in an experiment who are exposed to the independent variable introduced by the researcher, in contrast to the control group, which is not subjected to this variable but whose experience is the same in all other respects.

Extended family A family in which two or more generations of the same kinship line live together.

Externalization The process through which people create cultural products, such as social institutions, which then become "external" to the producers.

Fad A temporary form of conduct that is followed enthusiastically by large numbers of people.

False consciousness A subjective understanding of one's situation that does not accord with the objective facts of that situation.

Family A relatively permanent group of people related by ancestry, marriage, or adoption, who live together and form an economic unit, and whose adult members assume responsibility for the young.

Family of orientation The family into which one is born.

Family of procreation The family that we create for ourselves as opposed to the family of orientation into which we are born.

Fashion A currently accepted style of appearance or behavior.

Fecundity The biological potential for bearing a number of children, in contrast to fertility, the actual number of births.

Fertility Refers to the actual number of births to the average woman of childbearing age in a given society, in contrast to fecundity, the potential number of births.

Feudalism A relatively closed system of social stratification in which a landowning class exploits the mass of peasants and in which the rights and responsibilities of the classes are specified by tradition.

Folk society A term used by Robert Redfield to distinguish small, traditional societies from "urban" or large, modern societies.

Folkways The ordinary usages and conventions of everyday life; conformity to such norms is expected but violations are not regarded as immoral.

Formal operational stage A stage of cognitive development at which intelligence is sufficiently developed to deal with abstract, hypothetical, and formal thought.

Formal organization A large social group that is deliberately and rationally designed to achieve specific objectives.

Formal sanction A social reward or punishment that is applied in an organized and patterned way (such as a graduation ceremony or an execution).

Function Any consequence that a given component in a social system has, either for the system as a whole or for some other component within it. A function is usually assumed to contribute to the overall stability of the system.

Functionalist perspective A theoretical perspective on society that emphasizes the functional interrelations of the various elements in a social system, and the contributions that these elements make toward social order.

Functional prerequisite An important social requirement that must be fulfilled if society is to function effectively.

Gemeinschaft A term used by Ferdinand Tönnies to describe a small community characterized by intimate, face-to-face contact, strong feelings of group loyalty, and a commitment to tradition.

Gender Refers to the cultural concepts of masculinity and femininity that a society creates around the biological facts of maleness and femaleness.

Generalization A statement about the recurrent relationships between particular variables.

Generalized other An internalized concept of the expectations of society as a whole.

Genocide The extermination of an entire population.

Gesellschaft A term used by Ferdinand Tönnies to describe a society marked by impersonal contacts, an emphasis on individualism rather than group loyalty, and a lack of commitment to traditional values.

Group A collection of people interacting together in an orderly way on the basis of shared expectations about each other's behavior.

Growth rate A statistical measure reflecting changes in population size; it represents the number of births minus the number of deaths and is usually expressed as an annual percentage.

Hawthorne effect The contamination of an experiment by changes in the subjects' behavior resulting from their assumptions about what the researcher is trying to prove.

Heterosexuality Sexual acts or feelings directed toward members of the opposite sex.

Homogamy Marriage between people with similar social characteristics.

Homo sapiens The modern human species (literally "man, the wise").

Homosexuality Sexual acts or feelings directed toward members of the same sex.

Horizontal mobility A change from one social status to another that is roughly equivalent.

Horticultural society A society relying for its subsistence primarily on the hoe cultivation of domesticated plants.

Human ecology The study of the interrelationship between human groups and their total environment.

Hunting and gathering society A society relying for its subsistence on such food as its members are able to hunt and gather; there is no domestication of plants and animals.

Hypothesis A tentative statement that predicts a relationship between variables.

Id In Freudian theory, the reservoir of drives present in the individual at birth and throughout life.

Ideal culture Culture as it is expressed in the values and norms that people claim to believe in, rather than as expressed in their actual practices.

Ideal type An abstract description, constructed by the sociologist from observations of a number of real cases in order to reveal their essential features.

Ideology A set of beliefs that justifies the interests (or supposed interests) of those who hold it; the dominant ideology in any society legitimates the existing social order.

Illegitimate birth Birth to unmarried parents.

Incest Socially forbidden sexual intercourse with close relatives.

Incest taboo A powerful social prohibition on sexual intercourse with specific categories of kinfolk.

Independent variable A variable that causes a change or variation in another variable, termed the dependent variable.

Industrial society A society relying for its subsistence primarily on mechanized production.

Informal sanction A social reward or punishment that is applied through the spontaneous reactions of other people (such as a pat on the back or a gesture of disapproval).

Ingroup The group to which an individual belongs and feels loyalty, as opposed to any outgroup to which the individual does not belong.

Innovation In the sociology of science, the discovery of new scientific knowledge. In the sociology of deviance, a form of deviant behavior that occurs when people accept socially approved goals but resort to socially disapproved means of achieving them.

Instinct A complex pattern of behavior that is genetically determined and appears in all normal members of a species under identical conditions.

Institution A stable cluster of values, norms, statuses, roles, and expectations that develop around a basic need of a society.

Institutionalized discrimination Discrimination, often subtle and informal, that deeply pervades social customs and institutions.

Integration In social theory, the tendency for the various elements in culture and society to be interlinked and interdependent. In Parsonian theory, the process by which newly differentiated institutions are linked together once more. In the sociology of race and ethnic relations, the free and unrestricted association of members of different groups.

Interactionist perspective A theoretical perspective on society that focuses on the micro order and emphasizes the social interaction between individuals.

Interest group An organization or group of people that attempts to influence political decisions that might affect its members.

Intergenerational mobility A change in the social status of family members from one generation to the next.

Internalization The socialization process through which people absorb cultural knowledge, making it part of their "internal" consciousness and personality.

Invention The combination or new use of existing knowledge to produce something that did not exist before.

IQ (Intelligence Quotient) test A test that measures certain aspects of intelligence by comparing the performance of a subject with the rest of that subject's age group.

Kinship A network of people related by common ancestry, adoption, or marriage.

Labeling theory A theory that explains deviant behavior in terms of a process through which some people successfully apply the label of "deviant" to others.

Latent functions The unrecognized and unintended consequences of some element in a social system.

Law A rule that is formally enacted by a political authority and is backed by the power of the state.

Learning A change in an individual's thought, emotion, or behavior that results from previous experience.

Legal-rational authority Authority that is legitimated by explicit rules and procedures that define the rights and obligations of those who exercise it.

Legitimacy In political sociology, the term refers to a generally held belief that a particular political system is a valid and justified one.

Legitimate birth Birth to parents who are married.

Life chances Probabilities of benefiting from the opportunities that a society offers.

Life cycle The biological and social sequence of birth, childhood, maturity, old age, and death.

Life expectancy The average number of years that a newborn person in a given population can expect to live.

Life span The maximum length of life possible in a given species.

Linguistic relativity Refers to the fact that different languages dissect and organize reality in somewhat different ways, so that speakers of a particular language interpret the world through the unique forms that their language supplies.

Lobbying The practice of trying to persuade decision makers to adopt policies that favor one's own interests.

Looking-glass self The reflection of the self that is provided by the reactions of others to one's behavior.

Macro order The large-scale structures and processes of society.

Magic Rituals that attempt to harness supernatural powers for human ends.

Manifest functions The obvious and intended consequences of some element in a social system.

Marriage A socially approved sexual union of some permanence between two or more individuals.

Mass hysteria A form of collective behavior involving widespread and contagious anxiety, usually caused by an unfounded belief.

Mass media Forms of communication, such as television and newspapers, that reach a large audience without any personal contact between the senders and receivers of the messages.

Master status The most socially significant of an individual's various statuses (usually an occupational status).

Material culture The artifacts or physical objects created by human beings.

Matriarchal family One in which the wife has superior authority in family matters.

Matrilineal system A family system in which descent and inheritance are reckoned through the female side of the family.

Matrilocal residence pattern A family system in which a married couple is expected to live with the family of the wife.

Mechanical solidarity A form of social cohesion found primarily in small-scale preindustrial societies and based on the basic similarity of the members.

Megalopolis A virtually unbroken urban tract consisting of two or more metropolises.

Methodology A system of rules, principles, and procedures that regulates scientific investigation.

Metropolis An urban area including a city and its surrounding suburbs.

Micro order The small-scale processes that constitute the ongoing life of a society.

Migration rate A statistical measure, usually expressed as the number of immigrants or emigrants per thousand members of a given population.

Military industrial complex An informal system of mutual contact and influence between high officials in the Pentagon and major U.S. corporations.

Millenarian movement A religious movement that prophesies a cataclysm within the immediate future.

Minority group A group of people who, because of their physical or cultural characteristics, are differentiated from others in their society and treated unequally.

Mob An emotionally aroused crowd bent on violent action.

Modernization The process of economic and social transformation brought about by the introduction of industrialism into a society.

Monogamy A marriage form in which a person may not marry more than one other person at a time.

Monopoly In economic sociology, a single firm that dominates an industry.

Mores Powerful norms that are regarded as morally significant; violations are considered a serious matter.

Multilinear evolution Refers to a theory that sociocultural evolution may take different forms and directions in different societies.

Multiple-nuclei theory A theory that modern cities are typically organized around a number of specialized areas, each of which influences the character and development of the surrounding neighborhood.

Negative sanction A social punishment for disapproved behavior.

Neolocal residence pattern A family system in which a married couple establishes a new place of residence away from the families of the husband and the wife.

Nonmaterial culture Refers to social products that do not have a physical existence, such as language, customs, or religions.

Nonverbal communication Meaningful interaction between people that takes place through the use of symbols other than language.

Norm A shared rule or guideline that prescribes the appropriate behavior for people in a given situation.

Normal science A term used to describe a process of scientific innovation in which knowledge is steadily increased.

Nuclear family A family consisting of husband, wife, and their dependent children.

Objectivation The process by which cultural products are seen as having an existence and reality independent of those who produced them.

Objectivity Strictly speaking, a mode of interpreting reality in such a way that personal, subjective judgments are eliminated. In practice, objectivity refers to thought sufficiently disciplined to minimize distortions caused by personal bias.

Oligarchy Rule by a few people.

Oligopoly A situation that exists when a few firms dominate an industry.

Open system A system of social stratification in which social mobility is widely available.

Organic solidarity A form of social cohesion found primarily in large industrial societies and based on the differences between the members, which make them interdependent.

Outgroup A group to which an individual does not belong, as opposed to the ingroup to which the individual belongs and feels loyalty.

Panic A form of collective behavior in which a group of people, faced with an immediate threat, react in a fearful, uncoordinated, and irrational way.

Paradigm A set of concepts, methods, and assumptions shared by a community of scientists and guiding research in their discipline.

Participant observation A case-study method in which the researcher takes part in the activities of the people who are being studied.

Particular other An internalized concept of the expectations of specific other people.

Pastoral society A society relying for its subsistence primarily on domesticated herd animals.

Patriarchal family One in which the husband has superior authority in family matters.

Patrilineal system A family system in which descent and inheritance are reckoned through the male line of the family.

Patrilocal residence pattern A family system in which a married couple is expected to live with the family of the husband.

Peer group Companions and associates of equivalent social status and usually of similar age.

Personality The fairly stable patterns of thought, feeling, and action that are typical of an individual.

Pluralism In political sociology, the diffusion of power among various groups and interests. In the sociology of race and ethnic relations, a situation in which different groups live in mutual respect while maintaining their own identities.

Political order The institutionalized system through which some individuals and groups acquire and exercise power over others.

Political party A collectivity of people organized for the specific purpose of gaining legitimate control of government.

Polyandry A marriage form in which a wife may have more than one husband at the same time.

Polygamy A marriage form in which a person of one sex may be married to two or more persons of the opposite sex at the same time.

Polygyny A marriage form in which a husband may have more than one wife at the same time.

Population In demography, the total collectivity of individuals in a designated social unit, usually a society. In survey research, the total category of persons on which the survey is based and from which any sample is drawn.

Positive sanction A social reward for approved behavior.

Postindustrial society An advanced form of society said to be currently emerging and to be based on sophisticated technology and increased leisure time.

Power The ability to control the behavior of others, even in the absence of their consent.

Power elite A small network of powerful and influential individuals who are alleged to make the most important political decisions in American society.

Preindustrial society A society that does not rely for its subsistence on mechanized production but concentrates instead on hunting and gathering, pastoralism, horticulture, or agriculture.

Prejudice A "prejudged" negative attitude, often directed at individuals because they are members of a negatively valued group.

Preoperational stage A stage of cognitive development in which intelligence is insufficiently developed to perform basic logical operations.

Prestige The respect enjoyed by individuals or groups as a result of their social status.

Primary deviance Deviant behavior that is temporary, trivial, or concealed, and thus is not regarded as deviant by the actor or by significant other people.

Primary group A group consisting of a small number of people who interact in direct, intimate, and personal ways.

Primary industry Economic activity devoted to the gathering and extracting of undeveloped natural resources.

Primary socialization The basic socialization that takes place in the early years of life.

Priority dispute A dispute about which scientist made a particular discovery first.

Profane In the sociology of religion, anything that is not sacred.

Profession An occupation requiring some knowledge of and training in an art or science.

Projection Attributing to others characteristics that one is unwilling to recognize in oneself.

Propaganda Information or viewpoints designed to persuade an audience to adopt a particular opinion.

Property The rights that an owner of an object has in relation to others who are not owners of the object.

Prostitution The relatively indiscriminate exchange of sexual favors for economic gain.

Public A substantial number of people with a shared interest in some issue on which there are differing opinions.

Public opinion The sum of the decisions of the members of a public on a particular issue.

Race A large number of people who, for social or geographical reasons, have interbred over a long period of time and who as a result share visible physical characteristics and regard themselves and are regarded by others as a biological unity.

Racism The domination and exploitation by one group of another group that is seen as different and inferior.

Random sample A sample of individuals drawn from a larger population in such a way that every member of the population has an equal chance of being selected.

Rationalization The process by which traditional, spontaneous methods of social organization are replaced by abstract, explicit, carefully calculated rules and procedures.

Real culture Culture as it is expressed in people's actual practices rather than in what they claim to believe in.

Rebellion In the sociology of deviance, a form of deviance that occurs when people reject both approved social goals and means and substitute new, disapproved goals and means instead; in political sociology, an uprising against authority.

Reference group A group to which people refer when making evaluations of themselves and their behavior.

Relative deprivation The inability to maintain the standards of living customary in a society. More generally, the sense, derived from comparison with other people, that one lacks the resources or rewards that are usual in the society.

Religion A system of communally held beliefs and practices that are oriented toward some sacred, supernatural realm.

Replication The process of repeating a research study to verify its findings.

Representative democracy A form of government in which people appoint representatives who are responsible for making decisions on their behalf.

Resocialization Socialization that constitutes a sharp break with past experience and involves the internalization of radically different norms and values.

Respondent A person actually surveyed in the course of survey research.

Retreatism In the sociology of deviance, a form of deviance that occurs when people reject both socially approved goals and the socially approved means of achieving them.

Revolution The overthrow of existing political and sometimes other institutions and the radical reconstruction of the political order.

Riot A violent and destructive collective outburst.

Rising expectations A situation in which people who have accepted existing conditions in the past feel that it is their right to enjoy better conditions in the future.

Ritual An established form of procedure, particularly in religious ceremonies.

Ritualism In the sociology of deviance, a form of deviance that occurs when people abandon social goals but compulsively enact the approved means of achieving them.

Role The part a person occupying a particular status plays in society.

Role conflict A situation in which a person plays two or more roles whose requirements are difficult to reconcile.

Role expectation The generally accepted social norms that define how a particular role ought to be played.

Role performance The actual behavior of a person playing a particular role.

Role set A cluster of roles attached to a particular status.

Role strain A situation in which conflicting demands are built into the same role, or in which a person for some other reason cannot meet role expectations.

Role taking Taking or pretending to take the roles of other people, and thus seeing the world from their perspective.

Routinization The process by which a relatively informal, spontaneous social group or movement is transformed into a formal, rationalized, bureaucratized one.

Rumor Information that is transmitted informally from anonymous sources.

Sacred That which inspires awe, reverence, or deep respect.

Sample A small number of individuals drawn from a larger population.

Sanction A social reward or punishment for approved or disapproved behavior.

Scapegoating The placing of the blame for one's troubles on an individual or group incapable of offering resistance.

Science The logical, systematic methods by which reliable, empirical knowledge of nature is obtained, and the actual body of knowledge accumulated by these methods.

Scientific revolution A process of scientific innovation which involves a radical change in the way scientists conceptualize their subject matter.

Secondary deviance Deviant behavior that is regular or habitual and is regarded as deviant by both the actor and significant other people.

Secondary group A group consisting of a number of people who have few if any emotional ties with one another and who come together for a specific, practical purpose.

Secondary industry Economic activity devoted to the manufacture of goods from raw materials.

Sect A marginal religious organization that tends to be dogmatic, fundamentalist, and to recruit its members by conversion.

Sector theory A theory that modern cities typically grow outward from a center in wedge-shaped sectors, with each sector containing a different type of land use.

Secularization The process by which traditional religious beliefs and institutions lose their influence in society.

Self An individual's conscious experience of a distinct, personal identity that is separate from all other people and things.

Self-fulfilling prophecy A prediction about some personal or social behavior that influences the actual behavior, so that the prophecy is confirmed by the result that it has caused.

Sensorimotor stage A stage of cognitive development in which intelligence is expressed only in terms of sensory and physical contact with the environment.

Sexism An ideology or belief system that legitimizes sexual inequalities by assuming that these inequalities are based on inborn characteristics.

Sex role The learned patterns of behavior expected of the sexes in any society.

Sibling One's brother or sister.

Small group A group that contains sufficiently few members for the participants to relate to one another as individuals.

Social change The alteration in patterns of social structure, social institutions, and social behavior over time.

Social construction of reality The process by which definitions of reality are socially created, objectified, internalized, and then taken for granted.

Social control The mechanisms and processes by which a society ensures that its members generally behave in expected and approved ways.

Social Darwinism A theory that different societies and social groups are better fitted for survival than others, and consequently become more advanced or dominant.

Social inequality A situation in which people have different access to social rewards because of their personal or group characteristics.

Social interaction The process by which people act toward or respond to other people.

Socialism A political and economic system in which, ideally, classes are eliminated and production is for social benefit rather than private profit; the means of economic production are publicly owned but private ownership of consumer items is permitted.

Socialization The process of social interaction through which people acquire personality and learn the way of life of their society.

Social learning theory A theory of learning that relies on behaviorist principles but recognizes that some learning is incidental or the result of imitation, even though no obvious rewards or punishments are present.

Social mobility Movement from one status to another in a stratified society.

Social movement A large number of people who have joined together to bring about or resist some social or cultural change.

Social psychology The scientific study of the influence of social context on human personality and behavior.

Social sciences A related group of disciplines that study various aspects of human behavior.

Social stratification The structured inequality of entire categories of people, who have different access to social rewards as a result of their statuses in the social hierarchy.

Social structure The organized relationships between the basic components of a social system.

Society A group of interacting individuals sharing the same territory and participating in a common culture.
Sociocultural evolution The tendency of societies to evolve from simple to complex forms as their subsistence strategies become more efficient.
Socioeconomic status (SES) A measure of social status that takes into account a complex of factors, such as educational background, place of residence, and income.
Sociology The scientific study of human society and social behavior.
Spurious A term used to refer to a correlation between variables that is purely coincidental, not causal.
State The institution that successfully claims a monopoly of the legitimate use of force within a given territory.
Statics Refers to the phenomenon of social order and stability.
Status A socially defined position in society.
Stereotype A rigid mental image that summarizes whatever is believed to be typical of a group or category.
Stigma A mark of social disgrace.
Stratified random sample A sample obtained by dividing a population into various categories and then drawing a random sample from each category.
Subculture A group that shares in the overall culture of a society but also has its own distinctive values, norms, and life-style.
Subjectivity The tendency to see the world from a viewpoint that derives from the observer's own opinions, attitudes, and experiences.
Superego In Freudian theory, the internalized moral authority of society within the self; the superego is roughly equivalent to conscience.
Surplus wealth Wealth over and above that necessary to meet the basic needs of its producers.
Symbol Anything that can meaningfully represent something else, such as a word, a gesture, or a flag.
Symbolic interaction The interaction between people that takes place through symbols, such as signs, gestures, and language.

Taboo A powerful social belief that a particular act is utterly loathsome and disgusting.
Technocracy Rule by technical experts.
Technological determinism The theory that the technology available to a society is an important determinant of its social structure and even its history.
Technology The practical applications of knowledge about nature.
Tertiary industry Economic activity devoted to the provision of services rather than the extraction of raw materials or the manufacture of goods.
Theodicy An emotionally satisfying religious explanation for the great problems of human existence, such as suffering, death, and the meaning of life.
Theoretical perspective A broad, generalized assumption or set of assumptions about society and social behavior that provides an overall orientation for the examination of specific problems.
Theory A statement that organizes a set of concepts in a meaningful way by explaining the relationship between them.
Total institution A place of residence where the inmates are confined for an entire period of their lives, are cut off from the rest of society, and are under the almost absolute control of the administrative authorities.
Traditional authority Authority that is legitimated by ancient custom.
Triad A group consisting of three people.

Unilinear evolution Refers to a theory that sociocultural evolution follows the same course in all societies.

Value conflict Basic disagreement between groups over goals, ideals, policies, or other expressions of values.
Value freedom Refers to the position that sociologists can and should exclude personal judgments and biases from their work.
Value judgment A personal, subjective opinion based on the values of the observer.
Values Socially shared ideas about what is good, right, and desirable.
Variable A characteristic that can vary from one person, group, or context to another (such as age, race, intelligence, and violent behavior).
Verstehen Subjective interpretation of a social actor's behavior and intentions.
Vertical mobility A change to a higher or lower social status than the individual had initially.
Veto groups Strong interest groups that try to protect their interests by blocking proposals of other groups that might encroach on those interests.

White-collar crime Crimes committed by "respectable" persons of high status, frequently in the course of their occupations.

Zero population growth (ZPG) A situation in which population size remains stable over time.

References

ADORNO, THEODORE W., et al. 1950. *The Authoritarian Personality.* New York: W. W. Norton.

ALBERT, ETHEL M. 1963. "Women of Burundi: a study of social values," *in* Denise Paulme (ed.), *Women of Tropical Africa.* Berkeley, Calif.: California University Press.

ALLISON, PAUL D., and JOHN A. STEWARD. 1974. "Productivity differences among scientists: evidence for cumulative advantage." *American Sociological Review,* 39, pp. 596–606.

ALLPORT, GORDON W., and LEO J. POSTMAN. 1947. *The Psychology of Rumor.* New York: Holt, Rinehart and Winston.

ANDERSON, CHARLES H. 1974a. *The Political Economy of Social Class.* Englewood Cliffs, N.J.: Prentice-Hall.

———. 1974b. *Toward a New Sociology,* rev. ed. Homewood, Ill.: Dorsey Press.

APA Monitor. 1974. "Homosexuality dropped as mental disorder." 5, February, pp. 1, 9.

ARGYLE, MICHAEL, and J. DEAN. 1965. "Eye contact, distance, and affiliation." *Sociometry,* 28, pp. 289–304.

ARIES, PHILLIPE. 1962. *Centuries of Childhood: A Social History of Family Life.* New York: Alfred A. Knopf.

ARMER, J. MICHAEL. 1968. "Inter-society and intra-society correlations of occupational prestige." *American Journal of Sociology,* 74, pp. 28–63.

ASCH, SOLOMON. 1955. "Opinions and social pressure." *Scientific American,* 193, pp. 31–35.

ATHANASIOU, ROBERT, et al. 1972. "Sex." *Psychology Today,* 4, pp. 39–52.

AUCHINCLOSS, KENNETH. 1970. "The ravaged environment." *Newsweek,* 26, pp. 30–32.

BALES, ROBERT F. 1950. *Interaction Process Analysis: A Method for the Study of Small Groups.* Cambridge, Mass.: Addison-Wesley.

———. 1953. "The equilibrium problem in small groups," *in* Talcott Parsons et al. (eds.), *Working Papers in the Theory of Action.* Glencoe, Ill.: Free Press.

———. 1970. *Personality and Interpersonal Behavior.* New York: Holt, Rinehart and Winston.

———, and FRED L. STRODTBECK. 1951. "Phases in group problem solving." *Journal of Abnormal and Social Psychology,* 46, pp. 485–495.

BALL, DONALD W. 1968. "Toward a sociology of telephones and telephoners," *in* Marcello Truzzi (ed.), *Sociology and Everyday Life.* Englewood Cliffs, N.J.: Prentice-Hall.

BALSWICK, JACK O., and CHARLES W. PEEK. 1971. "The inexpressive male, a tragedy of American society." *Family Life Coordinator,* 20, pp. 363–368.

BALTZELL, E. DIGBY. 1958. *The Philadelphia Gentleman.* Glencoe, Ill.: Free Press.

BANDURA, ALBERT, and RICHARD H. WALTERS. 1963. *Social Learning and Personality Development.* New York: Holt, Rinehart and Winston.

BARBER, THEODORE, et al. 1969. "Five attempts to replicate the experimenter bias effect." *Journal of Consulting and Clinical Psychology,* 3, pp. 1–6.

BARNETT, H. G. 1953. *Innovation: The Basis of Cultural Change.* New York: McGraw-Hill.

BARRY, HERBERT, MARGARET K. BACON, and IRVIN CHILD. 1957. "A cross-cultural survey of some sex differences in socialization." *Journal of Abnormal and Social Psychology,* 55, pp. 327–332.

BARTELL, GILBERT. 1970. "Group sex among the mid-Americans." *Journal of Sex Research,* 6, May, pp. 113–130.

———. 1974. "Group sex among the middle Americans," *in* James R. Smith and Lynn G. Smith (eds.), *Beyond Monogamy.* Baltimore, Md.: Johns Hopkins Press.

BATES, ALAN P., and JOSEPH JULIAN. 1975. *Sociology: Understanding Human Behavior.* Boston: Houghton Mifflin.

BEACH, FRANK A. (ed.). 1965. *Sex and Behavior.* New York: Wiley.

BECKER, HOWARD S. 1953. "Becoming a marijuana user." *American Journal of Sociology,* 59, November, pp. 235–242.

———. (ed.). 1963a. *The Other Side.* New York: Free Press.

———. 1963b. *Outsiders: Studies in the Sociology of Deviance*. New York: Free Press.

BELL, DANIEL. 1967a. "Notes on the postindustrial society, I." *The Public Interest*, 6, pp. 24–35.

———. 1967b. "Notes on the postindustrial society, II." *The Public Interest*, 7, pp. 102–118.

———. 1973. *The Coming of Postindustrial Society*. New York: Basic Books.

BELL, DERRICK A. 1973. "Racism in American courts." *California New Law Review*, 61, pp. 165–203.

BELL, ROBERT R. 1964. "Some factors related to the sexual satisfaction of the college-educated wife." *Family Life Coordinator*, 13, pp. 43–47.

BELLAH, ROBERT N. 1970. *Beyond Belief*. New York: Harper & Row.

BEM, SANDRA, and DARYL BEM. 1970. "We're all nonconscious sexists." *Psychology Today*, 4, p. 22.

BEN-DAVID, JOSEPH. 1971. *The Scientist's Role in Society*. Englewood Cliffs, N.J.: Prentice-Hall.

BENEDICT, RUTH. 1934. *Patterns of Culture*. Boston: Houghton Mifflin.

BENJAMIN, HARRY, and R. E. L. MASTERS. 1964. *Prostitution and Morality*. New York: Julian Press.

BENNET, EDWARD M., and LARRY R. COHEN. 1959. "Men and women: personality patterns and contrasts." *Genetic Psychology Monographs*, 59, pp. 101–155.

BENNIS, WARREN G. 1966. *Changing Organizations*. New York: McGraw-Hill.

BERELSON, BERNARD, and GARY G. STEINER. 1964. *Human Behavior: An Inventory of Scientific Findings*. New York: Harcourt, Brace, and World.

BERGEL, ERGON E. 1962. *Social Stratification*. New York: McGraw-Hill.

BERGER, BENNET M. 1961. "The myth of suburbia." *Journal of Social Issues*, 17, pp. 38–49.

BERGER, PETER L. 1963. *Invitation to Sociology: A Humanistic Perspective*. New York: Doubleday.

———. 1964. "Some general observations on the problem of work," *in* Peter L. Berger (ed.), *The Human Shape of Work*. New York: Macmillan.

———. 1969a. *A Rumor of Angels: Modern Society and the Rediscovery of the Supernatural*. New York: Doubleday.

———. 1969b. *The Sacred Canopy: Elements of a Sociological Theory of Religion*. New York: Doubleday.

———, and THOMAS LUCKMANN. 1963. *The Social Construction of Reality*. New York: Doubleday.

BERLE, A. A., and G. C. MEANS. 1933. *The Modern Corporation and Private Property*. New York: Macmillan.

BERLIN, BRENT, and PAUL KAY. 1969. *Basic Color Terms: Their Universality and Evolution*. Berkeley, Calif.: University of California Press.

BERNARD, JESSIE. 1956. *Remarriage: A Study of Marriage*. New York: Dryden.

BERNARD, L. L. 1924. *Instinct*. New York: Holt, Rinehart and Winston.

BERNSTEIN, BASIL. 1971. *Class, Codes, and Control*. London: Routledge & Kegan Paul.

BERREMAN, GERALD D. 1960. "Caste in India and the United States." *American Journal of Sociology*, 66, pp. 120–127.

———. 1973. *Caste in the Modern World*. Morristown, N.J.: General Learning Press.

BERRY, R. STEPHEN. 1970. "The chemistry and cost: perspectives on polluted air—1970." *Bulletin of the Atomic Scientists*, 26, pp. 2, 34–41.

BIEBER, IRVING, et al. 1962. *Homosexuality: A Psychoanalytic Study*. New York: Basic Books.

BIRDWHISTELL, RAY L. 1970. *Kinesics and Context*. Philadelphia: Pennsylvania University Press.

BIRENBAUM, ARNOLD, and EDWARD SAGARIN. 1973. "The deviant actor maintains his right to be present: the case of the nondrinker," *in* Arnold Birenbaum and Edward Sagarin (eds.), *People in Places: The Sociology of the Familiar*. New York: Praeger.

BLAU, PETER M. 1963. *The Dynamics of Bureaucracy*, rev. ed. Chicago: University of Chicago Press.

———. 1964. *Exchange and Power in Social Life*. New York: Wiley.

———, and OTIS DUDLEY DUNCAN. 1967. *The American Occupational Structure*. New York: Wiley.

———, and MARSHALL W. MEYER. 1971. *Bureaucracy in Modern Society*, 2nd ed. New York: Random House.

———, and W. RICHARD SCOTT. 1962. *Formal Organizations*. San Francisco: Chandler.

BLAUNER, ROBERT. 1964. *Alienation and Freedom*. Chicago: University of Chicago Press.

———. 1972. *Racial Oppression in America*. New York: Harper & Row.

BLOOD, ROBERT O. 1962. *Marriage*. New York: Free Press.

BLUMBERG, ABRAHAM S. 1967. *Criminal Justice*. Chicago: Quadrangle.

BLUME, MARSHALL E., et al. 1974. "Stock ownership in the United States: characteristics and trends." *Survey of Current Business* (U.S. Department of Commerce), 54, pp. 16–40.

BLUMER, HERBERT. 1951. "Collective behavior," *in* Alfred McLung Lee (ed.), *New Outline of the Principles of Sociology*. New York: Barnes & Noble.

———. 1962. "Society as symbolic interaction," *in* Arnold Rose (ed.), *Human Behavior and Social Processes: An Interactionist*

Approach. Boston: Houghton Mifflin.

———. 1969. *Symbolic Interactionism: Perspective and Method.* Englewood Cliffs, N.J.: Prentice-Hall.

BLUMSTEIN, PHILIP, and PEPPER SCHWARTZ. 1974. "The acquisition of sexual identity: the bisexual case." Paper presented at the Annual Meetings of the American Sociological Association, August 25–29, Montreal, Canada.

BOTT, ELIZABETH. 1971. *Family and Social Network.* New York: Free Press.

BOULDING, KENNETH E. 1964. *The Meaning of the Twentieth Century: The Great Transition.* New York: Harper & Row.

BOWLBY, JOHN. 1969. *Attachment and Loss,* Vol. 1. New York: Basic Books.

BRIM, ORVILLE G., et al. (eds.). 1970. *The Dying Patient.* New York: Russell Sage Foundation.

BRINTON, CRANE. 1960. *The Anatomy of Revolution.* New York: Random House.

BRONFENBRENNER, URIE. 1970. *Two Worlds of Childhood.* New York: Russell Sage Foundation.

BROPHY, J. E., and T. L. GOOD. 1970. "Teachers' communication of differential expectations for children's classroom performance: some behavioral data." *Journal of Educational Psychology,* 61, p. 356.

BROWN, ROGER. 1965. *Social Psychology.* New York: Free Press.

BRYANT, JAMES H. 1965. "Apprenticeships in prostitution." *Social Problems,* 12, Winter, pp. 278–297.

BUCKLEY, W. 1958. "Social stratification and the functional theory of social differentiation." *American Sociological Review,* 23, pp. 369–375.

BUCKNER, H. T. 1970. "The transvestic career path." *Psychiatry,* 33, pp. 381–389.

BUMPASS, LARRY, and CHARLES WESTOFF. 1970. "Unwanted births and U.S. population control." *Family Planning Perspectives,* 2, pp. 9–11.

BURGESS, ERNEST W., and PAUL WALLIN. 1973. *Engagement and Marriage.* Philadelphia: Lippincott.

BURGOON, JUDEE K., and STEPHEN B. JONES. 1976. "Toward a theory of personal space expectations and their violations." *Human Communication Research,* 2, pp. 131–146.

BURNET, F. M. 1966. "Men or molecules, a tilt at molecular biology." *The Lancet,* 1, pp. 37–39.

BURNETTE, ROBERT. 1971. *The Tortured Americans.* Englewood Cliffs, N.J.: Prentice-Hall.

BURNHAM, JAMES. 1941. *The Managerial Revolution.* New York: John Day.

CAMPBELL, ERNEST Q., and C. NORMAN ALEXANDER. 1964. "Peer influences on adolescent educational aspirations and attainment." *American Sociological Review,* 29, pp. 58–75.

CANTRIL, HADLEY. 1940. *The Invasion from Mars.* Princeton, N.J.: Princeton University Press.

———. 1963. *The Psychology of Social Movements.* New York: Wiley.

CAPLOW, THEODORE. 1954. *The Sociology of Work.* Minneapolis, Minn.: University of Minnesota Press.

CENTERS, RICHARD. 1949. *The Psychology of Social Class.* Princeton, N.J.: Princeton University Press.

———, BERTRAM H. RAVEN, and AROLDO RODRIGUES. 1971. "Conjugal power structure: a reexamination." *American Sociological Review,* 36, pp. 264–277.

CHAGNON, NAPOLEON A. 1967. "Yanamamö social organization and warfare," *in* Morton Fried, Marvin Harris, and R. Murphy (eds.), *War: The Anthropology of Armed Conflict and Aggression.* New York: Doubleday.

———. 1968. *Yanamamö: The Fierce People.* New York: Holt, Rinehart and Winston.

CHAMBLISS, WILLIAM J. 1973. "The Saints and the Roughnecks." *Society,* 11, pp. 24–31.

CHANDLER, JOHN J. 1969. "Perspectives on Poverty: An International Comparison." *Monthly Labor Review,* 92, pp. 55–62.

CHEEK, WILLIAM F. 1970. *Black Resistance before the Civil War.* Beverly Hills, Calif.: Glencoe Press.

CHINOY, ELY. 1955. *The Automobile Worker and the American Dream.* New York: Doubleday.

CHOMSKY, NOAM. 1957. *Syntactic Structures.* The Hague: Mouton.

———. 1968. *Language and Mind.* New York: Harcourt Brace Jovanovich.

———. 1971. "The case against B. F. Skinner." *The New York Review of Books,* 17, pp. 18–24.

CHURCH, FRANK. 1973. "Will they usher in a new world order?" *Center Magazine,* 6, pp. 15–18.

CICOUREL, AARON, and JOHN I. KITSUSE. 1963. "A note on the use of official statistics." *Social Problems,* 11, pp. 131–139.

CLAIBORN, W. L. 1969. "Expectancy effects in the classroom: a failure to replicate." *Journal of Educational Psychology,* 60, p. 377.

CLARK, BURTON R. 1960. "The 'cooling-out' function in higher education." *American Journal of Sociology,* 65, pp. 567–576.

———. 1962. *Educating the Expert Society.* San Francisco: Chandler.

———, and MARTIN TROW. 1966. "The organizational context," *in* Burton R. Clark and Martin Trow (eds.), *College Peer Groups: Problems and Prospects for Research.* Chicago: Aldine.

CLARK, KENNETH. 1965. *Dark Ghetto.* New York: Harper & Row.

CLAUSEN, JOHN A., et al. 1968. "Perspectives on child socialization," *in* John A. Clausen (ed.), *Socialization and Society.* Boston: Little, Brown.

CLINARD, MARSHALL B. 1974. *Sociology of Deviant Behavior,* 4th ed.

Englewood Cliffs, N.J.: Prentice-Hall.

CLOWARD, RICHARD A., and LLOYD E. OHLIN. 1960. *Delinquency and Opportunity: A Theory of Delinquent Gangs.* New York: Free Press.

COHEN, ALBERT K. 1955. *Delinquent Boys: The Culture of the Gang.* New York: Free Press.

______. 1959. "The study of social disorganization and deviant behavior," *in* Robert K. Merton, Leonard Broom, and Leonard S. Cottrell (eds.), *Sociology Today: Problems and Prospects.* New York: Basic Books.

______. 1966. *Deviance and Control.* Englewood Cliffs, N.J.: Prentice-Hall.

______, and HAROLD M. HODGES, JR. 1963. "Characteristics of the lower-blue-collar classes." *Social Policy,* pp. 61–67.

COHN, NORMAN. 1962. *The Pursuit of the Millenium.* New York: Oxford University Press.

COLE, JOHNATHAN R., and STEPHEN COLE. 1972. "The Ortega hypothesis." *Science,* 178, pp. 368–375.

COLEMAN, JAMES C. 1976. *Abnormal Psychology and Modern Life,* 5th ed. Glenview, Ill.: Scott, Foresman.

COLEMAN, JAMES S. 1961. *The Adolescent Society.* New York: Doubleday.

______, et al. 1966. *Equality of Educational Opportunity.* Washington, D.C.: Government Printing Office.

COLEMAN, RICHARD F., and BERNICE L. NEUGARTEN. 1971. *Social Status in the City.* San Francisco: Jossey-Bass.

COLES, ROBERT. 1969. Testimony Before the Select Committee on Nutrition and Human Needs of the U.S. Senate, February.

COLLINS, RANDALL. 1971. "A conflict theory of sexual stratification." *Social Problems,* 19, pp. 3–12.

______. 1974. *Conflict Sociology: Toward an Explanatory Science.* New York: Academic Press.

Commission on Population Growth and the American Future. 1972. *Population and the American Future: The Report of the Commission on Population Growth and the American Future.* Washington, D.C.: Government Printing Office.

COMMONER, BARRY. 1971. *The Closing Circle.* New York: Alfred A. Knopf.

Congressional Quarterly, "White collar crime: huge economic and moral drain," 29, 1971 pp. 1047–1049.

COOK, M. 1970. "Experiments on orientation and proxemics." *Human Relations,* 23, pp. 61–76.

COOLEY, CHARLES HORTON. 1902. *Human Nature and the Social Order.* New York: Scribner's.

COOPER, A. J. 1969. "A clinical study of 'coital anxiety' in male potency disorders." *Journal of Psychometric Research,* 13, pp. 143–147.

COSER, LEWIS A. 1956. *The Functions of Social Conflict.* Glencoe, Ill.: Free Press.

______. 1962. "Some functions of deviant behavior and normative flexibility." *American Journal of Sociology,* 68, pp. 172–179.

CRANE, DIANA. 1969. "Social structure in a group of scientists: a test of the 'invisible colleges' hypothesis." *American Sociological Review,* 34, pp. 335–351.

CRESSEY, DONALD R. 1969. *Theft of the Nation: The Structure and Operations of Organized Crime in America.* New York: Harper & Row.

CROSSMAN, RICHARD (ed.). 1952. *The God That Failed.* New York: Bantam.

CUTRIGHT, PHILLIP. 1967. "Inequality: a cross-national analysis." *American Sociological Review,* 32, pp. 562–578.

DAHL, ROBERT. 1961. *Who Governs?* New Haven, Conn.: Yale University Press.

DAHRENDORF, RALF. 1958. "Toward a theory of social conflict." *The Journal of Conflict Resolution,* 11, pp. 170–183.

D'ANDRADE, ROY G. 1966. "Sex differences and cultural institutions," *in* Eleanor E. Maccoby (ed.), *The Development of Sex Differences.* Palo Alto, Calif.: Stanford University Press.

DANK, BARRY M. 1971. "Coming out in the gay world." *Psychiatry,* 34, May, pp. 180–197.

DARLEY, JOHN M., and BIBB LATANÉ. 1968. "Bystander intervention in emergencies: diffusion of responsibility." *Journal of Personality and Social Psychology,* 8, pp. 377–383.

DAVIES, JAMES C. 1962. "Toward a theory of revolution." *American Sociological Review,* 27, pp. 5–18.

DAVIS, ALAN J. 1968. "Sexual assaults in the Philadelphia prison system." *Transaction,* 6, pp. 28–35.

DAVIS, FRED. 1961. "Deviance disavowal: the management of strained interaction by the visibly handicapped." *Social Problems,* 9, pp. 120–132.

DAVIS, JAMES H. 1969. *Group Performance.* Reading, Mass.: Addison-Wesley.

DAVIS, KINGSLEY. 1932. "The sociology of prostitution." *American Sociological Review,* 2, pp. 744–755.

______. 1940. "Extreme social isolation of a child." *American Journal of Sociology,* 45, pp. 554–564.

______. 1947. "Final note on a case of extreme isolation." *American Journal of Sociology,* 50, pp. 432–437.

______. 1948. *Human Society.* New York: Macmillan.

______. 1965. "The urbanization of the human population." *Scientific American,* 312, pp. 41–53.

______. 1967. "Population policy: will current programs succeed?" *Science,* 158, pp. 730–739.

______. 1976a. "Sexual behavior," *in* Robert K. Merton and Robert Nisbet (eds.), *Contemporary Social Problems.* New York: Harcourt Brace Jovanovich.

______. 1976b. "The world's population crisis," *in* Robert K. Merton and Robert Nisbet (eds.), *Contemporary Social Problems,* 3rd ed. New York: Harcourt Brace Jovanovich.

______, and WILBERT E. MOORE. 1945. "Some principles of stratification." *American Sociological Review,* 10, pp. 242–249.

DAVIS, NANETTE J. 1971. "The prostitute: developing a deviant identity," *in* James M. Henslin (ed.), *Studies in the Sociology of Sex.* New York: Appleton-Century-Crofts.

DENFIELD, DUANE, and MICHAEL GORDON. 1974. "The sociology of mate swapping: or the family that swings together clings together," *in* James R. Smith and Lynn G. Smith (eds.), *Beyond Monogamy.* Baltimore, Md.: Johns Hopkins Press.

DENNIS, WAYNE. 1960. "Causes of retardation among institutionalized children: Iran." *Journal of Genetic Psychology,* 96, pp. 47–59.

______, and PERGROUHI NAJARIAN. 1957. "Infant development under environmental handicap." *Psychological Monographs,* 71, pp. 1–3.

DENTLER, ROBERT A., and LAWRENCE J. MONROE. 1961. "Social correlates of early adolescent theft." *American Sociological Review,* 26, pp. 733–743.

DE TOCQUEVILLE, ALEXIS. 1954, originally published 1835. *Democracy in America II,* Phillips Bradley (ed.). New York: Random House.

DEUTSCHER, IRWIN. 1973. *What We Say, What We Do: Sentiments and Acts.* Glenview, Ill.: Scott, Foresman.

DIAMOND, MILTON. 1965. "A critical evaluation of the ontogeny of human sexual behavior." *Quarterly Review of Biology,* 40, pp. 147–173.

DJILAS, MILOVAN. 1957. *The New Class: An Analysis of the Communist System.* New York: Praeger.

DOBRINER, WILLIAM. 1958. *The Suburban Community.* New York: Putnam's.

DOLESCHAL, EUGENE, and NORAH KLAPMUTS. 1973. *Toward a New Criminology.* Hackensack, N.J.: National Council on Crime and Delinquency.

DOMHOFF, G. WILLIAM. 1967. *Who Rules America?* Englewood Cliffs, N.J.: Prentice-Hall.

______. 1971. *The Higher Circles.* New York: Random House.

DUBERMAN, MARTIN. 1974. "The bisexual debate." *New Times,* 2, pp. 34–41.

DURKHEIM, EMILE. 1954, originally published 1912. *The Elementary Forms of Religious Life,* Joseph W. Swain (trans.). Glencoe, Ill.: Free Press.

______. 1964a, originally published 1893. *The Division of Labor in Society,* George Simpson (trans.). Glencoe, Ill.: Free Press.

______. 1964b, originally published 1897. *Suicide.* Glencoe, Ill.: Free Press.

DUVERGER, MAURICE. 1954. *Political Parties.* New York: Wiley.

EASTON, DAVID, and JACK DENNIS. 1969. *Children in the Political System.* New Haven, Conn.: Yale University Press.

______, and ROBERT D. HESS. 1962. "The child's changing political world," *Midwest Journal of Political Science,* pp. 229–246.

Economic Report of the President, 1974. Washington, D.C.: Government Printing Office.

EHRLICH, PAUL R. 1970. *The Population Explosion: Facts and Fiction.* Palo Alto, Calif.: Zero Population Growth.

______, and ANNE H. EHRLICH. 1972. *Population/Resources/Environment: Issues in Human Ecology.* San Francisco: W. H. Freeman.

______, and JOHN P. HOLDREN. 1971. "Avoiding the problem." *Saturday Review,* 54, p. 56.

EITZEN, D. STANLEY. 1974. *Social Structure and Social Problems in America.* Boston: Allyn and Bacon.

EKMAN, PAUL, and WALLACE V. FRIESEN. 1971. "Constraint across cultures in the face and emotion." *Journal of Personality and Social Psychology,* 17, pp. 214–219.

ELKINS, STANLEY M. 1963. *Slavery: A Problem in American Institutional and Intellectual Life.* New York: Grosset & Dunlap.

ELLIS, ALBERT. 1970. "Group marriage: a possible alternative?" *in* Herbert A. Otto (ed.), *The Family in Search of a Future.* New York: Appleton-Century-Crofts.

ELLUL, JACQUES. 1964. *The Technological Society.* New York: Alfred A. Knopf.

EMPEY, LAMAR T., and MAYNARD ERICKSON. 1966. "Hidden delinquency and social status." *Social Forces,* 44, pp. 546–554.

EPSTEIN, CYNTHIA F. 1976. "Sex roles," *in* Robert K. Merton and Robert Nisbet (eds.), *Contemporary Social Problems.* New York: Harcourt Brace Jovanovich.

ERBE, WILLIAM. 1964. "Social involvement and political activity: a replication and elaboration." *American Sociological Review,* 29, 198–215.

ERICKSON, MAYNARD L. 1971. "The group context of delinquent behavior." *Social Problems,* 19, pp. 114–129.

______. 1973. "Group violations, socioeconomic status and official delinquency." *Social Forces,* 52, pp. 41–52.

ERIKSON, ERIK H. 1964. *Childhood and Society.* New York: W. W. Norton.

ERIKSON, KAI T. 1966. *Wayward Puritans: A Study in the Sociology of Deviance.* New York: Wiley.

ETZIONI, AMITAI. 1961. *A Comparative Analysis of Complex Organizations.* Glencoe, Ill.: Free Press.

______. 1964. *Modern Organizations.* Englewood Cliffs, N.J.: Prentice-Hall.

______ (ed.). 1969. *The Semi-Professions and Their Organization.* New York: Free Press.

______. 1972. "Human beings are not very easy to change after all." *Saturday Review,* 55, pp. 45–47.

______, and CLYDE NUNN. 1974. "The public appreciation of science in contemporary America." *Daedalus,* 103, pp. 191–205.

FARBER, JERRY. 1970. *The Student as Nigger.* New York: Simon and Schuster.

FARRINGTON, BENJAMIN. 1949. *Greek Science, II.* London: Penguin.

FEAGIN, JOE R. 1972. "Poverty: we still believe that God helps those that help themselves." *Psychology Today,* 6, pp. 101–110.

FELIPE, N., and R. SOMMER. 1966. "Invasions of personal space." *Social Problems,* 14, pp. 206–214.

FESTINGER, LEON, H. W. RIECKEN, and STANLEY SCHACTER. 1956. *When Prophecy Fails.* New York: Harper & Row.

FIEDLER, FRED. 1969. "Style or circumstance: the leadership enigma." *Psychology Today,* 2, pp. 38–43.

FIREY, WALTER. 1947. *Land Use in Central Boston.* Cambridge, Mass.: Harvard University Press.

FITZGERALD, ERNEST. 1973. "The Pentagon as the enemy of capitalism." *World,* 2, pp. 18–21.

FORD, CLELLAN S., and FRANK A. BEACH. 1951. *Patterns of Sexual Behavior.* New York: Harper & Row.

FOX, THOMAS G., and S. M. MILLER. 1966. "Economic, political, and social determinants of mobility: an international cross-sectional analysis." *Acta Sociologica,* 9, No. 1–2, pp. 76–93.

______, and S. M. MILLER. 1965. "Inter-country variations: occupational stratification and mobility." *Studies in Comparative International Development,* 1, pp. 3–10.

FREEDMAN, M. 1975. *Personal Definition and Psychological Function.* New York: Harper & Row.

FRIED, MORTON. 1967. *The Evolution of Political Society.* New York: Random House.

FRIEDENBERG, EDGAR. 1969. "What do schools do?" *This Magazine Is About Schools,* 3, pp. 24–37.

GAGNON, JOHN, and WILLIAM SIMON (eds.). 1967. *Sexual Deviance.* Chicago: Aldine.

______, and WILLIAM SIMON. 1973. *Sexual Conduct: The Social Sources of Human Sexuality.* Chicago: Aldine.

GALBRAITH, JOHN KENNETH. 1966. *The Affluent Society.* Boston: Beacon.

______. 1967. *The New Industrial State.* New York: Signet.

______. 1971. *The New Industrial State,* 2nd ed. Boston: Houghton Mifflin.

______. 1973. *Economics and the Public Purpose.* Boston: Houghton Mifflin.

GALLMAN, ROBERT E. 1969. "Trends in size distribution in wealth in the nineteenth century: some speculation," *in* Lee Soltow (ed.), *Six Papers on the Size Distribution of Wealth and Income.* New York: Columbia University Press.

GANDY, PATRICK, and ROBERT DEISHER. 1970. "Young male prostitutes." *Journal of the American Medical Association,* 212, pp. 1661–1666.

GANS, HERBERT J. 1962a. "Urbanism and suburbanism as ways of life," *in* Arnold M. Rose (ed.), *Human Behavior and Social Processes.* Boston: Houghton Mifflin.

______. 1962b. *The Urban Villagers.* New York: Free Press.

______. 1967. *The Levittowners: Way of Life and Politics in a New Suburban Community.* New York: Pantheon.

______ (ed.). 1968. *People and Plans: Essays on Urban Problems and Solutions.* New York: Basic Books.

______. 1973. *More Equality.* New York: Pantheon.

GARDNER, R. ALLEN, and BEATRICE GARDNER. 1969. "Teaching sign language to a chimpanzee." *Science,* 165, pp. 664–672.

GARFINKEL, HAROLD. 1956. "Conditions of successful degradation ceremonies." *American Journal of Sociology,* 61, pp. 420–424.

______. 1964. "Studies of the routine grounds of everyday activities." *Social Problems,* 11, pp. 225–250.

______. 1967. *Studies in Ethnomethodology.* Englewood Cliffs, N.J.: Prentice-Hall.

______. 1970. "The ethnomethodological paradigm," *in* Hans Peter Dreitzel (ed.), *Recent Sociology No. 2: Patterns of Communicative Behavior.* London: Macmillan.

GEERTZ, CLIFFORD. 1968. "The impact of the concept of culture on the concept of man," *in* Yehudi A. Cohen (ed.), *Man and Adaptation: The Cultural Present.* Chicago: Aldine.

GEPHART, WILLIAM J. 1970. "Will the real Pygmalion please stand up?" *American Educational Research Journal,* 7, pp. 473–474.

GESELL, ARNOLD. 1940. *The First Five Years of Life: A Guide to the Study of the Preschool Child.* New York: Harper & Row.

GINTIS, HERBERT. 1971. "Education and the characteristics of worker productivity." *American Economic Review,* 61, pp. 266–279.

GLASER, BARNEY G., and ANSELM L. STRAUSS. 1965. *Awareness of Dying.* Chicago: Aldine.

______, and ANSELM L. STRAUSS. 1968. *Time for Dying.* Chicago: Aldine.

GLENN, NORVAL D. 1974. "Income inequality in the United States," *in* Joseph Lepreato and Lionel S. Lewis (eds.), *Social Stratification.* New York: Harper & Row.

GLOCK, CHARLES Y., and RODNEY STARK. 1965. *Religion and Society in Tension.* Chicago: Rand McNally.

______, and RODNEY STARK. 1966. *Christian Beliefs and Anti-Semitism.* New York: Harper & Row.

______, and RODNEY STARK. 1968. *American Piety: The Nature of Religious Commitment.* Berkeley, Calif.: University of California Press.

GLUECK, SHELDON, and ELEANOR GLUECK. 1956. *Physique and De-*

linquency. New York: Harper & Row.

GOCKEL, GALEN L. 1969. "Income and religious affiliation: a regression analysis." *American Journal of Sociology,* 74, pp. 632–646.

GOFFMAN, ERVING. 1959. *The Presentation of the Self in Everyday Life.* New York: Doubleday.

———. 1961. *Asylums: Essays on the Social Situation of Mental Patients and Other Inmates.* Chicago: Aldine.

———. 1963a. *Behavior in Public Places.* New York: Free Press.

———. 1963b. *Stigma: Notes on the Management of Spoiled Identity.* Englewood Cliffs, N.J.: Prentice-Hall.

———. 1966. *Encounters.* Indianapolis, Ind.: Bobbs-Merrill.

———. 1967. *Interaction Ritual: Essays on Face-to-Face Behavior.* New York: Doubleday.

———. 1969. *Strategic Interaction.* Philadelphia: University of Pennsylvania Press.

———. 1971. *Relations in Public.* New York: Basic Books.

———. 1974. *Frame Analysis: An Essay on the Organization of Experience.* New York: Harper & Row.

GOLD, MARTIN. 1970. *Delinquent Behavior in an American City.* Belmont, Calif.: Brooks/Cole.

GOLDBERG, PHILIP. 1968. "Are women prejudiced against women?" *Trans-Action,* 5, pp. 28–30.

GOLDFARB, WILLIAM. 1945. "Psychological privation in infancy and subsequent adjustment." *American Journal of Orthopsychiatry,* 15, April, pp. 247–253.

GOLDSMITH, EDWARD, et al. 1972. "Blueprint for survival." *The Ecologist,* 2, pp. 2–6.

GOODE, WILLIAM J. 1956. *The Family.* Englewood Cliffs, N.J.: Prentice-Hall.

———. 1959. "The theoretical importance of love." *American Sociological Review,* 24, pp. 38–47.

———. 1963. *World Revolution and Family Patterns.* New York: Free Press.

———. 1965. *After Divorce.* New York: Free Press.

GOODMAN, PAUL. 1970. "High school is too much." *Psychology Today,* 4, pp. 25–34.

GORDON, MILTON M. 1961. "Assimilation in America: Theory and reality." *Daedalus,* 90, pp. 363–365.

GORING, CHARLES. 1913. *The English Convict.* London: His Majesty's Stationery Office.

GOUGH, KATHLEEN E. 1959. "The Nayars and the definition of marriage." *Journal of the Royal Anthropological Institute,* 89, pp. 23–34.

GOULDNER, ALVIN W. 1970. *The Coming Crisis of Western Sociology.* New York: Avon.

———, and TIMOTHY SPREHE. 1965. "Sociologists look at themselves." Transaction, 2, pp. 42–44.

GRAHAM, HUGH DAVIS, and TED ROBERT GURR. 1969. *Violence in America: Historical Perspectives.* New York: Bantam.

GREELEY, ANDREW M. 1974. *Ethnicity in the United States.* New York: Wiley.

GREEN, MARK J. 1972. "The high cost of monopoly." *The Progressive,* pp. 15–19.

GREEN, RICHARD, and JOHN MONEY. 1969. *Transsexualism and Sex Reassignment.* Baltimore, Md.: Johns Hopkins Press.

GREENBERG, SELIG. 1957. "Why women live longer than men." *Harper's,* 215, October, pp. 70–73.

GREENFIELD, SIDNEY M. 1965. "Love and marriage in modern America: a functional analysis." *The Sociological Quarterly,* 6, pp. 361–377.

GREENSTEIN, FRED I. 1965. *Children and Politics.* New Haven, Conn.: Yale University Press.

———. 1968 "Political socialization." *International Encyclopaedia of the Social Sciences.*

GREENWALD, HAROLD. 1958. *The Call Girl.* New York: Ballantine.

———. 1970. *The Affluent Prostitute: A Social and Psychological Study.* New York: Walker.

GREENWOOD, E. 1962. "Attributes of a profession," *in* S. Nosow and W. H. Form (eds.), *Man, Work and Society.* New York: Basic Books.

GREER, SCOTT A. 1962. *The Emerging City: Myth and Reality.* New York: Free Press.

GRIFFITH, BELVER C., and NICHOLAS C. MULLINS. 1972. "Coherent social groups in scientific change." *Science,* 177, September 15, pp. 959–964.

GROSS, NEAL. 1953. "Social class identification in the urban community." *American Sociological Review,* 18, pp. 398–404.

HACKER, HELEN. 1951. "Women as a minority group." *Social Forces,* 30, pp. 60–69.

HADDEN, JEFFREY K. 1970. "Clergy involvement in civil rights." *The Annals,* 387, pp. 118–127.

HAGSTROM, WILLIAM O. 1965. *The Scientific Community.* New York: Basic Books.

———. 1974. "Competition in science." *American Sociological Review,* 39, pp. 1–18.

HALL, EDWARD T. 1959. *The Silent Language.* New York: Doubleday.

———. 1966. *The Hidden Dimension.* New York: Doubleday.

———, and MILDRED R. HALL. 1976. "The sounds of silence," *in* Jeffrey E. Nash and James P. Spradley (eds.), *Sociology: A Descriptive Approach.* Chicago: Rand McNally.

HALL, PETER M., and JOHN P. HEWITT. 1970. "The quasi-theory of communication and the management of dissent." *Social Problems,* 18, pp. 17–27.

HARE, A. PAUL. 1962. *Handbook of Small Group Research.* Glencoe, Ill.: Free Press.

______, et al. (eds.). 1965. *Small Groups: Studies in Social Interaction.* New York: Alfred A. Knopf.

HARLOW, HARRY F. 1958. "The nature of love." *American Psychologist,* 13, pp. 673–685.

______. 1965. "The affectional systems." *in* Allan Schrier *et al.* (eds.), *Behavior of Nonhuman Primates: Modern Research Trends.* New York: Academic Press.

______, and MARGARET K. HARLOW. 1962. "Social deprivation in monkeys." *Scientific American,* 207, November, pp. 137–147.

______, and R. R. ZIMMERMAN. 1959. "Affectional responses in the infant monkey." *Science,* 130, pp. 421–423.

HARRIS, C. D., and EDWARD L. ULLMAN. 1945. "The nature of cities," *The Annals of the American Academy of Political and Social Science,* 242, pp. 7–17.

HARRIS, LOUIS. 1973. *The Anguish of Change.* New York: W. W. Norton.

HARRIS, MARVIN. 1974. *Cows, Pigs, Wars, and Witches: The Riddles of Culture.* New York: Random House.

______. 1975. *Culture, People, and Nature: An Introduction to General Anthropology,* 2nd ed. New York: T. Y. Crowell.

HARTLEY, EUGENE. 1946. *Problems in Prejudice.* New York: King's Crown Press.

HARTLEY, RUTH E. 1970. "American core culture: changes and continuities," *in* Georgene H. Seward and Robert C. Williamson (eds.), *Sex Roles in a Changing Society.* New York: Random House.

HAUSER, PHILIP M. (ed.). 1969. *The Population Dilemma,* 2nd ed. Englewood Cliffs, N.J.: Prentice-Hall.

HEILBRONER, ROBERT. 1967. *The Worldly Philosophers,* 3rd ed. New York: Simon and Schuster.

HENRY, JULES. 1963. *Culture Against Man.* New York: Random House.

HENSLIN, JAMES M. 1968. "Trust and the cab driver," *in* Marcello Truzzi (ed.), *Sociology and Everyday Life.* Englewood Cliffs, N.J.: Prentice-Hall.

______. 1975. *Introducing Sociology.* New York: Free Press.

______, and MAE A. BRIGGS. 1971. "Dramaturgical desexualization: the sociology of the vaginal examination," *in* James M. Henslin (ed.), *Studies in the Sociology of Sex.* New York: Appleton-Century-Crofts.

HERBERG, WILL. 1960. *Protestant, Catholic, Jew.* New York: Doubleday.

HERRICK, NEAL W. 1972. "Who's unhappy at work and why." *Manpower,* 4, pp. 2 –7.

HEUSSENSTAMM, FRANCES K. 1971. "Bumper stickers and cops." *Transaction,* 8, pp. 32–33.

HEWITT, JOHN P., and PETER M. HALL. 1973. "Social problems, problematic solutions, and quasi-theories." *American Sociological Review,* 38, pp. 367–374.

______, and RANDALL STOKES. 1975. "Disclaimers." *American Sociological Review,* 40, pp. 1–11.

HILLIER, E. T. 1933. *Principles of Sociology.* New York: Harper & Row.

HINDELANG, MICHAEL J. 1971a. "Age, sex, and the versatility of delinquent involvements." *Social Problems,* 18, pp. 522–535.

______. 1971b. "The social versus solitary nature of delinquent involvement." *British Journal of Criminology,* 11, pp. 167–175.

HIRSCHI, TRAVIS. 1969. *Causes of Delinquency.* Berkeley, Calif.: University of California Press.

HITLER, ADOLF. 1948. *Mein Kampf,* Ralph Mannheim (trans.). Boston: Houghton Mifflin.

HOBBES, THOMAS. 1958 originally published 1598. *Leviathan.* New York: Liberal Arts Press.

HODGE ROBERT W., and DONALD J. TREIMAN. 1968. "Class identification in the United States." *American Journal of Sociology,* 73, pp. 535–547.

______, PAUL M. SIEGEL, and PETER H. ROSSI. 1964. "Occupational prestige in the United States, 1925–1963." *American Journal of Sociology,* 70, pp. 286–302.

______, D. TREIMAN, and PETER H. ROSSI. 1966. "A comparative study of occupational prestige," *in* R. Bendix and S. M. Lipset (eds.), *Class, Status, and Power,* 2nd ed. New York: Free Press.

HOFSTADTER, RICHARD. 1955. *Social Darwinism in American Thought.* Boston: Beacon.

HOLLANDER, EDWIN P. 1964. *Leaders, Groups, and Influence.* New York: Oxford University Press.

HOLLINGSHEAD, AUGUST B. 1949. *Elmstown's Youth.* New York: Wiley.

______, and FREDERICK REDLICH. 1958. *Social Class and Mental Disorder.* New York: Wiley.

HOLT, JOHN. 1964. *How Children Fail.* New York: Pitman.

______. 1972. "The little red prison." *Harper's,* 244, June, pp. 80–82.

HOMANS, GEORGE. C. 1961. *Social Behavior: Its Elementary Forms.* New York: Harcourt, Brace, and World.

HOOKER, EVELYN. 1957. "The adjustment of the male overt homosexual." *Journal of Projective Techniques,* 21, pp. 18–31.

______. 1962. "The homosexual community," in *Proceedings of the XVI International Congress of Applied Psychology,* Vol. 2, *Personality Research.* Copenhagen: Munksgaard.

______. 1965. "An empirical study of some relations between sexual patterns and gender identity in male homosexuals," *in* John Money (ed.), *Sex Research—New Developments.* New York: Holt, Rinehart and Winston.

______. 1969. "Parental relations and male homosexuality in patient and nonpatient samples." *Journal of Consulting and Clinical Psychology,* 33, pp. 140–142.

HORNER, MATINA. 1968. "Sex differences in achievement motivation and performance in competitive and noncompetitive situations." Doctoral dissertation, University of Michigan.

______. 1969. "Fail: bright women." *Psychology Today,* 3, p. 36ff.

______. 1972. "Toward an understanding of achievement-related conflicts in women." *Journal of Social Issues,* 29, pp. 157–175.

HOROWITZ, IRVING LOUIS. 1967. *The Rise and Fall of Project Camelot.* Cambridge, Mass.: MIT Press.

HORTON, PAUL B., and CHESTER L. HUNT. 1972. *Sociology,* 3rd ed. New York: McGraw-Hill.

______, and GERALD R. LESLIE. 1974. *Social Problems.* New York: McGraw-Hill.

HOWE, FLORENCE. 1971. "Sex role stereotypes start early." *Saturday Review,* 54, pp. 76–82.

HOWE, LOUISE KAPP. 1973. "Women in the workplace." *the Humanist,* 33, pp. 21–25.

HOYT, HOMER. 1939. *The Structure and Growth of Residential Neighborhoods in American Cities.* Washington, D.C.: Federal Housing Authority.

HUMPHREYS, LAUD. 1970. *Tearoom Trade: Impersonal Sex in Public Places,* Chicago: Aldine.

______. 1971. "New styles in homosexual manliness." *Transaction,* 8, pp. 38–46.

______. 1972. *Out of the Closets: The Sociology of Homosexual Liberation.* Englewood Cliffs, N.J.: Prentice-Hall.

HUNT, MORTON. 1959. *The Natural History of Love.* New York: Alfred A. Knopf.

______. 1974. *Sexual Behavior in the 1970's.* New York: Dell.

HUNTER, FLOYD. 1953. *Community Power Structure.* Chapel Hill, N.C.: University of North Carolina Press.

HUTTON, J. H., 1963. *Caste in India: Its Nature, Functions, and Origins,* 4th ed. London: Oxford University Press.

HYMAN, HERBERT. 1969. *Political Socialization: A Study in the Psychology of Political Behavior.* New York: Free Press.

HYMAN, HERBERT H., and CHARLES R. WRIGHT. 1971. "Trends in voluntary associational memberships of American adults: replication based on secondary analysis of national sample surveys." *American Sociological Review,* 23, April, pp. 191–206.

INKELES, ALEX. 1950. "Social stratification and mobility in the Soviet Union: 1940–1950." *American Sociological Review,* 15, pp. 465–479.

______, and PETER H. ROSSI. 1956. "National comparisons of occupational prestige." *American Journal of Sociology,* 66, July, pp. 329–339.

______, and DAVID H. SMITH. 1974. *Becoming Modern: Individual Change in Six Developing Countries.* Cambridge, Mass.: Harvard University Press.

JACKSON, DONALD. 1974. "Justice for none." *New Times,* 2, January 11, pp. 48–57.

JACKSON, ELTON F., and HARRY J. CROCKETT, JR. 1964. "Occupational mobility in the United States: a point estimate and a trend comparison." *American Sociological Review,* 24, pp. 5–15.

JACKSON, PHILIP. 1968. *Life in Classrooms.* New York: Holt, Rinehart and Winston.

JACOBS, JANE. 1961. *The Death and Life of Great American Cities.* New York: Random House.

JACOBY, NEIL H. 1970. "The multinational corporation." *Center Magazine,* 3, pp. 37–55.

JANIS, IRVING L. 1972. *Victims of Groupthink.* Boston: Houghton Mifflin.

JENCKS, CHRISTOPHER, et al. 1972. *Inequality: A Reassessment of the Effect and Schooling in America.* New York: Basic Books.

JENSEN, ARTHUR. 1969. "How much can we boost IQ and scholastic achievement?" *Howard Educational Review,* 39, pp. 273–274.

JOHNSON, DONALD M. 1945. "The 'phantom anesthetist' of Mattoon: a field study of mass hysteria." *Journal of Abnormal and Social Psychology,* 40, pp. 175–186.

JOHNSON, ROGER T., et al. 1973. "Cooperation and competition in the classroom." *The Elementary School Journal,* 74, pp. 172–184.

JOLLY, CLIFFORD L., and FRED PLOG. 1976. *Physical Anthropology and Archaeology.* New York: Alfred A. Knopf.

KAHL, JOSEPH A. 1957. *The American Class Structure.* New York: Holt, Rinehart and Winston.

______. 1961. *The American Class Structure,* 2nd ed. New York: Holt, Rinehart and Winston.

KATCHER, ALLAN. 1955. "The discrimination of sex differences by young children." *Journal of Genetic Psychology,* 87, September, pp. 131–143.

KATZ, MARLAINE L. 1972. "Female motive to avoid success: a psychological barrier or a response to deviance." Manuscript, School of Education, Stanford University, Palo Alto, Calif.

KAUFMAN, RICHARD F. 1970. *The War Profiteers.* Indianapolis, Ind.: Bobbs-Merrill.

KAYSON, CARL. 1972. "The computer that printed W*O*L*F." *Foreign Affairs,* 50, July, pp. 663–666.

KELLER, HELEN. 1903. *The Story of My Life.* New York: Doubleday.

KENISTON, KENNETH. 1970. "Youth: a new stage of life." *American Scholar,* 39, Autumn, pp. 631–654.

KETCHEL, MELVIN M. 1968. "Fertility control agents as a possible solution to the world population problem." *Perspectives in Biology and Medicine,* 11, pp. 687–703.

KEYSERLING, MARY DUBLIN. 1970. *Women's role in contemporary society: Report of the New York City Commission on Human Rights,* September 21–25.

KING, WAYNE. 1974. "Demand for divorce brings laws to make it easier and cheaper." *The New York Times,* January 5, p. 16.

KINSEY, ALFRED C., et al. 1948. *Sexual Behavior in the Human Male.* Philadelphia: W. B. Saunders.

______, et al. 1953. *Sexual Behavior in the Human Female.* Philadelphia: W. B. Saunders.

KIRK, DUDLEY. 1971. "A new demographic transition," in Study Committee of the National Academy of Sciences, *Rapid Population Growth: Consequences and Policy Implications.* Baltimore, Md.: John Hopkins Press.

KIRKHAM, GEORGE L. 1971. "Homosexuality in prison" *in* James M. Henslin (ed.), *Studies in the Sociology of Sex.* New York: Appleton-Century-Crofts.

KITWANGER, EVELYN M., and PHILIP H. HAUSER. 1967. *Education and Income Differentiations in Mortality, United States, 1960.* Chicago: University of Chicago Population Center.

KLAPP, ORIN. 1969. *Collective Search for Identity.* New York: Holt, Rinehart and Winston.

KLEIN, RUDOLF. 1972. "Growth and its enemies." *Commentary,* 53, pp. 37–45.

KLUCKHOHN, CLYDE. 1948. "An an anthropologist views it," *in* Albert Deutch (ed.), *Sex Habits of American Men.* New York: Prentice-Hall.

______. 1962. "Universal categories of culture," *in* Sol Tax (ed.), *Anthropology Today: Selections.* Chicago: University of Chicago Press.

KOGAN, N., and WALLACH, M. A. 1964. *Risk Taking: A Study in Cognition and Personality.* New York: Holt, Rinehart and Winston.

KOHLBERG, LAWRENCE. 1966. "A cognitive-developmental analysis of children's sex-role concepts and attitudes," *in* Eleanor E. Maccoby (ed.), *The Development of Sex Differences.* Palo Alto, Calif.: Stanford University Press.

______. 1969. "Stage and sequence: the cognitive-developmental approach to socialization," *in* David A. Goslin (ed.), *Handbook of Socialization Theory and Research.* Chicago: Rand McNally.

KOHN, M. L. 1963. "Social class and parent-child relationships: an interpretation." *American Journal of Sociology,* 68, pp. 471–480.

______. 1969. *Class and Conformity.* Homewood, Ill.: Dorsey Press.

KOHN, PAUL M. 1973. "Relationships between expectations of teachers and performance of students." *Journal of School Health,* 18, October, pp. 498–503.

KOLKO, GABRIEL. 1962. *Wealth and Power in America: An Analysis of Social Class and Income Distribution.* New York: Praeger.

KOMAROVSKY, MIRRA. 1962. *Blue-Collar Marriage.* New York: Random House.

______. 1973. "Cultural contradictions and sex roles: the masculine case." *American Journal of Sociology,* 78, pp. 873–884.

KOMISAR, LUCY. 1971. "The image of woman in advertising," *in* Vivian Gornick and Barbara K. Moran (eds.), *Women in Sexist Society: Studies in Power and Powerlessness.* New York: Basic Books.

KORNHAUSER, WILLIAM. 1966. " 'Power elite' or 'veto groups'?" *in* Reinhard Bendix and Seymour Martin Lipset (eds.), *Class, Status, and Power,* 2nd ed. New York: Free Press.

KOTTAK, CONRAD PHILLIP. 1974. *Anthropology: Exploration of Human Diversity.* New York: Random House.

KRAUSS, IRVING. 1964. "Sources of educational aspirations among working class youth." *American Sociological Review,* 29, pp. 867–879.

KROEBER, A. L. 1937. "Diffusionism," *in* Edward Seligman and Alvin Johnson (eds.), *The Encyclopaedia of the Social Sciences,* Vol. III. pp. 139–142.

KUBLER-ROSS, ELISABETH. 1969. *On Death and Dying.* New York: Macmillan.

______. 1972. "Facing up to death." *Today's Education,* 16, pp. 30–32.

KUHN, MANFORD, and THOMAS S. MCPARTLAND. 1954. "An empirical investigation of self-attitudes." *American Sociological Review,* 19, pp. 68–76.

KUHN, THOMAS S. 1962. *The Structure of Scientific Revolutions.* Chicago: University of Chicago Press.

KUNEN, JAMES S. 1973. "The rebels of '70." *The New York Times Magazine,* October 28, p. 22.

KUZNETS, SIMON. 1953. *Share of Upper Income Groups in Income and Savings.* New York: National Bureau of Economic Research.

LA BARRE, WESTON. 1954. *The Human Animal.* Chicago: University of Chicago Press.

LAMPMAN, ROBERT. 1962. *The Share of the Top Wealth Holders in National Wealth.* Princeton, N.J.: Princeton University Press.

LANDIS, JUDSON T. 1962. "A comparison of children from divorced and nondivorced unhappy marriages." *Family Life Coordinator,* 11, pp. 61–65.

LANE, DAVID. 1971. *The End of Inequality? Stratification Under State Socialism.* Baltimore, Md.: Penguin.

LANGTON, KENNETH P., and M. KENT JENNINGS. 1967. "Peer group and school in the socialization process." *American Political Science Review,* 61, pp. 751–758.

LANTERNARI, VITTORIO. 1963. *Religions of the Oppressed: A Study of Modern Messianic Cults.* New York: Alfred A. Knopf.

LAPIERE, RICHARD T. 1934. "Attitudes versus action." *Social Forces,* 13, pp. 230–237.

LASSITER, ROY L. 1966. *The Association of Income and Educational*

Achievement. Gainesville, Fla.: University of Florida Press.

LASSWELL, HAROLD D. 1936. *Politics: Who Gets What, When, and How.* New York: McGraw-Hill.

LATANÉ, BIBB, and JOHN M. DARLEY. 1968. "Group inhibition of bystander intervention." *Journal of Personality and Social Psychology,* 8, pp. 377–383.

———, and JOHN M. DARLEY. 1969. "Bystander apathy." *American Scientist,* 57, pp. 244–268.

———, and JEAN A. RODIN. 1969. "A lady in distress: inhibiting effects of friends and strangers on bystander intervention." *Journal of Experimental Social Psychology,* 5, pp. 189–202.

LEACOCK, ELEANOR. 1969. *Teaching and Learning in City Schools.* New York: Basic Books.

LE BON, GUSTAVE. 1960. *The Mind of the Crowd.* New York: Viking.

LEE, RICHARD B. 1968. "What hunters do for a living, or how to make out on scarce resources," *in* Richard B. Lee and Irvin De Vore (eds.), *Man the Hunter.* Chicago: Aldine.

LEMERT, EDWIN M. 1951. *Social Pathology.* New York: McGraw-Hill.

———. 1967. *Human Deviance, Social Problems, and Social Control.* Englewood Cliffs, N.J.: Prentice-Hall.

———. 1974. "Beyond Mead: the societal reaction to deviance." *Social Problems,* 21, pp. 457–468.

LENSKI, GERHARD. 1966a. *Power and Privilege: A Theory of Social Stratification.* New York: McGraw-Hill.

———. 1966b. *The Religious Factor.* New York: Doubleday.

———, and JEAN LENSKI. 1974. *Human Societies,* 2nd ed. New York: McGraw-Hill.

LERNER, M. J., and C. H. SIMMONS. 1966. "Observer's reaction to the 'innocent victim': compassion or rejection?" *Journal of Personality and Social Psychology,* 4, pp. 203–210.

LESLIE, GERALD R., and ARTHUR H. RICHARDSON. 1956. "Family versus campus influence in relation to mate selection." *Social Problems,* 4, pp. 117–121.

LEVINE, JANEY, et al. 1973. "Subway behavior," *in* Arnold Birenbaum and Edward Sagarin, *People in Places: The Sociology of the Familiar.* New York:Praeger.

LÉVI-STRAUSS, CLAUDE. 1966. *The Savage Mind.* Chicago: University of Chicago Press.

LEWIS, OSCAR. 1966. "The culture of poverty." *Scientific American,* 215, pp. 19–25.

———. 1968. *La Vida.* New York: Vintage.

LEZNOFF, MAURICE, and WILLIAM W. WESTLEY. 1956. "The homosexual community." *Social Problems,* 3, pp. 257–263.

LIAZOS, ALEXANDER. 1972. "The poverty of the sociology of deviance: nuts, sluts, and preverts." *Social Problems,* 20, pp. 103–120.

LIEBOW, ELLIOT. 1967. *Tally's Corner: A Study of Negro Streetcorner Men.* Boston: Little Brown.

LIENHARDT, GODFREY. 1966. *Social Anthropology.* London: Oxford University Press.

LINDESMITH, ALFRED R., A. L. STRAUSS, and N. K. DENZIN. 1975. *Social Psychology,* 4th ed. New York: Holt, Rinehart & Winston.

LINTON, RALPH. 1936. *The Study of Man.* New York: Appleton-Century-Crofts.

———. 1945. *The Cultural Background of Personality.* New York: Free Press.

LIPSET, SEYMOUR MARTIN. 1959a. *"Democracy and working-class authoritarianism." American Sociological Review,* 24, pp. 482–501.

———. 1959b. *Political Man.* New York: Doubleday.

———. 1959c. "Some social prerequisties for democracy: economic development and political legitimacy." *American Political Science Review,* 53, pp. 74–86.

———. 1973. "Commentary: social stratification research and Soviet scholarship," *in* Murray Yanovitch and Westley A. Fischer (trans. and eds.), *Social Stratification and Mobility in the USSR.* White Plains, N.Y.: International Arts and Sciences Press.

———, and REINHARD BENDIX. 1959. *Social Mobility in Industrial Society.* Berkeley, Calif.: University of California Press.

LOCKWOOD, DAVID. 1956. "Some notes on 'The Social System'." *British Journal of Sociology,* 7, p. 2.

LOFLAND, JOHN. 1969. *Deviance and Identity.* Englewood Cliffs, N.J.: Prentice-Hall.

LOMBROSO, CESARE. 1911. *Crime: Its Causes and Remedies.* Boston: Little, Brown.

LOWIE, ROBERT H. 1940. *Introduction to Cultural Anthropology.* New York: Holt, Rinehart and Winston.

LUNDBERG, FERDINAND. 1968. *The Rich and the Super-Rich.* New York: Bantam.

LYND, ROBERT S., and HELEN M. LYND. 1929. *Middletown: A Study in American Culture.* New York: Harcourt Brace Jovanovich.

MACCOBY, ELEANOR, and CAROL JACKLIN. 1974. *The Psychology of Sex Differences.* Palo Alto, Calif.: Stanford University Press.

MALINOWSKI, BRONISLAW. 1922. *The Argonauts of the Western Pacific.* New York: Dutton.

———. 1926. *Crime and Custom in Savage Society.* New York: Harcourt, Brace and Company.

———. 1948. *Magic, Science and Religion and Other Essays.* Glencoe, Ill.: Free Press.

MANKOFF, MILTON. 1971. "Societal reaction and career deviance: a critical analysis." *Sociological Quarterly,* 12, pp. 204–218.

MARX, GARY T. 1967. *Protest and Prejudice.* New York: Harper & Row.

MARX, KARL. 1964a. *Economic and Political Manuscripts of 1844.* New York: International Publishing.

______. 1964b, originally published 1848. *Selected Writings in Sociology and Social Philosophy,* T. B. Bottomore and Maximilian Rubel (eds.). Baltimore, Md.: Penguin.

______. 1967, originally published 1843. *Critique of Hegel's Philosophy of Right. in* Lloyd D. Easton and Kurt Guddat (trans. and eds.), *Writings of the Young Marx on Philosophy and Society.* New York: Doubleday.

______. 1967, originally published 1867–1895. *Das Capital.* New York: International Publishers.

______. 1969, originally published 1852. "The eighteenth brumaire of Louis Napoleon," *in Karl Marx: Selected Works,* Vol. 1. Moscow: Progress Publishers.

______, and FRIEDRICH ENGELS. 1970. *Selected Works,* Vol. 3. Moscow: Progress Publishers.

MASTERS, WILLIAM H., and VIRGINIA E. JOHNSON. 1970. *Human Sexual Inadequacy.* Boston: Little Brown.

______, and VIRGINIA E. JOHNSON. 1975. *The Pleasure Bond: A New Look at Sexuality and Commitment.* Boston: Little, Brown.

MATZA, DAVID. 1964. *Delinquency and Drift.* New York: Wiley.

MAUGH, THOMAS H. 1974. "Marijuana: the grass may no longer be greener." *Science,* 74, pp. 683–685.

MAYER, J. P. 1943. *Max Weber and German Politics.* London: Faber & Faber.

MAYO, ELTON. 1966. *Human Problems of an Industrial Civilization.* New York: Viking.

MCBRIDE, G., et al. 1965. "Social proximity effects of GSR in adult humans." Journal of Psychology, 61, pp. 153–157.

MCCARTHY, JOHN D., and MAYER N. ZALD. 1973. *The Trend of Social Movements in America.* Morristown, N.J.: General Learning Press.

MCDONALD, DONALD. 1970. "Militarism in America." *Center Magazine,* 3, pp. 12–33.

MCGEE, REECE. 1975. *Points of Departure.* Hinsdale, Ill.: Dryden Press.

MCINTOSH, MARY. 1968. "The Homosexual Role." *Social Problems,* 16, pp. 182–192.

MCIVER, ROBERT M. 1942. *Social Causation.* New York: Ginn & Company.

MCKEE, J., and A. SHERRIFFS. 1956. "The differential evaluation of males and females." *Journal of Personality,* 25, pp. 357–371.

MCKEE, MICHAEL, and IAN ROBERTSON. 1975. *Social Problems.* New York: Random House.

MEAD, GEORGE HERBERT. 1934. *Mind, Self, and Society: From the Standpoint of a Social Behaviorist.* Charles W. Morris (ed.). Chicago: University of Chicago Press.

MEAD, MARGARET. 1935. *Sex and Temperament in Three Primitive Societies.* New York: Dell.

______. 1970. *Culture and Commitment.* New York: Doubleday.

MEADOWS, DONNELLA H., et al. 1972. *The Limits to Growth.* New York: New American Library.

MEANS, GARDINER S. 1970. "Economic concentration," *in* Maurice Zeitlin (ed.), *American Society Inc.* Chicago: Markham.

MEDALIA, NAHUM Z., and OTTO N. LARSEN. 1958. "Diffusion and belief in a collective delusion: the Seattle windshield pitting epidemic." *American Sociological Review,* 23, pp. 221–232.

MELMAN, SEYMOUR. 1970. *Pentagon Capitalism: The Political Economy of War.* New York: McGraw-Hill.

MENDELSOHN, ROBERT, and SHIRLEY DOBIE. 1970. "Women's self-conception: a block to career development." Manuscript, LaFayette Clinic, Department of Mental Health, Detroit, Michigan.

MERTON, ROBERT K. 1938. "Social structure and anomie." *American Sociological Review,* 3, pp. 672–682.

______. 1942. "Science and technology in a democratic order." *Journal of Legal and Political Science,* 1, pp. 115–126.

______. 1949. "Discrimination and the American creed," *in* Robert M. McIver (ed.), *Discrimination and National Welfare.* New York: Harper.

______. 1968. *Social Theory and Social Structure,* 2nd ed. New York: Free Press.

______. 1973. *Sociology of Science: Theoretical and Empirical Investigations,* Norman W. Storer (ed.). Chicago: University of Chicago Press.

MICHELS, ROBERT. 1967, originally published 1911. *Political Parties.* New York: Free Press.

MIDDLETON, RUSSELL. 1962, "Brother-sister and father-daughter marriage in ancient Eygpt." *American Sociological Review,* 27, pp. 103–111.

MILES, RUFUS E., JR. 1971. "Man's population predicament." *The Population Bulletin,* 26, pp. 4–39.

MILGRAM, STANLEY. 1973. *Obedience to Authority: An Experimental View.* New York: Harper & Row.

MILLAR, RONALD. 1974. *The Piltdown Man.* New York: St. Martin's Press.

MILLER, HERMAN P. 1972. "Recent trends in family income," *in* Gerald W. Thielbar *et al.* (eds.), *Issues in Social Inequality.* Boston: Little, Brown.

MILLER, S. M. 1960. "Comparative social mobility." *Current Sociology,* 9, pp. 1–72.

______. 1964. "The outlook of working class youth," *in* Arthur P. Shostak and William Gomberg (eds.), *Blue-Collar World: Studies of the American Worker.* Englewood Cliffs, N.J.: Prentice-Hall.

MILLER, WALTER. 1958. "Lower class culture as a generating milieu of gang delinquency." *Journal of Sociological Issues,* 14, pp. 5–19.

MILLS, C. WRIGHT. 1956. *The Power Elite.* New York: Oxford University Press.

______. 1959. *The Sociological Imagination.* New York: Oxford University Press.

MILLS, THEODORE. 1967. *The Sociology of Small Groups.* Englewood Cliffs, N.J.: Prentice-Hall.

MITFORD, JESSICA. 1973. *Kind and Usual Punishment.* New York: Alfred A. Knopf.

MONEY, JOHN, and ANKE A. EHRHARDT. 1972. *Man and Woman, Boy and Girl.* Baltimore, Md.: Johns Hopkins Press.

MOONEY, JAMES. 1965. *The Ghost-Dance Religion and Sioux Outbreak of 1890.* Chicago: University of Chicago Press.

MOORE, BARRINGTON. 1958. *Political Power and Social Theory.* Cambridge, Mass.: Harvard University Press.

MOORE, WILBERT E. 1960. "A reconsideration of theories of social change." *American Sociological Review,* 25, pp. 810–818.

MOSCA, GAETANO. 1939. *The Ruling Class.* New York: McGraw-Hill.

MOUNIN, GEORGES. 1976. "Chimpanzees, language, and communication." *Current Anthropology.* 17, pp. 1–22.

MOYNIHAN, DANIEL PATRICK. 1965. *The Negro Family: The Case for National Action.* Washington, D.C.: Office of Policy Planning and Research, U.S. Department of Labor.

MULKAY, MICHAEL, J. 1972. *The Social Process of Innovation: A Study in the Sociology of Science.* New York: Macmillan.

MUMFORD, LEWIS. 1961. *The City in History.* New York: Harcourt Brace Jovanovitch.

MURDOCK, GEORGE P. 1934. *Our Primitive Contemporaries.* New York: Macmillan.

______. 1935. "Comparative data on the division of labor by sex." *Social Forces,* 15, pp. 551–553.

______. 1945. "The common denominator of cultures," *in* Ralph Linton (ed.), *The Science of Man and the World Crisis.* New York: Columbia University Press.

______. 1949. *Social Structure.* New York: Macmillan.

______. 1957. "World ethnographic sample." *American Anthropologist,* 54, August, pp. 664–687.

MYRDAL, GUNNAR. 1944. *An American Dilemma.* New York: Harper & Row.

National Advisory Commission on Civil Disorders (Kerner Commission). 1968. *Report of National Advisory Commission on Civil Disorders.* New York: Bantam.

National Commission on Marijuana and Drug Abuse. 1973. *Marijuana: A Signal of Misunderstanding.* Washington, D.C.: U.S. Government Printing Office.

National Education Association. 1968. *Ability Grouping: Research Summary 1968-se.* Washington, D.C.: NEA Research Division.

NEWCOMB, THEODORE. 1958. "Attitude development as a function of reference groups: the Bennington study," *in* Guy E. Swanson *et al.* (eds.), *Readings in Social Psychology.* New York: Holt, Rinehart and Winston.

NEWTON, ESTHER. 1972. *Mother Camp: Female Impersonation in America.* Englewood Cliffs, N.J.: Prentice-Hall.

NISBET, ROBERT A. 1953. *The Quest for Community.* New York: Oxford University Press.

______. 1969. *Social Change and History.* New York: Oxford University Press.

______. 1970. *The Social Bond.* New York: Alfred A. Knopf.

NIXON, RICHARD M. 1971. "Remarks of the President at the Republican Governors' Conference." Washington, D.C.: Office of the White House Press Secretary.

NOEL, DON. 1968. "The Theory of the Origin of Ethnic Stratification." *Social Problems,* 160.

NORUM, G. A., et al. 1967. "Seating patterns and group tasks." *Psychology in the Schools,* 1967, No. 4, p. 3.

NOVAK, MICHAEL. 1971. "White ethnic." *Harper's,* 243, pp. 44–50.

OAKLEY, ANN. 1974. *The Sociology of Housework.* New York: Pantheon.

OELSNER, LESLIE. 1972. "Scales of justice." *The New York Times News Service,* September.

OGBURN, WILLIAM F. 1950. *Social Change.* New York: Viking.

OPHULS, WILLIAM. 1974. "The scarcity society." *Harper's,* 246, pp. 47–52.

ORNATI, OSCAR. 1966. *Poverty Amid Affluence.* New York: Twentieth Century Fund.

ORUM, ANTHONY, and ROBERTA COHEN. 1973. "The development of political orientations among black and white children." *American Sociological Review,* 38, February, pp. 62–74.

ORWELL, G. 1949. *1984.* New York: New American Library.

OWEN, D. R. 1972. "The 47 XYY male: a review." *Psychological Bulletin,* 78, pp. 209–233.

PAINE, NATHANIEL. 1897. "Early American broadsides 1680–1800." *Proceedings, American Antiquarian Society,* 1897.

PARETO, VILFREDO. 1935. *Mind and Society.* New York: Harcourt Brace Jovanovitch.

PARK, ROBERT E., ERNEST W. BURGESS, and R. D. MCKENZIE. 1925. *The City.* Chicago: University of Chicago Press.

PARKE, ROBERT, JR., and PAUL C. GLICK. 1967. "Prospective changes in marriage and family." *Journal of Marriage and the Family,* 29, pp. 249–256.

PARKIN, FRANK. 1971. *Class Inequality and the Social Order.* London: McGibbon & Kee.

PARSONS, TALCOTT. 1937. *The Structure of Social Action.* New York: McGraw-Hill.

______. 1940. "An analytic approach to the theory of social stratification." *American Journal of Sociology,* 45, pp. 841–862.

———. 1951. *The Social System.* Glencoe, Ill.: Free Press.

———. 1954. "The professions and social structure," *in* Talcott Parsons (ed.), *Essays in Sociological Theory.* New York: Free Press.

———. 1961. "Some considerations on the theory of social change." *Rural Sociology,* 26, pp. 219–239.

———. 1966. *Societies: Evolutionary and Comparative Perspectives.* Englewood Cliffs, N.J.: Prentice-Hall.

———, and ROBERT F. BALES. 1953. *Family, Socialization, and Interaction Process.* Glencoe, Ill.: Free Press.

PATTERSON, M. L., et al. 1971. "Compensatory reactions to spatial intrusion." *Sociometry,* 34, pp. 114–121.

PEDERSON, D. M. 1973. "Developmental trends in personal space." *Journal of Psychology,* 83, pp. 3–9.

PHETERSON, GAIL I., et al. 1971. "Evaluation of the performance of women as a function of their sex, achievement, and personal history." *Journal of Personality and Social Psychology,* 19, pp. 114–118.

PIAGET, JEAN. 1950. *The Psychology of Intelligence.* London: Routledge & Kegan Paul.

———. 1954. *The Construction of Reality in the Child.* New York: Basic Books.

———, and BARBEL INHELDER. 1969. *The Psychology of the Child.* New York: Basic Books.

PILIAVAN, IRVIN, and SCOTT BRIAR. 1964. "Police encounters with juveniles." *American Journal of Sociology,* 70, pp. 206–214.

PITZER, KENNETH S. 1971. "Science and society: some policy changes are needed." *Science,* 1972, 172, pp. 223–226.

PLATERIS, ALEXANDER A. 1970. *Increases in Divorces: United States—1967.* Washington, D.C.: U.S. Department of Health, Education, and Welfare.

PLUMB, J. H. 1971. "The Great Change in Children." *Horizon,* 13, Winter, pp. 4–13.

POLANYI, MICHAEL. 1951. *The Logic of Liberty.* London: Routledge & Kegan Paul.

POLSKY, NED. 1964. *Hustlers, Beats, and Others.* Chicago: Aldine.

POMEROY, WARDELL B. 1965. "Some aspects of prostitution." *Journal of Sex Research,* 1, pp. 177–187.

———. 1972. *Dr. Kinsey and the Institute for Sex Research.* New York: Harper & Row.

POPPER, KARL R. 1959. *The Logic of Scientific Discovery.* New York: Basic Books.

PORTER, JOHN. 1968. "The future of upward mobility." *American Sociological Review,* 33, pp. 5–19.

POWERS, THOMAS. 1971. "Learning to die." *Harper's,* 242, pp. 72–80.

PREMACK, DAVID. 1970. "The education of Sarah." *Psychology Today,* 4, pp. 55–58.

President's Commission on Law Enforcement and the Administration of Justice. 1967. *The Challenge of Crime in a Free Society.* Washington, D.C.: U.S. Government Printing Office.

President's Commission on Obscenity and Pornography. 1970. *Report of the President's Commission on Obscenity and Pornography.* New York: Bantam.

PRICE, DEREK J. DE SOLLA. 1963. *Big Science, Little Science.* New York: Columbia University Press.

PROVENCE, S., and LIPTON, R. C., 1962. *Infants in Institutions.* New York: International Universities Press.

RADCLIFFE-BROWN, A. R. 1935. "On the concept of functionalism in the social sciences." *American Anthropologist,* 37, pp. 394–402.

———. 1952. *Structure and Function in Primitive Society.* Glencoe, Ill.: Free Press.

RAINWATER, LEE. 1964. "Marital satisfaction in four cultures of poverty." *Journal of Marriage and the Family,* 26, pp. 457–466.

———. 1966. "Some aspects of lower class sexual behavior." *Journal of Social Issues,* 22, pp. 96–108.

———, RICHARD P. COLEMAN, and GERALD HANDEL. 1959. *Working Man's Wife.* Chicago: Oceana Publications.

RAPER, ARTHUR. 1933. *The Tragedy of Lynching.* Chapel Hill, N.C.: University of North Carolina Press.

REDFIELD, ROBERT. 1941. *The Folk Culture of Yucatan.* Chicago: University of Chicago Press.

———. 1953. *The Primitive World and Its Transformation.* Ithaca, N.Y.: Cornell University Press.

REISCHAUER, ROBERT D., ROBERT W. HARTMAN, and DANIEL J. SULLIVAN. 1973. *Reforming School Finances.* Washington, D.C.: Brookings Institution.

REISS, ALBERT J., JR. 1961. "The social integration of peers and queers." *Social Problems,* 9, pp. 102–120.

———, et al. 1961. *Occupation and Social Status.* New York: Free Press.

REISS, IRA L. 1968. "How and why America's sex standards are changing." *Transaction,* 5, pp. 26–32.

———. 1971. *The Family System in America.* New York: Holt, Rinehart and Winston.

RIENOW, ROBERT, and LEONA TRAIN RIENOW. 1969. *Moment in the Sun.* New York: Ballantine.

RIESMAN, DAVID. 1961. *The Lonely Crowd.* New Haven, Conn.: Yale University Press.

RILEY, MATILDA W., and ANNE FONER (eds.). 1969. *Aging and Society: A Sociology of Age Stratification,* 3 vols. New York: Russell Sage Foundation.

RIST, RAY C. 1970. "Student social class and teacher expectations: the self-fulfilling prophecy in ghetto education." *Harvard Educational Review,* 40, pp. 411–451.

———. 1973. *The Urban School: A Factory for Failure.* New York: Doubleday.

ROBERTS, JOAN L. 1970. *Scene of the Battle: Group Behavior in Urban Classrooms.* New York: Doubleday.

ROBERTSON, IAN. 1973. "Education in South Africa: a study in the influence of ideology on educational practice." Unpublished doctoral dissertation, Harvard University.

______. 1976. "Social stratification," *in* David E. Hunter and Phillip Whitten (eds.), *The Study of Anthropology.* New York: Harper & Row.

ROETHLISBERGER, FRITZ J., and WILLIAM J. DICKSON. 1939. *Management and the Worker.* Cambridge, Mass.: Harvard University Press.

ROSE, ARNOLD M. 1967. *The Power Structure.* New York: Oxford University Press.

ROSE, PETER I. 1974. *They and We: Racial and Ethnic Relations in the United States,* 2nd ed. New York: Random House.

ROSENGRANT, T. 1973. "The relationship of race and sex on proxemic behavior and source credibility." Paper presented at the International Communication Association Convention, Montreal, April.

ROSENTHAL, D. 1970. *Genetic Theory and Abnormal Behavior.* New York: McGraw-Hill.

ROSENTHAL, M. 1971. "Where rumor raged." *Transaction,* 8, February, pp. 34–43.

ROSENTHAL, ROBERT. 1966. *Experimenter Effects in Behavioral Research.* New York: Appleton-Century-Crofts.

______. 1969. "Empirical versus decreed validation of clocks and tests." *American Educational Research Journal,* 6, November, pp. 689–691.

______, and LENORE JACOBSON. 1968. *Pygmalion in the Classroom: Teacher Expectation and Pupils' Intellectual Development.* New York: Holt, Rinehart and Winston.

ROSS, H. LAWRENCE. 1965. "Uptown and downtown: a study of middle class residential areas." *American Sociological Review,* 30, pp. 255–259.

ROSS, JAMES B., and MARY M. MCLAUGHLIN (eds.). 1949. *The Portable Medieval Reader.* New York: Viking.

ROSSIDES, DANIEL W. 1976. *The American Class System.* Boston: Houghton Mifflin.

ROSZAK, THEODORE. 1969. *The Making of a Counter-Culture: Reflections on the Technocratic Society and Its Youthful Opposition.* New York: Doubleday.

ROUSSEAU, JEAN JACQUES. 1950, originally published 1762. *The Social Contract.* New York: E. P. Dutton.

RUBOVITS, P. C., and A. L. MAEHR. 1971. "Pygmalion analyzed: toward an explanation of the Rosenthal-Jacobson findings." *Journal of Personality and Social Psychology,* 19, pp. 197–203.

______, and A. L. MAEHR. 1973. "Pygmalion black and white." *Journal of Personality and Social Psychology,* 25, pp. 210–218.

RUNCIMAN, WILLIAM G. 1966. *Relative Deprivation and Social Justice.* London: Routledge & Kegan Paul.

RUSSELL, M. A. HAMILTON. 1971. "Cigarette smoking: natural history of a dependence disorder." *British Journal of Medical Psychology,* 44, pp. 1–16.

SAFILIOS-ROTHSCHILD, CONSTANTINE. 1974. *Women and Social Policy.* Englewood Cliffs, N.J.: Prentice-Hall.

SAGARIN, EDWARD. 1973. "The good guys, the bad guys, and the gay guys." *Contemporary Sociology,* 2, pp. 3–13.

______. 1975. *Deviants and Deviance.* New York: Praeger.

SAHLINS, MARSHALL. 1972. *Stone Age Economics.* Chicago: Aldine.

SAMPSON, ANTHONY. 1973. *The Sovereign State of ITT.* Greenwich, Conn.: Fawcett.

SAPIR, EDWARD. 1929. "The status of linguistics as a science." *Language,* 5, pp. 207–214.

SCANZIONI, JOHN H. 1971. *The Black Family in Modern Society.* Boston: Allyn and Bacon.

SCHEFF, THOMAS J. 1966. *Being Mentally Ill: A Sociological Theory.* Chicago: Aldine.

SCHNEIDER, HERBERT. 1952. *Religion in 20th Century America.* Cambridge, Mass.: Harvard University Press.

SCHUMAN, HOWARD. 1974. "Are whites really more liberal? Blacks aren't impressed." *Psychology Today,* 8, pp. 82–86.

SCHUR, EDWIN M. 1965. *Crimes Without Victims—Deviant Behavior and Public Policy.* Englewood Cliffs, N.J.: Prentice-Hall.

SCHUTZ, ALFRED. 1962. *Collected Papers, I: The Problem of Social Reality.* The Hague: Martinus Nijhoff.

SCOTT, MARVIN B., and STANFORD M. LYMAN. 1968. "Accounts." *American Sociological Review,* 33, pp. 46–62.

______. 1971. *Labeling Deviant Behavior: Its Sociological Implications.* New York: Harper & Row.

SEARS, ROBERT R., ELEANOR E. MACCOBY, and HARRY LEVIN. 1957. *Patterns of Child Rearing.* Evanston, Ill.: Row, Peterson.

SEEMAN, MELVIN. 1959. "On the meaning of alienation." *American Sociological Review,* 24, pp. 783–789.

SEGAL, RONALD, 1973. "Everywhere at home, at home nowhere." *Center Magazine,* 6, pp. 8–14.

SELLIN, THORSTEN. 1938. *Culture Conflict and Crime.* New York: Social Science Research Council.

SELVIN, HANAN C., and WARREN O. HAGSTROM. 1960. "Determinants of support for civil liberties." *British Journal of Sociology,* 11, March, pp. 51–73.

SELZNICK, GERTRUDE JAEGER, and STEPHEN STEINBERG. 1969. *The Tenacity of Prejudice.* New York: Harper & Row.

SELZNICK, PHILIP. 1943. "An approach to a theory of bureaucracy." *American Sociological Review,* 8, pp. 47–54.

SEWELL, WILLIAM H. 1971. "Inequality of opportunity for higher education." *American Sociological Review,* 36, pp. 793–808.

SEYMOUR, WHITNEY N. 1973. "Social and ethical considerations in assessing white collar crime." *American Criminal Law Review,* 11, pp. 821–834.

SHAFER, WALTER E., et al. 1967. in *Delinquency and the Schools.* The President's Commission on Law Enforcement and Administration of Justice, Task Force Report: Delinquency and Youth Crime. Washington, D.C.: U.S. Government Printing Office.

SHAW, CLIFFORD R., and HENRY D. MCKAY. 1929. *Delinquency Areas.* Chicago: University of Chicago Press.

SHELDON, WILLIAM H. 1940. *The Varieties of Human Physique.* New York: Harper.

______, et al. 1949. *Varieties of Delinquent Youth.* New York: Harper & Row.

SHERIF, MUZAFER. 1956. "Experiments in group conflict." *Scientific American,* 195, pp. 54–58.

SHERRILL, ROBERT. 1970. "The war machine." *Playboy,* 17, pp. 134, 214–228.

SHIBUTANI, TAMOTSU. 1966. *Improvised News: A Sociological Study of Rumor.* Indianapolis, Ind.: Bobbs-Merrill.

SHORT, JAMES F., and F. IVAN NYE. 1957. "Reported behavior as a criterion of delinquent behavior." *Social Problems,* 5, pp. 207–213.

SILBERMAN, CHARLES E. 1970. "Murder in the classroom: how the public schools kill dreams and mutilate minds." *The Atlantic,* 225, June, pp. 82–94.

______. 1971. *Crisis in the Classroom: The Remaking of American Education.* New York: Random House.

SILLS, DAVID L. 1957. *The Volunteers.* Glencoe, Ill.: Free Press.

SIMMEL, GEORG. 1904. "The sociology of conflict," Albion Small (transl.). *American Journal of Sociology,* 9, p. 490 ff.

______. 1955. *Conflict and the Web of Group Affiliations,* Kurt Wolff (transl.). Glencoe, Ill.: Free Press.

SIMMONS, JACK L. 1969. *Deviants.* Berkeley, Calif.: Glendessary Press.

SIMPSON, GEORGE E. and J. MILTON YINGER. 1972. *Racial and Cultural Minorities: An Analysis of Prejudice and Discrimination,* 4th ed. New York: Harper & Row.

SINGH, J. A. L., and ROBERT M. ZINGG. 1942. *Wolf Children and Feral Man.* New York: Harper & Row.

SJOBERG, GIDEON. 1960. *The Preindustrial City.* New York: Free Press.

SKINNER, B. F. 1971. *Beyond Freedom and Dignity.* New York: Alfred A. Knopf.

SKOLNICK, JEROME H. 1969. *The Politics of Protest.* New York: Simon and Schuster.

SLATER, PHILIP E. 1955. "Role differentiation in small groups," *in* A. Paul Hare *et al.* (eds.), *Small Groups: Studies in Social Interaction.* New York: Alfred A. Knopf.

______. 1970. *The Pursuit of Loneliness: American Culture at the Breaking Point.* Boston: Beacon.

SMELSER, NEIL J. 1962. *Theory of Collective Behavior.* New York: Free Press.

______. 1963. *The Sociology of Economic Life.* Englewood Cliffs, N.J.: Prentice-Hall.

______. 1967. *Sociology: An Introduction.* New York: Wiley.

______. 1973. "Toward a theory of modernization," *in* Amitai Etzioni and Eva Etzioni-Halevy (eds.), *Social Change: Sources, Patterns, and Consequences.* New York: Basic Books.

SMITH, ADAM. 1910. *The Wealth of Nations.* London: Dent.

SMITH, LILLIAN. 1949. *Killers of the Dream.* New York: W. W. Norton.

SOMMER, R. 1965. "Further studies of small group ecology." *Sociometry,* 28, pp. 337–348.

SORENSEN, ROBERT. 1973. *Adolescent Sexuality in Contemporary America.* Cleveland: World.

SOROKIN, PITIRIM A. 1927. *Social Mobility.* New York: Harper.

______. 1937. *Social and Cultural Dynamics.* New York: American Books.

______. 1941. *The Crisis of our Age.* New York: E. P. Dutton.

SPECTOR, MALCOLM, and JOHN I. KITSUSE. 1973. "Social problems: a re-formulation." *Social Problems,* 21, pp. 145–159.

SPENGLER, OSWALD. 1926, originally published 1918, 1922. *The Decline of the West.* New York: Alfred A. Knopf.

SPITZ, RENÉ A. 1945. "Hospitalism: an inquiry into the genesis of psychiatric conditions in early childhood," *in* Anna Freud *et al.* (eds.), *The Psychoanalytic Study of the Child.* New York: International Universities Press.

SRINIVAS, M. N., et al. 1959. "Caste: a trend report and bibliography." *Current Sociology,* 8, pp. 135–151.

SROLE, LEO, et al. 1962. *Mental Health in the Metropolis.* New York: McGraw-Hill.

STAMPP, KENNETH. 1956. *The Peculiar Institution.* New York: Alfred A. Knopf.

STARK, RODNEY, and CHARLES Y. GLOCK. 1965. "The new denominationalism." *Review of Religious Research,* 7, pp. 8–17.

______, et al. 1971. *Wayward Shepherds: Prejudice and the Protestant Clergy.* New York: Harper & Row.

STEIN, MAURICE R. 1964. *The Eclipse of Community: An Interpretation of American Studies.* New York: Harper & Row.

STERN, MICHAEL. 1974. "Continued job declines threaten city economy." *The New York Times,* July 21, p. 1, 40.

STERN, PHILIP M. 1969. "How 381 super-rich Americans managed not to pay a cent in taxes last year." *The New York Times Magazine,* 118, p. 30 ff.

———. 1972. "Uncle Sam's welfare program—for the rich." *The New York Times Magazine,* p. 28.

———. 1973. *The Rape of the Taxpayer.* New York: Random House.

STEWARD, JULIAN H. 1956. "Cultural evolution." *Scientific American,* 194, pp. 70–80.

STOKES, RANDALL, and JOHN P. HEWITT. 1976. "Aligning actions." *American Sociological Review,* 41, pp. 838–849.

STONER, J. A. F. 1961. "A comparison of individual and group decisions involving risk." Unpublished master's thesis, Massachusetts Institute of Technology.

STORER, NORMAN W. (ed.). 1973. *Sociology of Science: Theoretical and Empirical Investigations.* Chicago: University of Chicago Press.

STOUFFER, SAMUEL A. 1955. *Communism, Conformity, and Civil Liberties.* New York: Doubleday.

SUMNER, WILLIAM GRAHAM. 1906. *Folkways.* Boston: Ginn & Co.

SUTHERLAND, EDWIN H. 1939. *Principles of Criminology.* Philadelphia: Lippincott.

———. 1940. "White collar criminality." *American Sociological Review,* 5, pp. 1–12.

SUTTLES, GERALD. 1970. *The Social Order of the Slum.* Chicago: University of Chicago Press.

SYMONDS, CAROLYN. 1971. "Sexual mate swapping: violation of norms and reconciliation of guilt," *in* James M. Henslin (ed.), *Studies in the Sociology of Sex.* New York: Appleton-Century-Crofts.

TAEUBER, IRENE B. 1960. "Japan's demographic transition reexamined." *Population Studies.* 14, pp. 28–39.

TAYLOR, CARL, et al. 1965. *India's Roots of Democracy.* London: Longman's.

TAYLOR, GORDON RATTRAY. 1970. *Sex in History.* New York: Vanguard.

TAYLOR, IAN, et al. 1973. *The New Criminology.* London: Routledge & Kegan Paul.

THOMPSON, N. L., et al. 1971. "Personal adjustment of male and female homosexuals and heterosexuals." *Journal of Abnormal Psychology,* 78, pp. 237–240.

THOMPSON, VICTOR. 1961. *Modern Organizations.* New York: Alfred A. Knopf.

THORNDIKE, ROBERT L. 1968. "Review of Pygmalion in the classroom." *American Educational Research Journal,* 5, pp. 708–711.

TOFFLER, ALVIN., 1970. *Future Shock.* New York: Random House.

TÖNNIES, FERDINAND. 1957, originally published in 1887. *Community and Society.* East Lansing, Mich.: Michigan State University Press.

TOURAINE, ALAN. 1971. *The Post-Industrial Society.* New York: Random House.

TOURNEY, G., et al. 1975. "Hormonal relationships in homosexual men." *American Journal of Psychiatry.* 132, pp. 288–290.

TOYNBEE, ARNOLD. 1946. *A Study of History.* New York: Oxford University Press.

TREIMAN, D. J., and K. TERRELL. 1972. "The role of education in status attainment: a comparison of the United States and Britain." Paper delivered at the annual meeting of American Sociological Association, September, New Orleans.

TREVOR-ROPER, H. R. 1967. *Religion, Reformation and Social Change.* London: Macmillan.

TRUZZI, MARCELLO. 1968. "Lilliputians in Gulliver's land: the social role of the dwarf," *in* Marcello Truzzi (ed.), *Sociology and Everyday Life.* Englewood Cliffs, N.J.: Prentice-Hall.

TUMIN, MELVIN M. 1953. "Some principals of stratification: a critical analysis." *American Sociological Review,* 18, pp. 378–394.

———. 1955. "Rewards and task orientations." *American Sociological Review,* 20, pp. 419–423.

———. 1963. "On inequality." *American Sociological Review,* 28, pp. 19–26.

TURNER, RALPH H. 1962. "Role taking: process versus conformity," *in* Arnold Rose (ed.), *Human Behavior and Social Processes: An Interactionist Approach.* Boston: Houghton Mifflin.

———. 1964. "Collective behavior," *in* Robert E. L. Faris (ed.), *Handbook of Modern Sociology.* Chicago: Rand McNally.

———, and LEWIS M. KILLIAN. 1972. *Collective Behavior,* 2nd ed. Englewood Cliffs, N.J.: Prentice-Hall.

TUSSING, A. DALE. 1974. "The dual welfare system." *Society,* 11, pp. 50–57.

UDRY, J. RICHARD. 1971. *The Social Context of Marriage.* Philadelphia: Lippincott.

U'REN, MARJORIE B. 1971. "The image of women in textbooks," *in* Vivian Gornick and Barbara K. Moran (eds.), *Women in Sexist Society: Studies in Power and Powerlessness.* New York: Basic Books.

U.S. Bureau of the Census. 1973., *Current Population Reports,* Series -60, No. 500–88, June. Washington, D.C.: U.S. Government Printing Office.

U.S. Department of Health, Education, and Welfare. 1972. *Infant Mortality Rates: Socioeconomic Factors.* Rockville, Md.: National Center for Health Statistics.

U.S. News and World Report. 1974. "The drive to open up more careers for women." 76, January, pp. 69–70.

VAN DEN BERGHE, PIERRE L. 1963. "Dialectic and functionalism: toward a theoretic synthesis." *American Sociological Review,* 28, pp. 695–705.

VANDER ZANDEN, JAMES W. 1972. *American Minority Relations: The Sociology of Racial and Ethic Groups,* 3rd ed. New York: Ronald.

VEBLEN, THORSTEIN. 1922. *The Instinct of Workmanship.* New York: Huebsch.

VERNON, RAYMOND. 1971. *Sovereignty at Bay: The Multinational Spread of U.S. Enterprises.* New York: Basic Books.

VOSS, HARWIN L. 1966. "Socio-economic status and reported delinquent behavior." *Social Problems,* 13, pp. 314–324.

WAGLEY, CHARLES, and MARVIN HARRIS. 1964. *Minorities in the New World.* New York: Columbia University Press.

WALKER COMMISSION. 1968. *Rights in Conflict: The Violent Confrontation of Demonstrators and Police in the Parks and Streets of Chicago during the Week of the Democratic National Convention of 1968.* Washington, D.C.: U.S. Government Printing Office.

WALLERSTEIN, JAMES S., and CLEMENT J. WYLE. 1947. "Our law-abiding law breakers." *Federal Probation,* 25, pp. 107–112.

WALTERS, JAMES, and NICK STINNETT. 1971. "Parent–child relationships: a decade review of research." *Journal of Marriage and the Family,* 33, pp. 70–111.

WALTON, JOHN. 1966. "Discipline, method, and community power: a note on the sociology of knowledge." *American Sociological Review,* 31, pp. 684–689.

WARNER, W. LLOYD, and PAUL S. LUNT. 1941. *The Social Life of a Modern Community.* New Haven, Conn.: Yale University Press.

______, et al. 1949. *Social Class in America.* New York: Harper.

WARREN, CAROL A. B. 1974. *Identity and Community in the Gay World.* New York: Wiley.

WATSON, J. B. 1924. *Behavior.* New York: Norton.

WATSON, PETER J., and MARTHA MEDNICK. 1970. "Race, social class, and the motive to avoid success in women." *Journal of Cross-Cultural Psychology,* 1, pp. 284–291.

WATTENBURG, BEN J., and RICHARD M. SCAMMON. 1967. *This U.S.A.* New York: Simon and Schuster.

WEBER, MAX. 1922. *Economy and Society,* Ephraim Fischoff *et al.* (transl.), 1968. New York: Bedminster Press.

______. 1946. *From Max Weber: Essays in Sociology,* H. H. Gerth and C. Wright Mills (trans./eds.). New York: Oxford University Press.

______. 1951. *The Religion of China.* New York: Free Press.

______. 1952. *Ancient Judaism.* New York: Free Press.

______. 1958a. *The Protestant Ethic and the Spirit of Capitalism.* New York: Scribner's.

______. 1958b. *The Religion of India.* New York: Free Press.

______. 1963. *The Sociology of Religion.* Boston: Beacon Press.

WEINBERG, MARTIN S. 1965. "Sexual modesty, social meanings, and the nudist camp." *Social Problems,* 12, pp. 311–318.

WEINBERG, M., and C. J. WILLIAMS. 1974. *Male Homosexuals: Their Problems and Adjustments.* New York: Oxford University Press.

WEITZMAN, LENORE J., et al. 1972. "Sex role socialization in picture books for preschool children." *American Journal of Sociology,* 77, pp. 1125–1149.

WHITE, LESLIE A. 1959. *The Evolution of Culture.* New York: McGraw-Hill.

______. 1969. *The Science of Culture.* New York: Farrar, Strauss, & Giroux.

WHITE, RALPH K., and RONALD O. LIPPITT. 1960. *Autocracy and Democracy.* New York: Harper & Row.

WHITE, THEODORE. 1969. *The Making of the President, 1968.* New York: Atheneum.

WHYTE, WILLIAM F. 1943. *Street-Corner Society: The Social Structure of an Italian Slum.* Chicago: University of Chicago Press.

WHYTE, WILLIAM H. 1956. *The Organization Man.* New York: Simon and Schuster.

WIESNER, JEROME B. 1973. "Technology is for mankind." *Technology Review,* May, pp. 10–13.

WILENSKY, H. L. 1964. "The professionalization of everyone?" *American Journal of Sociology,* 70, pp. 137–158.

WILLIAMS, JAY R., and MARTIN GOLD. 1972. "From delinquent behavior to official delinquency." *Social Problems,* 20, pp. 209–229.

WILLIAMS, ROBIN M., JR. 1964. *Strangers Next Door.* Englewood Cliffs, N.J.: Prentice-Hall.

______. 1970. *American Society: A Sociological Interpretation,* 3rd ed. New York: Alfred A. Knopf.

WILSON, JAMES Q. 1975. "Lock 'em up." *The New York Times Magazine,* March 9, pp. 11, 44–48.

WINICK, CHARLES, and PAUL M. KINSIE. 1971. *The Lively Commerce: Prostitution in the United States.* Chicago: Aldine.

WIRTH, LOUIS. 1931. "Culture conflict and misconduct." *Social Forces,* 9, pp. 484–492.

______. 1938. "Urbanism as a way of life." *American Journal of Sociology,* 44, pp. 8–20.

______. 1945. "The problem of minority groups," *in* Ralph Linton (ed.), *The Science of Man in the World Crisis.* New York: Columbia University Press.

WISE, DAVID. 1973. *The Politics of Lying.* New York: Random House.

WOMACK, JOHN, JR. 1972. "The Chicanos." *The New York Review of Books,* 19, No. 3, August 31, pp. 12–18.

WORSLEY, PETER. 1957. *The Trumpet Shall Sound.* London: MacGibbon & Kee.

WRONG, DENNIS H. 1959. "The functional theory of stratification: some neglected considerations." *American Sociological Review,* 24, pp. 772–782.

______. 1961. "The oversocialized conception of man in modern sociology." *American Sociological Review,* 26, pp. 183–193.

YANKELOVITCH, DANIEL. 1972. *The Changing Values on Campus: Political and Personal Values on Campus.* New York: Washington Square Press.

______. 1974. *The New Morality: A Profile of American Youth in the Seventies.* New York: John D. Rockefeller III Fund.

YARROW, L. J. 1963. "Research in dimensions of early maternal care." *Merrill-Palmer Quarterly,* 9, pp. 101–114.

Yearbook of the American Churches. 1971. New York: Council Press.

YORBURG, BETTY. 1974. *Sexual Identity: Sex Roles and Social Change.* New York: Wiley.

YOUNG, JOCK. 1971. *The Drugtakers.* London: Paladin.

ZANGWILL, ISRAEL. 1933. *The Melting Pot.* New York: Macmillan.

ZIMBARDO, PHILIP G. 1969. "The human choice: individuation, reason, and order vs. deindividuation, impulse, and chaos." *Nebraska Symposium on Motivation,* 17, pp. 237–307.

ZINKIN, TAYA. 1962. *Caste Today.* London: Oxford University Press.

ZURCHER, LOUIS A. 1970. "The 'friendly' poker game: a study of an ephemeral role." *Social Forces,* 49, pp. 173–186.

Acknowledgments

UNIT OPENERS

1. *The Fourteenth of July* (detail), Pablo Picasso. The Solomon R. Guggenheim Museum of Art, Thannhauser Collection.

2. *Dance* (First Version), Henri Matisse, 1909. Oil on canvas, 8′ 6½″ × 12′ 9½″. Collection, The Museum of Modern Art, New York, Gift of Nelson A. Rockefeller in honor of Alfred H. Barr, Jr.

3. *Willis Avenue Bridge,* Ben Shahn, 1940. Tempera on paper over composition board, 23″ × 31⅜″. Collection, The Museum of Modern Art, New York, Gift of Lincoln Kirstein.

4. *La Familia Pinzon,* Fernando Botero. Museum of Art, Rhode Island School of Design, Nancy Sayles Day Collection of Modern Latin American Art.

5. *Preparedness* (detail), Roy Lichtenstein. The Solomon R. Guggenheim Museum of Art.

CHAPTER 1

1.0 Guy Gillette, Photo Researchers
1.1 Burt Glinn, Magnum
1.2 *In order from left to right:* Ronny Jacques, Photo Researchers; Ken Heyman; Judith Aronson; Marc Riboud, Magnum
1.3–1.5 The Bettmann Archive
1.6 Brown Brothers
1.7 The Bettmann Archive
1.8 and 1.9 The Granger Collection
1.10 and 1.11 American Sociological Association
1.12 Ben Martin, TIME Magazine © Time, Inc.
1.13 Joe Munroe, Photo Researchers
1.14 Katrina Thomas, Photo Researchers
1.15 Larry Mulvehill, Photo Researchers
1.16 *top* Leonard Freed, Magnum; *bottom* John Henry Sullivan, Jr., Photo Researchers
1.17 S. M. Lipset and E. C. Ladd, Jr., "The Politics of American Sociologists," *American Journal of Sociology.* Copyright © 1972 by the University of Chicago Press.
Box p. 5, From *Invitation to Sociology* by Peter Berger. Copyright © 1963 by Peter L. Berger. Reprinted by permission of Doubleday & Company, Inc.
Reading p. 26, From *Invitation to Sociology* by Peter Berger. Copyright © 1963 by Peter L. Berger. Reprinted by permission of Doubleday & Company, Inc.

CHAPTER 2

2.0 Paul Fusco, Magnum
2.1 Steve Karp, Black Star
2.2 The New York Public Library
2.3 United Press International
2.4 Howard Petrick, Nancy Palmer Photo Agency
2.5 *both* United Press International

CHAPTER 3

3.0 June Lundborg
3.1 George Holton, Photo Researchers
3.2 *In order from left to right:* Jen and Des Bartlett, Photo Researchers; Stanley N. Botwick, Photo Researchers; Toni Angermayer, Photo Researchers
3.3 Flip Schulke, Black Star
3.4 John Launois, Black Star
3.5 Carl Frank, Photo Researchers
3.6 *top,* C. C. Bonnington, Woodfin Camp; *bottom,* Malcolm S. Kirk, Peter Arnold
3.7 *left,* Mathias Oppersdorff; *right,* Claus Meyer, Black Star
3.8 Joseph Martin, Scala, New York
3.10 Hamilton Wright, Photo Researchers
Box p. 69, Helen Keller, *The Story of My Life.* Copyright © 1903 Doubleday & Company.

Reading p. 75, Ralph Linton, *The American Mercury*. Reprinted by permission.

CHAPTER 4

4.0 Ray Ellis, Photo Researchers
4.1 Charles Gatewood
4.3 Constance Stuart, Black Star
4.4 Mathias Oppersdorff
4.5 Loren McIntyre, Woodfin Camp
4.6 Mathias Oppersdorff
4.7 Kenneth Murray, Nancy Palmer Photo Agency
4.8 The Metropolitan Museum of Art, George A. Hearn Fund, 1956
4.9 *left,* Malcolm Kirk, Peter Arnold; *right,* Raimondo Borea
Reading p. 93, Philip Zimbardo, "The Pathology of Imprisonment." Published by permission of Transaction, Inc. from *Society,* Vol 9 #4, Copyright © 1972 by Transaction, Inc.

CHAPTER 5

5.0 Susan McCartney, Photo Researchers
5.1 *In order from left to right:* Claus Meyer, Black Star; Morton Beebe & Associates, Photo Researchers; Reni Burri, Magnum
5.2 Alice Kandell, Rapho, Photo Researchers
5.3 Courtesy, Harry Harlow, Wisconsin Primate Laboratory
5.4 Jan Lukas, Rapho, Photo Researchers
5.5 The Bettmann Archive
5.6 George Roos, Peter Arnold
5.8 Erika Stone, Peter Arnold
5.9 Beryl Goldberg
5.10 Ken Heyman
5.12 Fritz Goro, Time-Life Picture Agency © TIME, Inc.

CHAPTER 6

6.0 Courtesy Vista/Alabama/Brown
6.1 From *Social Psychology,* Fourth Edition by Alfred R. Lindesmith, Anselm L. Strauss and Norman K. Denzin. Copyright 1949, 1956 by Dryden Press, © 1968, Holt, Rinehart and Winston, Inc., and © 1975 by The Dryden Press, A Division of Holt, Rinehart and Winston. Reprinted by permission of Holt, Rinehart and Winston.
6.3 Jan Lukas, Rapho, Photo Researchers
6.4 Abagail Heyman, Magnum
6.6 *left,* Serge de Sazo, Rapho, Photo Researchers; *right,* United Press International
6.7 and 6.8 Bill Stanton, Magnum
6.9 Ken Heyman
6.10 *left,* Simon Cherpitel, Magnum; *right,* Larry Mulvehill, Photo Researchers
6.11 Joel Gordon
6.12 Charles Gatewood
6.13 John Moss, Photo Researchers
6.14 B. D. Vidibar, Photo Researchers

CHAPTER 7

7.0 Ernest Baxter, Black Star
7.1 Beryl Goldberg
7.2 Larry Mulvehill, Photo Researchers
7.3 *top left,* Paul Fusco, Magnum; *top right and bottom,* Jim Amos, Photo Researchers
7.5 Bruce Roberts, Rapho, Photo Researchers
7.6 From H. Guetzkow (ed.), *Groups, Leadership and Men* (Pittsburgh: Carnegie Press, 1951). Reprinted by permission.
7.8 Copyright © 1975 Ziff-Davis Publishing Company. Reprinted by permission of *Psychology Today Magazine.*
7.9 Ken Heyman
7.10 Reprinted with permission from *The Washington Monthly.*
7.13 Timothy Egan

CHAPTER 8

8.0 Eugene Anthony, Black Star
8.1, both Charles Gatewood
8.2 Virginia Hamilton
8.3 Charles Gatewood
8.4 The Bettmann Archive
8.6 Ken Heyman
8.7 Marc Riboud, Magnum
8.10 George W. Gardner
8.12 James Sempepos
Box p. 162, Nathanael West, *Miss Lonelyhearts.* Copyright 1933 by Nathanael West, © 1960 by Laura Perelman. Reprinted by permission of New Directions Publishing Corporation.
Table p. 168, Adapted with permission of Macmillan Publishing Co., Inc. from *Social Theory and Social Structure* by Robert K. Merton. Copyright © 1968, 1967 by Robert K. Merton.
Reading p. 183, William Chambliss, "The Saints and the Roughnecks." Published by permission of Transaction, Inc. from *Society,* Vol 11 #1, Copyright © 1973 by Transaction, Inc.

CHAPTER 9

9.0 United Press International
9.1 Ron Sieg
9.3 *In order from left to right:* P. Jones-Griffiths, Magnum; John Marmaras, Woodfin Camp; Loren McIntyre, Woodfin Camp; Ken Heyman; Malcolm S. Kirk, Peter Arnold; Chester Higgins, Jr., Rapho, Photo Researchers
9.4 and 9.5 Scala, New York
9.7 The Bettmann Archive
9.8 Ron Sieg

9.9 Charles Gatewood
9.10 Arthur Tress, Photo Researchers
9.11 Copyright © Institute for Sex Research, Inc.
9.12 Scala, New York
9.14 United Press International
Box p. 209, Studs Terkel, *Working*. Copyright © 1974 by Pantheon Books, a Division of Random House, Inc.

CHAPTER 10
10.0 Fred Lyon, Photo Researchers
10.1 *left*, Jack Corn, Documerica, EPA; *right*, Peter Vandermark, Stock, Boston
10.2 Bruce Roberts, Rapho, Photo Researchers
10.3 Hodge, Seigel, and Rossi, "Occupational Prestige in the United States," *American Journal of Sociology*. Copyright © 1964 The University of Chicago Press.
10.4 Dorien Leigh, Ltd., Black Star
10.5 Inge Morath, Magnum
10.6 United Press International
10.7 Charles Gatewood
10.8 J. H. Retina et al., "Income and Stratification Ideology," *American Journal of Sociology*. Copyright © 1970 The University of Chicago Press.
10.9 George Holton, Photo Researchers
Reading p. 234, Ian Robertson, "Social Stratification" in David E. Hunter & Phillip Whitten (eds.) *The Study of Anthropology*, Copyright © 1976 by Harper & Row, Publishers, Inc.

CHAPTER 11
11.0 George W. Gardner
11.4 From *The American Class System* by Daniel W. Rossides. Copyright © 1976 by Houghton Mifflin Company. Reprinted by permission of the publisher.
11.5 Richard Pipes, Nancy Palmer Photo Agency
11.6, both George W. Gardner
11.7 *left;* Joel Gordon; *right*, James Sempepos
11.9, both James Carroll
11.10 *In order from left to right:* James H. Karales, Peter Arnold; Bruce Davidson, Magnum; Rachel Cowan; Don Rutledge, Black Star; Joel Gordon; Don Getsug, Rapho, Photo Researchers
11.11 J. H. Retina et al., "Income and Stratification Ideology," *American Journal of Sociology*. Copyright © 1970 The University of Chicago Press.
Reading p. 258, From *Blaming the Victim*, by William Ryan. Copyright © 1971 by William Ryan. Reprinted by permission of Pantheon Books, a Division of Random House, Inc.

CHAPTER 12
12.0 Charles Moore, Black Star
12.1 The Bettmann Archive
12.2 *In order left to right:* Don Getsug, Rapho, Photo Researchers; Georg Gerster, Rapho, Photo Researchers; Mathias Oppersdorff; Paolo Koch, Rapho, Photo Researchers; Paolo Koch, Rapho, Photo Researchers; Minoru Aoki, Rapho, Photo Researchers; Hubertus Kanos, Rapho, Photo Researchers; Yorum Lehmann, Peter Arnold; Joan Menschenfreund; A. Topping, Rapho, Photo Researchers; Bernard G. Silberstein, Rapho, Photo Researchers; Mathias Oppersdorff; Chester Higgins, Rapho, Photo Researchers; Emil Schulthess, Black Star; John Veltri, Rapho, Photo Researchers; R. B. Hott, Photo Researchers
12.3 United Press International
12.4 The Bettmann Archive
12.5 *left*, Max Tharpe, Black Star; *top right*, Gerhard E. Gscheidle, Peter Arnold; *bottom right*, Norris McNamara, Nancy Palmer Photo Agency
12.6 The Bettmann Archive
12.8 *In order left to right:* The Bettman Archive; Danny Lyon, Magnum; Danny Lyon, Magnum; Bruce Davidson, Magnum; Stephen Shames; Black Star
12.9 George Ballis, Black Star
12.10 United Press International
12.11 Charles Gatewood

CHAPTER 13
13.0 Elliott Erwitt, Magnum
13.1 Ginger Chih, Peter Arnold
13.2 Reprinted from *Social Forces*, 15 (May, 1935). "Comparative Data on the Division of Labor by Sex" by George P. Murdock. Copyright © The University of North Carolina Press.
13.3 Reprinted from *Social Forces*, 30 (October, 1951). "Women as a Minority Group" by Helen Mayer Hacker. Copyright © The University of North Carolina Press.
13.5 The New Morality: A Profile of American Youth in the 70's by Daniel Yankelovich, Inc. Copyright 1974 by the JDR 3rd Fund. The study on which this book is based was jointly funded by the Edna McConnell Clark Foundation, the Carnegie Corporation of New York, the Hazen Foundation, the JDR 3rd Fund, and the Andrew E. Mellon Foundation.
13.6 United Press International
13.7 Abram G. Schoenfeld, Photo Researchers
13.8 *top*, Steve Eagle, Nancy Palmer Photo Agency; *bottom*, Marcia Kay Keegan, Peter Arnold
13.9 *left*, Courtesy, International Labour Office, Geneva; *right*, Photo Researchers

13.10 *top,* Suzanne Szasz, Photo Researchers; *bottom,* Charles Harbutt, Magnum
Box p. 307, Betty and Theodore Roszak (eds.) *Masculine and Feminine,* 1970. Courtesy of Harper & Row, Publishers, Inc.
Reading p. 310, This excerpt from "The Changing Door Ceremony: Notes on the Operation of Sex Roles," by Laurel Richardson Walum is reprinted from *Urban Life & Culture* Vol. 2, No. 4 (Jan. 1974) pp. 506–515 by permission of the Publisher, Sage Publications, Inc.

CHAPTER 14
14.0 Joel Gordon
14.1 Inger McCabe, Rapho, Photo Researchers
14.2 (a), (d) Tom Pix, Peter Arnold; (b) A. Marciano; (c) Yoram Kahana, Peter Arnold; (e) Leonard Freed, Magnum
14.3 Beryl Goldberg
14.4 Bruce Roberts, Rapho, Photo Researchers
14.6 Culver Pictures
14.7 The Metropolitan Museum of Art, Bequest of Catherine Lorillard Wolfe, 1887.
14.8 Marc St. Gil, Documerica, EPA
14.10 Charles Gatewood
14.11 Copyright © 1975 Ziff-Davis Publishing Company. Reprinted by permission of *Psychology Today Magazine.*
Box p. 333, Copyright © 1966, by The Atlantic Monthly Company, Boston, Mass. Reprinted with permission.
Reading p. 337, Copyright © by Jessie Bernard from *The Future of Marriage* by Jessie Bernard. Originally published by the World Publishing Company, used with permission of Thomas Y. Crowell Company, Inc.

CHAPTER 15
15.0 Rachel Cowan
15.1 Charles Gatewood
15.4 George W. Gardner
15.5 Joel Gordon
15.6 *top,* Jodi Reston, Photo Researchers; *bottom,* Susan Johns, Rapho, Photo Researchers
15.7 Margot Granitsas, Photo Researchers
15.8 Stephen Collins, Photo Researchers
15.9 Charles Harbutt, Magnum
15.10 Bob Weiss Associates for *Fortune* Magazine.
15.12 Bettye Lane, Nancy Palmer Photo Agency
15.13 Copyright © 1975 by *The Chicago Tribune.* World Rights Reserved.
Box p. 359 Copyright © 1968 by The New York Times Company. Reprinted by permission.

CHAPTER 16
16.0 Mathias Oppersdorff
16.1 (a) Loren McIntyre, Woodfin Camp; (b) Alex Borodulin, Peter Arnold; (c) Judith Aronson; (d) Slim Aarons, Photo Researchers; (e) Björn Bölstad, Peter Arnold; (f) F. D. Siemens, Photo Researchers
16.2 Scala, New York
16.3 Reprinted with permission from the 1975 Britannica Book of the Year. Copyright 1975 by Encyclopaedia Britannica, Inc.
16.4 Paolo Koch, Rapho, Photo Researchers
16.5 and 16.6 The Bettmann Archive
16.7 Victor Engelbert, Photo Researchers
16.8 Scala, New York
16.9 From *Sociology of Religion* by Glenn M. Vernon. Copyright 1962 by McGraw-Hill. Used with permission of McGraw-Hill Book Company.
16.10 Betty Cheetham, Magnum
16.11 Copyright © 1968 by The Regents of the University of California, reprinted by permission of the University of California Press.
16.12 Don Rutledge, Black Star

CHAPTER 17
17.0 Ken Heyman
17.1 The Bettmann Archive
17.2 The New York Public Library
17.4 Philippe Halsman, Magnum
17.6 The Bettmann Archive
17.7 The New York Public Library
17.8 *top left,* Georg Gerster, Rapho, Photo Researchers; *top right,* Bruce Roberts, Rapho, Photo Researchers; *bottom,* Ted Spiegel, Black Star
17.9 *left,* The Bettmann Archive; *right,* Georg Gerster, Rapho, Photo Researchers
17.10 Louis Harris and Associates for polls in 1966, 1971, and 1972. Copyright © 1975 by the Chicago Tribune. World Rights Reserved.
Box p. 406, From *The Pursuit of Loneliness* by Philip Slater. Copyright © 1970 by Philip E. Slater. Reprinted by permission of Beacon Press.

CHAPTER 18
18.0 Georg Gerster, Rapho, Photo Researchers
18.1 *In order left to right:* Bruce Roberts, Rapho, Photo Researchers; Ken Heyman; Michal Heron, Woodfin Camp; George W. Gardner; Raimondo Borea; Cornell Capa, Magnum; Werner H. Müller, Peter Arnold; Ken Heyman
18.2 George Rodger, Magnum

18.3 *From top to bottom:* Marc & Evelyne Bernheim, Woodfin Camp; Ken Heyman; Ingbert Grüttner, Peter Arnold
18.4 From *The American Class System* by Daniel W. Rossides. Copyright © 1976 by Houghton Mifflin Company. Reprinted by permission of the publisher.
18.5 Ken Heyman
18.7 Robert A. Isaacs, Photo Researchers
18.8 Paolo Koch, Rapho, Photo Researchers
18.9 Dennis Stock, Magnum
18.10 Ken Heyman
18.12 George W. Gardner

CHAPTER 19
19.0 Richard Kalvar, Magnum
19.1 Cornell Capa, Magnum
19.2 *In order left to right:* p. 438 Marc Riboud, Magnum; Gerhard E. Gscheidle, Peter Arnold; United Press International; Henriques, Magnum; Collection, J.A.F./Paris, Magnum p. 439 The New York Public Library; Margaret Bourke-White, Time-Life Picture Agency © TIME, Inc.; The Bettmann Archive; United Press International
19.3 Tony Howarth, Woodfin Camp
19.4 and 19.6 United Press International
19.7 Bill Stanton, Magnum
19.8 *left,* Rhoda Galyn, Photo Researchers; *right,* Weinman, Magnum
19.9 United Press International
19.10 Adapted with permission of Macmillan Publishing Co., Inc. from *Culture and Social Character* by Seymour Lipset and Leo Lowenthal (eds.). Copyright © 1967 by The Free Press, a Division of The Macmillan Company.
19.11 Ken Heyman
19.12 Eve Arnold, Magnum
19.15 Rene Burri, Magnum
19.16 The Bettmann Archive

CHAPTER 20
20.0 Larry Mulvehill, Photo Researchers
20.1 Brown Brothers
20.3 Copyright, 1976, by Harcourt Brace Jovanovich, Inc., adapted and reproduced with their permission from "The World's Population Crisis" by Kingsley Davis in *Contemporary Social Problems* by Robert K. Merton and Robert Nisbet.
20.4 The Bettmann Archive
20.5 John Zoiner, Peter Arnold
20.6 From "World Resources and the World Middle Class" by Nathan Keyfitz. Copyright © 1976 by Scientific American, Inc. All rights reserved.
20.7 Yoram Kahana, Peter Arnold
20.8 Marc Riboud, Magnum
20.12 Henri Cartier-Bresson, Magnum
20.13 Werner H. Müller, Peter Arnold
20.10, 20.14, and Box p. 473, *The Limits to Growth: A report for THE CLUB OF ROME'S Project on the Predicament of Mankind,* by Donella H. Meadows, Dennis L. Meadows, Jørgen Randers, William W. Behrens III. A Potomac Associates book published by Universe Books, New York, 1972. Graphics by Potomac Associates.

CHAPTER 21
21.0 Courtesy, Jan Jachniewicz, The Chase Manhattan Bank
21.1 Georg Gerster, Rapho, Photo Researchers
21.2 Mathias Oppersdorff
21.3 United Press International
21.5 Joe Munroe, Photo Researchers
21.7 and 21.8 Georg Gerster, Rapho, Photo Researchers
21.9 Reprinted from "The Nature of Cities" by Chauncy D. Harris and Edward L. Ullman in Volume 242 (November, 1945) of *The Annals* of The American Academy of Political and Social Science. Copyright © 1945.

CHAPTER 22
22.0 Gerhard E. Gscheidle, Peter Arnold
22.1 The Bettmann Archive
22.2 Hiroji Kubota, Magnum
22.3 Courtesy, Capital Records
22.5 Joe Munroe, Photo Researchers
22.6 Brown Brothers
22.7 (a) Ken Heyman; (b) Raimondo Borea; (c) Ken Heyman; (d) Charles Harbutt, Magnum
22.8 The Bettmann Archive
22.9 Joel Gordon
22.10 The Bettmann Archive
Reading p. 535, From *My Lai* 4, by Seymour M. Hersh. Copyright © 1970 by Seymour M. Hersh. Reprinted by permission of Random House, Inc.

CHAPTER 23
23.0 Bob Fitch, Black Star
23.1 Library of Congress
23.2 Barbara Kirk, Peter Arnold
23.3 Beryl Goldberg
23.4 The Bettmann Archive
23.5 *top,* United Press International; *bottom;* John Bryson, Rapho, Photo Researchers
23.6 The Bettmann Archive
23.8 Scheler, *Stern,* Black Star
23.9 Bettye Lane, Photo Researchers

Index

aborigines, 320, 370, 547
absolute deprivation, 251
account, 122
achieved status, 79, 217, 218
Acton, William, 196
adolescence, 112
Adorno, Theodore W., 275, 276
advertising, 305–306, 425
aggregates, 139
Agnew, Spiro, 179
agricultural societies, 85, 440–441
Albert, Ethel M., 200
Alexander, C. Norman, 357
alienation, 372, 416–418
aligning actions, 122
Allison, Paul D., 397
Allport, Gordon W., 287, 515
American Association for the Advancement of Science, 394
American Indian Movement, 282
American Library Association, 305
American Medical Association, 450
American Psychiatric Association, 204
American Revolution, 436, 460
Anderson, Charles H., 240, 425, 459
Anglo-conformity, 286
animism, 368
anomalies, 396
anomie, 168–169, 412, 414
anthropology, 10, 262, 541–543
anticipatory socialization, 110–111
antisemitism, 275–276
Apartheid, 268, 235–237
Arapaho, 190
Arapesh, 56, 292
Argyle, Michael, 126
Aries, Phillipe, 112
Armer, J. Michael, 220
Asch, Solomon, 145–146
ascribed status, 79, 217, 218
Ash, Roberta A., 534
assimilation, 267, 268
Athanasiou, Robert, 197
Auchincloss, Kenneth, 488
authoritarian personality, 275–276
authority, 436–440
automation, 251, 431
automobile, 425, 549–550

Bales, Robert F., 141, 145, 294, 295
Ball, Donald W., 127
Balswick, Jack O., 307
Baltzell, E. Digby, 224, 373
Bandura, Albert, 101
Bane, Mary J., 360
Barber, Theodore, 349
Barry, Herbert, 292
Bart, Pauline, 25
Bartell, Gilbert, 334
Bates, Alan P., 25, 393
Bates, Daniel G., 92
Bay of Pigs, 145
Beach, Frank A., 189, 190–192, 200, 211, 291, 292
Beatles, 516–518
Becker, Howard S., 115, 127–128, 162, 171–172, 182
behaviorism, 101, 205
Bell, Daniel, 432, 555, 556
Bell, Derrick A., 178
Bellah, Robert N., 384
Bem, Daryl, 306
Bem, Sandra, 306
Ben-David, Joseph, 390
Bendix, Reinhard, 219, 224, 229, 233, 250
Benedict, Ruth, 74
Benjamin, Harry, 205, 206, 208
Bennet, Edward M., 297
Bennis, Warren G., 157
Bensman, Joseph, 509
Berelson, Bernard, 143
Berg, Ivar, 363
Bergel, Ergon E., 223
Berger, Bennet M., 499
Berger, Peter L., 4, 5, 25, 26–27, 136, 137, 416; on religion, 367, 368–9, 385, 387
Berle, A. A., 220
Berlin, Brent, 71
Bernard, Jessie, 334, 336, 337–339
Bernard, L. L., 97
Bernstein, Basil, 356
Berreman, Gerald D., 223
Berry, R. Stephen, 488
bias, 22–24
Bieber, Irving, 204
bilateral family, 322, 325
Birdwhistell, Ray, 123–124
Birenbaum, Arnold, 127, 137
birth rate, 470
black Americans, 266, 268, 271, 276, 277, 279, 301, 325–326, 482, 527–528
Blau, Peter M., 152, 154, 159, 249, 250, 251, 354
Blauner, Robert, 269, 431
Blood, Robert O., 328
Blume, Marshall E., 238
Blumer, Herbert, 119, 523
Blumstein, Philip, 205
body language, 123–124
body types, 167
Bott, Elizabeth, 248
Bottomore, T. B., 233
Boulding, Kenneth E., 486
Bowlby, John, 100
Brazil, 267, 268
Briar, Scott, 113, 177
Brim, Orville G., 113

Brinton, Crane, 462, 464
Britain, 267, 342–343, 420, 447; stratification in, 223–224
Bronfenbrenner, Urie, 109
Brophy, J. E., 349
Brown vs Board of Education, 280
Brown, Dee, 287
Brown, Roger, 137, 142
Bryant, James H., 208
Buckley, W., 229
Buckner, H. T., 203
Buddhism, 368, 369, 370, 378
Bumpass, Larry, 482
bureaucracy, 149–158, 346–347
Burgess, Ernest W., 16, 329, 502, 506
Burgoon, Judee K., 126
Burnette, Robert, 282
Burnham, James, 220
Burundi, 267, 268
busing, 361
bystander apathy, 129–131

Cadwallader, Mervyn, 333
Caesar, Julius, 437, 552–553
Calvin, John, 34
Calvinism, 369, 377–379
Campbell, Angus, 335
Campbell, Ernest Q., 357
Canada, 420, 502
cannibalism, 61, 85
Cantril, Hadley, 521, 527
capitalism, 35, 377–379, 420–422, 424–427, 444
Caplow, Theodore, 416
cargo cults, 377
case study, 40–41
caste, 215; in India, 222–223; in U.S., 217; in South Africa, 217, 234–236
categories, 139–140
Catholic Church, 194–196, 370, 373, 374–375, 378, 379
Catholics, 328, 382–383
Centers, Richard, 241, 242, 301
central tendency, 31
Chagnon, Napoleon A., 65
Chambliss, William J., 177, 183–185
Chandler, John J., 239
charisma, 437, 439
Chavez, Cesar, 283
Cheek, William F., 279
Cherokee, 282
Cheyenne, 62
Chicago School, 15, 502, 504
Chicanos. *See* Hispanic Americans
childhood, 112
childhood isolation, 98–101
Chile, 45, 427, 450, 451
China, 225, 230, 345, 348, 351, 414, 423, 424, 425
Chinese Americans, 273, 277, 284
Chinoy, Ely, 250
Chomsky, Noam, 102
Christianity, 297, 321, 368–370, 373–375, 377, 379–383
chromosomes, 167, 291
church and sect, 380, 382–383
Churchill, Winston S., 437, 439
Cicourel, Aaron, 357
city, 493–509; history of, 494–496; central cities and suburbs, 499–500; city planning, 501–522; growth patterns, 506–508
civil religion, 384
Civil Rights Acts, 358
civil rights movement, 281, 531
Clark, Burton R., 349, 350, 352
class, 217–218; in U.S., 237–255; in Britain, 223–224; and religion, 372–373; and education, 355–362. *See also* social stratification.
class conflict, 12, 216, 226
class consciousness, 226
Clinard, Marshall B., 182
closed system, 217
Cloward, Richard A., 169
coercion, 436
cognitive development, 105–107
Cohen, Albert K., 169, 170, 181, 271
Cohen, Larry R., 297
Cohn, Norman, 376
Cole, Johnathan R., 397
Cole, Stephen, 397
Coleman, James C., 189
Coleman, James S., 250, 349, 358, 360–362
Coleman, Richard F., 242
Coles, Robert, 356
collective behavior, 511–537; theory of, 513–514; types of, 514–530; and social movements, 531–533; and social change, 553
collective consciousness, 412
Collins, Randall, 296, 354
colonialism, 227, 267, 268, 270, 351, 373
communism, 230, 371, 372, 424, 444, 445
community, 458–459, 494, 502–504
Comte, Auguste, 12, 15, 540, 541
concentric-zone theory, 506–507
conditioning, 101, 303
conflict perspective, 18–19; on deviance, 171–173; on education, 353–358; on race relations, 269–270; on sex roles, 295–296; on the state, 443–445; on social change, 546–547; on social stratification, 226, 229–230, 232
conflict theory, 18–19, 21–22, 556
conformity, 145–146, 168
controls, 32, 35
Cook, M., 126
Cooley, Charles Horton, 102, 104
Cooper, A. J., 196
corporations, 240, 424–428, 451, 454–455, 458–460
correlations, 30–31
Coser, Lewis A., 18, 146, 181, 554
counterculture, 67–68, 371, 515–518
courts, 176–179, 272, 278, 280, 359
courtship, 327–329
Cressey, Donald R., 175
crime, 173–180
Crockett, Harry J., 250
Crossman, Richard, 371
crowding, 125
crowds, 523–528
crusades, 374
cult, 379–380
cultural anthropology, 10
cultural change, 71–72; 551–552
cultural deprivation, 360–361
cultural integration, 67–68
cultural relativism, 66
cultural transmission theory, 169–171
cultural universals, 64
culture, 51–75, 356, 357, 359, 360–361, 377
culture lag, 403, 549
culture of poverty, 252, 254
Curie, Elliott, 92
Cutright, Phillip, 239
cyclical theories, 543–545

Dahl, Robert, 458, 464
Dahrendorf, Ralf, 231, 545, 547, 554
Daley, Richard, 456
D'Andrade, Roy G., 292
Dank, Barry M., 204
Darley, John M., 130
Darwin, Charles, 52, 53, 97, 270, 398, 399–400, 542
Davies, James C., 460
Davis, Alan J., 205
Davis, Fred, 162

Davis, James H., 141, 159
Davis, Kingsley, 16; on isolated children, 99; on population, 474, 486 491; on sexual behavior, 189, 200, 210; on science, 401, 402; on urbanization, 493
Davis, Nanette J., 208
Dean, J., 126
death, 113, 133–135
death rate, 291, 471
de facto discrimination, 277–278
Deisher, Robert, 205
de jure discrimination, 277–278
democracy, 445–449
democratic socialism, 424, 450
demographic transition, 479–482
demography, 470–473
Denfield, Duane, 334
Dennis, Jack, 450
Dennis, Wayne, 100
denomination, 379
Dentler, Robert A., 176
dependent variable, 30
de Toqueville, Alexis, 412
Deutscher, Irving, 273
developmental school, 101–2, 105–7
developmental socialization, 111
deviance, 161–185; nature of, 161–174; and social control, 164–165; theories of, 166–173; and crime, 173–180; consequences of, 180–181
Dewey, John, 346
Dewey, Thomas E., 37
Diamond, Milton, 292
Dickson, William J., 35, 153, 419
dictatorship, 446
differential association theory, 169–171
diffusion, 72, 552
disclaimers, 122
discovery, 72, 551
discrimination, 273–274, 277–278. *See also* prejudice; segregation.
division of labor, 292–293, 301–302, 316–317, 410–414, 417
divorce, 329–332
Djilas, Milovan, 225
Dobie, Shirley, 297
Doleschal, Eugene, 176, 249
Domhoff, G. William, 240, 244, 257, 455–456, 460, 465
double standard, 195, 198
Douglas, Jack D., 182
dramaturgy, 20, 120–121, 128–129
drives, 57, 189
drugs, 172, 306
Duberman, Martin, 205
Duncan, Otis Dudley, 250, 251
Durkheim, Emile, 13–14, 16, 89, 362, 545, 548; on anomie, 168, 412, 414; on deviance, 165, 180; on religion, 367, 369–371; on suicide, 41–43; on division of labor, 412, 414; on social solidarity, 89, 412, 414
dyad, 142–143
dysfunction, 18, 153–154, 180, 269

Easton, David, 450
ecclesia, 379
ecological approach, 63; to society, 82; to culture, 62–64; to cities, 504–508. *See also* ecology; human ecology
ecological crisis, 390
ecology, 486–490. *See also* ecological approach
economics, 10
economy, 409–433
ecosystem, 487
ectomorph, 165
education, 341–363; in U.S., 343–50; functions of, 350–353; and social mobility, 353–355; and equal opportunity, 355–362. See also: schools
egalitarian family, 322, 325
ego, 103
Ehrhardt, Anke A., 189, 292
Ehrlich, Anne H., 481, 488, 491
Ehrlich, Paul R., 481, 488, 491
Einstein, Albert, 394, 395
Eisenhower, Dwight D., 458
Eitzen, D. Stanley, 326, 384 459
Ekman, Paul, 123
Elkin, Frederick, 115
Elkins, Stanley M., 279
Ellis, Albert, 334
Ellis, Havelock, 188
Empey, LaMar T., 176
endogamy, 217, 266, 322, 325
endomorph, 165
Engels, Friedrich, 371, 373, 444, 546
England. *See* Britain
Epstein, Cynthia F., 295
equality, 449–450; of opportunity, 358-362
Equal Rights Amendment, 308
equilibrium, 17, 545
Erbe, William, 456
Erickson, Maynard L., 176, 177
Erikson, Erik H., 112, 115
Erikson, Kai T., 162, 165, 182
Eskimo, 61, 62, 70, 75, 282, 321
ethical issues, 45–46
ethnic groups, 263–329, 381
ethnicity, 263
ethnocentrism, 64–65, 269, 275, 282, 351, 365, 367
ethnography, 10
ethnomethodology, 20
Etzioni, Amitai, 148, 159, 345, 390, 416, 556
Etzioni-Halevy, Eva, 556
Evans, Robert R., 534
Evolution, biological, 53–54, 202, 399, 401. *See also* human species; Darwin
Evolution, cultural and social, 12, 228, 231-232, 541–543, 545–546. *See also* sociocultural evolution
exchange theory, 20
exogamy, 321
experiment, 35–36
expressive role, 295

fad, 518–520
false consciousness, 226, 271, 272, 297
family, 106, 303–304, 315–339; functions of, 317–318; patterns, 318–322; changes in, 323–324; future of, 332–335; in U.S., 325–334. *See also* marriage; kinship
family planning, 484–485
Fanon, Franz, 287
Farber, Jerry, 347
Farrington, Benjamin, 390
fascism, 275, 371. *See also* Nazi Germany
fashion, 518
Fava, Sylvia F., 508
Feagin, Joe R., 254
fecundity, 470
Felipe, N., 126
feral children, 98–99
fertility, 470
Festinger, Leon, 40, 145
feudalism, 218–219, 223, 226–227, 444
Fiedler, Fred, 144
field experiment, 35
Firey, Walter, 507
Fitzgerald, Ernest, 460
folk society, 89
folkways, 58
Ford, Clellan S., 189, 190–192, 200, 211, 291
Ford, Gerald R., 550, 551
formal organizations, 147–158; and bureaucracy, 149–154; and oligarchy, 155–157; future of, 157–158

Fox, Thomas G., 224, 251
Frankel, Linda, 25
Freedman, M., 203
French Revolution, 436, 462–463, 512
Freud, Sigmund, 102, 103–4, 115, 188, 399
Fried, Morton, 440, 543
Friedenberg, Edgar, 347
Friesen, Wallace V., 123
functionalism, 14, 16–18, 21–22
functionalist perspective, 16–18; on culture, 61–62; on deviance, 168, 180–181; on education, 350–353; on family, 317–318, 323–324, 327; on sex roles, 294–296; on the state, 442–443; on social change, 546–547, 554; on stratification, 228–229, 232
functional prerequisite, 81

Gagnon, John, 189, 211, 204
Galbraith, John Kenneth, 405, 425, 426
Gallman, Robert E., 238
Gandhi, M., 437, 439
Gandy, Patrick, 205
Gans, Herbert J., 238, 257, 326, 499, 500, 501, 504, 508
Garfinkel, Harold, 20, 119, 120, 126, 171
Geertz, Clifford, 52
Geis, Irving, 47
Gemeinschaft, 89, 502
gender, 290
generalization, 7, 30
generalized other, 105
genocide, 268, 282
Genovese, Kitty, 129
Gephart, William J., 349
Gesell, Arnold, 303
Gesellschaft, 89, 502
Getty, John P., 240
Ghost Dance, 376
Gintis, Herbert, 354
Gist, Noel P., 508
Glaser, Barney G., 113, 133–134
Glazer, Myron, 47
Glenn, Norval D., 238
Glick, Paul C., 328
Glock, Charles, 381, 383, 387
Glueck, Eleanor, 167
Glueck, Sheldon, 167
Gockel, Galen L., 247
Goffman, Erving, 20, 41; on dramaturgical approach, 120–122, 128, 137; on deviance, 162, 171; on total institutions, 179–180
Gold, Martin, 176
Goldberg, Philip, 298
Goldfarb, William, 100
Goldsmith, Edward, 488
Goldwater, Barry, 156, 453
Good, T. L., 349
Goode, William J., 247, 323–327, 331
Goodman, Paul, 347
Gordon, Michael, 334
Gordon, Milton M., 286
Goring, Charles, 167
Gornick, Vivian, 309
Gough, Kathleen E., 320
Gouldner, Alvin W., 16, 554, 556
Graham, Hugh Davis, 279
Greeley, Andrew M., 284
Green, Mark J., 433
Green, Richard, 292
Greenberg, Selig, 291
Greenfield, Sidney M., 326
Greenstein, Fred I., 450
Greenwald, Harold, 206
Greenwood, E., 416
Greer, Germaine, 309
Greer, Scott A., 92, 504, 509
Griffith, Belver C., 394
groups, 80–81, 139–159; small groups, 141–146; leadership in, 143–144; decisions in, 144–145; conformity in, 145–146; reference groups, 147; ingroups and outgroups, 146–147. *See also* bureaucracy; formal organizations; peer groups; primary groups; secondary groups
groupthink, 144–145
Guevara, Che, 371, 460
Gurr, Ted Robert, 279
Guzzardi, Walter, 354

Hacker, Helen, 295
Hagedorn, Robert, 47
Hagstrom, William O., 352, 397, 398
Hall, Edward T., 125, 135
Hammond, Philip E., 47
Handel, Gerald, 115
Hare, A. Paul, 141
Hare Krishna movement, 381
Harlow, Harry F., 100, 189
Harlow, Margaret K., 100
Harris, Chauncy D., 507
Harris, Marvin, 62–63, 74, 266, 374–375
Hartley, Eugene, 276
Hartley, Ruth E., 303
Hauser, Philip H., 248
Hauser, Philip M., 487
Hawthorne effect, 35-36. *See also* Western Electric experiments
headhunting, 85
health, 247–248
Heilbronner, Robert, 475
Heller, Celia, 233
helping others, 129–131
Henry, Jules, 348
Henslin, James M., 61, 127, 128–129, 211
Herberg, Will, 384
Herrick, Neal W., 418
Hersch, Seymour M., 535–537
Hess, Robert D., 450
Heussenstamm, Frances K., 177–178
Hewitt, John P., 122
Hillier, E. T., 123
Hindelang, Michael J., 176
Hinduism, 222–223, 368, 369, 370, 373, 378
Hirschi, Travis, 176
Hispanic Americans, 271, 279
Hitler, Adolf, 273, 437, 446
Hobbes, Thomas, 443, 460
Hodge, Robert, W., 220, 221, 242
Hodges, Harold M., 271
Hofstadter, Richard, 421
Holdren, John, 482
Hollander, Edwin P., 141, 159
Hollingshead, August B., 242
Holt, John, 347
Homans, George C., 20
homogamy, 328
homosexuality, 45–46, 191–192, 195–197, 199–203, 207
Hooker, Evelyn, 203, 204
Hopi, 71
horizontal mobility, 218
Horner, Matina, 298
Horowitz, Irving Louis, 45, 92
horticultural societies, 84–85, 410, 440
hospitals, 128–129, 133–135
Howe, Louise Kapp, 302
Hoyt, Homer, 507
Huff, Darrell, 47
Hull, Raymond, 155
human ecology, 487
human sacrifice, 85
human species, 52–57, 316–317. *See also* evolution, biological
Humphreys, Laud, 45–46, 203, 205, 211
Hunt, Morton, 196, 197, 198, 203
Hunter, David E., 235
Hunter, Floyd, 458

hunting and gathering societies, 82–83, 440
hurting others, 131–133
Hutton, J. H., 223, 233
Hutton, James, 399
Huxley, T. H., 399
Hyman, Herbert, 450
hypothesis, 43

id, 102
ideal type, 150, 420, 440
ideology, 223-226, 271–273, 296–299, 542, 548–549
illiteracy, 344
impression management, 121
incest taboo, 189–191, 199, 272, 318–319
independent variable, 30
India, 42–43, 267, 384; sacred cows, 63; population, 484–485; caste system, 222–223
Indians, American. *See* Native Americans
industrialism, 87, 410, 429
industrialization, 11, 412, 487
industrial societies, 87–91, 232, 323–324, 429–431, 441
ingroup, 146–147
Inhelder, Barbel, 115
Inkeles, Alex, 25, 220
innovation, 72, 168, 395–401, 352–353, 551–552
instinct, 56–57, 97
institutional discrimination, 278, 281, 285
institutions, 81, 82–91
instrumental role, 295
intelligence, 357–358, 359
interactionist perspective, 20–21, 117–119; some applications, 127–135; on the development of self, 104–105; on deviance, 171–173; on sex roles, 310–311
interaction, social, 20–21, 117–135
interest groups, 240, 450–451, 454–455, 457
intergenerational mobility, 218–219, 250–251
interviews, 37–38
invention, 72, 551–552
IQ tests, 357–359
Ireland, 374
Islam, 321, 368, 370, 378

Jacklin, Carol N., 291, 292
Jackson, Donald, 178
Jackson, Elton F., 250
Jackson, Philip, 348
Jacobs, Jane, 501, 506
Jacobson, Lenore, 363
Jacoby, Neil H., 427
Janis, Irving L., 144, 145
Japan, 42, 480
Japanese Americans, 271, 284
Jefferson, Thomas, 278, 345, 384
Jehova's Witnesses, 379, 381
Jencks, Christopher, 247, 356, 362, 363
Jennings, M. Kent, 450
Jensen, Arthur, 357
Jews, 262–263, 266, 268, 275–276, 297, 328, 382, 383
Johnson, Donald M., 522
Johnson, Lyndon B., 447, 449, 550
Johnson, Roger T., 348
Johnson, Virginia E., 196
Jones, Stephen B., 126
Judaism, 321, 368, 379
Julian, Joseph, 393
juvenile delinquency, 169–171, 174, 176–177, 183–185

Kahl, Joseph A., 250
Katchadourian, Herant P., 211
Katcher, Allan, 303
Katz, Marlaine L., 298
Kaufman, Richard S., 459
Kay, Paul, 71
Kayson, Carl, 489
Keller, Helen, 69
Kelley, D. M., 387
Keniston, Kenneth, 112
Kennedy, John F., 145, 345, 384, 439, 440, 550, 551
Kenya, 271
Keraki, 61, 63
Ketchel, Melvin M., 486
Keyfitz, Nathan, 476
Killian, Lewis M., 526, 534
King, Martin Luther, 439
King, Wayne, 331
Kinsey, Alfred C., 188, 189, 191, 196–198, 202–203
Kinship, 316–324. *See also* family
Kinsie, Paul M., 206, 211
Kirk, Dudley, 480
Kirkham, George L., 205
Kitsuse, John I., 357, 532
Kitwanger, Evelyn M., 248
Klapmuts, Norah, 176, 249
Klapp, Orin, 519
Klein, Rudolf, 489
Kluckhohn, Clyde, 73, 191, 192
Knowles, Louis L., 287
Koestler, A., 371
Kogan, N., 144
Kohlberg, Lawrence, 102, 304
Kohn, M. L., 249
Kolko, Gabriel, 251
Komarovsky, Mirra, 247, 248, 308
Komisar, Lucy, 306
Kornhauser, William, 455, 460
Kottak, Conrad Phillip, 192
Krauss, Irving, 357
Kroeber, A. L., 552
Kubler-Ross, Elisabeth, 113, 115
Kuhn, Manford, 102
Kuhn, Thomas S., 396, 397, 398, 407
Ku Klux Klan, 274, 531
Kunen, James S., 68
Kuznets, Simon, 238
Kwakiutl, 61

La Barre, Weston, 200
labeling, 171–173, 183–185, 349, 357
laboratory experiment, 35
Labovitz, Sanford, 47
Ladd, Everett C., 23
laissez faire, 421
Lampman, Robert 238
Landis, Judson T., 330
Landon, Alfred, 36
Lane, David, 225
Langton, Kenneth P., 450
language, 68–71, 356
Lanternari, Vittorio, 376
LaPiere, Richard T., 273
Larsen, Otto N., 523
Lassiter, Roy L., 250
Laswell, Harold D., 435
Latané, Bibb, 130, 131
latent functions, 18
law, 58, 442
Leacock, Eleanor, 349
leadership, 143
learning, 101–102
Le Bon, Gustave, 525–526
Lee, Alfred McClung, 529
Lee, Elizabeth Bryant, 529
Lee, Richard B., 83
legal system, 176–179. *See* law; crime; courts
legitimacy, political, 223, 297, 436–440
legitimate birth, 316, 318
Lemert, Edwin M., 171, 172
Lenin, Nikolai, 371
Lenski, Gerhard, 92, 228, 231–232, 233, 238, 382, 387, 402, 440, 445, 543
Lenski, Jean, 84, 89, 92, 440, 445, 543
Lerner, M. J., 130

Levine, Janey, 127
Levi-Strauss, Claude, 71
Lewis, Oscar, 252
Leznoff, Maurice, 203
Liazos, Alexander, 161, 172
liberty, 449–450
Liebow, Elliot, 41
Lienhardt, Godfrey, 270
life chances, 237, 239
life cycle, 111–113, 371
life expectancy, 248, 471
life span, 471
Lightfoot, John, 399
Lincoln, Abraham, 275, 384, 445
Lindesmith, Alfred R., 118, 135
linguistic relativity, 70–71
Linton, Ralph, 57, 64, 65, 75, 79, 552
Lippitt, Ronald O., 143
Lipset, Seymour Martin, 23, 219, 224, 225, 229, 233, 250, 271, 447, 452, 455
Lipton, R. C., 100
lobbying, 450–451
Locke, John, 460
Lockwood, David, 545
Lofland, John, 172
Lombroso, Cesare, 166
looking-glass self, 104
Lowenthal, Leo, 455
Lowie, Robert H., 67
Luckmann, Thomas, 136, 137, 384
Lundberg, Ferdinand, 243
Lunde, Donald T., 211
Lunt, Paul S., 241
Lyell, Charles, 399
Lyman Stanford M., 122
lynching, 277, 281, 284, 526–527
Lynd, Helen M., 40, 250
Lynd, Robert S., 40, 250

Maccoby, Eleanor E., 291, 292, 309
macro order, 22
Madge, John H., 47
Maehr, A. L., 349
Mafia, 157, 175
magic, 368
Malinowski, Bronislaw, 61, 321
Malthus, Thomas, 475
mana, 368
manifest function, 18
Mankoff, Milton, 173
Mao Tse-Tung, 371, 372, 437, 439, 440, 546
marijuana, 127–128, 172–173
marriage, 316, 318–322, 334. *See also* family; kinship; courtship
Martian invasion, 521
Marx, Karl, 12–13, 14, 16, 18, 73, 95, 271, 297, 350, 371, 377, 401, 403, 433, 545; on alienation, 372, 416–417; on bureaucracy, 149; on class, 219–220, 229–230; on class conflict, 216, 444, 546; on communism, 424, 444; on economy, 210, 409, 444; on ideology, 225–226, 548; on the state, 445; critiques of, 230, 445
mass hysteria, 521–523
mass media, 110, 305–306
master status, 80, 171
Masters, William H., 196
Masters, R. E. L., 205, 206, 208
material culture, 51
Matras, Judah, 233
matriarchal, 322
matrilocal, 322, 323
matrilineal, 322
Matza, David, 177
Maugh, Thomas H., 172
Mayo, Elton, 36, 419, 420
McBride, G., 126
McCarthy, John D., 531
McCarthy, Joseph, 165
McCartney, Paul, 516–518
McDonald, Donald, 459
McGee, Reece, 368
McGovern, George, 156, 453
McIntosh, Mary, 202
McIver, Robert M., 550
McKay, Henry D., 169
McKee, J., 297
McKee, Michael, 189
McKenzie, R. D., 506
McPartland, Thomas S., 102
Mead, George Herbert, 14, 15, 20, 100; on self and symbolic interaction, 105, 112
Mead, Margaret, 292, 403, 556
Meadows, Donnella H., 432, 473, 481, 482, 490, 491
mean, 31
Means, G. C., 220
Means, Gardiner S., 425
mechanical solidarity, 89, 412
Medalia, Nahum Z., 523
median 31
Mednick, Martha, 298
Melman, Seymour, 458, 459, 465
melting pot, 279, 286, 351
Mendelsohn, Robert, 297
mental disorder, 163, 204, 248, 306
Merton, Robert K., 15, 16, 17, 18, 61, 154, 353, 474, 491, 546, 554; on anomie and deviance, 168–169; on prejudice and discrimination, 271–272, 273, 275; on science, 394–395, 397, 400, 407
mesomorph, 165
methodology, 29–47. *See also* research
Mexican Americans. *See* Hispanic Americans
Mexico, 472, 477
Meyer, Marshall W., 152
Michels, Robert, 155–156, 159, 454
micro order, 119, 127–135
Middleton, Russell, 200
migration, 471–472
Miles, Rufus E., 472
Milgram, Stanley, 131–133
military-industrial complex, 458–460. *See also* Pentagon; corporations
Millar, Ronald, 400, 407
millenarian movements, 375–376, 429
Miller, Herman P., 238
Miller, S. M., 224, 251, 357
Miller, Walter, 170
Mills, C. Wright, 7, 15, 16, 18, 25, 46, 239, 545; on sociological imagination, 5; on power elite, 454, 455, 456, 460, 465
Mills, Theodore, 141
minority group, 266–267, 295
Mitford, Jessica, 177, 182
Mob, 526–527
mode, 31
modernization, 429–432
Money, John, 189, 292
monogamy, 321, 323, 325, 332, 334
monopoly, 421
monotheism, 368
Monroe, Lawrence J., 176
Mooney, James, 376
Moore, Barrington, 332
Moore, Wilbert E., 228, 229, 540
Moran, Barbara K., 309
mores, 58
Morgan, Lewis Henry, 541
Mormons, 325, 379
Mosca, Gaetano, 454
Mounin, Georges, 68
Moynihan, Daniel Patrick, 326
Mulkay, Michael, 401, 407
Mullins, Nicholas C., 394
multiple-nuclei theory, 507
Mumford, Lewis, 495, 504
Mundugamor, 292

Murdock, George P., 64, 200, 293, 320, 321, 336, 440, 552
My Lai, 535–537
Myrdal, Gunnar, 278

Nader, Ralph, 220, 433
Najarian, Pergrouhi, 100
Nash, Jeffrey E., 138
nature-nurture debate, 97–98
national character, 96
National Commission on Civil Disorders, 528
National Commission on Marijuana and Drug Abuse, 172, 173
National Commission on Population Growth and the American Future, 483–484, 491, 494, 498
National Education Association, 349
National Rifle Association, 450
National Teachers Association, 345
native Americans, 66, 192, 268, 269, 271, 282, 345, 375–376
natural science, 7
Navajo, 71
Nayar, 320
Nazi Germany, 262–263, 268, 276, 345, 395
neolocal, 322, 323, 325
Neugarten, Bernice L., 242
Newcomb, Theodore, 147
New Guinea, 4, 62, 90
Newton, Esther, 203
Nisbet, Robert, 92, 170, 474, 491, 550
Nixon, Richard M., 80, 254, 427, 437, 440, 447, 449, 450, 484, 550, 551
nonmaterial culture, 51
nonverbal communication, 123–126
norms, 57–59, 394–395
Norum, G. A., 126
Novak, Michael, 285
Nunn, Clyde, 390
Nye, F. Ivan, 176

Oakley, Ann, 298
obedience to authority, 131–133
objectivity, 22–24
observational studies, 38–41
occupations, 414–416
O'Dea, Thomas, 387
Oelsner, Leslie, 178
Ogburn, William F., 401–403, 549, 552, 556
Ohlin, Lloyd E., 169
oligarchy, 446; iron law of, 155–157
oligopoly, 421
open system, 217
operational definition, 43
Ophuls, William, 555
opinion polls, 285
organic solidarity, 412
organized crime, 175
Ornati, Oscar, 248
Orwell, George, 70–71
outgroup, 146–147
overpopulation, 390
oversocialized conception, 114
Owen, D. R., 167

Paine, Nathaniel, 282
panics, 520
paradigm, 396–397, 400–401
Pareto, Vilfredo, 454
Park, Robert E., 151, 502, 506
Parke, Robert, 328
Parkin, Frank, 225
Parkinson, C. Northcote, 155, 159
Parkinson's Law, 155
Parsons, Talcott, 15, 16, 17, 61, 81, 226, 415, 540, 543; on sex roles, 294–295; on social order, 545; on social change, 545–546, 554
participant observation, 40–41
particular other, 105
pastoral societies, 83–84, 410, 440
patriarchal, 322, 323
patrilineal, 322
patrilocal, 322, 323
Patterson, M. L., 125
Pavlov, Ivan, 101
Pederson, D. M., 126
Peek, Charles W., 307
peer group, 109–110, 349–350, 357
pelvic examination, 128–129
Pentagon, 447, 458–460
personality, 95, 96, 97–98; authoritarian, 275–276; effects of isolation on, 98–101; and sex roles, 300–301
personal space, 125–126
Peter, Lawrence J., 155
Peter Principle, 155
Petras, John W., 309
Pettigrew, Thomas E., 360
Pheterson, Gail I., 298
physical proximity, 125–126
Piaget, Jean, 102, 105–107, 115
Pilbeam, David R., 74
Piliavan, Irvin, 177
Piltdown Man, 400
pimp, 208
Pitzer, Kenneth S., 390
Plains Indians, 66. *See also* Native Americans
Plateris, Alexander A., 331, 334
Plog, Fred, 92
Plumb, J. H., 112
pluralism, 267, 268, 280, 286
Polanyi, Michael, 398
political parties, 452–454
political science, 10
political sociology, 435–465. *See also* power; state; democracy; interest groups; political parties; revolutions; military-industrial complex
pollution, 404, 488, 489–490
Polsky, Ned, 41
polyandry, 321
polygamy, 322, 323, 373
polygyny, 320, 321
polytheism, 368
Pomeroy, Wadell B., 203, 208
Popper, Karl R., 396
population, 469–491; rapid growth of, 475–479; dynamics of 470–474; demographic transition, 479–482; in U.S., 482–484; and social change, 550
pornography, 9, 198, 199
Porter, John, 250
postindustrial society, 430–432
Postman, Leo, 515
poverty, 251–256
power, 220, 239–240, 435–440
power elite, 239, 454, 456, 460
Powers, Thomas, 113
preindustrial societies, 81–91, 231–232, 323, 495–496
prejudice, 273–277, 383
Presidential Commission on Law Enforcement and the Administration of Justice, 75, 178
Presidential Commission on Obscenity and Pornography, 199
prestige, 220, 240, 353; prestige ratings, 221
Prewitt, Kenneth, 287
Price, Derek J. de Solla, 393, 394
primary deviance, 171
primary groups, 80, 140–141
primary industry, 414–415
primary socialization, 110
primates, 53
priority disputes, 398
prisons, 93, 179–180, 207
Pritchard, James, 270
profane, 367

professions, 343, 415–416
Project Camelot, 44–45
projection, 277–278
propaganda, 529
property, 420–421, 443
prostitution, 205–210
Protestant ethic thesis, 35, 377–397
Protestantism, 375
Protestants, 328, 382–383
Provence, S., 100
psychoanalysis, 103
psychology, 10; of development, 97–107; of learning, 101–102; of prejudice, 275–277; of sex differences, 291, 303–304, 306–307
puberty rites, 371
public opinion, 529–531
Puerto Ricans, 283
puritans, 34–35, 165, 379

questionnaires, 37–38

race, 329, 362–363
race relations, 261–287. *See also* prejudice; discrimination; minority groups; ethnic groups
racism, 269–273
Radcliffe-Brown, A. R., 61
Rainwater, Lee, 301
random sample, 37
Raper, Arthur, 527
rationalization, 149–150
Raza Unida, 283
rebellion, 169
Redfield, Robert, 89, 488
reference groups, 147
reflexes, 57
Reischauer, Robert D., 346
Reiss, Albert J., 205, 220, 240
Reiss, Ira L., 326
relative deprivation, 251
religion, 247, 343, 365, 387, 429; sacred and profane, 367; world religions, 368–370; functions, 371; functional equivalents, 371–372; and conflict, 372–377; and social change, 377–378; church and sect, 379–380, 382–383; in U.S., 380–384; future of, 384–386
research, 29, 352–353, 393, 404–406; methods, 35–45
resocialization, 111
resource depletion, 481–482, 488–490
retreatism, 168
revolutions, 9, 230, 429, 440, 460–461. *See also* American Revolution; French Revolution
Richardson, Ken, 363
Rienow, Leona Train, 488
Rienow, Robert, 488
Riesman, David., 239, 455
Riley, Matilda W., 113
riot, 280, 527–528
Rist, Ray C., 349, 355
ritual, 367, 370, 371
ritualism, 168
Roach, Jack, 257
Roberts, Joan L., 346
Robertson, Ian, 189, 223, 228, 232–4, 234–6
Rockefeller, John D., 421
rock music, 279
Rodin, Jean A., 130, 131
Roethlisberger, Fritz J., 35, 153, 419
role, 79, 289; in social interaction, 119–120; role expectation, 79; role performance, 80, 119–120, 128–129; role conflict, 80; role strain, 80; role taking, 105, 118
romantic love, 9, 320, 326–327, 332
Roosevelt, Franklin D., 36, 439
Rose, Arnold M., 460
Rose, Peter I., 282, 287
Rosengrant, T., 126
Rosenthal, D., 204
Rosenthal, M., 514
Rosenthal, Robert, 349, 363
Ross, H. Lawrence, 499
Rossi, Peter H., 220
Rossides, Daniel W., 240, 242, 243, 246, 257, 414
Roszak, Betty, 307
Roszak, Theodore, 68, 74, 148, 307
Rousseau, Jean Jacques, 443–444, 460
Rubovits, P. C., 349
rumor, 514–518
Runciman, William G., 224
Russel, M. A. H., 172
Russia. *See* Soviet Union
Ryan, William, 258–259
Rytina, Joan H., 228, 225

sacred, 367
sacred cows, 63
Safilios-Rothschild, Constantine, 294
Sagarin, Edward, 127, 137, 171, 203
Sahlins, Marshall, 83
sample, 36-38
Sampson, Anthony, 427, 465
San, 82, 66, 262
sanctions, 59, 165
Sapir, Edward, 70
Scammon, Richard M., 343
Scanzioni, John H., 301
scapegoat, 276
Schafer, Walter E., 357
schools, 58-61, 108-109, 235, 304-305, 346-353. *See also* education
Schur, Edwin M., 172, 174
Schutz, Alfred, 135
Schwartz, Pepper, 205
science, 17-18, 389-407, 430; norms of, 394-395; institutionalization of, 390-394; innovation in, 395-401; social control of, 404-406; and technology, 389-390, 401-403
Scott, Marvin B., 122
Scott, W. Richard, 152, 154
Sears, Robert R., 292
secondary deviance, 171
secondary groups, 81, 140-141
secondary industry, 414-415
sect, 379, 380
sector theory, 507
secularization, 384-386
Seeman, Melvin, 416
segregation, 358-361. *See also* discrimination; race relations.
self, 102-105, 118-124, 128-129
self-fulfilling prophecy, 271, 348-349
Sellin, Thorsten, 170
Selvin, Hanan C., 352
Selznick, Gertrude Jaeger, 271, 276, 352
Selznick, Philip, 154
Seventh Day Adventists, 379
Sewell, William H., 355
sexism, 296-299
sex roles, 289-311, 316-317, 332; in U.S., 293-294, 299-308; cross-cultural, 292-294; division of labor by, 292-293, 301-302; psychology of, 291, 303-304, 306-307
sexual behavior, 57, 162, 187-211, 271, 332, 334; nature of, 187-192; cross-cultural, 189-192; in U.S., 192-199. *See also* homosexuality; incest; prostitution
Seymour, Whitney N., 178
Shaw, Clifford R., 169
Sheldon, William H., 167
Sherif, Muzafer, 146, 147
Sherriffs, A., 297
Sherrill, Robert, 458, 459
Shibutani, Tamotsu, 515, 534

Shinto, 369, 370
Short, James F., 176
Shoshone, 56
siblings, 318
Siegel, Paul M., 220
Silberman, Charles E., 345, 363
Sills, David L., 154
Simmel, Georg, 141, 502, 547
Simmons, C. H., 130
Simmons, Jack L., 161
Simon, William, 189, 204, 211
Simpson, George E., 267, 273, 287
Singh, J. A. L., 99
Sjoberg, Gideon, 496
Skinner, B. F., 101
Skolnick, Arlyne, 336
Skolnick, Jerome H., 92, 336
Slater, Philip E., 74, 143, 406
slavery, 270, 278, 279, 280, 373, 402–403
Smelser, Neil J., 425, 429, 433, 513–514, 528, 534, 553, 554
Smith, Adam, 412, 421
Smith, Lillian, 277
social change, 11, 17, 18, 403–404, 513, 539–556; theories of, 541–547; sources of, 547–553
social class. *See* class; caste; social stratification
social construction of reality, 135–136
social control, 58–59, 164–165, 414
social Darwinism, 542
social differentiation, 215, 289
socialization, 95–115, 248–249, 317, 342, 356, 403; agencies of, 108–110; political, 450; and self, 101–103; types of, 110–111; and sex roles, 302–306
socialism, 230, 420, 422, 424, 444–445
socialist societies, 218
social inequality, 215–216; in U.S., 237–259; and education, 353–362. *See also* class; caste; social stratification
social learning, 101, 204–205
social mobility, 218–219; in India, 222–223; in Britain, 223–224; in Soviet Union, 224–245; in U.S., 249–251; and education, 353–355
social movements, 512, 531–533
social problems, 532–533
social psychology, 10, 15
social science, 7, 10–11
social stratification, 215–236; elements of, 217–221; ideology and, 225–228; theories of, 228–232; in Britain, 223–224; in South Africa, 234–236; in Soviet Union, 224–225; in U.S., 237–255. *See also* class; caste; social inequality.
social structure, 78–81; in preindustrial societies, 82–87, 89–91; in industrial societies, 85–91
social system, 17
society, 51–52, 77–93
sociobiology, 399
sociocultural evolution, 82. *See also* evolution, cultural and social
socioeconomic status, 220
sociological imagination, 5–7
sociology, 3–25
Sommer, R., 126
Sorensen, Robert, 197, 198
Sorokin, Pitirim A., 89, 170, 249, 544
South Africa, 217, 226, 234–236, 268
Soviet Union, 244–245, 294, 420, 422–423, 427, 445
Spears, David, 363
Spector, Malcolm, 532
Spencer, Herbert, 12–13, 14, 16, 17, 542
Spengler, Oswald, 544
Spitz, René A., 100
Spradley, James P., 137
Sprehe, Timothy, 16
spurious correlations, 32
Srinivas, M. N., 223
Srole, Leo, 248
Stampp, Kenneth, 373
Standard Consolidated Area, 497
Standard Metropolitan Statistical Area, 497
Stark, Rodney, 381, 382, 383
state, 435, 440–445
statistical terms, 31
status, 78–79, 119–120, 217, 218–219, 222, 223, 540
Stein, Maurice R., 504
Steinberg, Rafael, 151
Steinberg, Stephen, 271, 276, 352
Steiner, Gary G., 143
stereotype, 275
Stern, Michael, 500
Stern, Philip M., 240, 256, 257
Steward, Julian H., 397, 543
stigma, 162
Stokes, Randall, 122
Stoner, J. A. F., 144
Storer, Norman W., 407
Stouffer, Samuel A., 143
stratified random sample, 37
Strauss, Anselm, 113, 118, 133, 134
streaking, 33
Strodtbeck, Fred L., 145
structural-functionalism, 17. *See also* functionalism
subcultures, 67–68, 170–171, 357, 361, 381
suicide, 41–43, 306
Sumner, William Graham, 15
superego, 103
supernatural, 365, 368
survey, 36-38
Sutherland, Edwin H., 169–170, 174
Suttles, Gerald, 504
Swanson, Guy, 556
Switzerland, 267
symbol, 68, 118–119
symbolic interaction, 20-21, 22, 115–119, 117–135. *See also* interactionist perspective
Szasz, Thomas, 182

tables, 39
taboo, 58, 187. *See also* incest
Taeuber, Irene B., 480
Tanzania, 267
Taoism, 369, 370, 378
Tasaday, 56
Taylor, Carl, 223
Taylor, Frederick Winslow, 418
Taylor, Gordon Rattray, 195
Taylor, Ian, 167
Tchambuli, 292
technocracy, 405
technological determinism, 401–403
technology, 389–390, 401–406, 549–550
Terkel, Studs, 209, 433
Terrel, K., 224
tertiary industry, 431
theism, 368
Theodore, Athena, 309
theoretical perspectives, 16–21. *See also* conflict perspective; functionalist perspective; interactionist perspective
theory, 16, 29
Thomas, W. I., 135, 271
Thompson, N. L., 203
Thompson, Victor, 154
Thorndike, Robert L., 349
Toffler, Alvin, 157, 403, 407, 425, 556
Tönnies, Ferdinand, 89, 502
total institution, 111, 179–180
totalitarianism, 446
totem, 370
Touraine, Alan, 432
Tourney, G., 204
Toynbee, Arnold, 544

transvestism, 203
Treiman, Donald J., 220, 224, 242
Trevor-Roper, H. R., 375
triad, 142
Trow, Martin, 350
Truman, Harry S, 37
Truzzi, Marcello, 127
Tumin, Melvin M., 229
Turner, Ralph H., 120, 515, 516, 534
Tussing, A. Dale, 255

Udry, J. Richard, 328, 331
Uganda, 267, 271, 553
Ullman, Edward L., 507
urban ecology, 505–508
urbanism, 502–504
urbanization, 430, 493–496
urban renewal, 501–502
urban sociology, 493–509
U'Ren, Marjorie B., 305

value, 59–61, 194–196, 248, 430, 477, 485
value freedom, 14
value judgment, 24
Van den Berghe, Pierre L., 231, 554
Vander Zanden, James W., 266, 269
variable, 30–31
Veblen Thorstein, 153, 401
Vernon, Raymond, 425
Verstehen, 34–35
vertical mobility, 218
veto groups, 455, 460
Viditch, Arthur, 509
Vietnam War, 382, 449, 535–537
Voss, Harwin L., 176

Wagley, Charles, 266
Wallace, A. R., 398
Wallach, M. A., 144
Wallerstein, James S., 176
Wallin, Paul, 329
Walters, Richard H., 101
Walton, John, 240, 458
Walum, Laurel Richardson, 310–311
Ward, Lester, 15
Warner, W. Lloyd, 241, 242
war on poverty, 345
Warren, Carol A. B., 203
Washington, George, 384
Watergate, 157, 178, 240, 449, 451
Watson, John B., 97, 101
Watson, Peter J., 298
Wattenberg, Ben J., 343
wealth, 220, 238–239
Weber, Max, 14, 16, 20, 153, 155, 156, 158, 548; on bureaucracy, 149–152; on class, 220; on Protestant ethic, 34–35, 377–379, 548; on political sociology, 435–440
Weinberg, Martin S., 127
Weinberg, M., 203
Weitzman, Lenore J., 305
welfare, 254–256
Western Electric Experiments, 35–36, 152–153, 419
Westhoff, Charles, 482
Westley, William M., 203
White, Leslie A., 200, 402
White, Ralph K., 143
white-collar crime, 174
white ethnics, 279, 284–285
Whorf, Benjamin, 70
Whyte, Theodore, 516
Whyte, William F., 40
Whyte, William H., 154
Wiesner, Jerome B., 390
Wilensky, H. L., 416
Williams, Jay R., 176
Williams, L. J., 203
Williams, Robin M., 59–61, 74, 92
Wilson, James Q., 180
Wilson, Edmund O., 399
Winch, Robert F., 336
Winick, Charles, 206, 211
Wirth, Louis, 170, 266, 502–503, 504
Wise, David, 449
witches, 165, 374–375
Womack, John, 283
women's liberation movement, 19, 240, 297, 308, 514. *See also* sex roles
work, 410
Worsely, Peter, 376, 534
Wrong, Dennis H., 114, 229, 491
Wyle, Clement J., 176

Xhosa, 376

Yanamamö, 63, 65
Yankelovitch, Daniel, 299, 418, 457
Yarrow, L. J., 100
Yinger, J. Milton, 267, 273, 287
yippies, 515–516
Yorburg, Betty, 291, 301, 309
Young, Jock, 172

Zald, Meyer N., 531
Zangwill, Israel, 279
zero population growth, 473
Zimbardo, Philip G., 93, 130
Zimmerman, R. R., 100
Zingg, Robert M., 99
Zinkin, Taya, 223
Zurcher, Louis A., 127